30th Pacific Asia Conference on Language, Information and Computation 2016 (PACLIC 30)

Seoul, South Korea
28 – 30 October 2016

Editors:

Jong C. Park
Jin-Woo Chung

ISBN: 978-1-5108-3466-8

Printed from e-media with permission by:

Curran Associates, Inc.
57 Morehouse Lane
Red Hook, NY 12571

Printed by Curran Associates, Inc. (2017)

Association for Computational Linguistics
209 N. Eighth Street
Stroudsburg, Pennsylvania 18360

Phone: 1-570-476-8006
Fax: 1-570-476-0860

acl@aclweb.org

Additional copies of this publication are available from:

Curran Associates, Inc.
57 Morehouse Lane
Red Hook, NY 12571 USA
Phone: 845-758-0400
Fax: 845-758-2633
Email: curran@proceedings.com
Web: www.proceedings.com

Proceedings of the 30th Pacific Asia Conference on Language, Information and Computation

edited by

Jong C. Park,
KAIST

Jin-Woo Chung,
KAIST

October 28-30, 2016

Acknowledgments

PACLIC 30 is organized by Korean Society for Language and Information (KSLI), Korea Advanced Institute of Science and Technology (KAIST), and Institute for the Study of Language and Information at Kyung Hee University (ISLI), under the auspices of PACLIC Steering Committee.

This work was supported by the NRF (National Research Foundation of Korea) Grant funded by the MOE (Ministry of Education).

Welcome & Acknowledgments

Welcome to the 30th Pacific Asia Conference on Language, Information and Computation (PACLIC30)!

We are really happy to have you all here at Kyung Hee University. Ever since 1995, the PACLIC has been a meeting place for researchers working on language and related fields. We have tried to share our research results in the field of theoretical and computational linguistics. It has been a favorite conference for many theoretical and computational linguists in the Pacific-Asia region as well as around the world. This year is no exception. We have researchers from various regions including Europe, the United States, and Middle East.

In addition to regular paper and poster presentations, we have three exceptional plenary talks and five invited papers on 'interesting issues of language and computing', respectively. The three plenary talks will be given by Stefan Müller from Freie Universität Berlin, Goran Nenadic from University of Manchester, and Anoop Sarkar from Simon Fraser University. The five invited papers are delivered by Jae-Woong Choe from Korea University, Shirley Dita from De La Salle University, Yasunari Harada from Waseda University, Chu-Ren Huang from The Hong Kong Polytechnic University, and Hongyong Liu from University of Macau. We thank all these plenary speakers and invited papers for the contribution. The selection process of regular papers and posters has been highly competitive with the acceptance rate of only 26.9% (29 papers) for oral presentation and 28.7% (31 posters) for poster presentation from the total 108 submitted papers. This can ensure the high quality of the oral presentations as well as posters.

Together with the distinguished plenary speakers and invited papers and high quality papers and posters, I have a strong belief that all the participants will greatly benefit from each other, sharing stimulating ideas, discussing provoking suggestions, lightening the direction of our linguistic research in future, and so forth.

This conference would not be possible without the support and efforts from many people, including program members and reviewers, organizers, volunteers, and sponsors. I would especially like to thank the Program Committee Chair, Prof. Jong C. Park, who tackled the many tasks associated with planning a program for the conference with enthusiasm and efficiency. In particular, many thanks go to Sanghoun Song for designing and maintaining the conference website and helping to coordinate the efforts of the Organizing Committee. I also thank student staff members Rok Sim, Okgi Kim, SeulKee Park, and graduate students at Kyung Hee University for their time and efforts to make everything for this conference run smoothly. We also thank the National Research Foundation of Korea, Institute for the Study of Language and Information at Kyung Hee University, Korean Society for Language and Information, and Korea Advanced Institute of Science and Technology for the generous financial and logistics support for the conference.

We hope you enjoy the conference and your stay in Kyung Hee, Seoul!

Jong-Bok Kim

PACLIC 30 Organization Committee Chair

Preface

The 30th Pacific Asia Conference on Language, Information and Computation (PACLIC 30) is held at Kyung Hee University in Seoul on (Friday) 28 October – (Sunday) 30 October 2016. The conference is co-hosted by the Korea Society of Language and Information, Institute for the Study of Language and Information at KHU, and Korea Advanced Institute of Science and Technology. The PACLIC series of conferences emphasize the synergy of theoretical analysis and processing of language, and provide a forum for researchers in different fields of language study in the Pacific-Asia region to share their findings and interests in the formal and empirical study of languages. Organized under the auspices of the PACLIC Steering Committee, PACLIC 30 continues our long standing collaborative efforts among theoretical and computational linguists in the Pacific-Asia region.

This year, we received 108 paper submissions that represent healthy diversity, with authors from 22 countries, which include Australia, Cambodia, China, Czech Republic, Denmark, France, Hong Kong, India, Indonesia, Ireland, Israel, Italy, Japan, Korea, New Zealand, Philippines, Russia, Taiwan, Thailand, United Kingdom, United States, and Vietnam (80.2% from 13 countries in Asia Pacific, 11.7% from 7 countries in Europe, 6.1% from the United States, and 2.0% from the Middle East). We wish to extend our deep thanks to all the authors for submitting papers to PACLIC 30 and for their contributions.

We would also like to thank 53 Program Committee members for writing over 327 reviews and for making the final paper selection possible among 108 submissions in total. After receiving acceptance letters for either oral or poster presentations, however, some authors of accepted papers chose to withdraw their submissions or to change their presentation modes afterwards. As a result, we have 29 papers for oral presentation (26.9% acceptance rate) and 31 papers for poster presentation (55.6% acceptance rate). Each submission was reviewed by at least three reviewers to ensure that all accepted papers meet the high quality standards of the PACLIC conference. We are extremely grateful to the Program Committee members for all their hard work, without which the preparation of this program would not have been possible at all.

We are delighted to have three plenary keynote speeches and five invited papers addressing different aspects of language and computing in PACLIC 30. The three keynote speeches are given by Stefan Müller from Freie Universität Berlin, Goran Nenadic from University of Manchester, and Anoop Sarkar from Simon Fraser University. The five invited papers are delivered by Jae-Woong Choe from Korea University, Shirley Dita from De La Salle University, Yasunari Harada from Waseda University, Chu-Ren Huang from The Hong Kong Polytechnic University, and Hongyong Liu from University of Macau. These plenary and invited papers will not be only informative but also enlightening to the audience, leading to many innovative research ideas in the future. We would like to thank General Chair Hee-Rahk Chae and the Steering Committee for their valuable help and advice. We also wish to extend our appreciation to Organization Chair Jong-Bok Kim and the Organization Committee members, for their exceptional dedication and coordination in their work.

We hope that you enjoy the conference!

Jong C. Park

PACLIC 30 Program Committee Chair

PACLIC 30 Organizers

Steering Committee:

Hee-Rahk Chae, Hankuk University of Foreign Studies, Seoul
Chu-Ren Huang, The Hong Kong Polytechnic University, Hong Kong
Rachel Edita O. Roxas, National University, Manila
Maosong Sun, Tsinghua University, Beijing
Benjamin T'sou, City University of Hong Kong, Hong Kong
Kei Yoshimoto, Tohoku University, Sendai
Min Zhang, Soochow University, Suzhou

Conference Chair:

Hee-Rahk Chae, Hankuk University of Foreign Studies

Organization Committee Chair:

Jong-Bok Kim, Kyung Hee University

Organization Committee:

Sang-gu Kang, Hansung University
Dongsik Lim, Hongik University
Sanghoun Song, Incheon National University

Program Committee Chair:

Jong C. Park, KAIST

Program Committee Members:

Wirote Aroonmanakun, Chulalongkorn University
Stephane Bressan, National University of Singapore
Kuang-Hua Chen, National Taiwan University
Hsin-Hsi Chen, National Taiwan University
Eng Siong Chng, Nanyang Technological University
Sae Youn Cho, Kangwon National University
Sung-Kwon Choi, ETRI
Jin-Woo Chung, KAIST
Siaw-Fong Chung, National Chengchi University
Beatrice Daille, Laboratoire d'Informatique de Nantes Atlantique
Shirley Dita, De La Salle University
Minghui Dong, Institute for Infocomm Research
Guohong Fu, Heilongjiang University
Wei Gao, Qatar Computing Research Institute

Helena Hong Gao, Nanyang Technological University
Yasunari Harada, Waseda University
Choochart Haruechaiyasak, National Electronics and Computer Technology Center
Munpyo Hong, Sungkyunkwan University
Shu-Kai Hsieh, National Taiwan Normal University
Byeongchang Kim, Catholic University of Daegu
Jung-Jae Kim, Institute for Infocomm Research
Oi-Yee Kwong, The Chinese University of Hong Kong
Yong-Hun Lee, Chungnam National University
Youngjoo Lee, Seoul Women's University
Dongsik Lim, Hongik University
Yuji Matsumoto, Nara Institute of Science and Technology
Hye-Jin Min, NAVER
Mathieu Morey, Paul Sabatier University - Toulouse III
Yoshiki Mori, University of Tokyo
Natchanan Natpratan, Kasetsart University
Ponrudee Netisopakul, KMAKE LAB
Jian-Yun Nie, Universit de Montral
Makoto Okada, Osaka Prefecture University
Chutamanee Onsuwan, Thammasat University
Ryo Otoguro, Waseda University
Cecile Paris, CSIRO - ICT Centre
Long Qiu, Institute for Infocomm Research
Bali Ranaivo-Malancon, MALINDO
Byong-Rae Ryu, Chungnam National University
Samira Shaikh, State University of New York - University at Albany
Pornsiri Singhapreecha, Thammasat University
Sanghoun Song, Incheon National University
Virach Sornlertlamvanich, SIIT, Thammasat University
Keh-Yih Su, Academia Sinica
Takenobu Tokunaga, Tokyo Institute of Technology
Aline Villavicencio, Universidade Federal do Rio Grande do Sul
Jiun-Shiung Wu, National Chung Cheng University
Cheng-Zen Yang, Yuan Ze University
Satoru Yokoyama, Tohoku University
Liang-Chih Yu, Yuan Ze University
Jiajun Zhang, Institute of Automation Chinese Academy of Sciences
Hai Zhao, Shanghai Jiao Tong University
Michael Zock, CNRS-LIF

Program Committee Coordinator:

Jin-Woo Chung, KAIST

Table of Contents

Keynote Speeches

Invited Papers

Oral Presentation Papers

Poster Presentation Papers

Keynote Speeches

The CoreGram Project: Theoretical Linguistics, Theory Development and Verification

Stefan Müller
Freie Universität Berlin
St.Mueller@hu-berlin.de

Abstract

The German Grammar group develops a fully formalized and computer-processable set of grammars that share a set of constraints, that is, they have a common core (see also Müller, 2013 for an overview). Some very general con-straints hold for all grammars, some for subgroups of languages.

Currently we work on:

1. German (Germanic, SFB 632, A6, Müller, 2007; Müller and Ørsnes, 2011),
2. Danish (Germanic, DFG MU 2822/2-1, Ørsnes, 2009; Müller, 2009; Müller and Ørsnes, 2011; Müller and Ørsnes, In Preparation),
3. Persian (Indo-Iranian, DFG/ANR MU 2822/3-1, Müller, 2010, Müller und Ghayoomi, 2010),
4. Maltese (Semitic, Müller, 2009),
5. Mandarin Chinese (Sino-Tibetian, DFG MU 2822/5-1, Lipenkova, 2008; Müller and Lipenkova, 2009),
6. Spanish (Romance, SFB 632, A6),
7. French (Romance, SFB 632, A6),
8. Yiddisch (Germanic, Müller and Ørsnes, 2011) and
9. Hindi.

The approach to developing the core grammar is bottom-up in that we do not assume a genetically determined Universal Grammar and try to prove its existence in language after language. Rather we treat every language in its own right and try to generalize over sets of languages only later. Some of this knowledge might be part of an UG in the above sense, but we do not make any claims on this issue.

We also do not make an explicit core-periphery distinction while working on individual languages. Rather what belongs to the core is determined empirically by comparing languages. If we find a phenomenon in more than one language and think that it is correct to describe the phenomenon by the same means, the respective representations are kept in one file that is used by the respective grammars. This results in a grouping of languages that share the same code, with files containing very general constraints being used by all languages.

Inferring Methodological Meta-knowledge from Large Biomedical Corpora

Goran Nenadic
University of Manchester
gnenadic@manchester.ac.uk

Abstract

Large amounts of biomedical corpora have emerged from different sources, including scientific literature, lab notes, patents and electronic health records. Most of the efforts in biomedical text mining have focused on the extraction and linkage of specific facts, such as molecular interactions, links between genes and diseases, or patients' symptoms. Such facts are rarely contextualised using the associated scientific or professional methodology (e.g. what methods were used to detect particular interaction, or to diagnose a particular disease). However, methods are the vital, but often neglected, under-pinning of science and practice. Given enough data, the ability to extract methodological knowledge would allow us to "infer" common (and possibly best) practice for a given task, and thus indeed learn from vast amount of text. This is obviously a complex task that involves identification, representation and linking of steps in associated methods, requiring a series of NLP methods such as temporal information extraction and discourse analysis. In this talk we will explore finding out what methods are being used to do what experiment from the literature, or to infer what clinical pathways patients have followed, based on the notes in their electronic health records. We will illustrate some of the work in the context of bioinformatics (e.g. recovering a general view of the methods described in the literature) and clinical practice (e.g. reconstruction of patient journeys). We will also discuss how feasible this task is given the known issues with the lack of reported details needed for understanding and reproducibility of associated methods (i.e. how much of a method is indeed present in the literate or clinical records).

The Challenge of Simultaneous Speech Translation

Anoop Sarkar
Simon Fraser University
anoop@sfu.ca

Abstract

Simultaneous speech translation attempts to produce high quality translations while at the same time minimizing the latency between production of words in the source language and translation into the target language. The variation in syntactic structure between the source and target language can make this task challenging: translating from a language where the verb is at the end increases latency when translating incrementally into a language where the verb appears after the subject.

In this talk I focus on a key prediction problem in simultaneous translation: when to start translating the input stream. I will talk about two new algorithms that together provide a solution to this problem. The first algorithm learns to find effective places to break the input stream. In order to balance the often conflicting demands of low latency and high translation quality, the algorithm exploits the notion of Pareto optimality. The second algorithm is a stream decoder that incrementally processes the input stream from left to right and produces output translations for segments of the input. These segments are found by consulting classifiers trained on data created by the first algorithm.

We compare our approach with previous work and present translation quality scores (BLEU scores) and the latency of generating translations (number of segments translated per second) on audio lecture data from the TED talks collection.

Invited Papers

The Significance of Background Information in Acceptability Judgements of Korean Sentences

Jae-Woong Choe
Korea University
jchoe@korea.ac.kr

Abstract

Linguists in the Generative Linguistics tradition typically rely on their own intuition as a native speaker for their core data. This practice has continually been challenged to be more rigorous in their data collection methodology, and Experimental Syntax is an effort to address the issue.

The purpose of this presentation is to discuss whether some background information of the subjects might affect the acceptability judgments of the subjects, mostly naive native speakers. It is well established, following the sociolinguistic research, that native speakers' use of language might be influenced by some social factors like age, gender, class, and others.

The data to be discussed in the presentation are drawn from acceptability judgments on sentences by Korean native speakers, and comprise 68,158 data points, gathered from 302 native speakers with 574 stimulus sentences (around 240 items per subject). The background information that was collected includes factors like sex, age, dialect, and previous exposure to linguistics classes ('familiarity').

We discuss in detail some statistical issues to be dealt with for any proper treatment of the data, focusing on their distributional characteristics. The results show that the 'familiarity' factor largely plays a marginally significant role in the distribution of the data.

Measuring Diversified Proficiency of Japanese Learners of English

Yasunari HARADA
Faculty of Law, Waseda University
Nishi-Waseda 1-6-1, Shinjuku-ku
Tokyo 169-8050, Japan
harada@waseda.jp

Abstract

Japan is faced with an imminent challenge of cultivating 'global human resources', as the whole society delves into the global information society. The Course of Study defined by the Ministry of Education, Culture, and Sports and Technology (MEXT) of the Japanese government has emphasized communicative competence and / or 'communication skills' as a focus of the foreign language subjects (e.g., English) since 1900's and the Courses of Study for most other subject also mention similar needs. During the academic year of 2014, the Educational Reform Working Group within the leading Liberal Democratic Party proposed the use of TOEFL iBT as an obligatory part of university entrance examination procedures. Furthermore, in 2015, MEXT advised the consideration of utilizing existing 4-skills English language proficiency tests that external test publishers have made available in Japan. Pearson offers various English tests that are automatically scored. Its spoken English test, Versant English Test, uses automated speech recognition and technologies. Versant Writing Test measures reading and writing skills and is scored automatically by using Latent Semantic Analysis. Approximately 60 first-year students at the undergraduate School of Law at Waseda University took Versant English Test and Versant Writing Test four times and the sores are compared to those of Oxford Placement English Test that the same students took three times. Oxford Quick Placement Test is designed to measure vocabulary, collocation, and grammar through reading-based multiple choice tasks. The present study reports results of analyses of these test scores and estimated CEFR levels, and then investigates challenges that Japanese learners and teachers of English are facing.

Credits

Parts of the materials in this paper are presented orally in (Suzuki, Morishita and Harada, 2016 a). Materials presented here in English have previously been published in Japanese in (Suzuki, Morishita and Harada, 2016 b) and (Harada & Morishita, 2013).

References

Suzuki, M., Morishita, M. & Harada, Y. (2016 a). Application of Language Technology to Language Assessment: Measuring Different Aspects of Language Proficiency of Japanese Learners of English with Different Automated Tests. Spring Joint Conference of English Linguistics Society of Korea and Korean Society for Language and Information, Kyung Hee University, Seoul.

Suzuki, M., Morishita, M. & Harada, Y. (2016 b). Application of Language Technology to Language Assessment: Measuring different aspects of language proficiency of Japanese learners of English with different automated tests"(in Japanese), IEICE Technical Report TL2016-9 / NLC-9, vol. 116, No. 77, pp. 41-46, Institute for Electronic and Communications Engineers,.

Harada, Y., & Morishita, M. (2013). Language processing and proficiency of Japanese learners of English: Versant English Test and Oxford Quick Placement Test (in Japanese). IEICE Technical Report, TL2013-14, 1–6.

Endurant vs Perdurant: Ontological Motivation for Language Variations

Chu-Ren Huang
Department of Chinese and Bilingual Studies
The Hong Kong Polytechnic University
churen.huang@polyu.edu.hk

Abstract

Modern ontology focuses on the shared structure of knowledge representation and sheds light on underling motivations of human conceptual structure. This paper addresses the issue of whether ontological structures are linguistically represented, and whether such conceptual underpinning of linguistic representation may motivate language variations. Integrating our recent work showing that the most fundamental endurant vs. perdurant ontological dichotomy is grammaticalized in Chinese and on comparable corpus based studies of variations of Chinese, I will explore the possibility that this basic conceptual dichotomy may in fact provide the motivation of changes of perspectives that underlies language variations. I will also discuss possible implication this approach has in accounting for other language changes and variations such as light verb's argument taking, incorporation, loss of case/agreement, and English –er/-ee asymmetry. In the process, the will resolve three linguistic puzzles and eventually show that the endurant/perdurant dichotomy may in fact be the conceptual basis of the hitherto undefined +N (i.e. nouny) vs. +V (i.e. verby) features prevalent in linguistics. Based on this proposal, the variations involving various types of denominalization and deverbalization can be accounted for.

1. Motivation: Three Linguistic Puzzles

This paper starts with three seemingly unrelated linguistic puzzles and will end in proposing a common solution to these puzzles, in spite of the fact that these puzzles are very different in nature and varies greatly at the linguistic levels where they occur. By showing that the perdurant/endurant ontological dichotomy offers common solution to these puzzles, I will further demonstrate that the same dichotomy can motivate a range of well-known facts in language changes and variations.

1.1. Three Linguistic Puzzles

The three puzzles belong to different domains. The first puzzle involves a common cross-linguistic phenomenon, the second puzzle is language specific, while the last is a meta-linguistic one.

(1) Why do we refer to a flight that did take off at 10:10 the 10:10 flight?

(2) Why 醫院病人 *yi1yuan4 bing4ren2* 'hospital patient' is not an acceptable expression in Mandarin Chinese?

(3) What does linguists mean by 'nouny' and 'verby'?; or
What does +N, +V stand for when linguistic theories claim that nouns are [+N, -V], and adjectives are [+N, +V]?

These puzzles are explicated further below.

Why 1 A flight that is scheduled for10:10 typically takes off earlier or later, and rarely takes off at exactly 10:10. For instance, it could be delayed and took off at 10:28. However, in any language, it is simply not possible to inquire about information related to this flight, such as the arrival time, by referring to the flight with it factually true 10:28 taking off time? Why are we linguistically obliged to refer it the 10:10 flight while we know that it is not true that it took off at 10:10 (and in fact a different flight might have taken off at 10:10)?

Why 2 NN compound are common and productive in Mandarin Chinese and a wide range of NN compounds are attested, such as 'school teacher' 學校老師 *xue2xiao4 lao3shi1*, 'hotel chef' 酒店廚師 *jiu3diao4 cu1shi*, or 'primary school student' 小

學學生 *xiao3xue1 xue1sheng*. Mandarin speakers, however, balk at and strongly dis-prefer 'hospital patient' 醫院病人 *yi1yuan4 bing4ren2*, and would prefer 醫院的病人 *yi1yuan4 de bing4ren2.* But why not and why does the addition of 的 *de* make the expression acceptable even though the semantic relations of between two component nouns seem to be similar.

Why 3 A fundamental architecture shared by a few linguistic theories is the use of +/- N, and +/-V features, often referred to as being nouny or verby. These are supposed to be more fundamental than grammatical categories as nouns are defined as a [+N, -V] category, adjectives as [+N, +V], verbs as [-N, +V], and adverbs as [-N, -V]. However, what does +N mean? A paraphrase of nouns have noun-like properties is a tautology. Since the definition of nouns depends on the +N features, yet the definition of the +N feature requires that we know what a noun is. Furthermore, deverbal nouns and denominal verbs, among other categorical shifts, are common in all languages. It is not unreasonable to expect that they retain some features of their original category, but does this make them nounier or verbier? Can they be both +N and +V (but this by definition means they are adjectives, which they clearly are not)? And most of all, is there any theoretical, empirical or cognitive ramification of this seemingly tautological stipulation?

1.2. Outline of the paper

After introducing the three linguistic puzzles, I will introduce the ontological dichotomy of endurant vs. perdurant (aka continuant vs. occurrent) and suggest why this dichotomy may be relevant for the three puzzles. In section three, following Huang (2015), I will show how this dichotomy is grammaticalized in Chinese. In particular, I argue that in Mandarin Chinese, sortal classifiers denote endurant properties, while measure words denote perdurant properties; and that 的 *de0* has a main function to mark perdurant relations. In section four, I explore some possible accounts of language variations based on this ontological dichotomy, including light verb selection variations in World Chineses, emergence of classifiers in Chinese, (verbal) incorporation involving VO and SO compounds in Chinese, and lose of gender and case in Middle English; as well as the lexical gaps in -ernominalization in English. I propose answers to the three puzzles in section 5. And section 6 will be the conclusion.

2. Endurant/Perdurant in Ontology

2.1 Endurant vs. Perdurant

Ontology in the application of information science and knowledge engineering is the shared system of knowledge representation (e.g. Gruber 1995). This shared system is often represented in terms of conceptual atoms and relations. One of the most fundamental issues in ontology construction the first binary bifurcation of all conceptual atoms. This seemingly simple decision will dictate the fundamental design of the knowledge system, as it entails the underlying conceptual or informational criteria for creating different branches in the knowledge system. We can find in the literature on ontology extensive discussion in philosophical, logical, linguistic, and cognitive theories before making commitment to this first bifurcation (e.g. Guarino 1998, and Gurino and Welty 2002 for DOLCE, Niles and Pease 2001 for SUMO, and Sminth and Grenon 2004 for Basis Formal Ontology (BFO)). Hence the fact that many upper ontologies adopt the endurant/perdurant dichotomy for this primary classification is significant. This dichotomy in fact relies crucially on relevance of time: a concept which can be defined independent of time is endurant; and a concept which must be defined dependent of time is perdurant. In terms of referning to entities, they correspond to what is called continuant and occurrent in philosophy. Hence the implication is that it is NOT the shape or other perceivable physical properties, but rather the entity's continuity of existence in time that plays a central role in conceptual classification of our knowledge systems. Although the logic primacy and cognitive necessity of such a stipulation seems well-motivated, one may wonder if such an abstract concept may play a role in the daily usage of language.

Before exploring their link to linguistic data, it is important to note that the time (in)dependency can be judged from pure physical/logical necessity (as in formal ontology) or based on (human) conceptualization (as in linguistic ontology). BFO, for instance, allows two types of ontologies to describe the same information content: three-dimensional SNAP ontologies without temporal dimension, which are therefore like snapshots; and four-dimensional SPAN ontologies incorporating spatiotemporal information (Grenon and Smith 2004). DOLCE, on the other hand, apply the endurant/perdurant dichotomy to entities only (Gangemi et al. 2003). This design feature can be illustrated by the DOLCE upper ontology (adapted from Gangemi et al 2003, and 2010) and given Figure 1 below. A different way to realize the edurant/perdurant dichotomy is BFO's basic bifurcation of continuant/occurrent, as illustrated Figure 2 (adapted from Smith 2012).

2.2 Interim Summary: Endurant/Perdurant

I summarize in three different ways the endurant vs. perdurant dichotomy as the foundation for the account to be proposed in this paper.

First, in intuitive and somewhat simplistic terms, referring entities are typically considered to be endurants; and processes are typically perdurants Endurants are hence noun-like and perdurants more verb-like.

Second, in terms of conceptual atoms, an endurant is "(the concept of) an entity which has spatial components but is not dependent on a specific time frame of occurrence." e.g. Hilary Clinton in 2008 and in 2016 are the save person. A perdurant is "(the concept of) an entity which has a time element crucially associated with its meaning." E.g. Clinton's 2008 and 2016 campaigns are two different campaigns.

Third, from conceptualization (or ontological representation) perspectives, and largely following Gernon and Smith (2004), an endurant ontology is SNAP ontology, where objects requires three-dimensional representation but can be described independent of time. And a perdurant ontology is SPAN ontology, where objects are given four (or higher) dimensional representation, and possible variations at different temporal point is integral part of the object being described.

2.3 Towards an Answer to Puzzle 1

Given the endurant vs. perdurant dichotomy, we are now able to differentiate the two different temporal references involved in the first puzzle, the 10:10 flight that took off at 10:28:

The 10:28 taking off time is the **perdurant** property of the event. Its relevance and validity is dependent on a specific timeframe of the occurrence of the event (e.g. 6 October, 2016). Hence to use this temporal reference, the speaker must both specify explicitly the particular the timeframe of the event as well as have specific knowledge of the parochial time reference. S/he also needs to establish that the listeners have the same reference and the same knowledge. It is easy to see that such level of shared reference and knowledge is not easy to establish.

The temporal reference of 10:10, as in 'a 10:10 flight', is the **endurant** property shared by all events belonging to this type. A 10:10 flight is 'the same' today, tomorrow, and the day after; regardless of when the flight actually take off each day as long as it is scheduled as such. Being a 10:10 flights is the shared endurant property of all such event episodes. More importantly, this 'enduring' property is conceptually robust for people to establish and share without further explication. This similarly applies to rigid designators. We refer to Hilary Clinton as a endurant even though we know that Clinton in 2008 and in 2016 have many different properties exactly because the reference is enduring and easy to establish for human conceptualization; while any other time-dependent reference can be easily lost track of by different participants in conceptualization, e.g. perdurant.

3. The Chinese classifier system: Linguistically encodes Endurant/Perdurant contrast

In this section, we follow the ontological account of Huang (2015), which adopts the generalizations of the linguistics system of Chinese classifiers presented in Ahrens and Huang (2016), as in Figure 3.

3.1 Sortal Classifier Denotes Endurant Properties

Ahrens and Huang (2016) identify two different sub-types in the syntactic classifier system of Chinese and call the first type 'sortal classifiers'. These are the prototypical Chinese classifiers Chinese, and individual classifiers in (4) are in turn the most prototypical sortal classifiers.

(4) a. 一張破破爛爛的紙
yi1_zhang1_po4po4lan4lan4_de_zhi3
one_CL_tattered_DE_paper
'one piece of tattered paper'

b. 那張缺腿的椅子
na4_zhang1_que1tui3_de_yi3zhi
that_CL_leg-missing_DE_chair
'that chair with a missing leg'

It is important to note that previous literature on classifiers in Chinese typically assumes that they establish different noun classes according to the physical properties, such as shapes, of the referents (e.g. Tai 1994). Huang (2015) showed that this is not the necessary conceptual motivation. In (4a), a piece of tattered or torn paper no longer retains the sheet like shape property purported to be selected by the classifier 張 *zhang1*. Similarly, a chair with a missing leg no longer poses the typical physical features purportedly selected by the classifier. The classifiers seem to select conceptual classes that are not affected by specific occurring events. In other words, sortal classifiers pick up the time independent property of being paper/chair regardless of the physical state of the referent at a certain time. I.e., they encode endurant properties We also picked the polysemous 張 *zhang1* to underline the fact that the classifier system is linguistically conventionalized and not dependent on the specific actual physical properties a particular classifier refer to.

3.2 Measure Words Denote Perdurant Properties

The other sub-class of the syntactic classifier system involves measure words, according to Ahrens and Huang (2016). These are the syntactic classifiers that are known not to select the nouns they modify. The example chosen involves a standard measure word

(5) 這一塊一公斤的肉，煮熟後只剩不到 600 公克
zhe4_yi1_kuai4_yi1_gong1jin1_de0_rou4zhu3shou2_hou4_zhi3_sheng4_bu2dao4_600_gong1ke4
this_one_CL_one_kilogram_DE_meat,
cooked_after_only_left_less_600_gram
'This piece meat of one kilogram only weighs less than 600 grams after being cooked.'

(5) shows that the property selected by a measure word is time dependent. Note the weight differs before and after cooking in (5), even though the weights belong to the same piece of meat. Hence, the measure words pick up a perdurant property of the object, unlike sortal classifier. This is one of the reasons why sortal classifiers have selectional restrictions (as they refer explicitly to a particular group of endurant entities); but measure words cannot (as the property they refer to is not a constant property of an entity). Huang (2015) hence argue that the sortal classifier vs. measure word dichotomy in Chinese classifier system is the grammaticalization of the endurant/perdurant ontological contrast.

The presence of 的 *de0* in (5) also underlines a well-known but never explained generalization that insertion of 的 *de0* (DE-insertion) is allowed after measure words but not after sortal classifiers.

3.3 Linguistic expression of ontological notions

Huang (2015) observes that although the fact that DE-insertion is not allowed after sortal classifiers suggests that its presence is linked to non-endurant properties, there are some exceptions.

(6) a. (一)大張(的)紙 yi1_da4_zhang1_de_zhi3
'a sheet of big paper'
b. (一)小張(的)紙 yi_xiao3_zhang1_de_zhi3
'a sheet of small paper'
c. 一張大紙 yi1_da4_zhang1_de_zhi3
'a sheet of big paper'
b. 一張小紙 yi_xiao3_zhang1_de_zhi3
'a sheet of small paper'

What (6)a-d show very crucially is that DE-insertion is allowed only with the rare cases when a sortal classifier is internally modified. Since such internal modification assigning specific physical properties to the sortal classifier, we assume that it acquires time-dependent properties and hence allows DE-insertion. This hypothesis is supported by the fact that DE-insertion is not allowed when modification is applied to the noun and not the classifier (hence does not change the endurant property of the sortal classifier).

Last, this generalization nicely applies to Chao's (1968) observation of a minimal contrast pair of compound nouns with or without 的 *de0*.

(7) a. 白花油 *bai2hua1you2*
white_flower_oil
'Pak Fah Yeow[A brand of Chinese herbal oil]'
b. 白花的油 *bai2hua1_de_you2*
white_flower_DE_oil
'A(n) (essential) oil made from a white flower'

(7a), without 的 *de0*, refers to an endurant which does not necessarily have any relation with white flowers (白花) but is established by convention. (7b), with 的 *de0*, however, requires the 'occurring' of the white flower. Based on this, Huang (2015) concluded that

> DE-insertion is allowed only when the M selects perdurant properties and that in general, DE-insertion does not change the meaning of perdurant D-M compounds

We can further hypothesize that DE-insertion marks the shift to a SPAN (four-dimensional) ontological view, and hence underlines time-dependent properties. This is also consistent with the analysis that modifier constructions with 的 *de0* has intersective reading, as well as the fact that 的 *de0* marks relevant clauses in Chinese (e.g. Huang and Shi 2016). To account for both generalizations, the shift to SPAN ontological view marked by 的 *de0* license the meaning where the pre- and post- 的 *de0* element must be present and interpreted at the same temporal point.

3.4 Possible Answer to **Why 2**

The ontological account of 的 *de0* above offers a solution to our second puzzle. Being a patient in a hospital is time-dependent (i.e. perdurant) property. That is, we do not expect being sick to be an inherent property of a person, unlike the other properties quoted above (e.g. being a chef, student, or teacher). Hence the presence of 的 *de0* is strongly preferred to mark the perdurant property of a patient in the hospital as in 醫院*的*病人. Without 的 *de0*, 醫院病人 is not ungrammatical yet creates semantic dissonance.

(8) a. 小學老師 *xiao3xue2 lao3shi1*
'elementary school teacher'
b.小明媽媽 *xiao3ming2 ma1ma1*
'XiaoMing's Mom'
c.小明老師 *xiao3ming2 lao3shi1*
'Teacher XiaoMing'
d.小明的老師 *xiao3ming2 de0 lao3shi1*
'XiaoMing's teacher'

In fact the perdrant/endurant contrast nicely predict the distribution and interpretation of NN's with(out) 的 *de0*, as shown above. The interpretation of (8c) and (8d) is the most crucial example fact. For NN without 的 *de0* both occupational (8a) and possessive (8b) readings are acceptable, both endurant. However, in contrast with (8b), the relations between XiaoMing and his teacher cannot be expressed without 的 *de0*, as it is a perdurant relation dependent on specific tempo-spatial constraints. The only endurant interpretation available for (8c) without 的 *de0* is an appositional one, where XiaoMing is the name of the teacher.

4. Ontological Basis of Language Variations

Given the fact that the endurant/perdurant time-dependency contrast is linguistically encoded and allow us to resolve two of the linguistic puzzles posed, I will explore the possibility of its contribution to language variations as a step toward solution of the meta-linguistic puzzle 3.

4.1 Incorporation: Chinese VR and VO compounds

The emergence of VR Compounds in Chinese (cf. Liu 2002) during the Northern and Southern Dynasties (CE 420-589) is one of the major grammatical changes in the history of Chinese language. In this process, phrasal 'verb + complement' units become incorporated VR compounds and gradually acquire ability to take direct object over time, but at different pace for different verbs.

Interestingly, we now see a similar process in action with the emergence of VO compounds in Mandarin Chinese for both in Mainland China and Taiwan (Jiang and Huang 2016). In this process, phrasal 'verb + object' units become incorporated VO compounds and gradually acquire ability to take direct object over time. However, intriguingly, this process is happening at different paces for different verbs and for different Chinese varieties. In general, the VO incorporation process seems to be faster in Taiwan Mandarin then Mainland Mandarin.

Verb-noun incorporation is an important linguistic topic from both synchronic and diachronic perspectives and has been extensively studied. Mithun (1984), for instance, describes incorporation as coalescence of nouns and verbs. She later (Mithun1986) claims that incorporation involves reduction of noun classes and incorporated nouns, like nouns in other compounds, do no refer but qualify or narrow the scope of the host verb. And Jacques (2012) claims that denominalization leads to incorporation

Re-interpreting the positions laid out by both Mithun and Jacques, we can assume that in incorporation, there is a conceptual shift of the R/O unit in terms of losing endurant meaning. That is, they lose the ability to refer independent of time and now becomes part of a time-dependent 'occurring' to the extent of allowing the new perdurant entity to predicate a new class of endurant arguments.

Based on the above generalizations, we envision the conceptual motivation of VO incorporation as follows. O gradually loses its time-independent properties and become more dependent on V because of their highly collocating occurrence to the extent that:

-O is no longer an endurant and hence cannot stand by itself and the V-O sequence losing one dimension of its event structure (still SPAN, but lost the ability to represent a dependent participants)

-Increasing Transitivity: As VO becomes fully incorporate ands strongly perdurant (as a new predicate), it evolves to differentiate itself from the event structure (ontological representation) of the original V by acquiring the ability to add another dimension i.e. ability to take another argument or a participants as a new dimension in the ontology).

It is important to note that this account motivates the decrease in transitivity, a common phenomenon in grammaticalization, as the switch from endurant to perdurant of a participant (and its merge with an extisitng perdurant V), a simple binary conceptual switch. This way, we can also view the variations of whether the incorporated verbs (VO) can take argument or not as ontologically motivated in terms of whether to add another dimension or not to the newly formed event structure. We can even speculate that the reason why Taiwan Mandarin incorporated VO is more likely to take additional object because its being conservative and has the tendency of maintaining the original transitivity or dimensions of event structure (Jiang and Huang 2016).

The emergence of the VR compound can in fact be described similarly as R typically is the property of an endurant object/theme. Hence the incorporation of R also reduces an endurant.

4.2 Case and Infection Loss in Middle English

Another well-known and well-studied case of historical change is the loss of case and inflection in Middle English. Note that both case (agreement) and inflection are in fact dependent on the concept of time. Inflection marks time directly, while case agreement allows an endurant to be linked to a perdurant and be associated with time dependency. Hence the loss of inflection and case simplifies the grammatical representation of ontological information by reducing the time dependent dimensions. I.e. it reduces the associated perdurant properties on an endurant entity.

4.3 Variations in Light Verb Selection in World Chineses

In a series of studies based on comparable corpora from Mainland China and Taiwan, Huang et al. (2014) and Jiang et al. (2015, 2016) showed that that the light verb 進行 *jing4xing2* 'to proceed' and some similar light verbs have different constraints on taking eventive nominals objects.

(9)a 進行研究 jing4xing2 yan2jiu4
'to carry on research'

b.進行 議案/議程 *jing4xing2 yi4an4/yi4cheng2*
'to carry on (in a meeting) discussion items/agenda'

In general, when such variations occur, light verbs in the Mainland Mandarin variant take only deverbal nouns, but NOT event nouns. That is (9a) will be used but (9b) not accepted. In Taiwan Mandarin, however, both (9a) and (9b) are commonly used and accepted.

In this context, our basic assumption is that as light verbs lack eventive content, it needs to take an object with eventive information. In the ontological view, this means that verbs represents four or higher dimension SPAN ontology but light verbs misses some essential dimension (esp. in terms of participants). Recall Chierchia's (1984) account of deverbal nouns as turning events into a referring entity but allowing the eventive information of argument structure to be preserved. In other words, a deverbal noun loses the dimension of time but retains the dimensions of participants. Hence, in terms of eventive or ontological information, light verbs and deverbal nouns complement each other. Non-derived event nouns, however, are *bona fide* nouns and should be endurants and time-independent by default. Note that the above discussion of light verb + deverbal noun combination assumes that they are both perdurant but with missing dimension(s) in SPAN ontological representation and hence can be unified to fill in the missing information. Hence a possible account of this variation is that these two variants differ in whether to allow the non-derived event noun to be viewed as perdurants and provide the kind of time-dependent participant information to complement that of the light verbs. And in this particular case, the Taiwan variant allows the non-derived noun to provide perdurant information while the Mainland variant does not. Note that this analysis is compatible with the VO variations that we discussed earlier, as one possible account (e.g. Huang 1990) of the VO's ability to take additional participants is in fact that O is encoded with eventive participant role information.

4.4 Emergence of Classifiers in Chinese

It is well known that Num+Measure Phrases occur after head nouns in Old Chinese and that they moved to pre-nominal position to develop the current classifier system in Mandarin Chinese. However, what motivated such change if their functions are similar in enumerating the noun?

(10) 陳文子有**馬十乘** (Confucius Analects 論語)

'Chen Wenzi used to have 40 horses (=horses enough to drive 10 quadriga).'...[He abandoned them to emigrate from a deteriorating staete.]

(11) 昔者吾先君中行穆子**皮車十乘**，不憂其薄也，憂德義之不足也。今主君有**革車百乘**，不憂德義之薄也，唯患車之不足也。(XinXu 新序)

'Our deceased king ...owned 10 quadriga (chariots)...; Now my lord owns 100 quadriga (chariots)..'

What has been generally observed is that in Old Chinese, there were fewer Measure words, they occur less often, and are less versatile in collocation. This is in contrast with the modern classifier system, which is pretty much required in a noun phrase, occurs frequently and typically can select multiples nouns. Careful reading of the two examples (10) and (11) involving the Measure word 乘 *cheng2* 'quadriga, chariot paired with four horses' and similar post-nominal measure words gives us good hints. One characteristic that jumped out in these examples is that all three instances of Num+Measure are describing a particular time-dependent event of ownership. And this seems to be true of most of the attested Old Chinese examples of post nominal Num+Measure phrases. Note also that 乘 *cheng2* can only measure either chariots or horses, not other nouns. The reason is self-evident as this is exactly what 乘 *cheng2* means and dependent on the actual event of pairing a chariot with four horses. In other words, this measuring is event-dependent, hence can only measure the two participants of the event. This particular usage is therefore conceptually perdurants, referring to a specific SPAN ontology where an event is measured. It does NOT select any other endurants that is not involved in the event and is different from the modern classifier system.

Based on the above analysis and on what we know about the Mandarin classifier system, we can speculate that the move of the Num+Measure from post-nominal to pre-nominal position is motivated by its functional shift from perdurant to endurant. That is, from measuring a specific time/event dependent relation to representing an endurant property shared by a class nouns. It is this differentiation of function that allows new pre-nominal position to emerge and eventually making the less grammaticalized post-verbal usage less favorable. Such account is in fact consistent with the residual use of post-nominal measure phrases in time-specific counting situation and with the existence of transitional period when both pre- and post- nominal measure phrases were used.

4.5 *-er*/-ee Asymmetry in English

The last set of variations I will look at is the lexical gaps in the participant nominalization in English involving suffixes *-er or -ee*. It is well known that there are gaps in terms of the nominalization of agent/patient applying this pair of suffixes. However, they were simply assumed to be lexical idiosyncrasies and do not require explanation in previous studies. In general, the *-er* normalization is more frequently attested but there are some exceptions:

(12) Agent Gaps

a. *Awarder/Awardee

b. *Granter/Grantee

(13) Patient Gaps

a. Presenter/*Presentee
b. Hijacker/ *hijackee
c. Robber/*Robbee
d. Preacher/*Preachee
e. Famer/*Farmee
f. Eater/*Eatee
g. Caretaker/*Caretakee

Of course there are many additional historical and morpho-phonological reasons for some gaps. However, a generalization emerges after examining a range of data, including additional examples that strongly prefer *-er* affix and not listed here. That is, with either *-er* or *-ee*, the attested nominalized forms have endurant interpretations. For instance, an awardee is a time-independent meaning, regardless of when s/he got the award, is always the awardee (of the prize/award). The person who presented the award, however, has the property of presenting the award only on that particular occasion. Hence the property of giving an award is perdurant. This also explains why there are many more words with *-er* affixes than *-ee* affixes. It is typically much easier to derive the enduring property of doing X when the participant is the actor/agent. E.g. it is much easier to conceptualize someone involving and engaging in the act of hijacking having that as an enduring property but very difficult to conceptualizing a person with the time-independent inherent property of being hijacked. In short, since the participant nominalization involving the conceptual manipulation of individualization, the identified individual must be endurant. Hence, for a participant nominalization to occur, the participant's involvement in an event can be able to be viewed as enduring. This conceptual necessity nicely accounts for the gaps and asymmetries in *-er/-ee* nominalization.

5. Conclusion

In this paper, I started with exploration of the nature of three linguistic puzzles and went through arguments for the necessity to present and preserve the endurant/perdurant dichotomy in language. I further demonstrated how the dichotomy is grammaticalized in the Chinese language. Lastly, I try to account for a few phenomena in language variations with the endurant/perdurant dichotomy. There is now one last meta-linguistic puzzle to be resolved in this conclusion. That is, what does +N/Nouny or +V/Verby represents?

It should be clear from the data and account presented above that I will propose that the +N feature stands for endurant properties, and the +V feature stands for perdurant properties. In other words, being nouny is referring to the time-independent properties of the linguistic element and being verby is referring to the time dependent properties of a linguistic element. And in fact, as mentioned, being endurant/perdurant does not necessary refer to the actual physical properties of the entity but could also refer to the (linguistic) perspectives of how we view the entities.

Hence, we use our fundamental conceptual bifurcation of time-dependency to conventionalize linguistic categories (i.e. using the N and V features to defined the PoS's). However, once the linguistics categories are conventionalized, we can then change our perspectives on the relevance of time-dependency for any linguistic element. The goal of this paper is to suggest that this simple change of perspective can be viewed as the conceptual motivation of a wide range of language variations in terms of lexical derivation, categorical changes, incorporation/transitivity, grammaticalization, and even variations among different variants. Although the accounts presented here is sketchy and somewhat speculative in a few cases, I hope our work will encourage more future work on the conceptual motivation for language changes and variations. I believe such ontology-driven accounts have the potential of unearthing the underlining mechanisms of linguistic variations and provide a more coherent and predictive account of language changes and variations in the future.

Acknowledgments

An earlier partial version of this paper was present at the 4th VariAMU workshop at PolyU and as part of a talk at National Taiwan University. I would like to thank the audience, especially colleagues from LPL-CNRS, Hong Kong PolyU, and NTU for their helpful comments. I would like to thank the support of PolyU-PKU Joint Research Centre on Chinese Linguistics, as well as the Kyunghee University organizers of the 30th PALCIC for their support for research on and presentation of this paper. Any remaining errors are, of course, mine.

Figure I: DOLCE Upper Ontology: Entities

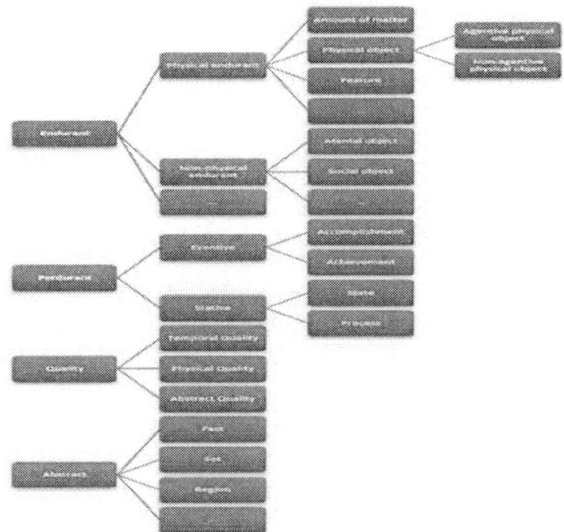

Figure 2: Basic Formal Ontology (BFO) Upper Ontology

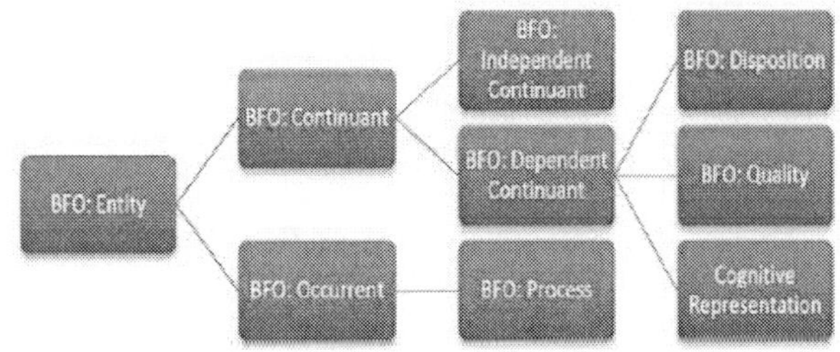

Figure 3: Chinese Classifier System (Ahrens and Huang 2016)

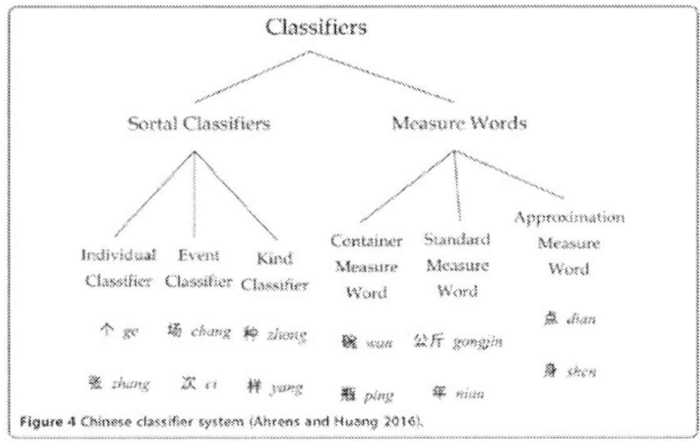

Figure 4 Chinese classifier system (Ahrens and Huang 2016).

References

Ahrens, K. and C.-R. Huang. 2016. Classifiers. In Huang and Shi (2016). Pp. xxx-yyy. Cambridge University Press

Aikhenvald, A. Y.. 2003. Classifiers: A typology of noun categorization devices. Oxford: Oxford Univ. Press.

Aikhenvald, A. Y. 2001. Classifiers. Oxford Bibliographies in Linguistics. Oxford University Press.

Chao, Y.R. 1968. A Grammar of Spoken Chinese. Berkeley: University of California Press.

Chao, Y.R. 1955. Notes on Chinese Grammar and Logic. In Philosophy East and West, Vol. 5, No. 1, pp. 31-41.

Chierchia, G. 1984. Topics in the Syntax and Semantics of Infinitives and Gerunds. University of Massachusetts Ph.D. Dissertation.

Chou, Y.-M. and C.-R. Huang. 2010. Hantology: conceptual system discovery based on orthographic convention. In Huang et al. (Eds.), Ontology and the Lexicon: A Natural Language Processing Perspective (pp. 122-143). Cambridge: Cambridge University Press.

Gangemi, A., N. Guarino, C. Masolo, and A. Oltramari. 2003. Sweetening Ontologies with DOLCE. AI Magazine. 24.3.13-24.

Gangemi, A., N. Guarino, C. Masolo, and A. Oltramari. 2010. Interfacing WordNet with DOLCE: towards OntoWordNet. In Huang et al. (2010) pp. 36-52.

Grenon, P. and B. Smith. 2004 SNAP and SPAN: Toward Dynamic Spatial Ontology. Spatial Cognition and Computation. 4.1.69-103.

Gruber, T. 1995. Toward Principles for the Design of Ontologies Used for Knowledge Sharing. *International Journal of Human-Computer Studies*. 43 (5-6). 907–928.

Guarino, N. 1998. Some Ontological Principles for Designing Upper-Level Lexical Resources. In Proceedings of the First International Conference on Language Resources and Evaluation, 527–534.

Guarino, N., and C. Welty. 2002. Evaluating Ontological Decisions with ONTOCLEAN. Communications of the ACM 45(2): 61–65.

Her, O.-S., and C.-T. Hsieh. 2010. On the Semantic Distinction between Classifiers and Measure Words in Chinese. Language and Linguistics. Vol. 11, No. 3, pp. 527-551.

Huang, C.-R. and D. Shi. 2016. A Reference Grammar of Chinese. Cambridge University Press.

Huang, C.-R, and S.-K. Hsieh. 2015. Chinese lexical semantics: from radicals to event structure. In William S.-Y. Wang and Chao-Fen Sun (Eds.), The Oxford Handbook of Chinese Linguistics (pp. 290-305).New York: Oxford University Press.

Huang, C.-R. 2015. Notes on Chinese grammar and ontology: the endurant/perdurant dichotomy and Mandarin D-M compounds. *Lingua Sinica*. *1*(1). http://link.springer.com/article/10.1186/s40655-015-0004-6

Huang, C.-R., J. Lin, H. Xu, and M. Jiang. 2014. Corpus-based Study and Identification of Mandarin Chinese Light Verb Variations. The Workshop on Applying NLP Tools to Similar Languages, Variations, and Dialects (VarDial), at the 25th International Conference on Computational Linguistics. Dublin, Ireland. 23 August.

Huang, C.-R,黄居仁。2013. 關於「的」的功能一致性研究。沈陽（主編），《走向當代前沿科學的現代漢語語法研究》，北京：商務印書館，頁 129-135。

Huang, C-.R. et al. 2010. Ontology and the Lexicon. Cambridge University Press.

Huang, C.-R., and K. Ahrens. 2003. Individuals, kinds and events: classifier coercion of nouns. In: Language Sciences. Vol. 25, No. 4, pp. 353-373.

Huang, C.-R. 1990. A unification-based LFG analysis of lexical discontinuity. *Linguistics*. *28*(2). 263-307.

Jacques, G. 2012. From Denominal Derivation to Incorporation. Lingua. 122.1207-1231.

Jiang, M., and C.-R. Huang. 2016. Constructional Correspondences of Transitivity of Mandarin VO Compounds: A corpus-based study. Paper presented at the 24rd annual conference of the International Association of Chinese Linguistics (IACL). 17 August. Beijing Language and Culture University, Beijing, China.

Jiang, M., D. Shi and C.-R. Huang. 2016. Transitivity in Light Verb Variations in Mandarin Chinese -- A Comparable Corpus-based Statistical Approach. To be presented at the 30th Pacific Asia Conference on Language Information and Computation (PACLIC). 28-30 Octobber, Kyunhee University. Seoul, Korea.

Jiang, M., J. Lin, and C.-R. Huang. 2015. *A comparable corpus-based study of VO compound variations between Mainland and Taiwan Mandarin. Presented at* the 23rd annual conference of the International Association of Chinese Linguistics (IACL). 26-28 August. Hanyang University, Seoul, Korea.

Li, C. N., S. A. Thompson. 1981. Mandarin Chinese: A Functional Reference Grammar.

Liu, C. 劉承慧. 2002. 漢語動補結構歷史發展. 台北：翰盧圖書出版有限公司.

Mithun, M. 1986. On the Nature of Noun Incorporation. Language. 62.1-32-37.

Mithun, M. 1984. The Evolution of Noun Incorporation. Language. 60.4.847.894.

Niles, I. and A. Pease. 2001. Towards a Standard Upper Ontology. Proceedings of the international conference on Formal Ontology in Information Systems. Pp. 2-9.

Smith, B., 2012. On classifying material entities in Basic Formal Ontology. *Interdisciplinary Ontology. Proceedings of the Third Interdisciplinary Ontology Meeting*. Keio University Press 1-13

Smith, B. and P. Grenon. 2004. The Cornucopia of Formal-Ontological Relations. Dialectica, 58.3.279-296.

Tai, J.H-Y. 1994. Chinese classifier systems and human categorization. In In Honor of William S-Y. Wang: Interdisciplinary Studies on Language and Language Change. Edited by Matthew Y. Chen and Ovid J.L. Tzeng. Taipei: Pyramid Press. pp. 479-494.

The syntax of the Chinese excessive resultative construction

LIU Hongyong
hongyongliu@umac.mo
University of Macau

This paper offers an affectedness-based analysis of the Chinese excessive resultative construction, which typically describes events of affectedness consisting of two participants, a theme participant and a scale participant measuring the degree of affectedness. In such an event, the theme participant is created or affected according to a beforehand prescribed value (e1) on a scale, while the process of the event results in an actual value (e2) on the same scale. The realized value may or may not be identical to the prescribed value. When the two values do not coincide (e2>e1), the 'more than expected' excessive resultative interpretation arises. This analysis crucially hinges upon the assumption that there is a covert comparison between two values on the same scale. If such a comparison cannot be established within a resultative construction, the excessive meaning will not arise.
Keywords: affectedness, resultative, excessive, comparison

1. Introduction

Back in 1990, Lu (1990) observed that there is a special type of resultative construction in Mandarin Chinese, which is different from other types of Chinese resultatives in both form and meaning. The following illustrative examples are given in Lu (1990).

(1) a.	qiang	qi	ai	le.
	wall	build	low	PFT
	'The wall was built lower than expected.			
b.	zhaopian	fang	xiao	le.
	photo	enlarge	small	PFT
	'The photo was enlarged less than expected.			

They are special in three ways. First, the subject must be the patient of the verb, and the predicate is invariantly in the form of a bare verb plus a bare adjective. Secondly, the sentence final perfective aspect marker *le* is obligatory. Thirdly, all the examples in (1) have a "more than expected" excessive meaning.

We will offer an affectedness-based analysis of the Chinese excessive resultative construction, trying to answer the following questions:

(2) a. How does the 'more than expected' reading arise?
b. Why do some excessive resultatives also have a normal resultative reading?
c. Why is the *bi*-phrase ('than expected') not able to show up?
d. Why is the sentence final *le* obligatory?

2. An affectedness-based analysis of the construction

2.1 Beavers' (2011) theory of affectedness

Beavers (2011) proposed that change is an inherently relational concept involving both a theme participant that undergoes the change and a scale participant defining the process of the change over time (following Kennedy and Levin 2008). According to this scalar model of change, all types of change can be defined as a transition of a theme along a scale that defines the change. Beavers (2011) defined an operator *result'* to capture this notion of affectedness:

(3) For all dynamic predicates $ø$, themes x, events e, states g, and scales s:
$[[ø\ (x,s,e) \wedge result'\ (x,s,g,e)] \longleftrightarrow [ø\ (x,s,e) \wedge SOURCE\ (x,b_c,e) \wedge GOAL\ (x,g,e)]]$
(This says for event e described by $ø$, g is the target state of theme x on scale s iff x transitions to g by the end of e from a contextually determined state b_c at the beginning of e.) (Beavers 2011: 351)

Beavers then showed that this scalar model of change can offer a unified analysis of different types of affectedness such as motion, change-of-state, and creation/consumption:

(4) John wiped the table clean. (scale of cleanliness of the table)

$\exists e \exists s[wipe'($**john**$, s,$ **table**$, e) \wedge result'\ ($**table**$,s,$**clean**$,e)]$

- *wipe'*(**john**, *s*, **table**, *e*) says that this is a wiping event of the table by John along a scale of cleanliness;
- *result'* (**table**,*s*,**clean**,*e*) says that the table transitions from some initial point of cleanliness to some subsequent degree clean on *s*.

(Beavers 2011: 351)

The most apparent advantage of this scalar model of change is that it manages to account for the double telicity effect. The following examples are given in Beavers (2011: 349) to show that the theme and the scale participants jointly determine the telicity of the sentence:

(5) a. Bill dimmed the lights half dim in/?for five minutes.
b. Bill dimmed lights half dim for/??in five minutes.
c. Bill dimmed the lights dimmer and dimmer for/??in five minutes.

The theme and the scale participants in (5a) are both specific, so the sentence is telic; in (5b) the scale participant is specific, but the theme is not, so the sentence is atelic; in (5c) the theme is specific, but the scale participant is vague, so the sentence is atelic.

2.2 The meaning of the Chinese excessive resultative construction

Adopting Beavers' (2011) scalar model of affectedness, we can analyze the semantics of the Chinese excessive resultative construction as follows:

(6)	maoyi	zhi	da	le.
	sweater	knit	large	PFT

'The sweater was knitted larger than expected.'

$\exists e \exists s\ [knit'($**sweater**$, s, e) \wedge result'\ ($**sweater**$,s,$**more-than-expected**$,e)]$

- *knit'*(**sweater**, *s*, *e*) says that there is a knitting event of the sweater along a scale of size;
- *result'* (**sweater**,*s*,**more-than-expected**,*e*) says that the sweater's actual size on the scale exceeds an expected size.

There are two end points in the event described in (6). The first end point is the completion of the sweat knitting, and the second end point is the actual size of the sweater surpassing the expected size. The first end point is related to the theme participant, and the second point is related to the scale participant.

We have also noticed that the Chinese excessive resultative construction exemplifies a very special type of events of affectedness. First, the two values compared are not the initial

(SOURCE) state and the final (GOAL) state. Rather, what is compared is the final state and an expected or desired state. This can be best illustrated by the following ambiguous sentence.

(7) shengzi jian duan le.
rope cut short PFT
a. 'The rope was cut short.'
b. 'The rope was cut shorter than expected.'

There are two readings with (7). Relevant to the two readings are three values of the length of the rope: (i) the initial length of the rope before the cutting event; (ii) the final length of the rope after the cutting event; (iii) the desired length of the rope set by the agent before the cutting event. This example shows that what count in the excessive resultative construction are the final state and the expected state.

With these differences in mind, we are now able to summarize the complex event described by the excessive resultatives as follows:

(8) A theme participant, serving as the grammatical subject, was affected by a covert (not phonetically realized) agent to such an extent that the degree associated with the final result has surpassed an expected degree which is set by the agent before the onset of the action. The dimension of the comparison and its direction are determined by the action denoted by the verb.

The description in (8) informs us of several significant points about the construction:

(9) a. First, the subject of the construction must be a theme, which differentiates the excessive resultatives from other types of resultatives such as the passives and the BA-construction.
b. Secondly, an expected value about the final state of the theme must have been set before the action.
c. Thirdly, the prescribed value will be compared with the actual value associated with the final state of the affected theme at the end of the action. The resultative clause is in fact a comparative construction, although there is no degree morphology found in the construction.
d. Fourthly, the initial state of the theme is irrelevant in this construction.

3. The reason for the potential ambiguity

With this in mind, we can come back to example (7) and explore why it is ambiguous. Take the following as another example:

(10) toufa jian duan le.
hair cut short PFT
a. Her hair was cut short.
b. Her hair was cut shorter.
c. Her hair was cut shorter than expected.

This sentence could be uttered in the following two contexts:

(11) a. Mary's hair was originally 150 centimeters long. She wanted her hair to be 100 centimeters long. She went to a barber's shop and had a haircut. After the haircut, her hair became 20 centimeters long.

b. Mary's hair was originally 150 centimeters long. She wanted her hair to be 100 centimeters long. She went to a barber's shop and had a haircut. After the haircut, her hair became 120 centimeters long.

Example (10) can be uttered to describe either of the two scenarios, but (10) is ambiguous in three different ways. In the two scenarios, the truth value of (10) totally depends on which interpretation in intended. To determine the truth value of (10), we need to pay attention to four degrees: $d_{initial}$; d_{final}; d_{ideal}; d_c.

(12) a. $d_{initial}$: Mary's original hair length (150cm)
b. d_{final}: May's final hair length (20cm in Scenario I/120cm in Scenario II)
c. d_{ideal}: May's intended hair length (100cm)
d. d_c: the hair length which is considered short by the general public (30cm)

Interpretations	Scenario I	Scenario II
a. $d_{final} < d_c$	T (20cm < 30cm)	F (120cm $\nless$ 30cm)
b. $d_{final} < d_{initial}$	T (20cm < 150cm)	T (120cm < 150cm)
c. $d_{final} < d_{ideal}$	T (20cm < 100cm)	F (120cm $\nless$ 100cm)

For interpretation (a), the adjective *short* refers to the property of the final state of the hair. Unless the final length of the hair is really considered to be short by the general public, (11) cannot be true. For example, In Scenario II, although the final length of Mary's hair is less than the original length, but the hair of the 120cm length is still far from short hair, according to the general assumption about short hair. Therefore, (11) cannot be true for Scenario II under the interpretation of (11a). For interpretation (b), (11) would sound most natural if a differential phrase such as *yidian* 'a little', *xuduo* 'much' , *bushao* 'too much' is added at the sentence final position. For interpretation (c), as long as the final length of the hair is less than the expected length, (11) will be true. In Scenario II, 120cm is more than 100cm; therefore (17) is false under this reading. The correct way to describe this situation is (13).

(13) toufa jian chang le.
hair cut long PFT
*a. Her hair was cut long.
*b. Her hair was cut longer.
c. Her hair was cut to an extent which is longer than expected.

Different from (11), example (13) has only one meaning, that is the excessive resultative interpretation. The reason for the lack of ambiguity in (13) is transparent. First, the cutting event will not lead to the result that the hair becomes long, so interpretation (a) is not available. Secondly, the hair cutting event determines the dimension of comparison (LENGTH) and its direction (SHORTNESS). Therefore, interpretation (b) is also not available. The only interpretation associated with *jian chang le* is the excessive resultative interpretation.

The 'more than expected" reading can be further highlighted by the use of the optional differential phrase. For example,

(14) a. maoyi zhi chang le san limi.
sweater knit long PFT three centimeter
'The sweater was knitted three centimeters longer than expected.'
b. maoyi xi chang le san limi.
sweater wash long PFT three centimeter
'The sweater was three centimeters longer than it had been after washing.'

The meaning of (21a) is that the actual final length of the sweater is three centimeters longer than the intended length set before the knitting event. Since the verb *zhi* 'knit' is a verb of creation. It does not make sense to talk about the original length of the sweater. This example is different from the hair cutting example. If we change the verb of creation *zhi* 'knit' to the verb of affection such as *xi* 'wash', then we will have the 'longer than the original length" reading rather than the "longer than expected" reading. This is due to the fact that before the washing event it is unusual for the agent to set an intended length of the sweater as the result of the washing event, so the "more than expected" reading is absent from (21b). The only standard of comparison to anchor the differential phrase *san limi* 'three centimeters' is the original length of the sweater.

The two examples in (21) give us a hint of what verbs can occur in the excessive resultative construction. Only those verbs which denote actions that can lead to an intended degree on a scale are able to occur in the excessive resultatives. The most typical, as Shen and Peng (2010) observed, is verbs of creation. Before creating something, the agent at least should have a plan in mind about the final state of the theme. Apart from verbs of creation, some ordinary affected verbs can also occur in the excessive resultatives. For example,

(15) a. zhuozi tai gao le.
table raise high PFT
'The table was raised higher than expected.'
b. denglong gua ai le.
lantern hang low PFT
'The lantern was hung lower than expected.'

4. The obligatory use of the sentence final perfective aspect marker

We have proposed that the sentence final *le* in the excessive resultative construction is a perfective aspect marker. In this section, we are going to defend this proposal from three aspects: the negative imperative sentence, the exclamatory sentence, and the availability of differential measure phrases.

Lu (2003: 182) pointed that there are two types of negative imperative sentences in Mandarin, differentiated by the verb class. For example,

(16) a. bie he!
don't drink
'Don't drink!'
b. [bie he] le!
don't drink SFP
'Don't drink any more!'
*c. bie bing!
don't get.sick
d. bie [bing le]!
don't sick PFT
'Don't get sick!'

The verb *he* 'drink' is a verb associated with an agent who can control the action of drinking, but the verb *bing* 'get sick' is a verb associated with an agent who cannot control the action leading to the result of getting sick.

- This difference reflects in the different behaviors of (16a) and (16c).
- By uttering (16a), the speaker can order the listener not to drink the liquid in sight, but nobody can be ordered not to get sick; therefore, (16c) is ungrammatical. However, (16c) will be saved if the sentence final *le* is added, as in (16d).
- By uttering (16b), the speaker can order the listener not to drink the liquid any more. The sentence final *le* indicates a change-of-state from the drinking state to the non-drinking state. The purpose of (16b) is to stop the continuation of the state of drinking.
- In contrast, (16d) aims at reminding the listener not to run into the undesirable state of getting sick.
- It is clear that what is negated in (16d) is the imagined state *bing le* 'getting sick'. This does not apply to (16b), since *he le* 'having drunk' could not be the imagined state being negated. This is the reason why we choose to treat *le* as SFP in (16b), but PFT in (16d).

Looking back at the Chinese excessive resultative construction, we found that it follows the pattern of the verb *bing* 'get sick'. For example,

(17) a. *maoyi bie zhi da.
sweater don't knit large
Intended meaning: 'Don't get the sweater knitted larger than expected.'
b. maoyi bie zhi da le.
sweater don't knit large PFT
'Don't get the sweater knitted larger than expected.'

Similar to example (16d), (17b) aims at reminding the listener not to run into the undesirable state of getting the sweater larger than expected.

If we compare the negative imperative sentence with the declarative sentence, we can see more clearly that the sentence final *le* is a perfective aspect marker, which marks the completion of the surpassing event. In the declarative sentence *maoyi zhi da le*, definitely the action of knitting the sweater is completed, and the actual size turns out to be larger than expected. But in (17b), the completion of the knitting event is irrelevant, since the sentence can be uttered before or in the knitting process. In this case, the sentence final *le* scopes only over the surpassing event, but not over the knitting event.

We also find that the sentence final *le* in the excessive resultative construction shares similarities with the *le* in exclamatory sentences in the form of "NP+tai+A+le!" For example,

(18) a. wan tai da!
bowl too big
'The bowl is too big.'
b. wan tai da le!
bowl too big PFT
'The bowl is too much bigger than expected.'

Without the sentence final *le*, (18a) is a simple exclamatory sentence with a positive adjective *da* 'big'. In contrast, the sentence final *le* turns (18b) into a comparative sentence, comparing the actual size of the bowl and a much smaller size expected before the speaker seeing the bowl in sight.

5. The syntactic derivation of the excessive resultative construction

Although the linear sequence of the excessive resultative construction is quite simple (in the form of NP+V+A+*le*), its syntax is quite complicated. We can use the following example to illustrate our syntactic analysis of the excessive resultative construction.

(19) denglong gua gao le.
lantern hang high PFT
'The lantern was hung higher than expected.'

The verb *gua* 'hang' is a two-place predicate. In the excessive resultatives, the transitive verb has to undergo the ergative shift, turning the transitive verb into an unaccusative verb. The theme cannot be assigned the accusative case by the verb, so it has to move to the subject position to get the nominative case. We can diagram the syntax of (19) as follows:

The higher AspP encodes the hanging event, and the lower AspP encodes the result. SpecDegP hosts the differential measure phrase. We will temporarily assume that the standard of the comparison is a covert PP, serving as the adjunct of DegP. Now we need to think about SpecAspP, the position for the subject of the predicate *gao-le*. We would argue that SpecAspP is a PRO, controlled by the subject of the main clause, and the whole construction of (20) is a control construction. The aspect marker *le* in the resultative clause, similar to the English infinitive tense marker *to*, does not have the case assigning ability. This suggests that the perfective aspect marker *le* should be further divided into two types: the perfective aspect marker le_1 occurring in the matrix clause has the ability to assign the nominative case, and the perfective aspect marker le_2 occurring in the embedded clause cannot assign case.

(20)

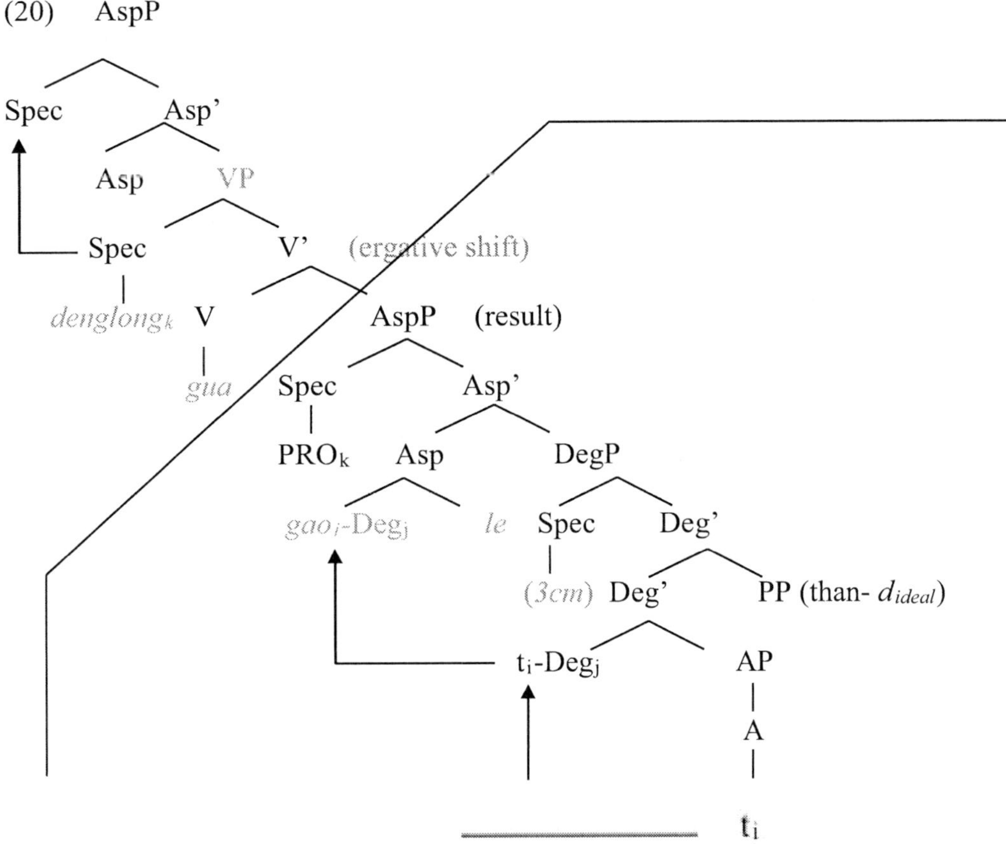

It remains a puzzle why the *than*-phrase in (20) cannot show up. We have observed that the than-phrase *bi wo qiwangde* can occur within the *de*-resultative clause. For example, in (21a), the *than*-phrase occurs after the resultative marker, but without this resultative marker, the than-phrase cannot occur, as in (21b).

(21) a. toufa jian de bi wo qiwangde duan le liang limi.
hair than RES than 1sg expect short PFT 2cm
'My hair was cut two centimeters shorter than expected.'
b. *toufa jian bi wo qiwangde duan le liang limi.
hair than than 1sg expect short PFT 2cm
Intended meaning 'My hair was cut two centimeters shorter than expected.'

According to Gu & Guo (2015), *toufa* forms a comitative construction with *bi wo qiwangde*, and the comitative construction serves as the subject of the comparative construction. (21a) shows that *toufa* can be fronted and serves as the subject of the matrix clause. The movement can only be accounted for by taking *jiande* as a raising verb. The verb *jian* is originally a transitive verb, but with the resultative suffix *de*, it becomes a raising verb, taking a clause as its complement, similar to the syntactic behavior of the typical English raising verb *seem*. The raising is triggered by case, because the perfective aspect *le* in the embedded clause is argued to lack the case assigning ability, *toufa* has to be raised to the subject position of the matrix clause to get the nominative case. The nominalized phrase *wo qiwangde* gets the accusative case from the preposition *bi*. As argued in Gu & Guo (2015), the subject of the comparative construction is a comitative phrase. Since the perfective aspect marker does not have the case assigning ability, the comitative phrase cannot be case-marked; therefore, it has to be empty.

6. Conclusion

This paper offers an affectedness-based analysis of the Chinese excessive resultative construction. Such a construction typically describes events of affectedness consisting of two participants, a theme participant and a scale participant measuring the degree of affectedness. The sentence final perfective aspect marker *le* in this construction is to encode the completion of the action of an implicit comparison. This paper looks at comparative constructions being used as embedded resultatives. The analysis offered in this paper might not only expand our current understanding of the operations involved in the syntactic computation of Chinese comparative constructions, but also shed some new light on how different languages encode the comparative meaning in embedded resultative clauses.

References

Beavers, John. 2011. On Affectedness. *Natural Language and Linguistic Theory* 29: 335-370.

Gu, Yang, and Guo Jie. 2015. On the internal structure of comparative constructions: From Chinese and Japanese to English. In *Chinese Syntax in a Cross-linguistic perspective*. eds. A.Li, A. Simpson & D. Tsai, 334-374. Oxford: OUP.

Kennedy, Christopher, and Beth Levin. 2008. Measure of change: The adjectival core of degree achievements. In *Adjectives and adverbs: Syntax, semantics, and discourse*, eds. Louise McNally and Chris Kennedy, 156–182. Oxford: Oxford University Press.

Lu, Jianming. 1990. 'VA le' shubu jiegou yuyi fenxi [A Semantic Analysis of the Excessive Resultative 'VA le' in Chinese] *Hanyu Xuexi* [Chinese Language Learning] 1: 1-6.

The grammar and semantics of disjuncts in World Englishes

Shirley Dita
De La Salle University, Manila
shirley.dita@dlsu.edu.ph

Abstract

Adverbs have become the ragbag in grammar in which all uncategorized items are relegated. Over the years, there have been several studies (e.g., Biber et al., 1999; Halliday, 1994; Hasselgard, 2010; Huddleston & Pullum, 2002; Quirk et al., 1985; Sinclair, 1990) that looked into the syntactic and semantic functions of adverbs. This paper focuses on what Quirk et al. (1985) call 'disjuncts' (which refer to the overt expression of an author's or speaker's attitudes, feelings, judgments, or commitment concerning the message. There are various terminologies in literature that have emerged: 'stance adverbs', 'conjunctive adjuncts', 'evaluative adjuncts', 'sentence adverbs', to name a few. The common denominator of all these adverbs is that, syntactically, they occupy the most peripheral position in the clause and that, semantically, they distinguish how the propositional content of the clause relates to the context.

Using 12 matching corpora of the International Corpus of English (ICE), that is, 5 from the Inner Circle (Australia, Canada, Great Britain, Ireland, New Zealand) and 7 from the Outer Circle (East Africa, Hong Kong, India, Jamaica, Nigeria, the Philippines, and Singapore), the present study aims at presenting the findings on the frequency and distribution of disjuncts across world Englishes.

This study supports the disagreement on the labelling of disjuncts as presented in literature in terms of their functions by showing evidence of such claims. Further, it argues that there exist several semantic functions apart from what are presented in literature and that - these functions are culture-specific.

Oral Presentation Papers

A "Maximal Exclusion" Approach to Structural Uncertainty in Dynamic Syntax

Tohru Seraku
Dept. of Japanese Interpretation & Translation
Hankuk University of Foreign Studies
seraku@hufs.ac.kr

Abstract

"Case" and "grammatical function" are central to syntactic theories, but rigorous treatments of these notions in surface-oriented grammars like Dynamic Syntax (DS) are pending. Within DS, it is simply held that a case particle resolves structural uncertainty (i.e., unfixed node) in the course of incremental tree update. We model the relation between "case" and "grammatical function" with special reference to Japanese. In this language, the nominative case particle *ga* normally marks a "subject" NP, but it may mark an "object" NP. Moreover, *ga* may occur more than once within a single clause. We will address these issues by proposing the "maximal exclusion" approach to structural uncertainty.

1 Introduction

"Case" and "grammatical function" are central to any syntactic theories; a number of constructions exhibit unique case-marking patterns and linguistic generalisations are often stated with reference to grammatical function (Keenan and Comrie, 1979). Rigorous accounts of these concepts, however, are pending in "surface-oriented" grammars such as Dynamic Syntax (DS) (Kempson et al., 2001). The aim of this article is to clarify the relation between case and grammatical function in formal-grammar terms, with examples drawn from Japanese.

As will be stated in §2, the case-marking system of Japanese challenges surface-oriented grammars. In particular, DS, which explicates the mechanism whereby a string of words is parsed online and a structure is progressively built up, has not seriously tackled the relation between case and grammatical function (see §3). In this article, we advance the DS formalism from the perspective of "maximal exclusion" so that it models the relation between case and grammatical function in Japanese (see §4). We then apply this account to further data relating to "Major Subject Constructions" (see §5).

2 Case and Grammatical Function

In this article, we construe case and grammatical function in line with Comrie (1989).

Firstly, "case" is a morphological category. In Japanese, a case particle is typically attached to a noun (or a nominalised element).

(1) *Ken-ga* *ringo-o* *tabe-ta*
K-NOM apple-ACC eat-PAST
'Ken ate an apple.'

In (1), *ga* indicates that *Ken* bears a nominative case, while *o* indicates that *ringo* 'apple' bears an accusative case.

Secondly, "grammatical function" refers to a relation which an NP in a sentence has with respect to the predicate in the sentence. Examples include "subject," "object," and so on. These are abstract concepts, and they are identified based on syntactic tests in each language/dialect.

The focus of our enquiry is "subject." Keenan (1975) offers a set of universal "subject"-properties, although "subject" is captured gradably depending upon properties observed. The standard tests for subjecthood in Japanese are as follows (Kishimoto, 2004; Tsujimura, 2013; Tsunoda, 2009):

- α is a subject if it may be a target of a certain "honorification" operation.
- α is a subject if it may be an antecedent of the reflexive anaphor *jibun* 'self.'

Let us illustrate the former property with (2).

(2) *sensei-ga* *ringo-o* *otabeninat-ta*
teacher-NOM apple-ACC eat.HON-PAST
'That teacher ate an apple.'

In (2), the honorific form *otabeninat* 'eat' elevates the referent of *sensei* 'teacher.' *Sensei* is thus said to be a subject of the predicate *otabeninat*.

For some frameworks, grammatical function is a primitive concept. In Lexical-Functional Grammar, SUB, OBJ, etc. are postulated as "attributes" in the attribute-value matrices (Dalrymple, 2001). On the other hand, Dynamic Syntax (DS) dispenses with such primitive concepts; grammatical functions are defined structurally, as in the grammar models that have been developed in Chomsky (1965, 1995), etc. For instance, "subject" is structurally designated as follows: an element on the argument node which is immediately dominated by the root node is said to be a "subject" of the predicate in this structure.

(3) Schematic tree-structure

root

argument (subject) predicate

In DS, no serious attention has been paid to the issue of how case relates to grammatical function,[1] and it has been simply assumed that the nominative particle *ga* marks a subject NP (Cann, et al. 2005; Seraku, 2013). This stipulation may hold of (1)-(2), but it is unsustainable due to the following facts (Kuno, 1973; NKK, 2009; Shibatani, 1978):

- *Ga* may mark an object NP.
- *Ga* may occur several times in a single clause.
- A subject NP may be marked with *ni*, a dative particle (see §4.6).

These properties are not found in all verbs; the *ga*-marking of an object NP, for instance, is normally possible only with "stative" predicates (Koizumi, 2008; Kuno, 1973). The first two properties are illustrated in (4). (See §4-§5 for further data.)

(4) *watashi-ga* *ringo-ga* *tabe-tai* (*koto*)[2]
I-NOM apple-NOM eat-want (COMP)
'I want to eat an apple.'

This single clause has two occurrences of *ga*.[3] The second NP *ringo* 'apple' is not a subject because it lacks the "subject-properties," unlike *sensei* in (2) (Koizumi, 2008: 142-5). On the other hand, *ringo* in (4) is characterised as an object NP according to syntactic tests for objecthood (Kishimoto, 2004). Therefore, the simple correspondence between *ga* and "subject" cannot deal with data like (4), as has been a residual issue within DS.

3 Dynamic Syntax (DS)

3.1 Basics

DS models the process whereby the parser takes a string of words and gradually builds up a **semantic** structure. This mapping is direct in that syntactic structure is **not** postulated at any level. Within DS, "dynamic" refers to "online parsing," and "syntax" refers to an abstract system that maps a string onto a semantic structure in a progressive manner (Cann et al., 2005; Kempson et al., 2001, 2011).

For an illustration, the parse of the whole string (5) creates the semantic structure (6).

(5) *Ken-ga* *ne-ta*
K-NOM sleep-PAST
'Ken slept.'

(6) Final state (ignoring tense)

sleep'(Ken') : t

Ken' : e *sleep'* : e→t

Each node conveys information about (i) semantic content such as *Ken'* and (ii) semantic type such as e ("entity" type). The node decorated with *Ken'* is at a "subject" position; a subject node is a type-e daughter of the root node in a propositional tree.

[1] An exception is Nakamura et al. (2009), which will be surveyed in §5. Kiaer (2014) also handles relevant data, but the formal details of her account are not clear.

[2] Without *koto*, (4) would sound better with the topic particle *wa* in place of the first instance of *ga* due to "exhaustivity" (Kuno, 1973). Such meaning disappears in embedded clauses, and scholars thus often put *koto* at the end of sentence. For the interests of brevity, we do not follow this practice in the rest of this article.

[3] *Ga* in *ringo-ga* is interchangeable with the accusative particle *o* in (4). The interchangeability is affected by various factors such as "style" and "transitivity" (Iori, 1995; Noda, 1996: 264-5), with cross-speaker variations (Shibatani, 1978: 230-2).

A tree is binary; a left-hand node is an argument node, and a right-hand node is a functor node. For instance, the right daughter of the root in (6) is a functor node, which takes the type-e content *Ken'* and returns the type-t content *sleep'*(*Ken'*).

A tree update starts with the AXIOM (7).

(7) AXIOM

?t

At this initial stage, there is only a root node, and it is annotated with ?t. ?t is a "requirement" that this node will be decorated with a type-t content. The parser executes **general** and **lexical** actions to meet requirements until no outstanding requirements are left in the tree.

General action. General actions are tree update actions whose applications are not triggered by the parse of a lexical item. If *Ken-ga ne* in (5) is parsed, it yields the semantic tree (8).

(8) Parsing *Ken-ga ne*

?t

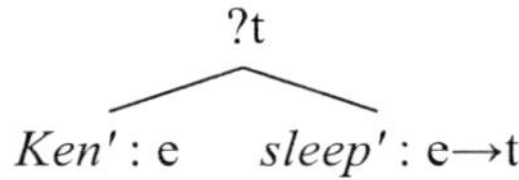

As each daughter node is specified for content and type, the parser may perform functional application. This is not lexically triggered, and it is formalised as the general action ELIMINATION. The execution of this action outputs (6). (The tense suffix *-ta* is disregarded in this article.)

Lexical action. Each lexical item encodes a set of actions for tree update. Consider (9).

(9) *ne-ta*
sleep-PAST
'Someone (or a salient person) slept.'

Japanese is a "pro-drop" language; argument NPs may be covert as long as they are retrievable in context. It is then assumed in DS that the parse of a verb projects a propositional template. For instance, *ne* 'sleep' encodes a set of actions to project the propositional template (10).

(10) Parsing *ne*

?t

U : e   *sleep'* : e→t

A subject node is decorated with a metavariable U, a placeholder to be saturated. If Ken is a salient person in context, U is saturated as *Ken'*.

3.2 Structural Uncertainty

Each node is assigned a label for a node position, with the "tree-node" predicate *Tn* which takes a numeral as argument (Cann et al., 2005).

(11) Node-Position Labelling

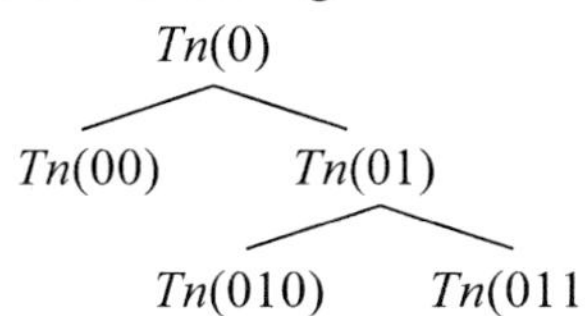

When a node is assigned a numeral "α," its left daughter is assigned "α0" and its right daughter "α1." Since the root receives "0," its left daughter receives "00" and its right daughter "01."

Let us then introduce LOCAL *ADJUNCTION, a general action to posit a node whose position in a tree is initially uncertain and needs to be resolved within a local structure.

(12) LOCAL *ADJUNCTION

?t, *Tn*(0)

Ken' : e, $<\uparrow_{01*}>$(*Tn*(0))

In $<\uparrow_{01*}>$(*Tn*(0)), "1*" is an arbitrary succession of "1" (including none). $<\uparrow_{01*}>$(*Tn*(0)) means: if you go up from an argument node by one node (and optionally keep going up through functor nodes), you will reach the root node, as marked with *Tn*(0) (Blackburn and Meyer-Viol, 1994). In (12), the dashed line visually displays structural uncertainty. $<\uparrow_{01*}>$(*Tn*(0)) indicates that this node is at some argument position within a local structure although the exact position is uncertain at this point.

Structural uncertainty may be fixed in two ways: (i) the general action of UNIFICATION (see §4.2) or (ii) lexical actions encoded in a case particle. As for (ii), it has previously been held that the parse of a case particle resolves an unfixed node (Cann et al., 2005; Seraku, 2013). The nominative particle *ga*, for instance, has been assumed to resolve an unfixed node as a "subject" node. (This analysis is similar to the "constructive case" analysis within LFG (Nordlinger, 1998).)

This past DS analysis of case particles, however, encounters the problem mentioned in the paragraph around (4). In the next section, we will abandon this previous view of case particles, and propose an alternative approach.

4 A "Maximal Exclusion" Approach

4.1 Informal Sketch

It has been held in DS that a case particle **uniquely determines** a landing site for an unfixed node (Cann et al., 2005). In this article, we propose that a case particle reduces the range of landing sites by **maximally excluding** potential sites modulo the limitations imposed by each case particle.

(13) Proposal: General Claim

- a. A case particle excludes all landing sites for an unfixed node but a few candidates.
- b. Such "candidates" differ depending on the type of a case particle.

Thus, a case particle may not immediately resolve an unfixed node. If the number of potential landing sites is reduced to one, however, it will amount to immediate resolution. (13) is consonant with the central DS view: a tree is gradually built up, with various constraints posited by general and lexical actions constraining the way the tree grows.

Concerning (13)b, we assume (14) for *ga*.

(14) Proposal: Nominative Particle *Ga*

- a. *Ga* excludes all but a subject node **and** an object node.
- b. If the above exclusion has already occurred, further exclusion occurs: exclude all but a subject node **or** an object node (not both).

(14) will be illustrated in §4.2-§4.5 (and formalised in the Appendix). Further, other case particles than *ga* are briefly discussed in §4.6.

4.2 Nominative Particle (Part I)

Suppose the parser processes the string (15). At the time of parsing *Ken*, the tree (16) has been built up. (Other *Tn*-statements than *Tn*(0) are omitted in this and subsequent tree displays.)

(15) *Ken-ga* *ne-ta*
K-NOM sleep-PAST
'Ken slept.'

(16) Parsing *Ken*

?t, *Tn*(0)

Ken' : e, $\langle\uparrow_{01*}\rangle(Tn(0))$

$\langle\uparrow_{01*}\rangle(Tn(0))$ specifies the set of constraints (17).

(17) $\{\langle\uparrow_0\rangle(Tn(0)), \langle\uparrow_{01}\rangle(Tn(0)), \langle\uparrow_{011}\rangle(Tn(0)) \ldots\}$

Recall that $\langle\uparrow_0\rangle(Tn(0))$ refers to a subject position, $\langle\uparrow_{01}\rangle(Tn(0))$ refers to an object position, and so on. Thus, (17) indicates that an unfixed node may be fixed at **any** argument position within a local tree.

The next element is *ga*. According to (14)a, *ga* excludes all but a subject and an object node.

(18) Parsing *Ken-ga*

?t, *Tn*(0)

Ken' : e, $\langle\uparrow_{0(1)}\rangle(Tn(0))$

"(1)" in $\langle\uparrow_{0(1)}\rangle(Tn(0))$ means that the presence of "1" is optional, as delineated in (19).

(19) $\{\langle\uparrow_0\rangle(Tn(0)), \langle\uparrow_{01}\rangle(Tn(0))\}$

Unlike (17), (19) indicates that an unfixed node may be fixed at a subject or an object node (but not other nodes). In this way, the parse of *ga* tightens the constraint $\langle\uparrow_{01*}\rangle(Tn(0))$ to $\langle\uparrow_{0(1)}\rangle(Tn(0))$.

The rest of the process is as usual: the parse of *ne* 'sleep' yields the tree (20) (cf., (10)).

(20) Parsing *Ken-ga ne*

?t, *Tn*(0)

U : e, $\langle\uparrow_0\rangle(Tn(0))$ *sleep'* : e→t

Ken' : e, $\langle\uparrow_{0(1)}\rangle(Tn(0))$

The intransitive verb *ne* creates a subject node, which is marked with $\langle\uparrow_0\rangle(Tn(0))$. UNIFICATION, then, merges this subject node with the unfixed node. (UNIFICATION is a general action to combine a description of an unfixed node with that of a fixed node of the same type; see §3.2.)

(21) UNIFICATION

?t, *Tn*(0)

Ken' : e, $\langle\uparrow_0\rangle(Tn(0))$ *sleep'* : e→t

ELIMINATION (i.e., functional application) outputs the final state; see (6) in §3.1.

4.3 Nominative Particle (Part II)

Let us turn to example (22).

(22) *Ken-ga* *ringo-o* *tabe-ta*
K-NOM apple-ACC eat-PAST
'Ken ate an apple.'

After *Ken-ga* is processed (see (18)), the parse of *ringo-o* engenders (23). (The parse of *o* resolves an unfixed node at an object position; see §4.6.)

(23) Parsing *Ken-ga ringo-o*

?t, *Tn*(0)

Ken' : e, $<\uparrow_{0(1)}>(Tn(0))$?(e→t)

apple' : e

The parse of *tabe* 'eat' then builds a propositional template, as in (24).

(24) Parsing *Ken-ga ringo-o tabe*

?t, *Tn*(0)

Ken' : e, $<\uparrow_{0(1)}>(Tn(0))$ U: e   ?(e→t)

apple' : e   *eat'* : e→(e→t)

The parse of *tabe* creates a subject node. This node is compatible with the constraint $<\uparrow_{0(1)}>(Tn(0))$ of the unfixed node. Thus, UNIFICATION may be run, merging the description of the unfixed node with that of the subject node. After ELIMINATION is run, the final state emerges.

(25) UNIFICATION + ELIMINATION

eat'(*apple'*)(*Ken'*) : t, *Tn*(0)

Ken' : e   *eat'*(*apple'*) : e→t

apple' : e   *eat'* : e→(e→t)

4.4 Nominative Particle (Part III)

Let us then examine (26), repeated from (4).

(26) *watashi-ga ringo-ga tabe-tai*
I-NOM apple-NOM eat-want
'I want to eat an apple.'

The parse of *watashi-ga* is as usual, and the parse of the next item *ringo* 'apple' yields (27). (*Sp'* is informally used for the content of *watashi* 'I.')

(27) Parsing *watashi-ga ringo*

?t, *Tn*(0)

Sp' : e, $<\uparrow_{0(1)}>(Tn(0))$ *apple'* : e, $<\uparrow_{01*}>(Tn(0))$

In (27), the exclusion stated in (14)a occurs. Thus, according to (14)b, the parser excludes all potential landing sites for an unfixed node but a subject or an object position. If the parser chooses to exclude all but an **object** position, $<\uparrow_{01}>(Tn(0))$ is posited at the unfixed node for *ringo*. That is, the unfixed node for *ringo* is resolved as the object node.

(28) Parsing *watashi-ga ringo-ga*

?t, *Tn*(0)

Sp' : e, $<\uparrow_{0(1)}>(Tn(0))$?(e→t)

apple' : e, $<\uparrow_{01}>(Tn(0))$

The remainder of the parse process is as outlined in the last subsection.

At the stage (27), the parser could have excluded all but a **subject** position as a landing site for the unfixed node for *ringo*. If this exclusion happened, the unfixed node for *watashi* would be licensed at an object position, giving rise to the interpretation 'An apple wants to eat me.' This tree update itself is legitimate, but the resulting interpretation would be blocked on semantic grounds.

In this respect, noteworthy is (29).

(29) *Ken-ga Naomi-ga sukida*
K-NOM N-NOM like
a. 'Ken likes Naomi.'
b. 'Naomi likes Ken.'

The parse of *Ken-ga Naomi* outputs (30).

(30) Parsing *Ken-ga Naomi*

?t, *Tn*(0)

Ken' : e, $<\uparrow_{0(1)}>(Tn(0))$ *Naomi'* : e, $<\uparrow_{01*}>(Tn(0))$

In parsing *ga* in *Naomi-ga*, if the parser chooses to put $<\uparrow_{01}>(Tn(0))$ at the unfixed node for *Naomi*, the node is resolved as the object node. This leads to the "a"-interpretation. If $<\uparrow_{0}>(Tn(0))$ is posited at the unfixed node for *Naomi*, the node is resolved as the subject node, and the "b"-reading arises.

4.5 Nominative Particle (Part IV)

The proposed account is still not complete. The *ga*-marking of an object NP is usually allowed only by stative predicates (see §2). Thus, (31), where *kat* 'buy' is an action verb, is ungrammatical.

(31) **Ken-ga ringo-ga kat-ta*
K-NOM apple-NOM buy-PAST
Int. 'Ken bought an apple.'

The account developed thus far does not rule (31) out because the possibility of the *ga*-marking of an object NP is dependent on the type of predicate.

We thus assume that if *ga* marks an object NP, this case-marking fact is recorded, which will be checked by a forthcoming predicate. In (31), when *ringo-ga* is parsed, it puts ?NMO at an object node.

(32) Parsing *Ken-ga ringo-ga*

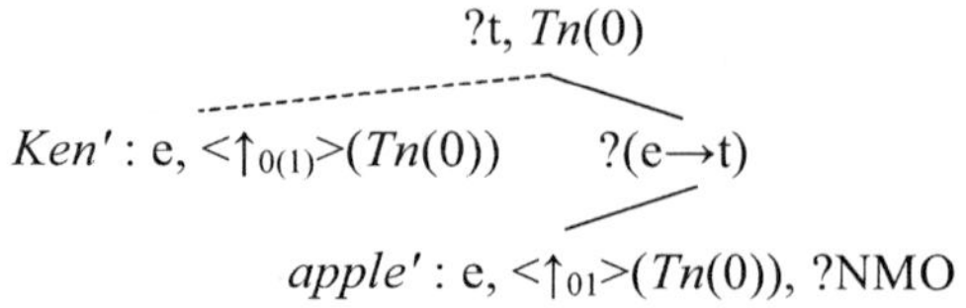

?t, *Tn*(0)

Ken' : e, $\langle\uparrow_{0(1)}\rangle(Tn(0))$?(e→t)

apple' : e, $\langle\uparrow_{01}\rangle(Tn(0))$, ?NMO

?NMO (Nominative Marking of Object) must be checked by a predicate that allows the *ga*-marking of an object NP. (This constraint is encoded in the entries for stative predicates.) In (31), *kat* 'buy' disallows such *ga*-marking. ?NMO is thus not met, and (31) becomes ungrammatical.

The above idea is summarised in (33); see also the Appendix for formalisation.

(33) Proposal: Record of Object Marking
If *ga* excludes all but an object node, the object node is annotated with ?NMO.

4.6 Other Case Particles

According to our general proposal (13), a case particle excludes all landing sites for an unfixed node but a few candidates, and such candidates are encoded in each particle. Below, we touch on the accusative particle *o* and the dative particle *ni*.

The accusative particle *o* typically marks an NP which bears the semantic role "theme"; see *ringo* 'apple' in (22). The accusative particle *o* may also mark an NP bearing the semantic role "path" (34) or "departure site" (35) (NKK, 2009: 67-70).

(34) *Ken-ga sono-yama-o koe-ta*
K-NOM that-mountain-ACC pass-PAST
'Ken passed that mountain.'

(35) *Ken-ga ie-o de-ta*
K-NOM house-ACC leave-PAST
'Ken left a house.'

In the light of the "double-*o* constraint" (Harada, 1973), Shibatani (1978: 289-92) shows that the *o*-marked NPs as in (34)-(35) have the grammatical function of "object." Setting aside complex issues,[4] we thus hold that *o* always marks an object NP.

(36) Proposal: Accusative Particle *O*
O excludes all but an object node.

(36) amounts to immediately resolving an unfixed node as an object node. So, as far as *o* is concerned, our "maximal exclusion" approach converges with the "unique-determination" approach (Cann et al., 2005; Seraku, 2013).

The dative particle *ni* usually marks an indirect-object NP (37), but in some environments, *ni* may mark a subject NP (38).

(37) *Ken-ga Naomi-ni ringo-o age-ta*
K-NOM N-DAT apple-ACC give-PAST
'Ken gave an apple to Naomi.'

(38) *Ken-ni eigo-ga wakaru*
K-DAT English-NOM understand
'Ken understands English.'

From the "maximal exclusion" perspective, then, we assume (39).

(39) Proposal: Dative Particle *Ni*
a. *Ni* excludes all but a subject node **and** an Indirect Object (IO) node.
b. If such exclusion has already been present, further exclusion occurs: exclude all but a subject node **or** an IO node (not both).

Two caveats are in order. First, the *ni*-marking of a subject NP is not possible with all predicates, and the possibility of such *ni*-marking must be encoded in each predicate (Shibatani, 1978: 224).[5] Second, although *ni* appears in other contexts (NKK, 2009), *ni* in these environments would be characterised as postpositions, such as *ni* 'at' and *ni* 'to.'

In this section, we have re-considered the role of case particles in structure building from the angle of "maximal exclusion."[6]

[4] First, *o* may mark an adverbial element (Mihara, 1994). This use of *o* would be an instance of the postposition *o*. Second, *o* is said to appear in "small clauses" or "ECM" constructions, but their theoretical status is contentious (Kawai, 2008; Kuno, 1976).

[5] The set of predicates allowing "SUB-*ni* OBJ-*ga*" is a proper subset of the set of predicates allowing "SUB-*ga* OBJ-*ga*" (Kuno, 1973: §4). ("SUB" means a subject NP, and "OBJ" an object NP.) For predicates allowing the *ni*-marking of SUB, we assume: if *ni* excludes all but a subject node, the subject node is annotated with ?DMS (Dative Marking of Subject); cf., (33).

[6] Case particles also appear in head-internal relatives (Kuroda, 2005). Within DS, this construction has been analysed in Seraku (2013), and our account of *ga*, *o*, and *ni* is compatible with Seraku's analysis.

5 Further Issues

Turning back to multiple occurrences of *ga*, let us explore MSC (Major Subject Construction) of the type (40) (Kuroda, 1992: 248). Noda (1996: 257-9) mentions other kinds of MSC, but (40) represents the most discussed type of MSC.

(40) *Ken-ga imouto-ga yasashii*
K-NOM younger.sister-NOM sweet
'Ken's younger sister is sweet.'

The first *ga*-marked item *Ken*, often called "major subject," acts as a possessor NP of the second *ga*-marked item *imouto* 'younger sister.' In fact, some scholars claim to derive (40) from (41), where *no* in *Ken-no* is a genitive case particle (e.g., Kuno's (1973: §3) "subjectivisation").

(41) *Ken-no imouto-ga yasashii*
K-GEN younger.sister-NOM sweet
'Ken's younger sister is sweet.'

5.1 Previous DS Account

In DS, Nakamura et al. (2009) focusses on the type of MSC shown in (40). (They do not address the data in §4.4-§4.5.) Their analysis is as follows:

- *Ga* does not resolve structural uncertainty, but just lets the parser return to the root node.
- Before a second *ga*-marked item is parsed, the general action of GENERALISED ADJUNCTION sets an unfixed ?t-node, under which a second *ga*-marked item is parsed.
- A second *ga*-marked item is a relational noun which creates a complex structure, into which the unfixed node for the first *ga*-marked item is incorporated by means of UNIFICATION.

In their analysis, while an unfixed node for the first *ga*-marked item requires that it be fixed in a **local** tree, an unfixed node introduced by GENERALISED ADJUNCTION requires that it be fixed **anywhere** in the whole tree. Presumably to avoid this problem, Nakamura et al. (2009: 114) resort to "structural abduction" (Cann et al., 2005: 256). But such an abduction step cannot occur in their proposed tree, since it ends up identifying the unfixed node for the first *ga*-item with that for the second *ga*-item, leading to inconsistency of node descriptions. Thus, their analysis is formally illegitimate.

5.2 Alternative DS Account

Our alternative account holds that *ga* is ambiguous between *ga* (14) and *ga* for "major subject" which we will propose by utilising Seraku and Ohtani's (2016) analysis of the genitive particle *no*.

Let us illustrate the analysis of *no* with (42). The parse of *Ken-no* derives the tree state (43).

(42) *Ken-no hon*
K-GEN book
'Ken's book' ('a book which Ken possesses,' 'a book which Ken wrote,' etc.)

(43) Parsing *Ken-no*

$Ken' : e \quad \curvearrowright \quad U_{R(Ken', U)} : e$

$U_{R(Ken', U)}$ must be saturated with a semantic content in relation R to *Ken*. R is contextually specified as a "possession" relation, for example. The curved arrow represents a "LINK" relation (Cann et al., 2005: Ch. 3). LINK connects two structures, given a shared term like *Ken'*. When the next item *hon* 'book' is parsed, the tree is updated into (44).

(44) Parsing *Ken-no hon*

$Ken' : e \quad \curvearrowright \quad book'_{POSS(Ken', book')} : e$

$book'_{POSS(Ken', book')}$ denotes a book which stands in a possession relation to Ken.[7]

A metavariable $U_{R(Ken', U)}$ is used in (43) since *Ken-no* itself may denote an entity.

(45) *Ken-no/*-ga*
K-GEN/-NOM
'Ken's'

For *Ken-no*, $U_{R(Ken', U)}$ is saturated pragmatically (rather than by the parse of *hon* 'book' as in (42)).

Another notable point is that *imouto* 'younger sister' in (40) is a relational noun which takes an individual x and denotes the sister(s) of x. We view "relational nouns" broadly so as to include nouns for which a relation can be contextually set out.

(46) *Ken-ga ie-ga goukada*
K-NOM house-NOM gorgeous
'Ken's house is gorgeous.'

We will thus define the actions encoded in *ga* (for major subjects) by reflecting the following:

[7] Formally, terms are expressed in the epsilon calculus: (ϵ, x, *book'*(x)&*poss'*(x)(*Ken'*)) for $book'_{POSS(Ken', book')}$.

- A post-*ga* NP must be overtly present.
- A post-*ga* NP is a "relational" noun (at least, for the type of MSC illustrated in (40)).

Our contention is that the parse of *Ken-ga* in (40) yields the tree (47).

(47) Parsing *Ken-ga*

$?t, Tn(0)$

$Ken' : e$ $\quad ?e, ?\exists x.Fo(x_{R(x, Ken')}), <\uparrow_{01*}>(Tn(0))$

$?\exists x.Fo(x_{R(x, Ken')})$ requires that this node will be decorated with a content in relation *R* to *Ken'*. (*Fo* is a "formula" predicate (Cann et al., 2005).) This requirement lacks a metavariable U, and data such as *Ken-ga* in (45) are ruled out. The requirement is fulfilled by the parse of *imouto* 'younger sister,' as shown in (48). $a'_{SISTER(a', Ken')}$ denotes an individual *a'* who is in a sister relation to Ken.[8]

(48) Parsing *Ken-ga imouto*

$?t, Tn(0)$

$Ken' : e$ $\quad a'_{SISTER(a', Ken')} : e, <\uparrow_{01*}>(Tn(0))$

The rest of the parse process is as outlined in §4.2. The final state is given in (49).

(49) Parsing *Ken-ga imouto-ga yasashii*

$sweet'(a'_{SISTER(a', Ken')}) : t, Tn(0)$

$Ken' : e$ $\quad a'_{SISTER(a', Ken')} : e$ $\quad sweet' : e \rightarrow t$

Note that the tree update triggered by the parse of a major subject may occur more than once. For instance, the parse of *Ken-ga imouto-ga se* in (50) gives rise to (51), where $b'_{HEIGHT(b', a')}$ represents the height of the individual who is the sister of Ken.[9]

(50) *Ken-ga imouto-ga se-ga takai*
K-NOM sister-NOM height-NOM high
'Ken's younger sister's height is high.'

(51) Parsing *Ken-ga imouto-ga se*

$?t, Tn(0)$

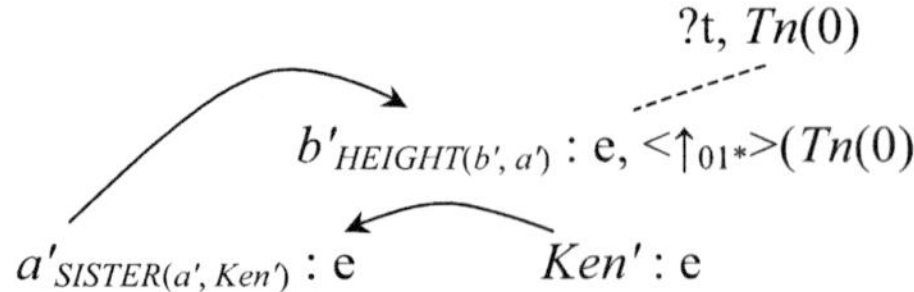

$b'_{HEIGHT(b', a')} : e, <\uparrow_{01*}>(Tn(0))$

$a'_{SISTER(a', Ken')} : e$ $\quad Ken' : e$

[8] Formally, (ι, x, *sister'*(*Ken'*)(x)).

[9] Formally, (ι, x, *height'*(ι, y, *sister'*(*Ken'*)(y))(x)).

Further, $a'_{SISTER(a', Ken')}$ is composed reflecting the order in which *Ken* is first parsed and then *imouto* 'younger sister' follows. Consider (52).

(52) * *imouto-ga Ken-ga yasashii*
sister-NOM K-NOM sweet
Int. 'Ken's younger sister is sweet.'

(52) is ruled out since *Ken* cannot denote a relation, unlike *imouto*, which denotes the relation *SISTER* so that composite terms like $a'_{SISTER(a', Ken')}$ are created.

As a residual issue, *ga* may be used as a genitive particle, but such examples are archaic (Frellesvig, 2011). Although our treatment of *ga* (for major subjects) allows (53), it is not obvious if we should posit further constraints to block such examples. (It is also notable that in many Ryukyuan languages, the nominative particles have the genitive-marking function, too (Tohyama and Seraku, in press).)

(53) *warera-ga michi*
we-GEN road
'Our road' (with an archaic flavour)

6 Conclusion

We have presented a maximal-exclusion approach to structural uncertainty. It is an open issue if this approach is applicable to data on languages other than Japanese (Koizumi, 2008: 142). It would also be essential to explore if the proposed view of case may be incorporated into other "realistic" grammar models (Sag and Wasow, 2011).

Appendix. Entries for Case Particles

A lexical entry specifies a set of actions to be run in conditional format (Cann et al., 2005). For space reasons, the entry for *ga* alone is presented here.

IF $\quad e, <\uparrow_{01*}>(Tn(0))$
THEN IF $\quad <\uparrow_{01*}><\downarrow_{1*0}>(Tn(U), \exists x.Tn(x), <\uparrow_{0(1)}>(Tn(0)))$
THEN put($<\uparrow_0>(Tn(0))/<\uparrow_{01}>(Tn(0))$, ?NMO)
ELSE put($<\uparrow_{0(1)}>(Tn(0))$)
ELSE abort

Acknowledgments

This article largely benefitted from the comments provided by the three anonymous PACLIC referees, Ruth Kempson, and Akira Ohtani. This work was supported by the Hankuk University of Foreign Studies Research Fund of 2016.

References

Blackburn, P. and Meyer-Viol, W. 1994. Linguistics, logic and finite trees. *Logic Journal of the IGPL* 2 (1), 3-29

Cann, R., Kempson, R., and Marten, L. 2005. *The Dynamics of Language*. Oxford: Elsevier.

Chomsky, N. 1965. *Aspects of the Theory of Syntax*. Cambridge, MA: MIT Press.

Chomsky, N. 1995. *Minimalist Program*. Cambridge, MA: MIT Press.

Comrie, B. 1989. *Language Universals and Linguistic Typology*, 2nd edn. Chicago, IL: The University of Chicago Press.

Dalrymple, M. 2001. *Lexical Functional Grammar*. New York: Academic Press.

Frellesvig, B. 2011. *A History of the Japanese Language*. Cambridge: Cambridge University Press.

Harada, S.-I. 1973. Counter equi-NP deletion. *Annual Bulletin Research Institute of Logopaedics and Phoniatrics* 7, 113-48.

Iori, I. 1995. "Ga shitai" to "o shitai." *Nihongo Kyoiku* 86, 52-64.

Kawai, M. 2008. Alleged small clauses in Japanese. *Toronto Working Papers in Linguistics* 28, 89-105.

Keenan, E. 1975. Towards a universal definition of "subject." In Li, C. (ed.) *Subject and Topic*. New York: Academic Press, pp. 303-33.

Keenan, E. and Comrie, B. 1977. Noun phrase accessibility and universal grammar. *Linguistic Inquiry* 8 (1), 63-99.

Kempson, R., Gregoromichelaki, E., and Howes, C. (eds.) 2011. *The Dynamics of Lexical Interfaces*. Stanford, CA: CSLI Publications.

Kempson, R., Meyer-Viol, W., and Gabbay, D. 2001. *Dynamic Syntax*. Oxford: Wiley-Blackwell.

Kiaer, J. 2014. *Pragmatic Syntax*. London: Bloomsbury Publishing.

Kishimoto, H. 2004. Transitivity of ergative-marking predicates in Japanese. *Studies in Language* 28 (1), 105-36.

Koizumi, M. 2008. Nominative object. In Miyagawa, S. and Saito, M. (eds.) *The Oxford Handbook of Japanese Linguistics*. Oxford: Oxford University Press, pp. 141-64.

Kuno, S. 1973. *The Structure of the Japanese Language*. Cambridge, MA: MIT Press.

Kuno, S. 1976. Subject raising. In Shibatani, M. (ed.) *Syntax and Semantics*, Vol. 5. New York: Academic Press, pp. 17–41.

Kuroda S.-Y. 1992. What can Japanese say about government and binding? In Kuroda, S.-Y. (ed.) *Japanese Syntax and Semantics*. Dordrecht: Kluwer, pp. 40-52.

Kuroda, S. Y. 2005. *Nihongo-kara Mita Seisei Bunpou*. (Generative grammar from the viewpoint of Japanese) Tokyo: Iwanami Shoten.

Mihara, K. 1994. *Nihongo-no Tougo Kouzou*. (Syntactic structure of Japanese) Tokyo: Shohakusha.

Nakamura, H., Yoshimoto, K., Mori, Y., and Kobayashi, M. 2009. Multiple subject construction in Japanese. In Hattori, H. et al. (eds.) *New Frontiers in Artificial Intelligence (LNAI 5447)*. Dordrecht: Springer, pp. 103-18.

NKK (Nihongo Kijyutsubunpou Kenkyuukai). 2009. *Gendai Nihongo Bunpou*, Vo. 2. (The grammar of modern Japanese) Tokyo: Kuroshio Publishers.

Noda, T. 1996. "*Wa*" *to* "*Ga*." ("Wa" and "ga") Toyko: Kuroshio Publishers.

Nordlinger, R. 1998. *Constructive Case*. Stanford, CA: CSLI Publications.

Sag, I. and Wasow, T. 2011. Performance-compatible competence grammar. In Borsley, R. and Borjars, K. (eds.) *Non-transformational Syntax*. Oxford: Wiley-Blackwell, pp. 359-77.

Seraku, T. 2013. *Clefts, Relatives, and Language Dynamics*. DPhil thesis, University of Oxford.

Seraku, T. and Ohtani, A. 2016. The word-order flexibility in Japanese novels. In Ogata, T. and Akimoto, T. (eds.) *Computational and Cognitive Approaches to Narratology*. Hershey, PA: IGI Global, pp. 213-44.

Shibatani, M. 1978. *Nihongo-no Bunseki*. (The analysis of Japanese) Tokyo: Taishukan Publishing Company.

Tohyama, N. and Seraku, T. in press. Towards a description of the case system of Yoron Ryukyuan. *International Journal of Okinawan Studies*.

Tsujimura, N. 2013. *An Introduction to Japanese Linguistics*, 3rd edn. Oxford: Wiley-Blackwell.

Tsunoda, T. 2009. *Sekai-no Gengo-to Nihongo*, 2nd edn. (The languages of the world and Japanese) Tokyo: Kuroshio Publishers.

Korean Language Resources for Everyone

Jungyeul Park
Department of Linguistics
University of Arizona
Tucson, AZ 85721
jungyeul@email.arizona.edu

Jeen-Pyo Hong
NAVER LABS
NAVER Corporation
Republic of Korea
jeenpyo.hong@navercorp.com

Jeong-Won Cha
Department of Computer Engineering
Changwon National University
Republic of Korea
jcha@changwon.ac.kr

Abstract

This paper presents open language resources for Korean. It includes several language processing models and systems including morphological analysis, part-of-speech tagging, syntactic parsing for Korean, and standard evaluation Korean-English machine translation data with the Korean-English statistical machine translation baseline system. We make them publicly available to pave the way for further development regarding Korean language processing.

1 Introduction

This paper presents open language resources (LRs) for Korean. We provide necessary data, models, tools, and systems to analyze Korean sentences. It includes the whole working pipeline from part-of-speech (POS) tagging to syntactic parsing for Korean. We also provide the Korean-English statistical machine translation (SMT) baseline system and newly created standard data for MT evaluation. All LRs described in this paper will be publicly available under the MIT License (MIT).

2 Korean Language

Korean is an agglutinative language in which "words typically contain a linear sequence of MORPHS" (Crystal, 2008). Words in Korean (*eojeols*), therefore, can be formed by joining content and functional morphemes to indicate such meaning. These *eojeols* can be interpreted as the basic segmentation unit and they are separated by a blank space in the Korean sentence. Let us consider the sentence in (1). For example, *unggaro* is a content morpheme (a proper noun) and a postposition *-ga* (a nominative case marker) is a functional morpheme. They form together a single word *unggaro-ga* ('Ungaro + NOM'). For convenience sake, we add - at the beginning of functional morphemes, such as *-ga* for NOM to distinguish between content and functional morphemes. The nominative case marker *-ga* or *-i* may vary depending on the previous letter - vowel or consonant. A predicate *naseo-eoss-da* also consists of the content morpheme *naseo* ('become') and its functional morphemes (*-eoss* 'PAST' and *-da* 'DECL').

3 Morphological analysis and POS tagging

Numerous studies pertaining to morphological analysis and POS tagging for Korean have been conducted over the past decades (Cha et al., 1998; Lee and Rim, 2004; Kang et al., 2007; Lee, 2011). Most morphological analysis and POS tagging for Korean have been conducted based on an *eojeol*. In the system of Korean POS taggers, a morphological analysis is generally followed by a POS tagging step. That is, all possible sequences of morphological segmentation for a given word are generated during the morphological analysis and the *possible* (or best) correct sequences are then selected during POS tagging.

ESPRESSO, a Korean POS tagger described in Hong (2009) is publicly available[1]. It greatly improves the accuracy of POS tagging using POS patterns of words in which it obtains up to 95.85% ac-

[1]Note that there is another resource with the same name (Pantel and Pennacchiotti, 2006).

(1) a. 프랑스의 세계적인 의상 디자이너 엠마누엘 웅가로가 실내 장식용 직물 디자이너로 나섰다.

b. *peurangseu-ui segyejeok-in uisang dijaineo emmanuel unggaro-ga silnae jangsikyong*
France-GEN world class-REL fashion designer Emanuel Ungaro-NOM interior decoration
jikmul dijaineo-ro naseo-eoss-da.
textile designer-AJT become-PAST-DECL.
'The world class French fashion designer Emanuel Ungaro became an interior textile designer.'

Figure 1: Example of the Korean sentence

Input:
프랑스의 세계적인 의상 디자이너 엠마누엘 웅가로가 실내 장식용 직물 디자이너로 나섰다.

Output:

프랑스의	BOS	프랑스/NNP+의/JKG
세계적인		세계/NNG+적/XSN+이/VCP+ㄴ/ETM
의상		의상/NNG
디자이너		디자이너/NNG
엠마누엘		엠마누엘/NNP
웅가로가		웅가로/NNP+가/JKS
실내		실내/NNG
장식용		장식용/NNG
직물		직물/NNG
디자이너로		디자이너/NNG+로/JKB
나섰다.	EOS	나서/VV+었/EP+다/EF+./SF

Figure 2: Input and output examples of ESPRESSO for Korean POS tagging

curacy for Korean. Figure 2 shows the input and output formats of ESPRESSO for Korean POS tagging. Even though ESPRESSO can yield several output formats, we only show the Sejong corpus-like format in this paper, in which we use the format for the input of syntactic analysis. While ESPRESSO indicates BOS and EOS (the beginning and the end of a sentence, respectively), the actual Sejong corpus does not contain BOS and EOS labels. The original Sejong morphologically analyzed corpus annotates the sentence boundary using the markup language.

We use Sejong POS tags, the mostly used POS tag information for Korean. Figure 3 shows the summary of the Sejong POS tag set and its mapping to the Universal POS tag (Petrov et al., 2012). We convert the XR (non-autonomous lexical root) into the NOUN because they are mostly considered as a noun or a part of noun (*e.g. minju*/XR ('democracy')). The current Universal POS tag mapping for Sejong POS tags is based on a handful of POS patterns of Korean words. However, combinations of words in Korean are very productive and exponential. Therefore, the number of POS patterns of the word does not converge as the number of words increases. For example, the Sejong Treebank contains about 450K words and almost 5K POS patterns. We also test with the Sejong morphologically analyzed corpus which contains over 10M words. The number of POS patterns does not converge and it increases up to over 50K. The wide range of POS patterns is mainly due to the fine-grained morphological analysis results, which shows all possible segmentations divided into lexical and functional morphemes. These various POS patterns indicate useful morpho-syntactic information for Korean. For example, Oh et al. (2011) predicted function labels (phrase-level tags) using POS patterns that would improve dependency parsing results.

Sejong POS	description	Universal POS
NNG, NNP, NNB, NR, XR	Noun related	NOUN
NP	Pronoun	PRON
MAG,	Adverb	ADV
MAJ	Conjunctive adverb	CONJ
MM	Determiner	DET
VV, VX, VCN, VCP	Verb related	VERB
VA	Adjective	ADJ
EP, EF, EC, ETN, ETM	Verbal endings	PRT
JKS, JKC, JKG, JKO, JKB, JKV, JKQ, JX, JC	Postpositions (case markers)	ADP
XPN, XSN, XSA, XSV	Suffixes	PRT
SF, SP, SE, SO, SS	Punctuation marks	PUNC (.)
SW	Special characters	X
SH, SL	Foreign characters	X
SN	Number	NUM
NA, NF, NV	Unknown words	X

Figure 3: POS tags in the Sejong corpus and their 1-to-1 mapping to Universal POS tags

4 Syntactic analysis

Statistical parsing trained from an annotated data set has been widespread. However, while there are manually annotated several Korean Treebank corpora such as the Sejong Treebank (SJTree), only a few works on statistical Korean parsing have been conducted.

4.1 Phrase structure parsing

For previous work on constituent parsing, Sarkar and Han (2002) used an early version of the Korean Penn Treebank (KTB) to train lexicalized Tree Adjoining Grammars (TAG). Chung et al. (2010) used context-free grammars and tree-substitution grammars trained on data from the KTB. Choi et al. (2012) proposed a method to transform the word-based SJTree into an entity-based Treebank to improve the parsing accuracy. There exit several phrase structure parsers such as Stanford (Klein and Manning, 2003), Bikel (Bikel, 2004), and Berkeley (Petrov and Klein, 2007) parsers (either lexicalized or unlexicalized) that we can train with the Treebank.

For phrase structure parsing, we provide a parsing model for the Berkely parser.[2] Choi et al. (2012) tested Stanford, Bikel, and Berkeley parsers and the Berkeley parser shows the best results for phrase structure parsing for Korean. The input sentence of phrase structure parsers is generally the tokenized sentence. It can be obtained by performing the segmentation task for a word. Each segmented morpheme becomes a leaf node in the phrase structure. Therefore, we use the tokenization scheme based on POS tagging. Figure 4 shows the input and output formats for the Berkeley parser. As preprocessing tools, we provide `MakeBerkeleyTestIn` and `MakeBerkeleyTestWithPOSIn`. They convert ESPRESSO's output into the Berkely parser's input by tokenizing the Korean sentence with or without POS information, respectively.

[2] `https://github.com/slavpetrov/berkeleyparser`

4.2 Dependency parsing

For previous work on dependency parsing for Korean, Chung (2004) presented a model for dependency parsing using surface contextual information. Oh and Cha (2010), Choi and Palmer (2011) and Park et al. (2013) independently developed a parsing model from the Korean dependency Treebank. They converted automatically the phrase-structured Sejong Treebank into the dependency Treebank. To convert into dependency grammars, Park et al. (2013) summarized as follows.

We, first, assign an anchor for nonterminal nodes using bottom-up breadth-first search. An anchor is

Input:
프랑스 의 세계 적 이 ㄴ 의상 디자이너 엠마누엘 웅가로 가 실내 장식 용 직물 디자이너 로 나서 었 다 .

Output:

```
(S (NP-SBJ (NP (NP-MOD (NNP 프랑스) (JKG 의)
              (NP (VNP-MOD (NNG 세계) (XSN 적) (VCP 이) (ETM ㄴ))
                  (NP (NP (NNG 의상))
                      (NP (NNG 디자이너)))))
                          (NP-SBJ (NP (NNP 엠마누엘))
                                  (NP-SBJ (NNP 웅가로) (JKS 가))))
   (VP (NP-AJT (NP (NP (NP (NNG 실내))
                           (NP (NNG 장식) (XSN 용)))
                       (NP (NNG 직물)))
                   (NP-AJT (NNG 디자이너) (JKB 로)))
       (VP (VV 나서) (EP 었) (EF 다) (SF .))))
```

Figure 4: Input and output examples for Korean phrase structure parsing

the lexical terminal node where each nonterminal node can have as a head node. We use lexical anchor rules described in Park (2006) for the SJTree. Lexical anchor rules distinguish dependency relations. We assign only the lexical anchor for nonterminal nodes and finding dependencies in the next step. Lexical anchor rules give priorities to the rightmost child node, which inherits mostly the same phrase tag. Exceptionally, in case of "VP and VP" (or "S and S"), the leftmost child node is assigned as an anchor. Then, we can find dependency relations between terminal nodes using the anchor information as follows:

1. The head is the anchor of the parent of the parent node of the current node.

2. If the anchor is the current node and

   (a) if the parent of the parent node does not have another right sibling, the head is itself.

   (b) if the parent of the parent node have another right sibling, the head if the anchor of the right sibling.

Results from the conversion can allow to train existing dependency parsers. Figure 5 presents an example of the original Sejong Treebank (above) and its automatically-converted dependency representation.[3] The address of terminal nodes (underneath) and the anchor of nonterminal node (on its right) are arbitrarily assigned for dependency conversion algorithm using lexical head rules. The head of the terminal node 1 is the node 4, which is the anchor of the parent of the parent node (NP:4). The head of the terminal node 4 is the node 6 where the anchor of its ancestor node is changed from itself (NP-SBJ:6). The head of the terminal node 11 is itself where the anchor of the root node and itself are same (S:11).

The parsing model of MaltParser (Nivre et al., 2006) is provided for dependency parsing for Korean.[4] As preprocessing tools, we provide `MakeMaltTestIn`. It converts ESPRESSO's output into the MaltParser's input by generating required features for MaltParser. Figure 6 shows example of the input and the output of MaltParser. We use the data format of CoNLL-X dependency parsing, described in Figure 7 (partially presented). See `http://ilk.uvt.nl/conll` for other information about the data format of CoNLL-X that MaltParser requires. From word and POS information, we convert them into features that MaltParser requires for Korean dependency parsing.

[3]The figure originally appeared in Park et al. (2013) with minor errors, and we corrected them.

[4]`http://www.maltparser.org`

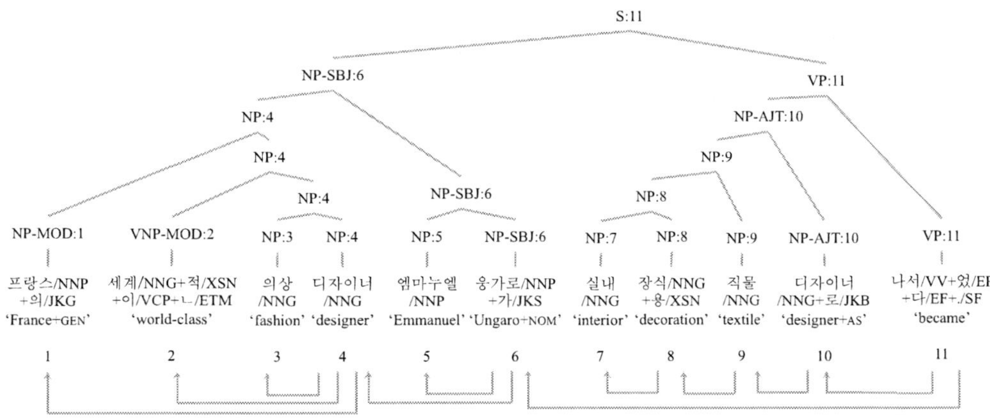

Figure 5: Example of the original Sejong Treebank (above) and its automatically-converted dependency representation (below)

4.3 Discussion on parsing for Korean

In previous work on parsing for Korean, either phrase structure or dependency parsing, while Park et al. (2013) proposed the 80-10-10 corpus split for training, development and evaluation, others often used cross validation (Oh and Cha, 2010; Choi et al., 2012; Oh and Cha, 2013).

For phrase structure parsing, Choi et al. (2012) obtained up to 78.74% F_1 score. For dependency parsing, Oh and Cha (2013) obtained 87.03% (10-fold cross validation) and Park et al. (2013) up to 86.43% (corpus split) by using external case frame information.

Currently, we distribute only parsing models instead of parsers and training data themselves because of following reasons. First, the Sejong Treebank that we use to train and evaluate is not allowed to be distributed by third parties. Corpus users should ask directly to National Institute of the Korean Language[5] for their own usage. Therefore, it would be easy that we only make current parsing models publicly available instead of actual training data. Second, multilingualism becomes more and more important. Many natural language processing (NLP)-related works rely on a single system to deal with multiple languages homogeneously. Berkeley parser and MaltParser in which we provide parsing models have been developed for many other languages and users can easily obtain their up-to-dated parsing systems and models for several other languages.

We provide parsing models trained only on the training data, which can be subject to the baseline parsing system for Korean to be compared in future work. Table 1 presents the current baseline parsing results using phrase structure grammars by the Berkeley parser. We performed 5-fold and 10-fold cross-validation as well as corpus split evaluation for comparison purpose. We also tested both cases in which Berkeley parser selects POS tags by itself during the parsing task (parser) and we provided gold POS tags before parsing (gold). Reported results are improved compared to Choi et al. (2012) because we have corrected syntactic and POS tagging errors in the Sejong Treebank for the current work. Since results between different evaluation methods are not statistically significant, we propose to use 80-10-10 corpus split evaluation using the current distributed parsing model. For the current baseline parsing results using dependency grammars trained using corpus split, Park et al. (2013) reported that MaltParser on the Sejong Treebank can obtain 85.41% for the unlabeled attachment score (UAS). We provide the development data (10% of the corpus) and the evaluation data set (last 10%) as well as the parsing model (trained on first 80% of the corpus) for phrase-structure and dependency parsing.

[5] http://www.korean.go.kr

Input:

1	프랑스의	프랑스	NNP	NNP+JKG	JKG
2	세계적인	세계적이	NNG+XSN+VCP	NNG+XSN+VCP+ETM	ETM
3	의상	의상	NNG	NNG	_
4	디자이너	디자이너	NNG	NNG	_
5	엠마누엘	엠마누엘	NNP	NNP	_
6	웅가로가	웅가로	NNG	NNG+JKS	JKS
7	실내	실내	NNG NNG	_	
8	장식용	장식용	NNG	NNG	_
9	직물	직물	NNG	NNG	_
10	디자이너로	디자이너	NNG	NNG+JKB JKB	
11	나섰다.	나서	VV	VV+EP+EF+SF	EP|EF|SF

Output :

1	프랑스의	프랑스	NNP	NNP+JKG	JKG	4	NP-MOD	_	_
2	세계적인	세계적이	NNG+XSN+VCP	NNG+XSN+VCP+ETM	ETM	4	VNP-MOD	_	_
3	의상	의상	NNG	NNG	_	4	NP	_	_
4	디자이너	디자이너	NNG	NNG	_	6	NP	_	_
5	엠마누엘	엠마누엘	NNP	NNP	_	6	NP	_	_
6	웅가로가	웅가로	NNG	NNG+JKS	JKS	11	NP-SBJ	_	_
7	실내	실내	NNG	NNG	_	8	NP	_	_
8	장식용	장식용	NNG	NNG	_	9	NP	_	_
9	직물	직물	NNG	NNG	_	10	NP	_	_
10	디자이너로	디자이너	NNG	NNG+JKB	JKB	11	NP-AJT	_	_
11	나섰다.	나서	VV	VV+EP+EF+SF	EP|EF|SF	0	ROOT	_	_

Figure 6: Input and output examples for Korean dependency parsing

column	name	description
3	LEMMA	Lexical morphemes, where functional morphemes are excluded from FORM.
4	CPOSTAG	POS tags for lexical morphemes.
5	POSTAG	Fine-grained part-of-speech tag.
6	FEATS	POS tags for functional morphemes.

Figure 7: Data format of CoNLL-X dependency parsing for Korean

	5-fold	10-fold	80-10-10
parser	84.90	84.83	84.34
gold	85.88	85.75	85.12

Table 1: Baseline phrase structure parsing results

5 Statistical Machine Translation

Actually, statistical machine translation (SMT) for Korean has not been frequently investigated. Previous work on SMT involving Korean often suffers from the lack of openly available bilingual language resources. Lee et al. (2006) used a Korean-English bilingual sentence-aligned corpus which contains 41,566 sentences and 190,418 eojeols. It was manually collected from travel guide books. Xu et al. (2009) used an in-house collection of Korean-English parallel documents. Unfortunately, they did not present the size, or the domain of the corpus. Hong et al. (2009) used about 300K sentences which were collected from the major bilingual news broadcasting sites and randomly selected 5,000 sentence pairs from the Sejong parallel corpus for tuning, development and evaluation. Chung and Gildea (2009) collected the Korean-English parallel data from news websites and used subsets of the parallel corpus consisting of about 2M words and 60K sentences on the English side. Tu et al. (2010) carried out an experiment on Korean-Chinese translation. The training corpus contains about 8.2M Korean words and 7.3M Chinese words. Most of the datasets in previous work are independently collected from various sources and more than anything else they are not currently publicly accessible.

5.1 Tokenization for Korean SMT

For Korean SMT, we tokenize Korean words based on morphological analysis instead of directly using words themselves by which we empirically found that we are able to get the best results for Korean SMT rather than other unsupervised syllable-based tokenization method described in Chung and Gildea (2009). In addition, by tokenizing Korean sentences based on morphological analysis, we can deal with compound words, in which they appear frequently in Korean. Such compounds may be written with or without a blank and they easily lead to the lexicon sparsity problem in SMT. In many cases, compound words become out-of-vocabulary words (OOV) if they do not appear in training data.

5.2 Korean-English parallel data

There are several existing Korean-English parallel data. Sejong parallel data are available directly from National Institute of the Korean Language and News Commentary data are available from the Korean parallel data site[6]. Sejong parallel data are from various sources including novels, government document, and transcribed speech documents. News Commentary data had been crawled from Yahoo! Korea[7] and Joins CNN[8] during 2010-2011. There are also several Korean-English parallel data from OPUS (Tiedemann, 2012)[9,10]. OPUS parallel corpora consist of movie subtitles (OpenSubtitles 2012, 2013, and 2016), technical documents (GNOME, KDE4, and Ubuntu) and religious texts (Tanzil). Since there are alignment errors, we use only some of parallel data from OPUS, in which we judged them to be proper enough to use. For example, PHP data from OPUS, in which the language identification task fails in the corpus, are not utilized. We summarize the brief statistics of currently available parallel corpora in Table 2. Note that the size indicates the number of words of the target language (English).

	size	description
Sejong parallel	0.8M	various
News commentary	2.3M	newswire
OpenSubtitles (OPUS)	3.5M	subtitles
Technical (OPUS)	0.4M	technical
Tanzil (OPUS)	2.8M	religious

Table 2: Previous Korean-English parallel data. These are publicly available.

Actually, there is no standard evaluation data for Korean-English machine translation. Previously existing parallel corpora are mostly automatically created without human intervention and judgment, and there exists inevitable sentence alignment errors. These errors make existing parallel corpora for Korean be difficult to use as standard evaluation data. Moreover, they are not written for translation studies and they might contain translation gaps between source and target languages, which still make them use as proper evaluation data for machine translation. Therefore, we decide to create new evaluation data for Korean-English machine translation (MT). Junior High English evaluation data for Korean-English machine translation (JHE) are the Korean-English parallel corpus which contains sentences from English reading comprehension exercises for Junior high students. We extracted Korean-English sentences from English reference materials and we manually aligned them to build a parallel data. We manage to produce a set of parallel sentences with high precision alignment, for the sake of future evaluation tasks. The average number of words in the sentence is 12 words in Korean, and it contains various topic including news articles, short stories, letters and advertisements. Table 3 describes the statistics of the newly created evaluation data. They are originally written in English (about 60%) and Korean (40%), and they are translated into counterpart languages. Since they are from educational materials, they keep well formal equivalence between source languages and their translation. We believe that JHE data should be suitable to evaluate the correctness and the robustness of MT systems for Korean regardless of their domain.

5.3 Baseline system for SMT

Table 4 shows results on machine translation using existing parallel corpora (Korean into English).

[6] http://site.google.com/koreanparalleldata

[7] https://www.yahoo.co.kr

[8] http://www.joins.com

[9] http://opus.lingfil.uu.se

[10] Accessed on 22 April 2016.

	sentences	words	
dev	720	7,608	8,702
eval	720	7,491	8,529
		(Korean)	(English)

Table 3: Junior High English evaluation data for Korean-English machine translation

	internal	JHE
Sejong parallel	1.34	4.48
News commentary	9.12	**7.92**
OpenSubtitles (OPUS)	7.67	6.60
Technical (OPUS)	10.45	0.92
Tanzil (OPUS)	14.95	0.96
News + OpenSubtitles	8.85	8.18

Table 4: Extrinsic evaluation results for the quality of the existing parallel corpora

Internal results presents BLEU scores (an automatic metric for evaluating the quality of machine-translated text) using held-out data from their own corpus (each 1,000 sentences for development and evaluation datasets, respectively). JHE results presents BLEU scores using JHE evaluation data. Bad internal results on the Sejong parallel corpus are understandable because they consist of various sources and held-out data can be a quite different domain from training data. While parallel data of specific domains such as technical and religious can obtain good internal results, it is very difficult to expect to equivalent results on texts of the general domain. We tested all possible combinations with Sejong, News, and OpenSubtitles and only News + OpenSubtitles improves the result. We provide the baseline SMT system using Korean-English News commentary and OpenSubtitles data for future comparison purpose.

6 Summary

In this paper, we present following data, models, tools, and systems for Korean:

- ESPRESSO for sentence segmentation, morphological analysis and POS tagging.
- Berkeley parser models for phrase structure syntactic parsing.
- A pipeline script from ESPRESSO to the Berkeley parser: `MakeBerkeleyTestIn` and `MakeBerkeleyTestWithPOSIn`.
- MaltParser models for dependency analysis.
- A pipeline script from ESPRESSO to MaltParser: `MakeMaltTestIn`.
- Baseline Korean-English SMT system using News commentary data and OpenSubtitles.
- Junior High English evaluation data for Korean-English machine translation.

Everyone's Korean language resources described in this paper is available at `https://air.changwon.ac.kr/software/everyone`.

7 Conclusion and Future Perspectives

In this paper, we provided the entire working pipeline for Korean from POS tagging to syntactic analysis. We also described the standard evaluation data and the baseline system for Korean-English statistical machine translation. We hope that these language resources for Korean will pave the way for further development regarding Korean language processing for everybody. For future work, we are planning to distribute other NLP-related systems and models for Korean such as named entity recognition (NER) and semantic role labeling (SRL).

Acknowledgments

We would like to thank the anonymous reviewers for their valuable comments.

References

[Bikel2004] Daniel M. Bikel. 2004. *On the Parameter Space of Generative Lexicalized Statistical Parsing Models*. Ph.D. thesis, University of Pennsylvania.

[Cha et al.1998] Jeong-Won Cha, Geunbae Lee, and Jong-Hyeok Lee. 1998. Generalized Unknown Morpheme Guessing for Hybrid POS Tagging of Korean. In *Proceedings of the Sixth Workshop on Very Large Corpora*, Montreal, Quebec, Canada.

[Choi and Palmer2011] Jinho D. Choi and Martha Palmer. 2011. Statistical Dependency Parsing in Korean: From Corpus Generation To Automatic Parsing. In *Proceedings of the Second Workshop on Statistical Parsing of Morphologically Rich Languages*, pages 1–11, Dublin, Ireland. Association for Computational Linguistics.

[Choi et al.2012] DongHyun Choi, Jungyeul Park, and Key-Sun Choi. 2012. Korean Treebank Transformation for Parser Training. In *Proceedings of the ACL 2012 Joint Workshop on Statistical Parsing and Semantic Processing of Morphologically Rich Languages*, pages 78–88, Jeju, Republic of Korea. Association for Computational Linguistics.

[Chung and Gildea2009] Tagyoung Chung and Daniel Gildea. 2009. Unsupervised Tokenization for Machine Translation. In *Proceedings of the 2009 Conference on Empirical Methods in Natural Language Processing*, pages 718–726, Singapore. Association for Computational Linguistics.

[Chung et al.2010] Tagyoung Chung, Matt Post, and Daniel Gildea. 2010. Factors Affecting the Accuracy of Korean Parsing. In *Proceedings of the NAACL HLT 2010 First Workshop on Statistical Parsing of Morphologically-Rich Languages*, pages 49–57, Los Angeles, CA, USA. Association for Computational Linguistics.

[Chung2004] Hoojung Chung. 2004. *Statistical Korean Dependency Parsing Model based on the Surface Contextual Information*. Ph.D. thesis, Korea University.

[Crystal2008] David Crystal. 2008. *Dictionary of Linguistics and Phonetics*. Wiley-Blackwell, the langua edition.

[Hong et al.2009] Gumwon Hong, Seung-Wook Lee, and Hae-Chang Rim. 2009. Bridging Morpho-Syntactic Gap between Source and Target Sentences for English-Korean Statistical Machine Translation. In *Proceedings of the ACL-IJCNLP 2009 Conference Short Papers*, pages 233–236, Suntec, Singapore. Association for Computational Linguistics.

[Hong2009] Jeen-Pyo Hong. 2009. *Korean Part-Of-Speech Tagger using Eojeol Patterns*. Master's thesis. Changwon National University.

[Kang et al.2007] Mi-Young Kang, Sung-Won Jung, Kyung-Soon Park, and Hyuk-Chul Kwon. 2007. Part-of-Speech Tagging Using Word Probability Based on Category Patterns. *Computational Linguistics and Intelligent Text Processing (Lecture Notes in Computer Science)*, 4394:119–130.

[Klein and Manning2003] Dan Klein and Christopher D. Manning. 2003. Accurate Unlexicalized Parsing. In *Proceedings of the 41st Annual Meeting of the Association for Computational Linguistics*, pages 423–430, Sapporo, Japan. Association for Computational Linguistics.

[Lee and Rim2004] Do-Gil Lee and Hae-Chang Rim. 2004. Part-of-Speech Tagging Considering Surface Form for an Agglutinative Language. In *The Companion Volume to the Proceedings of 42st Annual Meeting of the Association for Computational Linguistics*, pages 130–133, Barcelona, Spain. Association for Computational Linguistics.

[Lee et al.2006] Jonghoon Lee, Donghyeon Lee, and Gary Geunbae Lee. 2006. Improving phrase-based Korean-English statistical machine translation. In *Proceeding of: INTERSPEECH 2006 - ICSLP, Ninth International Conference on Spoken Language Processing*, Pittsburgh, PA, USA.

[Lee2011] Jae Sung Lee. 2011. Three-Step Probabilistic Model for Korean Morphological Analysis. *Journal of KIISE:Software and Applications*, 38(5):257–268.

[Nivre et al.2006] Joakim Nivre, Johan Hall, and Jens Nilsson. 2006. MaltParser: A Data-Driven Parser-Generator for Dependency Parsing. In *Proceedings of the Fifth International Conference on Language Resources and Evaluation (LREC'06)*.

[Oh and Cha2010] Jin-Young Oh and Jeong-Won Cha. 2010. High Speed Korean Dependency Analysis Using Cascaded Chunking. *Korean Simulation Journal*, 19(1):103–111.

[Oh and Cha2013] Jin-Young Oh and Jeong-Won Cha. 2013. Korean Dependency Parsing using Key Eojoel. *Journal of KIISE:Software and Applications*, 40(10):600–6008.

[Oh et al.2011] Jin Young Oh, Yo-Sub Han, Jungyeul Park, and Jeong-Won Cha. 2011. Predicting Phrase-Level Tags Using Entropy Inspired Discriminative Models. In *International Conference on Information Science and Applications (ICISA) 2011*, pages 1–5.

[Pantel and Pennacchiotti2006] Patrick Pantel and Marco Pennacchiotti. 2006. Espresso: Leveraging Generic Patterns for Automatically Harvesting Semantic Relations. In *Proceedings of the 21st International Conference on Computational Linguistics and 44th Annual Meeting of the Association for Computational Linguistics*, pages 113–120, Sydney, Australia. Association for Computational Linguistics.

[Park et al.2013] Jungyeul Park, Daisuke Kawahara, Sadao Kurohashi, and Key-Sun Choi. 2013. Towards Fully Lexicalized Dependency Parsing for Korean. In *Proceedings of The 13th International Conference on Parsing Technologies (IWPT 2013)*, Nara, Japan.

[Park2006] Jungyeul Park. 2006. *Extraction automatique d'une grammaire d'arbres adjoints à partir d'un corpus arboré pour le coréen*. Ph.D. thesis, Université Paris 7 - Denis Diderot.

[Petrov and Klein2007] Slav Petrov and Dan Klein. 2007. Improved Inference for Unlexicalized Parsing. In *Human Language Technologies 2007: The Conference of the North American Chapter of the Association for Computational Linguistics; Proceedings of the Main Conference*, pages 404–411, Rochester, New York. Association for Computational Linguistics.

[Petrov et al.2012] Slav Petrov, Dipanjan Das, and Ryan McDonald. 2012. A Universal Part-of-Speech Tagset. In *Proceedings of the Eighth International Conference on Language Resources and Evaluation (LREC-2012)*, pages 2089–2096, Istanbul, Turkey. European Language Resources Association (ELRA).

[Sarkar and Han2002] Anoop Sarkar and Chung-Hye Han. 2002. Statistical Morphological Tagging and Parsing of Korean with an LTAG Grammar. In *Proceedings of the 6th International Workshop on Tree Adjoining Grammars and Related Formalisms (TAG+ 6)*, pages 48–56, Venice, Italy.

[Tiedemann2012] Jörg Tiedemann. 2012. Parallel Data, Tools and Interfaces in OPUS. In *Proceedings of the Eighth International Conference on Language Resources and Evaluation (LREC-2012)*, pages 2214–2218, Istanbul, Turkey. European Language Resources Association (ELRA).

[Tu et al.2010] Zhaopeng Tu, Yang Liu, Young-Sook Hwang, Qun Liu, and Shouxun Lin. 2010. Dependency Forest for Statistical Machine Translation. In *Proceedings of the 23rd International Conference on Computational Linguistics (Coling 2010)*, pages 1092–1100, Beijing, China. Coling 2010 Organizing Committee.

[Xu et al.2009] Peng Xu, Jaeho Kang, Michael Ringgaard, and Franz Och. 2009. Using a Dependency Parser to Improve SMT for Subject-Object-Verb Languages. In *Proceedings of Human Language Technologies: The 2009 Annual Conference of the North American Chapter of the Association for Computational Linguistics*, pages 245–253, Boulder, Colorado. Association for Computational Linguistics.

Secondary Predicates in Native and Nonnative Grammars

Enchao Shi
California State University,
Northridge
18111 Nordhoff Street
English Department, CSUN
Northridge, U.S.A.
enchao.shi@csun.edu

Abstract

The typical measurement by which the nature of second language grammars is evaluated is the input of native speakers. This paper reports on data from Mandarin speakers of English (n = 19), with an average of 10;3 (year;month) length of residence in the U.S., and native American English speakers (n = 19), and looks at how they dealt with causatives, resultatives, and depictives under four experimental conditions. It was found that native participants did not always behave reliably; they altered, swung, and oscillated just like nonnative counterparts, and there were multiple cases where their fluctuation rates were way higher than those of the latter. Such variances were brought about by the effects of construction, task, or modality. These results cast doubt on the common practice of assessing second language grammars in terms of native intuitions and call on researchers to reconsider the assumption that second language grammars that are legitimate must be native-like.

1 Introduction

It goes without saying that adult second language (L_2) learning differs from child first language (L_1) development, owing to various identifiable disparities in cognition and maturation between the two groups. From this truism follows the logical question, for generative second language acquisition (SLA) researchers, how much of the initial state or the biologically determined precursor contributes to the acquisition of a language later in life. Previously, the issue was explored by inquiries into the developmental processes until about two decades ago when researchers started to seriously consider what it is that adults can ultimately know about the target language that are not true of their native languages. Much in line with the developmental research, results gleaned from empirical and longitudinal studies that focus on the final L_2 state, suggest, or in many cases conclude, that older learners attain different grammars than native speakers. For those born and raised in the target language setting, language development is, from the onset, controlled by UG (Universal Grammar) principles and parameters. Mature learners are subjected to all kinds of undesirable elements none of which occurs to child learners (for a review, see White$_a$, 2003), leading them to the mastery of L_2 grammars full of anomalies and aberrations.

The present experiment questions whether it is enough to measure L_2 grammars against native grammars (for discussion, see Mack, 1997) and shows that native speakers vary in behavior just as much as nonnative speakers, depending on the grammatical features under analysis and the experimental conditions. The typical comparative native-nonnative studies with an eye to pinning down the biological influence bear little fruit if it is true that the final state of the model subjects lacks the supposed uniformity in the knowledge of the target grammar, which, according to Chomsky (1986, 1988, 1993), is not something in dispute. What is not being investigated is the causes of the native variations (see Shi, 2014; Shi$_a$, in progress).

A large number of the generative L_2 studies conclude that there is something amiss about L_2 grammars, for their bearers deviate from the natives whose use of the target language is reliable and consistent. In an influential study involving proficient English speakers of first languages of Korean, Chinese, Indonesian, and Dutch, Schachter (1990) found that these subjects, unlike the native controls, did not always recognize errors in sentences like *What did Susan visit the store that had t in stock?

The extent to which an L_2 group succeeded was correlated with whether its native grammar instantiated the Subjacency constraint (Chomsky, 1981) as English did. Schachter takes this as support for her Incompleteness Hypothesis; namely "incompleteness will turn out to be an essential property of any adult second language grammar" (pp. 118-119).

Johnson et al. (1996) also found from 10 Chinese speakers of English, who had on average lived in the U.S. for 6.45 years, that their abilities to recognize morphosyntactic errors from auditorily presented sentences were lower (54.2% accurate) than the native speakers (98.3% accurate). This indicates, to the researchers, that L_2 grammars of the nonnative-born speakers are "not native in determinacy" (p. 343).

In an experiment on English psych verbs (*interest, disappoint*) and container verbs (e.g., *decorate, cover*), Juffs (1996) retrieved both production and comprehension data that informed him that the Chinese college students, with no living experience in an English-speaking environment, lagged behind native speakers in consistency, which tended to improve as a function of the increased proficiency level. While low- and intermediate-level learners had trouble producing or processing sentences like "The broken vase disappointed John," those at the advanced level did as well as the English speakers.

Chen (2005), in search of the association of verbs *consider, find* to various complement syntactic frames, uncovered a gradient preference pattern for Mandarin speakers of English: tensed clause > infinitive clause > small clause. The finding was based on a set of within-group statistical analyses conducted to the L_2 group. Assuming the lack of preference for the natives, the found preference pattern from the nonnatives suggested, to Chen, that it must be L_2 grammars that were faulty, since native speakers, being native, could not go wrong.

It is not that generative L_2 researchers are oblivious of or blindsided by the fact that native speakers, due to internal as well as circumstantial variables, can falter or fail to comply with the grammatical rules when called upon. For example, in the above study by Schachter (1990), she acutely noted the unusual poor performance by the English-speaking participants on the Wh-movement sentences that "had been piloted on other natives and performance has been much higher" (p. 111). As an explanation, Schachter speculated that the piloted subjects were "graduate students majoring in linguistics" (fn 19). In Johnson et al.'s (1996) error-detection experiment, if we remove the chance responses, based on their formula (p. 343), from the native group data, its accuracy rate would drop to 96.6 percent, from the reported 98.2 percent. In the study of Chen (2005), there was a case where native speakers showed more variations, based on her computations of standard deviations, on the use of *consider/find THAT*, than nonnative speakers. But spotting such variabilities from native speakers is one thing and taking it into account is another. As has been shown time and again, native variance is largely viewed as inconsequential, reflective of the accidental glitches, and therefore dismissible.

This experiment, a mixed design, aims to do the reverse of what has been typically done; that is, to demonstrate L_2 grammar is not as flawed as previously thought, provided that the random and experimental errors are carefully identified. The problem, which has been long neglected, is a methodological one – the use of native speakers as the sole yardstick to determine the nature of second language grammars. The null hypothesis tested is that speakers who acquire the target language natively therefore do not vary in linguistic competence; they as natives can always be counted on being up to par when it comes to the measurement of grammatical knowledge.

Nativeness may well be correlated with birthplace, but linguistic competence is not. To tap into the components of the faculty of language (Chomsky, 1972, p. 27; 1986, pp. 16-17; 1998, p. 115), we ought to rethink the current research procedure. One alternative being explored here is to hold off the input effects as a pernicious confounding variable, so that no subject group is at unwarranted advantage. To that end, the study tested, under contrasting conditions, a set of infrequent yet robust syntactic frames: causatives, resultatives, and depictives. The idea behind the design was that by displacing subjects from their "comfort zone" into a "leading edge" (Rispoli, 2003, p. 819), we are able to take a better look into their inner grammar proper. The independent variables of interest are three: construction (3 levels: causatives, resultatives, depictives), task (4 levels: Guided Production, Combining-Clause, Grammaticality Judgment, Interpretation Task), and modality (2 levels: production, comprehension). The construction effects are examined by holding the modality and task effects neutral. To factor in the influence of task and modality, pairs of group data from the comparable tasks or modalities are analyzed. And finally, to see if the key variables (modality × task) interact, tasks from different modalities are compared in pairs. The null hypothesis is rejected just in case the empirical data shows that those who speak English day in and day out fail to deliver the expected outcome on tasks presented under various conditions. They show tendencies to respond to the intricate properties of constructions, tasks, or modalities as opposed to their grammatical knowledge in ways of nonnative speakers.

1.1 Causatives, Resultatives, and Depictives

Accounts have been put forward for causatives, resultatives, and depictives, commonly known as secondary predicates (see Shi, 2003; Hale and Keyser, 2002; Levin and Rappaport Hovav, 1995; Jackendoff, 1990; Chomsky, 1981). The underlying framework for the present experiment is a combination of Distributed Morphology (Matushansky and Marantz, 2013; Embick and Noyer, 2007; Harley and Noyer, 2003; Marantz, 1997) and Lexical Argument Structure (Hale and Keyser, 1993, 2002). (1) illustrates the three constructions under analysis:

(1) a. The stories about animals interested Mary.
b. Sally could have complained herself calm.
c. The invited speaker delivered the speech drunk.

(1a) is a causative in contrast to a periphrastic structure, in that it consists of a single tensed predicate whereas the latter two predicates (*The stories about animals made Mary interested*). Mandarin for the most part allows the bi-clause causatives.

As a resultative, (1b) comprises a main verb and a secondary (resultant) predicate, as shown in (2):

(2) $[_{v}\ V^0\ [_{AP/PP}\ DP\ A^0/P^0\ ]]$

Semantically, a resultative expresses a cause-event leading to a result-event (Rothstein, 2006; Rappaport Hovav and Levin, 2001; Simpson, 1983, 2006; Washio, 1997; Hoekstra, 1988, 1992; Napoli, 1992; Roberts, 1988; Williams, 1980; Green, 1973; Halliday, 1967). Resultatives in the study fall into seven subtypes classified based on the syntactic categories of the main verbs, which are given in (3).[1]

(3) a. The defendant kicked the victim unconscious.
b. The little boy ate himself sick.
c. George joked himself out of his job.
d. Sally would sleep her headache away.
e. The waiter could quickly wipe the water off the table.
f. The sodas broke open.
g. The hiker followed the stars out of the forest.

(3a) and (3b) both are headed by transitive verbs except that "eat" can alternate as an intransitive. Verbs in (3c, d), inherently monadic, take a fake NP (3c) or an unselected DP (3d) as part of the secondary predications. "Wipe" of (3e), a two-place predicate, takes an unconventional DP "the water." (3f) involves an unaccusative "break," where the surface DP is the subject of the secondary predicate "open." Unlike the rest, (3g) is a subject resultative, in that the abstract subject of the secondary predication PRO co-refers to the main-clause subject.

Mandarin resultatives splits into *de*-resultatives and V-V resultatives (see, e.g., Huang et al., 2009; Huang, 2006; Zhang, 2001; Cheng, 1997; Sybesma, 1997; Cheng and Huang, 1995; Zou, 1994). Neither matches the resultatives in English. While the *de*-constructions roughly correspond to the English canonical, bi-clausal resultatives (*The defendant kicked the victim until he became unconscious*), the V-V structures are rarely observed in English (see Shi_b, in progress). Besides, Mandarin has causative resultatives (Huang, 1988) or inverted readings (Li, 1998); neither is possible for today's English.

Depictives (1c) is distinct from resultatives; a secondary resultative functions as a complement to the matrix verb, a depictive an adjunct that is predicated of an argument of the primary predication (for differences, see Rothstein, 2006; Schultze-Berndt and Himmelmann, 2004; Rapoport, 1999; Stowell 1991; Hoekstra, 1988; Halliday, 1967). For convenience, let us take a depictive construction to be (4),

(4) $[\ DP_i\ [_{VP}\ V\ DP_j]\ [PRO_{i/j}\ DepP\ ]]$

[1] These are the actual resultatives produced under GP condition by Mandarin speakers of English, with minor modifications like use of a pronoun instead of a proper noun.

where indexing means co-reference. Two types of depictives were investigated: subject depictives (5a) and object depictives (5b), and with an unaccusative main verb, the object was fronted (5c).

(5) a. The invited speaker$_i$ delivered the speech drunk$_i$.
b. She bought the furniture$_i$ unpainted$_i$.
c. The package$_i$ arrived broken$_i$.

A depictive is well-formed if the attribute identified by the depictive phrase holds at the time of the main event, or (5c) is false if it means something other than *the package was broken when it arrived.*

Depictives as an independent secondary predicate has not found its way into Mandarin (see Zhang, 2001, for a different view), although it does occasionally show depictive elements (for distinction, see Himmelmann and Schultze-Berndt, 2006).

In terms of the abstractness determined by the frequency effect, we see a hierarchy for English: causatives > resultatives > depictives, where the least frequent and hence the least accessible is the last. Chinese differs: resultatives > causatives > depictives. Mandarin resultatives is far more productive than English resultatives (Huang et al., 2009; Huang, 2006; Li, 1998; Sybesma, 1997), its causatives is substantially less so (Thompson, 1973), and depictives is merely absent (Shi$_b$, in progress, 2003).

2 Method[2]

2.1 Participants

Nineteen Mandarin speakers of English (9 males, 10 females), between the ages of 26 and 48 ($M = 37.3$), were tested, along with nineteen native-born American college students[3] (4 males, 15 females), between the ages of 17 and 41 ($M = 27.4$). The nonnatives were recruited based on a set of criteria, including a consecutive period of 5 living years in the U.S. and a college education. As it turned out, they had an average of over 10 years living experience (range 5-17) and were employed in the mainstream workplace in America. All participated voluntarily.

[2] The data reported here is part of a more comprehensive experiment (see Shi, 2003).

[3] One native participant was a college graduate.

2.2 Tasks

Participants were subjected to two production and two comprehension tasks. For each of the 30 Guided Production (GP) test items, they first read a narrative of about 3-line long and then answered a question, using words provided, in all possible ways (e.g., *The chef boiled the lobster alive; The lobster was alive when the chef boiled it*). On the Clause-Combining (CC) task (30 items), subjects converted bi-clauses (*Sam drank until there is nothing left in the bottle of whisky*) into mono-clauses (*Sam drank the bottle empty*), using key words given. Of the two, GP was more demanding, given that subjects were asked to produce multiple answers. Also, for CC, they were allowed to leave a question blank.

The Grammaticality Judgment (GJ) task asked subjects to assess a total of 81 items for grammaticality on a scale of -3 to +3, with zero = no judgment. The analyses given below were based on 47 (2 causative, 2 inchoative, 16 resultatives, 13 canonical resultatives, 8 depictives, 6 canonical depictives) and the rest were fillers (ill-formed sentences) or sentences that turned out to be structural ambiguous, which then did not enter into the analyses. In choosing a numeral other than +3, subjects were instructed to identify the problem site by underlining the relevant word(s). The Interpretation task (IT) is the mirror image of the CC task. Participants matched mono-clauses with bi-clauses as paraphrases. Some items were 3-way ambiguous (resultative, object depictive, subject depictive) (6 items), others 2-way ambiguous (resultative and object depictive) (3 items), and still the others 1-way ambiguous (resultative) (5 items). As was designed, IT was relatively more challenging than GJ since multiple semantic recognitions forced participants to reconstruct more than one underlying representation.

The experiment tested 105 verbs or verb-pairs under three to four conditions and the analyses here are based on 96 of them: 6 causative verbs, 60 resultative verb-pairs, 30 depictive verb-pairs.[4] All tasks were individually administered in a paper and pencil format, with no time limit. Subjects were requested to carry out the tasks on their own.

[4] Three depictive verb-pairs tested under GP and four under CC were removed from the analyses for being potentially interpretable as conditionals or concessive/causals. Two causative inchoative verbs tested under GJ were also removed.

2.3 Results

Previously, it has been attested in study after study that while the natives fell victim to random errors, the nonnatives erred systematically (e.g., Kweon and Bley-Vroman, 2011; Chen, 2005; Papp, 2000; Johnson et al., 1996; Juffs, 1996). Of all the plausible explications, one that stands out in particular, albeit rarely noted, is that such native-nonnative disparities reflect more of the properties of the linguistic variables being tested, which inadvertently give the monolinguals an unfair head start. So it would be not just interesting but essential to see whether the presumed perfect or near-perfect native performance still prevails in the absence of such advantages.

Causatives, resultatives, and depictives are posited to be the linguistic features, which are vibrant in positive evidence and yet low in frequency, hence providing us with a unique testing ground for the native systematic variance and the native-nonnative difference.

2.3.1 Causatives

The causative constructions were studied under three conditions. Table 1 enumerates the means and sigmas (standard deviations *s.d.*), for the groups, of the verbs tested: *disappoint, interest* (GP), *bore, frustrate* (CC), *lengthen, awake* (GJ). Based on a

	GP		CC		GJ	
	M	σ	*M*	σ	*M*	σ
NS	1.79	.42	1.42	.77	11.26	1.94
NNS	1.63	.6	.95	.62	10.11	2.11

Table 1. Causative Means and *s.d.*

one-factor ANOVA with repeated measures, conditional variabilities were robustly found from both groups. The native speakers (NS) shifted in performance, beyond chance, from task to task, $F(2, 56) = 376.4$, $p < .05$, partial $\eta^2 = .96$ and so did the nonnative speakers (NNS), $F(2, 56) = 267.15$, $p < .05$, partial $\eta^2 = .94$. Interestingly, between the two, it was the NS that wobbled at a higher rate. Regardless, for both groups over 94% of the total behavioral variance was caused by the general task effects. This evidence strongly suggests that knowing causatives does not always guarantee its use, which is true of every subject irrespective of where he or she was born. Take the native speakers as an example. They all (100%) composed the target causative sentence using *disappoint* under GP, but only 58% did so using *frustrate* under CC.

No significant difference was found between the groups for any given task, based on three independent-sample *t*-tests,[5] with the alpha being set at .02 or one-third usual .05 alpha to offset alpha inflation. This evidence doubtless is unfavorable to Juffs's findings, according to which Chinese participants should have flunked no matter what conditions they were tested under.

2.3.2 Resultatives

In Table 2, group averages are given of the resultative data elicited from four tasks. If a group behaves

	GP	CC	GJ	IT
	M	*M*	*M*	*M*
NS	7.11 (1.76)	13.37 (1.21)	78.21 (9.07)	10.84 (1.46)
NNS	3.37 (1.7)	12.05 (2.25)	76.68 (10.78)	11.89 (1.37)

Table 2. Resultative Means and *s.d.* (in brackets)

as though it is controlled by the experimental conditions under which it is measured, then a large *F* value arises from a one-way repeated measures ANOVA. This is precisely what was in fact obtained, $F(3, 54) = 1020.41, p < .05$, partial $\eta^2 = .98$ (L_1 group), and $F(3, 54) = 713.58, p < .05$, partial $\eta^2 = .98$ (L_2 group). The findings clearly showed that neither group was good at breaking the conditional barriers; all subjects responded in accordance with

[5] All *t*-tests conducted in the experiment were two-tailed.

the task intricacies as opposed to what they knew about the target language. To illustrate, the native participants created 5 resultatives using *eat-sick* (*The boy ate himself sick*) under GP, compared with 14 using *work-to death* (*Mark worked himself to death*) under CC, despite the fact that both main verbs came from the same categorial class a.k.a transitive and selected the same type of secondary predicates. Had the native grammars been as steady and fast, unaffected by the circumstantial vagaries, as has been shown again and again in the literature, we would not have seen variations in performance of such magnitude.

Equally surprising is the finding that of the four conditions, the monolinguals outperformed the bilinguals only under GP, $t(36) = 3.35$, $p < .01$ (near one-fourth of normal .05 alpha), and this native merit was cancelled out under IT, where the reverse was found, $t(36) = 2.39$, $p > .01$.[6] This rather unexpected result could be explained away as an effect of positive transfer, but this possibility diminishes in face of the aforementioned differences in Mandarin-English resultatives. Additionally, it would leave unexplained the native-nonnative congruence attested under the CC and GJ conditions ($p > .01$).

2.3.3 Depictives

If the notion that a legitimate L_2 grammar must be native-like is sound, then depictives gives us reasons to contemplate the possibility that it is not. Due to the effects of input frequency and crosslinguistic differences, persistent L_2 aberrations should readily come along, parting from the native benchmark. This prediction has not quite panned out, as seen in Table 3. The depictive data, in contrast to the resultative data, appeared to be more homogeneous, with smaller standard deviations across groups. But a one-factor ANOVA for repeated measures ascertained that this visual impression was not what it seemed. Both groups demonstrated sensitivities to the challenges imposed by individual tasks, causing them to behave chancily. As before, it was the natives that were plagued by such unwarranted variabilities, $F(3, 54) = 860.56$, $p < .05$, partial $\eta^2 = .98$ (natives); $F(3, 54) = 435.96$, $p < .05$, partial $\eta^2 = .96$ (nonnatives). A series of two-sample t-test revealed that the two groups differed drastically under GP ($p = .0097$) and IT ($p = .000$), but they were indistinguishable under CC ($p = .61$) and GJ ($p = .08$).

As shown in Table 1, 2 and 3, the native means for causative, resultative and depictive productions under CC are 1.42, 13.37, and 2.74 and the nonnative means are .95, 12.05, and 2.53. According to a one-way repeated measures ANOVA, the natives did not treat the three constructions evenly, $F(2, 36) = 851.09$, $p < .05$, partial $\eta^2 = .98$, and neither did the nonnatives, $F(2, 36) = 306.71$, $p < .05$, partial $\eta^2 = .95$. The results indicate that not only did the conditions contribute to variable behaviors but also the constructions. With everything else being equal, one thing that is quite clear is that in assessing whether nonnative grammars are up to native par, one should take as little risk as possible of overlooking the effects of tasks and linguistic variables. Studies that hinge on a single trial or banal linguistic features undermine both their internal and external validity (see Cook and Campbell, 1979). They most likely fail to shed light on the research questions under probe, let alone be fit to generalize beyond the data at hand.

	GP	CC	GJ	IT
	M	*M*	*M*	*M*
NS	4 (1.41)	2.74 (1.28)	40.32 (4.32)	6.32 (2.38)
NNS	2.58 (1.77)	2.53 (1.26)	37 (6.86)	3.11 (1.29)

Table 3. Depictive Means and *s.d.* (in brackets)

[6] The between group difference was a bit short of the critical value of 2.43.

2.3.4 Variations Within or Between a Modality

What has been presented is the overall group variances in the production and comprehension of causatives, resultatives, and depictives. What happens if the modality effect or the task effect is partialed out? At the minimum, it is of import to know whether performance disparities would remain when tasks are isolated from the modality so that they do not covary, and if the two variables interact, how it proceeds across the two groups.

Let us first look at causatives. This time we focus on the production data and see if there is still task-induced variation without the comprehension mode as a covariate. Four causative verbs were analyzed: *disappoint, interest, bore, frustrate*, under GP and CC. The NS group achieved means of 1.79 (GP) and 1.42 (CC) and the NNS group means of 1.63 (GP) and 0.98 (CC) (Table 1). The production tasks were found not to affect the groups in the same way, based on two paired t-tests. The natives, whether to create causatives from scratch (e.g., *The stories about animals interested her*) or from bi-clauses (e.g., *The lecture was so long that Jack became bored → The lecture bored Jack*), performed consistently, $t(18) = 1.9$, $p > .025$, but the nonnatives did not, $t(18) = 3.34$, $p < .025$. Note that the two groups did not deviate or coincide across tasks to the same extent; the Mandarin speakers fell way below expectations under CC. Among all other plausible culprits, one that seems particularly relevant is that this was a lexical problem, as identified by Pinker (1989); namely, lexical knowledge tends to vary greatly from speaker to speaker, "no two alike" (p. 2). Under CC, for example, L_2 subjects succeeded 14 times (74%) with *bore*, compared to 4 times (21%) with *frustrate*.

In the case of resultatives, a broad modality-within, task-related difference was found. The natives as well as the nonnatives excelled under the CC condition, compared with the GP condition according to a set of paired t-tests ($p < .025$). All subjects, regardless of whether English was their first or second language, had a higher success chance to combine (6a) into (6b) than to ab initio construct (6c, d) based on brief narratives. The same was

(6) a. Margaret screamed and as a result she became sore in her throat.
b. Margaret screamed herself hoarse.
c. Sara read herself angry.[7]
d. Bill could have watered the plants flat.[8]

found for resultatives under the comprehension mode; subjects, native and nonnative, did substantially better under the less stressful GJ condition, than the more stressful IT condition ($p < .025$).

The effects of tasks relative to depictives were a bit murky for both of the groups. For the natives, though they used distinct strategies in dealing with tasks of a given modality at $p = .025$, the putative influence was not forthcoming. In comprehension, for example, they judged, as anticipated, better on GJ than IT, but in production they were more successful ($p < .025$) at constructing depictives without cues (7a, b) than modifying a canonical depictive (7c) into a depictive (7d). The experimental group

(7) a. Robert opened the window wet.[9]
b. The package arrived broken.[10]
c. Bob sold his car when it was new.
d. Bob sold his car new.

showed no production-related task effect ($p > .025$). For the comprehension tests, they met the expectation, being more accurate on GJ than IT ($p < .025$). All statistics were based on paired t-tests with alpha set at .025.

We have by far seen 16 cases where tasks alone, implemented in identical or different modes, either enhanced or inhibited the activation of the sought grammatical knowledge. The other 2 cases showed no task effect in production, one concerning the NS group that treated causatives under GP and CC blindly and the other the NNS group that handled depictives under GP and CC indiscriminately. Out of the total 16 cases of task-related variations, the natives showed more variances in 5 cases, whereas the nonnatives showed only in one case.

This opens up a crucial question of whether a task effect still holds across modalities or whether task and modality interact. To see this, we reexamined the resultative data collected in the CC production mode and the IT comprehension mode. Two paired-sample t-tests were conducted. Results show that the English-speaking subjects were more sensitive to the effects of task and modality, $t(18) = 5.9$, $p < .025$; they were more proficient at producing than identifying resultatives. By contrast, the Mandarin speakers of English were indifferent, whether to combine bi-clauses into resultatives or to match target sentences with resultative readings, $t(18) = .33$, $p > .025$.

[7] For (6c), no sample was obtained from either of the groups.

[8] Three from L_1 group yielded (6d), out of a total of 19, whereas none from L_2 group succeeded.

[9] For (7c), only two subjects from each group provided the target depictive construction.

[10] For (7d), L_1 group outstripped L_2 group; it collectively created 9 depictives in contrast to 3 by the nonnative group.

This result is at odds with the widely reported findings on two fronts. First, if variable behavior was ever found as a function of tasks, it should be retrieved from the second language learners only, as has been shown in Chen (2005), Kong (2005), White (2003_b), Lardiere (1998a, 1998b), Johnson et al. (1996), Sorace (1993). Natives by definition are sticklers for grammatical rules. Second, if a group could care less about whether to produce or to judge, it must be the one whose members speak English their whole lives. What was uncovered in the present study is the opposite; it was the nonnatives that were more of rule enforcers than the natives in composing or parsing resultatives.

The finding that the native-born subjects were likely to fluctuate could be confirmed provided that the similar depictive data was attested. To that end, let us compare the relevant data under CC and IT through two paired *t*-tests. As it turned out, only the natives performed in an unbalanced manner; they, while performing at a rate of 70% in recognizing depictive readings, did so at a rate of 46% in recreating depictives, $t(18) = 5.9$, $p < .025$. In contrast, the nonnatives barely altered between the two modalities, $t(18) = .33, p > .025$. To reiterate, it was not once but twice that the native controls showed mixed performances – constructing more than identifying resultatives, but identifying more than constructing depictives. The same failed to be found from the nonnatives. This suggests the possibility that the receptive vs. productive knowledge was not exactly the same insofar as the two groups were concerned.

To summarize, both the experimental and the control groups were found to vary along the lines of construction, task, and modality. The overall task effects were found, with mixed between-group differences. For causatives, all subjects shifted in performance across tasks and the natives did so to a greater extent. Within a given task, no difference whatsoever was ever found between the groups, under both modalities. On resultatives, both groups were identified with the similar task-based variations. Between the two, the natives prevailed under GP and the nonnatives under IT, but the two did not differ under CC and GJ. For depictives, similar task-related variance was found from both L_1 and L_2 groups, but the former outstripped the latter under the GP and IT conditions.

When holding the modality constant, subjects still varied across tasks. On resultatives, both groups behaved variably between tasks under a single modality. This pattern was nevertheless not found for depictives. Only the native participants were observed to switch strategies between GP and CC. On the comprehension side, the controls did better under GJ than IT and, the reverse was true of the experimental group. For the interactive effects, we see that the English speakers produced under CC more resultative samples than identified under IT, whereas the Mandarin speakers treated them all the same. On depictives, the same asymmetric performance pattern was found for both groups. Like the natives who did better under IT than under CC, the nonnatives showed the same pattern.

3 Conclusion

The major finding of the study is that speakers of English, as an L_1 or L_2, are not unsusceptible to the variability problem. By measuring the linguistic knowledge and the extraneous factors under which such knowledge is elicited, it shows the ties of the failures of activating knowledge to the unduly interference of tasks, constructions, or modalities. Contra the previous research, native speakers, just like their nonnative counterparts, are found to shift linguistically, not occasionally but most of the time. Where the bilinguals are spared, the monolinguals still succumb to the modality effects in both the resultative and depictive cases. Given all this, it is hard not to reject the null hypothesis and argue that native speakers do vary in linguistic competence. Generative L_2 researchers have barely paid attention to this aspect, whose only interest seems to be in the extent to which L_2 grammars correspond to L_1 grammars. The native-like requirement is difficult to reconcile with the following two facts: (1) the natives alter, swing, oscillate to a greater extent than the nonnatives; (2) nonnative grammars different from native grammars are still permitted in UG. This should be enough for us to rethink about the widely accepted research practice whereby L_2 grammars are assessed exclusively through the lens of the native norm or what Mack (2003) calls the *monolingual-comparison approach*. Instead, second language grammars should be, first and foremost, evaluated with respect to UG principles and operations and the input effects. L_2 intuitions, no matter how nonnative-like, could still tell us about the UG involvement in adult L_2 development.

References

Marina Yueh-cheng Chen. 2005. English Prototyped Small Clauses in the Interlanguage of Chinese/Taiwanese Adult Learners. Second Language Research 21(1): 1-33.

Lisa L-S Cheng. 1997. Resultative Compounds and Lexical Relational Structure. Chinese Languages and Linguistics III: Morphology and Lexicon. Taiwan.

Lisa L-S Cheng and C.-T. James Huang. 1995. On the Argument Structure of Resultative Compounds. In M. Chen and O. Tzeng (Eds.), In Honor of William Wang: Interdisciplinary Studies on Language and Language Change, 187-221. Pyramid Press, Taipei.

Noam Chomsky. 1972. Language and Mind (Enlarged Edition). Harcourt Brace Jovanovich, San Diego.

Noam Chomsky. 1981. Lectures on Government and Binding. Foris, Dordrecht.

Noam Chomsky. 1986. Knowledge of Language: Its Nature, Origin, and Use. Fraeger Publishers, Westport, CT.

Noam Chomsky 1988. Language and Problems of Knowledge: The Managua Lectures. MIT Press, Cambridge, MA.

Noam Chomsky 1993. Language and Thought. Moyer Bell, Wakefield, RI.

Noam Chomsky. 1998. Some Observations on Economy in Generative Grammar. In Pilar Barbosa, Danny Fox, Paul Hagstrom, Martha McGinnis, and David Pesetsky (Eds.), Is the Best Good Enough? 115-128. MIT Press, Cambridge, MA.

Thomas D. Cook and Donald T. Campbell. 1979. Quasi-experimentation: Design Analysis Issues for Field Settings. Houghton Mifflin, Boston.

David Embick and Rolf Noyer. 2007. Distributed Morphology and the Syntax-Morphology Interface. In Gillan Ranchand and Charles Reiss (Eds.), The Oxford handbook of linguistic interfaces, 289-324. Oxford University Press, Oxford, UK.

Georgia M. Green. 1973. A Syntactic Syncretism in English and French. In B. B. Kachru, R. B. Lees, Y. Malkiel, A. Pietrangeli, and S. Saporta (Eds.), Issues in Linguistics: Papers in Honor of Henry and Renee Kahane. University of Illinois Press, Chicago.

Ken Hale and Jay Keyser. 1993. On Argument Structure and the Lexical Expression of Syntactic Relations. In Ken Hale and Jay S. Keyser (Eds.), The View from Building 20: Essays in Linguistics in Honor of Sylvain Bromberger, 53-109. MIT Press, Cambridge, MA.

Ken Hale and Jay Keyser. 2002. Prolegomenon to a Theory of Argument Structure. MIT Press, Cambridge, MA.

Heidi Harley and Rolf Noyer. 2003. Distributed Morphology. In Lisa Cheng and Rint Sybesma (Eds.), The Second Glot International State-of-the-Article Book: The Latest in Linguistics, 467-496. Mouton de Gruyter, Berlin.

M. A. K. Halliday. 1967. Notes on Transitivity and Theme in English, Part I. Journal of Linguistics, 3(1): 37-81.

Nikolaus P. Himmelmann and Eva F. Schultze-Berndt. 2006. Issues in the Syntax and Semantics of Participant-oriented Adjuncts. In Nikolaus P. Himmelmann and Eva F. Schultze-Berndt (Eds.), Secondary Predication and Adverbial Modification: The Typology of Depictives, 1-68. Oxford University Press, Oxford, UK.

Teun Hoekstra. 1988. Small Clause Results. Lingua, 74 (203): 101-39.

Teun Hoekstra. 1992. Aspect and Theta-Theory. In I. M. Roca (Ed.), Thematic Structure: Its Role in Grammar, 145-74. Mouton de Gruyter, Berlin.

Ray Jackendoff. 1990. Semantic Structures. MIT Press, Cambridge, MA.

C.-T James Huang. 1988. Wǒ Pǎo de Kuài and Chinese Phrase Structure. Language, 64(2): 274-311.

C.-T James Huang. 2006. Resultatives and Unaccusitives: A Parametric View. Bulletin of the Chinese Linguistic Society of Japan 253: 1-43.

C.-T James Huang, Y.-H Audrey Li, and Yafei Li. (2009). The Syntax of Chinese. Cambridge University Press, Cambridge, UK.

Jacqueline S. Johnson, Kenneth D. Shenkman, Elissa L. Newport, and Douglas L. Medin. 1996. Indeterminacy in the Grammar of Adult Language Learners. Journal of Memory and Language, 35(3): 335-352.

Alan Juffs. 1996. Semantics-Syntax Correspondences in Second Language Acquisition. Second Language Research, 13(2): 177-221.

Stano Kong. 2005. The Partial Access of Universal Grammar in Second Language Acquisition: An Investigation of the Acquisition of English Subjects by L1 Chinese Speakers. Journal of East Asian Linguistics, 14(3): 227-265.

Soo-Ok Kweon and Robert Bley-Vroman. 2011. Acquisition of the constraints on *wanna* contraction by advanced second language learners: Universal grammar and imperfect knowledge. Second Language Research 27(2): 207-228.

Donna Lardiere. 1998_a. Case and Tense in the 'Fossilized' Steady State. Second Language Research, 14(1): 1-26.

Donna Lardiere. 1998_b. Dissociating syntax from morphology in a divergent L2 end-state grammar. Second Language Research, 12(4): 359-375.

Beth Levin and Malka Rappaport Hovav. 1995. Unaccusativity: At the Syntax-Lexical Semantics Interface. MIT Press, Cambridge, MA.

Yafei Li. 1998. Chinese Resultative Constructions and the Uniformity of Theta Assignment Hypothesis. In Jerome L. Packard (Ed.), New Approaches to Chinese

Word Formation: Morphology, Phonology and the Lexicon in Modern and Ancient Chinese, 285-310. Mouton de Gruyter, Berlin.

Molly Mack. 1997. The Monolingual Native Speaker: Not a Norm, but Still a Necessity. Studies in the Linguistics Sciences, 27(2): 113-146.

Molly Mack. 2003. The Phonetic Systems of Bilinguals. In Marie T. Banich and Molly Mack (Eds.), Mind, Brain, and Language, 309-349. Lawrence Erlbaum Associates, Publishers, Mahwah, New Jersey.

Alec Marantz. 1997. No Escape from Syntax: Don't Try Morphological Analysis in the Privacy of Your Own Lexicon. In Alexis Dimitriadis (Ed.), Proceedings of the 27th Annual Penn Linguistics Colloquium. Pennsylvania Working Papers in Linguistics 4, Philadelphia.

Ora Matushansky and Alec Marantz. 2013. Distributed Morphology Today. MIT Press, Cambridge, MA.

Donna Jo Napoli. 1992. Secondary Resultative Predicates in Italian. Journal of Linguistics, 28(1), 53-90.

Szilvia Papp. 2000. Stable and Developmental Optionality in Native and Non-native Hungarian Grammars. Second Language Research, 16(2): 173-200.

Steven Pinker. 1989. Learnability and Cognition. MIT Press, Cambridge, MA.

Tova R. Rapoport. 1999. Structure, Aspect, and the Predicate. Language, 75(4): 653-77.

Malka Rappaport Hovav and Beth Levin. 2001. An Event Structure Account of English Resultatives. Language, 77(4): 766-797.

Matthew Rispoli. 2003. Changes in the Nature of Sentence Production During the Period of Grammatical Development. Journal of Speech, Language, and Hearing Research, 46(4): 818-830.

Ian Roberts. 1988. Predicative APs. Linguistic Inquiry, 19(4): 703-10.

Susan Rothstein. 2006. Secondary Predication. In Martin Everaert and Henk van Riemskijk (Eds.), The Blackwell Companion to Syntax, Volume I, 209-233. Blackwell, UK.

Jacquelyn Schachter. 1990. On the Issue of Completeness in Second Language Acquisition. Second Language Research, 6(2): 93-124.

Eva Schultze-Berndt and Nikolaus P. Himmelmann. 2004. Depictive Secondary Predicates in Crosslinguistic Perspective. Linguistic Typology 8(1): 59-131.

Enchao Shi. 2003. Second Language Grammar and Secondary Predication. Tucson: University of Arizona Ph.D. Dissertation.

Enchao Shi. 2014. Optionality in Second Language Grammar. In C.-T. James Huang and Feng-his Liu (Eds.), Peaches and Plums, 353-378. Academia Sinica, Taipei.

Enchao Shi$_a$. (in progress). Nativelikeness and Second Language Mini*G*. California State University, Northridge.

Enchao Shi$_b$ (in progress). Subject Resultatives and Mandarin Clause Structure. California State University, Northridge.

Jane Simpson. 1983. Resultatives. In Lori Levin, Malk Rappaport, and Annie Zaenen (Eds.), Papers in Lexical-Functional Grammar, 143-57. Indiana, Bloomington: Indiana University Linguistics Club.

Jane Simpson. 2006. Depictives in English and Warlpiri. In Nidolaus P. Himmelmann and Eva F. Schultze-Berndt (Eds.), Secondary Predication and Adverbial Modification: The Typology of Depictives, 69-106. Oxford University Press, Oxford, UK.

Antollena Sorace. 1993. Incomplete vs. Divergent Representations of unaccusativity in Near-Native Grammars of Italian. Second Language Research, 9(1): 22–48.

Tim Stowell. 1991. Small Clause Restructuring. In Robert Freidin (Ed.), Principles and Parameters in Comparative Grammar, 182-218. MIT Press, Cambridge, MA.

Rint Sybesma. 1997. Why Chinese Verb-Le Is a Resultative Predicate. Journal of East Asian Linguistics, 6(3): 215-261.

Sandra A. Thompson. 1973. Transitivity and Some Problems with the Ba Construction in Mandarin Chinese. Journal of Chinese Linguistics, 1(2): 208-221.

Ryuichi Washio. 1997. Resultatives, Compositionality and Language Variation. Journal of East Asian Linguistics 6(1): 1-49.

Lydia White. 2003$_a$. Second Language Acquisition and Universal Grammar. Cambridge University Press, Cambridge, UK.

Lydia White. 2003$_b$. Fossilization in Steady State L2 Grammars: Persistent Problems with Inflectional Morphology. Bilingualism: Language and Cognition, 6(2): 129-141.

Edwin Williams. 1980. Predication. Linguistic Inquiry 11(1): 203-38.

Niina Zhang. 2001. The Structures of Depictives and Resultative Construction in Chinese. In G. Jdger, A. Strigin, C. Wilder and N. Zhang (Eds.), ZAS working papers in linguistics 22: 191-221.

Ke Zou. 1994. Resultative V-V Compounds in Chinese. MIT working papers in linguistics 22: 1-23. Cambridge, MA.

A Generalized Framework for Hierarchical Word Sequence Language Model

Xiaoyi Wu, Kevin Duh, Yuji matsumoto
Nara Institute of Science and Technology
Computational Linguistics Laboratory
8916-5 Takayama, Ikoma, Nara Japan
{xiaoyi-w,kevinduh,matsu}@is.naist.jp

Abstract

Language modeling is a fundamental research problem that has wide application for many NLP tasks. For estimating probabilities of natural language sentences, most research on language modeling use n-gram based approaches to factor sentence probabilities. However, the assumption under n-gram models is not robust enough to cope with the data sparseness problem, which affects the final performance of language models.

At the point, Hierarchical Word Sequence (abbreviated as HWS) language models can be viewed as an effective alternative to normal n-gram method. In this paper, we generalize HWS models into a framework, where different assumptions can be adopted to rearrange word sequences in a totally unsupervised fashion, which greatly increases the expandability of HWS models.

For evaluation, we compare our rearranged word sequences to conventional n-gram word sequences. Both intrinsic and extrinsic experiments verify that our framework can achieve better performance, proving that our method can be considered as a better alternative for n-gram language models.

1 Introduction

Probabilistic Language Modeling is a fundamental research direction of Natural Language Processing. It is widely used in various application such as machine translation (Brown et al., 1990), spelling correction (Mays et al., 1990), speech recognition (Rabiner and Juang, 1993), word prediction (Bickel et al., 2005) and so on.

Most research about Probabilistic Language Modeling, such as Katz back-off (Katz, 1987), Kneser-Ney (Kneser and Ney, 1995), and modified Kneser-Ney (Chen and Goodman, 1999), only focus on smoothing methods because they all take the n-gram approach (Shannon, 1948) as a default setting for modeling word sequences in a sentence. Yet even with 30 years worth of newswire text, more than one third of all trigrams are still unseen (Allison et al., 2005), which cannot be distinguished accurately even using a high-performance smoothing method such as modified Kneser-Ney (abbreviated as MKN).

An alternative solution is to factor the language model probabilities such that the number of unseen sequences are reduced. It is necessary to extract them in another way, instead of only using the information of left-to-right continuous word order.

In (Guthrie et al., 2006), skip-gram (Huang et al., 1993)[1] is proposed to overcome the data sparseness problem. For each n-gram word sequence, the skip-gram model enumerates all possible word combinations to increase valid sequences. This has truly helped to decrease the unseen sequences, but we should not neglect the fact that it also brings a greatly increase of processing time and redundant contexts.

In (Wu and Matsumoto, 2014), a heuristic approach is proposed to convert any raw sentence into a hierarchical word sequence (abbreviated as

[1]The k-skip-n-grams for a sentence $w_1, ...w_m$ is defined as the set $\{w_{i_1}, w_{i_2}, ...w_{i_n} | \Sigma_{j=1}^{n} i_j - i_{j-1} < k\}$.

HWS) structure, by which much more valid word sequences can be modeled while remaining the model size as small as that of n-gram. In (Wu and Matsumoto, 2015) (Wu et al., 2015), instead of only using the information of word frequency, the information of direction and word association are also used to construct higher quality HWS structures. However, they are all specific methods based on certain heuristic assumptions. For the purpose of further improvements, it is also necessary to generalize those models into one unified structure.

This paper is organized as follows. In Section 2, we review the HWS language model. Then we present a generalized hierarchical word sequence structure (GHWSS) in Section 3. In Section 4, we present two strategies for rearranging word sequences under the framework of GHWSS. In Sections 5 and 6, we show the effectiveness of our model by both intrinsic experiments and extrinsic experiments. Finally, we summarize our findings in Section 7.

2 Review of HWS Language Model

In (Wu and Matsumoto, 2014), the *HWS* structure is constructed from training data in an unsupervised way as follows:

Suppose that we have a frequency-sorted vocabulary list $V = \{v_1, v_2, ..., v_m\}$, where $C(v_1) \geq C(v_2) \geq ... \geq C(v_m)$[2].

According to V, given any sentence $S = w_1, w_2, ..., w_n$, the most frequently used word $w_i \in S (1 \leq i \leq n)$ can be selected[3] for splitting S into two substrings $S_L = w_1, ..., w_{i-1}$ and $S_R = w_{i+1}, ..., w_n$. Similarly, for S_L and S_R, $w_j \in S_L (1 \leq j \leq i-1)$ and $w_k \in S_R (i+1 \leq k \leq n)$ can also be selected, by which S_L and S_R can be splitted into two smaller substrings separately. Executing this process recursively until all the substrings become empty strings, then a tree $T = (\{w_i, w_j, w_k, ...\}, \{(w_i, w_j), (w_i, w_k), ...\})$ can be generated, which is defined as an *HWS structure* (Figure 1).

In an HWS structure T, assuming that each node depends on its preceding n-1 parent nodes, then special n-grams can be trained. Such kind of n-grams are defined as *HWS-n-grams*.

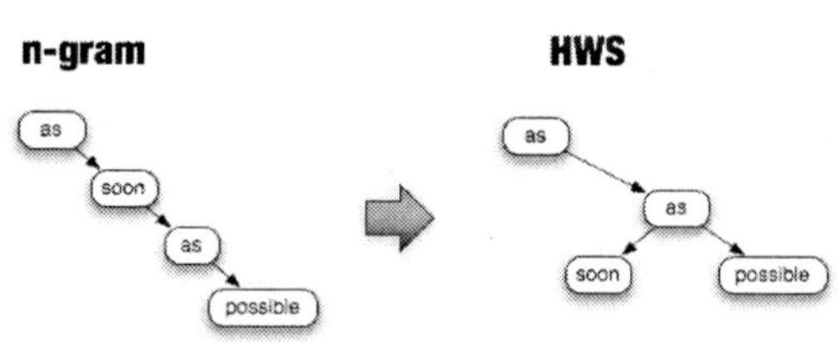

Figure 1: A comparison of structures between HWS and n-gram

The advantage of HWS models can be considered as *discontinuity*. Taking Figure 1 as an example, since n-gram model is a continuous language model, in its structure, the second 'as' depends on 'soon', while in the HWS structure, the second 'as' depends on the first 'as', forming a discontinuous pattern to generate the word 'soon', which is closer to our linguistic intuition. Rather than 'as soon ...', taking 'as ... as' as a pattern is more reasonable because 'soon' is quite easy to be replaced by other words, such as 'fast', 'high', 'much' and so on. Consequently, even using 4-gram or 5-gram, sequences consisting of 'soon' and its nearby words tend to be low-frequency because the connection of 'as...as' is still interrupted. On the contrary, the HWS model extracts sequences in a discontinuous way, even 'soon' is replaced by another word, the expression 'as...as' won't be affected. This is how the HWS models relieve the data sparseness problem.

The HWS model is essentially an n-gram language model based on a different assumption that a word depends upon its nearby high-frequency words instead of its preceding words. Different from other special n-gram language models, such as class-based language model (Brown et al., 1992), factored language model(FLM) (Bilmes and Kirchhoff, 2003), HWS language model doesn't use any specific linguistic knowledge or any abstracted categories. Also, differs from dependency tree language models (Shen et al., 2008) (Chen et al., 2012), HWS language model constructs a tree structure in an unsupervised fashion.

In HWS structure, word sequences are adjusted so that irrelevant words can be filtered out from contexts and long distance information can be used

[2] $C(v)$ represents the frequency of v in a certain corpus.

[3] If w_i appears multiple times in S, then select the first one.

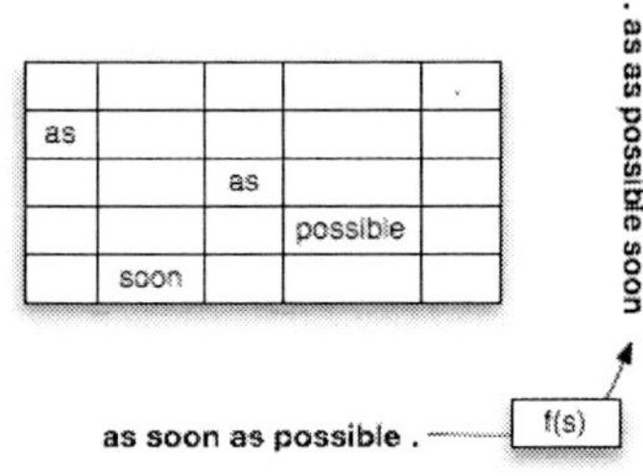

Figure 2: An Example of Generative Hierarchical Word Sequence Structure

for predicting the next word, which make it more effective and flexible in relieving the data sparseness problem. On this point, it has something in common with structured language model (Chelba, 1997), which firstly introduced parsing into language modeling. The significant difference is, structured language model is based on CFG parsing structures, while HWS model is based on pattern-oriented structures.

3 Generalized Hierarchical Word Sequence Structure

Suppose we are given a sentence $s = w_1, w_2, ..., w_n$ and a permutation function $f : s \rightarrow s'$, where $s' = w'_1, w'_2, ..., w'_n$ is a permutation of s. For each word index $i(1 \leq i \leq n, w_i \in s)$, there is a corresponding reordered index $j(1 \leq j \leq n, w'_j \in s', w'_j = w_i)$.

Then we create an $n \times n$ matrix A. For each row j, we fill cell $A_{j,i}$ with w_i. We define the matrix A as the **generalized hierarchical word sequence structure** (abbreviated as **GHWSS**) of the sentence s. An example is shown in Figure 2.

In a GHWSS, given any word $w \in \{A_{j,i} | w'_j = w_i\}$, the words in its higher rows are $X = \{A_{k,m} | k < j, 1 \leq m \leq n, w'_k = w_m\}$, in which the nearest two neighbors of w are $\hat{l} = A_{k_l,\hat{m}_l}(k_l < j, \hat{m}_l = \underset{1 \leq m < i}{\operatorname{argmin}}(i - m))$ and $\hat{r} = A_{k_r,\hat{m}_r}(k_r < j, \hat{m}_r = \underset{i < m \leq n}{\operatorname{argmin}}(m - i))$ respectively[4]. Then we assume that w depends on $\hat{w} = \hat{l}$ if $k_l > k_r$ or $\hat{w} = \hat{r}$ if $k_l < k_r$. For example, in Figure 2, given the word 'soon', its higher rows $X = \{as, as, possible, .\}$, in which the nearest neighbors of 'soon' are $\hat{l} = as$ and $\hat{r} = as$, since the second 'as' is closer to 'soon' vertically, we assume 'soon' depends the second 'as' in this GHWSS.

Further, for the word $A_{1,i}$, we define that it depends on symbol '$\langle s \rangle$'. We also use the symbol '$\langle /s \rangle$' to represent the end of generation.

For each word $w = A_{j,i}$, if we assume that it only depends on its previous few words in its dependency chain, then we can achieve special n-grams under the GHWSS. Taking Figure 2 as the example, we can train 3-grams like {($\langle s \rangle$, $\langle s \rangle$, .), ($\langle s \rangle$, ., as), (., as, as), (as, as, possible), (as, possible, $\langle /s \rangle$), (as, as, soon), (as, soon, $\langle /s \rangle$)}.

In (Wu and Matsumoto, 2015), it is verified that the performance of HWS model can be further improved by using directional information. Thus, in this paper, we defaultly use directional information to model word sequences. Then the above 3-grams should be {($\langle s \rangle$, $\langle s \rangle$, .), ($\langle s \rangle$, .-R, $\langle /s \rangle$), ($\langle s \rangle$, .-L, as), (.-L, as-L, $\langle /s \rangle$), (.-L, as-R, as), (as-R, as-L, soon), (as-L, soon-L, $\langle /s \rangle$), (as-L, soon-R, $\langle /s \rangle$), (as-R, as-R, possible), (as-R, possible-L, $\langle /s \rangle$), (as-R, possible-R, $\langle /s \rangle$) and the probability of the whole sentence 'as soon as possible .' can be estimated by the product of conditional probabilities of all these word sequences.

4 Two Strategies for constructing GHWSS

Once a permutation function f is implemented, the GHWSS of any sentence can be constructed. Thus, the performance of GHWSS is totally determined by how to implement the function f for rearranging word sequences.

Since n-gram models assume that a word depends on its previous n-1 words, the function f of n-gram methods can be considered as the identity permutation. For each word w_i, we fill cell $A_{i,i}$ with w_i, then the n-gram method is a special case of GHWSS.

In this section, we propose two kinds of methods for implementing function f under GHWSS.

4.1 Word Frequency Based Method

Step 1. Calculate word frequencies from training data and sort all words by their frequency. Assume we get a frequency-sorted list $V = \{v_1, v_2, ..., v_m\}$, where $C(v_j) > C(v_{j+1}), 1 \leq j \leq m - 1$. [5]

[4] There is no $\hat{l}$ when $i = 1$, while no $\hat{r}$ when $i = n$.

[5] $C(v_j)$ represents the frequency of v_j.

Step 2. According to V, for each sentence $s = w_1, w_2, ..., w_n$, we permute it into $s' = w_1', w_2', ..., w_n'(w_k' = v_x, w_{k+1}' = v_y, 1 \leq k \leq n-1, 1 \leq x \leq y \leq m)$.

Then the GHWSS constructed by the permutation s' is equivalent to that of frequency-based HWS method.

4.2 Word Association Based Method

Step 1. For each sentence s in corpus D, we convert it into s', in which each word only appear once.

Step 2. For each word w_i in the corpus $D' = \{s_i' | 1 \leq i \leq |D|\}$, we count its frequency $C(w_i)$ and its cooccurrence with another word $C(w_i, w_j)$.

Step 3. For each original sentence $s \in D$, we initiate an empty list X and set the beginning symbol '$\langle s \rangle$' as the initial context c[6].

Step 4. For each word $w \in s$, we calculate its word association score with context c. In this paper, we use T-score[7] as the word association measure.

$$T(c, w) = (C(c, w) - \frac{C(c) \times C(w)}{V}) \div \sqrt{C(c, w)} \quad (1)$$

Then we add the i-th word $\hat{w}$ with the maximum score to list X[8] and use it to split s into two substrings $s_l = w_1, ..., w_{i-1}$ and $s_r = w_{i+1}, ..., w_n$.

Step 5. We set $\hat{w}$ as the new context c'. For each word in s_l, we calculate its word association score with c' and add the word with the maximum score to list X[9] and use it to divide s_l into two smaller substrings. Then we apply the same process to the substring s_r.

Execute Step4 and Step5 recursively until anymore substrings cannot be divided, then the original sentence s is permuted as list X, by which GHWSS of s can be constructed.

5 Intrinsic Evaluation

We use two different corpus: **British National Corpus** and **English Gigaword Corpus**.

British National Corpus (BNC) [10] is a 100 million word collection of samples of written and spoken English from a wide range of sources. We use all the 6,052,202 sentences (100 million words) for the training data.

English Gigaword Corpus [11] consists of over 1.7 billion words of English newswire from 4 distinct international sources. We choose the *wpb_eng* part (162,099 sentences, 20 million words) for the test data.

As preprocessing of the training data and the test data, we use the tokenizer of NLTK (Natural Language Toolkit) [12] to split raw English sentences into words. We also converted all words to lowercase.

To ensure the openness of our research, the source code used in the following experiments is available on the internet.[13]

As intrinsic evaluation of language modeling, perplexity (Manning and Schütze, 1999) is the most common metric used for measuring the usefulness of a language model. However, since we unsupervisedly 'parse' the test sentence s into a GHWSS structure before we estimate its probability, its conditional entropy is actually $H(s|T(s))$, where $T(s)$ represents the GHWSS assigned to the test sentence s. Consequently, our method has much lower perplexity. It's not appropriate to directly compare the perplexity of GHWSS-based models to that of n-gram models.

Also, perplexity is not necessarily a reliable way of determining the usefulness of a language model since a language models with low perplexity may not work well in a real world application. Thus, for intrinsic evaluation, we evaluate models only based on how much they can *actually relieve the data sparseness problem* (reduce the unseen sequences).

In (Wu and Matsumoto, 2014), **coverage score** are used to perform this kind of evaluation. The word sequences modeled from training data are defined as TR, while that of test data as TE, then the coverage score is calculated by Equation (2). Obviously, the higher coverage score a language model can achieve, the more it can relieve the data sparseness problem (reduce the unseen sequences).

[6] Since $\langle s \rangle$ appears only once in each sentence, we set $C(\langle s \rangle)$ as the size of corpus.

[7] V stands for the total number of words in corpus.

[8] If $\hat{w}$ appears multiple times in s, then select the first one.

[9] If the context word c' also appears in s_l, then we regard it as the word with the maximum score and add it to X directly.

[10] http://www.natcorp.ox.ac.uk

[11] https://catalog.ldc.upenn.edu/LDC2011T07

[12] http://www.nltk.org

[13] https://github.com/aisophie/HWS

Table 1: Performance of Various Word Sequences

Models	Coverage		Usage		F-score	
	Unique	Total	Unique	Total	Unique	Total
bi-gram	**46.471**	83.121	12.015	76.336	**19.093**	79.584
frequency-based-bi	46.066	89.730	**12.019**	86.937	19.064	88.312
tscore-based-bi	45.709	**89.949**	11.872	**87.252**	18.848	**88.580**
tri-gram	27.164	51.151	5.626	40.191	9.321	45.013
frequency-based-tri	**36.512**	72.432	**8.546**	67.221	**13.850**	69.729
tscore-based-tri	36.473	**72.926**	8.501	**67.382**	13.788	**70.045**

$$score_{coverage} = \frac{|TR \bigcap TE|}{|TE|} \quad (2)$$

If all possible word combinations are enumerated as word sequences, then considerable coverage score can be achieved. However, the processing efficiency of a model become extremely low. Thus, **usage score** (Equation (3)) is also necessary to estimate how much redundancy is contained in a model.

$$score_{usage} = \frac{|TR \bigcap TE|}{|TR|} \quad (3)$$

A balanced measure between coverage and usage is calculated by Equation (4).

$$F\text{-}Score = \frac{2 \times coverage \times usage}{coverage + usage} \quad (4)$$

In this paper, we use the same metric to compare word sequences modeled under GHWSS framework with normal n-gram sequences.

The result is shown in Table 1 [14]. According to the results, for total word sequences, which actually affect the final performance of language models, GHWSS-based methods have obvious advantage over the normal bi-gram model. As for tri-grams, the GHWSS-based methods can even improve around 25%.

6 Extrinsic Evaluation

For the purpose of examining how our models work in the real world application, we also performed extrinsic experiments to evaluate our method. In this paper, we use the reranking of n-best translation candidates to examining how language models work in a statistical machine translation task.

We use the French-English part of TED talk parallel corpus for the experiment dataset. The training data contains 139,761 sentence pairs, while the test data contains 1,617 sentence pairs. For training language models, we set English as the target language.

As for statistical machine translation toolkit, we use **Moses system**[15] to train the translation model and output 50-best translation candidates for each French sentence of the test data. Then we use 139,761 English sentences to train language models. With these models, 50-best translation candidates are reranked. According to these reranking results, the performance of machine translation system is evaluated, which also means, the language models are evaluated indirectly. In this paper, we use the following measures for evaluating reranking results[16].

BLEU (Papineni et al., 2002): BLEU score measures how many words overlap in a given candidate translation when compared to a reference translation, which provides some insight into how good the fluency of the output from an engine will be.

METEOR (Banerjee and Lavie, 2005): METEOR score computes a one-to-one alignment between matching words in a candidate translation and a reference.

TER (Snover et al., 2006): TER score measures the number of edits required to change a system output into one of the references, which gives an indication as to how much post-editing will be required

[14] "Unique" means counting each word sequence only once in spite of the amount of times it really occurs.

[15] http://www.statmt.org/moses/

[16] We use open source tool **multeval** (https://github.com/jhclark/multeval) to perform the evaluation.

Table 2: Performance on French-English SMT Task Using Various Word Arranging Assumptions

Models	BLEU	METEOR	TER
tri-gram	31.3	33.5	49.0
frequency-based-tri	31.5	**33.6**	48.6
tscore-based-tri	**31.7**	**33.6**	**48.5**

on the translated output of an engine.

We use GHWSS word rearranging strategies to perform experiments and compared them to the normal n-gram strategy. For estimating the probabilities of translation candidates, we use the modified Kneser-Ney smoothing (MKN) as the smoothing method of all strategies. As shown in Table 2, GHWSS based strategies outperform that of n-gram on each score.

7 Conclusion

In this paper, we proposed a generalized hierarchical word sequence framework for language modeling. Under this framework, we presented two different unsupervised strategies for rearranging word sequences, where the conventional n-gram strategy as one special case of this structure.

For evaluation, we compared our rearranged word sequences to conventional n-gram word sequences and performed intrinsic and extrinsic experiments. The intrinsic experiment proved that our methods can greatly relieve the data sparseness problem, while the extrinsic experiments proved that SMT tasks can benefit from our strategies. Both verified that language modeling can achieve better performance by using our word sequences rearranging strategies, which also proves that our strategies can be used as better alternatives for n-gram language models.

Further, instead of conventional n-gram word sequences, our rearranged word sequences can also be used as the features of various kinds of machine learning approaches, which is an interesting future study.

References

B. Allison, D. Guthrie, L. Guthrie, W. Liu, and Y Wilks. 2005. *Quantifying the Likelihood of Unseen Events: A further look at the data Sparsity problem*. Awaiting publication.

S. Banerjee and A. Lavie. 2005. Meteor: An automatic metric for mt evaluation with improved correlation with human judgments. In *Proceedings of the acl workshop on intrinsic and extrinsic evaluation measures for machine translation and/or summarization*, pages 65–72.

S. Bickel, P. Haider, and T. Scheffer. 2005. Predicting sentences using n-gram language models. In *Proceedings of the conference on Human Language Technology and Empirical Methods in Natural Language Processing*, pages 193–200.

J. A. Bilmes and K. Kirchhoff. 2003. Factored language models and generalized parallel backoff. In *Proceedings of the 2003 Conference of the North American Chapter of the Association for Computational Linguistics on Human Language Technology*, volume 2, pages 4–6.

P.F Brown, J Cocke, S.A Pietra, V.J Pietra, F Jelinek, J.D Lafferty, R.L Mercer, and P.S Roossin. 1990. A statistical approach to machine translation. *Computational linguistics*, 16(2):79–85.

P. F. Brown, P. V. Desouza, R. L. Mercer, V. J. D. Pietra, and J. C. La. 1992. Class-based n-gram models of natural language. *Computational linguistics*, 18(4):467–479.

C. Chelba. 1997. A structured language model. In *Proceedings of ACL-EACL*, pages 498–500.

S. F. Chen and J. Goodman. 1999. An empirical study of smoothing techniques for language modeling. *Computer Speech and Language*, 13(4):359–393.

W. Chen, M. Zhang, and H Li. 2012. Utilizing dependency language models for graph-based dependency parsing models. In *Proceedings of the 50th Annual Meeting of the Association for Computational Linguistics*, volume 1, pages 213–222.

D. Guthrie, B. Allison, W. Liu, and L. Guthrie. 2006. A closer look at skip-gram modeling. In *Proceedings of the 5th international Conference on Language Resources and Evaluation*, pages 1–4.

X. Huang, F. Alleva, H.W. Hon, M.Y. Hwang, and K. F. Lee. 1993. The sphinx-ii speech recognition system: an overview. 7(2):137–148.

S. Katz. 1987. Estimation of probabilities from sparse data for the language model component of a speech recognizer. *Acoustics, Speech and Signal Processing*, 35(3):400–401.

R. Kneser and H. Ney. 1995. Improved backing-off for m-gram language modeling. *Acoustics, Speech, and Signal Processing*, 1:181–184.

C. D. Manning and H. Schütze. 1999. *Foundations of statistical natural language processing*. MIT Press.

E. Mays, F. J. Damerau, and R. L. Mercer. 1990. Context based spelling correction. *Information Processing and Management*, 27(5):517–522.

K. Papineni, S. Roukos, T. Ward, and W.J. Zhu. 2002. Bleu: a method for automatic evaluation of machine translation. In *Proceedings of the 40th annual meeting on association for computational linguistics*, pages 311–318.

L. Rabiner and B.H. Juang. 1993. *Fundamentals of Speech Recognition*. Prentice Hall.

C. E. Shannon. 1948. A mathematical theory of communication. *The Bell System Technical Journal*, 27:379–423.

L. Shen, J. Xu, and R.M. Weischedel. 2008. A new string-to-dependency machine translation algorithm with a target dependency language model. In *ACL*, pages 577–585.

M. Snover, B. Dorr, R. Schwartz, L. Micciulla, and J. Makhoul. 2006. A study of translation edit rate with targeted human annotation. In *Proceedings of association for machine translation in the Americas*, pages 223–231.

X. Wu and Y. Matsumoto. 2014. A hierarchical word sequence language model. In *Proceedings of The 28th Pacific Asia Conference on Language*, pages 489–494.

X. Wu and Y. Matsumoto. 2015. An improved hierarchical word sequence language model using directional information. In *Proceedings of The 29th Pacific Asia Conference on Language*, pages 453–458.

X. Wu, Y. Matsumoto, K. Duh, and S. Hiroyuki. 2015. An improved hierarchical word sequence language model using word association. In *Statistical Language and Speech Processing*, pages 275–287.

Processing English Island Sentences by Korean EFL Learners

Yeonkyung Park
Hannam University
70 Hannamro, Daedeok-gu
Daejeon 306-791, Korea
withbyk@gmail.com

Yong-hun Lee
Chungnam National University
99 Daehak-ro, Yuseong-gu
Daejeon 305-764, Korea
yleeuiuc@hanmail.net

Abstract

This paper took an experimental approach and investigated how Korean EFL learners process the English island constructions. Since there are some controversies on the existence of the island effects in Korean, the L1 transfer effect may make it difficult for the Korean EFL learners to learn island constructions in English. To examine if the difference between English and Korean affects the acquisition of English island constructions, four different types of target sentences were made for English island phenomena: Complex-NP, whether, subject, and adjunct island. The acceptability scores of Korean EFL learners were measured with Magnitude Estimation (ME). Then, the collected data were statistically analyzed. The analysis results showed that, unlike previous studies, the Korean EFL learners correctly identified all of the English island constructions. This finding showed that the island status of the Korean language did not affect the acquisition of island constructions in English.

1 Introduction

Since Ross's identifications of island constraints in English (Ross, 1967), there have been a lot of debates on the existence of island constraints in other languages. Some languages were believed to contain some island effects, while other languages (e.g. Chinese, Korean, or Japanese) were doubtful about the existence of island effect.

The status of island effects of the L1 (the mother tongue) also may influence the acquisition of L2, since it was well-known that the knowledge of L1 might influence the acquisition of L2, which was known as the L1 transfer effects (Selinker, 1969; Odlin, 1989; 2003). Korean students learn English as Foreign Language (EFL), since English is not an official language in Korean. There have been some controversies on the existence of island constraints in Korean. Some have argued for the presence of island effects (Lee 1982, Han 1992, Hong 2004), while others have argued against it (Sohn 1980, Kang 1986, Suh 1987, Hwang 2007).[1] Then, the question is whether the island status of Korean may influence the acquisition of the constructions in English. To answer this question is also crucial from the psycholinguistic point of view, since there might be different psycholinguistic or cognitive processes when people produce or understand the island constructions in their native language (L1) and another language (L2).

In order to investigate whether the L1 transfer effects also appear in the acquisition of English island constructions, an experiment was designed where the acceptability scores of the Korean EFL learners were measured with the ME method. Then, the collected data were statistically analyzed with R.

This paper is organized as follows. In Section 2, previous studies are reviewed. Section 3 includes the experimental design, research materials and research method. Section 4 enumerates the analysis

[1] Similar kinds of controversies exist also for Japanese. Nishigauchi (1990) and Watanabe (1992) claimed that there were island constraints in Japanese, but Ishihara (2002) and Sprouse et al. (2011) mentioned that this language had no island constraint.

results. Section 5 contains discussions, and Section 6 summarizes this paper.

2 Previous Studies

2.1 Island Effects in Korean

Since Ross (1967) identified the island constraints in English, there have been a lot of studies on the existence of island phenomena in other languages. These previous studies focused on examining if the island constraints existed in their languages and why the language escaped the island constraints when the language did not show the island phenomena.

Korean is no exception. There have been lots of previous studies on the island constraints also in Korean, but there are two opposite positions in the previous approaches. Some claimed that Korean has island constraints (Lee 1982; Han 1992; Hong 2004; Park, 2001, 2009). Hong (2004) proposed two diagnostics for syntactic movements: island and intervention effects. He mentioned that Korean also has an island effects. Park (2001) and Park (2009) claimed that matrix sluicing in Korean was island-sensitive, through examining the sluicing constructions in Korean.

On the other hand, other scholars claimed that there is no island effect in Korean (Sohn, 1980; Kang, 1986; Suh, 1987; Hwang, 2007; Chung, 2005; Yoon, 2011, 2012; Kim, 2013). Yoon (2011, 2012) identified two novel environments where *wh*-phrases had no island effects: the declarative intervention contexts and the embedded contexts. Kim (2013) investigated *wh*-islands in the relative clauses, and he claimed that the fact that Korean escaped the island constraint could be explained by a semantico-pragmatic constraint.

2.2 Experimental Approaches to Islands

Recently, as computer technology and statistical tools develop, many researchers had an interest in measuring native speakers' intuition on syntactic data objectively and scientifically (Bard, Robertson, and Sorace, 1996; Schütze, 1996; Cowart, 1997; Keller, 2000). This research method was also applied into the study of island constructions, and lots of fruitful facts have been discovered through experimental approaches.

Sprouse et al. (2012), for example, adopted an experimental approach to island constructions and examined native speakers' intuition. They adopted 2×2 factor combinations in (1) and investigated four types of island constraints using the sentences in (2)-(5) (Sprouse et al., 2012:87-8).

(1) Factor Combinations
- a. NON-ISLAND | MATRIX
- b. NON-ISLAND | EMBEDDED
- c. ISLAND | MATRIX
- d. ISLAND | EMBEDDED

(2) Whether islands
- a. Who __ thinks that John bought a car?
- b. What do you think that John bought __ ?
- c. Who __ wonders whether John bought a car?
- d. What do you wonder whether John bought __ ?

(3) Complex NP islands
- a. Who __ claimed that John bought a car?
- b. What did you claim that John bought __?
- c. Who __ made the claim that John bought a car?
- d. What did you make the claim that John bought __?

(4) Subject islands
- a. Who __ thinks the speech interrupted the TV show?
- b. What do you think __ interrupted the TV show?
- c. Who __ thinks the speech about global warming interrupted the TV show?
- d. What do you think the speech about __ interrupted the TV show?

(5) Adjunct islands
- a. Who __ thinks that John left his briefcase at the office?
- b. What do you think that John left __ at the office?
- c. Who __ laughs if John leaves his briefcase at the office?
- d. What do you laugh if John leaves __ at the office?

Along with these target sentences, they measured the acceptability scores of 173 native speakers. Through the experiments and their analysis, they obtained the following results (Sprouse et al. 2012:100).

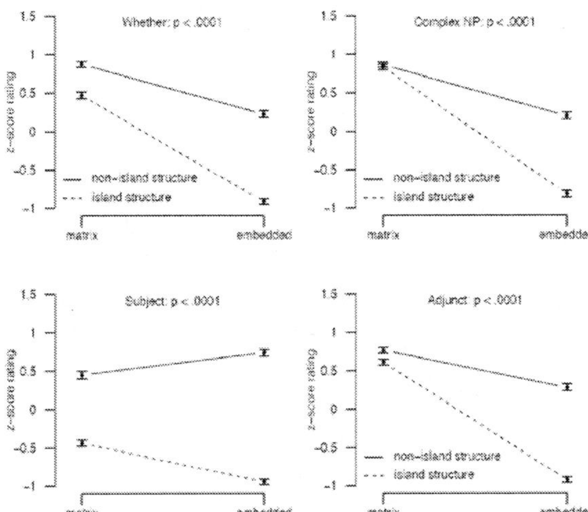

Figure 1: Analysis Results in Sprouse et al. (2012)

These analysis results illustrated (i) that native speakers showed more acceptability for non-island structures than island structures both in matrix and embedded causes and (ii) that the differences of acceptability scores became greater in embedded clauses rather than matrix clauses. All of these observations demonstrated that there were clearly island effects in English.

There were also some studies on the acquisition of the English island constructions by the Korean EFL learners. For example, Kim B. (2015) studied the acquisition of English island constructions by Korean-English bilinguals with an experimental approach and their statistical analysis. Sixty-three Korean-English bilinguals and sixty native speakers of English participated in the experiments. Here, bilinguals were either US-born or Korea-born who moved to the U.S. between ages 0 to 14. Based on their ages of arrival (AoA) to the U.S., bilinguals were divided into three groups: Heritage (AoA 0-5), Early (AoA 6-10), and Late (AoA 11-14). The experimental study demonstrated that all the group of speakers clearly distinguished four types of island constraints in Figure 1 (i.e., Complex NP, Whether, Subject, and Adjunct). However, the intuition of Heritage speakers were the closest to the intuitions of native speakers and the Early group was closer to natives though the group were far from the natives. The study also showed that the Late group was very far from both natives and the Heritage group. These results illustrated that, as the AoA was later, the L1 transfer effects might be stronger and the effects made it difficult for the EFL learners to learn the island constructions in the target language (here, English).

Although this study succeeded to demonstrate that the L1 transfer effects became stronger as the AoA was later, this study focused on the behaviors of the Heritage speakers. Accordingly, the study did not contain enough data which were obtained from the EFL students who resided in Korean. It is also necessary to conduct a similar experiment for the EFL students who resided in Korean.

Kim H. (2015) conducted such an experiment. In her studies, a total of fifty students participated in the experiment, who resided in Korean. Their proficiency level were classified with the TOEIC (Test Of English for International Communication), and the students with more than 750 points were included in the experiment. She adopted 5-points Likert scale to measure the acceptability scores of the Korean EFL learners. She also included four types of island constructions in Figure 1 and analyzed the data with ANalysis Of VAriance (ANOVA). Through the analysis, she found that the Korean EFL learners clearly identified the Whether island and the Subject island constraints but they did not identify the Complex NP island and the Adjunct island constraints.

Although her study was meaningful in that the experiment was conducted to the students who resided in Korean, there might be some problems which could be raised from the measurement of the acceptability scores for the Korean EFL learners. As mentioned in several previous studies (such as Bard et al., 1996; Schütze, 1996; Cowart, 1997; Keller, 2000), Likert scale has several problems compared with the ME method, to be used in the acceptability judgment tasks.[2] First, Likert scale has limited resolution. For example, if native speakers may feel that a sentence is somewhere between 4 and 5 (something like 4.5), gradient ratings are not available in the latter method. However, the former permits as much resolution as the raters wish to employ. Second, the latter

[2] Lee (2013) contained a detailed discussion on the differences between ME and Likert scales in the acceptability judgment task (intuition tests). Lodge (1981) mentioned that this ME had several advantages over the category scaling (the Likert scale). Although there are some claims that the Likert scales are available in the acceptability judgment task, this paper follows previous studies (Lodge, 1981; Johnson, 2008) and adopted ME in the experiment.

method uses an ordinal scale, and there is no guarantee that the interval between * and ** (ungrammatical) represents the same difference of impressions as that between ? and ?? (between grammatical and ungrammatical). The former method, on the other hand, provides judgments on an interval scale for which averages (mean value, *m*) and standard deviations (*sd*) can be more legitimately used. Third, the latter limits our ability to compare results across the experiments. The range of acceptability for a set of sentences has to be fitted to the scale, and what counts as ?? for one set of sentences may be quite different from what counts as ?? for another set of sentences. Accordingly, another type of measuring method was necessary to solve this problem. This paper adopted the ME method to solve the problems of the Likert scale.

3 Research Method

3.1 Research Question and Hypothesis

Through the experimental study, this paper wanted to investigate if the Korean EFL learners identified four types of island constraints in Figure 1.

Our research questions are as follows.

(6) Research Questions
  a. Do the Korean EFL learners clearly identify four types of island constraints in English?
  b. If the answer is 'no', which island constraints in English do they clearly identify and which ones are not identified?

For these questions, we made the following hypotheses.

(7) Hypothesis
  a. If there is no or little L1 transfer effect, the Korean EFL learners will clearly identify all of (four types of) the island constraints.
  b. If there is a L1 transfer effect, the Korean EFL learners will not clearly identify at least one of the island constraints.

To examine these hypotheses, an experiment was designed as follows.

3.2 Materials

To closely examine the English island constraints by the Korean EFL learners, the first thing to do was to make target sentences. This paper basically followed the factor combinations in (1), following the study in Sprouse et al. (2012). Accordingly, the following two factors were used in the experiment: Island constraint (Absence vs. Presence) and Location of *wh*-word (Matrix clause vs. Embedded clause). Since two factors were adopted and each factor had two values, the experiment had a 2×2 design.

First of all, basic target sentences were made with the sentences in (3) and the sentences in Pearl and Sprouse (2014), but a lexical items were slightly changed. These four sentences matched with the corresponding sentences in (3), and they contained the factor combinations in (1).

Along with these target sentences, the same number of filler sentences was made. The half of the filler sentences were constructed based on the structure of the target items. However, they were not related with the island constraints. The others were composed of the filler sentences that had no relation with the purpose of the experiment. Among them, some sentences were grammatical and others were ungrammatical. At the end, a total of 128 sentences were constructed in the experiments (4 island types×4 sentence types×4 repetitions).

After all the target and filler sentences were constructed, random numbers were generated with the R function (from 1 to 128; 64 target sentences and 64 fillers), and each sentence was given the generated random numbers. Then, the sentences were given to the participants after the sentences were sorted based on the random number.

3.3 Procedure

The data for a total of 20 native speakers were collected from the experiment. All the participants (m=23.40, sd=1.23) resided in and around Daejeon area, South Korea. All of them were either current university students or graduates of universities in Korea.

All the participants were first asked to fill out a simple one-page survey that contains biographical information such as age, gender, and dialect(s), together with the consent form for participating in the experiment. Then they were asked to proceed to take the main task.

The main task used in the experiment was an acceptability judgment task using Magnitude Estimation (ME; Lodge, 1981; Johnson, 2008).

There are two types of ME methods: numerical estimates and line drawing. However, as Bard et al. (1996) pointed out, the participants sometimes think of numeric estimates as academic test scores, and so they tend to limit their responses to a somewhat categorical scale, rather than using a ratio scale as intended in the magnitude estimation.

Accordingly, the current study adopted a line drawing method in which the participants were asked to draw different lengths of lines to indicate the naturalness (acceptability) of a given sentence (after reading the given sentence). An acceptability judgment task (also known as native speakers' intuition test) was used in the study since this method is known to be a psychological experiment which can be used to get the subconscious knowledge of native speakers in a given language (Carnie, 2012). In the main task, participants were required to draw a line for the given sentence, according to the degree of naturalness of the given sentence.

4 Statistical Analysis

4.1 Normality Tests and Regression Analysis

After all the data were collected from acceptability judgment tasks, the values were extracted for target sentences Then, the normality tests (Baayen, 2008; Gries, 2013; Lee, 2016) were performed to check whether parametric tests were available or not. If the distributions of the data follow the normal distribution, the parametric tests are available, such as *t*-tests, ANOVAs, or (ordinary) linear regression tests. However, if the distributions do not follow the normal distribution, the non-parametric tests must be applied such as Wilcoxon tests, Friedman tests, or generalized linear regression tests.

When the normality tests were performed, it was found that all the data sets did not follow the normal distribution. Some were positively skewed, and other sets had a slightly bimodal distribution. Consequently, non-parametric tests had to be used in the analysis of our data.

After the normality tests were performed, a (generalized) regression test (GLM) was performed. According to Agresti (2007), a generalized regression test is available when the distribution does not follow the normal distribution. Thus, the test was adopted to examine how each factor affects the acceptability of the sentences.

4.2 Complex NP Islands

Table 1 illustrated the analysis results of the GLM analysis.

	Estimate	*sd*	*t*	*p*
(Intercept)	145.1844	2.9011	50.045	<<<.001
CLAUSE	-0.1406	2.9011	-0.048	0.9614
ISLAND	17.3594	2.9011	5.984	<<<.001
CLAUSE:ISLAND	5.4719	2.9011	1.886	0.0602

Table 1: GLM Analysis Results for Complex NP

As you can see in this table, the factor CLAUSE was not significant (p=.9614), but the factor ISLAND was highly significant (p<.001). The interaction between these two factors was marginally significant (p=.0602).

Figure 2 showed us an effect plot for this island constraint.

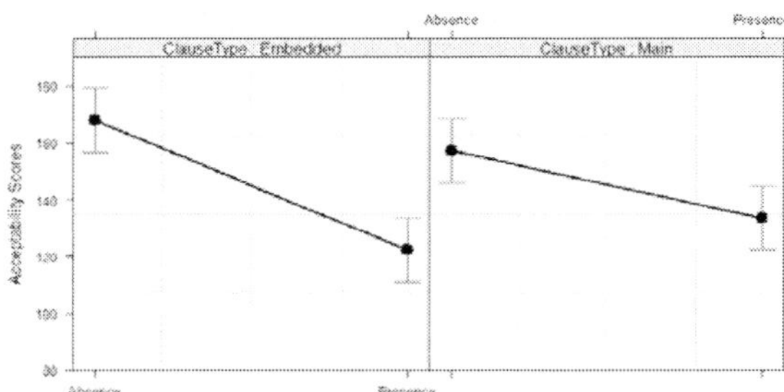

Figure 2: Interaction Plot for Complex NP

As you can see in this interaction plot, the overall acceptability scores became lower when the island constraint existed (i.e., Presence). The difference in the acceptability scores was bigger in the Embedded clause than in the Matrix clause. It implies that the Differences-in-Differences (DD) scores may have the plus values and that the Korean EFL learners surely identify the Complex NP island constraints in English.

4.3 Whether Islands

Table 2 illustrated the analysis results of the GLM analysis.

	Estimate	*sd*	*t*	*p*
(Intercept)	135.153	3.115	43.388	<<<.001
CLAUSE	-8.459	3.115	-2.716	.00698
ISLAND	12.641	3.115	4.058	<<<.001
CLAUSE:ISLAND	6.066	3.115	1.947	.05239

Table 2: GLM Analysis Results for Whether

As you can see in this table, both factors CLAUSE and ISLAND were significant (p=00698 and p<.001 respectively). The interaction between these two factors was marginally significant (p=.05239).

Figure 3 showed us an effect plot for this island constraint.

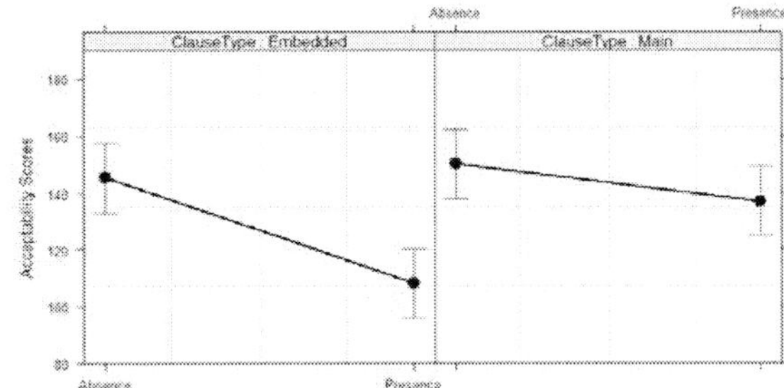

Figure 3: Interaction Plot for Whether

As you can see in this interaction plot, the overall acceptability scores became lower when the island constraint existed (i.e., Presence). The difference in the acceptability scores was bigger in the Embedded clause than in the Matrix clause. It implies that the DD scores may have the plus values and that the Korean EFL learners surely identify the Whether NP island constraints in English.

4.4 Subject Islands

Table 3 illustrated the analysis results of the GLM analysis.

	Estimate	*sd*	*t*	*p*
(Intercept)	123.2594	2.9104	42.351	<<<.001
CLAUSE	-3.0656	2.9104	-1.053	.293
ISLAND	21.3656	2.9104	7.341	<<<.001
CLAUSE:ISLAND	-0.1094	2.9104	-0.038	.970

Table 3: GLM Analysis Results for Subject

As you can see in this table, the factor CLAUSE was not significant (p=.293), but the factor ISLAND was highly significant (p<.001). The interaction was not significant (p=.970).

Figure 4 showed us an effect plot for this island constraint.

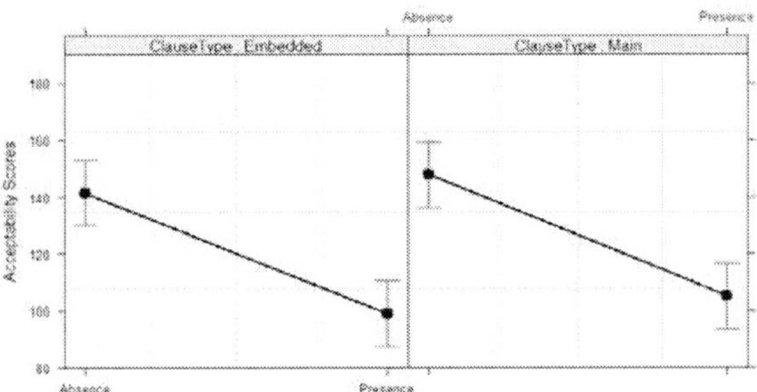

Figure 4: Interaction Plot for Subject

As you can see in this interaction plot, the overall acceptability scores became lower when the island constraint existed (i.e., Presence). The difference in the acceptability scores was bigger in the Embedded clause than in the Matrix clause. It implies the DD scores may have the plus values and that the Korean EFL learners surely identify the Subject island constraints in English.

4.5 Adjunct Islands

Table 5 illustrated the analysis results of the GLM analysis.

	Estimate	*sd*	*t*	*p*
(Intercept)	138.006	2.907	47.468	<<<.001
CLAUSE	-3.306	2.907	-1.137	0.256
ISLAND	13.931	2.907	4.792	<<<.001
CLAUSE:ISLAND	2.819	2.907	0.970	0.333

Table 5: GLM Analysis Results for Adjunct

As you can see in this table, the factor CLAUSE was not significant (p=.256), but the factor ISLAND was highly significant (p<.001). The interaction was not significant (p=.333).

Figure 6 showed us an effect plot for this island constraint.

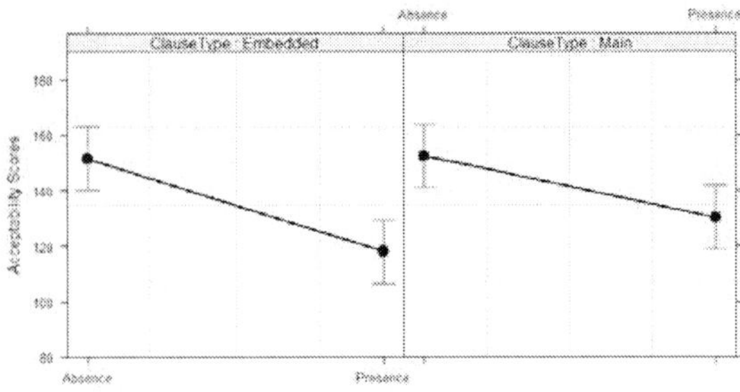

Figure 6: Interaction Plot for Adjunct

As you can see in this interaction plot, the overall acceptability scores became lower when the island constraint existed (i.e., Presence). The difference in the acceptability scores was bigger in the Embedded clause than in the Matrix clause. It implies that the DD scores may have the plus values and that the Korean EFL learners surely identify the Adjunct island constraints in English.

5 Discussion

The analysis results in Section 4.2-4.5 illustrated different aspects that Kim H. (2015) observed in her experimental studies. In her study, she found that the Korean EFL learners clearly identified the Whether island and the Subject island constraints but they did not identify the Complex NP island and the Adjunct island constraints. However, in this study, the Korean EFL learners clearly identified all of the island constraints.

Then, where did the differences come from? There may be two types of sources which made the differences. The first one might come from the methods of measuring the acceptability scores. Kim H. (2015) used a 5-point Likert scales, while this paper adopted the ME method. Although the Likert scales were widely used in previous studies, they had some shortcomings as mentioned in Section 2.2. Even though we did not take the problems into consideration, the ME method had more fine-grained scales than the Likert scale. Accordingly, more fine-grained differences in the acceptability scores were represented in the ME method, whereas the differences might be lessened or neutralized in the Likert scale, especially in the Complex NP and the Adjunct island constraints. The second origin came from the statistical method. In Kim H. (2015), the collected data were analyzed with z-transformation. Originally, the Likert scale was an ordinal variable (Lee, 2016). Consequently non-parametric tests had to be applied. In order to solve the problem, Kim H. (2015) employed a z-transformation, which made the ordinal variables like the ratio variables. However, z-transformation was also a transformation. That is, the data might be distorted during the transformation processes. This paper, on the other hand, did not apply any kind of transformation to the collected data. Since the acceptability scores were ratio variables (Lee, 2016), the normality tests were applied. Since the result was that the distributions did not follow the normal distributions, GLM methods were applied. Therefore, no transformation was adopted here, and the data were not distorted. Accordingly, the analysis results in this paper could be said to be more accurate than those in Kim H. (2015).

Now, let's see what answers can be provided to the research questions in (6) and Hypothesis in (7) along with the analysis results.

For the first question, the analysis results said that the Korean EFL learners clearly identified four island constraints in English, which was different from the analysis results in Kim H. (2015). For two hypotheses in (7), it could be said that there was no or little L1 transfer effect, since the Korean EFL learners clearly identified four island constraints in English. This implies that the unstable status of island constructions in Korean did not affect the acquisition of island construction in English.

6 Conclusion

In this paper, it was closely examined how the Korean EFL learners identified the English island constructions. Four types of island constructions (Complex NP, Whether, Subject, and Adjunct) were taken, and two linguistic factors (CLAUSE and ISLAND) were taken in the analysis, which made the experiment have a 2×2 design.

Based on this design, an acceptability judgment task was performed, where the data for 20 Korean native participants were collected with the ME method. After the experiments, all the values were extracted for target sentences and they were analyzed with R.

Through the experiments, it was found that the Korean EFL learners correctly identified all of the English island constructions. This finding showed that the island status of the Korean language did not affect the acquisition of island constructions in English.

References

Akira Watanabe. 1992. Wh-in-situ, Subjacency, and Chain Formation, MIT Occasional Papers in Linguistics 2. MIT Press, Cambridge, MA.

Alan Agresti. 2007. An Introduction to Categorical Data Analysis. John Wiley & Sons, Hoboken, NJ.

Andrew Carnie. 2012. Syntax: A Generative Introduction. 3rd Edition. Blackwell, Oxford.

Boyoung Kim. 2015. Sensitivity to Islands in Korean-English Bilingualism. Doctoral dissertation. University of California at San Diego.

Bum-Sik Park. 2001. Island-insensitive Sluicing. Harvard Studies in Korean Linguistics, 9: 669-682.

Bum-Sik Park. 2009. Island Sensitivity in Ellipsis and Its Implications for Movement. Studies in Generative Grammar, 19(4):599- 620 .

Carson Schütze. 1996. The Empirical Base of Linguistics: Grammaticality Judgments and Linguistic Methodology. University of Chicago Press, Chicago, IL.

Chungmok Suh. 1987. WH-constructions in Korean. Top Press, Seoul.

Daeho Chung. 2005. Why is HOW in Korean Insensitive to Islands?: A Revised Nominal Analysis. Studies in Modern Grammar, 39:115-131.

Ellen Bard, Dan Robertson, and Antonella Sorace, 1996. Magnitude Estimation of Linguistic Acceptability. Language, 72:32-68.

Frank Keller. 2000. Gradient in Grammar: Experimental and Computational Aspects of Degrees of Grammaticality. Doctoral dissertation. University of Edinburgh.

Harald Baayen. 2008. Analyzing Linguistic Data: A Practical Introduction to Statistics Using R. Cambridge University Press, Cambridge.

Heeju Hwang. 2007. Wh-Phrase Questions and Prosody in Korean. Proceedings of 17th Japanese/Korean Linguistics. Stanford, CA: CSLI.

Hey-Jin Kim. 2015. Aspects of Sentence Processing Island Structures in English by Korean Learners of English. Dongkuk University.

Ho-Min Sohn. 1980. Theme-prominence in Korean. Korean Linguistics, 2:2-19.

Hyo-Sang Lee. 1982. Asymmetry in Island Constrains in Korean, ms., University of California at Los Angeles

Ilkyu Kim. 2013. Rethinking 'Island Effects' in Korean Relativization. Language Sciences, 38:59–82

Jeong-Me Yoon. 2011. Wh-island Effects of Wh-in-situ Questions in Korean. Studies in Generative Grammar, 21(4): 763-778.

Jeong-Me Yoon. 2012. Wh-island Effects in Korean Wh-in-Situ Questions. Korean Journal of Linguistics, 37(2):357-382.

John Ross. 1967. Constraints on Variables in Syntax. Doctoral dissertation, Massachusetts Institute of Technology.

Jon Sprouse, Mathews Wagers, and Colin Phillips. 2012. A Test of the Relation between Working Memory Capacity and Syntactic Island Effects. Language, 88:82–123

Jon Sprouse, Shin Fukuda, Hajime Ono, and Robert Kluender. 2011. Reverse Island Effects and the Backward Search for a Licensor in Multiple Wh-questions. Syntax 14:179–203.

Jong-Im Han. 1992. Syntactic Movement Analysis of Korean Relativization. Language Research, 28:335–357.

Keith Johnson. 2008. Quantitative Methods in Linguistics. Blackwell, Oxford.

Larry Selinker. 1969. Language Transfer. General Linguistics 9(2):67-92.

Milton Lodge. 1981. Magnitude Scaling: Quantitative Measurement of Opinions. Sage Publications, Beverley Hills, CA.

Shinichiro Ishihara. 2002. Invisible but Audible Wh-scope Marking: Wh-constructions and Deaccenting in Japanese. Proceedings of the Twenty-first West Coast Conference on Formal Linguistics, 180-193

Stephan Th. Gries. 2013. Statistics for Linguistics with R: A Practical Introduction. Guyter: Berlin.

Sun-Ho Hong. 2004. On the Lack of Syntactic Effects in Korean WH-Questions. The Linguistic Association of Korea Journal, 12(3):43-57.

Taisuke Nishigauchi. 1990. Quantification in the Theory of Grammar. Kluwer Academic Publishers, Dordrecht.

Terence Odlin. 1989. Language Transfer. Cambridge University Press, Cmabridge.

Terence Odlin. 2003. Cross-linguistic Influence. In Doughty, Catherine and Michael Long (eds.) The Handbook of Second Language Acquisition, 436-386. Blackwell, New York.

Wayne Cowart. 1997. Experimental Syntax: Applying Objective Methods to Sentence Judgments. Sage Publications, Thousands Oaks, CA.

Yong-hun Lee. 2013. Experimental Approach to Multiple Case Constructions in Korean. Language and Information, 17(2): 29-50.

Yong-hun Lee. 2016. Corpus Linguistics and Statistics Using R. Hankook Publishing Company, Seoul.

Young-Se Kang. 1986. Korean Syntax and Universal Grammar. Doctoral dissertation, Harvard University.

Multiple Emotions Detection in Conversation Transcripts

Duc-Anh Phan, Hiroyuki Shindo, Yuji Matsumoto
Graduate School of Information and Science
Nara Institute of Science and Technology
8916-5, Takayama, Ikoma, Nara, 630-0192, Japan
{phan.duc_anh.oq3, shindo, matsu}@is.naist.jp

Abstract

In this paper, we present a method of predicting emotions from multi-label conversation transcripts. The transcripts are from a movie dialog corpus and annotated partly by 3 annotators. The method includes building an emotion lexicon bootstrapped from Wordnet following the notion of Plutchik's basic emotions and dyads. The lexicon is then adapted to the training data by using a simple Neural Network to fine-tune the weights toward each basic emotion. We then use the adapted lexicon to extract the features and use them for another Deep Network which does the detection of emotions in conversation transcripts. The experiments were conducted to confirm the effectiveness of the method, which turned out to be nearly as good as a human annotator.

1 Introduction

Along with the trend of "Affective Computing", the task of Emotion Detection in text has received much attention in the recent years. However, very little research has been working on the detection of multiple emotion simultaneously. Instead, most of them make simple assumption that emotions are mutually exclusive and focus on multi-class classification. In fact, the nature of human emotion is complicated: emotions have connections, some are opposite of each other, while some occur together at the same time, resonate and create another emotional state - dyads (Plutchik, 1980)

The survey by Dave and Diwanji (2015) predicted the need for Emotion Detection in *streaming data and the study of emotion flow during chatting*. In this paper, we tackle the simplified version of this task by detecting the emotions in *conversation*. The corpus we used is made of conversations among movie characters, who take turns in the conversation. Those turns are called utterances, which are then manually annotated in a multi-label manner.

Emotion detection in conversation is essentially different from identifying emotions in news headlines (Strapparava and Mihalcea, 2007) or Tweets (Bollen et al., 2011) where each instance is independent of each other. Generally, the expression of Emotion in general depends on the words being used. However, it also quite depends on the grammar structure and syntactic variables such as: negations, embedded sentence, and the type of sentence - question, exclamation, command or statement (Collier, 2014). Therefore, similar to the detection of emotions of sentences in a paragraph, the context information of the whole conversation and what is said in the previous utterance should be taken into consideration. The extraction of context features will be further explained in sub-section 4.3.1

Unlike other works (Li et al., 2015; Wang et al., 2015) where small sets of basic emotions are used, we annotated the dataset using the notion of Plutchik's basic emotion and dyads (1980). This eases the annotators' task since it offers annotators with wider range of emotion labels (8 basic and 23 combinations) to choose from.

Previous research often relied on a list of 6 basic emotions (Ekman et al., 1987) with some variants. However, this notion fails to show conflict side of some emotions. For example, people should not

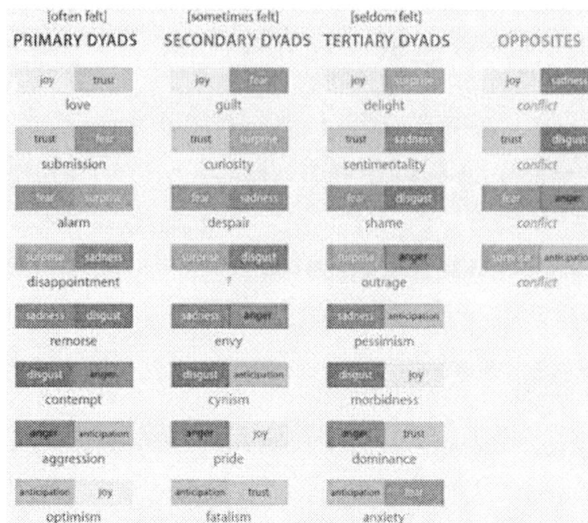

Figure 1: Plutchik's basic emotion and dyads - image taken from `http://twinklet8.blogspot.jp`

feel happiness and sadness from the same incident altogether. Furthermore, Ekman's basic emotions are the result of observation made on human facial expressions so applying such notion in text classification task seems irrelevant. Newer works relies on dimensional representation using valence-arousal space (Calvo and Mac Kim, 2013; Yu et al., 2015)

Plutchik (1980) suggested 4 axes of bipolar **basic emotions**: Joy - Sadness, Fear - Anger, Trust - Disgust, Surprise - Anticipatation. These primary emotions may blend to form the full spectrum of human emotional experience. The new complex emotions formed by them are called **dyads** (Figure 1). Plutchik's notion reasonably explains the connection between emotions. Some emotions will not occur at the same time since they are on the opposite side of the axis. Complex emotions can also be viewed as combinations of primary ones. The idea enables us to approach emotion detection in a more comprehensive manner. In the future, we may address not only complicating mixture of emotions but also the intensity of each of them.

In this paper, we propose a three steps method for the detection of emotions in conversation: 1)Building Emotion Lexicon from Wordnet (Miller, 1995). 2) Using simple Neural Network to adapt the lexicon to the training data. 3) Using Deep Network with features extracted from adapted lexicon and classify the multi-label corpus.

The remainder of the paper is organized as follows. Section 2 summarizes related work on emotion detection. Section 3 discusses the nature of our dataset and explains the annotating scheme. Section 4 proposes our approach which includes the 3 steps mentioned above. Section 5 evaluates the lexicon, the effectiveness of the adapted lexicon and the proposed method in general. Section 6 gives the conclusion and discusses future work.

2 Related Work

Most of the work in the field tried to define a small set of emotions (D'Mello et al., 2006; Yang et al., 2007) which involved only 3 and 4 emotional states respectively. Another work by Hasegawa et al. (2013) performed a *multi-class* classification on dialog data from Twitter in Japanese. They automatically labeled the obtained dialogs by using emotional expression clues, which is similar to our collocation list explained in sub-section 3.3. We propose a more comprehensive approach by exploiting Plutchik's notion which covers the full spectrum of human emotions to work on challenging multi-label conversation corpus.

Having the same notion, Buitinck et al. (2015) proposed a simple Bag of Words approach and tuned RAKEL for multi-label classification for movie reviews. We go further and work on conversation data where the exchange between characters and the context of the whole dialog are of great importance. The closest to our work is Li et al. (2015) on paragraphs and documents which tried to improve the sentence-level prediction of some special emotions which, due to data sparseness and inherent multi-label classification, were very hard to predict. They incorporated label dependency among labels and context dependency into the graph model to achieve such goal. However, their work is for paragraphs in Chinese. In our case, we take advantages of Deep Neural Network to capture the abstract representation of context information.

Our system is different from previous methods in four main ways:

- Plutchik's notion of primary emotions and dyads is incorporated in our system and provides scalability to address more than just primary emotions if needed in the future.

- We bootstrapped the lexicon and then adapted it to the training data which improved the classification result
- The proposed method includes 2 neural networks, one for adapting the lexicon and the other for multi-label classification of emotions.
- We use a set of manually constructed features instead of word-embedding directly for the Neural Network. The reason for that is further discussed in sub-section 4.3.1

3 Corpus, Dataset & Annotation Scheme

3.1 Movie Dialog Corpus

The Cornell Movie Dialog dataset [1] was originally used for understanding the coordination of linguistic style in dialogs (Danescu-Niculescu-Mizil and Lee, 2011). It includes in total 304,713 utterances (turns in conversation) out of 220,579 conversational exchanges between 10,292 pairs of 9,035 movie characters from 617 movies. The annotating scheme is as follows:

- One utterance may hold zero, one or more emotions at the same time. The list of emotions to assign includes Plutchik's 8 basic emotions and 23 dyads. The sytem will treat the dyads as combination of basic emotions. In case an utterance holds no emotion, it should be annotated with "None"
- The annotators need to assign the whole utterance which may have two or more sentences inside with a set of all emotions expressed inside it. There may be cases where confict emotions according to Plutchik's notion appear simultaneously in the same utterance.

The followings are some statistics of the corpus: total of 11,610 utterances, 10,008 of which are in the training data , 1,602 others are in the testing data, the average number of label per utterance is 1.29. We separated the *training data* which was annotated by only one annotator and the *testing data* which was annotated by all three annotators.

[1] http://www.mpi-sws.org/~cristian/Cornell_Movie-Dialogs_Corpus.html

3.2 Inter-Annotator Agreement

One of the most common Inter-Annotator Agreement measurement is the Kappa statistics (Cohen, 1960). Bhowmick et al. (2008) suggested a Kappa-based measurement for multi-class classification. However, none of them are applicable to our multi-label corpus because their ways of computing causes hypothetical probability of chance agreement P_e to be greater than 1 since there are cases where two or more labels are annotated to a given instance. Therefore, we measure the Kappa statistics for each emotion class and then average them as shown in Table 1. The survey by Artstein and Poesio (2008) suggested that low kappa scores are often observed in multi-label annotating tasks even when the annotators do not make much use of the ability to assign multiple tags.

Some strong emotions: "Anger", "Fear", "Surprise" have better agreement scores as they have indicators such as question marks and excalmation forms. Nevertheless, they are easier for human to identify because they are the basic emotions that we - human inherits from animals. They are the emotions that trigger the "fight or flight" and "stop and examine" response. (Plutchik, 1980)

Due to the time constraint, we had neither the time to show annotators the movies footage nor an adequate amount of sessions to work together and seek a better degree of agreement. Because the annotators only worked with the text data, it was very difficult for them to visualize the situation and make correct judgment.

3.3 ISEAR dataset for Collocation features

We also use ISEAR dataset [2] for the process of producing collocation features. In the ISEAR datase, student respondents, both psychologists and non-psychologists, were asked to report situations in which they had experienced 7 major emotions. Five out of them are completely identical to the basic emotions of Plutchik's . In each case, the questions covered the way they had appraised the situation and how they reacted. Therefore, to our belief, this dataset would provide good collocation features for the 5 identical emotions of our corpus. We mine

[2] http://www.affective-sciences.org/researchmaterial

Emotion class	Kappa Stat
Anger*	0.300
Fear*	0.303
Disgust*	0.127
Trust	0.102
Joy*	0.101
Sadness*	0.131
Surprise	0.575
Anticipation	0.110
Average (by class)	0.219
No. of utterances	1,602

* indicates that these emotions are also in ISEAR dataset

Table 1: Kappa Agreement score.

this dataset for words which frequently appear together with one emotion. If a word also appears in other emotions situation, it loses its place as the indicator toward one specific emotion and we discard it from the collocation list. The use of this collocation list in our work is closely similar to emotional expression clues in (Hasegawa et al., 2013).

4 The Proposed Method

4.1 Bulding Lexicon

Using Lexicon is proven to provide significant improvement in identifying the emotion conveyed by a word (Mohammad, 2012). Therefore, in our case, we built a new lexicon, each lexical item of which displays not only its association with Plutchik's basic emotions but also how strong the association is.

We define the primary emotions and dyads in Plutchik's theories as the seeds of our lexicon. Throughout Wordnet, we search for *synonyms, hypernyms, hyponyms* of the seeds. A reverse lemmatisation is necessary to retrieve related verbs, adjectives and adverbs and their derived forms (verb forms and comparative, superlative adjectives) of the seeds. We keep tracks of the original nouns and the seeds where the new words were derived from (Table 2). Note that sometimes a word was derived from different nouns and seeds, which suggests mixed emotional states.

Each lexical item in the lexicon has a vector of values on each axis of the basic emotions: Joy - Sadness, Fear - Anger, Trust - Disgust, Surprise - Anticipatation . We manually assign the primary emotions with a value vector of 1, 0 or -1 and the dyads with 0.5, 0 or -0.5, depending on the axes they belong. For example, "joy" came from the axis of Joy-Sadness, thus, its vector is [1,0,0,0] while the vector for "sadness" is [-1,0,0,0] (Table 3). The dyad "love" came from primary emotions "joy" and "trust", hence its vector is [0.5,0.5,0,0]. It is to be noted that the minus sign only indicates that the emotion is on the other side of the axis. It is not a suggestion of negative emotion in any case.

Words	Original Nouns - **Seeds**
joy	(primary)- **joy**
sadness	(primary)- **sadness**
fear	(primary)- **fear**
love	(dyad)- **love**
benevolent	benevolence- **love**
worship	worship-**fear** , worship-**love**

Table 2: Wordnet expansion.

In addition, we calculate the wup similarity (Wu and Palmer, 1994) between a new word and the seed it came from, based on the depth of the two senses in the Wordnet taxonomy and that of their Least Common Subsumer.

$$wup(word, seed) = \frac{2 * dep(lcs)}{dep(word) + dep(seed)} \tag{1}$$

We assumed that the higher the similarity, the closer emotional state of the word to the seed. Thus, the value vector of a word is the sum of the products of each seed vector and the similarity between the word and such seed.

$$\begin{aligned} vector(word) = \textstyle\sum_{k=1}^{n} vector(seed_k) \\ \times wup(word, seed_k) \end{aligned}. \tag{2}$$

For example, in the case of the word "worship", we first calculate the wup scores between the word and its two seeds: fear and love (Table 2). Next, they are multiplied by the vectors of the seeds fear-[0,0,1,0] and love-[0.5,0.5,0,0], and then summed up to get the result (Table 3).

4.2 Adapting Lexicon to Training data

We understand that a lexicon bootstrapped from a general domain resource such as Wordnet has its effectiveness limited when it is applied on a specified

Words	J-S	T-D	F-A	S-An
joy	1	0	0	0
sadness	-1	0	0	0
fear	0	0	1	0
love	0.5	0.5	0	0
benevolent	0.47	0.47	0	0
worship	0.14	0.14	0.29	0

Table 3: Value vector of some words. (*J-S: Joy-Sadness, T-D: Trust-Disgust, F-A: Fear-Anger, S-A: Surprise-Anticipation*)

domain. In order to partly solve this problem, we built a simple neural network with one input layer and one output softmax layer.

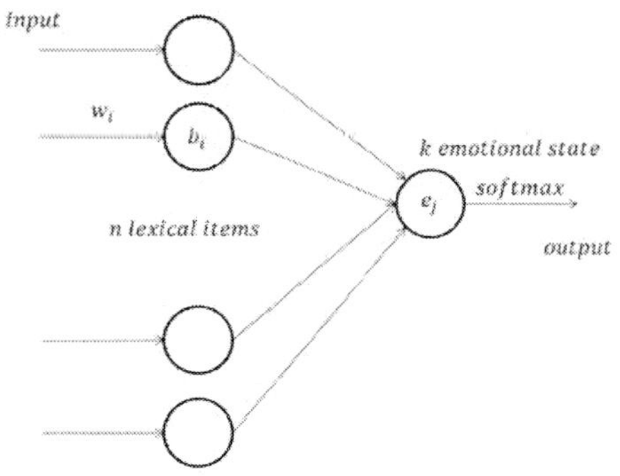

Figure 2: Adapting lexicon for emotional state e_j

The input to the network is the Bag-of-Words features of the training data. We then steps by steps, try to do binary classification on the basic emotion e_j. Let each node of the network be corresponding to each lexical item in the Lexicon. The biases a node b_i are initialized according to the value of each lexical items in the lexicon while the weights w_i are randomly initialized. After each step, we update the biases and weights and then repeat the process for the whole 8 basic emotions. Figure 2 shows the structure of the network. We use the log-likelihood as the cost function for the network input: $C = -\ln(a_y^L)$ where a^L is the output of the final layer and y is the desired output. In the end, we updated the lexicon with new values from the network. We will discuss about the improvements made by the network later in section 5.

4.3 Deep Network for Multi-label Classification

4.3.1 Features Extraction

The process of feature selection for the network is an heuristic one. We initially used a lot of features and then through logistic regression, unimportant features such as the genre of the movie or n-grams features were filtered out.

The core part of the extraction process is to take advantages of the lexicon to transform an utterance to a vector of values expressing the tendency towards each emotion state. This task is done in a rule-based manner (Algorithm 1 and Figure 3). Each word in the utterance is mapped to the lexicon to retrieve the value vector. The representation vector of an utterance is the sum vector of all the word inside it. The negation and word dependency are also taken into account when we calculate the sum with the help of NLTK (Bird et al., 2009) dependency parsing.

Data: Movie Dialogs
Result: Tendency Features
$utterance\_value \leftarrow 0$
foreach *word in utterance* **do**
  $value \leftarrow retrieve\_from\_lexicon(word)$
  $dependencies \leftarrow$
  $check\_dependency(word, utterance)$
  if *value & check_negation(dependencies)* **then**
    $value \leftarrow -value$
  end
  $utterance\_value += value$
end

Algorithm 1: Tendency Features extracting algorithm

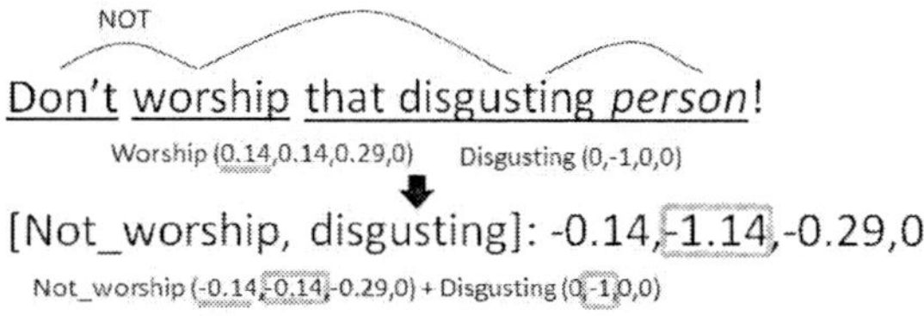

Figure 3: Extracting tendency features

Each utterance in the dataset is presented by the following compact set of 22 features:

1. The sum vector of the current utterance which suggest the *local tendency*.

2. The sum vector of all the utterances in the lexicon that appear in the conversation which provides the *context of the conversation*.

3. The sum vector of the previous utterance in the conversation which also provides the *context of previous exchange* (of what triggered the current emotion).

4. The *polarity* (negative/ positive) score of the sentence.

5. *Features* such as: length, is_it_a_question, is_it_an_exclamatory_sentence.

6. *Collocation features* which indicate the number of appearances of words inside the ISEAR collocations list.

The reason for us to use extracted features is that it is very hard to capture the context of both the conversation and previous exchange using direct word-embedding. While using a recurrent neural network can solve the latter, it is a challenge to address the first. Each conversation has different number of utterances, it may hurt the performance of the system and result in network architecture complexity if we use a non-fixed size window to monitor all the utterances in a same conversation.

4.3.2 Building the Deep Network

The structure of the network is built as shown in Figure 4. The raw input is generalized to produce a small set of features. These features are fed to the network as input layer. We have 2 fully connected hidden layers and an output layer. Since the task is a multi-label classification problem where softmax cannot be used,the output layer is change into sigmoid we add a set of threshold values (one for each basic emotions). Only the labels, whose output values greater than the threshold are considered valid. The thresholds are randomly initialized and then updated after each epochs the same way we updated the biases and weights. In our implementation of the network, Theano (Bastien et al., 2012) was used to take advantages of GPU computing power.

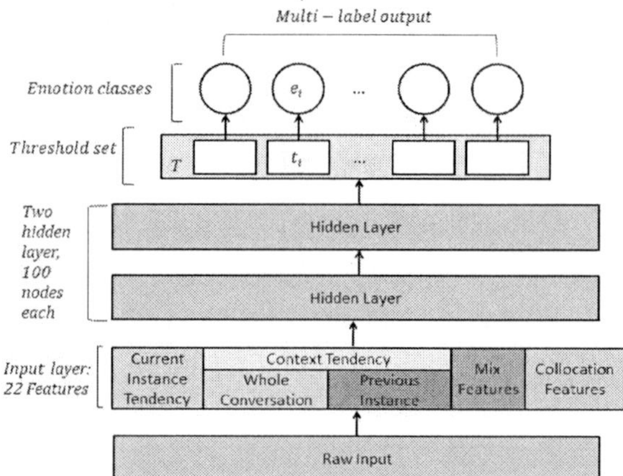

Figure 4: Structure of the Deep Network

The global cost function, similar to Zhang and Zhou (2006), is defined to reward the system for right predictions and severely punish for wrong ones in equation 3.

$$E = \sum_{i}^{m} = \frac{1}{|Y_i||\bar{Y}_i|} \sum_{(k,l)\in Y_i \times \bar{Y}_i} \exp\left(-(c_k^i - c_l^i)\right) \tag{3}$$

Let X be the set of all m instances. Let $Y = \{1, 2, .., Q\}$ be the set of all possible labels, Y_i is the set of true labels for ith instance x_i and $\bar{Y}_i$ is the set of the labels not belong to x_i. Obviously, $Y_i \cup \bar{Y}_i = Y$. We define E as the global cost function of the network. c^i is the set of actual outputs of the model for input x_i, each label has its own output. c_k^i is the output of label k belongs to the set of true labels, $k \in Y_i$. Meanwhile, c_l^i is the output of label l for $l \in \bar{Y}_i$. The difference $c_k^i - c_l^i$ measure the output of the system between the labels, which an instance belong to and which it doesn't. Naturally, we want this difference to be as big as possible.

5 Experiments

5.1 Experiment Setting

Corpus

As mention above, we used the annotated movie dialog corpus for testing our method. For the **gold standard** of the test data, we applied the majority rules on the annotation. If one emotion is annotated by two or more annotators, we accept it as a true label for the utterance.

Evaluation Metrics In our study, 4 common evaluation metrics which have been popularly used in multi-label classification problems (Godbole and Sarawagi, 2004; Li et al., 2015) are employed to measure the performance of our system to the baselines. Let Y_i be set of true labels for a given sample, then Y_i' is the set the labels predicted by a system. Let m be the total number of samples.

1. *Hamming score* or accuracy in multi-label classification, gives the degree of similarity between the ground truth set of labels and the predicted set of labels.

$$Hammingscore = \frac{1}{N}\sum_{i}^{N}\frac{|Y_i \cap Y_i'|}{|Y_i \cup Y_i'|} \quad (4)$$

2. *Precision:* the fraction of correctly predicted labels over all the predicted labels in the set.

$$Precision = \frac{1}{N}\sum_{i}^{N}\frac{|Y_i \cap Y_i'|}{|Y_i'|} \quad (5)$$

3. *Recall:* the fraction of correctly predicted labels over all the true labels in the set.

$$Recall = \frac{1}{N}\sum_{i}^{N}\frac{|Y_i \cap Y_i'|}{|Y_i|} \quad (6)$$

4. *F1-measure:* the harmonic mean of Precision and Recall. In our study, we gave equal importance to Precision and Recall.

$$F1 = \frac{2 * precision * recall}{precision + recall} \quad (7)$$

5.2 Experimental Results

To evaluate the system, we tried to replicate other works and applied them on our new corpus. A similar work is Buitinck et al. (2015) which use the same Plutchik's basic emotions and work on multi-label data. We used similar Meka's [3] RAkEL method and Bag-of-Words approach as the first baseline. We understand that Buitinck et al. (2015)'s system is fine-tuned for their corpus, therefore, it is a little unfair to apply it to our corpus and make comparison. Therefore, the second baseline is Meka's DBPNN which is reported as generally having better accuracy than RAkEL (Fernandez-Gonzalez et al., 2015).

We decided that the most important baseline is the human annotation. We calculated the evaluation metrics based on the annotation made by each annotator against the gold standard and averaged the result by the total number of annotators. Another baseline is our own system using the lexicon before adaptation. Figure 5 compares the performance of our system to the baselines.

vs. Bag-of-Words Approaches: Our system, with and without lexicon adaptation performed remarkably better than the simple approaches using Meka's DBPNN and RAkEL. It exceeded the better DBPNN significantly in *Hamming Score* by 7.28 and 7.19, *Recall* by 12.85 and 5.95, *F1-measure* by 7.33 and 4.33 respectively. We argue that the context features played as an important factor here.

Lexicon Adaptation vs. No Adaptation: We can clearly see the improvements made by the adaptation on our system in *Recall and F1-measure*,which are increased by 6.9 and 3.0. This confirmed the necessity of the adaptation step.

vs. Human Annotator: This is the most important baseline, which explains how well our system performs in comparison with a Human Annotator. Please note that these values are averaged by the total number of annotators after the judgment made by each annotator are compared to the gold standard. Our system is slightly worse than a Human Annotator in all 4 metrics by 0.43 in *Hamming Score*, 0.79, 1.67, 1.69 in *Precision, Recall and F1-measure* respectively.

These results confirmed the performance of our method which is slightly worse than such of an human annotator. On the other hand, our method is more efficient than simple Bag-of-Words approaches. We also confirmed the improvement made by the Lexicon Adaptation step to our system.

Classification result for each emotion class: Table 4 shows the distribution of emotion classes and reports the classification result of each emotion class in the corpus. Imbalance can be seen among classes in the corpus. We observed the expected "All-No-Recurrence" problem for minority classes of Joy and Sadness (high accuracy and near zero F1) as the corpus is unbalanced. "Surprise" is the class with the highest Agreement score (Table 1), it also

[3] http://meka.sourceforge.net/#about

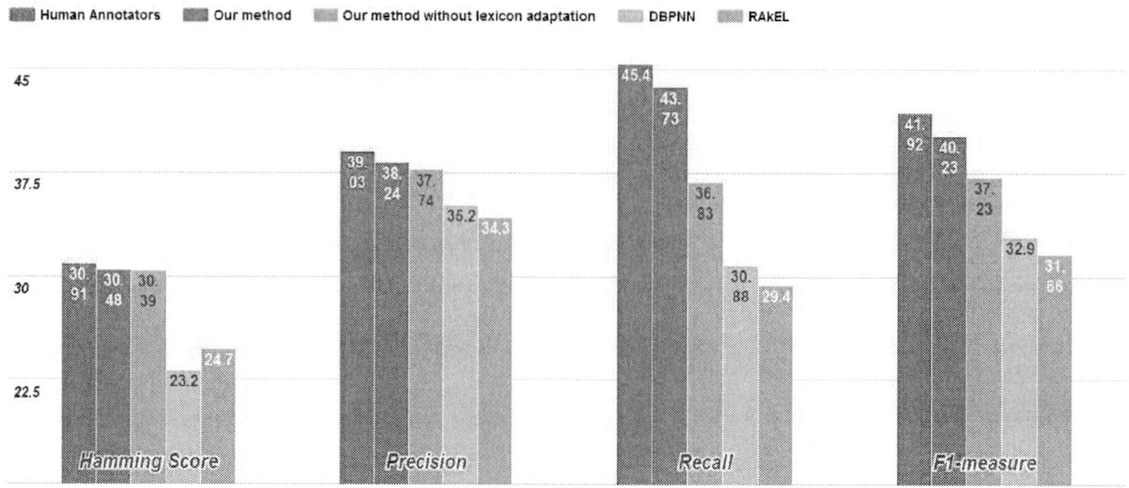

Figure 5: Evaluation of the system vs four baselines: 1) Human Annotators, 2) The system without lexicon adaptation, 3) DBPNN 4) RAkEL

Emotion	Percentage	Accuracy	F1
Anger	18.48%	0.615	0.265
Fear	16.52%	0.70	0.285
Disgust	16.52%	0.65	0.275
Trust	13.35%	0.69	0.313
Joy	5.56%	0.92	0.01
Sadness	5.18%	0.92	0.01
Surprise	17.01%	0.605	0.34
Anticipation	38.72%	0.395	0.27

Table 4: Accuracy and F1 for each emotion class.

achieves the highest F1 among other classes. While "Anticipation" class is a dominant class in the corpus, it suffers from low Agreement score. As a consequence, the classification result for this class is also not high. From this result, we can hope that in the future when movie footage are included, not only the agreement score but the system performance will also go up as well.

6 Conclusion & Future Work

In this paper, we propose our method of detecting and classifying emotions from a conversation corpus. The corpus is a set of movie dialogs annotated with multi-label emotions following Plutchik's notion of basic emotions and dyads. Our method involves building a lexicon from Wordnet using some seed emotion words, adapting the lexicon to the corpus, extracting a feature set from the input and classifying the emotions accordingly with the help of a deep neural network. The experiments show that our method's power to detecting emotion is comparable to that of a human annotator. However, one may argue that the disagreement among annotators may have affected the result. As discussed above, we hope to solve this problem by including the movies' footage in our annotating scheme.

At the time of the submission, we are adding the footages as well as improving annotating scheme to have higher Kappa statistics and evaluate again our method. Once finished, the corpus will be published for other researchers to use. In the future, we also want to further exploit the method by incorporating emotion detection on voices and images and monitoring complex emotions other than the basic ones and their intensity.

Acknowledgments

This research was supported by CREST project of Japan Science and Technology Agency. We are grateful to our colleagues from Computational Linguistics Lab, NAIST, Japan who provided insights and expertise that greatly assisted the research. We also thank the reviewers for their valuable comments that further improved our work.

References

Ron Artstein and Massimo Poesio. 2008. Inter-coder agreement for computational linguistics. *Computational Linguistics*, 34(4):555–596.

Frédéric Bastien, Pascal Lamblin, Razvan Pascanu, James Bergstra, Ian J. Goodfellow, Arnaud Bergeron, Nicolas Bouchard, and Yoshua Bengio. 2012. Theano: new features and speed improvements. Deep Learning and Unsupervised Feature Learning NIPS 2012 Workshop.

Plaban Kr Bhowmick, Pabitra Mitra, and Anupam Basu. 2008. An agreement measure for determining inter-annotator reliability of human judgements on affective text. In *Proceedings of the Workshop on Human Judgements in Computational Linguistics*, pages 58–65. Association for Computational Linguistics.

S Bird, E Klein, and E Loper. 2009. Nltk book.

Johan Bollen, Huina Mao, and Alberto Pepe. 2011. Modeling public mood and emotion: Twitter sentiment and socio-economic phenomena.

Lars Buitinck, Jesse Van Amerongen, Ed Tan, and Maarten de Rijke. 2015. Multi emotion detection in user-generated reviews. In *Advances in Information Retrieval*, pages 43–48. Springer.

Rafael A Calvo and Sunghwan Mac Kim. 2013. Emotions in text: dimensional and categorical models. *Computational Intelligence*, 29(3):527–543.

J Cohen. 1960. Kappa: Coefficient of concordance. *Educ. Psych. Measurement*, 20:37.

Gary Collier. 2014. *Emotional expression*. Psychology Press.

Cristian Danescu-Niculescu-Mizil and Lillian Lee. 2011. Chameleons in imagined conversations: A new approach to understanding coordination of linguistic style in dialogs. In *Proceedings of the Workshop on Cognitive Modeling and Computational Linguistics, ACL 2011*.

Saurin Dave and Hiteishi Diwanji. 2015. Trend analysis in social networking using opinion mining a survey.

Sidney K D'Mello, Scotty D Craig, Jeremiah Sullins, and Arthur C Graesser. 2006. Predicting affective states expressed through an emote-aloud procedure from autotutor's mixed-initiative dialogue. *International Journal of Artificial Intelligence in Education*, 16(1):3–28.

Paul Ekman, Wallace V Friesen, Maureen O'Sullivan, Anthony Chan, Irene Diacoyanni-Tarlatzis, Karl Heider, Rainer Krause, William Ayhan LeCompte, Tom Pitcairn, Pio E Ricci-Bitti, et al. 1987. Universals and cultural differences in the judgments of facial expressions of emotion. *Journal of personality and social psychology*, 53(4):712.

Pablo Fernandez-Gonzalez, Concha Bielza, and Pedro Larranaga. 2015. Multidimensional classifiers for neuroanatomical data. In *ICML Workshop on Statistics, Machine Learning and Neuroscience (Stamlins 2015)*.

Shantanu Godbole and Sunita Sarawagi. 2004. Discriminative methods for multi-labeled classification. In *Advances in Knowledge Discovery and Data Mining*, pages 22–30. Springer.

Takayuki Hasegawa, Nobuhiro Kaji, Naoki Yoshinaga, and Masashi Toyoda. 2013. Predicting and eliciting addressee's emotion in online dialogue. In *ACL (1)*, pages 964–972.

Shoushan Li, Lei Huang, Rong Wang, and Guodong Zhou. 2015. Sentence-level emotion classification with label and context dependence. In *Proceedings of the 53rd Annual Meeting of the Association for Computational Linguistics and the 7th International Joint Conference on Natural Language Processing (Volume 1: Long Papers)*, pages 1045–1053, Beijing, China, July. Association for Computational Linguistics.

George A Miller. 1995. Wordnet: a lexical database for english. *Communications of the ACM*, 38(11):39–41.

Saif Mohammad. 2012. Portable features for classifying emotional text. In *Proceedings of the 2012 Conference of the North American Chapter of the Association for Computational Linguistics: Human Language Technologies*, pages 587–591. Association for Computational Linguistics.

Robert Plutchik. 1980. A general psychoevolutionary theory of emotion. *Theories of emotion*, 1:3–31.

Carlo Strapparava and Rada Mihalcea. 2007. Semeval-2007 task 14: Affective text. In *Proceedings of the 4th International Workshop on Semantic Evaluations*, pages 70–74. Association for Computational Linguistics.

Zhongqing Wang, Sophia Lee, Shoushan Li, and Guodong Zhou. 2015. Emotion detection in code-switching texts via bilingual and sentimental information. In *Proceedings of the 53rd Annual Meeting of the Association for Computational Linguistics and the 7th International Joint Conference on Natural Language Processing (Volume 2: Short Papers)*, pages 763–768, Beijing, China, July. Association for Computational Linguistics.

Zhibiao Wu and Martha Palmer. 1994. Verbs semantics and lexical selection. In *Proceedings of the 32nd annual meeting on Association for Computational Linguistics*, pages 133–138. Association for Computational Linguistics.

Changhua Yang, Kevin Hsin-Yih Lin, and Hsin-Hsi Chen. 2007. Emotion classification using web blog corpora. In *Web Intelligence, IEEE/WIC/ACM International Conference on*, pages 275–278. IEEE.

Liang-Chih Yu, Jin Wang, K Robert Lai, and Xue-jie Zhang. 2015. Predicting valence-arousal ratings of words using a weighted graph method. *Volume 2: Short Papers*, page 788.

Min-Ling Zhang and Zhi-Hua Zhou. 2006. Multilabel neural networks with applications to functional genomics and text categorization. *Knowledge and Data Engineering, IEEE Transactions on*, 18(10):1338–1351.

Long-distance anaphors and the blocking effect revisited: An East Asian perspective

Hyunjun Park
Chinese Language and Literature
Chungbuk National University
Cheongju, South Korea 28644
tudorgepark@gmail.com

Abstract

A major claim in the literature is that a distribution of anaphoric elements either obeys or disobeys locality conditions. In addition, it has long been noted that the presence of a first (or second) person pronoun intervening between Chinese *ziji* and a higher potential antecedent blocks long-distance binding. However, this paper proposes that a third person antecedent can be a blocker in a given discourse, based on Kuno and Kaburaki's (1977) system. If this is on the right track, the blocking effect in East Asian languages, especially Chinese *ziji*, Korean *caki*, and Japanese *zibun*, can be accounted for with a unified treatment.

1 Introduction

Anaphoric elements are generally claimed to fall into two types: those that obey locality conditions and those that do not. Reflexives in English and their counterparts in East Asian languages, especially Chinese, Japanese, and Korean, display characteristics of one or other type. For example, while the English reflexive *himself* can only be felicitously used when bound within the same clause, as in (1), the Chinese reflexive *ziji* in (2) can ambiguously refer to the matrix subject, the intermediate subject, or the lowest subject across the clause boundary, which has been called a long-distance anaphor.

(1) John$_3$ thinks Tom$_5$ knows Bill$_7$ likes himself$_{*3/*5/7}$.

(2) Zhangsan$_3$ renwei Lisi$_5$ zhidao Wangwu$_7$
Zhangsan think Lisi know Wangwu
xihuan ziji$_{3/5/7}$.
like self
'Zhangsan$_3$ thinks Lisi$_5$ knows Wangwu$_7$ likes self$_{3/5/7}$.'
(Cole et al. 1990:1)

The long-distance anaphor *ziji* also shows this seemingly idiosyncratic property in some specific contexts. The presence of a first (or second) person pronoun intervening between *ziji* and the higher potential antecedent blocks its long-distance binding, which refers to a blocking effect, as exemplified in (3).

(3) Zhangsan$_3$ renwei wo$_5$ zhidao Wangwu$_7$
Zhangsan think I know Wangwu
xihuan ziji$_{*3/*5/7}$.
like self
'Zhangsan$_3$ thinks that I$_5$ know that Wangwu$_7$ likes him$_{*3}$/me$_{*5}$/himself$_7$.'
(Cole et al. 1990:15)

(4) Chelswu$_3$-nun nay$_5$-ka caki$_{3/*5}$-lul
Chelswu-Top I-Nom self-Acc
cohaha-n-ta-ko sayngkakha-n-ta.
like-Pres-Decl-Comp think-Pres-Decl
'Chelswu$_3$ thinks I$_5$ like him$_3$/myself$_{*5}$.'
(Cole et al. 1990:19)

However, no comparable cases, in which a blocking effect is triggered by the presence of first (or second) person pronoun, have been reported for the Korean long-distance anaphor *caki*.[1] A question

[1] It has long been accepted that a feature mismatch between potential antecedents does not induce the blocking effect for

arises at this point about the status of a blocking effect. Cross-linguistically, is it a universal or particular property of the languages? The purpose of this paper is to offer a unified account of long-distance anaphors including blocking effects among East Asian languages.

The organization of the paper is as follows. In section 2, I review the previous analyses of blocking effects with the long-distance binding of Chinese *ziji*. Then, in section 3, I introduce various counter-examples to the existing accounts. And in section 4, a unified account is given in order to accommodate blocking effects of Japanese *zibun* and Korean *caki*. Section 5 summarizes my findings and conclusions, with a discussion of some predictions that follow from the current analysis.

2 What has been said about blocking effects with *ziji* in Chinese

Huang and Liu (2001) argue that the blocking effect of the long-distance bound *ziji* can be attributed to the notion of logophoricity. They further reason that the blocking effect is induced in terms of conflicting perspectives, especially first or second person, when binding between *ziji* and its potential antecedents operates across an intermediate antecedent of different person, as illustrated in (5) and (6).

(5) *[3 [1 ... ziji ...]]

(6) *[3 [2 ... ziji ...]]

the long-distance binding of Japanese *zibun*, as shown in (i) and (ii).

(i) Taroo$_3$-wa watasi$_5$-ga zibun$_{3/5}$-o sukida-to omotte-riu.
Taroo-Top I-Nom self-Acc like-Comp think-Pres
'Taroo$_3$ thinks that I$_5$ like him$_3$/myself$_5$.'

(ii) John$_3$-ga watasi$_5$-ga Bill$_7$-ni zibun$_{3/5/7}$-no sigoto-o
John-Nom I-Nom Bill-Dat self Gen job-Acc
sa-seta to omotte-iru-
do-Cau Comp think-Pres
'John$_3$ thinks that I$_5$ made Bill$_7$ do zibun$_{3/5/7}$'s work.'
(Aikawa 1993:163)

However, the existence of the blocking effect of *zibun* has been reported recently by Nishigauchi (2014) while Cole et al. (1990) and Han and Storoshenko (2012) still claim that Korean *caki* is not subject to the blocking effect at all. I will return to this issue in section 3.

Huang and Liu propose, following Kuno's (1972) direct discourse representation hypothesis, that sentences containing logophoric *ziji* in reported discourse can be paraphrased in terms of direct discourse, by assuming that the source of *ziji* in indirect speech is basically equivalent to the first person pronoun *wo* 'I' in direct speech.[2] As pointed out by Clements (1975), the use of logophoric pronouns is quite similar to that of first person forms in the sense that logophoric pronouns refer to the internal speaker in reported discourse while first person pronouns refer to the external speaker in present discourse. To see how this works, consider the following examples.

(7) a. Zhangsan$_3$ juede Lisi$_5$ zai piping ziji$_{3/5}$.
Zhangsan think Lisi at criticize self
'Zhangsan$_3$ thinks that Lisi$_5$ is criticizing him$_3$/himself$_5$.'

b. Zhangsan$_3$ juede, "Lisi$_5$ zai piping wo$_3$."
Zhangsan think Lisi at criticize me
'Zhangsan$_3$ thinks, "Lisi$_5$ is criticizing me$_3$."'

(8) a. Zhangsan$_3$ juede wo$_5$ zai piping ziji$_{*3/5}$.
Zhangsan think I at criticize self
'Zhangsan$_3$ thinks that I$_5$ am criticizing him$_{*3}$/myself$_5$.'

b. Zhangsan$_3$ juede, "wo$_5$ zai piping wo$_3$".
Zhangsan think I at criticize me
'Zhangsan$_3$ thinks, "I$_5$ am criticizing me$_3$."'
(Huang and Liu 2001:161-2)

In (7a), the logophoric *ziji* referring to the reported speaker *Zhangsan* can be turned into the first person pronoun *wo* 'I' as the actual speaker in the direct discourse, as shown in (7b), without perspective clash between *Zhangsan* and *Lisi* since they are both a third party. Thus, the logophoric use of *ziji* is licensed in the indirect discourse. On the other hand, as shown in (8b), there are two instances of the first person *wo* 'I' when the logophoric *ziji* is paraphrased in the direct discourse.

[2] Kuno (1972) observes that the source of *zibun* in (i) is the first person pronoun *boku* in the direct representation of John's internal feeling, as shown in (ii).

(i) John$_3$-wa, Mary$_5$-ga zibun$_3$-o mita toki-wa byooki datta.
John-Top Mary-Nom self saw when-Top sick was
'John$_3$ was sick when Mary$_5$ saw him$_3$.'

(ii) John: "Boku-wa Mary-ga boku-o mita toki-wa
I-Top Mary-Nom I-Acc saw when-Top
byooki datta."
'I was sick when Mary saw me.'
(Kuno 1972:180-1)

The two *wo* 'I' are anchored in different sources, namely the external speaker and the internal speaker *Zhangsan* respectively and such a reading is not acceptable due to the perspective conflict it would cause. This is the reason Huang and Liu give to explain why a logophoric reading of *ziji* is blocked.

In addition, Pan (2001) claims that the blocking effect of *ziji* is not symmetrical in that intervening first and second person pronouns may block third person potential antecedents from long-distance binding *ziji*, while third person potential antecedents do not necessarily block first or second person pronouns from long-distance binding *ziji*. Here are the relevant judgments.

(9) a. Wo_3 bu xihuan $Lisi_5$ guan $ziji_{3/5}$
I not like Lisi interfere self
de shi.
DE matter
'I_3 don't like $Lisi_5$ interfering in my_3 (own) business.'
b. $Lisi_3$ bu xihuan wo_5 guan $ziji_{*3/5}$
Lisi not like I interfere self
de shi.
DE matter
'$Lisi_3$ does not like me_5 interfering in my_5 (own) business.'
(Pan 2001:283)

The first person pronoun as the matrix subject in (9a) is a possible antecedent. However, in (9b), the third person *Lisi* in the matrix subject position is excluded from being a candidate of long-distance antecedents in such a sentence because of a conflicting feature agreement. Hence, a logophoric reading of *ziji*, in Huang and Liu's (2001) system[3], is blocked here.

3 Another type of blocker

As already pointed out above, the canonical view on blocking effects of Chinese *ziji* has been accounted for in terms of either presence or absence of person feature agreement. In particular, a first or second person pronoun induces blocking effects, but not a third person pronoun. However, a closer look reveals a much different situation, as shown in (2) and (3), repeated below.

(10) $Zhangsan_3$ renwei $Lisi_5$ zhidao $Wangwu_7$
Zhangsan think Lisi know Wangwu
xihuan $ziji_{3/5/7}$.
like self
'$Zhangsan_3$ thinks $Lisi_5$ knows $Wangwu_7$ likes $self_{3/5/7}$.'

(11) $Zhangsan_3$ renwei wo_5 zhidao $Wangwu_7$
Zhangsan think I know Wangwu
xihuan $ziji_{*3/*5/7}$.
like self
'$Zhangsan_3$ thinks that I_5 know that $Wangwu_7$ likes him_{*3}/me_{*5}/$himself_7$.'

All the candidates of long-distance binding in (10) are a third person and there is no blocking effect. On the other hand, there is a person feature disagreement among the candidates in (11) and it would give rise to the blocking effect. Obviously, however, the blocker is not the first person pronoun *wo* 'I' but the third person proper noun *Wangwu*.[4] Let us look at the following contrast.

[3] Contrary to what Huang and Liu argue, Pan (2001:290) points out that the logophoric interpretation cannot properly accommodate the peculiar properties of long-distance bound *ziji* including the blocking effect. The following evidence seems to point in that direction.
(i) $Kofi_3$ nya be me_5-kpɔ $yè_3$.
Kofi know Comp Pro-see Log
'$Kofi_3$ knew that I_5 had seen him_3.' (Clements 1975: 170)
As we can see above, the blocking effect does not occur in logophoric environments at all. See Park (2015b) for further discussion.

[4] There has been a great diversity of opinion about what really triggers the blocking effects in the long-distance binding of *ziji*. Many authors agree that blocking can be induced entirely by the existence of an intervening first or second person pronoun, but not a third person antecedent. However, how can we explain what is different between the following sentences.
(i) $Zhangsan_3$ cong $Lisi_5$ nar tingshuo naben shu
Zhangsan from Lisi there hear that-CL book
hai-le $ziji_{3/*5}$.
hurt-Perf self
'$Zhangsan_3$ heard from $Lisi_5$ that that book hurt $him_{3/*5}$.'
(Pan 2001:291)
(ii) $Zhangsan_3$ cong wo_5 nar tingshuo $ziji_{3/*5}$ de erzi
Zhangsan from I there hear self DE son
de-le jiang.
get-Pref prize
'$Zhangsan_3$ heard from me_5 that his_3/my_{*5} son didn't win the prize.'
The first person pronoun *wo* 'I' in (ii) looks the same as the third person *Lisi* yet does not act as blocker for the long-distance binding of *ziji* in (i).

(12) Zhangsan$_3$ renwei wo$_5$ zhidao Wangwu$_7$
Zhangsan think I know Wangwu
xihuan ziji$_{*3/??5/7}$.
like self
'Zhangsan$_3$ thinks that I$_5$ know that Wangwu$_7$ likes him$_{*3}$/me$_{??5}$/himself$_7$.'

(13) Zhangsan$_3$ renwei Wangwu$_5$ zhidao wo$_7$
Zhangsan think Wangwu know I
xihuan ziji$_{*3/*5/7}$.
like self
'Zhangsan$_3$ thinks that Wangwu$_5$ knows that I$_7$ like him$_{*3*5}$/myself$_7$.'

(Cole et al. 2006:63)

The biggest difference between (12) and (13) is the fact that the third person antecedent *Wangwu* blocks the first person pronoun *wo* 'I' from binding *ziji* in (12) while a first person antecedent does in (13). To be more exact, the blocker of the long-distance binding in (12) is the third person *Wangwu* and the same role in (13) is carried by the first person pronoun *wo* 'I'. If this account is on the right track, the approach that long-distance binding of *ziji* is blocked exclusively by the presence of a first or second person needs to be reviewed. Here are the relevant data.

(14) Zhangsan$_3$ zhidao Lisi$_5$ gaosu-guo ni$_7$
Zhangsan know Lisi tell-Guo you
youguan ziji$_{*3/5/*7}$ de gongzuo.
about self DE work
'Zhangsan$_3$ knew that Lisi$_5$ told you$_7$ about his$_{*3/5}$your$_{*7}$ work.'

(15) Zhangsan$_3$ shuo Lisi$_5$ gen ni$_7$ tan-guo
Zhangsan say Lisi with you talk-Guo
ziji$_{*3/5/*7}$ de shi.
self DE business
'Zhangsan$_3$ said that Lisi$_5$ talked about his$_{*3/5}$your$_{*7}$ business with you$_7$.'

(16) Zhangsan$_3$ renwei Lisi$_5$ cong wo$_7$ nar
Zhangsan think Lisi from I there
tingshuo-le ziji$_{*3/5/*7}$ de fenshu.
hear-say-Perf self DE score
'Zhangsan$_3$ thinks Lisi$_5$ heard from me$_7$ his$_{*3/5}$my$_{*7}$ score.'

(17) Zhangsan$_3$ zhidao Lisi$_5$ zai wo$_7$ jia xi
Zhangsan know Lisi at I home develop
ziji$_{*3/5/*7}$ de zhaopian.
self DE photo
'Zhangsan$_3$ knew that Lisi$_5$ was developing his$_{*3/5}$my$_{*7}$ picture(s) at my home.'

(Pan 2001:281)

As we can see in (14) through (17), the first and second person pronouns cannot bind *ziji* whereas the intermediate antecedent can. Nonetheless, that they have been treated as blocking elements is not reasonable. The following example is acceptable as well.

(18) Zhangsan$_3$ cong wo$_5$ nar tingshuo
Zhangsan from I there hear-say
laoshi$_7$ ma-le ziji$_{3/*5/7}$.
teacher criticize-Perf self
'Zhangsan$_3$ heard from me$_5$ that the teacher$_7$ criticized him$_3$/me$_{*5}$/himself$_7$.'

In (18), *ziji* can be bound by both third person antecedents, but not by the first person pronoun.

Huang and Liu (2001) have argued that licensing long-distance binding in Chinese is characterized as the logophoric use of *ziji* and thus the blocking effect can be accounted for by means of logophoric effects such as Kuno's direct discourse representation hypothesis as the logophoric pronoun *yè* in Ewe is generally used in reported context while it is replaced by a first person form in direct speech. However, there is no logophoric effect in (19).[5]

(19) Zhangsan$_3$ de biaoqing gaosu wo$_5$
Zhangsan DE expression tell me
ziji$_{3/*5}$ shi guwude.
self is innocent
'Zhangsan's$_3$ expression tells me$_5$ that he$_3$/I$_{*5}$ am innocent.'

(Cole et al. 2006:37)

In (19), not only can *ziji* refer to the matrix subject over the intervening first person pronoun but it also occurs in the absence of a logophoric environment.

Besides, third person interveners may serve as a blocker, as shown in (21).

---

[5] An anonymous reviewer pointed out that grammaticality of the antecedents of the anaphors in sentences (19) through (26) can be influenced by the predicates. I definitely agree with the reviewer's comment that the predicate semantics should be considered in the analysis. Nonetheless, I would argue that the verbs used in those examples are utterance verbs, as in (19) through (25), and an attitude verb, as in (26), which makes attitude holders to serve as the antecedent of logophors in the embedded clauses.

(20) Mama$_3$ shuo jia chuqu-de nüer$_5$
mother say marry go.out-DE daughter
yijing hui lai ziji$_{3/*5}$-de jia le.
already return come self-DE home Asp
'Mother$_3$ said that the married daughter$_5$ had already come back to her$_{3/*5}$ home.'

(21) Mama$_3$ shuo jia chuqu-de nüer$_5$
mother say marry go.out-DE daughter
yijing hui qu ziji$_{*3/5}$-de jia le.
already return go self-DE home Asp
'Mother$_3$ said that the married daughter$_5$ had already gone back to her$_{*3/5}$ home.'
(Liu 1999:39)

The lower subject *nüer* 'daughter' in (21) can be reported by the external speaker as the empathy locus, in Kuno and Kaburaki's (1977) system, to which deictic elements such as 'come' and 'go' should refer.[6] Only *nüer* 'daughter' in this case, not *mama* 'mother', can be the antecedent for *ziji* and thus blocks long-distance binding *mama* 'mother', which means that the *nüer* 'daughter' functions as a blocker. The same situation occurs in Korean and Japanese, as shown in (22) through (25).

(22) Emeni$_3$-nun sicip-ka-n ttal$_5$-i
mother-Top marry-go.out-Adn daughter-Nom
caki$_{3/*5}$ cip-ulo tola-o-ass-tako
self home-to return-come-Past-Comp
malha-yss-ta.
say-Past-Decl
'Mother$_3$ said that the married daughter$_5$ had already come back to her$_{3/*5}$ home.'

(23) Emeni$_3$-nun sicip-ka-n ttal$_5$-i
mother-Top marry-go.out-Adn daughter-Nom
caki$_{*3/5}$ cip-ulo tola-ka-ass-tako
self home-to return-go-Past-Comp
malha-yss-ta.
say-Past-Decl
'Mother$_3$ said that the married daughter$_5$ had already gone back to her$_{*3/5}$ home.'

(24) Haha$_3$-wa yomeni itta musume$_5$-ga
mother-Top marry go.out daughter-Nom
zibun$_{3/*5}$-no ie-ni modotte ki-ta-to
self-Gen home-to return.come-Past-Comp
hanasi-ta.
say-Past
'Mother$_3$ said that the married daughter$_5$ had already come back to her$_{3/*5}$ home.'

(25) Haha$_3$-wa yomeni itta musume$_5$-ga
mother-Top marry go.out daughter-Nom
zibun$_{*3/5}$-no ie-ni modotte it-ta-to
self-Gen home-to return.go-Past-Comp
hanasi-ta.
say-Past
'Mother$_3$ said that the married daughter$_5$ had already gone back to her$_{*3/5}$ home.'

The blocking effect related to an empathy locus is also found in the environments with clausemate long-distance anaphors, as pointed out by Huang and Liu (2001) and Cole et al. (2006). Here is the example.[7]

(26) Zhangsan renwei Lisi zhidao Wangwu
Zhangsan think Lisi know Wangwu
ba ziji$_1$ de shu song-gei-le
BA self DE book give-to-Perf
Ziji$_2$ de pengyou.
self DE friend
'Zhangsan thinks that Lisi knows that Wangwu gave self's books to self's friends.'
(Cole et al. 2006:61)

In (26), there are two occurrences of long-distance *ziji*, *ziji*'s books and *ziji*'s friends, in the same clause. The two *zijis* referring to the books and the friends should be bound to the same antecedent. Thus, the sentence can only mean that Zhangsan thinks that Lisi knows that Wangwu gave Zhangsan's book to Zhangsan's friends, or that Zhangsan thinks that Lisi knows that Wangwu gave Lisi's books to Lisi's friends.[8] Either way, the blocker will be a third person referent. This kind of blocking effect can be seen in Japanese and Korean as well, as shown in (27) and (28) respectively.

(27) Naomi$_3$-wa Ken$_5$-ga zibun-no kuruma-de
Naomi-Top Ken-Nom self-Gen car-by

[6] Liu (1999:39-40) claims that the contrast between (20) and (21) can be accounted for in terms of one of logophoric effects like PIVOT in Sells' (1987) term. However, this paper, along the lines of Oshima (2004, 2007), argues that long distance bindings in East Asian languages, especially of Chinese *ziji*, Korean *caki*, and Japanese *zibun*, should be accounted for by the notions of logophor and empathy.

[7] This example was first discovered by Pan (1997).

[8] It can be explained in terms of Kuno's (1987:207) Ban on Conflicting Empathy Foci: A single sentence cannot contain logical conflicts in empathy relationships.

zibun-no ie-ni kaetta to itta.
self-Gen home-to returned Comp said
'Naomi$_3$ said that Ken$_5$ had returned to her$_3$ home in her$_3$ car.'
'Naomi$_3$ said that Ken$_5$ had returned to his$_5$ home in his$_5$ car.'
*'Naomi$_3$ said that Ken$_5$ had returned to his$_5$ home in her$_3$ car.'
*'Naomi$_3$ said that Ken$_5$ had returned to her$_3$ home in his$_5$ car.' (Iida 1996:81)

(28) John-i$_3$ Bill-i$_5$ caki-uy emma-ka
John-Nom Bill-Nom caki-Gen mother-Nom
caki-lul silhehanta-ko sayngkakhanta-ko
self-Acc hate-Comp think-Comp
malhayssta.
said
'John$_3$ said that Bill$_5$ thought that his$_3$ mother hates him$_3$.'
'John$_3$ said that Bill$_5$ thought that his$_5$ mother hates him$_5$.'
*'John$_3$ said that Bill$_5$ thought that his$_3$ mother hates him$_5$.'
*'John$_3$ said that Bill$_5$ thought that his$_5$ mother hates him$_3$.' (Park 2014)

4 Blocking effect revisited

As described in the preceding section, what licenses the long-distance binding, in Huang and Liu's (2001) system, is the logophoric reading of *ziji* and the existence of the blocking effect is caused by the result of the shifting of long-distance bound *ziji* from the speaker-referring *wo* 'I' in the direct discourse. The examples between (7) and (8) illustrate this claim, repeated below.

(29) a. Zhangsan$_3$ juede Lisi$_5$ zai piping ziji$_{3/5}$.
Zhangsan think Lisi at criticize self
'Zhangsan$_3$ thinks that Lisi$_5$ is criticizing him$_3$/himself$_5$.'
b. Zhangsan$_3$ juede, "Lisi$_5$ zai piping wo$_3$."
Zhangsan think Lisi at criticize me
'Zhangsan$_3$ thinks, "Lisi$_5$ is criticizing-me$_3$."'

(30) a. Zhangsan$_3$ juede wo$_5$ zai piping ziji$_{*3/5}$.
Zhangsan think I at criticize self
'Zhangsan$_3$ thinks that I$_5$ am criticizing him$_{*3}$/myself$_5$.'
b. Zhangsan$_3$ juede, "wo$_5$ zai piping wo$_3$".
Zhangsan think I at criticize me
'Zhangsan$_3$ thinks, "I$_5$ am criticizing me$_3$."'
(Huang and Liu 2001:161-2)

Huang and Liu consider that two instances of *wo* 'I' occurring in the same clause would refer to two different individuals, either the reporter or the internal speaker and thus it can result in a blocking effect. However, as pointed out by Chen (2009), actually their analysis induces a distortion of the truth-condition content of the source sentence, as shown in (31).

(31) a. Zhangsan$_3$ juede, "Lisi$_5$ zai piping wo$_3$".
Zhangsan think Lisi at criticize I
'Zhangsan$_3$ thinks, "Lisi$_5$ is criticizing me$_3$."'
b. Zhangsan$_3$ juede, "ni$_5$ zai piping wo$_3$".
Zhangsan think you at criticize I
'Zhangsan$_3$ thinks, "You$_5$ are criticizing me$_3$."'
c. Zhangsan$_3$ juede, "ta$_5$ zai piping wo$_3$".
Zhangsan think he at criticize I
'Zhangsan$_3$ thinks, "He$_5$ is criticizing me$_3$."'
(Chen 2009: 477-8)

Presumably, a logophoric *ziji* can be paraphrased by using a first person pronoun *wo* 'I' in the direct discourse such as (30b), (31a), (31b), and (31c) but a first person in the reported discourse should also be replaced by an individual referring to an external speaker such as *Lisi* in (31a), *ni* 'you' in (31b), *ta* 'he' in (31c), not *wo* 'I' in (30b). Intuitively, this is correct. Here is the relevant judgment in Ewe.

(32) a. Kofi$_3$ gblɔ na wo$_5$ be yè$_3$-a-dyi
Kofi speak to Pro that Log-T-seek
ga-a na wo$_5$
money-D for Pro
'Kofi$_3$ said to them$_5$ that he$_3$ would seek the money for them$_3$.'
b. Kofi$_3$ gblɔ na wo$_5$ be: ma-dyi
Kofi speak to Pro that Pro-seek
ga-a na mi
money-D for Pro
'Kofi$_3$ said to them$_5$: "I'll seek the money for you."' (Clements 1975: 152)

The second person plural pronoun *mi* 'you' in the direct discourse, as in (32b), is replaced by the third person plural form *wo* 'them' in the reported speech, as in (32a) even though the logophoric pronoun *yè* is replaced by the first person pronoun *ma* 'I' in the direct speech. Hence, the reconstruction of Huang and Liu shown in (30b) is not appropriate.

This would correspond precisely to the logophoric reading of Japanese *zibun*, as illustrated in (33).

(33) a. ?*Taroo$_3$-wa boku$_5$-ga zibun$_3$-ni
Taroo-Top I-Nom slef-Dat
o-kane-o kasi-te kure-ta koto-o
money-Acc lend Benef-Past that-Acc
sukkari wasure-ta rasii.
completely forget-Past seem
'Taroo seems to have completely forgotten that I had done favor to loan self money.'
b. Taroo: "Takasi-ga boku-ni o-kane-o
Taroo: Takashi-Nom I-Dat money-Acc
kasi-te kure-ta."
lend benef-Past
'Taroo: "Takashi did the favor of lending me money."'
(Nishigauchi 2014: 199)

The first person pronoun *boku* 'I' of the reported discourse in (33a) is derived from the third party *Takashi*, the external speaker, with respect to the virtual speaker, using Huang and Liu's (2001) term, *Taroo* in (33b), not the first person pronoun. Thus, there are not two occurrences of the first person pronoun *wo* 'I', contrary to Huang and Liu's claim.

Additionally, it would be no surprise that a logophoric pronoun does not exhibit the blocking effect, since a logophoric pronoun obligatorily denotes the attitude holder that serves as its referent in the scope of an attitude predicate and since the antecedent of a logophoric pronoun is strictly restricted to third persons. Here are the relevant examples, repeated below from footnote 3.

(34) Kofi$_3$ nya be me$_5$-kpɔ yè$_3$.
Kofi know Comp Pro-see Log
'Kofi$_3$ knew that I$_5$ had seen him$_3$.'
(Clements 1975: 170)

(35) Me$_3$-se tso Kofi$_5$ gbɔ be yè$_5$-xɔ
Pro-hear from Kofi side that Log-receive
nunana.
gift
'I$_3$ heard from Kofi$_5$ that he$_5$ had received a gift.' (Clements 1975: 158)

The first person pronoun *me* 'I' in (34) cannot block the third person matrix subject *Kofi* from binding *yè*. On the other hand, the first person pronoun *me* 'I' as the matrix subject in (35) cannot be bound by the logophoric pronoun *yè*. The examples of Korean counterparts below demonstrate convincingly that the property of a logophoric pronoun is not related to a blocking effect.

(36) Chelswu$_3$-nun nay$_5$-ka caki$_{3/*5}$-lul
Chelswu-Top I-Nom self-Acc
po-n-kes-ul al-ass-ta.
see-Adn-Comp-Acc know-Past-Decl
'Chelswu$_3$ knew that I$_5$ had seen him$_3$/myself$_{*5}$.'

(37) Na$_3$-nun Chelswu$_5$-lopwute caki$_{*3/5}$-ka
I-Top Chelswu-from self-Nom
senmwul-ul pat-ass-tako
gift-Acc receive-Past-Comp
ttul-ess-ta.
hear-Past-Decl
'I$_3$ heard from Chelswu$_5$ that *I$_3$/he$_5$ had received a gift.'

As a matter of fact, the first person pronoun in Chinese does not always serve as a blocker against long-distance binding in a given context, as shown in (38).

(38) Lisi$_3$ shengpa wo$_5$ chaoguo ziji$_{3/*5}$.
Lisi worry I surpass self
'Lisi$_3$ was afraid that I$_5$ would surpass him$_3$/myself$_{*5}$.' (Pollard and Xue 2001: 321)

In (38), *ziji* can take the matrix subject *Lisi* as its antecedent rather than the first person pronoun *wo* 'I' within the same clause. This is because *Lisi* here is the attitude holder that serves as the antecedent of logophoric *ziji* in the scope of an attitude predicate. At this point, it should be noted that a logophoric reading can co-occur with a first person pronoun, as illustrated in (39) through (41), respectively Ewe, Japanese, and Korean.

(39) Ama$_3$ se be me$_5$-kpɔ yè$_3$ le asi-a me.
Ama hear that Pro-see Log at market-D in
'Ama$_3$ heard that I$_5$ had seen her$_3$ at the market.' (Clements 1975: 158)

(40) Taroo$_3$-wa boku$_5$-ga zibun$_3$-o but-ta
Taroo-Top I-Nom self-Acc hit-Past

koto-o mada urande-i-ru.
fact-Acc still resent-Asp-Pres
'Taroo$_3$ still resents that I$_5$ hit him$_3$.'
(Kuno 1978: 212)

(41) Chelswu$_3$-nun nay$_5$-ka caki$_{3/*5}$-lul
Chelswu-Top I-Nom self-Acc
piphanha-yess-tako sayngkakha-n-ta.
criticize-Past-Comp think-Pres-Decl
'Chelswu$_3$ thinks that I$_5$ criticized him$_3$/*myself$_5$.'

On the other hand, an empathic reading of long-distance binding can exhibit the blocking effect[9], as shown in (42) and (43), respectively Japanese and Korean.

(42) *Taroo$_3$-wa boku$_5$-ga zibun$_3$-ni kasi-ta
Taroo-Top I-Nom self-Dat lend-Past
okane-o nakusite-simat-ta rasii.
money-Acc lose-end.up-Past it.seems
'It seems that Taroo$_3$ lost the money I$_5$ lent to him$_3$.' (Kuno 1978: 213)

(43) *Hyengsa$_3$-nun nay$_5$-ka caki$_3$ pwumo-lul
detective-Top I-Nom self parents-Acc
salhayha-n phaylyunpem-i-lako
kill-Adn reprobate-being-Comp
sayngkakha-n-ta.
think-Pres-Decl
'The detective$_3$ thinks that I$_5$ am a reprobate who killed his (*the detective's$_3$) parents.'
(Park 2015a: 193)

It is worth noting that there is no attitude holder associated with the reported attitude in (42). Moreover, the empathic use of long-distance binding can empathize with the person in a given context in terms of the external speaker even in the attitude report, such as (43).[10] These observed facts seem to indicate that logophoric use of long-distance binding does not exhibit the blocking effect. The relevant data from Chinese support this claim.

(44) Ta$_3$ shuo ni$_5$ mingming zhidao Mary$_7$
he say you clearly know Mary
bu hui xihuan ziji$_{3/5/7}$.
not will like self
'He$_3$ said you$_5$ knew clearly that Mary$_7$ wouldn't like him$_3$/you$_5$/herself$_7$.'
(Xu 1993:136)

(45) Zongtong$_3$ qing wo$_5$ zuo zai ziji$_{3/*5}$
president ask I sit at self
de shenbian.
DE side
'The president$_3$ asked me$_5$ to sit beside him$_3$/himself$_{*5}$.' (Pollard and Xue 2001: 321)

In (44), there is no blocking effect in spite of the mismatch of person features among the subjects of the three clauses. In addition, (45) shows that not only does *ziji* not occur in the scope of an attitude predicate at all, there is no blocking effect either.

5 Conclusion

Huang and Liu (2001) have argued that the blocking effect of long-distance binding in Chinese can be accounted for in terms of logophoricity and the direct discourse representation hypothesis. Furthermore, they claim that the mismatch of person features among possible antecedents induces the blocking effect. However, this paper proposes that a third person, in addition to a first or a second person, can be an antecedent and that the blocking effect is closely related to empathic use of long-distance anaphors, especially in East Asian languages such as Chinese, Korean and Japanese.

[9] Empathy theory in linguistics was first introduced by Kuno and Kaburaki (1977:628). The key notion of empathy is defined as follows:
(i) Empathy is the speaker's identification, with varying degrees (ranging from degree 0 to 1), with a person who participates in the event that he describes in a sentence.
To capture how the empathic use of Japanese *zibun* works in a sentence, see Oshima (2007). It is beyond the scope of this paper to explain how the alternative solution through empathy works with respect to a blocking effect of long-distance anaphors and the relationship, as an anonymous reviewer pointed out, between logophors and indexicals. I leave these issues to future research.

[10] An anonymous reviewer suggests that long-distance *ziji* is, or has a use as, a logophor and the felicitous use of *ziji* as a logophor is constrained by the factor of empathy. However, the domain of empathic use in long-distance binding should, I think, be separated from that of logophoric use even though empathic use occasionally overlaps the logophoric use in logophoric environments, as the Korean example in (43). Furthermore, given *ziji* is only characterized as a logophor, the following example cannot be appropriately accounted for by means of logophoricity.
(i) John$_3$ mingling Bill$_5$ [S PRO gei ziji$_{3/5}$ guahuzi].
John order Bill to self shave
'John$_3$ ordered Bill$_5$ to shave him$_3$/himself$_5$.'
(Pan 2001: 291)

Acknowledgements

I am grateful to the three anonymous reviewers of PACLIC 30 for their helpful comments and suggestions on the earlier version of the paper. All the remaining errors are, of course, my own.

References

Aikawa, Takako. 1993. Reflexivity in Japanese and LF-analysis of zibun-binding. Ph.D. dissertation, The Ohio State University.

Chen, Hsiang-Yun. 2009. Logophoricity and ziji. In Y. Xiao, ed., *Proceedings of the 21st NACCL*, pages 464-481. Smithfield: Bryant University.

Clements, George N. 1975. The logophoric pronoun in Ewe: Its role in discourse. *Journal of West African Languages* 2: 141-177.

Cole, Peter, Gabriella Hermon, and Li-May Sung. 1990. Principles and parameters of long-distance reflexives. *Linguistic Inquiry* 21: 1-22.

Cole, Peter, Gabriella Hermon, and C.-T. James Huang. 2006. Long-distance anaphors: an Asian perspective. In *SYNCOM*. Blackwell Publishers.

Han, Chung-hye and Dennis Ryan Storoshenko. 2012. Semantic binding of long-distance anaphor *caki* in Korean. *Language* 88: 764-790.

Huang, C.-T. James and C.-S. Luther Liu. 2001. Logophoricity, attitudes, and *ziji* at the interface, In *Long-distance reflexives: Syntax and semantics 33*, ed. by Peter Cole, Gabriella Hermon, and C.-T. James Huang, 141-195. New York: Academic Press.

Iida, Masaya. 1996. *Context and Binding in Japanese*. Stanford: CSLI.

Kuno, Susumu. 1972. Pronominalization, reflexivization, and direct discourse. *Linguistic Inquiry* 3: 161-195.

Kuno, Susumu. 1978. *Danwa no bunpoo* [Grammar of discourse]. Tokyo: Taishukan.

Kuno, Susumu. 1987. *Functional syntax: Anaphora, discourse and empathy*. Chicago: University of Chicago Press.

Kuno, Susumu and Etsuko Kaburaki. 1977. Empathy and syntax. *Linguistic Inquiry* 8: 627-672.

Liu, Chensheng. 1999. Anaphora in Mandarin Chinese and binding at the interface. Ph.D. thesis, UC Irvine.

Nishigauchi, Taisuke. 2014. Reflexive binding: awareness and empathy from a syntactic point of view. *Journal of East Asian Linguistics* 23: 157-206.

Oshima, David Y. 2004. *Zibun* revisited: empathy, logophoricity, and binding. *University of Washington Working Papers in Linguistics* 22: 175-190.

Oshima, David Y. 2006. Perspectives in reported discourse. Ph.D. dissertation, Stanford University.

Oshima, David Y. 2007. On empathic and logophoric binding. *Research on Language and Computation* 5: 19-35.

Pan, Haihua. 1997. *Constraints on reflexivization in Mandarin Chinese*. New York: Garland Publishing, Inc.

Pan, Haihua. 2001. Why the blocking effect? In *Long-distance reflexives: Syntax and semantics 33*, ed. by Peter Cole, Gabriella Hermon, and C.-T. James Huang, 279-316. New York: Academic Press.

Park, Hyunjun. 2015a. Logophor, empathy, and long-distance anaphors in East Asian languages. Ph.D. dissertation, City University of Hong Kong.

Park, Hyunjun. 2015b. Pan's (2001) puzzle revisited. In *Proceedings of the 29th Pacific Asia Conference on Language, Information and Computation* (PACLIC 29), pages 212-220.

Park, Hyunjun. 2016. Another type of blocker. Talk given at the 24th Annual Conference of the International Association of Chinese Linguistics (IACL-24). Beijing Language and Culture University, Beijing, China.

Park, Yangsook. 2014. Indexicals and the long-distance reflexive *caki* in Korean. In *Proceedings from SALT XIV*. CLS Publications.

Pearson, Hazel. 2013. The sense of self: Topics in the semantics of *de se* expressions. Ph.D. dissertation, Harvard University.

Pollard, Carl and Ping Xue. 2001. Syntactic and non-syntactic constraints on long-distance binding. In P. Cole, C.-T. J. Huang, and G. Hermon, eds., Long-distance reflexives, vol.33 of Syntax and semantics, pages 317-342. New York: Academic Press.

Sells, Peter. 1987. Aspects of logophoricity. *Linguistic Inquiry* 18: 445-479.

Wang, Yingying and Haihua Pan. 2014. A note on the non-de se interpretation of attitude reports. *Language* 90: 746-754.

Wang, Yingying and Haihua Pan. 2015. Empathy and Chinese long-distance reflexive *ziji*-remarks on Giorgi (2006, 2007). *Natural Language and Linguistic Theory*.

Xu, Liejiong. 1993. The long-distance binding of *ziji*. *Journal of Chinese Linguistics* 21: 123-142.

Yoon, Jeong-Me. 1989. Long-distance anaphors in Korean and their cross-linguistic implications. In *Papers from the 25th Annual Meeting of the Chicago Linguistic Society*, ed. by Caroline Wiltshire, Randolph Graczyk, & Music Bradley, pages 479-495. Chicago: Chicago Linguistic Society.

Developing an Unsupervised Grammar Checker for Filipino Using Hybrid N-grams as Grammar Rules

Matthew Phillip Go
De la Salle University
2401 Taft Avenue,
Manila, Philippines
matthew_phillip_go@dlsu.edu.ph

Allan Borra
De la Salle University
2401 Taft Avenue,
Manila, Philippines
allan.borra@dlsu.edu.ph

Abstract

This study focuses on using hybrid n-grams as grammar rules for detecting grammatical errors and providing corrections in Filipino. These grammar rules are derived from grammatically-correct and tagged texts which are made up of part-of-speech (POS) tags, lemmas, and surface words sequences. Due to the structure of the rules used by this system, it presents an opportunity to have an unsupervised grammar checker for Filipino when coupled with existing POS taggers and morphological analyzers. The approach is also customized to cover different error types present in the Filipino language. The system achieved 82% accuracy when tested on checking erroneous and error-free texts.

1. Introduction

According to the philosopher and educator Kevin Browne, poor grammar implies two negative sentiments towards the writer: either he is not intelligent or he just does not care about his writing any better. Backing on this problem, there has been many researches and advances in the field of computer-aided grammar checking such as Microsoft Word, Google Docs, Grammarly, LanguageTool, and Ginger. These software solutions can detect syntactical errors such as spelling, punctuation, word forms, and word usages. However, most of these solutions have focused on the English language. There has been very few works in the Filipino language despite being a language of at least 100 million people[1]. Additionally, it is difficult to use an existing grammar checker system of one language and apply it on another since the system would have its specific design and functionalities tackling the unique phenomena of its target language.

The Filipino language, just like any other language, has its own unique phenomena which serve as a challenge in developing its own grammar checker system. It has a 'large vocabulary of root, borrowed, and derived words' caused by the arrival and/or colonization of foreign countries including: Spain, USA, and China in the Filipino land[2]. It also has a high degree of inflection and uses variety of affixes to change the part-of-speech of a root word (ex. root: *tira* 'live [on a house]', *tira* + *han* = *tirahan* 'house') or change the focus and aspect of a verb (*tirhan* 'live' – neutral aspect/object focus, *titira* 'will live' – contemplative aspect/ actor focus, *tumira* 'lived' – perfective aspect/ actor focus. Another linguistic phenomenon in Filipino is its free-word order structure. Filipino sentences, in its natural form, follow the predicate-subject sentence format (ex. *Masaya ako* – word-per-word is translated as 'Happy I') or as subject-predicate sentence format (ex. *Ako ay masaya* – word-per-word is translated as 'I [none] happy') where the word *ay* acts as a lexical marker and is usually placed after the subject and before the predicate. In the Filipino language, direct objects, adjectives and adverbs may also be written as phrases and including prepositional phrases, they also follow the free-word order and not being limited to just one position in the sentence (Ramos, 1971). For example, the sentence 'Mark ate an apple.' can be translated to: *Si Mark ay kumain ng mansanas.*, *Kumain si Mark ng mansanas.*, and *Kumain ng mansanas si Mark.* As seen in the last two translations, the direct object phrase *ng mansanas* 'apple' can be placed directly after the verb or after the subject yet both produce the exact same meaning.

[1]http://www.philstar.com/headlines/2016/01/03/1538653/philippines-population-seen-hit-104m

[2] http://ffemagazine.com/the-origin-of-the-filipino-language-wikang-filipino/

As of this writing, there are still no grammar-checking software systems for Filipino that is publicly available that cover broad-range of grammatical errors. This fact may be associated with the complex structure of the Filipino language which makes it difficult in constructing (error) grammar rules. Among the few existing grammar checkers in Filipino are: Panuring Pampanitikan (PanPam) by Jasa et al. (2007) and Language Tool for Filipino (LTF) by Oco & Borra (2011). PanPam is a syntax and semantics-based grammar checker for Filipino that makes use of error patterns as rules and lexical functional grammar as its parsing algorithm. LTF, on the other hand, uses a rule file containing error patterns in the form of regular expressions and part-of-speech tags and a dictionary file in detecting its errors and providing corresponding suggestions. Although these systems, especially LTF, could distinctly recognize grammatical errors from correct text by using error patterns, the main concern with these systems is that the parser rules, dictionaries, affix-to-root-word mappings, word-to-part-of-speech mappings, error patterns, and other files are manually defined which is a very tedious task to cover the entire language and all possible errors in it especially that the language is ever growing and the number of errors committed by writers are directly proportional to it. This concern is evident on the systems' presented limitations and results where only a small subset of errors was covered.

In other languages such as English, there are existing works such as Lexbar (Tsao & Wible, 2009), EdIt (Huang et al., 2011), Google books n-gram corpus as grammar checker (Nazar & Renau, 2012), and Chunk-based grammar checker for translated sentences (Lin et al., 2011) which are unsupervised grammar checker systems that make use of grammatically correct texts, their corresponding part-of-speech (POS) tags, and/or lemmas converted into n-gram sequences and used as grammar rules.

The Lexbar application (Tsao & Wible, 2009) generated hybrid n-grams, which are n-grams composed of words, POS tags, and lemmas. These hybrid n-grams are generated from actual tagged word sequences. For example, given phrases such as 'from her point of view' and 'from his point of view', the system will be able to generate the hybrid rule 'from *[dps]*[3] point of view'. This rule can be used to flag the phrase 'from my point of view' as grammatically correct and the phrase 'from him point of view' as incorrect. The Lexbar app was only tested on substitution-correctable errors. The EdIt system (Huang et al., 2011) also made use of hybrid n-grams (called *pattern rules*) as grammar rules but only generates the rules such as *'play ~ role* in *[Noun]'*, *'play ~ role* in *[V-ing]'*, and *'look forward* to *[V-ing]*[4] ' from specific lexical collocations such as *'play ~ role'* and *'look forward'*. These types of rules tackle much more specific error types in English. The key difference of EdIt with Lexbar is that it only limits the number of POS tokens in an n-gram rule to one while Lexbar can have one or more POS tokens such as the rule: 'from *[dps] [nn0]*[5]' derived from the phrases like 'from his house' and 'from her balcony'. EdIt applied its rules in detecting errors correctable by substitution, insertion, and deletion. Both Lexbar and EdIt used weighted Levenshtein edit distance algorithm in prioritizing its suggestions.

This research aims to build an unsupervised grammar checker system for Filipino using hybrid n-grams as grammar rules following a similar format as Lexbar's grammar rules. These rules will be used to detect grammatical errors in Filipino and provide suggestions such as substitution, insertion, deletion, merging, and unmerging extending the existing suggestions made by both Lexbar and EdIt.

2. Filipino Linguistic Phenomena

Aside from the free-word order structure in Filipino, there are other linguistic phenomena such as being morphologically rich, existence of compound words, and the rule in Filipino: "*Kung ano ang bigkas, siyang sulat*" 'Spell as you pronounce it' (Ortograpiyang Pambansa, 2013).

There are at least 50 affixes and other morphologies such as partial reduplication, full reduplication, and compounding that are used in Filipino. These morphologies are categorized into three: *inflectional* – changes in word form that 'accompany case, gender, number, tense, person, mood, or voice that have no effect in the word's part-of-speech'; *derivational* – changes in

[3] *dps* is the part-of-speech (POS) tag for possessive pronouns such as his, her, my, their, etc in the CLAWS5 tagset.
[4] *V-ing* is the POS tag for verbs followed by –ing in the CLAWS5 tagset.
[5] *nn0* is the POS tag for neutral nouns in the CLAWS5 tagset.

word form that changes the word's part-of-speech category; and *compounding* – 'where independent words are concatenated in some way to form a new word' (Bonus, 2003). See Table 1 for some of the different forms of the root word *kain* 'eat'.

Word	Translation
Verbs	
ikakain	will just eat
ikain	just eat
ipakain	feed
ipapakain	will feed
kainin	eat (something)
kinain	ate (something)
kinakain	eating (something)
kumain	(somebody) eating
Nouns	
hapagkainan	eating/dinner table
kainan	eating place
kakainan	eating place (where do-er will go later)
kinakainan	eating place (where do-er is right now)
pagkain	food
Adjective	
palakain	loves eating

Table 1: Different forms of *kain* 'eat'

There are also affixes that are separated by a hyphen (-) from its root word or morpheme (ex. *mang-akit* 'to entice' from the root *akit* 'entice'). There are also cases wherein addition or insertion of an affix to a word could alter the spelling of its base form (ex. The prefix *pang-* + *palit* 'change' = *pamalit* 'item for changing'). However, not all affixes and reduplication can be applied to any word. For instance, the root word *luto* 'cook' can use 'nag-' as prefix but *kain* 'eat' cannot. It should also be noted that there are assimilated words from English in Filipino wherein affixes are also appended to it (ex. *magce-cellphone* 'will use a cellphone', *i-file* 'to file (a document)'). The Filipino language also has its own set of compound words. There are two ways to combine words together, either with the use of a hyphen (ex. *halo-halo* '(a type of Filipino dessert)' from the word *halo* 'mix', and *kisap-mata* 'instant' from the words *kisap* 'blink' & *mata* 'eye') or just combining them as is (ex. *kapitbahay* 'neighbor' from the words *kapit* 'hold onto' & *bahay* 'house', and *hanapbuhay* 'livelihood' from the words *hanap* 'find' & *buhay* 'life') (Paz, 2003).

Another important linguistic phenomenon in Filipino is the rule: "*Kung ano ang bigkas, siyang sulat"* 'Spell as you pronounce it' (Ortograpiyang Pambansa, 2013). As the rule states, the words in Filipino are usually spelled as they are pronounced with some exceptions. This phenomenon simplifies the way Filipino words are spelled out (ex. Filipinized form of 'computer' as *kompyuter)* but also causes some spelling confusion which will be discussed in the next section.

3. Error Types

In understanding the error types that exist in Filipino writing, three references were used: The Cambridge Learner Corpus (Nicholls, 1999), Wikapedia (2015), and a parallel corpus of 1252 erroneous-and-correct word and phrase pairs from sentences written by Filipino university students.

The Cambridge Learner Corpus contains 16 million words from English examination scripts by learners of English containing different types of errors. The corpus categorized the error types into general and specific errors. The proponents noticed that some error categories would have its Filipino counterpart such as wrong form used, missing word/phrase, word/phrase needs replacing, unnecessary word/phrase, punctuation errors, countability errors, determiner agreement, incorrect verb inflection, spelling errors, and other error categories also exist in Filipino.

Wikapedia (2015) is a booklet created by the Presidential Communications Development and Strategic Planning Office of the Philippines containing correct usage of affixes, words, and phrases in Filipino which people may find confusing. One example described in the book would be the use of *ng*, a function word defining possession (ex. *aso ng kapitbahay* 'dog of neighbor') and in a direct object phrase (ex. *kumain ng mansanas* 'ate an apple') vs the use of *nang* which is commonly used before an adverb (ex. *kumain nang mabilis* 'ate fast'). The usage of these two words is confusing because it is pronounced almost exactly the same. Other examples contained in the booklet are proper usage of affixes and words, morphophonemics, usage of hyphens and spaces, and others.

After analyzing the parallel corpus of 1252 erroneous-correct word/phrase pairs, it is found that majority of the errors fall under spelling errors, incorrect usage of affixes/reduplication which is mostly caused by usage of hyphens and spaces, and wrong word usage.

It is observed that one reason the students made spelling errors is because of the way a word is pronounced which is usually simplified for conversational use. Some of these simplified words, see Table 2, are still not accepted in formal Filipino writing which cause spelling errors. Another cause of spelling errors is the confusion whether to spell an English borrowed word in its English version or convert it to its Filipinized spelling version.

There were many instances of affix errors where the students were confused whether a word is an affix of a word, a separate word, or if there should be a hyphen between the affix and the root word. A few of the affix errors also show the confusion of students in selecting an appropriate affix of a verb when used for a certain focus and/or aspect. See Table 3.

The students also committed several mistakes in identifying which word to use in certain situations which is caused by unfamiliarity with Filipino syntax rules. See Table 4.

Other errors that exist in the parallel corpus include the lack of space between words (ex. *pa rin* 'still' incorrectly written as *parin*), compound words that was separated by a space (ex. *araw-araw* 'everyday' incorrectly written as *araw araw*) and punctuation errors where some commas or periods are missing.

Correct Word	Misspelled as	Reason
noon 'before'	*nuon*	Pronounciation
mayroon 'have'	*meron*	Pronounciation
anong 'what'	*anung*	Pronounciation
iyong	*yung*	Pronounciation
tingnan 'look'	*tignan*	Pronounciation
kumpanya 'company'	*companya*	Filipinization
iskolarship 'scholarship'	*scholarship*	Filipinization
risertser 'researcher'	*researcher*	Filipinization

Table 2: Spelling Errors

Correct Word	Misspelled as	Reason
Pangkain 'used for eating'	Pang kain	Extra Space
Tagtuyo 'drought'	Tag-tuyo	Extra Hyphen
Ikawalo 'eighth'	Ika-walo	Extra Hyphen
i-predict 'to predict'	ipredict	Missing Hyphen
mas malaki 'bigger'	masmalaki	Missing Space
inilagay sa kahon 'placed in a box'	*nilagay* sa kahon	Incorrect Affix used for a verb focus

Table 3: Affix Errors

Confused between:	
ng 'of'	*nang* '(function word before an adverb)'
may 'has (used before nouns, verbs, adjectives and adverbs)'	*mayroon* 'has (used before grammatical particles, personal pronouns, and adverbs of place'
suffix *–ng* 'used in place of *na* if word preceding it ends in a vowel	*na* '(type of grammatical particle)'

Table 4: Wrong Word Usage

4. Overview of the Grammar Checker

The grammar checker named Gramatika that is discussed in this paper utilizes the existing implementation of the Lexbar application by Tsao & Wible (2009) and extends it to cover more error types, some of which are unique in the Filipino language. It uses n-grams as rules, commonly referred to as hybrid n-grams, from grammatically correct texts consisting of words, POS tags, and lemmas to detect grammatical errors and provide suggestions containing possible corrections. The production of POS tags, and lemmas can be produced by existing POS taggers and morphological analyzers[6] for Filipino making the system unsupervised such that new grammatically correct texts can be fed through these systems and to Gramatika to easily increase the number of grammar rules.

[6] See Rabo & Cheng (2006) and Bonus (2003)

4.1 Rules Learning

Even though Gramatika also uses hybrid n-grams similar to Lexbar's (Tsao & Wible, 2009) and slightly similar to EdIt's (Huang et al., 2011), the approach in deriving the hybrid n-grams is different. Gramatika uses a clustering approach as opposed to Lexbar's pruning and EdIt's collocations-based approaches. The n-gram sizes used as rules range from 2 to 7. For example, given an incorrect phrase *para sa bata ang laruan ni iyon.* '?that? toy is for the kid', if Gramatika has the hybrid 7-gram *'para_sa [NNC] [DTC] [NNC] na [PRO].'* [7], then it can immediately suggest to change the word *ni* '(a grammatical particle used before a personal proper noun)' to *na* '(a grammatical particle used around adjectives, pointing pronouns, and others)' which produces the corrected version: *para sa bata ang laruan na iyon* 'that toy is for the kid' which is a more appropriate suggestion than the suggestion produced by the trigram *[NNC] ni [NNP]* [8] to change *iyon* to a proper noun (ex. Mark) producing the corrected version: *para sa bata ang laruan ni Mark* 'Mark's toy is for the kid'. The use of larger n-gram sizes increases the context from which a suggestion can be based from.

In the clustering approach, all n-gram sequences are retrieved from grammatically correct texts and are stored in the database. During the storing process, the frequency of all POS tag sequences is counted. POS tag sequences exceeding the threshold of 2 are retrieved and the word n-grams are grouped as clusters. For each n-gram clusters, the module checks if there are any token slot that can be generalized to POS level. For example, if a cluster has the instances *nagpunta sa bayan* 'went to the town' and *bumisita sa bahay* 'visited the house', the first and third tokens can be *generalized* because it meets the minimum difference threshold of 2. This produces the hybrid n-gram *[VBTS] sa [NNC]* which can be used to flag the phrase *umupo sa silya* 'sat on the chair' as grammatically correct or used to detect grammatical errors. The n-gram rules are stored in the database as sequences of words, POS tags, lemmas, and a Boolean sequence denoting which token slots are *generalized*. This is done to allow Gramatika to provide word-specific suggestions and to also identify the appropriate transformed word to a specific POS -lemma mapping.

[7] Based from the Rabo & Cheng (2006) tag set, NNC = common noun, DTC = determiner for common nouns, PRO = pronoun pointing to an object

[8] NNP = proper noun

4.2 Error Detection

In detecting grammatical errors and producing suggestions based on the hybrid n-grams, a weighted Levenshtein edit distance algorithm is used. This algorithm is commonly used in spell checking to compute how many edits it will take to convert a potentially misspelled word to a correct word in the dictionary. It has also been used by EdIt (Huang et al., 2011) in providing corrections by substitution, insertion, and deletion. In Gramatika, the edit distance algorithm is extended to detect errors and provide suggestions correctable by substitution, insertion, deletion, spelling correction, unmerging, and merging. The error types that exists in Filipino are grouped based on the six suggestion types, see Table 5.

Correction	Error Types
Substitution	Affix/Form errors, wrong word/punctuation usage (includes preposition, determiners, and others)
Spelling Correction	Misspelled words, misuse/lack of hyphens
Insertion	Missing words and punctuations
Deletion	Unnecessary words and punctuations
Unmerging	Incorrectly merged words requiring unmerging of words or removal of hyphens
Merging	Incorrectly unmerged word requiring removal of space or insertion of hyphen between texts

Table 5: Correction and Error Types

In producing suggestions, Gramatika parses the input, which is POS and lemma-tagged, into n-grams starting from size 7 down to 2. For each input n-gram, it retrieves hybrid n-gram rules "similar" to the input n-gram from the database. A rule is considered "similar" to an input n-gram if at least *n–2* POS tokens of it are equal to the POS tokens in the input n-gram. Three sizes of the rules are also retrieved for each input n-gram: rules that are of equal size to the input n-gram to be used for substitution and spelling correction suggestions, rules that are one token size larger to produce insertion and unmerging suggestions, and rules that are one token size smaller to produce deletion and merging suggestions. If an input n-gram is "equal" to a rule n-gram of the same size, then it is considered grammatically correct, which is denoted by an edit distance value of 0. "Equal" tokens, in this context, are defined as tokens having the same POS tag if the POS tag of the rule n-gram token is *generalized* or tokens that are equal in surface word level.

A substitution suggestion is outputted when all tokens in the rule n-gram except one are equal to its respective tokens in the input n-gram in the same index. The unequal token is categorized depending on its error type: affix errors or wrong word usage. In detecting affix errors, the system checks if the lemma of the unequal input token is equal to the respective rule token. If the lemmas are equal but the words and/or POS tags are not equal, then it is assumed that there is an affix usage error with respect to the rule n-gram used. For example, given the input *kumain siya bukas* 'he ate tomorrow' is compared against the rule n-gram *[VBTF] [PRS] bukas*[9], where one instance of the POS tag *[VBTF]* is the word *kakain* 'will eat', since *kumain* 'ate' and *kakain* has the same lemma *kain* 'eat', the error is classified as an affix usage error which will produce a suggestion 'Change *kumain* to *kakain*' to produce the phrase *kakain siya bukas* 'He will eat tomorrow'. For wrong word usage errors, Gramatika suggests that the unequal rule token should replace the unequal input token. Consider the example: *Bumili si bata ng laruan* '?the? child bought a toy'. It is considered grammatically incorrect because the word *si* is used as a determiner for proper nouns. Using the trigram rule *[VBTS] ang [NNC]*[10], the correct determiner for common nouns *ang* will be suggested to replace the incorrect word *si*. Corresponding edit distance values will be assigned to the outputted substitution suggestions as seen in Table 6.

Error Type	Weight	Error Type	Weight
Incorrect Affix/ Form	0.6	Wrong Word Same POS	0.8
Spelling Error	0.65	Wrong Word Diff. POS	0.95
Incorrectly Merged	0.7	Missing Word	1.0
Incorrectly Unmerged	0.7	Unnecessary Word	1.0

Table 6: Edit Distance Values

A spelling suggestion is similar to the substitution suggestion criteria where in all tokens except one should be equal to its respective tokens. The unequal tokens are compared using a character-level edit distance algorithm. If it meets the spelling difference threshold, then the token in the rule n-gram is outputted as a spelling correction suggestion. This approach is slightly similar to the traditional way of spell checking which is dictionary look up, but this uses context in providing an appropriate suggestion. For example, given the input *Bakt ?*, using dictionary look-up alone, two possible suggestions can be produced: *Bakat* 'a mark/trace' or *Bakit* 'why'. Using a context-based approach and the rule *[PRQ] ?*[11] where the word *bakit* is an instance of the POS tag *[PRQ]*, Gramatika will suggest the word *Bakit* to form the correct sentence *Bakit?* 'Why?'. This suggestion is assigned an edit distance value of 0.65, as seen in Table 6.

An insertion suggestion is outputted when all tokens in the input n-gram find their corresponding equal tokens in the rule n-gram and one token from the rule n-gram does not have a matched token. For example, given the input n-gram *a b d* and rule n-gram *a b c d*, tokens *a, b,* and *d* are equal tokens and *c* does not have a match which is outputted as an insertion suggestion. This suggestion is given an edit distance value of 1.0, as seen in Table 6.

A deletion suggestion is outputted when all tokens in the rule n-gram find their corresponding equal tokens in the input n-gram and one token from the input n-gram does not have a matched token. This one token will be suggested to be deleted. This suggestion is also given an edit distance value of 1.0, as seen in Table 6.

An unmerging suggestion is outputted when n-1 tokens in the input n-gram are equal to its respective tokens in the rule n-gram leaving one token in the input n-gram and two adjacent tokens in the rule n-gram without matching equal tokens. The system concatenates the two adjacent tokens in the rule n-gram together using a hyphen or removal of the space and checks if it equates to the spelling of the input token. If equal, then an unmerging suggestion is produced. For example, given the input four-gram *a b cd e*, and rule five-gram *a b c d e*, the tokens *a, b,* and *e* are equal tokens. After which, the tokens *c* and

[9] VBTF = contemplative verb, PRS = singular pronoun
[10] VBTS = perfective verb, NNC = common noun

[11] PRQ = question/interrogative pronoun

d in the rule n-gram is concatenated, since it equals the token *cd* in the input n-gram, then the unmerging suggestion is outputted. This suggestion is given an edit distance value of 0.7, as seen in Table 6.

A merging suggestion is outputted when n - 1 tokens in the rule n-gram are equal to its respective tokens in the input n-gram leaving one token in the rule n-gram and two adjacent tokens in the input n-gram without matching equal tokens. The system concatenates the two adjacent tokens in the input n-gram together using a hyphen or removal of the space and checks if it equates to the spelling of the rule token. If yes, then a merging suggestion is produced. For example, given the input five-gram *a b c d e*, and rule four-gram *a b cd e*, the tokens *a, b,* and *e* are equal tokens. After which, the tokens *c* and *d* in the input n-gram is concatenated, since it equals the token *cd* in the rule n-gram, then a merging suggestion is outputted. This suggestion is also given an edit distance value of 0.7, as seen in Table 6.

It should be noted that the edit distance values used are arbitrary and is mainly used for prioritization of suggestions only as the edit distance threshold is set to 1. In cases that there would be ties in terms of edit distance values (ex. three *wrong word different POS tag* suggestions), the frequency of how many times each suggestion is produced by the n-gram rules is also considered.

5. Results and Analysis

The Gramatika system is tested on 70 phrases (35 erroneous and 35 error-free) retrieved from PanPam (Jasa et al., 2007) Wikapedia (2015), translated documents by Filipino university students, and news articles. A small corpus of 2,668 complex sentences which consists of 70,312 tokens (14,575 unique tokens) is used in training of the n-gram rules which result to 83% accuracy, 93% precision, and 71% recall. Table 7 shows a summary of figures. 18 out of 25 erroneous phrases were marked as erroneous, and 23 out of 25 error-free phrases were marked as error-free.

Sentences	Correctly Flagged	Incorrectly Flagged	Total
Erroneous	25	10	35
Error-free	33	2	35
Total	58	12	70

Table 7: Grammar Checking Results

This result shows significant potential for an unsupervised grammar checker that currently only uses a small corpus of grammatically correct sentences.

In detecting errors, the system was able to produce word-specific suggestions for most errors except for one instance: *Noong 2006, mananalo ang* 'Last 2006, (something/someone) will win', having a verb aspect/tense and adverb of time disagreement, where the system only suggest to replace the word *mananalo* 'will win' with any perfective verb *[VBTS]* because it did not have the word- POS-lemma mapping *nanalo* 'won'-[VBTS] *panalo* 'win'. Other detected errors with produced word suggestions include affix errors (ex. *linaan* – root word *laan* 'allot' cannot use the infix '-in-' -> *naglaan* 'alloted'), wrong word usages (ex. *nang* vs *ng*, *para_sa* vs *para_kay*), spelling errors (ex. *kikumpara* -> *kinukumpara* 'comparing', *lalake* -> *lalaki* 'man', *nag-simula* -> *nagsimula* 'started', *nagka-loob* -> *nagkaloob* 'given', *skolar* -> *iskolar* 'scholar', *pwesto* -> *puwesto* 'position'), merging/unmerging errors (ex *maka kuha* -> *makakuha* 'to get', *parin* -> *pa rin* 'still'), and missing punctuation (ex. *Mayo 31 2016* -> *Mayo 31, 2016* 'May 31, 2016').

Gramatika failed to produce correct suggestions for some erroneous inputs because of several reasons. One reason is that some tags in the Rabo & Cheng (2006) tag set are *too* generalized. For instance, the sequence *para sa Mark* 'for the Mark' was incorrectly flagged as grammatically correct which is supposedly *para kay Mark* 'for Mark' because *para sa* is used for common nouns and proper nouns of place. This occurred because all proper nouns only use the tag [NNP] and an n-gram rule *para_sa [NNP]* was produced from phrases with proper nouns of place such as *para sa Amerika,* and *para sa Taiwan.* Another reason is that some words or phrase sequences were not part of the training corpus. For example, the phrase *taga Manila siya* was not corrected to *taga-Manila siya* 'He's from Manila' because the word *taga-Manila* was not in the database, thus preventing a merging suggestion. The system also failed to detect the grammatical error in the phrase *Maganda si.* 'is beautiful.' which can be corrected as *Maganda si Maria.* 'Maria is beautiful.' because the corpus sentences were all complex sentences and thus the correction for the simple sentence was not produced. The system also incorrectly flagged the phrase *na bibigay ang* where *bibigay* is an invalid contemplative form *[VBTF]* of the word *bigay* 'give' which is supposedly *magbibigay* 'will give' because there is no *magbibigay-[VBTF]-bigay* mapping in the database. This is caused by the word *bibigay* being given the tag *[VBTF]* since it follows the partial reduplication rule for the said tag and the hybrid sequence *na [VBTF] ang* being considered grammatically-correct based from sequences such as *na gagampanan ang* 'will take the role of'.

The system performed well in correctly flagging error-free phrases even though many of the words were not in the training corpus. This result can be attributed to the POS tags of the input phrases and the *generalized* rules. For instance, the phrase *ang pagtakbo ng mayor* 'mayor's candidacy' was flagged correctly because of the n-gram rule *ang [NNC] ng [NNC]* that came from instances such as *ang kulay ng apoy* 'fire's color', *ang proseso ng produksyon* 'production's process'. However, there are two instances wherein the system incorrectly flagged error-free phrases: *Siya ay masaya.* 'She is happy' because simple sentences that contain the word *ay* did not occur in the training corpus and *Kinuha ko ito dito.* 'I got it from here' because neither the word sequence *ko ito* nor the POS sequence *[PRS] [PRO]* is not in the n-gram rules.

6. Summary & Future Works

This paper presents an unsupervised grammar checker system for Filipino that uses grammatically correct texts as grammar rules in the form of hybrid n-grams. It achieved 83% accuracy, 93% precision, and 71% recall in detecting broad-range of grammar errors in Filipino using only a small corpus of 2,668 sentences which can potentially be further improved as the size and variety of training sentences increases.

Future works for this system includes exploring other tag sets or modifying existing ones to create more specific tag groups for the system to avoid errors caused by tag groups that are *too* general. Corpus size may also be increased to produce more n-gram rules and word- POS-lemma mappings used for grammar checking.

Acknowledgment

This research work is supported by the Department of Science & Technology – Philippines and De la Salle University – Manila as part of its Interdisciplinary Signal Processing for Pinoys: Software Applications for Education (ISIP:SAFE) research program.

References

Chung-Chi Huang, Mei-Hua Chen, Shih-Ting Huang, Jason Chang (2011). EdIt: A Broad-coverage Grammar Checker Using Pattern grammar. In Proceedings of the 49th Annual Meeting of the Association for Computational Linguistics: Human Language Technologies (p. 26-31).

Consuelo J. Paz. (2003). Compounding Old and New Words in Filipino. University of the Philippines.

Diane Nicholls. 1999. The Cambridge Learner Corpus – error coding and analysis for lexicography and ELT. Cambridge University Press.

Don Erick Bonus. 2003. The Tagalog Stemming Algorithm (TagSA). Master's Thesis. De la Salle University, Manila.

Michael Jasa, Justin O. Palisoc, and Martee M. Villa. 2007. Panuring Pampanitikan (PanPam): A Sentence Syntax and Semantic Based Grammar Checker for Filipino. Undergraduate Thesis. De La Salle University, Manila.

Nathaniel Oco and Allan Borra. 2011. A Grammar Checker for Tagalog using LanguageTool. Proceedings of the 9th Workshop on Asian Language Resources Collocated with IJCNLP 2011.

Nai-Lung Tsao & David Wible. 2009. A Method for Unsupervised Broad-Coverage Lexical Error Detection and Correction. Proceedings of the NAACL HLT Workshop on Innovative Use of NLP for Building Educational Applications, p. 51-54.

Nay Yee Lin, Khin Mar Soe, and Ni Lar Thein. 2011. Developing a chunk-based grammar checker for translated English sentences. In Proceedings of PACLIC-2011 (p. 245-254).

Ortograpiyang Pambansa. 2013. Komisyon sa Wikang Pilipino.

Rogelio Nazar & Irene Renau. 2012. Google Books N-gram Corpus used as a Grammar Checker. Proceedings of the EACL 2012 Workshop on Computational Linguistics and Writing, p. 27–34.

Teresita V. Ramos. 1971. Makabagong Bararila ng Pilipino. Rex Book Store.

Vladimir Rabo and Charibeth K. Cheng. (2006). TPOST: A Template-based Part-of-Speech Tagger for Tagalog. Journal of Research in Science, Computing, and Engineering, 3(1).

Wikapedia (2015), Manila: Lexmedia Digital Corporation.

Supervised Word Sense Disambiguation with Sentences Similarities from Context Word Embeddings

Shoma Yamaki, Hiroyuki Shinnou, Kanako Komiya, Minoru Sasaki
Ibaraki University, Department of Computer and Information Sciences
4-12-1 Nakanarusawa, Hitachi, Ibaraki JAPAN 316-8511
16nm724r@vc.ibaraki.ac.jp
{hiroyuki.shinnou.0828, kanako.komiya.nlp, minoru.sasaki.01}
@vc.ibaraki.ac.jp

Abstract

In this paper, we propose a method that employs sentences similarities from context word embeddings for supervised word sense disambiguation. In particular, if N example sentences exist in training data, an N-dimensional vector with N similarities between each pair of example sentences is added to a basic feature vector. This new feature vector is used to train a classifier and identification. We evaluated the proposed method using the feature vectors based on Bag-of-Words, SemEval-2 baseline as basic feature vectors and SemEval-2 Japanese task. The experimental results suggest that the method is more effective than the method with only basic vectors.

1 Introduction

Conventionally, the meaning of a word has been represented using a high-dimensional sparse Bag-of-Words (BoW) vector. Recently, there has been considerable interest in word embeddings, where words meanings are represented by low-dimensional and dense vectors using deep learning. With word embeddings, the distance between words can be measured more precisely than that provided by a vector based on the BoW model. Therefore, word embeddings has been used effectively for various natural language processing tasks. With regard to word sense disambiguation (WSD) tasks, some studies have considered that the word embeddings comprise embeddings of word senses(Chen et al., 2014)(Neelakantan et al., 2014)(Sakaizawa and Komachi, 2015)(Bhingardive et al., 2015);however, these studies only consider unsupervised WSD. To the best of our knowledge, the only study that addresses supervised WSD with word embeddings is by Sugawara(Sugawara et al., 2015). In Sugawara's method, one BoW-based vector and one vector based on context word embeddings (CWE) are merged, and they are used for training a classifier and identification. The method proposed by Sugawara is more effective than the method that only uses a vector based on the BoW model. However, we have found two problems with this method. First, it restricts the position of the word in the context. Second, it includes function words. In this paper, we propose a method that addresses both problems. Specifically, if N example sentences exist in training data, an N-dimensional vector that consists of the similarities between each pair of example sentences is added to a basic feature vector. This new feature vector is used for training a classifier and identification. The similarity between sentences is calculated using CWE. This solves the first problem. In addition, the proposed method only uses content words to calculate similarities between example sentences, which solves the second problem. We used SemEval-2 Japanese task to compare Sugawara's method and the proposed method. We found that the proposed method demonstrated higher precision. Furthermore, we performed experiments with basic features used in SemEval-2 baseline system and determined that the proposed method gave better results.

2 Word Embedding for WSD

Feature vectors can be created using the words around a target word in a sentence. This method can present a context of the target word with the vector in a binary representation. Therefore, unknown words cannot be handled.

To address this problem, superordinate concepts in a thesaurus are used because it provides the similarities between different words.

Thus, using a thesaurus is effective for WSD. In this paper, we propose to increase the accuracy of WSD using word embedding as a thesaurus.

3 Sentences Similarities

Sugawara's supervised WSD method represents features using one vector based on the BoW model and another vector that consists of CWE (the context is five words before and after a target word). For example, when the five words before a target word are $(w_{-5}, w_{-4}, w_{-3}, w_{-2}, w_{-1})$ and the five words after the target word are $(w_1, w_2, w_3, w_4, w_5)$, the features vector comprises a binary vector based on the BoW model $(1, 0, 0, 1, 0, \cdots, 1)$ and a vector with word embeddings $(v_{w-1}, v_{w-2}, \cdots, v_{w4}, v_{w5})$ as shown in Figure 1. Sugawara's experimental results suggested that word embeddings useful for WSD. However, we found following 2 problems in his method;

1. It restricts a position of a word in the context.

2. It includes function words.

Therefore, we propose a method that uses the similarities between example sentences from word embeddings to address these problems.

The similarities between two sentences are defined as the average of the cosine of each word embedding in sentences, then i-th sentence (V_i) and j-th sentence (V_j) in training data, and the similarities between V_i and V_j are expressed as follows:

$$V_i = (\boldsymbol{v}_{wi-1}, \boldsymbol{v}_{wi-2}, ..., \boldsymbol{v}_{wi4}, \boldsymbol{v}_{wi5})$$

$$V_j = (\boldsymbol{v}_{wj-1}, \boldsymbol{v}_{wj-2}, ..., \boldsymbol{v}_{wj4}, \boldsymbol{v}_{wj5})$$

$$sim(i, j) = \frac{\sum_{\boldsymbol{v}_{iw}}^{\boldsymbol{V}_i} \sum_{\boldsymbol{v}_{jw}}^{\boldsymbol{V}_j} cos(\boldsymbol{v}_{iw}, \boldsymbol{v}_{jw})}{|\boldsymbol{V}_i| \cdot |\boldsymbol{V}_j|}$$

When only content words are used to calculate similarities, all function words are removed from V_i, V_j.

4 Proposed Method

The proposed method employs a new features vector comprising the basic vector and a vector using the similarities between example sentences with word embedding. As mentioned previously, Sugawara's method employs a features vector comprising a vector based on the BoW model and a vector comprising CWE. However, the proposed method employs a new features vector comprising a vector based on the BoW model and a vector comprising the similarities between sentences from CWE (Figure 2).

In our experiments, we denote the method that includes content words and function words in features words to calculate similarities as "Proposed Method (1)" and the method that does not include function words as "Proposed Method (2)."

5 Features with Thesaurus

The grain size of thesaurus is the important problem in WSD (Shinnou et al., 2015). On the other hand, concepts of words are continuance because distance between words can be calculated with word embeddings. Therefore, it is assumed that using word embedding instead of thesaurus can increase accuracy of WSD.

We implement the SemEval-2 baseline system as a general method using thesaurus. The training algorithm is linear SVM (Support Vector Machine) and features are following twenty things (PoS; Part of Speech, w_i; a word positioned in context)

```
e1=2 previous word, e2=the PoS,
e3=the sub PoS,
e4=1 previous word, e5=the PoS,
e6=the sub PoS,
e7=target word, e8=the PoS,
e9=the sub PoS,
e10=1 following word, e11=the PoS,
e12=the sub PoS,
e13=2 following word, e14=the PoS,
e15=the sub PoS,
e16=relation,
e17=ID of 2 previous word
```

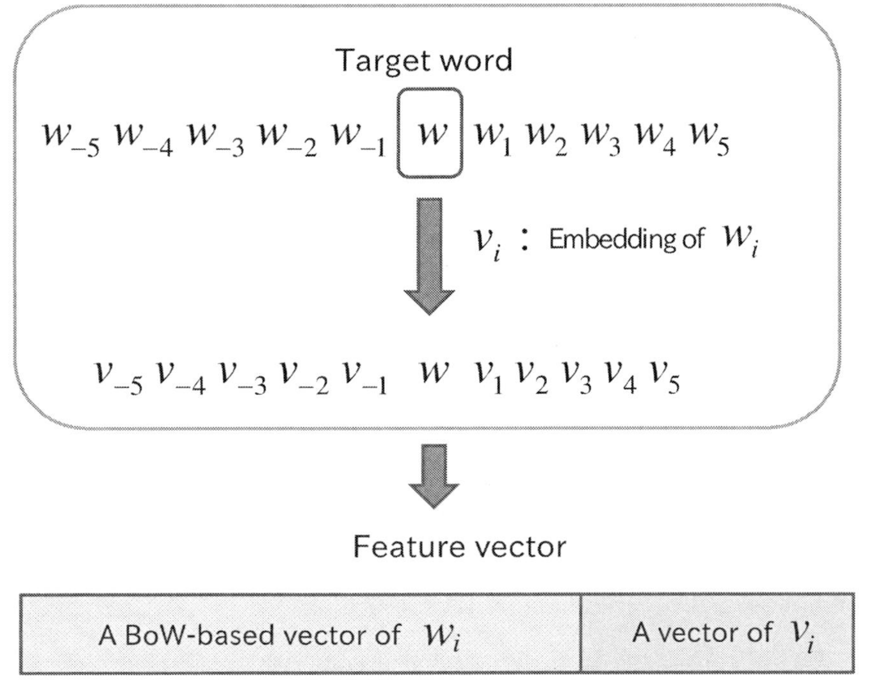

Figure 1: Feature vector in Sugawara's method

```
    in thesaurus,
e18=ID of 1 previous word
    in thesaurus,
e19=ID of 1 following word
    in thesaurus,
e20=ID of 2 following word
    in thesaurus
```

We use only the five character ID in thesaurus although both of the four and five character ID are used in the conventional baseline system. Moreover, the features vector for `e17, e18, e19, e20` are multiple because there are several ID for one word.

This features can be divided into two features; non-thesaurus features from `e1` to `e16` (std-0) and thesaurus features from `e1` to `e20` (std-1). We use two vectors based on std-0 and std-1 as the basic vectors to create the new features vector that the each of basic vectors and the similarities vector are merged. The new features vector are used in the experiments to confirm whether it can increase accuracy of WSD using word embeddings instead of thesaurus.

6 Experiments

6.1 Set-up

We used the SemEval-2 Japanese task in the experiments. This data consists of fifty multivocals. Fifty training data and fifty test data are for each multivocals. Both of training data and test data are adopted morpheme analysis and saved as XML format.

Word embeddings are 200-dimensional vectors calculated by word2vec [1] with Japanese articles in wikipedia.

We used the linearSVC of scikit-learn[2] to make the classifier and set its normalize parameter C to 1.0 .

In addition, we defined content words to the words whose the part of speech is noun, verb, adjective or adverb.

6.2 Results

First, we performed an experiment to confirm that Sugawara's method is to determine whether it is valid for the SemEval-2 Japanese task. The accu-

[1] https://code.google.com/p/word2vec/

[2] http://scikit-learn.org/stable/index.html

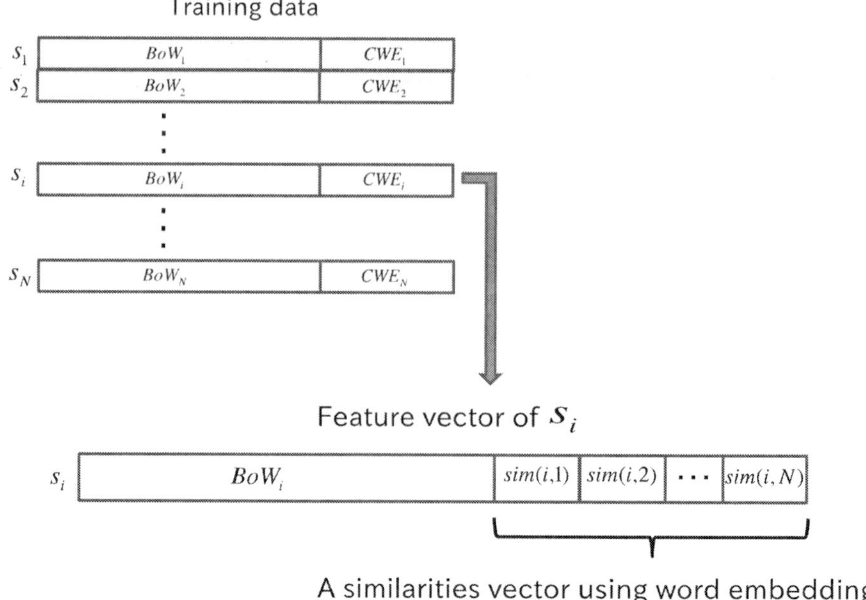

Figure 2: Features vector of training data in the proposal method

racy of the BoW features and the BoW+CWE features are shown in Table 1.

features	accuracy
BoW	0.716
BoW + CWE	0.745

Table 1: Result of the BoW and the BoW+CWE

The result suggested that the method can obtain higher accuracy than the BoW.

Second, we performed an experiment to compare the method using the BoW+CWE and our proposed method. The result is shown in Table 2.

features	accuracy
BoW + CWE	0.745
Proposal method (1)	0.753
Proposal method (2)	0.754

Table 2: Result of the BoW+CWE and the proposed method

The result suggested that the proposed method can obtain better accuracy than the BoW+CWE method. It was found that the proposed method (2) has obtained higher accuracy than proposed method (1). The accuracy for each of the target words is summarized in Table 4. The numbers in bold represents the maximum values for each of the target words, and the underlined numbers represents the number of the strictly larger by comparing the proposed method and the BoW+CWE.

Likewise, the experimental result using std-0 and std-1 as the basic vectors are shown in Table 3

features	accuracy
std-0	0.757
std-1	0.769
std-0 + similarities	0.761
std-1 + similarities	0.771

Table 3: Accuracy of std-0, std-1 and similarities

The result suggested that using the vectors comprising the each of basic vectors and the similarities vector can be obtained the higher accuracy than only using the basic vector. The accuracy for each of the target words is summarized in Table 5.

7 Discussions

We performed the experiment using the vectors based on the BoW, std-0 and std-1 as the basic vectors, it was found that the vector merged the basic vectors and sentence similarities vectors can produce higher accuracy than only the basic vectors. By comparing the result of BoW+CWE and the proposed method for each of the target words, the proposed method got strictly higher accuracy than the BoW+CWE in sixteen words and got lower accuracy in twelve words. Furthermore, by comparing the result of the std-0 and the proposed method, the proposed method got strictly higher accuracy than std-0 in ten words and got lower accuracy in three words. Likewise, by comparing the result of std-1 and the proposed method, the proposed method got higher accuracy in five words and got lower accuracy in one word. Therefore, the proposed method is considered to be effective in improving accuracy of WSD.

By comparing the result of the proposed method (1) and (2) in Table 4, the proposed method (1) got higher accuracy than the proposed method (2) in three words and got lower accuracy in four words. The accuracy rate of the method (2) was higher than the method (1) by 0.001. Therefore, we found that the superiority of the proposed method (2) was very slight.

A purpose of this experiment is to confirm whether that using word embeddings instead of a thesaurus can improve the accuracy of WSD. According to the accuracy rate in Table 3, the accuracy of the std-1 (0.769) is lower than the accuracy of the std-0 + similarities (0.761). This result suggested that the method using thesaurus is more effective for WSD than the method using the similarities between example sentences. However, it is assumed that the method using word embeddings instead of a thesaurus can improve the accuracy of WSD because of following reasons; there are a lot of methods other our proposing, and the quality of word embeddings depend on quality and quantity of text corpora.

8 Conclusion

In this paper, we have proposed a method that uses sentences similarities from CWE for supervised WSD. Specifically, if N example sentences exist in training data, an N-dimensional vector with N similarities between each pair of example sentences is added to a basic feature vector. We performed experiments with basic features used in a SemEval-2 baseline system and determined that the proposed method gave more accurate results than a previous method with only the basic features vector. The results suggested that the proposed method improves the accuracy of WSD. In future, we plan to confirm whether the method can further improve WSD by using word embeddings trained from other text corpora.

References

Sudha Bhingardive, Dhirendra Singh, V Redkar Murthy, Hanumant Redkar, and Pushpak Bhattacharyya. 2015. Unsupervised Most Frequent Sense Detection using Word Embeddings. In *HLT-NAACL-2015*, pages 1238–1243.

Xinxiong Chen, Zhiyuan Liu, and Maosong Sun. 2014. A Unified Model for Word Sense Representation and Disambiguation. In *EMNLP-2014*, pages 1025–1035.

Arvind Neelakantan, Jeevan Shankar, Alexandre Passos, and Andrew McCallum. 2014. Efficient Non-parametric Estimation of Multiple Embeddings per Word in Vector Space. In *EMNLP-2014*, pages 1059–1069.

Yuya Sakaizawa and Mamoru Komachi. 2015. Pragraph vector wo mochiita kyoushi nashi gogi aimaisei kaishou no kousatsu (in japanese). In *NLP 2015*, P1-29.

Hiroyuki Shinnou, Minoru Sasaki, and Kanako Komiya. 2015. Gogi aimaisei kaishou ni okeru thesaurus riyou no mondai bunseki (in japanese). In *NLP 2015*, P1-15.

Hiromu Sugawara, Hiroya Takamura, Ryohei Sasano, and Manabu Okumura. 2015. Context Representation with Word Embeddings for WSD. In *PACLING-2015*, pages 149–155.

Table 4: Accuracy of the each target words (1)

target words	BoW	BoW+CWE	proposed method (1)	proposed method(2)
相手 (aite)	**0.82**	**0.82**	**0.82**	**0.82**
会う (au)	0.60	0.70	0.70	0.70
上げる (ageru)	0.36	0.36	0.44	0.42
与える (ataeru)	0.64	0.64	0.66	0.68
生きる (ikiru)	**0.94**	**0.94**	**0.94**	**0.94**
意味 (imi)	0.38	0.52	0.64	**0.68**
入れる (ireru)	0.72	**0.74**	**0.74**	**0.74**
大きい (ookii)	**0.94**	**0.94**	**0.94**	**0.94**
教える (oshieru)	0.22	0.34	0.38	0.38
可能 (kanou)	0.68	**0.74**	0.62	0.60
考える (kangaeru)	**0.98**	**0.98**	**0.98**	**0.98**
関係 (kankei)	0.82	0.88	**0.96**	**0.96**
技術 (gijutsu)	0.84	0.84	**0.86**	**0.86**
経済 (keizai)	**0.98**	**0.98**	**0.98**	**0.98**
現場 (genba)	0.74	0.74	0.74	0.74
子供 (kodomo)	0.60	0.54	0.44	0.42
時間 (jikan)	0.86	0.84	**0.88**	**0.88**
市場 (shijou)	0.58	**0.64**	0.60	0.60
社会 (shakai)	**0.86**	**0.86**	**0.86**	**0.86**
情報 (jouhou)	0.70	0.76	0.82	0.82
進める (susumeru)	0.44	0.58	0.86	0.86
する (suru)	0.54	0.66	**0.72**	**0.72**
高い (takai)	0.86	0.86	0.86	0.86
出す (dasu)	0.40	0.46	0.40	0.40
立つ (tatsu)	0.46	0.50	0.58	**0.60**
強い (tsuyoi)	**0.92**	**0.92**	**0.92**	**0.92**
手 (te)	**0.78**	**0.78**	**0.78**	**0.78**
出る (deru)	0.62	**0.66**	0.58	0.58
電話 (denwa)	0.78	0.78	0.78	0.78
取る (toru)	0.24	0.26	**0.32**	**0.32**
乗る (noru)	0.56	0.58	0.60	0.60
場合 (baai)	0.86	**0.88**	0.84	0.84
入る (hairu)	**0.66**	**0.66**	**0.66**	**0.66**
はじめ (hajime)	0.90	**0.96**	**0.96**	**0.96**
始める (hajimeru)	0.78	0.80	0.78	0.78
場所 (basho)	0.94	**0.96**	**0.96**	**0.96**
早い (hayai)	0.58	0.66	0.62	0.62
一 (ichi)	**0.92**	**0.92**	**0.92**	**0.92**
開く (hiraku)	**0.90**	**0.90**	0.88	0.88
文化 (bunka)	**0.98**	**0.98**	**0.98**	**0.98**
他 (hoka)	**1.00**	**1.00**	**1.00**	**1.00**
前 (mae)	0.66	0.76	**0.78**	**0.78**
見える (mieru)	0.60	0.60	0.58	0.58
認める (mitomeru)	0.80	0.80	0.78	0.78
見る (miru)	**0.80**	**0.80**	**0.80**	**0.80**
持つ (motsu)	0.64	0.74	0.76	0.76
求める (motomeru)	**0.76**	0.74	0.74	**0.76**
もの (mono)	**0.88**	**0.88**	**0.88**	**0.88**
やる (yaru)	0.94	**0.96**	**0.96**	**0.96**
良い (yoi)	0.36	0.40	0.38	0.38
average	0.716	0.745	0.753	0.754

Table 5: Accuracy of each target words (2)

target words	std-0	std-1	std-0 + similarities	std-1 + similarities
相手 (aite)	0.78	0.80	0.78	0.80
会う (au)	0.88	0.92	0.90	0.92
上げる (ageru)	0.44	0.52	0.48	0.56
与える (ataeru)	0.76	0.70	0.74	0.70
生きる (ikiru)	0.94	0.94	0.94	0.94
意味 (imi)	0.48	0.44	0.46	0.46
入れる (ireru)	0.74	0.74	0.74	0.74
大きい (ookii)	0.94	0.94	0.94	0.94
教える (oshieru)	0.36	0.52	0.40	0.52
可能 (kanou)	0.68	0.64	0.68	0.64
考える (kangaeru)	0.98	0.98	0.98	0.98
関係 (kankei)	0.96	0.96	0.96	0.96
技術 (gijutsu)	0.84	0.82	0.84	0.82
経済 (keizai)	0.98	0.98	0.98	0.98
現場 (genba)	0.74	0.76	0.74	0.76
子供 (kodomo)	0.60	0.62	0.60	0.60
時間 (jikan)	0.86	0.84	0.86	0.86
市場 (shijou)	0.52	0.56	0.52	0.56
社会 (shakai)	0.86	0.86	0.86	0.86
情報 (jouhou)	0.86	0.84	0.86	0.84
進める (susumeru)	0.92	0.92	0.92	0.92
する (suru)	0.64	0.72	0.66	0.72
高い (takai)	0.86	0.88	0.86	0.88
出す (dasu)	0.40	0.50	0.42	0.50
立つ (tatsu)	0.52	0.50	0.52	0.52
強い (tsuyoi)	0.92	0.90	0.92	0.90
手 (te)	0.78	0.78	0.78	0.78
出る (deru)	0.52	0.52	0.52	0.52
電話 (denwa)	0.84	0.78	0.80	0.78
取る (toru)	0.26	0.28	0.26	0.28
乗る (noru)	0.78	0.78	0.78	0.78
場合 (baai)	0.84	0.84	0.84	0.84
入る (hairu)	0.54	0.56	0.54	0.56
はじめ (hajime)	0.88	0.88	0.88	0.88
始める (hajimeru)	0.88	0.86	0.88	0.86
場所 (basho)	0.90	0.96	0.92	0.96
早い (hayai)	0.70	0.70	0.72	0.72
一 (ichi)	0.92	0.90	0.92	0.90
開く (hiraku)	0.78	0.84	0.80	0.84
文化 (bunka)	0.98	0.98	0.98	0.98
他 (hoka)	1.00	1.00	1.00	1.00
前 (mae)	0.76	0.76	0.76	0.76
見える (mieru)	0.68	0.70	0.68	0.70
認める (mitomeru)	0.76	0.82	0.78	0.82
見る (miru)	0.78	0.78	0.78	0.78
持つ (motsu)	0.78	0.80	0.78	0.80
求める (motomeru)	0.64	0.76	0.68	0.76
もの (mono)	0.88	0.88	0.88	0.88
やる (yaru)	0.96	0.96	0.96	0.96
良い (yoi)	0.56	0.54	0.56	0.54
average	0.757	0.769	0.761	0.771

HSSA Tree Structures for BTG-based Preordering in Machine Translation

Yujia Zhang[1,2], **Hao Wang**[1] **and Yves Lepage**[1]
[1]Graduate School of Information, Production and Systems
Waseda University, Kitakyushu, Fukuoka 808-0135, Japan
[2]School of Computer Engineering and Science,
Shanghai University, Shanghai 200444, China
{ashley.zhang@moegi., oko_ips@ruri., yves.lepage@}waseda.jp

Abstract

The Hierarchical Sub-Sentential Alignment (HSSA) method is a method to obtain aligned binary tree structures for two aligned sentences in translation correspondence. We propose to use the binary aligned tree structures delivered by this method as training data for preordering prior to machine translation. For that, we learn a Bracketing Transduction Grammar (BTG) from these binary aligned tree structures. In two oracle experiments in English to Japanese and Japanese to English translation, we show that it is theoretically possible to outperform a baseline system with a default distortion limit of 6, by about 2.5 and 5 BLEU points and, 7 and 10 RIBES points respectively, when preordering the source sentences using the learnt preordering model and using a distortion limit of 0. An attempt at learning a preordering model and its results are also reported.

1 Introduction

One of the major common challenges for machine translation (MT) is the different order of the same conceptual units in the source and target languages. In order to get a fluent and adequate translation in the target language, the default phrase-based statistical machine translation (PB-SMT) system implemented in MOSES has a simple distortion model using position (Koehn et al., 2003) and lexical information (Tillmann, 2004) to allow reordering during decoding. Other solutions exist: e.g., the distortion model in (Al-Onaizan and Papineni, 2006) handles n-gram language model limitations; Setiawan et al. (2007) propose a function word centered syntax-based (FWS) solution; Zhang et al. (2007) propose a reordering model integrating syntactic knowledge. Also, other models than the phrase-based model have been proposed to address the reordering problem, like hierarchical phrase-based SMT (Chiang, 2007) or syntax-based SMT (Yamada and Knight, 2001).

Preordering (Xia and McCord, 2004; Collins et al., 2005) has been proposed primarily to solve the problems encountered when translating between languages with widely divergent syntax, for instance, from a subject-verb-object (SVO) language (like English and Mandarin Chinese) to a subject-object-verb (SOV) language (like Japanese and Korean). Preordering is a pre-processing task that aims to rearrange the word order of a source sentence to fit the word order of the target language. It is separated from the core translation task. Recent approaches (DeNero and Uszkoreit, 2011; Neubig et al., 2012; Nakagawa, 2015) learn a preordering model based on Bracketing Transduction Grammar (BTG) (Wu, 1997) from parallel texts to score permutations by using tree structures as latent variables. They build the needed tree structures and the preordering model (i.e., a BTG) at the same time using word alignments. However it is needed to check whether a given sentence can fit the desired tree structures.

It seems of course more difficult to build both the tree structures and the preordering model at the same time than to build only a preordering model if the tree structures are given. In this paper, we rapidly obtain tree structures using word-to-word associations taking advantage of the hierarchical sub-sentential alignment (HSSA) method (Lardilleux et al., 2012). This method computes a recursive binary segmentation in both languages at the same

S He enjoys beautiful scenery in Kyoto .

S' He Kyoto in beautiful scenery enjoys .

T 彼は京都で美しい景色を楽しむ。

Figure 1: Example of preordering.

time, judging whether two spans with the same concepts in both languages are inverted or not. We conduct oracle experiments to show that these tree structures may be beneficial for PB-SMT. We then use these tree structures as the training data to build a preordering model without checking the validity by modifying the top-down BTG parsing method introduced in (Nakagawa, 2015). Oracle experiments show that if we reorder source sentences exactly, translation scores can be improved by around 2.5 BLEU points and 7 RIBES points in English to Japanese) and 5 BLEU points and 10 RIBES points in Japanese to English. Experiments with our tree structures show that better RIBES scores can be easily obtained.

The rest of this paper is organized as follows: Section 2 describes related work in preordering and BTG-based preordering. Section 3 shows how to obtain tree structures using word-to-word associations. Section 4 reports oracle preordering experiments. Section 5 gives a method to build a preordering model using tree structures. Section 6 presents the results of our experiments and their analysis.

2 Related Work

2.1 Preordering for SMT

Preordering in statistical machine translation (SMT) converts a source sentence S, before translation, into a reordered source sentence S', where the word order is similar to that of the target sentence T (Figure 1).

Preordering can be seen as an optimization problem, where we want to find the best reordered source sentence that maximizes the probability among all possible reordering of the sentence.

$$\hat{S'} = \underset{S' \in \gamma(S)}{\operatorname{argmax}} P(S'|S) \qquad (1)$$

$\hat{S'}$ represents the best reordered source sentence, and $\gamma(S)$ stands for the set of all possible reordering of the source sentence.

Syntax-based preordering based on the existence parsers has been proposed to pre-process the source sentences by using automatically learned rewriting patterns (Xia and McCord, 2004). Several methods have been proposed methods, such as constituent parsing by automatically extracting preordering rules from a parallel corpus (Xia and McCord, 2004; Wu et al., 2011) or by creating rules manually (Wang et al., 2007; Han et al., 2012), or dependency parsing with automatically created rules (Habash, 2012; Cai et al., 2014) or manually generated rules (Xu et al., 2009; Isozaki et al., 2010).

Another trend of research is to try to solve the preordering problem without relying on parsers. Tromble and Eisner (2009) propose sophisticated reordering models based on the Linear Ordering Problem. Visweswariah et al. (2011) learn a preordering model by similarity with the Traveling Salesman Problem. Lerner and Petrovs (2013) present a source-side classifier-based preordering model. Several pieces of research (DeNero and Uszkoreit, 2011; Neubig et al., 2012; Nakagawa, 2015) are mainly about using tree structures as latent variables for preordering models. This is detailed in the next subsection.

2.2 BTG-based Preordering

BTG-based preordering is based on Bracketing Transduction Grammar (BTG), also called Inversion Transduction Grammar (ITG) (Wu, 1997). Whereas Chomsky Normal Form of context-free rules has two types of rules ($X \rightarrow X_1X_2$ and $X \rightarrow x$) and the grammar is monolingual, BTG has three types of rules, Straight, Inverted and Terminal, to cope with the possible correspondences between a source language and a target language.

Straight keeps the same order in the source and the target languages; Inverted exchanges the order; Terminal just stands for the production of a non-terminal symbol both in the source and target languages. The corresponding tree structures are illustrated in Figure 3 from (a) to (c) in the same order. The parse tree obtained by applying a BTG to parse a pair of sentences, provides the necessary information to reorder the source sentence in conformity to the word order of the target sentence, as it suffices to

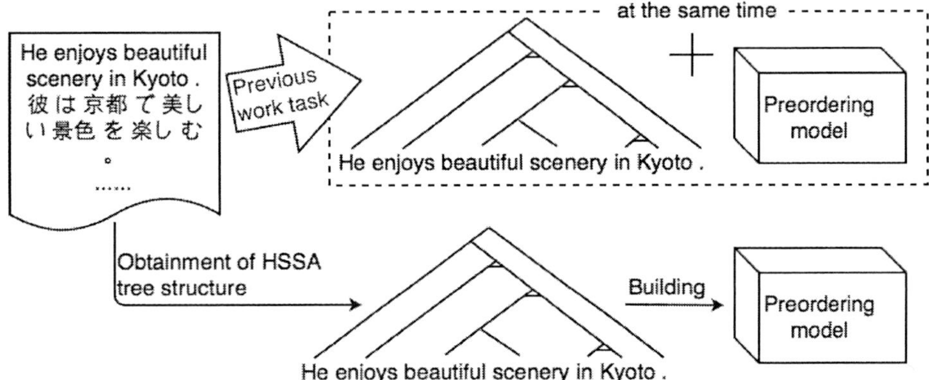

Figure 2: The difference between previous methods (Neubig et al., 2012; Nakagawa, 2015) and our proposed method when building a preordering model. In previous work, the tree structures and the preordering model should be deduced at the same time from the parallel text. Our work firstly produces the tree structures from parallel text, and then computes a preordering model.

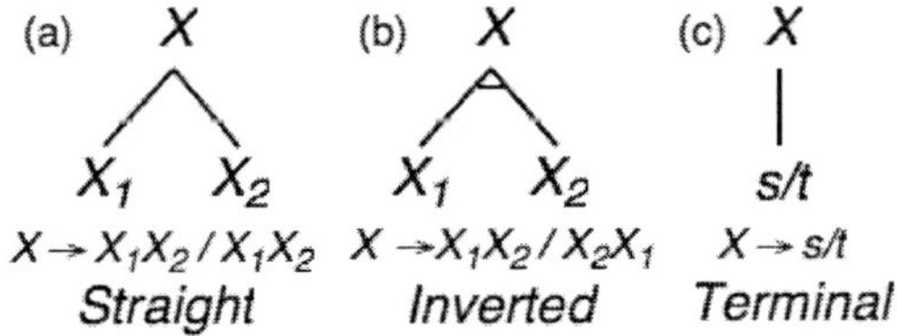

Figure 3: Tree structures related to bracketing transduction grammar.

read the type of rules applied, straight or inverted.

Neubig et al. (2012) present a discriminative parser using the derivations of tree structures as underlying variables from word alignment with the parallel corpus. However, the computation complexity is $O(n^5)$ for a sentence length of n because the method guesses the tree structure using the Coke-Younger-Kasami (CYK) algorithm, which complexity is $O(n^3)$. In order to reduce complexity, Nakagawa (2015) proposes a top-down BTG parsing approach instead of the bottom-up CYK algorithm. The computation complexity reduces to $O(kn^2)$ for a sentence length of n and a beam width of k.

Both methods need to predict the possible tree structures for each sentence when building the preordering model. Word alignments are used to check whether a pair of sentences can yield a valid tree structure.[1] Predicting tree structures while building the preordering model at the same time is difficult. In the present paper, we propose to directly generate the tree structures from the word-to-word association matrices, and to use these tree structures to build the preordering model afterwards. Figure 2 illustrates the differences between the two previous methods and our proposed method.

3 Obtaining HSSA Tree Structures

In our proposed method, the tree structures are obtained by using soft alignment matrices and recursively segmenting these matrices with Ncut scores (Zha et al., 2001) using the hierarchical sub-sentential alignment (HSSA) method (Lardilleux et al., 2012).

The HSSA method delivers tree structures which are similar to parse trees obtained by the application of a BTG. Figure 4 shows that segmenting along the second diagonal with the HSSA method corresponds to an Inverted rule in the BTG formalism and that segmenting according to the first diagonal corresponds to Straight. The column $S_p.\overline{S_p}$[2] and the row $T_p.\overline{T_p}$ of the matrix in Figure 4 are related to part of the source sentence and part of the target sentence respectively.

The HSSA method uses soft alignment matrices

[1] A sentence pair which cannot be represented by a BTG tree structure is: $B_2D_4A_1C_3$ to $A_1B_2C_3D_4$.

[2] The symbol "." stands for the concatenation of word strings.

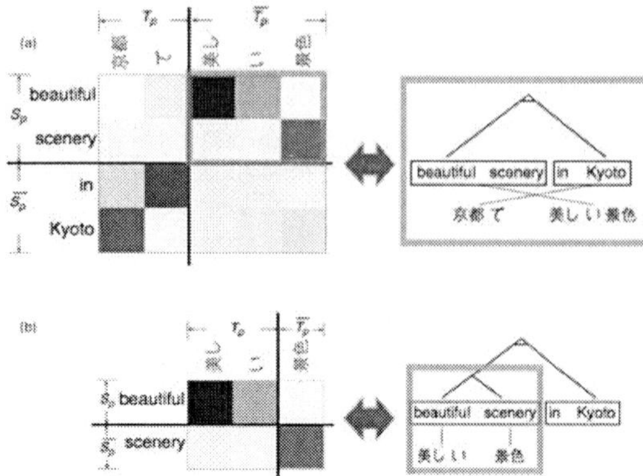

Figure 4: Hierarchical sub-sentential alignment and generation of tree structures. (a) a best segmentation according to the second diagonal in the soft alignment matrix using the HSSA method coresponds to an Inverted rule in the BTG formalism; (b) a best segmentation according to the main diagonal corresponds to a Straight rule. (b) is a sub-part in (a) to illustrate recursivity.

where each cell for a source word s and a target word t has a score $w(s,t)$ computed as the geometric mean of the word-to-word translation probabilities in both directions (see Equation (2)). In Figure 4, the saturation of the cells represents the score $w(s,t)$: the darker the color, the higher the score.

$$w(s,t) = \sqrt{p(s|t) \times p(t|s)} \tag{2}$$

Each segmentation iteration segments the soft alignment matrix in both horizontal and vertical directions to decompose the matrix recursively into two corresponding sub-parts. There are two cases: the two sub-parts follow the main diagonal, (S_p, T_p) and $(\overline{S_p}, \overline{T_p})$, this is similar to the BTG rule Straight (see Figure 4(b)); or they follow the second diagonal, $(S_p, \overline{T_p})$ and $(\overline{S_p}, T_p)$, this is similar to the BTG rule Inverted (see Figure 4(a)). In order to decide for the segmentation point and for the direction in a submatrix $(X, Y) \in \{S_p, \overline{S_p}\} \times \{T_p, \overline{T_p}\}$, Ncut scores (Zha et al., 2001) of crossing points in the matrix $(S_p.\overline{S_p}, T_p.\overline{T_p})$ are calculated in both directions.

$$W(X,Y) = \sum_{s \in X, t \in Y} w(s,t) \tag{3}$$

$$\text{cut}(X,Y) = W(X,\overline{Y}) + W(\overline{X},Y) \tag{4}$$

$$\begin{aligned}\text{Ncut}(X,Y) = & \frac{\text{cut}(X,Y)}{\text{Ncut}(X,Y) + 2 \times W(X,Y)} \\ & + \frac{\text{cut}(\overline{X},\overline{Y})}{\text{Ncut}(\overline{X},\overline{Y}) + 2 \times W(\overline{X},\overline{Y})}\end{aligned} \tag{5}$$

One tree structure for one sentence is generated with sub-sentential alignments at the same time by remembering the best segmentation point of each iteration in a sentence, using the HSSA method. In our proposed method, all the tree structures obtained from a training bilingual corpus become a training data set to learn a preordering model. The HSSA approach allows to get tree structures easily and rapidly, by using only a parallel corpus and the word-to-word associations obtained from it. No further annotation is needed.

4 Oracle Experiments: Upper Bounds

So as to check whether our proposed method is promising, in a first step, we perform oracle experiments. The purpose is to determine the upper bounds that can be obtained in translation evaluation scores. This will offer a judgment on the theoretical effectiveness of utilizing tree structures generated by the hierarchical sub-sentential alignment method.

In the oracle experiments, we apply the HSSA method on the sentence pairs of the test set to obtain their tree structures and then use these tree structures to reorder the source sentences of the test set. In a real experiment, this is impossible, because the target sentence, and hence the soft alignment matrices are unknown.

To reorder the words in a source sentence, as explained above, we recursively traverse the tree structure in a top-down manner. The order of the words in the source sentence is changed according to the types of nodes encountered in the tree structures. When the type of node is Straight, the two spans in the source sentence keep the original order; when it is Inverted, the two spans in the source sentence are inverted. After reordering, the alignment between the reordered source sentence and the target sentence follows the main diagonal, up to the cases where one word corresponds to several words. Figure 5 shows an example.

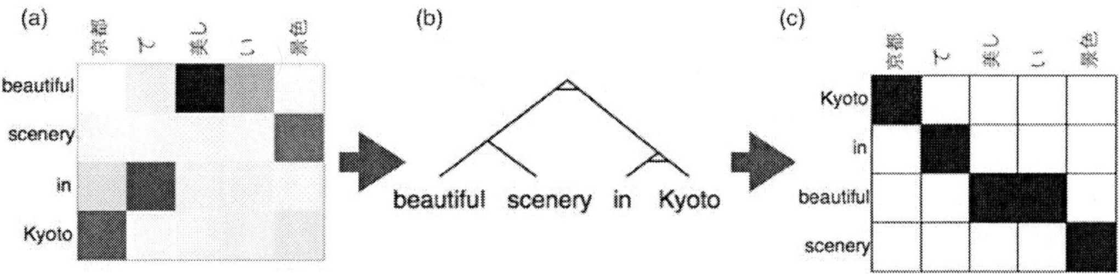

Figure 5: Example for oracle experiment. (a) a soft alignment matrix between a source sentence (left) and a target sentence (above); (b) a tree structure with Straight or Inverted nodes; (c) the alignment between the reordered source sentence and the target sentence. The arrow from (a) to (b) represents the generation of tree structures from word-to-word associations by use of the HSSA method; the arrow from (b) to (c) is reordering. In the oracle experiment, this is applied on test data. In a real experiment, this is applied on test data and development data, while the scheme given in Figure 6 is applied on the test data.

After reordering all source sentences in the training, tuning, and test sets, a standard PB-SMT system is built as usual with the reordered source sentences in place of the original sources sentences, and with their corresponding target sentences.

5 Building and Applying a Preordering Model

A preordering model is built by using the tree structures obtained on the parallel corpus used as training data for machine translation, as its training data. On test data, i.e., source sentences alone, the role of the pre-ordering model is to guess a new order for the words of the source sentences in the absence of corresponding target sentences. Figure 6 illustrates the process of building the preordering model with the tree structures obtained as explained in Figure 1 from the sentence pairs of the training data of a machine translation system. We now present a method to learn and apply a preordering model. This method is a modification of the top-down BTG parsing method presented in (Nakagawa, 2015). The main difference is that, in our present configuration, tree structures are available from a parallel corpus.

In Nakagawa's method, word alignments are used to predict the tree structures, so that, after segmenting one span into two, whether a word in one of two spans aligns to another word in the other span is checked in each iteration. However, in our configuration, we are able to directly get the separating points because we know the tree structure produced by the HSSA method.

The best derivation $\hat{d}$ for a sentence is important for both learning and applying a preordering model. Because one derivation leads to one parse tree, finding the best derivation can be regarded as finding the best parse tree. To assess the quality of a parse tree, we compare it with the tree structure output by the HSSA method. The best parse tree is the tree with the maximal score defined by the following formula:

$$\hat{d} = \underset{d \in D(T)}{\operatorname{argmax}} \sum_{m \in \text{Nodes}(T)} \sigma(m) \qquad (6)$$

where d represents one derivation in the set of all possible derivations $D(T)$ for the tree structure T; m represents one node in the set of nodes $\text{Nodes}(T)$ of the tree structure T, and $\sigma(m)$ represents the score of the node.

The score of a node in a tree structure is computed by applying the perceptron algorithm (Collins and Roark, 2004), i.e., by taking each node of trees as a latent variable (Nakagawa, 2015). This algorithm is an online learning algorithm, and processes nodes in an available tree structure one by one, by using the following formula to calculate the score of each node $\sigma(m)$:

$$\sigma(m) = \Lambda \cdot \Phi(m), \quad m \in \text{Nodes}(T)$$

where $\Phi(m)$ represents the feature vector of this node, and Λ represents the vector of feature weights.

Due to iterated binary decomposition, an increasing number of iterations for one sentence results in many derivations that wait for being checked

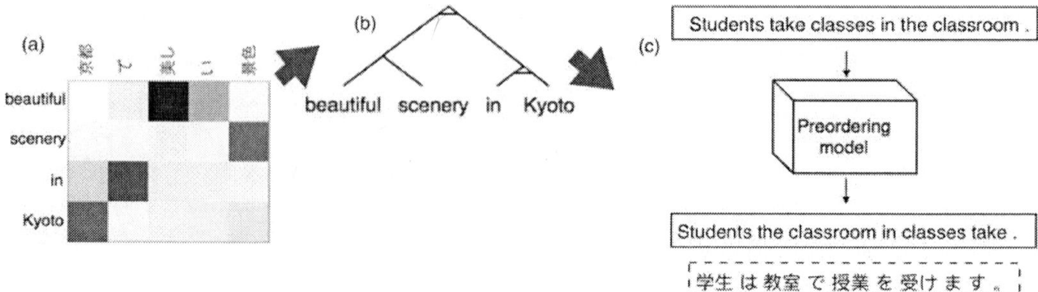

Figure 6: Example of building and applying preordering model using tree structures as the reference. (a), (b) and the arrow from (a) to (b) are the same with Figure 5. The difference is that both (a) and (b) generating from only a training set. (c) a sentence from test set becomes a target-like source sentence in the solid line and in dotted line it shows corresponding target sentence. The arrow from (b) to (c) represents building preordering model.

whether they are the best ones or not, both while building and while applying the preordering model. In order to control the size of the search space, a beam search is used.

We need to enable the system to output $\hat{d}$ to become as similar as possible as the derivation d found in the tree structure obtained by the HSSA model while building the preordering model. To do so, we learn the feature vectors and adjust their weight vectors by using the Expectation–Maximization (EM) algorithm on the training data. In the end, we obtain a preordering model with features and corresponding weights.

We then apply the preordering model on all the source sentences of all three data sets, training, tuning, and test, to reorder their words. A standard PB-SMT system is then built as usual with reordered source sentences in place of the original sources sentences, and with their corresponding target sentences.

6 Experiments

6.1 Experimental Settings

We build our PB-SMT systems in a standard way using the Moses system (Koehn et al., 2007), KenLM for language modelling (Heafield, 2011), and standard lexical reordering model (Koehn et al., 2005). This lexical reordering model allows local reordering with a given distortion limit during decoding. The default of the distortion limit in Moses is 6. When set to 0, the system does not perform any lexical reordering.

	Sentence Pairs	Words	
		Japanese	English
Train	330,000	6.09 M	5.91 M
Tune	1,235	34.4 k	30.8 k
Test	1,160	28.5 k	26.7 k

Table 1: Number of sentences and words in the training, tuning and test sets of the KFTT corpus.

The language pair we work on is Japanese–English in both directions. The data sets are the training, tuning and test sets from the Kyoto Free Translation Task (KFTT) corpus.[3] In this corpus, Japanese sentences have been segmented and tokenized by KyTea.[4] Table 1 gives statistics on these data sets.

For the generation of tree structures, word-to-word associations are extracted from the training set andused to the hierarchical sub-sentential alignment method, are extracted only from the training set.

For our preordering model, we carried out experiments by following the experimental settings reported in (Nakagawa, 2015) with a beam search of 20, a number of iteration of 20 and 100,000 sentences pairs as preordering training extracted at random from the training set. We use three kinds of features, LEX, POS, and CLASS. LEX consists in the lexical items inside a given window around the current word in the source language. POS are the parts-of-speech of the lexical items of the LEX fea-

[3] http://www.phontron.com/kftt/index.html
[4] http://www.phontron.com/kytea/

ture words. The CLASS features are their semantic classes. The POS tagging information is provided by KyTea for Japanese, and the Lookahead Part-Of-Speech Tagger (Tsuruoka et al., 2011) for English.[5] We use the Brown clustering algorithm (Brown et al., 1992; Liang, 2005) for word class information in English and Japanese.

6.2 Evaluation Metrics

In order to evaluate the efficiency of reordering, we use a modified version of the Fuzzy Reordering Score (FRS) (Talbot et al., 2011) and Kendall's τ (Kendall, 1938) as intrinsic evaluation metrics. The modified version of FRS (see Equation (7)) is inspired by (Nakagawa, 2015) because only two words are considered and the indices of the first and the last words are also considered (Neubig et al., 2012).

$$\text{mod FRS} = \frac{B}{|S| + 1} \tag{7}$$

B represents the number of word bigrams which appear in both the reordered sentence and the golden reference, and $|S|$ represents the length of the source sentence S in words.

We also change the formula for calculating Kendall's τ to a normalized Kendall's τ following (Isozaki et al., 2010). Equation (8) gives the definition.

$$\text{norm } \tau = 1 - \frac{E}{|S| \times (|S| - 1)/2} \tag{8}$$

E represents the number of not increasing word pairs and $|S| \times (|S| - 1)/2$ is the total number of pairs.

Being a metric to evaluate the quality of machine translation, RIBES (Isozaki et al., 2010) is an extrinsic metric in our work. However, given the fact that RIBES takes order into account, it can also be considered an intrinsic metric in our work. As a matter of fact, RIBES bases on the computation of FRS and τ.

In addition, we of course use BLEU (Papineni et al., 2002) for the evaluation of machine translation quality as it is the de facto standard metric.

[5] http://www.logos.ic.i.u-tokyo.ac.jp/~tsuruoka/lapos/

6.3 Experimental Results and Analysis

Table 2 shows the evaluation results in all intrinsic evaluation metrics (modified FRS and normalized τ), the intrinsic and extrinsic evaluation metric (RIBES) and in the extrinsic evaluation metric (BLEU). We use all these metrics in the language pair English–Japanese in both directions. In both directions, the seven other BLEU scores are all statistically significantly different (p-value < 0.05) from the BLEU score of the baseline system with a distortion limit of 6.

For the oracle experiments, all the scores are much higher than those of the baseline. The smallest improvement in extrinsic evaluation is in RIBES, around 6.5, when dl is equal to 6 in the language pair English to Japanese, but the difference is still statistically significant. The increase in BLEU scores is 4 points with a distortion limit of 0 and 3 points with a distortion limit of 6 in English to Japanese, 7 points with distortion limit of 0 and 5.5 points with distortion limit of 6 in Japanese to English, which is statistically significant. We also compare the results of the oracle experiments when the distortion limit is 0 to the baseline with a default distortion limit of 6. We get almost 2.5 BLEU point improvement in English to Japanese and 5 BLEU point improvement in Japanese to English. The oracle experiments outperform Nakagawa's top-down BTG parsing method, except in FRS and normalized τ scores for the language pair English to Japanese.

These results demonstrate the theoretical effectiveness of utilizing the tree structures generated by the HSSA method. In other words, the tree structures automatically generated using the HSSA method CAN benefit PB-SMT systems.

Our preordering model tries to reproduce the results of the oracle experiments. The scores for intrinsic evaluation metrics in both directions are better than those of the baseline, with large improvement. We obtain slight but statistically significant increases in the extrinsic evaluation with the same distortion limit. However, when compared to the baseline system with a default distortion limit of 6, the PB-SMT systems with a distortion limit of 0 that were built with our preordering models still lag behind, by around 1 BLEU point in English to Japanese and less than 0.5 BLEU point in Japanese

	Language pair	Intrinsic		Intrinsic & Extrinsic		Extrinsic	
		mod FRS	norm τ	RIBES		BLEU	
				dl = 0	dl = 6	dl = 0	dl = 6
Baseline	en-ja	51.12	73.99	65.83	68.10	19.45	21.51
Tree-based		66.12	83.08	69.31	70.11	20.43	21.97
Top-down		75.59	87.68	71.56	72.28	22.56	23.31
Oracle		66.60	87.39	75.17	74.74	23.75	24.23
Baseline	ja-en	59.41	72.98	64.87	65.87	16.01	18.10
Tree-based		64.87	80.14	66.23	66.63	17.55	18.76
Top-down		66.40	81.45	68.53	68.69	19.10	19.07
Oracle		68.18	85.81	75.44	75.18	23.20	23.87

Table 2: Intrinsic and extrinsic evaluation scores in English to Japanese and Japanese to English (mod FRS is the modified Fuzzy Reordering Score; norm τ is normalized Kendall's τ; dl stands for distortion limits). Baseline is a default PB-SMT system; Tree-based is our proposed preordering model; Top-down is the top-down BTG parsing-based reordering model; Oracle is an oracle system that uses HSSA tree structures obtained for the test set. The gray cells indicate the results to compare in translation: systems with preordering methods and with a distortion limit of 0 should be compared with the corresponding baseline system with a default distortion limit of 6; other results are given for completeness.

to English. However, the comparison is in favor of our system (preordering, distortion limit 0) in RIBES by 1 point. This seems natural as RIBES is a metric for machine translation which takes reordering into account.

The reasons for these mitigated results are listed below. Firstly, our preordering models do not simulates the HSSA method so well, because this method considers all words in the two parts at hand, while the learning models we used rely only on the features of two words in the beginning and the ending position of each part. Secondly, there may be several segmentation points with similar Ncut values when building the tree structures. We choose only one. To memorize other alternatives, the use of forests instead of trees would be required. Memorizing these alternatives may lead to larger increases in evaluation scores.

7 Conclusion

In this paper, we firstly automatically generate tree structures using the hierarchical sub-sentential alignment (HSSA) method. These tree structures are equivalent to parse trees obtained by Bracketing Transduction Grammars (BTG). Secondly, based on these tree structures, we build a preordering model. Thirdly, using this preordering model, source sentences are reordered. In an oracle experiment, we show that we may expect to outperform a baseline system with the default distortion limit of 6 by 2.5 (English to Japanese) or 5 (Japanese to English) BLEU points if we are able to reorder the text sentences exactly, without the need of any distortion limit. Other experiments show that tree structures generated by the HSSA method help in getting better RIBES scores than a baseline system without preordering.

In future work, we will try different features, times of iteration and sizes of beam. In addition, we would also like to try to the use of forest structures instead of tree structures.

Acknowledgements

The second author is supported in part by China Scholarship Council (CSC) under CSC Grant No. 201406890026. We would like to thank Tetsuji Nakagawa for his most helpful comments on the experiment setting details.

References

Yaser Al-Onaizan and Kishore Papineni. 2006. Distortion models for statistical machine translation. In *Proceedings of the 21st International Conference on Computational Linguistics and the 44th annual meeting of the Association for Computational Linguistics*, pages 529-536, Sydney, Australia, July. Association for Computational Linguistics.

Peter F. Brown, Peter V. deSouza, Robert L. Mercer, Vincent J. Della Pietra, and Jenifer C. Lai. 1992. Class-based n-gram models of natural language. *Computational linguistics*, 18(4): 467-479.

Jingsheng Cai, Masao Utiyama, Eiichiro Sumita, and Yujie Zhang. 2014. Dependency-based Pre-ordering for Chinese-English Machine Translation. In *Proceedings of the 52nd Annual Meeting of the Association for Computational Linguistics*, pages 155-160, Baltimore, MD, USA, June. Association for Computational Linguistics.

David Chiang. 2007. Hierarchical Phrase-Based Translation. *Computational Linguistics*, 33(2): 201-228.

Michael Collins and Brian Roark. 2004. Incremental Parsing with the Perceptron Algorithm. In *Proceedings of the 42nd Annual Meeting on Association for Computational Linguistics*, pages 111-118, Barcelona, Spain, July. Association for Computational Linguistics.

Michael Collins, Philipp Koehn, and Ivona Kučerová. 2005. Clause Restructuring for Statistical Machine Translation. In *Proceedings of the 43rd Annual Meeting of the Association for Computational Linguistics*, pages 531-540, Ann Arbor, MI, USA, June. Association for Computational Linguistics.

John DeNero and Jakob Uszkoreit. 2011. Inducing Sentence Structure from Parallel Corpora for Reordering. In *Proceedings of the 2011 Conference on Empirical Methods in Natural Language Processing*, pages 193-203, Edinburgh, Scotland, UK, July. Association for Computational Linguistics.

Nizar Habash. 2012. Syntactic Preprocessing for Statistical Machine Translation. In *Proceedings of the 11th Machine Translation Summit (MT-Summit)*, pages 215-222, Copenhagen, Denmark, September.

Dan Han, Katsuhito Sudoh, Xianchao Wu, Kevin Duh, Hajime Tsukada, and Masaaki Nagata. 2012. Head Finalization Reordering for Chinese-to-Japanese Machine Translation. In *Proceedings of SSST-6, Sixth Workshop on Syntax, Semantics and Structure in Statistical Translation*, pages 57-66, Jeju, Korea, July. Association for Computational Linguistics.

Kenneth Heafield. 2011. KenLM: Faster and Smaller Language Model Queries. In *Proceedings of the 6th Workshop on Statistical Machine Translation*, pages 187-197, Edinburgh, Scotland, UK, July. Association for Computational Linguistics.

Hideki Isozaki, Katsuhito Sudoh, Hajime Tsukada, and Kevin Duh. 2010a. Head Finalization: A Simple Reordering Rule for SOV Languages. In *Proceedings of the Joint 5th Workshop on Statistical Machine Translation and Metrics MATR*, pages 244-251, Uppsala, Sweden, July. Association for Computational Linguistics.

Hideki Isozaki, Tsutomu Hirao, Kevin Duh, Katsuhito Sudoh, and Hajime Tsukada. 2010b. Automatic Evaluation of Translation Quality for Distant Language Pairs. In *Proceedings of the 2010 Conference on Empirical Methods in Natural Language Processing*, pages 944-952, MIT, Massachusetts, USA, October. Association for Computational Linguistics.

Maurice G Kendall. 1938. A new measure of rank correlation. *Biometrika* 30(1/2): 81-93.

Philipp Koehn, Franz Josef Och, and Daniel Marcu. 2003. Statistical Phrase-Based Translation. In *Proceedings of the 2003 Conference of the North American Chapter of the Association for Computational Linguistics on Human Language*, pages 48-54, Edmonton, Canada, May-June. Association for Computational Linguistics.

Philipp Koehn, Amittai Axelrod, Alexandra Birch Mayne, Chris Callison-Burch, Miles Osborne, and David Talbot. 2005. Edinburgh System Description for the 2005 IWSLT Speech Translation Evaluation. In *2005 International Workshop on Spoken Language Translation*, pages 68-75, Pittsburgh, PA, USA, October.

Philipp Koehn, Hieu Hoang, Alexandra Birch, Chris Callison-Burch, Marcello Federico, Nicola Bertoldi, Brooke Cowan, Wade Shen, Christine Moran. 2007. Moses: Open Source Toolkit for Statistical Machine Translation. In *Proceedings of the 45th annual meeting of the ACL on interactive poster and demonstration sessions*, pages 177-180, Prague, Czech Republic, June. Association for Computational Linguistics.

Adrien Lardilleux, François Yvon, and Yves Lepage. 2012. Hierarchical Sub-sentential Alignment with Anymalign. In *Proceedings of the 16th annual conference of the European Association for Machine Translation (EAMT 2012)*, pages 279-286, Trento, Italy, May.

Uri Lerner and Slav Petrovs. 2013. Efficient Top-Down BTG Parsing for Machine Translation Preordering. In *Proceedings of the 2013 Conference on Empirical Methods in Natural Language Processing*, 513-523, Seattle, Washington, USA, October. Association for Computational Linguistics.

Percy Liang. 2005. Semi-supervised learning for natural language. Ph.D. Dissertation. Massachusetts Institute of Technology.

Tetsuji Nakagawa. 2015. Efficient Top-Down BTG Parsing for Machine Translation Preordering. In *Proceedings of the 53rd Annual Meeting of the Association for Computational Linguistics and the 7th International Joint Conference on Natural Language Processing*, pages 208-218, Beijing, China, July. Association for Computational Linguistics.

Graham Neubig, Taro Watanabe, and Shinsuke Mori. 2012. Inducing a Discriminative Parser to Optimize Machine Translation Reordering. In *Proceedings of the 2012 Joint Conference on Empirical Methods in Natural Language Processing and Computational Natural Language Learning*, pages 843-853, Jeju Island, Korea, July. Association for Computational Linguistics.

Kishore Papineni, Salim Roukos, Todd Ward, and Wei-Jing Zhu. 2002. BLEU: a Method for Automatic Evaluation of Machine Translation. In *Proceedings of the 40th Annual Meeting of the Association for Computational Linguistics (ACL)*, pages 311-318, Philadelphia, PA, USA, July. Association for Computational Linguistics.

Hendra Setiawan, Min-Yen Kan and Haizhou Li. 2007. Ordering Phrases with Function Words. In *Proceedings of the 45th Annual Meeting of the Association of Computational Linguistics*, pages 712-719, Prague, Czech Republic, June. Association for Computational Linguistics.

David Talbot, Hideto Kazawa, Hiroshi Ichikawa, Jason Katz-Brown, Masakazu Seno, and Franz J Och. 2011. A Lightweight Evaluation Framework for Machine Translation Reordering. In *Proceedings of the 6th Workshop on Statistical Machine Translation*, pages 12-21, Edinburgh, Scotland, UK, July. Association for Computational Linguistics.

Christoph Tillmann. 2004. A unigram orientation model for statistical machine translation. In *Proceedings of the 2004 Human Language Technology Conference of the North American Chapter of the Association for Computational Linguistics (Short Papers)*, pages 101-104, Boston, MA, USA, May. Association for Computational Linguistics.

Roy Tromble and Jason Eisner. 2009. Learning Linear Ordering Problems for Better Translation. In *Proceedings of the 2009 Conference on Empirical Methods in Natural Language Processing*, pages 1007-1016, Singapore, August. Association for Computational Linguistics.

Yoshimasa Tsuruoka, Yusuke Miyao, and Junichi Kazama. 2011. Learning with Lookahead: Can History-Based Models Rival Globally Optimized Models?. In *Proceedings of the Fifteenth Conference on Computational Natural Language Learning*, pages 238-246, Portland, Oregon, USA, June. Association for Computational Linguistics.

Karthik Visweswariah, Rajakrishnan Rajkumar, and Ankur Gandhe. 2011. A Word Reordering Model for Improved Machine Translation. In *Proceedings of the 2011 Conference on Empirical Methods in Natural Language Processing*, pages 486-496, Edinburgh, Scotland, UK, July. Association for Computational Linguistics.

Chao Wang, Michael Collins, and Philipp Koehn. 2007. Chinese syntactic reordering for statistical machine translation. In *Proceedings of the 2007 Joint Conference on Empirical Methods in Natural Language Processing and Computational Natural Language Learning*, pages 737-745, Prague, June. Association for Computational Linguistics.

Dekai Wu. 1997. Stochastic Inversion Transduction Grammars and Bilingual Parsing of Parallel Corpora. *Computational Linguistics*, 23(3): 377-403.

Xianchao Wu, Katsuhito Sudoh, Kevin Duh, Hajime Tsukada, and Masaaki Nagata. 2011. Extracting Preordering Rules from Predicate-Argument Structures. In *Proceedings of the 5th International Joint Conference on Natural Language Processing*, pages 29-37, Chiang Mai, Thailand, November.

Fei Xia and Michael McCord. 2004. Improving a statistical MT system with automatically learned rewrite patterns. In *Proceedings of the 20th international conference on Computational Linguistics*, pages 508-515, Geneva, Switzerland, August. Association for Computational Linguistics.

Peng Xu, Jaeho Kang, Michael Ringgaard, and Franz Och. 2009. Using a Dependency Parser to Improve SMT for Subject-Object-Verb Languages. In *Human Language Technologies: The 2009 Annual Conference of the North American Chapter of the ACL*, pages 245-253, Boulder, Colorado, June. Association for Computational Linguistics.

Kenji Yamada and Kevin Knight. 2001. A Syntax-based Statistical Translation Model. In *Proceedings of the 39th Annual Meeting on Association for Computational Linguistics*, pages 523-530, Toulouse, France, July. Association for Computational Linguistics.

Hongyuan Zha, Xiaofeng He, Chris Ding, Horst Simon, and Ming Gu. 2001. Bipartite Graph Partitioning and Data Clustering. In *Proceedings of the tenth international conference on Information and knowledge management*, pages 25-32, Atlanta, Georgia, USA, November. Association for Computational Linguistics.

Dongdong Zhang, Mu Li, Chi-Ho Li, and Ming Zhou. 2007. Phrase Reordering Model Integrating Syntactic Knowledge for SMT. In *Proceedings of the 2007 Joint Conference on Empirical Methods in Natural Language Processing and Computational Natural Language Learning*, pages 533-540, Prague, Czech Republic, June. Association for Computational Linguistics.

The Manner/Result Complementarity in Chinese Motion Verbs Revisited

Lei Qiu
Graduate School of International Cultural Studies, Tohoku University Aoba-ku Kawauchi 41, Sendai City, 980-8576, Japan
School of Foreign Languages, Huaiyin Normal Univerisity 111 Changjiang West Road, Huaian, 223300, Jiangsu, China
conniegiulei@163.com

Abstract

Rappaport Hovav and Levin (1998, 2010) propose manner/result complementarity hypothesis (MRC), i.e. verbs can not lexicalize manner and result simultaneously at a time. As to the encoding of motion events, Levin et al. (2009) also claim that manner of motion verbs across languages simply lexicalize manner and no direction is entailed. However, three basic motion verbs in Chinese--*zǒu* 'walk', *pǎo* 'run' and *fēi* 'fly', which are regarded as prototypical manner of motion verbs but also seem to lexicalize directed motion when used in some constructions. Then the questions are: do these verbs lexicalize direction of motion and are they counterexamples of the MRC? The answers to the questions are important as they can provide cross-linguistic evidence for or against the MRC hypothesis and reveal the possible lexicalization patterns of motion verbs in Chinese. Based on evidence gained from a series of linguistic tests, this study argues that on the one hand different from views of Levin et al. (2009), the three manner of motion verbs can indeed lexicalize directed motion, but on the other hand they never encode the manner and direction of motion simultaneously and thus they are not counterexamples of the MRC.

1 Introduction

Are there any constraints on the complexity of verb meaning? Can we explain verbs' varied grammatical behaviors by looking at their meaning? At least to lexical semanticists, the answers to both questions are "yes". As advocates of lexical semantic approach, Rappaport Hovav and Levin (2010) propose that verbs' ontological categorization constrains the complexity of verb meaning and the lexical property of a verb associated with its ontological type is important to determining or constraining its argument expressions. Based on their observation of the meaning components lexicalized in ontologically different types of verbs and their distinct grammatical behaviors, Rappaport Hovav and Levin (1998, 2010) suggest a systematic lexical gap in verbal meaning: manner and result meaning components can not be encoded simultaneously and thus the two meaning components are in complementary distribution. Though the proposal of this hypothesis is primarily based on English data, Rappaport Hovav and Levin (2010) also claim that the manner/result complementarity is cross-linguistically relevant.

Lexicalization patterns of motion verbs in Chinese have been studied mainly based Talmy's framework of motion events (Talmy, 1985, 2000). Among many other studies, Lin (2011) investigates lexicalized meaning in Chinese motion verbs in the light of the MRC in particular. Based on her observation of the syntactic distribution of Chinese motion verbs, Lin (2011) argues that the lexicalization patterns of motion verbs in Chinese conform to the MRC. However, some inconsistent grammatical behaviors of three basic motion verbs *zǒu* 'walk', *pǎo* 'run' and *fēi* 'fly' are neglected by previous researchers. The three verbs, though all regarded as manner of motion verbs by researchers, also behave like directed motion verbs in some constructions. For example, the three verbs can be found in subject inversion construction, as in (1)---a property they share with directed motion verbs such as *lái* 'come' and *qù* 'go' in (2), but not with other manner of motion verbs such as *tiào* 'jump' and *pá* 'crawl' in (3), as without getting combined with other path morphemes manner of motion verbs generally can not be used in this construction. (Yuan, 1999)

(1) a. *Zǒu le yī gè xuésheng.*
walk ASP one CL student
A student left.

b. *Fēi le yī zhī gēzi.*
fly ASP one CL pigeon
A pigeon flew away.

(2) a. *Lái le yī gè zhíyuán.*
come ASP one CL employee
Here came an employee.

b. *Qù le yī gè lǎo shī.*
go ASP one CL teacher
There went a teacher.

(3) a. **Tiào le yī gè xiǎohaí.*
jump ASP one CL child
(Intended) a child jumped.

b. **Pá le yī tiáo máomáochóng.*
crawl ASP one CL catepillar
(Intended) A caterpillar crawled.

Then questions arise: do these verbs lexicalized directed motion in these cases; are these verbs counterexamples of the MRC? The answers to the questions are important as they can provide direct evidence for or against the cross-linguistic validity of the MRC. The present study intends to have a closer look at the lexicalized meaning and grammatical behaviors of these three motion verbs and determine whether they are counterexamples of the MRC in order to further check the cross-linguistic validity of the hypothesis on one hand, and to reveal the possible lexicalization patterns of motion verbs in Chinese on the other. In the following part, the main tenets of the MRC will be presented in Section 2. Previous studies on lexicalization patterns of Chinese motion verbs will also be briefly reviewed in Section 3 before the three motion verbs *zǒu* 'walk' *pǎo* 'run' and *fēi* 'fly' are discussed in detail in Section 4. Section 5 concludes the whole study.

2 The manner/result complementarity as a lexical constraint

Assuming the argument realization of a verb is largely determined by event structure decomposition, in particular the association between event schemas and verb roots, Rappaport Hovav and Levin (1998, 2010) propose the ontological categorization of verb roots such as manner and result determines the way the root integrates into an event schema and that a root can only be associated with a single position in an event, as is illustrated in (4). Since manner and result roots occupy distinct positions in event schemas: manner roots are modifiers of the primitive predicate ACT and result roots are arguments of BECOME, the MRC follows.

(4) a. [x ACT<MANNER>]

b. [[x ACT] CAUSE [y BECOME <RESULT>]]

Rappaport Hovav and Levin (2010) also refine the semantic notions of manner and result verbs as involving non-scalar and scalar changes. In both change-of-state and motion domains result verbs involve scalar changes, as they lexicalize change in the value of some scalar attribute, while manner verbs lexicalize non-scalar changes which are complex and cannot be characterized by an ordered set of values of a single attribute.

The MRC is claimed to be grammatically relevant as manner and result verbs show distinct argument realization patterns and aspectual features. For example, manner rather than result verbs allow unspecified or unsubcategorized objects. While manner verbs are generally atelic activity verbs, result verbs associated with two-point scales are necessarily punctual and telic. Even result verbs involving multiple-point scales can be interpreted telically without supporting context. (Rappaport Hovav, 2014)

3 Previous studies on the lexicalization patterns of Chinese motion verbs

Rappaport Hovav and Levin's proposal of the MRC is also consonant with Talmy's well-known classification of motion verbs based on what semantic component--path vs. manner--is conflated into the verb. Lexicalization patterns of Chinese motion verbs have been studied mainly based on Talmy's framework. However, as Lin (2011) points out, motion verbs in Chinese are classified primarily via an intuition-based semantic grouping, so there are some controversies over some less prototypical motion verbs. For example, in Guo and Chen (2009), *zuā n* 'squeeze/get into' and *diào* 'fall' are classified as manner of motion verbs but directed motion verbs in Lamarre (2008). Some motion verbs such as *dēng* 'climb' and *táo* 'escape' are also cited as counterexamples of the MRC to encode both manner and direction of motion (Ma, 2008; Shi, 2014). Therefore it is necessary to reexamine the classification of Chinese motion verbs based on systematic and consistent criteria.

Based on the lexical property of manner and result verbs suggested by Rappaport Hovav and Levin (2010), Lin (2011) introduces several tests to identify manner or direction of motion verbs via their syntactic distribution. For example, according to Lin (2011), manner and direction of motion verbs exhibit different compatibility with other elements expressing manner or result: only manner of motion verbs are compatible with a variety of result and path phrases and only directed motion verbs can be modified by various manner adverbials or co-occur with a variety of manner verbs. As illustrated in (5), *tiào* 'jump' as a manner verb is compatible with a variety of path and result phrases such as *chū* 'exit' and *duàn tuǐ* 'break legs'. Nevertheless, it can not be modified by adverbials or verbs expressing other manners such as *gǔn* 'roll' or *pá* 'crawl'.

(5) a. *Tā tiào-chū-le shuǐkēng*
he jump-exit-ASP puddle
'He jumped out of the puddle.'
b. *Tā tiào-duàn-le tuǐ*
he jump-break-ASP leg
'His leg was broken as a result of his jumping.' (Peck et al., 2013, p.683)
c. * *Tā gǔn/pá tiào*
he roll/crawl jump
(Intended) 'He jumped by rolling /crawling.'

However, directed motion verbs show contrastive grammatical behaviors. For example, directed motion verb *huí* 'recede', as illustrated by Lin (2011) in (6), can co-occur with a variety of manner verbs such as *gǔn* 'roll' and *tiào* 'jump', but it is incompatible with path or result phrases which are not related to the path lexicalized in the verb itself.

(6) a. *Dírén tiào/gǔn-zhe huí guānwài*
enemy jump/roll-IMP return pass.outside
'The enemy returned to the outside of the pass jumping/rolling'
b. **Dírén huí-lèi le*

enemy return-be.tired ASP

(Intended) 'The enemy became tired as a result of returning'

(Lin, 2011, p.37)

As can be seen, linguistic tests introduced by Lin (2011) can distinguish manner of motion and directed motion verbs in Chinese in a consistent manner so far. However, when we check the actual uses of the three manner of motion verbs *zǒu* 'walk' *pǎo* 'run' and *fēi* 'fly', they also pose a problem to Lin's tests: though in their basic uses they can pass the tests for manner of motion verbs, in some other cases their syntactic distribution just contradicts the property of manner of motion verbs. For example, as prototypical manner of motion verbs, they are not expected to co-occur with other manner verbs, since verbs specifying different manners should not be compatible. Nevertheless, as illustrated in (7), in their actual uses they can co-occur with other manner verbs. In (7a) *zǒu* 'walk' co-occurs with another manner verb *piāo* 'float', in (7b) *pǎo* 'run' also co-occurs with another manner verb *gǔn* 'roll' and in (7c) *fēi* 'fly' follows another manner verb *tī* 'kick'.

(7) a. *Qìqiu piāo-zǒu le.*
balloon float-walk ASP
'The balloon flew away.'

b. *Píqíu gǔn-pǎo le.*
rubber ball roll-run ASP
'The rubber ball rolled away.'

d. *Xiézi beì tī-fēi le.*
shoe PASS kick-fly ASP
'The shoe was kicked away.'

The inconsistent grammatical behaviors of these verbs illustrated in (7), together with the evidence that they can enter subject inversion construction as mentioned in Introduction section force us to ask whether they can indeed encode direction of motion and then contribute to counterexamples of the MRC. Following the tenets of the MRC and Lin's (2011) study I will look at the semantics and grammatical behaviors of these verbs in detail to clarify their ontological status in next section.

4 Case studies of motion verbs *zǒu* 'walk' *pǎo* 'run' and *fēi* 'fly'

In this section, the lexicalized meaning components and the grammatical properties of the three motion verbs *zǒu* 'walk' *pǎo* 'run' and *fēi* 'fly' will be looked at in detail. Besides using Lin's linguistic tests to distinguish manner verbs from result verbs, I will also take the aspectual property of manner and direction of motion verbs into account, as different aspectual features of manner and result verbs are also crucial to their syntactic distribution. As mentioned in Section 3, Rapapport Hovav and Levin (2010) suggest distinct scalar notions underlying manner and result verbs. In case of motion verbs, manner of motion verbs encode non-scalar changes, they are atelic. Directed motion verbs can be further divided into two subtypes depending on whether they entail two-point or multi-point scalar changes: verbs lexicalizing two-point scalar changes are necessarily telic and punctual and verbs lexicalizing multi-point scales have either telic or atelic readings depending on contexts.

4.1 *zǒu* 'walk' *pǎo* 'run' and *fēi* 'fly' used as manner of motion verbs

In their basic uses, there is no doubt that the three verbs show hallmarks of manner verbs. As they lexicalize non-scalar changes, they are necessarily atelic and compatible with durative time adverbial. As illustrated in (8a), *zǒu* 'walk' is compatible with durative time adverbial *sān gè xiǎoshí* 'three hours'. In (8b) *fēi* 'fly' can be used with durative time adverbial *sān tiān* 'three days'.

(8) a. Tā zǒu le sān gè xiǎoshí
he walk ASP three CL hour
'He walked for three hours.'

b. *Xiǎoniǎo fēi le sāntiān*
little bird fly ASP three days
'The little bird flew for three days'

Since they do not entail any direction or result information, they can take as their complements varied result and path phrases. As illustrated in (9a), *pǎo* 'run' is compatible with both upward and downward directions. It is also shown that in (9b) *fēi* 'fly' can take *duàn* 'break (wings)' and in (9c) *pǎo* 'run' can take *dīu xié* 'lose shoes' as their resultant complements respectively.

(9) a. *Zhànshi měitiān pǎo-shàng-pǎo-xià*
soldier everyday run-ascend-run-descend
'Soldiers run up and down everyday.'

b. *Tā-men de chìbǎng dōukuài fēi-duàn le*
they-PL DE wings almost fly-break ASP
'They (pigeons) almost broke their wings as a result of flying (continuously)'

c. *Tā pǎo-dīu xiézi le*
he run-lose shoe ASP
'He lost his shoes as a result of running'

To conclude, it can be seen that in their basic uses the lexicalized meaning and grammatical behaviors of the three verbs conform to the property of manner of motion verbs.

4.2 *zǒu* 'walk' *pǎo* 'run' and *fēi* 'fly' used as directed motion verbs

As mentioned in previous sections, the three verbs can be found to exhibit grammatical behaviors distinct from manner of motion verbs, as they can be used in subject inversion construction and they can also follow another manner of motion verb to form a verbal compound without contradiction. Focusing on the two specific cases, this section uses a series of syntactic and semantic tests to check what lexical meaning they actually encode and to clarify their ontological status.

First, I will show when the three motion verbs are used in subject inversion constructions they only encode directed motion and their manner of motion sense is dropped out. In Chinese, it is generally accepted by scholars (Huang, 1990; Li, 1990; Yu, 1995) that verbs which are used with perfective aspectual marker in subject inversion construction are prototypical unaccusative verbs. These verbs generally describe non-volitional change-of-state/location of the theme. As illustrated in (10a), the verb *sǐ* 'die' describing a non-volitional change of state is unaccusative verb, so it can be used in the subject inversion construction. Nevertheless in (10b) *chàng* 'sing' expressing a volitional action is an unergative verb, so it can not be used in the construction.

(10) a. *Sǐ le yí gè rén*
die ASP one CL person
'A person died.'

b. **Chàng le yí gè rén.*
Sing ASP one CL person
(Intended) 'A person sang.'

Though generally manner of motion verbs are regarded as unergative verbs which without getting combined with other path morphemes can not enter the subject inversion construction, the three verbs can be used in the construction, as shown in the example sentences of (1).

With regard to these cases I suggest that these verbs entail only the directed motion as 'being away from the reference object'. Crucially as is shown by their grammatical properties in this construction, they lose their manner meaning components. First, when they are used in this construction, they lose the atelic aspectual feature of manner verbs and encode punctual and telic changes. The examples in (11) show that they are not compatible with durative aspectual marker *zhe*.

(11) *a. *Zǒu zhe yí gè xuésheng*
walk DUR one CL student
(Intended) 'A student is leaving.'

*b. *Pǎo zhe yí gè fànrén*
run DUR one CL prisoner
(Intended) 'A prisoner is running away'

*c. *Fēi zhe yí zhī gēzi*
fly DUR one CL pigeon
(Intended) 'A pigeon is flying away.'

In addition, when the three verbs are used in subject inversion construction they can not be modified by subject-oriented manner adverbials, as shown in (12). This also indicates that the manner of motion sense of the verbs is dropped out and they encode only the directed motion.

(12) *a. *Xùnsù de zǒu le yí gè xuésheng*
swiftly DE walk ASP one CL student
(Intended) 'A student left swiftly'.

*b. *Pīnmìng de pǎo le yí gè fànrén*
desperately DE run ASP one CL prisoner
(Intended) 'A prisoner ran away desperately'

*c. *Mǐnjié de fēi le yì zhī gēzi*
nimbly DE fly ASP one CL pigeon
(Intended) 'A pigeon flew away nimbly'

Furthermore, the subject inversion construction is not the only construction in which the tree verbs behave like directed motion verbs. They can also follow another verb specifying different manner to form a verbal compound. Based on Chinese morphology when two verbs co-occur to form a verbal compound there are two types of possible relationship between the two verbs. One type is that the two verbs hold a coordinating relation and they express synonymous information such as ji à ng-lu ò 'descend-fall'. Nevertheless in case of examples in (7) the two verbs express different manners of motion and they are not synonymous, so the possibility of adopting this explanation has been ruled out.

The other type of relation is that the two verbs form a resultative verbal compound, in which the first verb (V1) specifies the manner or cause of the action and the second verb (V2) indicates the result of the action. As for motion events, the two juxtaposing verbs form directional verbal compound (henceforth DVC) in which the first verb usually specifies the manner or cause of the motion and the second verb expresses the direction of motion. If it is true for the two juxtaposing verbs in (7), the verbs holding V1 position *piāo* 'float', *gǔn* 'roll' and *tī* 'kick' should specify the manner of motion, and the verbs occupying the V2 position *zǒu* 'walk' and *pǎo* 'run' should describe the direction of the motion. The contrastive semantic entailments of example sentences in (13) and (14) show that it is indeed the case. As shown in (13), the manner of motion verbs *piāo* 'float', *gǔn* 'roll' and *tī* 'kick' do not entail displacement of the theme. In the sentence of (13a), *piāo* 'float' describes that flags were floating on the top of the pole where flags were tied and thus no displacement was possible. Similarly, in (13b) *gǔn* 'roll' and *tī* 'kick' describe actions in place, so there is no displacement either.

(13) a. *Qígān shàng piāo zhē xiǎo qí*
flagpole LOC float IMP small flag
'small flags were floating on the top of the pole'

b. *Tā zài yuándì gǔn/tī*
he at original place kick/roll
'He rolled/kicked in place.'

However, when *zǒu* 'walk' *pǎo* 'run' and *fēi* 'fly' are added following these verbs to form verbal compounds, displacement of the theme as 'being away from the deictic object' is entailed. In (14a) *piāo-zǒu* 'float-walk' entails that the flags floated away and they were not on the top of the pole anymore. Similarly, the verbal compounds *gǔn-pǎo* 'roll-run' and *tī-fēi* 'kick-fly' also entail the themes have left the deictic object, as illustrated in (14b) and (14c).

(14) a. *Xiǎo qí piāo-zǒu le,*

small flat float-walk ASP,
*dàn tā hái zài qígān shàng.
but it still at flagpole LOC
'Flags floated away, #but they were still on the top of the pole.'

b. *Píqíu gǔn-pǎo le,*
rubber ball roll-run ASP
*dàn tā hái zài yuándì.
but it still at original place
'The rubber ball rolled away, #but it still stays at its original place.'

c. *Xiézi bèi tī-fēi le,*
shoe PASS kick-fly ASP
*dàn xiézi hái zài jiǎo shàng
but shoe still at foot LOC
'The shoe was kicked off, #but it was still on the foot.'

Furthermore, distinct lexical entailments can also be attested by looking at the aspectual features of these DVCs. As illustrated in (15), when the three verbs are used as V2 to form DVCs, these DVCs are incompatible with the progressive aspectual marker *zhèngzài*. This indicates that though all the components verbs of these DVCs are typically atelic, these DVCs have lost their atelic aspectual feature and telic change is entailed.

(15) a. **Qìqiu zhèngzài piāo-zǒu.*
balloon PROG float-walk
(Intended) 'The ballon is floating away.'

b. **Píqíu zhèngzài gǔn-pǎo.*
rubber ball PROG roll-run
(Intended) 'The rubber ball is rolling away'

c. **Xiézi zhèngzài bèi tī-fēi.*
shoe PROG PASS kick-fly
(Intended) 'The shoe is being kicked off.'

The change of aspectual feature can also be supported by the contrastive readings of the post-verbal adverbial 'for X time' when it co-occurs with only the manner verbs in V1 position or with the DVCs. To be specific, as in (16) when the manner verbs holding V1 position co-occur with a post-verbal adverbial 'for X time', there is only an atelic process reading.

(16) a. *Qìqiu piāo le yī xiǎoshí le.*
balloon float PERF one hour ASP
'The balloon has floated for an hour.'

b. *Píqíu gǔn le yī fēnzhōng le.*
rubber ball roll PERF one minute ASP
'The rubber ball has rolled for a minute.'

c. *Xiézi bèi tī le yī fēnzhōng le.*
shoe PASS kick PERF one minute ASP
'The shoe has been kicked for a minute.'

In contrast, when the post-verbal adverbial 'for X time' co-occurs with the DVCs, the time period indicated by the adverbial only has a 'after X time' reading which specifies the length of time the result state of 'being away from the deictic object' holds; see (17). This further indicates that the DVC as a whole describes a two-point scalar change.

(17) a. *Qìqíu piāo-zǒu le yī xiǎoshí le.*
Balloon float-walk PERF one hour ASP
'It had been an hour since the balloon floated away.'

b. *Píqíu gǔn-pǎo le yī fēnzhōng le.*
rubber ball roll-run PERF one minute ASP
'It had been a minute since the rubber ball rolled away.'

c. *Xiézi bèi tī-fēi le yī fēnzhōng le.*
shoe PASS kick-fly PERF one minute ASP
'It had been a minute since the shoe was kicked off.'

Thus it is safe to believe that the change of the aspectual feature from atelic to telic is attributed to the three verbs holding V2 position. The puzzling problem that the three verbs violate Lin's linguistic tests for manner of motion verb is also clear now. In these cases, the three verbs do not encode the manner of motion at all, but only express the direction of the motion. That's why they can co-occur with another manner of motion verb without contradiction.

Summarizing, when the three prototypical manner of motion verbs exhibit different grammatical behaviors, they also lexicalize distinct meaning components. To be specific, when used in subject inversion constructions and when they follow another manner of motion verb to form a DVC, they lose their manner sense and lexicalize only the sense of directed motion.

4.3 Two distinct senses of *zǒu* 'walk' *pǎo* 'run' and *fēi* 'fly' in complementary distribution

Some may argue the directed motion sense of the three motion verbs may not be the lexical entailment of the verb, and it may be derived from the meaning of the construction they are found in or from other pragmatic factors. In Section 4.2 the directed motion sense of the three verbs has been examined based on two typical constructions in Chinese, so it is natural to assume that the directed motion sense is derived from the constructions. In addition, Levin et al. (2009) argue that cross-linguistically manner of motion verbs share the same type of verb root: they all specify only the manner of motion and the sense of directed motion arises from pragmatic factors. However, I suggest neither case is true for the three motion verbs in Chinese. The directed motion sense is not derived from other elements of the sentence and it is indeed the lexicalized meaning in the verbs because the three verbs can have directed motion reading even though they are not used in the two constructions and without pragmatic support from context. For example, as illustrated in (18), without any contextual support the simple sentence with the verb *zǒu* 'walk' as its only verb is ambiguous. It has two possible interpretations: either 'I am capable of walking.' or 'I can leave'. Therefore, it can be seen that the directed motion sense is not derived from the two constructions; rather it is because the three verbs can possibly lexicalize directed motion that they can enter the two constructions.

(18) *Wǒ néng zǒu le*

I can walk ASP

a. 'I am capable of walking.'

b. 'I can leave.'

Interestingly, with the former reading 'I am capable of walking' the verb *zǒu* 'walk' only encodes the manner of motion and for the latter reading 'I can leave' the verb only lexicalizes directed motion as 'leaving the deictic center'. Though the verb can potentially encode both manner and direction of motion, the sentence never entails 'I can leave by walking'. In fact, it is just the direct evidence for the MRC as a general principle constraining how much meaning a verb can possibly lexicalize. Following Levin and Rappaport Hovav (2013), a lexicalized meaning component is one which is entailed across all uses of a verb. Though the three motion verbs can potentially lexicalize manner and result, but there is never a single use of the verb which entails both meaning components together. The MRC is a valid cross-linguistic principle that constrains the possible lexicalization patterns of the lexicon.

5 Conclusion

Focusing on three Chinese motion verbs *zǒu* 'walk', *pǎo* 'run' and *fēi* 'fly' [1], this study investigates the lexicalization patterns of Chinese motion verbs. Different from the view of Levin et al. (2009) that manner of motion verbs only lexicalize the sense of manner, I suggest the three Chinese motion verbs can indeed lexicalize direction of motion. However, they never encode manner and direction of motion simultaneously and thus do not falsify the MRC. As far as the actual uses are concerned the lexicalization pattern of these three verbs confirms the validity of MRC as a significant observation about how much meaning can be lexicalized in a verb.

Note

[1] An anonymous reviewer suggests more Chinese verbs with similar lexicalization patterns be investigated. Though there is little agreement upon the classification of some less prototypical motion verbs, e.g, *táo* escape, *luò* fall, *dēng*, ascend, these verbs hardly fall into the same group as the three verbs discussed in this paper. The complexity of the lexicalization patterns of Chinese motion verbs is probably due to the diachronic development of Chinese language, in particular its typological evolvement from verb-framed language to satellite-framed language (Lamarre, 2008; Shi, 2014). I have to leave those verbs for future research.

References

Chen, Liang and Jiansheng Guo. 2009. Motion events in Chinese novels: Evidence for an equipollently-framed language. Journal of Pragmatics, 41:1749-1766.

Huang, C-T. James. 1990 Two kinds of transitive verbs and two kinds of intransitive verbs in Chinese In Proceedings of the Second International Conference on Chinese Teaching, ed, Ting-Chi Tang et al., 39–59. Taipei: World Chinese Press.

Lamarre, Christine. 2008. The linguistic categorization of deictic direction in Chinese: With reference to Japanese. In Space in languages of China: Cross-linguistic, synchronic and diachronic perspectives, ed. Dan Xu, 69-98. Dordrecht: Springer.

Levin, Beth, and Malka Rappaport Hovav. 1995. Unaccusativity: At the syntax-lexical semantics interface. Cambridge: MIT Press.

Levin, Beth, John Beavers and Shiao Wei Tham. 2009. Manner of motion roots across languages: Same or different? Handout, Workshop on roots, University Stuttgart, Germany, June, 2009.

Levin, Beth, and Malka Rappaport Hovav. 2013. Lexicalized meaning and manner/result complementarity. In Studies in the composition and decomposition of event predicates. ed. Boban Arsenijevic, Berit Gehrke, Rafael Marin, 49-70. Dordrecht: Springer.

Li, Y.-H. Audre. 1990. Order and Constituency in Mandarin Chinese. Dordrecht: Kluwer Academic.

Lin, Jingxia. 2011. The encoding of motion events in Chinese: Multi-morpheme motion constructions. Stanford: Ph.D. dissertation, Stanford University.

Ma, Yunxia. 2008. The Development of Chinese path verbs and motion event expressions. Beijing: Zhongyang minzu daxue Presss.

Peck, JeeYoung, Jingxia Lin, and Chaofen Sun. 2013. Aspectual classification of Mandarin Chinese verbs: A perspective of scale structure. Language and Linguistics, 14(4): 663-700.

Rappaport Hovav, Malka, and Beth Levin. 1998. Building verb meanings. In The projection of argument structures: Lexical and compositional Factors, ed. M. Butt and W. Geuter, 97-134. Stanford, CA: CSLI Publications.

Rappaport Hovav, Malka, and Beth Levin. 2010. Refections on manner/result complementarity. In Syntax, lexical semantics, and event structure, ed, Edit Doron, Malka Rappaport Hovav, and Ivy Sichel, 21-38. Oxford: Oxford University Press.

Rappaport Hovav, M. 2014. Building Scalar Changes, in The Syntax of Roots and the Roots of Syntax, ed, A. Alexiadou, H. Borer, and F. Sch¨afer, 259-281. Oxford: Oxford University Press.

Shi, W., and Wu, Y. Which way to move: The evolution of motion expressions in Chinese. Linguistics, 52(5):1237-1292.

Talmy, Leonard. 1985. Lexicalization patterns: Semantic structure in lexical forms. In Language typology and syntactic description 3: Grammatical categories and the lexicon, ed. Timothy Shopen, 57-149. Cambridge: Cambridge University Press.

Talmy, Leonard. 2000. Toward a cognitive semantics, volume II: Typology and process in concept structure. Cambridge: MIT Press.

Yuan, B. 1999. Acquiring the unaccusative /unergative distinction in a second language: Evidence from English-speaking learners of L2 Chinese. Linguistics, 37: 275-296

Yu, Ning. 1995. Towards a definition of unaccusative verbs in Chinese. In Proceedings of the 6th North American Conference on Chinese Linguistics, ed, Jose Camacho and Lina Choueiri, 339–353. Los Angeles: University of South California.

Yet Another Symmetrical and Real-time Word Alignment Method: Hierarchical Sub-sentential Alignment using F-measure

Hao Wang, Yves Lepage
Graduate School of Information, Production and Systems
Waseda University
2-7 Hibikino, Wakamatsu-ku, Kitakyushu, Fukuoka, 808-0135, Japan
{oko_ips@ruri., yves.lepage@}waseda.jp

Abstract

Symmetrization of word alignments is the fundamental issue in statistical machine translation (SMT). In this paper, we describe an novel reformulation of Hierarchical Sub-sentential Alignment (HSSA) method using F-measure. Starting with a soft alignment matrix, we use the F-measure to recursively split the matrix into two soft alignment sub-matrices. A direction is chosen as the same time on the basis of Inversion Transduction Grammar (ITG). In other words, our method simplifies the processing of word alignment as recursive segmentation in a bipartite graph, which is simple and easy to implement. It can be considered as an alternative of *grow-diag-final-and* heuristic. We show its application on phrase-based SMT systems combined with the state-of-the-art approaches. In addition, by feeding with word-to-word associations, it also can be a real-time word aligner. Our experiments show that, given a reliable lexicon translation table, this simple method can yield comparable results with state-of-the-art approaches.

1 Introduction

Since most of state-of-the-art Statistical Machine Translation (SMT) approaches require word-to-word aligned data on a parallel corpus, word alignment is a fundamental issue to perform this task rapidly. In order to extract translation fragments for various purposes, e.g., word pairs (Brown et al., 1988), phrase pairs (Koehn et al., 2003), hierarchical rules (Chiang, 2005), tree-to-tree correspondences (Zhang et al., 2007), reliable and accurate word aligners are essential.

There exist several problems in state-of-the-art methods for word alignment. Present word alignment approaches are usually based on IBM models (Brown et al., 1993), which parameters are estimated using the Expectation-Maximization (EM) algorithm. Sometimes, they are augmented with an HMM-based model (Vogel et al., 1996). Since IBM Models is the restriction to one-to-many alignments, some multi-word units cannot be correctly aligned. It is necessary to train models in both directions, and merge the outcome of mono-directional alignments using some symmetrization methods can overcome this deficiency to some degree.

It results, even using the standard open source tool aligner, called `GIZA++`[1] (Och, 2003), which consist of the widely used IBM models and their extensions, still will spend lots of time to obtain word alignments. A recent development of word alignment approach `fast_align`[2] (Dyer et al., 2013), based on the variation of the IBM model 2, has been reported faster than baseline `GIZA++` but with comparable results. However, both mentioned approaches generate asymmetric alignments. In order to obtain the symmetrical word alignments, these approaches symmetrize the alignments in both forward and reverse directions using a symmetrization heuristic called *grow-diag-final-and* (Och, 2003). Starting with the intersection alignment points that occur in both of the two directional alignments, *grow-diag-final-and* expands the alignment in the union of

[1] http://www.statmt.org/moses/giza/GIZA++.html
[2] https://github.com/clab/fast_align

the alignment in either of the two directional alignments. Although it has been shown to be most effective for phrase extraction for phrased-based SMT (Wu and Wang, 2007), there lacks a principled explanation.

Recently, development in mining large parallel patent or document collections increase the needs in fast methods for word alignment. Besides, in the real scenario of Computer Assisted Translation (CAT) (Kay, 1997), in conjunction with SMT system (Farajian et al., 2014) for translation or post-editing (reference) (Guerberof, 2009), real-time word alignment methods become necessary.

In this paper, we propose a novel method based on the use of F-measure for symmetrization of word alignment, at the same time which can be regarded as an real-time word alignment approach. We justify this approach with mathematical principles. The paper is organized as follows: in Section 2, we discuss the motivation. In Section 3, we summarize the related work like Viterbi alignment and inversion transduction grammar. In Section 4, we formulate our method and give a mathematical justification. The Section 5 reports experiments and results. Finally, we give some conclusion and points for the future research.

2 Motivation

There exist several purposes that drive us to introduce such a new method which differs the previous approach. Absolutely, time cost is the first our consideration. Consider the case when huge parallel documents are handed to the computer. It will be a very interesting question that how to align these parallel sentences in a large number of documents while have spent the minimal time. Nowadays, since most of the public available word aligners are based on EM algorithm in order to get the global optimal alignments, the real-time cost of the processing of word alignment can not be estimated.

Another realistic problem is, in the most real situation of machine translation task, a bilingual lexicon dictionary even longer phrase translation fragments table is given or available, while reusing the pre-built knowledge base, rather than aligning data using some machine learning technique to guess the probable Viterbi alignment again, is a more advisable solution to employ a real-time aligner to align words automatically.

There are also some drawbacks of the previous approach likes IBM models and their variations. All these models are based on restricted alignments in the sense that a source word can be aligned to at most one target word. This constraint is necessary to reduce the computational complexity of the models, but it makes it impossible to align phrase in the target language (English) such as *"a car"* to a single word in the source language (Japanese/Chinese) "車/车". Beside, a variation of IBM model 2 was used in `fast_align`. It introduces a "tension" to model the overall accordance of word orders, but it has proved by (Ding et al., 2015) that it performs not well when applied to the very distinct language pairs, e.g., English and Japanese.

3 Related Work

3.1 Viterbi alignment and symmetrization

The basic idea of the previous approaches is to develop a model treating the word alignment as a hidden variables (Och, 2003), by applying some statistical estimation theory to obtain the most possible/Viterbi alignments. The problem of translation can be defined as:

$$Pr(f_1^J|e_1^I) = \sum_{a_1^J} Pr(f_1^J, a_1^J|e_1^I) \qquad (1)$$

Here we use the symbol $Pr(\cdot)$ to denote general probability distributions. a_1^J is a "hidden" alignment which is mapping from a source position j to a target position a_j. It is always possible to find a best alignment by maximizing the likelihood on the given parallel training corpus.

$$\hat{a}_1^J = \text{argmax}_{a_1^J} Pr(f_1^J, a_1^J|e_1^I) \qquad (2)$$

Since Viterbi alignment model is based on conditional probabilities, it only returns one directional alignment in each direction ($F \rightarrow E$ and vice-versa). In other words, this process is asymmetric. The complementary part of Viterbi alignment model before phrase extraction is *grow-diag-final-and*, in which the symmetrical word alignments are generated using simple growing heuristics. Given two sets of alignments $\hat{a}_1^J$ and $\hat{b}_1^J$, in order to increase the

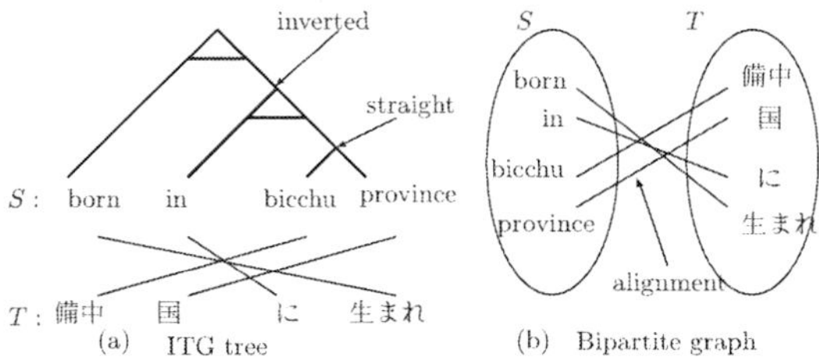

Figure 1: Alignments representations using ITG and bipartite graph. None of the structure contains cycles. The Japanese phrase 備中 国 に 生まれ means *born in bicchu province* in English.

quality of the alignments, they combine $\hat{a}_1^J$ and $\hat{b}_1^J$ into one alignment matrix A using *grow-diag-final-and* algorithm.

A widely used approach to get word alignments is estimating the alignment using IBM models because word alignments are the by-production of estimating lexicon translation probabilities. However, this generative story looks like a "*chicken or the egg*" problem. On the one hand, given alignments with probabilities it is possible to compute translation probabilities. On the other hand, if knowing which words are a probable translation of another one makes it possible to guess which alignment is probable and which one is improbable.

3.2 ITG-based word alignment

Since the search space of word alignment will grow exponentially with the length of source and target sentences (Brown et al., 1993), Wu (1997) proposed an approach to constraining the search space for word alignment, namely inversion transduction grammars (ITG). Generally, ITG is a family of grammars in which the right part of the rule is either two non-terminals or a terminal sequence. ITG is a special case of synchronous context-free grammar, also called Bracketing Transduction Grammar (BTG). There are three simple generation rules, S (straight), I (inverted) and terminal (T).

$$S: \quad \gamma \rightarrow [XY] \tag{3}$$

$$I: \quad \gamma \rightarrow < XY > \tag{4}$$

$$T: \quad \gamma \rightarrow w = (s, t) \tag{5}$$

The algorithm used by (Wu, 1997) synchronously parses the source and the target sentence to build a synchronous parse tree. This ITG tree indicates the same underlying structure but the ordering of constituents may be different. Due to its simplicity and effectiveness of modelling bilingual correspondence, ITG can be used to model the bilingual sentences in very distinct ordering. In fact, an ITG-style Tree is a bitree consists of one tree in the source side and another tree in the target side (see Figure 1.a), here, two trees are compressed as a single tree. Besides, an ITG-style Tree is also able to be displayed in a soft alignment matrix (see Figure 2) with the representation of bipartite graph (see Figure 1.b) .

3.3 Hierarchical sub-sentential alignment

Hierarchical sub-sentential alignment (HSSA) is yet another alignment approach, introduced by (Lardilleux et al., 2012). This method does not rely on the EM algorithm as other alignment models. With a recursive binary segmentation process of searching the segment point in a soft alignment matrix (as Figure 2) between a source sentence and its corresponding target sentence, this approach aims to minimize *Ncut* score (Zha et al., 2001), which can yield acceptable and accurate 1-to-many or many-to-1 word alignments.

In order to build soft alignment matrices before the step of aligning words, Lardilleux et al. (2012) employed `Anymalign`[3] to obtain the prepared translation table of lexicon translation probabilities. Since the training times and the quality of translation table changed considerably depending on the timeouts for `Anymalign`, an easy and fair comparison to state-of-the-art approaches is difficult.

Given the grey-scale graph of soft alignment, Hierarchical Sub-sentential Alignment (hereafter referred to as HSSA) approach takes all cells in the soft alignment matrix into consideration and seeks the precise criterion for a good partition same as image segmentation. It makes use of a popular modern clustering algorithm called *normalized cuts* (Zha et al., 2001; Shi and Malik, 2000), i.e., spectral clustering, or $Ncut$ for short, to binary segment the matrix recursively.

In the following section, we will refine the proposal of hierarchical sub-sentential alignment. We will not use the notion of *Ncut*, so as to give a sim-

[3]https://anymalign.limsi.fr/

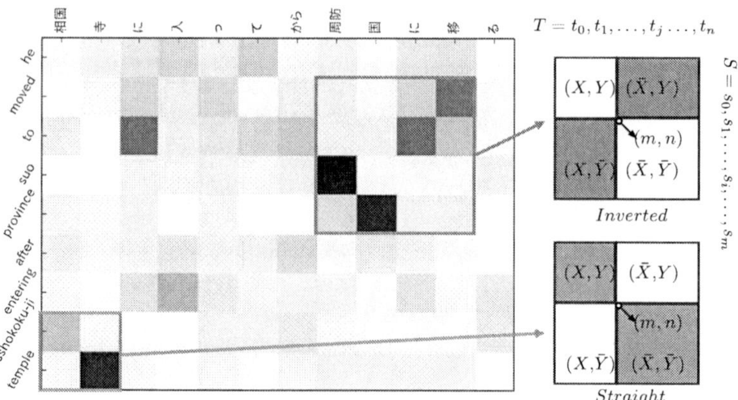

Figure 2: Translation strengths on a logarithmic scale in a English-Japanese sentence pair matrix as a grey graph.

ple and convincing justification using F-measure for this symmetrical word alignment approach.

4 Proposed Method

4.1 Soft alignment matrices

We propose to regard the alignment associations between a source sentence S and a target word T as a contingency matrix (Matusov et al., 2004; Moore, 2005) as in Figure 2, noted as $\mathcal{M}(I, J)$, in which I is the length of source sentence in words and J for target side. We define a function w which measuring the strength of the translation link between any source and target pair of words (s_i, t_j). The symmetric alignment between word s_i and t_j presents a greyed cell (i, j) in this matrix. In this paper, the score $w(s_i, t_j)$ is defined as the geometric mean of the bidirectional lexical translation probabilities $p(s_i|t_j)$ and $p(t_j|s_i)$. For a given sub-sentential alignment $A(X,Y) \subseteq I \times J$, we define the weight of this alignment W(X,Y) as the summation of association scores between each source and target words of a block (X, Y) in such a matrix.

$$W(X,Y) = \sum_{s \in X} \sum_{t \in Y} w(s,t) \tag{6}$$

Since we have to calculate all cells in the block (X, Y), the time complexity here is in $O(I \times J)$.

4.2 Reformulation: from Ncut to F-measure

Ncut can be computed as the following formula same as in (Zha et al., 2001), :

$$Ncut(X,Y) = \frac{cut(X,Y)}{cut(X,Y)+2 \times W(X,Y)} + \frac{cut(\overline{X},\overline{Y})}{cut(\overline{X},\overline{Y})+2 \times W(\overline{X},\overline{Y})}$$

$$cut(X,Y) = W(X,\overline{Y}) + W(\overline{X},Y) \tag{7}$$

Actually, minimizing $Ncut(X, Y)$ is equivalent to maximizing the arithmetic mean of the F-measure (also called F-score) of X relatively to Y and $\bar{X}$ relatively to $\bar{Y}$. It can be derived as following. In general, F_1-measure (Kim et al., 1999) of block (X, Y) is defined as the harmonic mean of precision P and recall R:

$$\frac{1}{F_1(X,Y)} = \frac{1}{2} \times \left(\frac{1}{P(X,Y)} + \frac{1}{R(X,Y)}\right) \tag{8}$$

To interpret sentence pair matrices as contingency matrices, it suffices to read trans- lation strengths as reflecting the contribution of a source word to a target word and reciprocally. With this interpretation, the precision (P) and the recall (R) for two sub-parts of the source and the target sentences can easily be expressed using the sum of all the translation strengths inside a block. These two measures can thus be defined as following Equations.

$$P(X,Y) = \frac{W(X,Y)}{W(X,Y) + W(X,\overline{Y})} \tag{9}$$

$$R(X,Y) = \frac{W(X,Y)}{W(X,Y) + W(\overline{X},Y)} \tag{10}$$

Now, it suffices to replace precision and recall by their values in terms of cut to derive the following formula.

$$\frac{1}{F_1(X,Y)} = \frac{1}{2} \times (\frac{W(X,Y)+W(X,\overline{Y})}{W(X,Y)} + \frac{W(X,Y)+W(\overline{X},Y)}{W(X,Y)}) \quad (11)$$

$$= \frac{2 \times W(X,Y)+W(\overline{X},Y)+W(X,\overline{Y})}{2 \times W(X,Y)} \quad (12)$$

$$= \frac{2 \times W(X,Y)+cut(\overline{X},Y)}{2 \times W(X,Y)} \quad (13)$$

By using Equation 13 and Equation 7, for (X, Y), we obtain:

$$F_1(X,Y) = 1 - \frac{W(\overline{X},Y)+W(X,\overline{Y})}{2 \times W(X,Y)+W(\overline{X},Y)+W(X,\overline{Y})} \quad (14)$$

$$= 1 - Ncut_{left}(X,Y) \quad (15)$$

In a contingency matrix, where balanced F_1-score can be used regularly for binary classification, especially on the scenario of binary segmentation of bilingual sentence pair under the ITG framework. With this interpretation, for the *straight* case of ITG, we can get the F_1-score for the remaining block $(\overline{X}, \overline{Y})$ as,

$$F_1(\overline{X},\overline{Y}) = 1 - Ncut_{right}(X,Y) \quad (16)$$

Absolutely, an equivalent way of writing is:

$$Ncut(X,Y) = 2 \times [1 - \frac{F_1(X,Y)+F_1(\overline{X},\overline{Y})}{2}] \quad (17)$$

To summarize, minimizing *Ncut* equals finding the best point with the maximum value in the matrix of arithmetic means of F_1-score. This in fact makes sense intuitively if we look for the best possible way for parts of the source and target sentences to correspond. These parts should cover one another in both directions as much as possible, that is to say, they should exhibit the best recall and precision at the same time.

4.3 Reducing time complexity

In order to reduce the time complexity in calculate the value of W($\overline{X}$,$\overline{Y}$), we make use of a specialized data structure for fast computation. For each given sentence pair, a summed area table (SAT) was created for fast calculating the summation of cells in the corresponding soft alignment matrix $\mathcal{M}(I, J)$. The preprocessing step is to build a new $(I+1, J+1)$ matrix $\mathcal{M}'$, where each entry is the sum of the sub-matrix to the upper-left of that entry. Any arbitrary sub-matrix sum can be calculated by looking up and mixing only 4 entries in the SAT.

Assume X, Y starts from point (i_0, j_0), where $X, \bar{X}$ and $Y, \bar{Y}$ are splitting at i_1 and j_1 separately. We have,

$$W(X,Y) = \sum_{\substack{i_0 < i < i_1 \\ j_0 < j < j_1}} w(i,j)$$
$$= \mathcal{M}'(i_1, j_1) - \mathcal{M}'(i_0, j_1) - \mathcal{M}'(i_1, j_0) + \mathcal{M}'(i_0, j_0)$$

Time complexity here is reduced from $O(I \times J)$ to $O(1)$ when calculating the summation of cells in the block of X, Y, and similar to the remaining. Due to data sparsity, a simple Laplace smoothing was used here to handle the unseen alignments with a very small smoothing parameter $\alpha = 10^{-7}$.

5 Experiments

5.1 Alignment Experiments

We evaluate the performance of our proposed methods. We conduct the experiments on KFTT corpus[4], in which applied Japanese-to-English word alignment. We report the performance of various alignment approach in terms of precision, recall and alignment error rate (AER) as (Och, 2003) defined. The quality of an alignment $A = \{(j, a_j)|a_j > 0\}$ is then computed by appropriately redefined precision and recall measures:

$$Recall = \frac{|A \cap S|}{|S|}, Precision = \frac{|A \cap P|}{|P|}, S \subseteq P \quad (18)$$

and the following alignment error rate:

$$AER(S, P; A) = 1 - \frac{|A \cap S| + |A \cap P|}{|A| + |S|} \quad (19)$$

The details are shown in Table 1. Figure 3 plots the average run-time of the currently available alignment approaches as a function of the number of input English-French sentence pairs. The HSSA approach is far more efficient. In total, aligning the

[4]http://www.phontron.com/kftt/index.html

			#	MatchRef	Prec	Rec	AER
Ref			33,377				
`GIZA++`	+	GDFA	31,342	18,641	59.48	55.85	42.39
`fast_align`	+	GDFA	25,368	14,076	55.49	42.17	52.08
`GIZA++`	+	HSSA	43,257	15,209	35.16	45.57	60.31
`fast_align`	+	HSSA	43,070	14,950	34.71	44.79	60.89

Table 1: Word alignments comparison on Japanese-English data in terms of matches number, precision, recall and alignment error rate (AER). GDFA: an abbreviation of *grow-diag-final-and*. HSSA: an abbreviation of hierarchical sub-sentential alignment.

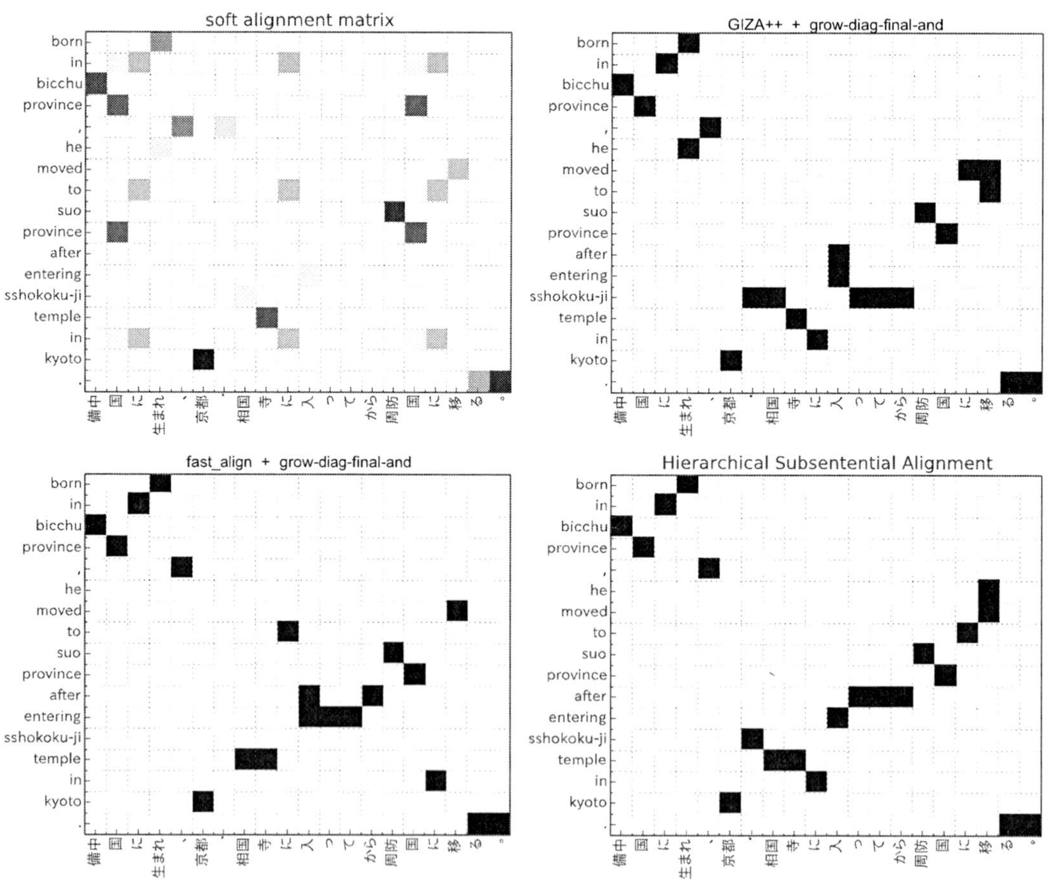

Figure 3: Comparison of alignments output by various tools. The test sentence pair is sampled from KFTT corpus. We fed HSSA with the lexical translation table relying on the output of `GIZA++`. In this example, our proposed approach (`GIZA++ + HSSA`) generates a better alignment than `GIZA++ + GDFA` or `fast_align + GDFA`.

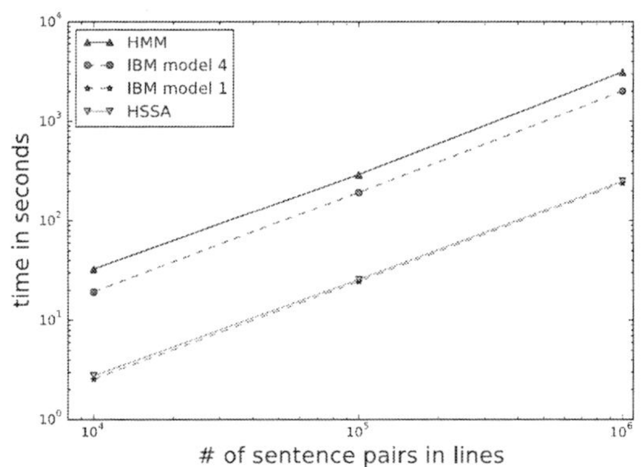

Figure 4: Average word alignment run-time (in seconds) as a function of the size of a corpus (in sentence pairs). Remember that, given the lexical translation probabilities, HSSA runs only in one iteration.

10K sentence pairs in the corpus completed in nearly 20 second with the HSSA approach but required more time with the other EM-based approaches.

In Table 1, Precision of our proposed approach are lower than baseline system, but Recall are better than fast_align + GDFA. However, it has been proved (Fraser and Marcu, 2007; Ganchev et al., 2008) that AER does not imply a better translation accuracy (see Table 3).

5.2 Translation Experiments

In this section, we first describe the data used in our experiments. We then perform to extract the lexical translation probabilities. Finally, we conduct translation experiments using both the baseline system (GIZA++) and the system using HSSA approach combined with to show, given a reliable lexical translation table for soft alignment matrix, the effectiveness of our proposed integrated system. We also investigate the time cost and the influence on the SMT frameworks.

In order to evaluate the proposed method, we conducted translation experiments on two corpora: Europarl Corpus and KFTT corpus. For English-Japanese (en-ja) and Japanese-English (ja-en), we evaluated on the KFTT corpus. For English-Finnish (en-fi), Spanish-Portuguese (es-pt) and English-French (en-fr), we measure the translation metrics

	Train	Tune	Test
Europarl v7	183K	1K	2K
KFTT	330K	1.2K	1.2K

Table 2: Statistics on the parallel corpus used in the experiments (K=1,000 lines).

on Europarl Corpus v7[5]. The baseline systems are using GIZA++ to train as generally.

In our experiments, standard phrase-based statistical machine translation systems were built by using the Moses toolkit (Koehn et al., 2007), Minimum Error Rate Training (Och, 2003), and the KenLM language model (Heafield, 2011). Default training pipeline for phrase-based SMT in is adopt with default *distortion-limit* 6. For the evaluation of machine translation quality, some standard automatic evaluation metrics have been used, like BLEU (Papineni et al., 2002), NIST (Doddington, 2002) and RIBES (Isozaki et al., 2010) in all experiments. When compared with the baseline system (GIZA++ + GDFA), there is no significant difference on the final results of machine translation between using the alignments output by the proposed approach and GIZA++.

6 Conclusion

In this paper, we studied an ITG-based bilingual word alignment method which recursively segments the sentence pair on the basis of a soft alignment matrix. There are several advantages in our proposed method. Firstly, when combining the proposed method with word association probabilities (lexical translation table), it is more reasonable to obtain symmetrical alignments using the proposed method rather than *grow-diag-final-and*. In other words, this method provides an alternative to *grow-diag-final-and* for symmetrization of word alignments. It achieves a similar speed compared to the simplest IBM model 1. Second, HSSA points a new way to real-time word alignment. For the tasks of processing same domain document, HSSA makes it possible to reuse the pre-built crossing-language information, likes bilingual lexical translation table. In our experiment, it has demonstrated that our proposed method achieves comparable accuracies compared

[5] http://www.statmt.org/europarl/

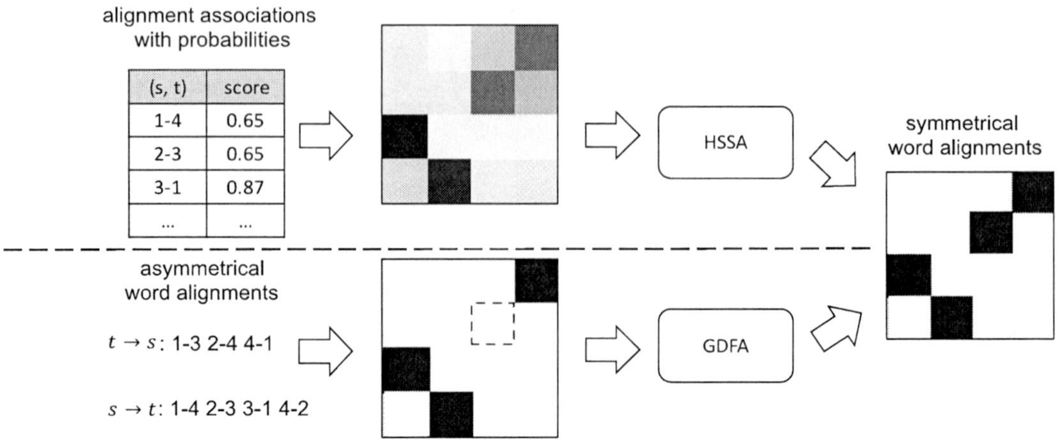

Figure 5: Our proposed approach starts from alignment associations with some probabilities, which is different from the standard phrase-based SMT pipeline.

				BLEU	NIST	TER	WER	RIBES
en-fr	`GIZA++`	+	GDFA	54.40	9.483	34.37	30.19	91.22
	`GIZA++`	+	HSSA	**54.42**	9.542	34.07	30.08	91.25
	`fast_align`	+	GDFA	54.10	9.438	34.63	30.45	91.14
	`fast_align`	+	HSSA	54.05†	9.417	34.72	30.58	91.11
es-pt	`GIZA++`	+	GDFA	49.34	9.182	35.97	31.74	90.62
	`GIZA++`	+	HSSA	49.32	8.980	36.99	32.44	90.30
	`fast_align`	+	GDFA	**49.70**	92.06	35.46	31.30	90.79
	`fast_align`	+	HSSA	49.51	9.203	35.59	31.38	90.79
en-fi	`GIZA++`	+	GDFA	**36.61**	6.608	47.08	41.36	87.03
	`GIZA++`	+	HSSA	35.15‡	6.448	47.71	42.18	86.60
	`fast_align`	+	GDFA	36.11	6.669	46.69	41.29	87.01
	`fast_align`	+	HSSA	35.88†	6.492	47.32	41.69	86.75
en-ja	`GIZA++`	+	GDFA	**21.59**	5.632	74.12	74.99	68.10
	`GIZA++`	+	HSSA	21.22	5.585	74.26	73.30	67.84
	`fast_align`	+	GDFA	20.80‡	5.592	74.50	74.33	68.13
	`fast_align`	+	HSSA	21.23	5.590	74.35	75.48	68.01
ja-en	`GIZA++`	+	GDFA	**18.78**	5.730	71.25	68.30	65.87
	`GIZA++`	+	HSSA	18.38	5.659	70.61	68.40	65.53
	`fast_align`	+	GDFA	18.23	5.628	71.26	68.01	65.25
	`fast_align`	+	HSSA	18.24	5.659	70.61	68.27	65.46

Table 3: Comparison of translation results using various configurations, `GIZA++` or `fast_align` with *grow-diag-final-and* (GDFA) or hierarchical subsentential alignment (HSSA). Bold surfaces indicate the best BlEU score in each group. No significant difference between directly `GIZA++` + GDFA with our proposed method except en-fi. Statistical significantly difference in BLEU score at ‡: $p < 0.01$ and †: $p < 0.05$ compared with `GIZA++` + GDFA.

with a state-of-the-art baseline. Finally, compared with original HSSA, the advantages of our implementation includes well-formulated, shorter computation times spent, armed with smoothing technique.

For future work, we think of designing a beam-search variation to make it possible to generate several parsing derivations during recursive segmentation. This will allow us to investigate recombinations of different derivations in order to obtain more possible alignments.

Acknowledgments

This work is supported in part by China Scholarship Council (CSC) under the CSC Grant No.201406890026. We also thank the anonymous reviewers for their insightful comments.

References

Peter F. Brown and John Cocke and Stephen A. Della-Pietra and Vincent J. Della-Pietra and Frederick Jelinek and Robert L. Mercer and Paul Rossin. 1988. A Statistical Approach to Language Translation. *Proceedings of the International Conference on Computational Linguistics (COLING).*

Peter F. Brown, Vincent J. Della Pietra, Stephen A Della Pietra and Robert L. Mercer 1988. The mathematics of statistical machine translation: Parameter estimation. *Computational linguistic.* volume 19 (2): pp.263–311. MIT Press

M. Amin Farajian, Nicola Bertoldi and Marcello Federico. 2014. Online word alignment for online adaptive machine translation. *EACL.* 84.

Philipp Koehn. 2003. Statistical machine translation. *Cambridge University Press* , 2009.

Percy Liang, Ben Taskar and Dan Klein. 2006. Alignment by agreement. *Proceedings of the main conference on Human Language Technology Conference of the North American Chapter of the Association of Computational Linguistics.* Association for Computational Linguistics.

Franz Josef Och and Hermann Ney. 2003. A systematic comparison of various statistical alignment models. *Computational linguistic.* 29.1: pp.19-51

Och, Franz Josef, and Hermann Ney. "A systematic comparison of various statistical alignment models." .

Philipp Koehn, Franz Josef Och and Daniel Marcu. 2003. *Statistical phrase-based translation.* Proceedings of the 2003 Conference of the North American Chapter of the Association for Computational Linguistics on Human Language Technology-Volume 1. Association for Computational Linguistics.

Kuzman Ganchev, Joao V Grac a and Ben Taskar. 2008. Better alignments= better translations? *ACL-08: HLT.* Association for Computational Linguistics. page 986.

Martin Kay 1997. The proper place of men and machines in language translation. *machine translation,* 12, 1-2. Springer. pp.3–23

Min Zhang, Hongfei Jiang and AiTi Aw and Jun Sun and Sheng Li and Chew Limu Tan. 2003. A tree-to-tree alignment-based model for statistical machine translation. *MT-Summit-07.* pp.535–542

Chenchen Ding, Masao Utiyama and Eiichiro Sumita. 2015. Improving fast align by Reordering. *Proceedings of the 2015 Conference on Empirical Methods in Natural Language Processing.*

David Chiang. 2005. A hierarchical phrase-based model for statistical machine translation. *Proceedings of the 43rd Annual Meeting on Association for Computational Linguistics.* Association for Computational Linguistics.

Kishore Papineni, et al. 2002. BLEU: a method for automatic evaluation of machine translation. *In Proceedings of the 40th annual meeting on association for computational linguistics. Association for Computational Linguistics.* p. 311-318.

Philipp Koehn, et al. 2007. Moses: Open source toolkit for statistical machine translation. *Proceedings of the 45th annual meeting of the ACL on interactive poster and demonstration sessions.* Association for Computational Linguistics, 2007.

Adrien Lardilleux, François Yvon and Yves Lepage. 2012. Hierarchical sub-sentential alignment with Anymalign. *16th annual conference of the European Association for Machine Translation (EAMT).*

Stephan Vogel, Hermann Ney and Christoph Tillmann. 1996. HMM-based word alignment in statistical translation. *Proceedings of the 16th conference on Computational linguistics*-Volume 2. Association for Computational Linguistics.

George Doddington. 2002. *Automatic evaluation of machine translation quality using n-gram co-occurrence statistics.* Proceedings of the second international conference on Human Language Technology Research. Morgan Kaufmann Publishers Inc.

C Dyer, V Chahuneau and NA Smith 2013. A Simple, Fast, and Effective Reparameterization of IBM Model. *Proceedings of the Conference of the North American Chapter of the Association for Computational Linguistics: Human Language Technologies.* pp.644-649.

Ashok K. Chandra, Dexter C. Kozen, and Larry J. Stockmeyer. 1981. Alternation. *Journal of the Association for Computing Machinery,* 28(1):114–133.

Hongyuan Zha, Xiaofeng He, Chris Ding, Horst Simon, and Ming Gu. 2001. Bipartite graph partitioning and data clustering. *In Proc. of the 10th international conference on Information and knowledge management*, pages 25–32, Atlanta.

Franz Josef Och. 2003. *Minimum error rate training in statistical machine translation.*. Proceedings of the 41st Annual Meeting on Association for Computational Linguistics-Volume 1. Association for Computational Linguistics.

Hua Wu and Haifeng Wang. 2007. Comparative study of word alignment heuristics and phrase-based SMT. *Proceedings of the MT Summit XI.*

Alexander Fraser and Daniel Marcu. 2007. Measuring word alignment quality for statistical machine translation. *Computational Linguistics*. 33(3)

Dekai Wu. 1997. Stochastic inversion transduction grammars and bilingual parsing of parallel corpora. *Computational linguistics*.23.3: pp.377–403.

Jianbo Shi and Jitendra Malik 2000. Normalized cuts and image segmentation. *Pattern Analysis and Machine Intelligence, IEEE Transactions on*.22.8. IEEE. pp.888–905

Hongyuan Zha, Xiaofeng He, Chris Ding and Horst Simon and Ming Gu. 2001. Bipartite graph partitioning and data clustering *Proceedings of the tenth international conference on Information and knowledge management*. Association for Computational Linguistics. pp.25–32.

Evgeny Matusov, Richard Zens, and Hermann Ney. 2004. Symmetric word alignments for statistical machine translation. *Proceedings of the 20th international conference on Computational Linguistics*. Association for Computational Linguistics. pp.219.

J. Makhoul, F. Kubala, R. Schwartz and R. Weischedel,. 1999. Performance measures for information extraction. *In Proceedings of DARPA broadcast news workshop*. pp. 249-252.

J. Makhoul, F. Kubala, R. Schwartz and R. Weischedel,. 1999. Performance measures for information extraction. *In Proceedings of DARPA broadcast news workshop*. pp. 249-252.

Jae Dong Kim, Ralf D. Brown, Peter J. Jansen and Jaime G. Carbonell. 2005. Symmetric probabilistic alignment for example-based translation. *In Proceedings of the Tenth Workshop of the European Assocation for Machine Translation (EAMT-05)*, May.

Robert C Moore. 2005. *Association-based bilingual word alignment. Proceedings of the ACL Workshop on Building and Using Parallel Texts*. Association for Computational Linguistics,

Ana Guerberof 2009. Productivity and quality in MT post-editing *MT Summit XII-Workshop: Beyond Translation Memories: New Tools for Translators MT.*

Hideki Isozaki, Tsutomu Hirao,Kevin Duh, Katsuhito Sudoh and Hajime Tsukada. 2010. Automatic evaluation of translation quality for distant language pairs. *Proceedings of the 2010 Conference on Empirical Methods in Natural Language Processing.* Association for Computational Linguistics. pp. 944–952.

Kenneth Heafield. 2011. KenLM: Faster and smaller language model queries *Proceedings of the Sixth Workshop on Statistical Machine Translation*. Association for Computational Linguistics.

Event Based Emotion Classification for News Articles

Minglei Li, Da Wang, Qin Lu, Yunfei Long
Computing Department, The Hong Kong Polytechnic University,
Hung Hom, Hong Kong
{csmli, csluqin, csylong}@comp.polyu.edu.hk
danwang.km@connect.polyu.hk

Abstract

Reading of news articles can trigger emotional reactions from its readers. But comparing to other genre of text, news articles that are mainly used to report events, lack emotion linked words and other features for emotion classification. In this paper, we propose an event anchor based method for emotion classification for news articles. Firstly, we build an emotion linked news corpus through crowd-sourcing. Then we propose a CRF based event anchor extraction method to identify event related anchor words that can potentially trigger emotions. These anchor words are then used as features to train a classifier for emotion classification. Experiment shows that our proposed anchor word based method achieves comparable performance to bag-of-word based method and it also performs better than emotion lexicon features. Combining anchor words with bag-of-words can increase the performance by 7.0% under weighted F-score. Evaluation on the SemEval 2007 news headlines task shows that our method outperforms most of other methods.

1 Introduction

Emotion classification from text, an extension of sentiment analysis, aims at assigning emotional labels to a given text. It has wide applications such as customer review (Pang et al., 2002), emotion based recommendation (Cambria et al., 2011), emotional human-computer interaction (Hollinger et al., 2006), eLearning (Rodriguez et al., 2012), etc. It is also important to understand reader's emotion reactions for reading news articles as they may trigger emotionally charged reactions which may lead to serious social and political consequences. However, news articles are normally used to describe recent events. To maintain objectivity, writers normally avoid using subjectivity and emotion-linked words. Thus, current works on emotion analysis, which use more social media type of text, would not work well for news text.

Generally speaking, emotion classification can be done either at document level or at sentence level. In this paper, we focus on document level emotion classification for news articles. Due to the nature of new articles, we need to address two main issues: 1) How to obtain sufficiently high quality labeled news corpus for training and prediction; and 2) How to identify suitable features for this genre of text. To address the first issue, we make use of the crowdsourcing method to obtain labeled data for a set of news articles provided in ACE 2005 (Walker et al., 2006) and through appropriate filtering, to obtain a reasonably good emotion-labeled corpus. To address the second issue, we first investigate the commonly used features for emotion prediction, including N-gram, Part-Of-Speech (POS), and emotion lexicons (Lin et al., 2007). However, these features, suited for sentence level classification, seem to be noisy for document level classification. Since news articles mainly describe a specific event and based on psychological studies that event can trigger emotions (Cacioppo and Gardner, 1999), we further explore event related features for emotion classification. Our hypothesis is that for news articles, a specific set of event linked anchor words can trigger emotions of readers and are therefore more important than most of the other words which may not have relations to emotions. Here the anchor word means the keyword of an event, such as *"die", "accident", "bomb"*, etc. Our proposed approach identifies event anchor words and use them as features for emotion classification. The main steps involved in event anchor word extraction involves three steps: First, we make use of the ACE 2005 data as our raw source corpus where event information was already annotated and crowdsourcing is used to obtain emotion linked labels for the news articles. Second, we use the annotated event information to train a CRF model for event anchor words extraction. Last, the extracted event anchor words can then be used as features to train a classifier for emotion prediction. This is different from lexicon based method because lexicon based method relies on externally prepared knowledge. In contrast, anchor words are automatically extracted from training data to be used as features. The main contributions of this work include:

1. The construction of an important annotated resource for event based emotion analysis based on ACE 2005 English news articles which can be made available to the research community.
2. The identification of more suitable features for document level emotion classification of news articles without emotion lexicon, and a feasible feature extraction method, which can also be used by other event based applications. The proposed features are more effective than emotion lexicon features and can improve the performance when combined with the bag-of-word features.

The rest of the paper is organized as follows: Section 2 discusses related works for emotion classification. Section 3 introduces the construction of the annotated corpus as a training data resource. Section 4 presents our event anchor word extraction and emotion analysis framework. Section 5 gives performance evaluation. The conclusion and future work are summarized in section 6.

2 Related Works

Any method on emotion analysis must rely on an emotion model to provide a framework for emotion classification. Emotion models can be characterized as discrete models and coordinate based models. Discrete models include the most commonly used six emotions (Ekman, 1993), the eight emotion model (Plutchik, 1980), Ortonys 22 emotions (Ortony, 1990), and Xu's seven emotion models (Xu and Lin, 2008), etc. Dimension based models include evaluation-activation based models (Whissell, 1989) and valence-arousal based models (Russell, 1980; Mehrabian, 1996; Wang et al., 2015), which is widely used for emotion classification. When using dimension based models, emotion prediction becomes a regression problem to predict the values in the two axis (Wu et al., 2013). When using discrete models, emotion prediction becomes a multi-class classification problem, which is the most commonly used methods in literature. This two representation methods are well compared in (Calvo and Mac Kim, 2013).

One of the problems that hinder emotion analysis is the lack of training data. Annotated emotion corpus is relative scarce compared to other NLP tasks. Manually labeled emotion corpora include SemEval 2007 for news headlines (Strapparava and Mihalcea, 2007), RenCECps for blogs in both sentence and document levels (Quan and Ren, 2009), and NLP&CC 2013 for Chinese microblogs. Because of the rapid development of social networks, many studies also try to automatically construct emotion corpus from the web using reader added emotion tags as labels. Lin crawled a news article corpus based on the emotion related tags by readers from Yahoo!s news (Lin et al., 2007). Hashtags, emoticons, and emoji characters are also used as naturally annotated labels to construct large emotion corpus from social media (Bandhakavi et al., 2014; Mohammad et al., 2013; Wang et al., 2012). However, these naturally annotated labels often contain noise. A recent trend is to make use of crowdsourcing to obtain annotated data. Crowdsourcing can be reliable if some control strategies are properly used. Example of resources obtained by crowdsourcing include lexicons constructed by Hutto (2013) and Mohammad (2013).

Emotion classification can be categorized into 1) rule based methods and machine learning based methods. As an example of rule based systems, the work by Chaumartin (2007) uses a set of hand crafted rules based on common knowledge to analyze the emotions of news headlines. In another system, Strapparava (2008) represents each emotion and text using latent semantic analysis (LSA) and analyzes the corresponding emotion based on the similarity between the text and the corresponding emotions. Machine learning based methods, on the other hand, heavily rely on the availability of training data as well as good feature selection methods. Mohammad shows that the combined using of emotion lexicon and N-gram features is more effective than N-gram feature only (Mohammad, 2012). Quan makes use of emotional words based features and tries to apply them to different classifiers such as SVM, Naive Bayes, and decision trees for sentence level blog emotion classification (Quan and Ren, 2009). Based on word embedding, Chen uses a sentence vector in combination with ML-KNN for microblog data (Chen et al., 2014). Inspired by Poria (2014) that uses dependency features and CRF model, a segment-based method is proposed to extract sentence segments using dependency trees and the semi CRF model is used to label emotions of all the segments, and then the log linear model is used to infer the final emotion of the whole sentence (Wang, 2014). Similar idea is adopted by Wen (2014) where the data mining technique class sequential rules (CSR) mining is used to analyze the emotion of the whole microblog containing several sentences.

Based on psychological studies that events can trigger emotions (Cacioppo and Gardner, 1999), many studies propose event based emotion prediction methods. Tokuhisa extracts events that can trigger emotions from the web based on emotion words and uses k-NN to predict new text for dialogs (Tokuhisa et al., 2008). Extending from Tokuhisa (2008), Vu constructs an event corpus by first defining a set of seed events and then extends it using boot-strapping (Vu et al., 2014). Lee builds an emotion linked event corpus from Chinese stories (Lee et al., 2014). Li proposes a system to detect and extract the cause event in microblogs, and uses these events as features to train a classifier for emotion prediction in microblogs (Li et al., 2014).

3 Corpus Construction

In order to serve the objective of our work for event based emotion prediction on news articles, we need to first prepare an appropriate training data which is currently not available. With consideration of resources, we choose to use the crowsourcing platform to annotate the data.

3.1 Data Source

The raw data comes from the Automatic Content Extraction 2005 (ACE 2005), a complete set of multi-language training data for the ACE 2005 evaluation (Walker et al., 2006). In this work, we only use the English collection of Automatic Content Extraction 2005 (ACE 2005)[1] which contains 754 English texts collected from newswire (18.57%), broadcast news (39.79%), broadcast conversation (9.15%), web log (18.30%), UseNet newsgroups/discussion forum (8.22%), and conversational telephone speech (5.97%). Though not all of these texts are news articles, they are all descriptions about events, consistent for our event based emotion analysis for news articles. So we simply name this set of the data as the news articles in the rest of this paper.

The news articles dataset was originally created by the Linguistic Data Consortium (LDC) prepared for event identification. The news articles dataset already have annotated event related information such as the anchor words for events, event types and event subtypes. For example, in the below sentence, *114 people were wounded in Tues-day's southern Philippines airport*, it contains an event about *injury*. The event anchor word is *"wounded"* while the event type and subtype are *"Life"* and *"Injure"* correspondingly. This dataset is quite appropriate to serve as the training data for our work because it is highly related with event description. However, there is no emotion related annotation that can be used directly as training data for emotion analysis.

3.2 Data Annotation

In order to use this collection as training data, we need to identify the emotion associated with each article. For annotation, we choose the most commonly used emotion model (Ekman, 1993), which includes six discrete emotion labels: *anger, disgust, fear, joy, sadness, and surprise*, respectively. We also add the category, *neutral*, to be used for those articles which may not trigger any emotion. This label is partic-

[1] http://www.itl.nist.gov/iad/mig/tests/ace/2005/

ularly suitable for news articles. Naturally, different people may have different emotions even when reading the same text. Therefore, to eliminate bias by a single crowdsourcing contributor, we request each article to be annotated by 5 contributors. Obviously, there may be different labels given by different annotators. The principle is to use the majority as the label for each article. If the result has no majority, the filtering process after crowdsourcing is initiated. The annotation platform used is CrowdFlower[2]. To ensure quality of annotation, a quality control (QC) mechanism is included in CrowdFlower to prevent people from randomly labeling the text (and also possibly eliminate people who have low English proficiency). Inspired by Hutto (2014), the QC process is conducted through a four step process as described below:

1. A subset H of eight articles are labeled by the research team as the ground truth for QC purpose. We asked 3 persons in the research team to serve as experts to annotate a selected set of articles independently. The articles which received the same labels by all three people are used as the ground truth for future usage.

2. We choose a subset H_t (6 articles) from H as quality test data and the contributors who correctly labelled 80% in H_t are qualified for future batches of work. Here correctness means the label given by the contributor is the same as the ground truth.

3. In the real annotation tasks, we randomly pick one instance from H in every batch of 6 articles to test whether they are doing random labeling. Results by those who wrongly labeled the test instances are discarded and the person will not be given new tasks. Even though this added redundancy costs more for annotation, it gives us more assurance of the quality of acquired data.

4. After completing the annotation for each article, the annotators are asked to briefly give rationales for their choice of label. We randomly check the written responses to ensure that the contributors are not making random choices.

[2]http://www.crowdflower.com/

Type	**Pattern**	**%(Number)**	Non-Neutral
1	5,0,0,0,0	3.18%(24)	1.59%(12)
2	4,1,0,0,0	11.14%(84)	6.23%(47)
3	3,2,0,0,0	9.81%(74)	6.63%(50)
4	3,1,1,0,0	22.68%(171)	15.78%(119)
5	2,2,1,0,0	22.81%(172)	10.08%(76)
6	2,1,1,1,0	26.13%(197)	20.42%(154)
7	1,1,1,1,1	4.24%(32)	-
Sum		100.00%(754)	60.74%(458)
Fleiss Kappa		0.212	

Table 1: Crowdsourcing based annotation result

Table 1 shows the distribution of the seven types of patterns in the annotation result (including the articles in H. Different annotators may give the same article different labels. The first pattern (5,0,0,0,0) means that all five annotators gives an identical emotion label. The second pattern (4,1,0,0,0) means 4 people give the same label whereas one person gives a different label. The pattern (1,1,1,1,1) means that every annotator give it a different emotion label. The labels for text in H are also refined through the labels given by the contributors. The 3rd column in **Table 1** shows the distribution percentage (%) and total articles number (Number) and the last column shows the percentage for data that have one major label and falls into the non-neutral categories. Out of the 7 possible patterns, only 3.18% of data falls into Type 1, the best scenario where the same label is given by all annotators. In Type 7, everyone gives a different label and 4.24%(32 articles) of data falls into this category.

We use Fleiss Kappa value to evaluate the consistence between different contributors and the value of 0.212 indicates a fair agreement. The relatively low value of Fleiss Kappa indicates the difficulty in emotion annotation because emotions is very subjective depends a lot on the annotators. This is particularly true for event linked emotions as they can be dependent on the annotators' background and preferences such as religions, political stands, etc. Since emotion classification is naturally multilabeled and personal variations are also natural, we consider the data quality is reasonably good. However, for training purpose, we further filter the data and only retain those which have a major shared emotion. We consider five of the patterns to have a major shared emotion including Type 1 to Type 4 and type 6. If the major label is the neutral label, however, the data will be removed. In other words, only the articles that has non-neutral labels are used as training data. In fact, in our data, 22.28% percent of annotated data falls into the neutral class which is only natural for news type of text. Obviously, this is very different for text from social media. The Type 5 pattern indicates two major emotion labels with equal numbers. Only if one of the major labels is neutral, the data is retained. Finally, we obtain 458 (60.74% of 754) articles with an improved Fleiss Kappa value of 0.214 (fair agreement), which is slightly better than the original 754. The distribution of the 6 emotion classes for the 458 articles are listed in **Table 2**. Note that the ratio of the largest set to the smallest set is about 3.2. Compare to other genre of text, the training data is not so skewed as the emotion labels in social media based corpus (Chen et al., 2014). To support research in emotion analysis. We make the annotated data available.[3]

Major emotion	Number	Percentage%
Fear	41	9.0
Sadness	114	24.9
Disgust	36	7.9
Surprise	115	25.1
Anger	61	13.3
Joy	91	19.9
Sum	458	100.00

Table 2: Emotion distribution of obtained data

4 Our Proposed Method

Our method for classification consists of two parts: the first part is anchor word extraction and the second part is the appropriate classification method for emotion classification.

4.1 Anchor Word Extraction

Many emotion prediction methods use NLP related features such as N-gram, POS tags, and position information of lexical sequences because they can be easily extracted to train classifiers. The ACE 2005 data contains many annotated latent information can potentially be useful for event identification. The annotated data in ACE 2005 at the summarization level includes topic, event type, event subtype, and event anchor word, etc. However, without appropriate method to extract latent information for testing data, they cannot be used. Because of this reason, other than lexical features which we can extract using NLP tools, most of the annotation information in ACE 2005 are not used as it is difficult to automatically infer event related summary information. We choose to focus our attention on extract event anchor words (anchors for short) as our features because they are easier to extract. Generally speaking we can consider event anchor word extraction as a kind of keyword extraction. The only difference is that the keyword here is linked to certain event (indicated by actions), and thus events provide the cues to identify the corresponding anchors.

Problem definition: Given a text sequence, $X = \{x_1, x_2, \ldots, x_n\}$ where x_i is a corresponding word and n is the number of words in X. Our goal is to find one or more words $x_j, \ldots, x_k$ used to describe the event in X. This problem can be converted into a sequential labeling problem. The objective of sequential labeling is to find the corresponding label sequence $Y = \{y_1, y_2, \ldots, y_n\}$ where $y_i \in \{0, 1\}$; 0 means not an anchor word; 1 otherwise. As this is a typical sequential labeling problem, the Conditional Random Field (CRF) algorithm can be used for anchor word extraction, the same method used by Zhang for keyword extraction (Zhang, 2008). The most important performance issue for CRF is feature construction. In our algorithm, we consider a context window of 2 on both sides of an anchor. Since we can easily use NLP tools to identify POS tags, features considered for anchor words include both the context words and their POS tags. The CRF model is trained using our 754 news articles which already contain the anchor annotation.

4.2 Classifier for Emotion Classification

Popularly used supervised machine learning methods for classification include Nave Bayes, k-NN, SVM, random forest, etc.. Study by (Fernandez-Delgado et al., 2014) shows that, among the reviewed 179 classifiers, random forest achieves the best result, closely followed by SVM. Since this work focuses on the effectiveness of our proposed

[3] https://github.com/MingleiLI/ACE2005_emotion_corpus

features rather than a classifier, we simply choose SVM as our classifier because it is widely used for multiclass classification. We further adopt the one-vs-all strategy for multiclass classification.

4.3 Features Used for Emotion Classification

To train an emotion classifier, we investigate the following features which are potentially useful. All features are considered using a context window of 5. In addition to an anchor word, the 2 words on each side of the anchor are included.

1. **F1: Frequency of anchors** - Occurrences of an identified anchor word in an article.
2. **F2: Word similarity** - Similarity between anchors and all the other words in the article. The motivation is if more words with similar meaning occur, the emotion tendency is more apparent. Similarity calculation is based on Lin's similarity module of WordNet, which is based on information content (Pedersen et al., 2004).
3. **F3: Frequency of POS tag of anchors** - Occurrences of POS tags of anchors.
4. **F4: Frequency of POS tag of context** - Occurrences of POS tag of context words. context words are not used because our training dataset is small.

Based on the above features, we form different feature sets to evaluate the effectiveness of these features and select the best one.

5 Performance Evaluation

Evaluations are conducted for both the event anchor word extraction and the selection of features in emotion prediction.

5.1 Evaluation on Anchor Word Extraction

Since anchor words are used to identify events, anchor word extraction can use all the 754 news articles as training data. The Stanford POS tagger is used for POS tagging[4]. CRF++[5] is used for event anchor extraction. As the training data is relatively small, 10-fold, 5-fold and 3-fold cross validation are conducted to see the effect of data size to anchor extraction performance. Results are shown in **Table 3**:

[4]http://nlp.stanford.edu/software/tagger.shtml

[5]http://taku910.github.io/crfpp/

Fold num	precision	recall	accuracy	F-score
10	82.17	63.50	97.30	71.64
5	82.07	62.17	97.24	70.75
3	81.96	59.86	97.14	69.19

Table 3: Event anchor word extraction result

Table 3 shows that the size of training dataset does affect performance. However, the difference is mostly on recall. From 3-fold to 10-fold, the increase in F-score is only little over 2% when the training data size is increased by about 35%. Close examination found that the extracted anchors are very stable. In other words, they are very similar under similar event types and similar topics. Thus, they are very good representatives. For example, if a news text is about *injury*, it is highly likely that the text would contain anchor words such as *wounded* or *injured*. Anchor extraction is a special kind of keyword extraction, yet its performance is much better compared to the state-of-art keyword extraction (Hasan and Ng, 2014) which has F-score of 31.7% on news articles. In addition, event anchor extraction is different because general keyword extraction focuses on extracting only a few keywords for the whole article while anchor extraction focuses on on extracting keyword more at the sentence level where the event is described. Ultimately, we care if the extracted anchors do serve as good features for emotion classification.

5.2 Evaluation on Emotion Classification

We use LibSVM (Chang and Lin, 2011) as the SVM tool. Three sets of experiments are conducted. The first set tests the performance of different anchor based feature groups in emotion classification. The second set tests the effectiveness of our selected features compared to features used by other methods for emotion classification. We conduct the third set of experiments by applying our method to the publicly available dataset used in the SemEval 2007 task for emotion classification. This dataset is on news headlines which should also be qualified as event-based data (Strapparava and Mihalcea, 2007). In the **first** set of experiments, we use the 458 news articles as training and a 10-fold cross validation is used for testing. Out of the 4 feature presented in Section 4.1

(F1 to F4), our test plan tries four feature groups to explore the best feature combination as shown in **Table 5**. In the first feature group (FG1), only anchor words are used. The other three groups use the basic anchor words to be combined with an additional single feature. **Table 5** gives the F-score of the 4 feature groups with details on the performance of each emotion type. The Weighted F-scores in the last row is the micro average of individual F-scores.

Feature Group	F1	F2	F3	F4
FG1	Y			
FG2	Y	Y		
FG3	Y		Y	
FG4	Y			Y

Table 4: Feature combinations

Emotion	FG1	FG2	FG3	FG4
Fear	12.9	**21.8**	13.8	12.4
Sadness	44.4	36.0	**46.0**	40.6
Disgust	**6.50**	3.2	5.3	0.0
Surprise	**36.4**	31.1	29.5	22.4
Anger	18.8	15.9	**19.9**	14.5
Joy	30.0	27.0	**31.8**	30.2
Weighted F-score	**30.3**	26.5	29.5	24.7

Table 5: Performance of different feature combinations

Table 5 shows that the best feature group is FG1 which takes only anchor text using frequency as the feature. The POS tags of context words (FG4) is the noisiest and produces the worst result. The use of the additional POS tags for anchor words (FG3) does not give overall better result. Yet, it gives better performance in 3 emotion types. Compared to the other two features, it is the least noisy because the performance degradation is less than 1%. This may be because frequency information is already used by FG1, and the frequency of POS tags of anchors are largely represented. It is interesting to see that context word does not give overall gain in performance except in the Fear emotion type. We can generally conclude that using POS tags do not translate into overall performance improvement. The F2 similarity feature degrades the performance maybe because this similarity is based on semantic similarity, not emotional similarity. In conclusion, anchor word as single feature achieves the best performance and thus we only use anchor words in the following experiments.

In the **second** set of experiments, we compare our event anchor based (EA) features to features used by other works for emotion classification using news articles. The features used by other methods include (1) lexicon feature based method (LF) which simply use a given emotion lexicon as features; (2) Bag of word (BOW) (Mohammad, 2012); (3) LF plus BOW based method (LF+BOW) that combines BOW and LF by increasing the weight of words that occur in the emotion lexicon, and (4) feature combination of event anchor words with BOW (EA+BOW) which does not use any external knowledge. The lexicon for LF is from WordNet-Affect (Strapparava and Valitutti, 2004). The parameters of SVM are the same for all SVMs used in this experiment. The result of F-score is shown in **Table 6**.

Table 6 shows that LF achieves the worst result which indicates that classification based only on an externally provided lexicon is not enough for document level emotion classification. BOW and EA use training data supplied information without any external knowledge and achieve much better result than LF as they are learning based methods. Our event anchor word based EA method achieves 75.1% better result than lexicon feature and slightly better performance than BOW based method. In this experiment, the size of the anchor words is 890, far smaller than the size of BOW at 13,793. This indicates that fewer effective features can actually achieve comparable result. As combined features, LF+BOW achieves better result than BOW (when LF in BOW is given more emphasis), which is consistent with the result of (Mohammad, 2012). In EA+BOW, anchor words in the bag of words are also given extra weight, and the performance is increased by 2.1% compared to BOW, which translates to 7.0% improvement over using BOW alone and also 4.9% improvement over using LF+BOW. The experiment shows that event anchors are more effective features than emotion lexicon and bag-of-words for news article emotion classification. This validates our assumption that news articles trigger emotions through specific set of event anchor words. Just a note that experiments show that increasing the frequency LF or EA in LF+BOW and EA+BOW by 3 achieves the best result.

Emotion	LF	BOW	EA	LF+ BOW	EA+ BOW
Fear	4.0	20.3	12.9	**20.4**	18.4
Sadness	17.5	41.5	44.4	39.5	**48.5**
Disgust	6.5	4.7	6.5	**7.3**	4.7
Surprise	20.8	28.8	30.4	28.8	**30.8**
Anger	11.1	24.7	18.8	24.6	**30.2**
Joy	27.1	35.9	30.1	**40.6**	32.5
Weighted F-score	17.3	30.2	30.3	30.8	**32.3**

Table 6: Results on Crowdsourcing Annotated Data

The **third** set of experiments are conducted on the SemEval 2007 data to test the usefulness of our proposed anchor feature. The SemEval 2007 affective task contains 1,000 annotated news headlines for testing and 250 annotated headlines as development data (though labelled, but too small to be used as training data). The dataset is similar in genre although has much less content. In this experiment, we directly use the event anchor words extracted in the second set of experiment as the feature set. To make easy comparison to other methods on the same dataset, our classifier is trained using the 250 validation dataset and test on the 1,000 test dataset for both the EA method and the EA+BOW method. We list the top three systems in SemEval 2007 labeled by SWAT, UA and UPAR7. We also compare with the DepecheMood (DM) method (Staiano and Guerini, 2014) which uses emotion lexicon as simple features. Their emotion lexicon contains aroun thirty seven thousand terms from 25.3K crowd-annotated news. The performance evaluation in terms of F-score is shown in **Table 7**

Emotion	SWAT	UA	UPA R7	DM	BOW	EA	EA+ BOW
Fear	18.3	**20.1**	4.7	32	13.4	16.2	13.4
Sadness	17.4	1.8	30.4	40	29.9	**35.6**	27.9
Disgust	0	0	0	0	0	0	0
Surprise	11.8	**15.0**	2.3	16	6.9	10.6	14.6
Anger	7.1	**16.0**	3.0	0	0	12.4	12.6
Joy	14.9	4.2	11.9	30	34.5	16.8	**37.6**
Weighted F-score	14.5	8.6	11.9	**27.1**	22.0	18.7	**25.0**

Table 7: Results on News Headline Data

Table 7 shows that both of our methods (EA+BOW and EA) perform better than the top three performers of SemEval 2007 task with a large margin and BOW performs 17.6% better than EA news headlines are too short to identify anchor words. Secondly, the news sources of ACE is different from the news headlines in SemEval 2007. So the anchor word extracted from ACE may not cover the news headlines well. EA+BOW, however performs better (13.6% improvement) than BOW only, which indicates the usefulness of event anchors. However, comparing to the DM method, we are still behind by about 2.1%. This may be because we have only 890 anchor words extracted from only 754 news articles and the training data size of our method is only 250 news headlines, whereas the lexicon of DM comes from 25.3K documents and their lexicon size is 37K.

6 Conclusion and Future Work

In this paper, we propose a novel method to make use of event anchor words as features for emotion classification in news articles. The use of event anchor words is based on the intuition that a small set of semantically relevant features should be more useful than a large set of noisy features. Experimental results show that anchor words are indeed quite effective. Another contribution of this work is the establishment of an important annotated resource for event based emotion analysis based on the ACE 2005 English dataset. The first limitation of this work is that the dataset used to extracted event anchors is relatively small. The second limitation is anchor words associated with events may not be sufficient to represent an event as an emotionally linked event may also be related to other attributes such as who, when, where, and others. In the future, we can extend the method on a larger dataset and explore the use of topics, event types, and other information to further improve the performance.

Acknowledgments

This work is supported by HK Polytechnic University (PolyU RTVU and CERG PolyU 15211/14E).

References

Anil Bandhakavi, Nirmalie Wiratunga, Deepak P, and Stewart Massie. 2014. Generating a Word-Emotion Lexicon from #Emotional Tweets. In *Proceedings of the Third Joint Conference on Lexical and Computational Semantics (*SEM 2014)*, pages 12–21. 00000.

John T. Cacioppo and Wendi L. Gardner. 1999. Emotion. *Annual review of psychology*, 50(1):191–214. 01223.

Rafael A. Calvo and Sunghwan Mac Kim. 2013. Emotions in text: dimensional and categorical models. *Computational Intelligence*, 29(3):527–543.

Erik Cambria, Amir Hussain, and Chris Eckl. 2011. Taking refuge in your personal sentic corner. pages 35–43. Citeseer.

Chih-Chung Chang and Chih-Jen Lin. 2011. LIBSVM: a library for support vector machines. *ACM Transactions on Intelligent Systems and Technology (TIST)*, 2(3):27. 21969.

Franois-Rgis Chaumartin. 2007. UPAR7: A knowledge-based system for headline sentiment tagging. pages 422–425. Association for Computational Linguistics.

Tao Chen, Ruifeng Xu, Qin Lu, Bin Liu, Jun Xu, Lin Yao, and Zhenyu He. 2014. A Sentence Vector Based Over-Sampling Method for Imbalanced Emotion Classification. In *Computational Linguistics and Intelligent Text Processing*, pages 62–72. Springer.

Paul Ekman. 1993. Facial expression and emotion. *American psychologist*, 48(4):384.

Manuel Fernandez-Delgado, Eva Cernadas, Senen Barro, and Dinani Amorim. 2014. Do we Need Hundreds of Classifiers to Solve Real World classification problems. *Journal of Machine Learning Research*, Microtome Publishing, No. 15, pp. 3133-3181 , 2014.:3133–3181.

Kazi Saidul Hasan and Vincent Ng. 2014. Automatic Keyphrase Extraction: A Survey of the State of the Art. *Proceedings of the 52nd Annual Meeting of the Association for Computational Linguistics (Volume 1: Long Papers)*, 1:1262–1273. 00006.

Geoffrey A Hollinger, Yavor Georgiev, Anthony Manfredi, Bruce A Maxwell, Zachary A Pezzementi, and Benjamin Mitchell. 2006. Design of a social mobile robot using emotion-based decision mechanisms. pages 3093–3098. IEEE.

C. J. Hutto and Eric Gilbert. 2014. VADER: A parsimonious rule-based model for sentiment analysis of social media text. In *Proceedings of the Eighth International Conference on Weblogs and Social Media, ICWSM 2014, Ann Arbor, Michigan, USA, June 1-4, 2014*. 00010.

Sophia Lee, Shoushan Li, and Chu-Ren Huang. 2014. Annotating Events in an Emotion Corpus. *Proceedings of the Ninth International Conference on Language Resources and Evaluation (LREC-2014)*. 00000.

Chengxin Li, Huimin Wu, and Qin Jin. 2014. Emotion Classification of Chinese Microblog Text via Fusion of BoW and eVector Feature Representations. In *Natural Language Processing and Chinese Computing*, pages 217–228. Springer.

Kevin Hsin-Yih Lin, Changhua Yang, and Hsin-Hsi Chen. 2007. What emotions do news articles trigger in their readers? pages 733–734. ACM.

Albert Mehrabian. 1996. Pleasure-arousal-dominance: A general framework for describing and measuring individual differences in temperament. *Current Psychology*, 14(4):261–292.

Saif M Mohammad and Peter D Turney. 2013. Crowdsourcing a wordemotion association lexicon. *Computational Intelligence*, 29(3):436–465.

Saif M Mohammad, Svetlana Kiritchenko, and Xiaodan Zhu. 2013. NRC-Canada: Building the state-of-the-art in sentiment analysis of tweets. *arXiv preprint arXiv:1308.6242*.

Saif Mohammad. 2012. Portable features for classifying emotional text. In *Proceedings of the 2012 Conference of the North American Chapter of the Association for Computational Linguistics: Human Language Technologies*, pages 587–591. Association for Computational Linguistics.

Andrew Ortony. 1990. *The cognitive structure of emotions*. Cambridge university press.

Bo Pang, Lillian Lee, and Shivakumar Vaithyanathan. 2002. Thumbs up?: sentiment classification using machine learning techniques. pages 79–86. Association for Computational Linguistics.

Ted Pedersen, Siddharth Patwardhan, and Jason Michelizzi. 2004. WordNet:: Similarity: measuring the relatedness of concepts. In *Demonstration papers at HLT-NAACL 2004*, pages 38–41. Association for Computational Linguistics. 01145.

Robert Plutchik. 1980. A general psychoevolutionary theory of emotion. *Emotion: Theory, research, and experience*, 1(3):3–33.

Soujanya Poria, Erik Cambria, Grgoire Winterstein, and Guang-Bin Huang. 2014. Sentic patterns: Dependency-based rules for concept-level sentiment analysis. *Knowledge-Based Systems*, 69:45–63.

Changqin Quan and Fuji Ren. 2009. Construction of a blog emotion corpus for Chinese emotional expression analysis. pages 1446–1454. Association for Computational Linguistics.

Pilar Rodriguez, Alvaro Ortigosa, and Rosa M. Carro. 2012. Extracting emotions from texts in e-learning environments. In *Complex, Intelligent and Software Intensive Systems (CISIS), 2012 Sixth International Conference on*, pages 887–892. IEEE. 00021.

James A Russell. 1980. A circumplex model of affect. *Journal of personality and social psychology*, 39(6):1161.

Jacopo Staiano and Marco Guerini. 2014. Depeche Mood: a Lexicon for Emotion Analysis from Crowd Annotated News. *Proceedings of the 52nd Annual Meeting of the Association for Computational Linguistics (Volume 2: Short Papers)*, 2:427–433. 00000.

Carlo Strapparava and Rada Mihalcea. 2007. Semeval-2007 task 14: Affective text. In *Proceedings of the 4th International Workshop on Semantic Evaluations*, pages 70–74. Association for Computational Linguistics.

Carlo Strapparava and Rada Mihalcea. 2008. Learning to identify emotions in text. pages 1556–1560. ACM.

Carlo Strapparava and Alessandro Valitutti. 2004. WordNet Affect: an Affective Extension of WordNet. volume 4, pages 1083–1086.

Ryoko Tokuhisa, Kentaro Inui, and Yuji Matsumoto. 2008. Emotion classification using massive examples extracted from the web. pages 881–888. Association for Computational Linguistics.

Hoa Trong Vu, Graham Neubig, Sakriani Sakti, Tomoki Toda, and Satoshi Nakamura. 2014. Acquiring a Dictionary of Emotion-Provoking Events. *Proceedings of the 14th Conference of the European Chapter of the Association for Computational Linguistics, volume 2: Short Papers*, pages 128–132. 00000.

Christopher Walker, Stephanie Strassel, Julie Medero, and Kazuaki Maeda. 2006. ACE 2005 multilingual training corpus. *Linguistic Data Consortium, Philadelphia*. 00057.

Wenbo Wang, Lu Chen, Krishnaprasad Thirunarayan, and Amit P. Sheth. 2012. Harnessing twitter" big data" for automatic emotion identification. In *Privacy, Security, Risk and Trust (PASSAT),2012 International Confernece on Social Computing (SocialCom)*, pages 587–592. IEEE.

Jin Wang, K. Robert Lai, Liang-Chih Yu, and Xue-jie Zhang. 2015. A locally weighted method to improve linear regression for lexical-based valence-arousal prediction. In *Affective Computing and Intelligent Interaction (ACII), 2015 International Conference on*, pages 415–420. IEEE.

Zengfu Wang. 2014. Segment-based Fine-grained Emotion Detection for Chinese Text. *CLP 2014*, page 52.

Shiyang Wen and Xiaojun Wan. 2014. Emotion Classification in Microblog Texts Using Class Sequential Rules. In *Proceedings of the Twenty-Eighth AAAI Conference on Artificial Intelligence, July 27 -31, 2014, Qubec City, Qubec, Canada.*, pages 187–193.

Cynthia Whissell. 1989. The dictionary of affect in language. *Emotion: Theory, research, and experience*, 4(113-131):94.

Bin Wu, Erheng Zhong, Derek Hao Hu, Andrew Horner, and Qiang Yang. 2013. Smart: Semi-supervised music emotion recognition with social tagging. In *SIAM International Conference on Data Mining*, pages 279–287. SIAM.

Linhong Xu and Hongfei Lin. 2008. Constructing the Affective Lexicon Ontology [J]. *Journal of the China Society for Scientific and Technical Information*, 2:006.

Chengzhi Zhang. 2008. Automatic keyword extraction from documents using conditional random fields. *Journal of Computational Information Systems*, 4(3):1169–1180. 00063.

The interaction of politeness systems in Korean learners of French

Darcy Sperlich
Department of Applied Language Studies
National Kaohsiung University of Applied Sciences
Kaohsiung, Taiwan R.O.C.
darcy.sperlich@kuas.edu.tw

Jaiho Leem
Department of French
Yonsei University
Seoul, South Korea
jhl@yonsei.ac.kr

Eui-Jeen Ahn
Department of French
Yonsei University
Seoul, South Korea
ejeen.ahn@gmail.com

Abstract

This paper investigates how the French second person pronouns, *tu* and *vous*, are acquired by Korean learners of French. This is specifically approached from an interlanguage pragmatics research viewpoint, focusing upon the status of the learners' pragmalinguistic and sociopragmatic knowledge (whether they are explicit or implicit). It is hypothesized that Korean learners of French will face difficulties acquiring *vous*, but not with *tu* due to the similarities between French and Korean second person pronoun use in requests, mediated by their implicit/explicit knowledge. Using a discourse completion task and an error correction task, the findings support the hypothesis, showing the interplay between language transfer and their second language developmental status. Moreover, this was detectible by using a combination of tasks which allows pinpointing of knowledge used. The implications for explicit/implicit knowledge status in relation to the use of pragmatic knowledge are discussed against the degree of control learners have over *tu* and *vous*.

1 Introduction

One has a full understanding of how to be polite in one's own language, however when acquiring another language it is often the case that the first (L1) and second language (L2) express politeness norms differently. Furthermore, as politeness is embedded within a language's grammar system, language learners must have the grammatical competence along with the pragmatic knowhow to select and use politeness expressions appropriately in the target language being acquired.

The focus of this article is to investigate the system of politeness surrounding French *tu* and *vous*, from a Korean learner of French's perspective. The acquisition of *tu*/*vous* is no easy matter; syntactically it may be straightforward to acquire two pronominal forms and use them grammatically, pragmatically however it is very difficult as your grammatical competence will not be much assistance to you in selecting the appropriate form for the situation you might find yourself in (to be discussed). Moreover, this may be compounded by influence from your first language which may not have the politeness concepts the target language has, as illustrated by the below examples (the meanings follow the English):

1a) Do you know what time it is?
1b) Vous avez l'heure?
You have the time
1c) ø/nuh myutsiinji ah-seyo/-ni?
ø/you what time-INT know-HON Q/non-HON Q

In addressing someone when making a request, the English example (1a) shows there are no *tu*/*vous* forms used to indicate politeness, rather politeness here can be framed via choice of structures (e.g., *Would you mind telling me*... versus the above). French on the other hand (1b), uses *tu*/*vous* to express politeness according to whom you are addressing (simplified, *tu* is 'friendly' while *vous* is more 'respectful' – to be discussed), while Korean has an alternation between *nuh* and the null pronoun (the latter for more polite situations) in similar circumstances to French.[1]

Thus, it appears that in requests, Korean and French follow similar patterns in that the pronominal is selected according to the context, allowing for a strong possibility of observing Korean L1 influence on Korean learners' L2 French. Formally, the research question pursued in this article is thus: will there be positive transfer from Korean regarding the acquisition of French *tu* (i.e., they will use it correctly early on given similarities with *nuh*), and negative transfer regarding the acquisition of *vous* (i.e., they will use it incorrectly early on given the parallels drawn with the Korean null pronoun)? To the best of our knowledge, studies on the L2 acquisition of *tu*/*vous* in French have been largely restricted to Anglophone speakers (to be discussed), and there have yet to be studies involving speakers of Asian languages with complex politeness systems (e.g., Korean) thus filling an obvious gap in the field.

Theoretically, this study fits within the research program of interlanguage pragmatics (Bardovi-Harlig, 1999), here specifically focusing on the pragmalinguistic and sociopragmatic knowledge of learners surrounding *tu*/*vous*. Following the canonical definitions of Leech (1983) and Thomas (1983), pragmalinguistic knowledge is concerned with the use of linguistic forms to produce speech acts, while sociopragmatic knowledge is concerned with the appropriate use of those speech acts in context. Moreover, the investigation involves interlanguage transfer (in terms of failure; Thomas, 1983) and considers the conditions that might promote them (Takahashi, 2000).

In sum, Korean learners of French *tu*/*vous* acquisition necessarily covers both pragmalinguistic and sociopragmatic competence, as the learner must successfully assess the situation in order to convey their intended intention in the L2 using the appropriately selected form, while dealing with possible language transfer from their L1 Korean.

2 Politeness in French and Korean

The politeness systems of Korean and French are vastly different, yet there appears to be similarities in use surrounding the use of singular second person pronouns in both languages to express politeness.[2] To be very clear, we do not claim the systems are the same, and we do not focus on other areas of politeness (such as terms of address, honorifics, etc.) – our targeted focus is on the politeness alternations in singular second person pronouns.

Drawing from the literature (Gardner-Chloros, 1991; Peeters, 2004; Liddicoat, 2006; Coveney, 2010), the basic facts about *tu* and *vous* in French are that they are singular second person pronouns (*vous* is also plural). In a simplistic sense, *tu* is understood (by language learners at least) that it is used in informal situation (such as with friends), while *vous* is used in formal situations (such as talking to a police officer). In other words, following Brown and Gilman (1960), there is a power versus solidarity dimension (*vous* related to the former, *tu* to the latter). However, scholars such as Morford (1997) and Van Compernolle (2013) have pointed out that this is an overly simplistic understanding of *tu*/*vous*, as there are deep and complex social indexes that *tu* and *vous* are related to, which Brown and Gilman (1960) fail to capture (e.g., use of *vous* to create distance with someone familiar). Moreover, the factors that affect the use of *tu*/*vous* include age, sex, and gender of the interlocutors of the conversation, among others (see Morford, 1997, for further discussion).

The Korean system on the other hand has different social indexes to that of *tu*/*vous* in French; however, it does alternate between two address forms according to who is being addressed. These two forms are the null pronoun, basically used for formal situations, and *nuh*, used for informal situations (Sohn, 1999; Oh, 2011; Lee, 2014). The indexes underlying their use will obviously be different to French, but as pointed out earlier both languages share similarities between how they perform requests, in that in a formal

[1] Korean is more complicated than this, as it is also possible to use a null pronoun in a 'tu' context, as well as a term of address. The key is that *nuh* cannot be used for polite terms of address to a social superior, while there is no overt Korean counterpart of *vous*. This will be addressed more with our own data gathered from native Korean speakers.

[2] That is, between *tu*/*nuh*, however *vous* has no corresponding second person pronoun in Korean – a null pronoun is used instead (or a term of address).

situation *vous*/null pronoun are likely to be used, while *tu*/*nuh* appear more frequently in informal situations.[3]

3 Challenges acquiring *tu* and *vous*

Firstly, there have been no studies done on Korean learners of French acquiring *tu*/*vous*, hence the review draws from the literature that mainly focuses on Anglophone learners of French. These studies' main focus is on the sociolinguistic aspects of *tu*/*vous*, namely the sociopragmatics concerning their appropriate use in context, and how that is developed within a classroom/learning abroad environment. Moreover, many studies take a qualitative approach to understanding *tu*/*vous*, using interviews and learner reports to understand the learner thinking behind their *tu*/*vous* use. Thus, through reviewing important works in this area will we come to appreciate what difficulties Korean learners of French might face and how this will help inform our research focus.

The basic theme underlining these studies is that the acquisition of *tu*/*vous* is not straightforward, it is difficult to control and it needs to be addressed specifically in the learners' French language program if they hope to improve their simplistic understanding of *tu*/*vous*. This is multiplied by the fact that textbook treatment of *tu*/*vous* is usually limited to (along the lines) '*tu* is used among friends/people you know and *vous* is used with people you don't know/ more formal situations', noted in the literature (e.g., Van Compernolle, 2014). To check if this is indeed the case of French textbooks used in Korea, three popular textbooks (*Campus 1*, *Festival 1* and *Le Français Contemporain*) were surveyed and found equally to have the same issues.

The problems with acquiring *tu*/*vous* were noted at least two decades ago, for example an early study by Swain and Lapkin (1990) found that French immersion students studying in Canada had significantly different use of *tu*/*vous* compared to that of native speakers – attributed to the restrictions of a classroom environment. This was further supported by Lyster (1994) who pointed out that the classroom is limited in assisting the acquisition of sociolinguistic features of *tu*/*vous*, which requires native speaker interaction. In this vein, there have been studies in learner abroad contexts which trace the development of *tu*/*vous* of students in France (e.g., Kinginger and Farrell, 2004) noting the obvious improvements (given the native speaker input) while noting the struggles of the learners.

A teaching intervention study by Liddicoat (2006) found that beginner learners' of French understanding of *tu*/*vous* was poor, but after a 7 week course on *tu*/*vous* their knowledge increased greatly. Van Compernolle (2013) found similar results in learners' *tu*/*vous* development from a rigid rule based system to a flexible context dependent system. In another study by Van Compernolle et al. (2011) through a synchronous computer-mediated communication course of 12 weeks, it was noted that the grammatical competence of the learners was not related to their pragmatic competence surrounding *tu*/*vous*. This was seen by a degree of alteration between *tu*/*vous* use, showing at least the learners were not fully aware of the sociopragmatic effects of *tu*/*vous* use (further supporting what McCourt, 2009, found). Thus, it is possible to improve learners' *tu*/*vous* understanding in class conditions by giving students the needed pragmatic focus.

It can be seen that learners' control of forms is related to their pragmatic/sociolinguistic knowledge they have. Then, it is natural to consider how stable this knowledge source is given their *tu*/*vous* use variation. Dewaele (2002; 2004) studied learner reports of when they use *tu*/*vous* and found much more variation than native French speakers. In considering this lack of control, Dewaele hypothesized that learners must have a degree of grammatical competence before they have the relevant sociolinguistic knowledge developed. Moreover, Dewaele noted that learners' knowledge is necessarily explicit in the beginning, thus leading to the inconsistency. Implicit knowledge is well known for its role in automated language production, its development essential for L2 learners' development towards native-like proficiency (Ellis, 2009), as from the outset L2 knowledge is first explicit. This division of knowledge seems to suggest that it is a major factor that learners must develop in order to obtain native-like competence in *tu*/*vous* use.

It is this distinction that this study seizes

[3] This will be examined briefly with our own data in the results section.

upon, however not concerned with the grammatical knowledge but the knowledge state of the aforementioned pragmalinguistic and sociopragmatic divisions. That is, if Deweale is on the right track in attributing the explicit/implicit knowledge distinction to the learner's inconsistent use of *tu/vous*, then we can investigate this in-depth by considering their knowledge state of the pragmatic realm. Moreover, as the study is focused on interlanguage pragmatics, how language transfer interacts with the status of these knowledge sources is another key factor, as Deweale (2004) noted that even though some of his learners' L1 had a *tu/vous* system, this in fact did not assist very much with their understanding of *tu/vous* in their L2 French. These factors in acquisition will be the focus in the discussion after the results have been analyzed.

4 Methodology

This study utilizes two tasks to elicit *tu/vous* use and interpretation, a traditional discourse completion task (DCT) and an error correction task (ECT). These two tasks are used to elicit both the productive and receptive skills of the participants. This breaks from sociolinguistic orientated investigations (such as Belz and Kinginger, 2002; Kinginger and Farrell, 2004; Kinginger and Belz, 2005) using learner reports and learner interviews in order to provide a quantitative approach to whether or not language transfer is affecting their L2 French (more in line with Deweale, 2002; 2004).

The DCT consists of 8 situations (4 of which are distracters), two of which target a *vous* elicitation, and the other two elicit *tu*, an example of this below in (2):

(2) David est perdu dans Paris. Il veut aller à la tour Eiffel. Il veut demander son chemin à un monsieur en costume. Qu'est-ce qu'il dit?
David is lost in Paris. He wants to go to the Eiffel tower. He wants to ask the direction to a gentleman in suit. What does he say?

The second task is an error correction task, which specifically focuses on pragmatic appropriateness. Namely, participants are provided with a grammatical sentence (12 situations, 6 being distracters), however with an in/appropriate *tu/vous*, as (3) below.[4]

(3) David voit que son ami a l'air préoccupé. Il veut lui demander à quoi il pense: *À quoi pensez-vous?*
David sees that his friend is anxious. He wants to ask what he's thinking: *What are you thinking?*

There are 54 Korean learner of French participants (age range 20-30). They completed a standardized proficiency test, indicating their levels range from A2 to C1.[5] A French (N=30, age range 19-69) and Korean (N=30, age range 19-58) control group were established to understand the politeness strategies used in these two L1s.[6]

The DCT was scored as receiving '0' for a correct use of *tu/vous*, '1' for an incorrect use (or missing the pronoun, which is incorrect), and '0.5' for a use that was almost correct, e.g., the verb was modified for *tu* but the pronoun did not occur. If the participant avoided *tu/vous* use, this was excluded from the marking process (to be discussed). In the error correction task, '0' was given for a correct change to *tu/vous*, and '1' for an incorrect change. The test was completed in a lab-like setting, taking roughly 30 minutes to complete overall.

5 Results

The results of the DCT and ECT can be seen in Figure 1 below, for the Korean learners of French only. It shows three important pieces of information, the proficiency level, DCT and ECT overall performance, which can be tracked per participant. The left x-axis represents the scoring for the proficiency test, while the right x-axis lists the total percentage correct for the DCT and ECT. As a guiding example, participant 37 scored 66 in the language proficiency test, and performed at ceiling level in the DCT and ECT. Turning to the

[4] The participants were also tested in English in similar situations to understand their politeness strategies used. In fact, English is their L2 while French is their L3; however L2 refers to here as any language acquired after their first.
[5] Test provided by *Language Trainers*.
[6] The French and Korean native speaker groups performed as expected, at ceiling level. That is, both groups used the pronouns as described previously.

results, firstly, the DCT shows significant differences between the Korean learners of French (KLF) and French native speakers (FNS), KLF *m* = .07, *sd* = .14; FNS *m* = .00, *sd* = .00; *t* = 3.38, *p* = .001. FNS perform at ceiling level, while the KLF perform well but show some difficulties are present. The difference between the two groups are much more marked in the ECT, KLF *m* = .42, *sd* = .30; FNS *m* = .07, *sd* = .12; *t* = 7.52, *p* < .001. Thus, these results show that there is a definite difference between the two tasks which will be discussed.

Upon further investigation, the *vous* conditions in the DCT are done worse than the *tu* conditions when avoidance is factored in. What this means, is that currently in the above figure for the DCT cases where the pronoun is not used, this is not scored. Avoiding a piece of language one has difficulty with is a classic strategy, and to be sure this is not the adopted strategy by our FNS who clearly prefer using a pronoun. Therefore, recoding all avoidance cases to incorrect yields significant mean differences (*vous m*= .17, *tu m*= .07, *t*= 2.142 *p*= .035). Thus, avoidance of the *vous* form and its incorrect use occur more than with such cases involving *tu*. This will be further discussed.

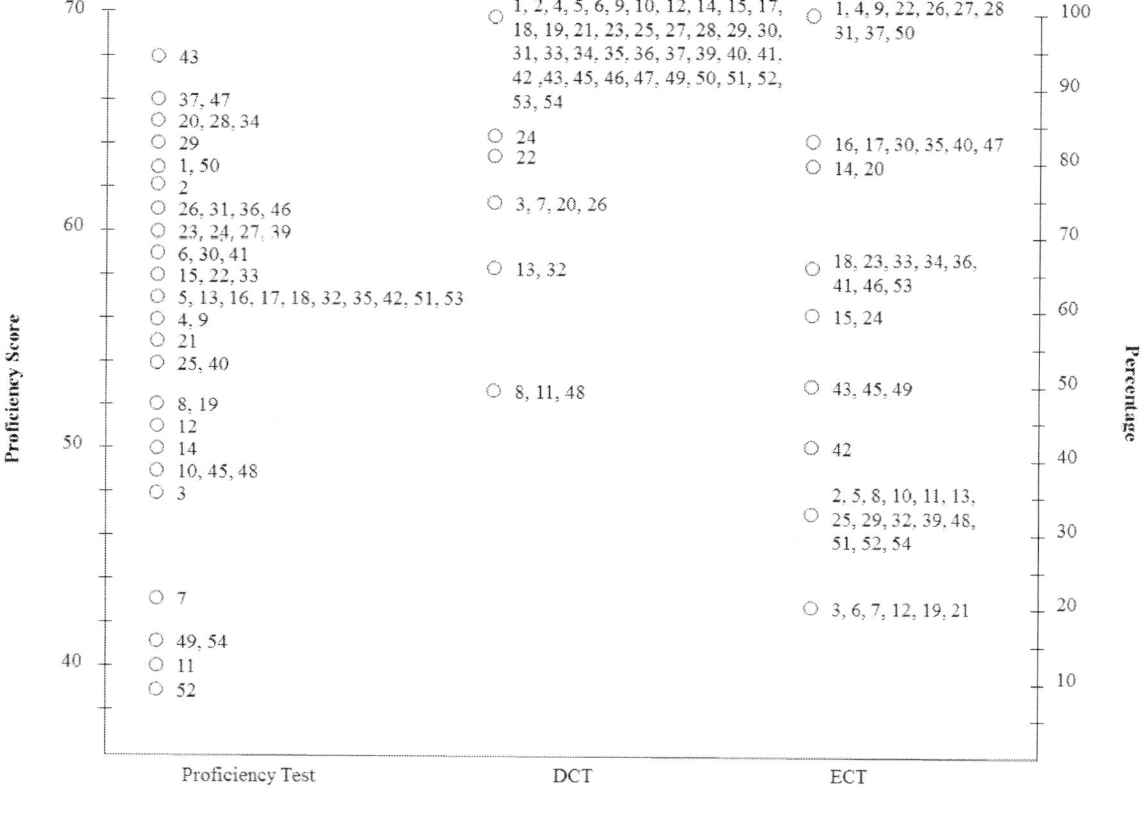

Figure 1. Participant Results in Three Tests

Finally in Korean, the null pronoun/*nuh*/term of address (such as 'teacher') used in Korean, our DCT results show that while null pronouns and terms of address are spread around in both 'tu' and 'vous' conditions, *nuh* is used in the less formal 'tu' condition, and does not occur in the 'vous' condition (Fisher's Exact, *p*< .001). Thus, Korean has the option to express 'closeness' with *nuh* and has been shown to be used to that effect, paralleling the use of *tu* in French.[7]

[7] The exact conditions of when null pronoun/*nuh*/term of

6 Discussion

The data analysis has revealed two important issues:

1. Why is there a performance difference between the DCT and ECT?
2. Within the DCT, why is there a difference between *vous* and *tu* treatment?

The latter issue is dealt with first, as it is relatively straightforward. As discussed previously, French and Korean are similar in the manner that both languages use a pronoun of address in familiar request situations (*tu* and *nuh* respectively). Learners with a lower proficiency perform well with *tu*, which can be attributed to their L1 strategies. This is also seen at the advanced levels as well (the border between transfer residue and full acquisition of *tu* is difficult to tell), thus it appears that the L1 transfer has been positive in nature, facilitating the acquisition of *tu*.

Applying this logic to *vous*, the transfer is instead negative in nature due to two patterns observed. Firstly, there are more cases of avoidance occurring at the lower levels than the higher levels (r= -.336, p= .016), being that no pronoun is used – in line with the Korean L1 strategy of polite request. Interestingly, in lieu of subject pronoun-dropping (which would result in ungrammaticality in French), some lower-level participants instead opt to establish reference via a strategy present in their L2 English (and L1 Korean), using something like 'Excuse me sir'. The higher proficiency groups have the pronoun occurring, but vary between *tu*/*vous* use, before *vous* use is stabilized at the highest proficiency level. In sum, using a null pronoun is ungrammatical in French, ruling out L1 transfer of this as the learners advance. Thus, in the 'vous' condition we see more use of terms of address before *vous* is more fully acquired, while in the 'tu' condition more use of *tu* is attributed to the availability of *nuh* due to the similarity of the L1 Korean politeness strategy *nuh* use in the same situation.

Moving back to the first question, it is hypothesized the difference in performance can be attributed to how the tasks tap the relevant knowledge sources, as well as the implicit/explicit status of this knowledge. The two knowledge sources dealt with are the pragmalinguistic and sociopragmatic knowledge surrounding *tu*/*vous*, whereby the DCT (productive) taps both knowledge sources more while the ECT focuses more on the sociopragmatic competence.

Concentrating on the ECT first, the responses are more variable than the DCT. Therefore, it can be argued that the knowledge source the learners draw upon is not implicit in nature, as implicit knowledge is needed in order for consistent language use (Ellis, 2009). This knowledge is thus explicit in nature, resulting in variable performance. Those learners that performed better (reliably correct) were at a higher proficiency level, furthering this hypothesis that the knowledge drawn upon is explicit at the lower levels. This knowledge source has been identified here as the sociopragmatic competence of the learner, which this task draws more from. Compared to the DCT, the ECT is not a productive task and therefore does not 'engage' the learner as much as the DCT does. What this means is that the ECT simply provides the form for the learners to read, without them having to produce it. In this way, their pragmalinguistic knowledge is not being assessed as much as the DCT because they do not have to choose from a variety of forms in order to produce the relevant piece of language. The sociopragmatic knowledge use is more focused on in the ECT because the learner should take into account more the situational context and assess the presented sentence against that context. It is clear from the DCT that all the learners have the grammatical knowhow surrounding *tu*/*vous* (in that sentences are not subjectless), but the ECT makes it very clear that many of the learners are not able to identify whether or not the *tu*/*vous* usage is correct against the presented situation. Therefore, the sociopragmatic knowledge is relied on more in the ECT task, and the consistency of responses can be attributed to the implicit/explicit nature of that sociopragmatic knowledge.[8]

---

address occurs go beyond the scope of this article and should be a target of future research.

[8] If the sociopragmatic knowledge is indeed explicit, then this would help explain the cases of variability seen in the DCT. On another note, the pragmalinguistic knowledge status has

To summarize the differences seen between the DCT and ECT, the DCT engages both pragmalinguistic and sociopragmatic knowledge more due to its productive nature.[9] The ECT on the other hand relies more on the sociopragmatic competence of the learner as it focuses more upon the contextual appropriateness of the sentence to the situation. This has resulted in more varied answers (learners have not noticed the errors as their awareness is not at a high level), allowing us to conclude that their sociopragmatic competence is not at the same level (lower) as their pragmalinguistic competence, which appears to be the case and finds support from the literature discussed.

So far, language transfer and knowledge source have been discussed, however the disconcert between implicit and explicit knowledge requires further discussion in how our observations reconcile with that of the literature. Dewaele (2002) in his research of *tu/vous* acquisition commented that L2 learners rely much more on their declarative memory system (equated to explicit knowledge), which can be seen more in the early stages of acquisition. Moreover, explicit memory use is related to variability in answers, as consistent production is related to implicit knowledge (Ellis 2009). Deweale's observations fall along the lines of Paradis (2004; 2009), who argues strongly for a non-interface division of knowledge types in L2 learners. Generally taken, implicit competence is understood through Paradis (2004; 2009) as knowledge that learners are unaware of yet that leads them to systematic language performance while explicit knowledge is understood as the knowledge that learners are aware of but not leading to the same systematic performance.

Thus, Dewaele (2002; 2004) hypothesizes that grammatical and sociolinguistic knowledge of *tu/vous* at the beginning of acquisition is explicit, and at the later stages of acquisition this knowledge shifts to implicit knowledge, based in the implicit memory. In relation to the data gathered here, some amendments are made to deal with the pragmatic-orientated data. Regarding the lower proficiency levels, both pragmalinguistic and sociopragmatic knowledge are explicit. At the intermediate levels, the pragmalinguistic knowledge shifts to the implicit mode, while sociopragmatic knowledge is explicit. Finally, at the advanced levels both knowledge types used are implicit.

Such a differentiation in knowledge at the implicit/explicit level neatly captures three different groups as can be seen in Figure 1; explicitly the higher proficiency learners have 100% correct performance in both the DCT and ECT, leading to the suggestion that both sources of knowledge are implicit. The intermediate and lower proficiency levels on the other hand share inconsistent answers in the ECT, but not in the DCT, thus the intermediate learners have implicit pragmalinguistic knowledge (like the advanced group) but their sociopragmatic knowledge is explicit (like the lower level learners). With the lower level learners, due to their inconsistency in the DCT, it is suggested that their pragmalinguistic knowledge is explicit (given the variety of strategies used, and inconsistent *tu/vous* use).

However, this might not be a completely correct characterization of the sociopragmatic knowledge along implicit/explicit grounds. Importantly, as it has been oft discussed in the literature (as reviewed) it is difficult to develop sociopragmatic knowledge in the classroom, especially with *tu/vous* given their complex social indexes. Thus, the best way to develop this implicit knowledge of *tu/vous* is to live in a native French speaking environment for some time. Therefore, at this stage we cannot rule out that the advanced proficiency learners' sociopragmatic knowledge is in fact explicit – however this needs to be reconciled with the explicit knowledge of the lower proficiency learners which leads to variability not seen in the advanced learners.

The answer may lie with Paradis (2004: 35-36), who argues that explicit knowledge may resemble implicit knowledge at an advanced stage. What this means is that learners have sped-up access to their explicit knowledge to the degree its processing resembles that of implicit knowledge. While appealing, explicit knowledge use is associated with inconsistency, and it is not clear that this 'advanced' explicit knowledge is related to

---

yet to be mentioned – if it is explicit at the lower levels, coupled with language transfer, then the product is inconsistent selection of forms, which is seen.

[9] Learners have the opportunity to bring both their implicit and explicit knowledge to the fore in both tasks.

consistent language use as implicit knowledge is.

7 Pedagogical Implications

The question of how to teach *tu/vous* in the classroom has been discussed by scholars such as Lyster (1994), Liddicoat (2006) and Van Compernolle (2014). Clearly, *tu/vous* are not just mere pronouns of reference but encode extremely important sociolinguistic information that must be used carefully in communication. It does not appear from the literature that there is an advantage of having a T/V system in a learner's L1 in their quest to acquire the L2, as demonstrated here. In the case of Korean learners of French, it is advisable to explicitly cover the preference for a *tu/vous* pronoun in a request, noting that request strategies transferred from Korean are not likely to encourage successful communication in French – especially surrounding *vous*. Our data shows that the sociopragmatic understanding of *vous* is successfully acquired at the advanced level (and *tu* earlier on), however this surely should occur much earlier on as if one cannot address someone with the most suitable pronoun in a request, then there is a chance for the request to fail its communicative function due to the addressee's perception of the pronoun's politeness suitability. In more general SLA terms, there needs to be a stronger focus in the classroom on such important phenomena as surely speaking somewhat ungrammaticality will be overlooked as long as a learner is able to address someone using the correct term. Of course, whether one would want to adopt a Sociocultural Theory methodology as espoused by Van Compernolle (2014) depends on one's classroom training and resources at hand; for this we provide no insight apart from the call that pronominal systems encoding important sociolinguistic information need to be consistently addressed in the classroom in order to facilitate their earlier understanding.

8 Conclusion

The politeness system behind *tu* and *vous* is undeniably complex, and presents clear difficulties to learners from any language due to the complex variables involved. However, the focused approach taken by this study unravels a little more of this complexity involving L2 learners; with Korean learners of French, it is clear that the acquisition of *tu* presents little difficulty due to positive transfer, while *vous* acquisition is clearly more problematic due to negative transfer. Moreover, the explicit/implicit state of the learners' pragmalinguistic and sociopragmatic knowledge are further factors affecting the use and interpretation of *tu/vous* – discovered using different task types. In conclusion, the *tu/vous* investigation presented here represents a piece of the puzzle regarding learner acquisition of these forms, the approach here adding to the literature from a non-Anglophone point-of-view.

Acknowledgements

We would like to thank the reviewers for their constructive comments, all the participants who made this study possible, Madame Berangère Lesage for her French language support and a Ministry of Science and Technology (Taiwan R.O.C.) grant 105-2914-I-151-004-A1 awarded to the first author which has partially supported this research.

References

Bardovi-Harlig, Kathleen. 1999. Exploring the interlanguage of interlanguage pragmatics: A research agenda for acquisitional pragmatics. *Language Learning* 49(4): 677-713.

Belz, Julie A. & Celeste Kinginger. 2002. Cross-linguistic development of address form use in telecollaborative language learning: two case studies. *Revue Canadienne des Langues Vivantes* 59 (2): 189-214.

Brown, Roger and Albert Gilman. 1960. The pronouns of power and solidarity. In T.A. Sebeok (Ed.), *Style in Language* (pp. 252-281). Cambridge, MA: MIT Press.

Compernolle, Rémi van. 2013. From verbal protocols to cooperative dialogue in the assessment of second language pragmatic competence. *Intercultural Pragmatics* 10(1): 71-100.

Compernolle, Rémi van. 2014. *Sociocultural Theory and L2 Instructional Pragmatics*. Bristol: Multilingual Matters.

Compernolle, Rémi van, Lawrence Williams & Claire McCourt. 2011. A corpus-driven study of second-person pronoun variation in L2 French synchronous computer-mediated communication. *Intercultural Pragmatics* 8(1): 67-91.

Coveney, Aidan. 2010. Vouvoiement and tutoiement: Sociolinguistic reflections. *Journal of French Language Studies* 20(2): 127-150.

Dewaele, Jean-Marc. 2002. Variation, chaos et système en interlangue française. *Acquisition et Interaction en Langue Étrangère* 17: 143-167.

Dewaele, Jean-Marc. 2004. *Vous* or *tu*? Native and non-native speakers of French on a sociolinguistic tightrope. *International Review of Applied Lingusitics in Language Teaching* 42: 383-402.

Ellis, Rod. 2009. Implicit and explicit learning, knowledge and instruction. In Rod Ellis, Shawn Loewen, Catherine Elder, Rosemary Erlam, Jenefer Philp and Hayo Reinders (Eds.), *Implicit and Explicit Knowledge in Second Language Learning, Testing and Teaching* (pp. 3-25). Bristol: Multilingual Matters.

Gardner-Chloros, Penelope. 1991. Ni tu ni vous: principes et paradoxes dans l'emploi des pronoms d'allocution en français contemporain. *Journal of French Language Studies* 1: 139-155.

Kinginger, Celeste and Julie A. Belz. 2005. Socio-cultural perspectives of pragmatic development in foreign language learning. *Intercultural Pragmatics* 2: 369-421.

Kinginger, Celeste and Kathleen Farrell. 2004. Assessing development of metapragmatic awareness in study abroad. *Frontiers: The interdisciplinary Journal of Study Abroad* 10(2): 19-42.

Lee, Narah. 2014. A reconsideration of the omission of first and second person subjects in modern spoken Korean: Focusing on the pragmatic meanings of the overt subject expressions. *Dahmhwa-wa inji [Discourse and Cognition]* 21(3): 145-163.

Leech, Geoffrey. 1983. *Principles of Pragmatics*. New York: Longman.

Liddicoat, Anthony J. 2006. Learning the culture of interpersonal relationships: Students' understanding of personal address forms in French. *Intercultural Pragmatics* 3(1): 55-80.

Lyster, Roy. 1994. The effect of functional-analytic teaching on aspects of French immersion students' sociolinguistic competence. *Applied Linguistics* 15: 263-287.

McCourt, Claire. 2009. Pragmatic variation among learners of French in real-time chat communcation. In R. Oxford & J. Oxford (Eds.), *Second langauge Teaching and Learning in the Net Generation* (pp. 143-154). Honolulu: University of Hawai'i.

Morford, Janet. 1997. Social indexicality in French pronominal address. *Journal of Linguistic Anthropology* 7(1): 3-37.

Oh, Myungki. 2011. A pragmatic/sociolinguistic approach to 2nd person pronominal in English and Korean. *Hyundai Munbup yungoo [Studies in Modern Grammar]* 66: 273-289.

Paradis, Michel. 2004. *A Neurolinguistic Theory of Bilingualism*. Amsterdam: John Benjamins.

Paradis, Michel. 2009. *Declarative and Procedural Determinants of Second Languages*. Amsterdam: John Benjamins.

Peeters, Bert. 2004. To ou vous? *Zeitschrift für französische sprache und literatur* 114(1): 1-17.

Sohn, Ho-Min, 1999. *The Korean Language*. Cambridge University Press: Cambridge.

Swain, M. and S. Lapkin. 1990. Aspects of the sociolinguistic performance of early and late French immersion students. In R. Scarcella, E. Andersen & S. Krashen (Eds.), *Developing Communicative Competence in a Second Language* (pp. 41-54). New York: Newbury House.

Takahashi, Satomi. 2000. Transfer in interlanguage pragmatics: New research agena. *Studies in Languages and Cultures* 11: 109-28.

Thomas, Jenny. 1983. Cross-cultural pragmatic failure. *Applied Linguistics* 4: 91-112.

Integrating Word Embedding Offsets into the Espresso System for Part-Whole Relation Extraction

Van-Thuy Phi
Nara Institute of Science and Technology
Computational Linguistics Laboratory
8916-5 Takayama, Ikoma, Nara Japan
phi.thuy.ph8@is.naist.jp

Yuji Matsumoto
Nara Institute of Science and Technology
Computational Linguistics Laboratory
8916-5 Takayama, Ikoma, Nara Japan
matsu@is.naist.jp

Abstract

Part-whole relation, or *meronymy* plays an important role in many domains. Among approaches to addressing the part-whole relation extraction task, the Espresso bootstrapping algorithm has proved to be effective by significantly improving recall while keeping high precision. In this paper, we first investigate the effect of using fine-grained subtypes and careful seed selection step on the performance of extracting part-whole relation. Our multitask learning and careful seed selection were major factors for achieving higher precision. Then, we improve the Espresso bootstrapping algorithm for part-whole relation extraction task by integrating word embedding approach into its iterations. The key idea of our approach is utilizing an additional ranker component, namely *Similarity Ranker* in the Instances Extraction phase of the Espresso system. This ranker component uses embedding offset information between instance pairs of part-whole relation. The experiments show that our proposed system achieved a precision of 84.9% for harvesting instances of the part-whole relation, and outperformed the original Espresso system.

1 Introduction

A major information extraction task is relation extraction, whose goal is to predict semantic relations between entities or events expressed in the structured or unstructured text. There are several different kinds of semantic relations that connect two or more concepts. Among those semantic relations, *part-whole* relation, or *meronymy* plays an important role in many domains and applications. Extracting part-whole relations in the text is also a crucial step towards applications in several fields, such as Information Extraction, Web/Text Mining and Ontology Building. Such systems often need to recognize part-whole relations for better understanding semantic relationships between concepts. Therefore, in our research, we aim at extraction of part-whole relation. We are interested in relations between entities in the newswire domain.

Among approaches to addressing the part-whole relation extraction problem, the Espresso bootstrapping algorithm (Pantel and Pennacchiotti, 2006) has proved to be effective by significantly improving recall while keeping high precision. Espresso is a well-known bootstrapping algorithm that uses a set of seed instances to induce extraction patterns for the target relation and then acquire new instances in an iterative bootstrapping manner. Nevertheless, it has a bias, called *semantic drift,* to select unrelated instances if a polysemous instance has been extracted as the iteration proceeds.

Recently, Mikolov et al. (2013) have introduced the skip-gram text modeling architecture. It has been shown efficiently to learn meaningful distributed representations of terms from unannotated text. The vectors have some of the semantic characteristics in element-wise addition and subtraction. For example, the result of a vector subtraction vec("*Madrid*") - vec("*Spain*") is close to vector subtraction vec("*Paris*") - vec("*France*"). That is an example of *the country to capital city* relationship. It indicates that the embedding offsets represent the shared semantic relation between the two word pairs.

The example above raises a question whether we can apply those semantic characteristics for part-whole relation? In this paper, we would like to address two important questions:

1. Is Word2Vec model appropriate for pairs of part-whole relation? That is, we investigate typical instances of part-whole relation to measure their similarities by cosine distance.

2. How to integrate Word2vec model efficiently into the Espresso system?

The details of our contribution are as follows:

- We apply the Espresso bootstrapping algorithm for part-whole relation, and study the effect of using careful seed sets and fine-grained subtypes on the performance of extracting part-whole relation.

- We investigate similarities between two instances of the part-whole relation. Then, we integrate an additional ranker component into the Espresso bootstrapping algorithm to improve the performance when using iterative bootstrapping process and reduce semantic drift phenomenon for extracting part-whole relation. That ranker component uses similarity score between embedding offsets to keep similar instances in each iteration.

To the best of our knowledge, ours is the first study to integrate word embedding approach in a bootstrapping algorithm for part-whole relation extraction task.

2 Related Work

In this section, we provide an overview of previous studies related to relation extraction problem. Approaches for relation extraction are divided into three classes: rule-based methods, supervised methods, and semi-supervised and unsupervised methods.

The first approach is usually used in domain-specific tasks. Systems which use this one rely on some linguistic rules to capture patterns in text. Patterns are manually defined for a particular semantic relation. Hearst (1992) describes the usage of lexico-syntactic patterns for extracting *"is-a"* relations, for example, *"such as"*, *"including"*, *"especially"*, etc. However, the author notes that this method does not work well for some other kinds of relations, for example, meronymy (part-whole relation).

Supervised approaches for relation extraction are divided into feature-based methods and kernel methods. In feature-based methods, syntactic and semantic features can be extracted from the text given a set of positive and negative relation examples. Kambhatla (2004) employs Maximum Entropy model to combine diverse lexical, syntactic and semantic features derived from the text in relation extraction. Zhou et al. (2005) explore various features in relation extraction using Support Vector Machine (SVM). They report that chunking information contributes to most of the performance improvement from the syntactic aspect. In kernel methods, a kernel is used to calculate the similarity between two objects. Kernel-based relation extraction methods were first attempted by Zelenco et al. (2003). They devise contiguous subtree kernels and sparse subtree kernels for recursively measuring the similarity of two parse trees to apply them to binary relation extraction. Bunescu and Mooney (2005) present a different kernel based on the shortest path between two relation entities in the dependency graph. Zhao and Grishman (2005) define a feature-based composite kernel to integrate diverse features for relation extraction. Girju et al. (2006) present a domain independent approach for the automatic extraction of part-whole relation. Their method discovers the lexico-syntactic patterns and the semantic classification rules needed for the disambiguation of these patterns.

Annotated data is lacking and expensive to create in large quantities, therefore making semi-supervised or unsupervised techniques is desirable. Early semi-supervised learning and bootstrapping methods are DIPRE (Brin, 1999) and Snowball (Agichtein and Gravano, 2000). They rely on a few learning collections for making the use of bootstrapping for gathering syntactic patterns that express relations between the two entities in a large web-based text corpus. Ittoo and Bouma (2013) use a minimally-supervised approach to extract part-whole relations from text iteratively. Wikipedia is the knowledge base, from which they first select a seed set of reliable patterns. Other works include Espresso bootstrapping algorithm (Pantel and Pennacchiotti, 2006), TextRunner (Yates et al., 2007).

3 Part-Whole Relation Extraction Task

The part-whole relation is a relationship between the parts of things and the wholes which comprise them. We are interested in relations between two entities in the English newswire domain. If the entities X and Y are related in such a manner that X is one of the constituents of Y, then there is a part-whole relation between X and Y. In the context of knowledge representation and ontologies, the study of part-whole relations has three axioms (Rector et al., 2005):

- Transitive - "*parts of parts are parts of the whole*" - If A is part of B and B is part of C, then A is part of C.
- Reflexive - "*Everything is part of itself*" - A is part of A.
- Antisymmetric - "*Nothing is a proper part of its parts*" - if A is part of B and A != B then B is not part of A.

Given a piece of text that contains two entity mentions, the goal of part-whole relation extraction task is to decide whether that text contains part-whole relation between the two entities. Let the triple T = *(arg1, P, arg2)* denote a part-whole relation, where *arg1* and *arg2* are two entities contained in text, and:

- *P* is a lexical pattern,
- *(arg1, arg2)* is an instance, where *arg1* represents the part and *arg2* represents the whole, or vice versa.

4 Our Approach

One problem of supervised approach is that it requires large amounts of annotated data. Therefore, we choose a bootstrapping method. In this approach, we only need a few high-precision examples as the input.

In this section, we first describe how we apply the Espresso bootstrapping algorithm for part-whole relation. We focus on seed selection since it is one of the most important steps in bootstrapping algorithms. Then, we propose an effective method for integrating word embedding approach into the Espresso system, after similarity between instances of part-whole relation were investigated.

4.1 The Espresso Bootstrapping Algorithm for Part-Whole Relation

Currently, Espresso (Pantel and Pennacchiotti, 2006) is well known as an efficient algorithm for extracting pairs of entities in a particular relationship. It is a pattern-based and minimally supervised bootstrapping algorithm of extracting lexical-semantic relations. It takes as input a few seed instances and iteratively learns surface patterns to acquire more instances. The Espresso bootstrapping algorithm iterates between the following 3 phases:

1. Pattern Induction: Induce a set of patterns *P* that connects the seed instances in a given corpus. Patterns may be surface text patterns or lexico-syntactic patterns.

2. Pattern Ranking/Selection: Create a pattern ranker, and select the top-k patterns by pattern reliability score. The reliability of a pattern p, $r_\pi(p)$ is average strength of association across input i in the set of instances *I*, weighted by the reliability of each instance i:

$$r_\pi(p) = \frac{\sum_{i \in I}(\frac{pmi(i,\, p)}{max_{pmi}} * r_{\iota(i)})}{|I|} \quad (1)$$

where $r_\iota(i)$ is the reliability of instance i (defined below) and max_{pmi} is the maximum pointwise mutual information between all patterns and all instances. The value of $r_\pi(p)$ ranges from [0, 1], and the reliability of the manually provided seed instances are $r_\iota(i) = 1$. The pointwise mutual information (PMI) between instance *i = (x, y)* and pattern *p* is measured using the following formula:[1]

$$pmi(i,\, p) = log\frac{|x,\ p,\ y|}{|x,\ *,\ y||*,\ p,\ *|}$$

where $|x,\ p,\ y|$ is the frequency of pattern p linked with the instance (x, y). Then, $pmi(i,\, p)$ is multiplied with the discounting factor used in (Pantel and Ravichandran, 2004) to mitigate a bias towards infrequent events.

[1] In that formula, the asterisk (*) represents a wildcard.

3. Instance Extraction: Retrieve from the corpus the set of instances *I* that match any of the patterns in *P*, then create an instance ranker, and select the top-m instances by the instance reliability score. Calculating the reliability of an instance is similar to calculating the reliability of a pattern. The reliability of an instance i, $r_{\iota(i)}$, is defined as:

$$r_{\iota(i)} = \frac{\sum_{p \in P}(\frac{pmi(i,p)}{max_{pmi}} * r_{\pi}(p))}{|P|} \tag{2}$$

A reliable instance should be highly associated with as many reliable patterns as possible. Espresso iterates the above three phases several times until stopping criteria are met.

Unfortunately, like other bootstrapping algorithms, Espresso is prone to *semantic drift*. This phenomenon often occurs when ambiguous or unrelated terms and/or patterns are acquired and then dominate the iterative process (Curran et al., 2007). Ranking patterns and instances by their reliability is an effective way to avoid semantic drift (Equations (1) and (2)). However, bootstrapping is indeed a seed set expansion, therefore selecting good seeds is the most important step to reduce semantic drift. Moreover, semantic drift still occurs in later iterations if the seed set is not good.

To cover the variety of part-whole relation, we classify its subtypes systematically before the seed selection step. There are several subtypes of part-whole relation mentioned in previous ontological studies. In WordNet, part-whole relation is classified into 3 basic subtypes: *Stuff-of*, *Member-of*, and *Part-of*. Chaffin et al. (1988) defined 7 subtypes of part-whole relation, namely *Component-Object, Member-Collection, Portion-Mass, Stuff-Object, Feature-Activity, Place-Area*, and *Phase-Process*. In recent research, Keet and Artale (2008) identified 8 subtypes of part-whole relation. From their taxonomy, Mereological (or transitive) relations include *Involved-In, Located-In, Contained-In*, and *Structured-Part-Of*; while Meronymic (or intransitive) relations consist of *Member-Of, Constituted-Of*, and *Sub-Quantity-Of*.

We reorganize subtypes of part-whole relation as follows:

1. **Component-Of**: or Part-Of; between integrals and their functional components, e.g. *(finger, hand)*.

2. **Member-Of**: between a physical object (or role) and an aggregation (team or organization, etc.), e.g. *(player, team)*.

3. **Portion-Of**: or Sub-Quantity-Of; between amounts of matter or units, e.g. *(oxygen, water)*.

4. **Stuff-Of**: or Substance-Of, or Constituted-Of; between a physical object and an amount of matter, e.g. *(steel, car)*.

5. **Located-In**: between an entity and its 2-dimensional region, e.g. *(Tokyo, Japan)*.

6. **Contained-In**: between an entity and its 3-dimensional region, e.g. *(chip, processor)*.

7. **Phase-Of**: or Involved-In, or Feature-Activity; between a phase and a process, e.g. *(chewing, eating)*.

8. **Participates-In**: between an entity and a process, e.g. *(enzyme, reaction)*.

Basically, our classification is similar to Keet and Artale's taxonomy, which also contains subtypes in other ontological studies. However, we normalize name of subtypes, to find a coherent name set over studies, for example, in WordNet or in (Chaffin et al., 1988).

Seed Selection: We use the following strategy to select seeds for part-whole relation:

- First, for each subtype, we find unambiguous lexical patterns that always convey a part-whole relation, for example, "*a component of*", "*consist of*", etc.

- Then, we search for instances pairs (e.g. Wikipedia dataset) connected by patterns above.

- We select at most 5 instances for each subtype. The most frequent pairs are selected, and we try to select pairs that do not overlap each other. Also, we try not to extract the same instances crossing over the subtypes.

Then, we use simultaneously all the instances to perform the Espresso bootstrapping algorithm for part-whole relation extraction task.

4.2 Similarity Between Instances of Part-Whole Relation

One interesting feature of Word2vec model is that the vectors conserve some of the semantic characteristics in operations regarding the semantic information that they capture, for example, *the country to capital city relationship*: vec("*Madrid*") - vec("*Spain*") ≈ vec("*Paris*") - vec("*France*"), or *gender relationship*: vec("*woman*") - vec("*man*") ≈ vec("*queen*") - vec("*king*"). They indicate that the embedding offsets actually represent the shared semantic relation between the two word pairs.

Can we apply those characteristics for part-whole relation, for example, vec("*pedal*") - vec("*bike*") ≈ vec("*engine*") - vec("*car*")? To answer this question, we investigate typical instances of part-whole relation to measure their similarities by cosine distance. Our calculation is mainly based on the recently proposed Word2vec model. We use *word2vec* tool, and pre-trained vectors published by Google.[2] The model contains 300-dimensional vectors for 3 million words and phrases.

The Word2vec model gives us a vector for each word. To measure the similarity between two instances of part-whole relation, for example, *(pedal, bike)* and *(engine, car)*, we first compute the embedding offsets between two terms in instances, that is, calculate vec("*pedal*") - vec("*bike*") and vec("*engine*") - vec("*car*"). Then, we calculate the cosine distance between those embedding offsets. Here, the bigger the cosine value is, the more similar the two instances will be.

Two instances	**Similarity by cosine distance**
(husband, marriage) & *(wife, marriage)*	0.852828
(Paris, France) & *(Beijing, China)*	0.536129
(pedal, bike) & *(engine, car)*	0.347589

Table 1: Similarities between two instances of part-whole relation

In Table 1, we show the similarities between two instances of the part-whole relation. The part-whole relation is a combination of several subtypes; therefore, it is more complicated than other semantic relations. From the results in Table 1, we can see that instances of part-whole relation are quite similar by cosine distance: vec("*husband*") - vec("*marriage*") ≈ vec("*wife*") - vec("*marriage*"); vec("*pedal*") - vec("*bike*") ≈ vec("*engine*") - vec("*car*"), etc. That means the instance *(husband, marriage)* is close to the instance *(wife, marriage)*, the instance *(pedal, bike)* is close to the instance *(engine, car)*, etc., in semantic space. Therefore, we can leverage such characteristic to apply for part-whole relation extraction task.

4.3 Integrating Word Embedding Offsets into the Espresso Bootstrapping Algorithm

In the Espresso bootstrapping algorithm, ranking instances in Instance Extraction phase is very important. The Espresso system creates an instance ranker to keep only high-confidence instances at this phase, as they are used as seed instances for the next iteration.

By using word embedding approach, our purpose is to keep high-precision over iterations for part-whole relation extraction task. The key idea of our approach is utilizing an additional ranker component, namely *Similarity Ranker* in the Instances Extraction phase of the Espresso system. We still use the reliability of instances in the first ranker. Similarity Ranker operates when the instance ranker is completed. It takes top-m instances from the instance ranker as the input and returns top-n instances as the output. This ranker component uses cosine distance as the *similarity score* between instance pairs of part-whole relation to measure their similarities, and remove unrelated instances in each iteration.

The details of our approach are described in the following:

- An additional ranker is used in Instance Extraction phase, namely *Similarity Ranker*.
- We assume that each instance of part-whole relation is represented by the embedding offset between its terms, for example, the instance (*pedal, bike*) corresponds to: vec("*pedal*") - vec("*bike*").
- *Similarity Ranker* takes top-m instances from the instance ranker as the input. For each new instance, our ranker calculates average similarity score between this instance and previous instances. The similarity score of an instance i,

[2]https://code.google.com/p/word2vec/

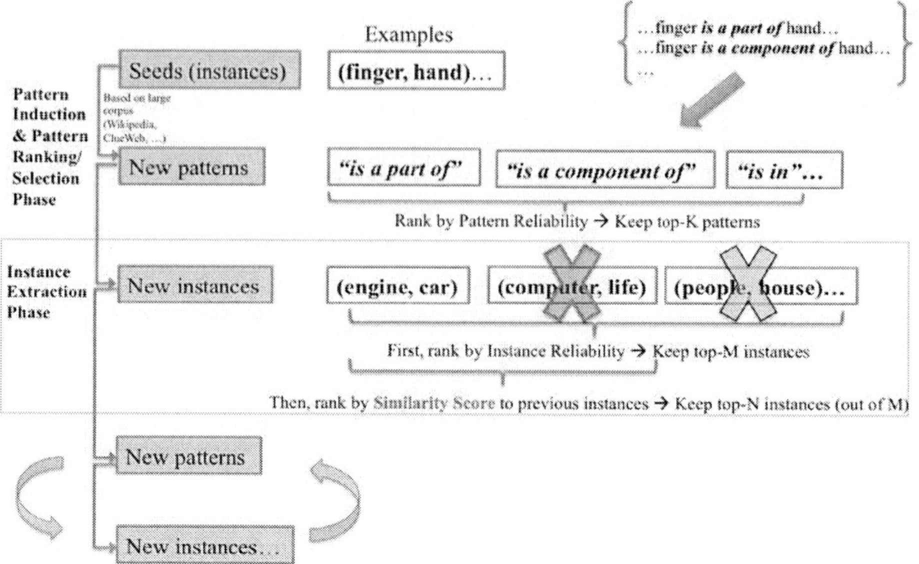

Figure 1: Illustration of our proposed model (Espresso + Word2vec)

SIM(i), is defined as:

$$SIM(i) = \frac{\sum_{j \in I_{Previous}} Cos\_sim(i,j)}{|I_{Previous}|}$$

where $Cos\_sim(i,j)$ is the cosine similarity between two instances, and $I_{Previous}$ is the set of extracted instances.

- If a particular term does not appear in Word2vec model, we use the average vector of its tokens to represent it. For example, if Word2vec model can not recognize the phrase "*Japanese car*", this term corresponds to (vec("*Japanese*") + vec("*car*")) / 2. And in the worst case, if the token "*Japanese*" or the token "*car*" does not appear in Word2vec model, the similarity score of the term "*Japanese car*" is 0.

- Then, m instances are ranked by their similarity score to old instances. Similarity Ranker discards all but the top-n instances as input for the subsequent iteration.

Figure 1 provides an illustration of our proposed model. In Instance Extraction phase, the Espresso bootstrapping algorithm ranks instances first by instance reliability, and removes unrelated pairs, e.g. *(people, house)*. Then, the Similarity Ranker ranks the remaining instances and keeps top-n instances that have the highest similarity score. In our illustration, the instance *(computer, life)* is eliminated to keep high-precision over iterations.

5 Experiments

In this section, we present the results of the Espresso bootstrapping algorithm, and our proposed method (Espresso + Word2vec) on the task of extracting part-whole relations.

Below we describe the systems used in our empirical evaluation of the new proposed model.

- **ESP**: The original *Espresso* algorithm without careful selection of seeds. In this system, part-whole relation is not classified into subtypes and instances are selected randomly.

- **ESP_W2V**: Our proposed method (Espresso + Word2vec) for integrating word embedding approach in the *Espresso* algorithm. Instances are selected randomly. We perform two experiments for two different seed sets, and calculate the average precisions.

- **ESP***: The original *Espresso* algorithm with the careful seed selection step in Section 4.1.

- **ESP*_W2V**: Our proposed method for integrating word embedding approach in the *Espresso* algorithm, with the careful seed selection step.

5.1 Data

We use *ReVerb Extractions 1.1 dataset* as a knowledge-base for our task. ReVerb (Fader et al., 2011) is a program that automatically identifies and extracts binary relationships from English sentences. It contains a set of *(x, r, y)* extraction triples of binary relations (part-whole and other relations), for example, *(bananas, be source of, potassium)*.

A collection of 15 million high-precision ReVerb extractions is available for academic use.[3] The following statistics are the number of distinct tuples, argument strings, and relation strings in the data set: 14,728,268 triples, 2,263,915 instances, and 664,746 patterns.

5.2 Evaluation Method

Our evaluation method is similar to the one introduced by Pantel and Pennacchiotti (2006). We measure the precision of systems by evaluating instances in their output manually. For each instance, we assign a score of 1 if it is correct, 0 if it is incorrect, and 1/2 if it is ambiguous. An example of ambiguous instances is *(energy, economic growth)*. The Cohen's kappa coefficient on our task was 0.689. In total, 4080 instances (6 experiments * 680) were annotated per judge.

5.3 The Espresso System with Careful Seed Selection

As mentioned before, we classify systematically part-whole relation into 8 subtypes before seed selection step to cover the variety of this relation. Then, we select at most 5 instances for each subtype and use this seed set to perform the Espresso bootstrapping algorithm for part-whole relation extraction task. We denote this system by *ESP**.

In total, 35 instances are manually selected as the seed set for our problem. Table 2 lists examples of the seeds.

We experimentally set the number of instances and patterns that the system keeps in each iteration.

[3] http://reverb.cs.washington.edu

Seed	Subtype
(iron, hemoglobin)	Component-Of
(the committee, the president)	Member-Of
(caffeine, coffee)	Portion-Of
(paper, trees)	Stuff-Of
(Shanghai, China)	Located-In
(references, request)	Contained-In
(treatment, surgery)	Phase-Of
(students, class)	Participates-In

Table 2: Sample seeds used for part-whole relation

The parameters for the Espresso bootstrapping algorithm are as follows:

- In the 1st iteration: keep top-10 patterns and top-100 instances.

- In next iterations: keep top-5 patterns and top-20 instances.

We perform experiments with the random selection of seeds (*ESP* system), to compare the effect of the careful seed selection step in the Espresso bootstrapping algorithm. In contrast to the careful seed selection step, we do not separate subtypes of part-whole relation. Each seed set contains 35 instances selected randomly such that those instances always convey part-whole relation. Part-whole relation is single-type in those experiments. The results of the *ESP* system is the average precision when we conduct experiments with two different seed sets of part-whole relation. Each seed set contains 35 instances selected randomly.

The results are reported in Table 3. We evaluated the results after 30 iterations since the precision was nearly constant. At this point, 680 instances were extracted by both systems. The *ESP* system achieved a precision of 74.3%, while the precision of instances harvested by the *ESP** system is 83.3%. We extracted new instances keeping them in different subtypes to be non-overlapping, this can be consider as a kind of multi-task learning. The results show that multi-task learning and seed selection are effective ways to get high precision.

SYSTEM	INSTANCES	CORRECT INSTANCES	AMBIGUOUS INSTANCES	PRECISION
ESP	680 680	466 482	65 60	74.3%[a]
ESP_W2V	680 680	493 563	54 45	78.5%[a]
ESP*	680	549	35	83.3%
ESP*_W2V	680	554	47	**84.9%**

[a] The result of this system is the average precision when we perform two experiments with two random seed sets of part-whole relation.

Table 3: System performance for part-whole relation extraction task

5.4 Our Proposed System (Espresso + Word2vec)

In this experiment, we present the result of our proposed system for integrating word embedding offsets into the Espresso system. We use the careful seed set in the previous experiment to perform our system for part-whole relation extraction task. The parameters for our proposed system are as follows:

- In the 1st iteration: keep top-10 patterns and top-100 instances (the same as in previous experiment).
- In next iterations: keep top-5 patterns; for instances, keep top-100 by instance reliability, then keep top-20 (out of 100) by similarity score (similar to the previous experiment).

One problem of Word2vec model is that it tends to select very similar instances to given instances, for example, *(team, seven players)*, *(team, six players)*, *(team, three players)*, etc. Therefore, we keep only one of them that has the highest instance reliability in each iteration.

We denote the system in this experiment by *ESP*_W2V*. Then, we evaluated the results after 30 iterations. At this point, 680 instances were extracted. The *ESP*_W2V* system achieved a precision of 84.9%. It outperformed *ESP** system, which is reported 83.3% precision.

We also conduct another experiment for integrating word embedding approach into the Espresso system, without careful seed selection step. That is, we use random seed sets (the same for ESP system) in a new system, which is denoted by *ESP_W2V*. The results of the *ESP_W2V* system is the average precision when we conduct experiments with two different seed sets. From Table 3, we can see that the precision is increased from 74.3% (*ESP* system) to 83.3% (*ESP** system) by using careful selection of seeds, and improved from 78.5% (*ESP_W2V* system) to 84.9% (*ESP*_W2V* system) by integrating word embedding approach into the Espresso system.

All above results showed that our proposed system (Espresso + Word2vec) can keep high-precision over iterations, and outperformed the original Espresso system for part-whole relation extraction.

6 Conclusion and Future Work

In this paper, we considered the part-whole relation extraction task. Subtypes of part-whole relation are separated before seed selection step to cover the variety of this relation. We evaluated 4 systems (6 experiments: 2 for ESP, 2 for ESP_W2V, 1 for ESP* and 1 for ESP*_W2V) to show that by using fine-grained subtypes of part-whole relation and careful seed selection step, the precisions were increased (74.3/83.8 - 78.5/84.9). That is, multi-task learning and seed selection are factors for achieving higher precision. To improve the performance of extracting part-whole relation, we integrated word embedding approach into the Espresso system. Our results illustrated that the proposed model can keep high-precision (84.9%) over iterations, and it outperformed the original Espresso system (74.3/78.5 - 83.3/84.9). We plan to set thresholds in the *Similarity Ranker* to get more accurate results. Our system can be extended for extracting other binary relations.

References

Eugene Agichtein and Luis Gravano. 2000. Snowball: Extracting relations from large plain-text collections. In *Proceedings of the fifth ACM conference on Digital libraries*, pages 85–94. ACM.

Sergey Brin. 1999. Extracting patterns and relations from the world wide web. In *The World Wide Web and Databases*, pages 172–183. Springer.

Razvan C Bunescu and Raymond J Mooney. 2005. A shortest path dependency kernel for relation extraction. In *Proceedings of the conference on Human Language Technology and Empirical Methods in Natural Language Processing*, pages 724–731. Association for Computational Linguistics.

Roger Chaffin, Douglas J Herrmann, and Morton Winston. 1988. An empirical taxonomy of part-whole relations: Effects of part-whole relation type on relation identification. *Language and Cognitive processes*, 3(1):17–48.

James R Curran, Tara Murphy, and Bernhard Scholz. 2007. Minimising semantic drift with mutual exclusion bootstrapping. In *Proceedings of the 10th Conference of the Pacific Association for Computational Linguistics*, volume 6.

Anthony Fader, Stephen Soderland, and Oren Etzioni. 2011. Identifying relations for open information extraction. In *Proceedings of the Conference on Empirical Methods in Natural Language Processing*, pages 1535–1545. Association for Computational Linguistics.

Roxana Girju, Adriana Badulescu, and Dan Moldovan. 2006. Automatic discovery of part-whole relations. *Computational Linguistics*, 32(1):83–135.

Zhou GuoDong, Su Jian, Zhang Jie, and Zhang Min. 2005. Exploring various knowledge in relation extraction. In *Proceedings of the 43rd annual meeting on association for computational linguistics*, pages 427–434. Association for Computational Linguistics.

Marti A Hearst. 1992. Automatic acquisition of hyponyms from large text corpora. In *Proceedings of the 14th conference on Computational linguistics-Volume 2*, pages 539–545. Association for Computational Linguistics.

Ashwin Ittoo and Gosse Bouma. 2013. Minimally-supervised extraction of domain-specific part–whole relations using wikipedia as knowledge-base. *Data & Knowledge Engineering*, 85:57–79.

Nanda Kambhatla. 2004. Combining lexical, syntactic, and semantic features with maximum entropy models for extracting relations. In *Proceedings of the ACL 2004 on Interactive poster and demonstration sessions*, page 22. Association for Computational Linguistics.

C Maria Keet and Alessandro Artale. 2008. Representing and reasoning over a taxonomy of part–whole relations. *Applied Ontology*, 3(1):91–110.

Tomas Mikolov, Ilya Sutskever, Kai Chen, Greg S Corrado, and Jeff Dean. 2013. Distributed representations of words and phrases and their compositionality. In *Advances in Neural Information Processing Systems*, pages 3111–3119.

Patrick Pantel and Marco Pennacchiotti. 2006. Espresso: Leveraging generic patterns for automatically harvesting semantic relations. In *Proceedings of the 21st International Conference on Computational Linguistics and the 44th annual meeting of the Association for Computational Linguistics*, pages 113–120. Association for Computational Linguistics.

Patrick Pantel and Deepak Ravichandran. 2004. Automatically labeling semantic classes. In *HLT-NAACL*, volume 4, pages 321–328.

Alan Rector, Chris Welty, Natasha Noy, and Evan Wallace. 2005. Simple part-whole relations in owl ontologies.

Alexander Yates, Michael Cafarella, Michele Banko, Oren Etzioni, Matthew Broadhead, and Stephen Soderland. 2007. Textrunner: open information extraction on the web. In *Proceedings of Human Language Technologies: The Annual Conference of the North American Chapter of the Association for Computational Linguistics: Demonstrations*, pages 25–26. Association for Computational Linguistics.

Dmitry Zelenko, Chinatsu Aone, and Anthony Richardella. 2003. Kernel methods for relation extraction. *The Journal of Machine Learning Research*, 3:1083–1106.

Shubin Zhao and Ralph Grishman. 2005. Extracting relations with integrated information using kernel meth ods. In *Proceedings of the 43rd Annual Meeting on Association for Computational Linguistics*, pages 419–426. Association for Computational Linguistics.

An Experimental Study of Subject Properties in Korean Multiple Subject Constructions (MSCs)

Ji-Hye Kim
Baird University College
Soongsil University
Seoul, Korea
psychlg@gmail.com

Eunah Kim
College English Program
Seoul National University
Seoul, Korea
eakim2@gmail.com

James Hye-Suk Yoon
Department of Linguistics
University of Illinois,
Urbana-Champaign
U.S.A.

Abstract

Yoon (2008, 2009) claimed that there are two distinct Subjects in Multiple Subject Constructions (MSCs) in Korean. The crux of his argument hangs on reinterpreting the traditionally proposed subject diagnostics as distinguishing between the Grammatical Subject (GS) and the Major Subject (MS) in MSCs. The claimed diagnostics for GS and MS were examined experimentally in MSCs and corresponding Single Subject Constructions (SSCs). We found that: (i) MS diagnostics and GS diagnostics were differentiated even in SSCs and (ii) there was no statistically significant difference between MS and GS diagnostics in MSCs. Implications of these findings are discussed.

1 Introduction: MSCs and Subjecthood in Korean

Sentences in Korean where more than one Subject-like NP carries nominative case are known as Multiple Nominative Constructions (MNCs) or Multiple Subject Constructions (MSCs) (cf. 1 below).

(1) a. *Cheli-ka* *nwun-i* *khu-ta.*
Cheli-NOM eye-NOM big-DECL
'Cheli's eyes are big.'
Cheli-NOM father-NOM rich-DECL

b. *Cheli-ka* *apeci-ka* *hoysa-ka* *pwuca-ta.*
Cheli-NOM father-NOM compnay-NOM
rich.DECL
'It is Cheli whose father's company is rich.'

A debate concerning MSCs is whether they possess more than one Subject, as the name MSC implies, or has a single Subject with multiple NPs carrying nominative case on the surface, as the name MNC implies. The latter position is defended in works such as Yoon 1986, Yoon 1989, Hong 1991, Park 1995, Schütze 2001, etc., while the former position finds advocacy in works such as Park 1973, Teng 1974, Youn 1990, Cho 2000, Lee 1997, Heycock 1993, Kang 2002, Yoon 2004, 2007, 2008, 2009, 2015, etc.

To make headway on this debate we need to first establish the properties that diagnose subjecthood. The following are some of the subjecthood diagnostics proposed in the literature (Yoon 1986, Hong 1991, 1994, Youn 1990, etc.)

(2) Subject Diagnostics in Korean[1]

a. Controller of optional plural-marking (i.e., Plural Copying)
b. Controller of subject honorification (i.e., Honorific Agreement)
c. Controller of PRO in complement (obligatory) control

† We thank Yong-hun Lee for statistical consultation.

[1] There are additional subject diagnostics proposed in the previous studies. However, we mention only 6 diagnostics tested in this study. For more discussion of comprehensive subject diagnostics, see Kim et al (2015)'s experimental study or Yoon (1986), Hong (1991, 1994) or Youn (1990).

d. Antecedent of (subject-oriented) anaphors
e. Controller of PRO in adjunct control
f. Controller of null coordinate subjects[2]

In sentences with a single Subject, or SSCs, the subject properties shown in (2) will be controlled by the unique Subject nominal. If MSCs are characterized by multiple Subjects, we expect the situation to be different.

Under Yoon's (2008, 2009) proposal, MSCs have two different types of Subjects. The nom-marked NP immediately preceding the predicate (e.g., *nwun-i* in 1a) is the Grammatical Subject, while the initial NP that carries nom-marking (e.g., *Cheli-ka* in 1a) is the Major Subject. Yoon hypothesized that the subject properties controlled by the unique Subject NP in an SSC will be distributed between the Major Subject and the Grammatical Subject in MSCs.

Specifically, Yoon proposes that among the list of subject properties in (2), (2a), (2b), (2c) and (2d) are properties controlled by the GS, whereas (2e) and (2f) are controlled by the MS in MSCs. The reason for this particular split is that the Major Subject is a Subject-*qua*-Pivot, while the Grammatical Subject is a Subject-*qua*-Prominent Argument, in the sense of Falk 2006.

A significant shortcoming of previous studies on MSCs, including the studies by Yoon, is that the key claims are based on the intuition of researchers. Since MSCs are not common and require particular contexts to be felicitous, it is important to test these theoretical claims on a large scale with naïve speakers. However, we know of only a few experimental studies on MSCs. In addition, the previous experimental studies based on Yoon's approach (Kim et al. 2015, Lee et al. 2015, and Kim et al., in progress) focused on testing the validity of one or two chosen subject diagnostics, but not that of the entire set of GS vs. MS diagnostics. This is what we propose to do in this paper.

[2] This diagnostic was referred as Coordinated Null Subject Deletion (CD) in this study, following Kim et al (2015), to avoid confusion with what it refers to in the previous study.

2 Research Method

2.1 Research Questions and Hypotheses

The research question of the current study is the following: Do native Korean speakers distinguish between GS and MS in MSCs in terms of subject properties as proposed in Yoon (2008, 2009)?

Assuming Yoon's proposals, we hypothesize the following:

Hypothesis 1: In SSCs, all 6 diagnostics in (2) should be controlled by the unique Subject nominal.
Hypothesis 2: In MSCs, the subject properties will be distributed between the GS (2a-d) and MS (2e,f).

2.2 Participants

Forty Korean native speakers (age range: 23~38) residing in and near Seoul, South Korea, who are either current university students or graduates, participated in the experiment.

2.3 Task, Materials, and Procedure

The main task was an acceptability judgment using Magnitude Estimation (ME), in which the participants were asked to draw different lengths of lines (range:0 to 150mm) to indicate the perceived degree of naturalness (acceptability) of a given sentence.[3]

The test materials consisted of 40 sentences: 20 target sentences (4 conditions × 5 tokens) and 20 filler sentences. Since we have six diagnostics, 240 sentences were used in the experiments.

The target sentence types had a 2×2 design, crossing sentence type (SSC vs. MSC) with the NP that is intended as the controller of a given subjecthood diagnostic (NP1 vs. NP2). In MSCs, NP1 is the Major Subject while NP2 is the Grammatical Subject. In SSCs that match MSCs, NP1 is the Possessor of NP2 which we take to be the unique Subject NP.

The 4 conditions are illustrated below in (3) with relevant examples, with respect to diagnostic of Honorific Agreement, a GS diagnostic.

[3] See Kim et al (2015) for the rationale of using ME for acceptability judgment tasks.

(3) Target Sentences

a. Type 1: $[NP1]_{poss}$ $[NP2]_{nom}$ $Subj.Diag_{[controlled\ by\ NP2]}$ (SSC+NP2)

a'. Cheli-uy(NP1) **apenim-i(NP2)**
C-GEN father-NOM
pwuca-i-**si**-ta
rich-cop-HON-DECL

b. Type 2: $[NP1]_{poss}$ $[NP2]_{nom}$ $Subj.Diag_{[controlled\ by\ NP1]}$ (SSC+NP1)

b'. **Apenim-uy(NP1)** ankyengthey-ka(NP2)
father-GEN glass.frame-NOM
kwuksan-i-**si**-ta
Korean.made-cop-HON-DECL

c. Type 3: $[NP1]_{nom}$ $[NP2]_{nom}$ $Subj.Diag_{[controlled\ by\ NP2(GS)]}$ (MSC+NP2)

c'. Cheli-ka(NP1) **apenim-i(NP2)**
C-NOM father-NOM
pwuca-i-**si**-ta
rich-cop-HON-DECL

d. Type 4: $[NP1]_{nom}$ $[NP2]_{nom}$ $Subj.Diag_{[controlled\ by\ NP1(MS)]}$ (MSC+NP1)

d'. **Apenim-i(NP1)** ankyengthey-ka(NP2)
father-NOM glass.frame-NOM
kwuksan-i-**si**-ta
Korean.made-cop-HON-DECL

Specific predictions of our experiment are as follows:

Prediction 1) Type 1 sentences should be acceptable while Type 2 sentences should be unacceptable for all subject diagnostics, because NP1 in SSCs is not a Subject.

Prediction 2) Type 3 sentences should be acceptable and Type 4 should be unacceptable for GS diagnostics (i.e., 2a-2d).

Prediction 3) Type 3 sentences should be unacceptable and Type 4 should be acceptable for MS diagnostics (i.e, 2e or 2f).

2.4 Statistical Analysis

After the experiment was conducted, all the scores were extracted for the target sentences. Then, three factors were encoded as follows for statistical analysis.

Factor	Value
DIAGTYPE	GS, MS
CONSTTYPE	SSC, MSC
CONTROLLERTYPE	SSC: Possessor (NP1), Subject (NP2) MSCs: GS (NP1), MS (NP2)

Table 1: Encoded Factors

Since the data did not follow normal distribution with the normality tests, a non-parametric GLM analysis was adopted in order to examine how each factor affected the acceptability scores.[4]

For each combination of two factors in Table 1, a GLM was performed with Gaussian distributions. Also, a statistical analysis was performed to determine how CONTROLLERTYPE distinctions played a role in the acceptability scores in SSCs and MSCs.

3 Results

3.1 SSC: GS Diagnostics

While analyzing the results, we found that GS vs. MS diagnostics behave differently not just in MSCs, but also in SSCs. Therefore, we will separate the diagnostics for both construction types.

Figure 1 illustrates the distributions of acceptability scores in SSCs with 4 GS diagnostics. Here 'Possessor' is NP1, while 'Subject' is NP2. The y-axis represents the length of the lines (in mm) that participants drew for the target sentences (range: 0~150mm).

[4] If the collected data follow the normal distribution, parametric tests such as t-test, ANOVA, or ordinary regression analysis can be applied; otherwise, non-parametric tests such as Mann-Whitney tests, Wilcoxon tests, Friedman tests, and/or Generalized Linear Model (GLM) should be applied (Gries 2013, Lee 2016).

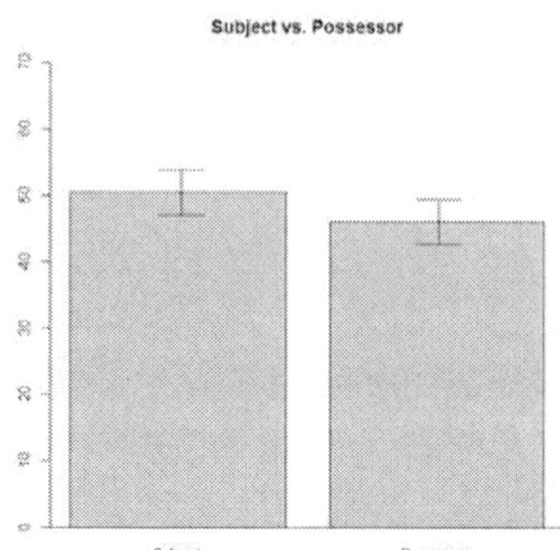

Figure 1: Bar Plots for 'GS diagnostics in SSC'

As you can see, the average acceptability score for 'Subject' was slightly higher than that of 'Possessor.' Though the differences between the two groups were not clear in Figure 1, which is descriptive statistics, the results of the GLM analysis in Table 2 below show that they were statistically significant (p<.001).[5]

	Estimate	Standard Error	*T*	*P*
(Intercept)	48.2889	0.5341	90.413	.000 ***
AGREETYPE	-2.1456	0.5341	-4.017	.000 ***

Table 2: Regression Analysis Results

Similarly, the interaction plot in Figure 2 below shows that the acceptability score for 'Subject' was higher than those of 'Possessor.' The non-overlapping 95% CIs as indicated in the interaction plot in Figure 2 shows that the difference is significant. The significantly higher acceptability scores for 'Subject' than those of 'Possessor' is consistent with Prediction 1.

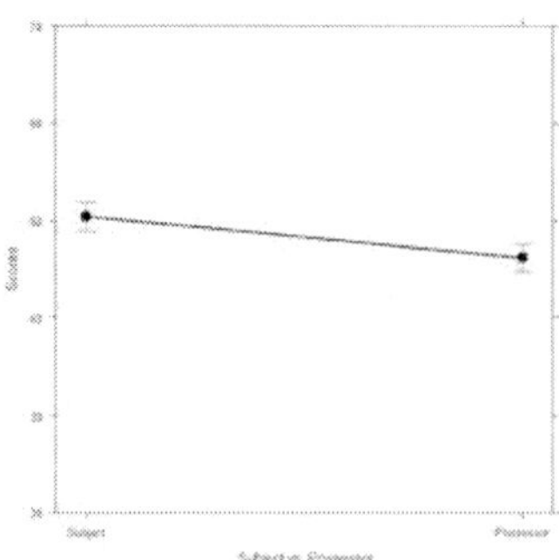

Figure 2: Interaction Plot

[5] While the bar plots indicate the results of descriptive statistics, the GLM and the interaction effect plot provide results from inferential statistics.

3.2 SSC: MS Diagnostics

The distributions of acceptability scores in SSC with MS diagnostics are illustrated in Figure 3.

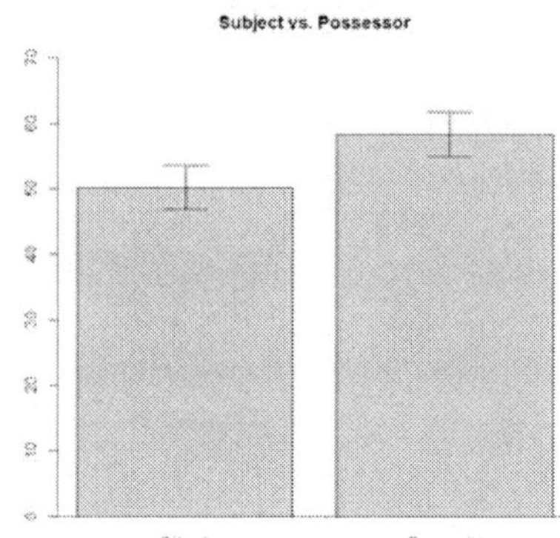

Figure 3: Bar Plots for 'MS diagnostics in SSC'

The acceptability scores for 'Possessor' were higher than those of 'Subject.' The GLM analysis in Table 3 shows that the differences were statistically significant (p<.001).

	Estimate	Standard Error	*t*	*p*
(Intercept)	54.3246	0.6938	78.299	.000 ***
CONTROLLERTYPE	4.0989	0.6938	5.908	.000 ***

Table 3: Regression Analysis Results

Similarly, the interaction plot in Figure 4 below shows that the 95% CIs of the 'Possessor' and the 'Subject' did not overlap.

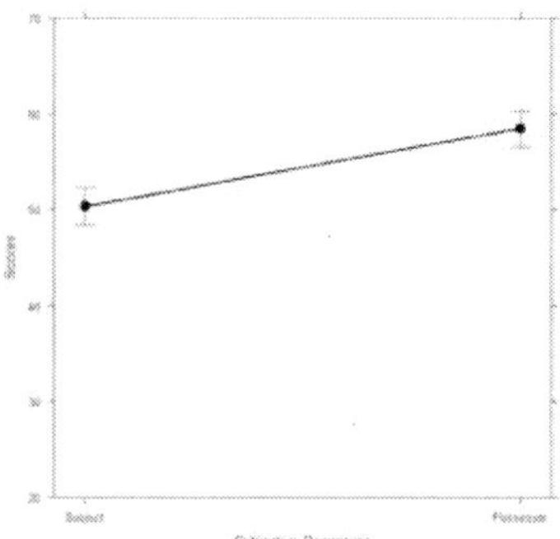

Figure 4: Interaction Plot

3.3 MSC: GS Diagnostics

The acceptability scores for MSCs were lower overall compared to that for SSCs.[6] Perhaps because of the overall lower degree of acceptability, the difference between NP1 (Major Subject) and NP2 (Grammatical Subject) was less pronounced than in SSCs.

Figure 5 shows the acceptability scores for GS and MS with GS diagnostics. While the acceptability score for 'GS' (NP2) was slightly higher than those of 'MS' (NP1), the 95% CIs clearly overlapped.

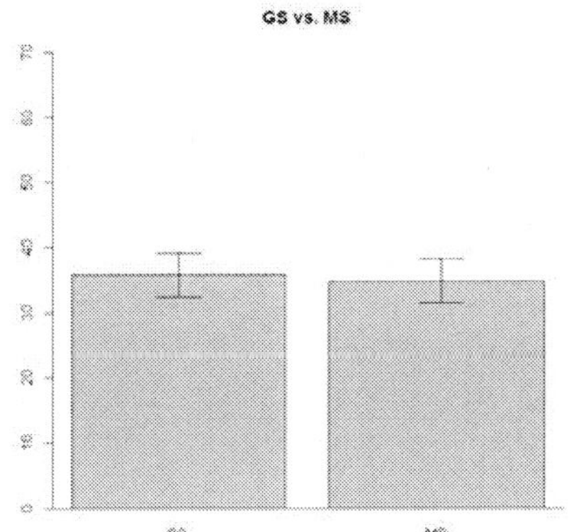

Figure 5: Bar Plots for 'GS diagnostics in MSC'

The inferential statistics (the GLM analysis in Table 4 and the interaction plot in Figure 6) indeed suggest that there was no significant difference between the acceptability score for 'GS' and that for 'MS'.

	Estimate	Standard Error	*t*	*p*
(Intercept)	32.0058	0.4162	76.897	.000 ***
CONTROLLERTYPE	-0.3842	0.4162	-0.923	.356

Table 4: Regression Analysis Results

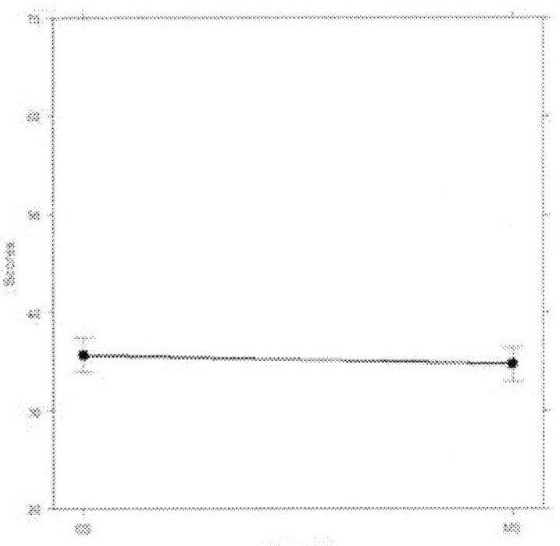

Figure 6: Interaction Plot

3.4 MSC: MS Diagnostics

Figure 7 shows the acceptability scores for GS and MS with MS diagnostics. As can be seen in the Figure, the acceptability scores for 'MS' (NP1) and those for 'GS' (NP2) were not very different.

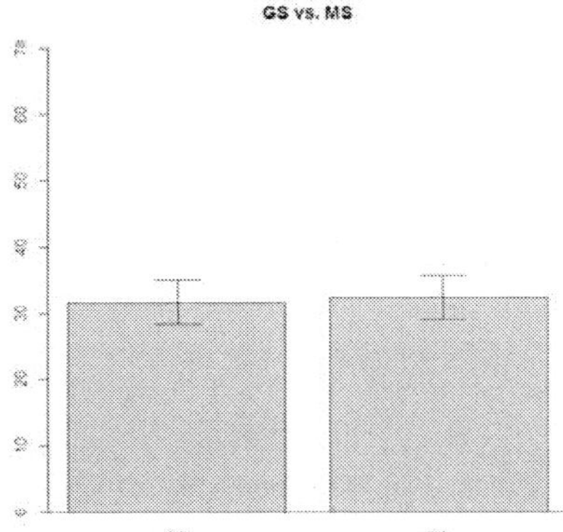

Figure 7: Bar Plots for 'MS diagnostics in MSC'

The results of GLM analysis (Table 5) and the interaction plot (Figure 8) show that the difference between the two conditions was not statistically significant.

	Estimate	Standard Error	*t*	*p*
(Intercept)	35.2086	0.6205	56.746	.000 ***
Fator1	0.4886	0.6205	0.787	.431

Table 5: Regression Analysis Results

[6] While the mean score for grammatical SSCs was generally higher than 50 on a 0-145 scale, MSCs were mostly rated below 50 in the scale. This could reflect many factors, one being that MSCs are felicitous in particular contexts, unlike SSCs but no context was given in the task. Another is that MSCs are marked constructions that are not commonly used.

We do not think that the lower ratings mean that MSCs are ungrammatical but only that they may not sound as natural out of context to untrained subjects. Given the decades of attention paid to them in both traditional and contemporary linguistic research, they clearly inhabit the grammatical landscape of Korean.

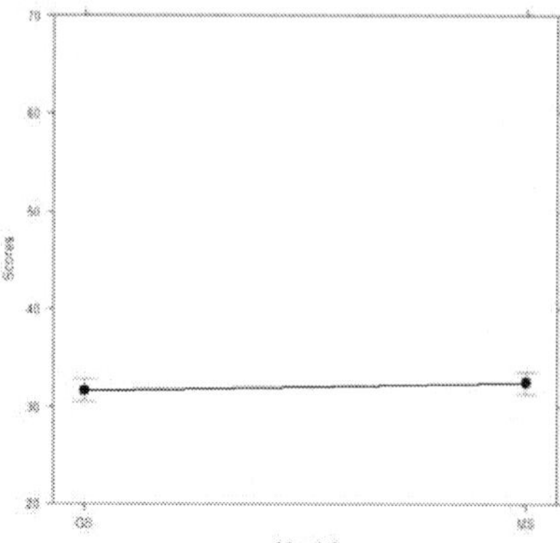

Figure 8: Interaction Plot

4 Discussion

We hypothesized that in SSCs, sentences where the Subject (NP2) controls the subject diagnostics would be acceptable while those where the Possessor (NP1) does should be unacceptable, regardless of the type of subject diagnostic (**Prediction 1**). However, the results diverged from the prediction in two ways. First, SSCs where the Possessor (NP1) controls subject diagnostics were not judged unacceptable. The overall acceptability rating of such sentences was even higher than MSCs, for example. Secondly, SSCs where the Possessor controls a given diagnostic were judged to be better than those where the Subject (NP2) does so for certain subject diagnostics (i.e., Plural Copying (PC) and Adjunct Control (AC)). Thus, Prediction 1 was not fully supported by the results.

For MSCs, **Prediction 2** (that sentences where GS diagnostics are controlled by NP2 but not NP1 would be acceptable) was not supported statistically. Likewise, **Prediction 3** (that sentences where MS diagnostics are controlled by NP1 but not NP2 would be acceptable) was not supported statistically either. However, the overall numerical results were in the direction of the two predictions.

Since the SSC condition constitutes the baseline against which the results of the MSC condition can be evaluated, we turn to SSCs first. We predicted that the Possessor (NP1) should not control any subject property, but it came close to the Subject (NP2) with respect to the GS subject properties and actually surpassed the latter with the MS subject properties. How could we understand these results?

One possibility is that the properties that Yoon and others picked as subject properties in Korean (in 2) are not valid, at least when considered as a group. Among them, it seems that the MS properties (as a group) are even less likely than the GS properties to be subject properties, since the Possessor, a non-Subject, outperformed the Subject in a statistically significant manner with these diagnostics. And while the Subject outperformed the Possessor (in a statistically significant manner, to boot) for GS properties, SSCs where the Possessor 'wrongly' controlled these properties were judged to be fairly well-formed. So, even the GS properties as a group may not be valid to diagnose all and only Subjects in Korean. We need to examine the validity of each diagnostic separately. Doing so may reveal that the set of true subject diagnostics is a much smaller subset of the GS diagnostics.[7]

A different way to understand the results is to try to make sense of them in light of the fact that the non-subject nominal in SSCs that was able to usurp some subject properties is the Possessor of the Subject. The reason this is important is the following.

While we have been writing about Subjects as if they were theoretical primitives, in many syntactic traditions subjecthood is a derived notion. Subjects are defined in terms of structural prominence (i.e., Subject is the highest nominal in an A-position that asymmetrically c-commands other nominals). Understood this way, a surface Subject controls Subject Agreement in a language because the nominal is in the right configuration to be the minimal controller (via relations such as Agree) of the category that bears Subject Agreement.

Now, it is well-known that the Possessor of a Subject can scope or bind out of the Subject in certain circumstances in certain languages, perhaps because Specifiers can optionally c-command out of the constituent they are in (Kayne 1994).

What this means is that the behavior of the Possessor-of-Subject may not be representative of how non-Subject nominals behave in general because the Possessor-of-Subject can usurp certain properties of the Subject by virtue of being able to

[7] Previous studies (Kim et al, 2015; Lee et al, 2015; Kim et al, forthcoming) found that individual diagnostics actually fared better. In particular, Obligatory Control (OC) and Reflexive Binding (RB) were fairly robust in being controlled by GS but not MS properties in both SSCs and MSCs.

c-command out of the Subject constituent. In an approach where subject behavior derives from a nominal having the highest structural prominence, the Possessor-of-Subject would actually have to be considered a Subject.

Therefore, rather than coming to a hasty conclusion that the majority of the properties identified in the literature as diagnosing Subjects in Korean needs to be discarded because the Possessor-of-Subject can sometimes control them, we need to contrast Subjects with non-Subject nominals other than its Possessor.

Nevertheless, it is disturbing to find that the Possessor-of-Subject outperforms the Subject with respect to the so-called MS subject properties (Adjunct Control (AC) and Coordinated Null Subject Control/Coordinate Null Subject Deletion (CD)). This possibly means that these are not valid in diagnosing Subjects in a given structure. Anything with enough contextual salience may be able to control these properties.

Turning to MSCs, the surprising results with SSCs indicate that no reliable conclusion about the question of subjecthood can be made pending a full and comprehensive investigation of the necessary and sufficient conditions of subjecthood in SSCs where a variety of non-subject nominals are systematically compared with the unique Subject. Therefore, the fact that the pattern of results in MSCs tended in the direction of the claims made in Yoon (2008, 2009) cannot be interpreted as indicating anything definitive about whether MSCs are characterized by the presence of multiple Subjects, with relevant subject properties distributed between the two types of Subjects.

A further problem with the current experiment is that since the subjects were presented with both SSC and MSC conditions, the ratings of MSCs could reflect judgments given in comparison with SSCs. And because of the lower ratings, any differences that emerged did not lend themselves to statistical significance. To fix this problem, we should test SSCs and MSCs separately in future experiments. Increasing the number of subjects might be able to give more robust results.

5 Conclusion

The current study investigated how two different types of subjecthood diagnostics (GS diagnostics and MS diagnostics) behaved in SSCs and MSCs, respectively. Though additional experiments are needed, we can tentatively come to the following conclusions.

First, among the proposed subjecthood diagnostics, those we classified as MS diagnostics are probably not valid subjecthood diagnostics at all (cf. Hong 1991, 1994 for a similar position).

Second, even among the remainder (that is, the set of GS diagnostics), there may be diagnostics that do not identify all and only Subjects. In particular, some of these diagnostics may be applicable to structural Subjects and Possessors contained within them.

Third, because of the ability of the Possessor-of-Subject to usurp the properties of the Subject (by optionally c-commanding out of the Subject, we assume), we need to investigate the question of subject diagnostics by contrasting Subjects with non-Subject nominals other than its Possessor.

Finally, because the question of subjecthood diagnostics has not been settled for SSCs, we cannot have a definitive answer to the question of whether MSCs are characterized by the presence of multiple Subjects, with subject properties distributed between the different types of Subjects. The (dis)confirmation of the theoretical proposals put forth in Yoon (2008, 2009) cannot be achieved without first traversing these prior steps.

References

Beom-Mo Kang. 2002. Pemcwu Mwunpep: Hankwuke-uy Hyengthaylon, Thongsalon, Thaipnonlicek Uymilon (Categorial Grammar: The Morphology, Syntax, and Type-Logical Semantics of Korean). Korea University Press, Seoul.

Byung-Soo Park. 1973. On the Multiple Subject Constructions in Korean. Linguistics, 100:63-76.

Byung-Soo Park. 2001. Constraints in Multiple Nominative Constructions in Korean: A Constraint-based Lexicalist Approach. The Journal of Linguistic Science, 20:147-190.

Caroline Heycock and Young-suk Lee. 1989. Subjects and Predication in Korean and Japanese. Language Research, 25(4): 755-792.

Carson Schütze. 2001. On Korean 'Case Stacking': The Varied Functions of the Particles *-ka* and *-lul*. The Linguistic Review, 18:193-232.

Cheong Youn. 1990. A Relational Analysis of Korean Multiple Nominative Constructions. Doctoral dissertation, State University of New York at Buffalo.

Eunah Kim, Ji-Hye Kim, and Yong-hun Lee. In progress. Honorific Agreement and Plural Copying as Subject Diagnostics in Korean: An Experimental Approach.

Ik-Hwan Lee. 1987. Double Subject Constructions in GPSG. Harvard Studies in Korean Linguistics II:287-296.

James Hye-Suk Yoon. 1986. Some Queries Concerning the Syntax of Multiple Subject Constructions in Korean. Studies in the Linguistic Sciences 16: 215-236, Department of Linguistics, University of Illinois, Urbana-Champaign.

James Hye-Suk Yoon. 2004. Non-nominative (Major) Subjects and Case-stacking in Korean. In Peri Bhaskararao and Karumuri VenkataSubbarao (eds.), Non-nominative Subjects, volume 2:265-314. Mouton de Gruyter, Berlin.

James Hye-Suk Yoon. 2008. Subjecthood and Subject Properties in Multiple Subject Constructions. Talk presented at the East Asian Linguistics Seminar, Oxford University, Oxford.

James Hye-Suk Yoon. 2009. The Distribution of Subject Properties in Multiple Subject Constructions. Proceedings of Japanese/Korean Linguistics, 64-83. CSLI, Stanford, CA.

James Hye-Suk Yoon. 2015. Double Nominative and Double Accusative Constructions. In Lucien Brown and Jaehoon Yeon (eds.), The Handbook of Korean Linguistics, First Edition. 79-97. John Wiley & Sons, Inc., New York.

James Hye-Suk Yoon. 2007. Raising of Major Arguments in Korean and Japanese. Natural Language and Linguistic Theory, 25:615-653.

Ji-Hye Kim, Yong-hun Lee and Eunah Kim. 2015. Obligatory Control and Coordinated Deletion as Korean Subject Diagnostics: An Experimental Approach. Language and Information, 19(1):75-101.

Jong-Yurl Yoon. 1989. On the Multiple *–ka* and *–lul* Constructions in Korean. Harvard Studies in Korean Linguistics III:383-394. Hanshin Publishing Company, Seoul.

Kayne, Richard. 1994. The Antisymmetry of Syntax. Cambridge: MIT Press.

Ki-Sun Hong. 1991. Argument Selection and Case-Marking in Korean. Doctoral dissertation, Stanford University.

Ki-Sun Hong. 1994. Subjecthood in Korean. Language Research 30. 99-136.

Shou-Hsin Teng. 1974. Double Nominatives in Chinese. Language, 50:455-473.

Stefan Th. Gries. 2013. Statistics for Linguistics. 2nd Edition. Mouton de Gruyter, Berlin.

Yong-hun Lee, Eunah Kim, and Ji-Hye Kim. 2015. Reflexive Binding and Adjunct Control as Subject Diagnostics in Korean: An Experimental Approach. Studies in Language 31.2: 427-449.

Yong-hun Lee. 2016. Corpus Linguistics and Statistics with R (written in Korean). Hankook Publishing Company, Seoul.

Focal Prominence Underlying Distribution of Mandarin Minimizers

I-Hsuan Chen
Department of Chinese and Bilingual Studies
The Hong Kong Polytechnic University
Department of Linguistics
University of California, Berkeley

ihsuanchen@berkeley.edu

Abstract

This corpus study of the distribution of Mandarin minimizer negative polarity items connects word order patterns and focal constructions. The OV word order pattern is claimed to be a focal construal. However, the corpus analysis shows the majority of them stay in VO. This distribution is constrained by the information structure of Mandarin word order patterns and negative constructions. The requirement of focal prominence is clearly reflected in the types of co-occurring modifiers in VO and OV. This study of minimizers shows how emphatic pragmatic inferences are construed through the interaction between focal construction, negation, and numeral phrases.

Key words: minimizers, negation, focus, word order, Mandarin Chinese

1 Introduction

This paper investigates Mandarin information structure entailed in word order and various types of negation through analyzing the distribution of Mandarin minimizers. 'One'-phases are the main source of minimizes in East Asian numeral classifier languages, which is the presence of numeral classifiers. As shown in (1), the 'one'-phrase, a combination of a numeral, a classifier or measure word, and a noun, is used as a negative polarity item (NPI) for emphasizing negation, instead of being used for denoting the actual quantity.

(1) [yí lì liángshí] dōu/ yě bú làngfèi
one CLF[1] food FOC/ FOC NEG waste
'(They) did not waste even a bit of food.'

Minimizers form a class of strong NPIs and induce strong scalar inferences (Giannakidou 2011, Israel 2011). The minimizers behave different requirements in VO and OV, as discussed in Section 2.

2 The Distribution of Minimizers in Two Word Order Patterns in Modern Mandarin

The Modern Mandarin 'one'-phrase data have been collected from *Chinese Gigaword*[2]. The combination of 'one'-phrases and three types of negation are examined based on two types of word orders, OV and VO. The three types of negation include the generic/ stative negator *bù*, the negator for negating the instantiation of an event *méi*, and the existential negative predicate *méiyǒu* 'there be not' (Li and Thompson 1981). The three negators are used in different environments. *Bù* is the most general and neutral form of negation. It is used for simple denial of assertions and for refusal, as shown (2) and (3) *Bù* negator does not involve

[1] Abbreviations: 3.sg: 3rd person singular, ASP: aspect, CLF: classifier, EXT: existential predicate, FOC: focus, LOC: locative, MW: measure word, NEG: negation, negative, PASS: passive, PFV: perfective, POSS: possessive, PRF: perfect, REL: relative.

[2] The *Chinese Gigaword Corpus* contains approximately 1.1 billion Chinese characters. The data come from two main sources. One is from Taiwan's Central News Agency (around 700 million characters) and the other is from China's Xinhua News Agency (around 400 million characters).

completion regardless of the time frame, past or present.

(2) tā bù cōngmíng
he NEG smart
'He is not smart.'

(3) tā bù dúshū
he NEG study
'He does/did not study.'

When instantiation of events is concerned, the negator *méi* is used. The form *méi* is used when the main verb of the sentence is *yǒu*. *Yǒu* has a number of different meanings, such as existential, possessive, perfective, presentational, and assertive (Cheng 1978, Huang 1987, Tsai 2004). The existential verb *yǒu* can be optionally omitted when the negator *méi* appears. This study concerns two major functions of the negative predicate *méi(yǒu)*. The first one is negating the instantiation of an event, as shown in (4). *Méi* in (4) negates the instantiation of the drinking event. This function is different from the generic/ stative negator *bù*. As shown in (5), *bù* negates habituals or states.

(4) tā méi hē jiǔ
he NEG drink wine
'He didn't drink wine.'

(5) tā bù hē jiǔ
he NEG drink wine
'He doesn't drink wine.'/ 'He refused to drink wine.'

The other major function of the negator *méi(yǒu)* is the negation of the existential verb *yǒu*, which is the main focus in this study. As in (6), the negator *méiyǒu* includes both negation and an existential verb. The existential verb *yǒu* is optional when *méi* appears.

(6) méi yǒu shuǐ le
NEG.EXT there be water PFV
'There is no more water.'

This section concerns the interaction between 'one'-phrases as minimizers and the three types of negation, stative or generic *bù*, event-non-instantiation negator *méi*, and existential negative predicate *méiyǒu*. In terms of syntactic positions, *bù* and non-existential *méi* follow the subject and precede the verb, while existential negative predicate *méiyǒu* generally precedes the NP whose existence is being introduced. Its position is the same as its positive counterpart, existential predicate *yǒu*. The Mandarin existential construction is shown (7), where the existence of 'one person' is introduced by existential predicate *yǒu*. It is also possible to have a locative NP preceding *yǒu* (Huang 1987), as in (8). Due to the specific arrangement of the existential verb and the unaccusative subject in the Mandarin existential construction, the NP in the position of the unaccusative subject patterns like the object in the canonical VO order. As in (7) and (8), the 'one'-phrases are preceded by an existential verb. Following Huang's (1987) analysis of Mandarin existential sentences, this analysis include V subject/ subject V in this broader definition of VO/ OV construction due to the shared properties between them. The combination of an existential verb followed by a postverbal NP is labeled as VO order for the purpose of comparing how word order influences the interpretation of minimizers under the scope of various negators. When the focus construction is involved, the NP whose existence is concerned precedes the existential predicate, as shown in (9). Analogously, the combination of a preverbal NP and the existential predicate is labeled as OV order.

(7) **yǒu** [yí ge rén] hěn tǎoyàn nǐ
EXT.V one CLF person very dislike you
'There is a person who dislikes you very much.'

(8) zhuō shàng **yǒu** [yì běn xiǎoshuō]
table top EXT.V one CLF novel
hěn yǒuqù
very interesting
'There is a novel on the table which is very interesting.'

(9) zhuō shàng [yì běn shū] yě méi **yǒu**
desk top one CLF book FOC NEG EXT.V
'There is not even a book on the desk.'

The three types of negation have different influences on 'one'-phrases as minimizers regarding their distribution in different word order patterns. The three types can be divided into two groups based on the principle of existentiality because minimizers have a particular relation with existential constructions. The following discussion will begin with non-existential negators *bù* and *méi* and continue to the existential negative predicate *méiyǒu*.

2.1 'One'-phrases as minimizers under non-existential negation

For each of the non-existential negators *bù* and *méi*, the two combinations of **NEG-v...'one'** and **'one'...NEG-v** are collected from the corpus. The former targets 'one'-phrases in VO, while the latter targets 'one'-phrases in OV. Mandarin OV has been regarded as a focal construction (Tsai 2004, Zhang 2000). Thus it should be ideal for minimizers since they attract focal prominence for inducing inferences (Israel 2011). The distribution of the 'one'-phrases as minimizers in the two word orders based on *Chinese Gigaword* are summarized in Figure 1.

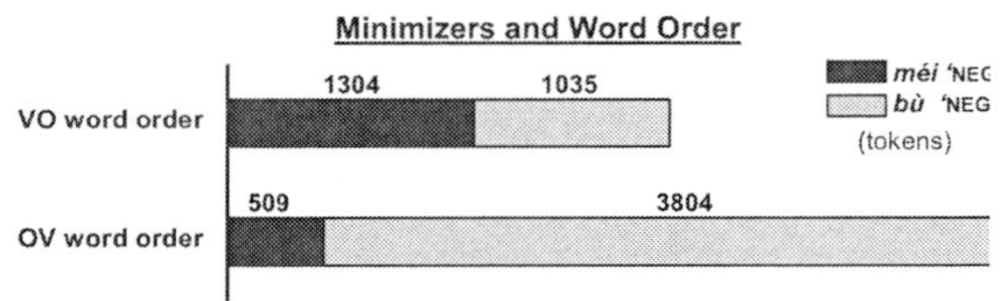

Figure 1: 'One'-phrases as minimizers in VO and OV under non-existential negation

Notably, the overall number of 'one'-phrases as minimizers in OV outnumbers that in VO. It should be mentioned that the genres from *Chinese Gigaword* are restricted to newspaper and press releases. In other words, the 'one'-phrases as minimizers here are collected from written Chinese, which is stylistically formal. SVO is normally preferred in a formal style. Even given the restriction of genres, however, there are still more tokens in OV than in VO, as indicated in Figure 1. The association between minimizers and OV in Modern Mandarin should be more prominent when the genres expand to include colloquial Mandarin.

The asymmetry of VO and OV orders in terms of accommodating 'one'-phrases as minimizers is reflected in how the minimizers behave in the two orders. The 'one'-phrases with negator *bù* or *méi* in VO may be interpreted in various ways. The interpretation as minimizers is only one of these ways. In Modern Mandarin, the inclusion of a classifier in numeral phrases has become mandatory. Classifiers overtly specify the basic unit of the object since they denote some prominently perceived or imputed properties of the entity to which associated nouns refer, as defined in Allan (1977). They are compatible with the concept of a minimal unit and express the concept overtly. For example, the classifiers in (10) and (11) designate the smallest atomic unit, and the measure words in (12) and (13) refer to the smallest quantity. With the classifiers, the 'one'-phrases unambiguously profile the minimal unit of a scale, which is the foundation for inducing scalar inferences.

(10) Kàn bú dào [yì zhāng yǒushànd miànkǒng]
see NEG ASP one CLF friendly face
'did not see even one friendly face'

(11) méi liú guò [yì dī lèi]
NEG tear ASP one drop tear
'hasn't even shed a tear'

(12) bù hē [yì kǒu shuǐ]
NEG drink one MW(mouth) water
'did not drink even one mouthful of water'

(13) méi hē qúnzhòng [yì zhōng jiǔ]
NEG drink people one MW wine
'hasn't drunk a cup of wine from the people'

In addition to the function of minimizers, 'one'-phrases can also function as indefinite referential expressions under negation in VO, as in (14), where the 'one'-phrase is the object of the verb. The 'one'-phrase emphasizes the indefiniteness instead of the quantity of the denotatum; this is reflected in the corresponding English translation '**a** NP'. In the referential function, the numeral 'one' cannot be substituted with other numerals because 'one' cannot contrast with other numerals.

(14) wǒ bù [xiǎng chéngwéi]$_v$ [yí wèi zhèngzhì lǐngxiù]$_o$
I NEG want become one CLF political leader
'I don't want to become a political leader.'

The 'one'-phrase under negation in VO can also be a canonical numeral phrase denoting quantity, as in (15). In this case, the numeral 'one' can be used to contrast with other numerals. The numeral 'one' can be replaced with other numerals.

(15) zhōngguó wending bù yīng xì yú [yì rén]
China stability NEG should tie at one person
'The stability of China should not be tied to one person.'

These different interpretations of 'one'-phrases show that VO under negation can have various interpretations. A minimizer reading is not guaranteed.

However, when 'one'-phrases appear under negation in OV, they are unambiguously understood as minimizer NPIs, as in (16).

(16) song le tā sì běn shū, tā [yì běn] dōu méi kàn wán
give PRF he four CLF book he one CLF

FOC NEG read ASP
'...gave him four books. He did not finish even one book.'

No tokens from the corpus show that 'one'-phrases in the preverbal object position are used as indefinite referential expressions or quantity-denoting phrases. This is because the focus of the preverbal object position in OV forces 'one'-phrases to be interpreted as minimizers. Based on the data so far, asymmetry between VO and OV can be clearly observed. The following sections will discuss asymmetric requirements for Mandarin minimizers in VO and OV.

2.1.1 Collocation of *rènhé* 'any' and minimizers in VO and OV

The distribution of minimizers in Modern Mandarin clearly illustrates the asymmetry of OV and VO in terms of securing a minimizer NPI reading. Since VO is open to multiple interpretations, additional mechanisms, such as the occurrence of *rènhé* 'any', guarantee the minimizer reading. Mandarin *rènhé* is functionally similar to English NPI *any*. In VO, when *rènhé* 'any' is added to a 'one'-phrase under negation, the 'one'-phrase must be understood as a minimizer NPI, as shown in (17).

(17) qùnián méi mǎi **rènhé** [yì běn shū]
last year NEG buy any one CLF book
'last year did not buy any book'

Interestingly, both *rènhé* 'any' and minimizers are polarity items. Each of them can be used alone for scalar readings. When *rènhé* 'any' and the minimizer appear in VO, their associated NPs have prosodic prominence or emphatic stress. This indicates that they profile an extreme value in an ordered set of alternatives. Since both of them occur in a scalar construal, they induce similar scalar inferences. Although the subtle differences between the two types of polarity items are hard to distinguish in the VO, it is clear that the combination of two polarity items as in (17) has a stronger emphatic effect. Importantly, such a combination must be an NPI. It does not allow alternative interpretations.

In contrast, the 'one'-phrases under negation in OV are not ambiguous in nature. In this case, the addition of *rènhé* 'any' does not help much in terms of turning the 'one'-phrases into minimizers. Following this logic, there should be fewer cases of *rènhé* 'any' modifying 'one'-phrases in OV. The prediction turns out to be true, as reflected in the difference regarding the frequency of co-occurrence of *rènhé* 'any' with 'one'-phrases in VO and OV. As in Figure 2, *rènhé* 'any' appears mostly in VO, itis barely found in OV.

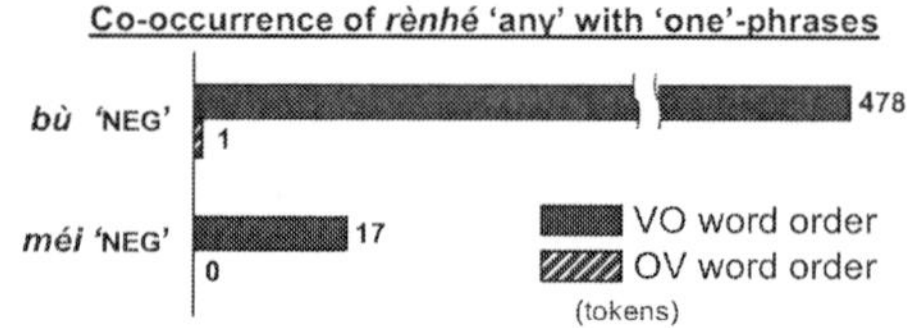

Figure 2: Co-occurrence of *rènhé* 'any' and 'one'-phrases as minimizers in VO and OV

The sharp contrast of the occurrences of *rènhé* 'any' in the two word orders again shows that the information structure of OV can ensure that 'one'-phrases under negation are understood as minimizers, while VO may need additional elements to make a minimizer reading unambiguous. The addition of the NPI *rènhé* 'any' to 'one'-phrases can be viewed as a strategy to fully distinguish the minimizer function from other readings of 'one'-phrases in VO.

2.1.2 Requirement of focus particles for minimizers in OV

In Modern Mandarin, the type of focus in OV becomes overtly specified. The 'one'-phrases as minimizers in OV are now accompanied by the focus-sensitive scalar particles, *yě* and *dōu*. The involvement of scalar particles is the result of creating maximal distinction between various types of focus carried in the OV construction. The great majority of the 'one'-phrases as minimizers in OV co-occur with the scalar particles, as shown in Figure 3.

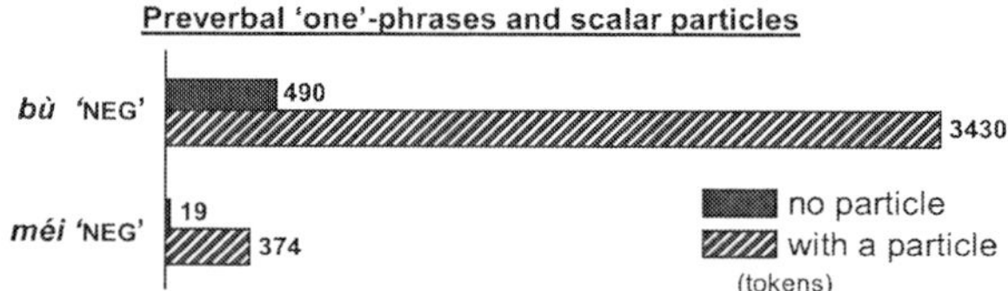

Figure 3: Involvement of the scalar particles in OV order containing 'one'-phrases as minimizers

The 'one'-phrases which lack a scalar particle have two properties. First, this class of minimizers is more archaic, and may be viewed as vestiges from earlier periods of Chinese which characterize the formal style. Second, preverbal 'one'-phrases without scalar particles tend to appear in parallel clauses, as shown in (18). The parallel clauses are normally used in slogans for stylistic formal symmetry. This type of 'one'-phrases also sounds formal because they look as though they are imitations of archaic forms.

(18) [yí tàng bù bái zǒu] ,

one trip NEG in vain walk

[yí jù bù bái wèn]
one sentence NEG in vain ask
'not have any trip for nothing and not ask a sentence for nothing'

The preverbal 'one'-phrases without scalar particles thus have their own syntactic and pragmatic characteristics, departing from typical contemporary use. As indicated in Figure 3, the majority of the preverbal minimizers occur with the scalar particles. The canonical form of minimizers in OV is shown in (19) and (20), where the occurrence of the particles clearly indicates scalar focus and reinforces the scalar nature of their associated 'one'-phrases.

(19) [yì píng] **yě** bù liú
one bottle FOC NEG keep
'Don't keep even a single bottle.'

(20) jiālǐde niú yang [yì zhī]
in the house cow sheep one CLF
dōu méi sǔnshī
FOC NEG lose
'...did not lose even a single cow or sheep'

2.1.3 VO-OV asymmetry in acceptance of Double-object construction

Although OV is apparently a more ideal place for minimizer 'one'-phrases as minimizers, there are still a fair number of them in VO, as shown in Figure 3. This is partly due to the syntactic constraints of OV. VO allows the Mandarin double object construction. As shown in (21) and (22), the double object construction involves the form, Subj V Obj_1 Obj_2, where the 'one'-phrase (Obj. 2) is the direct object of the verb. The focal stress of the two examples falls on the 'one'-phrase, which indicates that the 'one'-phrase is used as an emphatic NPI. However, OV can accommodate only one object argument. In OV, the preposed object must be the direct object.

(21) méi hē women$_1$ [yì kǒu shuǐ]$_2$ què
NEG drink us one mouth water but
xiàng qīn xiōngdì yíyàng guānxīn
alike close brother same care about
'(He) did not drink a mouthful of our water, but treated us like his close brothers'

(22) dàjiā kǔ gàn wǔ nián，
everyone hard work five year
méi yào guójiā$_1$ [yì fēn qián]$_2$
NEG ask for country one cent money
'Everyone worked hard for five years and did not ask the country for even a cent.'

OV can only accommodate one preverbal object. In contrast, VO is relatively flexible to take 'one'-phrases as minimizers occurring in a variety of constructions, such as a double-object construction.

This section has discussed the distribution of minimizers under non-existential negation, which reveals their tendency to occur in OV word order.

3 'One'-phrases as minimizers with existential negation

When 'one'-phrases appear with the existential negative predicate of *méiyǒu*, the 'one'-phrases as minimizers do not show a tendency toward OV. This distribution is unlike the distribution under non-existential negation. In the context of *méiyǒu*, the majority of 'one'-phrases as minimizers (13,650 tokens) appear in VO, while fewer than 3,000 tokens are found in OV. Such a vast difference suggests that existential negation has a remarkable influence on the distribution of 'one'-phrases as minimizers in the two word order patterns. The distribution implies that Mandarin existential constructions should be able to provide informative conditions in semantics and pragmatics for 'one'-phrases to be interpreted as minimizers. With respect to the syntactic properties, the existential constructions in VO are compatible with a variety of predicate constructions which cannot fit into OV. Due to the syntactic characteristics, the existential constructions in VO can accommodate a larger diversity of constructions involving minimizers as compared with those in OV.

Mandarin existential sentences can occur in a more complicated structure involving more than one VP. For example, sentences (23) and (24) contain two verbs, as a subtype of existential presentative sentences. This type of sentence is labeled as "realis descriptive clauses" by Li and Thompson (1981). It is analyzed as a serial verb construction and it has two properties. First, the direct object of the existential verb must be indefinite. Second, its discourse function is to present or introduce an NP to be further described. As in (23), the NP 'one person' is an indefinite referential expression, followed by a descriptive clause. The indefinite numeral phrase 'one tree' in (24) is provided with more details by its following adjectival predicate.

(23) yǒu [yí ge rén] qiāo mén
EXT.V one CLF person knock door
'There is someone knocking on the door.'

(24) yuànzi yǒu [yì kē shù] hěn gāo
court yard EXT.V one CLF tree very high
'There is a tree in the yard which is very tall.'

Huang (1987) further proposes a general form of Mandarin existential sentences as repeated in (25). Position II is reserved for existential predicates. The grammatical subject generally appears in Position I. Position III is for the NP whose existence is being asserted. Position IV is filled by an expression of predication, which is a descriptive clause or phrase. The expression in Position IV has to be semantically related to the NP in Position III.

(25) ...(NP)...EXT.V...NP...(XP)...
Position I II III IV

The general form not only applies to positive existential predicates, but also to existential negation *méiyǒu*. For instance, the 'one'-phrase introduced by *méiyǒu* in (26) is followed by a verb phrase which provides relevant details. In sentence (27), the whole VP following the 'one'-phrase functions as a restrictive clause specifying the property concerned in the discussion.

(26) **méiyǒu** [yí ge huànzhě de
EXT.V one CLF patient POSS
jiǎnyàn jiéguǒ] chéng yángxìng
inspection result show positive
'Not a single patient has positive results'

(27) jiānglái **méiyǒu** [yí ge guójiā]
future EXT.V one CLF country
néng bǎohù tā de huánjìng
can protect 3.SG POSS environment
'There will not be a country that can protect its environment in the future.'

In the data from *Chinese Gigaword*, when 'one'-phrases as minimizers appear with existential negation *méiyǒu*, the majority of them are followed by a phrase of predication. However, the "complicated" existential construction involving more than one predicate can only appear in VO. According to the corpus data, the generalization is that in OV the NP as the preverbal object cannot be followed by any predicative phrases. If there is any modification for the denotatum of the preverbal 'one'-phrase, it has to precede the noun of the 'one'-phrase. As in (28), the adjective occurs between the classifier and the noun.

(28) lián [yí wèi **zhōngguó**
even one CLF Chinese
liúxuéshēng] dōu méiyǒu
overseas student FOC EXT.NEG
'There is not even a single Chinese overseas student.'

Examples (29) and (30) illustrate the different requirements regarding modification in the two word orders. Predicative clauses and relative clauses appear in different syntactic positions to modify 'one'-phrases as minimizers. Predicative clauses have to immediately follow 'one'-phrases, whereas relative clauses with the relative marker *de* precede 'one'-phrases. In (29), the 'one'-phrase as minimizer in VO is followed by an expression of predication in boldface. If it is paraphrased using OV, the phrase of predication has to be expressed by a relative clause. In Modern Mandarin, a relative clause is marked by *de* at the end, as underlined in (30).

(29) yóuqí shì liánhéguó méiyǒu [yí
specifically FOC UN EXT.NEG one
ge huìyuán guó] **kěyǐ dàibiǎo táiwān**
CLF member country can represent Taiwan
'Specifically in the United Nations, there is no member country that can represent Taiwan.'

(30) yóuqí shì liánhéguó , [yí ge
specifically FOC United Nations one CLF
kěyǐ dàibiǎo táiwān **de** huìyuán guó]
can represent Taiwan REL member country
yě /dōu méiyǒu
FOC/FOC EXT.NEG
'Specifically in the United Nations, there is not even a single member that can represent Taiwan.'

Relative clauses can also modify 'one'-phrases as minimizers in VO, as shown in (31). However, in some cases the strategy of modification is not ideal in VO. For example, if (27) is paraphrased with a relative clause in VO, the grammatical acceptability becomes a problem, as in (32), which is even rejected by some native speakers. The ungrammaticality of (33) shows that the position between the unit word and the noun in VO is not an ideal position for relative clauses modifying 'one'-phases as minimizers.

(31) yóuqí shì liánhéguó , méiyǒu
specifically FOC United Nations EXT.NEG
[yí ge kěyǐ dàibiǎo táiwān de
one CLF can represent Taiwan REL
huìyuán guó]
member country

'Specifically in the United Nations, there is not a member country that can represent Taiwan.'

(32) ??jiānglái **méiyǒu** [yí ge néng bǎohù
future EXT.NEG one CLF can protect
tā de huánjìng de guójiā]
3.SG POSS environment REL country
'There will not be a country that can protect its environment in the future.'

(33) *jiānglái **méiyǒu** [néng bǎohù tā
future EXT.NEG can protect 3.SG
de huánjìng de yí ge guójiā]
POSS environment REL one CLF country
Intended reading: 'There will not be a country that can protect its environment in the future.'

The awkwardness of (32) can mainly be attributed to three reasons. First, it is difficult to trace the referent of the third person pronoun in the cases where the pronoun precedes its referent. Second, Mandarin sentences generally do not allow the phonological clash of multiple *de*, which have various functions such as a possessive or a relative clause marker. Third, existential constructions profile the NP introduced by the existential verbs in the information structure. This profiled NP is foregrounded with focal prominence. The intervention of a long relative clause may decrease the focal prominence assigned by the existential predicate. The preference of a predicative clause over a relative clause in VO is reflected in the corpus data, where up to 95% of the 'one'-phrases as minimizers in VO are followed by an expression of predication. The use of relative clauses for modifying minimizers is relatively not productive.

Relative clauses are rarely found in VO, and also seldom appear to modify 'one'-phrases as minimizers in OV. As shown in (34)-(35), the 'one'-phrases normally do not have additional modification. The information relevant to the denotatum of 'one'-phrases is normally provided in earlier contexts. For example, the numeral 'one'-classifier combination in (35) is associated with the 'tent' appearing in the previous clause. Notably, the majority of the 'one'-phrases as minimizers in OV order have the noun omitted in the corpus data. Since the classifier alone is sufficient to delimit the basic unit of its associated noun, the noun which appears earlier in the context does not need to be repeated. The way the preverbal minimizers behave in the corpus data also reveals a special property of the OV construction. Since the preverbal object of the OV construction has focal prominence, the preverbal object with a focus stress tends to be a small unit, which can make the prosodic prominence more salient. In addition to the prosodic emphasis, the basic component of 'one'-phrases without additional modification also increases the semantic prominence of the minimizer by narrowing the focus to the 'one'-phrase only.

(34) tā rúguǒ zuò zài jiā lǐ
he if sit at home in
[yí piào] yě méiyǒu
one vote FOC NEG.EXT
'If he sits at home, there will not be even a single vote (for him).'

(35) yào shēnlǐng wǔ bǎi dǐng zhàngpéng
want apply for five hundred CLF tent
[yì dǐng] yě méiyǒu
one tent CLF NEG.EXT
'...plan to apply for five hundred tents, but there is not even a single one.'

Based on corpus data, the preverbal 'one'-phrases as minimizers are generally not newly introduced information in the discourse. As shown in (36), the first clause clearly conveys a negative proposition, but the preverbal 'one'-phrase in the second clause repeats the information for the sake of emphasis and reinforcement.

(36) méiyǒu rén xià qù，[yí ge]
NEG.EXT person down go one CLF
yě méiyǒu
YE NEG.EXT
'Nobody went down, not even a single one.'

The discussion so far concerns how the information structure of OV and VO is reflected in the syntactic constraints of the *méiyǒu* existential construction. The differences of 'one'-phrases with negation *méiyǒu* in VO and OV are summarized in (37).

(37) 'One'-phrases as minimizers in existential constructions

	VO	OV
'one'-phrase followed by another expression of predication	√	x
'one'-phrase modified by a relative clause (*yi*-CLF RC N)	√	√

Although both predicative phrases and relative clauses can be used to provide further information for 'one'-phrases, relative clauses are preferred. The preference of one strategy over the other is relevant to the issue of profiling the element of which the existence is concerned. In OV, the 'one'-phrases have the tendency to remain as a basic numeral phrase without extra modifiers. This is for the purpose of foregrounding the 'one'-phrases as minimizers both phonologically and semantically. Even though the three strategies of providing further information of the 'one'-phrases are all legitimate, the actual use in the corpus shows that the choice of the form for modification is determined by the principle of maximally foregrounding the focused elements. Among the three modification strategies, the existential construction with a predicative phrase in VO has most tokens. This type of modification satisfies the emphatic nature of minimizers because the NP immediately following the existential predicate is profiled in the information structure. The principle of profiling important information provides an answer as to why 'one'-phrases as minimizers under existential negation do not show a tendency toward OV.

4 Conclusion

The semantics and pragmatics of OV support the minimizer reading of preverbal object phrases, so OV should be ideal for Mandarin 'one'-phrases as minimizers. Following this line, it predicts that in Modern Mandarin the majority of 'one'-phrases as minimizers should occur in OV. On the contrary, this turns out not to be the case because the majority of 'one'-phrases as minimizers still stay in VO when under existential negation. This study solves the puzzle by showing that the distribution of 'one'-phrases as minimizers in VO and OV is linked with their co-occurring negators. The property of existentiality of negation can divide Mandarin negation into two types. In the environment of non-existential negation, there are more 'one'-phrases as minimizers appearing in OV than in VO. However, when they occur with existential negation, the vast majority of them stay in VO. The distribution in which VO outnumbers OV in the existential constructions has remained unchanged since Old Chinese. This phenomenon of 'one'-phrases staying in VO is due to the semantic and syntactic characteristics of the existential constructions. The 'one'-phrases under existential negation in VO can receive sufficient focal prominence, which is required for the interpretation of minimizers. In order to maximize the focal prominence, most of the 'one'-phrases as minimizers remain in the basic form, leaving other information in the preceding context.

In sum, this paper presents a corpus analysis on the distribution of Mandarin minimizers. The results not only show the crucial function of focal constructions in inducing emphatic inferences from negative polarity items, but also explain how information structure shapes the distribution and interpretation of numeral phrases.

Acknowledgments

The author would like to thank reviewers for their insightful feedback and Hong Kong Polytechnic University for the research support.

References

Allan, Keith. 1977. Classifiers. *Language* 53 (2): 285-311.

Cheng, Robert L. 1978. Tense interpretation of four Taiwanese modal verbs. In *Proceedings of Symposium on Chinese Linguistics, 1977 Linguistic Institute of the Linguistic Society of America*, ed. by Robert L. Cheng, Ying-chi Li, and Ting-chi Tang, 243-266. Taipei: Student Book Co.

Giannakidou, Anastasia. 2011. Positive polarity items and negative polarity items: variation, licensing, and compositionality. In *Semantics: An international handbook of natural language meaning*, ed. by Claudia Maienborn, Klaus von Heusinger, and Paul Portner, 1660-1712. Berlin: Mouton de Gruyter.

Huang, C-T, James. 1987. Existential sentences in Chinese and (in)definiteness. In *The Representation of (In)definiteness*, ed. by Eric J. Reuland and Alice G.B. ter Meulen, 226-253. Cambridge, MA: MIT Press.

Israel, Michael. 2011. *The Grammar of Polarity: Pragmatics, Sensitivity and the Logic of Scales*. Cambridge: Cambridge University Press.

Li, Charles N., and Sandra A. Thompson. 1981. *Mandarin Chinese: A functional reference grammar*. University of California Press, Berkeley.

Tsai, Wei.-Tien Dylan. 2004b. Tan 'you ren', 'you-de ren', he 'you-xie ren' [On 'a person', 'some of the people', and 'some people' in Chinese]. *Hanyu Xuebao* 漢語學報 [Chinese Linguistics] 2004 (2): 16-25.

Zhang, Ning. 2000. Object shift in Mandarin Chinese. *Journal of Chinese Linguistics* 28 (2).201-246.

Planting Trees in the Desert: Delexicalized Tagging and Parsing Combined

Daniel Zeman,⋆ David Mareček,⋆ Zhiwei Yu,† and Zdeněk Žabokrtský⋆
⋆ Charles University, Prague, Czechia
† Shanghai Jiaotong University, Shanghai, China
{zeman|marecek|zabokrtsky}@ufal.mff.cuni.cz
jordanyzw@sjtu.edu.cn

Abstract

Various unsupervised and semi-supervised methods have been proposed to tag and parse an unseen language. We explore delexicalized parsing, proposed by (Zeman and Resnik, 2008), and delexicalized tagging, proposed by (Yu et al., 2016). For both approaches we provide a detailed evaluation on Universal Dependencies data (Nivre et al., 2016), a de-facto standard for multi-lingual morphosyntactic processing (while the previous work used other datasets). Our results confirm that in separation, each of the two delexicalized techniques has some limited potential when no annotation of the target language is available. However, if used in combination, their errors multiply beyond acceptable limits. We demonstrate that even the tiniest bit of expert annotation in the target language may contain significant potential and should be used if available.

1 Introduction

Dependency parsing is an important step in language analysis, useful for downstream applications such as machine translation or question answering. Unfortunately, it is not an easy task. Successful parsers rely on dependency treebanks annotated by language experts. While at least small treebanks are becoming available for an increasing number of languages, the world's languages will not be covered any soon. The number of languages for which at least a small treebank is available lies probably somewhere between 50 and 100 (we are aware of treebanks for 56 languages). At the same time, the number of world's languages is usually estimated between 4,000 and 7,000; and 398 languages are reported to have more than 1 million speakers (Lewis et al., 2016). In order to parse the treebankless languages, several techniques have been developed.

(Hwa et al., 2004) projected dependency trees across bilingual word alignments in a parallel corpus. They used a few target-language rules to improve the target trees.

(Zeman and Resnik, 2008) proposed *delexicalized parsing*, a method that trains a parsing model on part-of-speech tags only, ignoring lexical information. The trained model is then used to parse data in a related language for which POS tags are available. It is assumed that POS-tagged data are cheaper and easier to obtain for new languages than treebanks are. Such claim is probably justified, yet it does not provide any immediate solution in the case that no annotated resources are available for the target language.

(McDonald et al., 2011) evaluated their multi-source delexicalized transfer using POS tags predicted by the projected part-of-speech tagger of (Das and Petrov, 2011). This tagger relies only on labeled training data for English, and uses a parallel corpus (Europarl) to project the tags across word alignment. Both (Zeman and Resnik, 2008) and (McDonald et al., 2011) notice that varying treebank annotation styles are a major obstacle to meaningful evaluation of any cross-linguistic transfer.

Projection across bitexts is the central approach in many published experiments with POS tagging of low-resource languages.

(Yarowsky and Ngai, 2001) project POS tags

from English to French and Chinese via both automatic and gold alignment, and report substantial improvement of accuracy after using de-noising post-processing. (Fossum and Abney, 2005) extend this approach by projecting multiple source languages onto a target language.

(Das and Petrov, 2011) use graph-based label propagation for cross-lingual knowledge transfer, and estimate emission distributions in the target language using a loglinear model. (Duong et al., 2013) choose only automatically recognized "good" sentences from the parallel data, and further apply self-training.

(Agić et al., 2015) learn taggers for 100 languages using aligned Bible verses from The Bible Corpus (Christodouloupoulos et al., 2010).

Besides approaches based on parallel data, there are also experiments showing that reasonable POS tagging accuracy (close to 90 %) can be reached using quick and efficient prototyping techniques, such as (Cucerzan and Yarowsky, 2002). However, such approaches rely on at least partial understanding of the target language grammar, and on the availability of a dictionary, hence they do not scale well when it comes to tens or hundreds of languages (Cucerzan and Yarowsky experiment with two languages only).

In contrast, (Yu et al., 2016) train a tagging model on language-independent meta-features and transfer it directly to a target language in a fashion similar to the delexicalized parsing; they call their approach *delexicalized tagging*. They use neither parallel corpora nor any target-language dictionary, rules or other expert knowledge. They compute meta-features on large raw corpora, and they make tagged texts of 107 languages available for download.[1]

2 Delexicalized Tagging

(Yu et al., 2016) describe 17 features they extract for each word type in each source and target language. The features describe statistical properties of the word type in a large raw corpus. They are not directly tied to the lexicon of any particular language.

[1]Note that a pre-requisity of delexicalized tagging is that word boundaries in the target text are easily detectable. Hence the method is not suitable for languages that do not use inter-word spacing, such as Chinese, Japanese or Thai.

Languages for which POS-tagged data is available can be used as source languages. A classifier is trained to learn the correspondence between feature vectors and POS tags. The classifier is then directly applied to feature vectors of the target language, and assigns a POS tag to each target word type.

(Yu et al., 2016) experiment with various classifiers and report that *support vector machines* (SVM) with radial kernel (Boser et al., 1992) gave the best results on their data; therefore we use SVM in our experiments, too.

A prerequisite to delexicalized tagging is a common tagset for both the source and the target languages. (Yu et al., 2016) use the Google Universal POS (set of 12 tags) (Petrov et al., 2012). We use an extended version of this tagset, used in the Universal Dependencies project[2] (Nivre et al., 2016). With 17 tags it is still reasonably coarse-grained, which is advantageous for such a resource-poor method.

The 17 tags are `NOUN`, `PROPN` (proper noun), `VERB`, `AUX` (auxiliary verb), `ADJ` (adjective), `ADV` (adverb), `PRON` (pronoun), `DET` (determiner), `NUM` (numeral), `ADP` (adposition i.e. pre- or postposition), `CONJ` (coordinating conjunction), `SCONJ` (subordinating conjunction), `PART` (particle), `INTJ` (interjection), `SYM`, `PUNCT` and `X` (unknown).

2.1 Features

We use the same 17 features[3] as (Yu et al., 2016), which we describe below. Let C be a corpus and c_i the i-th token in the corpus. $N = |C|$ = the number of tokens in the corpus C. $f(w) = |\{i : c_i = w\}|$ = the absolute word frequency, i.e. number of instances of the word type w in the corpus C. Similarly, $f(x, y)$ is the absolute frequency of the word bigram xy. $Pre(w) = \{x : \exists i\,(c_i = w) \wedge (c_{i-1} = x)\}$ is the set of word types that occur at least once in a position preceding an instance of w. Analogously, $Next(w)$ denotes the set of word types following w in the corpus. $Context(w) = \{x, y : \exists i\,(c_{i-1} = x) \wedge (c_i = w) \wedge (c_{i+1} = y)\}$ denotes the set of contexts surrounding w, and $Subst(w) = \{y : Context(y) \cap Context(w) \neq \emptyset\}$ is the set of words that share a context with w.

1. *word length* – the number of characters in w

[2]`http://universaldependencies.org/`

[3]Software at `github.com/ufal/deltacorpus`.

2. *log frequency* – logarithm of the relative frequency of w in C

$$\log \frac{f(w)}{N}$$

3. *is number* – binary value based on the Unicode character property *digit*

4. *is punctuation* – binary value based on the Unicode character property *punctuation*

5. *relative frequency after number*

$$\log \frac{|i : c_i = w \wedge is\_number(c_{i-1})|}{f(w)}$$

6. *relative frequency after punctuation*

$$\log \frac{|i : c_i = w \wedge is\_punctuation(c_{i-1})}{f(w)}$$

7. *how many different words appear before* w: $|Pre(w)|$

8. *how many different words appear after* w: $|Next(w)|$

9. *how many different words in* C *share a context with* w: $|Subst(w)|$

10. *preceding word entropy*

$$PN = \sum_{y \in Pre(w)} f(y)$$

$$\sum_{y \in Pre(w)} -\frac{f(y)}{PN} \log \frac{f(y)}{PN}$$

11. *following word entropy*

$$NN = \sum_{y \in Next(w)} f(y)$$

$$\sum_{y \in Next(w)} -\frac{f(y)}{NN} \log \frac{f(y)}{NN}$$

12. *substituting word entropy*

$$SN = \sum_{y \in Subst(w)} f(y)$$

$$\sum_{y \in Subst(w)} -\frac{f(y)}{SN} \log \frac{f(y)}{SN}$$

13. *weighted sum of pointwise mutual information (PMI) of* w *with the preceding word* – collect all words y in C that precede w, then calculate their PMI values with w and sum PMIs weighted by the joint probability of the pair

$$\frac{\sum_{y \in Pre(w)} f(w, y) \times \log \frac{N \times f(w,y)}{f(w) \times f(y)}}{N}$$

14. *weighted sum of PMI of* w *with the following word* – fully analogous to the previous feature

15. *pointwise mutual information between* w *and the most frequent preceding word*

$$MaxP = \arg\max_{y \in Pre(w)} f(y)$$

$$\log \frac{N \times f(w, MaxP)}{f(w) \times f(MaxP)}$$

16. *pointwise mutual information between* w *and the most frequent following word* – fully analogous to the previous feature

17. *entropy of suffixes following the root of* w – First we collect counts of suffixes $count(suffix)$ in C whose length range from 1 to 4 and counts of corresponding roots (words without suffixes) $count(root)$ in C. For each word, we find the border between root and suffix by maximization of the product $f(root) \times f(suffix)$. Then, we compute conditional entropy over all suffixes given the root.[4]

3 Delexicalized Parsing

The idea of delexicalized parsing is that a given sequence of parts of speech has often the same preferred dependency structure regardless of language. To illustrate this, consider the bilingual example in Figure 1. The mapping between the words in the two sentences is not 1-1. However, the words they have in common have identical part-of-speech tags and the dependency relations are also shared.

The POS tags are the key here. We can remove the words from the training data and show only the

[4] The underlying intution is that some POSs tend to participate in derivation and inflection more often than others. Obviously, our root/suffix segmentation is only an approximation.

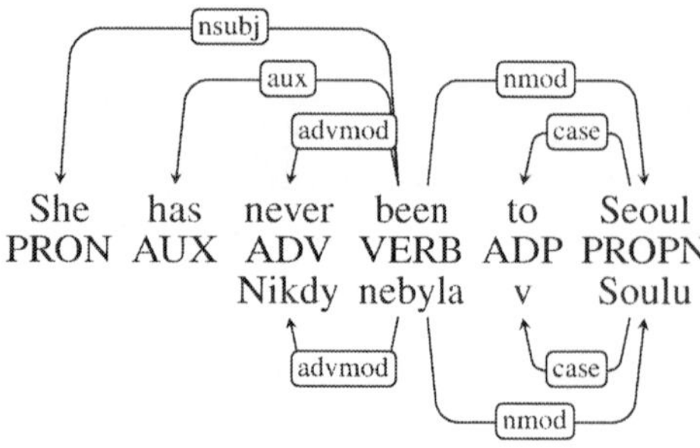

Figure 1: English and Czech sentence with equivalent meaning and shared dependencies.

POS tags to the parser when training the parsing model. Such model will be less accurate because it will lack important lexical information such as verb valency. However, at the same time it will be applicable to multiple languages. Obviously, the more closely related the languages are to the source (training) language, the better.

While a common tagset is a prerequisite to delexicalized tagging, for parsing we assume a common dependency style, i.e. the set of relation types and guidelines for their attachment.[5] Fortunately, Universal Dependencies define a harmonized annotation style for all languages and we do not have to consider annotation differences, unlike (McDonald et al., 2011) and other previous work.

4 Data and Experimental Setup

In order to increase comparability of our results to (Yu et al., 2016), we use the same W2C corpus (Majliš and Žabokrtský, 2012) to extract feature vectors (we use at most the first 20 million tokens from the WEB section in each language).

Unlike (Yu et al., 2016), we take the POS-tagged data for SVM training and evaluation from the Universal Dependencies collection (Nivre et al., 2016). UD is also used to train and evaluate delexicalized parsers. We work with the following 29 UD languages:[6] Basque (eu), Bulgarian (bg), Croatian (hr), Czech (cs), Danish (da), Dutch (nl), English (en), Estonian (et), Finnish (fi), French (fr), German (de), Greek (el), Hebrew (he), Hindi (hi), Hungarian (hu), Indonesian (id), Irish (ga), Italian (it), Latin (la), Norwegian (no), Persian (fa), Polish (pl), Portuguese (pt), Romanian (ro), Slovenian (sl), Spanish (es), Swedish (sv), Tamil (ta). For experiments that do not involve delexicalized tagging we also report results on Ancient Greek (grc), Arabic (ar), Gothic (got) and Old Church Slavonic (cu).[7]

The first 30,000 tokens of the training data of each language were used to train the SVM classifier for delexicalized tagging. Each token was considered one training instance (i.e., n occurrences of a word w result in n identical instances). In addition we trained several mixed models based on multiple source languages ($N \times 30,000$ tokens). (Yu et al., 2016) observe that it is really significant how much similar the source and the target languages are. Hence we trained specialized models for several groups of Indo-European languages (Germanic – ger, Romance – rom, and Slavic – sla), one model of agglutinating languages (agl: Hungarian, Finnish, Estonian, Basque), one general model for Indo-European languages (ine) and one model based on all languages. We always excluded the target language from the source mix. While the first three groups are motivated by genetic relatedness, the *agl* group is based on surface properties because we have few related languages in the collection.

In the case of delexicalized parsing, we compare several scenarios, depending on what is the source of the part-of-speech tags used in parsing models: gold-standard, predicted by a supervised tagger and predicted by a delexicalized tagger. To speed up experimentation, the parser is trained only on the first 5,000 sentences of the training section of the given language. In the case of multi-source transfer, all the source languages are merged first (interlaced, so that all languages can participate), then the first 5,000 sentences are taken. We use the Malt Parser (Nivre and Hall, 2005) with the `stacklazy` algorithm; it is reasonably fast to train and it allows for non-projective dependencies.

[5] The common style is only required for evaluation of the results using some labeled data. When the technique is applied to a truly unknown language, the target annotation style will be naturally inherited from the source language.

[6] We use the UD release 1.2 and exclude languages that are not represented in W2C and also Arabic (because of vowel diacritics and tokenization in UD not matching W2C) and Japanese (because of its non-trivial word segmentation).

[7] There are languages with more than one treebank and we use numeric indices to distinguish the extra treebanks in our results: fi_1 for the FinnTreeBank, la_1 and grc_1 for the PROIEL treebanks, and la_2 for the Index Thomisticus Treebank.

	source								
target	base	self	all	ine	ger	rom	sla	agl	c7
bg	37	87	57	58	61	56	**67**	45	50
cs	42	82	60	59	52	46	**63**	45	54
da	30	83	63	67	**70**	58	48	42	55
de	30	83	58	60	**63**	58	46	39	51
el	36	88	**62**	**62**	51	54	51	40	55
en	30	81	56	58	**62**	54	49	48	52
es	31	89	69	72	72	**79**	56	40	61
et	49	73	**51**	48	47	37	47	**51**	45
eu	42	78	**52**	45	41	40	42	46	44
fa	48	89	**47**	39	34	27	**47**	42	42
fi	41	74	**49**	**49**	46	42	**49**	**49**	43
fi_1	35	73	46	47	40	36	42	**48**	41
fr	33	89	73	73	63	**78**	52	41	65
ga	38	84	**58**	56	57	51	49	45	57
he	38	81	**42**	37	34	29	39	34	38
hi	30	85	**51**	45	50	43	46	35	48
hr	41	84	56	60	51	41	**65**	49	52
hu	37	79	51	49	**55**	51	43	37	46
id	42	82	**50**	47	42	41	47	42	44
it	34	86	58	51	56	**74**	53	38	55
la	30	74	**49**	39	34	26	40	43	43
la_1	20	79	**35**	28	23	17	33	22	29
la_2	37	89	50	47	44	39	52	**53**	50
nl	28	83	62	61	**65**	60	44	44	61
no	29	87	66	65	**70**	56	48	44	49
pl	45	80	60	59	48	47	**64**	46	53
pt	36	89	67	67	62	**75**	60	40	51
ro	36	75	**58**	56	47	55	50	39	51
sl	36	78	**62**	60	52	45	**62**	45	53
sv	30	80	65	68	**71**	53	53	46	59
ta	42	69	**37**	33	30	25	35	36	32

Table 1: POS tagging accuracy using the SVM classifier, measured on UD 1.2 development data. The "base" column shows baseline results. The "self" column contains results of a classifier trained on the target language. In the remaining columns the target language was always excluded from the source language set. Various combinations of source languages were tested: all, Indo-European, Germanic, Romance, Slavic, a mix of agglutinating languages, and the "c7" combination from (Yu et al., 2016) (but UD 1.2 does not contain Catalan and Turkish, so our mix contains a maximum of 5 languages, minus the source: bg, de, el, hi, hu).

5 Evaluation

Table 1 summarizes the results of delexicalized tagging on UD 1.2 development data. The "base" column presents results of a baseline tagger that tags everything except punctuation and numbers as NOUN. The general tendency is that Romance and Germanic languages, with their higher proportion of function words, have lower baseline accuracy than Slavic and Uralic languages. At the same time, languages with low baseline score often (but not always) witness high accuracy of the SVM tagger. For high-baseline languages the classifier brings only moderate improvement, and in two cases (Persian and Tamil) it does not beat the baseline at all.

The "self" column gives results of a classifier trained on the target language (but training data is still different from test data). It can be understood as an estimate of the upper bound of achievable results.

The rest of the table shows classifiers trained on various combinations of source languages. The grouping is done the same way as for tagging, although there are other options, e.g. the KLcpos3 metric proposed by (Rosa and Žabokrtský, 2015). We have confirmed the hypothesis that if there are multiple closely related source languages available, the more distant languages are better left out. All Slavic, Germanic and Romance languages (except Romanian) achieve the best scores with classifiers trained on their respective groups (the target language always excluded from training). This can be explained by different distribution of parts of speech: Slavic languages do not have articles, hence the 'DET' tag is much less frequent than in Germanic and Romance languages. The replacement of case morphology by prepositions is even more pervasive in Romance than in Germanic languages. And so on.

For the other target languages, training on all available source languages seems to be the best recipe in most cases. For example Hindi, an Indo-European language, is not so close to its relatives (at least w.r.t. the features that we measure) that we could base the classifier solely on Indo-European languages from our collection. However, using the labeled Hindi data to tag Urdu, Punjabi or Gujarati is likely to be more successful.

Table 2 summarizes the unlabeled attachment score (UAS) of delexicalized parsing based on POS tags predicted by the supervised tagger from UDPipe (Straka et al., 2016). There are three exceptions: the columns "gold", "lex" and "l20" use lexicalized parsing models. In addition, "gold" uses gold-standard POS tags.

For some languages the difference between us-

	self				source				
target	gold	lex	delex	120	single best			multi best	
ar	80	80	70	58	**he:50**	got:49	pl:48	sla:45	rom:45
bg	84	88	84	51	sl:73	cs:72	hr:70	**sla:76**	ine:71
cs	81	80	73	55	**hr:62**	bg:60	sl:60	sla:61	ine:60
cu	87	83	77	60	**got:73**	grc$_1$:69	la$_1$:57	ger:68	ine:67
da	84	78	72	54	no:63	bg:61	sv:59	**ger:66**	ine:66
de	81	75	67	51	sv:54	sl:53	bg:53	**sla:59**	ger:57
el	80	80	73	60	hr:59	sl:59	ro:51	**sla:63**	ine:62
en	84	81	71	56	sv:55	de:54	fr:52	**all:58**	ger:58
es	76	81	72	59	it:68	fr:65	ro:54	**rom:70**	ine:69
et	88	82	78	53	fi:65	hu:64	pl:63	**agl:75**	all:64
eu	78	73	66	53	**hu:45**	hi:41	et:39	sla:44	ine:43
fa	83	80	68	55	grc$_1$:47	he:46	sl:45	**sla:49**	all:44
fi	78	74	65	42	da:49	fi$_1$:47	et:45	**all:52**	agl:51
fi$_1$	73	69	65	45	fi:54	**la:49**	et:44	all:48	ine:47
fr	81	80	73	59	es:66	it:65	bg:57	**rom:67**	all:65
ga	78	73	70	58	**he:57**	id:53	ro:51	all:57	rom:56
got	82	77	73	58	**cu:67**	grc$_1$:66	la$_1$:54	sla:66	all:62
grc	72	68	59	45	grc$_1$:50	**got:49**	la:47	all:47	ine:47
grc$_1$	74	72	67	33	**got:62**	grc:52	la$_1$:49	sla:57	ine:56
he	84	81	76	59	id:55	es:54	ro:51	**rom:57**	all:57
hi	91	89	82	60	ta:55	hu:53	et:43	**agl:56**	all:47
hr	83	77	72	51	sl:57	cs:55	bg:54	**sla:61**	ine:60
hu	79	74	70	62	sv:54	bg:53	et:47	**sla:54**	all:53
id	82	79	70	58	**hr:57**	he:54	bg:48	sla:57	rom:53
it	87	86	79	64	es:74	fr:72	ro:59	**rom:76**	all:73
la	62	55	47	31	**grc$_1$:54**	cu:52	la$_1$:51	all:53	sla:52
la$_1$	72	69	58	43	**grc$_1$:56**	got:56	cu:54	sla:50	all:49
la$_2$	72	71	65	38	la:44	pl:44	hr:44	**sla:47**	ine:47
nl	73	71	68	53	de:52	pt:52	el:52	**ine:54**	all:53
no	87	84	72	42	sv:61	hr:61	bg:60	**ine:66**	ger:66
pl	87	83	78	62	sl:69	hr:67	bg:63	**sla:73**	all:69
pt	78	84	76	67	**it:69**	es:69	fr:66	all:68	rom:68
ro	76	66	62	53	it:59	id:58	es:56	**rom:62**	ine:61
sl	88	83	79	56	cs:70	hr:65	bg:62	**sla:75**	ine:69
sv	86	81	73	49	no:64	da:63	en:62	**ger:69**	ine:65
ta	80	66	63	50	hi:46	hu:44	eu:40	**agl:50**	all:48

Table 2: Unlabeled attachment score of delexicalized parsers on the UD 1.2 test data. Gold-standard tags were used in the "gold" column, and tags predicted by UDPipe everywhere else. The "gold", "lex" and "120" columns are lexicalized. Parsers in "120" are trained on 20 labeled sentences; highlighted figures indicate languages where the delexicalized parser did worse than "120".

ing gold and predicted tags is not large (surprisingly, in three cases the predicted tags even outperform the gold standard). However, the UDPipe tagger was trained only on UD data and thus we observe a much larger drop in Romanian and Tamil—two tiny treebanks, too small to train a good tagger.

The "self/delex" column illustrates how much we lose by removing the lexical values of the words. Finally, we present scores of the three best-performing source languages, and two source language combinations. Again, genetically related languages tend to stick together and the scores could be used as an interesting language-typological metric, even if the correllation is less pronounced than with tagging. Sometimes the type of text plays a more important role. E.g. the treebanks from the PROIEL project (cu, got, grc_1 and la_1) work well together despite being from different language groups. They contain similar texts (Bible) and their annotation is harmonized to a greater extent than the rest of UD.

It is not surprising that the best possible source is usually a mix of languages (note that this cannot be attributed to larger training data, which is always limited to 5,000 sentences). Some of the UAS values look promising and certainly outperform unsupervised parsing. Yet there are two important factors that hold back excessive optimism. First, the results in Table 2 are based on a *supervised* tagger. Replacing it by the delexicalized tagger does not work for us. We do not show the scores in the table but they are generally under 20% and effectively useless. The number of tagging errors may not seem so disastrous, but their distribution is too random for the downstream parsing model to build upon the tags. Delexicalized tagging is reasonably good at distinguishing function words from content words but it often fails to tell apart nouns and verbs—a distinction that affects the entire structure of a dependency tree, whose root node is usually a verb.

The second factor lies in the "l20" column, which shows scores of a lexicalized parser trained on just 20 manually annotated sentences. (Zeman and Resnik, 2008) were able to show that their delexicalized transfer in their setup (with quite different data and parser from ours) was worth 1,546 manually annotated sentences. However, the learning curve of Malt Parser on UD data is much steeper in the beginning, making it harder for semi-supervised approaches to compete. Our results are rarely equivalent to more than 200 sentences of lexicalized data. In nine cases (highlighted red in the table) the delexicalized parser does not even outperform the "l20" result. This is certainly not good news for the delexicalized techniques, but there is a positive message, too: whenever some knowledge of the target language is available, use it. If a native speaker is available, ask him for help—even if he does not know anything about linguistics! The data you obtain may look ridiculously small, but they will probably get you further than expected.

6 Conclusion

We have investigated two techniques of cross-linguistic model transfer, known as delexicalized tagging and parsing. We evaluated them thoroughly on a common dataset, Universal Dependencies v1.2.

We have confirmed that models are more easily transferred between phylogenetically related languages—a hypothesis that is very natural, yet it could not be confirmed in the previous work, working with treebanks whose annotation style was not harmonized across languages (a famous finding of (McDonald et al., 2011) was that Danish was in fact the worst possible source language for Swedish).

We have also exposed the limits of the two methods. Each technique in isolation looks moderately promising, especially if only the intrinsic scores are considered. However, they fail terribly when used in combination. Since the learning curve of modern dependency parsers is quite steep, we argue that it is more advantageous to ask a native speaker to annotate just a small dataset, rather than trying to transfer models from other languages. We agree with (Yu et al., 2016) that such an approach does not scale well to tens or hundreds of languages, and a native speaker may not always be available, but it is a path that should not be ignored. Alternatively, one may want to employ Wiktionary crawling-based techniques such as (Sylak-Glassman et al., 2016) to acquire lexical knowledge about new languages.

Acknowledgments

The work was supported by the grants 15-10472S and 14-06548P of the Czech Science Foundation, and by the EU project H2020-ICT-2014-1-644402.

References

Željko Agić, Dirk Hovy, and Anders Søgaard. 2015. If all you have is a bit of the Bible: Learning pos taggers for truly low-resource languages. In *The 53rd Annual Meeting of the Association for Computational Linguistics and the 7th International Joint Conference of the Asian Federation of Natural Language Processing (ACL-IJCNLP 2015)*.

Bernhard E. Boser, Isabelle M. Guyon, and Vladimir N. Vapnik. 1992. A training algorithm for optimal margin classifiers. In *Proceedings of the Fifth Annual Workshop on Computational Learning Theory*, COLT '92, pages 144–152, New York, NY, USA. ACM.

Christos Christodouloupoulos, Sharon Goldwater, and Mark Steedman. 2010. Two decades of unsupervised pos induction: How far have we come? In *Proceedings of the 2010 Conference on Empirical Methods in Natural Language Processing*, EMNLP '10, pages 575–584.

Silviu Cucerzan and David Yarowsky. 2002. Bootstrapping a multilingual part-of-speech tagger in one person-day. In *Proceedings of the 6th Conference on Natural Language Learning - Volume 20*, COLING-02, pages 1–7.

Dipanjan Das and Slav Petrov. 2011. Unsupervised part-of-speech tagging with bilingual graph-based projections. In *Proceedings of the 49th Annual Meeting of the Association for Computational Linguistics: Human Language Technologies*, pages 600–609, Portland, Oregon, USA, June.

Thành Duong, Steven Bird, Paul Cook, and Pavel Pecina. 2013. Simpler unsupervised POS tagging with bilingual projections. In *Proceedings of the 51st Annual Meeting of the Association for Computational Linguistics*, number Volume 2: Short Papers, pages 634–639, Sofija, Bulgaria.

Victoria Fossum and Steven P. Abney. 2005. Automatically inducing a part-of-speech tagger by projecting from multiple source languages across aligned corpora. In Robert Dale, Kam-Fai Wong, Jian Su, and Oi Yee Kwong, editors, *Natural Language Processing - IJCNLP 2005, Second International Joint Conference, Jeju Island, Korea, October 11-13, 2005, Proceedings*, volume 3651 of *Lecture Notes in Computer Science*, pages 862–873. Springer.

Rebecca Hwa, Philip Resnik, Amy Weinberg, Clara Cabezas, and Okan Kolak. 2004. Bootstrapping parsers via syntactic projection across parallel texts. *Natural Language Engineering*, 1(1):1–15.

M. Paul Lewis, Gary F. Simons, and Charles D. Fennig, editors. 2016. *Ethnologue: Languages of the World, Nineteenth edition*. SIL International, Dallas, Texas.

Martin Majliš and Zdeněk Žabokrtský. 2012. Language richness of the web. In *Proceedings of the 8th International Conference on Language Resources and Evaluation (LREC 2012)*, pages 2927–2934, İstanbul, Turkey.

Ryan McDonald, Slav Petrov, and Keith Hall. 2011. Multi-source transfer of delexicalized dependency parsers. In *Proceedings of Empirical Methods in Natural Language Processing (EMNLP)*.

Joakim Nivre and Johan Hall. 2005. Maltparser: A language-independent system for data-driven dependency parsing. In *In Proc. of the Fourth Workshop on Treebanks and Linguistic Theories*, pages 13–95.

Joakim Nivre, Marie-Catherine de Marneffe, Filip Ginter, Yoav Goldberg, Jan Hajič, Christopher Manning, Ryan McDonald, Slav Petrov, Sampo Pyysalo, Natalia Silveira, Reut Tsarfaty, and Daniel Zeman. 2016. Universal dependencies v1: A multilingual treebank collection. In *Proceedings of the 10th International Conference on Language Resources and Evaluation (LREC 2016)*, pages 1659–1666, Portorož, Slovenia.

Slav Petrov, Dipanjan Das, and Ryan McDonald. 2012. A universal part-of-speech tagset. In *Proceedings of the 8th International Conference on Language Resources and Evaluation (LREC 2012)*, pages 2089–2096, İstanbul, Turkey.

Rudolf Rosa and Zdeněk Žabokrtský. 2015. Klcpos3 - a language similarity measure for delexicalized parser transfer. In *Proceedings of the 53rd Annual Meeting of the Association for Computational Linguistics and the 7th International Joint Conference on Natural Language Processing (Volume 2: Short Papers)*, pages 243–249, Stroudsburg, PA, USA. Association for Computational Linguistics.

Milan Straka, Jan Hajič, and Jana Straková. 2016. UDPipe: Trainable pipeline for processing CoNLL-U files performing tokenization, morphological analysis, POS tagging and parsing. In *Proceedings of the Tenth International Conference on Language Resources and Evaluation (LREC 2016)*, Portorož, Slovenia.

John Sylak-Glassman, Christo Kirov, and David Yarowsky. 2016. Remote elicitation of inflectional paradigms to seed morphological analysis in low-resource languages. In *Proceedings of the Tenth International Conference on Language Resources and Evaluation (LREC 2016)*, Portorož, Slovenia, may.

David Yarowsky and Grace Ngai. 2001. Inducing multilingual pos taggers and np bracketers via robust projection across aligned corpora. In *Proceedings of the Second Meeting of the North American Chapter of the Association for Computational Linguistics on Language Technologies*, NAACL '01, pages 1–8.

Zhiwei Yu, David Mareček, Zdeněk Žabokrtský, and Daniel Zeman. 2016. If you even don't have a bit of Bible: Learning delexicalized POS taggers. In *Proceedings of the 10th International Conference on Language Resources and Evaluation (LREC 2016)*, pages 96–103, Portorož, Slovenia.

Daniel Zeman and Philip Resnik. 2008. Cross-language parser adaptation between related languages. In *Workshop on NLP for Less-Privileged Languages, IJCNLP*, Hyderabad, India.

Recurrent Neural Network Based Loanwords Identification in Uyghur

Chenggang Mi[1,2], **Yating Yang**[1,2,3], **Xi Zhou**[1,2], **Lei Wang**[1,2], **Xiao Li**[1,2] **and Tonghai Jiang**[1,2]
[1]Xinjiang Technical Institute of Physics and Chemistry of Chinese Academy of Sciences, Urumqi, 830011, China
[2]Xinjiang Laboratory of Minority Speech and Language Information Processing, Xinjiang Technical Institute of Physics and Chemistry of Chinese Academy of Sciences, Urumqi, 830011, China
[3]Institute of Acoustics of the Chinese Academy of Sciences, Beijing, 100190, China
{micg, yangyt, zhouxi, wanglei, xiaoli, jth}@ms.xjb.ac.cn

Abstract

Comparable corpus is the most important resource in several NLP tasks. However, it is very expensive to collect manually. Lexical borrowing happened in almost all languages. We can use the loanwords to detect useful bilingual knowledge and expand the size of donor-recipient / recipient-donor comparable corpora. In this paper, we propose a recurrent neural network (RNN) based framework to identify loanwords in Uyghur. Additionally, we suggest two features: inverse language model feature and collocation feature to improve the performance of our model. Experimental results show that our approach outperforms several sequence labeling baselines.

1 Introduction

Most natural language processing (NLP) tools rely on large scale language resources, but many languages in the world are resource-poor. To make these NLP tools widely used, some researchers have focused on techniques that obtain resources of resource-poor languages from resource-rich languages using parallel data for NLP applications such as syntactic parsing, word sense tagging, machine translation, semantic role labeling, and some cross-lingual NLP tasks. However, high quality parallel corpora are expensive and difficult to obtain, especially for resource-poor languages like Uyghur.

Lexical borrowing is very common between languages. It is a phenomenon of cross-linguistic influence (Tsvetkov et al., 2015a). If loanwords in resource-poor languages (e.g. Uyghur) can be identified effectively, we can use the bilingual word pairs as an important factor in comparable corpora building. And comparable corpora are vital resources in parallel corpus detection (Munteanu et al., 2006). Additionally, loanwords can be integrated into bilingual dictionaries directly. Therefore, loanwords are valuable to study in several NLP tasks such as machine translation, information extraction and information retrieval.

In this paper, we design a novel model to identify loanwords (Chinese, Russian and Arabic) from Uyghur texts. Our model based on a RNN Encoder-Decoder framework (Cho et al., 2014). The Encoder processes a variable length input (Uyghur sentence) and builds a fixed-length vector representation. Based on the encoded representation, the decoder generates a variable-length sequence (Labeled sequence). To optimize the output of decoder, we also propose two important features: inverse language model feature and collocation feature. We conduct three groups of experiments; experimental results show that, our model outperforms other approaches.

This paper makes the following contributions to this area:

- We introduce a novel approach to loanwords identification in Uyghur. This approach increases F1 score by 12% relative to traditional approach on the task of loanwords detection.

- We conduct experiments to evaluate the performance of off-the-shelf loanwords detection tools trained on news corpus when applied to loanwords detection. By utilizing in-domain and out-of-domain data.

- For integrate these crucial information for better loanwords prediction, we combine two features into the loanwords identification model, so that we can use more important information to select the better loanword candidate.

The rest of this paper is organized as follows: Section 2 presents the background of loanwords in Uyghur; Section 3 interprets the framework used in our model; Section 4 introduces our method in detail. Section 5 describes the experimental setup and the analysis of experimental results. Section 6 discusses the related work. Conclusion and future work are presented in Section 7.

2 Background

Before we present our loanwords detection model, we provide a brief introduction of Uyghur and loanwords identification in this section. This will help build relevant background knowledge.

2.1 Introduction of Loanwords

A loanword is a word adopted from one language (the donor language) and incorporated into a different, recipient language without translation. It can be distinguished from a calque, or loan translation, where a meaning or idiom from another language is translated into existing words or roots of the host language. When borrowing, the words may have several changes to adopt the recipient language:

- Changes in meaning. Words are occasionally improved with a different meaning than that in thc donor languagc
- Changes in spelling. Words taken into different recipient languages are something spelled as in the donor language. Sometimes borrowed words retain original (or near-original) pronunciation, but undergo a spelling change to represent the orthography of the recipient language.
- Changes in pronunciation. In cases where a new loanword has a very unusual sound, the pronunciation of the word is radically changed.

2.2 Loanwords in Uyghur

Uyghur is an official language of the Xinjiang Uyghur Autonomous Region, and is widely used in both social and official spheres, as well as in print, radio and television, and is mostly used as a lingua franca by other ethnic minorities in Xinjiang. Uyghur belongs to the Turkic language family, which also includes languages such as the more distantly related Uzbek. In addition to influence of other Turkic languages, Uyghur has historically been influenced strongly by Person and Arabic and more recently by Mandarin Chinese and Russian (Table 1).

Loanwords in Uyghur not only include named entities such as person and location names, but also some daily used words.

2.3 Challenges in Loanwords Identification in Uyghur

Spelling Change When Borrowed From Donor Languages

To adopt the pronunciation and grammar in Uyghur, spelling of words (loanwords) may change when borrowed from donor languages. Changes of spelling have a great impact on the loanwords identification task.

Russian loanwords in Uyghur:
"radiyo"[1]-"радио"("radio")
Chinese loanwords in Uyghur:
"koi"-"块" ("kuai")

Suffixes of Uyghur Words Affect the Loanwords Identification

A Uygur word is composed of a stem and several suffixes, which can be formally described as:

$$Word = stem + suffix_0 + suffix_1 + ... + suffix_N \quad (1)$$

If we just use the traditional approaches such as edit distance, in some cases, these algorithms cannot give us sure results, for example, the length of suffixes equal even greater than the original word's length.

Data Sparsity Degrades the Performance of Loanwords Identification Model

[1]In this paper, we use Uyghur Latin Alphabet.

Chinese loan words in Uyghur [in English]	Russian loan words in Uyghur [in English]
shinjang(新疆) [Xinjiang]	tElEfon(телефон) [telephone]
laza(辣子) [hot pepper]	uniwErsitEt(университет) [university]
shuji(书记) [secretary]	radiyo(радио) [radio]
koi(块) [Yuan]	pochta(почта) [post office]
lengpung(凉粉) [agar-agar jelly]	wElsipit(велосипед) [bicycle]
dufu(豆腐) [bean curd]	oblast(область) [region]

Table 1: Examples of Chinese and Russian Loanwords in Uyghur.

Loanwords detection can be reformulated as a sequence labeling problem. Most sequence labeling tools (such as CRFs-based, HMM-based etc.) are built on large scales labeled data, lack of available labeled language resource makes decrease of performance on loanwords identification in Uyghur using above "off-the-shelf" tools.

3 Methodology

Recent development of deep learning (representation learning) has a strong impact in the area of NLP (natural language processing). According to traditional approaches, extraction of features often requires expensive human labor and often relies on expert knowledge, and these features usually cannot be expended in other situations. The most exciting thing of deep learning is that features used in most traditional machine learning models can be learned automatically.

In this section, we first introduced the most popular deep learning models used in this paper, then, we involved in the details of this model.

3.1 Recurrent Neural Network

RNNs (Recurrent Neural Networks) are artificial neural network models where connections between units form a directed cycle (Jaeger, 2002). This creates an internal state of the network which allows it to exhibit dynamic temporal behavior. RNNs can use their internal memory to process arbitrary sequences of inputs. This makes them show great promise in many NLP tasks.

The most important feature of a RNN model is that the network contains at least one feed-back connection, so the activations can flow round in a loop. That makes the networks very suited for tasks like temporal processing and sequence labeling.

3.2 RNN Encoder-Decoder Framework

In this section, we give a brief introduction of the RNN Encoder-Decoder framework, which was proposed by (Cho et al., 2014a) and (Sutskever et al., 2014). We build a novel architecture that learns to identify loanwords in Uyghur texts based on this framework.

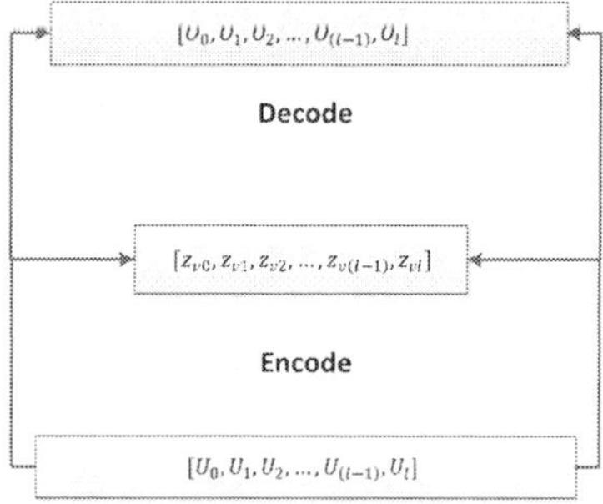

Figure 1: The Encoder-Decoder Framework Used in Loanword Identification Model.

$U_0, U_1, U_2, ..., U_{l-1}, U_l$ is a sequence of Uyghur words, $O_0, O_1, O_2, ..., O_{l-1}, O_l$ is a sequence of labels (loanword or not), and $Z_{v0}, Z_{v1}, Z_{v2}, ..., Z_{v(l-1)}, Z_{vl}$ is a sequence of vector representation of Uyghur words. The bold face "Encode" and "Decode" are two processes of encoder and decoder in our loanword identification model, respectively (Figure 1).

Encoder

In the RNN Encoder-Decoder framework, a sentence is firstly transformed into a sequence of vectors $x = (x_1, x_2, ..., x_l)$, then the encoder reads x as a vector $\vec{c}$. The most common approach is to use an RNN such that

$$h_t = f(x_t, h_{t-1}) \tag{2}$$

And

$$c = q(h_1, h_2, ..., h_{l-1}, h_l) \tag{3}$$

where $h_t \in \gamma$ is a hidden state at time t, and $\vec{c}$ is a vector generated from the sequence of the hidden states. f and q are some nonlinear functions. For instance, the Long-Short Term Memory (LSTM) is used as f, and $q(h_1, h_2, ..., h_{l-1}, h_l)$ as h_t.

Decoder

In RNN framework, the decoder is often used to predict the next word y_t given the context vector $\vec{c}$ and all the previously predicted words $y_1, y_2, ..., y_{t-1}$. In other words, the decoder defines a probability over the identification y_t by decomposing the joint probability into the ordered conditionals:

$$p(y) = \prod_{t=1}^{l} p(y_t | \{y_1, y_2, ..., y_{t-1}\}, \vec{c}) \tag{4}$$

4 Loanwords Identification

To make our loanwords identification model stronger, we also proposed several features as the additional knowledge of RNN. These features can be derived from monolingual corpus. In this section, we present two features firstly, then, we introduce the decoding part of our model.

4.1 Features

Inverse Language Model Feature

A language model is a probability distribution over sequences of words in NLP. Traditionally, language models are widely used in applications such as machine translation, speech recognition, part-of-speech tagging, parsing, and information retrieval. For example, in statistical machine translation, language models are used to improve the fluency of generated texts (Lembersky et al., 2012)

$$p(e|f) \propto p(f|e)p(e) \tag{5}$$

$p(e|f)$ indicates the translation model, which means the probability that the source string e is the translation of the target string f; $p(e)$ is the language model, which indicates the probability that the string e appeared in target language.

Usually, there are different pronunciation systems between donor language and recipient language. Different pronunciation rules can be represented by different character-based language models. In our paper, we propose an inverse language model (ILM) to constraint the output of loanword identification system.

N-gram Model

N-gram is a contiguous sequence of n items from a given text. An n-gram model models natural language sequences using the statistical properties of n-grams. Practically, an n-gram model predicts x_i based on $x_{i-(n-1)}, ..., x_{i-1}$. This can be indicated by probability terms as

$$p(x_i | x_{i-(n-1)}, ..., x_{i-1}) \tag{6}$$

When used in language modeling, independent assumptions are made so that each item word replies on its last $n-1$ words.

Inverse Language Model

As mentioned above, we can use a character-based language model to indicate a pronunciation system. Although a loanword may adapt the pronunciation of recipient language when borrowing, there are still some differences exist, and these differences usually reflect features of donor language pronunciation system. Accordingly, we computed the inverse language model feature as following

$$p_{ilm} = (1 - \lambda_1 p_{uyg}) + \lambda_2 p_{dnr} \tag{7}$$

Where p_{uyg} is the language model probability of a given character sequence in Uyghur, p_{dnr} is the language model probability of above sequence in donor languages. λ_1 and λ_2 are weights which can be obtained during model optimization. Language model probabilities are all based on n-gram models.

Collocation Feature

Unlike Chinese, some words (e.g. person names) are written separately. For detect loanwords effectively, we proposed a collocation feature, which measures the co-occurrence probability of two words.

The frequency of words is a simple but effective metric in NLP. In this paper, we use a probability of words co-occurrence to measure the composition of several parts of a possible loanword. Similar to language model, we also use smooth mechanism to alleviate the data sparseness.

Another metric used in our collocation extraction is the skip-gram language model (SGLM), which has the ability to model semantic relations between words, and capture a form of compositionality. We represent words by distributed representation encoded in the hidden layers of neural networks. Given a word, the context can be learned by the model. In our model, we can apply the SGLM to predict a loanword (such as Chinese person names in Uyghur texts) based on one part of it.

$$p_{clc1} = \max \sum_{-k \le j-1, j \le k}^{l} \log p(w_{t+j}|w_t) \tag{8}$$

For example, if we indicate v as a function that maps one part of a loanword w to its n-dimensional vector representation, then

$$\begin{aligned} &v(\text{“}jinping\text{”}) - v(\text{“}shi\text{”}) + v(\text{“}zEmin\text{”}) \\ &\approx v(\text{“}jyang\text{”}) \end{aligned} \tag{9}$$

The symbol $\approx$ means its right hand side must be the nearest neighbor of the value of the left hand side.

4.2 Decoding

In this paper, we use a beam search decoder as the basic framework, a neural network and two features are also integrated into it. Two features used in this model are as two re-rankers to filter out incorrect outputs.

$$\begin{aligned} s(o|w) = &\log p_{rnn}(o|w) \\ &+ \mu_1 \log p_{ilm}(w_{c1...ck}) \\ &+ \mu_2 \log p_{clc}(w) \end{aligned} \tag{10}$$

Where μ_1 and μ_2 are parameters which determine how much inverse language model and collocation model are weighted. According to our model, several characteristics are captured when loanwords identification. $p_{rnn}(o|w)$ is the most important part in our framework, some information that difficult to define by human can be learned automatically by the RNN model. Different language has a different pronunciation system. In our loanwords identification task, we use the inverse language model of characters to highlight the probability of a loanword $p_{ilm}(w_{c1...ck})$. For loanwords such as person names which have been separated by blank spaces, we predict their contexts according to themselves. In our method, we integrated both inner word information and information between words into the decoder.

5 Experiments and Results

We conduct experiments to evaluate our loanword identification model. According to the tasks defined in this paper, these experiments can be divided into two types: 1) in-domain experiments; 2) cross-domain experiments. We train the loanword identification model using a small set of training data, and evaluate the performance of our model with three held out test sets for each language.

5.1 Setup and Datasets

We evaluate our approach on three donor languages: Chinese, Russian and Arabic. In our approach, loanword identification models are trained on Uyghur news corpora. Test sets used in our experiments include in-domain test sets and cross-domain test sets. Since we are very familiar with Chinese and Russian, we labeled several types of Chinese (Chn) and Russian (Rus) loanwords in Uyghur test sets, such as person names, locations, and other daily used words. For Arabic loanwords (Arab), we labeled them in test set manually. Because we have limited knowledge about Arabic, we just labeled some person names and locations. We collected some relatively regular corpora from news websites in Chinese[2] , Russian[3] and Arabic[4] to train the language models, respectively.

We built the recurrent neural network which used in our loanword identification model on the open source deep learning software Deeplearning4j[5]. For

[2]http://www.people.com.cn/

[3]http://sputniknews.ru/

[4]http://arabic-media.com/arabicnews.htm

[5]http://deeplearning4j.org

Languages	TR-Set	DE-Set	TE-Set
Uyghur	10,000 * 3	1,000 * 3	1,000 * 3
Chinese	\	1,000	\
Russian	\	1,000	\
Arabic	\	1,000	\

Table 2: Statistic of Corpora.

the inverse language model, we used a java version language model tool which was implemented by ourselves. For the collocation extraction feature, we trained a model based on the word2vec, which was proposed by Tomas Mikolov, and a java version is also implemented in Deeplearning4j toolkits.

To evaluate the performance of loanword identification models, several metrics are used in our experiments:

$$R = \frac{A}{A+C}, P = \frac{A}{A+B}, F1 = \frac{2 \star R \star P}{P+R} \quad (11)$$

$P(Precision)$ indicates the percentage of loanwords found that match exactly the spans found in the evaluations data (test set);

$R(Recall)$ means the percentage of loanwords defined in the corpus that were found in the same location;

$F1$ can be interpreted as the harmonic mean of P and R.

5.2 Experiments and Analysis

For validate the effectiveness of our loanword identification model, we first compare our model (RNN-based model) with other loanword detection models, including CRFs-based model (CRFs) (Lafferty et al., 2001), the identification model based on string similarity (SSIM) (Mi et al., 2013), classification-based identification model (CBIM) (Mi et al., 2014). We suggest two important features in this paper to optimize the output of our loanword identification model, affection of these features are evaluated on identification performance. Loanwords can exist in any domains in a language; therefore, we also conduct experiments on texts in several domains.

Evaluation on Loanword Identification Models

In this part, we introduce the experiment results on four models, then we analysis the reasons.

From the Table 3 we can found that the performance of RNN based model outperforms other three approaches, we summarized possible reasons as follow: 1) CRFs model rely heavily on labeled data, because we only have limited training examples, the CRFs model achieved lowest performance among four models; 2) SSIM model based on two string similarity algorithms: edit distance and the common substring, compare with the RNN model, SSIM has a limited ability of generalization, and cannot capture semantic information in Uyghur texts, so the SSIM achieved a relative low performance; 3) Several information including above two algorithms are integrated into the CIBM model, and consider the loanwords identification as a classification problem, the performance of CIBM model outperforms the CRFs model and SSIM model. However, like the SSIM model, there is almost no semantic information and limited generalization ability, therefore, the performance of CIBM model cannot achieve or outperform the RNN based model.

Evaluation on Features Used in RNN-based Model

Features used in our model optimized the output of loanword identification. We show the experimental results on combination of features: $RNN+f0$ (no additional feature used), $RNN+f1$ (inverse language model feature used), $RNN+f2$ (collocation feature used) and $RNN+f1+f2$ (both inverse language model feature and collocation feature are used).

In Table 4, $RNN+f1$ combines the inverse language model information into loanword identification model, which apply the local feature in our task, so the performance of $RNN+f1$ outperforms the basic RNN model and $RNN+f2$. $RNN+f2$ integrated the collocation information into the model, and the generation ability of the model only rely on RNN, therefore, the performance of $RNN+f2$ only outperform the basic RNN model. The $RNN+f1+f2$ not only combine the generalization ability into the model, but also the local feature ($f1$) and global feature ($f2$). So

Languages	P-Chn	R-Chn	F1-Chn	P-Rus	R-Rus	F1-Rus	P-Arab	R-Arab	F1-Arab
CRFs	69.78	62.33	66.35	71.64	63.25	67.18	72.50	65.32	68.72
SSIM	66.32	77.28	71.38	75.39	70.02	72.61	73.76	67.51	70.50
CIBM	78.82	68.30	73.18	81.03	73.22	76.93	75.22	70.71	72.90
RNNs	**78.97**	**79.20**	**79.08**	**82.55**	**75.93**	**79.10**	**83.26**	**77.58**	**80.32**

Table 3: Experimental Results on Loanword Identification Models.

Languages	P-Chn	R-Chn	F1-Chn	P-Rus	R-Rus	F1-Rus	P-Arab	R-Arab	F1-Arab
RNN+f0	77.65	67.89	72.44	78.02	68.33	72.85	78.38	70.96	74.49
RNN+f1	78.86	70.32	74.35	81.94	70.65	75.88	81.12	71.52	76.02
CIRNN+f2	78.79	69.54	73.88	81.35	71.28	75.98	80.76	70.20	75.11
RNN+f1+f2	**78.97**	**79.20**	**79.08**	**82.55**	**75.93**	**79.10**	**83.26**	**77.58**	**80.32**

Table 4: Evaluation on Features Used in RNN-based Model.

the $RNN + f1 + f2$ model achieved the best performance.

Evaluation on Cross-domain Corpora

We evaluate our model in two domains on different test sets: $RNNLIS + NEWS$ and $RNNLIS + ORAL$.

In Table 5, the experimental results on news ($RNNLIS + NEWS$) which is similar with our training examples are outperform the results on oral test set ($RNNLIS + ORAL$). This may be no doubt. Amazingly, we found that performance of $RNNLIS + ORAL$ is just a little worse compared with $RNNLIS + NEWS$. A possible reason is that our model can learn representation of knowledge beyond given training examples.

5.3 Discussion

In our experiments, we try to identify Chinese, Russian and Arabic loanwords in Uyghur texts. We found that results on Arabic loanwords identification achieved the best performance. There are two possible reasons. First, most of loanwords labeled in the training examples for Arabic loanwords identification are person names; therefore, it is relatively easy to find them out. Second, Persian has exerted some influence on Arabic, and borrowing much vocabulary from it. Meanwhile, Uyghur has historically been influenced strongly by Persian, so Arabic loanwords in Uyghur may have the similar pronunciation system with Arabic. These two reasons contribute to Arabic loanwords identification in Uyghur.

We have limited number of labeled corpus, so a competitive identification result cannot be expected if a traditional approach is used (such as the CRF). Our proposed RNN Encoder-Decoder framework can learn features automatically and use its internal memory to process arbitrary sequences of inputs. Additionally, two features inverse language model and collocation can constraint the output of identification model. Therefore, our model achieved the best performance.

Loanword identification models are all trained on news corpora, so in cross-domain (news and oral) experiments, results in news are outperform results in oral. We analysis the results, and found that several errors including spelling error are exist in oral corpora, and these errors may affect the performance of our model.

6 Related work

There has been relatively few previous works on loanwords identification in Uyghur. Our work is inspired by two lines of research: (1) recurrent neural network; (2) loanwords detection.

6.1 Recurrent Neural Network

In recent years, the Recurrent Neural Network has proven to be highly successful in capturing semantic information in text and has improved the results of several tasks in NLP area. (Socher et al., 2013) uses

Languages	P-Chn	R-Chn	F1-Chn	P-Rus	R-Rus	F1-Rus	P-Arab	R-Arab	F1-Arab
RNNLIS+NEWS	**78.97**	**79.20**	**79.08**	**82.55**	**75.93**	**79.10**	**83.26**	**77.58**	**80.32**
RNNLIS+ORAL	75.23	76.44	75.83	78.11	70.59	74.16	80.03	76.42	78.18

Table 5: Evaluation on Cross-Domain Corpora.

a recursive neural network to predict sentence sentiment. (Luong et al., 2013) generates better word representation with recursive neural network. (Cho et al., 2014a) proposed a RNN encoder-decoder model to learn phrase representations in SMT. (Irsoy et al., 2014) introduce a deep recursive neural network, and evaluate this model on the task of fine-grained sentiment classification. (Liu et al., 2014) propose a recursive recurrent neural network to model the end-to-end decoding process for SMT; experiments show that this approach can outperform the state-of-the-art baseline. (Yao et al., 2013) optimized the recurrent neural network language model to perform language understanding. (Graves , 2012) apply a RNN based system in probabilistic sequence transduction.

6.2 Loanwords Detection

In general, word borrowing is often concerned by linguists (Chen, 2011; Chen et al., 2011a). There are relatively few researches about loanwords in NLP area. (Tsvetkov et al., 2015a) and (Tsvetkov et al., 2016) proposed a morph-phonological transformation model, features used in this model are based on optimality theory; experiment has been proved that with a few training examples, this model can obtain good performance at predicting donor forms from borrowed forms. (Tsvetkov et al., 2015) suggest an approach that uses the lexical borrowing as a model in SMT framework to translate OOV words in a low-resource language. For loanwords detection in Uyghur, string similarity based methods were often used at the early stage (Mi et al., 2013). (Mi et al., 2014) propose a loanword detection method based on the perceptron model, several features are used in model training.

7 Conclusion

We have presented an approach to identify loanwords (Chinese, Russian and Arabic loanwords) in Uyghur texts, our model based on the RNN Encoder-Decoder framework. We also suggested two important features: inverse language model and collocation feature to optimize the output of our loanword identification model. Experimental results show that our model achieves significant improvements in loanwords detection tasks. In the future, we plan to further validate the effectiveness of our approach on more languages, especially on languages with rich morphology.

Acknowledgments

We sincerely thank the anonymous reviewers for their thorough reviewing and valuable suggestions. This work is supported by the West Light Foundation of The Chinese Academy of Sciences under Grant No.2015-XBQN-B-10, the Xinjiang Key Laboratory Fund under Grant No.2015KL031 and the Strategic Priority Research Program of the Chinese Academy of Sciences under Grant No.XDA06030400.

References

Shiming Chen. 2011. New Research on Chinese Loanwords in the Uyghur Language. *N.W.Journal of Ethnology*, pages 176-180, 28(1).

Yan Chen and Ping Chen. 2011. A Comparison on the methods of Uyghur and Chinese Loan Words. *Journal of Kashgar Teachers College* pages 51-55, 32(2).

Kyunghyun Cho, Bart van Merriënboer, Dzmitry Bahdanau and Yoshua Bengio. 2014. On the properties of neural machine translation: Encoder-decoder approaches. In *Proceedings of the Eighth Workshop on Syntax, Semantics and Structure in Statistical Translation (SSST-8)*, pages 103-111, October 25, Doha, Qatar. Association for Computational Linguistics.

Kyunghyun Cho, Bart van Merriënboer, Caglar Gulcehre, Dzmitry Bahdanau, Fethi Bougares, Holger Schwenk and Yoshua Bengio. 2014. Learning Phrase Representations using RNN Encoder – Decoder for Statistical Machine Translation. In *Proceedings of the 2014 Conference on Empirical Methods in Natural Language Processing (EMNLP 2014)*, pages 1724-1734, October 25-29, Doha, Qatar. Association for Computational Linguistics.

Alex Graves. 2012. Sequence Transduction with Recurrent Neural Networks. In *Proceedings ICML Representation Learning Workshop,* Edinburgh, Scotland.

Ozan Irsoy and Claire Cardie. 2012. Deep Recursive Neural Networks for Compositionality in Language. In *Proceedings of the 2014 Conference on Advances in Neural Information Processing Systems (NIPS 2014),* pages 2096-2104, December 8-13, Montréal, Canada.

Herbert Jaeger. 2002. A tutorial on training recurrent neural networks, covering BPPT, RTRL, EKF and the "echo state network" approach. *GMD-Forschungszentrum Informationstechnik.*

John Lafferty, Andrew McCallum and Fernando Pereira. 2001. Conditional Random Fields: Probabilistic Models for Segmenting and Labeling Sequence Data. In *Proceedings of the Eighteenth International Conference on Machine Learning (ICML 2001),* pages 282-289, June 28-July 2, Bellevue, Washington, USA.

Gennadi Lembersky, Noam Ordan and Shuly Wintner. 2012. Language Models for Machine Translation: Original vs. Translated Texts. *Computational Linguistics,* pages 799-825, 38(4). Association for Computational Linguistics.

Shujie Liu, Nan Yang, Mu Li and Ming Zhou. 2014. A Recursive Recurrent Neural Network for Statistical Machine Translation. In *Proceedings of the 52nd Annual Meeting of the Association for Computational Linguistics (ACL 2014),* pages 1491-1500, June 23-25, Baltimore, Maryland, USA. Association for Computational Linguistics.

Thang Luong, Richard Socher and Christopher Manning. 2013. Better Word Representations with Recursive Neural Networks for Morphology. In *Proceedings of the Seventeenth Conference on Computational Natural Language Learning (CoNLL 2013),* pages 104-113, August 8-9, Sofia, Bulgaria. Association for Computational Linguistics.

Chenggang Mi, Yating Yang, Xi Zhou, Xiao Li and Mingzhong Yang. 2013. Recognition of Chinese Loan Words in Uyghur Based on String Similarity. *Journal of Chinese Information Processing,* pages 173-179, 27(5).

Chenggang Mi, Yating Yang, Lei Wang, Xiao Li and Kamali Dalielihan. 2014. Detection of Loan Words in Uyghur Texts. In *Proceedings of the 3rd International Conference on Natural Language Processing and Chinese Computing (NLPCC 2014),* pages 103-112, December 5-9, Shen Zhen, China.

Dragos Stefan Munteanu and Daniel Marcu. 2006. Extracting Parallel Sub-Sentential Fragments from Non-Parallel Corpora. In *Proceedings of the 21st International Conference on Computational Linguistics and 44th Annual Meeting of the ACL (COLING-ACL 2006),* pages 81-88, July 17-21, Sydney, Australia. Association for Computational Linguistics.

Richard Socher, Alex Perelygin, Jean Wu, Jason Chuang, Christopher D. Manning, Andrew Ng and Christopher Potts. 2013. Recursive Deep Models for Semantic Compositionality Over a Sentiment Treebank. In *Proceedings of the 2013 Conference on Empirical Methods in Natural Language Processing (EMNLP 2013),* pages 1631-1642, October 18-21, Seattle, Washington, USA. Association for Computational Linguistics.

Ilya Sutskever, Oriol Vinyals and Quoc V. Le. 2014. Sequence to Sequence Learning with Neural Networks. In *Proceedings of the 2014 Conference on Advances in Neural Information Processing Systems (NIPS 2014),* pages 3104-3112, December 8-13, Montréal, Canada.

Yulia Tsvetkov, Waleed Ammar and Chris Dyer. 2015. Constraint-Based Models of Lexical Borrowing. In *Proceedings of the 2015 Conference on Human Language Technologies: The 2015 Annual Conference of the North American Chapter of the ACL (NAACL-HLT 2015),* pages 598-608, May 31-June 5, Denver, Colorado.

Yulia Tsvetkov and Chris Dyer. 2016. Cross Lingual Bridges with Models of Lexical Borrowing. *Journal of Artificial Intelligence Research* pages 63-93, 55(2016).

Yulia Tsvetkov and Chris Dyer. 2015. Lexicon Stratification for Translating Out-of-Vocabulary Words. In *Proceedings of the 53rd Annual Meeting of the Association for Computational Linguistics and the 7th International Joint Conference on Natural Language Processing (Short Papers)(ACL-IJCNLP 2015),* pages 125 - 131, July 26-31, Beijing, China.

Kaisheng Yao, Geoffrey Zweig, Mei-Yuh Hwang, Yangyang Shi and Dong Yu. 2013. Recurrent Neural Networks for Language Understanding. In *Proceedings of 14th Annual Conference of the Inter national Speech Communication Association (INTERSPEECH 2013),* pages 2524-2528, August 25-29, Lyon, France.

Solving Event Quantification and Free Variable Problems in Semantics for Minimalist Grammars

Yu Tomita
Department of Informatics, SOKENDAI
National Institute of Informatics
tomita@nii.ac.jp

Abstract

In this paper, I will focus on the event quantification and free variable problems in semantics for Minimalist Grammar formalism, with which both Montagovian compositional semantics and neo-Davidsonian event semantics are compatible. In the literature, two operations of the formalism, MERGE and MOVE, are considered to correspond to semantic operations. MERGE corresponds to functional application or predicate conjunction, whereas MOVE determines a quantifier scope. In these semantic frameworks for Minimalist Grammar, however, the event quantification and free variable problems remain unsolved. Here I first propose a compositional event semantics for a subset of the formalism without MOVE and show that compositional event semantics is a key to solving the event quantification problem. Then, I extend the result to the formalism enriched with MOVE, and show that it is unnecessary to add any free variables or assignment functions.

1 Introduction

Minimalist Grammars (MGs), a grammar formalism which first appeared in (Stabler, 1997), have two operations, MERGE and MOVE[1]. The former combines two expressions into another expression. The latter extracts a subconstituent from a complex expression and remerges them. MGs are compatible with both Montagovian compositional semantics (Montague, 1976; Heim and Kratzer, 1998) and neo-Davidsonian event semantics (Parsons, 1990; Larson and Segal, 1995). In the literature, MERGE corresponds to functional application in Montagovian compositional semantics (Kobele, 2006, 2012) or predicate conjunction in neo-Davidsonian event semantics (Hunter, 2010a,b), respectively, whereas MOVE determines quantifier scope.

The previous studies (Hunter, 2010b; Kobele, 2006) assume the interaction between MOVE operation and quantification, which requires semantic expressions to contain free variables or assignment functions. The problems we have to consider here are the event quantification problem (Winter and Zwarts, 2011), which remains unanswered in (Hunter, 2010a), and the problem with free variables (Kobele, 2006).

This paper contains the following sections. In section 2, I introduce a tiny subset of MGs, and I will take up Montagovian and neo-Davidsonian semantic frameworks following (Hunter, 2010a). Then, in section 3, I will show that MOVE-free MG introduced in section 2 has the event quantification problem and I introduce a neo-Davidsonian logical form invented by (Champollion, 2015), which is compatible with pure functional application, showing that this framework can solve the event quantification problem. In section 4, I try to extend the proposal to full MG, considering the relationship between determination of quantifier scope and movement operation without adding any free variables or assignment functions.

[1] In this paper, I ignore the operation ADJOIN, which is added to MGs in (Frey and Gärtner, 2002; Hunter, 2010a,b), and should be considered in further studies.

2 MOVE-free MGs

In this section, we will look at MOVE-free MG and its semantics following (Hunter, 2010a). For the moment, we can ignore MOVE and its corresponding semantic operation.

Let V be a finite set of *phonological expressions* (or *strings*) containing the empty string ε and $B = \{\mathsf{c}, \mathsf{d}, \mathsf{n}, \mathsf{v}, ...\}$ be a set of *selection features*. B (selectees) determines $B_{=} = \{=\mathsf{b} \mid \mathsf{b} \in B\}$ (selectors). Let $\{:, ::\}$ be the set of expression markers. In the following, we assume $s, t \in V^*$, $\S_1, \S_2 \in \{:, ::\}$, $\mathsf{g}, \mathsf{b}, \mathsf{b}_i \in B$ for $0 \leq i$.

A MOVE-free MG G is a 4-tuple $\langle V, B, Lex, \mathsf{v}\rangle$ where Lex is a finite subset of $V \times \{::\} \times (B_{=}^* \times B)$. Given G, the set of expressions $Expr$ is a union of the set of *lexical expressions*, namely, Lex and a subset of $V^* \times \{:\} \times (B_{=}^* \times B)$. The latter expressions marked with ':' are called *complex expressions*. MERGE is an operation to derive a sentence. It combines two expressions into a complex expression by saturating =b with b. There are two cases of MERGE: the complement merge case (MERGE_1) and the specifier merge case (MERGE_2). If the expression carrying =b is indicated by '::', then MERGE_1 is applied; otherwise, MERGE_2 is applied.

(1) $$\frac{s :: =\mathsf{b}_1 ... =\mathsf{b}_n\mathsf{g} \qquad t \S_1 \mathsf{b}_1}{st : =\mathsf{b}_2 ... =\mathsf{b}_n\mathsf{g}} \ \text{MERGE}_1$$

(2) $$\frac{s : =\mathsf{b}_1 ... =\mathsf{b}_n\mathsf{g} \qquad t \S_1 \mathsf{b}_1}{ts : =\mathsf{b}_2 ... =\mathsf{b}_n\mathsf{g}} \ \text{MERGE}_2$$

A derivation is complete when the expression has the distinguished feature v only. An example derivation for *Brutus stabbed Caesar* is shown in Figure 1.

2.1 Semantics for the MOVE-free MG

Let us discuss semantics for a G next. The sentence (3) has semantic representations as shown in (4). Montagovian compositional semantics (henceforth compositional semantics) yields the semantic representation (4a). On the other hand, neo-Davidsonian event semantics (henceforth event semantics) composes a more complicated logical form (4b).

(3) Brutus stabbed Caesar

(4) a. $\textbf{stab}(\textbf{b})(\textbf{c})$

b. $\exists e.\textbf{stabbing}(e) \wedge \textbf{stabbee}(\textbf{c})(e) \wedge \textbf{stabber}(\textbf{b})(e)$

We here call $\exists e$ an event quantifier. Note that this paper uses e both as an event variable and as the type for individuals. An event variable e has semantic type v, whereas every individual has type e. Let S be a set of *semantic expressions* (or *semantic components*). In the following sections, strings and expression markers are omitted in derivations.

2.1.1 Compositional Semantics

In the compositional semantics, each lexical expression has a semantic component, as in the following entries:

(5)
Brutus::d, $\textbf{b}$
Caesar::d, $\textbf{c}$
stabbed::=d =d v, $\lambda xy.\textbf{stab}(x)(y)$

MERGE combines two semantic expressions. We here suppose that MERGE involves functional application of two semantic components. If P and Q are semantic components assigned to expressions, then the general scheme involved in MERGE is as shown in (6).

(6) $$\frac{=\mathsf{b}_1 ... =\mathsf{b}_n\mathsf{g}, P \qquad \mathsf{b}_1, Q}{=\mathsf{b}_2 ... =\mathsf{b}_n\mathsf{g}, P\,Q}$$

The truth condition for the semantic expression comes from itself.

2.1.2 Event Semantics

Hunter (2010a) proposes an event semantic framework incorporated into MOVE-free MG. In this framework, each feature in a lexical item is annotated with semantic constants, as in the following entries:

(7)
Brutus::$\langle$d, $\textbf{b}\rangle$
Caesar::$\langle$d, $\textbf{c}\rangle$
stabbed::$\langle$=d, $\textbf{stabbee}\rangle\langle$=d, $\textbf{stabber}\rangle$ $\langle$v, $\textbf{stabbing}\rangle$

We here call semantic expressions assigned to selectees *main predicates*, which have type $\langle v, t\rangle$, and those assigned to selectors *thematic relations*, which have type $\langle e, vt\rangle$.

The general schema involved in MERGE operation is shown in (8)

(8) $$\frac{\langle =\mathsf{b}_1, \theta_1\rangle ... \langle =\mathsf{b}_n, \theta_n\rangle\langle \mathsf{g}, P\rangle \qquad \langle \mathsf{b}_1, Q\rangle}{\langle =\mathsf{b}_2, \theta_2\rangle ... \langle =\mathsf{b}_n, \theta_n\rangle\langle \mathsf{g}, P \& \theta_1(Q)\rangle}$$

where $P \& R = \lambda e.P(e) \wedge R(e)$. We here call this compositional scheme *predicate conjunction*. If the

$$\dfrac{\dfrac{\texttt{stabbed::=d =d v} \quad \texttt{Caesar::d}}{\texttt{stabbed Caesar:=d v}}\text{MERGE}_1 \quad \texttt{Brutus::d}}{\texttt{Brutus stabbed Caesar:v}}\text{MERGE}_2$$

Figure 1: Derivation of *Brutus stabbed Caesar*

sentential expression denotes a predicate P, its type is $\langle v, t\rangle$ and its truth condition is $\exists e.[P(e)]$.

3 Event Quantification Problem

In this section, we will consider the event quantification problem in semantics for G. One of the incompatibilities between event semantics and compositional semantics comes from the fact that quantificational arguments obligatorily take scope over event quantifier, as suggested in (Fry, 2005). For example, a sentence (9) has a reading in (10a), but not (10b). In other words, since *nobody* is a quantifying expression $\lambda k.\neg\exists x.k\,x$, it cannot take scope under the event quantifier.

(9) Nobody walked

(10) a. $\neg\exists z.\exists e.\mathbf{walking}(e) \wedge \mathbf{walker}(z)(e)$

b. $\exists e.\neg\exists z.\mathbf{walking}(e) \wedge \mathbf{walker}(z)(e)$

In the compositional scheme of (Hunter, 2010a), however, quantifying determiner phrases merged into a verb phrase must take scope under the event quantifier. The question then arises: how can quantifying expressions such as *nobody* take scope over the event quantifier via the compositional scheme for event semantics?[2]

3.1 Compositional Event Semantics for MOVE-free MG

To avoid the event quantification problem, we here adopt the proposal in (Champollion, 2015) to MOVE-free MG. First, the main predicates contain an event quantifier and have a GQ type over events $\langle vt, t\rangle$, rather than $\langle v, t\rangle$. This means that sentences and verb phrases are assumed to take $\lambda e.\top$ to produce a proposition.

(11) $P_{\textbf{doing}} = \lambda f.\exists e.f(e) \wedge \mathbf{doing}(e)$

Second, a separate semantic component for giving thematic relations to an argument is assigned to each selector feature.

[2] A solution in Abstract Categorial Grammar is illustrated in (Winter and Zwarts, 2011).

(12) $\theta_{\mathbf{r}} = \lambda MNf.[M(\lambda x.[N(\lambda e.[f(e) \wedge \mathbf{r}(x)(e)])])]$

Here, $\mathbf{r}$ is a thematic relation constant. The overall semantic expressions assigned to each lexical item are shown in Table 1.

Then, we can compose the argument and main predicate via pure functional application without giving rise to the event quantification problem. MERGE checks features in two expressions, applying a semantic component assigned to the selector feature to an argument.

(13) $$\frac{\langle =\mathsf{b}_1, \theta_{\mathbf{r}1}\rangle \ldots \langle =\mathsf{b}_n, \theta_{\mathbf{r}n}\rangle\langle \mathsf{g}, P\rangle \qquad \langle \mathsf{b}_1, Q\rangle}{\langle =\mathsf{b}_2, \theta_{\mathbf{r}2}\rangle \ldots \langle =\mathsf{b}_n, \theta_{\mathbf{r}n}\rangle\langle \mathsf{g}, (\theta_{\mathbf{r}1}Q)P\rangle}$$

Here the arguments have GQ type $\langle et, t\rangle$. If the argument has only selectee feature, MERGE involves functional application of the semantic component $\theta_{\mathbf{r}1}Q$ to the main predicate P. For example, the logical form for the sentence (9) is derived in the following way:

(14) $$\frac{\langle =\mathsf{d}, \theta_{\textbf{walker}}\rangle\langle \mathsf{v}, P_{\textbf{walking}}\rangle \qquad \langle \mathsf{d}, Q_{\textbf{nobody}}\rangle}{\langle \mathsf{v}, (\theta_{\textbf{walker}}\, Q_{\textbf{nobody}})\, P_{\textbf{walking}}\rangle}$$

where

$$\begin{aligned}\theta_{\textbf{walker}} &= \lambda MNf.[M(\lambda x.[N(\lambda e.[f(e) \wedge \\ &\quad \mathbf{walker}(x)(e)])])], \\ Q_{\textbf{nobody}} &= \lambda k.\neg\exists z.k\, z, \\ P_{\textbf{walking}} &= \lambda f.\exists e.f(e) \wedge \mathbf{walking}(e),\end{aligned}$$

and

$$\begin{aligned}(\theta_{\textbf{walker}}\, Q_{\textbf{nobody}})\, P_{\textbf{walking}} = \lambda f.\neg\exists z.\exists e.f(e) \wedge \\ \mathbf{walking}(e) \wedge \\ \mathbf{walker}(z)(e).\end{aligned}$$

When the sentential expression denotes a predicate P, its truth condition is $P(\lambda e.\top)$.

In summary, I considered the event quantification problem in MOVE-free MG. In the next section, I will expand the proposed idea into full MG enriched with MOVE.

Table 1: Examples of lexical expressions for a subset of MGs

Brutus::$\langle$d, $\lambda k.k\,\mathbf{b}\rangle$

Caesar::$\langle$d, $\lambda k.k\,\mathbf{c}\rangle$

everyone::$\langle$d, $\lambda k.\forall x.k\,x\rangle$

someone::$\langle$d, $\lambda k.\exists y.k\,y\rangle$

nobody::$\langle$d, $\lambda k.\neg\exists z.k\,z\rangle$

walked::$\langle$=d, $\lambda MNf.[M(\lambda x.[N(\lambda e.[f(e) \wedge \mathbf{walker}(x)(e)])])]\rangle\langle$v, $\lambda f.\exists e.f(e) \wedge \mathbf{walking}(e)\rangle$

stabbed::$\langle$=d, $\lambda MNf.[M(\lambda x.[N(\lambda e.[f(e) \wedge \mathbf{stabbee}(x)(e)])])]\rangle$
$\langle$=d, $\lambda MNf.[M(\lambda x.[N(\lambda e.[f(e) \wedge \mathbf{stabber}(x)(e)])])]\rangle\langle$v, $\lambda f.\exists e.f(e) \wedge \mathbf{stabbing}(e)\rangle$

4 Full MG and the Problem with Free Variables

The question we have to consider next is a problem with free variables. In the literature, MOVE operations in MGs require free variables or assignment functions in a semantic system. But the semantic components containing free variables or using assignment functions can cause some problems (Jacobson, 2015; Kobele, 2006). In this paper, however, we will observe that compositional event framework does not require any free variable or assignment function for MOVE.

4.1 A Minimalist Grammar Enriched with MOVE

Let $F = \{$o, q, ...$\}$ be a set of *licensing features*, where F and B are disjoint sets. F determines $F_+ = \{$+f $\mid$ f $\in F\}$ (licensors) and $F_- = \{$-f $\mid$ f $\in F\}$ (licensees). Let Syn be the set of *feature bundles* $(B_= \cup F_+)^* \times B \times (F_-)^*$. We assume f $\in F$, $\phi \in (B_= \cup F_+)^*$, $\chi \in (B \times F_-^*)$, $\psi \in F_-^+$ and $\alpha_i, \beta_i \in (V^* \times F_-^+)$ for $0 \leq i$. For instance, +f$\phi\chi$, b$\psi \in$ Syn.

A *Minimalist Grammar* G is a 5-tuple $\langle V, B, F, Lex,$ c$\rangle$ where Lex is a finite subset of $V \times \{::\} \times$ Syn. Given G, the set of expressions $Expr$ is a union of Lex and a subset of $(V^* \times \{:\} \times \text{Syn}) \times (V^* \times F_-^+)^*$. A complex expression can contain a sequence of subconstituents, each of which is a tuple of sequences of strings and licensees. There are two operations to derive a sentence: MERGE and MOVE. Each operation is defined in Figure 2.

MERGE_1 and MERGE_2 are essentially same as in MOVE-free MG we discussed earlier, except that the subconstituents can occur in each expression. The nonfinal merge case (MERGE_3) takes two expressions into one expression with an additional subconstituent, without concatenation of strings in expressions. The last two cases of MERGE (MERGE_4 and MERGE_5) realize covert movement. In these cases, where a feature bundle contains a distinguished licensee feature -q, the way of concatenation of strings is the same as MERGE_1 and MERGE_2, leaving a phonologically vacuous subconstituent for covert movement[3].

A specifier move case (MOVE_1) applies to an expression which contains a licensing feature +f and a subconstituent with an unchecked feature -f and concatenates two strings in one expression, whereas a nonfinal move case (MOVE_2) only checks their features.

A derivation is complete when the expression has the distinguished feature c only and involves no subconstituent. Additional examples of lexical expressions are shown in Table 2.

4.2 Variable-Free Semantics for full MG

I may now proceed to semantics of full MG. In a similar fashion to MOVE-free MG, a semantic component is assigned to each selector =b and selectee (followed by a sequence of licensees) χ. No semantic component is assigned to a licensor +f.

Additional lexical expressions for full MG include complementizer heads such as the one shown in (15).

(15) ε :: $\langle$=v, $\lambda Nf.N\,f\rangle\langle$c, $\lambda e.\top\rangle$

They have no thematic relation. Instead, complementizer heads provide $\lambda e.\top$ to make the logical form closed.

[3]Torr and Stabler (2016) have introduced essentially same operations for Directional Minimalist Grammar.

$$\frac{s :: \texttt{=b}\phi\chi \qquad t ?_1 \texttt{b}, \alpha_1 ... \alpha_m}{st : \phi\chi, \alpha_1 ... \alpha_m} \text{MERGE}_1 \qquad \frac{s : \texttt{=b}\phi\chi, \alpha_1 ... \alpha_m \qquad t ?_1 \texttt{b}, \beta_1 ... \beta_n}{ts : \phi\chi, \alpha_1 ... \alpha_m \beta_1 ... \beta_n} \text{MERGE}_2$$

$$\frac{s ?_1 \texttt{=b}\phi\chi, \alpha_1 ... \alpha_m \qquad t ?_2 \texttt{b}\psi, \beta_1 ... \beta_n}{s : \phi\chi, \alpha_1 ... \alpha_m (t, \psi) \beta_1 ... \beta_n} \text{MERGE}_3 \text{ (where } \psi \neq \texttt{-q})$$

$$\frac{s :: \texttt{=b}\phi\chi \qquad t ?_1 \texttt{b -q}, \alpha_1 ... \alpha_m}{st : \phi\chi, (\varepsilon, \texttt{-q}) \alpha_1 ... \alpha_m} \text{MERGE}_4 \qquad \frac{s : \texttt{=b}\phi\chi, \alpha_1 ... \alpha_m \qquad t ?_1 \texttt{b -q}, \beta_1 ... \beta_n}{ts : \phi\chi, \alpha_1 ... \alpha_m (\varepsilon, \texttt{-q}) \beta_1 ... \beta_n} \text{MERGE}_5$$

$$\frac{s : \texttt{+f}\phi\chi, \alpha_1 ... \alpha_i (t, \texttt{-f}) \alpha_{i+1} ... \alpha_m}{ts : \phi\chi, \alpha_1 ... \alpha_i \alpha_{i+1} ... \alpha_m} \text{MOVE}_1 \qquad \frac{s : \texttt{+f}\phi\chi, \alpha_1 ... \alpha_i (t, \texttt{-f}\psi) \alpha_{i+1} ... \alpha_m}{s : \phi\chi, \alpha_1 ... \alpha_i (t, \psi) \alpha_{i+1} ... \alpha_m} \text{MOVE}_2$$

$\phi \in (B_= \cup F_+)^*$; $\chi \in (B \times F_-^*)$; $\psi \in F_-^+$; $\alpha_i, \beta_i \in (V^* \times F_-^+)$ for $0 \leq i$; $0 \leq m, n$

Figure 2: Operation for MGs enriched with MOVE

Table 2: Additional examples of lexical expressions for full MG

everyone::$\langle \texttt{d -q}, \lambda k.\forall x.k\, x \rangle$
someone::$\langle \texttt{d -q}, \lambda k.\exists x.k\, x \rangle$
man::$\langle \texttt{n}, \lambda y.\textbf{man}(y) \rangle$
who::$\langle \texttt{d -o}, \lambda ky.k\, y \rangle$
ε::$\langle \texttt{=v}, \lambda Nf.N\, f \rangle \langle \texttt{c}, \lambda e.\top \rangle$
ε::$\langle \texttt{=v}, \lambda NfW.(W\, N)\, f \rangle \langle \texttt{+o}, \emptyset \rangle \langle \texttt{=n}, \lambda hky.(h\, y) \wedge (k\, y) \rangle \langle \texttt{n}, \lambda e.\top \rangle$
ε::$\langle \texttt{=v}, \lambda NV.V\, N \rangle \langle \texttt{+q}, \emptyset \rangle \langle \texttt{v}, \emptyset \rangle$

The compositional scheme for full MG is as follows. MERGE_3, MERGE_4 and MERGE_5 involve functional application of an argument Q and a semantic component assigned to selector R, but not a main predicate P. As a result, a moving subconstituent has a semantic representation $R\,Q$.

(16) $$\frac{\langle \texttt{=b}, R \rangle \Phi \langle \chi, P \rangle, \Psi_1 \qquad \langle \texttt{b}\psi, Q \rangle, \Psi_2}{\Phi \langle \chi, P \rangle, \Psi_1 \langle \psi, R\,Q \rangle \Psi_2}$$

Here, $\Phi \in ((B_= \times \mathcal{S}) \cup (F_+ \times \{\emptyset\}))^*$ and $\Psi_1, \Psi_2 \in (F_-^+ \times (\mathcal{S} \cup \{\emptyset\}))^*$. MOVE_1 checks licensing features, obligatorily applying functional application if a moving subconstituent contains a licensee -f.

(17) $$\frac{\langle \texttt{+f}, \emptyset \rangle \Phi \langle \chi, P \rangle, \Psi_1 \langle \texttt{-f}, Q \rangle \Psi_2}{\Phi \langle \chi, P\,Q \rangle, \Psi_1 \Psi_2}$$

If a moving subconstituent contains a sequence of licensee features, MOVE_2 is applied. In this case, functional application is optional.

(18) $$\frac{\langle \texttt{+f}, \emptyset \rangle \Phi \langle \chi, P \rangle, \Psi_1 \langle \texttt{-f}\psi, Q \rangle \Psi_2}{\Phi \langle \chi, P \rangle, \Psi_1 \langle \psi, Q \rangle \Psi_2}$$

(19) $$\frac{\langle \texttt{+f}, \emptyset \rangle \Phi \langle \chi, P \rangle, \Psi_1 \langle \texttt{-f}\psi, Q \rangle \Psi_2}{\Phi \langle \chi, P\,Q \rangle, \Psi_1 \langle \psi, \emptyset \rangle \Psi_2}$$

Here I suppose $P\,\emptyset = P$. I now discuss compositional event semantics for MOVE, such as wh-movement and Quantifier Raising.

4.2.1 Wh-Movement

In MG, a wh-phrase can move to the highest position of the clause which it first merged. For example, a nominal expression *man who everyone stabbed* is supposed to have the following structure:

(20) man [who [everyone stabbed ~~who~~]]

Figure 3 shows the derivation of the expression *man who everyone stabbed*. Before *who* is moved to its surface position, phonetically null complementizer is merged with the clause to form the nominal expression[4].

[4]Since the semantic component of *who* has type $\langle et, et \rangle$, if θ_r would have type $\langle \langle et, t \rangle, \langle \langle vt, t \rangle, \langle vt, t \rangle \rangle \rangle$, functional application of θ_r with *who* causes type mismatch. Therefore, I suppose θ_r has type $\langle \langle et, \gamma \rangle, \langle \langle vt, t \rangle, \langle vt, \gamma \rangle \rangle \rangle$, where γ ranges over the semantic types.

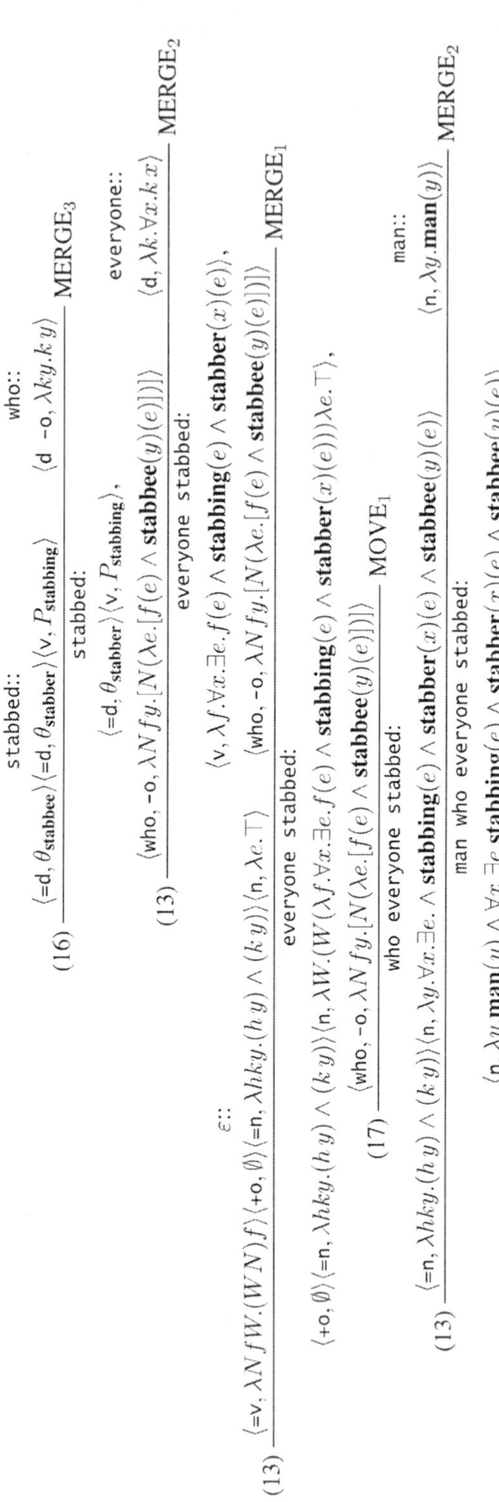

Figure 3: Derivation of *man who everyone stabbed*

4.2.2 Quantifier Raising

Since (May, 1977), quantificational determiner phrases such as *everyone* and *someone* are supposed to be raised as if they were wh-phrases. This Quantifier Raising (QR) is different from wh-movement in terms of QR does not affect word order. Moreover, if a sentence contains more than one quantifier, it can have semantic ambiguity due to QR. For instance, the sentence (21) has two readings, surface scope reading (22a) and inverse scope reading (22b).

(21) Someone stabbed everyone

(22) a. $\exists y.\forall x.\exists e.\mathbf{stabbing}(e) \wedge \mathbf{stabbee}(x)(e) \wedge \mathbf{stabber}(y)(e)$

b. $\forall x.\exists y.\exists e.\mathbf{stabbing}(e) \wedge \mathbf{stabbee}(x)(e) \wedge \mathbf{stabber}(y)(e)$

In the proposed framework, both readings are derivable with additional entries shown in (23).

(23)
everyone::$\langle$d -q, $\lambda k.\forall x.k\,x\rangle$
someone::$\langle$d -q, $\lambda k.\exists x.k\,x\rangle$
ε::$\langle$=v, $\lambda NV.V\,N\rangle\langle$+q, $\emptyset\rangle\langle$v, $\emptyset\rangle$

Figure 4 shows the derivation of *someone stabbed everyone* with inverse scope reading. Here I adopt the QR analysis. All quantificational determiner phrases covertly move to higher positions of the sentence than the positions where the determiners are merged, without changing word order. The proposed idea is similar to the *delta QP* analysis in (Ikuta, 2015). In his analysis, a phonologically vacuous head Δ has two features [+topic] and [+focus] to invoke movement of arguments, such as QR and topic/focus movement. Here I suppose that each phonologically vacuous head carries a licensor feature +q only.

5 Comparison with Other Approaches

There are some previous works investigating MOVE and semantic operation. The comparison of my proposal with (Kobele, 2012; Hunter, 2010b) is summarized in Table 3.

In (Hunter, 2010a), typical quantificational determiner phrases like *everyone* do not actually appear. Hunter (2010b) proposes Insertion Minimalist Grammar and a QR analysis which can solve the

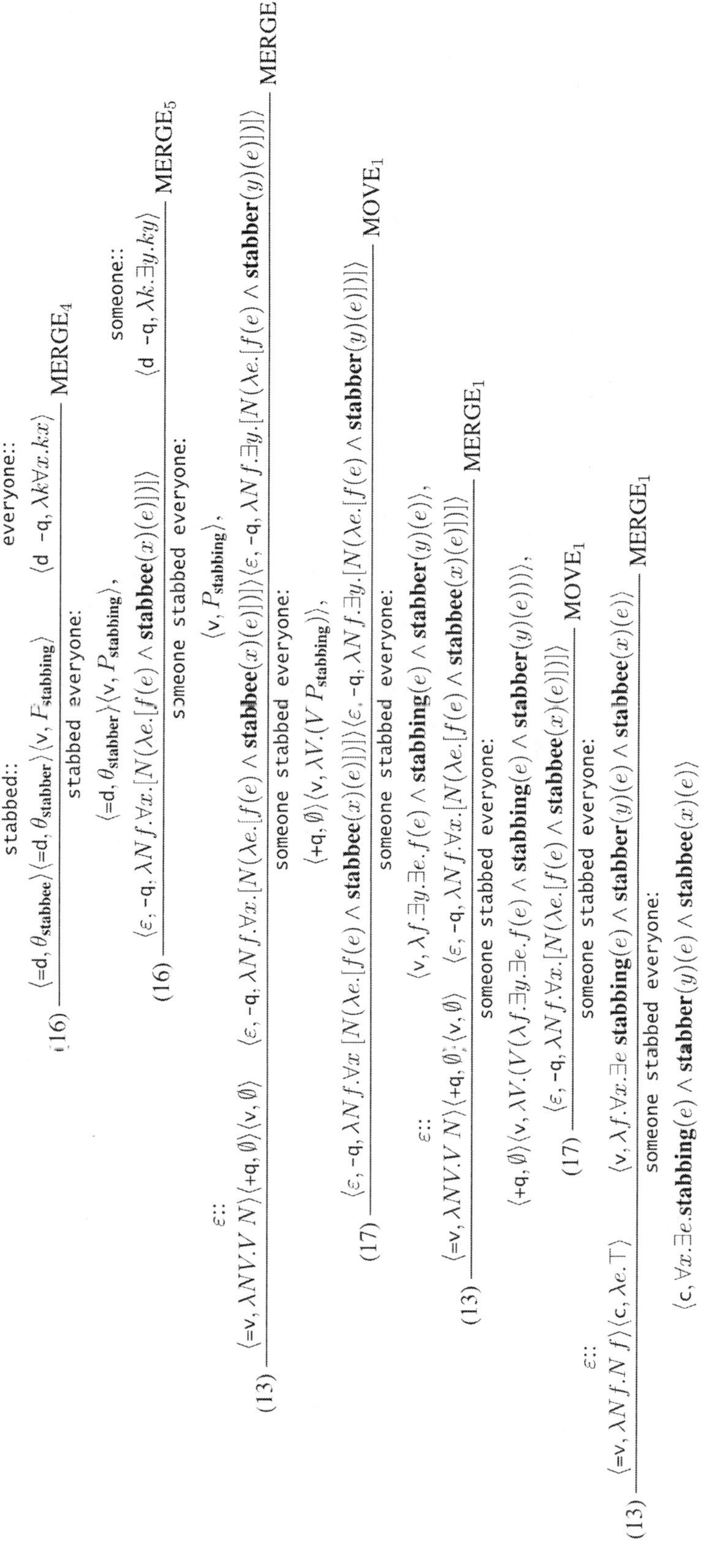

Figure 4: Derivation of *someone stabbed everyone*

Table 3: Comparison of semantic frameworks for MGs

	Event quantification problem	Problem with free variable
(Kobele, 2012)	(No event)	✓
(Hunter, 2010b)	✓	×
My proposal	✓	✓

event quantification problem. The problem with free variables, however, still remains.

A proposal in (Kobele, 2012) gives an interesting way to eliminate free variables in MG semantics. This paper shows that a compositional scheme (pure functional application) does not require any free variable or assignment function in MG semantics, due to just the event system which is not considered in (Kobele, 2012).

Besides those works on MGs, there are a few studies considering displacement operation and compositional semantics without free variables. Unger (2010) provides a variable-free semantics for a grammar formalism involving displacement operation similar to MOVE. She assumes that there is no correspondence between displacement and semantic operation. In contrast, I argue that MOVE corresponds to determination of a quantifier scope.

6 Conclusions

In this paper, I have illustrated a combination of compositional semantics and event semantics in MG formalism, showing that the compositional event semantic framework is the key to solve the event quantification problem. Moreover, I have given variable-free semantics for MG enriched with MOVE within the proposed scheme. This approach is different from any other previous works.

There is room for reconsidering compositional scheme and the semantic components to construct a complex sentence. The most important limitation lies in extraction from embedded clauses.

(24) a. Brutus saw a man who Caesar stabbed

b. Brutus saw a man who Longus thought Caesar stabbed

In the case of (24a), the meaning of an relative clause is derivable in the way I have shown in section 4.2.1. In the case of (24b), however, *who* moves out of two embedded clauses. If functional application of *who* to *Longus thought Caesar stabbed* is applied, then the thematic relation assigned to *who* might take the event variable associated with *thought*, not with *stabbed*. One way that we can think of to solve this puzzle is (i) successive-cyclic movement of *who* to *Caesar stabbed* involving functional application, and then (ii) employment of the thematic relation assigner for *thought* shown in (25), which is similar to the lifted thematic relation assigner proposed in (Champollion, 2015).

(25) $\theta_{\textbf{thinkee}} = \lambda WNVf.[W(\lambda e.[(V\ N)(\lambda o.[f(o) \wedge \textbf{thinkee}(e)(o)])])]$

(i) allows the semantic components for *who* to take the event variable associated with *stabbed*, not with *thought*. Then, inverse scope between two embedded clauses is derivable due to (ii) and the following lexical expressions.

(26)
$\mathsf{who}::\langle \mathsf{d}\ \text{-}\mathsf{o}\ \text{-}\mathsf{o}, \lambda ky.k\,y\rangle$
$\varepsilon::\langle \mathsf{=v}, \lambda NU.U\,N\rangle\langle \mathsf{+o}, \emptyset\rangle\langle \mathsf{d}, \emptyset\rangle$
$\varepsilon::\langle \mathsf{=v}, \lambda Nf.(N\,f)\,\lambda e.\top\rangle\langle \mathsf{+o}, \emptyset\rangle$
$\langle \mathsf{=n}, \lambda hky.(h\,y) \wedge (k\,y)\rangle\langle \mathsf{n}, \lambda o.\top\rangle$

However, there is a more complicated puzzle shown in (27) which is unsolvable with (i) and (ii).

(27) Brutus met a man who everyone thought nobody stabbed

Though *everyone* must take scope over *nobody*, this solution requires only inverse scope reading.

In conclusion, the current study is unable to treat some embedded clauses and quantifying expressions properly. Clearly, however, there may be other possible explanation of a multiple embedded clause. Additional works on the compositional event semantics would be helpful to solve this problem. This approach has the potential to account more semantic descriptions than those I have shown in this paper.

Acknowledgements

I appreciate Makoto Kanazawa and Hitomi Hirayama giving me helpful comments on the earlier versions of the present paper. I also thank the anonymous PACLIC reviewers for their comments. The earlier version of the paper was encouraged by comments offered at NII Logic Seminar. All errors are mine.

References

Champollion, Lucas. 2015. The interaction of compositional semantics and event semantics. *Linguistics and Philosophy* 38:31–66.

Frey, Werner, and Hans-Martin Gärtner. 2002. On the Treatment of Scrambling and Adjunction in Minimalist Grammars. In *Proceedings of formal grammar*, ed. Gerhard Jäger, Paola Monacheshi, and Gerald Penn, 41–52.

Fry, John. 2005. Resource-logical Event Semantics for LFG (Draft). Unpublished Manuscript.

Heim, Irene, and Angelika Kratzer. 1998. *Semantics in Generative Grammar*. Blackwell.

Hunter, Tim. 2010a. Deriving Syntactic Properties of Arguments and Adjuncts from Neo-Davidsonian Semantics. In *The Mathematics of Language*, ed. Christian Ebert, Gerhard Jäger, and Jens Michaelis, volume 6149, 103–116. Springer Berlin Heidelberg.

Hunter, Tim. 2010b. Relating movement and adjunction in syntax and semantics. Doctoral Dissertation, University of Maryland.

Ikuta, Toshikazu. 2015. Interactions between Quantifier Scope and Topic / Focus. In *Proceedings of the Florida Linguistics Yearly Meeting (FLYM) 2*.

Jacobson, Pauline. 2015. *Compositional Semantics*. Oxford: Oxford University Press.

Kobele, Gregory Michael. 2006. Generating Copies : An investigation into structural identity in language and grammar. Doctoral Dissertation, University of California, Los Angels.

Kobele, Gregory Michael. 2012. Importing Montagovian Dynamics into Minimalism. In *Logical Aspects of Computational Linguistics*, ed. Denis Béchet and Alexander Dikovsky, 103–118. Springer Berlin Heidelberg.

Larson, Richard, and Gabriel Segal. 1995. *Knowledge of Meaning*. Cambridge, MA: MIT Press.

May, Robert. 1977. The Grammar of Quantification. Doctoral Dissertation, Massachusetts Institute of Technology.

Montague, Richard. 1976. *Formal Philosophy, Selected Papers of Richard Montague*. New Haven: Yale University Press.

Parsons, Terence. 1990. *Events in the Semantics of English: A Study in Subatomic Semantics*. Cambridge, MA: MIT Press.

Stabler, Edward P. 1997. Derivational Minimalism. In *Logical Aspects of Computational Linguistics*, ed. Christian Retoré, 68–95. London, UK: Springer-Verlag.

Torr, John, and Edward P Stabler. 2016. Coordination in Minimalist Grammars : Excorporation and Across the Board (Head) Movement. In *Proceedings of the 12th International Workshop on Tree Adjoining Grammars and Related Formalisms (TAG+12)*, 1–17.

Unger, Christina. 2010. A computational approach to the syntax of displacement and the semantics of scope. Doctoral Dissertation, Universiteit Utrecht.

Winter, Yoad, and Joost Zwarts. 2011. Event Semantics and Abstract Categorial Grammar. In *The Mathematics of Language*, ed. Makoto Kanazawa, András Kornai, Marcus Kracht, and Hiroyuki Seki, volume 6878, 174–191.

Testing APSyn against Vector Cosine on Similarity Estimation

Enrico Santus[1], Emmanuele Chersoni[2], Alessandro Lenci[3], Chu-Ren Huang[1], Philippe Blache[2]
[1] The Hong Kong Polytechnic University, Hong Kong
[2] Aix-Marseille University
[3] University of Pisa
{esantus, emmanuelechersoni}@gmail.com
alessandro.lenci@unipi.it
churen.huang@polyu.edu.hk
blache@lpl-aix.fr

Abstract

In Distributional Semantic Models (DSMs), Vector Cosine is widely used to estimate similarity between word vectors, although this measure was noticed to suffer from several shortcomings. The recent literature has proposed other methods which attempt to mitigate such biases. In this paper, we intend to investigate APSyn, a measure that computes the extent of the intersection between the most associated contexts of two target words, weighting it by context relevance. We evaluated this metric in a similarity estimation task on several popular test sets, and our results show that APSyn is in fact highly competitive, even with respect to the results reported in the literature for word embeddings. On top of it, APSyn addresses some of the weaknesses of Vector Cosine, performing well also on genuine similarity estimation.

1 Introduction

Word similarity is one of the most important and most studied problems in Natural Language Processing (NLP), as it is fundamental for a wide range of tasks, such as *Word Sense Disambiguation* (WSD), *Information Extraction* (IE), *Paraphrase Generation* (PG), as well as the automatic creation of semantic resources. Most of the current approaches to word similarity estimation rely on some version of the Distributional Hypothesis (DH), which claims that words occurring in the same contexts tend to have similar meanings (Harris, 1954; Firth, 1957; Sahlgren, 2008). Such hypothesis provides the theoretical ground for Distributional Semantic Models (DSMs), which represent word meaning by means of high-dimensional vectors encoding corpus-extracted co-occurrences between targets and their linguistic contexts (Turney and Pantel, 2010).

Traditional DSMs initialize vectors with co-occurrence frequencies. Statistical measures, such as Positive Pointwise Mutual Information (PPMI) or its variants (Church and Hanks, 1990; Bullinaria and Levy, 2012; Levy et al., 2015), have been adopted to normalize these values. Also, these models have exploited the power of dimensionality reduction techniques, such as Singular Value Decomposition (SVD; Landauer and Dumais, 1997) and Random Indexing (Sahlgren, 2005).

These first-generation models are currently referred to as count-based, as distinguished from the context-predicting ones, which have been recently proposed in the literature (Bengio et al., 2006; Collobert and Weston, 2008; Turian et al., 2010; Huang et al., 2012; Mikolov et al., 2013). More commonly known as *word embeddings*, these second-generation models learn meaning representations through neural network training: the vectors dimensions are set to maximize the probability for the contexts that typically occur with the target word.

Vector Cosine is generally adopted by both types of models as a similarity measure. However, this metric has been found to suffer from several problems (Li and Han, 2013; Faruqui et al., 2016), such as a bias towards features with higher values and the inability of considering how many features are actually shared by the vectors. Finally, Cosine is affected by the hubness effect (Dinu et al., 2014; Schn-

abel et al., 2015), i.e. the fact that words with high frequency tend to be universal neighbours. Even though other measures have been proposed in the literature (Deza and Deza, 2009), Vector Cosine is still by far the most popular one (Turney and Pantel, 2010). However, in a recent paper of Santus et al. (2016b), the authors have claimed that Vector Cosine is outperformed by APSyn (Average Precision for Synonymy), a metric based on the extent of the intersection between the most salient contexts of two target words. The measure, tested on a window-based DSM, outperformed Vector Cosine on the ESL and on the TOEFL datasets.
In the present work, we perform a systematic evaluation of APSyn, testing it on the most popular test sets for similarity estimation - namely WordSim-353 (Finkelstein et al., 2001), MEN (Bruni et al., 2014) and SimLex-999 (Hill et al., 2015). For comparison, Vector Cosine is also calculated on several count-based DSMs. We implement a total of twenty-eight models with different parameters settings, each of which differs according to corpus size, context window width, weighting scheme and SVD application. The new metric is shown to outperform Vector Cosine in most settings, except when the latter metric is applied on a PPMI-SVD reduced matrix (Bullinaria and Levy, 2012), against which APSyn still obtains competitive performances. The results are also discussed in relation to the state-of-the-art DSMs, as reported in Hill et al. (2015). In such comparison, the best settings of our models outperform the word embeddings in almost all datasets. A pilot study was also carried out to investigate whether APSyn is scalable. Results prove its high performance also when calculated on large corpora, such as those used by Baroni et al. (2014).
On top of the performance, APSyn seems not to be subject to some of the biases that affect Vector Cosine. Finally, considering the debate about the ability of DSMs to calculate genuine similarity as opposed to word relatedness (Turney, 2001; Agirre et al., 2009; Hill et al., 2015), we test the ability of the models to quantify genuine semantic similarity.

2 Background

2.1 DSMs, Measures of Association and Dimensionality Reduction

Count-based DSMs are built in an unsupervised way. Starting from large preprocessed corpora, a matrix $M_{(m \times n)}$ is built, in which each row is a vector representing a target word in a vocabulary of size m, and each column is one of the n potential contexts (Turney and Pantel, 2010; Levy et al., 2015). The vector dimensions are counters recording how many times the contexts co-occur with the target words.
Since raw frequency is highly skewed, most DSMs have adopted more sophisticated association measures, such as Positive PMI (PPMI; Church and Hanks, 1990; Bullinaria and Levy, 2012; Levy et al., 2015) and Local Mutual Information (LMI; Evert, 2005). PPMI compares the observed joint probability of co-occurrence of w and c with their probability of co-occurrence assuming statistical indipendence. It is defined as:

$$PPMI(w,c) = max(PMI(w,c), 0) \quad (1)$$

$$PMI(w,c) = log\left(\frac{P(w,c)}{P(w)P(c)}\right) = log\left(\frac{|w,c|D}{|w||c|}\right) \quad (2)$$

where w is the target word, c is the given context, $P(w,c)$ is the probability of co-occurrence, and D is the collection of observed word-context pairs.
Unlike frequency, PPMI was found to have a bias towards rare events. LMI could therefore be used to reduce such bias and it consists in multiplying the PPMI of the pair by its co-occurrence frequency.
Since target words may occur in hundreds of thousands contexts, most of which are not informative, methods for dimensionality reduction have been investigated, such as truncated SVD (Deerwester et al., 1990; Landauer and Dumais, 1997; Turney and Pantel, 2010; Levy et al., 2015). SVD has been regarded as a method for noise reduction and for the discovery of latent dimensions of meaning, and it has been shown to improve similarity measurements when combined with PPMI (Bullinaria and Levy, 2012; Levy et al., 2015). As we will see in the next section, APSyn applies another type of reduction, which consists in selecting only the top-ranked

contexts in a relevance sorted context list for each word vector. Such reduction complies with the principle of cognitive economy (i.e. only the most relevant contexts are elaborated; see Finton, 2002) and with the results of behavioural studies, which supported feature saliency (Smith et al., 1974). Since APSyn was defined for linguistic contexts (Santus et al., 2016b), we did not test it on SVD-reduced spaces, leaving such test to further studies.

2.2 Similarity Measures

Vector Cosine, by far the most common distributional similarity metric (Turney and Pantel, 2010; Landauer and Dumais, 1997; Jarmasz and Szpakowicz, 2004; Mikolov et al., 2013; Levy et al., 2015), looks at the normalized correlation between the dimensions of two word vectors, w_1 and w_2 and returns a score between -1 and 1. It is described by the following equation:

$$cos(w_1, w_2) = \frac{\sum_{i=1}^{n} f_1 i \times f_{2i}}{\sqrt{\sum_{i=1}^{n} f_1 i} \times \sqrt{\sum_{i=1}^{n} f_2 i}} \quad (3)$$

where $f_i x$ is the *i*-th dimension in the vector *x*. Despite its extensive usage, Vector Cosine has been recently criticized for its hyper sensibility to features with high values and for the inability of identifying the actual feature intersection (Li and Han, 2013; Schnabel et al., 2015). Recalling an example by Li and Han (2013), the Vector Cosine for the toy-vectors $a = [1, 2, 0]$ and $b = [0, 1, 0]$ (i.e. 0.8944) is unexpectedly higher than the one for a and $c = [2, 1, 0]$ (i.e. 0.8000), and even higher than the one for the toy-vectors a and $d = [1, 2, 1]$ (i.e. 0.6325), which instead share a larger feature intersection. Since the Vector Cosine is a distance measure, it is also subject to the hubness problem, which was shown by Radovanovic et al. (2010) to be an inherent property of data distributions in high-dimensional vector space. The problem consists in the fact that vectors with high frequency tend to get high scores with a large number of other vectors, thus becoming universal nearest neighbours (Dinu et al., 2014; Schnabel et al., 2015; Faruqui et al., 2016).

Another measure of word similarity named APSyn [1] has been recently introduced in Santus et al. (2016a) and Santus et al. (2016b), and it was shown to outperform the vector cosine on the TOEFL (Landauer and Dumais, 1997) and on the ESL (Turney, 2001) test sets. This measure is based on the hypothesis that words carrying similar meanings share their most relevant contexts in higher proportion compared to less similar words. The authors define APSyn as the extent of the weighted intersection between the top most salient contexts of the target words, weighting it by the average rank of the intersected features in the PPMI-sorted contexts lists of the target words:

$$APSyn(w_1, w_2) = \sum_{f \epsilon N(F_1) \cap N(F_2)} \frac{1}{(rank_1(f) + rank_2(f))/2} \quad (4)$$

meaning: for every feature f included in the intersection between the top N features of w_1 and the top of w_2 (i.e. $N(f_1)$ and $N(f_2)$), add 1 divided by the average rank of the feature in the PPMI-ranked features of w_1 (i.e. $rank_1$) and w_2 (i.e. $rank_2$). According to the authors, N is a parameter, generally ranging between 100 and 1000. Results are shown to be relatively stable when N varies in this range, while become worst if bigger N are used, as low informative features are also introduced. Santus et al. (2016a) have also used LMI instead of PPMI as weighting function, but achieving lower results.

With respect to the limitations mentioned above for the Vector Cosine, APSyn has some advantages. First of all, it is by definition able to identify the extent of the intersection. Second, its sensibility to features with high values can be kept under control by tuning the value of N. On top of it, feature values (i.e. their weights) do not affect directly the similarity score, as they are only used to build the feature rank. With reference to the toy-vectors presented above, APSyn would assign in fact completely different scores. The higher score would be assigned to a and d, as they share two relevant features out of three. The second higher score would be assigned to a and c, for the same reason as above. The lower score would be instead assigned to a and b, as they only share one non-salient feature. In section 3.4, we briefly discuss the hubness problem.

[1] Scripts and information can be found at https://github.com/esantus/APSyn

2.3 Datasets

For our evaluation, we used three widely popular datasets: WordSim-353 (Finkelstein et al., 2001), MEN (Bruni et al., 2014), SimLex-999 (Hill et al., 2015). These datasets have a different history, but all of them consist in word pairs with an associated score, that should either represent word association or word similarity. WordSim-353 (Finkelstein et al., 2001) was proposed as a word similarity dataset containing 353 pairs annotated with scores between 0 and 10. However, Hill et al. (2015) claimed that the instructions to the annotators were ambiguous with respect to similarity and association, so that the subjects assigned high similarity scores to entities that are only related by virtue of frequent association (e.g. *coffee* and *cup*; *movie* and *theater*). On top of it, WordSim-353 does not provide the POS-tags for the 439 words that it contains, forcing the users to decide which POS to assign to the ambiguous words (e.g. [*white*, *rabbit*] and [*run*, *marathon*]). An extension of this dataset resulted from the subclassification carried out by Agirre et al. (2009), which discriminated between similar and associated word pairs. Such discrimination was done by asking annotators to classify all pairs according to the semantic relation they hold (i.e. identical, synonymy, antonymy, hypernymy, meronymy and none-of-the-above). The annotation was then used to group the pairs in three categories: similar pairs (those classified as identical, synonyms, antonyms and hypernyms), associated pairs (those classified as meronyms and none-of-the-above, with an average similarity greater than 5), and non-associated pairs (those classified as none-of-the-above, with an average similarity below or equal to 5). Two gold standard were finally produced: i) one for similarity, containing 203 word pairs resulting from the union of similar and non-associated pairs; ii) one for relatedness, containing 252 word pairs resulting from the union of associated and non-associated pairs. Even though such a classification made a clear distinction between the two types of relations (i.e. similarity and association), Hill et al. (2015) argue that these gold standards still carry the scores they had in WordSim-353, which are known to be ambiguous in this regard.

The MEN Test Collection (Bruni et al., 2014) includes 3,000 word pairs divided in two sets (one for training and one for testing) together with human judgments, obtained through Amazon Mechanical Turk. The construction was performed by asking subjects to rate which pair - among two of them - was the more related one (i.e. the most associated). Every pairs-couple was proposed only once, and a final score out of 50 was attributed to each pair, according to how many times it was rated as the most related. According to Hill et al. (2015), the major weakness of this dataset is that it does not encode word similarity, but a more general notion of association.

SimLex-999 is the dataset introduced by Hill et al. (2015) to address the above mentioned criticisms of confusion between similarity and association. The dataset consists of 999 pairs containing 1,028 words, which were also evaluated in terms of POS-tags and concreteness. The pairs were annotated with a score between 0 and 10, and the instructions were strictly requiring the identification of word similarity, rather than word association. Hill et al. (2015) claim that differently from other datasets, SimLex-999 inter-annotator agreement has not been surpassed by any automatic approach.

2.4 State of the Art Vector Space Models

In order to compare our results with state-of-the-art DSMs, we report the scores for the Vector Cosines calculated on the neural language models (NLM) by Hill et al. (2015), who used the code (or directly the embeddings) shared by the original authors. As we trained our models on almost the same corpora used by Hill and colleagues, the results are perfectly comparable.

The three models we compare our results to are: i) the convolutional neural network of Collobert and Weston (2008), which was trained on 852 million words of Wikipedia; ii) the neural network of Huang et al. (2012), which was trained on 990 million words of Wikipedia; and iii) the word2vec of Mikolov et al. (2013), which was trained on 1000 million words of Wikipedia and on the RCV Vol. 1 Corpus (Lewis et al., 2004).

Dataset	SimLex-999		WordSim-353		MEN	
Window	**2**	**3**	**2**	**3**	**2**	**3**
Cos Freq	0.149	0.133	0.172	0.148	0.089	0.096
Cos LMI	0.248	0.259	0.321	0.32	0.336	0.364
Cos PPMI	0.284	0.267	0.41	0.407	0.424	0.433
Cos SVD-Freq300	0.128	0.127	0.169	0.172	0.076	0.084
Cos SVD-LMI300	0.19	0.21	0.299	0.29	0.275	0.286
Cos SVD-PPMI300	**0.386**	**0.382**	**0.485**	**0.47**	**0.509**	**0.538**
APSynLMI-1000	0.18	0.163	0.254	0.237	0.205	0.196
APSynLMI-500	0.199	0.164	0.283	0.265	0.226	0.214
APSynLMI-100	0.206	0.182	0.304	0.265	0.23	0.209
APSynPPMI-1000	0.254	0.304	0.399	0.453	0.369	0.415
APSynPPMI-500	0.295	0.32	**0.455**	**0.468**	0.423	0.478
APSynPPMI-100	**0.332**	**0.328**	0.425	0.422	**0.481**	**0.513**
State of the Art						
Mikolov et al.	0.282		0.442		0.433	

Table 1: Spearman correlation scores for our eight models trained on RCV Vol. 1, in the three datasets Simlex-999, WordSim-353 and MEN. In the bottom the performance of the state-of-the-art model of Mikolov et al. (2013), as reported in Hill et al. (2015).

3 Experiments

In this section, we describe our experiments, starting from the training corpora (Section 3.1), to move to the implementation of twenty-eight DSMs (Section 3.2), following with the application and evaluation of the measures (Section 3.3), up to the performance analysis (Section 3.4) and the scalability test (Section 3.5).

3.1 Corpora and Preprocessing

We used two different corpora for our experiments: RCV vol. 1 (Lewis et al., 2004) and the Wikipedia corpus (Baroni et al., 2009), respectively containing 150 and 820 million words. The RCV Vol. 1 and Wikipedia were automatically tagged, respectively, with the POS tagger described in Dell'Orletta (2009) and with the TreeTagger (Schmid, 1994).

3.2 DSMs

For our experiments, we implemented twenty-eight DSMs, but for reasons of space only sixteen of them are reported in the tables. All of them include the pos-tagged target words used in the three datasets (i.e. MEN, WordSim-353 and SimLex-999) and the pos-tagged contexts having frequency above 100 in the two corpora. We considered as contexts the content words (i.e. nouns, verbs and adjectives) within a window of 2, 3 and 5, even though the latter was given up for its poor performances.

As for SVD factorization, we found out that the best results were always achieved when the number of latent dimensions was between 300 and 500. We report here only the scores for $k = 300$, since 300 is one of the most common choices for the dimensionality of SVD-reduced spaces and it is always close to be an optimal value for the parameter.

Fourteen out of twenty-eight models were developed for RCV1, while the others were developed for Wikipedia. For each corpus, the models differed according to the window size (i.e. 2 and 3), to the statistical association measure used as a weighting scheme (i.e. none, PPMI and LMI) and to the application of SVD to the previous combinations.

3.3 Measuring Word Similarity and Relatedness

Given the twenty-eight DSMs, for each dataset we have measured the Vector Cosine and APSyn between the words in the test pairs.

Dataset	SimLex-999		WordSim-353		MEN	
Window	**2**	**3**	**2**	**3**	**2**	**3**
Cos Freq	0.148	0.159	0.199	0.207	0.178	0.197
Cos LMI	0.367	0.374	0.489	0.529	0.59	0.63
Cos PPMI	0.395	0.364	0.605	0.622	0.733	0.74
Cos SVD-Freq300	0.157	0.184	0.159	0.172	0.197	0.226
Cos SVD-LMI300	0.327	0.329	0.368	0.408	0.524	0.563
Cos SVD-PPMI300	**0.477**	**0.464**	**0.533**	**0.562**	**0.769**	**0.779**
APSynLMI-1000	0.343	0.344	0.449	0.477	0.586	0.597
APSynLMI-500	0.339	0.342	0.438	0.47	0.58	0.588
APSynLMI-100	0.303	0.31	0.392	0.428	0.48	0.498
APSynPPMI-1000	0.434	0.419	0.599	0.643	0.749	0.772
APSynPPMI-500	**0.442**	**0.423**	**0.602**	**0.653**	**0.757**	**0.773**
APSynPPMI-100	0.316	0.281	0.58	0.608	0.703	0.722
State of the Art						
Huang et al.	0.098		0.3		0.433	
Collobert & Weston	0.268		0.494		0.575	
Mikolov et al.	0.414		0.655		0.699	

Table 2: Spearman correlation scores for our eight models trained on Wikipedia, in the three datasets Simlex-999, WordSim-353 and MEN. In the bottom the performance of the state-of-the-art models of Collobert and Weston (2008), Huang et al. (2012), Mikolov et al. (2013), as reported in Hill et al. (2015).

The Spearman correlation between our scores and the gold standard was then computed for every model and it is reported in Table 1 and Table 2. In particular, Table 1 describes the performances on SimLex-999, WordSim-353 and MEN for the measures applied on RCV Vol. 1 models. Table 2, instead, describes the performances of the measures on the three datasets for the Wikipedia models. Concurrently, Table 3 and Table 4 describe the performances of the measures respectively on the RCV Vol. 1 and Wikipedia models, tested on the subsets of WordSim-353 extracted by Agirre et al. (2009).

3.4 Performance Analysis

Table 1 shows the Spearman correlation scores for Vector Cosine and APSyn on the three datasets for the eight most representative DSMs built using RCV Vol. 1. Table 2 does the same for the DSMs built using Wikipedia. For the sake of comparison, we also report the results of the state-of-the-art DSMs mentioned in Hill et al. (2015) (see Section 2.5).

With a glance at the tables, it can be easily noticed that the measures perform particularly well in two models: i) APSyn, when applied on the PPMI-weighted DSM (henceforth, APSynPPMI); ii) Vector Cosine, when applied on the SVD-reduced PPMI-weighted matrix (henceforth, CosSVDPPMI). These two models perform consistently and in a comparable way across the datasets, generally outperforming the state-of-the-art DSMs, with an exception for the Wikipedia-trained models in WordSim-353.

Some further observations are: i) corpus size strongly affects the results; ii) PPMI strongly outperforms LMI for both Vector Cosine and APSyn; iii) SVD boosts the Vector Cosine, especially when it is combined with PPMI; iv) *N* has some impact on the performance of APSyn, which generally achieves the best results for *N*=500. As a note about iii), the results of using SVD jointly with LMI spaces are less predictable than when combining it with PPMI.

Also, we can notice that the smaller window (i.e. 2) does not always perform better than the larger one (i.e. 3). The former appears to perform better on SimLex-999, while the latter seems to have some advantages on the other datasets. This

Dataset	WSim (SIM)		WSim (REL)	
Window	**2**	**3**	**2**	**3**
Cos Freq	0.208	0.158	0.167	0.175
Cos LMI	0.416	0.395	0.251	0.269
Cos PPMI	0.52	0.496	0.378	0.396
Cos SVD-Freq300	0.240	0.214	0.051	0.084
Cos SVD-LMI300	0.418	0.393	0.141	0.151
Cos SVD-PPMI300	**0.550**	**0.522**	**0.325**	**0.323**
APSynLMI-1000	0.32	0.29	0.259	0.241
APSynLMI-500	0.355	0.319	0.261	0.284
APSynLMI-100	0.388	0.335	0.233	0.27
APSynPPMI-1000	0.519	0.525	0.337	**0.397**
APSynPPMI-500	**0.564**	**0.546**	**0.361**	0.382
PMI APSynPPMI-100	0.562	0.553	0.287	0.309

Table 3: Spearman correlation scores for our eight models trained on RCV1, in the two subsets of WordSim-353.

might depend on the different type of similarity encoded in SimLex-999 (i.e. genuine similarity). On top of it, despite Hill et al. (2015)'s claim that no evidence supports the hypothesis that smaller context windows improve the ability of models to capture similarity (Agirre et al., 2009; Kiela and Clark, 2014), we need to mention that window 5 was abandoned because of its low performance.

With reference to the hubness effect, we have conducted a pilot study inspired to the one carried out by Schnabel et al. (2015), using the words of the SimLex-999 dataset as query words and collecting for each of them the top 1000 nearest neighbors. Given all the neighbors at rank r, we have checked their rank in the frequency list extracted from our corpora. Figure 1 shows the relation between the rank in the nearest neighbor list and the rank in the frequency list. It can be easily noticed that the highest ranked nearest neighbors tend to have higher rank also in the frequency list, supporting the idea that frequent words are more likely to be nearest neighbors. APSyn does not seem to be able to overcome such bias, which seems to be in fact an inherent property of the DSMs (Radovanovic et al., 2010). Further investigation is needed to see whether variations of APSyn can tackle this problem.

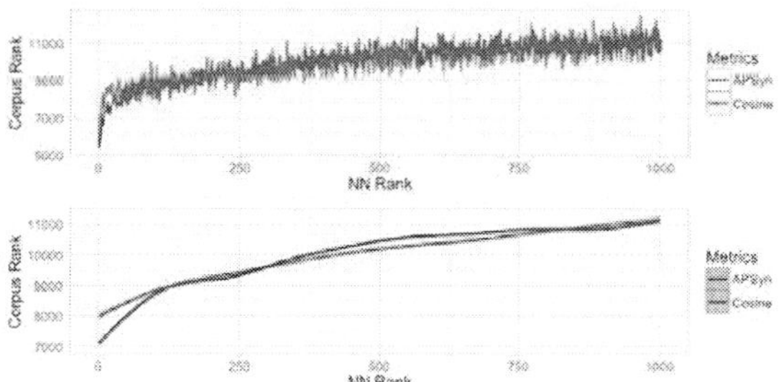

Figure 1: Rank in the corpus-derived frequency list for the top 1000 nearest neighbors of the terms in SimLex-999, computed with Cosine (red) and APSyn (blue). The smoothing chart in the bottom uses the Generalized Additive Model (GAM) from the *mgcv* package in *R*.

Finally, few words need to be spent with regard to the ability of calculating genuine similarity, as distinguished from word relatedness (Turney, 2001; Agirre et al., 2009; Hill et al., 2015). Table 3 and Table 4 show the Spearman correlation scores for the two measures calculated on the models respectively trained on RCV1 and Wikipedia, tested on the subsets of WordSim-353 extracted by Agirre et al. (2009). It can be easily noticed that our best models work better on the similarity subset. In particular, APSynPPMI performs about 20-30% better for the similarity subset than for the relatedness one (see Table 3), as well as both APSynPPMI and CosSVDPPMI do in Wikipedia (see Table 4).

Dataset	WSim (SIM)		WSim (REL)	
Window	**2**	**3**	**2**	**3**
Cos Freq	0.335	0.334	0.03	0.05
Cos LMI	0.638	0.663	0.293	0.34
Cos PPMI	0.672	0.675	0.441	0.446
Cos SVD-Freq300	0.35	0.363	-0.013	0.001
Cos SVD-LMI300	0.604	0.626	0.222	0.286
Cos SVD-PPMI300	**0.72**	**0.725**	**0.444**	**0.486**
APSynLMI-1000	0.609	0.609	0.317	0.36
APSynLMI-500	0.599	0.601	0.289	0.344
APSynLMI-100	0.566	0.574	0.215	0.271
APSynPPMI-1000	0.692	0.726	0.507	0.568
APSynPPMI-500	**0.699**	**0.742**	**0.508**	**0.571**
APSynPPMI-100	0.66	0.692	0.482	0.516

Table 4: Spearman correlation results for our eight models trained on Wikipedia, in the subsets of WordSim-353.

3.5 Scalability

In order to evaluate the scalability of APSyn, we have performed a pilot test on WordSim-353 and MEN with the same corpus used by Baroni et al. (2014), which consists of about 2.8B words (i.e. about 3 times Wikipedia and almost 20 times RCV1). The best scores were obtained with APSyn, N=1000, on a 2-window PPMI-weighted DSM. In such setting, we obtain a Spearman correlation of 0.72 on WordSim and 0.77 on MEN. These results are much higher than those reported by Baroni et al. (2014) for the count-based models (i.e. 0.62 on WordSim and 0.72 on MEN) and slightly lower than those reported for the predicting ones (i.e. 0.75 on WordSim and 0.80 on MEN).

4 Conclusions

In this paper, we have presented the first systematic evaluation of APSyn, comparing it to Vector Cosine in the task of word similarity identification. We developed twenty-eight count-based DSMs, each of which implementing different hyperparameters. PPMI emerged as the most efficient association measure: it works particularly well with Vector Cosine, when combined with SVD, and it boosts APSyn.

APSyn showed extremely promising results, despite its conceptual simplicity. It outperforms the Vector Cosine in almost all settings, except when the latter is used on a PPMI-weighed SVD-reduced DSM. Even in this case, anyway, its performance is very competitive. Interestingly, our best models achieve results that are comparable to - or even better than - those reported by Hill et al. (2015) for the state-of-the-art word embeddings models. In Section 3.5 we show that APSyn is scalable, outperforming the state-of-the-art count-based models reported in Baroni et al. (2014). On top of it, APSyn does not suffer from some of the problems reported for the Vector Cosine, such as the inability of identifying the number of shared features. It still however seems to be affected by the hubness issue, and more research should be carried out to tackle it. Concerning the discrimination between similarity and association, the good performance of APSyn on SimLex-999 (which was built with a specific attention to genuine similarity) and the large difference in performance between the two subsets of WordSim-353 described in Table 3 and Table 4 make us conclude that APSyn is indeed efficient in quantifying genuine similarity.

To conclude, being a linguistically and cognitively grounded metric, APSyn offers the possibility for further improvements, by simply combining it to other properties that were not yet considered in its definition. A natural extension would be to verify whether APSyn hypothesis and implementation holds on SVD reduced matrices and word embeddings.

Acknowledgments

This paper is partially supported by HK PhD Fellowship Scheme, under PF12-13656. Emmanuele Chersoni's research is funded by a grant of the University Foundation A*MIDEX. Thanks to Davis Ozols for the support with *R*.

References

Eneko Agirre, Enrique Alfonseca, Keith Hall, Jana Kravalova, Marius Paşca, and Aitor Soroa. 2009. A study on similarity and relatedness using distributional and wordnet-based approaches. In *Proceedings of Human Language Technologies: The 2009 Annual Conference of the North American Chapter of the Association for Computational Linguistics*, pages 19–27. Association for Computational Linguistics.

Luis Von Ahn and Laura Dabbish. 2004. Labeling images with a computer game. In *Proceedings of the SIGCHI conference on Human factors in computing systems*, pages 319–326. ACM.

Marco Baroni and Alessandro Lenci. 2010. Distributional memory: A general framework for corpus-based semantics. *Computational Linguistics*, 36(4):673–721.

Marco Baroni, Silvia Bernardini, Adriano Ferraresi, and Eros Zanchetta. 2009. The wacky wide web: a collection of very large linguistically processed web-crawled corpora. *Language resources and evaluation*, 43(3):209–226.

Marco Baroni, Georgiana Dinu, and Germán Kruszewski. 2014. Don't count, predict! a systematic comparison of context-counting vs. context-predicting semantic vectors. In *ACL (1)*, pages 238–247.

Yoshua Bengio, Holger Schwenk, Jean-Sébastien Senécal, Fréderic Morin, and Jean-Luc Gauvain. 2006. Neural probabilistic language models. In *Innovations in Machine Learning*, pages 137–186. Springer.

Elia Bruni, Nam-Khanh Tran, and Marco Baroni. 2014. Multimodal distributional semantics. *J. Artif. Intell. Res.(JAIR)*, 49(1-47).

John Bullinaria and Joe Levy. 2012. Extracting Semantic Representations from Word Co-occurrence Statistics: Stop-lists, Stemming and SVD. *Behavior Research Methods*, 44(890-907).

Kenneth Ward Church and Patrick Hanks. 1990. Word association norms, mutual information, and lexicography. *Computational linguistics*, 16(1):22–29.

Ronan Collobert and Jason Weston. 2008. A unified architecture for natural language processing: Deep neural networks with multitask learning. In *Proceedings of the 25th international conference on Machine learning*, pages 160–167. ACM.

Scott Deerwester, Susan T Dumais, George W Furnas, Thomas K Landauer, and Richard Harshman. 1990. Indexing by latent semantic analysis. *Journal of the American society for information science*, 41(6):391.

Felice DellOrletta. 2009. Ensemble system for part-of-speech tagging. *Proceedings of EVALITA*, 9.

Michel Marie Deza and Elena Deza. 2009. *Encyclopedia of distances*. Springer.

Georgiana Dinu, Angeliki Lazaridou and Marco Baroni 2014. Improving zero-shot learning by mitigating the hubness problem. *arXiv preprint arXiv:1603.09054*.

Stefan Evert. 2005. The statistics of word cooccurrences: word pairs and collocations.

Manaal Faruqui, Yulia Tsvetkov, Pushpendre Ratogi, and Chris Dyer. 2016. Problems With Evaluation of Word Embeddings Using Word Similarity Tasks. *arXiv preprint arXiv:1301.3781.*.

Christiane Fellbaum. 1998. *WordNet*. Wiley Online Library.

Lev Finkelstein, Evgeniy Gabrilovich, Yossi Matias, Ehud Rivlin, Zach Solan, Gadi Wolfman, and Eytan Ruppin. 2001. Placing search in context: The concept revisited. In *Proceedings of the 10th international conference on World Wide Web*, pages 406–414. ACM.

David Finton. 2002. Cognitive economy and the role of representation in on-line learning. Doctoral dissertation. University of Wisconsin-Madison.

John Rupert Firth. 1957. *Papers in linguistics, 1934-1951*. Oxford University Press.

Zellig S Harris. 1954. Distributional structure. *Word*, 10(2-3):146–162.

Felix Hill, Roi Reichart, and Anna Korhonen. 2015. Simlex-999: Evaluating semantic models with (genuine) similarity estimation. *Computational Linguistics*.

Eric H Huang, Richard Socher, Christopher D Manning, and Andrew Y Ng. 2012. Improving word representations via global context and multiple word prototypes. In *Proceedings of the 50th Annual Meeting of the Association for Computational Linguistics: Long Papers-Volume 1*, pages 873–882. Association for Computational Linguistics.

Mario Jarmasz and Stan Szpakowicz. 2004. Rogets thesaurus and semantic similarity1. *Recent Advances in Natural Language Processing III: Selected Papers from RANLP*, 2003:111.

Douwe Kiela and Stephen Clark. 2014. A systematic study of semantic vector space model parameters. In *Proceedings of the 2nd Workshop on Continuous Vector Space Models and their Compositionality (CVSC) at EACL*, pages 21–30.

Thomas K Landauer and Susan T Dumais. 1997. A solution to plato's problem: The latent semantic analysis theory of acquisition, induction, and representation of knowledge. *Psychological review*, 104(2):211.

Thomas K Landauer, Peter W Foltz, and Darrell Laham. 1998. An introduction to latent semantic analysis. *Discourse processes*, 25(2-3):259–284.

Omer Levy, Yoav Goldberg, and Ido Dagan. 2015. Improving distributional similarity with lessons learned from word embeddings. *Transactions of the Association for Computational Linguistics*, 3:211–225.

David D Lewis, Yiming Yang, Tony G Rose, and Fan Li. 2004. Rcv1: A new benchmark collection for text categorization research. *The Journal of Machine Learning Research*, 5:361–397.

Baoli Li and Liping Han. 2013. Distance weighted cosine similarity measure for text classification.. *Intelligent Data Engineering and Automated Learning -IDEAL 2013*: 611-618.

Tomas Mikolov, Kai Chen, Greg Corrado, and Jeffrey Dean. 2013. Efficient estimation of word representations in vector space. *arXiv preprint arXiv:1301.3781*.

Milos Radovanovic, Alexandros Nanopoulos and Mirjana Ivanovic. 2010. On the existence of obstinate results in vector space models. *Proceedings of SIGIR*:186-193.

Magnus Sahlgren. 2005. An introduction to random indexing. In *Methods and applications of semantic indexing workshop at the 7th international conference on terminology and knowledge engineering, TKE*, volume 5.

Magnus Sahlgren. 2008. The distributional hypothesis. *Italian Journal of Linguistics*, 20(1):33–54.

Enrico Santus, Tin-Shing Chiu, Qin Lu, Alessandro Lenci, and Chu-ren Huang. 2016. Unsupervised Measure of Word Similarity: How to Outperform Co-Occurrence and Vector Cosine in VSMs. *arXiv preprint arXiv:1603.09054*.

Enrico Santus, Tin-Shing Chiu, Qin Lu, Alessandro Lenci, and Chu-ren Huang. 2016. What a Nerd! Beating Students and Vector Cosine in the ESL and TOEFL Datasets. In *Proceedings of LREC*.

Helmut Schmid. 1994. Probabilistic part-of-speech tagging using decision trees. In *Proceedings of the international conference on new methods in language processing*, volume 12, pages 44–49. Citeseer.

Tobias Schnabel, Igor Labutov, David Mimmo and Thorsten Joachims. 2015. Evaluation methods for unsupervised word embeddings. In *Proceedings of EMNLP*.

Edward Smith, Edward Shoben and Lance Rips. 1974. Structure and process in semantic memory: A featural model for semantic decisions. *Psychological Review*, 81(3).

Joseph Turian, Lev Ratinov, and Yoshua Bengio. 2010. Word representations: a simple and general method for semi-supervised learning. In *Proceedings of the 48th annual meeting of the association for computational linguistics*, pages 384–394. Association for Computational Linguistics.

Peter D Turney and Patrick Pantel. 2010. From frequency to meaning: Vector space models of semantics. *Journal of artificial intelligence research*, 37(1):141–188.

Peter D Turney. 2001. Mining the web for synonyms: Pmi-ir versus lsa on toefl.

Recognizing Open-Vocabulary Relations between Objects in Images

Masayasu Muraoka* **Sumit Maharjan†** **Masaki Saito‡**
Kota Yamaguchi‡ **Naoaki Okazaki†** **Takayuki Okatani‡** **Kentaro Inui†**
IBM Research – Tokyo* Tohoku University†‡
mmuraoka@jp.ibm.com*
{sumit,okazaki,inui}@ecei.tohoku.ac.jp†
{msaito,kyamagu,okatani}@vision.is.tohoku.ac.jp‡

Abstract

How can we describe the relations between objects in a picture? As recent deep neural networks have exhibited impressive performance in identifying individual entities in a picture, in this study we turn our attention to recognize inter-object relations. To recognize open-domain relations, (a) we propose collecting relational concepts automatically from an image-text corpus. In addition, using collected relational instances, (b) we train a classifier to recognize inter-object relations. A relation recognition experiment conducted in our study suggests that relative information calculated from objects improves relation recognition effectively.

1 Introduction

Generating image descriptions draws considerable attention in the natural language processing and computer vision communities. Recent studies have addressed this task by using a Deep Neural Network (DNN) (Kiros et al., 2014; Karpathy and Fei-Fei, 2015; Vinyals et al., 2015; Donahue et al., 2015; Johnson et al., 2015). Even though these studies provide elegant end-to-end solutions, they essentially extract visual features trained for an object recognition task, and plug them into a (variant of) neural language model. In other words, these studies essentially utilize the language model to put the 'pieces' of recognized objects into a sentence.

*This work was conducted while the author was in Tohoku University.

Figure 1: Different relations between a man and skateboard.

One possible drawback of this approach is that these studies do not necessarily recognize the structure of objects in an image, whereas a sentence typically exhibits a syntactic/semantic structure. More specifically, they do not consider the spatial (positional, magnitude, tangent, etc.) or action relations between objects in an image. Therefore, it may be relatively easy to generate the description *a man rides on a skateboard* for Figure 1 (a) because the major relation between the person and skateboard is *ride_on*. In contrast, we need to focus on the positional relationship between the man and skateboard in Figure 1 (b), and verbalize the relationship as *hold* for generating the description *a man holds a skateboard*.

Now that DNN models have reached the level of a human's ability for recognizing objects, as shown in the ImageNet Large Scale Visual Recognition Challenge 2015 (ILSVRC2015) (He et al., 2015), we believe that the primary and important next step toward image understanding is to recognize relations between objects in an image. Recognizing relations between objects also opens up new applications such as image retrieval using a subject-verb-object (SVO) triplet (Farhadi et al., 2010), reasoning with relational knowledge grounded with both the image and text (Sadeghi et al., 2015), and enrichment of common-sense knowledge with visual information.

However, only a few studies have addressed relation recognition between objects. Elliott and de Vries (2015), Kong et al. (2014), and Lin et al. (2015) classified a pair of objects into a relation from a small number of manually-defined relations, but their types are restricted to positional ones (e.g., *close_to*, *on_top_of*, and *in_front_of*), not including other types of relations such as actions (e.g., *ride*, *throw*, and *eat*).

In this paper, we present the first approach for open-vocabulary relation recognition between objects in images. The contributions of this paper are two fold.

(a) We propose to automatically extract relation instances between objects in images, e.g., *ride_on*(PERSON, SKATEBOARD), using the IBM Model and the dependency information of descriptions.

(b) We train a classifier that recognizes relations between objects with novel features (e.g., positional or regional feature and more), and demonstrate the effectiveness through the experiments.

2 Related work

2.1 Relation recognition between objects

Elliott and de Vries (2015) proposed Visual Dependency Representation (VDR) to represent dependency relations between objects in images. VDR categorizes a relation of a pair of objects in five positional relations: *beside*, *above*, *below*, *on*, and *surrounds*. They reported that the VDR-based method could achieve a comparable performance to that using DNN. Although they did not evaluate the effectiveness of VDR in relation recognition, the results indicated the importance of identifying inter-object relations for description generation.

Kong et al. (2014) proposed the use of a Markov Random Field (MRF) for building a relational graph representing inter-object relations. A node in the graph denotes either an object in an image or a noun in a caption describing the image. MRF trains the mapping of objects to nouns. Their approach considers two types of relations (*close–to*, *on–top–of*) as the edge potential functions of MRF to capture a spatial relation between the objects. Extending the work of Kong et al. (2014), Lin et al. (2015) addressed a task for generating multiple sentences for indoor scenes, and built a scene graph from an image. In addition, they incorporated attribute expressions (e.g., the color and size of an object) to vertices of the graph in order to generate detailed descriptions of the scene. In their work, a relation is defined by eight labels (*next–to*, *near*, *top–of*, *above*, *in–front–of*, *behind*, *to–left–of*, *to–right–of*).

Unlike the previous work (Elliott and de Vries, 2015; Kong et al., 2014; Lin et al., 2015), we do not define relations in advance. Instead, we extract the vocabulary of relations between objects that are used frequently to describe the scenes of images in a dataset. This approach can naturally include action relations such as *look_at*, *throw*, and *eat*, which have never previously been explored.

The closest work to this paper is that by Aditya et al. (2015), in that they do not pre-define a relation vocabulary but instead extract relations from image descriptions. Their approach associates object categories (e.g., PERSON) with words (e.g., man) by using the WordNet hierarchy[1]. They extracted inter-object relation instances by applying a semantic parser named the XYZ Parser (formally named the K-parser)[2] to image descriptions.

Our approach is different from that of Aditya et al. (2015) in two aspects. Firstly, we bridge object categories and textual expressions by using an alignment model for statistical machine translation. As we will show in Section 5.3, our alignment model outperforms the method using the WordNet hierarchy. Secondly, they did not develop a relation recognizer between two image objects, but only extracted relation instances for constructing a knowledge base. In con-

[1] It is trivial to map an object category to textual expressions because category labels were originally defined in ImageNet dataset and taken from the WordNet hierarchy.

[2] `http://kparser.org`

The skateboarder is putting on a show using the picnic table as his state.
A skateboarder pulling tricks on top of a picnic table.
A man riding on a skateboard on top of a table.
A skate boarder doing a trick on a picnic table.
A person is riding a skateboard on a picnic table with a crowd watching.

Figure 2: An instance in the MS COCO dataset.

trast, we build a classifier that predicts a relation between a pair of objects.

2.2 Caption generation from images

Description generation is a fascinating application of image understanding. A number of studies applied DNNs for generating image descriptions with the availability of a large amount of training data (Karpathy and Fei-Fei, 2015; Vinyals et al., 2015; Donahue et al., 2015; Johnson et al., 2015, Kiros et al., 2014). A typical approach combines a Convolutional Neural Network (CNN) with a variant of a Recurrent Neural Network (RNN). We can view this approach as an instance of an *encoder-decoder model*, where an encoder (CNN) represents an input image with abstract features, and a decoder (RNN) realizes a sentence from the feature representation.

This architecture seemingly has the ability to recognize object categories as well as relations between objects in an image. However, the end-to-end models adopted in these studies make an analysis of the internal mechanism for generating image descriptions intractable. Furthermore, these models do not encode spatial relationships between image objects. Thus, no one has demonstrated that these studies really recognize relations between objects.

3 Dataset for image and description

We explore relations between objects using the MS COCO dataset (Lin et al., 2014)[3]. MS COCO is a large-scale collection of images depicting various objects in the scene, with an emphasis on the contextual relationship between multiple objects. The dataset was originally designed for various tasks including language generation, object segmentation, and context understanding between multiple objects. The dataset contains 328k images, distributed under the Creative Commons Attribution 4.0 License[4] and Flickr Terms of Use[5].

The dataset annotates objects with a single category (out of 80 categories) and a bounding box (e.g., the blue, green and yellow rectangles in Figure 2). A bounding box is represented by four values (x, y, w, h), where x and y represent the top-left coordinates of the bounding box, and w and h are the width and height, respectively, of the box. Throughout this work, we use the object categories and bounding boxes annotated in the dataset as the ground truth.

In addition, MS COCO includes five manually written descriptions (sentences) per image (see Figure 2). We utilize these image descriptions to discover relations between objects. For example, the third sentence in Figure 2 expresses the *ride_on* relation between *a man* and *a skateboard*. If we could ground the man with a yellow bounding box (PERSON) and *a skateboard* with a green box (SKATEBOARD), we could understand the meaning of $ride\_on(o_1, o_2)$ relation via the image: the object o_1 has a contact with o_2, and o_1 is usually located above o_2. Unfortunately, because the MS COCO dataset does not have alignments between images and words in its descriptions, we estimate the alignments, as will be explained in Section 5.1.

There are other publicly available datasets, such as the VLT2K (Elliott and Keller, 2013), PASCAL VOC (Everingham et al., 2014), Stanford 40 Actions (Yao et al., 2011), and HICO (Chao et al., 2015). Those datasets contain relation information, although the information restricts only positional or action ones: VLT2K has only positional relations, PASCAL VOC and Stanford 40 Actions contain action relations (e.g., *walking* and *running*), and HICO has human-object relations (e.g., *riding a bike*). We aim at a generic natural image understanding that might involve object-object relationships other than people, and we consider the MS

[3] http://mscoco.org/

[4] https://creativecommons.org/licenses/by/4.0/legalcode

[5] https://info.yahoo.com/legal/us/yahoo/utos/utos-173.html

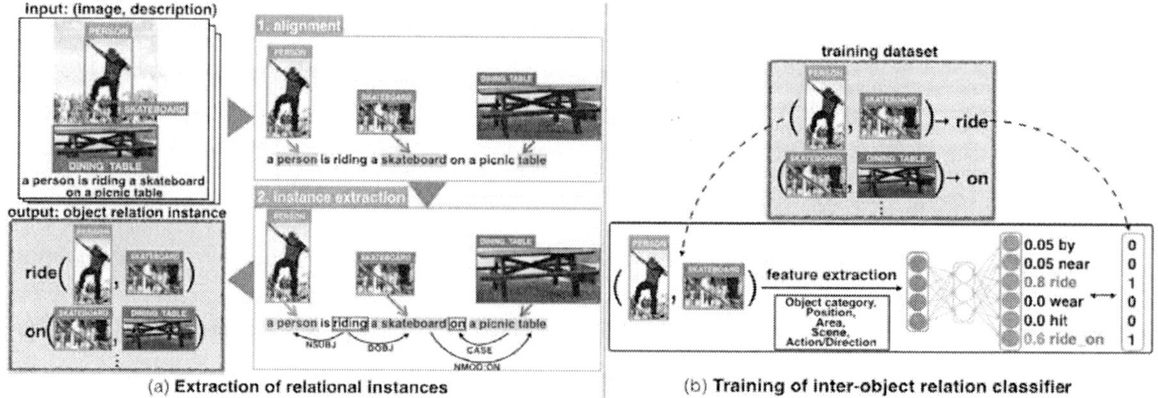

(a) Extraction of relational instances

(b) Training of inter-object relation classifier

Figure 3: Our approach to open-vocabulary relation recognition between image objects: (a) automatic acquisition of relation instances and (b) training of a classifier to recognize inter-object relations.

COCO dataset to be more appropriate for our purpose of open-vocabulary recognition.

4 Our approach

Figure 3 illustrates our approach. We first associate objects in an image with their corresponding expressions in the description, adapting an alignment model for statistical machine translation (Section 5.1). Using the alignments and dependency parses of image descriptions, we extract relation instances whose arguments are grounded to image objects, and whose relations include various expressions that are commonly perceived and described for two objects (Section 5.2). Unlike the previous rule-based approaches (Elliott and Keller, 2013; Elliott and de Vries, 2015; Kong et al., 2014; Lin et al., 2015), our approach does not require hand-crafted relation labels or manual annotations between objects.

Using the relation instances, we train a relation recognizer that predicts a relation for a given pair of unseen image objects (Section 6). The relation recognizer is modeled by a three-layer neural network, whose input provides various features for two given objects: object categories, relative coordinates and intersection areas, etc. The relation instances include multiple relations between the same pair of objects in the image because MS COCO involves five independent descriptions. For example, the relation between the PERSON and SKATEBOARD is described by *ride_on* and *ride* in Figure 2. Thus, we design the recognizer such that it can also handle multiple relations between a pair of objects rather than force a single relation as the ground truth.

5 Extracting relation instances

5.1 Aligning image objects and text

Although the MS COCO dataset contains only 80 object categories (e.g., PERSON or CAR), each object category is referred to by a number of expressions. For example, the object category PERSON can be described by *man*, *person*, *skateboarder*, *skate boarder*, etc., as shown in Figure 2. Thus, we need to identify the correspondences between objects in an image and their referring expressions in the dataset.

In this study, we cast the problem of object-word alignment as a translation task, where the input language is a set of object categories and the output language is a description. Here, we use the IBM Model (Brown et al., 1993) to obtain the translation probability $P(w|c)$, where c denotes an object category in an image and w denotes a word in its description. For instance, the IBM Model gives a higher probability for $P(w = man|c = \text{PERSON})$ after seeing the training instances:

PERSON, SKATEBOARD
a man is riding a skateboard

PERSON, DONUT
a man who is eating a donut

We use the GIZA++ (Och and Ney, 2003) implementation[6] to estimate the alignments.

[6] https://github.com/moses-smt/giza-pp

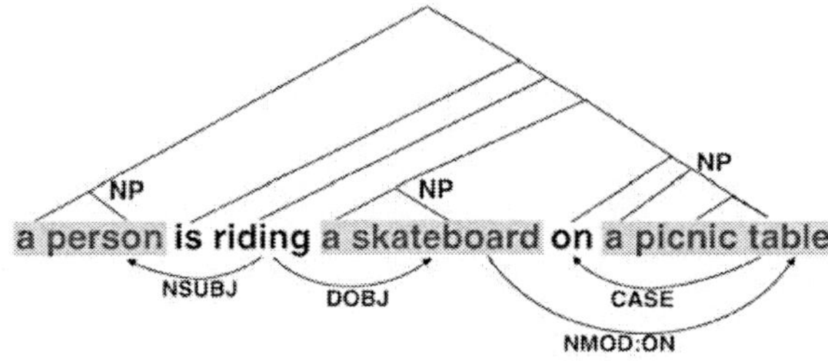

Figure 4: An output from the Stanford CoreNLP. The upper part depicts a phrase-structure tree, and the lower part shows a dependency tree. Phrases in blue represent noun phrases.

5.2 Extracting relation instances

We extract object-relation instances from a description with the image objects aligned. Suppose that we have a description that is aligned with the image objects.

a man/PERSON *riding*
a skateboard/SKATEBOARD
on a picnic table/DINING_TABLE

Here, we denote an object category in uppercase letters followed by a word and a slash. We extract two relation instances from the example:

ride(*a man*/PERSON,
a skateboard/SKATEBOARD),
on(*a skateboard*/SKATEBOARD,
a picnic table/DINING_TABLE)

Because PERSON, SKATEBOARD, and DINING_TABLE are associated with the objects in the image, the two relation instances describe the relations between PERSON and SKATEBOARD objects as *ride* and between SKATEBOARD and DINING_TABLE objects as *on*.

We design a method for extracting relation instances from dependency trees of image descriptions, inspired by the methods for Open Information Extraction (Schmitz et al., 2012; Nakashole et al., 2012; Xu et al., 2013; Moro and Navigli, 2013). We first parse a description using the Stanford CoreNLP (Manning et al., 2014)[7]. We find a set of the longest noun phrases (NPs) whose phrase structures are located at nodes of height no greater than three from their leaves (in blue in Figure 4)[8].

[7]We used Stanford CoreNLP 3.5.2.
`http://stanfordnlp.github.io/CoreNLP/`

[8]This finds noun phrases with four words at most.

Table 1: Result of object-word alignment.

	Precision	Recall	F1
IBM Model	**.880**	**.743**	**.806**
WordNet	.738	.565	.638

We extract inter-object relation instances using the following templates.

1. $v(o_1, o_2)$: $o_1 \xleftarrow{\text{nsubj}} v \xrightarrow{\text{dobj}} o_2$
   e.g., *ride*(*a man*, *a skateboard*)
2. $v\_p(o_1, o_2)$: $o_1 \xleftarrow{\text{nsubj}} v \xrightarrow{\text{nmod}} o_2 \xrightarrow{\text{case}} p$
   e.g., *ride_on*(*a man*, *a skateboard*)
3. $p(o_1, o_2)$: $o_1 \xrightarrow{\text{nmod}} o_2 \xrightarrow{\text{case}} p$
   e.g., *on*(*a skateboard*, *a picnic table*)

Templates 1 and 3 extract their example instances from Figure 4. Template 2 is used to extract the example from the sentence, "A man is riding on a skateboard." In Template 1, we attach a particle (compound:prt) if any to the verb for extracting *take_off*(*a man*, *the hat*) from the sentence, "A man is taking off the hat." In this way, we extracted 156,293 instances with 5,153 distinct relations from the MS COCO dataset.

5.3 Experiments

Table 1 reports the quality of the object-word alignments in terms of precision, recall, and F1. The performances were measured on a test set with 50 images that were sampled randomly from the MS COCO dataset; we annotated the gold-standard alignments for the 250 descriptions corresponding to the 50 images.

The alignment method presented in this paper achieved a reasonably high precision (0.880) despite its simplicity. Because we use only aligned descriptions as the source for relation extraction in Section 5.2, the precision is more important than the recall.

In contrast, the method using the WordNet hierarchy, which has been commonly used in previous work (Elliott and de Vries, 2015; Aditya et al., 2015), underperformed the presented alignment method. The recall of the WordNet method was relatively low because WordNet is prone to suffer from textual variations. For example, WordNet includes *skateboarder* as a descendant of the synset *person*, but does not include *skate border* nor *border*. The precision of the WordNet method was also lower than the IBM Model because some object categories

Table 2: The 10 most frequent relations extracted from the MS COCO dataset.

Relation	# of instances	Relation	# of instances
on	19,666 (12.58%)	of	4,096 (2.62%)
in	14,300 (9.15%)	next_to	3,974 (2.54%)
with	13,047 (8.35%)	ride	3,711 (2.37%)
hold	5,136 (3.29%)	sit_on	3,265 (2.09%)
at	4,345 (2.78%)	on_top_of	2,393 (1.53%)

(e.g., PERSON, FOOD, VEHICLE) are general concepts in WordNet and are mapped to general words (e.g., *building* and *group*) inappropriately.

5.4 Collected relation instances

Table 2 lists the 10 most frequent relations extracted from the MS COCO dataset. We can see from the table that our approach extracts not only spacial relations consisting of prepositions (e.g., *on* and *next_to*) but also predicative relations representing actions (e.g., *hold*, *ride* and *sit_on*).

Figure 5 visualizes some interesting examples of relations. A relation instance $r(o_1, o_2)$ consists of a relation expression r and objects o_1 and o_2 in the image. Each object o has the bounding box $(o.x, o.y, o.w, o.h)$. Therefore, we can compute the means and standard deviations of objects o_1 and o_2 that appear as the arguments of the relation r. In this way, we can visualize a rough interpretation of spatial relationships between objects referred to by the relation r.

In Figure 5, we normalize the image coordinates of all bounding boxes to the range of $[0, 1]$, and transform the position of o_2 to a relative coordinate with respect to o_1. The center of the ellipse in each visualization indicates the mean of the center of the objects. A bright ellipse represents the mean size of bounding boxes for the object, and a dark ellipse indicates the standard deviation of the center coordinates. For example, the visualization of *above*(o_1, o_2) reflects the meaning of *above* that the y-coordinate of o_1 is greater than that of o_2.

The previous work (Elliott and de Vries, 2015; Kong et al., 2014; Lin et al., 2015) pre-defined rules to represent relations. For example, the *above* relation holds if an object o_1 has a greater y-coordinate than that of o_2 and if no overlap exists between the two objects. We would like to stress here that we could acquire similar rules automatically from the statistics of a large-scale dataset with image annotations. In addition, it is non-trivial to define rules manually for action verbs such as *wear* or *eat*. These spatial relationships will be encoded as features for the relation recognizer described in the next section.

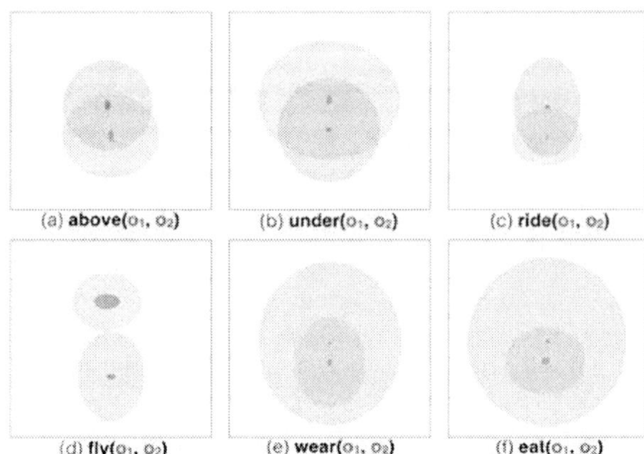

Figure 5: Visualization of positional relations between objects.

6 Recognizing inter-object relations

6.1 Relation recognizer

Using the relation instances acquired in the previous section, we train a classifier to recognize relations between two objects in an unseen image. Let R denote a set of relations extracted in Section 5.2. We model $P(r|o_1, o_2)$, the probability that two objects o_1 and o_2 have the relation $r \in R$ in the image. Note that multiple relations may hold true at the same time (e.g., *ride* and *ride_on*). Thus, we formalize the recognition task as a multi-label classification problem. We design a three-layer neural network[9] whose top layer uses the sigmoid activation function σ,

$$P(r|o_1, o_2) = \sigma(\boldsymbol{w}_r \cdot \boldsymbol{h}_{o_1,o_2} + b_r), \quad (1)$$

$$\boldsymbol{h}_{o_1,o_2} = \mathrm{ReLU}(H\boldsymbol{x}_{o_1,o_2} + \boldsymbol{b}_h). \quad (2)$$

Here, $\boldsymbol{x}_{o_1,o_2} \in \mathbb{R}^d$ is a feature vector for the two object o_1 and o_2. The matrix $H \in \mathbb{R}^{d \times h}$, vector $\boldsymbol{w}_r \in \mathbb{R}^d$, and bias terms $\boldsymbol{b}_h \in \mathbb{R}^h$, $b_r \in \mathbb{R}$ are the model parameters. $\mathrm{ReLU}(.)$ represents the leaky rectified linear unit function (Xu et al., 2015), $\mathrm{ReLU}(x) = \max(x, ax)$. We use the default slope

[9]We used Chainer (Tokui et al., 2015) to implement this network. http://chainer.org/

coefficient value $a = 0.2$. When predicting relations, we identify all relations $r \in R$ satisfying $P(r|o_1, o_2) \geq 0.5$. We found empirically that a hidden layer helps mitigate the difficulty of learning specific relations.

We compute the input vector $\boldsymbol{x}_{o_1,o_2}$ for the objects o_1 and o_2 by using the following features.

Category (160 dims) We encode a one-hot vector representing 80 categories of an object. We concatenate two one-hot vectors corresponding to the two objects ($2 \times 80 = 160$ dimensions in total).

Position (8 dims) Scaling the coordinates of every image in the range of $[0, 1]$, we encode the position of the center of the bounding box for o_1 and the relative position of o_2 with respect to o_1. In addition, we encode the sizes of the two objects.

Area (5 dims) We encode the following values as features: the areas of o_1 and o_2; the ratio of the area of o_1 to that of o_2; the area of the union of o_1 and o_2; and the ratio of the area of the intersection of o_1 and o_2 to that of the union of o_1 and o_2.

Scene (205 dims) We take the `fc8` layer of Place CNN (Zhou et al., 2014) to incorporate the scene of the image. We expect that this feature can capture a scene-specific relation, e.g., the *look_at* relation between PERSON and GIRAFFE objects when the scene of the image is in a zoo.

Action/Direction (20 dims) It may be difficult to identify a relation for a PERSON object with only the above features because there are high ambiguities among relations between a PERSON and the other object. For this reason, we made an attempt to manually annotate action states (*standing*, *walking*, *running*, *sitting/lying*, *unknown*) and directions (*left*, *right*, *frontal*, *back*, *unknown*) of a person. We asked nine experts to annotate, and assigned one annotator per image. The experts discussed the criteria of the annotation every time the need arose. We encode a one-hot vector representing the truths of 10 attributes per person (i.e., 20 features for two people). Because these features currently require manual annotations, we will explore the usefulness of these features in the experiment.

Concatenating the above features, we form a 398-dimensional vector $\boldsymbol{x}_{o_1,o_2}$ as the input for the neural network. A training instance consists of a tuple $(\boldsymbol{x}_{o_1,o_2}, \boldsymbol{y})$, where $\boldsymbol{y}$ represents a n-hot vector for the gold relations $\{r_1, r_2, \cdots r_n\}$ for the objects. In order to remove infrequent relations, we employ only the top 80% of the frequent relations in the extracted relation instances. In this way, we obtained 43,290 relation instances with 133 distinct relations ($|R| = 133$) for the experiments.

Table 3: Performance of object relation prediction.

	Precision	Recall	F1
Category only	.385	.149	.205
All features	.304	**.255**	**.250**
w/o Category	.241	.217	.199
w/o Scene	**.393**	.195	.241
w/o Action/Direction	.336	.218	.239
w/o Area	.302	.250	.243
w/o Position	.296	.246	.245

We initialized the model parameters randomly according to $\mathcal{N}(0, \sqrt{1/d})$ or $\mathcal{N}(0, \sqrt{1/h})$ (depending on the layer of the parameters). We determined the dimension of the hidden layer $h \in \{100, 200, 300, 400, 500\}$ such that it yielded the best performance on 10-fold cross validation. We used the cross-entropy loss function and RMSProp to train the model parameters.

6.2 Results

To the best of our knowledge, this is the first research to evaluate open-vocabulary relation recognition between image objects. Therefore, we built a test set by sampling 1,000 images randomly from those in the MS COCO dataset that were left unused in the training data. We annotate gold relations manually to the object pairs mentioned in the descriptions. The test set consists of 454 instances.

Table 3 shows the performance of relation recognition and the results of ablation tests that remove one of the five features types. The classifier that was trained with all features in Section 6 (*All features*) achieved a 0.250 F1 score whereas the one trained with only the object category feature (*Category only*) achieved a 0.205 F1 score. We can consider *Category only* as a language model since it uses only text information (i.e., object categories). Although the ablation test for *Category* also reveals the importance of the category information (a 0.051 reduction of F1 score), showing the largest contribution among five features, the difference of F1

Table 4: Top-1 result of object relation prediction.

	Precision	Recall	F1
Majority baseline	.282	.281	.281
Category only	.467	.495	.480
All features	.452	.474	.463
w/o Category	.342	.352	.347
w/o Scene	**.479**	**.520**	**.499**
w/o Action/Direction	.449	.469	.459
w/o Area	.441	.465	.453
w/o Position	.420	.436	.428

scores (0.045) between *All features* and *Category only* indicates the importance of spatial and visual features for recognizing relations between objects. We speculate the reason of the largest contribution of the *Category* feature is that, compared to the spatial or visual features, it can reduce relation candidates given two objects. We might be able to specify the relations if *Category* information (e.g., PERSON and SKATEBOARD) rather than the spacial or visual information (e.g., "o_1 is upper of o_2") is given when looking at a picture. The ablation test for *Action/Direction* shows that understanding the state of a person is also useful for recognizing relations.

We also evaluate the performance of relation recognition in terms of top-1 predictions, as it is important practically for the application of description generation to predict at least one true-positive relation. Defining a top-1 prediction as the relation r to which the classifier yielded the highest probability $P(r|o_1, o_2)$ of all relations, we regard a prediction as correct if the predicted relation r is included in the set of gold relations.

Table 4 reports the performance of the top-1 evaluation. We added a *Majority baseline* that always predicts the most frequent relation *on* in the training set. The full-feature model achieved a 0.463 F1 score. In contrast to our expectation, the best result of a 0.499 F1 score was obtained without the scene features. This is probably because the relation recognizer overfitted to the training data with the abstract features of the `fc8` layer of Place CNN, which may have the potential to discriminate against individual images. Removing the scene features, the relation recognizer could outperform the *Category only* baseline.

However, we also encounter pairs of image objects for which the proposed method cannot predict relations in principle. Figure 6 shows a typical ex-

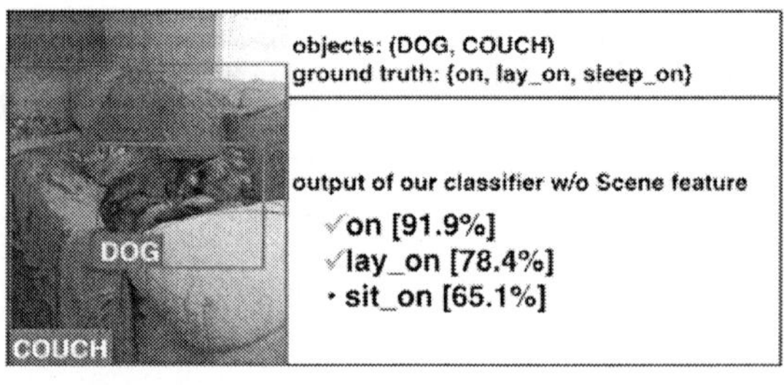

Figure 6: An example of our inter-object relation classifier. A green tick indicates that the relation is true (included in the gold labels).

ample of these instances. In this image, the dog is located around the center of the couch, but the spatial relationship is insufficient to describe the scene. Furthermore, we need to recognize the state of the dog in order to differentiate *sleep_on*, *lie_on*, and *sit_on*. It may be necessary to recognize the fine-grained properties about objects, e.g., whether or not the animal has its eyes closed.

7 Conclusion

In this paper, we presented the first approach for open-vocabulary relation recognition between objects in images. In order to extract expressions that refer specifically to relations between objects, we successfully adopted a word alignment model developed for statistical machine translation. Using the relation instances whose arguments are grounded to image objects, we could train a relation recognizer that predicts a relation for a given pair of objects in an image. The experimental results demonstrated that the spatial features contributed to the task of relation recognition.

An immediate future work would be further analysis to explore important features/attributes for relation recognition, e.g., features/attributes expressing an object, two objects, or the whole scene of an image. We plan to demonstrate the usefulness of relation recognition between image objects in applications including image description generation, image retrieval, and even image recognition with the commonsense knowledge extracted from the image descriptions.

Acknowledgments

We gratefully acknowledge anonymous annotators for annotating a large amount of gold labels within a limited time period. We thank anonymous reviewers for their thoughtful comments and suggestions. This research was supported by JSPS KAKENHI Grant Numbers JP15H01702, JP15H05318 and JP15H05919.

References

Somak Aditya, Yezhou Yang, Chitta Baral, Cornelia Fermüller, and Yiannis Aloimonos. 2015. From images to sentences through scene description graphs using commonsense reasoning and knowledge. *CoRR*, abs/1511.03292.

Peter F Brown, Vincent J Della Pietra, Stephen A Della Pietra, and Robert L Mercer. 1993. The mathematics of statistical machine translation: Parameter estimation. *Computational linguistics*, 19(2):263–311.

Yu-Wei Chao, Zhan Wang, Yugeng He, Jiaxuan Wang, and Jia Deng. 2015. HICO: A benchmark for recognizing human-object interactions in images. In *Proceedings of the IEEE International Conference on Computer Vision*, pages 1017–1025.

Jeffrey Donahue, Lisa Anne Hendricks, Sergio Guadarrama, Marcus Rohrbach, Subhashini Venugopalan, Kate Saenko, and Trevor Darrell. 2015. Long-term recurrent convolutional networks for visual recognition and description. In *Proceedings of the IEEE Conference on Computer Vision and Pattern Recognition (CVPR)*, pages 2625–2634.

Desmond Elliott and Arjen de Vries. 2015. Describing images using inferred visual dependency representations. In *Proceedings of the 53rd Annual Meeting of the Association for Computational Linguistics and the 7th International Joint Conference on Natural Language Processing (Volume 1: Long Papers)*, pages 42–52.

Desmond Elliott and Frank Keller. 2013. Image description using visual dependency representations. In *Proceedings of the 2014 Conference on Empirical Methods In Natural Language Processing (EMNLP)*, pages 1292–1302.

Mark Everingham, S. M. Ali Eslami, Luc Van Gool, Christopher K. I. Williams, John Winn, and Andrew Zisserman. 2014. The pascal visual object classes challenge: A retrospective. *International Journal of Computer Vision*, 111(1):98–136.

Ali Farhadi, Mohsen Hejrati, Mohammad Amin Sadeghi, Peter Young, Cyrus Rashtchian, Julia Hockenmaier, and David Forsyth. 2010. Every picture tells a story: Generating sentences from images. In *Computer Vision–ECCV 2010*, pages 15–29.

Kaiming He, Xiangyu Zhang, Shaoqing Ren, and Jian Sun. 2015. Deep residual learning for image recognition. *CoRR*, abs/1512.03385.

Justin Johnson, Andrej Karpathy, and Fei-Fei Li. 2015. Densecap: Fully convolutional localization networks for dense captioning. *CoRR*, abs/1511.07571.

Andrej Karpathy and Li Fei-Fei. 2015. Deep visual-semantic alignments for generating image descriptions. In *Proceedings of the IEEE Conference on Computer Vision and Pattern Recognition (CVPR)*, pages 3128–3137.

Ryan Kiros, Ruslan Salakhutdinov, and Richard S. Zemel. 2014. Unifying visual-semantic embeddings with multimodal neural language models. *CoRR*, abs/1411.2539.

Chen Kong, Dahua Lin, Mayank Bansal, Raquel Urtasun, and Sanja Fidler. 2014. What are you talking about? text-to-image coreference. In *The IEEE Conference on Computer Vision and Pattern Recognition (CVPR)*, pages 3558–3565.

Tsung-Yi Lin, Michael Maire, Serge Belongie, James Hays, Pietro Perona, Deva Ramanan, Piotr Dollár, and C Lawrence Zitnick. 2014. Microsoft COCO: Common objects in context. In *Computer Vision–ECCV 2014*, pages 740–755.

Dahua Lin, Sanja Fidler, Chen Kong, and Raquel Urtasun. 2015. Generating multi-sentence natural language descriptions of indoor scenes. In *Proceedings of the British Machine Vision Conference (BMVC)*, pages 93.1–93.13.

Christopher D. Manning, Mihai Surdeanu, John Bauer, Jenny Finkel, Steven J. Bethard, and David McClosky. 2014. The Stanford CoreNLP natural language processing toolkit. In *Proceedings of 52nd Annual Meeting of the Association for Computational Linguistics: System Demonstrations*, pages 55–60.

Andrea Moro and Roberto Navigli. 2013. Integrating syntactic and semantic analysis into the open information extraction paradigm. In *Proceedings of the 23th International Joint Conference on Artificial Intelligence*, IJCAI'13, pages 2148–2154.

Ndapandula Nakashole, Gerhard Weikum, and Fabian Suchanek. 2012. Patty: a taxonomy of relational patterns with semantic types. In *Proceedings of the 2012 Joint Conference on Empirical Methods in Natural Language Processing and Computational Natural Language Learning*, pages 1135–1145.

Franz Josef Och and Hermann Ney. 2003. A systematic comparison of various statistical alignment models. *Computational Linguistics*, 29(1):19–51.

Fereshteh Sadeghi, Santosh K Divvala, and Ali Farhadi. 2015. Viske: Visual knowledge extraction and question answering by visual verification of relation phrases. In *Proceedings of the IEEE Conference on Computer Vision and Pattern Recognition (CVPR)*, pages 1456–1464.

Michael Schmitz, Robert Bart, Stephen Soderland, Oren Etzioni, et al. 2012. Open language learning for information extraction. In *Proceedings of the 2012 Joint Conference on Empirical Methods in Natural Language Processing and Computational Natural Language Learning*, pages 523–534.

Seiya Tokui, Kenta Oono, Shohei Hido, and Justin Clayton. 2015. Chainer: a next-generation open source framework for deep learning. In *Proceedings of Workshop on Machine Learning Systems (LearningSys) in The Twenty-ninth Annual Conference on Neural Information Processing Systems (NIPS)*.

Oriol Vinyals, Alexander Toshev, Samy Bengio, and Dumitru Erhan. 2015. Show and tell: A neural image caption generator. In *Proceedings of the IEEE Conference on Computer Vision and Pattern Recognition (CVPR)*, pages 3156–3164.

Ying Xu, Mi-Young Kim, Kevin Quinn, Randy Goebel, and Denilson Barbosa. 2013. Open information extraction with tree kernels. In *Proceedings of the 2013 Conference of the North American Chapter of the Association for Computational Linguistics: Human Language Technologies*, pages 868–877.

Bing Xu, Naiyan Wang, Tianqi Chen, and Mu Li. 2015. Empirical evaluation of rectified activations in convolutional network. *CoRR*, abs/1505.00853.

Bangpeng Yao, Xiaoye Jiang, Aditya Khosla, Andy Lai Lin, Leonidas Guibas, and Li Fei-Fei. 2011. Human action recognition by learning bases of action attributes and parts. In *Proceedings of the IEEE International Conference on Computer Vision*, pages 1331–1338.

Bolei Zhou, Agata Lapedriza, Jianxiong Xiao, Antonio Torralba, and Aude Oliva. 2014. Learning deep features for scene recognition using places database. In *Advances in neural information processing systems*, pages 487–495.

Strong Associations Can Be Weak: Some Thoughts on Cross-lingual Word Webs for Translation

Oi Yee Kwong
Department of Translation
The Chinese University of Hong Kong
Shatin, N.T., Hong Kong
oykwong@arts.cuhk.edu.hk

Abstract

This paper discusses the implications of human word association norms on the modelling of word associations from large corpora and the relevance of different types of associations in the process of translation, with a focus on adjectives. It is observed that the proportion of paradigmatic responses found in English norms tends to be higher, whereas a clear preference for syntagmatic associations is exhibited in Chinese norms. Further comparison with corpus-based extracted associations, using various functions in the Sketch Engine, shows that collocational associations might be more effectively extracted, but there is also considerable individual variation for different words. It is suggested that although free associations elicited in isolated context serve to reveal a wide range of potential lexical relations, their usefulness and relevance in real language applications should consider the actual task and its information demand. A purpose-based approach to construct cross-lingual word webs for computer-aided translation is thus proposed.

1 Introduction

Many online dictionaries, thesauri and other lexical resources are now capable of providing users with flexible modes of searching and displaying lexical information. In particular, access by meaning is recognised as even more important than access by form. As Zock et al. (2010) remarked, word access in a dictionary is a search problem. The storage of information does not guarantee successful access, and adequate navigational means have to be provided. In other words, while lexical databases tend to contain rich information about words, their usefulness (to humans or to computers) will actually depend on how readily the right information could be retrieved at the right time for the right purpose.

The onomasiological approach for organising and retrieving lexical items starts with concepts and leads to forms, which is typically what thesauri are designed for. Word finding in this way often assumes an extensive inter-connection of words, which is largely inspired by psychological models of the mental lexicon (e.g. Aitchison, 2003; De Deyne et al., 2016). Enhancement of word access in electronic dictionaries thus focuses on identifying, capturing and making available a wide range of word associations to enable words to be searched via multiple routes.

To this end, empirical evidence from psycholinguistic data, especially word association norms, offers valuable information about the variety of associative relations and their relative significance in the mental word web (e.g. Joyce and Srdanović, 2008; Kwong, 2013). At the same time, computational linguists and lexicographers have attempted to model such relations and even the corresponding associative strengths (e.g. Church and Hanks, 1990; Kilgarriff et al., 2004), not necessarily as ambitious as to reconstruct the human mental lexicon, but often aiming to enhance lexical access with a mechanism taking advantage of the organisation of the mental word repository. For instance, even when a user fails to name the target word, as in the tip-of-the-tongue situation, he or she should be enabled to access the word by means of other closely associated words that can be thought of (e.g. Sinopaknikova and Smrž, 2006; Rapp and Zock, 2014; Zock et al., 2010).

A very wide range of associative relations have been revealed from word association norms, but as they are elicited in isolation, their readiness to be computationally modelled and their relevance in specific applications might vary. In this study, we further explore the implications from word association norms especially with respect to bilingual dictionary access. In Section 2, we first compare among several existing word association norms for the distribution of different associative types. In Section 3, we then investigate how thoroughly such associations could be modelled by various means and tools. In Section 4, we discuss the need and relevance of word associations in the context of a specific task, namely translation, and propose that word associations have to be flexibly utilised according to the nature of a task and thus its information demand. The study is concluded with future directions in Section 5.

The current investigation focuses on adjectives, which are relatively less addressed than nouns and verbs in related studies. In addition, the polysemy of adjectives bears significant implications on translation, and is worth studying for computer-aided translation.

2 Clues from Word Association Norms

The following word association norms were used: the Birkbeck Association Norms (Moss and Older, 1996) and the University of South Florida Association Norms (Nelson et al., 1998) for English, and the Hong Kong Chinese Association Norms (Kwong, 2013) for Chinese, labelled as BBK, USF, and HKC respectively.

Twenty adjectival stimuli found in both English datasets and with at least partial equivalents in the Chinese dataset were selected, as listed in the first column of Table 1 and Table 2 respectively.

2.1 Intra-lingual Comparison

In Table 1, the columns under BBK and USF show the number of responses appearing twice or more, referred to as non-single responses hereafter (F2), the number of responses appearing once only (F1), and the top response (Top 1) for individual stimuli in the two sets of norms.

Among the 20 stimuli, only 8 have the same top response in the two datasets (easy – hard, empty – full, good – bad, happy – sad, innocent – guilty, narrow – wide, obvious – clear, and strong – weak), all except one are antonym pairs. For the remaining cases, the top responses are more often syntagmatic in BBK, mostly the nouns that are typically modified by the corresponding adjectives (e.g. brittle – bone, precious – stone). In contrast, more paradigmatic top responses are found in USF, with many synonym pairs (e.g. broad – wide, calm – quiet, precious – valuable).

Among the non-single responses, overlapping items range from 2 to 5, with the percentage of overlap (with respect to BBK) reaching as much as 100% (Obvious) to 28.6% (Broad), averaging at 51.3%. There are also some unexpected observations. First, despite the vast difference in the number of participants, it is nevertheless natural to expect the bigger set of norms should more or less cover the smaller set, especially for the frequent responses. However, in 5 out of the 20 cases, the top response in BBK is not even found among the non-single responses in USF. Second, the distributions of the association types are also not uniform. As seen in Table 3, the proportions of adjectival and nominal responses in BBK are comparable, at 48.75% and 47.41% on average respectively. But in USF, adjectival responses almost double nominal ones, amounting to 61.30% and 32.65% on average respectively. This point will be further discussed in Section 2.3.

2.2 Cross-lingual Comparison

As mentioned, the corresponding stimuli selected from HKC are partial equivalents of the English stimuli. Hence the responses may only be associated with particular word senses possessed by the English words. As seen in Table 2, F2 and F1 for HKC stimuli are closer to BBK than USF, given the similar number of participants for the norming of individual stimuli in HKC and BBK.

English	**BBK**			**USF**			**Overlapping Responses**	
	F2	F1	Top 1	F2	F1	Top 1	N	Items
Active	5	22	Passive	21	40	Sports	2	Fit, Passive
Brittle	8	20	Bone	15	29	Peanut	4	Bone, Break, Fragile, Peanut
Broad	7	22	Bean	16	36	Wide	2	Shoulders, Wide
Calm	8	26	Water	14	38	Quiet	3	Peaceful, Quiet, Sea
Common	9	29	Land	23	40	Uncommon	3	Law, Place, Usual
Correct	4	21	Right	7	11	Wrong	2	Right, Wrong
Easy	5	18	Hard	8	23	Hard	4	Difficult, Hard, Rider, Simple
Empty	6	17	Full	11	22	Full	2	Box, Full
Good	3	24	Bad	8	17	Bad	2	Bad, Evil
Great	7	25	Weak	18	32	Big	2	Big, Good
Happy	6	22	Sad	8	19	Sad	2	Sad, Smile
Innocent	8	18	Guilty	16	9	Guilty	4	Bystander, Guilty, Man, Shy
Narrow	5	24	Wide	12	16	Wide	3	Mind, Thin, Wide
Obvious	5	24	Clear	19	45	Clear	5	Clear, Easy, Evident, Open, Obscure
Plain	7	53	Jane	20	45	Simple	3	Boring, Jane, Ordinary
Precious	6	19	Stone	23	32	Valuable	4	Gem, Jewel, Metal, Stone
Rare	7	33	Bird	27	37	Common	3	Extinct, Steak, Uncommon
Sharp	5	21	Knife	18	19	Point	4	Blunt, Edge, Knife, Point
Strong	5	25	Weak	11	20	Weak	3	Man, Muscle, Weak
Wise	7	16	Old	10	14	Smart	3	Knowledge, Old, Owl

Table 1 English Stimuli and Top Responses

Chinese	**HKC**		
	F2	F1	Top 1
積極 *ji1ji2 'active'*	8	29	進取 *jin4qu3 'aggressive'*
脆弱 *cui4ruo4 'brittle'*	5	25	心靈 *xin1ling2 'heart'*
廣泛 *guang3fan4 'broad'*	11	33	興趣 *xing4qu4 'interest'*
平靜 *ping2jing4 'calm'*	11	35	海 *hai3 'sea'*
普通 *pu3tong1 'common'*	9	28	平凡 *ping2fan2 'plain'*
正確 *zheng4que4 'correct'*	5	23	答案 *da2an4 'answer'*
容易 *rong2yi4 'easy'*	12	24	困難 *kun4nan2 'hard'*
空虛 *kong1xu1 'empty'*	5	23	寂寞 *ji4mo4 'lonely'*
良好 *liang2hao3 'good'*	12	26	表現 *biao3xian4 'performance'*
偉大 *wei3da4 'great'*	10	28	母親 *mu3qin1 'mother'*
快樂 *kuai4le4 'happy'*	8	35	開心 *kai1xin1 'joyful'*
單純 *dan1cun2 'innocent'*	13	29	天真 *tian1zhen1 'childlike'*
狹窄 *xia2zai2 'narrow'*	12	37	小巷 *xiao3xiang4 'alley'*
明顯 *ming2xian3 'obvious'*	5	45	突出 *tu1chu1 'outstanding'*
平凡 *ping2fan2 'plain'*	12	32	人 *ren2 'person'*
寶貴 *bao3gui4 'precious'*	4	21	時間 *shi2jian1 'time'*
罕見 *han4jian4 'rare'*	9	42	疾病 *zhi2bing4 'disease'*
尖銳 *jian1rui4 'sharp'*	7	28	問題 *wen4ti2 'question'*
強烈 *qiang2lie4 'strong'*	7	23	感覺 *gan3jue2 'feeling'*
明智 *ming2zhi4 'wise'*	5	21	選擇 *xuan3ze2 'choice'*

Table 2 Chinese Stimuli and Top Responses

As reported in Kwong (2013), collocational responses are abundant in the Hong Kong Chinese Association Norms, especially for abstract nouns and verbs. Also, there are quite a constant proportion of non-linguistic associations. It was thus suggested that the top responses for individual stimulus words may serve to inform the design of semantic lexicons, but the majority and infrequent responses may not even be properly qualified as weak associations. Nominal responses also make up the majority of responses in general, even for adjectival stimuli, although they also elicited relatively more adjectival, and paradigmatic, responses than stimuli of other parts of speech.

With respect to the selected stimuli in this study, Table 2 shows that the top responses are adjectives in only 7 out of the 20 cases (積極 active – 進取 aggressive, 普通 common – 平凡 plain, 容易 easy – 困難 hard, 空虛 empty – 寂寞 lonely, 快樂 happy – 開心 joyful, 單純 innocent – 天真 childlike, 明顯 obvious – 突出 outstanding). All other top responses are nouns (e.g. 偉大 great – 母親 mother, 狹窄 narrow – 小巷 alley). This is an interesting distribution especially when compared with the English norms.

Table 3 shows the proportions of non-single responses in the various association norms by part of speech (POS), with N for noun, A for adjective, and V for verb. As reported in Section 2.1, USF has many more adjectival responses than nominal responses compared to BBK, although both English norms show the dominance of adjectival or paradigmatic responses. For HKC, however, nominal responses dominate, followed by adjectives and verbs, with average proportion at 59.04%, 23.66% and 13.79% respectively.

		N (%)	A (%)	V (%)
BBK	**Avg**	**47.41**	**48.75**	**1.25**
	Max	88.89	100.00	25.00
	Min	0.00	11.11	0.00
USF	**Avg**	**32.65**	**61.30**	**4.07**
	Max	63.64	100.00	13.33
	Min	0.00	33.33	0.00
HKC	**Avg**	**59.04**	**23.66**	**13.79**
	Max	100.00	55.56	50.00
	Min	25.00	0.00	0.00

Table 3 POS Distribution of Responses

2.3 Word Associations across Languages

It can be readily observed from the above comparisons that English and Chinese speakers exhibit different patterns in what one might consider "strong" associations in their mental lexicons. Based on the selected adjectival samples, apparently English speakers tend to come up with more paradigmatic responses as the most strongly associated words, while syntagmatic responses (mostly nouns which are typically modified by the adjectives) are dominant among Chinese speakers. Considering all non-single responses, still more adjectival responses were elicited from English speakers than Chinese speakers. The adjectival responses, corresponding to paradigmatic relations, could be the relatively narrow synonymy or antonymy relations (e.g. good – bad), or broader conceptual semantic relations and contextual collocations (e.g. wise – old, innocent – shy). The differences and characteristics revealed from the association norms can be attributed to polysemy to a certain extent. It happens that the English stimuli are relatively more polysemous while the Chinese stimuli are often their partial equivalents only. For instance, "innocent" may mean "not guilty" or "simple-minded", while 單純 only covers the latter sense. The morphological properties of the two languages may also make a difference. The disyllabic Chinese words are often formed with two individual morphemes. When they are combined to form a word, very often the resulting word will have more specific meanings. With such additional constraints on the word sense, it may somehow limit the paradigmatic relations, making them less readily available than their syntagmatic or collocational counterparts. The grammatical system is apparently better defined in English where word classes or POS categories are relatively more clearly distinguished. Given the lack of morphology and various specific word formation mechanisms, categorial fluidity is more common in Chinese, and POS groups are less homogenous. For instance, Chinese adjectives may often function like adverbs to modify verbs (e.g. 廣泛 broad – 傳播 *chuan2bo1* 'communicate', which actually means "widely spread" when used together). This probably explains for the much higher proportion of verbal responses for the adjectival stimuli in the Chinese norms than the English norms. The above comparison thus suggests that modelling of word associations has to consider language difference and weigh various associative types accordingly.

3 Modelling of Word Associations

It is generally realised that while word association norms are important resources not only for understanding the mental lexicon but also as linguistic resources for a variety of applications, they are expensive to obtain, especially in large scale with reliable sampling. Computational modelling with large corpora is a natural way out. Most typically, Church and Hanks (1990) measured associative strength with mutual information. Wettler and Rapp (1993) relied on co-occurrence frequencies to model word associations, which tend to be biased toward syntagmatic associations. Lin (1998) extracted paradigmatically related words based on contextual similarity.

While human word association norms exhibit a wide range of associative relations, some of which are even non-linguistic and personal, we try to investigate the extent to which the linguistic ones can be effectively modelled. In this study, we make use of the Word Sketch function and the Thesaurus function in the Sketch Engine for the comparison. The Word Sketch function shows a one-page summary of the grammatical and collocational behaviour of words (Kilgarriff et al., 2004). The Thesaurus function produces a list of words occurring in similar contexts as the query word (Rychlý and Kilgarriff, 2007).

3.1 Corpus-based vs Human Associations

Collocations fall between free combinations and idioms (McKeown and Radev, 2000). Typically they refer to grammatically bound co-occurring words (e.g. modifier-head constructions). A more inclusive view will also consider broader semantic relations or topical associations. Thus collocations might involve words of the same or different word classes. On the contrary, paradigmatic associations always involve words of the same POS. Human responses in free word association norms, as seen above, encompass a wide range of both linguistic and non-linguistic relations.

In this comparison, we used the Word Sketch function and the Thesaurus function in the Sketch Engine (SkE), and compared the collocations and similar words extracted with the non-single responses for the selected stimuli in the various association norms. For English, we tested with the British National Corpus (BNC) and the ukWaC corpus. For Chinese, we used the ChineseTaiwanWaC (twWaC) corpus for the current purpose. The top 50 similar words returned by the Thesaurus function were considered, and all default *gramrel* relations in the corresponding Sketch Grammars were included for the Word Sketch function. Other parameters were kept at the default settings.

Table 4 shows the results for comparing the SkE extractions with the association norms. The first figure in each cell is the number of overlapping words, and the figure in brackets is the percentage of non-single responses in the association norms found in the SkE extraction results.

In general, the Thesaurus function tends to generate fewer words matching the association norms. For instance, with ukWaC, the Thesaurus function produces 3.55 words on average which are found among the association responses for a particular stimulus in USF, whereas the Word Sketch function produces 5.25 matching words on average. It should be noted that the number and the percentage presented in Table 4 are not necessarily linked to the same stimulus. Since the number of non-single responses is different across the stimuli, the one with most matching words are not always the one with the highest percentage of overlap. The two figures are presented to give a different reference point only.

Modelling with different corpora may make a difference, but with respect to the results in this study, the difference does not seem to be drastic. For instance, despite the considerable size difference between the two corpora, using BNC or ukWaC leads to similar overlapping with USF associations, although with slight variations.

One interesting observation from Table 4 is that while the Word Sketch function is in general more effective than the Thesaurus function in extracting word matching the association norms, the difference is more pronounced in the Chinese data. As discussed earlier, syntagmatic associations are more abundant for the adjectival stimuli in the Chinese norms, whereas the English norms exhibit a relatively higher proportion of paradigmatic responses, which probably accounts for the better modelling results by Word Sketch for Chinese.

	Thesaurus N(%)				Word Sketch N(%)	
	BNC vs USF	*ukWaC vs USF*	*ukWaC vs BBK*	*twWaC vs HKC*	*ukWaC vs USF*	*twWaC vs HKC*
Avg	3.40 (23.50)	3.55 (24.53)	1.15 (20.05)	1.65 (20.97)	5.25 (33.67)	3.35 (42.49)
Max	8.00 (50.00)	9.00 (50.00)	3.00 (60.00)	4.00 (50.00)	13.00 (60.00)	8.00 (85.71)
Min	0.00 (0.00)	0.00 (0.00)	0.00 (0.00)	0.00 (0.00)	2.00 (11.11)	1.00 (8.33)

Table 4 Comparing Corpus-based Associations and Human Responses

3.2 Extracting Associations from Corpora

One of the most closely related studies worked on Japanese. Joyce and Srdanović (2008) compared the lexical relationships observed in word association norms and those in the collocational and thesaural data extracted with the Sketch Engine. Six Japanese lexical items were selected, including two verbs, one adjective and three nouns. As expected, a rich variety of associative relations have been observed from the word association norms. While there was considerable overlap between the two resources, attention was drawn to the relations which were only found in the association norms but absent from the associations extracted by the Sketch Engine. More fine-grained sub-categories for typical associations, including even encyclopedic and cultural specific ones, were distinguished. The value of word association norms as linguistic resources was highlighted and it was suggested that they be incorporated in electronic dictionaries for a more comprehensive coverage to enhance association-based lexical access as has often been aspired.

In this study, we have focused on adjectives as the stimulus words. Grammatically they are supposed to form a homogenous group sharing most distributional features. However, when it comes to associations, individual variations are more than obvious. On the one hand, the computational extraction of associations is not equally or comparably effective for all stimuli. For instance, with Word Sketch on ukWaC and compared with USF, the number of matching words vary from 2 to 13. In the best case, 60% of overlap was found (e.g. for "brittle", matched associations include "peanut", "hard", "fragile", "dry", "crack", "hair", "stiff", "weak" and "bone"), whereas in the worst case, only 11.11% overlap could be achieved (e.g. for "great", only "big" and "little" could be matched). Similarly for the Chinese data, the overlapping ranges from 1 to 8, and in terms of percentage, it could be as poor as 8.33% (e.g. quite unexpectedly, for 容易 'easy', only 簡單 'simple' could be matched) to as good as 85.71% (e.g. the matched words for 強烈 'strong' include 反對 *fan3dui4* 'oppose', 慾望 *yu4wang4* 'desire', 要求 *yao1qiu2* 'request', 氣味 *qi4wei4* 'smell', 建議 *jian4yi4* 'suggest' and 感受 *gan3shou4* 'feeling').

Meanwhile, the relative association strengths found in the association norms and the extracted words are seldom in concord. Sometimes the results could be quite counter-intuitive as the following example.

If we try the Thesaurus function in the Sketch Engine, with "strong" as the query word, it turns out that "weak" is not a strongly associated item. With BNC, "weak" appears at the 34th position in the ordered list of similar words. With ukWaC, "weak" even comes at the 67th position. Hence larger corpora may not always produce the expected and desired results. Nevertheless, with both corpora, generating a thesaurus with "weak" as the query word unanimously gives "strong" as the foremost associated word.

4 Purpose-based Word Webs

Human word association norms contain many possible kinds of lexical relations. Some can be conveniently defined by linguistic means, such as paradigmatic relations and some syntagmatic relations. Broad conceptual relations need to be topically situated. In addition, there is always a considerable amount of personal associations. These are often single responses, and although they cannot be analysed linguistically, they are still cognitively salient at least to some individuals.

The last type of associations aside, the others can potentially be modelled from large corpora by various means. However, as seen from the above discussion, the effectiveness of such modelling varies. On the one hand, humans do not generate similar types of responses even for similar types of stimuli, or the strength of a particular type of response could be different across stimuli. On the other hand, associated words extracted from corpora do not always substantially match human responses, and even when there is overlap, the relative association strengths could find little correlation, if any at all.

What does such discrepancy imply on the modelling of word associations? Even norms with large samples and participants could only show the tip of an iceberg within the whole lexical repository. The issue is therefore not whether one could model the responses found in association norms. The more important question is what purpose the modelling is supposed to serve, and whether the results really serve the purpose. Free word association norms are elicited in isolation, but in real language applications one often works in a context. Hence amidst a sea of free associations, according to the task purpose and information demand, some associations must be more relevant and useful than others, and it is this subset of associations that the modelling should settle on. In other words, we need effective means to filter enormous word webs to allow flexible utilization of the word associations.

4.1 Enhancement of Dictionary Access

Studies in dictionary access have drawn on association norms, which inspire many attempts to provide adequate navigational means for dictionary users to access what they want, especially when they could only start with some fuzzy query. One such scenario is the tip-of-the-tongue problem, as Zock et al. (2010) suggested, in which case an extensively linked lexicon and making these links available is particularly essential.

The salience and interest in this area of research is also evident from the series of workshops on Cognitive Aspects of the Lexicon (CogALex). In the most recent CogALex workshop, there was a shared task addressing the lexical access problem with a bag of associated words (Rapp and Zock, 2014). Significant implications were drawn from word association norms, and systems were designed to model the intended word among an ordered list of candidates. Several applications were suggested, one of which is association-based machine translation, by translating meaning vectors into the target language and selecting the target language meaning vector and its corresponding linguistic phrase which is most similar to the source language meaning vector.

Nevertheless, while the idea of having more entry points for dictionary access is plausible, it is not always clear what precise associative relations are to be included and how it is to be implemented. After all, dictionary usage in practice often carries a purpose. We therefore propose a more user-oriented and purpose-based approach to the design of features to facilitate dictionary access and thus the modelling and inclusion of word associations in the process. We use translation as an example, and discuss how computer-aided translation may benefit from the comparison of word association data in this study.

4.2 A Scenario in Translation

In practical lexicography, the user profile is deemed particularly important in dictionary design (Atkins and Rundell, 2008). The content and presentation of a dictionary should be grounded on the purposes and proficiency, and thus the information demand, of the target users. During the 1980s, when computer-aided translation started to gain attention, the Translator's Workstation was proposed (Melby, 1982), where translators can work in an integrated environment with different resources at hand, including automatic dictionary lookup and the use of translation memory among others. By now most people will agree that word-for-word lookup is not all satisfactory and will not be sufficient in a real translation setting.

Let us consider a more realistic scenario, such as when a translation student needs to look up a bilingual dictionary to decide on how the phrase "strong allegation" should be rendered in Chinese. The adjective "strong" can be used in a wide range of context, and will be expressed differently in Chinese for "strong coffee", "strong man", "strong economy" and "strong emotion". Table 5 shows some more examples, which have not yet included cases where a disyllabic Chinese word encompassing the meaning of the adjective and the noun can be used, such as 濃茶 *nong2cha2* 'strong tea' and 強風 *qiang2feng1* 'strong wind'. It happens that "strong allegation" is not listed in the monolingual Macmillan English Dictionary or the bilingual dictionary available in Cambridge Dictionaries Online. The Word Sketch function does not list "allegation" for "strong" either. So is this a weak association, weak enough for it to be excluded from major lexical resources? But if this collocation is repeatedly found in real text, then it must be relatively stronger in some context. How can we enable the student to access the relevant lexical information then?

Strong	**N**
洪亮 *hong2liang4*	聲線 *sheng1xian4 'voice'*
有力 *you3li4*	證據 *zheng4ju4 'evidence'*
強健 *qiang2jian4*	體魄 *ti3po4 'body'*
深刻 *shen1ke4*	印象 *yin4xiang4 'impression'*
巨大 *ju4da4*	壓力 *ya1li4 'pressure'*
濃烈 *nong2lie4*	氣味 *qi4wei4 'smell'*

Table 5 Some Contexts for "Strong"

Two types of information demand thus arise from this scenario. First, the student will need to find out that in a different collocation, the word "strong" or the phrase "strong+N" will have to be expressed differently in Chinese, and what may be similar collocations as "strong allegation". Second, considering the register and context of the source text, the student will need to know what alternative expressions or (near-)synonyms might be available for his or her choice to render that group of collocations. The first question thus involves mainly decoding usage, requiring mostly collocational information, and the second question involves mainly encoding usage, concerning mostly with paradigmatic associations.

4.3 Bilingual vs Cross-lingual Associations

In fact the Sketch Engine has recently developed the Bilingual Word Sketch function (Baisa et al., 2014). The function allows lexicographers to compare collocations across translation equivalents, but as the developers pointed out, they are not the source and target languages as understood by translators. Moreover, as remarked by McKeown and Radev (2000), a concept expressed by way of a collocation in one language may not have a corresponding collocation in another language. Hence instead of bilingual associations, we propose cross-lingual word webs. Here we outline the steps needed for such word webs, illustrated with the "strong allegation" example, for which indirect means are needed to draw an association.

The first question is which sense of "strong" is most relevant here. Suppose we start with the adjective "strong", among the clusters of nouns which are typically modified by it, can we group "allegation" into one of these clusters? Using SkE to simulate the situation, we can get the nouns being modified with the Word Sketch function. At the same time, we use the Thesaurus function to find a list of similar words for "allegation". Comparing the two sets of words, "evidence" and "argument" are found in common. The second question is how one should render the corresponding meaning of "strong" in the target language, in this case Chinese. Based on the set of similar words (allegation, evidence, argument, and possibly others), a corresponding Chinese word web can be built in the reverse direction. With the equivalents based on a bilingual dictionary, groups of similar words and collocated adjectives can then be extracted from a Chinese corpus (not necessarily parallel to the English one). The resulting associations, which may include 指控 'allegation', 證據 'evidence', 理據 'rationale', 充分 'sufficient', 有力 'strong' and many others, could be of reference to the translator. The word web is expected to offer assistance by presenting possibilities like 有力的指控, 理據充足的指控 and 證據確鑿的指控 especially in the absence of "strong allegation" in dictionaries in the first place, and it is of course up to the translator to judge for their appropriateness in the specific context.

5 Conclusion and Future Work

Our comparison among word association norms and associations extracted from corpora has revealed discrepancy between (1) types of free association responses across languages, (2) words deemed closely related by humans and by statistics, and (3) relative association strengths in human responses and corpus-based associations. These observations bear important implications on modelling word associations and using them to enhance dictionary access. It is suggested that the usefulness and relevance of different associations depends on the actual task and its information demand, and purpose-based word webs are proposed. Future work includes more comparison of association norms, refinement of the modelling steps for cross-lingual word webs and their implementation for computer-aided translation.

Acknowledgments

The work described in this paper was supported by funding from the Faculty of Arts of the Chinese University of Hong Kong (Project No. 3132414).

References

Aitchison, J. (2003) *Words in the Mind: An Introduction to the Mental Lexicon*. Blackwell Publishers.

Atkins, B.T.S. and Rundell, M. (2008) *The Oxford Guide to Practical Lexicography*. New York: Oxford University Press.

Baisa, V., Jakubíček, M., Kilgarriff, A., Kovář, V. and Rychlý, P. (2014) Bilingual Word Sketches: the translate Button. In *Proceedings of the 16th EURALEX International Congress*, Bolzano, Italy, pp.505-513.

Church, K.W. and Hanks, P. (1990) Word Association Norms, Mutual Information, and Lexicography. *Computational Linguistics, 16(1)*:22-29.

De Deyne, S., Verheyen, S. and Storms, G. (2016) Structure and Organization of the Mental Lexicon: A Network Approach Derived from Syntactic Dependency Relations and Word Associations. In A. Mehler, A. Lücking, S. Banisch, P. Blanchard and B. Job (Eds.), *Towards a Theoretical Framework for Analyzing Complex Linguistic Networks*. Springer Berlin Heidelberg.

Joyce, T. and Srdanović, I. (2008) Comparing Lexical Relationships Observed within Japanese Collocation Data and Japanese Word Association Norms. In *Proceedings of the Workshop on Cognitive Aspects of the Lexicon*, Manchester, U.K., pp.1-8.

Kilgarriff, A., Rychlý, P., Smrz, P. and Tugwell, D. (2004) The Sketch Engine. In *Proceedings of EURALEX 2004*, Lorient, France.

Kwong, O.Y. (2013) Exploring the Chinese Mental Lexicon with Word Association Norms. In *Proceedings of the 27th Pacific Asia Conference on Language, Information and Computation (PACLIC 27)*, Taipei.

Lin, D. (1998) Automatic Retrieval and Clustering of Similar Words. In *Proceedings of the 36th Annual Meeting of the Association for Computational Linguistics and 17th International Conference on Computational Linguistics (COLING-ACL'98)*, Montreal, Canada, pp.768-774.

McKeown, K.R. and Radev, D.R. (2000) Collocations. In R. Dale, H. Moisl and H. Somers (Eds.), *A Handbook of Natural Language Processing*. Marcel Dekker.

Melby, A.K. (1982) Multi-Level Translation Aids in a Distributed System. In J. Horecký (Ed.), *COLING 82: Proceedings of the Ninth International Conference on Computational Linguistics*, Academia, Prague and North-Holland, Amsterdam, pp.215-220.

Moss, H. and Older, L. (1996) *Birkbeck Word Association Norms*. Hove, U.K.: Psychology Press.

Nelson, D. L., McEvoy, C. L. and Schreiber, T. A. (1998). The University of South Florida word association, rhyme, and word fragment norms. http://w3.usf.edu/FreeAssociation/.

Rapp, R. and Zock, M. (2014) The CogALex-IV Shared Task on the Lexical Access Problem. In *Proceedings of the 4th Workshop on Cognitive Aspects of the Lexicon*, Dublin, Ireland, pp.1-14.

Rychlý, P. and Kilgarriff, A. (2007) An efficient algorithm for building a distributional thesaurus (and other Sketch Engine developments). In *Proceedings of the 45th Annual Meeting of the ACL on Interactive Poster and Demonstration Sessions*, Czech Republic, pp.41-44.

Sinopalnikova, A. and Smrz, P. (2006) Knowing a word vs. accessing a word: WordNet and word association norms as interfaces to electronic dictionaries. In *Proceedings of the Third International WordNet Conference*, Korea, pp.265-272.

Wettler, M. and Rapp, R. (1993) Computation of word associations based on the co-occurrences of words in large corpora. In *Proceedings of the 1st Workshop on Very Large Corpora: Academic and Industrial Perspectives*, Columbus, Ohio, pp.84-93.

Zock, M., Ferret, O. and Schwab, D. (2010) Deliberate word access: an intuition, a roadmap and some preliminary empirical results. *International Journal of Speech Technology, 13(4)*: 201-218.

Dealing with Out-Of-Vocabulary Problem in Sentence Alignment Using Word Similarity

Hai-Long Trieu
Japan Advanced Institute of Science and Technology
trieulh@jaist.ac.jp

Le-Minh Nguyen
Japan Advanced Institute of Science and Technology
nguyenml@jaist.ac.jp

Phuong-Thai Nguyen
Vietnam National University, Hanoi, Vietnam
thainp@vnu.edu.vn

Abstract

Sentence alignment plays an essential role in building bilingual corpora which are valuable resources for many applications like statistical machine translation. In various approaches of sentence alignment, length-and-word-based methods which are based on sentence length and word correspondences have been shown to be the most effective. Nevertheless a drawback of using bilingual dictionaries trained by IBM Models in length-and-word-based methods is the problem of out-of-vocabulary (OOV). We propose using word similarity learned from monolingual corpora to overcome the problem. Experimental results showed that our method can reduce the OOV ratio and achieve a better performance than some other length-and-word-based methods. This implies that using word similarity learned from monolingual data may help to deal with OOV problem in sentence alignment.

Keywords: sentence alignment, out-of-vocabulary, word similarity, monolingual data

1 Introduction

Sentence alignment plays an important role in building bilingual corpora for statistical machine translation and many other tasks. Given documents from two languages, the task is to align sentences which are translations of each other. There are three main methods in sentence alignment including length-based, word-based, and the combination of the first two methods. Length-based methods were proposed in (Brown et al., 1991; Gale and Church, 1993). (Wu, 1994) and (Melamed, 1996) introduced methods based on word correspondences. Length-based and word-based methods were also combined to make hybrid methods (Moore, 2002; Varga et al., 2007).

Length-based methods which are only based on the number of words or characters in sentence pairs can run very fast but show a low accuracy. Meanwhile, word-based methods which use bilingual lexicon gain high accuracy, but heavily depend on available lexical resources. The length-and-word-based methods which combine length-based and word-based methods (Moore, 2002; Varga et al., 2007) do not depend on lexical resources and overcome the problem of low accuracy in length-based methods. Nonetheless, a drawback of these length-and-word-based methods which trained a bilingual dictionary using IBM models is the OOV problem.

In this work, we propose an approach to deal with the OOV problem in sentence alignment based on word similarity learned from monolingual corpora. Words that were not contained in the bilingual dictionaries were replaced by their similar words from the monolingual corpora. Experiments conducted on English-Vietnamese sentence alignment showed that using word similarity learned from monolingual corpora can help to reduce the OOV ratio and lead to an improvement in comparison with some other length-and-word-based methods.

We describe phases used in our method in Section 2. Experimental results and discussions are analysed in Section 3. An overview of related researches is discussed in Section 4, and conclusions are drawn in Section 5.

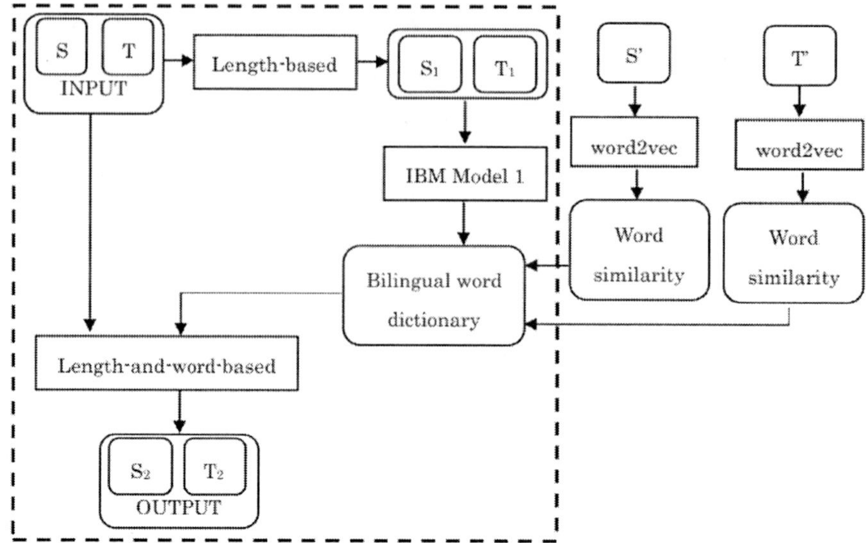

Figure 1: Phases in our model; *S*: the text of source language, *T*: the text of target language; S_1, T_1: sentences aligned by the length-based phase; S_2, T_2: sentences aligned by the length-and-word-based phase; *S'*, *T'*: monolingual corpora of the source and target languages, respectively. The components of the length-and-word-based method (Moore, 2002) are bounded by the dashed frame.

2 Method

In this section, we describe phases used in our method, which include four phases: the length-based phase, the training bilingual dictionaries, using word similarity to deal with the OOV problem, and the combination of length-based and word-based methods. The model is illustrated in Figure 1.

2.1 Length-based Phase

Let l_e and l_v be the lengths of English and Vietnamese sentences, respectively. Then, l_e and l_v varies according to Poisson distribution as follows:

$$P(l_v|l_e) = exp^{-l_v r} \frac{(l_e r)^{l_v}}{l_v!} \quad (1)$$

Where *r* is the ratio of the mean length of Vietnamese sentences to the mean length of English sentences.

As shown in (Moore, 2002), the length-based phase based on the Poisson distribution was slightly better than the Gaussian distribution proposed by (Brown et al., 1991).

$$P(l_v|l_e) = \alpha exp^{-\frac{log(\frac{l_v}{l_e}) - \mu)^2}{2\sigma^2}} \quad (2)$$

Where μ and σ^2 are the mean and variance of the Gaussian distribution, respectively. The length-based model based on the Poisson distribution was shown to be simpler to estimate than the model based on the Gaussian distribution which has to iteratively estimate the variance σ^2 using the expectation maximization (EM) algorithm.

Our model was based on the length-based model using the Poisson distribution.

2.2 Training IBM Model 1

Sentence pairs extracted from the length-based phase are then used to train IBM Model 1 (Brown et al., 1993) to build a bilingual dictionary.

Let e and v be English and Vietnamese sentences, respectively. The procedure of generating sentence v from a sentence e with the length of l_e is as follows:

1. Selecting a length l_v for the sentence v

2. For each word position j in $\{ 1..l_v \}$ of v:

(a) Selecting a word e_i in e
(b) For each pair (j, e_i): choosing a word v_j to fill the position j

$$P(v|e) = \frac{\epsilon}{(l_e+1)^{l_v}} \prod_{j=1}^{l_v} \sum_{i=0}^{l_e} tr(v_j|e_i) \quad (3)$$

Where ϵ is the uniform probability for all possible lengths of v.

2.3 Using Word Similarity to Deal with OOV

In the sentence alignment task based on word correspondences, bilingual dictionaries trained on IBM models can help to produce highly accurate sentence pairs when they contain reliable word pairs with a high percentage of vocabulary coverage. The OOV problem appears when the bilingual dictionary does not contain word pairs which are necessary to produce a correct alignment of sentences. The higher the OOV ratio, the lower the performance. The bilingual dictionary can also be expanded by training IBM models on available bilingual data. However, such resources are very rare especially for low-resource language pairs like English-Vietnamese. Meanwhile, monolingual data is easy to acquire in an abundant amount. We propose using word similarity learned from monolingual corpora to overcome the OOV problem.

Monolingual corpora of English and Vietnamese were used to train two word similarity models separately using a continuous bag-of-word model. In continuous bag-of-words models, words are predicted based on their context, and words that appear in the same context tend to be clustered together as similar words. We used word2vec (Mikolov et al., 2013), a powerful continuous bag-of-words model to train word similarity. The word2vec model can run very fast and enables to train continuous vector representations of words on large data sets.

The word similarity models were then used to enrich the bilingual dictionary.

1. Let $(e_i - v_j)$ be a word pair in the dictionary in which e_i is the English word, and v_j is the Vietnamese word.

2. Let

   (a) $sim(e_i) = \{e'_{i1}, ..., e'_{im}\}$
   (b) $sim(v_j) = \{v'_{j1}, ..., v'_{jn}\}$

   be sets of similar words of e_i and v_j, respectively.

3. The dictionary can be expanded as follows:

   (a) For e' in $sim(e_i)$: add pairs $(e' - v_j)$ to the dictionary
   (b) For v' in $sim(v_j)$: add pairs $(e_i - v')$ to the dictionary
   (c) $score(e' - v_j) = score(e_i - v_j) * cosine(e_i - e')$
   (d) $score(e_i - v') = score(e_i - v_j) * cosine(v_j - v')$

Where $score(a, b)$ is the word translation probability of the word pair (a, b) by training IBM Model 1. $cosine(a, b)$ is the cosine similarity between a and b from word similarity models.

The expanded dictionary can help to cover a higher ratio of vocabulary, which reduces the OOV ratio and improves overall performance.

2.4 Length-based and Word-based

The expanded dictionary was then combined with the length-based phase described in Section 2.1 to produce final alignments, which are described as follows:

$$P(e,v) = \frac{P_{1-1}(l_e, l_v)}{(l_e+1)^{l_v}} \left(\prod_{j=1}^{l_v} \sum_{i=0}^{l_e} tr(v_j|e_i)\right)\left(\sum_{i=1}^{l_e} f_u(e_i)\right) \quad (4)$$

Where f_u is the observed relative unigram frequency of the word in the text in the corresponding language.

3 Experiments

3.1 Setup

We conducted experiments on the sentence alignment task for English-Vietnamese, a low-resource language pair. We evaluated our method on the test set collected from the website.[1] After preprocessing the collected data, we conducted sentence alignment manually to achieve the reference data. We publish

[1]http://www.vietnamtourism.com/

these data sets on the website.[2] The statistics of these data sets are shown in Table 1.

Statistics	Test Data
Sentences (English)	1,705
Sentences (Vietnamese)	1,746
Average length (English)	22
Average length (Vietnamese)	22
Vocabulary Size (English)	6,144
Vocabulary Size (Vietnamese)	5,547
Reference Set	837

Table 1: Statistics of Test Corpus

In order to produce a more reliable bilingual dictionary, we added an available bilingual corpus to train IBM Model 1, which was collected from the IWSLT2015 workshop.[3] The dataset contains subtitles of TED talks (Cettolo et al., 2012). The IWSLT2015 training data is shown in Table 2.

Statistics	iwslt15
Sentences (English)	129,327
Sentences (Vietnamese)	129,327
Average length (English)	19
Average length (Vietnamese)	18
Vocabulary Size (English)	46,669
Vocabulary Size (Vietnamese)	50,667

Table 2: Statistics of the IWSLT15 Corpus

In the preprocessing steps, we tokenized these datasets using the tokenizer of Moses script[4] for English and JVnTextpro[5] for Vietnamese. The datasets were then lowercased. For Vietnamese, we conducted word segmentation using JVnTextpro.

For the sentence alignment algorithm, we reimplemented phases in the model (Moore, 2002) using Java.

To evaluate performance we used common metrics: Precision, Recall, and F-measure (Véronis and Langlais, 2000).

[2]https://github.com/nguyenlab/SentAlign-Similarity

[3]https://sites.google.com/site/iwsltevaluation2015/mt-track

[4]http://www.statmt.org/moses/?n=moses.baseline

[5]http://jvntextpro.sourceforge.net/

3.2 Training Word Similarity

In order to train word similarity models, we used English and Vietnamese monolingual corpora. For English we used the one-billion-words[6] dataset which contains almost 1B words. To build a huge monolingual corpus of Vietnamese, we extracted articles from the web (*www.baomoi.com*)[7]. The data set was then preprocessed to achieve 22 million Vietnamese sentences.

We used word2vec from gensim python[8] to train two word-similarity models on the monolingual corpora. We set the cbow model with configurations: window size=5, vector size=100, min count = 10. The word2vec trained model of Vietnamese is also available on the website.[2]

3.3 Result and Discussion

We compared our model with the two other length-and-word-based methods: M-align[9] (Moore, 2002) and Hun-align[10] (Varga et al., 2007). We showed how our method can deal with the OOV problem.

We setup the length-based phase's threshold to 0.99 to extract highest sentence pairs. Then in the length-and-word-based phase, we setup the threshold to 0.9 to ensure a high confidence. Experimental results are shown in Table 3.

Setup	M-align	Hun-align	OurMethod
Reference	837	837	837
Results	580	1373	609
Correct	412	616	433
Precision	71.03%	44.87%	71.10%
Recall	49.22%	73.60%	51.73%
F-measure	58.15%	55.75%	59.89%

Table 3: Experimental results. (*Reference, Results, Correct*: number of sentence pairs in reference set, results from systems, and correct sentences, respectively.)

Overall, the performance of our model slightly improved the M-align in all scores of precision, recall, and f-measure. Our model also gained higher

[6]http://www.statmt.org/lm-benchmark/

[7]http://www.baomoi.com/

[8]https://radimrehurek.com/gensim/models/word2vec.html

[9]http://research.microsoft.com/en-us/downloads/aafd5dcf-4dcc-49b2-8a22-f7055113e656/

[10]http://mokk.bme.hu/en/resources/hunalign/

performance than Hun-align. Although Hun-align can achieve the highest recall of 73.60% due to the approach that Hun-align constructs dictionaries, the method produced a number of error results, so this caused the lowest precision.

A problem of using the IBM Model 1 as in Moore's method was the OOV. When the dictionary cannot cover a high ratio of vocabulary, it decreases the contribution of the word-based phase. The average OOV ratio is shown in Table 4. In comparison with M-align, using word similarity in our model reduced the OOV ratio from 7.37% to 4.33% in English and from 7.74% to 6.80% in Vietnamese vocabulary. By using word similarity models we overcame the problem of OOV. The following discussion will show how the word similarity models helped to reduce the OOV ratio.

Setup	Test	M-align	Our Model
#vocab. en	1,705	27,872	28,371
#vocab. vi	1,746	25,326	25,481
OOV en	NA	7.37%	4.33%
OOV vi	NA	7.74%	6.80%

Table 4: Average OOV ratio.

We describe word similarity models using word2vec with examples. Tables 5 and 6 show examples of OOV words and their most similar words extracted from the word similarity models. The word similarity models can explore not only helpful similar words in terms of variants in morphology but also words that share the same meaning but different morphemes. There are useful similar words that can have the same meaning as the OOV words like word pairs ("*intends*" and "*aims*") or ("*honours*" and "*awards*"), ("*quát*", "*mắng*"), ("*ghe*", "*đò*"). However, because in the word2vec model words are predicted based on their context in terms of windows, some word pairs may contain different meanings like ("*bangkok*", "*jakarta*"), or ("*pagoda*", "*citadel*"), ("*phở*", "*cơm*"). Therefore extracting suitable similar words is also needed to be further investigated.

We show an example of how our method deals with the OOV problem in Table 7. The word pairs (*reunification-thống_nhất*) and (*impressively-mạnh_mẽ*) were not covered by the dictionary using IBM Model 1, and this became an example of

OOV Words	Similar Words	Cosine Similarity
intends	aims	0.74
intends	refuses	0.74
intends	plans	0.66
honours	honors	0.71
honours	prizes	0.65
honours	awards	0.62
bangkok	jerusalem	0.65
bangkok	jakarta	0.61
pagoda	temple	0.86
pagoda	tower	0.76
pagoda	citadel	0.73

Table 5: Examples of English Word Similarity Model

OOV Words	Similar Words	Cosine Similarity
quát (*to shout*)	mắng (*to scold*)	0.35
quát (*to shout*)	nạt (*to bully*)	0.32
hủy (*to destroy*)	hoại (*to ruin*)	0.50
hủy (*to destroy*)	dỡ (*to unload*)	0.42
hủy (*to destroy*)	phá (*to demolish*)	0.36
ghe (*junk*)	thuyền (*boat*)	0.64
ghe (*junk*)	xuồng (*whaleboat*)	0.61
ghe (*junk*)	đò (*ferry*)	0.56
phở (*noodle soup*)	cháo (*rice gruel*)	0.67
phở (*noodle soup*)	cơm (*rice*)	0.65

Table 6: Examples of Vietnamese Word Similarity Model. The italic words in brackets are corresponding English meaning which were translated by the authors.

Language	Sentence
English	since the reunification in 1975 , vietnam ' s architecture has been impressively developing .
Vietnamese	từ sau ngày đất_nước thống_nhất (1975) kiến_trúc việt_nam phát_triển khá mạnh_mẽ .
(*Translation*)	*After the country was unified (1975), vietnam's architecture has been developing rather impressively.*

Table 7: An example of English-Vietnamese OOV. The translations to English (italic) were conducted by the authors.

OOV Words	Similar Words	Cosine Similarity
reunification	independence	0.71
reunification	**unification**	**0.67**
reunification	peace	0.62
impressively	amazingly	0.74
impressively	**impressive**	**0.74**
impressively	exquisitely	0.72
impressively	brilliantly	0.71

Table 8: An example of similar word pairs trained on monolingual corpus

OOV. Examples of similar word pairs are shown in Table 8, and translation word pairs trained by IBM Model 1 are shown in Table 9. Because (*reunification-unification*) was a similar word pair, and the translation word pair (*unification-thống_nhất*) was contained in the dictionary, the new translation word pair (*reunification-thống_nhất*) was then created. Similarly, the new translation word pair (*impressively-mạnh_mẽ*) was created via the similar word pair (*impressively-impressive*) and the translation word pair (*impressive-mạnh_mẽ*). Table 10 shows induced translation word pairs. By using word similarity learned from monolingual corpora, a number of OOV words can be replaced by their similar words, which helped to reduce the OOV ratio and improve performance in overall.

4 Related Work

Sentence alignment is an essential task in natural language processing, which builds bilingual corpora, a valuable resource in many applications like statistical machine translation, word sense disambiguation, information retrieval, etc. The task can be solved based on the number of words or

Score	English	Vietnamese
0.597130	independence	độc_lập (*independent*)
0.051708	independence	sự_độc_lập (*independence*)
0.130447	**unification**	**thống_nhất** (*to unify*)
0.130447	unification	sự_thống_nhất (*unification*)
0.130446	unification	sự_hợp_nhất (*unify*)
0.551291	impressive	ấn_tượng (*impression*)
0.002927	**impressive**	**mạnh_mẽ** (*impressive*)
0.002440	impressive	kinh_ngạc (*amazed*)

Table 9: An example of bilingual dictionary trained by IBM Model 1 (*Score*: translation probability); the translations to English (italic) were conducted by the authors.

Score	English	Vietnamese
0.215471	reunification	thống_nhất (*to unify*)
0.369082	impressively	mạnh_mẽ (*impressive*)

Table 10: Induced translation word pairs; the translations to English (italic) were conducted by the authors.

characters(Brown et al., 1991; Gale and Church, 1993). These methods are fast and effective in some closed language pairs like English-French but achieve low performance in language pairs like English-Chinese. Word-based methods were proposed in (Kay and Röscheisen, 1993; Chen, 1993; Wu, 1994; Melamed, 1996; Ma, 2006), based on lexical resources. These methods showed better performance than length-based methods, but they depend on available linguistic resources, which are rare and expensive to achieve in almost all language pairs, especially in low-resource languages like English-Vietnamese. Hybrid methods which combine length-based and word-based methods as shown in (Moore, 2002; Varga et al., 2007) can overcome the low accuracy of length-based methods, and these methods also do not depend on lexical resources.

(Varga et al., 2007) proposed building bilingual corpora for medium-density languages. This can overcome the problem of the unavailability of bilingual resources of low-resource languages by building dictionaries and merge them to make a huge dictionary to cover a high ratio of vocabulary. However, because the method does not compute the score of word pairs in dictionaries, this leads to a low precision. Moore's method (Moore, 2002) can gain high accuracy, but the method has to deal with the OOV problem. Our model is similar to Moore's method, but we can overcome the OOV problem based on word similarity learned from monolingual corpora using a continuous bag-of-words model.

Continuous bag-of-words models were proposed in (Mikolov et al., 2013), which can learn word similarity on very monolingual data. The model also has been applied to learn phrase similarity on monolingual data to improve statistical machine translation (Zhao et al., 2015).

In using monolingual data for alignment tasks, (Trieu et al., 2014) proposed using word clustering trained on monolingual data to improve the Moore's method (Moore, 2002). In our model, we also based on word similarity learned from monolingual data, but we used a strong technique of word vector representation, word2vec, to learn word similarity. (Songyot and Chiang, 2014) proposed a method using word similarity from monolingual corpora to improve machine translation. In the work of (Songyot and Chiang, 2014), the word similarity is trained based on a word context model using a feedforward neural network and then applied to improve statistical machine translation.

The idea of using the word similarity model learned from monolingual data based on word2vec in our work is closed to the research of (Li et al., 2016). In (Li et al., 2016), the word similarity model is used to substitute rare words in neural machine translation. In our work, we adopted the word similarity model to overcome the out-of-vocabulary problem in sentence alignment.

5 Conclusion

In this work, we propose using word similarity to overcome the problem of OOV in sentence alignment. The word2vec model was trained on monolingual corpora to produce word-similarity models. These models were then combined with the bilingual word dictionary trained on IBM Model 1, which were integrated to length-and-word-based phase in a sentence alignment algorithm. Our method can reduce the OOV ratio with similar words learned from monolingual corpora, which leads to an improvement in comparison with some other length-and-word-based methods. Using word similarity trained on monolingual corpora based on a distributed word representation model like word2vec may help to reduce the OOV in sentence alignment. Some aspects of this work need to be more investigated in future work like: applying word similarity in sentence alignment in a large scale data; exploring the contribution of word2vec in this task like using both the cbow and skip-gram models. We also plan to further leverage monolingual corpora to sentence alignment and then apply to statistical machine translation, especially for low-resource languages.

References

Peter F Brown, Jennifer C Lai, and Robert L Mercer. 1991. Aligning sentences in parallel corpora. In *Proceedings of the 29th annual meeting on Association for Computational Linguistics*, pages 169–176. Association for Computational Linguistics.

Peter F Brown, Vincent J Della Pietra, Stephen A Della Pietra, and Robert L Mercer. 1993. The mathematics of statistical machine translation: Parameter estimation. *Computational linguistics*, 19(2):263–311.

Mauro Cettolo, Christian Girardi, and Marcello Federico. 2012. Wit3: Web inventory of transcribed and translated talks. In *Proceedings of the 16th Conference of the European Association for Machine Translation (EAMT)*, pages 261–268.

Stanley F Chen. 1993. Aligning sentences in bilingual corpora using lexical information. In *Proceedings of the 31st annual meeting on Association for Computational Linguistics*, pages 9–16. Association for Computational Linguistics.

William A Gale and Kenneth W Church. 1993. A program for aligning sentences in bilingual corpora. *Computational linguistics*, 19(1):75–102.

Martin Kay and Martin Röscheisen. 1993. Text-translation alignment. *Computational linguistics*, 19(1):121–142.

Xiaoqing Li, Jiajun Zhang, and Chengqing Zong. 2016. Towards zero unknown word in neural machine translation. In *Proceedings of the 25th International Conference on Artificial Intelligence*.

Xiaoyi Ma. 2006. Champollion: A robust parallel text sentence aligner. In *LREC 2006: Fifth International Conference on Language Resources and Evaluation*, pages 489–492.

I Dan Melamed. 1996. A geometric approach to mapping bitext correspondence. *arXiv preprint cmp-lg/9609009*.

Tomas Mikolov, Kai Chen, Greg Corrado, and Jeffrey Dean. 2013. Efficient estimation of word representations in vector space. *arXiv preprint arXiv:1301.3781*.

Robert C Moore. 2002. *Fast and accurate sentence alignment of bilingual corpora*. Springer.

Theerawat Songyot and David Chiang. 2014. Improving word alignment using word similarity. In *Proceedings of the 2015 Conference on Empirical Methods in Natural Language Processing*, pages 1840–1845.

Hai-Long Trieu, Phuong-Thai Nguyen, and Kim-Anh Nguyen. 2014. Improving moore's sentence alignment method using bilingual word clustering. In *Knowledge and Systems Engineering*, pages 149–160. Springer.

Dániel Varga, Péter Halácsy, András Kornai, Viktor Nagy, László Németh, and Viktor Trón. 2007. Parallel corpora for medium density languages. *Amsterdam studies in the theory and history of linguistic science series 4*, 292:247.

Jean Véronis and Philippe Langlais. 2000. Evaluation of parallel text alignment systems. In *Parallel text processing*, pages 369–388. Springer.

Dekai Wu. 1994. Aligning a parallel english-chinese corpus statistically with lexical criteria. In *Proceedings of the 32nd annual meeting on Association for Computational Linguistics*, pages 80–87. Association for Computational Linguistics.

Kai Zhao, Hany Hassan, and Michael Auli. 2015. Learning translation models from monolingual continuous representations. In *Proceedings of the 2015 Conference of the North American Chapter of the Association for Computational Linguistics: Human Language Technologies*.

A Pipeline Japanese Entity Linking System with Embedding Features

Shuangshuang Zhou **Koji Matsuda** **Ran Tian** **Naoaki Okazaki** **Kentaro Inui**
Graduate School of Information Sciences, Tohoku University
6-6 Aramaki Aza Aoba, Aobaku, Sendai, Miyagi 980-8579, Japan
{shuang,matsuda,tianran,okazaki,inui}@ecei.tohoku.ac.jp

Abstract

Entity linking (EL) is the task of connecting mentions in texts to entities in a large-scale knowledge base such as Wikipedia. In this paper, we present a pipeline system for Japanese EL which consists of two standard components, namely candidate generation and candidate ranking. We investigate several techniques for each component, using a recently developed Japanese EL corpus. For candidate generation, we find that a concept dictionary using anchor texts of Wikipedia is more effective than methods based on surface similarity. For candidate ranking, we verify that a set of features used in English EL is effective in Japanese EL as well. In addition, by using a corpus that links Japanese mentions to *Japanese* Wikipedia entries, we are able to get rich context information from Japanese Wikipedia articles and benefit mention disambiguation. It was not directly possible with previous EL corpora, which associate mentions to *English* Wikipedia entities. We take this advantage by exploring several embedding models that encode context information of Wikipedia entities, and show that they improve candidate ranking. As a whole, our system achieves 82.27% accuracy, significantly outperforming previous work.

1 Introduction

Entity Linking (EL), also known as wikification or named entity disambiguation, is the task of linking mentions in texts to entities in a large-scale knowledge base such as Wikipedia[1]. EL is useful in many NLP tasks such as information retrieval (Blanco et al., 2015), question answering (Khalid et al., 2008), searching digital libraries (Han et al., 2005), semantic search,[2] coreference resolution (Durrett and Klein, 2014; Hajishirzi et al., 2013), named entity recognition (Durrett and Klein, 2014) and knowledge base population (Suchanek and Weikum, 2013; Dredze et al., 2010).

However, development of Japanese EL has been slow, partly due to the lack of a publicly available Japanese EL corpus. Most previous Japanese EL systems link mentions to English Wikipedia (Furakawa et al., 2014; Nakamura et al., 2015; Hayashi et al., 2014), which might be less informative because there are about 0.44 million articles in Japanese Wikipedia that do not have correspondence in English. Recently, Jargalsaikhan et al. (2016) released a Japanese EL corpus in which mentions are linked to Japanese Wikipedia entries. In this paper, we investigate several techniques for developing a Japanese EL system, and evaluate on this newly released corpus.

An EL system first performs Named Entity Recognition to detect and classify spans of texts which are mentions to certain types of entities. Then, the system links the mentions to entries in Wikipedia. A major challenge here is the mention ambiguity; for example, given the sentence "*The I.B.M. is the world's largest organization dedicated to the art of magic.*", an EL system should associate "*I.B.M*" with the organization "*International Brotherhood of Magicians*", rather than the American technology and consulting company. An or-

[1] https://en.wikipedia.org

[2] https://stics.mpi-inf.mpg.de/

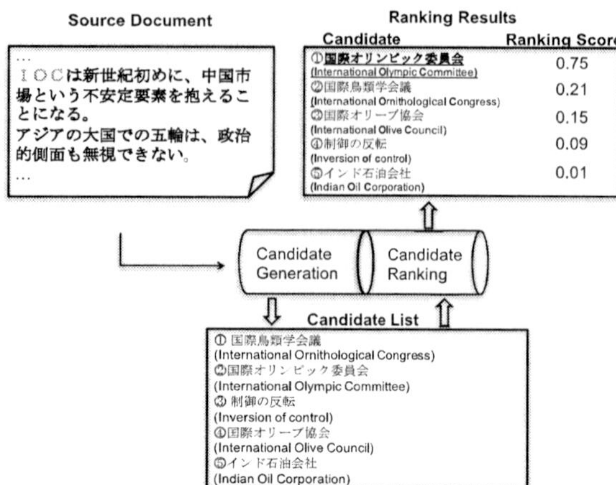

Figure 1: An Entity Linking system generates and ranks a list of candidate entities for the mention "*IOC*".

thodox approach to address this issue is a pipeline of two components, the **candidate generation** component which generates a candidate list of possible entities for each mention, and the **candidate ranking** component which ranks candidates according to multiple features (Figure 1). For candidate generation, another challenge is the variety of mentions. For example, both "*Big Blue*" and "*I.B.M.*" could refer to "*International Business Machines Corporation*".

We investigate several techniques from each component. For candidate generation, string matching between mentions and entity titles has been the main approach, but we find the recall of string matching not satisfactory; instead, a cross-lingual dictionary turns out to be effective in finding correct candidates (Section 3.1, Section 5.3). For candidate ranking, we explore a set of features used in English EL, and find it effective in Japanese EL as well (Section 3.2, Section 5.4). In addition, we apply several embedding models to encode context information of entities in Wikipedia articles, and show that the embeddings are useful features for disambiguating mentions in texts (Section 4, Section 5.4). This technique would not be directly possible in previous Japanese EL systems which link mentions in Japanese texts to English Wikipedia entries, because the embedding models should be trained on articles written in the same language as texts. As a whole, our system achieves 82.27% accuracy and significantly outperforms previous work (Section 5.5).

2 Related Work

English EL is a widely studied topic. There are several public corpora for English EL (Cucerzan, 2007; Yosef et al., 2011), and the TAC-KBP workshop has provided systematical evaluation on EL task in recent years (Ji et al., 2014).

To address mention ambiguity, previous works have explored advanced linguistic features (Bunescu and Pasca, 2006; Dredze et al., 2010; Zhang et al., 2011; Graus et al., 2012; Zhou et al., 2014) and link-based features (Milne and Witten, 2008; Han and Zhao, 2009; Kulkarni et al., 2009; Guo et al., 2011; Ratinov et al., 2011; Hoffart et al., 2011).

Embedding features have been actively used as well. For example, He et al. (2013) use neural networks to compute representations for entities and mentions directly from knowledge base; similarly, Sun et al. (2015) propose to model an entity by combining the sum of surface word vectors and the sum of category word vectors; Blanco et al. (2015) propose mapping entities into word embeddings by using entity descriptions; Hu et al. (2015) build entity hierarchy embedding by learning distance metric of category nodes in Wikipedia; Yang et al. (2014) and Lin et al. (2015) encode relational information by low-dimensional representations.

To counter the variety of mentions, previous English EL systems generate entity candidates by search engine (Dredze et al., 2010; Zhou et al., 2014; Graus et al., 2012), and/or utilize various resources such as Wikipedia disambiguation, Wikipedia redirection, Geonames, *etc.* (Dredze et al., 2010; Zhou et al., 2014).

On the other hand, research on Japanese EL has received less attention. Furakawa et al. (2014) focus on entity linking in academic fields, and link technical terms to English Wikipedia. Nakamura et al. (2015) link keywords in twitter texts to English Wikipedia, aiming at constructing a cross-language topic recognition system. Hayashi et al. (2014) study EL on both English and Japanese texts. In addition, there are several works on linking geopolitical entities in local news articles (Osada et al., 2015; Inoue et al., 2016; Seiya et al., 2015). For candidate generation, most previous Japanese EL systems simply use surface string matching (Osada et al., 2015; Inoue et al., 2016; Seiya et al., 2015).

3 System Architecture

In this section, we present our pipeline system for Japanese EL. The system takes Named Entity Recognition (NER) as input, and links the named entity mentions to Wikipedia articles as output. For NER, we simply use golden annotations in corpus.

Our system consists of two standard components: candidate generation and candidate ranking (Figure 1). In the candidate generation phase, our system generates a list of Wikipedia articles for each mention in text. For example, given a mention "*IOC*", the candidates which the mention can be linked to include Wikipedia articles titled "国際鳥類学会議 (*International Ornithological Congress*)", "国際オリンピック委員会 (*International Olympic Committee*)", *etc*. Then, in the candidate ranking phase, each Wikipedia article in the candidate list obtains a ranking score from a scoring function, which is constructed via supervised learning on a set of features. We pick the top-1 candidate from the ranking result as system output. For example, in Figure 1, "国際オリンピック委員会 (*International Olympic Committee*)" is output as the referent of "*IOC*". Details of the two components are described below.

3.1 Candidate Generation

If an EL system cannot include correct Wikipedia articles on lists in candidate generation, the next candidate ranking process will be in vain. Previous English EL systems usually generate a candidate list as long as possible. String matching between metion and article titles is a common method for candidate generation.

In this work, we use the simple and efficient `Simstring`[3] tool for calculating similarity and searching similar strings. The tool implements two similarity measures, the cosine similarity and overlap coefficient. We extract all Japanese Wikipedia titles into a database, and use `Simstring` to find all titles with similarity scores larger than a threshold for each mention.

Another approach to candidate generation is the **concept dictionary** (Spitkovsky and Chang, 2012). This approach gathers hyper-links that jump to each Wikipedia article, and regard the surface texts of hyper-links as possible mentions to the article. We call the surface texts of hyper-links **anchor texts**. For example, there are hyper-links in Wikipedia with surface texts "*IOC*", "*I.O.C*" and "*the Olympic Committee*", all jump to the article "国際オリンピック委員会 (*International Olympic Committee*)". Thus, "*I.O.C*" is an anchor text of the article. A concept dictionary is a collection of anchor texts.

[3]http://www.chokkan.org/software/simstring/

3.2 Candidate Ranking

We formulate the candidate ranking problem similar to Bunescu and Pasca (2006) and McNamee et al. (2009). Namely, we construct a scoring function $f(m, e)$ based on features extracted from mention m and candidate Wikipedia article e. We select candidate from a candidate list E, according to the ranking score:

$$\widehat{e} = \arg\max_{e \in E} f(m, e).$$

Therefore, the scoring function $f(m, e)$ should be trained such that the correct Wikipedia article $\widehat{e}$ is linked to the mention m. We use SVM^{rank} (Joachims, 2006) with linear kernel for training.

3.2.1 Feature Sets

In this section, we describe the features we use to construct the scoring function. These are powerful features used by state-of-the-art English EL systems, combined with several new embedding features. Table 1 shows a complete list. As a running example, we consider the following text snippet (translated from Japanese) surrounding a mention "*IOC*":

> ＩＯＣは新世紀初めに、中国市場という不安定要素を抱えることになる。アジアの大国での五輪は、政治的側面も無視できない。
>
> The **IOC** is facing the elements of instability from the market of China from the beginning of this new century. The Olympics at major Asian nations can never ignore this kind of political aspects.

In which, underlined words are annotated named entities.

Feature Type	Description	Example
String Similarity (S)	string similarity between mention and entity title	the Levenshtein edit-distance between "*IOC*" and "*International Olympic Committee*" is 11
Entity Popularity (P)	distribution of anchor texts in Wikipedia	68% of mention "*IOC*" in Japanese Wikipedia is linked to article "*International Olympic Committee*"
Bag-of-Word (Bw)	BoW similarity between text and Wikipedia article	words {"*face*", "*market*", ...} from text and {"*modern*", "*Olympic*", ...} from Wikipedia article
Bag-of-Entity (Be)	BoE similarity between text and Wikipedia article	entities {"*China*", "*Olympic*", ...} in text and {"*Olympic Games*", ...} in Wikipedia article
Word Vector (WV)	cosine similarity between sums of word vectors	cosine similarity between vector $\mathbf{w}_{face} + \mathbf{w}_{market} + \ldots$ for text and vector $\mathbf{w}_{modern} + \mathbf{w}_{Olympic} + \ldots$ for Wikipedia article
Entity Vector (EV)	cosine similarity between sums of entity vectors	cosine similarity between $\mathbf{e}_{China} + \mathbf{e}_{Olympic} + \ldots$ and $\mathbf{e}_{Olympic\_Games} + \ldots$
Paragraph Vector (PV)	cosine similarity between paragraph vectors	cosine similarity between paragraph vector for text and paragraph vector for Wikipedia article
Entity Category (Cate)	word in text is category of Wikipedia article	Wikipedia article "*International Olympic Committee*" belongs to categories "*Olympic movement*", "*Committees*"
Entity Class (Class)	overlap of Sekine's entity class	mention "*IOC*" in text and Wikipedia entry "*International Olympic Committee*" both labeled *Organization*

Table 1: Features for candidate ranking.

Correspondingly, we show a snippet of the Wikipedia article "国際オリンピック委員会 (*International Olympic Committee*)":

> 国際オリンピック委員会は、近代オリンピックを主催する団体であり、またオリンピックに参加する各種国際スポーツ統括団体を統括する組織である。2009年に国際連合総会オブザーバー資格を得たため国際機関の一つと思われている。

> International Olympic Committee is an organization sponsored by the modern Olympics, also is an organization that oversees the various international sports governing body to participate in the Olympic Games. It is believed to be one of the order to give the General Assembly of the United Nations observer status international organizations in 2009.

In which, underlined words are anchor texts (i.e. hyper-links).

We consider the following features.

String Similarity This type of features measures the string similarity between mentions and the titles of Wikipedia articles. We use several similarity measures explored in previous work (Graus et al., 2012; Dietz and Dalton, 2012), such as the Levenshtein edit distance and Jaccard coefficient score.

Entity Popularity This is the probability $p(e|m)$ of an anchor text m linking to a Wikipedia article e. The probability is estimated as:

$$p(e|m) = \frac{\#\text{ times of } m \text{ jumping to } e}{\#\text{ occurrence of anchor text } m}.$$

As discussed in Milne and Witten (2008), this probability reflects the "commonness" or "popularity" of a Wikipedia article.

Bag-of-Word Similarity This feature measures the similarity between texts surrounding the mention and the contents of the Wikipedia article. For example, we assess the similarity between the set of words {"*face*", "*market*", ...} taken from text, and the set of words {"*modern*", "*Olympic*", ...} taken from Wikipedia article. We consider several similarity measures such as cosine similarity of TF-IDF weights (Zheng et al., 2010) and Jaccard coefficient (Dietz and Dalton, 2012).

Bag-of-Entity Similarity This is similar to Bag-of-Word Similarity, except that we only take named entities from text and anchor texts from Wikipedia articles. For example, we assess the similarity between the set of entities {"*China*", "*Olympic*", ...} taken from text, and the set of anchor texts {"*Olympic Games*", ...} taken from Wikipedia article.

Embedding Similarity We construct vectors for texts and Wikipedia articles, and assess cosine similarity between the vectors. This feature also measures the similarity between texts and Wikipedia contents. We consider three types of vectors, namely the word vector (WV), entity vector (EV), and paragraph vector (PV). Details of the embedding models are described in Section 4.

Entity Category This feature counts how many words in category names of a Wikipedia article also appear in text. For example, the Wikipedia article "*International Olympic Committee*" belongs to categories "*Olympic movement*", "*Committees*", *etc.*, and some words in the category names, such as "*Olympic*", also appear in text. This feature reflects such overlaps.

Entity Class The corpus (Jargalsaikhan et al., 2016) we use in this work has annotated each named entity with a fine-grained entity class label, called Sekine's entity class (Sekine et al., 2002). On the other hand, Suzuki et al. (2016) released a system which automatically label Wikipedia articles with Sekine's entity classes. We use this system and assess overlap between the two entity class labels. For example, the Wikipedia article "*International Olympic Committee*" is assigned the class label "*Sports Organization Other*", whereas the mention"*IOC*" is annotated as "*International Organization*"; both of them are organizations. It has been shown that finer-grained entity class is useful for English EL (Ling and Weld, 2012; Ling et al., 2015).

4 Embedding Models

In this section, we describe the embedding models we use to construct vectors for texts and Wikipedia articles.

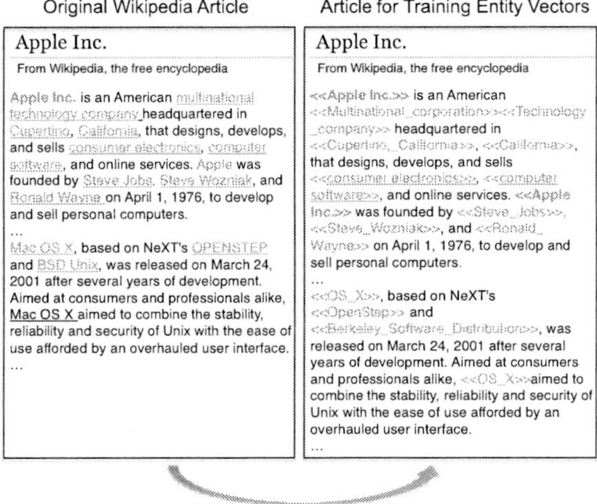

Figure 2: Training entity vectors from anchor texts.

4.1 Word Vector

We apply the `word2vec`[4] tool to Japanese Wikipedia for training word vectors. Then, we take sums of the word vectors to obtain document vectors.

4.2 Entity Vector

The Skip-gram model (Mikolov et al., 2013b) implemented by `word2vec` learns vectors by predicting context words from targets. We use this model to train vectors for Wikipedia articles, by regarding each anchor text as a target of the referent article, and words surrounding the anchor text as context. For example, in Figure 2 we replace all anchor texts with their referent articles (e.g. converting the hyper-link "*Mac OS X*" to $\langle\langle OS\_X \rangle\rangle$, representing the Wikipedia article "*OS X*"), and train vectors for the referent articles according to the converted document.

4.3 Paragraph Vector

The paragraph vector (Le and Mikolov, 2014) is a powerful unsupervised method of learning representations of arbitrary lengths of texts and has the advantages of simplicity and versatility. We use the Distributed Memory Model of Paragraph Vectors model to train paragraph vectors of texts and Wikipedia articles. The model is an extension of the

[4]https://code.google.com/p/word2vec/

CBoW model (Mikolov et al., 2013a) implemented in `word2vec`.

5 Experiments

In this section, we first introduce the evaluation data set. Then we evaluate the performance of candidate generation and the performance of each feature set on candidate ranking. Finally, we compare our system with the previous work (Jargalsaikhan et al., 2016).

5.1 Data set

We use a new released Japanese Wikification corpus (Jargalsaikhan et al., 2016), which consists of 340 newspaper articles from Balanced Corpus of Contemporary Written Japanese (BCCWJ).[5] Mentions in each document are annotated with fine-grained named entity class labels that are defined by Sekine Extended Named Entity Hierarchy (Sekine et al., 2002).[6] In this corpus, 19,121 mentions are linked to Wikipedia while 6,554 mentions do not reference Wikipedia articles. 7,118 distinct mentions were linked to 6,008 distinct entities totally. Because the corpus was built with recognized named entities, we omit the step of mention detection.

Since mentions are scattered in texts of the original corpus, in order to facilitate the system processing, we generate a single document that contains the composite of all mentions. Our new data set contains all information of mentions of which the format refers to the TAC-KBP data set. An example is shown in Figure 3. We obtain the information of a mention including mention ID, document ID, mention name, begin offset, end offset, entity class, entity linking mark, unique Wikipedia ID and unique Wikipedia title.

<mention id="PN1a_00002_T38">
<name>佐藤秀夫(Sato Hiteo)</name>
<docid>PN1a_00002</docid>
<beg>2687</beg>
<end>2691</end>
<entity class>Person</entity class>
<entity linking mark>A</entity linking mark>
<wikipedia id>2617934</wikipedia id>
<wikipedai title>佐藤秀夫(Sato
Hiteo)</wikipedia title>
</mention>

Figure 3: A mention snippet in data set.

5.2 Experimental Setup

We utilize 2016.3.5 Japanese Wikipedia dump as the referent Knowledge base. We tokenize and remove punctuations in documents by using a Japapense part-of-speech and morphological analyzer, Mecab.[7] We learn word embeddings, entity embeddings and paragraph vectors on this processed corpus. The word and entity vectors are learned by setting the dimensions d to 200, the size of context window c to 10 and the negative samples to 5. Meanwhile, the paragraph vectors are learned by setting the dimensions d to 400, the size of context window c to 5 and the negative samples to 5.

5.3 Evaluation of Candidate Generation

We evaluate our candidate generation methods on all mentions in the corpus (Jargalsaikhan et al., 2016). We normalize mention surfaces to eliminate the effect of half-width characters or full-width characters in the preprocessing step.

We compare cosine similarity and overlap coefficient with threshold of 0.7 and 0.9 respectively. We look up the concept dictionary with the mention and we can obtain Wikipedia articles from the results of entries. Table 2 shows the results of recall and average length of candidate lists. Here, recall means the percentage of mentions that have the gold entity in the candidate list. Moreover, we also compare the candidate list length because the more counts of candidates we have, the more time will be spend on candidate ranking.

According to the results in Table 2, we find that our concept dictionary based on anchor texts is suitable for the need of high-recall (91.98%) and short length (17.58). Moreover, we extend family names or given names of person to full names before searching on the concept dictionary, which will enhance the correct rate. After this extending step, we achieved the recall of 94.14% and the average number of candidates per list is 17.79.

[5] http://pj.ninjal.ac.jp/corpus_center/bccwj

[6] https://sites.google.com/site/extendednamedentityhierarchy/

[7] http://taku910.github.io/mecab/

Methods	Recall	AveLen
cosine(Threshold=0.9)	74.49%	1.58
overlap(Threshold=0.9)	66.68%	736.4
cosine(Threshod=0.7)	87.47%	27.12
overlap(Threshold=0.7)	68.01%	1750
anchor texts	91.98%	17.58
anchor texts (+extended)	94.14%	17.79

Table 2: Performance of candidate generation approaches on NonNIL mentions.

5.4 Feature Study

We conducted the feature study on each feature set by a 5-fold cross validation. We applied experiments on NonNILs, entities that exist in the Wikipedia. We begin with the string similarity feature set, added various features to it incrementally and reported their impact on performance.

From the results of Table 3, we found that our system obtained the performance with approximately 3 percents higher than previous work by only using string similarity features. Adding popularity features slightly further improved the performance.

We observed significant improvement when adding Bag-of-words features. However, only adding Bag-of-entities features led the performance to drop by about 9 percents. Adding both Bag-of-words and Bag-of-entities together, the system performance is improved to 84.88%.

Moreover, adding the features of fine-grained entity class is better than adding the category features. Therefore, we remove the category feature in the remaining experiments.

In addition, our system had slightly improved by adding entity embedding features. Here, features of entity vectors (EV) is more effective than features of word vectors (WV) by the accuracy of 0.64%. We also found that only using features of entity vectors (EV) is better using both word vectors (WV) and entity vectors (EV). The best performance of our system reached to 86.68% after adding features of paragraph vectors (PV).

5.5 System Performance

We made a 5-fold cross validation and calculated the average accuracy of each fold. Although we get the top-1 Wikipedia article from the ranking results, we need to determine that the mention in the text is a NonNIL or a NIL. NonNILs are entities that exist in the KB (Wikipedia) while NILs are entities that do not exist in the KB (Wikipedia).

In NIL labeling, we use two rules to make decisions. First, the mention will be labeled with NIL when there is no Wikipedia article for it. Second, the mention will be labeled with NIL when the ranking score of the top 1 candidate of the mention is below a threshold (heuristically set to 2.9).

Table 4 shows the accuracy of our system as well as a unsupervised method (Jargalsaikhan et al., 2016). Their method relies on the popularity of entities in the anchor texts of the mention, which is the same with our *Entity Popularity* feature. They also estimate probability distributions conditioned on a mention and its fine-grained semantic classes. We compared system performance of NILs and NonNILs while there is no comparison in the previous work (Jargalsaikhan et al., 2016). Our proposed system achieved a 82.27% accuracy across the 5-folds and outperform the previous unsupervised method by significant margins.

5.6 Error Analysis

For our candidate generation method, we found that some failure cases are caused by transliterating katakana from other languages. Since the abbreviation rules of Japanese are different from English, some failure cases are caused by lacking of resources to obtain specific abbreviations of Japanese characters.

Moreover, we found that exactly surface matching and high popularity have strong bias effects on incorrect entities. For example, a mention "*Japan*" may refer to the entity "Japan Television Network Corporation" in the sentence "There is a logo 'Old men can have beautiful life' in Beauty 7 (*Japan* 10:00PM)". However, the incorrect entity "*Japan* (Country)" is linked because of the bias effects. Furthermore, lacking of description words in Wikipedia is also a problem for our context based method.

Finally, we utilized the simple rules for NIL labeling instead of learning the characters of NILs. Talbe 4 shows our system performance on NILs is far from that of NonNILs. The weak NILs performance slightly affected the whole system performance because the counts of NonNILs is three times

Feature sets	Accuracy
Jargalsaikhan et al. (2016) Popularity	53.31%
StringSim (S)	56.13%
S+Popularity (P)	61.87%
S+P+Bag-of-words (Bw)	84.48%
S+P+Bag-of-entities (Be)	75.26%
S+P+Bw+Be	84.88%
S+P+Bw+Be+Entity Category (Cate)	84.77%
S+P+Bw+Be+Entity Class (Class)	85.54%
S+P+Bw+Be+Cate+Class	85.37%
S+P+Bw+Be+Class+Word Vectors (WV)	85.58%
S+P+Bw+Be+Class+Entity Vectors (EV)	86.22%
S+P+Bw+Be+Class+WV+EV	85.79%
S+P+Bw+Be+Class+EV+Paragraph Vectors (PV)	86.68%

Table 3: Performance on NonNILs by incremental feature study.

Methods	Acc(NonNILs)	Acc(NILs)	Acc(All)
Our system	86.95%	68.80%	82.27%
Jargalsaikhan et al. (2016) Popularity	–	–	53.31%
Jargalsaikhan et al. (2016) Popularity + Class	–	–	53.26%

Table 4: Comparing the system performance of the proposed method with an unsupervised method.

of NILs counts.

6 Conclusions and Future Work

In this paper, we constructed a pipeline Japanese EL system that consists of two standard components, candidate generation and candidate ranking. We build a concept dictionary to generate referent Wikipedia articles for Japanese mentions. Comparing with the methods based on surface similarity, the concept dictionary extracted from Wikipedia was verified more effective on generating candidate lists with high-recall and short length.

Moreover, we verified that the effectiveness of several feature sets on Japanese EL that have been used in English EL . We jointly learned a new entity representation model and improved the system performance by adding features based on the learned entity embeddings. We verified that word embeddings and paragraph vectors also effectively improve the system performance. All in all, our system overcome the previous work on the same data set with significant margins.

In future work, we plan to use the cross-lingual information retrieval technology to solve the transliteration problems between Japanese and English. We also consider developing methods to solve the problems of matching abbreviation mentions to Wikipedia articles on Japanese. Moreover, we intend to improve our system by leveraging advanced context embedding methods instead of using the sum of vectors, such as CNN (Convolutional Neural network), LTSM (Long Short Term Memory), etc.

In addition, we will connect mention detection component to our current system and construct an end-to-end Japanese EL system. Finally, we expect the effectiveness of our Japanese EL system on other NLP task, e.g. knowledge base population, question answering, etc.

References

Roi Blanco, Giuseppe Ottaviano, and Edgar Meij. 2015. Fast and space-efficient entity linking for queries. In *Proceedings of the Eighth ACM International Conference on Web Search and Data Mining*, pages 179–188. ACM.

Razvan C Bunescu and Marius Pasca. 2006. Using encyclopedic knowledge for named entity disambiguation. In *Proceedings of EACL*, volume 6, pages 9–16.

Silviu Cucerzan. 2007. Large-scale named entity disambiguation based on wikipedia data. In *Proceedings of EMNLP-CoNLL*, volume 7, pages 708–716.

Laura Dietz and Jeffrey Dalton. 2012. A cross document neighborhood expansion: Umass at tac kbp 2012 entity linking. In *Proceedings of Text Analysis Conference (TAC)*.

Mark Dredze, Paul McNamee, Delip Rao, Adam Gerber, and Tim Finin. 2010. Entity disambiguation for knowledge base population. In *Proceedings of the 23rd International Conference on Computational Linguistics*, pages 277–285.

Greg Durrett and Dan Klein. 2014. A joint model for entity analysis: Coreference, typing, and linking. *Proceedings of TACL*, 2:477–490.

Tatsuya Furakawa, Takeshi Sagara, and Akiko Aizawa. 2014. Semantic disambiguation for cross-lingual entity linking (in japanese). *Journal of Japan society of Information and Knowledge*, 24(2):172–177.

David Graus, Tom Kenter, Marc Bron, Edgar Meij, M Rijke, et al. 2012. Context-based entity linking-university of amsterdam at tac 2012.

Yuhang Guo, Guohua Tang, Wanxiang Che, Ting Liu, and Sheng Li. 2011. Hit approaches to entity linking at tac 2011. In *Proceedings of the Fourth Text Analysis Conference (TAC 2011)*. Citeseer.

Hannaneh Hajishirzi, Leila Zilles, Daniel S Weld, and Luke S Zettlemoyer. 2013. Joint coreference resolution and named-entity linking with multi-pass sieves. In *Proceedings of EMNLP*, pages 289–299.

Xianpei Han and Jun Zhao. 2009. Named entity disambiguation by leveraging wikipedia semantic knowledge. In *Proceedings of the 18th ACM conference on Information and knowledge management*, pages 215–224. ACM.

Hui Han, Hongyuan Zha, and C Lee Giles. 2005. Name disambiguation in author citations using a k-way spectral clustering method. In *Proceedings of the 5th ACM/IEEE-CS Joint Conference on*, pages 334–343. IEEE.

Yoshihiko Hayashi, Kenji Yamakuchi, Masaaki Nagata, and Takaaki Tanaka. 2014. Improving wikification of bitexts by completing cross-lingual information (in japanese). In *Proceedings of The 28th Annual Conference of the Japanese Society for Artificial Intelligence*, pages 1A2–2.

Zhengyan He, Shujie Liu, Mu Li, Ming Zhou, Longkai Zhang, and Houfeng Wang. 2013. Learning entity representation for entity disambiguation. In *Proceedings of ACL*, pages 30–34.

Johannes Hoffart, Mohamed Amir Yosef, Ilaria Bordino, Hagen Fürstenau, Manfred Pinkal, Marc Spaniol, Bilyana Taneva, Stefan Thater, and Gerhard Weikum. 2011. Robust disambiguation of named entities in text. In *Proceedings of EMNLP*, pages 782–792.

Zhiting Hu, Poyao Huang, Yuntian Deng, Yingkai Gao, and Eric P Xing. 2015. Entity hierarchy embedding. In *Proceedings of ACL-IJCNLP*, volume 1, pages 1292–1300.

Tatsukuni Inoue, Keigo Suenaga, Nagata Seiya, and Kenji Tateishi. 2016. Tagging geopolitical information on news article by using entity linking (in japanese). In *Proceedings of the Twenty-second Annual Meeting of the Association for Natural Language Processing*.

Davaajav Jargalsaikhan, Naoaki Okazaki, Koji Matsuda, and Kentaro Inui. 2016. Building a corpus for japanese wikificaiton with fine-grained entity classes. In *ACL student research workshop. to appear*.

Heng Ji, Joel Nothman, and Ben Hachey. 2014. Overview of tac-kbp2014 entity discovery and linking tasks. In *Proceedings of Text Analysis Conference (TAC2014)*.

Thorsten Joachims. 2006. Training linear svms in linear time. In *Proceedings of the 12th ACM SIGKDD international conference on Knowledge discovery and data mining*, pages 217–226. ACM.

Mahboob Alam Khalid, Valentin Jijkoun, and Maarten De Rijke. 2008. The impact of named entity normalization on information retrieval for question answering. In *Proceedings of Advances in Information Retrieval*, pages 705–710. Springer.

Sayali Kulkarni, Amit Singh, Ganesh Ramakrishnan, and Soumen Chakrabarti. 2009. Collective annotation of wikipedia entities in web text. In *Proceedings of the 15th ACM SIGKDD international conference on Knowledge discovery and data mining*, pages 457–466. ACM.

Quoc V Le and Tomas Mikolov. 2014. Distributed representations of sentences and documents. *arXiv preprint arXiv:1405.4053*.

Yankai Lin, Zhiyuan Liu, Maosong Sun, Yang Liu, and Xuan Zhu. 2015. Learning entity and relation embeddings for knowledge graph completion. In *Proceedings of AAAI*, pages 2181–2187.

Xiao Ling and Daniel S Weld. 2012. Fine-grained entity recognition. In *Proceedings of AAAI*.

Xiao Ling, Sameer Singh, and Daniel S Weld. 2015. Design challenges for entity linking. *Proceedings of TACL*, 3:315–328.

Paul McNamee, Mark Dredze, Adam Gerber, Nikesh Garera, Tim Finin, James Mayfield, Christine Piatko, Delip Rao, David Yarowsky, and Markus Dreyer.

2009. Hltcoe approaches to knowledge base population at tac 2009. In *Proceedings of Text Analysis Conference (TAC)*.

Tomas Mikolov, Kai Chen, Greg Corrado, and Jeffrey Dean. 2013a. Efficient estimation of word representations in vector space. *arXiv preprint arXiv:1301.3781*.

Tomas Mikolov, Ilya Sutskever, Kai Chen, Greg S Corrado, and Jeff Dean. 2013b. Distributed representations of words and phrases and their compositionality. In *Proceedings of Advances in neural information processing systems*, pages 3111–3119.

David Milne and Ian H Witten. 2008. Learning to link with wikipedia. In *Proceedings of the 17th ACM conference on Information and knowledge management*, pages 509–518. ACM.

Tatsuya Nakamura, Masumi Shirakawa, Takahiro Hara, and Shojiro Nishio. 2015. An entity linking method for closs-lingual topic extraction from social media (in japanese). In *Proceedings of DEIM Forum 2015*, pages A3–1.

Seiya Osada, Keigo Suenaga, Yoshizumi Shogo, Kazumasa Shoji, Tsuneharu Yoshida, and Yasuaki Hashimoto. 2015. Assigning geographical point information for document via entity linking (in japanese). In *Proceedings of the Twenty-first Annual Meeting of the Association for Natural Language Processing*, pages A4–4.

Lev Ratinov, Dan Roth, Doug Downey, and Mike Anderson. 2011. Local and global algorithms for disambiguation to wikipedia. In *Proceedings of ACL*, pages 1375–1384. Association for Computational Linguistics.

Nagata Seiya, Keigo Suenaga, Yoshizumi Shogo, Kazumasa Shoji, Yoshida ToruHaru, and Hashimoto KyoAkira. 2015. Application of geopolitical entity linking on documents (in japanese). In *Proceedings of the Twenty-first Annual Meeting of the Association for Natural Language Processing*.

Satoshi Sekine, Kiyoshi Sudo, and Chikashi Nobata. 2002. Extended named entity hierarchy. In *Proceedings of LREC*.

Valentin I Spitkovsky and Angel X Chang. 2012. A cross-lingual dictionary for english wikipedia concepts. In *Proceedings of LREC*, pages 3168–3175.

Fabian Suchanek and Gerhard Weikum. 2013. Knowledge harvesting from text and web sources. In *Proceedings of Data Engineering (ICDE)*, pages 1250–1253. IEEE.

Yaming Sun, Lei Lin, Duyu Tang, Nan Yang, Zhenzhou Ji, and Xiaolong Wang. 2015. Modeling mention, context and entity with neural networks for entity disambiguation. In *Proceedings of IJCAI*, pages 1333–1339.

Masatoshi Suzuki, Koji Matsuda, Satoshi Sekine, Naoaki Okazaki, and Kentaro Inui. 2016. Multi-label classification of wikipedia articles into fine-grained named entity types (in japanese). In *Proceedings of the Twenty-second Annual Meeting of the Association for Natural Language Processing*.

Bishan Yang, Wen-tau Yih, Xiaodong He, Jianfeng Gao, and Li Deng. 2014. Embedding entities and relations for learning and inference in knowledge bases. *arXiv preprint arXiv:1412.6575*.

Mohamed Amir Yosef, Johannes Hoffart, Ilaria Bordino, Marc Spaniol, and Gerhard Weikum. 2011. Aida: An online tool for accurate disambiguation of named entities in text and tables. *Proceedings of the VLDB Endowment*, 4(12):1450–1453.

Wei Zhang, Yan Chuan Sim, Jian Su, and Chew Lim Tan. 2011. Entity linking with effective acronym expansion, instance selection, and topic modeling. In *Proceedings of IJCAI*, volume 2011, pages 1909–1914.

Zhicheng Zheng, Fangtao Li, Minlie Huang, and Xiaoyan Zhu. 2010. Learning to link entities with knowledge base. In *Proceedings of NAACL*, pages 483–491. Association for Computational Linguistics.

Shuangshuang Zhou, Canasai Kruengkrai, Naoaki Okazaki, and Kentaro Inui. 2014. Exploring linguistic features for named entity disambiguation. *International Journal of Computational Linguistics and Applications*, 5(2):49.

Toward the automatic extraction of knowledge of usable goods

Mei Uemura, Naho Orita, Naoaki Okazaki and Kentaro Inui
Tohoku University, Japan
{mei.uemura, naho, okazaki, inui}@ecei.tohoku.ac.jp

Abstract

Knowledge of usable goods (e.g., *toothbrush is used to clean the teeth* and *treadmill is used for exercise*) is ubiquitous and in constant demand. This study proposes semantic labels to capture aspects of knowledge of usable goods and builds a benchmark corpus, USABLE GOODS CORPUS, to explore this new semantic labeling task. Our human annotation experiment shows that human annotators can generally identify pieces of information of usable goods in text. Our first attempt toward the automatic identification of such knowledge shows that a model using conditional random fields approaches the human annotation (F score 73.2%). These results together suggest future directions to build a large-scale corpus and improve the automatic identification of knowledge of usable goods.

1 Introduction

A rich body of information extraction techniques focuses on acquiring knowledge from a huge amount of text data (Nickel et al. 2016). This allows large-scale knowledge bases to cover a broad range of knowledge. However, an important subfield of knowledge is not fully addressed: knowledge about use of objects such that *hand sanitizer is used to kill bacteria* and *dental floss is used to remove plaque*. Every object that humans create has its own purpose and function. We call these pieces of information **knowledge of usable goods**. Knowledge of usable goods is ubiquitous and in constant demand. People use search engines to find information on effect caused by using a new product, its proper way to use, and so on.

Knowledge sources that contain such information would also be beneficial for various kinds of natural language processing tasks, such as question answering systems and textual entailment. However, knowledge of usable goods is not thoroughly covered by current knowledge bases because these resources focus on entities (e.g. person or organization) and their relations (e.g. *IsPresidentOf*). Section 4.3 shows the gap between kinds of knowledge available in the current knowledge bases and the ones that we aim to acquire.

To fill in this gap, this study proposes a set of semantic labels to capture knowledge of usable goods and builds a benchmark corpus, USABLE GOODS CORPUS, to explore the automatic extraction of such knowledge. This work begins with focusing on information of health care and household goods such as *air freshener*, *rice cooker*, and *nasal strip*.

We assume that one of the most important aspects of knowledge of usable goods is about effects caused by using/consuming them as in (1). [1]

(1) a. Fish-oils ... are known to reduce inflammation in the body, ... (`fish oil`)

b. Alcohol-based hand sanitizers are more effective at killing microorganisms than

[1] Throughout this paper, each typewriter word in a round bracket (e.g. `toothbrush`) indicates a name of a usable good that corresponds to the title of Wikipedia article.

soaps... (`hand sanitizers`)

c. BB cream and CC cream are both <u>tinted moisturizers</u> ... (`CC cream`)

d. ... the American Dental Association reports that <u>up to 80% of plaque can be eliminated</u> with this method. (`dental floss`)

Humans can easily understand what the effects of these goods are: fish-oils reduce inflammation in the body (1a), hand sanitizers kill microorganisms (1b), BB cream tints and moisturizes skin (1c), and dental floss eliminate plaque (1d). However, the automatic extraction of such knowledge is challenging in that these effects can be expressed in various ways such as a verb phrase (1a), gerund (1b), noun phrase (1c), and clause (1d). This poses a problem that superficial linguistic patterns would not help identifying these kinds of expressions. To gauge difficulties of the automatic acquisition of these pieces of information, we conduct human annotation (Section 4) and automatic identification experiments (Section 5).

The major contributions of this work are: (i) We define a set of semantic labels to capture knowledge of usable goods, suggesting a new semantic labeling task. (ii) We experimentally build a benchmark corpus (USABLE GOODS CORPUS) to explore the automatic extraction of knowledge of usable goods. The corpus and guidelines will be available when this paper is presented. (iii) We present our initial attempts toward the automatic extraction of such knowledge using a sequence labeling method. The results in this experiment provide measures to estimate the complexity of this task and suggest future directions to build a large-scale corpus.

2 Related work

To our knowledge, there is no resource that focuses on knowledge of usable goods. There are manually constructed and relatively accurate lexical resources such as WordNet (Miller 1995) and FrameNet (Baker et al. 1998), but their coverage is inevitably limited and these ontologies do not contain knowledge of our interest. Current large-scale knowledge bases focus on knowledge of entities and their relations, but the coverage of knowledge of usable goods is still sparse as shown in Section 4.3. OpenIE systems (Etzioni et al. 2011) such as TEXTRUNNER (Etzioni et al. 2008) and REVERB (Fader et al. 2011) extract a large number of relations such as ⟨*treadmill, burns, more calories*⟩ using lexico-syntactic patterns from massive corpora drawn from the Web. Though these systems cover a wide variety of relational expressions, they do not intend to extract information of usable goods.

As for extracting information of objects, there is a body of research on the acquisition of telic and agentive roles in the context of generative lexicon theory (Pustejovsky 1991). Pustejovsky proposes qualia structures that define prototypical aspects of word's meaning (Pustejovsky et al. 1993). Of four semantic roles in the qualia structures, the telic role describes the purpose or function of an object (e.g. *read* is a typical telic role for *book*). Computational approaches are suggested to automatically extract expressions of this role from text (Yamada et al. 2007, Cimiano and Wenderoth 2007), but these models tend to focus on taking paraphrases of "*using X*", rather than the expressions of purpose or function of objects. While the telic roles cover a broader range of expressions (probably due to the unspecified definition of telicity in the original theory), our work focuses on effects caused by using/consuming objects, standing as complementary to these previous studies.

Information extraction research in biomedical domains concerns effects caused by using drugs such that drug X causes adverse effect Y (Gurulingappa et al. 2012). This kind of information may overlap with what we aim to acquire, but ontologies in these studies are domain-specific such as protein interactions and adverse effects, contrary to our interest, which is more generic.

In summary, neither existing resources nor methods focus on knowledge of usable goods. In the next section, we propose a set of semantic labels that captures aspects of knowledge of usable goods.

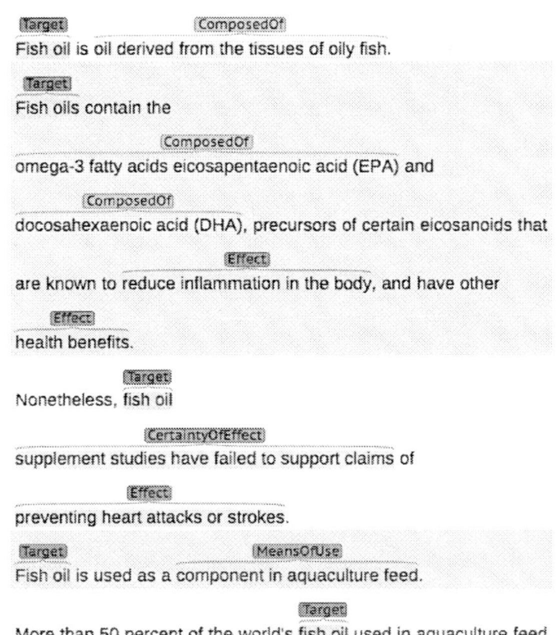

Figure 1: Assigned semantic labels for an excerpt from Wikipedia article on `fish oil` [3].

3 Semantic labels for capturing knowledge of usable goods

To capture aspects of knowledge of usable goods, we define semantic labels as in Table 1 based on observation of 25 Wikipedia lead sections on health care and household goods. The Wikipedia lead [4] is normally a summary of its most important contents, and therefore it may allow us to get rich information from relatively small amount of data.

As shown in (1), we assume that one of the most important aspects of knowledge of usable goods is about effects caused by the use of goods. We also observe that there are various kinds of information that express degree/certainty of effects and conditions for the occurrence of effects. Semantic labels in Table 1 are intended to capture these kinds of information. In addition to these semantic labels, we define a label TARGET for name and other expressions that refer to a usable good in the article. Names of usable goods essentially correspond to titles of Wikipedia articles, which refer to the topic of the text. Figure 1 shows how these labels are assigned to pieces of information about `fish oil`.

The annotation guidelines are designed to increase consistency. We define rules for segmentation in the guidelines, along with definition and examples of each label. To capture various linguistic expressions as illustrated in (1), we do not define a particular syntactic category for each label. All labels can take any type of linguistic constituent, but function words that do not contribute to the meaning are not included in each segment to avoid inconsistency. For example, we ask annotators mark *define the eyes* in *Eyeliner is a cosmetic used to define the eyes* as EFFECT (i.e., *to* is not included).

The set of semantic labels in Table 1 proposes a new semantic labeling task. To gauge the complexity of this task, we conduct human annotation experiment (Section 4) and automatic identification experiment (Section 5) as follows.

4 Annotation

We conduct a pilot annotation experiment to measure the complexity of this task. Measures of inter-annotator agreement and distributional analysis of the annotated data provide indications to improve the annotation schema for building a large-scale corpus in the future. This pilot corpus is also used for the automatic identification in Section 5. The following describes our annotation experiment in details.

4.1 Data: snippets from Wikipedia leads

We collect 200 English Wikipedia articles for annotation. Each article is about a health care or household goods such as *toothpaste*, *tea cosy*, and *dishwasher*. We choose these items using Ama-

[3]The phrase *precursors of certain eicosanoids* in Figure 1 is not COMPOSED OF for `fish oil` because this phrase just denotes an explanation of the constituents of `fish oil`, *omega-3 fatty acids eicosapentaenoic acid (EPA)* and *docosahexaenoic acid (DHA)* are constituents of `fish oil`.

[4]It is also known as the introduction of a Wikipedia article, the section before the table of contents and the first heading.

Label	Definition	Example
TARGET	expression referring to a target object, including aliases and pronouns	BB cream stands for blemish balm, blemish base (BB cream)
EFFECT	effect caused by using TARGET	to decorate and protect the nail plates (nail polish)
NULL EFFECT	description that states there is no EFFECT	The myth of its effectiveness (bear's grease)
DEGREE OF EFFECT	description that states a degree of EFFECT	poor substitute for protective clothing (barrier cream)
CERTAINTY OF EFFECT	description that states a certainty/reliability of EFFECT	a have not been proven to give lasting or major positive effects (anti-aging cream)
MEANS OF USE	description of how TARGET is used	is applied around the contours of the eye(s) (eye liner)
COMPOSED OF	material/ingredient that composes of TARGET	consisting mainly of triglycerides (egg oil)
PART OF	material/object that TARGET is a part of	Cinnamon is a spice obtained from the inner bark (cinnamon)
LOCATION	description of where TARGET is used	often used where sunlight can impair seeing (eye black)
TIME	description of when TARGET is used	soon after birth (kohl)
USER	description of who uses/receives EFFECT	mothers would apply kohl to their infants' eyes (kohl)
VERSION	different version of TARGET	It is distributed as a liquid or a soft solid (lip gloss)

Table 1: Semantic labels to capture knowledge of usable goods

zon categories and products lists. [5] All of chosen items are expressed as common nouns. We exclude any company-specific product.

We extract the lead section of each Wikipedia article for annotation. We use at most the first 5 sentences of the lead to even out the number of sentences, ending up 792 sentences in total from 200 lead snippets.

Each annotator annotates same 100 snippets using brat (Stenetorp et al. 2012). Figure 1 shows an example of annotation. In addition to these 100 snippets, one of the two annotators annotates another 100 snippets, resulting in 200 annotated snippets. We use this set of 200 annotated snippets as the gold standard dataset in the following automatic identification experiment.

4.2 Evaluation

Two annotators were given the guidelines and a short training on texts not included in the corpus. Their task is to annotate linguistic expressions that correspond to the semantic labels in Table 1.

Table 2 shows F scores for inter-annotator agreement. We compute these scores in two ways: (i) **strict match**: the starting and ending of the segment to be the same, (ii) **lenient match**: the starting and ending of the segment do not have to be the same but they overlap. We obtain Kappa coefficient of 0.57 in the lenient match, suggesting moderate agreement (Landis and Koch 1977). F score in the strict match (micro average 36.8%) seems to be reasonable because we give annotators unparsed raw text to explore the range of linguistic expressions. Most segmentation disagreements occur in deciding whether to include function words (e.g. *to protect skin* or *protect skin*).

Type of match	F-score (%)
lenient match (micro average)	**77.2**
lenient match (macro average)	52.5
strict match (micro average)	36.8
strict match (macro average)	27.1

Table 2: Inter-annotator agreement

In addition, there are label disagreements accounting for 20% of segment pairs that either partially or completely match. For example, one annotator marks *hair and skin care* in (2) as EFFECT and the other does so as MEANS OF USE, where both labels seem to be appropriate.

[5] https://www.amazon.com/gp/help/customer/display.html

Label	Annotator A	Annotator B
EFFECT	195 (31.7%)	189 (32.8%)
CERTAINTY OF EFFECT	32 (10.1%)	19 (3.3%)
DEGREE OF EFFECT	13 (2.1%)	13 (2.1%)
NULL EFFECT	0 (0.0%)	0 (0.0%)
MEANS OF USE	115 (18.7%)	59 (9.6%)
COMPOSED OF	98 (15.9%)	112 (19.4%)
PART OF	12 (1.9%)	14 (2.3%)
LOCATION	16 (2.6%)	26 (4.2%)
TIME	15 (2.4%)	16 (2.6%)
USER	19 (3.1%)	25 (4.1%)
VERSION	100 (16.2%)	103 (16.7%)
Total	616	576

Table 3: Numbers of the annotated labels

(2) It is used for topical applications such as <u>hair and skin care</u>. (`egg oil`)

This kind of disagreement may reflect differences in annotators' background knowledge. *Hair and skin care* does not explicitly denote the effect, but people usually have the relevant knowledge such that skin care improves skin elasticity.

The following (3) shows an example of disagreement between VERSION and COMPOSED OF.

(3) A wet wipe ... is a small moistened piece of <u>paper</u> or <u>cloth</u> ... (`Wet wipe`)

Paper and *cloth* in (3) could be VERSION of `wet wipe`, but they are also materials that compose of `wet wipe`. Both VERSION and COMPOSEDOF are valid in this example.

These examples of label disagreement suggest that single-label annotation would not be able to sufficiently capture the knowledge of usable goods. Allowing multi-labeling would be one direction for further improvement.

4.3 The distribution of the annotated data

We conduct distributional analysis to examine the extent to which the proposed semantic labels capture information of usable goods. Table 3 breaks up numbers of the annotated instances by two annotators. EFFECT results in the most frequent one, suggesting its significance at least in the domain of health care and household goods.

On the other hand, there are a few number of instances for CERTAINTY OF EFFECT, DEGREE OF EFFECT, NULL EFFECT, PART OF, LOCATION, TIME, and USER. This may due to the content of the Wikipedia leads. These kinds of more precise information would usually appear after the lead section. [6]

We further examine the syntactic distribution of EFFECT instances as in Table 4. The majority of EFFECT instances are represented as verb phrases and there is a variation in those instances such as *darken the eyelids* (`kohl`), *minimize shininess caused by oily skin* (`face powder`), *tones the face* (`face powder`), *reflect light at different angles* (`glitter`) and so on, in addition to typical causal expressions such as *causes anesthesia* (`anesthetic`), *prevent snoring* (`nasal strip`), and *promote oral hygiene* (`toothpaste`). An example of noun phrase in Table 4 suggests an interesting problem in that *lacquer* itself is a usable good but also means effect caused by using a nail polish. This kind of information structure has not been addressed in previous work on information extraction.

Overall, we find that 81.8% of instances occur with TARGET in the same sentence. The remaining cases involve long-distance dependencies across the sentence. This distribution suggests that we do not need to annotate the relation between TARGET and each label and we could exploit these inter-sentential relations in the automatic identification task. The following Section 5 shows our automatic identification experiment using this distributional property.

4.4 Comparison with current knowledge base

The above human annotation experiment shows that Wikipedia leads contain a reasonable amount of information on effects caused by us-

[6] Besides these semantic labels, there are other descriptions on the manufacturing process and history of usable goods as in (4).

(4) a. (herbal distillate) ... obtained by steam distillation or hydrodistillation (`herbal distillate`)

b. Modern perfumery began in late 19th century with the commercial synthesis (`perfume`)

Phrase type		# of instances	Example
Verb phrase	transitive	121 (60.8%)	... that can be applied to decorate and protect the nail plates (`nail polish`)
	intransitive	14 (7.0%)	It generally stays on longer than lipstick (`lip stain`)
Noun phrase		44 (22.1%)	Nail polish is a lacquer (`nail polish`)
Adjective phrase		19 (9.5%)	Choline is a water-soluble nutrient (`choline`)
Sentence		1 (0.5%)	... reports that up to 80% of plaque can be eliminated (`dental floss`)
Total		199	

Table 4: Syntactic distribution of EFFECT instances

ing goods. However, it is possible that existing knowledge bases might have already acquired such knowledge. To examine the coverage of the current knowledge base, we compare ConceptNet (Speer and Havasi 2012) with our corpus.

For comparison, we use 100 usable goods in our corpus such as *ice pack*, *hand sanitizer* and *perfume*. We then manually select 4 out of 39 pre-defined relations in ConceptNet that could be associated with effect expressions such as USED FOR, CAPABLE OF, CAUSES DESIRE, and CAUSES. Of 100 usable goods, 27 usable goods have pieces of knowledge that are expressed with the above relations such as ⟨*hand sanitizer*, CAUSES, *clean hand*⟩ and ⟨*Toothpaste*, CAPABLE OF, *help remove plaque*⟩.

In short, though ConceptNet contains information of our interest, the coverage is still not sufficient (27/100 usable goods). The automatic extraction of information of usable goods would help populate this kind of knowledge base. The next section shows our initial attempt toward the automatic extraction of knowledge of usable goods.

5 Sequence labeling model for identifying information of usable goods

This section presents our experiment for automatically identifying information of usable goods. The results provide baseline measures for this new semantic labeling task and suggest potential directions for improvement.

Section 4.3 shows that almost all instances in our corpus occur with TARGET in the same sentence. We exploit this distributional property by using TARGET words as a cue to find information of usable goods and pose this task as a sequence labeling problem. We use Conditional Random Fields (CRFs), a popular approach to solve sequence labeling problems (Lafferty et al. 2001). CRFsuite [7] is used as an implementation of CRF for our purpose.

5.1 Experimental Settings

The training and test data consists of 792 sentences from 200 Wikipedia snippets (see Section 4.1). We select the four most frequent labels in the corpus, EFFECT, MEANS OF USE, COMPOSED OF and VERSION, for evaluation.

For the data pre-processing, we first parse the raw text and assign a part of speech tag and a named entity tag to each word using Stanford CoreNLP (Manning et al. 2014). Then we add a semantic label to each word with BIO format (Beginning, Inside and Outside).

5.2 Features

Features shown in Table 5 are used for training. We use these features within a window of ±3 around the current word. Some of these features are used in combination with another feature as shown in Table 5.

In addition to standard features, we add three features to exploit the characteristics of this corpus: **Target**, **Disease** and **Repeat**. **Target** feature is true when the current word is same as the title of Wikipedia article. **Disease** feature is true when the current word is in a list of disease names that we create using Freebase (Bollacker et al. 2008). This feature is intended to capture effect expressions that include disease names such as *provoke allergy and asthma symptoms* (`air freshener`). **Repeat** feature is true when the current word has already been appeared in the sentence. This feature is intended to capture a parallel structure that is often used

[7] `http://www.chokkan.org/software/crfsuite/`

Feature	Definition	Example
Token	current word	Perfume
Lower	lowercased current word	perfume
POS	POS tag of the current word	NNS
NE	named entity type of the current word	O
Target	whether the current word is TARGET	True
Disease	whether the current word is a disease name	False
Repeat	whether the current word has been appeared in the sentence	False
Combination	**Definition**	**Example**
Token + Lower	current word and lowercased current word	(Perfume, perfume)
Token + POS	current word and its POS tag	(Perfume, NNS)
Lower + POS	lowercased current word and its POS tag	(perfume, NNS)
Disease + POS	POS tag and whether the current word is a disease name	(NNS, False)

Table 5: Features

to express VERSION and COMPOSED OF.

5.3 Evaluation

We compute precision, recall and F1 measure using ten fold cross validation. We compute these scores in two ways, lenient match and strict match as in the human annotation experiment (see Section 4.2). Table 6 shows results.

F score in the lenient match (73.2%) approaches the human annotation performance (81.9%). This suggests that the model is able to identify labels to some extent. For example, the model recognizes typical lexico-syntactic patterns such as *be used to* in *(wallpaper) is used to cover and decorate the interior walls* and *be designed to* in *(rice cooker) is designed to boil or steam rice*. Furthermore, the model captures various effect expressions such as an adjective phrase (5a), verb phrase (5b), and gerund (5c).

(5) a. Chandeliers are often ornate, and normally use... (`chandelier`)

b. A diuretic is any substance that promotes the production of urine. (`diuretic`)

c. An espresso machine brews coffee by forcing pressurized water near boiling point... (`espresso machine`)

On the other hand, the segmentation problem as discussed in the human annotation experiment influences the F score in the strict match (13.7%).

In sum, though there is the segmentation problem derived from the annotation, the results in the lenient match suggest that the model can identify information of usable goods to some extent. Improving the annotation schema and increasing the size of the corpus would be promising directions for future work.

6 Conclusion

This paper proposes semantic labels to capture aspects of knowledge of usable goods. We design annotation schema and build the benchmark corpus, USABLE GOODS CORPUS, based on the proposed semantic labels. Our human annotation experiment shows that (i) while there is the segmentation mismatch problem, human annotators can generally identify pieces of information of usable goods, and (ii) Wikipedia leads contain a reasonable amount of information on effects caused by using goods in contrast to the coverage of the current knowledge base. The automatic identification experiment shows that despite of the influence of the segmentation problem in the human annotation, the model can to some extent identify pieces of information of usable goods.

Our next steps are to alleviate the segmentation problem and increase the corpus size. With these goals in mind, we plan to revise the annotation schema as follows: (a) Some semantic labels do not seem to be important as seen in the statistics in Table 3. Reducing the variation of the semantic labels is a reasonable direction. (b) Defining a syntactic category for each label and giving annotators/models parsed text would increase consistency in the segmentation. (c) These simplifications (a,b) would allow us to

	Label	Precision (%)	Recall (%)	F score (%)
strict match	Effect	24.2	24.1	24.1
	Means of Use	10.3	4.9	6.6
	Composed of	13.0	13.0	11.4
	Version	15.9	8.5	11.1
	micro average	16.0	12.21	13.7
	macro average	20.2	15.4	17.4
lenient match	Effect	79.4	71.8	74.1
	Means of Use	75.0	58.1	60.2
	Composed of	71.8	60.6	63.1
	Version	75.9	64.6	66.5
	micro average	72.7	73.6	**73.2**
	macro average	51.9	39.2	41.7
Results in human annotation				
lenient match	micro average	81.9	81.9	81.9
	macro average	71.2	65.7	66.9

Table 6: 10-fold cross-validation

try crowdsourcing annotation to increase the size of the corpus.

Acknowledgements

This study is supported by CREST, JST and JSPS KAKENHI Grant Number JP15H05318.

References

Collin F Baker, Charles J Fillmore, and John B Lowe. The Berkeley FrameNet Project. In *Proceedings of the 17th International Conference on Computational Linguistics*, pages 86–90. Association for Computational Linguistics, 1998.

Kurt Bollacker, Colin Evans, Praveen Paritosh, Tim Sturge, and Jamie Taylor. Freebase: A Collaboratively Created Graph Database for Structuring Human Knowledge. In *Proceedings of ACM Special Interest Group on Management of Data*, pages 1247–1250, 2008.

Philipp Cimiano and Johanna Wenderoth. Automatic Acquisition of Ranked Qualia Structures from the Web. In *Proceedings of the 45th Annual Meeting of the Association for Computational Linguistics*, pages 888–895, 2007.

Oren Etzioni, Michele Banko, Stephen Soderland, and Daniel S. Weld. Open information extraction from the web. *Communications of the Association for Computing Machinery*, 51 (12):68–74, 2008.

Oren Etzioni, Anthony Fader, Janara Christensen, Stephen Soderland, and Mausam. Open Information Extraction: the Second Generation. In *Internartional Joint Conference on Artificial Intelligence*, pages 3–10, 2011.

Anthony Fader, Stephen Soderland, and Oren Etzioni. Identifying relations for open information extraction. In *Proceedings of the Conference on Empirical Methods in Natural Language Processing*, pages 1535–1545, 2011.

Harsha Gurulingappa, Abdul Mateen Rajput, Angus Roberts, Juliane Fluck, Martin Hofmann-Apitius, and Luca Toldo. Development of a benchmark corpus to support the automatic extraction of drug-related adverse effects from medical case reports. *Journal of biomedical informatics*, 45(5):885–892, 2012.

John D. Lafferty, Andrew McCallum, and Fernando C. N. Pereira. Conditional Random Fields: Probabilistic Models for Segmenting and Labeling Sequence Data. In *Proceedings of the Eighteenth International Conference on Machine Learning*, pages 282–289, 2001.

J Richard Landis and Gary G Koch. The Measurement of Observer Agreement for Categorical Data. *Biometrics*, 33(1):159–174, 1977.

Christopher D. Manning, Mihai Surdeanu, John Bauer, Jenny Finkel, Steven J. Bethard, and David McClosky. The Stanford CoreNLP Natural Language Processing Toolkit. In *Association for Computational Linguistics System Demonstrations*, pages 55–60, 2014.

George A Miller. Wordnet: a lexical database for English. *Communications of the Association for Computing Machinery*, 38(11):39–41, 1995.

Maximilian Nickel, Kevin Murphy, Volker Tresp, and Evgeniy Gabrilovich. A Review of Relational Machine Learning for Knowledge Graphs. *Proceedings of the Instute of Electrical and Electronics Engineers*, 104(1):11–33, 2016.

James Pustejovsky. The Generative Lexicon. *Computational linguistics*, 17(4):409–441, 1991.

James Pustejovsky, Peter Anick, and Sabine Bergler. Lexical Semantic Techniques for Corpus Analysis. *Computational Linguistics*, 19 (2):331–358, 1993.

Robert Speer and Catherine Havasi. Representing General Relational Knowledge in ConceptNet 5. In *Language Resources and Evaluation Conference*, pages 3679–3686, 2012.

Pontus Stenetorp, Sampo Pyysalo, Goran Topić, Tomoko Ohta, Sophia Ananiadou, and Jun'ichi Tsujii. BRAT: a Web-based Tool for NLP-Assisted Text Annotation. In *Proceedings of the Demonstrations at the 13th Eutopean Chapter of the Association for Computational Linguistics*, pages 102–107, 2012.

Ichiro Yamada, Timothy Baldwin, Hideki Sumiyoshi, Masahiro Shibata, and Yagi Nobuyuki. Automatic Acquisition of Qualia Structure from Corpus Data. *The Institute of Electronics, Information and Communication Engineers transactions on information and systems*, 90(10):1534–1541, 2007.

A Syntactic Approach to the 1st Person Restriction of Causal Clauses in Korean

Semoon Hoe
Department of Linguistics
Seoul National University
Seoul, Korea
geisthoe@gmail.com

Yugyeong Park
Department of Linguistics
Seoul National University
Seoul, Korea
yugyeongpark@gmail.com

Abstract

The main purpose of this paper is to provide a syntax-based analysis of the differences between the two Korean causal clauses, i.e. *ese*-clauses and *nikka*-clauses. Focusing on the various aspects of Mood distinction, we claim that *nikka* and *ese*-clauses can be analyzed as indicatives and subjunctives, respectively. Such an analysis enables us to provide syntactic explanations for issues—what we call the 1st person restriction of *ese*-clauses and its obviation—which might be considered merely semantic/pragmatic issues.

1 Main puzzle: The 1st person restriction of *ese*-clauses

Korean has two causal connectives, *-nikka* and *-ese* 'because'. In most cases, they can be used interchangeably without noticeable differences in their meanings:

(1) Pi-ka o-*ase*/*nikka* ttang-i cecnunta.
rain-Nom come-because ground-Nom wet
'Because it rains, the ground is getting wet.'

The two connectives, however, exhibit different distributions with respect to the main clause subject when they contain a Contrastive Topic (CT) marking: while *ese*-clauses display person restrictions on the main clause subject, *nikka*-clauses do not. In (2), for example, both *–ese* and *–nikka* allow CT-marking when the main clause subject is 1st person. In this case, the CT conveys the implied message that the speaker believes that *Hoya* cannot fulfill other conditions required for marriage, such as a full-time job position.

(2) a. pro_2 cip-***un*** sa-***se***, **na**$_1$-nun
pro house-CT buy-*ese* I-Top
Hoya$_2$-wa kyeolhonha-yss-ta.
Hoya-with marry-Past-Decl
b. pro_2 cip-***un*** sa-ss-***unikka***, **na**$_1$-nun
pro house-CT buy-Past-*nikka* I-Top
Hoya$_2$-wa kyeolhonha-yss-ta.
Hoya-with marry-Past-Decl
'I married Hoya because he (at least) bought a house.'

However, the two connectives behave differently when the main clause subject is not 1st person. As in (3a), an *ese*-clause does not allow CT-marking, when the main clause subject is 3rd person. We name this constraint *the 1st Person Restriction* (PR).

Unlike *ese*-clauses, *nikka*-clauses allow CT-marking regardless of whether the main clause subject is 1st person or not. In (3b), *Yuna* is the one who believes *Hoya* at least meets the minimum condition for marriage, but it is possible that he cannot fulfill any other conditions.[1]

(3) a. #pro_2 cip-***un*** sa-***se***, **Yuna**$_1$-nun
pro house-CT buy-because Yuna-Top
Hoya$_2$-wa kyeolhonha-yss-ta.
Hoya-with marry-Past-Decl
'Yuna married Hoya because he (at least) bought a house.'

[1] As far as we know, this kind of difference doesn't seem to be found in any other languages—even though some languages use two words for 'because' (e.g., German *denn* and *weil*).

b. pro_2 cip-***un*** sa-s*s*-***unikka,*** **Yuna**$_1$-nun
pro house-CT buy-Past-*nikka* Yuna-Top
$Hoya_2$-wa kyeolhonha-yss-ta.
Hoya-with marry-Past-Decl
'Yuna married Hoya because he (at least) bought a house.'

Note that an *ese*-clause displays this restriction only in cases where it contains a CT marker:

(4) pro_2 cip-***ul*** sa-***se,*** **na**$_1$**/Yuna**$_1$-nun
pro house-Acc buy-*ese* I/Yuna-Top
$Hoya_2$-wa kyeolhonha-yss-ta.
Hoya-with marry-Past-Decl
'I/Yuna married Hoya because he bought a house'

More surprisingly, PR can be circumvented when even one of the arguments in the *ese*-clause is co-indexed with the subject of the main clause. It is commonly claimed that as an applicative construction *-e cwu-* adds a *goal* argument of the beneficiary relation (Jung 2014, etc.). PR can be obviated due to a co-indexation of the goal argument with the main clause subject, as in (5).

(5) pro_2 cip-***un*** pro_1 sa-cwu-***ese,***
pro house-CT pro buy-give-because
na$_1$**/Yuna**$_1$-nun $Hoya_2$-wa kyeolhonha-yss-ta.
I/Yuna-Top Hoya-with marry-Past-Decl
'Yuna married Hoya because he (at least) bought a house for her.'

Just like (3b), the implied massage in (5) is that *Yuna* believes it is possible that *Hoya* meets the minimum condition for marriage, but he cannot fulfill other conditions. Thus, (3b) and (5) show that the unacceptability of (3a) cannot be attributed to a semantic/pragmatic anomaly.

2 Causal clauses and Contrastive marking

To explain PR, it is necessary to understand the CT-marking in causal clauses. As widely pointed out in the previous literature, CT-marking is restricted in embedded contexts: while it is allowed in a causal clause but not in a temporal/conditional clause: (e.g., Hara 2008, Tomioka 2015 for Japanese, Park & Hoe 2015, etc.)

(6) *Hangsang aitul-***un*** cip-ey
always children-CT house-to
o-*l ttay,* kay-ka cic-nun-ta.
come when dog-Nom bark-Pres-Decl
'When (at least) children come to our house, dogs always bark.' (based on Hara 2008)

(7) Sacangnim-un John-i ilpone-***nun***
president-Top John-Nom Japanese-CT
hal cul-a-*nikka/al-ase* chayonghay-ss-ta.
do can-because hire-Past-Decl
'Because John can speak (at least) Japanese, the president hired him.' (based on Hara 2008)

According to Hara (2008), a CT-marking conveys an implied message that some epistemic bearer (mostly the speaker of the 'utterance context' (C_U, hereafter)) entertains the possibility that the stronger scalar alternatives to the asserted proposition are false (e.g., it is possible that John cannot speak both Japanese and Korean in (7)). For such a scalar comparison, the use of CT requires some kind of epistemic bearer who has limited knowledge. Given this, Hara (2008) claims that CT-marking is licensed in causal clauses because causal clauses can fulfill the requirement about the epistemic bearer by introducing their own contexts.

The idea of introducing an additional context can also be supported by Davidson's (1963) primary reason. According to Davidson, doing something for a reason means doing something intentionally. Thus, to accept a rationalization of an action, we should be able to say what caused the agent to do the action (e.g., attractions, obligations, etc.). Davidson claims that when somebody does something for a reason, he must have a primary reason that consists of (i) a pro-attitude toward an action of a certain kind (e.g. desires come from moral believes, social conventions, etc.), and (ii) a belief that doing his action is of that kind, and (iii) this belief and desire cause him in the right way to do the action. In this way, the primary reason can be understood as a cause of the action. In order to accept only intentionally qualified causal relations, a kind of screening of the causal relation is added (expressed by "in the right way"). The relation between the reason/cause and its unintended outcomes cannot be qualified as a "right" causal relation. As exemplified in Davidson (1963), if someone turned on the light and by doing so he happened to alert the burglar in the room, the relation between the two events cannot be qualified as a right causal relation if the pro-attitude is supposed to be an intention. Given this, we can say that the use of causal clauses adds some additional context corresponding to the qualifying process. We call this additional context '*reason* context (C_R, hereafter)'.

If we accept Kaplanian context, a context can be construed as a tuple of indices identifying the contextual features such as an author, addressee, etc. In this way, C_U and C_R can be illustrated as in (8).

(8) a. utterance context (C_U) in main clauses:
<author (= speaker), addressee (=hearer), tense (=utterance time), location, ...>
b. *reason* context (C_R) in causal clauses:
<author (= subject of the main clauses), addressee, tense (= tense information of the main clauses), location, ...>

As in (8), the C_R is different from the C_U in that its author feature is associated with the subject of the main clause (see also Hara 2008).

3 Indicative vs. Subjunctive Mood

To explain PR, we claim that there's a correspondence between the two causal clauses and two different moods. In this section, we layout semantic and syntactic properties of mood distinction and provide some evidence.

3.1 Semantic Aspect

Anand & Hacquard (2009) (A&H, hereafter) show that only certain types of attitude verbs allow epistemic modals in their complement:

(9) a. John [believes, argues, assumed] that the Earth might be flat.
b. #John [hopes, wishes, commanded] that the Earth might be flat. (A&H 2009, (1))

According to A&H, in the complement of 'believe' type verbs, doxastic attitudes of *John* (that is the attitude holder) can license the embedded epistemic modal *might*. In contrast, in the complement of 'want' type verbs, since doxastic attitudes of the attitude holder are not involved, the embedded epistemic modal cannot be licensed. A&H argue that such a distinction is attributed to the mood distinction: while 'believe' type verbs select an indicative complement, 'want' type verbs select a subjunctive complement.

We assume that causal connectives introduce *modal* environments similar to attitude verbs. Recall Davidson's (1963) claim that primary reasons in causal relation always consist of a pro-attitude and belief related in the right way. Given this, we further claim that the two causal clauses are different in their moods: *nikka*-clauses and *ese*-clauses correspond to indicative and subjunctive mood, respectively.[2 3]

The supporting evidence for the current analysis can be found in the examples like (10). As in (10), while *nikka*-clauses allow epistemic modals, *ese*-clauses do not.

(10) The *speaker came to know that a bomb went off at the park ....*
a. Mina-ka cip-ey iss-e ya ha-*nikka*,
Mina-Nom home-Loc stay-have to-*nikka*
na-nun ansim-i-ta.
I-Top be.releived-Cop-Decl
'Because Mina must be home, I feel relieved.'
(ok) Circumstantial, (ok) Epistemic
b. Mina-ka cip-ey iss-e ya ha-*ese*,
Mina-Nom home-Loc stay-have to-*ese*
na-nun ansim-i-ta.
I-Top be.releived-Cop-Decl
'Because Mina must be home, I feel relieved.'
(ok) Circumstantial, *Epistemic

The modal *-e ya ha-* in (10a) can be interpreted as either circumstantially (i.e. 'Mina is obligated to stay at home due to the curfew hour. Thus, I am not worried about her safety') or epistemically (i.e. 'As far as I know, it is quite certain that Mina stays at home since she is very tired due to a long trip. Thus, I am not worried about her safety.'). In (10b), by contrast, *-e ya ha-* is interpreted only as a circumstantial modal.

3.2 Syntactic Aspect

On the syntactic side, various syntactic analyses have been proposed to explain the mood distinction concerning: finiteness, phi-feature agreements,

[2] Portner & Rubinstein (2012) show convincingly that despite a similar meaning, two relevant predicates can select a different complement with respect to moods (e.g. *vouloir* 'want'-subjunctive vs. *espérer* 'hope'-indicative in French, etc.). We refer to Portner & Rubinstein (2012) for more detailed discussion.

[3] Some might say that the subjunctive is not suitable for causal clauses since it has been discussed that its content cannot be regarded as a true statement (e.g. irrealis, non-veridicality, etc.). But this seems not always the case as evidenced by the cases like *prin* 'before'-subjunctive vs. *afu* 'after'-indicative in Greek (Giannakidou 2015) and so on. See also de Jonge (2001), A&H (2009) for alternatives regarding the semantic nature of the subjunctive mood.

temporal markers, designated verbal forms, special kinds of the complementizer, etc. However, Bianchi (2001, 2003) argues that many of them are just peripheral effects related to the finiteness, and that it is *context anchoring* that plays a crucial role to determine moods and finiteness (See also Amritavalli 2014).[4] In this regard, it can be said that the mood determination has to do with the context choice: which context can/should the materials in the complements be evaluated with? Based on Bianchi's (2001, 2003) analysis, we suggest (11).

(11) The taxonomy of (syntactic) Moods
  a. Indicative: All the context sensitive elements in the complements can be freely evaluated with the embedded context and/or C_U.
  b. Subjunctive
    (i) Internally Centered logophoric Subjunctive (**ILS**): In the C-T layer of the complements, the logophoric elements should be used and evaluated relative to the embedded context via *internal Logophoric anchoring* (*iLa*, hereafter).
    (ii) Non-Internally anchored Subjunctive (**NIS**): Compared to ILS, some regular expressions can be employed instead of the logophoric elements and they can be associated with the outer perspective sources.

As for the indicatives, it is generally assumed that the elements in the embedded clause can be freely evaluated with the C_U. In this regard, the Double Access Reading (DAR) of tense is well studied (Abusch 1997, Giorgi & Pianesi 1997, a. o).

(12) Double Access Reading
  a. John believed that Mary is pregnant.
  b. #Two years ago, John believed that Mary is pregnant. (Abusch 1997, a. o)

It is well-known that in some languages (e.g. English, Italian, French, Spanish, and many other), the embedded indicative tense is evaluated twice: once it is anchored to the C_U and once it is anchored to the 'attitude context (C_A, hereafter)'. As seen in (12), even if *John* believed *Mary's* pregnancy in the past, *Mary* should still be pregnant 'now'. Usually, this is understood as (13) (see Giorgi & Pianesi 1997 for more detailed discussion).

(13) a. The indicative complement can specify the *independent* tense, which can be directly evaluated with respect to C_U.
  b. On the contrary, it has been argued that DAR is not generally available in subjunctive complements.

Unfortunately, DAR is hard to test in our target sentences since it is not clear whether Korean belongs to the DAR language group or not (see Kim 2013 for details). However, (13a) may still be relevant since there is evidence to show that only *niikka*-clauses allow the independent tense.

(14) a. Pi-ka o-*ass-unikka*, ttang-i
  rain-Nom come-Past-*nikka* ground-Nom
  cec-ess-ta.
  wet-Past-Decl
  b. Pi-ka o-(*ass)-*ese*, ttang-i
  rain-Nom come-(*Past)-*ese* ground-Nom
  cec-ess-ta.
  wet-Past-Decl
  'The ground got wet, because it rained.'

Previous analyses point out that unlike *ese*-clauses, *nikka*-clauses are obligatorily marked with tense (e.g., Lee S. 1978; Lee, E. 1990; etc.). Also, the main clause and the *nikka*-clause can be independent from each other with respect to their temporal interpretations. Unlike *nikka*, the tense of the *ese*-clause relies on the temporal interpretation of the main clause (Park 2015: p.53). As many authors have proposed, if only the indicative clauses allow independent tense (Landau 2004, 2015; Giannakidou 2009, etc.), the contrast in (14) can be easily accounted for.

Unlike indicatives, Bianchi (2001, 2003) argues that subjunctives can be subdivided along the (un-)obligatory use of the logophoric elements at the C-T layer depending on how much the C-T layer can reflect the independent phi-agreements.

In this line, to support ILS, Bianchi discusses the Obligatory Control (OC, hereafter) originating from attitude verbs. It is widely assumed that some logophoric elements should be interpreted with respect to a certain perspectival relation regarding

[4] Accordingly, we can say that as long as the finiteness is verified, the impoverishment of verbal forms does not necessarily mean the absence of the subjunctive mood. As for the finiteness and the subjunctive mood in Korean, we refer to Lee (2009). See also Giannakidou (2009) and Yoon (2013) for more detailed discussions on the various patterns of the subjunctive mood.

SELF, PIVOT, SOURCE (Sells 1987) and so on. Bianchi argues that PRO is one of them as evidenced by sentences like (15); PRO should be co-indexed with the *addressee* of the C_A in (15).

(15) Object-oriented OC with an attitude verb
Yuna$_1$-ka Yumi$_2$-eykey [PRO$_{2/*1/*3}$
Yuna-Nom Yumi-Dat [PRO
aph-ey ancu-la]-ko myenglyengha-yss-ta.
front-in sit-Imp]-comp order-Past-Decl
'Yuna ordered Yumi to sit in the front row.'

In cases like (15), when the C_A is constituted by a 'want' type verb like *myenglyenghata* 'order', its external argument (*Yuna* in 15) corresponds to the *author* of the C_A, and its internal argument (*Yumi* in 15) corresponds to the *addressee* of the C_A (Bianchi 2003, Landau 2015, a. o.). Given this, Bianchi argues that if the denotation of PRO should be determined in terms of *iLa,* we can explain why PRO should be co-indexed with the argument(s) of the matrix attitude verbs. Furthermore, we can say that the semantic correlation discussed in section 3.1 still hold since the complement of 'want' type verbs should be subjunctive. 333

Roughly summarizing, what Bianchi argues is that the distribution of PRO is (partly) attributed to the subjunctive mood allowing *iLa* (see also Landau 2015 for a similar analysis). In this regard, we can also easily find evidence for the existence of NIS: when a 3rd person pronominal subject is employed in a supposed OC complement, it comes to allow a Non-OC reading (though rather marginal).

(16) Non-OC reading in NIS
a. Scenario (Seo & Hoe 2015)
Yumi, *is a class leader, and her home teacher,* Yuna, *transmits an order to another student,* Hoya, *through* Yumi.
b.(?)Yuna-nun Yumi-eykey [ku-ka aph-ey
Yuna-Top Yumi-Dat [he-Nom front-in
ancu-la]-ko myenglyeng-ha-yss-ta.
sit-Imp]-Comp order-Past-Decl
Int. 'A teacher ordered to Yumi that Hoya should sit in the front row.'

Under the scenario in (16a), (16b) is much more acceptable than (15) weakening the OC reading. With this, we can easily draw a conclusion that *iLa* is blocked in (16b) in the following way: as widely discussed, unlike PRO, regular pronominals cannot be licensed in ILS since a more articulated structure (regarding phi-agreement, for example) is required (Bianchi 2001, 2003, Landau 2004, 2015, etc.). But such a complement should still be subjunctive since it is selected by the 'want' type predicate. Thus, even though Korean lacks any other overt cues like phi-agreements, the use of an overt pronominal subject is enough to show that the complement in (16b) amounts to NIS rightly predicting the absence of *iLa*.

4 *Ese* vs. *Nikka*: Mood distinction

Up to this point, we have discussed two aspects of the mood distinction and provide some evidence to show that *ese*-clauses are identified with subjunctives while *nikka*-clauses are identified with indicatives. In this section, we further propose that such a distinction also holds in regard to *iLa*.

4.1 More on the *causal* relation.

As we have seen in section 2, Davidson (1963) claims that the relation between the action and the reason for doing something can be accepted only in the case such that it is qualified in a *right way*, and this is why we add the independent C_R. However, such a qualification is not freely given in relation to the C_R. Instead, we suggest that there should be a type of doxastic information included in causal clauses, and it is necessary to judge whether this information is qualified from the evidential bearer's perspective (cf. Hara 2008). We call this process *the judge requirement.*[5]

This poses one interesting question. As widely discussed, when a speaker utters a declarative sentence, the content in it should be regarded as true according to her doxastic information. If, then, the declarative sentence contains a causal clause, the following condition should hold, too.

(17) *Felicity condition of the causal relations:*
The speaker is certain about the judge requirement.

Notice that (17) is not trivially satisfied. As discussed, the C_R exists independently, and it plays a crucial role for the judge requirement. Thus, it is

[5] In propositional attitude environments related to C_A, all the (specific) individuals should be identified by the attitude holder via a suitable acquaintance relation (e.g. *de re/se/te*) (Anand 2006, a. o.). Similar to this, we may say that the judge requirement can be regarded as a suitable acquaintance relation between the evidential holder and the causal relation in the C_R.

possible to imagine situations where the speaker cannot be the proper Evidential Bearer (EB, hereafter) of the causal relation.

4.2 *Nikka* vs *Ese*: Judge requirement

Following Speas (2004), Tenny (2006) and others, we assume that Evid(ential) Phrase constitutes a perspectival relation in causal clauses (cf. evidential OP in Hara 2008). Based on this, we suggest that the Judge requirement is also provided through the EvidP.

Given all this, suppose that the default structure of *ese*-clauses is ILS. Then, we can say that since EB is responsible for a perspective relation, such a logophoric element should be controlled by *iLa* in *ese*-clauses.

To implement this idea, we assume that EvidP is located at the CP-peripheries and introduces EB. Additionally, to explain the obligatoriness of *iLa,* we adopt the *OP_{-log} binding* (Anand 2006) in the following manner: Anand (2006) argues that logophoric elements should be bound by a special kind of OP_{-log} by assuming that (i) as a bound variable (BV), the former contains the *uninterpretable log-*feature ([ulog], hereafter), and the latter can check and erase [ulog] in Chomsky's (1995) sense via a variable binding relation.

Along these lines, we propose that in ILS structures, the perspective sensitive elements in the C-T layer are just BVs which are born with [ulog]. This means that EBs in ILS should bear [ulog]. We further argue that OP_{-log} is introduced by the ILS SpeechAct phrase (SAP_{-ILS}, hereafter), which should be anchored to the *closest* context.[6]

(18) Structure of *ese*-clauses: OP_{-log} binding

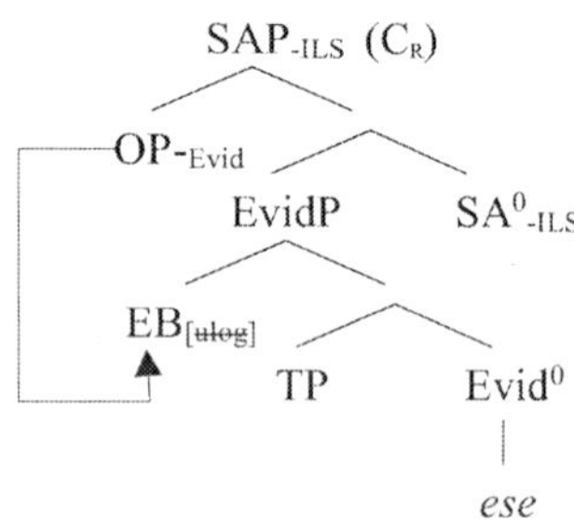

Since Anand (2006, 2009) argues that there are various kinds of OP_{-log}s with respect to the nature of the perspectives (e.g. $OP_{-SOURCE}$, OP_{-SELF}, OP_{-PIVOT}, etc), we assume the OP_{-Evid} is introduced at spec, SAP_{-ILS} in the causal clauses.

In (18), the embedded context should be C_R. Then, since the author of the C_R is picked out as the subject of the main clause (Hara 2008), we can predict that the EB should be identified with it.

As for *nikka*-clauses, however, indicatives are not sensitive to OP_{-log} binding. Instead, similar to the tense interpretation in DAR cases, any elements in *nikka*-clauses can be evaluated with the C_U directly. This implies, then, that EB in indicative *nikka* clauses can be freely associated with the speaker of the C_U.

5 Explanation of PR

Now, we can explain PR as follows. First, recall the licensing of the CT in causal clauses. As discussed, for CT to be interpreted, an epistemic bearer is required. Regarding the nature of causal clauses, we suggest that the epistemic barer of CT is determined along with the EB. As the CT information is one of the main sources for the judge requirement, it is fair to say that EB is responsible for the CT information.

One immediate question now arises: regarding the Epistemic licensing, how can the Felicity condition in (17) hold? We believe that this is the key property of PR.

In our target sentence like (19), if *Yuna* is used as the subject of the main clause, the EB of the *ese*-clause should be *Yuna*, the author of the C_R.

(19) #pro$_2$ cip-***un*** sa-***se,*** **Yuna**$_1$-nun
pro house-CT buy-because Yuna-Top
Hoya$_2$-wa kyeolhon-ha-yss-ta.
Hoya-with marry-Past-Decl.
'Yuna married Hoya because he (at least) bought a house.'

As proposed, the epistemic bearer of CT is picked out as *Yuna*, and as a result, the CT information should be vested in *Yuna*'s personal CT scale. What this means is that *Yuna* becomes the only person who can fulfill the judge requirement. Since such CT information is unilateral, even if it could be accepted in general, and thus be easily accommodated, it cannot be regarded as a mutual belief for all the relevant people, including the speaker. Thus, when the speaker utters (19), there is no way for her to be convinced of whether the causal connection is felicitous along with *Yuna*'s personal CT

[6] Notice that this does not mean that OP_{-log} bindings are not allowed in NIS or indicative complements.

scale. Therefore, the Felicity condition in (17) cannot be met in (19).

On the other hand, in cases like (20), the Felicity condition in (17) can trivially hold, since the EB is the speaker of the C_U.

(20) pro$_2$ cip-***un*** sa-***se***, **na**$_1$-nun
pro house-CT buy-because I-Top
Hoya$_2$-wa kyeolhonha-yss-ta.
Hoya-with marry-Past-Decl
'I married Hoya because he (at least) bought a house.'

Thus, we can explain why CT can be properly used in ILS causal clauses only if the subject of the main clause is the speaker herself.

As predicted, however, such a contrast is not found with *nikka*-clauses. Due to the lack of the *iLa* in indicative clauses, the EB of the *nikka*-clause can be determined as either the author of the C_R or the speaker of the C_U.

(21) pro$_2$ cip-***un*** sa-***ss-unikka***, **na**$_1$/
pro house CT buy Past because I/
Yuna$_1$-nun Hoya$_2$-wa kyeolhonha-yss-ta.
Yuna-Top Hoya-with marry-Past-Decl
'I/Yuna married Hoya because he (at least) bought a house.'

No matter who the subject of the main clause is, (17) does not pose any problem in (21).

6 The obviation of PR: NIS over ILS

In the previous section, we tried to explain PR based on the nature of the ILS structure. However, it brings one non-trivial question: as a subjunctive, should *ese*-clauses constitute ILS only? The answer seems negative concerning the obviation as seen in (22).

(22) pro$_2$ cip-***un*** pro$_1$ sa-***cwu-ese***, *[=5]*
pro house-CT pro buy-*give*-because
na$_1$/**Yuna**$_1$-nun Hoya$_2$-wa kyeolhonha-yss-ta.
I/Yuna-Top Hoya-with marry-Past-Decl
'I/Yuna married Hoya because he (at least) bought a house for her.'

If *ese*-clauses were confined to ILS, (22) cannot be accounted for. This indicates that the most plausible candidate for the grammaticality of (22) will be a NIS structure. To explain this, we propose (23).

(23) NIS over ILS in causal clauses
NIS can be selected only if ILS violates some *structurally* driven conditions.

In fact, (23) is reminiscent of the OC over Non-OC (Farkas 1992, Bianchi 2003; cf. Hornstein 2006; McFadden & Sundaresan 2016). Briefly speaking, its basic premise is that the OC structure is a default one, thereby it is preferred to Non-OC counterpart in general.

For instance, (15) is an OC structure with PRO as discussed above. However, it has been argued that Korean has a regular null pronoun, namely *pro*, too. Thus, given the existence of the structures like (16b), it is possible to say that (15) can be parsed as a Non-OC structure with *pro*; since there are no other distinctive markers as seen in (16b), the resulting phonological string with *pro* would become exactly the same as the one with PRO. However, (15) does not allow Non-OC reading at all.

OC over Non-OC is proposed to explain why OC structure is generally selected in cases like (15). In the relevant literature (e.g. Farkas 1992, Bianchi 2003; cf. McFadden & Sundaresan 2016), its motivation is usually tied to the assumption that OC structure has a less complex C T layer than the Non-OC counterpart in regard to phi-agreement and finiteness (but see Hornstein 2006 for an alternative based on 'parsing preference'). In this respect, the rationale behind OC over Non-OC can be understood in such a way that a more structurally economical construction should be selected unless there are clear reasons to block it.

Given the above-mentioned assumption that the OC-Non-OC pair is one instance of ILS-NIS pairs, we suggest that such a preference condition can be extended to all the ILS-NIS pairs as described in (23).

However, this raises another question: Why cannot the failure of the Felicity condition in (17) trigger the NIS over ILS?

Fortunately, there is evidence to show that pragmatically driven problems cannot be involved with the OC over Non-OC cases. In general, it has been argued that PRO in object-oriented OC should be interpreted *de te* (Anand 2006, Landau 2015, a. o.). In this regard, (15) should be construed with *de te* attitude; if *Yumi* does not recognize the fact that her conversational partner (that is the addressee of the reported speech context) is indeed *Yumi*, the sentence becomes unacceptable (Park 2011, Hoe 2014, etc.). However, in the Non-OC structure with an overt pronominal subject like (16b), a *de re* reading is also available (Hoe 2014). This can be interpreted as saying that *pro* in such a position—if possible—should allow a *de re* reading, as well (see also Sundaresan 2014). Then, if pragmatic factors like the unavailability of the *de te* can trigger (23), *pro* can replace PRO allowing a *de re* attitude. If this were the case, however, we would not be able to explain why (15) should be interpreted as *de te*, since the supposed Non-OC structure and (15) have the exact same phonological string as discussed above.

If this is on the right track, we can conclude that a certain structurally driven condition is violated in (22). Regarding this, we suggest (24).

(24) Anti-logophoricity (or Disjoint) Effects:
Non-logophoric pronouns in the scope of the OP_{-log} must be disjoint from the antecedent of a logophoric element.

In order to more fully understand this, let us consider (25) first.

(25) a. Kofi be ye-dzo.
Kofi say Log-leave
'Kofi$_1$ said Log$_{1/*2}$ left.'
b. Kofi be e-dzo.
Kofi say 3rd-leave
'Kofi$_1$ said 3rd$_{2/*1}$ left.' (Clements 1975)

As shown in (25), in environments where a logophor can be licensed, if a run-of-the-mill 3rd person pronoun is employed, it cannot refer to the individual that the logophor does (Koopman & Sportiche 1989, Bianchi 2003, Anand 2006, a. o.).

Along these lines, (24) can easily explain the obviation of PR in (22): a potential ILS structure is blocked due to (24) since the added goal argument is eventually co-indexed with the EB as illustrated in (26).[7] Thus, if an NIS structure is selected in (22), the Felicity condition in (17) can hold, thanks to the absence of *iLa*.

[7] We suspect that (24) in (26) has to do with Condition C violation: If the EB in (26) is a sort of BV, it cannot c-command any co-indexed (referential) DPs. However, the exact motivation of (24) is not clear to us yet. In particular, it has been pointed out that (24) does not arise uniformly in all subjunctive clauses or logophor licensing environments (Bianchi 2001, 2003, Landau 2015, a. o.). For example, in some languages (e.g. Italian, Hebrew, etc.), (24) is observed with an overt pronominal subject in Non-OC complements. But it is not found in Korean as seen in (16b), and this remains as yet unsolved (see Landau 2015 for more detailed discussion). We leave this for future research.

(26) Anti-logophoricity violation: ILS in (22)

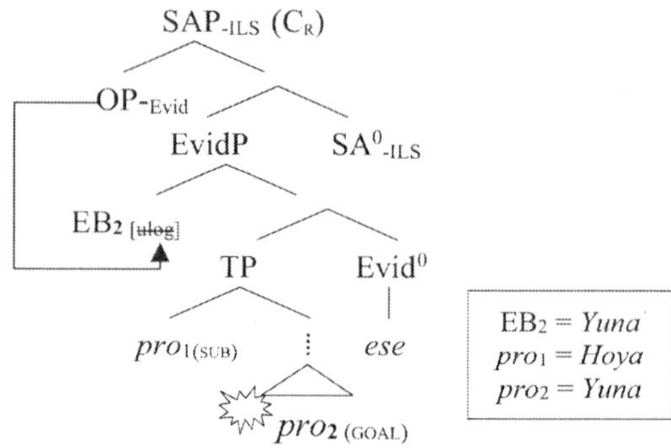

The example in (27) also buttresses this conclusion.

(27) pro$_{1/\#2}$ chaekimkam-***un*** iss-***ese***,
pro responsibility-CT exist- because
Yuna$_1$-nun Hoya$_2$-wa kyeolhonha-yss-ta.
Yuna-Top Hoya-with marry-Past-Decl
'Yuna married Hoya because she/#he (at least) has a sense of responsibility.'
(Park & Hoe 2015)

Logically, *pro* can denote the subject or the comitative argument of the main clause. However, PR is circumvented only when *pro* refers to the subject, allowing to obtain the proper CT interpretation.

7 Conclusions

In this paper, we have claimed that the differences between *nikka* and *ese*-clauses can be explained in terms of the mood distinction. To do so, we first assumed that causal clauses involve some epistemic step to qualify their causal connections. We then provided novel observations to show that when the CT marking is involved, *nikka* and *ese*-clauses differ with respect to who is responsible for the epistemic step. Finally, we claimed that this can be explained with syntactic phenomena, namely logophoric anchoring.

Acknowledgments

We are grateful to the audiences in ICKL-ISOKL 2015, KSLI-ELSK joint conference 2016 and LSK 60th Anniversary meeting 2016. We also thank the three anonymous reviewers for their comments and suggestions on the earlier version of the paper. Any remaining errors are, of course, our own.

References

Abush, Dorit. 1997. Sequence of tense and temporal de re. *Linguistics and Philosophy*, 20. 1-50.

Amritavalli, Raghavachari. 2014. Separating tense and finiteness: anchoring in Dravidian. *Natural Language and Linguistic Theory* 32, 283-306.

Anand, Pranav. 2006. *De de se*. Ph.D. Dissertation. MIT: Cambridge, Mass.

Anand, Pranav (2009) The cross-linguistic manifestations of de se expressions, Handout in Arche/CSMN Mini-course & Workshop: De Se Attitudes, CSMN, University of Oslo.

Anand, Pranav, and Valentine Hacquard. 2009. Epistemics with Attitude in *Proceedings of SALT 18*.

Bianchi, Valentina. 2001. *On Person Agreement*. Ms., Pisa, Scuola Normale Superiore.

Bianchi, Valentina. 2003. On finiteness as logophoric anchoring. In *Tense and point of view*, eds. by J. Gueron & L. Tasmovski, 213-246. Nanterre: Universite Paris X.

Chomsky, Noam. 1995. *The Minimalist Program*. Cambridge, MA: MIT Press.

Clements, George. 1975. The Logophoric Pronoun in Ewe: Its Role in Discourse. *The Journal of West African Languages*.

Davidson, Donald. 1963 Actions, reasons, and causes. *The journal of philosophy* 60, 685-700.

De Jonge, Bob. 2001. Spanish subjunctive mood. In *Adverbial modification: Selected papers from the Fifth Colloquium on Romance Linguistics*, 79-92.

Farkas, Donka. 1992. On obviation. *Lexical matters* 1, 85-109.

Giorgi, Alessandra, and Fabio Pianesi. 1997. *Tense and aspect*. Oxford: Oxford University Press.

Giannakidou, Anastasia. 2009. The dependency of the subjunctive revisited. *Lingua* 120, 1883–1908.

Giannakidou, Anastasia. 2015. *Evaluative subjunctive and nonveridicality*, Ms. University of Chicago. (To appear at *Mood, Aspect, Modality Revisited: New Answers to Old Questions*, University of Chicago Press.)

Hara, Yurie. 2008. Evidentiality of Discourse Items and Because-clauses, *Journal of Semantics* 25, 229-268

Hoe, Semoon. 2014. *A Study on Obligatory Control Constructions in Korean* (written in Korean). Doctoral Dissertation, Seoul National University.

Hornstein, Norbert. 2006. A short note on non-obligatory control. In *University of Maryland Working Papers in Linguistics*, eds. by N. Kazanina, et al., 39-46. UMWPiL.

Hwang, Hwa-Sang. 2008. The Semantic Function of Conjunctive Ending '-eoseo, -nikka' in Korean (written in Korean). *Kwukehak* [Korean Linguistics] 51.

Jung, Hyun Kyoung. 2014. *On the Syntax of the Applicative and Causative Constructions*. Ph.D. Dissertation, The University of Arizona.

Kim, Hyuna B. 2013. Pragmatic repair driven by indexicality. *Coyote Papers: Working Papers in Linguistics*. Department of Linguistics, University of Arizona.

Koopman, Hilda, and Dominique Sportiche. 1989. Pronouns, Logical Variables and Logophoricity in Abe. *Linguistic Inquiry* 20, 555-588.

Landau, Idan. 2004. The scale of finiteness and the calculus of control. *Natural Language & Linguistic Theory* 22, 811-877.

Landau, Idan. 2015. *A Two-Tired Theory of Control*. Cambridge, Mass.: MIT Press.

Lee, Eung-Kyeong. 1990. A study of Korean connectives (written in Korean). *Kwuke yenkwu* [Korean Research] 97.

Lee, Kum Young. 2009. *Finite Controls in Korean*. Doctoral Dissertation, University of Iowa.

Lee, Sang-Pok. 1978. About Korean connective endings (written in Korean). *Mal* 3. 59-80.

McFadden, Thomas, and Sandhya Sundaresan. 2016. *Failure to control is not a failure: it's pro*. Ms. (lingbuzz/002987)

Park, Jong-un. 2011. *Clause structure and null subjects*. Doctoral dissertation, Georgetown University.

Park, Yugyeong. 2015. *A grammar of mood and clausal adjunction in Korean*, Doctoral dissertation, University of Delaware.

Park, Yugyeong, and Semoon Hoe. 2015. Korean Causal Clauses and Point of View. A handout presented at ICKL & Harvard-ISOKL.

Portner Paul, and Aynat Rubinstein. 2012. Mood and contextual commitment. In *Proceedings of SALT 22*, 461-487.

Seo, Saetbyol, and Semoon Hoe. 2015. Agreement of a Point-of-Viewer and a Jussive Subject. *Studies in Generative Grammar* 25, 1-34.

Sohn, Sung-Ock S. 1992. Speaker-oriented and Event-oriented Causals: A comparative analysis of -nikka and -ese. *Korean Linguistics* VI, 83-93.

Speas, Margaret. 2004. Evidentiality, Logophoricity and the syntactic representation of pragmatic features, *Lingua* 114, 255-276.

Sundaresan, Sandhya. 2014. Making sense of silence: Finiteness and the (OC) PRO vs. pro distinction. *Natural Language and Linguistic Theory* 32, 59–85.

Tenny, Carol L. 2006. Evidentiality, experiencers, and the syntax of sentience in Japanese, *Journal of East Asian Linguistics*, 15. 245-288.

Tomioka, Satoshi. 2015. Embedded wa-phrases, predication, and judgment theory, *Natural Language and Linguistic Theory*, 33. 267-305.

Yoon, Suwon. 2013. Parametric variation in subordinate evaluative negation: Korean/Japanese versus others. *Journal of East Asian Linguistics* 22, 133–166

Towards a QUD-Based Analysis of Gapping Constructions

Sang-Hee Park
University at Buffalo, SUNY
sangheep@buffalo.edu

Abstract

In this paper I examine what have often been considered the syntactic properties of Gapping constructions (Ross, 1970) and show that they are in fact discourse-pragmatic in nature. I offer a novel analysis of Gapping constructions by extending recent Question Under Discussion (QUD)-based accounts in Head-Driven Phrase Structure Grammar (Ginzburg and Sag, 2000; Ginzburg, 2012).

1 Introduction

Gapping constructions are characterized by an initial, sentential clause (the *source clause*) and one or more non-initial gapped clauses in which a verb and, optionally, other material are missing (the *gapped clauses*). Some examples are given in (1).[1]

(1) a. Mary loves apples, and Tom, pears.
b. On Saturday, John bought a magazine, and on Sunday, a newspaper.
c. Kim played the guitar, Ray, the piano, and Sue, the bass.

The missing material in gapped clauses is interpreted as if it were there. In (1a), for example, the gapped clause is interpreted as 'Tom ate pears', receiving the interpretation of the missing material from the source clause.

In this paper I provide a novel approach to Gapping constructions that builds on recent QUD-based (Roberts, 1996/2012) accounts of non-sentential utterances in HPSG. In Section 2, I review three previous proposals and discuss their problems. In Section 3, I examine some widely accepted assumptions that have been used to characterize the syntax of Gapping constructions and show that they are not fully justified by empirical data. After discussing the relevance of Gapping constructions to QUD, I present a novel QUD-based analysis in Section 4. Section 5 concludes the paper.

[1] Commas are used to indicate a pause throughout this paper.

2 Previous Research

Previous approaches to Gapping constructions can be grouped into three types: deletion-based (Ross, 1970; Sag, 1976; Hartmann, 2000; Chaves, 2005), movement-based (Johnson, 2009; Johnson, 2014), and construction-based (Culicover and Jackendoff, 2005; Abeillé et al., 2013). A sample analysis is given in (2).

(2) a. [$_S$ Mary ate apples] and [$_S$ Tom ~~ate~~ pears]
b. Mary$_x$ ate$_y$ [$_{VP}$ t$_x$ t$_y$ apples] and [$_{VP}$ Tom t$_y$ pears]
c. [$_S$ Mary ate apples] and [$_{XP}$ Tom pears]

In the deletion-based approach, shown in (2a), gapped clauses have the same structure as their non-gapped counterparts, hence the same meaning. The missing material arises as the result of a deletion under identity with the corresponding material in the source clause. In the movement-based approach, shown in (2b), Gapping constructions are assigned a conjoined VP structure that yields the semantics of complete sentences, and the missing material arises as the result of an ATB-style movement of the verb. In the construction-based approach, shown in (2c), gapped clauses are treated as instances of a non-headed construction consisting of a set of phrasal remnants linked to an open proposition that contains the non-focused elements of the source clause.

Each of these approaches have their own problems, however. According to the deletion-based approach, gapped clauses have the syntactic structure of a sentence that includes no missing material. This predicts that gapped clauses would have the same distribution with their alleged non-gapped counterparts. As noted by Culicover and Jackendoff (2005, p.280), however, there are instances of gapped clauses that do not have grammatical non-gapped counterparts:

(3) a. Paul saw Leslie, but not Leslie (*saw) Paul.

b. You may have this cake, or him (*may have) that ice cream.

Note that the gapped clauses in (3a) and (3b) have the properties of non-finite categories: The gapped clause in (3a) is selected by a constituent negation that modifies non-sentential phrases, and the one in (3b) has an accusative subject. This suggests that the syntax of a given gapped clause is not equivalent to the syntax of its non-gapped counterpart.

So-called wide-scope readings of scopal operators (Siegel, 1984; McCawley, 1993) present a problem to the deletion-based and construction-based approaches alike. The phenomenon is illustrated by the example in (4), which has the two readings in (a) and (b), dubbed as *wide-* and *distributive*-scope readings, respectively.

(4) Ward can't eat caviar, and Sue, beans.

a. *Distributive-scope reading*
Ward can't eat caviar and Sue can't eat beans. (They have different allergies.)

b. *Wide-scope reading*
It can't be the case that Ward eats caviar and Sue eats beans. (That's not fair!)

The first, distributive-scope reading arises if the negation and modal are each interpreted twice, once within the source clause and once within the gapped clause; the second, wide-scope reading arises if the negation and modal are interpreted only once, taking the entire sentence within their scope.

In the deletion-based approach, gapped clauses are predicted to be semantically equivalent to their corresponding non-gapped clauses. This follows from the alleged syntactic equivalence between a gapped clause and the corresponding non-gapped clause. In the construction-based approach, the missing material is recovered from the non-focused part of the source clause, and this predicts two possibilities: For example, (4) would be interpreted as *Ward can't eat caviar and Sue can't eat beans* (if *can't* is not focused) or as *Ward can't eat caviar and Sue eats beans* (if *can't* is focused), which is semantically odd. Thus, the only acceptable readings that these approaches predict are distributive-scope readings; wide-scope readings remain entirely unexplained.

The difficulty of explaining wide scope readings is circumvented in the movement-based approach by "lowering" the conjunction from where it appears to be located. An example structure is given in (5).

(5) Ward$_x$ can't eat$_y$ [$_{\text{VP}}$ [$_{\text{VP}}$ t$_x$ t$_y$ caviar] and [$_{\text{VP}}$ Sue t$_y$ beans]]

But such an advantage comes at the cost of empirical perspicuity: Some instances of Gapping constructions do involve a conjoined TP:[2]

(6) a. Yesterday we went to the movies, and last Thursday, to the circus. (Sag, 1976, p.265)

b. To Robin, Chris gave the book, and to Leslie, the magazine. (Kubota and Levine, 2016)

The problem cannot be avoided by simply allowing Gapping constructions to be of two varieties, conjoined VPs or TPs. Consider the example in (7).

(7) She can't eat caviar, and he/him, beans.

This sentence can be understood to have a wide-scope reading ('It can't be the case that she eats caviar and he eats beans'), suggesting that the sentence is an instance of a conjoined VP. But the

[2]This type of data was first noted by Sag (1976).

availability of the nominative subject in the gapped clause suggests that a conjoined TP structure is involved. Given this, the fact that (7) can simultaneously have a nominative subject and a wide-scope reading creates a serious problem to the movement-based approach because a single instance of an expression cannot simultaneously be assigned two different structures.

Besides, the acceptability of instances of Gapping constructions does not always match that of their corresponding *wh*-questions, as has previously been noted (Culicover and Jackendoff, 2005, pp.274-275). Between (8a) and (8b), for example, only the latter incurs a violation of constraints on extraction.

(8) a. Robin believes that everyone pays attention to you when you speak French, and Leslie, German. (Culicover and Jackendoff, 2005, p.273)
   b. #Which language does Robin believe that everyone pays attention to you when you speak?

The contrast in acceptability like the one shown here suggests that the movement operation alleged to be involved in Gapping constructions has little empirical support.

3 Problems of some Common Assumptions

There are some widely held assumptions often used to characterize the syntax of Gapping constructions. In this section I discuss their problems and provide an alternative discourse-pragmatic account.

3.1 The Major Constituent Hypothesis

Since Hankamer (1973, p.18), it has been assumed that the remnants that occur in gapped clauses are syntactically constrained:

(9) The Major Constituent Hypothesis: A permissible remnant is either immediately dominated by the root clause or by some verbal head.

The Major Constituent Hypothesis is supported by the contrast in acceptability like the one shown by (10a) and (10b) (Examples and judgments are due to McCawley (1988, p.287)). Under this hypothesis, *proud* in (10a) does not qualify as a major constituent while *proud of it* in (10b) does.

(10) a. ??George became ashamed of the Washington family's past and Martha, proud. (= Martha became proud of the Washington family's past)
   b. George became ashamed of the Washington family's past and Martha, proud of it.

But a more representative set of data invalidates the Major Constituent Hypothesis. A first type of counterexamples involves remnants that are complements of a preposition, such as (11a-c) (Hudson, 1989, pp.59-64). Since P-complements do not qualify as major constituents, the acceptability of these sentences is inconsistent with the predictions generated under the Major Constituent Hypothesis.

(11) a. John thought about Jane, and Bill, Betty.
   b. Fred has been working on semantics, and Bill, syntax.
   c. Fred sat on a chair, Mary, a stool, and Bill, a bench.

Undoubtedly, there is a tendency for speakers to prefer major constituents as the remnants of Gapping, and some speakers do not fully accept sentences like (11a-c). This tendency is what Hankamer and others have tried to capture under their respective *syntactic* hypotheses. But instead, there is reason to seek an alternative, processing-oriented account. Steedman (1990) notes that the acceptability of sentences like (11-c) is more readily apparent when considered as an answer to questions such as those in (12).

(12) a. Which boy thought about which girl?
   b. Which student has been studying which specialization?
   c. Which person sat on where?

A second type of problematic data that has been around since McCawley (1993) involves N' remnants. These are are known as *determiner Gapping*:

(13) a. No dog ate Whiskas, and cat, Alpo (= *no* cat ate Alpo).
   b. The duck is dry, and mussels, tough (= *the* mussels are tough).
   c. Bob has read many magazines, and Mary, novels (= Mary has read *many* novels). (Reeve, 2014, p.354)

Other material within a noun phrase than a determiner can additionally go missing, as shown by (14) (Small caps indicates pitch accent).

(14) a. Many famous LINGUISTS have been DUTCH, and HISTORIANS, GREEK. (= *many famous* historians have been Greek)

b. Italian RED wines are OUTSTANDING, and WHITE wines, EXCELLENT. (= *Italian* white wines are excellent) (McCawley, 1993, p. 246)[3]

Sentences like these are easier to understand if the remnants and their correlates are marked by pitch accent. Again, this suggests that remnants only tend to be phrasal constituents and that there is no hard syntactic constraint on their category.

3.2 Restriction to symmetric coordination

Many theories assume that Gapping constructions are restricted to coordination (Jackendoff, 1971; Johnson, 2009):

(15) a. Some had eaten mussels and others shrimp.

b. *Some had eaten mussels because others shrimp. (Johnson, 2009, his judgment)

In the movement-based approach (Johnson, 2009; Johnson, 2014), where Gapping constructions are stipulated as conjoined VPs, (15b) is *ungrammatical* because coordination and subordination are incompatible. But Kehler (2002, Ch.4) considers such sentences *unacceptable*, and provides an explanation based on an independently motivated theory of coherence (Hobbs, 1985). For Kehler, the (un)acceptability of (15a) and (15b) are correlated with the types of coherence relation involved: While (15a) involves a Resemblance relation, (15b) involves a Cause-Effect relation[4]. He argues that reasoning with Resemblance relations provides a necessary means to recover the missing material. For example, in (15a) inferring a Resemblance relation between the source and gapped clauses amounts to equating *some* with *others*, *mussels* with *shrimp*, and *had eaten* with the missing material. In (15b), however, inferences leading to Resemblance relations are unavailable because a Cause-Effect relation is targeted.

Note, however, that there are instances in which the predictions of these accounts are not observed. Sentences in (16) are naturally occurring instances of Gapping constructions that involve subordination (drawn by a Google search).

(16) a. Truth is YOU will be in a position to hire ME, before I, YOU.[5]

b. No doubt THEY will find US, before WE, THEM.[6]

c. As for me all a little pup has to do is give me one of those sad, entreating looks and I am his prisoner, his pal, his confidant, and slave... Maybe WE love THEM, because THEY, US. (Statesville Daily Record from Statesville, North Carolina)[7]

The speakers I consulted for the judgment of these sentences reported that their acceptability is more obvious if there are pauses as the commas indicate and if the remnants and their correlates are marked by pitch accent. Such improved acceptability in the presence of prosodic cues is unexpected in the movement-based approach, or any theory that relies on any sort of a syntactic assumption. Kehler's analysis is not successful, either. For example, since his explanation for (15b) relies on the incompatibility between a Resemblance relation and a Cause-Effect relation to some degree, it is unclear how sentences like those in (16) would be analyzed.[8]

Alternatively, the (un)acceptability of examples considered so far in this section is expected if one assumes (i) that the missing material in a gapped clause is retrieved from the QUD (Roberts, 1996/2012) evoked by its source clause and (ii) that the ease with which a QUD is evoked and recovered

[3] McCawley judges (14b) as ungrammatical, but many speakers find it acceptable when there is contrastive pitch accent on the remnants and their correlates.

[4] Resemblance relations are a class of coherence relations that hold between sentences in which contrasting entities and properties are highlighted. (Kehler, 2002, pp.15-20)

[5] http://bit.ly/1TUTcx2

[6] http://bit.ly/1PUDHZA

[7] http://bit.ly/2bm6Ehi

[8] In fact, assuming Kehler's definition of Resemblance relations (Kehler, 2002, pp.15-20), nothing in principle prevents understanding (15b) as an instance of a Resemblance relation.

is a function of the ease with which contrastive topics and foci are construed (Hendriks, 2004).

3.3 Wide scope interpretations as the consequence of small coordination

In Section 2 it is noted that Gapping constructions that include missing scopal operators are ambiguous between wide- and distributive-scope readings (Siegel, 1984; McCawley, 1993). Examples in (4) and (13a) are repeated in (17a) and (17b), respectively.

(17) a. Ward can't eat caviar, and Sue, beans.
b. No dog ate Whiskas, and cat, Alpo.

These sentences can be understood to have the same meaning as their respective counterparts in (18) (= distributive-scope readings). But they can also have a reading in which the negation and modal apply to the entire conjunction (= wide-scope readings).

(18) a. Ward can't eat caviar and Sue can't eat beans.
b. No boy ate Whiskas and no cat ate Alpo.

In recent studies (Johnson, 2009; Kubota and Levine, 2016) wide-scope interpretations like those of (17a-b) have been identified as a problem in static compositional semantics: In this view, sentences like (17a-b) are problematic because there is a mismatch between the syntactic position of scopal operators and the position in which they receive the appropriate interpretation. For example, the negation and modal in (17a) are embedded within the first conjunct but can nevertheless be interpreted to take scope over the conjunction.

Johnson (2009) and Kubota and Levine (2016) propose to explain wide-scope interpretations on the basis of the observation that such interpretations are the result of the structural asymmetry between the source and gapped clauses, the latter containing missing material.[9] But the supposed generalization that the wide-scope phenomenon is bounded to coordinate structures that contain missing material has problems. Chaves (2007, p.89) provides examples in which an adverb in the first conjunct outscopes the entire coordination that does not contain missing material:

(19) a. I usually open the window and the dog starts barking.
usually(I open the window & the dog starts barking)
b. Kim probably is playing Juliet and Fred is playing Romeo.
probably(Kim is playing Juliet & Fred is playing Romeo)

Whitman (2010) offers similar examples that have other scopal operators:

(20) a. No one measures I.Q. when you apply for a job and you are then paired with employees of your mental ability.
neg(someone measures I.Q. when you apply for a job & then you are paired with employees of your mental ability)
b. They might have escaped and she didn't notice.
might(they have escaped & she didn't notice)

I argue, contra Johnson and Kubota-Levine, that wide-scope interpretations are the consequence of an asymmetry in the way subsequent conjuncts are interpreted in the discourse they occur in: The first conjunct updates the input context and yields a local context for the second conjunct, but not vice versa. In this dynamic view, it is predicted that the scope of an operator embedded in the first conjunct can reach into the second conjunct but the reverse would not be possible. This prediction is borne out in examples like (21): The scope of the negation in the second conjunct is conjunct-bound.

(21) Syntax is governed by rules of well-formedness which specify [which combinations are permissible and which not].

The examples considered so far show that conjunct-bound scope-taking is a default case and that it

[9] Johnson assumes that determiner Gapping like (18b) is dependent on the presence of a verbal "gap", but this is problematic, as Kubota and Levine point out:

(i) No dog barked or donkey brayed last night. (Kubota and Levine, 2016, (39b))

Kubota and Levine instead assume that determiner Gapping is dependent on the presence of a determiner gap only, hence correctly predict the felicity of (i). But they cannot handle data like (20a) as discussed below.

can be overridden by context-dependent processes (Chaves, 2007, p.89).

In order to allow scopal operators in a conjunct to outscope subsequent conjuncts from where they occur, one needs to adopt a dynamic semantic approach. To see this, consider the example in (22a) and its translation in (22b).

(22) a. Some boy$_x$ went to the army and his$_x$ girlfriend, the navy.

c. $\exists x(boy(x) \wedge go\text{-}to(x, army)) \wedge$
$\exists y(girlfriend(y, x) \wedge go\text{-}to(y, navy))$

In order for the pronoun in (22a) to be anaphorically linked to *Some boy* in the first conjunct, the existential quantifier must be given a wide scope over the conjunction. In Dynamic Predicate Logic (DPL) (Groenendijk and Stokhof, 1991), the free variable x in the second conjunct can be interpreted as bound by the co-indexed antecedent in the first conjunct without having to "raise" the antecedent.[10] This can be achieved by treating the existential and conjunction as dynamic operators, so that the value assigned to x in the fist conjunct remains available for the second conjunct.[11] The approach proposed here, if fully developed, would provide a simple, uniform treatment for various wide-scope phenomena without unnecessary complications.

4 A QUD-based analysis

In 3.1 and 3.2 of Section 3 it was observed that acceptable instances of Gapping constructions are those in which the connections between the remnants and their correlates are easily recognizable. Building on the insights from Levin and Prince (1986), I argue that such connections provide necessary information to recover a QUD evoked by the source clause of Gapping constructions. I assume that such a QUD is locally available in the pragmatics of the gapped clause in the form of a propositional abstract.

I adopt a construction-based HPSG grammar proposed by Ginzburg and Sag (2000) to model Gapping constructions. Informally, the strategy I adopt for the licensing of gapped clauses is to think of them as non-sentential utterances of underspecified category that provide an answer to the QUD introduced by their respective source clauses. To model the discourse context of Gapping constructions, I adopt Ginzburg's (2012) Dialogue GameBoard (DBG), an independently motivated feature used to model discourse. DGB provides a structured view of discourse by keeping track of which question gets introduced at a given point in discourse and which gets downdated. It is an object of type *dgb*, which specifies information about Maximal Question Under Discussion (MAX-QUD), which itself contains Focus Establishing Constituents (FEC) and Question (Q).

(23)
$$\begin{bmatrix} dgb & \\ \text{MAX-QUD} & \begin{bmatrix} \text{FEC} & \text{set(SemObj)} \\ \text{Q} & \text{Question} \end{bmatrix} \\ \ldots & \ldots \end{bmatrix}$$

Roughly speaking, elements within the FEC set correspond to focal utterances (defined as semantic objects), and the Q feature contains the question currently being discussed.[12]

The DGB of a source clause *Mary loves Paul* (as in *Mary loves Paul, and Sue, Bill*) is shown in (24).

(24) Uttering(May loves Paul) $\rightsquigarrow$
$$\begin{bmatrix} dgb & \\ \text{MAX-QUD} & \begin{bmatrix} \text{FEC} & \left\{ \begin{bmatrix} \text{SEM } m \end{bmatrix}, \begin{bmatrix} \text{SEM } p \end{bmatrix} \right\} \\ \text{Q} & \lambda y.\lambda x.love(x, y) \end{bmatrix} \end{bmatrix}$$

The AVM in (24) specifies the partial DGB of a discourse to which the sentence *Mary loves Paul* has just entered. There are two focal elements in the set, m and p introduced by *Mary* and *Paul*, respectively. These are recorded as possible correlates that would be matched with the focal elements of the incoming sentence. The value of Q in (24) is an open proposition which basically corresponds to the part of the sentence that is not focused.

I assume that source clauses are partial answers, and as such they allow a question to persist into

[10] Nothing hinges on the choice of DPL here, however. Any other type of dynamic semantics would in principle suffice.

[11] See Poesio and Zucchi (1992) and Wang et al. (2006) for a similar treatment for Telescoping and other similar phenomena.

[12] Cf. FEC is defined as a set of Locutionary Propositions in Ginzburg's (2012, pp.234-237) original formulation.

the upcoming discourse. This means that updating a given discourse by introducing a potential source clause to it would not result in downdating the relevant question in Q. Rather, an incoming gapped clause is entering into a context which has been created by its source clause and is still 'alive'.

Next, in (25) I introduce the constraints characterizing *gapped phrase*. The key idea here is that gapped clauses are resolved to the variables of the open proposition introduced by the source clause.

(25) *gapped phrase*:

$$\begin{bmatrix} \text{SYN} \mid \text{HEAD} \ \boxed{H} & \\ \text{MAX-QUD} & \begin{bmatrix} \text{FEC} & \left\{ \begin{matrix} \begin{bmatrix}\text{SEM } z_1\end{bmatrix},...,\begin{bmatrix}\text{SEM } z_n\end{bmatrix}, \\ \begin{bmatrix}\text{SEM } x_1\end{bmatrix},...,\begin{bmatrix}\text{SEM } x_n\end{bmatrix} \end{matrix} \right\} \\ \text{Q} & \boxed{Q} = \lambda y_n ... \lambda y_1 . [\Phi] \end{bmatrix} \\ \text{SEM} & \boxed{Q}(x_n, ..., x_1) \\ \text{DTRS} & \left\langle \begin{bmatrix} \text{SEM} & x_1 \\ \text{FEC} & \left\{ [\text{SEM } x_1] \right\} \end{bmatrix}, ..., \begin{bmatrix} \text{SEM} & x_n \\ \text{FEC} & \left\{ [\text{SEM } x_n] \right\} \end{bmatrix} \right\rangle \end{bmatrix}$$

$(n \geq 2)$

The SYN(TAX) | HEAD value of the mother is underspecified, and this allows gapped clauses to combine with connectives selecting a non-finite category like *as well as* and *and/but not*.

The constraints on MAX-QUD are partly from the source clauses. The objects in the FEC set correspond to the source clause's focal elements as well as the remnants of the gapped clauses that are also focal elements. $\boxed{Q}$ is an open proposition that corresponds to the unfocused part of the source clause (Φ) and a set of lambda variables.

The constraints on SEM ensure that the semantics of a given gapped clause is obtained on the basis of the propositional abstract $\boxed{Q}$ and the semantics of the daughters by applying beta reduction: It is computed by replacing the lambda variables $\lambda y_1 ... \lambda y_n$ in Q with the semantics of the daughters $x_n, ..., x_1$.

Lastly, the D(AUGH)T(E)RS list contains a list of signs that correspond to the remnants. It is specified that the semantics of the daughters must be structure-shared with the semantics of the objects within FEC, which ensures that there are no remnants are are not focal elements.

The structure in Figure 1 provides an analysis of an instance of *gapped phrase*, *Sue Bill*, that is introduced to the context updated by the source clause *Mary loves Paul*.

$$\begin{bmatrix} \text{MAX-QUD} & \begin{bmatrix} \text{FEC} & \left\{ \begin{matrix} \begin{bmatrix}\text{SEM } m\end{bmatrix}, \begin{bmatrix}\text{SEM } p\end{bmatrix} \\ \begin{bmatrix}\text{SEM } s\end{bmatrix}, \begin{bmatrix}\text{SEM } b\end{bmatrix} \end{matrix} \right\} \\ \text{Q} & \lambda y . \lambda x . love'(x, y) \end{bmatrix} \\ \text{SEM} & love(s, b) \end{bmatrix}$$

NP $\begin{bmatrix} \text{SEM} & s \\ \text{FEC} & \left\{ [\text{SEM } s] \right\} \end{bmatrix}$ — Sue

NP $\begin{bmatrix} \text{SEM} & b \\ \text{FEC} & \left\{ [\text{SEM } b] \right\} \end{bmatrix}$ — Bill

Figure 1: Gapped clause *Sue Bill*

Here s and b represent the semantics of the daughters, *Sue* and *Bill*, respectively. The FEC set contains the semantic objects introduced by the focal elements in the source clause, *Mary* and *Paul*. The semantics of the mother $love(s, b)$ is obtained by applying the propositional abstract to the semantics of the daughters.

The analysis I have proposed so far has a number of advantages. As is well-known, a given remnant and its correlate must establish contrastive foci (**Mary*$_x$ *loves apples and she*$_x$, *pears*). In my analysis, this is expected because the remnants and their correlates are required to be members of their respective FEC set (See (25)). Furthermore, the precise constraints on contrastive foci are motivated independently by theories of focus (Rooth, 1985; Büring, 2003), which allows us to have a simpler theory of Gapping.

Second, the current analysis does not require that a given remnant-correlate pair must satisfy some sort of structural parallelism: In (25) the head values of the daughters are not required to be identical to the head values of the respective focal elements. Thus, case-mismatch between a remnant and its correlate like the one in (26) is allowed.

(26) You may have this cake, or him, that ice cream.

Third, in the analysis I proposed, the semantics of gapped clauses is computed by beta-reducing a propositional abstract that contains lambda variables. Because lambda is order-sensitive, the impossibility of case-mismatch like the one shown in (27) is correctly predicted.

(27) #Casablanca was directed by Michael Curtiz, and Roman Polanski, Chinatown. (= Roman Polanski directed Chinatown)

One can think of the reason for the oddness of (27) intuitively: The gapped and source clauses are answers to two different questions, *Which movie was directed by which director?* and *Which director directed which movie?*, respectively. The proposed QUD-based analysis captures this intuition directly by requiring that the semantics of gapped clauses make reference to the structure of the QUD introduced by their respective source clauses.

5 Conclusion

In this work I proposed a QUD-based analysis of Gapping constructions integrated in a more general constraint on fragment utterances, following Ginzburg and Sag (2000) and Ginzburg (2012). The QUD-based constraint on Gapping constructions I proposed enables the semantics of gapped clauses to be constructed based on the semantics of the expressed information and the information retrieved from a contextually provided question under discussion. This QUD-based account correctly predicts the availability of subordinators and sub-phrasal remnants in certain cases of Gapping constructions, and the possibility of wide scope operators in various contexts, all of which pose serious challenges to previous accounts. Further research is required to investigate the precise effect of prosodic factors on acceptability.

Acknowledgments

I thank Rui Chaves, Jean-Pierre Koenig, and members of the Syntax-Semantics Research Group at the University at Buffalo for their comments and discussions that contributed to this work. I also thank the reviewers for their valuable suggestions. All remaining errors are solely mine.

References

Andrew Kehler. 2002. *Coherence, Reference, and the Theory of Grammar*. CSLI.

Anne Abeillé, Gabriela Bîlbîie, and Francois Mouret. 2013. A Romance perspective on Gapping constructions. In *Romance in Construction Grammar*, ed. H. Boas and F. Gonzalvez Garcia. Amsterdam: John Benjamins.

Craige Roberts. 1996/2012. Information structure in discourse: towards an integrated formal theory of pragmatics. *Semantics & Pragmatics* 5(6): 1-69.

Daniel Büring. 2003. On D-trees, beans and B-accents. *Linguistics and Philosophy*, 26:511-545.

Ivan A. Sag. 1976. Deletion and logical form. Ph.D. Dissertation. MIT.

James D. McCawley. 1988. *The Syntactic Phenomena of English*, Vol. 1. University of Chicago Press.

James D. McCawley. 1993. *Gapping with shared operators*. In D. A. Peterson (ed.), *Berkeley Linguistics Society*, 245-253. University of California, Berkeley, California.

Jason Merchant. 2004. Fragments and Ellipsis. *Linguistics and Philosophy*, 27:661–738.

Jerry Hobbs. 1985. On the Coherence and Structure of Discourse. CSLI-85-37.

Jeroen Groenendijk and Martin Stokhof. 1991. Dynamic Predicate Logic. *Linguistics and Philosophy* 14(1): 39–100.

John R. Ross. 1970. Gapping and the order of constituents. In M. Bierwisch and K. Heidolph (eds.), *Progress in Linguistics*, 249–259. The Hague: Mouton.

Jonathan Ginzburg and Ivan A. Sag. 2000. *Interrogative investigations: the form, meaning and use of English interrogatives*. Stanford: CSLI Publications.

Jonathan Ginzburg. 2012. *The Interactive Stance: meaning for conversation*. Oxford University Press, Oxford.

Jorge Hankamer. 1973. Unacceptable Ambiguity. *Linguistic Inquiry*, 4(1):17–68.

Katharina Hartmann. 2000. *Right Node Raising and Gapping: Interface conditions on prosodic deletion*. John Benjamins Publishing.

Kyle Johnson. 2009. Gapping is not (vP-) ellipsis. *Linguistic Inquiry*, 40(2):289–328.

Kyle Johnson. 2014. Gapping. Ms., University of Massachusetts, Amherst.

Linton Wang, Eric McCready, and Nicholas Asher. 2006. Information dependency in Quantificational Subordination. *Where Semantics Meets Pragmatics*. Oxford: Elsevier, 267–304.

Mark J. Steedman. 1990. Gapping as constituent coordination. *Linguistics and Philosophy* 13(2):207–263.

Massimo Poesio and Alessandro Zucchi. 1992. On Telescoping. *Proceedings of Semantics and Linguistic Theoty 2*.

Matthew Reeve. 2014. If there's anything cleft-ellipsis resembles, it's (pseudo)gapping. In R. E. Santana-LaBarge (ed.), *Proceedings of the 31st West Coast Conference on Formal Linguistics*, 351–360.

Muffy E. A. Siegel. 1984. Gapping and interpretation. *Linguistic Inquiry*, 15:523–530.

Nancy Levin and Ellen Prince. 1986. Gapping and causal implicature. *Papers in Linguistics*, 19, 351–364.

Neal Whitman. 2010. Deriving wide-scoping operators in an associative Lambek categorial grammar. LSA Annual Meeting Extended Abstracts.

Peter Culicover and Ray Jackendoff. 2005. *Simpler Syntax*. Oxford University Press.

Petra Hendriks. 2004. Coherence relations, ellipsis and contrastive topics. *Journal of Semantics*, 21(2): 133–153.

Ray S. Jackendoff. 1971. Gapping and related rules. *Linguistic Inquiry* 2(1):21–35.

Richard A. Hudson. 1989. Gapping and grammatical relations. *Journal of Linguistics*, 25(1):57–94.

Mats E. Rooth. 1985. Association with Focus. Ph.D. dissertation. University of Massachusetts, Amherst.

Rui P. Chaves. 2005. A linearization-based approach to gapping. *Proceedings of the 10th Conference on Formal Grammar and the 9th Meeting on Mathematics of Language*, 1–14. CSLI.

Rui P. Chaves. 2007. Coordinate Structures: constraint-based syntax-semantics processing. Ph.D. Dissertation. University of Lisbon.

Yusuke Kubota and Robert Levine. 2014. The scope anomaly of Gapping. In *Proceedings of NELS*, 44: 247–260.

Yusuke Kubota and Robert Levine. 2016. Gapping as hypothetical reasoning. *Natural Language and Linguistic Theory*, 34(1):107–156.

Poster Presentation Papers

Retrieval Term Prediction Using Deep Learning Methods

Qing Ma[†] **Ibuki Tanigawa**[†] **Masaki Murata**[‡]
[†] Department of Applied Mathematics and Informatics, Ryukoku University
[‡] Department of Information and Electronics, Tottori University
qma@math.ryukoku.ac.jp

Abstract

This paper presents methods to predict retrieval terms from relevant/surrounding words or descriptive texts in Japanese by using deep learning methods, which are implemented with stacked denoising autoencoders (SdA), as well as deep belief networks (DBN). To determine the effectiveness of using DBN and SdA for this task, we compare them with conventional machine learning methods, i.e., multi-layer perceptron (MLP) and support vector machines (SVM). We also compare their performance in case of using three regularization methods, the weight decay (L2 regularization), sparsity (L1 regularization), and dropout regularization. The experimental results show that (1) adding automatically gathered unlabeled data to the labeled data for unsupervised learning is an effective measure for improving the prediction precision, and (2) using DBN or SdA results in higher prediction precision than using SVM or MLP, whether or not regularization methods are used.

1 Introduction

Existing Web search engines have very high retrieval performance as long as the proper retrieval terms are input. However, many people, particularly children, seniors, and foreigners, have difficulty deciding on the proper retrieval terms for representing the retrieval objects,[1] especially in searches related to technical fields. Support systems are in place for search engine users that show suitable retrieval term candidates when clues such as their descriptive texts or relevant/surrounding words are given by the users. For example, when the relevant/surrounding words "computer", "previous state", and "return" are given by users, "system restore" is predicted by the systems as a retrieval term candidate. It is therefore necessary to develop various domain-specific information retrieval support systems that can predict suitable retrieval terms from relevant/surrounding words or descriptive texts in Japanese.

In recent years, on the other hand, deep learning/neural network techniques have attracted a great deal of attention in various fields and have been successfully applied not only in speech recognition (Li et al., 2013) and image recognition (Krizhevsky et al., 2012) tasks but also in NLP tasks including morphology & syntax (Billingsley and Curran, 2012; Hermann and Blunsom, 2013; Luong et al., 2013; Socher et al., 2013a), semantics (Hashimoto et al., 2013; Srivastava et al., 2013; Tsubaki et al., 2013), machine translation (Auli et al., 2013; Liu et al., 2013; Kalchbrenner and Blunsom, 2013; Zou et al., 2013), text classification (Glorot et al., 2011), information retrieval (Huang et al., 2013; Salakhutdinov and Hinton, 2009), and others (Seide et al., 2011; Socher et al., 2011; Socher et al., 2013b). Moreover, a unified neural network architecture and learning algorithm has also been proposed that can be applied to various NLP tasks including part-of-speech tagging, chunking, named entity recognition, and semantic role labeling (Collobert et al., 2011). How-

[1]For example, according to a questionnaire administered by Microsoft in 2010, about 60% of users had difficulty deciding on the proper retrieval terms. (http://www.garbagenews.net/archives/1466626.html) (http://news.mynavi.jp/news/2010/07/05/028/)

ever, there have been no studies on applying deep learning to information retrieval support tasks. It is therefore necessary to confirm whether deep learning is more effective than other conventional machine learning methods in this task.

Two objectives were cited above. One was to develop an effective method for predicting suitable retrieval terms and the other was to determine whether deep learning is more effective than other conventional machine learning methods, i.e., multi-layer perceptron (MLP) and support vector machines (SVM), in such NLP tasks. On this basis, Ma et al. (2014) proposed a method to predict retrieval terms in computer-related fields using machine learning methods with deep belief networks (DBN) (Hinton et al., 2006; Lee et al., 2009; Bengio et al., 2007; Bengio, 2009; Bengio et al., 2013). In small-scale experiments they showed that using DBN resulted in higher prediction precision than using either a multi-layer perceptron (MLP) or support vector machines (SVM). To evaluate their proposed method more reliably, the first thing we must do is scale up the experiments. In general, it is not easy to obtain large training data, particularly labeled data for supervised learning. Fortunately, deep learning consists of both unsupervised learning and supervised learning, and unlabeled data can be collected relatively easily. Second, since a number of regularization methods (Srivastava et al., 2014) have been adopted for improving the generalization performance of neural networks, we also need to conduct evaluations when regularization is used.

This study is an enhanced version of the previous work of Ma et al. (2014), and the retrieval terms were confined to computer-related fields as before. We implemented deep learning not only with the DBN as done in the previous work of Ma et al. (2014), but also with stacked denoising autoencoders (SdA) (Bengio et al., 2007; Bengio, 2009; Bengio et al., 2013; Vincent et al., 2008; Vincent et al., 2010). We conducted extensive experiments in which a large amount of unlabeled data was automatically collected from the Web (as a result, the amount of data and the number of labels used in this study were about ten times larger than those used in the previous study (Ma et al., 2014)), and then we compared the performance between DBN and SdA, and between DBN/SdA and conventional machine learning methods, in the respective cases of using or not using regularization methods, i.e., weight decay (L2 regularization), sparsity (L1 regularization), and dropout regularization.

Experimental results show that using SdA achieves the highest prediction precision among all the methods and that using both DBN and SdA produces higher prediction precision than that achieved using either MLP or SVM, when regularization methods are not used. On the other hand, when regularization methods are used MLP and DBN performance is improvement in some cases, whereas no performance improvement can be found in SdA. Whether or not regularization methods are used, however, the order of superiority among SdA, DBN, and MLP remains unchanged. The experimental results also show that adding automatically gathered unlabeled data to the labeled data for unsupervised learning is an effective measure for improving the prediction precision.

2 Data

In this section, we describe how the training and testing data were obtained and how the feature vectors of the inputs were constructed from the data for machine learning.

2.1 Labeled Data

For supervised learning and testing, a labeled data set consisting of pairs of inputs and their responses (or correct answers) — in our case, pairs of the relevant/surrounding words or descriptive texts and retrieval terms — is needed. The responses are typically called labels in supervised learning, so we call the retrieval terms labels here. Table 1 gives examples of these pairs, where the "Relevant/surrounding words" are those extracted from descriptive texts in accordance with the steps described in Subsection 2.3.

A total of 1,234 pieces of data labeled with 100 different labels (i.e., 1,234 pairs of inputs and labels) were manually collected from 22 computer terminology Web sites.

2.2 Unlabeled Data

Unlabeled data can be used for unsupervised learning and are obtained from the Web in an automatic manner. We respectively combine five words or

Labels (Retrieval terms)	Inputs (Descriptive texts or relevant/surrounding words; translated from Japanese)	
Graphics board	**Descriptive text**	Also known as: graphics card, graphics accelerator, GB, VGA. While the screen outputs the picture actually seen by the eye, the screen only displays as commanded and does not output anything if it does not receive a command. The graphics board is the device that outputs the commands. Two types of data exist that the graphics board needs to process on the PC: 2D (planar data) and 3D (three-dimensional data).
	Relevant/surrounding words	screen, picture, eye, displays, as commanded, command, device, two types exist, data, process, on the PC, 2D, planar data, 3D, three-dimensional data.
	Descriptive text	A device that provides independent functions for outputting or inputting video as signals on a PC or various other types of computers in the form of an expansion card (expansion board). The drawing speed, resolution, and 3D performance vary according to the chip and memory mounted on the card.
	Relevant/surrounding words	independent, functions, outputting, inputting, video, signals, PC, various other types, computer, expansion card, expansion board, drawing speed, resolution, 3D performance, chip, memory, mounted, card
Main memory	**Descriptive text**	A device that stores data and programs on a computer. Also known as the 'primary memory device'. Since main memory uses semiconductor elements to electrically record information, its operation is fast and it can read and write directly to and from the central processing unit (CPU). However, it has a high cost per unit volume and so cannot be used in large quantities.
	Relevant/surrounding words	device, stores, data, programs, on a computer, primary memory device, main memory, uses, semiconductor elements, electrically, record, operation, fast, read and write directly, central processing unit, CPU, cost, per unit volume, used, in large quantities.
	Descriptive text	Main memory is a device that temporarily stores data on a PC. Increasing the volume of the main memory is important in terms of increasing PC performance.
	Relevant/surrounding words	main memory, device, temporarily, stores, data, PC, volume, performance

Table 1: Examples of input-label pairs in the corpus.

parts of phrases とは (toha, "what is"), は (ha, "is"), というものは (toiumonoha, "something like"), については (nitsuiteha, "about"), and の意味は (noimiha, "the meaning of"), on the labels to form the retrieval terms (e.g., if a label is グラフィックボード (gurafikku boudo, "graphics board"), then the retrieval terms are グラフィックボード とは (gurafikku boudo toha, "what is graphics board"), グラフィックボード は (gurafikku boudo ha, "graphics board is"), etc.) and then use these terms to obtain the relevant Web pages by a Google search. Because data gathered in this way might have incorrect labels, i.e., labels that do not match the descriptive texts, we use them as unlabeled data. We obtained 25,000 pieces of data (i.e., inputs) in total.

2.3 Word Extraction and Feature Vector Construction

Relevant/surrounding words are extracted from descriptive texts in steps (1)–(4) below, and the inputs are represented by feature vectors in machine learning constructed in steps (1)–(6): (1) perform morphological analysis on the labeled data that are used for training and extract all nouns, including proper nouns, verbal nouns (nouns forming verbs by adding the word する (suru, "do")), and general nouns; (2)

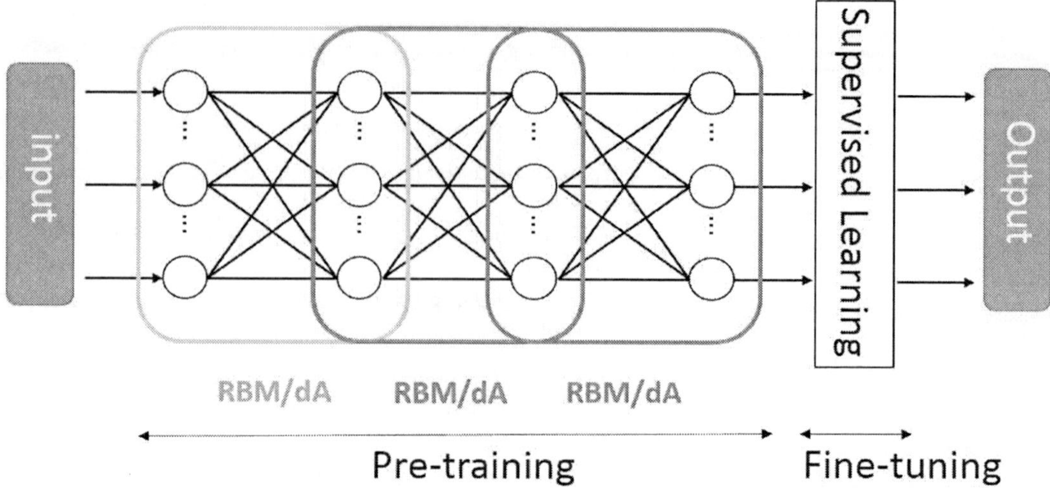

Figure 1: An example of deep neural networks consisting of DBN or SdA.

connect the nouns successively appearing as single words; (3) extract the words whose appearance frequency in each label is ranked in the top 30; (4) exclude the words appearing in the descriptive texts of more than 20 labels; (5) use the words obtained in the above steps as the vector elements with binary values, taking value 1 if a word appears and 0 if not; and (6) morphologically analyze all data described in Subsections 2.1 and 2.2, and construct the feature vectors in accordance with step (5).

3 Deep Learning and Regularization

Deep learning consists of unsupervised learning for pre-training to extract features and supervised learning for fine-tuning to output labels. Deep learning can be implemented by two typical approaches: using deep belief networks (DBN) (Hinton et al., 2006; Lee et al., 2009; Bengio et al., 2007; Bengio, 2009; Bengio et al., 2013) and using stacked denoising autoencoders (SdA) (Bengio et al., 2007; Bengio, 2009; Bengio et al., 2013; Vincent et al., 2008; Vincent et al., 2010). The same supervised learning method can be used with both of these approaches; i.e., both approaches can be implemented with a single-layer or multi-layer perceptron or other techniques (linear regression, logistic regression, etc.), while a different unsupervised learning method is used; i.e., a DBN is formed by stacking restricted Boltzmann machines (RBM), and an SdA is formed by stacking denoising autoencoders (dA) using a greedy layer-wise training algorithm. In this work, we use SdA as well as DBN, both of which use logistic regression for supervised learning.

Figure 1 shows an example of deep neural networks composed of three RBM or dA for pre-training and a supervised learning device for fine-tuning. Naturally the number of RBM/dA is changeable as needed. As shown in the figure, the hidden layers of the earlier RBM/dA become the visible layers of the new RBM/dA.

A number of regularization methods have been proposed to prevent overfitting and to improve the generalization performance. Weight decay (L2 regularization) is a method to prevent the weights from becoming too large by adding the sum of the squared weights to an error function, and sparsity (L1 regularization) is a method to help select features in sparse feature spaces by adding the sum of the absolute values of weights to an error function, which leads to many of the weights becoming zero. In contrast, dropout (Srivastava et al., 2014) is a method to train different models for each piece of a training data set by randomly removing units with probability p from input and hidden layers. At test time, all units are then always present (not removed) and their

Machine learning methods	Hyperparameters	Values
DBN	structure (hidden layers)	662, 992-662, **1103-882-662**[2], 1985, 1985-1985, 1985-1985-1985, 2646, 1985-2646, 1764-2205-2646
	ϵ of pre-training	0.05, 0.1, 0.5
	ϵ of fine-tuning	0.05, 0.1, 0.5
	epoch of pre-training	10, 50, 100
	stop of fine-tuning	when the training error (average of 0/1 loss) is below 0.03
SdA	structure (hidden layers)	662, 992-662, 1103-882-662, 1985, 1985-1985, 1985-1985-1985, 2646, 1985-2646, 1764-2205-2646
	ϵ of pre-training	0.05, 0.1, 0.5
	ϵ of fine-tuning	0.05, 0.1, 0.5
	epoch of pre-training	10, 50, 100
	stop of fine-tuning	when the training error (average of 0/1 loss) is below 0.03
MLP	structure (hidden layers)	662, 992-662, 1103-882-662, 1985, 1985-1985, 1985-1985-1985, 2646, 1985-2646, 1764-2205-2646
	ϵ	27 divisions between 10^{-2}-10^{0} in a logarithmic scale
	stop of training	when the training error (average of 0/1 loss) is below 0.03
SVM (Linear)	C	243 divisions between 10^{-6}-10^{6} in a logarithmic scale
SVM (RBF)	C	16 divisions between 10^{-4}-10^{4} in a logarithmic scale
	γ	15 divisions between 10^{-4}-10^{4} in a logarithmic scale
Bernoulli Naïve Bayes	additive smoothing	122 divisions between 10^{-6}-10^{0} in a logarithmic scale
	learning of prior probability	True, False

Table 2: Hyperparameters for grid search used in the comparative experiments of different training data sets and different machine learning methods without regularization.

weights are multiplied by 1-p.

4 Experiments

4.1 Experimental Setup

We used three data sets with different amounts of data (i.e., 1,134 labeled data; 1,134 labeled data + 13,000 unlabeled data; and 1,134 labeled data + 25,000 unlabeled data) for unsupervised learning, the same 1,134 labeled data for supervised learning, and the remaining 100 labeled data for testing. The

[2]As an example, the structure (hidden layers) **1103-882-662**, shown as bold in the table, refers to a DBN with a 1323-**1103-882-662**-100 structure, where 1323 and 100 respectively refer to dimensions of the input and output layers. These figures were set not in an arbitrary manner. The first three structures are decreasing (pyramid-like) size and all hidden layers were set to 3/6, 4/6, 3/4, and 5/6 times smaller than that of the input layer, i.e., $662 = 1323 \times 3/6$, $882 = 1323 \times 4/6$, $992 = 1323 \times 3/4$, and $1103 = 1323 \times 5/6$. The last three structures are increasing (upside down pyramid) size and all hidden layers were set to 8/6, 9/6, 10/6, and 12/6 times larger than that of the input layer, i.e., $1764 = 1323 \times 8/6$, $1985 = 1323 \times 9/6$, $2205 = 1323 \times 10/6$, and $2646 = 1323 \times 12/6$. The middle three structures were set in accordance with the recommendations of (Bengio, 2012) that using the same size works generally as well as or better than using a decreasing (pyramid-like) or increasing (upside down pyramid) size.

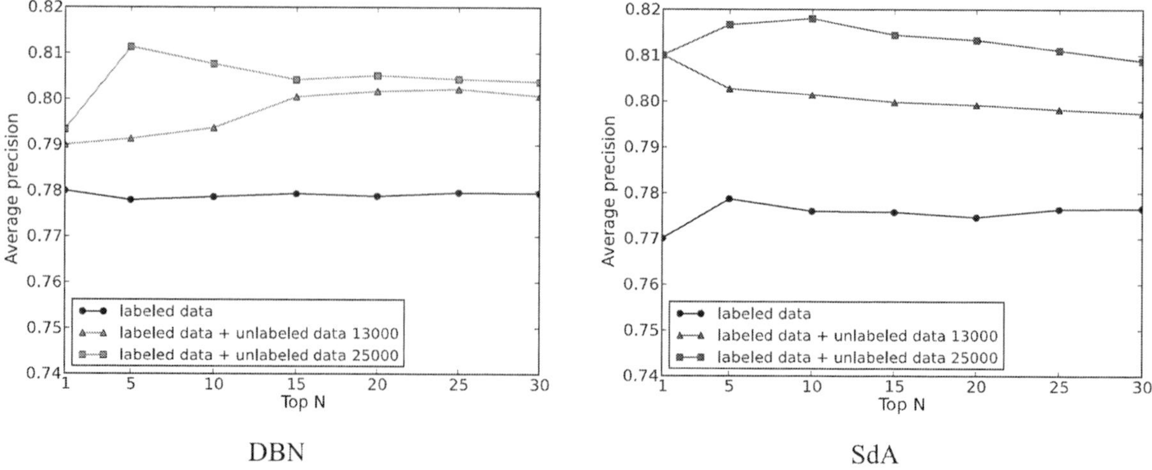

Figure 2: Average precision values obtained using different training data without regularization.

dimension of the feature vectors constructed from the 1,134 labeled training data in accordance with the steps in Subsection 2.3 was 1,323.

The optimal hyperparameters of the various machine learning methods used were determined by a grid search using 5-fold cross-validation on training data. To avoid unfair bias toward DBN/SdA during cross-validation due to DBN/SdA having more hyperparameters than MLP/SVM, we divided MLP/SVM hyperparameter grids more finely than that of the DBN/SdA so that they had the same hyperparameter combinations (hyperparameter sets) as those of DBN/SdA. Also, to avoid unfair bias toward DBN/SdA/MLP with regularization during cross-validation due to they having more hyperparameters than those without regularization, we divided DBN/SdA/MLP with no regularization hyperparameter grids more finely than those of the DBN/SdA/MLP with regularization so that they had the same hyperparameter combinations as those of DBN/SdA/MLP with regularization.

Table 2 shows the hyperparameters for grid search used in the comparative experiments of different training data sets and different machine learning methods without regularization. We therefore had 243 hyperparameter sets in total for these experiments. On the other hand, hyperparameters for grid search used in the comparative experiments with and without regularization are not shown in a table because of space limitations. In these experiments, the

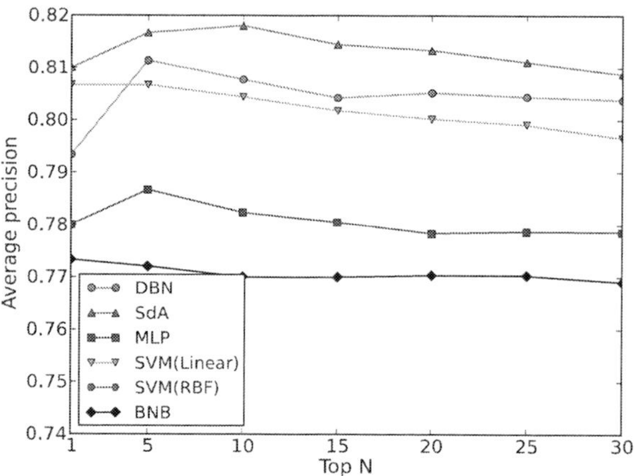

Figure 3: Average precision values obtained using different methods without regularization.

hyperparameters of DBN/SdA/MLP without regularization differ from those in Table 2. The differences were due to the above-cited measure we took to avoid unfair bias. As a result, we had 2,187 hyperparameter sets in total for these experiments.

4.2 Results

Figure 2 compares the testing data precision obtained with DBN and SdA when using different training data sets. The precision values are averages

	N=1	N=5	N=10
BNB	0.773	0.772	0.770
MLP	0.780	0.789	0.790
SVM (Linear)	0.807	0.807	0.804
SVM (RBF)	0.717	0.719	0.716
DBN	0.793	0.811	0.808
SdA	**0.810**	**0.817**	**0.818**

Table 3: Average precisions values obtained using different methods without regularization.

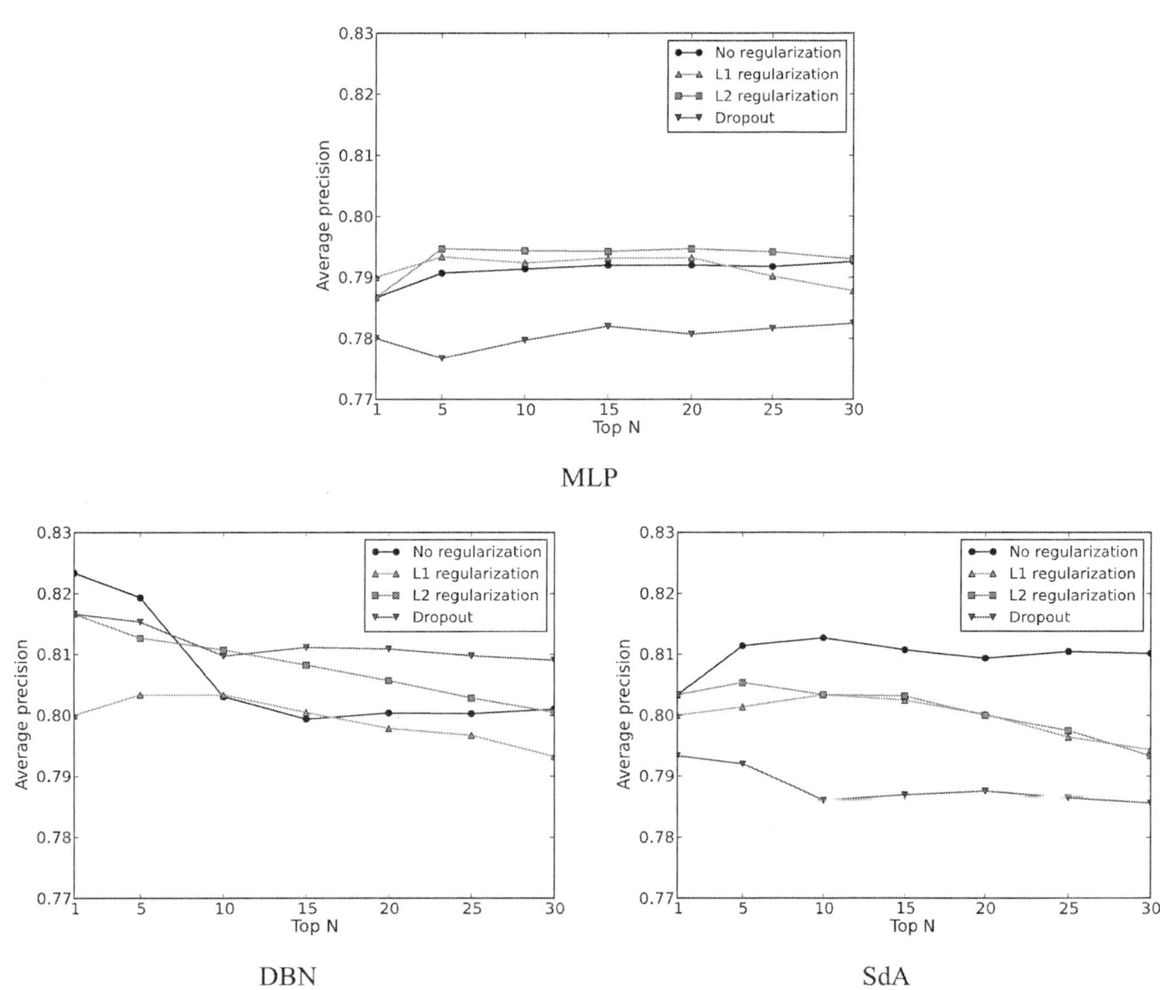

Figure 4: Comparison of average precision values obtained with and without regularization.

when using the top N sets of the hyperparameters in ascending order of the cross-validation errors, with N varying from 1 to 30. As shown in the figure, the precision of both DBN and SdA can be improved by adding the unlabeled data to the labeled data as training data, and both DBN and SdA have higher precision when using a larger amount of unlabeled data.

Figure 3 compares the testing data precision values obtained when using the largest data set (1,134 labeled data + 25,000 unlabeled data) for unsupervised learning, when using different learning meth-

	N=1	N=5	N=10
BNB	0.773	0.773	0.773
MLP	0.787	0.791	0.791
MLP with L1	0.790	0.793	0.792
MLP with L2	0.787	0.795	0.794
MLP with Dropout	0.780	0.777	0.780
SVM (Linear)	0.807	0.809	0.807
SVM (RBF)	0.730	0.737	0.735
DBN	**0.823**	**0.819**	0.803
DBN with L1	0.800	0.803	0.803
DBN with L2	0.817	0.813	0.811
DBN with Dropout	0.817	0.815	0.810
SdA	0.803	0.811	**0.813**
SdA with L1	0.800	0.801	0.803
SdA with L2	0.803	0.805	0.803
SdA with Dropout	0.793	0.792	0.789

Table 4: Average precision values obtained using different methods with and without regularization.

ods and Bernoulli Naïve Bayes (BNB), which is used as a baseline. We can see at a glance from the figure that the performance of SdA is superior to that of DBN and that both DBN and SdA are generally superior to BNB, MLP, and SVM. We should point out that the results for SVM (RBF) are not indicated in the figure because the precision values were lower than 0.74. Table 3 lists the specific average precision values obtained using different learning methods when N=1, 5, and 10.

Figure 4 and Table 4 compare the testing data precision values for MLP, DBN, and SdA with and without regularization[3]. The figure and table show that the performance of MLP and DBN improved in some cases by using regularization, whereas no performance improvement can be found for SdA. However, both DBN and SdA outperformed BNB, MLP and SVM whether regularization was used or not.

5 Conclusion

We presented methods to predict retrieval terms from relevant/surrounding words or descriptive texts in Japanese by using deep belief networks (DBN) and stacked denoising autoencoders (SdA). Experimental results based on a relatively large scale confirmed that (1) adding automatically gathered unlabeled data to the labeled data for unsupervised learning was an effective measure for improving the prediction precision, and (2) using either DBN or SdA definitely achieved higher prediction precision than that obtained using multi-layer perceptron (MLP), whether weight decay (L2 regularization), sparsity (L1 regularization), or dropout regularization was used. Both DBN and SdA achieved higher precision than Bernoulli Naïve Bayes (BNB) and support vector machines (SVM).

In the future, we plan to start developing various practical domain-specific systems that can predict suitable retrieval terms from the relevant/surrounding words or descriptive texts.

[3]It should be noted that the precision values obtained without regularization (shown in Figure 4 and Table 4) differ from those shown in Figure 3 and Table 3. This is because different numbers of hyperparameter sets were used for grid searching between the two experiments as described in Subsection 4.1.

Acknowledgments

This work was supported by JSPS KAKENHI Grant Number 25330368.

References

M. Auli, M. Galley, C. Quirk, and G. Zweig. 2013. Joint Language and Translation Modeling with Recurrent Neural Networks. EMNLP 2013, 1044–1054.

Y. Bengio, P. Lamblin, D. Popovici, and H. Larochelle.

2007. Greedy Layer-wise Training of Deep Networks. 153–160. NIPS 2006, 153–160.

Y. Bengio. 2009. Learning Deep Architectures for AI. Foundations and Trends in Machine Learning, 2(1):1–127.

Y. Bengio. 2012. Practical Recommendations for Gradient-Based Training of Deep Architectures. eprint arXiv1206.5533, 1–33.

Y. Bengio, A. Courville, and P. Vincent. 2013. Representation Learning: A Review and New Perspectives. IEEE Transactions on Pattern Analysis and Machine Intelligence, 35(8):1798–1828.

R. Billingsley and J. Curran. 2012. Improvements to Training an RNN Parser. COLING 2012, 279–294.

R. Collobert, J. Weston, L. Bottou, M. Karlen, K. Kavukcuoglu, and P. Kuksa. 2011. Natural Language Processing (Almost) from Scratch. Journal of Machine Learning Research,

X. Glorot, A. Bordes, and Y. Bengio. 2011. Domain Adaptation for Large-Scale Sentiment Classification: A Deep Learning Approach. ICML 2011, 513–520.

K. Hashimoto, M. Miwa, Y. Tsuruoka, and T. Chikayama. 2013. Simple Customization of Recursive Neural Networks for Semantic Relation Classification. EMNLP 2013, 1372–1376.

K. M. Hermann and P. Blunsom. 2013. The Role of Syntax in Vector Space Models of Compositional Semantics. ACL 2013, 894–904.

G. E. Hiton, S. Osindero, and Y. Teh. 2006. A Fast Learning Algorithm for Deep Belief Nets. Neural Computation, 18:1527–1554.

P. S. Huang, X. He, J. Gao, L. Deng, A. Acero, and L. Heck 2013. Learning deep structured semantic models for web search using clickthrough data. CIKM 2013, 2333–2338.

N. Kalchbrenner and P. Blunsom. 2013. Recurrent Continuous Translation Models. EMNLP 2013, 1700–1709.

A. Krizhevsky, I. Sutskever, and G. E. Hinton. 2012. ImageNet Classification with Deep Convolutional Neural Networks. NIPS 2012, 1097–1105.

H. Lee, R. Grosse, R. Ranganath, and A. Y. Ng. 2009. Convolutional Deep Belief Networks for Scalable Unsupervised Learning of Hierarchical Representations. ICML 2009, 609-616.

L. Li and Y. Zhao, et al. 2013. Hybrid Deep Neural Network - Hidden Markov Model (DNN-HMM) Based Speech Emotion Recognition. ACII 2013.

L. Liu, T. Watanabe, E. Sumita and T. Zhao. 2013. Additive Neural Networks for Statistical Machine Translation. ACL 2013, 791–801.

T. Luong, R. Socher, and C. Manning. 2013. Better Word Representations with Recursive Neural Networks for Morphology. ACL 2013, 104–113.

Q. Ma, I. Tanigawa, and M. Murata. 2014. Retrieval Term Prediction Using Deep Belief Networks. Paclic 2014.

S. J. Nowlan and G. Hinton. 1992. Simplifying Neural Networks by Soft Weight-sharing. Neural Computation, 4:474-493.

R. Salakhutdinov and G. E. Hinton. 2009. Semantic Hashing. International Journal of Approximate Reasoning, 50(7): 969-978.

F. Seide, G. Li, and D. Yu. 2011. Conversational Speech Transcription Using Context-Dependent Deep Neural Networks. INTERSPEECH 2011, 437-440.

R. Socher, E. H. Huang, J. Pennington, A. Y. Ng, and C. D. Manning. 2011. Dynamic Pooling and Unfolding Recursive Autoencoders for Paraphrase Detection. NIPS 2011, 801–809.

R. Socher, J. Bauer, C. D. Manning, and A. Y. Ng. 2013. Parsing with Computational Vector Grammars. ACL 2013, 455–465.

R. Socher, A. Perelygin, J. Y. Wu, and J. Chuang. 2013. Recursive Deep Models for Semantic Compositionality Over a Sentiment Treebank. EMNLP 2013, 1631–1642.

S. Srivastava, D. Hovy, and E. H. Hovy. 2013. A Walk-Based Semantically Enriched Tree Kernel Over Distributed Word Representations. EMNLP 2013, 1411–1416.

N. Srivastava, G. Hinton, A. Krizhevsky, H. Sutskever, and R. Salakhutdinov. 2014. Dropout: A Simple Way to Prevent Neural Networks from Overfitting. Journal of Machine Learning Research, 15:1929–1958.

M. Tsubaki, K. Duh, M. Shimbo, and Y. Matsumoto. 2013. Modeling and Learning Semantic Co-Compositionality through Prototype Projections and Neural Networks. EMNLP 2013, 130–140.

P. Vincent, H. Larochelle, Y. Bengio, and P. A. Manzagol. 2008. Extracting and Composing Robust Features with Denoising Autoencoders. ICML 2008, 1096–1103.

P. Vincent, H. Larochelle, I. Lajoie, Y. Bengio, and P. A. Manzagol. 2010. Stacked Denoising Autoencoders: Learning Useful Representations in a Deep Network with a Local Denoising Criterion. Journal of Machine Learning Research, 11:3371–3408.

W. Y. Zou, R. Socher, D. M. Cer, and C. D. Manning. 2013. Bilingual Word Embeddings for Phrase-Based Machine Translation. EMNLP 2013, 1393–1398.

Japanese Postverbal Constructions Revisited

Kohji Kamada
Chiba University/1-33, Yayoicho, Inage Ward, Chiba-shi, Chiba, 263-8522 Japan
k-kamada@chiba-u.jp

Abstract

There are two types of possible approaches to the derivation of Japanese Postverbal Constructions (JPVCs): (i) movement and (ii) base-generation. Certain base-generation analyses can account for properties of JPVCs that movement analyses fail to, such as split antecedency. These properties are explained by interface conditions and a licensing condition for adjoined elements, on the basis of the claim that postverbal elements are adjoined to preceding phrases by *external Merge*.

1 Introduction

Japanese is classified as a verb-final language. In colloquial speech, however, optional non-verbal elements can appear in the sentence-final position. This phenomenon, which I call Japanese Post-verbal Constructions (JPVCs), is shown in (1).[1]

(1) a. *Kinoo keiki-o tabe-masita, **Taro-ga**.*
yesterday cake-ACC ate Taro-NOM
'Taro ate cake yesterday.'
b. *Taro-ga keiki-o tabe-masita, **kinoo**.*
Taro-NOM cake-ACC ate yesterday

Taro-ga 'Taro-NOM' in (1a) and ***kinoo*** 'yesterday' in (1b), which appear postverbally, are here called postverbal elements (PVEs).[2]

There are two types of possible approaches to the derivation of JPVCs: (i) movement and (ii) base-generation. Movement analyses can be further classified into two types: (i-a) rightward movement and (i-b) leftward movement. The purpose of this paper is to argue against movement approaches.

The present paper is organized as follows. In section 2, I point out empirical problems with the arguments by Simon (1989) and Tanaka (2001): Simon (1989) claims that the JPVC is derived by rightward movement, and in Tanaka (2001) the derivation of the JPVC is purported to involve the operation of deletion after leftward movement. In section 3, I argue that PVEs are adjoined to phrases via *external Merge*, and that properties that movement analyses explain poorly can be accounted for by independently motivated principles, including interface conditions. Section 4 concludes the paper.

2 Previous Studies

In this section, I will first discuss a rightward movement analysis proposed by Simon (1989).[3] Then, I will take up Tanaka (2001) as an example of leftward movement analyses.[4] I will argue that neither movement analysis is tenable, pointing out several empirical problems with them.

2.1 A Rightward Movement Analysis

In the framework of government and binding theory, Simon (1989) claims that the JPVC is generated by rightward movement, and proposes that the PVE is moved rightward from a preverbal position and right-adjoined to a clause, as schematized in (2), where a trace of the PVE is indicated by *t*:

(2) $[_{CP}\,[_{CP} \ldots\ldots t_i \ldots\ldots]\ \mathbf{PVE}_i]$

The JPVC does not display the Right Roof Constraint (RRC) effect, as shown below:[5]

[1] The abbreviations I use in glossing the data are as follows: ACC=accusative, COMP=complementizer, FP=sentence-final particle, NOM=nominative, Q=question particle, TOP=topic.
[2] (Latent) postverbal elements are henceforth indicated by boldface.

[3] Kaiser (1999) and Takano (2014) also take rightward movement approaches. In the former, the JPVC is functionally analyzed, and in the latter, it is analyzed more phonologically and a crucial discussion is based on some data that seem to be very subtle. For these reasons, in 2.1 I focus on Simon (1989), who analyzes the JPVC more syntactically.
[4] Leftward movement analyses are also defended by Endo (1996), Whitman (2000), Abe (2004), Kurogi (2006), Watanuki (2006) and Takita (2011). Therefore, all of them face some similar problems concerning movement approaches.
[5] The RRC states that an element cannot move rightward out of the clause in which it is contained. (Ross, 1986)

(3) [CP t_i *Hanako-o aisiteiru koto*]-*ga hontoo*
Hanako-ACC love that -NOM true
desu, ***Taro$_i$-ga.***
is Taro-NOM
'That Taro loves Hanako is true.'

Simon (1989: 104) therefore claims that as shown in (4), "an element first adjoins to the S'[=CP] from which it originates, then to the next higher S'[=CP], and so on, until it reaches the highest S'[=CP] and adjoins to its right" (successive cyclic movement), assuming that the RRC is not active in Japanese.

(4) [CP1 [CP1 *Ken wa okusan ni* [CP2 [CP2 [CP3 [CP3 t_i
Ken-TOP wife to
yame-yoo to] t_i] *omotte-ru tte*] t_i]
(he) quit-will that (he) is-thinking that
itta no yo] ***kaisha$_i$-o.***
said FP company-ACC
'Ken told his wife that (he)'s thinking that (he)'ll quit his company.' (Simon, 1989: 102)

Because of just stipulating that the PVE should successive-cyclically move to the root, however, Simon (1989) fails to explain in a principled way why the PVE cannot stay in an embedded clause (i.e., a root phenomenon), as shown in (5):[6]

(5) *[CP *John-ga t_i tabe-ta* ***susi$_i$-o*** *koto*] *-wa*
John-NOM eat-PAST sushi-ACC COMP-TOP
hontoo desu.
true is
'That John ate sushi is true.'

Moreover, every movement analysis fails to cope with examples like the one in (6).[7] There, the PVE concurrently modifies *ringo* 'apple' and *mikan* 'orange', and the pronoun *karera* 'they' can refer to *Taro* and *Ken* (i.e., the so-called split antecedent phenomenon). If movement were involved in the derivation, no source structure for (6) would exist.

(6) *Taro-wa ringo-o, Ken-wa mikan-o,*
Taro-TOP apple-ACC Ken-TOP orange- ACC
tabe-masita, ***kinoo karera-ga katta.***
ate yesterday they-NOM bought
'Taro ate an apple and Ken ate an orange, which they bought yesterday.'

2.2 Leftward Movement Analyses

2.2.1 A Biclausal + Deletion Analysis

Tanaka (2001) assumes, following Kuno (1978), that the JPVC should be derived from two separate clauses that have no hierarchical relation, as schematized in (7).[8]

(7) [CP1 ...(*pro*)...... ....], [CP2 ....]

According to Tanaka (2001: 558-560), the first clause CP1 may or may not contain an empty pronoun *pro* as in (7), and in the second clause CP2, a "PVE" is left-adjoined to IP by scrambling in overt syntax as shown in (8a), which is the S-structure representation. Tanaka (2001) proposes further that the IP to which the PVE adjoins in the second clause is deleted under a certain identity condition, as diagrammed in (8b) with elided material indicated by strikeout:

(8) a. [CP2 [IP **PVE**$_i$ [IP.......... t_i........]]
b. [CP2 [IP **PVE**$_i$ [~~IP.......... t_i........~~]]

[6] At first glance, (i) seems to be an exception:
(i) [NP [*Dress kat-ta Ginza-de, tte yuu*] *uwasa*]-*o ki-ita.*
Dress bought Ginza-at Prt say rumor-ACC heard
'(I) heard the rumor that someone bought a dress on the Ginza.' Adapted from (Whitman, 2000: 465)
However, the underlined part in (i) should be regarded as direct speech, because *tte yuu* 'particle say' is usually used to quote what someone has said. (cf. Seraku, 2015)
[7] Another type of problematic example, shown in (i), is fully acceptable:
(i) [NP [CP Sonkeisiteiru] gakuseitati]-ga fueteimasu yo,
respect students -NOM increase FP
Tanaka sensei-o.
Tanaka teacher-ACC
'The number of the students who respect Mr. Tanaka is increasing.' Kamada (2013a: 459)

Under movement analyses, the PVE in (i) is purported to be extracted out of the object position within the relative clause, thereby violating the so-called complex NP constraint. For a discussion on the presence or absence of island effects observed in JPVCs, see Kamada (2009, 2013a,b), where the island effect is accounted for in terms of language processing (cf. Hagiwara & Soshi, 2004).
[8] Under a base-generation analysis, Kuno (1978) proposes that the JPVC is derived from two clauses by the ellipsis of relevant elements in each clause under an "identity condition." However, the ellipsis analysis has a critical flaw in the language processing in that the parser fails to recover the deleted "PVE" in the first clause before encountering the PVE. The same flaw is found in Takita (2011).

According to this analysis, the example in (9) is derived in the way illustrated in (10):

(9) *Kinoo Ken-ga kai-masita, **kuruma-o**.*
yesterday Ken-NOM bought car -ACC
'Ken bought a car yesterday.'

(10) a. [$_{IP}$ kinoo Ken-ga *pro* kai-masita],
[$_{IP}$ kinoo Ken-ga **kuruma-o** kai-masita]
b. kinoo Ken-ga *pro* kai-masita,
kuruma$_i$-o [$_{IP}$ kinoo Ken-ga t_i kai-masita].
c. kinoo Ken-ga *pro* kai-masita,
kuruma$_i$-o [$_{IP}$ ~~kinoo Ken-ga t_i kai-masita~~]

The example in (9) has an underlying structure as given in (10a), where an empty pronoun *pro* appears in the first clause and the PVE ***kuruma-o*** 'car-ACC' is base-generated in a canonical position in the second clause. Then, ***kuruma-o*** undergoes scrambling, and is left-adjoined to the IP in the second clause as illustrated in (10b). Finally, as shown in (10c), the remnant IP in the second clause is deleted.

Since the PVE undergoes leftward movement, it is possible to account for the absence of the RRC effect. Furthermore, Tanaka (2001) accounts for the root phenomenon by assuming that subordinate clauses cannot be repeated for certain pragmatic reasons:

(11) a. *[[*John-ga susi-o tabeta, John-ga*
John- NOM sushi-ACC ate, John- NOM
susi-o tabe-ta] *koto*]*-wa hontoo desu.*
sushi-ACC ate COMP TOP true is
'That John ate sushi is true.'
b. *[[*John-ga pro tabeta, John-ga*
John- NOM sushi-ACC ate, John- NOM
susi-o tabe-ta] *koto*]*-wa hontoo desu.*
sushi-ACC ate COMP TOP true is

Tanaka (2001) claims that (11b), which is supposed to be a source structure for (5), is ill-formed for the same reason as (11a) and that the example in (5) is hence impossible.

2.2.2 Problems with Tanaka (2001)

In this subsection, I will present three kinds of empirical problems encountered in Tanaka (2001). The first problem comes from the fact that adjuncts can appear postverbally, but they cannot undergo leftward movement (i.e., scrambling).

(12) *Ken-ga ie-o kai-masita, **sugoku ookii**.*
Ken-NOM house-ACC bought very large
'Ken bought a very large house.'

(13) ****Sugoku ookii**, Ken-ga ie-o kai-masita.*
Very large Ken-NOM house-ACC bought
'Ken bought a very large house.'

(14) *Ken-ga kai-masita, **ie-o**, **sugoku ookii**.*
Ken-NOM bought house-ACC very large
cf. *Ken-ga (*sugoku ookii) kai-masi-ta, **ie-o.***
Ken-NOM very large bought house-ACC

(15) a. *Ken-ga (**sugoku ookii**) **ie-o** kai-masita.*
Ken-NOM very large house-ACC bought
b. (***Sugoku ookii***) ***ie-o*** *Ken-ga kai-masita.*
very large Ken-NOM house-ACC bought
c. *Ken-ga **ie-o** (***sugoku ookii**) kai-masita.*
Ken-NOM house-ACC very large bought
d. ***Ie-o**, (***sugoku ookii,**) Ken-ga kai-masita.*
House-ACC very large Ken-NOM bought

Tanaka (2001) would claim that the examples in (12) and (14) are derived from sources that contain the relevant PVEs undergoing leftward movement, as in (13) and (15d).

Although examples like the one in (12) are not discussed at all in Tanaka (2001), it can be assumed that nonarguments should be scrambled such that (12) can be derived. In (13), therefore, ***sugoku ookii*** 'very large' moves leftward from a position inside the noun phrase *ie* 'house'. This movement, however, violates the Left Branch Condition (LBC), which states that an element is inhibited from moving out of the specifier position of DP/NP. That is, it is impossible to derive (13), which is a supposed source for (12). Therefore, there is no way for Tanaka's (2001) analysis to produce the acceptable example in (12).[9]

Next, let us turn to (14), where the adjunct follows the head noun. As shown in (15c, d), however, adjuncts are inhibited from following their head nouns when both the adjuncts and their heads appear preverbally. If the second clause in the source for (14) were (15d), (14) would be predicted to be unacceptable, which is not the case.

[9] An example like (12) would also challenge Simon (1989) unless the LBC is purported to be inactive in Japanese in the case of rightward movement.

Thus, as with the example in (12), (14) challenges Tanaka's (2001) analysis as well.[10]

Another problematic example is the one in (6), of which the second clause in the source might be (16):

(16) ****Kinoo*** ***karera-ga katta,*** *Taro-wa*
yesterday they-NOM bought Taro-TOP
ringo-o, *Ken-wa* *mikan-o, tabe-masita.*
apple-ACC Ken-TOP orange-ACC ate

As with (13), the relative clause is not allowed to undergo scrambling. Besides this, the underlying structure for (16) is not clear in the first place. Therefore, Tanaka (2001) cannot cope with (6).

The second problem concerns pronominal coreference.

(17) a. *Taro$_i$-no oji-ga homemasita,* ***kare$_i$-o.***
Taro-GEN uncle-NOM praised him
'Taro's uncle praised him.'
b.**Kare$_i$-o, Taro$_i$-no oji-ga t_i homemasita.*
him Taro-GEN uncle-NOM praised
'Him, Taro's uncle praised.'

In (17a), *Taro* and *kare* 'he' can be coreferential, whereas in (17b) they cannot. Tanaka (2001) would claim that the structure corresponding to the second clause in the source for (17a) should be (17b), where *kare-o* is left-adjoined to IP by scrambling. Thus, Tanaka (2001) incorrectly predicts that *Taro* cannot be an antecedent of ***kare*** in (17a).

The third problem is related to scope ambiguity.[11]

(18) a. *Dareka-ga subete-no-hon-o yomi-masita.*
someone-NOM all book-ACC read
'Someone read all books.'
someone >> all, *all >> someone
b. *Subete-no-hon-o yomi-masita,* ***dareka-ga.***
all book-ACC read someone-NOM
someone >> all, ?all >> someone

[10] Based on Merchant (2004), Watanuki (2006) claims that deletion of traces of scrambled phrases within remnant IPs makes ungrammatical extraction possible (island repair). The example in (14), however, remains to be accounted for, as the adjunct is still not allowed to follow the head noun even after the deletion of the remnant part as long as the underlying structure is biclausal (i.e., CP1 is independent of CP2).

[11] X >> Y indicates that X takes scope over Y.

In (18a), *dareka* 'someone' takes scope over *subete-no hon* 'all books', but not vice versa. By contrast, in (18b), either ***dareka*** or *subete-no-hon* may take scope over the other, although ***dareka*** preferentially takes scope over *subeteno-hon*. Since (18a) roughly corresponds to the second clause in the source, (18b) is incorrectly predicted to be unambiguous.

It may be worth noting in passing that Tanaka (2001) does not describe how to license scrambled elements, namely PVEs.

3 A Base-Generation Analysis

In the previous section, I pointed out empirical problems with movement analyses. I claim that the derivation of the JPVC involves no movement, thereby accounting for some properties peculiar to the JPVC, including the absence of the RRC effect, the split antecedent phenomenon, and scope ambiguity. In this section, I propose that PVEs are adjoined to phrases via *external Merge* (see, e.g., Chomsky, 2005), creating adjunction structures, as schematized below in (19).[12,13]

(19)

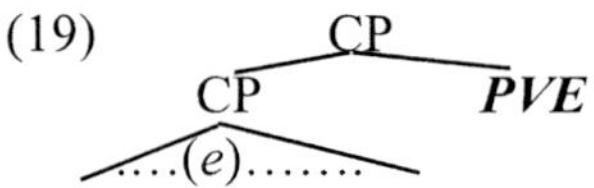

Here, I adopt the Licensing Condition (LC) originally proposed by Kamada (2015: 230), given in a slightly modified form in (20).

(20) The Licensing Condition for adjoined phrases (where X = any syntactic category):
A phrase α adjoined to XP is licensed only if α is associated with an element β such that
(i) α c-commands β, and

[12] Following Saito and Fukui (1998), I assume that order is introduced in Narrow Syntax (NS), although the Minimalist Program has assumed that there is no order in NS except for adjuncts (see Chomsky, 2004: 117ff.).

[13] Non-referential NPs (e.g., idiom chunks) can appear in a postverbal position. Hence, *pro* is inappropriate as a null argument (pace Tanaka, 2001). Accordingly, I follow Xu (1986) in proposing that the null argument *e* is underspecified, being an empty category that has no inherently specified features such as [+pronominal]. Under (21), the value of a null argument may be determined (for a discussion of functional determination of empty categories, see e.g., Chomsky, 1981, 1982; Xu, 1986; Pesetsky and Torrego, 2004; Adger and Ramchand, 2005).

(ii) α is non-distinct from β in terms of agreement-features.[14,15]

Furthermore, Kamada (2015: 230) proposes the Interpretive Rules (IRs) in (21).

(21) Interpretive Rules for adjoined phrases
Suppose that a phrase α is adjoined to XP (where X = any syntactic category) and is associated with an element β; then,
(i) α is construed as an element sharing properties with β [16] only if
a. α is an NP or a CP, and
b. α is non-distinct from β in terms of semantic features and semantic types.[17]
(ii) α is construed as a potential modifier of β only if α cannot be construed as an element sharing properties with β.

To show how the LC and the IRs apply to JPVCs, let us consider the examples in (1). In (1a), ***Taro-ga*** 'Taro-NOM' is adjoined to CP by *external Merge*, thereby c-commanding the null argument *e*. ***Taro-ga*** is non-distinct from *e* in terms of agreement features. Being associated with *e*, ***Taro-ga*** is licensed.[18] Furthermore, according to the IRs in (21), ***Taro-ga*** is construed as an argument of the verb *tabe* 'eat' because ***Taro*** and *e* are non-distinct in terms of semantic features and types. (1a) is thus acceptable. Even if ***Taro-ga*** were intended to correspond to *keiki-o* 'cake-ACC', for example, ***Taro-ga*** would not be associated with *keiki-o* (i.e., not licensed) because they have different Case features. By contrast, in the case where ***Taro-ga*** is intended to be connected with the verb *tabe*, ***Taro-ga*** is associated with the verb, which is non-distinct from ***Taro-ga*** in terms of agreement features, and hence ***Taro-ga*** is licensed. (21ii) in the IRs is applicable in this case, and thus ***Taro-ga*** is construed as a potential modifier of the verb. In Japanese, however, NPs are not allowed to modify verbs or verb phrases. It is therefore impossible to interpret ***Taro-ga*** as modifying the verb.

The example in (1b) does not contain *e*. The PVE ***kinoo*** 'yesterday' is licensed because it c-commands the VP without disagreement in terms of agreement features. (21ii) in the IRs allows the PVE to be construed as a modifier of the VP. Hence, (1b) is acceptable.

3.1 A Solution to the Problems with Movement Analyses

The base-generation of the PVE makes the RRC effect disappear. In this subsection, I consider another phenomenon that movement analyses cope with poorly. Let us first return to (12).

(12) *Ken-ga ie-o kai-masita, **sugoku ookii**.*
Ken-NOM house-ACC bought very large
'Ken bought a very large house.'

In (12), ***sugoku ookii*** 'very large' c-commands *ie-o* 'house-ACC', and they are non-distinct in terms of agreement features. Hence, the PVE is licensed. According to the IRs in (21), the PVE can be construed as a potential modifier of ***ie-o*** because ***sugoku ookii*** and *ie-o* are not non-distinct in terms of semantic features and semantic types.

Let us next re-consider (14), repeated below with a slight modification.

(14) *Ken-ga e kai-masita, **ie-o, sugoku ookii**.*
Ken-NOM bought house-ACC very large

Assume that the structure for multiple PVEs is schematized in (22), where the PVE is adjoined to CP by repeated *external Merge*.

(22)
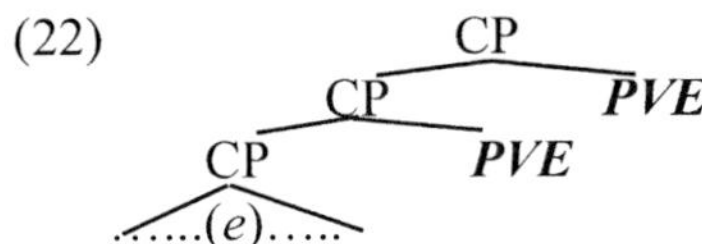

Based on (22), in (14), ***ie-o*** 'house-ACC' is licensed because it c-commands *e* and they are non-distinct in terms of agreement features. As with (1a), ***ie-o*** is construed as an argument of the verb *kau* 'buy'. As for ***sugoku ookii*** 'very large', it

[14] "Node A c-commands node B if neither A nor B dominates the other and the first branching node which dominates A dominates B." (Reinhart, 1976: 32)

[15] Agreement features include ϕ -features, Case features and honorific features.

[16] "α and β share properties including theta-roles (if any), referentiality, and semantic features/types unless semantic conflicts occur." (Kamada, 2015: 230n)

[17] "Concerning semantic types, if *α* is an NP, its semantic type may be <e> or < <e, t> t>, and if *α* is a CP, its semantic type may be <t> or <e, t>." (*ibid.*)

[18] In Kamada (2009), I propose that, in Japanese, Case features are interpretable (i.e., visible at the interfaces) only if they are morphologically realized as case particles such as *-ga* and *-o* in the phonological component. "Legibility conditions" (Chomsky, 2001) can thus be met.

c-commands ***ie-o***, and they are non-distinct in terms of agreement features. Thus, ***sugoku ookii*** is licensed. ***Sugoku ookii*** is neither an NP nor a CP, but an AP, and can hence be construed as modifying ***ie*** 'house'. (14) is therefore correctly predicted to be acceptable.

The LC in (20) and the IRs in (21) can also apply in the example in (6) where the PVE has split antecedents.[19] If the PVE in (6) merges with the topmost clause, thereby c-commanding both *ringo* 'apple' and *mikan* 'orange', it is licensed. Accordingly, the PVE can be construed as modifying *ringo* and *mikan* (see footnote 17). Concerning the coreferentiality of the pronoun *karera* 'they' with *Taro* and *Ken*, it is natural in Japanese that antecedents precede their pronoun.

Let us return to the example in (17a), reproduced as (23), where *e* is inserted.

(23) *Taro$_i$-no oji-ga e$_i$ home-masita,* ***kare$_j$-o***.
Taro-GEN uncle-NOM praised him
'Taro's uncle praised him.'

Recall that in (17a), *Taro* and *kare* 'he' can be coreferential. In (23), the PVE c-commands the null argument *e*, thereby being licensed. According to (21), the PVE is construed as an element sharing properties with *e* because they are non-distinct in terms of semantic features and semantic types.

(24) *Taro$_i$-no oji-ga kare$_i$-o home-masita.*
Taro-GEN uncle-NOM him praised

Just as *Taro* can be co-indexed with the overt pronoun *kare* in (24), so too can *Taro* be co-indexed with *e* in (23). There, the PVE ***kare*** can hence be interpreted as an element co-indexed with *Taro* (i.e., $i = j$). Note that since the PVE (i.e., ***kare-o***) in (23) occupies an A-bar position, no violation of the Binding Principle (C) occurs.

Next, let us turn to the scope ambiguity in (18b), reproduced as (25).

(25) *Subete-no-hon-o yomi-masita,* ***dareka-ga***.
all book-ACC read someone-NOM
someone >> all, ?all >> someone

Recall that as mentioned earlier, in (25), ***dareka*** 'someone' preferentially takes scope over *subeteno-hon* 'all books' but either ***dareka*** or *subete-no-hon* may take scope over the other. Before discussing this point, based on Aoun and Li (1993: 204) and Abe (2004: 57) (cf. Kural, 1997: 504), I propose a scope assignment rule in (26) to capture the fact that scrambling changes quantifier scope interpretation, as shown in (27).

(26) Scope Assignment Rule
QP_1 (quantifier phrase) may take scope over QP_2 only if (a) QP_1 c-commands QP_2 or (b) QP_1 c-commands the element co-indexed with QP_2.[20]

(27) *Subete-no-hon$_i$-o dareka-ga t$_i$ yomi-masita.*
all book-ACC someone-NOM read
someone >> all, all >> someone

In (27), the object is scrambled leftward to the initial position of the clause, and a scope ambiguity emerges. This ambiguity can be explained by the scope assignment rule in (26): *subete-no hon* 'all books' c-commands *dareka* 'someone', and hence the former takes scope over the latter in accordance with (26a); *dareka* c-commands the element co-indexed with *subete-no hon*, namely the trace of *subete-no hon*, and *dareka* can hence take wide scope in accordance with (26b).

Furthermore, the absence of ambiguity in (18a) also comes from the rule in (26). In (18a), ***dareka*** c-commands *subete-no hon*, whereas *subete-no hon* cannot c-command ***dareka***. Thus, ***dareka*** takes scope over *subete-no hon*, but not vice versa.

With this in mind, let us return to the example in (25), assuming that the structure for (25) is (25').[21] The object *subete-no hon-o* 'all books-ACC' may undergo scrambling because nothing prohibits the

[19] The coordinate structure in (i) illustrates that the PVE may be associated with more than one null argument if ***susi-o*** 'sushi-ACC' c-commands the two null arguments:
(i) *Taro-ga e tsukuri Ken-ga e tabe-masita,* ***susi-o***.
Taro-NOM make (and) Ken-NOM ate sushi-ACC
'Taro made and Ken ate sushi.'
It may be interesting to point out that in (i), the sushi that Ken ate should be the one Taro made, but in (ii), the sushi that Ken ate is not necessarily the one Taro made.
(ii) *Taro-ga susi-o tsukuri, Ken-ga susi-o tabe-masita.*
Taro-NOM sushi-ACC make (and) Ken-NOM sushi-ACC ate
'Taro made sushi and Ken ate sushi.'

[20] The element co-indexed with QP_2 may or may not be the trace of QP_2 (see Aoun and Li, 1993; Abe, 2004).

[21] As will be seen in 3.2, it is assumed that the verb is attached to the light verb, and then the complex *v* is adjoined to T at the interfaces.

object from being analyzed as a scrambled element unless syntactic principles are violated.[22]

The structure in (25') is compatible with the fact that (25) is scopally ambiguous: in (25'), the PVE c-commands the scrambled object *subete-no hon*, and the scrambled NP c-commands the null argument *e* that is co-indexed with the PVE via the IRs, which leads to the scope ambiguity in (25).

(25')

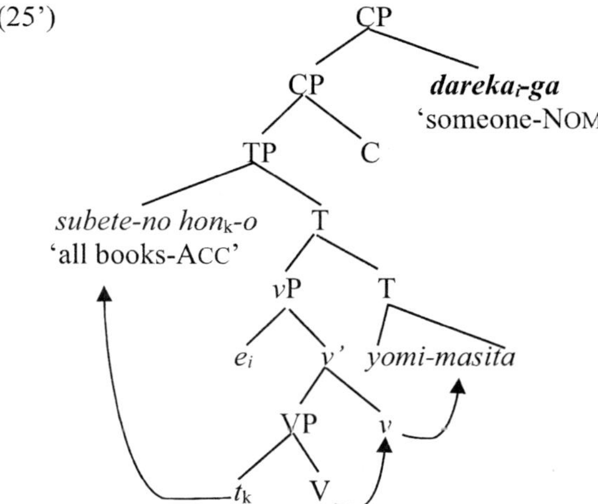

3.2 Interface Conditions

The proposed analysis thus far does not prohibit the PVE from adjoining to any projection via *external Merge* unless such adjunction is incompatible with bare phrase structure. As the examples in (28a, b) show, however, the PVE is not allowed to adjoin to *v*P or to TP. Before addressing this problem, I will discuss the head movement in detail.

(28) a. [*v*P adjunction] Impossible
*[$_{vP}$[$_{vP}$ *Ken-ga e tabe*] ***susi-o***] *-masita ka.*
Ken-NOM eat sushi-ACC -PAST Q
'Did Ken eat sushi?'
b. [TP adjunction] Impossible
*[$_{TP}$ [$_{vP}$ *Ken-ga e tabe*]*-masita*] ***susi-o*** *ka.*
Ken-NOM eat - PAST sushi-ACC Q
c. [CP adjunction] Possible
[$_{CP}$ [$_{TP}$[$_{vP}$ *Ken-ga e tabe*]*-masita*] *ka*] ***susi-o***
Ken-NOM eat- PAST Q sushi-ACC

[22] It is assumed that in Japanese, if necessary, nominative Case checking should be done in the specifier of *v*P without movement to the specifier of TP (see footnote 18, cf. Fukui, 1995; Kuroda, 1992). That is, a subject does not move to the specifier position of TP unless T has an EPP feature (cf. Miyagawa, 2001).

Let us first suppose that there are morphological restrictions on functional heads such as T. Based on the basic idea advanced in Stowell (1995: 278), I propose a condition on Tense as formulated in (29), which states that Tense must be amalgamated with the Verb at the interfaces. In other words, Tense can be given a proper interpretation only if Tense and the Verb amalgamate.

(29) The Output Condition on T (= Tense):[23]
T (= Tense) must be amalgamated with V at the interfaces—i.e., PHON and SEM.
(cf. Sakai, 2002: 5)

The amalgamation of T with V is realized on the assumption that V moves to T, as given in (30).

(30) V moves to T (= Tense) (Chomsky, 1986)

It is possible that complementizers in Japanese (e.g., *-ka, -to, -no, -koto*) may be regarded as bound morphemes just like the past tense morpheme *-masita* and morphological case particles such as *-ga*, because they cannot stand by themselves (cf. Whitman, 2000: 465). I therefore propose the following output condition on complementizers formulated in such a way that complementizers can be given a proper interpretation at the interfaces.

(31) The Output Condition on COMP in Japanese
A complementizer (COMP) that is phonetically non-null must be amalgamated with V adjoined to T at the interfaces.

Following van Riemsdijk (1998), I also adopt the Head Adjacency Principle as given in (32).

(32) The Head Adjacency Principle (HAP)[24]
A transformation process that affects two head positions must be Head Adjunction.

[23] PHON and SEM are interface levels; the former comprises phonetic forms accessed by sensorimotor systems and the latter comprises semantic forms accessed by conceptual-intentional systems.

[24] The complete definition of HAP given in van Riemsdijk (1998: 645) adds Head Substitution: "a head is moved into head position which is phonetically empty but which may contain Φ-features, thereby unifying the two morphosyntactic feature matrices."

Head Adjunction: Two phonetically identified [=realized] heads are joined, yielding an adjunction structure, in which case the two heads must be strictly linearly adjacent at the moment of application of the rule.
Adapted from (van Riemsdijk, 1998: 644-645)

Let us now return to the question of the syntactic position of the PVE. As shown above in (28), the PVE is not allowed to adjoin to *v*P or to TP.

In (28a), ***susi-o*** 'sushi-ACC' is adjoined to *v*P by *external Merge* as diagrammed in (33a), where the PVE intervenes between the verb *tabe* 'eat' and the past morpheme *-masita*. The verb cannot move to T because the HAP is not observed, and hence a violation of the output condition in (29) occurs.

In (28b), the PVE is adjoined to TP by *external Merge* as illustrated in (33b). There, the question particle *ka* is merged with TP, but the past tense morpheme amalgamated with the verb cannot move to the particle *-ka* because the PVE intervenes between them, and hence the output condition in (31) is violated.

(33) a. [TP[vP[vP *Ken-ga e tabe*] ***susi-o***]*-masita*] *ka*.

b. [TP[vP *Ken-ga e tabe*]*-masita*] ***susi-o*** *ka*.

c. [CP [TP[vP *Ken-ga e tabe*]*-masita*] *ka*] ***susi-o***

In (28c), the PVE is adjoined to CP by *external Merge* as given in (33c). The verb can move to T, and subsequently to C, because there are no elements intervening between the verb, T, and C. Thus, the interface conditions in (29) and (31) are satisfied, and the example is acceptable unless other principles are violated. Therefore, the system assumed here can account for why the PVE can never adjoin to *v*P or to TP.

It is worth noting in passing that if the verb moves to T and C before the PVE is adjoined to *v*P or TP (see e.g., Koizumi, 2000 for a discussion of head movement in Narrow Syntax), the above argument would be untenable. However, it remains possible to explain why the PVE can adjoin neither to *v*P nor to TP, if one follows Chomsky (1995) in adopting a condition on *external Merge* called the Extension Condition, as formulated in (34):

(34) Extension Condition (EC):
External Merge always applies at the root only.
Adapted from (Chomsky, 1995: 248)

The EC successfully excludes the possibility that the PVE adjoins to *v*P or TP after verb movement takes place. That is, if the verb moves to T and the PVE is subsequently adjoined to *v*P by *external Merge*, then the EC is violated because the *v*P at which *Merge* applied is no longer a root. The same is true in the case of TP-adjunction: the TP at which *Merge* could apply is not a root after it is merged with the C to which the verb moves. Therefore, whether or not verb movement takes place in Narrow Syntax, it is possible to rule out the adjunction of the PVE to *v*P and to TP.

3.3 A Root Phenomenon

PVEs cannot appear within subordinate clauses, as observed in (5), reproduced below with a slight modification.

(5) *[CP *John-ga e tabe-ta* ***susi–o*** *koto*] *-wa*
John-NOM eat-PAST sushi-ACC COMP-TOP
hontoo desu.
true is

The Output Condition in (31) requires that *koto* 'COMP' should be amalgamated with the complex T *tabe-ta* 'eat-PAST'. This amalgamation, however, is impossible due to the presence of ***susi-o*** between the two relevant elements. Hence, (5) violates (31). This is why the JPVC is restricted to a root clause.

4 Conclusion

In this paper, I demonstrated that properties specific to JPVCs such as a root phenomenon and split antecedency, which are poorly dealt with by movement analyses, receive a better account in terms of the LC, the IRs, and the interface conditions, claiming that the PVE is adjoined to preceding phrases via *external Merge*.

Acknowledgments

This work was supported by JSPS KAKENHI Grant Number 26370439. I would like to thank Masahiro Akiyama, Kazuaki Ezure and Tsuguro Nakamura as well as the three PACLIC 30 reviewers for their valuable comments.

References

Abe, Jun. 2004. On Directionality of Movement: A Case of Japanese Right Dislocation. Proceedings of the 58th Conference, The Tohoku English Literary Society, 54-61.

Adger, David and Gillian Ramchand. 2005. Merge and Move: Wh-Dependencies Revisited. Linguistic Inquiry 36, 161-193.

Aoun, Joseph and Yen-hui Audrey Li. 1993. Wh-movements in situ: Syntax or LF? Linguistic Inquiry 24: 199-238.

Chomsky, Noam. 1981. Lectures on Government and Binding. Dordrecht: Foris.

Chomsky, Noam. 1982. Some Concepts and Consequences of the Theory of Government and Binding. Cambridge, Mass.: MIT Press.

Chomsky, Noam. 1986. Barriers. Cambridge MA: The MIT Press.

Chomsky, Noam. 1995. The Minimalist Program. Cambridge, Mass.: MIT Press.

Chomsky, Noam. 2001. Derivation by Phase. In Michael Kenstowicz, (ed.) Ken Hale: A life in language. Cambridge, Mass: MIT Press. pp. 1-52.

Chomsky, Noam. 2004. Beyond Explanatory Adequacy. In Adriana Belletti (ed.), Structures and Beyond: The Cartography of Syntactic Structures, Volume 3. Oxford: Oxford University Press. pp. 104-131.

Chomsky, Noam. 2005. Three Factors in Language Design." Linguistic Inquiry 36, 1-22.

Endo, Yoshio. 1996. Right Dislocation. In Masatoshi Koizumi, Masayuki Oishi and Uli Sauerland (eds.), Formal Approaches to Japanese Linguistics 2, MIT Working Papers in Linguistics 29. Cambridge: Department of Linguistics, MIT. pp. 1-20.

Fukui, Naoki. 1995. Theory of Projection in Syntax. California: CSLI.

Heim, Irene and Angelika Kratzer. 1998. Semantics in Generative Grammar. Oxford: Blackwell.

Kaiser, Lizanne. 1999. Representing the Structure-Discourse Iconicity of the Japanese Post-Verbal Construction. In Darnell, Michael, Edith Moravcsik, Frederic Newmeyer, Michael Noonan, and Kathleen Wheatley (eds.), Functionalism and Formalism in Linguistics, Volume II: Case Studies. Amsterdam: John Benjamins Publishing Company. pp. 107-129.

Kamada, Kohji. 2009. Rightward Movement Phenomena in Human Language. Doctoral dissertation, the University of Edinburgh.

Kamada, Kohji. 2013a. The Island Effect in Postverbal Constructions in Japanese. Proceedings of the 27th Pacific Asia Conference on Language, Information and Computation (PACLIC 27): 459-466.

Kamada, Kohji. 2013b. Nihongo Kouchi Koubun to Gengo Shori [Japanese Postverbal Constructions and Language Processing]. Sophia Linguistica 61: 165-185.

Kamada, Kohji. 2015. English Right Dislocation. Proceedings of the 29th Pacific Asia Conference on Language, Information and Computation (PACLIC 29), 225-234.

Koizumi, Masatoshi. 2000. String Vacuous Overt Verb Rasing. Journal of East Asian Linguistics 9, 227-285.

Kuno, Susumu. 1978. Danwa no Bunpo (Discourse Grammar), Tokyo: Taishukan.

Kural, Murat. 1997. Postverbal Constituents in Turkish and the Linear Correspondence Axiom. Linguistic Inquiry 28, 498-519.

Kuroda, Shigeyuki. 1992. Japanese Syntax and Semantics, Collected Papers. Dordrecht: Kluwer Academic Publishers.

Kurogi, Akito. 2006. Nihongo Uhooten-ibun no kozoo ni tsuite: Sahooidoobunseki no kantenkara. (On Japanese Right Dislocation: from the point of view of a leftward movement analysis). Scientific Approaches to Language 5, Centre for Language Sciences, Kanda University of International Studies. pp. 213-231.

Merchant, Jason. 2004. Fragments and ellipsis. Linguistics and Philosophy 27.6: 661-738.

Miyagawa, Shigeru. 2001. The EPP, Scrambling, and Wh-in-Situ." In Michael Kenstowicz, (ed.) Ken Hale: A life in language. Cambridge, Mass: MIT Press. pp. 293-338.

Pesetsky, David and Esther Torrego. 2004. Tense, Case, and the Nature of Syntactic Categories. In Jacqueline Guéron and Jacqueline Lecarme (eds.), Syntax of Time. Cambridge, MA: MIT Press. pp. 495-537.

Reinhart, Tanya. 1976. The Syntactic Domain of Anaphora. Doctoral dissertation, MIT.

Ross, John, R. 1986. Infinite Syntax!, New Jersey: Ablex.

Saito, Mamoru and Naoki Fukui. 1998. Order in Phrase Structure and Movement. Linguistic Inquiry 29, 439-474.

Sakai, Hiromu. 2002. Seibutsugengogaku apuroochi-no kanoosei (The possibility of a biolinguistic approach). Handout of talk at the symposium titled ''Kokoro-no Kagakutosite-no Gengo Kenkyu (Linguistic research as a science of mind). at Kyushu University, 31 July 2002.

Seraku, Tohru 2015. A Dynamic Syntax Modelling of Postposing in Japanese Narratives. Proceedings of the 29th Pacific Asia Conference on Language, Information and Computation (PACLIC 29), 124-132.

Simon, Endo, Mutsuko. 1989. An analysis of the postposing construction in Japanese, Doctoral Dissertation, the University of Michigan.

Soshi, Takahiro and Hiroko Hagiwara. 2004. Asymmetry in Linguistic Dependency: Linguistic and Psychophysiological Studies of Japanese Right Dislocation. English Linguistics 21-2, 409-453.

Stowell, Tim. 1995 The Phrase Structure of Tense. In Johan Rooryck and Laurie Zaring (eds.) Phrase Structure and the Lexicon (Studies in Natural Language and Linguistic Theory). Dordrecht: Kluwer Academic Publishers, pp. 277-291.

Takita, Kensuke. 2011. Argument Ellipsis in Japanese Right Dislocation. In William McClure and Marcel den Dickken (eds.) Japanese/Korean Linguistics 18. Stanford CA: CSLI Publications, pp. 380-391.

Takano, Yuji. 2014. A Comparative Approach to Japanese Postposing. In Mamoru Saito (ed.) Japanese Syntax in Comparative Perspective. New York: Oxford University Press, pp. 139-180.

Tanaka, Hidekazu. 2001. Right-Dislocation as scrambling. Journal of Linguistics 37, 551-579.

van Riemsdijk, Henk. 1998. Head movement and adjacency. Natural Language and Linguistic Theory 16, 633-678.

Watanuki, Keiko. 2006. Nihongo-no Koochibun (Japanese postposing construction). Scientific Approaches to Language 5, Center for Language Sciences, Kanda University of International Studies. pp. 251-268.

Whitman, John. 2000. Right Dislocation in English and Japanese. In Ken-ichi Takami, Akio Kamio, and John Whitman (eds.) Syntactic and Functional Explorations in Honor of Susumu Kuno. Tokyo: Kuroshio Publishers, pp. 445-470.

Xu, Liejion. 1986. Free Empty Category. Linguistic Inquiry 17, 75-93.

Sentence Clustering using PageRank Topic Model

Kenshin Ikegami
Department of Systems Innovation
The University of Tokyo
Tokyo, Japan
kenchin110100@gmail.com

Yukio Ohsawa
Department of Systems Innovation
The University of Tokyo
Tokyo, Japan
ohsawa@sys.t.u-tokyo.ac.jp

Abstract

The clusters of review sentences on the viewpoints from the products' evaluation can be applied to various use. The topic models, for example Unigram Mixture (UM), can be used for this task. However, there are two problems. One problem is that topic models depend on the randomly-initialized parameters and computation results are not consistent. The other is that the number of topics has to be set as a preset parameter. To solve these problems, we introduce PageRank Topic Model (PRTM), that approximately estimates multinomial distributions over topics and words in a vocabulary using network structure analysis methods to Word Co-occurrence Graphs. In PRTM, an appropriate number of topics is estimated using the Newman method from a Word Co-occurrence Graph. Also, PRTM achieves consistent results because multinomial distributions over words in a vocabulary are estimated using PageRank and a multinomial distribution over topics is estimated as a convex quadratic programming problem. Using two review datasets about hotels and cars, we show that PRTM achieves consistent results in sentence clustering and an appropriate estimation of the number of topics for extracting the viewpoints from the products' evaluation.

1 Introduction

Many people buy products through electronic commerce and Internet auction site. Consumers have to use products' detailed information for decision making in purchasing because they cannot see the real products. In particular, reviews from other consumers give them useful information because reviews contain consumers' experience in practical use. Also, reviews are useful for providers of products or services to measure the consumers' satisfaction.

In our research, we focus on generating clusters of review sentences on the viewpoints from the products' evaluation. For example, reviews of home electric appliance are usually written based on the following the viewpoints: performance, design, price, etc. If we generate clusters of the review sentences on these viewpoints, the clusters can be applied to various uses. For example, if we extract representative expressions from clusters of sentences, we can summarize reviews briefly. This is useful because some products have thousands of reviews and hard to be read and understood.

There are various methods to generate clusters of sentences. Among several methods, we adopt probabilistic generative models for sentence clustering because the summarizations of clusters can be represented as word distributions. Probabilistic generative models are the methods that assume underlying probabilistic distributions generating observed data, and that estimate the probabilistic distributions from the observed data. In language modeling, these are called topic models.

Latent Dirichlet Allocation (LDA) (Blei et al., 2003) is a well-known topic model used in document clustering. LDA represents each document as a mixture of topics. A topic means a multinomial distribution over words in a vocabulary.

Unigram Mixture (UM) (Nigam et al., 2000) assumes that each document is generated by a multinomial distribution over words in a vocabulary, $\phi_k = (\phi_{k1}, \cdots, \phi_{kV})$, where V denotes the size of vocabulary and ϕ_{kv} denotes the appearance probability of v-th term in the k-th topic. UM estimates a multinomial distribution over topics, $\boldsymbol{\theta} = (\theta_1, \cdots, \theta_K)$, where θ_k denotes the appearance probability of k-th topic. After all, K+1 multinomial distributions, $\boldsymbol{\theta}$ and $\boldsymbol{\phi} = (\phi_1, \cdots, \phi_K)$ are estimated from the observed data, where K denotes the number of topics.

Using estimated $\boldsymbol{\theta}$ and $\boldsymbol{\phi}$, the probability that a document is generated from ϕ_k is calculated. This probability determines the clusters of the sentences.

In UM, $\boldsymbol{\theta}$ and $\boldsymbol{\phi}$ can be estimated by iterative computation. However, since $\boldsymbol{\theta}$ and $\boldsymbol{\phi}$ are initialized randomly, computation results are not consistent. In addition to this, the number of topics K has to be set as a preset parameter.

To estimate the appropriate number of topics, the average cosine distance ($AveDis$) of each pair of topics can be used (Cao et al., 2009). This measure is based on the assumption that better topic distributions have fewer overlapping words. However, to estimate the appropriate number of topics based on this measure, we need to set several numbers of topics and it takes much time to calculate.

In this paper, we introduce PageRank Topic Model (PRTM) to consistently estimate $\boldsymbol{\phi}$ and $\boldsymbol{\theta}$ using Word Co-occurrence Graphs. PRTM consists of 4 steps as follows:

1. Convert corpus W into a Word Co-occurrence Graph G_w.
2. Divide graph G_w into several communities.
3. Measure PageRank in each community and estimate multinomial distributions over words in a vocabulary $\boldsymbol{\phi}$.
4. Estimate a multinomial distribution over topics $\boldsymbol{\theta}$ as a convex quadratic programming problem assuming the linearity of $\boldsymbol{\phi}$.

Network structures have been applied to several Natural Language Processing tasks (Ohsawa et al., 1998) (Bollegala et al., 2008). For example, synonyms can be identified using network community detection method, e.g. the Newman method (Clauset et al., 2004) (Sakaki et al., 2007). In this research, we also apply the Newman method to detect communities of co-occurrence words in step 2. In step 3, we calculate the appearance probability of nodes using PageRank (Brin and Page, 1998). PageRank is the appearance probability of nodes in a network. In Word Co-occurrence Graph G_w, each node represents a word. Therefore, we regard a set of PageRank of nodes as $\boldsymbol{\phi}$. After that, $\boldsymbol{\theta}$ is estimated using a convex quadratic programming problem based on the assumption of the linearity of $\boldsymbol{\phi}$ in step 4. From these steps, reproducible $\boldsymbol{\phi}$, $\boldsymbol{\theta}$ and clustering results can be obtained because the Newman method, PageRank and the convex quadratic programming problem are not depending on random initialization of parameters.

There is another advantage to identify communities of co-occurrence words using the Newman method. The Newman method yields an optimized number of communities K in the sense it extracts communities to maximize Modularity Q. Modularity Q is one measure of the strength of division of a network structure into several communities. When modularity Q is maximized, the graph is expected to be divided into an appropriate number of communities.

Our main contributions are summarized as follows:

- Using PRTM, we estimate consistent multinomial distributions over topics and words. It enables us to get consistent computation results of sentence clustering.
- PRTM yields an appropriate number of topics, K, as well as the other parameters. It is more suitable to estimate the number of viewpoints from the products' evaluation than the average cosine distance measurement.

In this paper, we first explain our proposed method, PRTM, in section 2. We show the experimental results in section 3 and compare with related works in section 4. At last, we discuss our conclusions in section 5.

2 Proposed Method

In this section, we explain the Newman method and PageRank in subsection 2.1, 2.2. After that, we show our proposed method, PageRank Topic Model, in subsection 2.3.

2.1 Newman method

The Newman method is a method to detect several communities from a network structure (Clauset et al., 2004). The method puts together nodes to maximize Modularity Q. Modularity Q is defined as follows:

$$Q = \sum_{i=1}^{K}(e_{ii} - a_i^2) \quad (1)$$

where K is the number of communities, e_{ii} is the ratio of the number of edges in the i-th community to the total number of edges in the network, a_i is the ratio of the number of edges the i-th community from the other communities to the total number of edges in the network.

Modularity Q represents the density of connections between the nodes within communities. Therefore, the higher the Modularity Q is, the more accuratly the network is divided into communities. In the Newman method, communities are extracted by the following steps:

1. Assign each node to a community.
2. Calculate the increment in Modularity ΔQ when any two communities are merged into one community.
3. Merge the two communities, that score the highest ΔQ in the previous process, into one community.
4. Repeat step 2 and step 3 as long as Q increases.

2.2 PageRank

PageRank (Brin and Page, 1998) is the algorithm to measure the importance of each node in a network structure. It has been applied to evaluating the importance of websites in the World Wide Web. In PageRank, the transition probability matrix $H \in \mathbb{R}_+^{V \times V}$ is generated from network structure, where V denotes the number of nodes. H_{ij} represents the transition probability from node n_i to node n_j, a ratio of the number of edges from node n_i to node n_j to the total number of edges from node n_i. However, if node n_i does not have outgoing edges (dangling node), node n_i does not have transition to any other nodes. To solve this problem, matrix H is extended to matrix $G \in \mathbb{R}_+^{V \times V}$ as follows:

$$G = dH + (1-d)\frac{1}{V}\mathbf{1}^T\mathbf{1} \quad (2)$$

where d is a real number within [0, 1] and $\mathbf{1} \in \{1\}^V$. PageRank of node n_i, i.e. $PR(n_i)$, is calculated using matrix G as follows:

$$\boldsymbol{R}^T = \boldsymbol{R}^T G \quad (3)$$

where $\boldsymbol{R} = (PR(n_i), \cdots, PR(n_V))^T$. Equation (3) can be solved with the simultaneous linear equations or the power method.

2.3 PageRank Topic Model

In this subsection, we explain our proposed method, PageRank Topic Model (PRTM), to estimate a multinomial distribution over topics $\boldsymbol{\theta}$ and words in a vocabulary $\boldsymbol{\phi}$ using a Word Co-occurrence Graph. PRTM consists of 4 steps as shown in section 1. We explain them by following these steps.

Step 1: First, we convert a dataset into a bag of words. Each bag represents a sentence in the dataset. We define Word Co-occurrence Graph $G_w(V, E)$ as an undirected weighted graph where each vocabulary v_i is represented by a node $n_i \in V$. An edge $e_{ij} \in E$ is created between node n_i and node n_j if v_i and v_j co-occur in the bag of words.

Step 2: We apply the Newman method to graph G_w to extract communities $Com^{(k)}$, where $k = 1, \cdots, K$ and K denotes the number of communities. $Com^{(k)}$ is a set of nodes in G_w. From this results, we generate Word Co-occurrence SubGraph $G_w^{(k)}(V^{(k)}, E^{(k)})$. Although $V^{(k)}$ is the same as V of G_w, an edge $e_{ij}^{(k)} \in E^{(k)}$ is created if node n_i or n_j exists in $Com^{(k)}$. Figure 1 shows the relationship between $Com^{(k)}$ and $G_w^{(k)}$.

Step 3: We measure the importance of each node in $G_w^{(k)}$ with PageRank. Page et al. (1999) explained PageRank by the random surfer model. A random surfer is a person who opens a browser to any page and starts following hyperlinks. PageRank can be interpreted as the probability of a random surfer existence in nodes. In this case, a node $n_i^{(k)}$ represents vocabulary v_i. Therefore $PR(n_i^{(k)})$ represents the

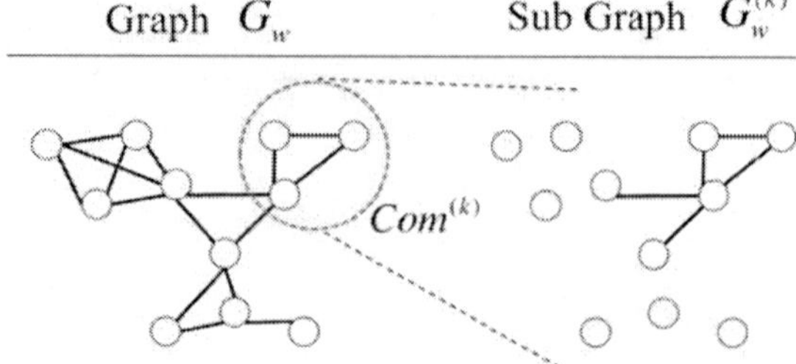

Figure 1: The relationship between $Com^{(k)}$ and $G_w^{(k)}$

appearance probability of word v_i in $G_w^{(k)}$. We regard $G_w^{(k)}$ as k-th topic and define multinomial distributions over words in a vocabulary ϕ_k as follows:

$$\begin{aligned} \phi_k &= (\phi_{k1}, \cdots, \phi_{kV}) \\ &= (PR(n_1^{(k)}), \cdots, PR(n_V^{(k)})) \end{aligned} \tag{4}$$

Step 4: We estimate a multinomial distribution over topics $\boldsymbol{\theta}$ using $\boldsymbol{\phi}$, that is estimated in Step 3. To estimate $\boldsymbol{\theta}$, we assume the linearity of $\boldsymbol{\phi}$ as follows:

$$\phi_{\cdot v} = \sum_{k=1}^{K} \phi_{kv}\theta_k \tag{5}$$

where $\phi_{\cdot v}$ denotes the appearance probability of v-th term in graph G_w. However, it is impossible to estimate a θ_k that satisfies Equation (5) in all of words in a vocabulary because each ϕ_k is independently estimated using PageRank.

Therefore, we estimate θ_k minimizing the following equation:

$$\begin{aligned} &\arg\min_{\boldsymbol{\theta}} L \\ &= \arg\min_{\boldsymbol{\theta}} \sum_{v}^{V} (\phi_{\cdot v} - \sum_{k=1}^{K} \phi_{kv}\theta_k)^2 \\ &\text{s.t. } \|\boldsymbol{\theta}\| = 1, \boldsymbol{\theta} \geq 0 \end{aligned} \tag{6}$$

By reformulating Equation (6), the following equation can be obtained:

$$\begin{aligned} &\arg\min_{\boldsymbol{\theta}} L \\ &= \arg\min_{\boldsymbol{\theta}} \frac{1}{2}\boldsymbol{\theta}^T Q \boldsymbol{\theta} + c^T \boldsymbol{\theta} \\ &\text{s.t. } \|\boldsymbol{\theta}\| = 1, \boldsymbol{\theta} \geq 0 \end{aligned} \tag{7}$$

where the (i, j)-th element of matrix $Q \in \mathbb{R}^{K \times K}$ denotes $2\boldsymbol{\phi}_i{}^T \boldsymbol{\phi}_j$ and the i-th element of vector c denotes $-2\boldsymbol{\phi}_{\cdot}{}^T \boldsymbol{\phi}_i$.

Equation (7) is formulated as a convex quadratic programming problem, of which a global optimum solution should be obtained.

The probability that document d is generated from k-th topic, i.e. $p(z_d = k|w_d)$, is calculated as follows:

$$\begin{aligned} p(z_d = k|w_d) &= \frac{p(w_d|k)p(k)}{\sum_{k'=1}^{K} p(w_d|k')p(k')} \\ &= \frac{\theta_k \prod_{v=1}^{V} \phi_{kv}^{N_{dv}}}{\sum_{k'=1}^{K} \theta_{k'} \prod_{v=1}^{V} \phi_{k'v}^{N_{dv}}} \end{aligned} \tag{8}$$

where N_{dv} denotes the number of v-th term in document d.

3 Experiments

In this section, we show the evaluation results of PRTM using real-world text data in comparison with UM and LDA. In subsection 3.1, we explain our test datasets and the measure used to evaluate sentence clustering accuracy. Furthermore, we present the conditions of UM and LDA in the same subsection. We show topic examples estimated by PRTM, UM, and LDA in subsection 3.2. In subsection 3.3, we compare the sentence clustering accuracy of PRTM with that of UM and LDA. In addition, we compare the estimated number of topics of PRTM with that of the average cosine distance measurement in subsection 3.4.

3.1 Preparation for Experiment

In the experiments, we used the following two datasets:

Hotel Reviews: This is Rakuten Travel[1] Japanese review dataset and has been published by Rakuten, Inc. In this dataset, there are 4309 sentences of 1000 reviews. We tokenized them using Japanese morphological analyzer, mecab[2], and selected nouns and adjectives. It contains a vocabulary of 3780 words and 19401 word tokens. During preprocessing, we removed high-frequency words appearing more than 300 times and low frequency words appearing less

[1] http://travel.rakuten.co.jp/
[2] http://taku910.github.io/mecab/

than two times. The sentences of this dataset were classified by two annotators. The annotators (humans) were asked to classify each sentence into six categories; "Service", "Room", "Location", "Facility and Amenity", "Bathroom", and "Food". We adopted these six categories because Rakuten Travel website scores hotels by these six evaluation viewpoints. In evaluation of sentence clustering accuracy, we used 2000 sentences from the total sentences which both the annotators classified into the same category.

Car Reviews: This is Edmunds[3] Car English review dataset and has been published by the " Opinion Based Entity Ranking " project (Ganesan and Zhai, 2011). In this dataset, there are 7947 reviews in 2009, out of which we randomly selected 600 reviews consisting of 3933 sentences. We tokenized them using English morphological analyzer, Stanford CoreNLP[4], and selected nouns, adjectives and verbs. It contains a vocabulary of 3975 words and 27385 word tokens. During preprocessing, we removed high-frequency words appearing more than 300 times and low frequency words appearing less than two times. All of the 3922 sentences were classified into eight categories by two annotators; "Fuel", "Interior", "Exterior", "Build", "Performance", "Comfort", "Reliability" and "Fun". We adopted these eight categories for the same reason as Hotel Review. There are 1148 sentences which both annotators classified into the same category and we used them in the evaluation of sentence clustering accuracy.

Evaluation: We measured Purity, Inverse Purity and their F_1 score for sentence clustering evaluation (Zhao and Karypis, 2001). Purity focuses on the frequency of the most common category into each cluster. Purity is calculated as follows:

$$Purity = \sum_i \frac{|C_i|}{n} \max_j Precision(C_i, L_j) \quad (9)$$

where C_i is the set of i-th cluster, L_j is the set of j-th given category and n denotes the number of samples. $Precision(C_i, L_j)$ is defined as:

$$Precision(C_i, L_j) = \frac{|C_i \cap L_j|}{|C_i|} \quad (10)$$

[3]http://www.edmunds.com/

[4]http://stanfordnlp.github.io/CoreNLP/

However, if we make one cluster per sample, we reach a maximum purity value. Therefore we also measured Inverse Purity. Inverse Purity focuses on the cluster with maximum recall for each category and is defined as follows:

$$InversePurity = \sum_j \frac{|L_j|}{n} \max_i Precision(L_j, C_i) \quad (11)$$

In this experiment, we used the harmonic mean of Purity and Inverse Purity, F_1 score, as clustering accuracy. F_1 score is calculated as follows:

$$F_1 = \frac{2 \times Purity \times InversePurity}{Purity + InversePurity} \quad (12)$$

Estimation of number of topics: To estimate the appropriate number of topics, we used the average cosine distance measurement ($AveDis$) (Cao et al., 2009). $AveDis$ is calculated using the multinomial distributions ϕ as follows:

$$corre(\phi_i, \phi_j) = \frac{\sum_{v=0}^{V} \phi_{iv}\phi_{jv}}{\sqrt{\sum_{v=0}^{V}(\phi_{iv})^2}\sqrt{\sum_{v=0}^{V}(\phi_{jv})^2}}$$
$$AveDis = \frac{\sum_{i=0}^{K}\sum_{j=i+1}^{K} corre(\phi_i, \phi_j)}{K \times (K-1)/2} \quad (13)$$

where V denote the number of words in a vocabulary and K denotes the number of topics.

If topic i and j are not similar, $corre(\phi_i, \phi_j)$ becomes smaller. Therefore, when the appropriate number of topics K is preset, that is all the topics have different word distributions, $AveDis$ becomes smaller.

Comparative Methods and Settings: We compared PRTM with UM and LDA in the experiments. UM can be calculated using several methods: EM algorithm (Dempster et al., 1977), Collapsed Gibbs sampling (Liu, 1994) (Yamamoto and Sadamitsu, 2005), or Collapsed Variational Baysian (Teh et al., 2006). In our experiments, topic and word distributions θ, ϕ were estimated using Collapsed Gibbs sampling for both the UM and LDA models. The hyper-parameter for all the Dirichlet distributions were set at 0.01 and were updated at every iteration. We stopped iterative computations when the difference of likelihood between steps got lower than 0.01.

cluster1			cluster2		
PRTM	UM	LDA	PRTM	UM	LDA
breakfast	breakfast	breakfast	bath	bath	breakfast
satisfaction	meal	satisfaction	wide	wide	service
very	satisfaction	support	care	care	absent
service	delicious	convenient	comfortable	good	location
meal	delicious	absent	big bath	absent	satisfaction
cluster3			**cluster4**		
PRTM	UM	LDA	PRTM	UM	LDA
good	station	breakfast	support	support	breakfast
location	convenient	reception	reception	reception	good
station	close	support	feeling	staff	satisfaction
cheap	location	satisfaction	reservation	check-in	very
fee	convenience-store	bath	good	kindness	shame
cluster5			**cluster6**		
PRTM	UM	LDA	PRTM	UM	LDA
different	reservation	support	absent	satisfaction	breakfast
bathing	plan	satisfaction	other	opportunity	wide
bathroom	non-smoking	breakfast	people	wide	station
difficult	preparation	reception	preparation	business-trip	absent
illumination	breakfast	very	voice	very	care

Table 1: Top 5th terms in each topic by PRTM, UM, and LDA. Each term has been translated from Japanese to English using Google translation.

3.2 Topic Examples

We used Hotel Reviews dataset and estimated words distributions ϕ by PRTM, UM, and LDA. All of the PRTM, UM, and LDA were given the number of topics $K = 6$.

In Table 1, we show the terms of top fifth appearance probabilities in each topic estimated. As we can see, PRTM and UM contain similar terms in cluster 1, 2, 3, and 4. For example, in cluster 1, both of PRTM and UM have terms, "breakfast" and "meal". Therefore its topic seems to be "Food." On the other hand, there are the same terms, "support" and "reception", in cluster 4. This topic seems to represent "Service." However, in LDA, the estimation seems to fail because all of the topics have similar words (e.g. the word "breakfast" exists in all the topics.) For these reasons, it is more suitable to assume that each sentence has one topic than to assume that it has multiple topics.

3.3 Sentence Clustering Accuracy

We evaluated sentence clustering accuracy comparing PRTM with UM and LDA on Hotel Review and Car Review datasets. By changing the number of topics K from 3 to 20, we trained topics and word distributions $\boldsymbol{\theta}$, ϕ with PRTM, UM, and LDA. We generated clusters of sentences by Equation (8) in PRTM and UM. In LDA, we decided the cluster of sentence using topic distributions of each sentence. The sentence clustering accuracy was evaluated by F_1 score on Purity and Inverse Purity. F_1 scores of UM and LDA were the mean values of the tests running ten times, because the computation results vary depending on randomly initialized $\boldsymbol{\theta}$ and ϕ.

We present sentence clustering accuracy for all the PRTM, UM, and LDA in Figure 2. As shown in Figure 2, PRTM outperformed UM when the number of topics is more than six in both the Hotel and Car Review datasets. For UM, F_1 score became highest when K was small and gradually decreased when K became larger. On the other hand,

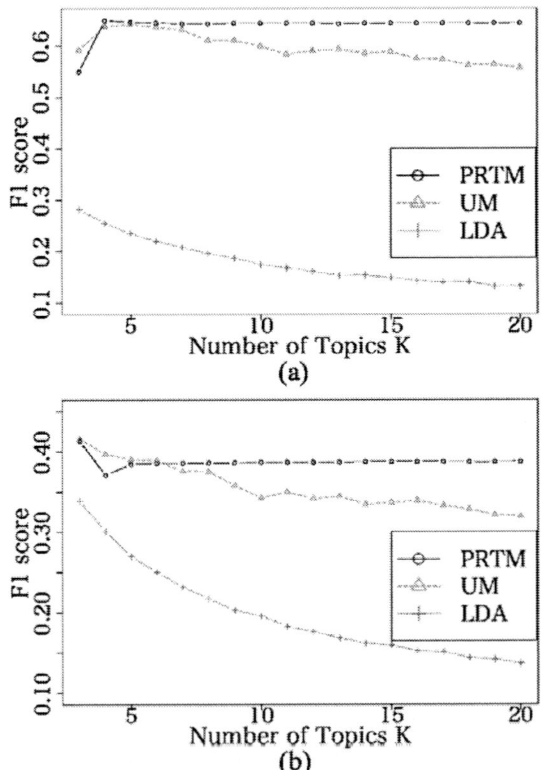

Figure 2: F_1 score comparison with different numbers of topics. (a) Hotel Reviews. (b) Car Reviews.

Number of Topics $K = 6$		
θ_k	PRTM	UM
θ_1	2.58×10^{-1}	3.11×10^{-1}
θ_2	2.54×10^{-1}	1.77×10^{-1}
θ_3	2.24×10^{-1}	1.71×10^{-1}
θ_4	1.68×10^{-1}	1.40×10^{-1}
θ_5	7.04×10^{-2}	1.27×10^{-1}
θ_6	2.70×10^{-2}	7.39×10^{-2}
Number of Topics $K = 12$		
θ_k	PRTM	UM
θ_1	2.52×10^{-1}	2.20×10^{-1}
θ_2	2.50×10^{-1}	1.23×10^{-1}
θ_3	2.17×10^{-1}	1.14×10^{-1}
θ_4	1.65×10^{-1}	9.58×10^{-2}
θ_5	6.94×10^{-2}	9.58×10^{-2}
θ_6	2.13×10^{-2}	7.34×10^{-2}
θ_7	1.79×10^{-2}	6.35×10^{-2}
θ_8	7.62×10^{-3}	6.03×10^{-2}
θ_9	2.28×10^{-4}	5.54×10^{-2}
θ_{10}	1.58×10^{-5}	4.02×10^{-2}
θ_{11}	1.28×10^{-5}	3.90×10^{-2}
θ_{12}	2.93×10^{-6}	1.83×10^{-2}

Table 2: The appearance probabilities θ_k comparison with $K = 6$ and $K = 12$. Sorted in descending order.

with PRTM, F_1 score did not decrease if K became larger. The F_1 scores of LDA were lower than PRTM and UM because it is not suitable for review sentence clustering as mentioned in subsection 3.2.

Table 2 shows the comparison of the appearance probabilities θ_k with the number of topics $K = 6$ and $K = 12$. Similar θ_k was estimated by PRTM and UM with $K = 6$. However, with $K = 12$, PRTM had the larger deviation of the θ_k from 2.93×10^{-6} to 2.52×10^{-1}. On the other hand, UM with $K = 12$ had the more uniform θ_k than PRTM. This large deviation of θ of PRTM prevents sentences in the same category from being divided into several clusters. This is the reason why the F_1 score of UM gradually decreased and PRTM achieved invariant sentence clustering accuracy.

3.4 Appropriate Number of Topics

PRTM yields an appropriate number of topics by maximization of Modularity Q. On the other hand, the appropriate number of topics in UM and LDA can be estimated using the average cosine distance ($AveDis$) measurement. Therefore, we compared Modularity of PRTM with $AveDis$ of UM and LDA with different numbers of topics. We trained topic and word distributions $\boldsymbol{\theta}$, $\boldsymbol{\phi}$, and estimated the optimal number of topics K with both of Hotel Reviews and Car Reviews. The $AveDis$ scores of UM and LDA were the mean values of the tests running three times for the same reason as subsection 3.3.

Figure 3 shows the experimental results. The $AveDis$ of UM got the smallest scores in $K = 47$ with Hotel Reviews and in $K = 47$ in Car Reviews. Furthermore, $AveDis$ of LDA decreased monotonically in the range of $K = 3$ to $K = 60$. On the other hand, the Modularity of PRTM got largest in $K = 7$ with Hotel Reviews and in $K = 6$ with Car Reviews. When we consider that Rakuten Travel website scores hotels by six viewpoints and that Edmunds website scores cars by eight viewpoints, the Modularity of PRTM estimates more appropriate number of topics than $AveDis$ of UM in review

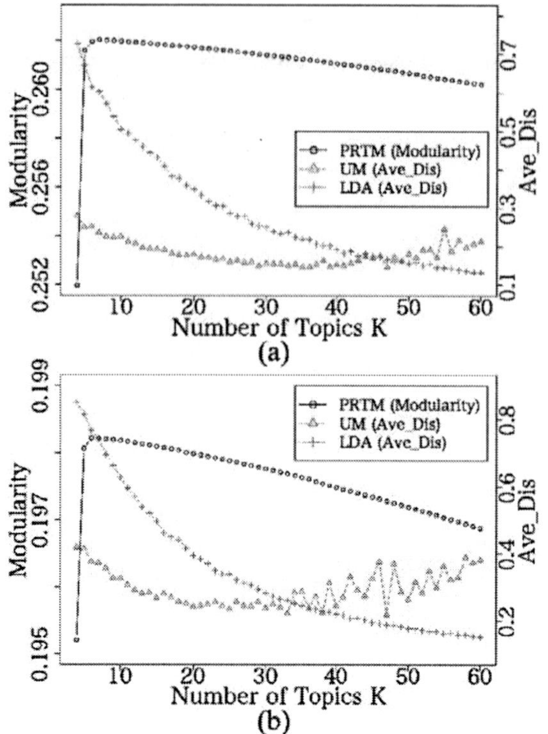

Figure 3: Modularity and Ave-Dis comparison with different numbers of topics. (a) Hotel Reviews. (b) Car Reviews.

datasets.

4 Related Work

There are several previous works of probabilistic generative models. Latent Dirichlet Allocation (LDA) (Blei et al., 2003) estimates topic distributions for each document and word distributions for each topic. On the other hand, Unigram Mixtures (UM) (Nigam et al., 2000) estimates a topic distribution for all the documents and word distributions for each topic. In both papers, their models are tested at document classification task using WebKB datasets which contain 4199 web sites and 23830 words in a vocabulary. Twitter-LDA (Zhao et al., 2011) has been presented to estimate more coherent topic from tweets which consist of less than 140 letters. In Twitter-LDA model, it is hypothesized that one tweet is regarded to be generated from one topic such as UM. Twitter-LDA is tested using over 1 million tweets which have over 20000 words in a vocabulary.

There are several benefits of using probabilistic generative models for sentence clustering as described in section 1. However, these probabilistic generative models need much amount of datasets to get consistent computation results. In our experiments, we used about 4000 sentences of reviews which are the same number of documents as in WebKB datasets. However, there are few words in a vocabulary since a sentence of reviews has fewer words than a website. Therefore, in UM and LDA, the computation results seriously depended on randomly-initialized parameters, and lower clustering accuracy was obtained than PRTM in our experiment. To get consistent computation results from short sentence corpus with probabilistic generative models, over 1 million sentences are needed for like the experiment in Twitter-LDA. However, our proposed method, PageRank Topic Model (PRTM), can get consistent multinomial distributions over topics and words with few datasets because the network structure analysis methods are not dependent on randomly-initialized parameters. Therefore, PRTM achieved higher sentence clustering accuracy than UM and LDA with few review datasets.

5 Conclusion

In this paper, we have presented PageRank Topic Model (PRTM) to estimate a multinomial distribution over topics θ and words ϕ applying the network structure analysis methods and the convex quadratic programming problem to Word -Co-occurrence Graphs. With PRTM, the consistent computation results can be obtained because PRTM is not denpendent on randomly-initialized θ and ϕ. Furthermore, compared to other approaches at the task of estimations of the appropriate number of topics, PRTM estimated more appropriate number of topics for extracting the viewpoints from reviews datasets.

Acknowledgments

This research was partially supported by Core Research for Evolutionary Science and Technology (CREST) of Japan Science and Technology Agency (JST).

References

Aaron Clauset, Mark EJ Newman and Cristopher Moore. 2004. Finding community structure in very large networks. *Physical review E*, 70(6):066111.

Arthur P. Dempster, Nan M. Laird, and Donald B. Rubin. 1977. Maximum likelihood from incomplete data via the EM algorithm. *Journal of the Royal Statistical Society, Series B (methodological)*, 39(1): 1–38.

Danushka Bollegala, Yutaka Matsuo, and Mitsuru Ishizuka. 2008. A Co-occurrence Graph-based Approach for Personal Name Alias Extraction from Anchor Texts. *In Proceedings of International Joint Conference on Natural Language Processing*: 865–870.

David M. Blei, Andrew Y. Ng and Michael I. Jordan. 2003. Latent Dirichlet allocation. *the Journal of machine Learning research*, 3: 993–1022.

Juan Cao, Tian Xia, Jintao Li, Yongdong Zhang, and Sheng Tang. 2009. A density-based method for adaptive LDA model selection. *Neurocomputing*, 72: 1775–1781.

Jun S. Liu. 1994. The collapsed Gibbs sampler in Bayesian computations with applications to a gene regulation problem. *Journal of the American Statistical Association*, 89(427): 958–966.

Kamal Nigam, Andrew K. McCallum, Sebastian Thrun, and Tom Mitchell. 2000. Text Classification from Labeled and Unlabeled Documents using EM. *Machine Learning*, 39(2/3): 61–67.

Kavita Ganesan and ChengXiang Zhai. 2011. Opinion-Based Entity Ranking. *Information Retrieval.*

Larry Page, Sergey Brin, Rajeev Motwani, and Terry Winograd. 1999. The pagerank citation ranking: Bringing order to the web. *Technical Report 1999-66, Stanford InfoLab. Previous number = SIDL-WP-1999-0120.*

Mikio Yamamoto and Kugatsu Sadamitsu. 2005. Dirichlet Mixtures in Text Modeling. *CS Technical report CS-TR-05-1, University of Tsukuba, Japan.*

Sergey Brin and Larry Page. 1998. The anatomy of a large-scale hypertextual Web search engine. *Computer Networks and ISDN Systems*, 30(17):107–117.

Takeshi Sakaki, Yutaka Matsuo, Koki Uchiyama and Mitsuru Ishizuka 2007. Construction of Related Terms Thesauri from the Web. *Journal of Natural Language Processing*, 14(2):3–31.

Wayne Xin Zhao, Jing Jiang, Jianshu Weng, Jing He, Ee-Peng Lim, Hongfei Yan, and Xiaoming Li. 2011. Comparing twitter and traditional media using topic models. *The annual European Conference on Information Retrieval*:338–349.

Yee W. Teh, David Newman, and Max Welling. 2006. A collapsed variational Bayesian inference algorithm for latent Dirichlet allocation. *In Advances in Neural Information Processing Systems*: 1353–1360.

Ying Zhao and George Karypis. 2001. Criterion functions for document clustering: Experiments and analysis. *Technical Report TR 01-40, Department of Computer Science, University of Minnesota, Minneapolis, MN.*

Yukio Ohsawa, Nels E. Benson, and Masahiko Yachida. 1998. KeyGraph: Automatic Indexing by Co-occurrence Graph based on Building Construction Metaphor. *In Proceedings of Advanced Digital Library Conference*: 12–18.

The Inner Circle vs. the Outer Circle or British English vs. American English

Yong-hun Lee
Chungnam Nation University
99 Daehak-ro, Gung-dong, Yuseong-gu
Daejeon 34134, S. Korea
yleeuiuc@hanmail.net

Ki-suk Jun
Hannam University
70 Hannam-ro, Ojoeng-dong, Daedeok-gu
Daejeon 34430, S. Korea
mango0322@naver.com

Abstract

In this paper, the use of two modals (*can* and *may*) in four varieties of English (British, India, Philippines, and USA) was compared and the characteristics of each variety were statistically analyzed. After all the sample sentences were extracted from each component of the ICE corpus, a total of twenty linguistic factors were encoded. Then, the collected data were statistically analyzed with R. Through the analysis, the following facts were observed: (i) India and Philippine speakers used *can* more frequently than natives, (ii) Three linguistic factors interacted with CORPUS, and (iii) The distinctions between American and British were more influential than those of the Inner Circle vs. the Outer Circle.

1 Introduction

As English has spread worldwide, new varieties of English have emerged and they got independent status accordingly. In order to systematically classify them, Kachru (1992) introduced the three concentric circles as way of conceptualizing this pluri-centricity. There should be a distinction between American English (AmE) and British English (BrE) as well.

Out of the varieties of English, we chose four different ones and statistically analyzed their properties. To this end, we picked out four components of the International Corpus of English (ICE; Greenbaum, 1996), which are the varieties of British, India, Philippines, and USA. Then, all the sentences with two modal auxiliaries *can* and *may* were extracted. Then, a total of twenty linguistic factors were encoded to the extracted ones, and the encoded data were statistically analyzed with R, with the theoretical basis of Competition Model (Bates and MacWhinney, 1982, 1989). In addition, two statistical analysis methods were adopted. One was a logistic regression with which the properties of each component were closely investigated. The other was a Behavior Profile (BP) analysis where the four components were clustered by their similarity.

In short, we selected two modal auxiliaries *can* and *may* for comparison for the following reasons. As several of the previous studies (Leech, 1969, Coates, 1983; Collins, 2009) pointed out, these two modal verbs have similar meanings, and the native speakers interchange them in similar contexts. However, the distributions of these two are systematic, even in native speakers' writings. Then, what happens in non-native speakers' counterparts and how can the phenomena be explained? We are to present one possible type of answer to these questions.

2 Previous Studies

2.1 World Englishes

The term 'World Englishes', not 'World English', refers to emerging localized/indigenized varieties of English, especially the varieties which have developed in territories influenced by the United Kingdom (Great Britain) or the United States. The primary goals of World Englishes are (i) to identify the varieties of English in diverse sociolinguistic contexts and (ii) to analyze how the sociolinguistic factors (histories, multi-cultural backgrounds and contexts of function) influence the use of English in different regions of the world.

There are several theoretical models to explain the spread of English, but the three concentric circles model by Kachru is probably the most influential one. In this model, the spread of English is classified and grouped into three different categories of regional varieties of English. These three categories are called the Inner Circle, the Outer Circle, and the Expanding Circle (Kachru, 1992:356). Figure 1 illustrates the three concentric circles.

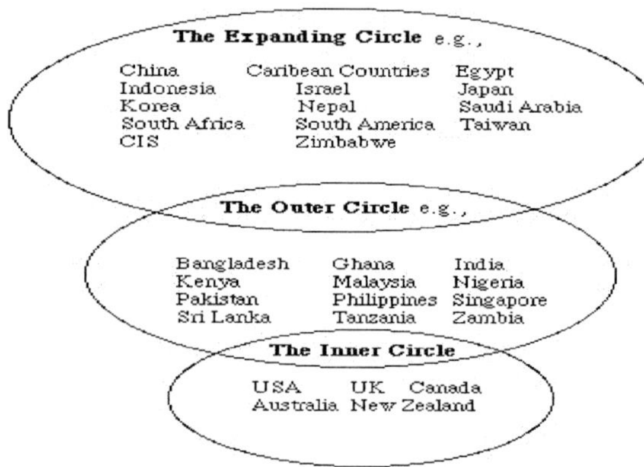

Figure 1: The Three Concentric Circles

The English varieties in each circle have their own characteristics.

The Inner Circle of English took shape first and spread across the world in the first diaspora. In this early spread of English, speakers from England carried the language to the colonies, such as Australia, New Zealand, North America, and so on. The English language in this circle represents the traditional historical and sociolinguistic bases in the regions where it is now used as English as the Native Language (ENL): the United Kingdom, the United States, Australia, New Zealand, Ireland, Canada, South Africa, and some of the Caribbean territories. In these countries, English is the native language or mother tongue for most people. The total number of English speakers in this circle is estimated to be as many as around 380 million.

The Outer Circle of English was made during the second diaspora of English, which diffused the language through the expansion of Great Britain. In the areas such as Asia and Africa, English is not the native language, but it serves as a useful lingua franca between various ethnic and language groups. Some people with higher education, the legislature and judiciary, national commerce, and others may speak English for practical purposes. The countries in this circle include India, Nigeria, Bangladesh, Pakistan, Malaysia, Tanzania, Kenya, non-Anglophone South Africa, the Philippines and others. The total number of English speakers is estimated to range from 150 million to 300 million.

The Expanding Circle includes the countries in which English plays no historical or governmental role but is widely used as a medium of international communication. This includes much of the rest of the world's population not categorized as either of the other two circles: China, Russia, Japan, most of Europe, Korea, Egypt, Indonesia, etc. It is difficult to estimate the total number of people in the Expanding Circle, but the estimates range from 100 million to one billion.

2.2 British English and American English

In addition to the three concentric circles in Kachru (1992), one of the most influential classifications of English is that of British English and American English.

British English (BrE) refers to the form of English primarily used in the Great Britain, but it includes all the dialects used in other areas which were the former colonies of Great Britain. Likewise, American English (AmE) is the form of English mainly used in the United States, but it includes all the dialects used in other areas like the former colonies of the United States.

As the Great Britain expanded its territories by colonization, the United States of America (USA) also established a few colonies in Asian countries. Accordingly, English in these countries was influenced by its superpower. Nowadays, as the influences of the USA increased in many other countries, the importance of AmE increased as well.

English in Australia, Canada, Ireland and New Zealand belongs to BrE. In addition, most of Africa (including Egypt and South Africa), South Asia (Pakistan, India, and Bangladesh), Malta, some countries in Southeast Asia (Myanmar, Singapore, Malaysia, and Thailand), and Hong Kong still use BrE. On the other hand, most of Eastern Europe (including Russia), most East

Asian countries excluding Hong Kong (China, Japan, and Korea), Philippines, most American countries (except Canada, Jamaica and the Bahamas), and some African countries (Liberia and Namibia) still use AmE.

There have been quite a few studies on the differences between BrE and AmE (McArthur, 2002; Tottie, 2002; Crystal, 2003; Hargraves, 2003; Peters, 2004; Algeo, 2006; Trudgill et al. 2013). The differences between these two types of English cover various areas including phonetics, phonology, morphology, syntax, semantics, and so on. However, most of the previous studies were focused on lexical differences and did not adopt any statistical methods in their analyses.

2.3 Competition Model

The Competition Model (CM), on which this paper is theoretically based, is a psycholinguistic theory of language acquisition and sentence processing. This model was developed by Elizabeth Bates and Brian MacWhinney. The most important idea of the CM is that the meaning of a language must be and can be interpreted by comparing a number of linguistic factors within a sentence. In addition, a language is acquired and/or learned through the competition of basic cognitive mechanisms with a rich linguistic environment.

The CM claims that human beings understand the meaning of a sentence by taking into account various factors, such as word order, morphology, and semantic characteristics (e.g. animacy), and so on. Thus, when people articulate a sentence, they unconsciously calculate the probabilities of each meaning and choose the one with the highest value.

We adopted this model as a theoretical basis because two modal auxiliaries *can* and *may* occur in similar linguistic environments and that they compete with each other. As a result of the competition, one of them is chosen as a winner in the given linguistic environments. The winner has more probability than the other in the given environments. Then, the question is which factor would decide the winner. We investigated the decision mechanisms with a statistical analysis.

3 Research Method

3.1 Research Procedure

Our research proceeded as follows. First, four corpora were selected from the ICE: British, India, Philippines, and USA. Each corpus included about 1 million of word tokens, and the composition of each corpus was nearly identical. They are listed as in Table 1. Next, all the sentences with the two modal auxiliaries were extracted from the four corpora, using NLPTools (Lee, 2007).

	The Inner Circle	The OuterCircle
BrE	Britain	India
AmE	USA	Philippines

Table 1: Classification of Four Corpora

Since there were so many sentences in each variety, we extracted 1,000 sentences per each corpus with random sampling. Then, twenty different linguistic factors were manually encoded into them, following Deshors (2010) and Deshors and Gries (2014). Lastly, a statistical analysis of the corpus data was done with the help of R (R Core Team, 2016).

3.2 Encoding Variables

Table 2 illustrates the encoded factors, used in this paper. Following Atkins (1987), each linguistic factor and its level are called ID tag and ID tag levels.

ID Tag Type	ID Tag	ID Tag Levels
Data	CORPUS	Britain, India, Philippines, USA
Morphological	FORM	*can, may*
	ELLIPTIC	yes, no
	VOICE	active, passive
	ASPECT	simple, progressive, perfect
	MOOD	indicative, subjunctive
	SUBJMORPH	adj., adv., common noun, proper noun, relative pronoun, noun phrase, etc.
	SUBJPERSON	1, 2, 3
	SUBJNUMBER	singular, plural
	SUBJREFNUMBER	singular, plural
Syntactic	NEG	affirmative, negated
	SENTTYPE	declarative, interrogative
	CLTYPE	main, coordinate, subordinate
Semantic	SENSE	epistemic, deontic, dynamic
	SPEAKERPRESENCE	weak, medium, strong
	VENDLER	accomplishment, achievement, process, state

	VERBSEMANTICS	abstract, general action, action incurring transformation, action incurring movement, perception, etc.
	REFANIM	animate, inanimate
	ANIMTYPE	animate, floral, object, place/time, mental/emotional, etc.
	USE	idiomatic, literal, metaphorical

Table 2: Encoded Factors and Predictors

The variables were used in the statistical analysis.[1]

3.3 Statistical Analysis

We also carried out a multi-factorial analysis, in which not only the effects of each factor but also the interactions among the factors are statistically analyzed. The multi-factorial analyses of linguistic data are supported by many studies in cognitive linguistics. Langacker (2000:3) mentioned that "to conceive of [linguistic] entities in connection with one another (e.g., for the sake of comparison, or to assess their relative position), not just as separate, isolated experiences. This is linguistically important because relationships figure in the meaning of almost all expressions, many of which (e.g., verb, adjectives, prepositions) designate relationships." Gries (2003) also conducted the multi-factorial analysis to analyze the distributions of particle placement in native speakers' English. Deshors (2014:11) also mentioned that "The multi-factorial approach also helps the authors make a connection between degrees of grammatical complexity of speakers' utterances and learners' lexical choices during second language production. For instance, they observe that *can* rather than *may* is more frequently used by French English learners (compared to native speakers) in more complex grammatical environments such as negated or subordinated linguistic contexts."

As a multi-factorial approach, we used a Generalized Linear Model (GLM) with logistic regression, since it is one of the simplest and most widely-adopted analyses. For regression analysis, Deshors (2014:11) mentioned that "Binary logistic regression is a confirmatory statistical technique that allows the analyst to identify possible correlations between the dependent and the independent factors/variables. Ultimately, this statistical approach allows us to see what factors influence learners' choices of *may* and *can*."

During the analysis process, a stepwise model selection procedure was adopted as follows. First, an initial model was constructed with all of the factors and their interactions. Second, a new model was constructed in which only one factor or one interaction was deleted from the previous model. Third, the newly constructed model was compared with the previous one with an ANalysis Of VAriance (ANOVA). Fourth, an optimal model was chosen according to some criteria such as significance testing or information ones: If a model m_1 contained a factor f or an interaction i but a model m_2 did not contain f or i, and (i) when the p-value of the ANOVA test was significant (p<.05), it implied that the factor f or an interaction i must NOT be deleted from the model and the model m_1 was selected consequently, and (ii) when the p-value of ANOVA was NOT significant (.05<p), it implied that the factor f or an interaction i can safely deleted from the model and the model m_2 was selected accordingly. The processes continued until all the factors and their interactions were scrutinized.

We also adopted another multi-factorial analysis, a Behavioral Profile (BP) analysis. It was developed by Gries and Otami (2010) and Gries (2010a), and it is a statistical method to examine the behavioral properties of each linguistic factor. The analysis represents the similarity or dissimilarity of the components with a dendrogram (the hierarchical agglomerative cluster analysis). It was originally used to analyze the synonymy and/or the antonymy in lexical semantics. However, the same method can also be used here, since the use of the modal constructions in the EFL learners' writings can be classified on a basis of the behavioral properties of linguistic factors.

4 Logistic Regression

4.1 The Analysis

The first step for the (binary) logistic regression was to set up an initial model. Table 3 shows the initial model of our study.

FORM~CORPUS+NEG+SENTTYPE+CLTYPE+SUBJMORPH+SUBJPERSON+SUBJNUMBER+VOICE+ASPECT+MOOD+SUBJREFNUMBER+SENSE+SPEAKER

[1] This process is called *operationalization*.

PRESENCE+USE+VERBSEMENATICS+REFANIM+ANIMTYPE+CORPUS:NEG+CORPUS:SENTTYPE+CORPUS:CLTYPE+CORPUS:SUBJMORPH+CORPUS:SUBJPERSON+CORPUS:SUBJNUMBER+CORPUS:VOICE+CORPUS:ASPECT+CORPUS:MOOD+CORPUS:SUBJREFNUMBER+CORPUS:SENSE+CORPUS:SPEAKERPRESENCE+CORPUS:USE+CORPUS:VERBSEMANTICS+CORPUS:REFANIM+CORPUS:ANIMTYPE

Table 3: Initial Model

Then, model selection procedures were applied (cf. Section 3.3) and the final (optimal) model was selected. Table 4 shows the final model.

FORM~CORPUS+SUBJMORPH+MOOD+SENTTYPE+CLTYPE+VENDLER+CORPUS:SUBJMORPH+CORPUS:SENTTYPE+CORPUS:VENDLER

Table 4: Final Model

As seen in Table 3 and Table 4, the six main factors and three interactions with CORPUS survived in the final model.

4.2 Analysis Results

With the final model obtained, all the main factors and their interactions with CORPUS were statistically analyzed as in Table 5. Here, '×' (not significant) is used when $0.1<p$; '.' (marginally significant) when $p<0.1$; '*' (significant) when $p<0.05$; '**' (very significant) when $p<0.01$; and '***' (highly significant) when $p<0.001$.

	df	deviance	AIC	LRT	*p*	
<none>		29195	29575			
CORPUS	3	1352.7	1470.7	40.15	9.926e-09	***
ELLIPTIC	1	1313.7	1435.7	1.16	0.2816880	
VOICE	1	1312.5	1434.5	0.00	0.9696053	
ASPECT	3	1316.6	1434.6	4.06	0.2549911	
MOOD	1	1323.9	1445.9	11.36	0.0007513	***
SUBJMORPH	8	1315.7	1423.7	3.21	0.9202972	
SUBJPERS	2	1313.9	1433.9	1.37	0.5034411	
SUBJNUM	1	1313.3	1435.3	0.83	0.3623101	
SUBJREFNUM	1	1312.8	1434.8	0.25	0.6186114	
NEG	1	1315.7	1437.7	3.14	0.0765925	.
SENTTYPE	2	1324.7	1444.7	12.22	0.0022183	**
CLTYPE	2	1320.0	1440.0	7.53	0.0231573	*
SENSE	2	1972.1	2092.1	659.55	<2.2e-16	
VENDLER	3	1324.8	1442.8	12.25	0.0065658	**
VERBSEM	8	1323.0	1431.0	10.50	0.2318564	
REFANIM	1	1313.1	1435.1	0.55	0.4579886	
ANIMTYPE	20	1332.1	1416.1	19.56	0.4854248	
USE	1	1312.5	1434.5	0.02	0.8965201	
CORPUS:ELLIPTIC	3	23068	23442	0.0	1	
CORPUS:VOICE	3	22852	23226	0.0	1	
CORPUS:ASPECT	6	24293	24661	0.0	1	
CORPUS:MOOD	2	23573	23949	0.0	1	
CORPUS:SUBJMORPH	13	40801	41155	11606.1	<2e-16	***
CORPUS:SUBJPERS	6	24438	24806	0.0	1	
CORPUS:SUBJNUM	3	26744	27118	0.0	1	
CORPUS:SUBJREFNUM	3	24726	25100	0.0	1	
CORPUS:NEG	3	23140	23514	0.0	1	
CORPUS:SENTTYPE	3	41594	41968	12399.0	<2e-16	***
CORPUS:CLTYPE	6	27321	27689	0.0	1	
CORPUS:SENSE	6	1156	1524	0.0	1	
CORPUS:VENDLER	8	37557	37921	8362.1	<2e-16	***
CORPUS:VERBSEM	19	25375	25717	0.0	1	
CORPUS:REFANIM	3	21554	21928	0.0	1	
CORPUS:ANIMTYPE	36	1169	1477	0.0	1	
CORPUS:USE	0	29195	29575	0.0		

Table 5: Analysis Results

The table demonstrates that five main factors and three interactions with CORPUS were statistically significant in the model. It also shows that one factor (SUBJMORPH) survives in the final model because of its interactions with the factor CORPUS.

Since we obtained the final model, it was possible to investigate how the speakers' use of *can* and *may* was different in the four components of the ICE corpus, with graphic representations.

Among the main factors, only one factor (i.e., CORPUS) was examined with a graphic tool. Figure 2 illustrates the association plot for CORPUS. As shown in the figure, the effects of a factor are represented by the baseline (the dotted line) and rectangles above and below it. Here, the baseline refers to the expected frequency of each value for a given factor. The width of the rectangle is proportional to the square root of the expected frequency, and the width of the rectangle to the standardized residual.

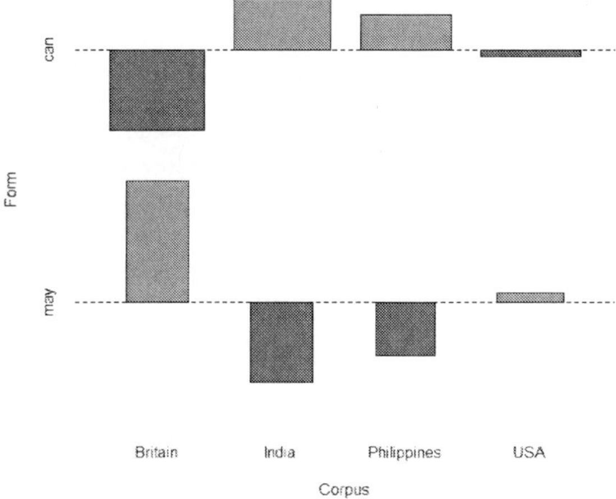

Figure 2: Association Plot for CORPUS

As this plot indicates, the ENL speakers (Britain and USA) use *may* more often and *can* less often than the ESL speakers (India and Philippines). In other words, the ESL speakers use *may* less frequently and *can* more frequently than the ENL speakers.

Figure 3 illustrates the effect plot for CORPUS: SUBJMORPH.

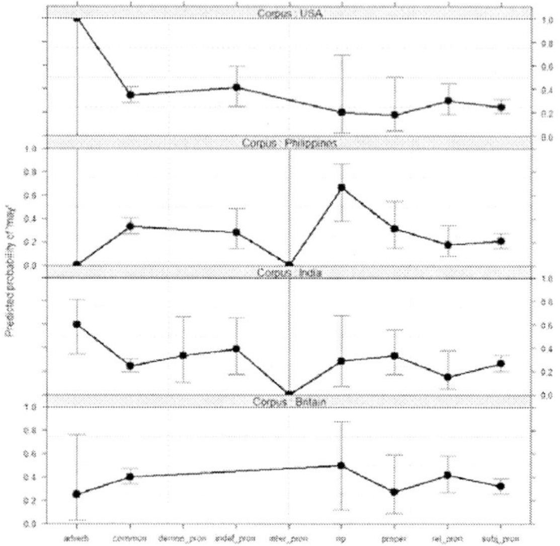

Figure 3: Effect Plot for CORPUS:SUBJMORPH

This plot demonstrates several facts about the use of *can* and *may* by different groups of speakers. When the subject is an 'adverb' (i.e., *here* or *there* [existential constructions]), USA and India use *may* more frequently than *can*, while Britain and Philippines demonstrate the opposite tendency. When the subject contains a 'common noun', all the groups of speakers prefer to use *can*. When the subject includes an 'NP', the Philippines learners prefer to use *may*, while the other three groups of speakers prefer to use *can*. For the three types of pronouns ('demon_pron (demonstrative pronoun)', 'indef_pron (indefinite pronoun)', and 'inter_pron (interrogative pronoun)'), only the Indian ESL speakers used all of them, whereas all the other speakers employed only some of them. When the subject contains a 'proper noun', a 'relative pronoun', or a 'subject (personal) pronoun', all the groups of speakers prefer to use *can*.

Figure 4 demonstrates the effect plot for CORPUS:SENTTYPE. As you can observe, in both types of sentences, the ENL speakers and the ESL speakers prefer to use *can* rather than *may*, but the probabilities of *may* increase when SENTTYPE is 'declarative', in both groups of speakers.

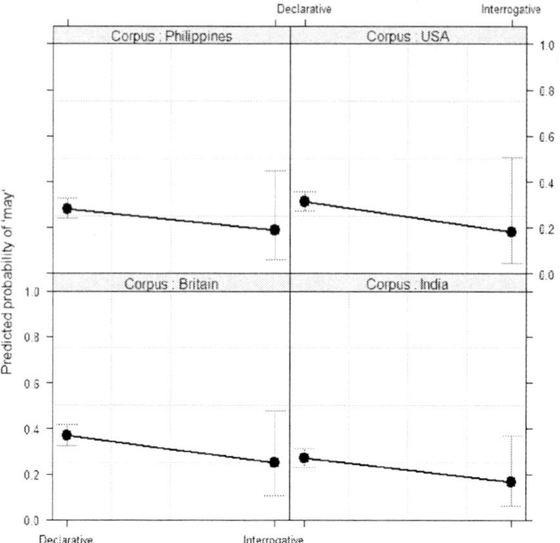

Figure 4: Effect Plot for CORPUS:SENTTYPE

Figure 5 shows the effect plot for CORPUS: VENDLER.

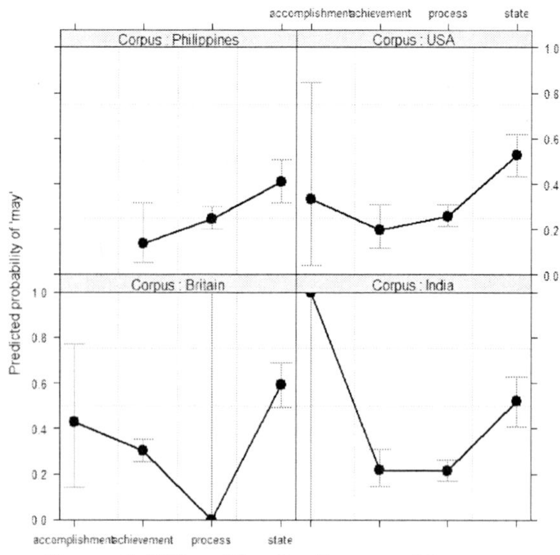

Figure 5: Effect Plot for CORPUS: VENDLER

This plot illustrates that all the groups of speakers prefer to use *may* more when the verbs represent 'accomplishment' or 'state' but that they prefer to use *can* when the verbs represent 'achievement' or 'process'.

5 The BP Analysis

As the analysis results in Section 4 show, four groups of speakers demonstrated different characteristics in using two modal auxiliaries *can* and *may*. Then, the question was whether the Inner/Outer distinctions influenced more or the AmE/BrE distinctions influenced more. To get the answer, a BP analysis was performed.

Among the factors in Table 2, the combination of CORPUS and FORM were chosen as a dependent variable and the other factors as independent ones. Figure 6 illustrates the dendrogram resulting from the analysis (multiscale bootstrap resampling clustering).

Here, the horizontal lines represent which component(s) is/are grouped with which component(s), and the vertical lines indicate the distance between these two groups. Two numeric values in the dendrogram refer to AU (approximately unbiased) *p*-value and BP (bootstrap probability) value for each cluster, respectively.

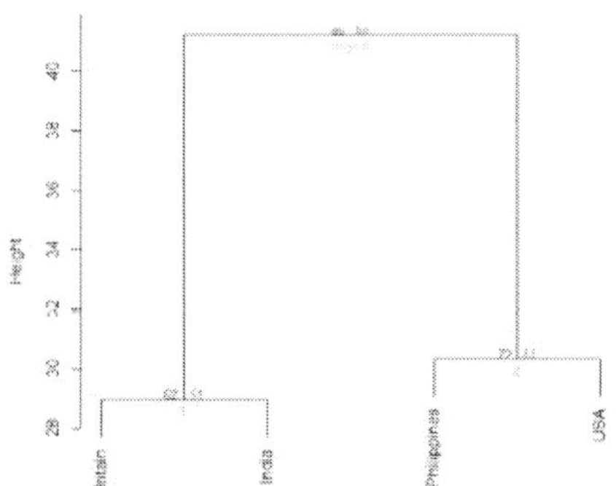

Figure 6: BP Analysis Result

This dendrogram represents which one is closer to which one.

As you can see, Britain and India were grouped together first. Likewise, Philippines and USA were grouped together first. Then, the two groups were combined together, to be represented as {{Britain, India}, {Philippines, USA}}. Though more complicated statistical analysis is necessary, the analysis result shows us the fact that the AmE/ BrE distinctions were more powerful than those of the Inner/ Outer Circle.

6 Discussion

In this paper, the use of two modal auxiliaries *can* and *may* was compared on a basis of the data extracted from the four components of the ICE corpus. Twenty linguistic factors were encoded to the sentences, and they were analyzed with a logistic regression and a BP analysis.

The analysis results in Section 4 and Section 5 reveal several facts about the use of two modal auxiliaries *can* and *may* in the four components.

The association plot in Figure 2 demonstrates the fact that the ENL speakers (British and USA) use *may* more often and *can* less often than the ESL speakers (India and Philippines). Namely, the ESL speakers use *may* less frequently and *can* more frequently than the ENL speakers. It also illustrates the possibility that the Inner/Outer Circle distinctions might be sharper than those of the BrE/AmE.

The analysis results in Figure 5 and the effect plots in Figure 3, Figure 4, and Figure 5 indicate that each component of the ICE corpus had its own characteristics, and three interactions with CORPUS (i.e., CORPUS:SUBJMORPH, CORPUS:SENTTYPE, and CORPUS:VENDLER) made each component unique in the use of the two modal auxiliaries.

The BP analysis in Figure 6 demonstrates that the AmE/BrE distinctions were more clear-cut than those of the Inner/Outer Circle. Note that the grouping of the components was made as {{Britain, India}, {Philippines, USA}}. If the Inner/Outer Circle distinctions were stronger than those of AmE/BrE, the grouping of the components would be made as {{Britain, USA}, {India, Philippines}}. The grouping of Figure 6 clearly shows that the AmE/BrE distinctions were more important than those of the Inner/Outer Circle in the four components of the ICE corpus.

7 Conclusion

In this paper, the sentences with two modal auxiliaries (*can* and *may*) were extracted from the four components of the ICE corpus (British, India, Philippines, and USA), and their uses were examined. After twenty linguistic factors were encoded to the sentences, the collected data were statistically analyzed with R.

Two statistical methods were adopted in the analysis. One was a logistic regression by which the properties of each ICE component were closely investigated. The other was a BP analysis where the four components were clustered with the similarity.

Through the analysis, the following three facts were observed: (i) India and Philippine speakers used *can* more frequently than natives, (ii) Three linguistic factors interacted with CORPUS, and (iii) The AmE vs. BrE differences were more influential than those of the Inner vs. Outer Circle.

References

Beryl Atkins. 1987. Semantic ID Tags: Corpus Evidence for Dictionary Senses. In Proceedings of the Third Annual Conference of the UW Centre for the New Oxford English Dictionary, 17-36.

Braj Kachru. 1992. The Other Tongue: English across Cultures. University of Illinois Press, Urbana, IL.

David Crystal. 2003. The Cambridge Encyclopedia of the English Language. Cambridge University Press, Cambridge.

Deshors, Sandra. 2014 Constructing Meaning in L2 Discourse: The Case of Modal Verbs and Sequential Dependencies. In Glynn, Dylan and M. Sjo..lin (eds.) Subjectivity and Epistenicity: Stance Strategies in Discourse and Narration, 329-348. Lund University Press, Lund.

Elizabeth Bates and Brian MacWhinney. 1982. Functionalist Approaches to Grammar. In Eric Wanner and Lila Gleitman (eds.) Language Acquisition: The State of the Art, 73–218. Cambridge University Press, Cambridge.

Elizabeth Bates and Brian MacWhinney. Functionalism and the Competition Model. In Brian MacWhinney and Elizabeth Bates (eds.) The Cross-linguistic Study of Sentence Processing, 3–73. Cambridge University Press, Cambridge.

Geoffrey Leech. 1969. Towards a Semantic Description of English. Indiana University Press, Bloomington.

Gunnel Tottie. 2002. An Introduction to American English. Wiley- Blackwell, Oxford.

Jennifer Coates. 1983. The Semantics of the Modal Auxiliaries. Croom Helm, London.

John Algeo. 2006. British or American English? Cambridge University Press, Cambridge.

Orin Hargraves. 2003. Mighty Fine Words and Smashing Expressions. Oxford University Press, Oxford.

Pam Peters. 2004. The Cambridge Guide to English Usage. Cambridge University Press, Cambridge.

Peter Collins. 2009. Modals and Quasi-modals in English. Rodopi, Amsterdam.

Peter Trudgill and Jean Hannah. 2013. International English: A Guide to Varieties of Standard English. 5th Edition. Routledge, London.

R Core Team. 2016. R: A Language and Environment for Statistical Computing. R Foundation for Statistical Computing, Vienna.

Ronald Langacker. 2000. Grammar and Conceptualization. Mouton, Berlin.

Sandra Deshors and Stefan Greis. 2014. A Case for the Multifactorial Assessment of Learner Language: The Uses of *May* and *Can* in French-English Interlanguage. In Dylan Glynn and Justyna Robinson (eds.), Corpus Methods for Semantics: Quantitative Studies in Polysemy and Synonymy, 179-204. John Bejamins, Amsterdam.

Sandra Deshors. 2010. Multifactorial Study of the Uses of *May* and *Can* in French-English Interlanguage. Ph.D. dissertation, University of Sussex.

Sidney Greenbaum. 1996. Comparing English Worldwide: The International Corpus of English. Claredon, Oxford.

Stefan Gries and Naoki Otani. 2010. Behavioral Profiles: A Corpus-based Perspective on Synonymy and Antonymy. ICAME Journal 34:121-150.

Stefan Gries. 2003. Multifactorial Analysis in Corpus Linguistics: A Study of Particle Placement. Continuum Press, London.

Stefan Gries. 2010a. Behavioral Profiles: A Fine-grained and Quantitative Approach in Corpus-based Lexical Semantics. The Mental Lexicon 5(3):323-346.

Stefan Gries. 2010b. Behavioral Profiles 1.01: A Program for R 2.7.1 and Higher.

Tom McArthur. 2002. The Oxford Guide to World English. Oxford University Press, Oxford.

Yong-hun Lee. 2007. Corpus Analysis and Their Applications Using NLPTools: Applications to Study of Language, English Education, and Development of English Textbooks. Cambridge University Press, Seoul.

A Correlation Analysis of English Particle Placement of Three East Asian EFL Learners' Writings

Ha-Eung Kim
Hannam University
70 Hannamro, Daedeok-gu
Daejeon 306-791, Korea
tankkh@hanmail.net

Gyu-Hyeong Lee
Hannam University
70 Hannamro, Daedeok-gu
Daejeon 306-791, Korea
gyuhyung73@naver.com

Yong-hun Lee
Chungnam Nat'l University
99 Daehak-ro, Yuseong-gu
Daejeon 305-764, Korea
yleeuiuc@hanmail.net

Abstract

This paper examines the English particle placements of EFL learners' writings in three East Asian countries (Chinese, Japan, and Korea). Three parts of the TOEFL11 corpus were chosen, and all the sentences with particles were extracted. The ICE-GB was chosen as a native speakers' English. Then, eleven linguistic factors were manually encoded. The collected data were analyzed with R. Correlation tests and a hierarchical clustering analysis was adopted. Through the analysis, the following two facts were observed: (i) each linguistic factor affected differently in four varieties of English and (ii) Japanese English was similar to native speakers' counterparts whereas Korean and Chinese formed another group.

1 Introduction

Linguistic alternation has been one of the interesting research areas in linguistics. Particle placement is one of such syntactic alternations. It refers to the linguistic phenomenon where a particle is located before or after the direct object (DO) in the phrasal verb constructions. [1] For example, let's see the following sentence (Gries, 1999:1).

(1) a. John *picked up* the book.
b. John *picked* the book *up*.

As you can see, the word order in (1a) is 'verb + particle + DO', whereas the order of (1b) is 'verb + DO + particle'.

There have been a lot of studies on this topic in traditional grammar and Chomskyan syntax. They have primarily focused on what linguistic factors determine the choice of alternations. Nowadays, as computer technology and statistics develop, there have been a few corpus-based studies to explain these syntactic phenomena with authentic corpus data and statistical analysis. Gries (1999, 2001, 2003) were such trials, and these studies adopted a multifactorial analysis to investigate the particle placement in the native speakers' writings. These studies also proposed several linguistics factors and the factors were encoded in the corpus data. These studies demonstrated that various linguistic factors and their interactions with the main factors significantly influenced the choice of alternations

This paper, however, adopted a monofactorial analysis to examine the particle placement in three Eat Asian EFL learners' writings (Korean, Chinese, and Japanese). The TOEFL11 corpus was used for the EFL learners' writings, and the ICE-GB corpus (the British component of the International Corpus of English; Nelson et al., 2002) was chosen for the native speakers' counterparts.

[1] Gries (1999) used the term *particle movement* while Gries (2001) used the term *particle placement*. The former adopted Chomsky's transformational-generative grammar approach (Chomsky, 1957, 1965) and thought that particle moved from one position to another. The latter did not presuppose such movement analysis. This paper adopted Gries' second approach and called the phenomena in (1) *particle placement*. That is, this paper did not presuppose the movement of particles. Instead, how various linguistic factors influenced the placement of particles was investigated with statistical tools.

From these four corpora (Chinese, Japanese, Korean, and ICE-GB), all the relevant sentences were extracted using the tag information. Then, eleven linguistic factors were manually encoded to these sentences. After the process, all the linguistic factors were statistically analyzed with R. Two different types of statistical analyses were adopted in the paper: correlation analysis and a hierarchical clustering. These statistical analyses demonstrated how each linguistic factor played a role in the choice of particle placement, in the four varieties of English.

This paper is organized as follows. In Section 2, three groups of previous studies are reviewed with a focus on corpus-based approaches. Section 3 is on the corpus data and research methods. Section 4 contains the analysis results of correlation analyses, and Section 5 the analyses results of a hierarchical clustering. Section 6 is for discussions, and Section 7 summarizes this paper.

2 Previous Studies

2.1 Studies in Traditional Grammar

There have been several studies on English particle placement in various linguistic fields: traditional grammar (Sweet, 1892; Jespersen, 1928; Kruisinga and Erades, 1953), Chomskyan transformational-generative grammar (Fraser, 1974, 1976; Den Dikken, 1992, 1995; Rohrbacher, 1994), cognitive grammar (Yeagle, 1983), discourse-functional approaches (Chen, 1986), psycholinguistically-oriented approaches (Hawkins, 1994), and so on.

In the traditional grammar, there have been lots of studies on English particle placement (Sweet, 1892; Jespersen, 1928; Kruisinga and Erades, 1953). Gries (1999:33) closely investigated the claims in previous studies and summarized them as in Table 1.

Here, *construction*$_0$ refers to the sentences with the order of 'verb + particle + DO' as in (1a), while *construction*$_1$ refers to the sentences with the order of 'verb + DO + particle' as in (1b). Table 1 enumerated 18 different linguistic factors and this table demonstrated that several different types of factors, not a single factor, actually influenced the choice of alternations.

Value for construction$_0$	Variable	Value for construction$_1$
Long DO	Length of the DO in words (Length W)	
Long DO	Length of the DO in syllables (LengthS)	
Complex	Complexity of the DO (Complex)	
	NP-Type of the DO: semi-pronominal (Type)	pronominal
Indefinite	Determiner of the DO (Det)	definite
No	Previous mention of the DO (Lm)	yes
Low	◄——Times of preceding mention of the DO (Topm)——►	high
High	◄——Distance to last mention of the DO (Dtlm/ActPC)——►	low
High	◄——News Value of the DO——►	low
Yes	(Contrastive) Stress of the DO	
Yes	Subsequent mention of the DO (Nm)	no
High	◄——Times of subsequent mention of the DO (Tosm)——►	low
How	◄——Distance to next mention of the DO (Dtnm/ClusSC)——►	high
	Overall frequency of the DO (Om)	
	following directional adverbial (PP)	yes
Yes	Prep of the following PP is identical to the particle (Part = Prep)	
	Register	
Idiomatic	◄——Meaning of the VP (Idiomaticity)——►	literal
Low	◄——Cognitive Entrenchment of the DO——►	high
Inanimate	Animacy of the DO (Animacy)	animate
Abstract	Concreteness of the DO (Concreteness)	concrete

Table 1: Variables That Govern the Alternation

Let's examine how these factors can be related with the choice of particle placement. For example, LENGTHW (the first factor in Table 1) refers to the length of DO in words. If the DO is long, native speakers tend to choose *construction*$_0$ rather than *construction*$_1$. If the DO is short, however, the native speakers tend to use *construction*$_1$ rather tahn *construction*$_0$. The factor DET, the fifth factor, refers to the determiner of the DO. If the determiner of DO is indefinite (such as *a* or *an*), native speakers tend to choose *construction*$_0$ rather than *construction*$_1$. If the determiner of DO is definite (such as *the*), native speakers prefer to use *construction*$_1$ rather than *construction*$_0$. Table 1 contains all the related factors which cover most of linguistic fields: phonology, syntax, semantics, pragmatics, and discourse analysis.

2.2 Gries' Corpus-based Approaches

Though it is fact that previous studies in traditional grammar surely contributed to the study of particle placement, their data exclusively relied on native speakers' intuition. Gries (2001, 2003) pointed out this problem and performed an analysis based on the corpus data.

Gries (2001:36-37) pointed out the problems of these previous approaches, and Gries (2001, 2003) employed a corpus-based analysis. They adopted both monofactorial analyses and multifactorial analyses.

In the monofactorial analyses, each linguistic factor was statistically analyzed. In these studies, the British National Corpus (BNC; Aston and Burnard, 1998) was taken, and all the sentences with phrasal verbs were extracted. Then, several linguistic factors were manually annotated, and the data were statistically analyzed. Two types of statistical analyses were taken. The first one is correlation analysis, and each factor was analyzed as follows (Gries, 2001:42).

Variable/Variable: *Value*	Correlation Coefficient
Complexity of the DO	γ =-0.85***
Idiomaticity of the VP	γ =-0.6***
Complex: *simple* NP	ϕ=0.522*** (λ=0.49)
NP Type of the DO	ϕ=0.492*** (λ=0.366)
Length of the direct object in syllables	r_{pbis}=-0.481 ***
Type: *lexical* NP	ϕ=0.47*** (λ=0.366)
Type: *pronominal* NP	ϕ=0.468*** (λ=0.32)
Complex: *intermediate* NP	ϕ=0.455*** (λ=0.412)
Distance to last mention of the DO	r_{pbis}=0.452 ***
Cohesiveness of the DO to the preceding discourse	r_{pbis}=0.429 ***
Length of the DO in words	r_{pbis}=0.423 ***
Times of preceding mention of the DO	r_{pbis}=0.414 ***
Last mention of the DO	ϕ=0.411*** (λ=0.387)
Overall mention of the DO	r_{pbis}=0.357 ***
Concreteness of the DO	ϕ=0.339*** (λ=0.314)
Idiomaticity: *idiomatic* VP	ϕ=-0.328*** (λ=0.253)
Determiner of the DO	ϕ=0.319*** (λ=0.206)
Idiomaticity: *literal* VP	ϕ=0.314*** (λ=0.268)
Register	ϕ=0.291*** (λ=0.263)
DET. *indefinite determiner*	ϕ=-0.288*** (λ=0.206)
Directional adverbial	following the DO
DET. *no determiner*	ϕ=0.232*** (λ=0.191)
Complex: *complex* NP	ϕ=-0.193*** (λ=0.077)
Times of subsequent mention of the DO	r_{pbis}=0.191 ***
Animacy of the DO	ϕ=0.166*** (λ=0.057)
Cohesiveness of the DO to the subsequent discourse	r_{pbis}=0.142 ***
Next mention of the DO	ϕ=0.104* (λ=0.072)
Distance to next mention of the DO	r_{pbis}=0.1*
Type: *semi-pronominal* NP	ϕ=0.092*** (λ=0)
Idiomaticity: *metaphorical* NP	ϕ==0.047 ns (λ=0.016)
Type: *proper name*	ϕ=0.023 ns (λ=0)
DET: *definite determiner*	ϕ=-0. 018 ns (λ=0)
Particle equals the preposition of the following PP	ϕ=0.003 ns (λ=0)

Table 2: Correlation Analysis in Gries (2001)

As you can observe in this table, Gries (2001) calculated the correlation coefficients for both each linguistic factor and each value for the factor. In addition to the correlation analysis, Gries (2001) also took a linear discriminant analysis (LDA), where factor loading of each factor was calculated.

Gries (2001, 2003) also employed multifactorial analyses, where all the linguistic factors in Table 1 were taken into consideration simultaneously. The studies used a Generalized Linear Model (GLM) to statistically analyze how each linguistic factor played a role in the choice of alternation. These studies also took a classification and regression tree (CART) and calculated the importance of each factor.

Gries (2001) and Gries (2003) were essentially different from the previous approaches, since (i) these studies were based on corpus data (naturally occurring data) and (ii) they statistically analyzed the collected data.

2.3 Lee et al. (2015) and Lee et al. (2016)

Following the analyses in Gries (2001, 2003), Lee et al. (2015) analyzed the particle placement in the Korean EFL learners' writings. The studies used the Korean component of the TOEFL11 corpus (which was the same corpus that this paper used) to extracted all the sentences with phrasal verbs. Then, eight linguistic factors were encoded into each extracted sentence, and the annotated data were statistically analyzed with GLM.

Through the analysis, it was demonstrated that Korean EFL learners employed a different strategy in the particle placement and that only some factors were used for the selection of constructions. Unlike native speakers, only four linguistic factors were significant in Korean EFL learners' writings (ANIMACY, PRONOMINALITY, CONCRETENESS, and LENGTH). It was also observed that there were some differences in the ratio of these two constructions (*construction$_0$* vs. *construction$_1$*) as the level of proficiency went up.

Lee et al. (2016) extended the scopes of study and statistically examined the particle placement of the EFL learners' writings in three East Asian countries (Chinese, Japanese, and Korean). They manually encoded eleven linguistic factors (Table 4) and statistically analyzed the data with R. The study also adopted a GLM analysis and statistically analyzed how each factor influenced the choice of alternation. The study also took the ICE-GB corpus as a reference corpus and compared the tendencies of the three EFL learners' writings with those of native speakers.

3 Research Method

3.1 Corpus

This study employed two types of data. The first one was the TOEFL11 corpus for the EFL learners (LDC Catalo No.: LDC2014T06), and the second one was the data in ICE-GB for the native speakers (as reference data set).

The TOEFL11 corpus was first released by the English Testing Service (ETS) in 2014. The corpus consists of essays written during the TOEFL iBT® tests in 2006-2007 (Blanchard et al., 2013). It contains 1,100 essays per each of the 11 native languages, totaling 12,100 essays. All of the essays were taken from the parts of TOEFL independent task, where test-takers were asked to write an essay in response to a brief writing topic. The essays were sampled as evenly as possible from eight different topics. The corpus also provides the score levels (Low/Medium/High) for each essay.

From the TOEFL corpus, three components were chosen: Chinese, Japanese, and Korean. The sizes of each component were as follows.

Level	Chinese	Japanese	Korean
High	102,293	67,404	95,066
Medium	228,331	194,716	202,531
Low	21,798	40,060	30,787
Total	352,422	302,180	328,384

Table 3: Corpus Size of Each Component

These texts were the target of the investigations.

The ICE-GB corpus contained both spoken and written components of native speakers in Great Britain. Its size was about 1 million (word) tokens. Among the corpus data in this corpus, only the written part was taken, since the data for three EFL corpora were written materials.

3.2 Procedure

The analysis in this paper proceeded as follows.

First, four corpora were chosen for the analysis: Chinese, Japanese, Korean and ICE-GB.

Second, each text in the three EFL corpora was POS tagged with the C7 CLAWS taggers.[2]

Third, all the sentences with particles were extracted using NLPTools (Lee, 2007).[3]

Fourth, since the number of extracted sentences in three EFL learners' corpora was about 1,000, exactly 1,000 sentences were randomly extracted from the ICE-GB corpus.

Fifth, eleven linguistic factors were encoded to each sentence.[4] They are enumerated in Table 4.[5]

Tag Type	ID Tag	ID Tag Level
Length	LENGTHS	
	LENGTHW	
Synatx	VOICE	active, passive
	NPTYPE	proper noun, lexical, semi-pronominal, pronominal
	DEFINITE	definite, indefinite, no determiner
	COMPLEX	simple, intermediate, complex
	PP	yes, no
	PART=PP	yes, no
Semantics	ANIMACY	animate, inanimate
	IDIOMACITY	literal, metaphorical, idiomatic
	CONCRETENESS	abstract, concrete

Table 4. Variables Used in the Analysis

Following the study of Atkins (1987), each linguistic factor and its level were called ID tag and ID tag levels respectively. These variables were used in the statistical analysis.

Finally, all the data were statistically analyzed using R.

4 Correlation Analysis

4.1 Preprocess

After all the sentences with the particles were extracted from each corpus and eleven linguistic factors were encoded to the extracted sentences, all the data were statistically analyzed using R (R

[2] You can easily use Free CLAWS WWW tagger in http://ucrel.lancs.ac.uk/claws/trial.html. For details of C7 tag sets, see Jurafsky and Martin (2009).

[3] In the C7 tag sets, particles have a tag RP. The reason why NLPTools was used here is that the software had a function which could extract the whole sentences with the given tag(s) (i.e., *_RP).

[4] This operation is called *operationalization* (Deshors, 2010, Deshors and Gries, 2014).

[5] As you can find in this table, all the factors which were related with the discourse properties were not included in the encoding process.

Core Team, 2016). Before the statistical analyses were performed based on Gries (2013) and Lee (2016), the sentences were classified into two groups, based on the transitive vs. intransitive use of phrasal verbs. This process was necessary since the particle placement occurred only in the transitive or ditransitive use of phrasal verbs.

The first statistical analysis which was taken was the correlational analysis. This paper followed the correlation analysis in Gries (2001:41), and the coefficients in Table 5 were determined depending on the measurement scale of the variables.

Variable	Correlation Coefficient
Categorical	ϕ, Cramer's V, and λ
Ordinal	γ (equaling Kendall's τ with correction for ties)
Interval	Pearson product-moment correlation

Table 5: Coefficients for Each Measurement Scale

These (monofactorial) correlation analyses were only taken in order to numerically examine how each linguistic factor influenced the choice of alternation.

Though this paper followed the analysis in Gries (2001), there were three differences between the analysis in Gries (2001) and those of this paper. First, though Gries (2001) provided the correlation coefficients for both each linguistic factor and each value for each linguistic factor, this paper provided the correlation coefficients only for each linguistic factor (not each value for the factor). This strategy was chosen since we were primarily interest in how each linguistic factor influenced the choice of alternation, not how the value for each linguistic factor was.[6] Second, Gries (2001) used Crammer's I, but this paper used Crammer's V instead. This difference was originated from the above strategy. Since Gries (2001) provided the coefficients for both each linguistic factor and each value for each linguistic factor, nominal data prevailed. Since this paper provided the correlation coefficients only for each linguistic factor (not each value for the factor), categorical data were abundant. Thus, Crammer's V was more appropriate in this paper. Third, the (correlation) coefficients for native speakers were provided for the data which were collected from the BNC corpus. However, this paper employed the ICE-GB corpus. In addition, as mentioned in Section 3.2, only 1,000 sentences were randomly extracted from the ICE-GB corpus. Accordingly, a comparison with Gries (2001) was impossible.

The following four tables illustrated the analysis results in the ICE-GB corpus and those of three components in the TOEFL corpus.

Variables	Correlation Coefficient
LENGTHS	r_{pbis}=0.587 ***
LENGTHW	r_{pbis}=0.542 ***
VOICE	ϕ=0.244 * (λ=0)
NPTYPE	γ=-0.819 ***
DEFINITE	V=0.215 ***
COMPLEX	γ=0.717 ***
PP	ϕ=0.1 * (λ=0)
PART=PP	ϕ=0.021 ** (λ=0)
ANIMACY	ϕ=0.3 *** (λ=0)
IDIOMACITY	V=-0.03 ***
CONCRETENESS	ϕ=-0.36 *** (λ=0.259)

Table 6: Correlation Analysis (English)

Variables	Correlation Coefficient
LENGTHS	r_{pbis}=0.684 ***
LENGTHW	r_{pbis}=0.645 ***
VOICE	ϕ=0.12 * (λ=0)
NPTYPE	γ=-0.912 ***
DEFINITE	V=0.169 ***
COMPLEX	γ=0.826 ***
PP	ϕ=0.07 * (λ=0)
PART=PP	ϕ=0.28 ** (λ=0)
ANIMACY	ϕ=0.017 *** (λ=0)
IDIOMACITY	V=-0.09 ***
CONCRETENESS	ϕ=-0.33 *** (λ=0.218)

Table 7: Correlation Analysis (Chinese)

Variables	Correlation Coefficient
LENGTHS	r_{pbis}=0.784 ***
LENGTHW	r_{pbis}=0.713 ***
VOICE	ϕ=0.068 * (λ=0)
NPTYPE	γ=-0.968 ***
DEFINITE	V=0.187 ***
COMPLEX	γ=0.933 ***
PP	ϕ=0.08 * (λ=0)
PART=PP	ϕ=0.015 ** (λ=0)
ANIMACY	ϕ=0.15 *** (λ=0)
IDIOMACITY	V=-0.15 ***
CONCRETENESS	ϕ=-0.32 *** (λ=0.174)

Table 8: Correlation Analysis (Korean)

[6] You might investigate the value for each linguistic factor in the analysis of Lee et al. (2016).

Variables	Correlation Coefficient
LENGTHS	r_{pbis}=0.636 ***
LENGTHW	r_{pbis}=0.577 ***
VOICE	ϕ=0.066 * (λ=0)
NPTYPE	γ=-0.938 ***
DEFINITE	V=0.066 ***
COMPLEX	γ=0.788 ***
PP	ϕ=0.12 * (λ=0)
PART=PP	ϕ=0.013 ** (λ=0)
ANIMACY	ϕ=0.28 *** (λ=0)
IDIOMACITY	V=0.07 ***
CONCRETENESS	ϕ=-0.23 *** (λ=0.126)

Table 9: Correlation Analysis (Japanese)

These tables demonstrated that each linguistic factor played a role differently in each variety of English.

In these four tables, the following three facts were observed. First, the absolute values for the coefficients in two factors (NPTYPE and COMPLEX) were over 0.7. We usually say that the relationship is strong if the coefficient is over 0.7. Accordingly, we could say that the relationship was strong in these two factors. Second, the absolute values for the coefficients in two factors (LENGTHS and LENGTHW) were between 0.3 and 0.7. We usually say that the relationship is moderate if the value is between 0.3 and 0.7. Consequently, we could say that the relationship was moderate in these two factors. Third, the values for the coefficients in the other factors were under 0.3. We usually say that the relationship is weak if the coefficient is under 0.3. Thus, we could say that the relationships were weak in the other factors.

A close comparison of these tables revealed (i) that the values of native speakers (English) were similar to those of Japanese EFL learners and (ii) that the values of Chinese EFL learners were similar to those of Korean EFL learners.

5 Agglomerative Clustering

In order to examine which one was close to which one, another statistical analysis was performed. The second statistical analysis was a hierarchical agglomerative clustering analysis.

Usually, the cluster analyses have been used to determine the similarity among the group members or the degree of granularity exhibited by the group members. In this paper, the tables of correlation coefficients were submitted into a hierarchical agglomerative cluster analysis, resulting in the dendrogram in the following figure.

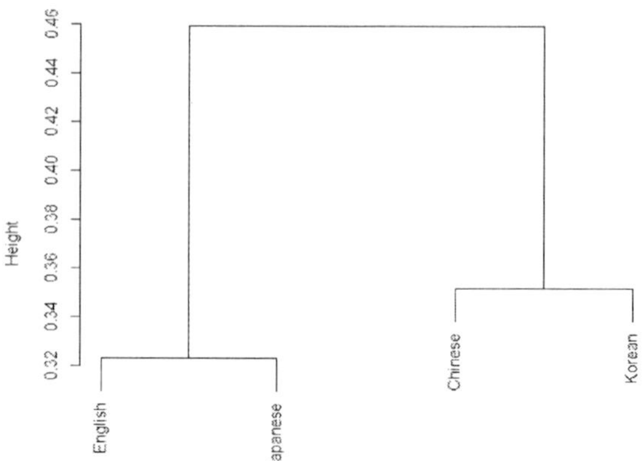

Figure 1: Cluster Dendrogram

Here, the horizontal lines indicate which one can be grouped with which one, and the vertical lines indicate the distance between the two groups.

This figure graphically illustrated the following facts. First, the correlation relationships of native speakers (i.e., English) were similar to those of Japanese EFL learners, which can be represented as {English, Japanese}. Second, the relationships of Chinese EFL learners were similar to those of Korean EFL learners, which can be represented as {Chinese, Korean}. Third, these two groups were amalgamated together to form a cluster {{English, Japanese}, {Chinese, Korean}}. The dendrogram in Figure 1 demonstrated (i) that the tendency of particle placement of Japanese EFL learners was close to that of native speakers and (ii) that the tendencies of particle placement of Chinese and Korean EFL learners were slightly far from that of native speakers.

6 Discussions

In this paper, the alternation of particle placement was closely examined in the native speakers' writings and the three EFL learners' writings.

From the three components of the TOEFL11 corpus and the ICE-GB corpus, all the sentences with phrasal verbs were extracted and eleven factors were manually encoded into the extracted sentences.

The correlation analyses between these eleven linguistic factors and the choice of alternation revealed the following facts. First, the coefficients in two linguistic factors (NPTYPE and NPTYPE) were strong since the coefficient is over 0.7. This means that the data points for these two linguistic factors were closely distributed to the regression lines for these factors. Second, the coefficients in two linguistic factors (LENGTHS and LENGTHW) were moderate since the coefficient was between 0.3 and 0.7. This means that the data points for these linguistic factors were moderately distributed to the regression lines for these factors. Of course, the coefficients of LENGTHS and LENGTHW were over 0.7 in Korean. This says that the relationship of these factors was strong in the Korean EFL learners' writings. Third, the coefficients in the other linguistic factors were weak since the values were under 0.3. This means that the data points for these linguistic factors were sparsely distributed to the regression lines for these factors.

Based on the results of correlation analysis, a hierarchical agglomerative clustering analysis was performed. This analysis was conducted in order to examine which one was close to which one. The analysis result was {{English, Japanese}, {Chinese, Korean}}, where the correlation relationships of native speakers (i.e., English) were similar to those of Japanese EFL learners and the relationships of Chinese EFL learners were similar to those of Korean EFL learners.

If it had been supposed that the EFL learners were severely influenced by the L1, the correlation analysis results would have been different. That is, if it had been supposed that the L1 transfer effects had involved in the choice of particle placement in the three EFL learners' writings (following the study of Oldin [1989, 2003]), the analysis result would have been {{English}, {Japanese, Chinese, Korean}}. The dendrogram in Figure 1 illustrated that more factors might be involved in the choice of particle placement constructions in the Japanese EFL learners, as Lee et al. (2016) mentioned. More study is necessary to investigate what linguistic or extra-linguistic factors influenced this kind of tendency.

7 Conclusion

This paper adopted a monofactorial analysis as in Gries (2001, 2003) to examine particle placement in three East Asian EFL learners' writings. For the comparison, two different types of corpora were chosen. The components of the TOEFL11 corpus was used for the EFL learners' parts (Chinese, Japanese, and Korean), and the ICE-GB corpus was chosen for the native speakers' parts. Then, all the relevant sentences were extracted using the tag information. After that, the eleven relevant factors were encoded to these sentences, and each factor and their interactions were statistically analyzed with R.

Through the correlation analysis, it was found that each linguistic factor influenced differently in four varieties of English. Through the hierarchical agglomerative clustering analysis, it was found that the correlation relationships of native speakers (i.e., English) were similar to those of Japanese EFL learners and the relationships of Chinese EFL learners were similar to those of Korean EFL learners.

However, we do NOT say that these differences between the native speakers and the three East Asian EFL learners come from only the L1 transfer effects. Another kind of complicated statistical analysis (such as another regression analysis with the native data and/or the analysis in Gries and Deshors (2015)) is necessary to examine if the L1 really influenced these factors and how much the L1 transfer effects are involved in these factors. Notwithstanding, this mentioning does not say that the analysis result in this paper is meaningless. The analysis results in this paper enumerate how much each linguistic factor influenced the choice of particle placement, and we can start our future research from this set of factors.

References

Bernhard Rohrbacher. 1994. English Main Verbs Move Never. The Penn Review of Linguistics, 18:145-159.

Beryl Atkins. 1987. Semantic ID Tags: Corpus Evidence for Dictionary Senses. In Proceedings of the Annual Conference of the UW Center for the New Oxford English Dictionary, 17-36. University of Waterloo, Waterloo, ON, Canada.

Bruce Fraser. 1974. The Phrasal Verb in English, by Dwight Bolinger. Language, 50:568-575.

Bruce Fraser. 1976. The Verb-Particle Combination in English. New York: Academic Press.

Daniel Blanchard, Joel Tetreault, Derrick Higgins, Aoife Cahill, and Martin Chodorow. 2013. TOEFL11: A corpus of non-native English. ETS RR-13-24. Prinston, NJ: Educational Testing Service.

Daniel jurafsky and James Martin. 2009. Speech and Language Processing: An Introduction to Natural Language Processing, Computational Linguistics and Speech Recognition. Prentice Hall, Upper Saddle Hill, NJ.

Etsko Kruisinga and Patrick Erades. 1953. An English Grammar. Vol. I. P. Noordhoff, Groningen.

Etsko Kruisinga and Patrick Erades. 1953. An English Grammar. Vol. I. Groningen: P. Noordhoff.

Gerald Nelson, Sean Wallis, and Bas Aarts. 2002. Exploring Natural Language: Working with the British Component of the International Corpus of English. John Benjamins Publishing Company, Amsterdam.

Guy Aston and Lou Burnard. 1998. The BNC Handbook. Exploring the British National Corpus with SARA. Edinburgh University Press, Edinburgh.

Gyu-hyoeng Lee, Ha-Eung Kim, and Yong-hun Lee. 2015. A Multifactorial Analysis of English Particle Movement in Korean EFL Learners' Writings. Proceedings of 19th Pacific Asian Conference on Language, Information, and Computation. Shanghai, China.

Henry Sweet. 1892. A New English Grammar. Clarendon Press, Oxford.

Henry Sweet. 1892. A New English Grammar. Oxford: Clarendon Press.

John Hawkins. 1994. A Performance Theory of Order and Constituency. Cambridge: Cambridge University Press.

Marcel Den Dikken. 1995. Particles: On the Syntax of Verb-Particle, Triadic, and Causative Constructions. Oxford: Oxford University Press.

Marcel Den Kikken. 1992. Particles. Holland Institute of Linguistics Dissertations. The Hague: Holland Academic Graphics.

Noam Chomsky. 1957. Syntactic Structures. Mouton, Berlin.

Noam Chomsky. 1965. Aspects of the Theory of Syntax. MIT Press. Cambridge.

Otto Jespersen. 1928. A Modern English Grammar on Historical Principles. George Allen and Unwin Ltd., London.

Otto Jespersen. 1928. A Modern English Grammar on Historical Principles. London: George Allen and Unwin Ltd.

Ping Chen. 1986. Discourse and Particle Movement in English. Studies in Language 10:79-95.

R Core Team. 2016. R: A Language and Environment for Statistical Computing. Vienna: R Foundation for Statistical Computing.

Rosemary Yeagle. 1983. The Syntax and Semantics of English Verb-Particle Constructions with off: A Space Grammar Analysis. Unpublished M.A. Thesis, Southern Illinois University at Carbondale

Sandra Deshors and Stefan Th. Gries. 2014 A Case for the Multifactorial Assessment of Learner Language: The Use of *May* and *Can* in French-English Interlanguage. In Dylan Glynn and Justyna Robinson (eds.), Corpus Methods for Semantics: Quantitative Studies in Polysemy and Synonymy, 179-204. John Benjamins Publishing Company, Amsterdam.

Sandra Deshors. 2010. Multifactorial Study of the Use of *May* and *Can* in French-English Interlanguage. Ph.D. dissertation. University of Sussex.

Stefan Th. Gries and Sandra Deshors. 2015. EFL and/vs. ESL? A Multi-level Regression Modeling Perspective on Bridging the Paradigm Gap. International Journal of Learner Corpus Research 1(1): 130–159.

Stefan Th. Gries. 1999. Particle movement: A Cognitive and Functional Approach, Cognitive Linguistics, 10(2):105-145.

Stefan Th. Gries. 2001. A Multifactorial Analysis of Syntactic Variation: Particle Movement Revisited. Journal of Quantitative Linguistics, 8(1):33-50.

Stefan Th. Gries. 2003. Multifactorial Analysis in Corpus Linguistics: A Study of Particle Movement. Continumm, London.

Stefan Th. Gries. 2013. Statistics for Linguistics with R: A Practical Introduction. Guyter, Berlin.

Terence Oldin. 1989. Language Transfer. Cambridge University Press, Cambridge.

Terence Oldin. 2003. Cross-linguistic Inference. In Catherine Doughty and Michael Long (eds.), The Handbook of Second Language Acquisition, 436-486. Blackwell, Oxford.

Yong-hun Lee, Ha-Eung Kim, and Gyu-hyoeng Lee. 2016. A Multifactorial Analysis of English Particle Placement in Three East Asian Countries. A Submitted Paper.

Yong-hun Lee. 2007. Corpus Analysis Using NLPTools and Their Applications: Applications to Linguistic Research, English Education, and Textbook Evaluation. Cambridge University Press, Seoul.

Yong-hun Lee. 2016. Corpus Linguistics and Statistics Using R. Hankook Publishing Company, Seoul.

The sources of new words and expressions in the Chinese Internet language and the ways by which they enter the Internet language

Aleksandr Sboev
Far Eastern Federal University
Vladivostok
Russian Federation
sboevalexander@mail.ru

Abstract

The given work is focused on the principal ways by which new words and expressions enter the Chinese Internet language, the sources of new meanings for old words and phrases; neologisms and chengyu with modified meaning and structure. Some new tendencies in developing of the Chinese Internet language, such as wide use of dialect-originated words, archaic characters and monosyllabic words, are introduced as well.

1 Introduction

The Internet brings some new ways of words formation in language. Apart from character-written words, in the Chinese Internet language there also can be words written with English letters, pinyin, punctuation marks and even pictures. As a matter of fact, the Internet language is a kind of a social dialect. It is mainly spread in the Internet environment and differs from the language of the classical information channels and the real environment. Moreover, it has two characteristic features: virtuality and temporality (Yu, 2013).

The relevance of the research topic is defined by the fact that the Internet as a means of spreading information and exchanging messages becomes increasingly important in the modern world. The Internet language is constantly developing: it is being enriched with completely new words and new meanings for already existing ones, as a consequence, there can be confusion in understanding and usage of them either by native or non-native speakers; therefore a thorough research into such vocabulary is necessary. In view of rapid development and spread of modern science and technologies, including the Internet technologies, and the growing influence of the Internet on different aspects of contemporary human's life, the research on the Internet language seems to be more important, so the Internet lexicon is what has been chosen as the subject.

The attempts to find out how new words and expressions penetrate into the Chinese Internet language and where they originate from, constitute a fresh study field in linguistics

Elaboration on the ways in which the vocabulary is evolving in the modern Chinese makes the research theoretically valuable.

It can also have a high practical value, as the results of the research introduced here could serve as valid materials for lectures and practical classes of Mandarin lexicology, and for working on Internet language dictionaries.

The purpose of the research is to reveal the principal ways by which new words and expressions enter the Chinese Internet language. Apart from Chinese Internet language, the author also has done some research on words that emerged in English and Russian Internet language by the same ways as in Chinese Internet language.

In the lexicon of the Internet language Chinese and non-Chinese, ancient and modern languages, Putonghua (Standard Chinese) and different dialects are exquisitely combined. It is like a 'jigsaw', different and numerous cuts of which have been put together by web-users, who had applied for it all power of their imagination and every piece of their knowledge (Zhang, 2014).

So, the principal sources of new words and expressions in the Internet language are introduced as below.

2 Dialect-originated words in the Chinese Internet language

All Chinese dialects are divided into 10 groups: guanhua, min, jin, wu, hakka, yue, xiang, gan, hui, pinghua (Zavyalova, 2010).

Nevertheless, the Internet has accelerated the process of integration: in the Internet language one can come across a great number of dialect-originated words regardless of where they are spread.

Dialects supplement the Standard Chinese and continually enrich the language on the whole. Each of the dialects in China is bound to a particular region, although web-users do not feel it when communicating online. Therefore many words from different dialects are widely used and becoming rather popular. For example, 粉 *fěn* 'pink' means 很 *hěn* 'very', as in the south min dialect 很 *hěn* is consonant to 粉 *fěn*, plus, the colour of pink itself symbolizes romanticism, kindness, love, so 粉 *fěn* has replaced 很 *hěn* rather quickly (Xu, 2013).

However, not all dialect-originated words can enter the common language and steadily fix in it. According to Xu Chaohui's point of view, to come into being in the common language a dialect-originated word should meet the two following conditions: 1) it should be easy to understand, memorize and use in speech; 2) it should go beyond the limits of the dialect it belongs to, be perfectly usable in everyday life. So, only highly expressive words are likely to enter the common language (Xu, 2013).

People from all over the country are permanently communicating with each other in the Internet space. As a result, a lot of dialect-originated words have entered the basic vocabulary of the Internet language (Zhang, 2010). Although web-users to communicate with each other mainly use the Standard Chinese, to accelerate the process of communication and to express one's region's particularity, in some cases they use dialect-originated words as well. Also web-users to show off their originality can deliberately use words from alien dialects.

Many dialect-originated words are written in the same way as words in Putonghua, the only difference between them lies in their pronunciation. As this cannot be noticed in writing, web-users write characters which pronunciations are near to the pronunciation of the given word in dialect, and therefore make a sound effect. Because of the fact that Chinese is famous for its numerous homonyms, when a person types a word on keyboard, he encounters more than one variant of characters of the word, so web-users in order to accelerate the process of communication choose the first variant in the list without consideration, sometimes implying a hidden sense. For example, in (1) a user chose 女银 *nǚ yín* instead of 女人 *nǚ rén*, because the latter is pronounced as the former in the north-east dialect, but the character 银 *yín* 'silver' itself is related to money (the left radical means 'money'), so the given word in the given context can imply two senses, one of which is 'mercantile girl' (Tang, 2010).

(1) 有个哥哥说这样子爱慕虚荣的女银不适合的
Yǒu gè gē gē shuō zhèi yàng zǐ ài mù xū róng de nǚ yín bù shì hé de
'One lad said that such girls, boasting of their positive sides, were really not suitable'.

Here are some more dialect-originated words that have entered the Internet language: 贼 *zéi* 'very' – belongs to the dialect group guanhua (Xu, 1999); 偶 *ǒu* 'I, my' – belongs to the dialect group wu (Xu 1999); 阿拉 *àla* 'I, my' – belongs to the Shanghai dialect of the dialect group wu (Xu, 1999).

Xinhua Internet Language Dictionary published in 2012 in Beijing contains 0.5% dialectisms (Wang, 2012).

English Internet language also has number of dialect-originated words, for example: cum 'ere – come here; o'er there – over there; 'em – them.

3 Use of archaic characters in the Chinese Internet language

Some characters, which were hardly ever used before, are becoming very popular in the Internet language today. The character 囧 is an example. In the Internet language the given character has lost its original meaning 'light (n/adj.)' and gained a new one 'sad, helpless, difficult'. The meaning is easy to work out, as the character's picture resembles a face of a depressed man.

Tang Lan once said that the three characteristics of each Chinese character are its spelling, meaning and pronunciation (Tang, 2005). But web-users in writing archaic characters save only their spelling and pronunciation but change their meaning. The new meaning is defined by meanings of radicals building the character.

As the character 槑 *méi* (original meaning is 'plum') consists of two 呆 *dāi* 'stupid', it has acquired the meaning of the word 很呆 *hěn dāi* 'very stupid' in the Internet language. It should be noted that with this meaning the word 槑 *méi* has been included in dictionaries of neologisms. (Wang, 2011)

The basic meaning of the character 靐 *bìng* is 'thunder'. The character consists of three 雷 *léi* which in the Internet language means 'shocking, stunning'. If three 雷 *léi* are gathered together, it means that a particular event or subject is extremely shocking, that is what 靐 *bìng* actually implies.

The word 煋 *xīng* has replaced 火星 *huǒ xīng* 'Mars' in the Internet language, and can be used instead of a sentence like (2) somewhere in a forum or chat as a reaction to an absurd saying or comment.

(2) 你火星来的吗？
Nǐ huǒ xīng lái de ma？
'Are you from Mars?'

The original meaning of the character 兲 *tiān* is the same as 天 *tiān* 'sky'. To work out the meaning of the former in the Internet language, one has to take out the upper and the lower parts of the character and put them together – 王八 *wáng bā* which means 'bastard, scoundrel'.

The original meaning of the character 巭 *bū* (or *pū*) is 工作人员 *gōng zuò rén yuán* 'working stuff'. But after the success of 'Kong Fu Panda', the film became a frequent topic in Internet forums and chats, so the character 巭 (it consists of 功 *gōng* and 夫 *fú* which combine as 功夫 'kong fu' has got the meaning of 有功夫的人 *yǒu gōng fú de rén* 'a person who can do kong fu' and come into wide use in the Internet.

The character 砳 *lè* is an onomatopoeia (imitates the sound of clashing of two rocks), and has acquired the meaning 'joy, happy' in the Internet language, because it sounds the same with 乐 *lè* 'happy' (Chinese General Political Propaganda Department, 2014).

Archaic characters compose 0.2% of the words in the Xinhua Internet Language Dictionary (Wang, 2012).

4 Monosyllabic (one-morpheme) words in the Chinese Internet language

The vocabulary of the modern Chinese in the process of development has gradually become disyllabic; most of monosyllabic words of the ancient Chinese have been replaced by their disyllabic variants; many polysyllabic words have been reduced to two syllables as well. But in the Internet language the situation is exactly opposite – more and more words are becoming monosyllabic (Lin, 2012).

One of typological features of Chinese is mutual exchangeability of a monosyllabic and disyllabic variant of one word. In the Chinese Internet language, as a result of realization of the economy principle in language, there has been the tendency to use only monosyllabic variants. Some monosyllabic words have come into use instead of di- and polysyllabic words with the same meaning. For example, one can come across such monosyllabic words as 晕 *yūn* instead of 搞不懂 *gǎo bù dǒng* 'to get confused, to feel faint'; 顶 *dǐng* instead of 支持 *zhī chí* 'to support'；赞 *zàn* instead of 赞同 *zàn tong* 'to put a like on smth, to praise'; 挂 *guà* instead of 失败 *shī bài* 'to fail'; 踩 *cǎi* instead of 反对 *fǎn duì* 'to oppose'; 萌 *méng* instead of 很可爱 *hěn kě ài* 'nice, lovely'; 晒 *shài* instead of 分享 *fēn xiǎng* 'to share'; 秀 *xiù* instead of 公开 *gōng kāi* 'open, public', etc. (Fu, 2013). It should be noted that the last three words are loaned: 萌 *méng* from Japanese (もえ moe), 晒 *shài* from English (share) and 秀 *xiù* from English too (show).

Monosyllabic words written with archaic characters introduced above, and words like 把 *bǎ*, 雷 *léi*, 汗 *hàn*, 倒 *dào*, 菜 *cài*, etc., introduced below, have obtained other meanings in the Internet language.

Xinhua Internet Language Dictionary contains 3.3% monosyllabic words (Wang, 2012).

5 New meanings for words, phrases, expressions in the Chinese Internet

The emergence of new things and new concepts results in emergence of new words and new meanings of the old words. The arrival of the computer and the Internet furthered this process. Old words which gain new meanings in the Internet language, make 7.3% of all the new words (Cao, 2012). A word form can remain the same, but some changes can occur within a meaning. The words created this way are not completely new words as they remain their spelling and pronunciation, just get a new meaning.

There are three basic ways of changing the word meaning: widening, narrowing and transfer of meaning (Sun, 2006). In the Internet language the most common way is the transfer of meaning. It is often based on comparison and association.

A figurative meaning partly keeps an original meaning but at the same time the meaning partly changes, thus the new meaning of the word is created.

恐龙 *kǒnglóng* – a basic meaning is 'a dinosaur', but in the Internet language this word means 'an ugly girl'. This new meaning has the following prehistory: 龙 *lóng* refers us to Zhuge Liang's wife named Huang Yueying. She was one of the ugliest women in Jingzhou, prefecture-level city in Hubei province. Zhuge Liang was called 孔明 *kǒngmíng*, thus people started respectfully call Huang Yueying 孔龙 *kǒnglóng*. Afterwards all the ugly women were called 孔龙 *kǒnglóng*, and because 孔 *kǒng* and 恐 *kǒng* morphemes are homonyms, the word 恐龙 *kǒnglóng* little by little replaced the word 孔龙 *kǒnglóng* (Internet "Dinosaur", 2014).

However, considerable number of words taking on new meanings in the Internet is common:

打铁 *dǎtiě* 'to forge', being homonym of 打贴 *dǎtiē* 'to post, to leave a message', in the Internet language gets a new meaning 'to post, to leave a message'.

灌水 *guànshuǐ* 'to irrigate' is a loan translation of the English word "flood" i.e. to leave lots of unimportant messages.

造砖 *zàozhuān* 'brick production' – 'to flame', i.e. to give blunt statements, assault interlocutor, and if it causes arguments between forum guests, it calls 拍砖 *pāizhuān* 'to advance an opinion'.

隔壁 *gébì* 'through the wall' – 'another topic on this forum'.

潜水 *qiánshuǐ* 'underwater diving' – 'to visit forum without leaving messages', which is similar to 'surf the net' in English.

Internet users sometimes replace their names or other people's names with food products names. For example, fans of a Chinese actress Li Yuchun's (李宇春) are called 玉米 *yùmǐ* 'corn', because 玉 *yù* sounds similar to 宇 *yǔ*, and 米 *mǐ* – to 迷 *mí* 'fan'. Fans of a singer named Zhang Liangying (张靓颖) are called 凉粉 *liángfěn* 'cold mung bean noodles', as 凉 *liáng* sounds similar to 靓 *liàng*, and 粉 *fěn* is a part of the word 粉丝 *fěnsī* 'fan'. Admirers of He Jie (何洁), an actress and a singer, are called 盒饭 *héfàn* 'food in container', because 盒 *hé* sounds similar to 何 *hé*, and 饭 *fàn* to 粉 *fěn*. About those who like all the three girls people say: 早上吃玉米，中午吃凉粉，晚上吃盒饭 *zǎoshang chī yùmǐ, zhōngwǔ chīl liángfěn, wǎnshang chī héfàn* 'he/she has corn for breakfast, noodles for dinner and food in container for supper'. These three girls were born in Chengdu (Sichuan province) so their admirers are called 成都小吃团 *chéngdū xiǎochītuán* 'a group of Chengdu light refreshments lovers' (Tang, 2010).

The morpheme 把 *bǎ* 'to keep, to grab' is used with meaning of 'to court, to flirt', e.g.: 把妹妹 *bǎmèimei* or 把美眉 *bǎměiméi* 'to court a girl'.

倒 *dǎo* 'to fall' is used with meaning of 晕倒 *yūndǎo* 'to faint away, to be shocked', which is caused by something unexpected or surprising (Zhang, 2010).

坛子 *tánzi* 'a jar' means 'forum', is formed from the word 论坛 *lùntán* 'forum' by omitting the morpheme 论 *lùn* and adding the derivational suffix 子 *zi*. The messages leaved top-down also have their own names – 楼上 *lóushàng* 'the previous post' и 楼下 *lóuxià* 'the next post'. And a person who created a topic is called 楼主 *lóuzhǔ* 'a topic starter'.

Some words, phrases and expressions used in popular movies, books, TV serials, advertisements, as well as said by famous figures, announcers, politicians etc., thanks to the resourcefulness of the Internet users get some new meanings in the Internet language. Here are some examples:

a) 理论准备不足 *lǐlùn zhǔnbèi bùzú*

People's Liberation Army National University of Defense Science and Technology professor Gong Fangbin was mocked in the Internet because of his article where he said: 中国不是惧怕民主，政治改革无法推进是因为"理论准备不足" *Zhōngguó bùshì jùpà mínzhǔ, zhèngzhì gǎigé wúfǎ tuījìn shì yīnwèi "lǐlùn zhǔnbèi bùzú*" 'China is not afraid of democracy, but political reforms won't turn into practice as we don't have enough theoretical training»'. So Internet users found the reason of all their problems and failures, they started to describe them like that: 不是惧怕结婚，而是很大程度上缘于理论准备不足 *Bùshì jùpà jiéhūn, érshì hěn dà chéngdù shàng yuányú lǐlùn zhǔnbèi bùzú* 'I'm not afraid of getting married, I just don't have enough theoretical training', a blogger wrote in his microblog. (The Top 10 Chinese Internet Memes of 2012).

b) 看星星 *kànxīngxīng*

A basic meaning is 'to look at the stars', but is the Internet this expression has a different meaning. The sources of this new meaning are the following: as in Chinese dormitories a student must come back strictly before certain time, those students who come late should write down the reason in a log book. So one of the students of Beijing Film Academy came late and to explain her delay wrote that 'she was looking at the stars'. After a time log entries got into the Internet and attracted user's attention. After that an expression 看星星 *kànxīngxīng* in the Internet language means 'a reason for evasion of business or a cause for being absent at school or at work '(Yu, 2013). For example, (3).

(3) 谁和我结伴去"看星星"去?

Sheí hé wǒ jiébàn qù "kànxīngxīng" qù?

'Who will keep me company and go 'looking at the stars'?'

c) 躲猫猫 *duǒmāomāo*

A basic meaning is 'to play hide-and-seek'. 28 January 2009 citizen Li Qiaoming was imprisoned. His cellmates treated Li very unkindly and often beat him. During another assault co-prisoners blindfolded him, and Li didn't survive. At the interrogation about the incident Li's cellmate said they were just playing hide-and-seek, and Li Qiaoming accidentally stroke himself against the wall and therefore died. After these events the expression 躲猫猫 *duǒmāomāo* began to be used for labeling different wordings people use to evade legal accountability. (Yu, 2013). For example, (4), (5).

(4) 检方调查男子看守所身亡，真相不会"躲猫猫"

Jiǎnfāng diàochá nánzǐ kānshǒusuǒ shēnwáng, zhēnxiàng bù huì "duǒmāomāo"

'The Prosecutor's Office opens an investigation into the circumstances of the death a man in a lock-up ward, and the true state of affairs won't be concealed'.

(5) 政府不应该和媒体玩躲猫猫

Zhèngfǔ bù yīnggāi hé méitǐ wán "duǒmāomāo"

'The government shouldn't 'play hide-and-seek' with mass media'.

d) 卖肾 *màishèn*

In 2012 a 17-year-old man decided to sell his own kidney to buy a new iPhone. This incident caused a surge of discussions in the Internet and now the word 卖肾 *màishèn* 'to sell the kidney' is used in the meaning 'to sell something in order to use the gained money for buying a new thing'. For example, (6).

(6) iPhone 6 要出了，又要卖肾了

iPhone 6 yàochū le, yòu yào màishèn le

'iPhone 6 is going on sale, I have to «sell my kidney» again'.

There are some words in the English and Russian Internet language that gain new meanings, for example: 'to freeze' means 'become temporarily locked because of system problems (of a computer screen)'.

Original meaning of the Russian word 'грузить' *gruzit'* is 'load', but in the Russian Internet language it means 'download' or 'upload'.

6 Chengyu with modified meaning and structure in the Chinese Internet language

The chengyu 不见不散 *bù jiàn bù sàn* 'not to party before seeing', having a positive connotation, with putting one comma obtains a different meaning in the Internet language: 不见，不散 *bù jiàn, bù sàn* 'not to see, not to party'; besides, the chengyu can be lexically altered, thus acquiring another sense: 一见就散 *yī jiàn jiù sàn* 'to party immediately after seeing' (Zhang, 2014).

The chengyu 娇生惯养 *jiāo shēng guàn yǎng* 'spoiled, effete' has a modified form in the Internet language – 娇身冠养 *jiāo shēn guān yǎng* 'Jiao keeps Guan' where 'Jiao' means 阿娇 *ā jiāo* 'A Jiao' (a stage name of a Chinese female singer) and 冠 *guān* means 陈冠希 *chén guānxī* 'Chen Guanxi' (a name of a Chinese male singer). This 'new' chengyu emerged after one scandalous photo of A Jiao and Chen Guanxi being together had released in the Internet (Cao, 2012).

In the Internet language there are some examples of 'new' chengyu created by replacing one of their components, and thus frequently acquiring a meaning opposite to the original one. For example, 如花似玉 *rú huā sì yù* 'to be like a flower and a jade' (refers to a beautiful woman) transforms into 如花撕玉 *rú huā sī yù* 'lit. to be like a flower tearing a jade' (refers to smth ugly and disgusting) (Cao, 2012).

The chengyu 奋发图强 *fèn fā tú qiáng* 'to work hard and enthusiastically in order to make (the country) powerful and flourishing' transforms into a homonymic one 粉发涂强 *fěn fā tú qiáng* '[referring to] girls who are mad about make-up' (粉 *fěn* – powder, rouge; 涂 *tú* – to paint (face), to smear).

The chengyu 一键钟情 *yī jiàn zhōng qíng* 'to fall in love at the first click' originates from the chengyu 一见钟情 *yī jiàn zhōng qíng* 'to fall in love at the first sight' (键 jiàn and 见 jiàn are homonyms), and is used in respect of people addicted to the Internet.

The chengyu 美丽动人 *měi lì dòng rén* 'beautiful and charming' refers to beautiful girls; a homonymic chengyu 美丽冻人 *měi lì dòng rén* 'lit. beautiful and frozen' is used in respect of girls who try to dress beautifully but not according to the weather.

Besides, there are some chengyu which can obtain new meanings without replacement of their lexical components. For example, the chengyu 火眼金睛 *huǒ yǎn jīn qíng* 'lit. fire eye, golden eye' is used when talking of a person who has a sharp eye and is capable to discriminate the truth from the lie. In modern Chinese the idiom is used in respect of a student whose perfect seeing enables him to successfully cheat on exams.

The chengyu 后起之秀 *hòu qǐ zhī xiù* means 'a young talent' (后起 *hòu qǐ* means 'young generation, youngsters, young'), but it has acquired a new meaning which is 'a student who was the last to get up from bed' (refers to lovers of sleep). In the given context the word 后起 *hòu qǐ* should be read according to the basic meanings of the first and the second characters: 后 - 'last', 起 - 'to get up' (Xu, 2013).

Xinhua Internet Language Dictionary contains 1.6% different types of idioms (Wang, 2012).

English spoken Internet users and Russian Internet users also create new idioms. For example, the idiom 'to rock smb's boat' means 'drive crazy', 'to grind gears' means 'enrage'.

Russian idioms 'аффтар жжет' *afftar zhzhot* means 'the topic's author wrote something interesting, absurd or shocked'.

7 Conclusion

Due to a great variety of ways by which new words enter the Internet language, the latter is dynamically developing. The Internet language is full of words originated from different dialect groups and used by web-users regardless of their own belonging to a particular dialect group. As a result, dialect-originated words are no longer regarded as such in the Internet language, and become a part of the basic vocabulary of the whole language, thus making it more expressive.

The other source of new words and expressions in the Internet language is new meanings for words written with archaic characters. To work out a new meaning, one has to read a character according to radicals building it from top to bottom (i.g., 嫑 *biáo*) or from left to right (i.g., 煋 *xīng*), or sometimes by associating a character with a certain image (i.g., 囧 *jiǒng*).

Words written with archaic characters as a rule are monosyllabic; use of monosyllabic words instead of di- and polysyllabic ones is one of tendencies in developing of the Internet language, and, besides, one of the sources of its lexical enrichment. Some monosyllabic words replace their synonymic variants with more than one morpheme; some constitute a part of a polysyllabic word.

Some words, when entering the Internet language, are gaining new meanings derived from the original meaning of a word, or created by semantic transfer based on metaphorical, metonymical, functional and associative connection with the original meaning.

The Internet language has its own chengyu which mostly are coined by replacing one of lexical components of existing chengyu. Some chengyu can obtain new meanings without any modifying in structure.

The sources of new lexis in the Chinese Internet language are numerous and different. For example, they can be events causing a particular reaction among web-users, posts on forums, sayings of different people, etc.

References

Cao Jin. 2012. An introduction to Internet language dissemination. Beijing: Tsinghua University Press.

Cao Qi. 2012. Language variations of the Chinese in the new period. Beijing: China Social Sciences Publishing House.

Fu Yifei. 2013. Comparative study of English and Chinese Internet language. Beijing: National Defense Industry Press.

General Political Propaganda Department. 2014. A selection of Internet language neologisms. Beijing: PLA Publishing House.

Internet "Dinosaur" // Baidu Baike. URL: http://baike.baidu.com/view/573964.htm (acceptance date: 13.07.2014)

Lin Gang. 2012. Pragmatic analysis of the language of Internet news. Nanjing: Nanjing University Press.

Sun Chang. 2006. Chinese Vocabulary. Beijing: Commercial Press.

Tang Lan. 2005. Chinese philology. Shanghai: Shanghai Ancient Books Publishing House.

Tang Weiying. 2010. New discussion about Internet language. Zhengzhou: Henan People's Publishing House.

Wang Junxi. 2011. Chinese new words dictionary: 2005-2010. Shanghai: Academia Press.

Wang Lei. 2012. Xinhua Internet Language Dictionary. Beijing: The Commercial Press.

Xu Baohua, Gongtian Yilang. 1999. Chinese dialect dictionary. Beijing: Zhonghua Book Company.

Xu Zhaohui. 2013. Study of contemporary modern words. Guangzhou: Jinan University Press.

Yu Zhiwei, Chen Liming. 2013. Discussion about new language of the Internet. Beijing: China Social Sciences Publishing House.

Zavyalova O. I. 2010. The great world of Chinese language. Moscow: Eastern Literature.

Zhang Yuling. 2014. Study of Internet language stylistic. Beijing: China Social Sciences Publishing House.

Zhang Yunhui. 2010. Internet language grammar and pragmatics. Shanghai: Academia Press.

Sentiment Clustering with Topic and Temporal Information from Large Email Dataset

Sisi Liu
Information Technology
James Cook University
Cairns, QLD 4870, Australia

Guochen Cai
Information Technology
James Cook University
Cairns, QLD 4870, Australia

Ickjai Lee
Information Technology
James Cook University
Cairns, QLD 4870, Australia

{Sisi.Liu1, Guochen.Cai}@my.jcu.edu.au; Ickjai.Lee@jcu.edu.au

Abstract

Sentiment analysis with features addition to opinion words has been an appealing area in recent studies. Some research has been conducted for finding relationship between sentiments, topics and temporal sentiment analysis. Nevertheless, Email sentiment analysis received relatively less attention due to the complexity of its structure and indirectness of its language. This paper introduces a systematic framework for sentiment clustering using topic and temporal features for large Email datasets. Interesting Email and sentiment distribution patterns are summarized and discussed with empirical results.

1 Introduction

The generation of enormous diversified data stream by social networking and communication contributes to the rapid development of text mining and its related area (Hao et al., 2013). Literature indicates that product reviews, Twitter corpus and news articles are common sources for conducting sentiment analysis (Ravi and Ravi, 2015), whereas Electronic mail (Email), as one of the most adapted means of communication and networking, is a rare option due to its complex structure and natural language characteristics (Tang et al., 2014). However, the efficiency, compatibility and ease of communication embed great business potential in Email messages (Tang et al., 2014), which is a promising and meaningful sentiment analysis subject.

Sentiment analysis is one of the most appealing areas in text mining among researchers. In the past few decades, sentiment analysis techniques, both machine learning approaches and statistical approaches, have improved significantly and been applied to various industries, such as stock market prediction, customer relationship management, and e-learning (Feldman, 2013; Liu, 2015; Ortigosa et al., 2014; Smailović et al., 2013). Herein, some researchers extend their studies to enriching sentiment analysis by adding additional features. For instance, Mei et al. (2007) propose a novel topic-sentiment mixture model using probabilistic testing for topic and sentiment discovery; Saif et al. (2012) show that adding semantic features results in more accurate sentiment classification. Additionally, Fukuhara et al. (2007) introduce the idea of generating time and sentiment graph using Dice coefficient probabilistic model. However, no qualitative and quantitative experiments have been undertaken for the evaluation of the proposed method.

This research paper develops a systematic scheme of approach for discovering sentiment distribution patterns from large Email corpus based on clustering results of topic and temporal information using bag-of-words model as distance matrix and DBSCAN (Ester et al., 1996) algorithm for clustering and pattern analysis, addressing the following contributions:

a) introducing a systematic scheme of approach composed of bag-of-words term weighting method and DBSCAN clustering algorithm for Email sentiment pattern discovery using topic and temporal information;

b) using Email corpus as data source for the effectiveness and feasibility test of the proposed framework;

c) discovering sentiment distribution and characteristics discovery in temporal categories and relationship between sentiment variance and topic categories.

2 Related Work

Sentiment analysis, a study of extracting and analyzing the implications of emotions, attitudes or opinions from natural language, has attracted researchers from diverse areas (Liu, 2015). Papers and articles on sentiment analysis published in recent years indicate a trend of more comprehensive view of conducting sentiment analysis, including feature enrichment, and sentiment visualization. Among them, research on sentiment with temporal or topic information is one of the most appealing targets.

As Liu (2015) illustrates in its definition of opinion, time is considered as a crucial factor in sentiment analysis as identifying pattern of sentiment changes from historical data assists in the trend prediction of the future, as well as the topic. Though some studies have been conducted on sentiment analysis with topic or temporal features, problems, such as limitations in the dataset options and no pattern display, remain unsolved (Diakopoulos et al., 2010; Fukuhara et al., 2007; Li and Liu, 2012; Mei et al., 2007). For example, Fukuhara et al. (2007) presented topic, timestamp and sentiment graph for news articles using coefficient model, even if the study was purely theoretical with insufficient experiments. Additionally, Mei et al. (2007) undertook experiments on discoverying relationship between topic and sentiment using topic-sentiment mixture model on webblogs; Diakopoulos et al. (2010) utilized Vox Civitas, an automated visual analytic tool, for extracting news from social media data stream, displaying topic and keyword trend. To the best of our knowledge, experiments using large Email data have not been proposed yet.

As for Email mining applications, reviews on previous articles reveal that information management and spam detection are heated study topics (Basavaraju and Prabhakar, 2010; Hangal et al., 2011; Tang et al., 2014; Whittaker and Sidner, 1996). For instance, Whittaker and Sidner (1996) highlighted the issue of Email overload and its negative influence on personal information management; Basavaraju and Prabhakar (2010) proposed a new approach for spam mail detection using semi-supervised learning algorithm. However, research on sentiment analysis using Email data is rare and leaves enormous space for refinement and improvement.

3 Framework

As illustrated in the previous section, a comprehensive and systematic framework is presented in this section. Figure 1 outlines major components and flow of the proposed scheme of approach. To be specific, the framework consists of several procedures, including data extraction, text preprocessing, feature selection and sentiment clustering.

Text preprocessing step incorporates basic Natural Language Processing (NLP) techniques, such as stop word removal and stemming. In feature selection process, topic, timestamp and opinion words are the feature options, in which topic is generated using keyword search and opinion words are generated using the English opinion lexicon (Liu et al., 2004). Sentiment clustering is composed of two substeps containing grouping data based on timestamp and classifying sentiment based on topic. DBSCAN algorithm is chosen to perform the clustering task for its efficiency in speed and effectiveness in handling noise (Ester et al., 1996).

3.1 Text Preprocessing

Text preprocessing aims at removing unnecessary information, such as punctuations and articles, and converting natural language into machine readable content. Tang et al. (2014) highlight the indispensability of Email data cleaning, whilst point out the complexity and limitation of the process. Herein, standard text preprocessing procedures for general NLP tasks have been applied.

In this study, Apache Lucene, an open-source NLP toolkit, is utilized for performing text normalization and filtering (Hatcher and Gospodnetic, 2004). Details are described as follows:

- First step: duplication removal and noise filtering. Assuming a dataset has been imported into

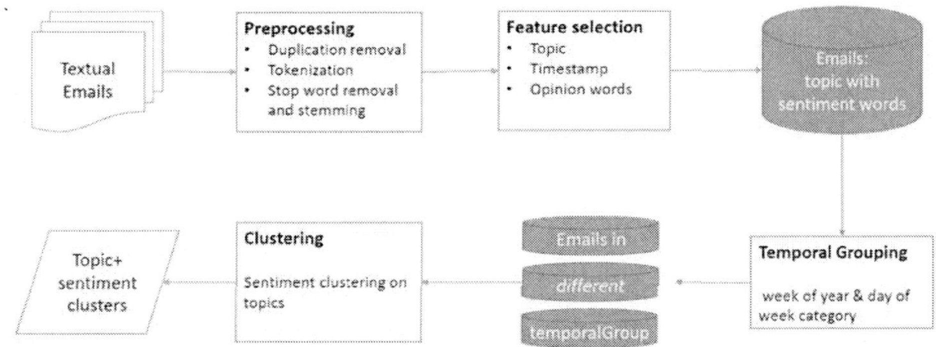

Figure 1: Framework for Email sentiment clustering in topic and temporal categories.

database, a query statement is required for retrieving the data. The implementation of SQL function *DISTINCT* and elimination of item with empty "subject" assist in the achievement of this process;

- Second step: tokenization. After retrieving the entire dataset from database, tokenizing each Email message through the implementation of *tokenize*() function for further processing;
- Third step: stop word removal and stemming. Filtering each Email message using *stopAnalyzer*() embedded in Apache toolkit removes common conjunctions, such as punctuation marks and articles, while iterating for stop word removal, simultaneously using *stem*() function for restoring words' original format, especially for verb and plural.

3.2 Feature Selection

Since the main aim of this research is to identify the sentiment distribution in accordance with topic and temporal classification, feature selection process is divided into three parts: topic word extraction, timestamp transformation and opinion words generation. Details of each feature category are discussed as follows.

Topic : feature extracted based on keyword search. A list of keywords matching topic category defined is generated manually. Querying column named *subject* in database returns a string containing subject data of each Email message. A comparison between the string and each keyword list is conducted for searching the corresponding category.

Timestamp : feature is generated through querying column named *data* in the database. Functions *getTime*() and *getTimeZone*() are implemented for converting temporal data into milliseconds with standard *UTC* timezone. For instance, date value "2016-04-02 11:12:28" is transformed into "1459559492612".

Opinion words : features identified on the basis of a well-defined English opinion lexicon (Liu et al., 2004) contain 2,046 positive words and phases, and 4,833 negative words and phases. Let $\mathcal{OW}$ be a collection of entire opinion lexicon, containing word $ow_1, ow_2, \ldots, ow_i$, then $\mathcal{OW} = \{ow_1, ow_2, \cdots, ow_i\}$ $i \in (6, 879)$. Sample positive and negative words chosen from the lexicon are shown in Table 1.

Positive Words	Negative Words
good	bad
thank	disgrace
worthy	overwhelm
flourishing	incomplete
delight	sick

Table 1: Positive and negative words representation from the English opinion words list (Liu et al., 2004).

At this stage, a sequence of opinion words based on its presence in each Email message is stored for future study (i.e. the inner sentiment changes); however, bag-of-words model is adopted as a term weighting method for distance matrix for sentiment clustering, which will be discussed in the following section. Each data item is transformed into feature representation after this procedure. A sample Email item is represented into:

$$< id, Topic, Timestamp, [ow_1, ow_2, ow_3, ow_4] >$$

3.3 Sentiment Clustering

Sentiment clustering is composed of two steps: grouping data based on timestamp and clustering sentiment based on topic. First step aims at clustering the entire dataset into different date categories with day and week labels using personalized Email temporal clustering algorithm. Second step clusters sentiment using DBSCAN clustering algorithm with bag-of-words term weighting method and Euclidean distance matrix in accordance with topic.

3.3.1 Grouping Data based on Timestamp

To investigate the Email distribution, an Email temporal clustering algorithm is applied to group Email messages into days under week category. The *Calendar* object embedded in Java is utilized for the comparison of timestamp with calendar and classification into day of the week. The pseudo code for *EmailTC* algorithm is presented in Algorithm 1. Due to the characteristics of *Calendar* object, the first day of week is defined as Sunday. Hence, the classification results start with day 1 representing Sunday and end with day 7 representing Saturday.

Algorithm 1 EmailTC

for each Email message $e_i \in \mathcal{E}$ **do**
    Get timestamp $\mathcal{T}$ from e_i
    Get Calendar object;
    Get week of year;
    Get day of week;
    Create group G_w for week of year;
    Create group G_d for day of week;
    if $\mathcal{T} \notin G_w$ **then**
        Create subgroup $Gsub_w$;
        Put e_i in $Gsub_w$;
        Put e_i in G_d;
    else
        Put e_i in G_w;
        if $\mathcal{T} \in G_d$ **then**
            Put e_i in G_d;
        end if
    end if
end for

3.3.2 Clustering Sentiments based on Topic

Revised DBSCAN algorithm (Ester et al., 1996) with bag-of-words term weighting scheme (see Equation 1) and Euclidean distance (see Equation 2) as distance matrix are implemented for conducting the clustering process. Bag-of-words model and Euclidean distance, though invented for decades, remain efficient and well-adopted in many studies.

$$\mathcal{BOW} = freqeuncy * ow_i, i \in OW_p. \quad (1)$$

$$Eu_(d) = \sqrt{(x_s - x_t)^2 + (y_s - y_t)^2} s, t \in (1, n). \quad (2)$$

In Equation 1, supposing OW_p represents a collection of all positive opinion words, bag-of-words approach computes the frequency of each positive word ow_i appeared. Herein, Equation 2 calculates the distance between positive words and negative words contained in each Email message.

As for the option of DBSCAN, its ability of noise handling and fast processing speed increases the utilization of DBSCAN in various applications (Ester et al., 1996). Furthermore, as DBSCAN follows the rule of density-reachablility based on $minPts$ and $epsilon$ parameters defined, it generates diversified number of clusters in accordance with different sentiment scaling. The pseudo code for revised DBSCAN algorithm is presented in Algorithm 2.

Note that as Ester et al. (1996)'s DBSCAN algorithm served as the foundation of the revised version in this paper, more details can be referred to (Ester et al., 1996), especially for the $expandCluster()$ that has not been written out in the pseudo code due to its complexity. By changing the two parameters $minPts$ and $epsilon$, clustering results are varied accordingly (see Algorithm 2). Therefore, implementation of DBSCAN without accurate $minPts$ and $epsilon$ normally involves trial and error testing (Ester et al., 1996).

4 Empirical Results and Discussion

Experiments are conducted on a subcollection of the large Enron Email corpus, which contains emails exchanged from business operation, personal com-

Algorithm 2 AlgoDBSCAN

Input: A collection of Email messages $\mathcal{E}$, $minPts$, $epsilon$.
Output: A collection of sentiment clusters $\mathcal{C}$ with a subset of Email messages $\{E_1, \cdots, E_i\} \in (T_1, T_j)$.

/ Set $\mathcal{E}$ to UNCLASSIFIED*/*
for each Email message $e_i \in \mathcal{E}$ **do**
    Mark e_i as Cluster point c_i;
    Compute $BOW1$ for e_i;
    Compute $Eu_{(d)}$ between e_i and other data $\in \mathcal{E}$;
    Compare $epsilon$ with $Eu_{(d)}$ to find $\mathcal{N}$ neighbors;
    if $\mathcal{N}$ is greater than $minPts$ **then**
        Form cluster c_i;
        Insert e_i into c_i;
        Add all messages $\in \mathcal{E}$ reachable using expandCluster function;
    else
        Assign e_i to noise;
    end if
    Insert c_i into $\mathcal{C}$;
end for
return $\mathcal{C}$

munication, commercial and advertising. Graphs on the Email message distribution on temporal classification and sentiment distribution are topic classification are to be displayed for the visualization of the sentiment patterns discovered. In addition, sentiment words frequency is illustrated using tag cloud and frequency table.

4.1 Dataset

As Email data cleaning is an independent area requiring deep learning and investigation (Tang et al., 2014), a database version of the Enron Email corpus generated by (Liu and Lee, 2015) (available at $http://www.ahschulz.de/enron-Email-data/enron-mysqldump_v5.sql.gz$) has been utilized. A collection of $32,716$ Email messages exchanged between January to May in 2001 has been extracted from the Enron corpus database for conducting our experiments. MySQL database and Eclipse IDE are incorporated for data extraction and feature selection. *15* topic phases, such as $BusinessDocument$, $GeneralOperation$ and etc., are set up manually for grouping the dataset into different categories. Among them, a special topic named $Other$ is defined for storing messages with no subject keyword matching. As for temporal feature, the entire dataset is classified into *22* weeks with each subdivided into *7* days. All features are extracted using method discussed in the previous sections. The structure of data with feature representation is indicated in the following sample fragments (see Figure 2).

<3038, Company Strategy, 984614400000, [available, pretty, works]>

<3039, Technical Issue, 984614400000, [benefits, appreciate, good, -bad, good]>

<3041, Other, 984614400000, [comprehensive, convenient, concise, -issues, -concerns, available, dedicated, available]>

Figure 2: Fragments of data with feature representations.

4.2 Email Distribution in Temporal Categories

Experiments on sentiment clustering are undertaken using DBSCAN algorithm that requires two parameters $minPts$ and $epsilon$. With reasonable assumption and several attempts, the results are generated with $minPts$ of 5 and $epsilon$ of 0.15. Therefore, the description of sentiment clusters is assumed to be similar to a 5 likert scale including *strongly positive, positive, neutral, negative and strongly negative*. The graphs and tables of detailed sentiment clustering results are to be displayed in the following section. As a temporal clustering is performed before sentiment clustering, Fig. 3 and Fig. 4 illustrate the distribution of Email messages and clustering results in temporal categories.

In the two figures, 5 months are divided into 22 weeks with each week having 7 days. Based on the results shown in Fig. 3 and Fig. 4, more Emails exchange between weekdays with an average of 202 mails, than weekends with an average of 23 mails. This result is coherent with common observation that proves the authenticity of the dataset. Furthermore, in Fig. 4, more clusters are discovered during weekdays that implies a variety of topic discussed during business days. More detailed analysis on sentiment clustering results is to be discussed in the fol-

Figure 3: The distribution of Email messages in temporal category.

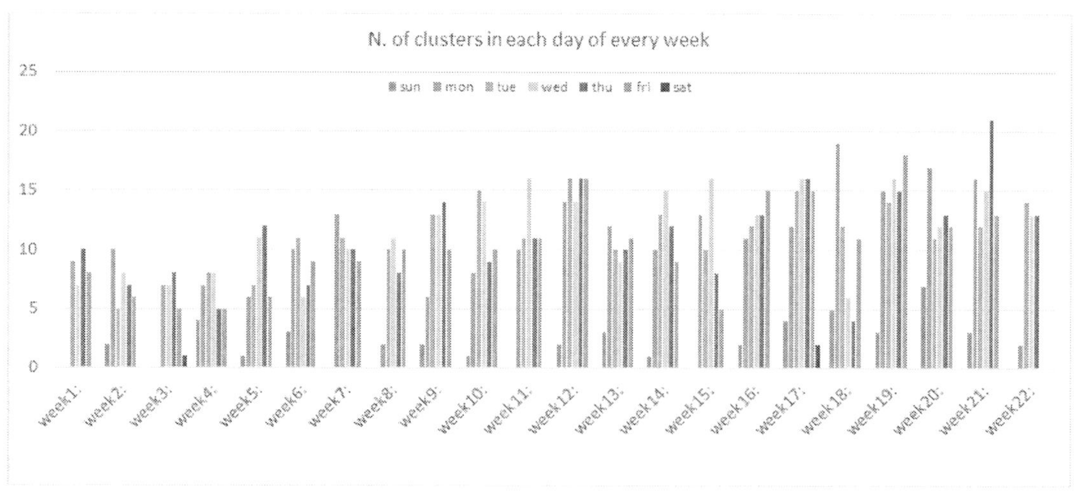

Figure 4: The distribution of Email clusters in temporal category.

lowing section.

4.3 Sentiment and Topic Clustering Results

As discussed in the previous section, sentiments are broadly categorized into five scales in accordance with the ratio of positive words and negative words. Since the research mainly focuses on finding distribution and patterns among sentiment clusters with topic and temporal information, accuracy of clustering results is not evaluated. The following two tables, Table 2 and Table 3, are generated using part of clustering results in week 4.

Due to the limitation of paper length, the above Table 2 summarizes some of the prominent clustering results with topic feature in each day. SP, P, $Neutral$, N, and SN represent for strongly positive, positive, neutral, negative and strongly negative, respectively. Individual cluster shows one topic

Day	Topic in sentiment clusters
Monday	Other-SP Private Issue-SP Commercial/Advertising-SP Company Strategy-SP General Operation-P Logistic Issue-NEUTRAL Other-SN
Tuesday	Private Issue-SP Other-SP Company Strategy-SP Logistic Issue-SP Other-P General Operation-P Logistic Issue-NEUTRAL Other-SN
Wednesday	Employee Training-SP Business Investment-SP Company Strategy-SP Company Project-SP Logistic Issue-SP Other-P General Operation-P Other-SN
Thursday	General Operation-SP Other-SP Employment Arrangement-SP Other-N Other-SN
Friday	General Operation-SP General Operation-P News/Press/Media-NEUTRAL Other-NEUTRAL Other-SN

Table 2: Sentiment clustering results in topic category in week 4.

with sentiments in that day. It appears that more positive clusters are discovered with various topics than negative clusters. Interestingly, some topics have both positive and negative clusters which indicates people's different views on the same topic that is coherent with human nature. Table 3 shows the corresponding items in some of the cluster.

The combination of two tables assists in the further justification of the option of DBSCAN input parameters and the sentiment result criteria. On one hand, objects are relevant in the corresponding cluster, while distinguished from others. For instance, Emails with more positive features are categorized into positive clusters, such as message id 73677 and message id 54522; while Emails with more negative features are categorized into negative clusters, such as message id 141463 and message id 180199. On the other hand, objects with different feature words are categorized into one cluster indicating a reasonable option of the $minPts$ parameter.

As an auxiliary to view the sentiments in details rather than a 5 likert scale, two tag cloud graphs (see Fig. 5 and Fig. 6) containing 100 positive and negative words and a table with 20 most frequently referred opinion words are displayed.

Positive	Frequency	Negative	Frequency
work	6767	issue	6896
support	3634	problem	3011
master	2448	limited	2865
thank	2207	risk	2818
lead	1762	crisis	2250
important	1489	concerns	2204
privileged	1277	vice	1763
respect	1262	error	1761
recommend	1220	debt	1410
helpful	1083	critical	1273

Table 4: Top 10 frequent opinion words.

Figure 5: Tag cloud for positive opinion words.

As shown in Table 4, positive words commonly used in Emails are work, support and master and negative words are issue, problem and limited. An applealing observation lies in the statistics that most

Clusters	Details
Cluster 1: (Other-SP)	⟨9948:Other-[like]⟩ ⟨24718:Other-[clear]⟩ ⟨34752:Other-[thank]⟩ ⟨47679:Other-[free]⟩ ⟨73677:Other-[available, good, significant]⟩ ⟨80082:Other-[love]⟩ ⟨103142:Other-[excel]⟩ ⟨103148:Other-[diligence, soft]⟩
Cluster 2: (Employment Arrangement-SP)	⟨24721:Employment Arrangement-[like, thank]⟩ ⟨33181:Employment Arrangement-[well, happy]⟩ ⟨54522:Employment Arrangement-[encouragement]⟩ ⟨80114:Employment Arrangement-[well, good]⟩ ⟨180206:Employment Arrangement-[works]⟩
Cluster 3: (Other-SN)	⟨120803:Other-[-curt]⟩ ⟨121264:Other-[-curt]⟩ ⟨141463:Other-[-miss, -miss, -miss]⟩ ⟨164561:Other-[-liars]⟩ ⟨164563:Other-[-hells]⟩ ⟨180199:Other-[-hedge, -issues, -hedge, -subjected]⟩

Table 3: Objects in sentiment clusters on topic category in week 4.

Figure 6: Tag cloud for negative opinion words.

negative words are nouns, while most positive words adjectives. Conclusion is to be summarized until more findings are discovered. However, a potential topic is developed for future study.

5 Conclusion and Future Work

In this research paper, we propose a robust and comprehensive framework for sentiment clustering with topic and temporal features using bag-of-words model as term weighting approach and revised DBSCAN algorithm for clustering. Features composed of topic, timestamp and opinion words are extracted for performing two experiments, including grouping Email messages into temporal categories and clustering sentiments based on topic, for discovering sentiment patterns.

Based on the summary of the clustering results, major findings are categorized into three points. First, the distribution of Email messages reveals more intense communication during weekdays and variety of topics. This pattern justifies the authenticity and originality of the Email corpus. Second, sentiment clustering results assist in the validation of the parameters chosen for the implementation of revised DBSCAN algorithm as clusters are distinguished from others as well as coherent within themselves. Also, feature words for generating sentiment clusters are with high similarity which implies a proper choice of the *epsilon* value. And finally, Table 4 lists the top 20 most commonly used opinion words with most of them related to business and management, which shows a linkage to the characteristics of the dataset.

References

M. Basavaraju and Dr. R. Prabhakar. 2010. A novel method of spam mail detection using text based clustering approach. *International Journal of Computer Applications*, 5(4):15–25.

Nicholas Diakopoulos, Mor Naaman, and Funda Kivran-Swaine. 2010. Diamonds in the rough: Social media visual analytics for journalistic inquiry. In *Visual Analytics Science and Technology (VAST), 2010 IEEE Symposium on*, pages 115–122. IEEE.

Martin Ester, Hans-Peter Kriegel, Jörg Sander, and Xiaowei Xu. 1996. A density-based algorithm for discovering clusters in large spatial databases with noise. In *Kdd*, volume 96, pages 226–231.

Ronen Feldman. 2013. Techniques and applications for sentiment analysis. *Communications of the ACM*, 56(4):82–89.

Tomohiro Fukuhara, Hiroshi Nakagawa, and Toyoaki Nishida. 2007. Understanding sentiment of people from news articles: Temporal sentiment analysis of social events. In *ICWSM*.

Sudheendra Hangal, Monica S Lam, and Jeffrey Heer. 2011. Muse: reviving memories using email archives. In *Proceedings of the 24th annual ACM symposium on User interface software and technology*, pages 75–84. ACM.

Ming C Hao, Christian Rohrdantz, Halldor Janetzko, Daniel A Keim, Umeshwar Dayal, Lars erik Haug, Meichun Hsu, and Florian Stoffel. 2013. Visual sentiment analysis of customer feedback streams using geo-temporal term associations. *Information Visualization*, page 1473871613481691.

Erik Hatcher and Otis Gospodnetic. 2004. Lucene in action.

Gang Li and Fei Liu. 2012. Application of a clustering method on sentiment analysis. *Journal of Information Science*, 38(2):127–139.

Sisi Liu and Ickjai Lee. 2015. A hybrid sentiment analysis framework for large email data. In *Intelligent Systems and Knowledge Engineering (ISKE), 2015 10th International Conference on*, pages 324–330. IEEE.

Bing Liu, Xiaoli Li, Wee Sun Lee, and Philip S Yu. 2004. Text classification by labeling words. In *AAAI*, volume 4, pages 425–430.

Bing Liu. 2015. *Sentiment analysis: Mining opinions, sentiments, and emotions*. Cambridge University Press.

Qiaozhu Mei, Xu Ling, Matthew Wondra, Hang Su, and ChengXiang Zhai. 2007. Topic sentiment mixture: modeling facets and opinions in weblogs. In *Proceedings of the 16th international conference on World Wide Web*, pages 171–180. ACM.

Alvaro Ortigosa, José M Martín, and Rosa M Carro. 2014. Sentiment analysis in facebook and its application to e-learning. *Computers in Human Behavior*, 31:527–541.

Kumar Ravi and Vadlamani Ravi. 2015. A survey on opinion mining and sentiment analysis: Tasks, approaches and applications. *Knowledge-Based Systems*, 89:14 – 46.

Hassan Saif, Yulan He, and Harith Alani. 2012. Semantic sentiment analysis of twitter. In *The Semantic Web–ISWC 2012*, pages 508–524. Springer.

Jasmina Smailović, Miha Grčar, Nada Lavrač, and Martin Žnidaršič. 2013. Predictive sentiment analysis of tweets: A stock market application. In *Human-Computer Interaction and Knowledge Discovery in Complex, Unstructured, Big Data*, pages 77–88. Springer.

Guanting Tang, Jian Pei, and Wo-Shun Luk. 2014. Email mining: tasks, common techniques, and tools. *Knowledge and Information Systems*, 41(1):1–31.

Steve Whittaker and Candace Sidner. 1996. Email overload: exploring personal information management of email. In *Proceedings of the SIGCHI conference on Human factors in computing systems*, pages 276–283. ACM.

On What an Adnominal Appendix Modifies in Korean Adjunct RDCs

Daeho Chung
Department of English Language and Culture,
Hanyang University, 55 Hanyangdaehak-lo, Sangnok-gu,
Ansan-si, Gyeonggi-do, Republic of Korea
cdaeho@hanyang.ac.kr

Abstract

This work addresses the question of how adnominal appendices in the adjunct right dislocation construction (ADJ-RDC) in Korean resolve their modification relation. The main points made in this paper are: (i) Ko's (2014, 2015) account in terms of assimilating the ADJ-RDC to a parasitic gap construction does not gain much support; (ii) a proximity based approach more adequately describes the facts; (iii) proximity can be overridden by focus information; and (iv) given a designated default focus position in Korean, the role of proximity can be subsumed under the role of focus. Thus, a unified focus based account is provided.

1 Introduction

This work addresses the question of how post-verbal adnominal adjuncts (ADAs in short) resolve their modification relation in Korean adjunct-type right dislocation constructions (ADJ-RDCs). To the best of my knowledge, Ko (2014, 2015) first brought up this issue seriously. She makes two interesting observations that Korean ADJ-RDCs display: They exhibit a subject-object asymmetry and a CED effect[1] when an ADA is associated with the head noun in the host clause. As the two properties are typically observed in the parasitic gap construction (PGC) as well, she assimilates the ADJ-RDC to a PGC and proposes a sideward movement analysis in which the so-called adjunct domain (composed of an adnominal phrase and its head noun) is concatenated with the host clause and the head noun moves sideward to the host clause. The current work illustrates, however, that the parallelism of ADJ-RDC and PGC is not compelling, neither theoretically nor empirically. Instead, this paper observes that some sort of proximity principle and focus information interplay to resolve the modification relation in the ADJ-RDC involving an ADA.

This paper is organized as follows. Section 2 briefly reproduces Ko's (2014, 2015) account in terms of assimilating the ADJ-RDC to a PGC. Section 3 shows that her account is not fully supported, despite apparent similarities between the two constructions. Section 4 tries to account for the restrictions that the ADJ-RDC displays in terms of interplay of a proximity principle and focus information. Section 5 suggests a unified focus-based analysis. Section 6 concludes the paper.

2 Ko's (2014, 2015) Concatenation & Sideward Movement Analysis

According to Ko (2014, 2015), an ADJ-RDC with an ADA results from a combination of two syntactic processes: concatenation and sideward movement.[2] First, the so-called adjunct domain that consists of an adnominal phrase and its head is concatenated with a host clause, along the lines of Hornstein and Nunes' (2008) analysis of adjunct structures. Then the head of the adjunct domain moves sideward to

[1] The CED (Condition on Extraction Domain) states that extraction is possible out of a complement, but not out of a subject or an adjunct (Huang 1982).

[2] Argument-type RDCs are differently derived in Ko (2014, 2015). They start with a mono-clausal structure and two movement operations apply to them: An argument that will eventually function as an appendix first undergoes a leftward movement to the specifier of a focus phrase, and then the remnant (the host clause) undergoes a leftward movement to the specifier of a topic phrase. Such a hybrid approach to RDCs may face an immediate problem as there exists a mixed form of appendices, as discussed in Chung (2015).

the host clause, analogously to Nunes' (2004) derivation of the PGC. For example, the ADJ-RDC in (1) has the derivational processes schematically illustrated in (2a, b):

(1) na-nun [han sonyen]-ul manna-ess-e
I-Top one boy-Acc meet-Pst-DE
[acwu ttokttok-hako calsayngki-n]
very smart-and handsome-RC
'I met a boy who is very smart and handsome.'

(2) a. **Concatenation**
I met ^ [[very smart and handsome] [a boy]]
b. **Sideward movement**
I [a boy]$_i$ met ^ [[very smart and handsome] e$_i$]

Ko (2014, 2015) observes that ADJ-RDCs, just like PGCs, display a subject-object asymmetry and a CED effect. Based on these observations, she proposes a sideward movement analysis of ADJ-RDCS with an ADA. She takes examples like (3) and (4) to show that ADJ-RDCs are sensitive to the grammatical function. An ADA can be associated with an object, but not with a subject. A similar restriction seems to apply in the licensing of a parasitic gap (PG), as shown in (5) and (6), where a PG can be associated with an object trace, but not with a subject trace.

(3) (adapted from Ko 2015, her (61)) *Subject-object asymmetry: relative clause*
Cheli-ka **Yengi-lul** manna-ess-e
C.-Nom Y.-Acc meet-Pst-DE
[$_{RC}$ **ppalkah-ko khun moca-lul ssu-n.**]
red-and big hat-Acc wear-RC
'Cheli met Yengi, who wears a big red hat.'
[who=Yengi; *who=Cheli]

(4) (adapted from Ko 2015, her (62)) *Subject-object asymmetry: genitive-marked phrase*
a. Cheli-ka **apeci-lul** manna-ess-e **Yengi-uy**
C.-Nom father-Acc meet-Pst-DE Y.-Gen
'Cheli met Yengi's father.'
b. ***Apeci-ka** Cheli-lul manna-ess-e
father-Nom C.-Acc meet-Pst-DE
Yengi-uy
Y.-Gen
'Yengi's father met Cheli.'

(5) (=Nunes 2004: 109, his (55a))
*I wonder [which man]$_i$ e$_i$ called you before you met PG$_i$.

(6) (=Nunes 2004, 95: his 16a))
[Which man]$_i$ did you file e$_i$ without reading PG$_i$.

Ko (2014, 2015) also points out that the ADJ-RDC and the PGC behave alike in that they both display a CED effect. An ADA can be associated with a direct object but not with an element embedded under it, as the contrast between (7) and (8) shows, which seems to be analogous to the contrast in PGCs between (9) and (10):

(7) (adapted from Ko 2015: 33, her (59)) *Lack of LBC*
Na-nun [__ cha]-lul pilliesse
I-Top car-Acc borrowed
[**Yengi-uy emma-uy**]
Y.-Gen mother-Gen
'I borrowed Yengi's mother's car.'

(8) (adapted from Ko 2015: 33, her (60)) *Emergence of LBC due to embedding*
*Na-nun [[__ **emma-uy**] cha-lul]
I-Top mommy-Gen car-Acc
pilli-ess-e **Yengi-uy**.
borrow-Pst-DE Y.-Gen
'I borrowed Yengi's mother's car.'

(9) (=Ko 2015: 31, her (57)) *PG and lack of CED effects*
a. PG+subject island
Which politician did [**pictures of ___**$_{PG}$] upset __ ?
b. PG+adjunct island
Which paper did you read __ [**before filing** ___$_{PG}$] ?

(10) (=Ko 2015: 31, her (58)) *Emergence of CED effects with PG*
a. *Which politician did you criticize __ [before [**pictures of ___**$_{PG}$] upset the voters]?
b. *Which book did you finally read __ [after leaving the bookstore [**without finding** ___$_{PG}$]]?

Under Ko's (2014, 2015) system, an ADA in the ADJ-RDC is to be associated with the object head in the host clause. The system works fine with the data up to now. However, it will be shown in the next section that the parallelism between the ADJ-RDC and PGC does not always hold.

3 Evidence against the ADA-PG Parallelism

This section will show that the parallelism between the ADJ-RDC and PGC claimed in Ko (2014, 2015) does not seem to be fully motivated. The subject-object asymmetry in particular is shown not to be compelling, neither theoretically nor empirically. (The CED effect will be briefly discussed later in Section 4.)

First, subject gaps do license PGs, given an appropriate structural relation. Although there exists a clear contrast between sentences like (5) and those like (6), the contrast may not be based on the grammatical function of the real gap. Notice that, as was observed by Taraldsen (1981) and Engdahl (1983), subject gaps (as well as object gaps) can license PGs, given an appropriate structural relation, as exemplified below:

(11) (=Engdahl 1983: 21, her (60))
Which Caesar did Brutus imply ___ was no good while ostensibly praising $\_\_\__{PG}$?

(12) (=Engdahl 1983: 21, her (61))
Who did you say John's criticism of $\_\_\__{PG}$ would make us think ____ was stupid?

In (11), the subject gap in the embedded clause can license the PG in the adjunct clause, if the *while* clause is regarded as being attached to the matrix VP, not to the embedded VP. Also in (12), the subject gap in the embedded clause can license the PG contained in the subject of a higher clause. Thus the licensing condition does not care about the grammatical function of the real gap. Rather an anti-c-command condition is respected, as was first proposed by Engdahl (1983). The real gaps in (11) and (12) do not c-command the PGs. As far as the PG licensing is not sensitive to the grammatical function of the real gap (at least not to an anti-subject condition), but to a structural (c-command) relation, the presumed parallelism between the ADJ-RDC and the PGC does not sustain.

Second, even if the grammatical function were assumed to be relevant, it would be hard to structurally capture the relevance under Ko's (2014, 2015) own structure. Notice that the structural relation that holds between a real gap and a PG in the PGC does not hold between an ADA and the associated head noun in the host clause, as schematically represented below:

(13) a. PGC

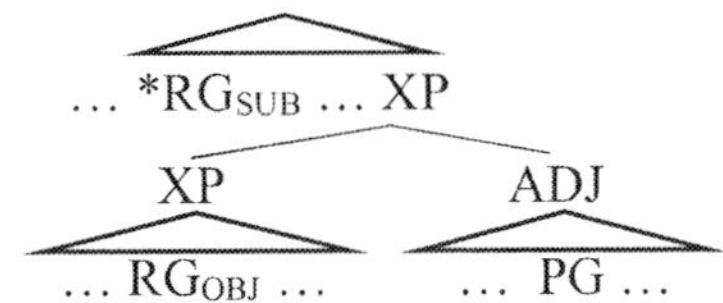

b. ADJ-RDC

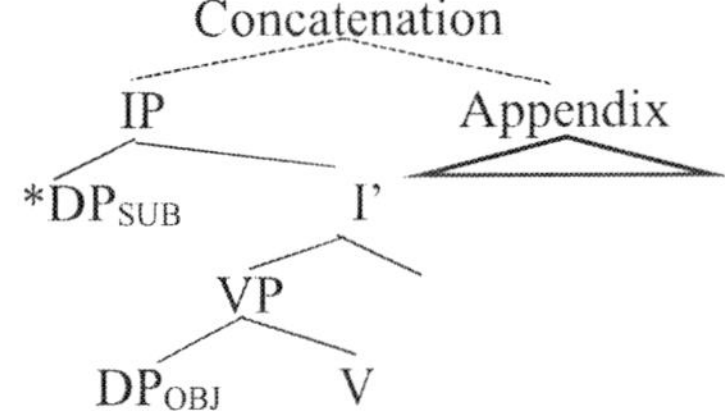

As illustrated in (13a), the 'subject-object asymmetry' in the PGC as observed in the contrast between (5) and (6) can be accounted for in terms of a structural relation, i.e., by an anti-c-command relation between the real gap and the PG. However, the presumed 'subject-object asymmetry' in the ADJ-RDC as observed in the contrast between (3) and (4) cannot be explained in this way with (13B). Notice that neither the subject nor the object c-commands the ADA in the structure.[3]

Third, empirically, the subject association reading is not absolutely banned. It is readily available, given pragmatically appropriate situations, as in (14) below, which is cited from Chung (2015: 750, his (24)):

(14) **ceysam-uy** **senswu-ka** kummeytal-ul
third-Gen player-Nom gold;medal-Acc
tta-ess- ta, [**hwuposenswu** **myengtan-ey-to**
win-Pst-DE backup;player list-to-even
mos-kki-ten]
not-belong-PNE
'A third player, who was not even listed as a backup player, won the gold medal.'

The ADA in (14), which is required to be predicated of a human being due to its pragmatic property, can

[3] This relation holds, no matter how 'concatenation' is interpreted, as far as the ADA (or more precisely the so-called adjunct domain) is concatenated with the whole of the host clause.

be associated with the subject, but not with the object. In contrast, in sentences like (3), where the ADA is potentially compatible with both subject and object, the ADA tends to be associated with the object. What is clear from the discussion is that the subject association is not absolutely banned, although the subject association is much more difficult when both subject and object can be potentially associated with the ADA.

Fourth, there are cases where the subject association is preferred or even uniquely available. Compare (15a) and (15b). The two are identical to each other, except that the object has undergone scrambling in the latter.

(15) a. Cheli-ka [**Yengi-lul**]
C.-Nom Y.-Acc
sangtayha-lke-ya,
compete;with-will-DE
[$_{RC}$ **kacang kyenghemmanh-un**].
most experienced-RC
'Cheli will compete with Yengi, who is the most experienced.'
[*who=Cheli; who=Yengi]

b. [Yengi-lul]$_i$ **Cheli-ka** e_i
Y.-Acc C.-Nom
sangtayha-lke-ya,
compete;with-will-DE
[$_{RC}$ **kacang kyenghemmanh-un**].
most experienced-RC
'Cheli will compete with Yengi, who is the most experienced.'
[who=Cheli; ??who=Yengi]

In a canonical SOV order, as in (15a), the subject association reading is hardly available. In an OSV order due to scrambling, as in (15b), however, the ADA is more readily associated with the subject: The object association is much more degraded. The contrast shows that the grammatical function does not matter in the modification relation in ADJ-RDCs.

There are even cases where the subject association is uniquely available. Consider the following dialogue:

(16) A: nwu-ka Yengi-lul
who-Nom Y.-Acc
sangtayha-lke-ya?
compete;with-will-QE
'Who will compete with Yengi?'

B: **Cheli-ka** e_j sangtayha-lke-ya,
C.-Nom compete;with-will-DE
[$_{RC}$ **kacang kyenghemmanh-un**].
most experienced-RC
'Cheli will compete with Yengi, who is the most experienced.'
[who=Cheli; *who=Yengi]

Cheli-ka in (16B) will receive information focus as it corresponds to the *WH*-phrase *nwu* 'who' in (16A). The object in (16B) is suppressed as it is given information from (16A). In such a case, the ADA is associated with the subject, but not with the suppressed object. Even when the object is overtly realized, the object association reading is hardly available, as shown in (17B) below:

(17) A: (=16A)
B: **Cheli-ka** Yengi-lul sangtayha-lke-ya,
C.-Nom Y.-Acc compete;with-will-DE
[$_{RC}$ **kacang kyenghemmanh-un**].
most experienced-RC
'Cheli will compete with Yengi, who is the most experienced.
[who=Cheli; *?who=Yengi]

To sum up, Ko's (2014, 2015) account of the restrictions that the ADJ-RDC display in terms of assimilating the ADJ-RDC to a PGC does not seem to be fully supported, despite some syntactic similarities between the two constructions. The subject-object asymmetry in particular does not hold, given appropriate pragmatic situations, discrediting Ko's (2014, 2015) derivation of the ADJ-RDC in terms of concatenation of a host clause plus an adjunct domain followed by a sideward head noun movement.

4 Proximity and Focus

What is then responsible for the facts discussed in the previous sections? It will be shown in this section that some sort of proximity principle plays an active role in the choice of the right element to be associated with the ADA. Another point to be made in this section is that the proximity principle can be overridden by focus.

ADAs in ADJ-RDCs seek to be associated with the closest possible focus element. Let us first consider the interpretation facts in (3), (4), and (15b), repeated below:

(3) (adapted from Ko 2015, her (61)) *Subject-object asymmetry: relative clause*
Cheli-ka **Yengi-lul** manna-ess-e
C.-Nom Y.-Acc meet-Pst-DE
[RC **ppalkah-ko khun moca-lul ssu-n**.]
red-and big hat-Acc wear-RC
'Cheli met Yengi, who wears a big red hat.'
[who=Yengi; *who=Cheli]

(4) (adapted from Ko 2015, her (62)) *Subject-object asymmetry: genitive-marked phrase*
a. Cheli-ka **apeci-lul** manna-ess-e **Yengi-uy**
C.-Nom father-Acc meet-Pst-DE Y.-Gen
'Cheli met Yengi's father.'
b. ***Apeci-ka** Cheli-lul manna-ess-e
father-Nom C.-Acc meet-Pst-DE
Yengi-uy
Y.-Gen
'Yengi's father met Cheli.'

(15) b. [Yengi-lul]$_i$ **Cheli-ka** e_i
Y.-Acc C.-Nom
sangtayha-lke-ya,
compete;with-will-DE
[RC **kacang kyenghemmanh-un**].
most experienced-RC
'Cheli will compete with Yengi, who is the most experienced.'
[who=Cheli; ??who=Yengi]

In (3) and (4), the objects are linearly closer to the ADAs than the subjects are. In contrast, in (15b), where the object has undergone scrambling, the subject becomes closer to the ADA. The ADAs are associated with the closer elements in the host clause. The association of an ADA with a head noun in the host clause is blocked or at least less preferred when another dependent intervenes between the head noun and the predicate. Thus the subject association reading in (3) and (4b) and the object association reading in (15b) are unavailable or drastically degraded.

In a similar vein, the strength of association in a dative construction changes depending on the word order variations. Consider the following examples:

(18) Cheli-ka Yengi-lul **Songi-eykey**
C.-Nom Y.-Acc S.-Dat
sokayha-ess-ta,
introduce-Pst-DE
[RC ppalkah-ko khun moca-lul ssu-n].
red-and big hat-Acc wear-RC
'Cheli introduced Yengi to Songi, who wears a big red hat.' [who=Songi; ?who=Yengi]

(19) Cheli-ka Songi-eykey **Yengi-lul**
C.-Nom S.-Dat Y.-Acc
sokayha-ess-ta,
introduce-Pst-DE
[RC ppalkah-ko khun moca-lul ssu-n].
red-and big hat-Acc wear-RC
'Cheli introduced Yengi to Songi, who wears a big red hat.' [?who=Songi ; who=Yengi]

In (18), which has an accusative-dative word order in the host clause, the ADA prefers to be associated with the dative element, which is closer to it. In contrast, in (19), where the order of the internal arguments is reversed, the ADA prefers to be associated with the accusative element, conforming to the proximity principle.

Also observe that the object association reading in (3) becomes severely degraded when an adjunct is added after the object, as shown in (20) below:

(20) *? Cheli-ka **Yengi-lul** hakkyo-eyse
C.-Nom Y.-Acc school-at
manna-ess-e
meet-Pst-DE
[RC **ppalkah-ko khun moca-lul ssu-n**.]
red-and big hat-Acc wear-RC
'Cheli met Yengi at school, who wears a big red hat.'

When neutrally uttered, (20) hardly produces an object association reading. (As will be discussed later in this section, this reading can reemerge when some manipulation is made as to the focus feature.) The low acceptability of (20) can be attributed to a proximity violation.

Let us now consider the case where the proximity principle appears to be violated, as in the examples like (14), (16) and (17), repeated below:

(14) **ceysam-uy senswu-ka** kummeytal-ul
third-Gen player-Nom gold;medal-Acc
tta-ess- ta, [**hwuposenswu myengtan-ey-to**
win-Pst-DE backup;player list-to-even
mos-kki-ten]
not-belong-PNE
'A third player, who was not even listed as a backup player, won the gold medal.'

(16) A: nwu-ka Yengi-lul
who-Nom Y.-Acc
sangtayha-lke-ya?
compete;with-will-QE
'Who will compete with Yengi?'

B: **Cheli-ka** e_j sangtayha-lke-ya,
C.-Nom compete;with-will-DE
[$_{RC}$ **kacang kyenghemmanh-un**].
most experienced-RC
'Cheli will compete with Yengi, who is the most experienced.'
[who=Cheli; *who=Yengi]

(17) A: (=16A)

B: **Cheli-ka** Yengi-lul sangtayha-lke-ya,
C.-Nom Y.-Acc compete;with-will-DE
[$_{RC}$ **kacang kyenghemmanh-un**].
most experienced-RC
'Cheli will compete with Yengi, who is the most experienced.
[who=Cheli; *?who=Yengi]

In these examples, the ADA appears to be associated with the subject, crossing over the object, violating the proximity principle.

Then the question that arises is why the violation of the proximity principle is tolerated in such examples. It seems to be the case that focus overrides the proximity principle. In (16B) and (17B), the subject bears an information focus feature, which is clear from the discourse context of a content question and answer pair. Thus, a more distant element can basically be associated with the ADA, when it receives focus. In sentences like (14) as well, focus seems relevant. Due to the pragmatic property, the expression *cey sam-uy X* 'a third X' generally receives focus. Notice that (14) becomes unacceptable if focus is forced to fall on the object, as shown in (21), which is identical to (14), except that the object receives a pitch accent, indicated by upper case letters:

(21) *?**ceysam-uy senswu-ka** KUMMEYTAL-ul
third-Gen player-Nom gold;medal-Acc
tta-ess- ta, [**hwuposenswu myengtan-ey-to**
win-Pst-DE backup;player list-to-even
mos-kki-ten]
not-belong-PNE
'A third player, who was not even listed as a backup player, won the gold medal.'

The association of the ADA with the subject becomes impossible when such a focus element intervenes between the two.

Likewise, the proximity principle that used to constrain sentences like (20) can be overridden by focus. Thus, the object or even the subject in (20) can come to be associated with the ADA, when focus falls on appropriate elements. Compare (20), with the dialogues in (22)~(24):

(22) A: Cheli-ka Yengi-lul **eti**-eyse
C.-Nom Y.-Acc where-at
manna-ess-ni?
meet-Pst-QE
'Where did Cheli meet Yengi?'

B: #Cheli-ka Yengi-lul **HAKKYO-eyse**
C.-Nom Y.-Acc school-at
manna-ess-e
meet-Pst-DE
[$_{RC}$ **ppalkah-ko khun moca-lul ssu-n**.]
red-and big hat-Acc wear-RC
'Cheli met Yengi at school, who wears a big red hat.' [*?who=Cheli, *? Who=Yengi]

(23) A: Cheli-ka **nwukwu-lul** hakkyo-eyse
C.-Nom who-Acc school-at
manna-ess-ni?
meet-Pst-QE
'Who Cheli meet at school?'

B: Cheli-ka **YENGI-lul** hakkyo-eyse
C.-Nom Y.-Acc school-at
manna-ess-e
meet-Pst-DE
[$_{RC}$ **ppalkah-ko khun moca-lul ssu-n**]
red-and big hat-Acc wear-RC
'Cheli met Yengi at school, who wears a big red hat.' [*?who=Cheli; Who=Yengi]

(24) A: **nwu-ka** Yengi-lul hakkyo-eyse
Who-Nom Y.-Acc school-at
manna-ess-ni?
meet-Pst-QE
'Who met Yengi at school?'

B: **CHELI-ka** Yengi-lul hakkyo-eyse
C.-Nom Y.-Acc school-at
manna-ess-e
meet-Pst-DE
[RC **ppalkah-ko khun moca-lul ssu-n**]
red-and big hat-Acc wear-RC
'Cheli met Yengi at school, who wears a big red hat.' [who=Cheli; *?who=Yengi]

When focus falls on the adjunct, as in (22B), neither the subject nor object association reading is available. However, when focus falls on the object as in (23B) or on the subject as in (24B), the proximity principle can be overridden, producing an object association reading or a subject association reading. These data indicate that an ADA tends to be associated with a focused element, even crossing an intervening non-focus element. Thus, the ADA association shows more respect to focus than to proximity.

The CED effect in the contrast between (7) and (8) can be accounted for by the proximity principle, as the closest candidate to be associated with the ADA will be the head noun, rather than the specifier or adjunct, as schematically represented below:

(25) [S … [XP YP$_{SPEC/ADJ}$ … X] …] [ADA]

As far as XP has a head final structure, X is closer to the ADA than its specifier or adjunct is. Thus, an ADA is more readily associated with the head than with the specifier or adjunct.

However, extra focus on a non-head element, e.g., on the specifier, obviates or at least weakens the CED effect, as exemplified in (26B) below:[4]

(26) A: **nwukwu-uy** yekwen-i
who-Gen passport-Nom
tonantangha-ess-ni?
be;stolen-Pst-QE
'Whose passport was stolen?'
B: **KIM KYOSWU-uy** yekwen-i
K. professor-Gen passport-Nom
tonantangha-ess-e,
be;stolen-Pst-DE
[nayil mikwuk-ulo ttena-ki-lo. ha-n]
tomorrow US-to leave-decide-RC
'Professor Kim's passport was stolen, (the person) who decided to leave for the States tomorrow.'

In (26B), *KIM KYOSWU* 'Professor Kim' is a specifier of the subject DP, but it can be associated with the ADA, as it receives focus. Of course, when focus falls on the head noun, such a CED obviation does not obtain, as shown below:

(27) A: Kim kyoswu-uy **etten mwulken**-i
K. professor-Gen which thing-Nom
tonantangha-ess-ni?
be;stolen-Pst-QE
'Which thing of Prof. Kim was stolen?'
B: #Kim kyoswu-uy **YEKWEN**-i
K. professor-Gen passport-Nom
tonantangha-ess-e,
be;stolen-Pst-DE
[nayil mikwuk-ulo ttena-ki-lo. ha-n]
tomorrow US-to leave-decide-RC
'Professor Kim's passport was stolen, (the person) who decided to leave for the States tomorrow.'

The focused head noun *YEKWEN* 'passport' blocks the association of the ADA with the specifier *Kim kyoswu* 'Prof. Kim'.

This section has observed the following two. First, proximity plays an active role in locating the associated head noun of the ADA in Korean ADJ-RDCs. The proximity based approach more adequately describes the modification relation than the grammatical function based approach. Second, proximity can be overridden by focus information

[4] Chung (2015) also points out that the CED can be violated, taking the following example:

(i) (=Chung 2015: 750, his (23))
a. [[Kim kyoswu-uy [ceyca]]-uy nonwmun]-i LI-ey
K. professor-Gen student-Gen article-Nom LI-in
silli-ess-ta.
get;published-Pst-DE
'Professor Kim's student's article was published in LI.'
b. [[e$_i$ [ceyca]]-uy nonwmun]-i LI-ey silli-ess-ta,
[Kim kyoswu-uy]$_i$

Focus falls on *ceyca* 'student' in (ib) to have the relevant reading. When *nonmwun* 'paper' or *LI* receives focus, however, such a CED obviation does not obtain.

such that an ADA can be associated with a more distant element when the latter receives focus.

5 A Unified Focus Based Explanation

It is worth asking whether there is any way to unify the proximity principle and the focus overriding effect. If there is any possibility to unify the two at all, the former has to be subsumed under the latter for the obvious reason that the proximity principle can be obviated. Then the question is whether the data covered by the proximity principle can be subsumed under the focus based approach. The answer seems to be positive, if it is assumed, basically following Kim (1985), Jo (1986), Lee (1992), and Park (2003), that there is a default focus position in Korean, i.e., the position that immediately precedes the verb.

In fact, it is widely held that in SOV languages the immediately pre-verbal element tends to have the greatest focus. According to Kim (1988), there are various SOV languages extensively distributed from Asia Minor through the Far Eastern region of the Eurasian Continent that follow this pattern: Dravidian languages (Telugu, Laccadive Malayalam, and Tamil), Indo-Aryan languages (Dogri, Bengali, Gujarati, and Hind-Urdu), Sino-Tibetan languages (Sherpa), Altaic languages (Turkish and Mongolian); and Altai-like languages (Japanese and Korean). (See also discussions made in Kuno 1978, Hankamer 1979, Erguvanlı 1984, Givón 1984, Comrie 1984, Herring and Paolillo 1995, among others.) Kim (1988) generalizes this tendency as the follows:[5]

(28) Linear Order Focus Hypothesis
If L is a rigid head-final language in its basic word order, the rhematic focus of a sentence of L is most likely in the position immediately preceding the finite verb. (Kim 1988: 150)

With the default focus position in mind, let us consider the following schematic structure that Korean ADJ-RDCs will take:

(29) [... α ... β ... γ Pred], [Appendix]

In a neutral situation, only γ will receive focus. Thus the ADA in the appendix position will be associated with γ. The facts described under the proximity principle in Section 4 will be dealt with in this way. When extra focus falls on α or β, however, the appendix can be associated with these focused elements, covering the focus overriding data discussed in Section 4.

6 Summary and Concluding Remarks

This work has illustrated that the ADJ-RDC/PGC parallelism is not compelling, weakening Ko's (2014, 2015) concatenation-followed-by-sideward-head-movement analysis of the Korean ADJ-RDC. Instead, proximity and focus are shown to play more active roles in the resolution of the modification relation in the ADJ-RDC. Furthermore, given the designated default focus theory proposed in Kim (1985) and Jo (1986) among others, the role of proximity can be subsumed under the role of information focus.

Various issues remain unaddressed in this paper. In particular, this work has not provided an exact syntactic structure of the ADJ-RDC, except pointing out that Ko's (2014, 2015) derivation based on the presumed parallelism between the ADJ-RDC and the PGC does not gain much support. Definitely further research needs to be conducted to decide whether all the facts described in this paper fit into one of the syntactic structures proposed thus far in the literature (See Ko 2015 for an excellent summary and references cited there) or if a new syntactic structure has to be provided.

Acknowledgments

I would like to thank Hee-Don Ahn, Heejeong Ko, Sun-Woong Kim, Myung-Kwan Park and three anonymous PACLIC paper reviewers for their valuable comments, suggestions and corrections on earlier versions of this work. Of course, all shortcomings are mine.

[5] At the latter part of the same article, Kim (1988) does not distinguish rigid and non-rigid head-final languages, as far as they are 'harmoniously head-final' languages of Greenberg's (1966) Type XXIII, and proposes a more neutral hypothesis, as follows:

(i) If a language has a harmoniously head-final property, the information flow principle will not apply beyond the verbal head of the sentence. (Kim 1988: 162)

According to (i), the default (primary) focus in SOV languages falls on the immediately pre-verbal position, while post-verbal elements are predicted not to bear focus.

References

Chung, Daeho. 2015. Some Notes on Ko's (2014b, 2015) Hybrid Approach to the Korean RDC. *Studies in Generative Grammar*, 25(3): 735-754.

Comrie, Bernard. 1984. Some Formal Properties of Focus in Modern Eastern Armenian. *Annual of Armenian Linguistics*, 5: 1-21.

Engdahl, Elisabet. 1983. Parasitic Gaps. *Linguistics and Philosophy* 6, 5-34.

Erguvanlı, Eeser. E. 1984. *The Function of Word Order in Turkish Grammar*. University of California Press, Berkeley.

Givón, Talmy. 1984. *A Functional-Typological Introduction Vol. 1*, John Benjamins Publishing Co, Philadelphia.

Greenberg, Joseph. H. 1966. Some Universals of Grammar with Particular Reference to the Order of Meaningful Elements. In Greenberg, Joseph. H. (ed.), *Universals of Language*. MIT Press, Cambridge, 73–113.

Hankamer, Jorge. 1979. *Deletion in coordinate Structures*. New York Garland Publishing, Inc.

Herring, Susan C. and John C. Paolillo. 1995. Focus Position in SOV Languages. In Downing, Pamela A. and Michael Noonan (eds.), *Word Order in Discourse*, John Benjamins Publishing Company, Philadelphia, 163-198.

Hornstein, Norbert and Jairo Nunes. 2008. Adjunction, Labeling, and Bare Phrase Structure. *Biolinguistics* 2: 57-86.

Huang, C.-T. James. 1982. Logical Relations in Chinese and the Theory of Grammar. Ph.D. diss., MIT.

Jo, Mi-Jeung. 1986. Fixed Word Order and the Theory of the Pre-Verbal Focus Projections in Korean. Ph.D. diss., Univ. of Washington.

Kim, Alan Hyun-Ok. 1985. The Grammar of Focus in Korean Syntax and its Typological Implications. Ph.D. diss., Univ. of Southern California.

Kim, Alan Hyun-Ok. 1988. Preverbal Focusing and Type XXIII Languages. In Hammond, Michael, Edith A. Moravscik and Jessica R. Wirth (eds.), *Studies in Syntactic Typology*. John Benjamins, Philadelphia, 149–171.

Ko, Heejeong. 2014. Remarks on Right Dislocation Construction in Korean: Challenges to bi-clausal analyses. *Language Research*, 50(2): 275-310.

Ko, Heejeong. 2015. Two Ways to the Right: A Hybrid Approach to Right-dislocation in Korean. *Language Research*, 51(1): 3-40.

Kuno, Susumu. 1978. *Danwa no Bunpo* (The Grammar of Discourse), Taishukan, Tokyo. [Written in Japanese]

Lee, Chungmin. 1992. (Pi)hancengseng/(Pul)thukcengseng tae Hwascey/Chocem—Kayche Chungwi/Tankye Chungwi Swulewato Kwanlyenhaye ((In)Definitness/(Non-)Specificity vs. Topic/Focus—In Relation to the Individual Level/ Stage Level Predicate). *Kwukehak* (Korean Linguistics), 22: 397-424. [Written in Korean]

Nunes, Jairo. 2004. *Linearization of Chains and Sideward Movement*. MIT Press.

Park, Cheol-Woo. 2003. *Hankwuke Cengpokwucoeyseuy Hwaceywa Chocem* (Topic and Focus in Korean Information Structure). Yeklak, Seoul. [Written in Korean]

Taraldsen, K. T. 1981. The Theoretical Interpretation of a Class of Marked Extractions. In Belletti, Adriana, Luciana Brandi and Luigi Rizzi (eds.), *Theory of Markedness in Generative Grammar*, Scuola Normale Superiore, Pisa, 475-516.

Automatic Identifying Entity Type in Linked Data

Qingliang Miao, Ruiyu Fang, Shuangyong Song, Zhongguang Zheng, Lu Fang, Yao Meng, Jun Sun
Fujitsu R&D Center Co., Ltd.
Chaoyang District, Beijing P. R. China 100027
{qingliang.miao,fangruiyu,shuangyong.song,zhengzhg,fanglu,meng yao,sunjun}@cn.fujitsu.com

Abstract

Type information is an important component of linked data. Unfortunately, many linked datasets lack of type information, which obstructs linked data applications such as question answering and recommendation. In this paper, we study how to automatically identify entity type information from Chinese linked data and present a novel approach by integrating classification and entity linking techniques. In particular, entity type information is inferred from internal clues such as entity's abstract, infobox and subject using classifiers. Moreover, external evidence is obtained from other knowledge bases using entity linking techniques. To evaluate the effectiveness of the approach, we conduct preliminary experiments on a real-world linked dataset from Zhishi.me [1]. Experimental results indicate that our approach is effective in identifying entity types.

1 Introduction

An increasing number of linked datasets is published on the Web. At present, there have been more than 200 datasets in the LOD cloud. Among these datasets, DBpedia (Bizer, C. *et al.*, 2009) and Yago (Suchanek, F.M. *et al.*, 2007) serve as hubs in LOD cloud. As the first effort of Chinese LOD, Zhishi.me (Niu, X. *et al.*, 2011) extracted RDF triples from three largest Chinese encyclopedia web sites i.e. Chinese Wikipedia, Baidu Baike[2] and Hudong Baike[3]. However, type information is incomplete or missing in these linked datasets. For example, more than 36% of type information is missing in DBpedia (Kenza Kellou-Menouer and Zoubida Kedad, 2012). Zhishi.me only uses the SKOS vocabulary to represent the category system and does not strictly define the "*rdf:type*" relation between instances and classes.

Type information is an important component of linked datasets. Knowing what a certain entity is, e.g., a person, organization, place, etc., is crucial for enabling a number of desirable applications such as query understanding (Tonon, A. *et al.*, 2013), question answering (Kalyanpur, A. *et al.*, 2011; Welty, C. *et al.*, 2012), recommendation (Lee, T. *et al.*, 2006; Hepp, M. 2008), and automatic linking (Aldo Gangemi *et al.*, 2012). Since it is often not feasible to manually assign types to all instances in a large linked data, automatic identifying type information is desirable. Furthermore, since open and crowd-sourced encyclopedia often contain noisy data, filtering out the incorrect type information is crucial as well (Heiko Paulheim and Christian Bizer, 2013).

Recently, more and more attention has been paid to extracting or mining type information from linked

[1] http://zhishi.me/

[2] http://baike.baidu.com/

[3] http://www.baike.com/

data. However, most of current techniques on obtaining type information are either language-dependent or inferring type information only from internal clues such as textual description of entity. Most existing work was mainly focused on mining entity type from internal clues, and missed out the point that the issue can be boosted by integrating external evidence. Our assumption is that given an entity e_1 without type information, if we can find an equivalent entity e_2 with type information, we can obtain the type information of e_1 directly.

In this paper, we investigate whether external evidence from other knowledge base could be helpful to entity type identification, and how to combine internal clues such as abstract, infobox and subject with external evidence. In particular, several learning features are extracted from entity abstract, infobox and subject, and then classifiers are trained to get entity type prediction models. Meanwhile, entity linking tools are utilized to link entities with external knowledge base e.g. DBpedia, where we can get type information. Finally, a voting mechanism is adopted to decide the final entity type. We have implemented our algorithms and present some experimental evaluation results to demonstrate the effectiveness of the approach.

The remainder of the paper is organized as follows. In the following section we review the existing literature on entity type identification. Then, we introduce the proposed approach in section 3. We conduct comparative experiments and present the results in section 4. At last, we conclude the paper with a summary of our work and give our future working directions.

2 Related Work

In the field of entity type inference, there are two dominant methods, namely, content-based (*Aldo Gangemi et al., 2012; Tianxing Wu et al., 2014*) and link-based methods (*Andrea Giovanni Nuzzolese et al., 2012; Heiko Paulheim and Christian Bizer, 2013*). Next we will introduce these methods respectively.

Content-based methods usually utilize entity descriptions such as abstract, infobox and properties to identify entity types. Several learning features are extracted from textual data and classification or clustering models are trained to predict entity types. For example, Aldo Gangemi et al., first extracted definitions from Wikipedia pages, used a natural language deep parser FRED to produce a logical RDF representation of definition sentences, and then select types and type-relations from the RDF graph based on graph patterns. Finally, a word sense disambiguation engine is used to identify the types of an entity and their taxonomical relations (*Aldo Gangemi et al., 2012*). Tianxing Wu et al., also mined type information from abstracts, infobox and categories of article pages in Chinese encyclopedia Web sites. They presented an attribute propagation algorithm to generate attributes for categories and a graph-based random walk method to infer instance types from categories of entities (*Tianxing Wu et al., 2014*). Man Zhu et al., transformed type assertion detection into multiclass classification of pairs of type assertions, and adopted Adaboost as the meta classifier with C4.5 as the base classifier (*Man Zhu et. al., 2014*). Kenza Kellou-Menouer and Zoubida Kedad utilized a density-based clustering algorithm to discovery types in RDF datasets. They first adopted Jaccard similarity to measure the closeness between two entities. In particular, they calculated the similarity between two given entities by considering their respective sets of both incoming and outgoing properties. Then entities are grouped according to their similarity (*Kenza Kellou-Menouer and Zoubida Kedad, 2015*).

Link-based methods can also be used in entity type assignment. For example, Heiko Paulheim and Christian Bizer proposed a heuristic link-based type inference mechanism. They used each link from and to an instance as an indicator for the resource's type. For each link, they use the statistical distribution of types in the subject and object position of the property for predicting the instance's types (*Heiko Paulheim and Christian Bizer, 2013*). Andrea Giovanni Nuzzolese et al., utilized k-Nearest Neighbor algorithm for classifying DBpedia entities based on the wikilinks (*Andrea Giovanni Nuzzolese et al., 2012*).

In this paper, we integrate content-based methods and external evidence to identify entity type. We views type identification as classification issue, and adopt classifiers to train type prediction models. Meanwhile, entity linking tools are adopted to link entities with external knowledge base, where we can get type information. Finally, we use a weighted voting approach to obtain the entity type.

3 The Approach

In this section, we will introduce the architecture of the system as shown in figure 1. The inputs of the system are entity data as illustrated in figure 2, the outputs are entity types. In particular the system consists of two parallel parts: (1) classification module; (2) entity linking module;

In classification module, we first extract entity definition from its abstract. And then, we extract several learning features from its definition, infobox, and subject. We choose several classification models to train the entity type prediction model.

In entity linking module, we first construct profile for each entity, and then entity linking tool (Qingliang Miao *et al.*, 2015) is used as a bridge to get entity type information from other linked data i.e. DBpedia. Finally, a voting mechanism is used to get the final answer. In particular, if these two models' results are different, we use entity linking based results as the final answer.

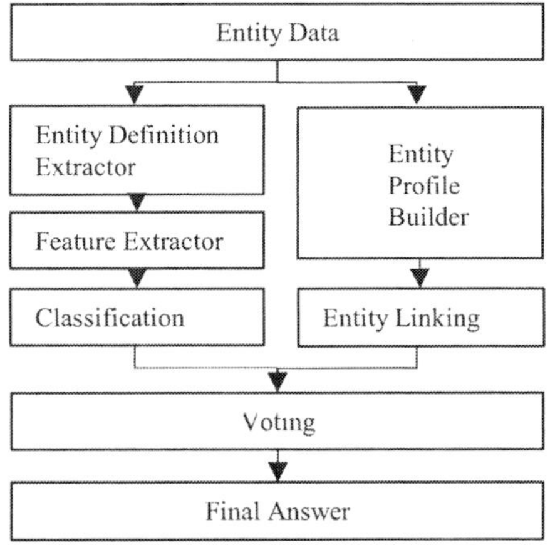

Figure 1: The workflow of the approach.

3.1 Classification based Model

In this section, we mainly introduce learning features and feature selection method.

In Linked Data, entities are usually descripted using Resource Description Framework (RDF)[4]. Each entity in Linked Data space is identified by a unique HTTP dereferenceable Uniform Resource Identifier (URI) and the relations of resources are described with simple subject-predicate-object triples. Figure 2 shows an example of entity "首尔/Seoul". The task of this research is to identify the type of the entity using existing information as illustrated in figure 2.

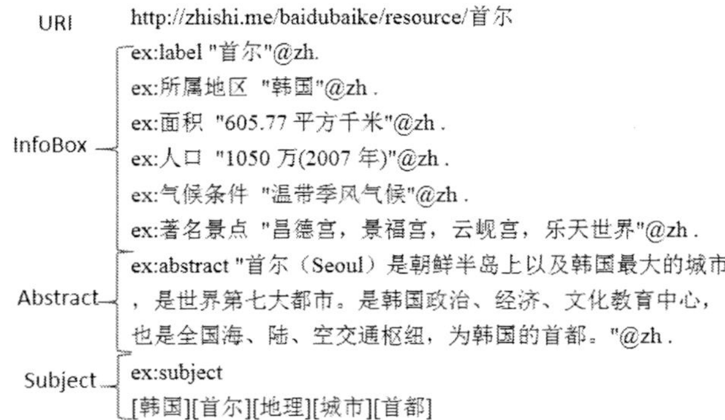

Figure 2: Linked Data example of entity "首尔/Seoul"

Pattern feature

Typically, the definition of an entity is in the first k sentences of its abstract. Inspired by (Aldo Gangemi *et al.*, 2012), we use a set of heuristics based on lexico-syntactic patterns to extract entity definition. The pattern features are derived from entity definition text in the form of "[entity] is/belongs [t_i] [$word_1 \ldots word_n$]", where t_i is the type keyword of entity type i and n is the distance between the key word t_i and the sentence's end. Table 1 shows some examples of the patterns.

Entity type	Patterns
Insect	<是.+虫>,<is.+insect>, <属于.+纲><belongs to.+species>
University	<是.+大学>,<是.+高校> <is.+university/college>
Game	<是.+游戏>,<is.+game>
City	<是.+城市>,<一座.+城市> <is.+city>
Scene	<是.+景点>,<是.+胜地>, <is.+attraction/scenic>

Table 1: Example of pattern features

Table 2 shows top 5 type keywords of each entity type. The type keyword set is obtained from encyclopedia and Chinese corpus and we will detail the process in next section. The type keywords are selected from keyword set manually. The feature vector based on pattern is Q_i, where N is the number of entity type. If the first k

[4] http://www.w3.org/RDF/

sentences x in abstract contain the patterns in Table 1, we set the value δ, otherwise the value is 0. In our experiment, we set δ =1.0 empirically. For example, the definition of "首尔/Seoul" we extracted from abstracts is "首尔（Seoul）是朝鲜半岛上以及韩国最大的城市". And the feature value for type "city" is δ and 0 for the other types.

$$Q_i = \begin{cases} \delta \text{ , if } f(x,t_i)=1; \\ 0, \text{ if } f(x,t_i)=0; \end{cases} i \in \{1,2,\ldots N\}$$

Keyword feature

Besides pattern features described above, we use keywords features as well. To ensure high coverage and quality of keywords for each type, we use rule base method and statistic based method to mine related keywords. For rule based method, we first collect entity description page with type information from three Chinese encyclopedia. Through analyzing description page, we extract 4 types of contents to construct keyword set, "*Title*", "*Alias*", "*Category*", and "*Related Entity*".

- Title: The titles in Chinese encyclopedia are used as labels for the corresponding entities directly.
- Alias: The alias in Chinese encyclopedia is used to represent the same entity. For example, [北京|北平|京师].
- Category: Categories describe the subjects of a given entity.
- Related Entities: In Chinese encyclopedia there are related entities of a given entity. For example, related entities of "大学(university)" are "北京大学(Peking university)", "清华大学 (Tsinghua University)

For statistic based method, we use word2vec model to obtain word vectors based on Chinese corpus and obtain similar word lists for each entity type. The final keyword list is obtained by a voting method. Table 2 shows the top 5 keywords for each type.

Entity type	Keywords
Insect	{昆虫,虫,物种,天敌,害虫}/{insect, species, predators, pets }
University	{大学,高校,校园,学院,分校}/{university, college, campus, branch}
Game	{游戏,电脑游戏,电子游戏,网络游戏,在线游戏}/{games, computer games, web game, online games }
City	{首都,大都市,城市,省会,城区}/{capital, metropolis, cities, provincial capital, urban}
Scene	{景点,名胜,旅游,景区,风景}/{attractions, scenic, tourism, scenic, scenery}
Politician	{政治家,政界,活动家,外交家,政客}/{ politician, activists, diplomats }
Song	{歌曲,歌词,演唱,歌名,曲目}/{song, lyrics, singing, song title, track }
Novel	{小说,短篇小说,科幻小说,武侠小说,传记}/{novel, short story, science fiction, martial arts novel, biography }
Cartoon	{动画,漫画,动画片,动画制作,电视}/{attractions, scenic, tourism, scenic, scenery}
Actor	{演员,导演,编剧,主演,剧情}/{actor, director, screenwriter, starring, drama}

Table 2: Top 5 keywords for each type

Infobox features

Since different entity types have different properties. For example, person has birthday and organization has locations. We extract property names from infobox and use them as infobox features. For example, in figure 1, property features of entity "首尔/Seoul" is "所属地区/region", "面积/area", "人口/population", "气候条件/climatic condition", "著名景点/famous scenery".

Subject features

Besides infobox features, we collect entity subject information from zhishi.me. Subject information contains many domain-specific terms, which are indicator of entity types. Table 3 shows some example of subject features. In this study, all these above features are binary features.

Entity	Subject features
颐和园/Summer Palace	{公园,景点,旅游}/{park, attraction, tourism}
静冈市/Shizuoka City	{日本,城市}/{japan, city}
面包超人 /Anpanman	{动画片,萌}/{cartoon, cute}

Table 3: Example of subject features

Feature selection

The learning features are all extracted empirically, therefore, effective feature selection is necessary. We design a feature selection scheme as below: we take 'maximum probability of a feature representing a category' as the indicator of the effectiveness of features, and remove features whose effectiveness is smaller than a threshold T. In our experiment, we set T=0.85 empirically based on the development set. The changing curve of F-measure and threshold T is shown in figure 3.

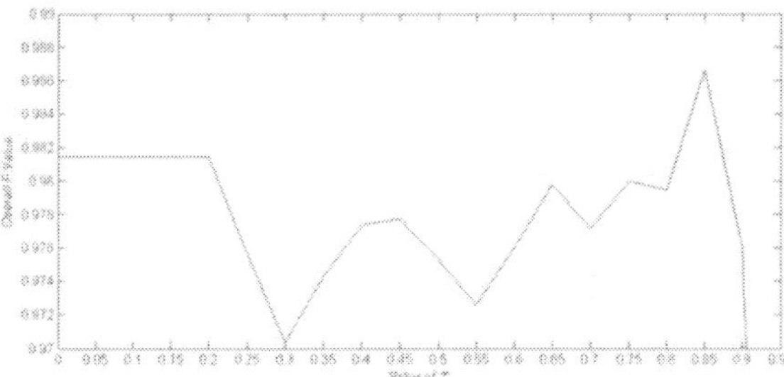

Figure 3: F-measure changes with threshold T.

3.2 Entity linking based Model

To use type information of DBpedia, we use entity linking tool to link entities with Chinese DBpedia. Since entities in Chinese DBpedia lack of "*rdf:type*" property, we use following steps to get type information.

Using "sameAs" relation

Since many entities in English DBpedia have "*rdf:type*" property, we can use "owl:sameAs" relation to obtain type information of Chinese DBpedia entities. For example, *<zhishi.me:伊斯兰堡>* is linked with *<zh.dbpedia:伊斯兰堡>* that is same as English DBpedia entity: *<en.dbpedia:Islamabad>*, and the type of *<en.dbpedia:Islamabad>* is *<dbo:City>*. Therefore, the type of *<zhishi.me:伊斯兰堡>* is city. Figure 4 illustrates the process.

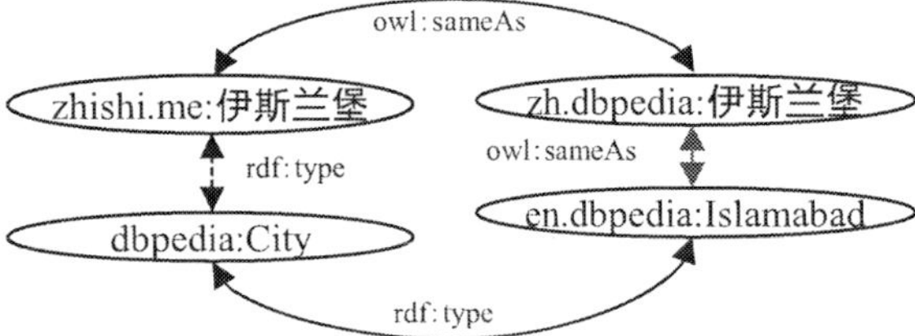

Figure 4: Example of "sameAs" relation.

Using redirect relation

In some cases, we can use redirect relation to obtain the type. Figure 5 shows an example. *<zhishi.me:青岛>* is same as *<zh.dbpedia:青岛>* and *<zh.dbpedia:青岛>*is redirected from *<zh.dbpedia:青岛市>*, and *<zh.dbpedia:青岛市>* is same as *<en.dbpedia:Qingdao>* whose type is city.

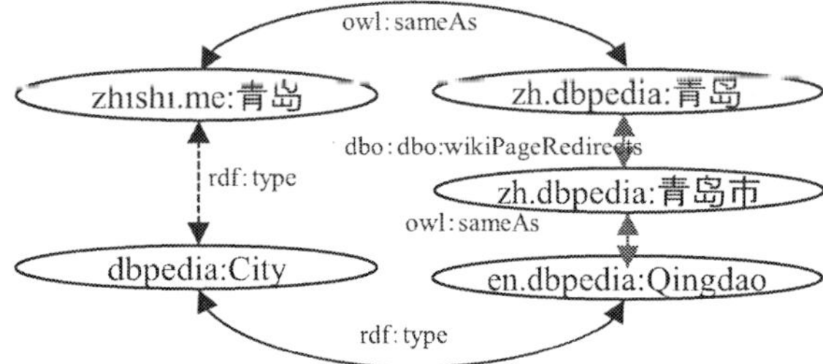

Figure 5. Example of "redirect" relation.

Using category information

Besides "sameAs" and "redirection" relation, we use entity category information to infer type information as well. Category information in DBPedia is usually a strong indicator for entity type. For example, person usually has category information "People_from_Beijing" or "People_born_1960s". Therefore, we can infer an entity's type from category. In particular, we use a simple method that match category information e.g. "People" with DBpedia ontology class.

Type mapping

Since the DBPedia Ontology (dbo) is different from type information in Zhishi.me, we have to map dbo with entity type in Zhishi.me. In particular, given a dbo type, we use a type mapping table shown in table 4 to find the corresponding type in Zhishi.me. We use entity linking tools to link Zhishi.me training data with DBPedia, and obtain the type mapping relation.

For example, if entity e_1 in Zhishi.me with type "Politician" is linked with e_2 in DBPedia with type "Governor", we can obtain a mapping relation between "Politician" and "Governor".

Type in Zhishi.me	Type in DBPedia
Insect	dbo:Insect
University	dbo:University
Game	dbo:ViedoGame
Politician	dbo:Politician;dbo:OfficeHolder dbo:Governor;dbo:Ambassador dbo:Chancellor
City	dbo:City;dbo:Capital;dbo:Town dbo:Settlement
Song	dbo:Song
Novel	dbo:Novel
Scene	dbo:NaturalPlace;dbo:Mountain dbo:Canal;dbo:Park
Cartoon	dbo:Cartoon;dbo:Comic dbo:TelevisionShow;dbo:Film
Actor	dbo:Actor;dbo:Artist

Table 4: Type mapping table

4 Experiment

In order to evaluate the effectiveness of the proposed approach, we conduct our experiments by using test data from JIST15 type identification challenge[5]. The data includes 1397 entities with type information and 500 unlabeled entities that are used as test data. There are 10 classes including insect, university, game, politician, city, song, novel, scene, cartoon and actor. The statistics of the data is shown in Table 5.

Entity Type	# training data	# testing data
Insect	124	41
University	157	42
Game	143	59
Politician	134	43
City	139	59
Song	139	59
Novel	150	51
Scene	130	60
Cartoon	134	38
Actor	147	48

Table 5: The statistics of the test data

Precision, Recall and F-measure are used as the evaluation metric. All of them are defined as follows where a_i is the number of URLs that are actually in label i and also predicted in label i, b_i is the number of URLs that are predicted in label i, c_i is the number of URLs that are actually in label i.

$$precision = \sum_{i=1}^{n} \frac{a_i}{b_i}$$

$$recall = \sum_{i=1}^{n} \frac{a_i}{c_i}$$

$$f-measure = \frac{2precision * recall}{precision + recall}$$

In experiment, we first evaluate the performance using internal information only, namely classification based method. And then we evaluate whether external knowledge is useful to improve type identification performance. We also compare with our method with state of the art method (Tianxing Wu. *et al.*, 2014).

In this experiment, we have compared with four classification algorithms, Naïve Bayes, Bayes Net, Random Forest and Support Vector Machine. Figure 6 shows experiment results, from which we can see *F-measure* is relative high in classification method, and Random Forest algorithm performs best among four classifiers and F-measure is above 0.98.This results indicate the learning features are very predictive for this task.

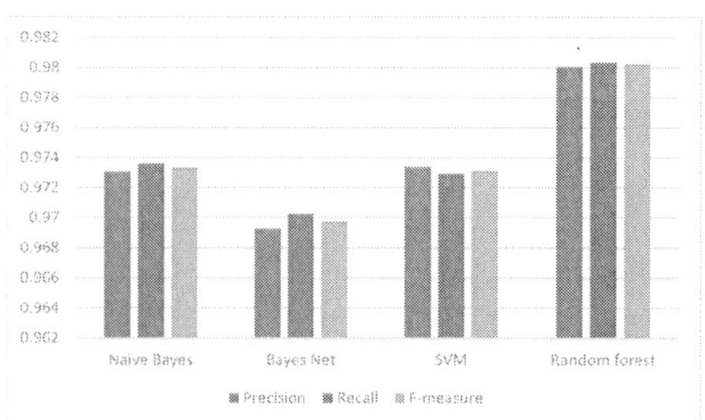

Figure 6: Experiment results on precision.

To evaluate whether external evidence derived from other knowledge base is helpful, we have built and compared two kinds of type identification methods, one with utilizing entity linking techniques and the other without.

[5] ttp://www.jist2015.org/index.php?m=list&a=index&id=48&skip=50

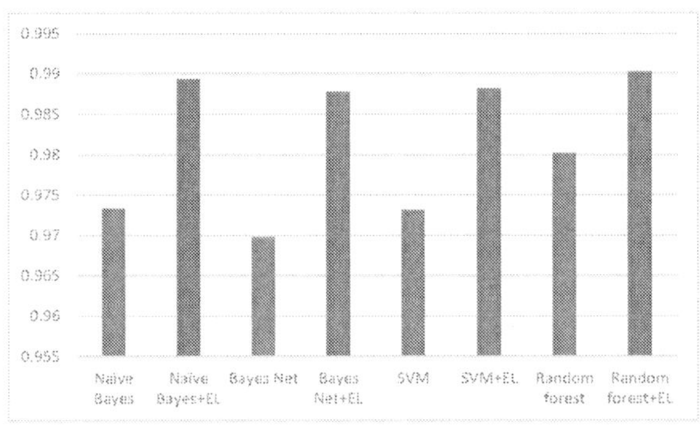

Figure 7: Experiment results of models with and without entity linking on f-measure.

Figure 7 shows the comparing results of type identification models with and without entity linking. From Figure 7 we can see that when incorporating entity linking results, the average *F-measure* can be improved by 1.5%. The improvement of *F-measure* is likely attributable to the external knowledge base. The improvement is not as much as expected. Through carefully analyze the results, we find two reasons. First, entity linking tools only link 40% entity in testing data. Second, most derived type from external knowledge base is consistent with classification results

In order to validate whether the improvement is significant, we adopt pair-wise t-tests on *F-measure*. For all t-tests, p-values are all less than 0.01, therefore the improvement is significant. We confirm that the improvement of *F-measure* is due to incorporating external evidence and we believe that it will achieve better results if we incorporate enough and high quality external evidence.

From the above analysis, it is evident that entity linking results can be incorporated as knowledge to improve the performance of entity type identification.

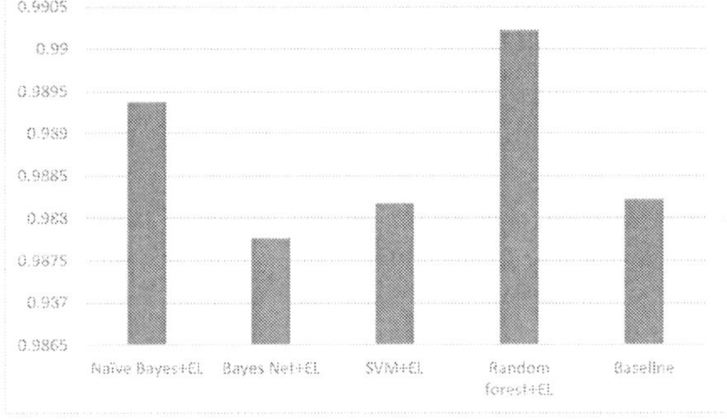

Figure 8: Experiment results of models with entity linking and baseline on f-measure

We also use state of the art method (*Tianxing Wu et al., 2014*) as baseline and conduct experiment to compare our method with the baseline. Figure 8 shows the experiment results. From figure 8 we can see our best performance (Random forest with entity linking) outperform state of the art method by 1.1%.

5 Conclusion

In this paper, we study entity type information identification from Chinese linked data and present a novel approach by integrating classification and entity linking techniques. In particular, entity type information is inferred from internal clues using classifiers. Moreover, external evidence is obtained from other knowledge bases through entity linking techniques. Experimental results on real-world datasets show the learning features we selected are predictive. Moreover, results indicate external evidence derived by entity linking techniques is helpful to type identification as well. We believe that this study is just the first step in type identification and much more work needs to be done to further explore the issue. In our ongoing work, we plan to improve entity tools to find more equivalent entities in external knowledge base. We also plan to reduce the amount of training data, which is time consuming to obtain, by using entity linking results. For example, type information obtained by entity linking techniques could be used as training data directly. Another direction is to harvest external evidence from broader resources, e.g. text or web tables, not just from linked data or knowledge base. For instance, in sentence "...including cities such as Birmingham, Montgomery, Huntsville...", if we know the type information of "Birmingham", we can infer other entities' type as well. Similarly, if we know the type of an entity, the other entity types in the same column can also be obtained by reasoning. At last, we plan to study fine grained type identification.

References

Aldo Gangemi, Andrea Giovanni Nuzzolese, Valentina Presutti, Francesco Draicchio, Alberto Musetti, and Paolo Ciancarini. Automatic typing of DBpedia entities, In Proceedings of the 11th International Semantic Web Conference, 2012, pp. 65-81.

Andrea Giovanni Nuzzolese, Aldo Gangemi, Valentina Presutti and Paolo Ciancarini, Type inference through the analysis of Wikipedia links, In Proceedings of the LDOW2012, 2012.

Bizer, C., Lehmann, J., Kobilarov, G., Auer, S., Becker, C., Cyganiak, R., Hellmann, S.: DBpedia-a Crystallization Point for the Web of Data. Web Semantics: Science, Services and Agents on the World Wide Web 7(3), 2009, pp. 154-165.

Heiko Paulheim and Christian Bizer, Type Inference on Noisy RDF Data, In Proceedings of the 12th International Semantic Web Conference, 2013, pp. 510-525.

Hepp, M.: GoodRelations: An ontology for describing products and services offers on the web. In: EKAW 2008, Vol. 5268, 2008, pp. 329-346.

Kalyanpur, A., Murdock, J.W., Fan, J., Welty, C.: Leveraging Community-built Knowledge for Type Coercion in Question Answering. In Proceedings of the 10th International Semantic Web Conference, pp. 144-156.

Kenza Kellou-Menouer and Zoubida Kedad, Discovering Types in RDF Datasets, In Proceedings of the 12th Extended Semantic Web Conference, 2015, pp. 77-81.

Lee, T., Chun, J., Shim, J., Lee, S. G.: An Ontology-based Product Recommender System for B2B Marketplaces. International Journal of Electronic Commerce 11(2), 2006, pp. 125-155.

Man Zhu, Zhiqiang Gao, and Zhibin Quan, Noisy Type Assertion Detection in Semantic Datasets, In Proceedings of the 13th International Semantic Web Conference, 2014, pp. 373-388.

Niu, X., Sun, X., Wang, H., Rong, S., Qi, G., Yu, Y.: Zhishi.me - Weaving Chinese Linking Open Data. In Proceedings of the 10th International Semantic Web Conference, pp. 205-220.

Qingliang Miao, Yao Meng, Lu Fang, Fumihito Nishino and Nobuyuki Igata, Link Scientific Publications using Linked Data. In Proceedings of the 9th IEEE International Conference on Semantic Computing, 2015.

Suchanek, F.M., Kasneci, G., Weikum, G.: Yago: a Core of Semantic Knowledge. In Proceedings of the 16th International Conference on World Wide Web, 2007 pp. 697-706.

Tianxing Wu, Shaowei Ling, Guilin Qi, and Haofen Wang, Mining Type Information from Chinese Online Encyclopedias, In Proceedings of the 4th Joint International Conference, 2014, pp 213-229.

Tonon, A., Catasta, M., Demartini, G., Cudr´e-Mauroux, P., Aberer, K.: TRank: Ranking Entity Types Using the Web of Data. In Proceedings of the 12th International Semantic Web Conference, pp. 640-656

Welty, C., Murdock, J.W., Kalyanpur, A., Fan, J.: A Comparison of Hard Filters and Soft Evidence for Answer Typing in Watson. In Proceedings of the 11th International Semantic Web Conference, pp. 243-256.

SMTPOST: Using Statistical Machine Translation Approach in Filipino Part-of-Speech Tagging

Nicco Nocon
De La Salle University
2401 Taft Avenue, Malate, Manila City
1004 Metro Manila, Philippines
noconoccin@gmail.com

Allan Borra
De La Salle University
2401 Taft Avenue, Malate, Manila City
1004 Metro Manila, Philippines
allan.borra@dlsu.edu.ph

Abstract

The field of Natural Language Processing (NLP) in the country has been continually developing. However, the transition between Tagalog to the progressing Filipino language left tools and resources behind. This paper introduces a Statistical Machine Translation Part-of-Speech (POS) Tagger for Filipino (SMTPOST), with the purpose of reviving, updating and widening the scope of technologies in the POS' tagging domain, catering to the changes made by the Filipino language. Resources built are comprised mainly of a tagset (218 tags), parallel corpus (2,668 sentences), affix rules (59 rules) and word-tag dictionary (309 entries). SMTPOST was tested to different tagsets and domains, producing 84.75% as its highest accuracy score, at least 3.75% increase from the available Tagalog POS taggers. Despite SMTPOST's utilization of Filipino resources and good performance, there are room for improvements and opportunities. Recommendations include a better feature extractor (preferably a morphological analyzer), an increase in scope for all of the resources, implementation of pre- and/or post-processing, and the utilization of SMTPOST research to other NLP applications.

1 Introduction

Natural Language Processing (NLP) is a field in computer science where it connects human language with technology. In the Philippines, NLP applications and resources have been continually expanding. Specifically, a project conducted by De La Salle University (DLSU), Manila in the span of three years developed numerous NLP products: from language resources such as lexicons, word corpora, tagsets and grammar rules, to tools such as Morphological Analyzers, Part-of-Speech (POS) Taggers, Grammar Checkers and Machine Translators (Chu, 2009). These outputs enabled DLSU to produce research papers and extended applications not only for the Filipino language, but also to English, marking these works as well-established at that time.

Focusing on POS tagging[1], Chu (2009) featured taggers from Miguel and Roxas' (2007) comparative study. These POS taggers were implemented on different approaches: PTPOST4.1 (Go, 2006) an extension from past PTPOST researches (Cortez et al., 2005; Flordeliza et al., 2005), is a probabilistic tagger implementing the Hidden Markov model, Viterbi algorithm, lexical and contextual probabilities; MBPOST (Raga and Trogo, 2006), a memory-based tagger; Tag-Alog (Fontanilla and Wu, 2006), a rule-based tagger; TPOST (Cheng and Rabo, 2004), a template-based tagger; and adding to the list, SVPOST (Reyes et al., 2011), a Support Vector Machines tagger. Despite developments of POS taggers in the country, the Filipino language's evolution requires constant updates on the tools and their resources. Without these updates, the products become outdated in the following factors: data contents, software usability, performance and availability. This paper addresses those issues through experimentation and creation of a new tagger using Statistical Machine Translation (SMT) for

[1] The process of indicating the Part-of-Speech (i.e. Nouns, Pronouns, Verbs, Adjectives, etc.) of a given word. In this case, the tagging process is automated.

the Filipino language. This research is also intended to provide aid in the understanding of Filipino POS, establish a Filipino tagset and support NLP products or processes (i.e. grammar checker, language parsing, speech processing, information retrieval, etc.) in their tasks.

In choosing an approach, the use of Hidden Markov Models, Viterbi Algorithm, and Machine Learning (Support Vector Machines, Perceptron, and the likes) has been recurrent to foreign languages. As a challenge and motivation for this research, instead of implementing widely used approaches, it has been set to start up new ventures on a potential tagger – ending up with selecting Statistical Machine Translation. SMT as a tagger is uncommon; as specified in its name, it is mainly used in translating one language to another. However, it is not limited to be used that way. Oda et al.'s (2015) work, used SMT for generating English and Japanese pseudo-codes from a given source code, intended to aid code understanding. Other samples are from the work of Mizumoto et al.'s (2011) Japanese error correction and Nocon et al.'s (2014) Filipino shortcut words normalizer. These examples, provided results that proved using SMT in different areas is feasible by supplying two types of data labeled as source (to be transformed) and target (transformed into).

As a data-driven approach, the method for this research leverages SMT by using pairs of word features (source) and POS tag counterparts (target), and translated Filipino Wikipedia data as input for training; while for POS tagging, words or sentences are accepted as input to be automatically transformed into features to match the generated model from training.

This paper mainly focuses on elaborating the creation of Statistical Machine Translation Part-of-Speech Tagger (SMTPOST). It is outlined in the following order: first is the methodology section in which the construction of SMTPOST is discussed; followed by test results and discussions, including analysis of SMTPOST's performance against other existing taggers; next, conclusion and recommendations; and finally, the list of references used.

2 Methodology

In order to create the Filipino Statistical Machine Translation Part-of-Speech Tagger (SMTPOST), the necessary resources and tools were built.

2.1 Language Resources

MGNN Tagset

From the Rabo Tagset (Cheng and Rabo, 2004), tag codes were modified and POS sub-categories were added such as common noun abbreviation, preposition, semi-colon tag and compound (combination of two or more POS) tags. An example for a compound tag, given the word *bagong* 'new', it has the frequency adverb (RBW) *bago* 'new' and the ligature (CCP) *-ng,* resulting to the compound RBW_CCP tag. The MGNN Tagset[2] consists of 218 tags, with 69 basic and 149 (currently used) compound tags.

Corpora

The parallel corpus used was collected from Wikipedia, containing Filipino word and POS tag pairs, with a total of 2,668 sentences or 70,312 (14,575 distinct) words. The parallel corpus was divided into two parts: training and testing data, following 80 (2,134 sentences/55,428 words) to 20 (534 sentences/14,884 words) ratio, respectively.

Additional corpora were gathered from TPOST (i.e. Biblical Text and Children Storybooks) for testing purposes. The numbers designated from their work's training and testing were followed.

All of these data were collected in English and then translated into Filipino by university students whom were supervised by a linguist in the specified language field. There were no specific rules in translating as long as they are consistent (sentences may be in predicate-subject or subject-predicate form), to apply Filipino conversational style and terminologies in the data. The POS counterpart was manually tagged using the MGNN Tagset for Wikipedia and Biblical Text (1) corpora, and Rabo Tagset for Biblical Text (2) and Children Storybooks. Taken from TPOST, Biblical Text (1) and (2) have the same word entries but differ in their POS tag counterparts.

Affix Rules

59 affix rules from Bonus (2003) were used as basis for feature extraction. Rules per affix: prefix, infix, and suffix are distributed in 42, 2 and 15 rules, respectively.

Word-Tag Dictionary

A dictionary containing 309 word and POS tag pair entries (updated from TPOST's predefined

[2] Can be accessed in http://goo.gl/dY0qFe

words) include word samples from each category. It acts as a database for determining words that have POS tags. TPOST used this resource in providing tags, but in this research, it was only used to mark words that are already in the dictionary as part of the feature extraction.

2.2 SMTPOST

SMTPOST's processes follows the framework shown at Figure 1. Processes with the '*' mark were done beforehand and are excluded during the tagging process.

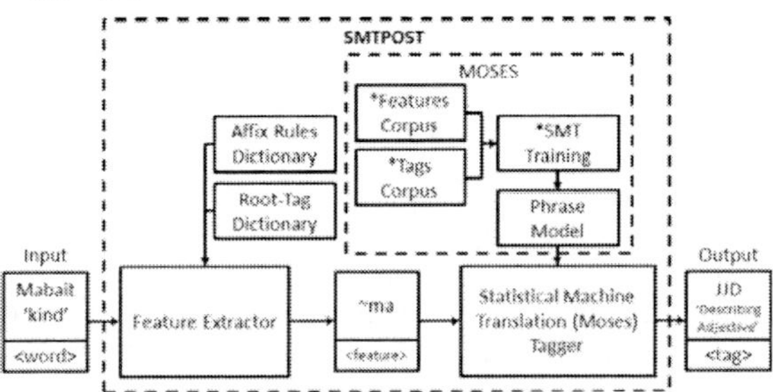

Figure 1. SMTPOST Framework

Feature Extractor (FEX)

FEX takes out word features (affixes) from a given text and inserts marker/s before the found affixes. Following TPOST's structure for extracting and marking features (see Table 1) with the addition of *:A* marker for abbreviations, *kumakain* 'eating' will result into *@um$ka* or in English *+ing*.

Word Feature Structure

(
  (
    (#<PDW>)* [:<Capitalized>](~<Prefix>)*
    (@<infix>)* (+<Suffix>)*
    ($<DuplicatedCharacters>)*
) [-] or *<word>
)

Feature Code	Description
#	Predefined Word
:F	1st letter Capitalized
:FS	1st word of Sentence
:A	Abbreviations
~	Prefix
@	Infix
+	Suffix
$	Duplicated Characters
-	Hyphen
*	No Features, whole word

Table 1. FEX Structure and Markers

The algorithm for extracting features was based from Cheng and Rabo's TPOST (2004), migrated from 2004 Java Server Pages into 2016 Java – intended to eliminate dependencies on other POS tagger programs. It utilizes the affix rules and word-tag dictionary to aid in the marking of word features. Using it on training and testing words passes the extracted affixes on as input for SMTPOST. Given this, the input data for SMTPOST is generalized instead of literal words.

Statistical Machine Translation (SMT)

SMT is a translation technique which uses statistical models as its heuristics. By setting a parallel corpus as training input, it determines the patterns and matches of both words and phrases, together with their probabilities. The SMT tagger was implemented using Moses [3] (including SRILM and GIZA++), a well-known and online available SMT tool.

In Moses, there are two main components namely, training and decoding. For training, it requires a set of data to learn from the source and target data. In this research, a Wikipedia parallel corpus was used; but before feeding the data to Moses, it underwent cleaning. Unnecessary characters (e.g. Äi1916 → 1916) and duplicate entries were omitted. At the same time, cleaning involves word correction (e.g. k0lumna → kolumna) and fixing tagging errors such as typographical errors (e.g. JJCC → JJC), incorrect tags (e.g. '.' = PMC → PMP) and tag casing (e.g. PRI_cCP → PRI_CCP).

The cleaned data was originally a word-tag parallel corpus. To generalize the data, word features were generated by running FEX to the words counterpart, producing the feature-tag parallel corpus. This monolingual feature-tag parallel corpus serves as the main data for training, setting word features as source and POS tags as target data.

Following the training pipeline, feeding the data into Moses generated the phrase-model. It contains phrase-table rules (features mapped with tags and their probabilities) with a total of 297,633 lines to be used in POS tagging.

Decoder on the other hand is the tagging proper. It uses the output of training (phrase-model) and sentence/s to be tagged. The accepted input for SMT are extracted features based from input sentence/s and by supplying them, SMT will be able to decode and determine the POS tag – SMTPOST's final output.

[3] http://statmt.org/moses/

Tagging using SMTPOST				
Domain	**Tagset**	**Training Sentences**	**Testing Sentences**	**Accuracy**
Wikipedia	MGNN	2,134	534	84.75%
Biblical Text (1)	MGNN	107	34	77.20%
Biblical Text (2)	Rabo	107	34	84.63%
Children Storybooks	Rabo	68	34	68.72%
Tagging using TPOST (Cheng and Rabo, 2004)				
Wikipedia	MGNN	2,134	534	23.33%
Biblical Text[4]	Rabo	107	34	81.65%
Children Storybooks[4]	Rabo	68	34	61.00%

Table 2. Testing Summary and Results

3 Results and Discussion

SMTPOST was tested through the following domains and tagsets (see Table 2). Additional information on the table are results using TPOST (Cheng and Rabo, 2004), for it is the closest one to the system – in terms of data and process. Data with at most 141 sentences or 2,658 (637 distinct) words per domain were reflected from the same reference in order to enable this research in showing the performance of SMTPOST based on TPOST's testing using different types of corpora.

On the first part of the table, results showed SMTPOST's 84.75% tagging accuracy, where in a total of 14,869 words, the number of correctly tagged, incorrectly tagged and untagged instances are the following: 12,601, 1,577 and 691, respectively. Biblical Text (1) against (2) fell from the line of 8 to 7, with 7.43% difference. This score was the effect of tag specifics and variations using MGNN Tagset, which enhanced the detail in capturing how words are used in a sentence – a deeper POS categorization for a certain word. To illustrate this point, given the words *akin* 'mine' and *aking* 'my', MGNN tags the two words as PRSP (possessive subject pronoun) and PRSP_CCP (possessive subject pronoun with the ligature *-ng*), respectively. On the other hand, Rabo Tagset will simply tag them both as PRSP. Based on the example above, it differentiates independent from dependent possessive pronouns through their single or combined POS tags than generalizing all that falls under a single POS sub-category. With this statement, even if Biblical Text (2) is close to the highest, the use of MGNN Tagset was favored than of Rabo's because of its well tag description for a word and was applied to the training of a modernized Filipino data. About the Children Storybooks domain, it performed poorly with 68.72%. The reason for this is that the data heavily contained proper and common nouns, resulting into a large number of words without features; unlike Wikipedia, the preceded case together with its limited training data prevented both the feature extractor and statistical heuristics from pulling up its accuracy score.

On the second part of the table, the Wikipedia corpus was tagged using TPOST and TPOST's testing results on Biblical Text and Children Storybooks were taken directly from the source for cross-referencing. Tagging the Wikipedia corpus produced 23.33% accuracy, exceedingly low as opposed to the other testing and domains. The testing revealed that similar to Children Storybooks, the Wikipedia corpus contains a heavy amount of nouns and complex terminologies (multiple affixes) which makes it difficult to tag and TPOST was unable to handle its complexity; thus exhibiting SMTPOST's exceptional tagging capabilities.

Comparing results from the two taggers, SMT showed that its results between the same tagset and domain surpassed the template-based approach. It implies that even though both uses generalized data, the use of probabilities in tagging is superior than TPOST's scoring heuristics. Furthermore, evaluation in terms of tagging speed was conducted to both taggers. On the same machine, TPOST tagged 534 sentences for 2 hours and 50 minutes while SMTPOST tagged them for only 26 seconds. Although TPOST's computations are simpler than SMTPOST, TPOST's scoring system were done during the tagging process; whereas, SMTPOST's computations were done during the training process, making the tagging similar to a lookup. Taking an ambiguous word for instance, both taggers will gather the candidate phrases (neighboring words) that will help distinguish the correct tag. After collecting the candidates,

[4] Results taken from Cheng and Rabo (2004) reference.

TPOST will compute how much each candidate fit with the ambiguous word; in contrast, SMTPOST searches for the candidate with the highest probability. Hence, the testing results showed that SMTPOST performs well when it comes to the correctness of its tag while maintaining its decent tagging speed in the process.

Aside from TPOST, SMTPOST was compared to other POS taggers shown at Table 3.

POS Tagger	Data Composition	Accuracy
PTPOST4.1	120,000 words (Miguel and Roxas, 2007)	78.30%
MBPOST		77.00%
Tag-Alog		72.50%
TPOST		70.00%
SVPOST	122,318 words (Reyes et al., 2011)	81.00%
SMTPOST	**70,312 words**	**84.75%**

Table 3. Comparison of POS Taggers

From the given scores, with just 70,312 words, SMTPOST's score exceeded the other taggers by at least 3.75%. The reason for this is other taggers used words for their training, whereas SMTPOST used features which are words in their generalized forms. The effect of using generalized data mainly widens the scope of the tagger, lessening out-of-vocabulary (OOV) words or words unrecognized by the system. For example, in SMTPOST's training data, *kumain* 'ate', *sumayaw* 'danced' and *tumalon* 'jumped' all contains the infix *-um-* *(@um)*. SMTPOST then creates a rule that whenever an extracted feature is *@um*, it will tag VBTS or past tense verb. When FEX process a word like *tumakbo* 'ran', it will output *@um* and through SMTPOST, it will be tagged as VBTS. Note that SMTPOST considers the probabilities of neighboring features or tags, and features may match words more than the previous examples given, for which both improves the tagging output.

Given the presented results, gaining the highest score among the other taggers demonstrated the utilization of SMT for tagging, at the same time the implementation of Filipino language, generation of word features and accurate generalizations as the basis for tagging were a success. To produce such results, SMTPOST is found to have its own set of advantages and disadvantages. One of the advantages is related to its tagging process, which makes use of generalized data instead of literal ones. Choosing this type of data extends the tagger's scope and lessens the instances of OOV words. Applying statistics as basis is equally as important, for it uses frequency and probability to determine the correct tags, even for phrases and ambiguous words. Moreover, SMTPOST has been tested with different domains, so adaptability is not a problem when its training data is modified.

On the other hand, disadvantages include a weak feature extractor and the lack of training data, hindering SMTPOST to tag complex feature combinations. Common features such as *~mag* 'to ...' (future tense), *~nag* '-d or -ed' (past tense) and *+ng* (a word with the ligature *-ng*) are helpful triggers in determining tags for any given word as long as those features appear in it. However, when mixed with additional features, the word features become complicated, thus resulting into errors. An example word feature *~mag~ka~sing+an* from *magkasingkahulugan* 'synonymous'; where the *~mag* prefix feature is present, but joined by other features such as the prefixes *~ka*, *~sing*, and suffix *+an*. Its distinctness made it out-of-vocabulary and as a result made SMTPOST unable to label a POS out of it. In relation to this, OOV features also appear on occurrences of nouns, foreign words, abbreviations and numbers (e.g. *:F*osaka*, **sweldo* 'salary', **box*, *:A*ceo*, **2016*) due to their empty word features – they are marked as "no features" or "whole word". In this case, SMTPOST's data failed to capture these types of words because they were already whole (or in their root) form and not affected by the generalized data. Nevertheless, these uncaptured words come with definite marker patterns which can be resolved through the use of pre- or post-processing tools, hinting on the usage of regular expressions or increase in language resources (pointing out to the corpora and word-tag dictionary).

Overall, in spite of imperfectly extracting word features, the accuracy of the system is high. Acknowledging this, certain and common patterns of words in Filipino were captured by the tagger, making different word variations with the same features most likely fall into one POS category.

4 Conclusion and Recommendations

SMTPOST proved that an unconventional Statistical Machine Translation approach can be used as a Part-of-Speech tagger in Filipino; addressing the factors about existing taggers' data contents, software usability, performance and availability. With 70,312 words from Wikipedia, its highest accuracy score produced 84.75%, at least 3.75% higher than the other existing taggers. Despite SMTPOST's high accuracy, there are some improvements needed. Recommended for future works are the following: use of a morphological analyzer for feature extraction; increase in scope for all of the resources, aiming at least 100,000 words for the parallel corpus and inclusion of other local and/or foreign languages; utilization of resources built by SMTPOST to other NLP applications; data checks for SMT, to make sure the correctness of the given word-tag pair data; software solutions for lessening complex feature and OOVs; implementation of additional techniques for pre- or post-processing; and finally, usability and availability extensions by using SMTPOST in a NLP software application or deploying it into the web as a service.

Acknowledgments

This research work is supported by the Philippine Council for Industry, Energy and Emerging Technology Research and Development (PCIEERD) of the Department of Science and Technology (DOST), Philippines as part of their research program entitled "Interdisciplinary Signal Processing for Pinoys: Software Applications for Education (ISIP:SAFE)".

References

Bonus, E. (2003). A Stemming Algorithm for Tagalog Words. De la Salle University, Manila.

Cheng, C. K., & Rabo, V. S. (2004). TPOST: A Template-Based, N-gram Part-of-Speech Tagger for Tagalog. Journal Research in Science, Computing and Engineering (JRSCE), 3(1).

Chu, S. (2009). Language Resource Development at DLSU-NLP Lab. The School of Asian Applied Natural Language Processing for Linguistics Diversity and Language Resource Development ADD-4: Language Resource Technology, Bangkok, Thailand, February 23-27, 2009.

Cortez, A., Navarro, D.J., Tan, R., & Victor A. (2005). PTPOST: Probabilistic Tagalog Part-of-Speech Tagger. De La Salle University, Manila.

Flordeliza, J., Go, K., & Miguel, D. (2005). PTPOST4.0: Probabilistic Tagalog Part of Speech Tagging. De La Salle University, Manila.

Fontanilla, G. K., Wu, H.W. (2006). Tag-Alog: A Rule-Based Part-Of-Speech Tagger For Tagalog. De La Salle University, Manila.

Go, K. (2006). PTPOST4.1 Probabilistic Tagalog Part of Speech Tagger. Class Project. De La Salle University, Manila.

Miguel, D., & Roxas, R. (2007). Comparative Evaluation of Tagalog Part-of-Speech Taggers. In Proceedings of the 4th National Natural Language Processing, De La Salle University, Manila, Philippines, June 14-16, 2007.

Mizumoto. T., Mamoru, K., Nagata, M., & Matsumoto, Y. (2011). Mining Revision Log of Language Learning SNS for Automated Japanese Error Correction of Second Language Learners. In Proceedings of the 5th International Joint Conference on Natural Language Processing, pp. 147-155, Chiang Mai, Thailand, November 8-13, 2011.

Nocon, N., Cuevas, G., Magat, D., Suministrado, P., & Cheng, C. (2014). NormAPI: An API for Normalizing Filipino Shortcut Texts. In Proceedings of the International Conference on Asian Language Processing 2014, pp. 207-210, Kuching, Sarawak, Malaysia, October 20-22, 2014. doi: 10.1109/IALP.2014.6973494

Oda, Y., Fudaba, H., Neubig, G., Hata, H., Sakti, S., Toda, T., & Nakamura, S. (2015). Learning to Generate Pseudo-code from Source Code using Statistical Machine Translation. In proceedings of the 30th IEEE/ACM International Conference on Automated Software Engineering (ASE 2015), pp. 574-584, Lincoln, Nebraska, USA, November 9-13, 2015.

Raga, R. Jr., & Trogo, R. (2006). Memory-Based Part-Of-Speech Tagger. De La Salle University, Manila.

Reyes, C. D. E., Suba, K. R. S., Razon, A. R., & Naval, P. C. Jr. (2011). SVPOST: A Part-of-Speech Tagger for Tagalog using Support Vector Machines. In Proceedings of the 11th Philippine Computing Science Congress, Ateneo de Naga University, Philippines.

From built examples to attested examples: a syntax-based query system for non-specialists

Ilaine Wang[1,2] **Sylvain Kahane**[1] **Isabelle Tellier**[2]
[1]MoDyCo (UMR 7114), CNRS
Université Paris Ouest Nanterre La Défense
i.wang@u-paris10.fr
sylvain@kahane.fr
[2]LaTTiCe (UMR 8094), CNRS, ENS Paris
Université Sorbonne Nouvelle – Paris 3
PSL Research University, USPC
isabelle.tellier@univ-paris3.fr

Abstract

Using queries to explore corpora is today routine practice not only among researchers in various fields with an empirical approach to discourse, but also among non-specialists who use search engines or concordancers for language learning purposes. While keyword-based queries are quite common, non-specialists are less likely to explore syntactic constructions. Syntax-based queries usually require the use of regular expressions with grammatical words combined with morphosyntactic tags, meaning that users need to master both the query language of the tool and the tagset of the annotated corpus. However, non-specialists such as language learners may prefer to focus on the output rather than spend time and efforts mastering a query language. To address this shortcoming, we propose a methodology including a syntactic parser and using common similarity measures to compare sequences of automatically produced morphosyntactic tags.

1 Introduction

A corpus, as a collection of texts used as a representative sample of a given variety of a language or genre, is often considered as a tool in itself. Whether the investigator adopts a corpus-based approach, testing preformed hypotheses against authentic data, or a corpus-driven approach, inducing hypotheses from observed regularities or exceptions, corpora are an invaluable resource from which examples of *real language use* can be extracted to support linguistic arguments.

As soon as corpora could be stored electronically, tools were built to make the most of them. Over the years, corpus linguistics has thus equipped itself with numerous tools to meet various needs. Concordancers, for instance, are used to observe keywords in context relying on keyword-based queries. However using tools does not only allow corpus exploitation but also determines what observations can be made from them: what can be inferred from corpora strongly depends on the possibilities that the tool offers (Anthony, 2013), and relying on keywords alone are a drawback for those who are interested in complex constructions and/or constructions which do not have a specific lexical marker. We will consider the case of relative clauses, as they are not marked by one specific lexical item but by the whole grammatical category of relative pronouns.

It is hardly possible today to search for complex structures without knowing how they are analysed in the annotated corpus, which implies that one masters at least both a query language and the tagset of the annotated corpus. These skills are common in the fields of Computational Linguistics and Natural Language Processing (NLP) but require tremendous effort from non-specialists such as language learners or teachers to be grasped.

In this article, we will first account for the need of the use of native corpora in language learning and the tools currently available to explore them. We will then present a processing chain which is based on the notion of syntactic similarity and takes into consideration the potential difficulties encountered by non-specialists.

2 Corpus Query

Language learners and teachers are generally not linguists and are seldom familiar with methods from the Computational Linguistics or NLP fields despite their growing interest for corpora. Having explained the whys and wherefores of the access to authentic data in language learning, we will present current tools used to interrogate corpora as well as their limits, especially when the query focuses on a syntactic construction.

2.1 The use of corpora in language learning and teaching

Native corpora are interesting resources for language learning as they represent for both teachers and learners collections of authentic data in which it is possible to observe what is considered as natural or usual in the target language (see Chambers (2005; 2010) or Cavalla (2015) for examples of uses of corpora to improve writing skills in French as a foreign language). Exposure to authentic data can be indirect (for instance through the study of concordance print-outs carefully chosen by the teacher beforehand) or it can be the outcome of a more direct process. The latter is particularly exploited in what Johns calls *Data-Driven Learning*, which considers language learners as "research workers whose learning needs to be driven by access to linguistic data" (Johns, 1991). Learners should therefore be active in their learning process, being able not only to formulate hypotheses but also to observe and analyse linguistic data to confirm or refute their hypotheses by themselves, and eventually formulate new hypotheses if necessary.

However, in practice, learners might consider that the benefit gained from a direct confrontation with authentic corpora is not worth either the time or the effort put into learning how to use corpus exploration tools. Boulton (2012) conducted experiments involving his university students using corpora and mentioned that "causes of concern focused on the complexity of the interface (the functions and the query syntax) and the time it took to conduct some queries.". One of the students even expressed the need to attend a course specifically dedicated to the use of corpus exploration tools. Based on the same conclusions, Falaise et al. (2011) proposed an adapted exploration tool for treebanks displaying an interface that is simple, minimalist (options are hidden) and user-friendly (using a graphical interface rather than a textual one). This simplification does not hinder the expression of elaborate and precise queries but does not solve the problem either. Although users spend less time mastering this kind of tool, they still need to know how data are encoded in the tagged corpus.

2.2 Current methods for corpus query

One of the most common methods in Corpus Linguistics consists in using concordancers to look at language as it is. These tools are increasingly used in the context of language teaching and include at least two main functions : on the one hand, concordancers bring to light general statistical properties of a text or corpus (displaying lists of words with their frequencies, distributions, collocations etc.) and on the other hand, they also allow more detailed analysis with KWIC (KeyWord In Context) concordances, showing the target word or sequence of words aligned in their original context. It should be pointed out that unlike queries used in search engines, the sequences of words given as input to a concordancer are generally n-grams, in other words, sequences of n strictly contiguous words with a fixed order. The implementation of *skipgrams*, or non-contiguous n-grams, in concordance tools is quite rare but can be found in tools that focus on the search for phraseological units such as ConcGram or Lexicoscope for French. Both systems take as inputs several words[1] called *pivots*, either directly input by the user or found through iterative associations. In the latter case, the tool takes a first pivot (or the first two for ConcGram) and searches for words with which it has the strongest co-occurrence rates; these words are then used in turn as pivots (up to four additional pivots) (Cheng et al., 2006; Kraif and Diwersy, 2012).

In all the above-mentioned cases, queries are based on words. However, it is possible to go beyond words by resorting to morphosyntactic tags directly. The matching of two segments such as "*the person who is sleeping*" and "*the jury which was*

[1]By *words* we are referring to inflected forms of a word, but also to the corresponding lemma. It is therefore up to the user to choose whether morphological variations should be considered or not.

locked up" which have no lexical units in common but which share the same syntactic structure can only be achieved with a pattern like "DET NOUN WH-PRO AUX VERB"[2]. This type of query is commonly used in linguistics, but producing such patterns requires users not only to know the tagset of the corpus but also, and maybe more importantly, to be able to associate a word with the right part-of-speech. Regular expressions are a good means to broaden the range of query possibilities but at the cost of more advanced learning to attain that level of abstraction. GrETEL, a tool developed by Augustinus et al. (2012), partly solves the problem as it offers the possibility to interrogate a treebank by automatically transforming an example of a syntactic structure into a query, in the same manner as our proposal. This process is designed to spare users from learning a complex query syntax, but is still aimed at linguists who know what they are looking for and are capable of configuring the query to fulfill their purpose.

While our methodology relies on the same idea as GrETEL, we wish to go one step further in opening corpus exploration tools to a broader public. With this aim in view, our processing chain must (1) reduce the complexity of the interface of the query system and (2) reduce the depth and variety of knowledge required from the user. Incidentally, even though it might seem more relevant to work with treebanks, our research problem only focuses on the use of corpora annotated with morphosyntactic tags. We chose not to make use of dependency or constituency links yet for the sake of genericity, for treebanks are still rare resources.

3 Methodology

3.1 Processing chain

As our main objective is to simplify the query formulation as much as possible for non-specialists, we propose a methodology which takes as input a simple example of a target syntactic construction written in natural language and "directly" retrieves other examples of that construction. Every step from the transformation of the input into a query to the ranking of relevant sentences is performed by automatic processes and therefore does not require any more knowledge than that necessary to validate (or invalidate) the output.

The complete processing chain detailed in Figure 1 and illustrating a query on relative clauses with "who" is divided into six steps:

1. the input of one or several segments by the user[3] and expressed in natural language;
2. the conversion of the initial input into an actual machine-interpretable query using an automatic (morpho)syntactic analyser or parser;
3. the syntactic similarity measure between the query and sentences from the tagged corpus;
4. the proposition of relevant sentences grouped by clusters according to the mode of research;
5. the selection by the user of the example which seems to be the closest to his/her input or to what he/she expected to see, thus refining the initial query (selecting a relevant example narrows the number of matches and increases precision as retrieved segments must be similar to both the query and each newly appointed relevant example[4]);
6. the output of segments belonging to the chosen cluster (through the selection of its most representative example in the previous step).

As this project is still being developed, we focus on the first three steps of the process in this paper.

3.2 Similarity as a flexible search method

As we have seen with the example of relative clauses, syntactic similarity cannot rely on sequences of lexical units only but should rather be described with syntactic patterns in the form of sequences of syntactic tags possibly associated with

[2]These part-of-speech tags do not belong to any specific tagset. They are purposely generic and we decided to use the tag VERB for the sake of illustrating the fact that the two segments are different in terms of grammatical categories (auxiliary and -ing verb on the one hand, verb and preposition on the other hand) but are *similar* in the sense that they are both verbal phrases.

[3]Steps requiring an intervention by the user are represented by shapes with thick dark contours and were reduced to the strict minimum in compliance with our objective.

[4]Steps 4 and 5 are iterative, allowing the user to refine the query until satisfaction.

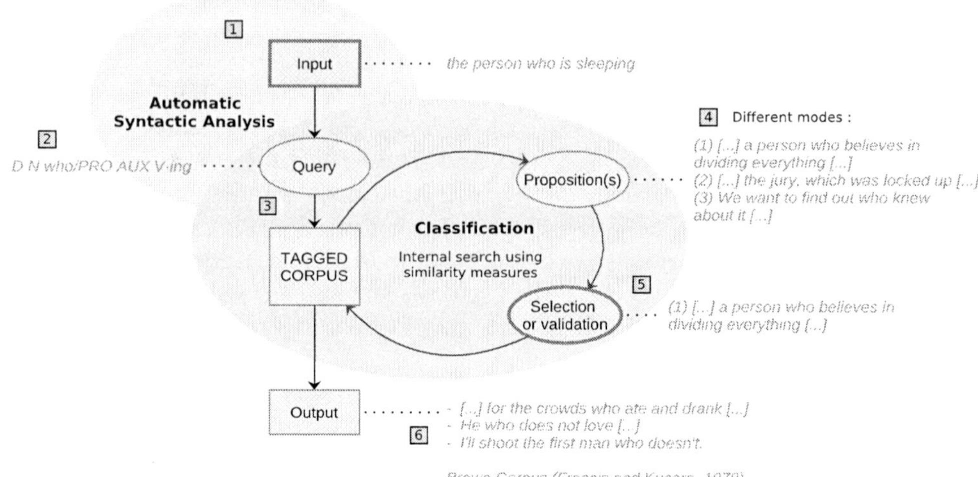

Figure 1: Flowchart of the process proposed for the syntactic query system

lexical units. The idea is to match instances of a syntactic construction while tolerating some variations in the vocabulary but also variations in the structure itself. Indeed, if we look at the propositions in step 4 of Figure 1, we notice that the first segment retrieved by the tool does not strictly match the query. The segment would be described by the sequence "`D N PRO V PREP V-ing`" while the query does not contain any preposition but the present progressive form of an intransitive verb. Despite these differences, this proposition is still relevant as it does display a relative clause and is similar enough to the initial query to be easily identified as such.

It is not self-evident for non-specialist users to define an efficient pattern, with a sufficiently high tolerance threshold to accept variations but low enough to keep a decent precision. We thus propose a method based on the similarity measure between an automatically defined pattern extracted from the input example(s) (the query) and examples from the corpus.

This methodology has a two advantages: it is more flexible than a query with regular expressions and it makes it possible to stay closer to data as it respects the bottom-up method supported by the *Data-Driven Learning* approach[5].

This flexibility also allows users to choose between different pre-defined options:

1. searching for similar segments with the same *grammatical* word(s), marked as relevant by the user (see the first proposition in step 4 of the flowchart);
2. searching for strongly similar segments but which do not contain the same *grammatical* word(s), marked as irrelevant by the user (see the second proposition, where "which" appears instead of "who");
3. searching for the same *grammatical* word(s), but in different contexts, in other words least similar sequences of tags (see proposition 3);
4. if lexical resources are available, searching for a semantically close *lexical* word could also be a possibility.

The second option could typically be used to search for structures such as relative clauses as they are characterised in English by the grammatical category of relative pronouns which have different surface forms among a finite list of possibilities. The

[5]As opposed to *data-based*, approaches called data-driven follow an inductive reasoning and start from the observation of regularities in data to formulate hypotheses or modify them.

tool must therefore be capable of identifying the category of relative pronouns but not necessarily try to match the one in the query, and more importantly, it must retrieve segments with variations in peripheral tags since the syntactic context could be quite different depending on the function of the pronoun (compare the constructions of *whom* and *whose* in "a few hundred people whom she knew" and "students whose interviews I discuss").

The first option gives outputs close to what can be retrieved through a concordancer, with the difference that the context also needs to be similar to that of the input query. As for the third option, it enables the user to search for other contexts of use of a specific word (or sequence of words), thus finding new functions for instance (see 4.3 for an example of an interesting case). Finally, option 4 would include the possibility to expand the query by using semantic similarity, as is commonly done in certain applications in information retrieval (search engines, question answering systems) where keywords can be replaced by synonyms or hyperonyms.

Users can choose between these options from the beginning if they are sufficiently aware of what they are searching for and sufficiently competent to identify it. Otherwise, they can determine what suits them better from observing the concrete examples presented for each option (in the same manner as in step 4 and from comparing to what they expected.

3.3 Similarity measures

We chose to use Jaccard and Dice coefficients, widely used in NLP to measure similarity, in particular between two words or two strings. In our case, these coefficients can be used to compare larger units, such as sequences of syntactic tags (`D N PRO AUX V-ing`) or sequences containing tags associated with their lexical units (`N who/PRO AUX V-ing`). We are also exploring the possibilities offered by edit distance (or Levenshtein distance), a metric which is not an actual similarity measure but can evaluate indirectly the distance (dissimilarity) between two objects: if the similarity is maximal, the distance is zero. This alternative is particularly interesting as the edit distance between two "words" (or sequences of tags) M and N is defined by the minimal cost necessary to transform M into N through specific operations, the insertion, the deletion or the substitution of a unit (a character if it is a string or a tag in a sequence of tags for instance).

Even more interesting is the possibility to weight the cost of each operation and thus to adapt the distance to our data. With this method it would then be possible to consider the removal of an adjective (or all modifiers) as costing less than the removal of a verb or a conjunction for instance.

4 Preliminary experiments

We are currently conducting experiments on Korean as a foreign language, simulating queries that could be made by a learner of Korean who has difficulties apprehending a grammatical structure and understanding the contexts in which it is used (Wang, 2016).

4.1 Data

We considered that learners were likely to use our tool when failing to fully understand sentences they encountered. We thus decided to use as inputs for our preliminary experiments sentences that are typically available to learners, that is to say those used to illustrate grammatical points in grammar books or language textbooks. Accordingly, sentences extracted from textbooks of levels 1, 2 and 3 (equivalent to roughly three years of study of Korean) from Yonsei University and Ewha Language Center were gathered to make a corpus of potential inputs to our tool. The structure of the sentences was compared to those from the Sejong Corpus (Kim, 2007), the reference corpus for Korean language. Tests were made on the monolingual morphosyntactically annotated part of the Sejong Corpus (a total of around 13.5 million tokens) and composed of samples from various genres, including written essays to transcriptions of spontaneous conversations.

4.2 Method

There are two essential prerequisites to enable a syntactic comparison between an input query and sentences from a corpus: firstly, an efficient automatic morphosyntactic tagger or parser must be used on the input, and secondly, the tagset used by the tagger and the one that was applied on the corpus must be identical (in the case of similar tagsets, adaptations should be done beforehand). In our case, we used an implemented version of KKMA[6], originally developed by the Intelligent Data System (IDS) Laboratory at Seoul National University and wrapped in KoNLPy[7] (Park and Cho, 2014). Among the five morphosyntactic analysers available in KoNLPy, KKMA was the slowest to run according to tests[8] but this flaw is not critical as KKMA would here be used to tag only one or a few sentences at most. Additionally, KKMA was trained on the Sejong Corpus, thus very few adaptations were needed to get perfectly matching part-of-speech tagsets.

내일은 맑**을지도 모릅니다.**
nay-il-un malk-**ul-ci-to mo-lup**-ni-ta.
'It is unsure if the weather is going to be clear tomorrow.'
↓
내일/NNG 은/JX 맑/VA **을지/EC 도/JX 모르/VV** ㅂ니다/EF ./SF

Figure 2: Example of input sentence

A typical input for our tool would be a sentence like the one in Figure 2: a sentence taken from Ewha's Korean Language textbook level 3-2, which has been segmented (essential for an agglutinative language like Korean) and annotated by KKMA. We set the morphemes illustrating the grammar point in bold. Likewise, users may eventually also have the possibility to show what morphemes seem to be their target, possibly in a simplified but similar manner as the matrix Augustinus et al. (2012) proposed for GrETEL, in which users are asked to choose if a word from the input is relevant or not and to what extent (relevant as POS, lemma or token). Sentences from Sejong Corpus are initially formatted the same way but would be output without tags so that users would really only see natural language sentences from input to output.

As for the technical aspect of our tool, different parameters were tested in our preliminary experiments:

- number of sentences as inputs: whether a single sentence was sufficient or if a greater number of sentences was more efficient;
- modes: whether the different options we described in this paper were relevant and viable;
- use of lexical units: whether we should include lexical units and take them into account in the similarity measure, or keep their part-of-speech tags only;
- similarity measure: whether a traditional similarity measure (such as Jaccard or Dice coefficients) is better than weighted edit distance or not;
- genres: whether all genres of texts or transcription types were relevant for our task, and which should be made default if any.

Current experiments focus on two differents types of grammar points of the Korean language which could be tricky to distant language learners: -(으)로 *-(u)lo*, the instrumental case particle which also fulfils different roles such as marking directions (학교**로** *hakkyo**lo*** 'in the direction of school') or the essive function (학생**으로** *haksayng**ulo*** 'as a student') and -(으)ㄹ지도 모르다 *-(u)lcito moluta*, a construction relying on several morphemes to express an epistemic modality (strong uncertainty).

4.3 Preliminary results

Results from our preliminary experiments are still too tentative to allow us to draw a clear conclusion on the most efficient parameters to represent input data or which measure should be applied and how.

However, we observed that:

- in most cases, one or two sentences given in input were sufficient to determine the context targeted. A greater number of sentences could be relevant if they all shared the same pattern, otherwise, it would only produce more confusion for the similarity measure;
- preliminary results from experiments on -(으)ㄹ지도 모르다 *-(u)lcito moluta* with the second option (same context, different

[6]http://kkma.snu.ac.kr/

[7]Korean Natural Language Processing in Python, an open source package supplying fundamental resources for Korean NLP. Experiments were run with KoNLPy 0.4.3.

[8]Time analysis and performance tests conducted by KoNLPy's development team are described on: http://konlpy.org/en/v0.4.4/morph/\#comparison-between-pos-tagging-classes

word(s)) confirm the ideas about why the different options could be theoretically interesting for the language learners we described in 3.2. Indeed, searching for a similar structure but a different morpheme retrieved sentences with -ㄴ/는지도 모르다 *-n/nuncito moluta* (see example (2a)), a structure absent from the textbooks we are working with despite a large number of occurrences in the Sejong Corpus and which is used to express a strong uncertainty as well, but without the prospective aspect of -(으)ㄹ 지도 모르다 *-(u)lcito moluta*. This second option also retrieves allomorphs and other close constructions, respectively observed in examples (2b) and (2c). In contrast, sentences such as (1) retrieved using the first option (same context, same word(s)) simply contain the exact same construction as the one given in the input[9], i.e -을지도 모르(다) *-ulcito molu(ta)*;

(1) "다이아몬드가 붙을지도 모르지."
*taiamontuka puth**ulcito moluci***

(2) a. 끝내 망가뜨리고 말는지도 모른다
*kkuthnay mangkattuliko mal**nuncito molu**nta*

b. 그럴지도 모른다
*kule**lcito molu**nta*

c. 기대만큼 될지는 모르겠지만
*kitaymankhum toy**lcinun molu**keysscinan*

– deleting all lexical units could prevent our tool from retrieving certain structures relying on a lexical word, typically, -(으)ㄹ 지도 모르다 *-(u)lcito moluta* which uses the verb 모르다 *moluta* 'to ignore'. Examples (3a) and (3b) were both retrieved using the second option but this time without lexical units. Only the sequence of POS (EC JX VV) has to be taken into account, resulting in very different constructions from the input. In the case of -(으)로 *-(u)lo*, deleting verbs of movement such as 가다 *kata* 'to go' or 내려오다 *naylyeota* 'to come down' could prevent our tool from discriminating between the directional function of the particle, often associated with such verbs, and other functions;

(3) a. 하긴 그렇기도 하겠네요
hakin kulehkito hakeyssneyyo
(POS-tagged form: 하긴/MAJ 그렇/VA 기**/EC** 도**/JX** 하**/VV** 겠/EP 네요/EF ./SF)

b. 이제 와서야 깨닫는다
icey waseya kkaytatnunta
(이제/MAG 오/VV 아서**/EC** 야**/JX** 깨닫**/VV** 는다/EF ./SF)

– edit distance has the advantage of retrieving sentences with similar length to the query, in our case, relatively short sentences, more likely to be of similar complexity as well. Other than that, no similarity measure seems to work better than another for now, but the weighting of edit distance costs could be refined with further experiments;

– experiments were only conducted on written texts (i.e samples from books, journals and newspapers). As searches focus on syntactic similarity instead of lexical words, all genres appear to be potentially relevant for language learners and allowing a search through all genres could raise awareness of extralinguistic factors such as the fact that newspapers and journals tend to be factual and do not contain as many occurrences of -(으)ㄹ 지도 모르다 *-(u)lcito moluta* as in books.

The performance of such a tool is difficult to evaluate in terms of information retrieval quantitative measures since each retrieved sentence shares some similarity with the input and could therefore be considered as relevant. If we choose to focus on the quality of the system and the relevancy of the output sentences for users, we should ensure that the processing chain is working efficiently, which can be jeopardised by errors such as wrong POS tags in the very first step of our proposal. In order to be less dependent on the performance of the tagger or the parser, future experiments will include a non-corrected version of the Sejong corpus. With this

[9] Sentences from examples (1) to (3) were all extracted from Sejong's journal samples and were all retrieved using the sentence from Figure 2 as input and Levenshtein as the similarity measure.

method, potential tagging errors on the input would also be present in the corpus and match, while corresponding correctly tagged sentences from the gold standard version would be used as outputs for ethical reasons.

5 Conclusion and perspectives

We have seen that at the core of our study lies the simplification of the access to rich resources such as annotated corpora for a non-specialist public. Although certain studies support the idea that the confrontation with authentic data is beneficial even at an early stage of the learning process (Holec, 1990; Boulton, 2009), the potential complexity of authentic data raises the question of learners' autonomy. This tool is designed to be used by university students as well as self-directed language learners but the guidance of a teacher might be crucial for beginners, especially as we chose to explore monolingual corpora only. This work focuses on the design of the tool but several extra options will be studied to tackle this problem, including the categorisation of each sample in terms of genre and readability degree, a color-coded grammar so that learners can easily distinguish and identify parts-of-speech (similar to what was proposed for FipsColor (Nebhi et al., 2010)) or even an integrated monolingual or multilingual dictionary so that unknown vocabulary does not add another layer of cognitive difficulty to the analysis of the output. These enhancements which operate both at the very beginning and at the end of the process are already implemented in numerous tools (not necessarily built for educational purposes).

A certain number of other treatments that we hope to present in the near future are considered, including steps 4 to 6 of our processing chain, notably the clustering of relevant sentences. This particular step is crucial in reducing the perceived complexity of corpus exploration as it allows the user to glance immediately at the *type* of output instead of being submerged by an overwhelming number of unsorted sentences (other than by alphabetical order of the preceding or following word). Each cluster would be represented by the example that seems to be the most representative of all members of the cluster (the *centroid*). We believe that this step could also discriminate the different uses of polysemous particles such as -(으)로 *-(u)lo* based on the dissimilarity of contexts (only examples from the same context would be in the same cluster).

We are not building a pedagogical tool in itself, but we believe that this program could in the end complement current pedagogical resources by offering an original focus on the grammatical constructions of the target language.

References

Anthony Laurence. 2013. A critical look at software tools in corpus linguistics. *Linguistic Research*, 30(2):141–161.

Augustinus L., Vandeghinste V. and Van Eynde F. 2012. Example-based treebank querying. *Proceedings of eighth international conference on Language Resources and Evaluation (LREC'2012)*, p. 3161–3167.

Boulton Alex. 2009. Testing the limits of data-driven learning : language proficiency and training. *ReCALL*, 21(1):37–54

Boulton Alex. 2012. Beyond concordancing : Multiple affordances of corpora in university language degrees. *Procedia-Social and Behavioral Sciences*, 34:33–38.

Cavalla Cristelle. 2015. Collocations transdisciplinaires : réflexion pour l'enseignement. *Le problème de l'emploi actif et/ou de connaissances passives des phrasèmes chez les apprenants de langues étrangères*, E.M.E & Intercommunication.

Chambers Angela. 2005. Integrating corpus consultation in language studies. *Language learning & technology*, 9(2):111–125.

Chambers Angela. 2010. L'apprentissage de l'écriture en langue seconde à l'aide d'un corpus spécialisé. *Revue française de linguistique appliquée*, XV, 9–20.

Cheng Winnie, Greaves Chris and Warren Martin. 2006. From n-gram to skipgram to concgram. *International journal of corpus linguistics*, 11(4):411–433.

Falaise Achille, Tutin Agnès and Kraif Olivier. 2011. Exploitation d'un corpus arboré pour non spécialistes par des requêtes guidées et des requêtes sémantiques. *Actes de la 18e conférence sur le Traitement Automatique des Langues Naturelles (TALN'2011)*, Montpellier, France.

Holec Henri. 1990. Des documents authentiques, pour quoi faire. *Mélanges Crapel*, 20:65–74.

Johns Tim 1990. Should you be persuaded: Two samples of data-driven learning materials. *Classroom Concordancing: English Language Research Journal*, 4:1–16.

Kim Hung-Gyu, Kang Beom-Mo and Hong Jungha 2007. 21st Century Sejong Corpora (to be) Completed. *The Korean Language in America*, 12, 31–42.

Kraif Olivier and Diwersy Sascha 2012. Le Lexicoscope : un outil pour l'étude de profils combinatoires et l'extraction de constructions lexico-syntaxiques. *Actes de la 19e conférence sur le Traitement Automatique des Langues Naturelles (TALN'2012)*, p. 399–406.

Nebhi Kamel, Goldman Jean-Philippe and Laenzlinger Christopher 2010. FipsColor : grammaire en couleur interactive pour l'apprentissage du français. *Actes de la 17e conférence sur le Traitement Automatique des Langues Naturelles (TALN'2010)*, Montréal, Canada.

Park Eunjeong L. and Cho Sungzoon 2014. KoNLPy: Korean natural language processing in Python. *Proceedings of the 26th Annual Conference on Human & Cognitive Language Technology*, Chuncheon, Korea.

Wang Ilaine. 2016. A syntax-based query system adapted to language learning and teaching. *American Association for Corpus Linguistics (AACL) and Technology for Second Language Learning (TSLL) Conference*, Ames, USA : Iowa State University. Poster presentation.

A Study of Valence & Argument Integration in Chinese Verb-Resultative Complement

Anran Li
Center for Chinese Linguistics, Peking University
li_anran@pku.edu.cn

Abstract

Verb resultative complement (VC) is a common structure of Chinese language with abundant forms of collocation. It makes much sense for VC research to analyze the general rules of argument integration in light of diversities of predicate & complement and the complexity of argument integration in the forming of VC with predicate & complement. This article has analyzed and summarized the existing research outcome of VC, and then gives further analyses thereby on argument integration process and multi-valence phenomena.

1 What's a Verb Resultative Complement?

Concept of "Verb-Resultative Complement (VC)" was initially brought out by Lv Shuxiang in 1980, who has defined it as a phrase verb consisting of "a main verb plus a resultative adjective or verb". Zhu Dexi has initiated later in 1982 that VC includes in a broader sense the structure of a predicate verb followed immediately by complements, i.e. either resultative complements as in "学会(xué huì, study and grasp)、吵醒(chǒo xǐng, make noise and awake)" or tendential complements as in "走来(zǒu lái, come up)、飘进(piāo jìn, float in)". Therefore VC is in brief a structure of a fore predicate (mostly a verb or an adjective) to indicate an action, plus a rear complement to indicate the result of such action.

2 Existing Studies of VC Valence

Verb valence is a hot theme in study of contemporary Chinese with popular academic concentrations, as VC is provided with not only distinct characteristics of verbs but also features of phrases, which has thus added more complexity in valence than normal verbs. Wherein, Huan Jinzhang in an early study (in 1993) has examined the collocations of "mono valence predicate + mono valence complement" and "bi valence predicate + mono valence complement". Despite the restrained scope of study, his article has initiated multi feasible dimensions to the study of VC valence, for example, looking into with co referral relations the valence alterations in predicate & supplement combination, or with argument's sequence of entering into a perspective field the argument integration & disappearance during VC integration: these are well inspiring for the studies later on.

Then, Guo Rui (1995) and Wang Hongqi (1995) have each brought out an analyzing scheme of VC valence in the book of *Study of Valence Grammar in Contemporary Chinese*, wherein Guo's introduction of location argument is well worthy of concentration. According to Guo, certain predicates and complements in VC can be added with a location argument, e.g. bi valence verbs like "来(lói, come)/去(qù, go)、走(zǒu, walk)/跑(pǒo, run)" and tri valence verbs like "挂(guà, hand)、放(fàng, lay)" can be all added with an argument of location or destination of the action. Introduction of the location argument is perfect for the actual valence demand of predicate and complement, but however is skipped in most studies.

According to Wang Hongqi (in 1995) who has brought out multi new concepts of VC, the complements' argument is virtual rather than ostensive for a VC with complement of a verb like "好(hǎo)、见(jiàn)、住(zhù)、动(dòng)、到(dào)"; and furthermore, the complement argument is just the predicate itself rather than a specific item or location for a VC with complement of verbs like "早(zǎo, early)/晚(wǎn, late)、快(kuài, fast)/慢(màn, slow)", ---- this is a persuasive viewpoint with compliance of actual language usages. However, Wang's article is imperfect for its over reliance on complement during classification, and its negligence in predicate's impact on valence of entire VC, and in alteration of valence form for one complement's collocating with various predicates.

Yuan Yulin (in 2001) has also given detailed analyses on VC valence. He has made in-depth study on categories of VC argument collocation and on access rules in argument assignment. Also he has classified the variations of VC valence into merged, eliminated, and co valences, and the outcome of argument integration into equal, decreased and increased valences. Terms he has defined are instructive for future studies, however, the article also reveals insufficiency in precise VC studies since it has focused on systems of argument integration.

Favored by plenteous outcome of previous studies, Shi Chunhong (in 2005) has initiated a more perfect new analysis plan, in which he has admitted Wang Hongqi's viewpoint that complement argument can be virtual and could be the predicate, and also numbered up various arguments when the predicate is a tri valence verb. His article has also specified a principle of boundary in argument integration, in addition to detailed functions of boundary principle during the process of argument integration & promotion when predicate and complement arguments are co or disjoint referential.

3 A Scheme of Chinese VC Valence Categories

No.	Predicate Valence	Complement Valence	VC Valence	Predicate Arguments x,y,z	Complement Arguments a,b,c	VC Arguments	Relationship of Predicate & Complement Arguments	Instance
1	1	1	1	Subject	Subject	Subject	co referential x & a	累病 lèi bìng (get tired out, resulting in illness)
2	1	1	2	Subject	Subject	Subject, Object	disjoint referential x & a	哭肿 kū zhǒng (cried badly and get eyes swollen)
3	1	1	1	Subject	Predicate	Subject	None	病久 bìng jiǔ (stay in illness for a long time)
4	2	1	1	Subject, Object	Subject	Subject	co referential x & a; disappeared y	看傻 kàn shǎ (see and get shocked)
5	2	1	2	Subject, Object	Subject	Subject, Object	co referential y & a	点亮 diǎn liàng (lighten)
6	2	1	2	Subject, Object	Subject	Subject, Object, Causer	disjoint referential x, y, a	砍钝 kǎn dùn (chop to get the axe or blade blunt)
7	2	2	2	Subject, Object	Subject, Object	Subject, Object	co referential x& a; co referential y &b	学会 xué huì (get learned)
8	2	2	2	Subject, Object	Subject, Object	Subject, Object	co referential x & a;	玩忘 wán wàng (play a lot /

							disappeared y	happily so that forget)
9	2	1	1	Subject, Object	Predicate	Subject	None	吃早 chī zǎo (eat early)
10	2	1	2	Subject, Object	Predicate	Subject, Object	None	抓住 zhuā zhù (catch, grasp)
11	3	1	1	Subject, Participator, Object	Subject	Subject	co referential x & a; disappeared y & z	教累 jiāo lèi (teach and get tired)
12	3	1	2	Subject, Participator, Object	Subject	Subject, Object	co referential y & a; disappeared z	教坏 jiāo huài (teach something bad)
13	3	2	3	Subject, Participator, Object	Subject, Object	Subject, Participator, Object	co referential y & a; co referential z &b	教会 jiāo huì (teach to get learned)
14	3	3	3	Subject, Participator, Object	Subject, Participator, Object	Subject, Participator, Object	co referential x & a; co referential y &b; co referential z &c	送给 sòng gěi (give to)
15	3	1	1	Subject, Participator, Object	Predicate	Subject	None	教晚 jiāo wǎn (teach late)
16	3	1	3	Subject, Participator, Object	Predicate	Subject, Participator, Object	None	教完 jiāo wán (done with teaching)
17	1	2	2	Subject	Subject, Location	Subject, Location	co referential x & a	活在 huó zài (live in)
18	2	2	3	Subject, Object	Subject, Location	Subject, Location, Object	co referential y & a	拖回 tuō huí (drag back)
19	2	1	1	Subject, Location	Subject	Subject	co referential x & a; disappeared y	走累 zǒu lèi (walk and get tired)
20	2	1	1	Subject, Location	Subject	Subject, Object	disjoint referential x & a; disappeared y	坐麻 zuò má (sit and get body numb)
21	2	2	2	Subject, Location	Subject, Object	Subject, Object	co referential x & a; disappeared y	跑丢 pǎo diū (run and get something lost)
22	2	2	2	Subject, Location	Subject, Location	Subject, Location	co referential x & a; co referential y &b	站在 zhàn zài (stand at)
23	2	1	1	Subject, Location	Predicate	Subject	None	住久 zhù jiǔ (live long)
24	3	1	1	Subject, Location, Object	Subject	Subject	co referential x & a; disappeared y & z	挂累 guà lèi (hang and get tired)
25	3	1	2	Subject, Location, Object	Subject	Subject, Object	co referential z & a; disappeared x	挂满 guà mǎn (hang and get fully distributed)
26	3	1	2	Subject, Location, Object	Subject	Subject, Object	co referential z & a; disappeared y	放歪 fàng wāi (lay in the slanting direction)

Viewpoints of each scholar share both coincidence and divarication in the study of Chinese VC categories. Here on basis of both existing and my personal induction and analyses, VC valences are categorized into 26 types as above[1].

Firstly, I agree with Guo Rui that verbs like "来(lái, come)/去(qù, go)、走(zǒu, walk)/跑(pǎo, run)" etc. are of bi valence as predicates, and those like "挂(guà, hang)、放(fàng, lay)" are of tri valence, because some of them are distinctly oriented and the target of action is indispensable for the verb valence, while others have to rely on specific space or fixed location to get itself done. Previously, most articles have neglected the collocable location argument for verb valence, and instead attribute them all to mono or bi valences, which is not rational.

Secondly, I agree partly with Wang Hongqi that argument of complement can be the predicate of VC, and complement shall mostly define if complement argument is the predicate. For example, "晚" (wǎn, late) as a complement means "later than specified or appropriate time", and is thus usually not used for specific person or thing. In a VC, be the collocated predicate is "睡" (shuì, sleep) of mono valence, "来" (lái, come) of bi valence, or "教" (jiāo, teach) of tri valence, the argument of "晚" is the predicate instead of anything else.

However, Wang's article has indicated that given with complement of "好、见、着、掉、住、动、到" etc., the argument of complement shall get virtual, which I won't however agree. Let's just take a look at their interpretations according to *Dictionary of Contemporary Chinese*:

1. 好(hǎo): attached after a verb, indicating it has been done or is perfect.
2. 见(jiàn): see, catch sight of.
3. 着(zháo): attached after a verb, indicting the target or result has been achieved.
4. 掉 (diào): attached after certain verbs, indicating the result of an action.
5. 住(zhù)$_1$: attached as a complement to a verb, indicating it is fixed or steady.
6. 住(zhù)$_2$: attached as a complement to a verb, indicating it is stopped or at rest.
7. 动(dòng): changing the original location or appearance of things.
8. 到(dào): attached as a complement to a verb, indicating the action has got its result.[2]

According to the interpretations above, targets of "好、着、掉、住$_1$、到" can be all viewed as the predicates of VCs, e.g. "（某动作）使得事物牢固" ([certain action] gets something fixed). Despite its indistinct interpretation, "见" as revealed by its roles in "看见(kàn jiàn)、听见(tīng jiàn)" etc. can be deemed as getting certain actions with a result, so its valence argument is also the predicate. On the other hand, for "住$_2$" and "动", be it indicating being stopped, at rest or changing the location, its target argument should be a specific subject argument, which is also the subject argument of predicate. Therefore, it is my opinion herein that argument of complement won't get virtual.

4 Valence Integration Process of Chinese VC

Obviously, VC predicate and complement arguments are often co referential. As languages would avoid repetitions as much as possible, co referential arguments would be definitely combined when they are united to form a VC, which is defined as "argument integration" herein. Meanwhile, as argument of certain complement is predicate, the predicate has met with valence demand of complement when forming the VC, and the complement is about provided with zero valence, the type of which is named as "complement of fake zero valence" herein.

In summary of the chart above, if complement's fake zero valence is deemed as a real zero valence, argument variations can be classified into two categories in the forming of VC:

[1] We use subject & object instead of agent & patient here because they can also be target, tool, location and some other arguments.

[2] All these interpretations are quoted from *Dictionary of Contemporary Chinese* version 2002.

1. After argument integration, quantity of VC arguments (C_{VR}) shall reduce no more in relative of quantities of predicate arguments (C_V) and complement arguments (C_R), i.e. $C_{VR} = C_V + C_R - C_{V\&R}$ ($C_{V\&R}$ is the quantity of co referential arguments of predicate and complement);
2. After argument integration, still quantity of VC argument shall reduce in relative of arguments of predicate and complement, i.e. $C_{VR} < C_V + C_R - C_{V\&R}$.

In the first category, argument integration is a simpler and regulated process. If predicate and complement have no co referential arguments, subject argument of predicate shall be projected before the predicate, and argument of complement projected after the complement. If they have, arguments shall be integrated first, then the subject argument of predicate shall be projected before predicate, and the object argument of predicate and argument of complement projected after the complement.

In the second category, occasions are sorted as following:

1. Predicate and complement have no location arguments:

Predicate Arguments x, y, z	Complement Arguments a, b, c	VC Arguments	Relationship in Arguments of Predicate & Complement	Instance
Subject, Object	Subject	Subject	co referential x & a, disappeared y	看傻 kàn shǎ (see and get shocked)
Subject, Object	Subject, Object	Subject, Object	co referential x & a, disappeared y	玩忘 wán wàng (play a lot / happily so that forget)
Subject, Object	Predicate	Subject	None	吃早 chī zǎo (eat early)
Subject, Participator, Object	Subject	Subject	co referential x & a, disappeared y & z	教累 jiāo lèi (teach and get tired)
Subject, Participator, Object	Subject	Subject, Object	co referential y & a, disappeared z	教坏 jiāo huài (teach something bad)
Subject, Participator, Object	Predicate	Subject	None	教晚 jiāo wǎn (teach late)

On normal occasions during VC integration, subject argument of predicate won't disappear, because the predicate verb is highly motional and vitalized; and be it co referential with the subject argument of complement or not, the agent subject shall be usually the agent of the whole VC. Meanwhile, as there implies that the execution of predicate verb has brought in the outcome of complement, complement object as receiver of resultative complement shall usually enjoy priority to be promoted as VC's object. If the complement has no object, then its subject shall enjoy priority to be promoted accordingly. During the promotion, predicate object which is not co referential with the subject or object of complement may be often sifted out, for when $C_{VR} < C_V + C_R - C_{V\&R}$, target concerned with predicate's object isn't a must for action provider and result receiver. For example in "玩忘" (wán wàng, play a lot / happily so that forget), two actions "玩" (play) and "忘" (forget) are involved with VC, their object arguments are co referential, and the provider of VC action is promoted as subject of VC. Now there remains only one idle valence digit in VC, so the object argument of either "玩" or "忘" should be sifted out since they are disjoint referential. Target of "忘" is more critical since the whole VC is about a psychological process, while that of "玩" isn't directly involved with whole VC and is thus sifted out.

However sometimes even if the argument of VC isn't fully occupied, the object argument of predicate may be also sifted out, because the causing even indicated by predicate verb may not only function on other items, --- it may also function on itself. For example in "看傻" (kàn shǎ, see and get shocked), the whole VC indicates a provider of action "看" (see) has received the result of "傻" (get shocked) from such process, which means the result of "看" has functioned directly onto the provider of the action "看". Therefore, only the provider of such action is directly involved with status of "看傻", while content of "看", which is not direct participator of process "傻", is sifted out during integration.

2. Predicate and complement have location arguments:

Predicate Arguments x, y, z	Complement Arguments a, b, c	VC Arguments	Relationship in Arguments of Predicate & Complement	Instance
Subject, Location	Subject	Subject	co referential x & a, disappeared y	走累 zǒu lèi (walk and get tired)
Subject, Location	Subject	Subject, Object	disjoint referential x & a, disappeared y	坐麻 zuò má (sit and get body numb)
Subject, Location	Subject, Object	Subject, Object	co referential x & a, disappeared y	跑丢 pǎo diū (run and get something lost)
Subject, Location	Predicate	Subject	None	住久 zhù jiǔ (live long)
Subject, Location, Object	Subject	Subject	co referential x & a, disappeared y & z	挂累 guà lèi (hang and get tired)
Subject, Location, Object	Subject	Subject, Object	co referential z & a, disappeared x	挂满 guà mǎn (hang and get fully distributed)
Subject, Location, Object	Subject	Subject, Object	co referential z & a, disappeared y	放歪 fàng wāi (lay in the slanting direction)

Arguments in the chart are sifted out similarly with the foregoing. If the complement is not a direction verb, the location or target location of predicate verb is less critical for the VC signification when compared with the action provider and result receiver, and would be sifted out when idle valence digit is insufficient. However there is one single exception: if the complement is "满" (mǎn, -ful), the predicate agent subject shall be sifted out instead during argument integration, and the location & object arguments of predicate shall be both preserved. This is because "满" is highly stateful, would decrease the procedural property of collocated predicate, and tends to indicate an immobile rather than dynamic processes. And on such occasions, it is the location and object arguments of predicate as direct participators of status that serves as necessary elements for completion of VC.

In summary of above, we can conclude that VC valence integration follows about such priorities:

VC Subject: predicate subject > predicate object

VC Object: complement object > complement subject > predicate object

Wherein, VC subject comes only from the original arguments of predicate, and the object mostly from original arguments of complement. The reason lies in that the predicate is the trigger of VC, and its subject is more vitalized and causative than the object, while complement is a result from predicate, and its object is less vitalized and more passive than the subject.

5 Multi-Valence of VC

Section II has mentioned some potential relations between arguments of VC and of its predicate & complement, however, this is far more complicated in actual language circumstances. Common multi-valences of VC are summarized and classified as following:

1. Multi-valence resulted from semantic differences of predicate or complement, e.g. "气死" (qì sǐ, get badly annoyed or annoyed to death), "饿死" (è sǐ, get badly starved or starve to death), and "跑丢" (pǎo diū, run and get something lost) etc.

Such predicates have usually dual types of usages: active and passive. For example in the *Dictionary of Contemporary Chinese* version 2002, "气(qì)" includes these two interpretations: "气 1：生气；发怒" (get angry; lose temper) and "气 2：使人生气" (get somebody annoyed). Wherein, we can recognize easily, "气 1" is a mono valence verb, while "气 2" is a bi valence verb, thus resulting in the two sentence patterns of "气死" as following:

(1) a. 周瑜气死了。

(Zhou Yu gets angry badly.)

b. 诸葛亮气死了周瑜。

(Zhuge Liang gets Zhou Yu annoyed rather badly till death.)

Complement on such occasions has also two potential valences. For example in "跑丢(pǎo diū)", "丢" can be of either bi valence, indicating get something lost, or mono valence, indicating get him/herself lost or dropped from teammates:

(2) a. 我跑丢了鞋。

(I run and get my shoes lost.)

b. 我跑丢了。

(I am dropped from my teammates.)

2. Some VCs gain more arguments via verb copy structures, e.g. "来早" (lái zǎo, come early) and "点亮" (diǎn liàng, lighten) etc.

"来" (lái, come) is a bi valence verb, while argument of "早" (zǎo, early) is just "来". On normal occasions, the location argument of "来" would be sifted out, but we may also get it into VC with a verb copy structure:

(3) a. 我来早了。

(I come here early.)

b. 我来学校来早了。

(I come to school early.)

"点(diǎn)" is a bi valence verb, and "亮(liàng)" indicates the status and could be collocated with only one argument. On normal occasions, the object of "点" and the subject of "亮" are co referential, however, if they are disjoint referential, a verb copy structure shall be relied on for signification:

(4) a. 我点亮了灯。

(I turn the light on.)

b. 我点烟花点亮了夜空。

(I lighten the dark sky with fireworks.)

3. Complement argument of VC may have various designatums, e.g. "练结实" (liàn jiē shi, exercise and get strong), "唱红" (chàng hóng, sing songs and get popular) and "哭醒" (kūxǐng, cry and get awaken).

It can be classified even further into two categories.

In Category I, various designatums of complement have meronymy. For example in "练结实", "结实" (strong) can refer to either the object argument of predicate "（我的）肌肉" (wǒ de jī ròu, [my] muscles), or generally the subject argument of predicate "我" (wǒ, me):

(5) a. 我练结实了。

(I do exercises and get strong.)

b. 我练结实了肌肉。

(I do exercises and get my muscles strong.)

In Category II, various designatums of complement are disconnected. For example in "哭醒"(kū xǐng), both "哭" and "醒" are mono valence verbs, involve only one subject argument, and can be however either co or disjoint referential.

(7) a. 宝宝哭醒了。

(The baby cries and gets him/herself awaken.)

b. 宝宝哭醒了妈妈。

(The baby cries and gets his/her mom awaken.)

4. Subject argument of VC may have various

designatums, e.g. "问倒" (wèn dǎo, beat with questions) and "撬断" (qiàoduàn, prize and break). On such occasions, the predicate is sometimes of tri valence, e.g. "问倒". When the VC has been formed, the subject of VC can be either the subject or the object of predicate:

(8) a. 我问倒了孩子们。

(I beat the children with questions.)

b. 这个问题问倒了孩子们。

(The question gets the children napping.)

On other occasions, arguments like methods or tools etc. may be involved, and such arguments can be either subject or object of VC. For example in "撬断(qiào duàn)", object argument of "撬" is the tool: if it acts as subject argument of VC, it shall be disjoint referential with subject argument of "断"; if acts as object argument, it shall be co referential with subject argument of "断"; and meanwhile, it may also disappear from VC:

(11) a. 铁棍撬断了保险杠。

(Bumper is prized and broken with an iron stick.)

b. 他撬断了铁棍。

(He prizes something with an iron stick and gets the stick broken.)

c. 他（用铁棍）撬断了保险杠。

(He prizes and gets the bumper broken [with an iron stick].)

In light of the four occasions above, Tao Hongyin's "Assumption of Dynamic Argument Structure" (in 2000) can be well demonstrated in VC.

Firstly, argument structure in a verb of high frequency is more tendential of unsteadiness: a high frequency verb tends to have multi interpretations, so is easily open to multi-valence category I; it is more flexible and is used fairly repeatedly, so is easily open to multi-valence category II and IV.

Secondly, a verb is more often combined with typical arguments and less often with non-typical ones. The ones which enter into VC valence are mostly highly typical arguments like subject, object and participator etc.

Thirdly, variation of argument structure would involve first the argument most adjacent to the core: provided with multi-valence in adding of arguments, priority shall be usually the subject or object arguments (they are more adjacent to the core), and then the location or tool arguments which are farther to the core if subject & object arguments are both available or if the predicate or complement itself cannot share valence with either arguments.

Furthermore, expansion of argument structure tends to have particular marks of sentence pattern, and multi-valence category II has provided the best instance: expansion of such VC argument structure has to rely on verb copying, or is otherwise illegal.

Finally, variation of sentence pattern is often in parallel with that of semantics: for example, multi-valence category I itself is based on semantic deviations of predicate or complement, and in multi-valence category 3, "宝宝哭醒了" (The baby cries and gets him/herself awaken.) indicates the status alteration of "宝宝" (baby) from "睡" (shuì, asleep) to "醒" (xǐng, awaken), while "宝宝哭醒了妈妈" (The baby cries and gets his/her mom awaken.) indicates status alteration of "妈妈" (mom) from "睡" to "醒".

As we can see, forming of a VC is fairly flexible, but meanwhile, all these forming are carried out as per a unique principle of integration.

6 Significations in Analyses & Study of Chinese VC Valences

In summary, the VC valence-argument integration methods, though fairly abundant, they have also rules available. Classification of common predicates and complements and summarization of rules in VC argument integration would help verifying the legality of VC sentences with computer. On the other hand, predicate and complement which enter into VC are often verbs, however conjunction of two verbs would form very abundant new structures, e.g. successive predicate structure, parallel

structure, predicate-object structure, and adverbial-core structure etc. Classification and study of VC valence methods would help identifying the features of VC argument integration, and thus eliminating ambiguities with computer.
Besides, since a series of predicate or complement with similar semantic fields are provided with relatively typical methods of argument integration, we may also generalize VC by calculating distances between words, and thus presume the property and semanteme of unregistered words, which would be also very helpful for auto analyses of these unregistered words.

Acknowledgments

I'd like to extend my sincere gratitude to my supervisor, Prof. Zhan Weidong, for his instructive advice on my thesis.
At the same time, this paper is supported by National Key Basic Research Program of China No.2014CB340504 and Major Project of Humanities & Social Science Fund of Ministry of Education of China No.15JJD740002.Thanks for their support.

Reference

Guo Rui, *VC Valence Structure & Component Integration*, Study of Valence Grammar in Contemporary Chinese [M], Beijing University Press, 1995.

Huang Jinzhang, *Logic Structure and Surface Syntax Phenomena of Behavior Type Potential Form V-R Predicate Sentences* [J], Study of Chinese Language & Literature, 1993(2).

Shi Chunhong, *Integration Process of Verb Resultative Argument Structure and Issues Concerned* [J], Chinese Teaching in the World, 2005(1).

Song Wenhui, *Study of Cognition in Verb Resultative Structure of Contemporary Chinese* [M], Beijing University Press, 2007.

Tao Hongyin, *A View of Dynamic Characters of Verb Argument Structure with Instance of "吃 (Eat)"* [J], Studies in Language and Linguistics, 2000(3).

Wang Hongqi, *Research of Valence in Verb Resultative Predicate-Complement Structure*, Study of Valence Grammar in Contemporary Chinese [M], Beijing University Press, 1995.

Yuan Yulin, *Analyses of VC Valence's Control & Restoration* [J], Chinese Language & Literature, 2001(5).

Dictionary Compiling Office, Institute of Linguistics, CASS, *Dictionary of Contemporary Chinese* [M], Commercial Press, 2002.

Lv Shuxiang, *Eight Hundred Words in Contemporary Chinese* [M], Commercial Press, Beijing, 1980.

Zhu Dexi, *Lecture Notes of Grammar* [M], Commercial Press, Beijing, 1982.

Phonological Principles for Automatic Phonetic Transcription of Khmer Orthographic Words

Makara Sok
Payap University / Chiang Mai, Thailand
makara_sok@hotmail.com

Larin Adams
Payap University / Chiang Mai, Thailand
larin.adams@gmail.com

Abstract

This paper explores phonological regularities in the Khmer language which can be used to convert Khmer words written in Khmer script into both phonemic and close phonetic transcriptions. They involve *series assimilation, vowel modification*, and *sound change rules* which govern how a word should be pronounced. Based on these rules, a Thrax grammar was written to produce word transcriptions which closely approximate actual speech.

1. Introduction

The Khmer writing system is known as one of the most complex scripts because of its large alphabet inventory and because symbols (orthographic characters) are strung together in complex ways to form a word. The script often does not represent the inherent vowels whose pronunciation is dependent on the series of the surrounding consonants. Huffman (1970) claimed that the Khmer writing system is far more regular than that of English--the sounds (i.e. the phonological structure) and the symbols (i.e. the writing system) closely fit together leaving little to less ambiguity. However, no attempt to model this alleged regularity currently exists. Pali/Sanskrit loanwords are of exception, for they have their own pronunciation rules. It is also worth noting that the majority of Khmer native roots are either monosyllabic or disyllabic which is the main focus of this project.

2. Khmer Orthography

According to the Ministry of Education of Youth and Sport, there are 33 consonants, 23 dependent vowels[1] and 13 independent vowels--excluding some deprecated characters. Khmer words are written from left to right, though vowels could go before, after, above and around the base consonant. Subscripts can be placed under a base consonant to form a consonant cluster. Two types of special diacritics are used where needed to change consonant series and/or modify its inherent or dependent vowel; they are usually placed above a consonant. The order of character writing could be arbitrary in handwriting, but electronically they are fixed by the Unicode consortium.

In this research, characters are ordered as the following:

C (S) (D1) (V) (F) (D2)

where:
- C -- any consonant
- S -- any subscript (Coeng[2] + C)
- D1 -- series shifter (◌៉/◌៊)
- V -- dependent/inherent vowel
- F -- any consonant in the final position
- D2 -- Bantoc (◌់)

The orthographic syllable structure here shows that a word could be composed of just a single consonant. Since the inherent vowel is invisible, the orthographic vowel is optional.

---

[1] In modern Khmer system, there are three additional vowels.

[2] ◌្ (U+17D2) renders any consonant after it as a subscript in monosyllabic words, and in disyllabic words, it functions as a syllable break.

3. Khmer Phonology

	Labial	Alveolar	Palatal	Velar	Glottal
Plosives	p	t	c	k	ʔ
Asp. Plosives[3]	p^h	t^h	c^h	k^h	
Implosives	ɓ	ɗ			
Fricatives	(f)[4]	s			h
Nasals	m	n	ɲ	ŋ	
Semi-vowels	w		j		
Lateral		l			
Trill		r			

Table 1: Consonant Phonemes

	Front		Central		Back	
High	i	ii	ɨ	ɨɨ	u	uu
Mid	e	ee	ə	əə	o	oo
Mid-Low		ɛɛ	a	aa	ɔ	ɔɔ
Low			ɑ	ɑɑ		

Table 2: Monophthong

Diphthongs: iə, ɨə, uə, ae, aɔ, ao, oa, ie, ea

4. Dataset and Methodology

The dataset used in this experimentation is obtained from the official fifth edition of the Khmer monolingual dictionary published by the Buddhist Institute of Cambodia in 1967. The dictionary contains around 17,000 entries, which could not be used right away. It had to be cleaned of duplicates and stray characters such as: "!, ?, and ៗ". Pali/Sanskrit loanwords were identified and then removed for this stage of the project, leaving only native words for the conversion process (see Figure 1 below). Rounded rectangular balloons with fix border lines contain description of source/content of data which was put though each process labeled in heptagon balloons. On the right side, the rounded rectangular balloons with dotted border lines describes actions taken. For instance, the data used in the first process "cleanup.rb" was obtained from "Chuon Nath 2.0. original" lexicon. The "cleanup.rb" is a Ruby code file which was written using regular expression to carry out two cleanup actions: "removing duplicates" and "removing prefix" from the lexicon.

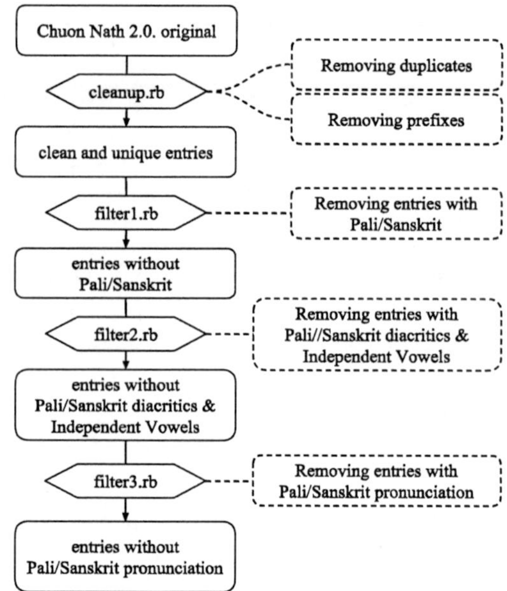

Figure 1: Data Cleanup

After the cleanup process, 11,109 words were identified as native words. The next step was to group words into their orthographic syllable structures: monosyllable disyllable, or double disyllable (see Section 6.3 below). There are four different types of disyllabic words, while there is only one type of monosyllabic words.

Grouping	Quantity
monosyllabic	3,969
disyllabic-type 1	1,249
disyllabic-type 2	815
disyllabic-type 3	769
disyllabic-type 4	864
double monosyllabic words	1,963
double disyllabic words	481
subtotal	10,110
remaining words[5]	999
Total	11,109

Table 3: Syllable Grouping

After preparing the dataset, character grouping and mapping were done. Then phonological regularities were explored and proposed.

In order to ensure the generated transcriptions are correct as expected, a set of validation data was built. 140 words were handpicked in order to assure that they cover all cases. Their expected phonemic transcription was taken from Headley's

[3] Ehrman (1972:4) included these aspirated consonants in the phonemic inventory.

[4] Only occurs in loan words.

[5] Any words which do not fit into the three groups were ignored, for they are compound words which is not yet covered at this stage.

Cambodian-English Dictionary (1997) and phonetic transcriptions were manually and carefully produced. The two outputs, phonemic and phonetic, generated by the grammar was then compared with the validation data. If the generated transcription match the validation data of the same orthographic word, it is considered as correct. Finally, phonemic transcriptions were automated for all 10,110 words in their respective syllable groups and compared with Headley's phonemic transcriptions.

5. Character Grouping and Mapping

Each orthographic consonant and vowel was mapped to an IPA character, while each diacritic was mapped to nothing. Consonants were grouped by their manner of articulations and series which would later be used to describe how the *series assimilation* works in initial consonant clusters.

- **Orthographic Consonants to Phonemes:**

Groupings		Mapping
Manner	**Series**	
Unaspirated Plosives	1st	ក > k
		ច > c
		ដ > ɗ
		ត > t
		ប > ɓ
		ប៉ > p *
		អ > ʔ
	2nd	គ > k
		ជ > c
		ឌ > ɗ
		ទ > t
		ប៊ > ɓ *
		ព > p
		អ៊ > ʔ *
Aspirated Plosives	1st	ខ > k^h
		ឆ > c^h
		ថ > t^h
		ឋ > t^h
		ផ > p^h
	2nd	ឃ > k^h
		ឈ > c^h
		ឍ > t^h
		ធ > t^h
		ភ > p^h
Fricatives	1st	ស > s
		ហ > h
	2nd	ស៊ > s *
		ហ៊ > h *
Nasals	1st	ង៉ > ŋ *
		ញ៉ > ɲ *
		ណ > n
		ម៉ > m *
	2nd	ង > ŋ
		ញ > ɲ
		ន > n
		ម > m
Approximants	1st	យ៉ > j *
		រ៉ > r *
		ឡ > l
		វ៉ > w *
	2nd	យ > j
		រ > r
		ល > l
		វ > w

Table 4: Character Grouping and Mapping

* marked consonants which have been modified by D1. These modification is done to fill in the

gap where certain consonants do not have the 1st/2nd series counterparts. For example,

- **Orthographic Vowels to Phonemes:**

Vowels	Series	
	1st	2nd
Inherent vowel	ɑɑ	ɔɔ
◌ា	aa	ie
◌ិ	eʔ	iʔ
◌ី	əj	ii
◌ឹ	əʔ	ɨʔ
◌ឺ	əə	ɨɨ
◌ុ	oʔ	uʔ
◌ូ	oo	uu
◌ួ	uə	uə
◌ើ	aə	əə
◌ឿ	ɨə	ɨə
◌ៀ	iə	iə
េ◌	ee	ee
ែ◌	ae	ɛɛ
ៃ◌	aj	ej
ោ◌	ao	oo
ៅ◌	aw	ɨw
◌ុំ	om	um
◌ំ	ɑm	um
◌ាំ	am	oam
◌ះ	ah	eah
◌ុះ	oh	uh
េ◌ះ	eh	eh
ោ◌ះ	ɑh	uəh

Table 5: Vowel Mapping

- **Diacritics (D1 and D2):**

D1 refers to one of the two series shifters: MUUSIKATOAN (U+17C9) and TRIISAP (U+17CA). The first changes the second series to the first series, and the later does the opposite.

D2, BANTOC (U+17CB), is placed on the final consonant to modified the vowel before it. Not any vowel could be modified by BANTOC. It is only applicable to the inherent vowel and the first dependent vowel (◌ា). See Table 6: Vowel Modification in section 6.3 below.

6. Orthography to Phonemic

One result of this process is a phonemic transcription which represent *careful speech.* It is important to note that it is always the case that the series of the consonant determines the series of the vowel attached to it. For instance, if the initial consonant is in the 1st series, the realization of the inherent vowel or the dependent vowel should also be in the 1st series. The same applies to the 2nd series initial consonant.

6.1. Monosyllable

Orthographic monosyllable structure:

C(S)(D1)(V)(D2)

The pronunciation rule is straight forward when the monosyllabic word does not contain initial consonant clusters or D1/D2 diacritics:

C	CF
CV	CVF

If an initial consonant cluster and/or D1/D2 diacritics are involved, special attention is needed. All syllable types of monosyllabic words containing initial consonant cluster and diacritic are listed below:

CS	CSF	CSFD2
CSV	CSVF	CSVFD2
CD1	CD1F	CD1FD2
CD1V	CD1VF	CD1VFD2
CSD1	CSD1F	CSD1FD2
CSD1V	CSD1VF	CSD1VFD2

In initial consonant clusters, there is a conflict of whether which series of the two consonants should be taken as the series of the cluster. Only when the series of the cluster is known, then the vowel attached to it would just follow. This is when *series assimilation* comes into play. Series Assimilation is a significant phenomenon in Khmer pronunciation which occurs in both monosyllabic and disyllabic words. The sonority hierarchy plays an important role in determining which series of the consonant cluster or the following syllable should be. The series of the least sonorous consonant (or in another word, strong consonantal) determines the series of the cluster regardless of its position in the cluster. Then the series of the vowel attached to it has to be in that same series. Note that the series of the syllable final consonant has no influence on the series of the vowel preceding it.

According to Hooper (1976:206) and Hogg and McCully (1983:33), the sonority hierarchy adapted to Khmer is as following: unaspirated plosives > aspirated plosives > fricatives > nasals > approximants (from the least sonorous to the most sonorous). Unaspirated plosives are the strongest consonant for they are the least sonorous, and the approximants are the weakest consonants for they are the most sonorous. Here are some examples:

(1)	ក្រាល 'to unroll'
character sequence:	ក ្ រ ា ល
character mapping:	k r aa/ie l
series of each character:	1 2 1/2 2
series of the cluster:	1
phonemic transcription:	/kraal/

(2)	ស្ពាន 'bridge'
character sequence:	ស ្ ព ា ន
character mapping:	s p aa/ie n
series of each character:	1 2 1/2 2
series of the cluster:	2
phonemic transcription:	/spien/

(3)	ព្រាល 'dim'
character sequence:	ព ្ រ ា ល
character mapping:	p r aa/ie l
series of each character:	2 2 1/2 2
series of the cluster:	2
phonemic transcription:	/priel/

(4)	ក្បាល 'head'
character sequence:	ក ្ ប ា ល
character mapping:	k ɓ aa/ie l
series of each character:	1 1 1/2 2
series of the cluster:	1
phonemic transcription:	/kɓaal/

Example (1) shows that the series of the cluster is 1st because ក /k/, an unaspirated plosive, is a stronger consonant (less sonorous) than រ /r/, an approximant; and the 1st series vowel is used. Example (2) illustrates the case a cluster of a fricative and a following less sonorous unaspirated plosive, the series of the cluster is 2nd; and the 2nd series vowel is used. Example (3) and (4) show the fact that if both consonant in the cluster are of the same series, the series of the cluster stay the same.

6.2. Disyllables

Orthographic disyllable structure:
Type 1: CN្+Monosyllabic Structure
Type 2: Cr+ Monosyllabic Structure
Type 3: C(D1)+ Monosyllabic Structure
Type 4: Cំ+Monosyllabic Structure

Where:
N -- any nasal consonant
r -- a subscript ្រ
ំ -- NIKAHIT, a vowel /ɑm/

Orthographically, disyllabic words are composed of two parts: a minor syllable and a major syllable (or a monosyllable which has previously been described). The major syllable no longer has *series assimilation* within its own syllable, but the series of the minor syllable does influence that of the major. The initial consonant of the minor syllable determines the series of the major syllable. It begins with a weak consonant.

For example,

(5)	សម្រាក 'to relax'
character sequence:	ស ម ្ រ ា ក
character mapping:	s m r aa/ie k
series of each character:	1 2 2 1/2 1
series of the minor-major:	1 1
phonemic transcription:	/sɑm.raak/

(6)	សម្គម 'skinny'
character sequence:	ស ម ្ គ ម
character mapping:	s m k m
series of each character:	1 2 2 2
series of the minor-major:	1 2
phonemic transcription:	/sɑm.kɔɔm/

Example (5) shows *series assimilation* cross syllable, while (6) illustrates just the opposite--dissimilation. The initial consonant (រ /r/) of the major syllable of example (5) is a weaker consonant, and (6) a stronger consonant--unaspirated stop គ /k/. The same rule applies to nasals (ង /ŋ/, ញ /ɲ/, ន /n/, ម /m/) as the initial consonant of the major syllable.

For example,

(7) សម្ងំ 'to remain quiet'

character sequence:	ស	ម	្	ង ំ
character mapping:	s	m		ŋ ɑm/um
series of each character:	1	2		2 1/2
series of the cluster:	1			1
phonemic transcription:	/sɑm.ŋɑm/			

A question may arise as to where the open central unrounded vowel /ɑ/ in the minor syllable of each example above came from. This is exactly a case of the inherent vowel, but it has undergone a special treatment whereby the inherent vowel /ɑɑ/ is shorten to only /ɑ/.

6.3. Vowel Modification (D2)

Two vowels, the inherent vowels /ɑɑ/ɔɔ/ and the first vowel ា /aa/ie/ can be modified by adding a diacritic, BANTOC "់", to it. The BANTOC is used to shorten as well as change the vowel quality completely. It is attached to certain final consonants, such as: -ក /-k/, -ច /-c/, -ត /-t/, -ង /-ŋ/, -ញ /-ɲ/, -ន /-n/, -ល /-l/, -ស /-h/, -ប /-p/.

	Syllable Structures	Vowel Modification
1st series	CFD2 CD1FD2 CSFD2 CSD1FD2	/ɑɑ/ is shortened to /ɑ/ where F = -ក/-ង/-ច/-ញ/-ត/ -ន/-ល/-ស/-ប
2nd series		/ɔɔ/ is changed to /uə/ where F = -ក/-ស /ɔɔ/ is changed to /u/ (elsewhere)
1st series	CFD2 CD1FD2 CSFD2 CSD1FD2	/aa/ is shortened to /a/ where F = -ក/-ង/-ច/-ញ/-ត/-ន/- ល/-ស/-ប
2nd series		/ie/ is changed to /ea/ where F = -ក/-ង/-ច/-ញ /ie/ is changed to /oa/ (elsewhere)

Table 6: Vowel Modification

6.4. Sound Change Rules

The following sound change rules were adapted from a manuscript and implemented in the phonemic transcriptions:

- Final devoicing: voice implosives become voiceless in a syllable final position.
- Final unreleased: aspirated plosives become unaspirated in a syllable final position
- Implosive devoicing: voiced implosives become voiceless plosives in the initial position before another consonant.
- Fricative backing: alveolar fricatives become glottal fricatives in the syllable final position.
- Plosive backing: voiceless velar plosives become voiceless glottal plosives in the syllable final position.
- Trill deletion: alveolar trills get deleted in the syllable final position.
- Nasal deletion: nasals are deleted before another nasal in the syllable final position.
- Vowel backing: open and open-mid front unrounded vowel becomes central open and open-mid central unrounded vowel in closed syllable.

7. Phonemic to Phonetic

The result of this process is the phonetic transcription which is close to rapid speech or how people normally talk. A set of rules was observed and identified as followed:

- Aspiration is the transition between the first and second member of the cluster when the first member is one of the unaspirated plosives /p/t/c/k/ and the second member is one of these /p/t/c/k/m/n/ɲ/l/w/j/s. (Huffman 1972:55, Filippi 2009:164)
- Schwa is the transition if /m/l/ occurs before another consonant or ɓ/ɗ/ʔ occurs after any consonant. (Filippi 2009:165)
- Any sonorant consonants become voiceless when occurs after an aspirated plosive. (Filippi 2009:144-145)

- Plosives and nasals in the final position do not have audible releases. (Filippi 2009:144-145)
- The minor syllables of disyllabic words are subject to extreme reduction in rapid colloquial speech. They are usually reduced to just Cə-. (Huffman 1972:59)
  - o Vowel of the minor syllable is reduced to a schwa [ə].
  - o /rɔ-/ is reduced to [rə-] or [lə-].
  - o /ɗɑ-/ and /sɑ/ are changed to [tə-].
  - o /ɓɑ-/ is changed to [pə-].
  - o /CrV-/ is reduced to [Cə-].
  - o /ʔVN-/ is reduced to [N̩-].
  - o /CVN-/ is reduced to [Cə].

8. Result

Based on the validation dataset of 140 selected words, the accuracy of phonemic transcription increases over time as more rules were added:

- character mapping: 2.14%
- series assimilation: 15%
- vowel modification: 50%
- sound change rules: 97.86%

The accuracy went up from 2.14% to 97.86%. The ~3% of errors is caused by the exception where certain words do not conform to any rules implemented.

Given that the phonemic transcription generated by the grammar satisfies the validation dataset, an attempt has been made to implement the grammar on the 10,110-word dataset in their respective syllable type. The results are:

Syllable Type	Accuracy Rate (%)
monosyllabic	99.06
disyllabic-type 1	98.32
disyllabic-type 2	97.06
disyllabic-type 3	96.62
disyllabic-type 4	98.61
Overall Accuracy Rate: 98.43%	

Table 7: Accuracy rate of the two syllable types

The accuracy rate of when the grammar was implemented on the monosyllabic and disyllabic words is comparable to the accuracy rate of when the grammar was implemented on the validation dataset. The phonetic rules are able to generate all 140 phonemic tokens.

The system was built using Thrax, a grammar compiler which compiles rules that consist of regular expression and context dependent rewrite rules into (FST) archive of weight finite state transducers. More rules can be added upon new encounters in order to improve the phonemic and phonetic transcription in an elegant way (Roark et. al. 2012:61).

9. Conclusion

The conversion does work as expected regardless of minor exceptional cases. There is always room of improvement. Pali/Sanskrit words should be studied and carefully incorporated into this current work.

Acknowledgements

I would like to express my very great appreciation to Dr. Larin Adams for his valuable contribution and patient guidance from the beginning to the end of this project. I would also like to thank Dr. Robert Batzinger for giving helpful advice and training me on how to do the data preparation using Ruby. My grateful thanks are also extended to Dr. Richard Sproat for introducing me to Thrax, to Dr. Thammanit Pipatsrisawat and Dr. Sopheakmungkol Sarin for their encouragement and help when I was struggling with Thrax grammar, and to Mr. Theeraphol Wattanavekin who helped me getting Thrax compiler up and running as well as providing instant support on Thrax when I needed it the most.

I would also like to extend my thanks to all professors and students at Payap University for providing helpful and constructive and helpful criticism on this project.

Finally, I wish to thank my mother and grandmother for their support emotionally and financially though out my study, without them I would not have come this far.

References

Chuon, Nath. 1967. Khmer-Khmer Dictionary. Phnom Penh: Buddhist Institute.

Ehrman, Madeline E., and Sos, Kern. 1972. Contemporary Cambodian: A Grammatical sketch. Washington. DC: Foreign Service Institute.

Filippi, Jean-Michael, and Hiep, Chanvichetr. 2009. ឯកសារណែនាំ អំពីសូរវិទ្យា Introduction to Phonetic. Phnom Penh: FUNAN.

Headley, Robert K., Rath Chim, and Ok Soeum. 1997. Modern Cambodian – English Dictionary. Kensington, Maryland: Dunwoody Press

Hogg, Richard M., and McCully, C. B.. 1987. Metrical Phonology: A coursebook. Cambridge: Cambridge University Press.

Hooper, Joan B. 1976. An introduction to Natural Generative Phonology. New York: Academic Press.

Huffman, Franklin E.. 1970. Cambodian System of Writing and Beginning Reader with Drills and Glossary. Adam Wood.

Huffman, Franklin E.. 1972. The Boundary between the Monosyllable and Disyllable in Cambodian. Lingua, 29.54-66.

Roark, Brian, Richard Sproat, Cyril Allauzen, Michael Riley, Jeffrey Sorensen and Terry Tai. 2012. The OpenGrm open-source finite-state grammar software libraries. In Proceedings of the ACL 2012 System Demonstrations, pp. 61-66.

The Unicode Consortium. 2015. The Unicode Standard, Version 8.0.0. Mountain View: CA http://www.unicode.org/versions/Unicode8.0.0/

On the Possessor Interpretation of Non-Agentive Subjects

Tomokazu Takehisa
Niigata University of Pharmacy and Applied Life Sciences
265-1 Higashijima, Akiha-ku, Niigata 956-8603, Japan

takehisa@nupals.ac.jp

Abstract

It has been observed that the relation of possession contributes to the formation of so-called adversity causatives, whose subject is understood as a possessor of an object referent. This interpretation is reflected at face value in some studies, and it is assumed there that the subject argument is introduced as a possessor in syntax. This paper addresses the question of whether the observed relation should be directly encoded as such and argues that the subject argument is introduced as merely an event participant whose manner is underspecified. Moreover, it argues that the possessor interpretation arises from inference based on both linguistic and extralinguistic contexts, such as the presence of a possessum argument. This view is implemented as an analysis making use of a kind of applicative head (Pylkkänen, 2008) in conjunction with the post-syntactic inferential strategy (Rivero, 2004).

1 Introduction

It is well known that in Japanese, some transitive subjects, in addition to the agentive reading, allow the reading where they do not instigate but rather undergo an event described by the verb phrase, thereby giving rise to an ambiguity, as in (1).[1]

(1) Taroo$_1$-ga {kare$_1$-no/ zibun$_1$-no/Ø$_1$}
T.-NOM he-GEN/ self-GEN/ pro
ude-o or-Ø-ta (>ot-ta)
arm-ACC √break-CAUS-PST
'Taroo broke his arm.'

That the ambiguity is real can be shown by the sentence in (2), where the second conjunct serves to ensure the subject is not an agent.

(2) Taroo$_1$-ga {kare$_1$-no/ zibun$_1$-no/Ø$_1$}
T.-NOM he-GEN/ self-GEN/ pro
ude-o or-Ø-ta (>ot-ta) kedo,
arm-ACC √break-CAUS-PST but
zibun$_1$-de-wa or-Ø-anak-at-ta
self-INST-TOP break-CAUS-NEG-DV-PST
'Taroo broke his arm, but he didn't break it himself.'

Moreover, direct passivization, which necessarily implies the presence of an agent, renders the non-agentive reading of the subject in (1) unavailable, as shown in (3):[2]

(3) *Taroo$_1$-niyotte {kare$_1$-no/ Ø$_1$} ude-ga
T.-by he-GEN/ pro arm-NOM
or-Ø-are-ta kedo,
√break-CAUS-PASS-PST but
kare.zisin$_1$-de-wa or-Ø-anak-at-ta
he.self-INST-TOP break-CAUS-NEG-DV-PST
'Taroo's arm was broken by him, but he didn't break it himself.'

[1] The following abbreviations are used: ACC = accusative, CAUS, C = causative, CL = classifier, COP = copula, DAT = dative, DV = dummy verb, GEN = genitive, INCH, I = inchoative, INST = instrumental, LOC = locative, NEG = negative, NML = nominalizer, NPST = nonpast, PASS = passive, pro = null pronoun, PST = past, TOP = topic, √verb = verbal root.

[2] In what follows, the "conjunction" test will be applied only when its application is crucial to prove the point.

Thus, these examples clearly demonstrate that the ambiguity is not illusionary and that the subject can have a reading significantly distinct from the agentive reading.

Inoue (1976) has shown that there are two conditions to be met in order to obtain the non-agentive—or, in her terms, experiential—reading of the subject: (i) the subject must appear with a verb that alternates in transitivity; (ii) there must be a "proximate" relation, typically that of inalienable possession, between the subject and an object.[3] These are well-established generalizations in the literature, and I do not discuss them in detail. Yet, since this paper focuses on the possessor interpretation of non-agentive subjects, I will illustrate that the possession condition does hold and it affects another dimension of interpretation: distributive and collective readings. Specifically, when plural subjects are non-agentive, only the distributive reading is available because each of the subject referents possesses a referent of the object (i.e., the possession condition). On the other hand, the collective reading is unavailable with non-agentive subjects unless some unusual context is given (e.g., subject referents share an inalienably possessed entity). Thus, under normal contexts, forcing the collective reading renders the non-agentive interpretation unavailable. Consider (4) and (5) below.

(4) Huta-ri-no kodomo$_1$-ga [Ø$_1$ ude]-o
    2-CL-GEN child-NOM pro arm-ACC
    or-Ø-ta (>ot-ta)
    √break-CAUS-PST
    'Two children broke their arms.'
    [distributive: agentive or non-agentive]
    [collective: agentive]

(5) Huta-ri-no kodomo$_1$-ga hito-kumi-de
    2-CL-GEN child-NOM 1-group-COP
    [Ø$_1$ ude]-o or-Ø-ta (>ot-ta)
    pro arm-ACC √break-CAUS-PST
    'A pair of two children broke their arms.'
    [collective: agentive]

Hence, despite the fact that the non-agentive subject in question has been called different names in the literature, it seems plausible to consider the property of being a possessor as its defining characteristic.

However, although it is clear that the non-agentive subject is understood as a possessor, the fact does not guarantee that the subject is linguistically encoded as such. Thus, this paper addresses the question of whether the relation of possession should be directly reflected in syntax when non-agentive subjects are available. Specifically, the paper argues against the view that the possessor interpretation is directly encoded in syntax by showing that approaches encoding the non-agentive subject as a possessor face insuperable difficulties. Instead, I argue that the subject is encoded as an event participant whose manner of participation is underspecified, and that the possessor interpretation results from inference based on linguistic and extralinguistic contexts, along with many interpretations that are possible with the subject in question.

The organization of the paper is as follows: in the next section, we will discuss problems with two major approaches under the subject-as-encoded-possessor view. In section 3, we will see how the subject-as-underspecified-argument view deals with the possessor interpretation and avoids the problems discussed in section 2. Section 4 concludes the paper.

2 Subject As Encoded Possessor

Two approaches are immediately conceivable as to the way possession is encoded in syntax, namely, DP-internal possession, as in (6), and predicative possession, represented by a low applicative phrase (ApplLP; Pylkkänen, 2008), as in (7).

(6) DP-internal, nominal possession

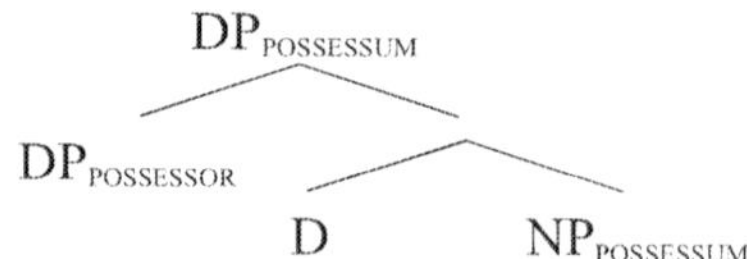

[3] Two terminological notes are in order: One is that Inoue (1976) calls the interpretation under discussion Experiencer, while other researchers call it different names such as Affectee, Possessor, Undergoer, etc. What we are concerned here is the fact that the argument bears the possessor interpretation. Moreover, although they involve lexical causatives and not syntactic causatives, the examples in the text should be regarded as cases of so-called adversity causative. This is because the causative morpheme *-(s)ase-* in adversity causatives, as in (i), can be regarded as the default realization of a lexical causative morpheme (Miyagawa, 1998).

(i) Taroo-ga tamago-o kusar-ase-ta
    T.-NOM egg-ACC rot-CAUS-PST
    '(His) eggs rotted on Taroo.'

(7) DP-external, predicative possession

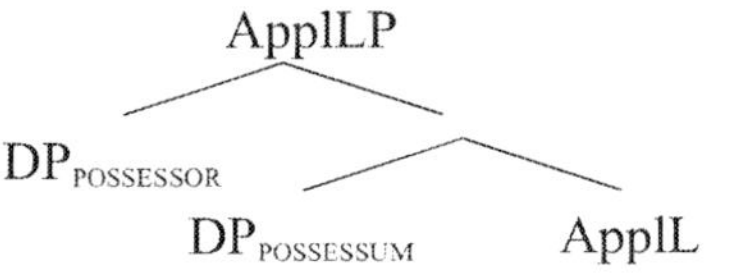

Both structures are inside the verbal domain, i.e., vP, and the possessor argument raises out of it into the subject position, i.e., SpecTP, as depicted in (8).

(8) [$_{TP}$ __ T [$_{vP}$ v [$_{\sqrt{P}}$ √ [$_{XP}$ DP$_{POSS'R}$ X]]]]
(where X is D or ApplL)

Hence, in both cases, possession is syntactically encoded and the subject argument is introduced as a possessor. In what follows, we will see problems with these approaches.

2.1 DP-internal Possession

As has been discussed in Deal (2014) recently, possessor raising does exist in natural languages. However, it is a controversial issue whether the process is available in Japanese. For instance, to argue for a possessor-raising analysis of non-agentive subjects, Hasegawa (2001) presents the following example.

(9) Hanako$_1$-ga {* kanozyo$_1$-no/*?zibun$_1$-no/Ø$_1$}
H.-NOM her-GEN self-GEN pro
ude-o or-Ø-ta (>ot-ta)
arm-ACC √break-CAUS-PST
'Hanako broke her arm.'
(Hasegawa, 2001: 19; her judgments)

In (9), pronouns or self-anaphors correferential with the subject cannot appear inside the possessum nominal. As she argues, this is parallel to the pattern observed in multiple nominative constructions, as given in (10), which are independently proposed to involve possessor raising (Ura, 2000).

(10) Hanako$_1$-ga {*kanozyo$_1$-no/*zibun$_1$-no/ Ø$_1$}
H.-NOM her-GEN self-GEN pro
asi-ga naga-k-Ø (>naga-i)
leg-NOM long-COP-NPST
'Hanako, her legs are long.'
(Hasegawa, 2001: 19; with minor changes)

If the non-agentive subject in (9) undergoes possessor raising, leaving a trace inside the possessum object, the unacceptable cases of (9) can be immediately explained.

However, in Takehisa (2003) I argue against the possessor-raising approach based on the same logic as Hasegawa invokes. Specifically, it is pointed out that, once pragmatically controlled, a sentence like (9) becomes acceptable.

(11) Koohun-no amari Hanako$_1$-wa
excitement-GEN excess H.-TOP
{kanozyo$_1$-no / zibun$_1$-no/ Ø$_1$ } asi-o
her-GEN self-GEN pro leg-ACC
or-Ø-ta (>ot-ta) koto-ni
√break-CAUS-PST NML-DAT
kizuk-anak-ar-ta (>-at-ta)
notice-NEG-COP-PST
'Due to too much excitement, Hanako didn't notice that she broke her leg.'

Another problem concerns the relation of proximity. While nouns of inalienable possession, which are predicates in their own right (Barker, 1995), are typical sources of possessor arguments, this is not always the case. Consider (12):

(12) Context: Taroo wore a long-sleeved shirt.
Taroo$_1$-ga Ø$_1$sode-o yabuk-Ø-ta (>yabui-ta)
T.-NOM pro sleeve-ACC √rip-CAUS-PST
'Taroo ripped his sleeve.'

For the non-agentive reading to be possible in (12), Taroo should be in a proximate relation with the shirt in such a way that he wore it at the time of ripping. Note that the shirt could be someone else's.

Even in cases where an inalienably possessed body-part is involved, an unusual context renders an unambiguous sentence acceptable with the non-agentive reading as well. For example, the English sentence in (13) is possible with the non-agentive, possessor reading of the subject under the context where John has Bill's arm transplanted. The same holds true for the Japanese counterpart. Again, the proximity condition must be satisfied and, as it seems, it can be satisfied extralinguistically.

(13) John broke Bill's arm.

Advocates for the possessor-raising approach might argue that it is still technically possible to assume the possessor argument generated inside the possessum nominal to account for (12) and (13). This is indeed true. However, if we entertain this possibility, the same analysis should be applicable to the sentence in (11) and any other example, and thus it would lose its predictive power in the end.

Moreover, even though it is technically possible to maintain the possessor-raising approach by assuming "stacked" possessors inside the possessum DP, the analysis has nothing to say about why the proximity condition holds. In particular, consider again the sentence in (12), where the possessum nominal is not relational. In this case, the possession relation involved can be contextually determined (Barker, 1995). However, as we have seen above, the relation imposed on the subject and the object in (12) is more restricted than that: they should be proximate.

2.2 DP-external Possession: Low Applicative

The possessor and the possessum arguments are mediated by a predicative element in DP-external possession, as represented in (7) above. In this paper, I follow Pylkkänen (2008) and assume that a low applicative head (ApplL) is responsible for a relation between individuals.

It is hard to distinguish between the possessor-raising approach and the low-applicative approach on the empirical ground. This is because, when one is possible, the other is also possible, sometimes with fancy tricks to explain away counterexamples. To the best of my knowledge, no knockdown arguments have been provided in this debate.

However, the example in (14) below, taken from Inoue (1976), cannot be accounted for under the low applicative approach. The verb involved is a change-of-location verb and it alternates in transitivity, as shown in (15) below.

(14) Hanako-ga te-ni toge-o
H-NOM hand-LOC needle-ACC
sas-Ø-ta (>sas-i-ta)
√stick-CAUS-PST
'Hanako had a needle stuck into her hand.'

(15) Hanako-no te-ni toge-ga
H-GEN hand-LOC needle-NOM
sas-ar-ta (>sas-at-ta)
√stick-INCH-PAST
'A needle stuck into Hanako's hand.'
(Inoue, 1976: 93ff., w/ minor changes)

Note that *ni* in these examples is a locative postposition. This is supported by the fact that the *ni*-marked phrase in (14) resists passivization even under the agentive interpretation of the subject.

(16) *Hanako-niyotte te-ga toge-o
H.-by hand-NOM needle-ACC
sas-Ø-are-ta
√stick-CAUS-PASS-PST
'A hand got a needle stuck into by Hanako.'

This clearly shows that the possessum argument in (14) is inside a PP. While a possessor-raising analysis can deal with this case easily because DP can be a postpositional object, analyses under the low applicative approach have no way to deal with a possessor argument related to PP-internal DPs.[4]

Another piece of evidence against the low applicative approach comes from interaction with resultative secondary predicates. Specifically, Pylkkänen (2008) discusses that a resultative predicate, which forms a small clause structure, serves to detect a low applicative structure. For instance, the verb *paint* can take double objects or form resultatives, as shown in (17)a and (17)b, respectively, but it cannot do both at the same time, as shown in (17)c.

(17) a. He painted me this flower.
b. He painted this flower blue.
c.* He painted me this flower blue.

According to Pylkkänen (2008), "[w]hile resultatives fail to cooccur with low applicatives, they easily combine with high applicatives" (Pylkkänen, 2008: 40). To explain this observation, she attributes the incompatibility of resultatives with low applicatives to the aspectual mismatch between the selectional restrictions of ApplLP, which selects for events, and the stative nature of the resultative phrase.

Applying this test to the English counterpart of adversity causatives yields (18) below, suggesting that non-agentive subjects are not introduced by ApplL.[5]

[4] Pylkkänen (2008: 59ff.) points out this problem in relation to Hebrew possessor datives and concludes that possessors related to PP-internal DPs must be distinct from those that are introduced by ApplL.

[5] Pylkkänen (1999, 2008) claims that English has no adversity causatives. Yet, (18) is a case of adversity causative.

(18) John broke his arm into two pieces, but he didn't break it himself.

When we turn to Japanese, we get the same result as in English. See (19).

(19) Taroo-ga ziko-de ude-o
T.-NOM accident-LOC arm-ACC
mapputatu-ni or-Ø-ta (>ot-ta)
two-COP √break-CAUS-PST
'Taroo broke his arm in two in the accident.'

Thus, it is safe to conclude that ApplL is not responsible for introducing non-agentive possessor subjects and they should receive a different treatment.

Lastly, the low applicative approach has one drawback on the conceptual ground: in cases where inalienably possessed nouns are involved, possession is doubly encoded by means of an ApplL head, which introduces a possessor argument in syntax, and an inalienably possessed noun, which is relational and takes a possessor argument. It is unclear why such double encoding is necessary. As it stands, this treatment is simply redundant.

Summarizing, the two approaches we have seen in this section face insuperable problems, and it can be concluded that neither possessor raising nor base generation by ApplL is involved in the possessor interpretation of non-agentive subjects.

3 Subject As Underspecified Argument

We have seen that approaches under the subject-as-encoded-possessor view, i.e., possessor raising and base generation by ApplL, fail to account for the distribution of non-agentive subjects. Moreover, we know that these non-agentive subjects bear the possessor interpretation, as demonstrated in (4). Given these, it seems plausible to pursue the possibility that possession is not directly encoded and the possessor interpretation of non-agentive subjects is derived by some other means.

Since non-agentive possessor subjects do not seem to bear any distinct interpretation other than that of possessor, I assume that they are mere event participant arguments, and also that they are introduced by the most underspecified version of argument-introducing head, which I take to be a version of high applicative (ApplH), as in (20).

(20) [[ApplH]] = $\lambda x.\lambda e.$ Participant(e,x)

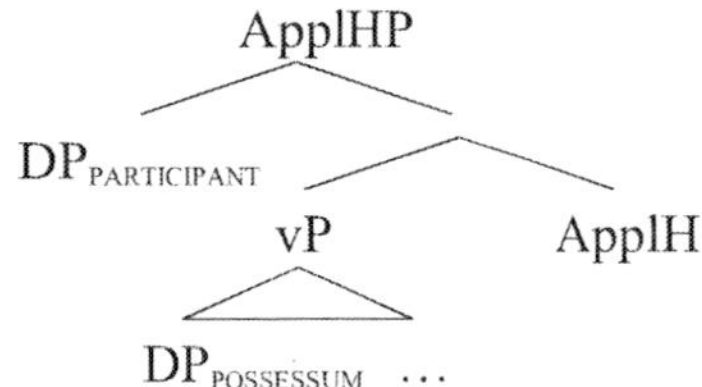

The high applicative head in (20) is different from those introducing arguments such as benefactives, malefactives, locatives, instrumentals, and the like, and its participant argument is underspecified with respect to the manner it participates in the event described by vP.

The underspecified argument is subject to enrichment by means of the post-syntactic inferential procedure, which Rivero (2004) calls the Ethical Strategy, at the C-I interface. Given that the C-I systems are the concept/context/inference systems (Reinhart 2006), I assume that inferences are made based on linguistic and extralinguistic contexts and the conceptual knowledge of higher-order generalizations about events.[6]

I further assume that, given the proto-agent/proto-patient dichotomy (Dowty, 1991), the underspecified event participant can be assumed to cause an event (i.e. a proto-agent property) or be affected in the event (a proto-patient property) as a starting point for inference and further inference derives the argument's readings. Thus, if the argument is assumed to cause the event, readings such as involuntary/accidental agent or (in)direct cause are derived depending on the context.[7] On the other hand, if it is assumed to be affected in the event, then readings such as benefactive, malefactive, undergoer, and the like are derived.

The possessor interpretation of non-agentive subjects, as in (2), can receive the same analysis. In this case, the presence of an inalienably possessed noun as an object argument contributes to the underspecified argument's construal as a possessor,

[6] The present analysis is in the same spirit of Ritter and Rosen's (1993) analysis of *have*, but it is different from theirs in that it adopts Dowty's (1990) proto-role theory in its implementation, instead of invoking complex predicate formation and its effect on the temporal dimension of the event.

[7] Note that the involuntary/accidental agent reading associated with an argument introduced by ApplH is distinct from the (volitional) agent reading, which is associated with an argument introduced by Voice (Kratzer, 1996).

on the condition that the possession relation is encoded linguistically, through binding, as in (11), or understood under the sufficiently rich extralinguistic context, as in (13).

Moreover, the underspecification approach in conjunction with the post-syntactic inferential strategy can give a natural account of the proximity condition as evidenced by (12), repeated below:

(21) Context: Taroo wore a long-sleeved shirt.
Taroo$_1$-ga Ø$_1$sode-o yabuk-Ø-ta (>yabui-ta)
T.-NOM pro sleeve-ACC √rip-CAUS-PST
'Taroo ripped his sleeve.'

Recall that, for the non-agentive reading to be possible in (21), Taroo should be in a proximate relation with the shirt in such a way that he wore it at the time of ripping, and moreover, that the shirt could be someone else's.

Under the present approach, the subject argument in (21) is asserted to be a participant of the event of ripping the shirt, and it can be assumed to cause the event or be affected in the event, as a starting point of inference. If the latter path is chosen, then the only way that the argument was affected is that it had some relation to another affected entity in the event. This is what explains the proximity condition.

Furthermore, the problems with low applicatives pointed out in section 2.2 dissolve, once you recognize ApplH is responsible for introducing the non-agentive subjects in (14), (18) and (19).

Therefore, the present approach solves all the problems reviewed in section 2, and hence it fares better than the possessor-raising approach and the low-applicative approach.

Further evidence for the subject-as-underspecified-argument view and against the subject-as-encoded-possessor view comes from the fact that the possessor interpretation is not restricted to examples like (2). It can be observed in examples as in (22).

(22) Indirect Cause and Possessor
Taroo$_1$-ga [Ø$_1$ kami]-o kir-Ø-ta (>kit-ta)
T.-NOM pro hair-ACC √cut-C-PST
(kedo zibun-de-wa kir-Ø-anak-ar-ta (>-at-ta))
but self-INST-TOP √cut-C-NEG-DV-PST
'Taroo had his hair cut.'
Lit.: 'Taroo cut his hair, but he didn't cut it himself.'

In (22), the subject argument is not an agent of the event, as evidenced by the second conjunct. Instead, it is construed as an indirect causer, or a higher cause in command of an unidentified direct cause of the event. More importantly, it is also a possessor.

Note that sentences like (22) cannot be equated with those like (2) above. They behave differently with respect to the Japanese version of *do so* replacement test, which serves to single out verbs which select a volitional subject, as shown by the following examples.

(23) Taroo$_1$-ga [Ø$_1$ kami]-o kir-Ø-ta (>kit-ta)
T.-NOM pro hair-ACC √cut-C-PST
Ziroo-mo soo si-ta
Z.-also so do-PST
'Taroo had his hair cut. Ziroo did so, too.'
[*Ziroo* as Indirect Cause/Possessor]

(24) Taroo$_1$-ga [Ø$_1$ ude]-o or-Ø-ta (>ot-ta).
T.-NOM pro arm-ACC √break-C-PST
Ziroo-mo soo si-ta.
Z.-also so do-PST
'Taroo broke his arm. Ziroo did so, too.'
[**Ziroo* as Possessor]

As shown above, the indirect cause/possessor subject can be volitional, while the pure possessor subject cannot.

What (22) and (23) show is that non-agentive subjects can have readings such as indirect cause, possessor and volition at the same time. This in turn suggests that the subject-as-encoded-possessor view is hard to maintain. Specifically, it appears impossible to encode possession in syntax in the case of non-agentive subjects with the indirect cause reading without introducing unlikely assumptions about indirect cause.

On the other hand, the underspecification approach, with the help of the post-syntactic inferential strategy, has a way to account for cases like (22), since it invokes the inferential procedure to derive various readings associated with the non-agentive subjects, which are event participants underspecified with respect to their manner of participation. [8]

[8] See Takehisa (2014) for more details.

4 Summary

This paper has compared the two views concerning the possessor interpretation of non-agentive subjects in Japanese lexical causatives: the subject-as-encoded-possessor view and the subject-as-underspecified-argument view. We have seen that the latter does not suffer from the problems the former does and hence is superior to the former. Specifically, the latter view is implemented as an analysis employing a particular type of high applicative (ApplH), which introduces an event participant whose manner is underspecified, in conjunction with the post-syntactic inferential strategy, originally proposed by Rivero (2004), which serves to enrich the interpretation of the underspecified argument.

Acknowledgments

I am grateful to Chigusa Morita and three anonymous reviewers for their invaluable comments, which helped clarify the manuscript. I am solely responsible for any errors and inadequacies contained herein.

References

Barker, Chris. 1995. *Possessive Descriptions*. CSLI Publication, Stanford.

Deal, Amy Rose. 2014. External Possession and Possessor Raising. Ms. UC Santa Cruz.

Dowty, David. 1991. Thematic Proto-roles and Argument Selection. *Language* 67(3):547–619.

Hasegawa, Nobuko. 2001. Causatives and the Role of v: Agent, Causer, and Experiencer. In Kazuko Inoue and Nobuko Hasegawa, eds., *Linguistics and Interdisciplinary Research*, pp.1–35.

Inoue, Kazuko. 1976. *Henkeebompoo-to Nihongo*, volume 2. Taishuukan, Tokyo.

Kratzer, Angelika. 1996. Severing the External Argument from its Verb. In Johan Rooryck and Lorie Zaring, eds., *Phrase Structure and the Lexicon*, pp.109-137. Kluwer Academic Publishers, Dordrecht.

Miyagawa, Shigeru. 1998. *(S)ase* as an Elsewhere Causative and the Syntactic Nature of Words. *Journal of Japanese Linguistics* 16: 67–110.

Pylkkänen, Liina. 1999. Causation and External Argument. *MIT Working Papers in Linguistics* 35:161–183.

Pylkkänen, Liina. 2008. *Introducing Arguments*. MIT Press, Cambridge, MA.

Reinhart, Tanya. 2006. *Interface Strategies*. MIT Press, Cambridge, MA.

Ritter, Elizabeth and Sara Thomas Rosen. 1993. Deriving Causation. *Natural Language and Linguistic Theory* 11(3):519–555.

Rivero, Maria Luiza. 2004. Datives and the Non-active Voice/Reflexive Clitics in Balkan Languages. In Olga Miseska-Tomic, ed., *Balkan Syntax and Semantics*, pp.237–267. John Benjamins, Amsterdam.

Takano, Yuji. 2011. Double Complement Unaccusatives in Japanese: Puzzles and Implications. *Journal of East Asian Linguistics* 20(3):229–254.

Takehisa, Tomokazu. 2003. Possession and Possessor Raising in Japanese. *McGill Working Papers in Lingusitics* 18(1):81–101.

Takehisa, Tomokazu. 2014. Non-selected Arguments and the Ethical Strategy. In Laura Teddiman, ed., *The 2014 CLA Proceedings*, pp.1–15.

Ura, Hiroyuki. 2000. *Checking Theory and Grammatical Functions in Universal Grammar*. Oxford University Press, Oxford.

Resources for Philippine Languages: Collection, Annotation, and Modeling

Nathaniel Oco[a], Leif Romeritch Syliongka[a], Tod Allman[b], Rachel Edita Roxas[a]
[a]National University
551 M.F. Jhocson St., Sampaloc, Manila, PH 1008
[b]Graduate Institute of Applied Linguistics
7500 W. Camp Wisdom Rd., Dallas, TX 75236
{nathanoco,lairusi,todallman,rachel_roxas2001}@yahoo.com

Abstract

In this paper, we present our collective effort to gather, annotate, and model various language resources for use in different research projects. This includes those that are available online such as tweets, Wikipedia articles, game chat, online radio, and religious text. The different applications, issues and directions are also discussed in the paper. Future works include developing a language web service. A subset of the resources will be made temporarily available online at: http://bit.ly/1MpcFoT.

1 Introduction

The Philippines is a country in Southeast Asia composed of 7,107 islands and 187 listed individual languages. Among these, 41 are listed as institutional, 73 are developing, 45 are vigorous, 13 are in trouble, 11 are dying, and 4 are already extinct[1]. These numbers highlight that there is a pressing need for a databank on Philippine languages. As highlighted in literature (Dita et al., 2009; Oco and Roxas, 2012), even those with high number of native speakers have limited available corpora. Towards addressing this scenario, we describe in this paper the collection, annotation, and modeling of various language resources.

The paper's structure is as follows: section 2 discusses initiatives in the country and the various language resources we collected; section 3 discusses annotation and documentation efforts; section 4 discusses language modeling; and we conclude our work in section 5.

2 Collection

Research works in language studies in the Philippines – particularly in language documentation and in corpus building – often involve one or a combination of the following: "(1) residing in the place where the language is spoken, (2) working with a native speaker, or (3) using printed or published material" (Dita and Roxas, 2011). Among these, working with resources available is the most feasible option given ordinary circumstances. Following this consideration, the Philippines as a developing country is making its way towards a digital age, which highlights – as Jenkins (1998) would put it – a "technological culture of computers". Organizations and educational institutions are making resources available in the Internet.

In the Philippines, documenting languages and making the resources public had been realized even before the turn of the millennium. For our collection initiatives, we derive inspiration from previous works. One of the projects is IsaWika (Roxas and Borra, 2000). It is an English-Filipino machine translator developed in 1999 that translates simple declarative sentences using the augmented transition network. Years after, the development of the Philippine component of the International Corpus of English or ICE-PHI (Bautista, 2004) started. It contains one million words of written and spoken Philippine English.

[1] Ethnologue Philippine language status profile for the Philippines: http://www.ethnologue.com/country/PH

Source	Language	Number of Articles
Inquirer	English	547
Manila Bulletin	English	1,333
Pang-Masa	Filipino	576
Pilipino Star Ngayon	Filipino	1,013
Rappler	English	779
The Philippine Star	English	1,011
Total		5,259

Table 1. Number of news articles collected

The written component contains non-printed texts such as non-professional writing and correspondence; and printed texts such as academic writing, reportage, instructional writing, persuasive and creative writing. On the other hand, the transcribed texts contain dialogues and monologues. One feature of the corpus is manual annotation – there are markup symbols to indicate the part-of-speech, the foreign and indigenous words, and paralinguistic devices.

The advent of ICE-PHI inspired the development of PALITO (Dita et al., 2009). An online corpus developed for purposes of pursuing various linguistic agendas, PALITO is a repository for religious and literary texts written in eight Philippine languages – Bikol, Cebuano, Hiligaynon, Ilocano, Kapampangan, Pangasinense, Tagalog, and Waray – and has a total word count of two million words. Aside from written texts, another component is the Filipino sign language (FSL) videos. The signs were illustrated in the form of actions and the videos cover the alphabet, number system, basic terms and expressions, and discourse. The 118 FSL videos have a combined file size of 224 million bytes.

The size of both ICE-PHI and PALITO highlights one limitation if collection was done manually – the low number of resources. In our initiative, we address this through automatic means. Current statistics put the number of Internet users to 44%[2], which makes social media and other online forms as viable sources of data, and one popular form is Twitter, a social networking site.

2.1 Tweets

For the current work, we continued the automatic collection of tweets started in a previous project (Oco et al., 2014b). A program was used to collect these online. A tweet is a short 140-character message delivered in Twitter. The program uses Twitter 4J[3] Java library and stores the following information in a database: Tweet ID; the tweet; date and time the tweet was sent; and geolocation where the tweet was sent.

The collection started last February 17, 2013 and a total of approximately 50 million tweets have been collected as of this writing. As tweets are considered an online chronicle of events and a repository of human opinion, they have been used to study Filipino voting behavior (Pablo et al., 2014) and analyze disasters such as the typhoon Haiyan (Soriano et al., 2016). In tandem with classification techniques such as sentiment analysis, tweets can be used in prediction and to help policy makers make informed decisions. It should be noted that we only collected those that are publicly available and those whose location is set, following ethical standards.

2.2 News Articles

Aside from tweets, we also collected news articles as they also represent actual language usage. Also a continuation of a previous project (Oco et al., 2014b), we are collecting from four news agencies (shown in Table 1). Calibre, an open source e-book management system[4] was used. As of this writing, a total of 5,259 articles have been collected, which are in .txt, .epub, and .pdf formats.

News articles provide a clear usage of the language. In a culturomics study (Ilao et al., 2011), cultural trends were studied using articles collected from more than ten Philippine tabloids and a computational model for language development was built.

2.3 Game Chat

An untapped source of valuable information is massively multiplayer online role-playing games (or MMORPG). They provide a venue for people to interact virtually. One of the popular MMORPG in the Philippines is Ragnarok. Also a continuation of a previous project (Oco et al., 2014b), we are collecting chat logs from this game using OpenKore[5] – a client and bot program made specifically for Ragnarok. Chats are classified into four: (1) A private chat [PM], which is a message sent to the character and can

[2] https://telehealth.ph/2015/03/26/internet-social-media-and-mobile-use-of-filipinos-in-2015/

[3] http://twitter4j.org/en/index.html

[4] http://calibre-ebook.com/

[5] http://www.openkore.com/index.php/Main_Page

only be read by the recipient of the message; (2) a public chat [C], which is a message sent by nearby characters and can be read by other nearby players; and (3) a shout [GM] and [S], which are game-wide message and can be read by everyone.

The chat logs can be used as training data in text normalization (Nocon et al., 2014b) and in cyber bullying detection (Cheng and Ng, 2016). The current log has 1,166,352 lines.

2.4 Wikipedia

Inspired by a previous study that collected English and Tagalog Wikipedia articles (Oco et al., 2014b), we also collected Wikipedia articles in other Philippine languages because of its popularity and availability. Embodiment of majority of the society, it is a multilingual Internet encyclopedia that is collaboratively edited by volunteers. Entire Wikipedias are publicly available through XML dumps and editions in Philippine languages exist. As a form of cleaning, we used an XML to text converter[6] to extract entries from XML dumps of the following languages: Bikol, Chavacano Zamboangeño, Ilokano, Kapampangan, Pangasinense, and Tagalog. Table 2 shows a sample text in the XML dump and its converted version, while Table 3 shows the word count of the converted text. A total of 7,304,254 words were collected. There is also an ongoing work to collect articles from the Cebuano, Hiligaynon, and Waray Wikipedias. Earlier projects utilized the Tagalog Wikipedia for purposes of code-switching point detection (Oco and Roxas, 2012). Another work (Syliongka and Oco, 2014) utilized Wikipedia articles as training data for named entity extraction.

XML dump	Extracted Text
<text xml:space="preserve">{{year navl{{PAGENAME}}}} Ang '''2005''' ay isang karaniwang taon na nagsisimula sa [[Sabado]] ayon sa [[Gregorian calendar]]. Ito ay hinirang na	Ang 2005 ay isang karaniwang taon na nagsisimula sa Sabado ayon sa Gregorian calendar. Ito ay hinirang na

Table 2. Sample XML dump

ISO Code	Word Count
bik	466,096
cbk	283,798
ilo	842,373
pag	127,492
pam	628,948
tgl	4,955,547
Total	7,304,254

Table 3. Summary of Wikipedia articles

ISO Code	Corpus Size (Words)
ceb	1,069,713
hil	291,370
ilo	1,003,392
tgl	1,104,035
Total	**3,468,510**

Table 4. Corpus size of Bible editions

2.5 Bible Editions

A number of religious organizations have put efforts to translate the Bible and made them available online in an effort to promote biblical teachings. One of these organizations is the Jehovah's Witness, which has more than 100,000 active members in the Philippines. It provides ePub versions of several Bible editions in their website[7]. To collect these, we used Calibre to convert the files to text files. The size of each edition is detailed in Table 4. The collection has a total size of 3,468,510 words. Bible editions have been used as training data in translation studies, language identification (Oco et al., 2013a; Oco et al., 2014a; Octaviano et al., 2015), and language clustering (Oco et al., 2013b).

2.6 Online Radio

Deviating from the usual text collection, we have also decided to start collecting audio files. A number of radio stations in the Philippines are already airing online. We used Screamer Radio[8] to record airings from radio stations. Figure 1 shows a sample screenshot of the program. More than 5,400 hours of music, commercials, and commentaries have been recorded in stereo format from three radio stations. The details are shown in Table 5. Screamer radio provides direct MP3 audio stream saving at 31kbps. These audio files could be used as training data for speech synthesis and automatic speech recognition (ASR). One study (Laguna and

[6] An XML to text converter by Evan Jones: http://www.evanjones.ca/software/wikipedia2text.html

[7] http://www.jw.org/en/publications/bible/

[8] http://www.screamer-radio.com/

Guevara, 2014), developed an audio language identification system for different Philippine languages.

3 Annotation and Documentation

Another corpus being developed consists of lexicons, grammars, and texts that are translated by a natural language generator (NLG) called Linguist's Assistant (LA) (Beale and Allman, 2011). LA is being used to build lexicons and grammars for many of the languages in the Philippines, and that data is being applied to thoroughly annotated semantic representations in order to generate initial draft translations of various educational, religious, and community development texts. LA has successfully been used to document many languages from a variety of language families, and it has produced high quality initial draft translations of a variety of texts in those languages (Allman et al., 2014). A new technique developed specifically for the Malayo-Polynesian languages of the Philippines was recently implemented (Allman, 2014), and an extensive Tagalog lexicon and grammar were developed. LA is now able to produce initial draft translations of a variety of texts in Tagalog. Experiments indicate that mother-tongue translators are able to edit those drafts into publishable form in approximately one fourth the time required for manual translation. The Tagalog grammar and lexicon are currently being expanded so that LA can produce initial draft translations of a wider variety of texts. Additionally, the Tagalog grammar and lexicon are being modified to accommodate another Malayo-Polynesian language named Ayta Mag-Indi. Because Tagalog and Ayta Mag-Indi are structurally very similar, the process of modifying the Tagalog grammar to accommodate Ayta Mag-Indi is proceeding very quickly. After only six meetings with an Ayta speaker, LA was able to produce an initial draft translation of a simple story in Ayta Mag-Indi. That same story required approximately 38 meetings with the Tagalog mother-tongue speaker. The work to expand the Ayta Mag-Indi grammar and lexicon will continue so that more texts can be translated. After the Ayta Mag-Indi work has been completed, the same process will be repeated with multiple Malayo-Polynesian languages. There are many potential uses for the resulting data and corpora. A few of these usages are detailed in the following sections.

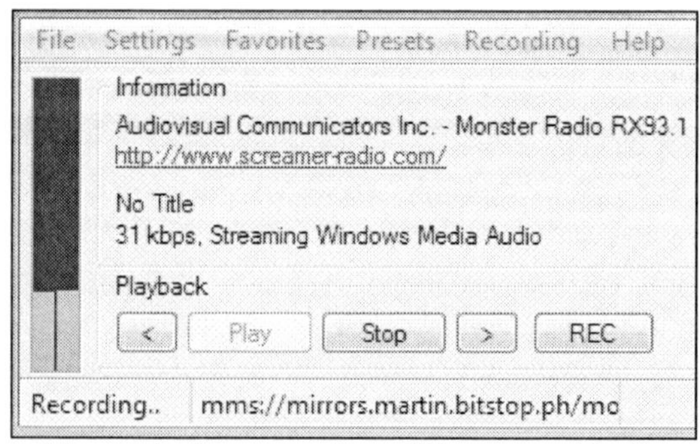

Figure 1. A screenshot of Screamer Radio

Description	Love Radio	Monster Radio	Yes FM
Frequency	90.7 MHz	93.1 MHz	101.1 MHz
Power	25 kW	25 kW	25 kW
Total File Size	19.7 GB	32.5 GB	
Total Length (hours)	2,532	1,869	1,075

Table 5. Details about the Radio Stations

3.1 MTBMLE

The Mother-Tongue Based Multilingual Education (MTBMLE) initiative mandates that many educational books and instructional documents be translated into all of the Philippine languages. After a lexicon and grammar have been developed for a particular language, LA is able to generate a translation of any document that has been converted into a semantic representation. Therefore LA could potentially facilitate the implementation of MTBMLE.

3.2 ASEAN-MT

The ASEAN Machine Translation project or ASEAN-MT (Nocon et al., 2014a) uses standard English as its interlingua. However, a problem will arise because English is impoverished in many areas (e.g., its pronominal system, its deictic and article systems, its tense system, etc.). The Tagalog texts produced by this project could be aligned with the associated semantic representations, and then the stochastic trainer for the Tagalog component of ASEAN-MT could be used to produce enriched English as the interlingua. Using enriched English as the interlingua will significantly improve the quality of the translations produced in the other ASEAN languages.

3.3 Linguistic Research

Having computational lexicons and grammars in a standardized format for many of the Philippine languages could prove invaluable to linguists, lexicographers, and translators throughout the country. Additionally the data could be used to determine language affinities, supplement cross-linguistic research, and bolster typological studies.

A tool that can be used by linguists for describing morphology, syntax, and semantics is beneficial (Beale et al., 2005). Anthropologists have noted that when a language is documented and texts are translated into the language, the speakers of the language are often motivated to preserve their language and expand its use.

4 Modeling

A number of the resources were modeled in terms of word n-grams and character n-grams. A word n-gram is n-slices of a sentence while a character n-gram is n-slices of a word. As an example, the list of 3-grams that can be generated from the word "language" are: {_la, lan, ang, ngu, gua, uag, age, ge_}. These language models provide information on frequently occurring words and phrases. The advent of data-centric computing made it possible for models to be used as training data in various tasks (Legaspi et al., 2008; Gavrila and Vertan, 2011). A number of text documents written in various languages have been used as training data in language identification (Oco et al., 2013a) and language clustering (Oco et al., 2013b).

5 Conclusion

In this paper, we presented our collective effort to collect, annotate, document, and model various language resources to address the pressing need for a databank on Philippine languages. We also detailed the different applications, issues, and directions.

The work can be extended by considering automatic annotation and making the resources available online as a language web service.

Acknowledgment

This work is supported in part by the Philippine Commission on Higher Education through the Philippine-California Advanced Research Institutes Project (no. IIID-2015-07).

References

Allman, T., S. Beale, and R. Denton. 2014. Toward an Optimal Multilingual Natural Language Generator: Deep Source Analysis and Shallow Target Analysis. Philippine Computing Journal, 9(1), pp. 55-63.

Allman, T. 2014. Linguist's Assistant: Gleaning Malayo-Polynesian Grammars from Small, Lightly Annotated Corpora. Paper presented at the 12th Philippine Linguistics Congress.

Bautista, M.L. 2004. An Overview of the Philippine Component of the International Corpus of English (ICE-PHI). Asian English, 7(2), pp. 8-26.

Beale, S., S. Nirenburg, M. McShane, and T. Allman. 2005. Document Authoring the Bible and for Minority Language Translation. Proceedings of MT Summit.

Beale, S. and T. Allman. 2011. Linguist's Assistant: A Resource for Linguists. Proceedings of the 9th Workshop on Asian Language Resources, pp. 41-49.

Cheng, C. and L. Anson Ng. 2016. Automated Role Detection in Cyberbullying Incidents. Proceedings of the 16th Philippine Computing Science Congress, pp. 85-92.

Dita, S., R.E. Roxas, and P. Inventado. 2009. Building Online Corpora of Philippine Languages. Proceedings of the 23rd Pacific Asia Conference on Language, Information and Computation, pp. 646-653.

Dita, S. and R.E. Roxas. 2011. Philippine Languages Online Corpora: Status, Issues, and Prospects. Proceedings of the 9th Workshop on Asian Language Resources, pp. 59-62.

Gavrila, M. and C. Vertan. 2011. Training Data in Statistical Machine Translation: The More the Better. Proceedings of Recent Advances in Natural Language Processing, pp. 551-556.

Ilao, J., R.C. Guevara, V. Llenaresas, E.A. Narvaez, and J. Peregrino. 2011. Bantay-Wika: Towards a Better Understanding of the Dynamics of Filipino Culture and Linguistic Change. Proceedings of the 9th Workshop on Asian Language Resources, pp. 10-17.

Jenkins, H. 1998. The Poachers and the Stormtrooper: Popular Culture in the Digital Age. Red Rock Eaters News.

Laguna, A.F.B. and R.C.L. Guevara. 2014. Experiments on Automatic Language Identification for Philippine Languages using Acoustic Gaussian Mixture Models. Proceedings of IEEE TENSYMP.

Legaspi, R., S. Kurihara, K. Fukui, K. Moriyama, and M. Numao. 2008. Proceedings of the 5th

International Conference on Information Technology and Applications, pp. 88-93.

Nocon, N., G. Cuevas, D. Magat, P. Suministrado, and C. Cheng. 2014a. NormAPI: An API for normalizing Filipino shortcut texts. Proceedings of the International Conference on Asian Language Processing.

Nocon, N. N. Oco, J. Ilao, and R.E. Roxas. 2014b. Philippine Component of the Network-based ASEAN Language Translation Public Service. Proceedings of the 7th International Conference on Humanoid, Nanotechnology, Information Technology, Communication and Control, Environment, and Management.

Oco, N. and R.E. Roxas. 2012. Pattern Matching Refinements to Dictionary-Based Code-Switching Point Detection. Proceedings of the 26th Pacific Asia Conference on Language, Information and Computation, pp. 229-236.

Oco, N., J. Ilao, R.E. Roxas, and L.R. Syliongka. 2013a. Measuring Language Similarity using Trigrams: Limitations of Language Identification. Proceedings of the 3rd International Conference on Recent Trends in Information Technology.

Oco, N., L.R. Syliongka, J. Ilao, and R.E. Roxas, 2013b. Dice's Coefficient on Trigram Profiles as Metric for Language Similarity. Proceedings of the 2013 International Conference Oriental COCOSDA held jointly with 2013 Conference on Asian Spoken Language Research and Evaluation (O-COCOSDA/CASLRE).

Oco, N., L.R. Syliongka, J. Ilao, and R.E. Roxas. 2014a. N-gram based Language Identification and Rule-based Grammar Checking. Proceedings of the 14th Philippine Computing Science Congress, pp. 244-250.

Oco, N., R. Sison-Buban, L.R. Syliongka, R.E. Roxas, and J. Ilao. 2014b. Ang Paggamit ng Trigram Ranking Bilang Panukat sa Pagkakahalintulad at Pagkakapangkat ng mga Wika [Trigram Ranking: Metric for Language Similarity and Clustering]. Malay, 26(2), pp 53-68.

Octaviano Jr., M., R. Fajutagana, C.M.L., J.D. Miñon, J.-A. Morano, R.C. Tinoco, and N. Oco. 2015. The use of Trigram Models in Classifying and Clustering different Philippine Languages. Proceedings of the 10th International Conference on Knowledge Information and Creativity Support Systems, pp. 546-552.

Pablo, Z.C., N. Oco, M.D.G. Roldan, C. Cheng, and R.E. Roxas. 2014. Toward an enriched understanding of factors influencing Filipino behavior during elections through the analysis of Twitter data. Philippine Political Science Journal, 35(2), pp. 203-224.

Roxas, R. and A. Borra. 2000. Computational Linguistics Research on Philippine Languages. Proceedings of the 38th Annual Meeting of the Association for Computational Linguistics.

Soriano, C.R., M.D.G. Roldan, C. Cheng, and N. Oco. 2016. Social media and civic engagement during calamities: The case of Twitter use during typhoon Yolanda. Philippine Political Science Journal, 37(1), pp. 6-25.

Syliongka, L.R. and N. Oco. 2014. Using Language Modeling and Data Association to Perform Named Entity Recognition. Proceedings of the 10th National Natural Language Processing Research Symposium, pp. 115-119.

Generating a Linguistic Model for Requirement Quality Analysis

Juyeon Kang
PROMETIL
42 avenue du Général de Croutte
31100 Toulouse, France
j.kang@prometil.com

Jungyeul Park
Department of Linguistics
University of Arizona
Tucson, AZ 85721
jungyeul@email.arizona.edu

Abstract

In this work, we aim at identifying potential problems of ambiguity, completeness, conformity, singularity and readability in system and software requirements specifications. Those problems arise particularly when they are written in Natural Language. We describe them from linguistic point of view but the business impacts of each potential error will be considered in system engineering context where our corpus come from. Several standards give the criteria on writing good requirements to guide requirement authors. These properties are linguistically observable because they appear as lexical, syntactic, semantic and discursive problems in documents. We investigate error patterns heavily used, by analyzing manually the corpus. This analysis is based on the requirements grammar that we developed in this work. We then propose an approach to identify them automatically by applying the rules developed from the error patterns to the POS tagged and parsed corpus. By using error annotated corpus, we can train the error model using CRFs and evaluate it. We obtain overall 79.17% F_1 score for the error label annotation task.

1 Introduction and Context

In order that a system is realized and become operational in real applications, it follows several stages of conception, development, production, use, support and retirement (ISO/IEC TR 24748-1, 2010). During the concept stage, we identify and document the stakeholder's needs in the system requirements specification (Hull et al., 2011). Writing clearly all required elements without ambiguities (Berry et al., 2003) in the specifications is an essential task before passing to the development stage (Galin, 2003; Bourque et al., 2004). According to the *2015 Chaos report* by the Standish Group[1], only 29% of projects was successful[2]. And 50% of the challenged projects is related to the errors from the Requirement Engineering and 70% of them comes from the difficulties of understanding of implicit requirements. All these errors do not lead to the failure, but generate useless information. It is well known that the costs to fix errors increase much more after that the product is built than it would if the requirements errors were discovered during the requirements phase of a project (Glas, 2002; Stecklein et al., 2004).

However, when writing or revising a set of requirements, or any technical document, it is particularly challenging to make sure that texts read easily and are unambiguous for any domain actor (Weiss, 1990; Grady, 2013). The previous experience shows that even with several levels of proofreading and validation, most texts still contain a large number of language errors (lexical, grammatical, semantic, style, etc.), and lack of overall cohesion and coherence. Risks emerge from poorly written texts, and from various forms of incoherence. For example, *Progressively heat the probe X27* relies too much on the operators knowledge and practice: what temperature should be reached and in how much time? A

[1] http://www.standishgroup.com

[2] They studied 50,000 projects around the world, ranging from tiny enhancements to massive systems re-engineering implementations.

wrong interpretation may lead to accidents and damages.

Tools controlling the authoring quality of requirements have been developed in the past with the use of templates or boilerplates meant to guide the technical writer. This is most notably the case for the RAT-RQA system[3] and of the RUBRIC system (Arora et al., 2013). Let us also cite two major CNL-based prototypes which are of much interest for requirement authoring: ACE (Fuchs, 2012), which stands for Attempto Controlled English. This system makes an in-depth language semantic analysis. It was initially designed to control software specifications, and has been used more recently in the semantic web. PENG (Processable English) (White and Schwitter, 2009) is a computer-processable controlled natural language system designed for writing unambiguous and precise specifications. These systems make heavy use of syntactic analysis, which is rather costly. A synthesis of CNL based systems is developed in (Kuhn, 2013).

We also find the systems of requirements quality analysis based on the shallow parsing techniques. First, SEMIOS system[4] is relevant for requirements where the language is complex and sometimes ill-formed. It detects several types of errors, lexical, syntactic and related to style. Error detection in this system depends on the discourse structure analysis. Second, (Berrocal Rojas and Barrantes Sliesarieva, 2010) proposes a software prototype for controlling if a requirement satisfies the criteria of the high quality requirement defined in DO-178b. This work focuses on the detection of inaccurate, non-verifiable and ambiguous elements in requirements by means of lexical (using WordNet and VerbNet) and syntactic analysis.

There are other interesting approaches and tools developed for automatically analyzing the requirements specifications but we do not develop all of them in this paper because of the lack of space. We invite the readers to consult (Gnesi et al., 2005; Fabbrini et al., 2001; Zapata Jaramillo, 2010).

The model that we propose identifies the potential errors in natural language requirements by applying error patterns rules to the POS tagged and syntactically parsed sentences. It depends on the requirements grammar that we elaborate from the requirements authoring guidelines. In §2, we introduce the essential constraints of authoring high quality requirements with examples, and in §3, develop the requirements grammar rules corresponding to each constraint. Errors patterns are also described in this section as they are induced by verifying if requirements are correctly written following the rules of the requirements grammar. The §4 describes the methods and results of our experiments elaborated for generating an adapted model of automatic error patterns labeling to requirements documents. The main contribution of the paper is as follows: (1) We define requirements grammar and their error patterns. (2) We create training and evaluation data for building an error pattern model and assigning error labels. To the best of the author's knowledge, it is the first time to achieve such results by using the automatically learned model from the training data set. It would be suitable for the general purpose error annotation for requirements authoring quality.

2 Requirements Authoring and Quality

Among technical documents, requirements are a central issue since they must comply with a high number of constraints of e.g. readability, lack of ambiguity and implicit data, feasibility, relevance, traceability, conformity and overall cohesion and coherence (Firesmith, 2003; Alred et al., 2012). The principles of the authoring quality of requirements are defined in different standards like IEEE 830-1998 (IEEE Recommended Practice for Software Requirements Specification), ISO/IEC/IEEE29148:2011 (Systems and software engineering – Life cycle processes – Requirements engineering), ARP4754A (Aerospace Recommended Practice) and also in the recommendations of INCOSE (Guide for Writing Requirements), IREB (International Requirements Engineering Board) and the controlled natural languages (e.g. ASD-STE 100[5]). The authoring constraints specify the syntax, the semantic along with the style and the lexical items that the technical authors must respect.

[3]http://www.reusecompany.com

[4]http://www.semiosapp.com

[5]Simplified Technical English, Aerospace and Defense, by Industries Association of Europe, Issue 5, 2010

In this paper, we focus on the five constraints (ambiguity, conformity, completeness, singularity, readability), considered as being the most critical by requirements authors, with examples and descriptions. All examples was extracted from our test corpus. It contains technical requirements and some of them are anonymized because of confidential problems. But they remains meaningful enough to show real problems in requirements texts.

We follow mainly the definitions of these constraints, proposed by the above mentioned standards and guidelines of IEEE and INCOSE.

2.1 Non-Ambiguity

An ambiguous term can convey several information which lead the requirement to different interpretations of what the system is expected to do. A requirement must be interpreted in only one way without ambiguities. The following examples contain a lexical ambiguity in (Req1) with the fuzzy adjective *standard* and a grammatical ambiguity in (Req2) with the combinator *or*.

- (Req1) *The maximum pressure loads at the standard operating temperature shall be 6.*
- (Req2) *The CPU system shall set these signals in output* ***or*** *shall send them directly to the platform.*

2.2 Conformity

A requirement must be written conforming to the standard structure and style defined by a company or a group of authors. Not respecting this standard increases the problem of understanding and makes difficult to identify the main requirements from the other types of sentences having a similar structure like procedures, instructions, recommendation, etc. The use of *should* instead of *shall* in (Req3) makes the requirement non mandatory.

- (Req3) *Paint coatings should also assist in the overall maintenance of the vehicle by providing easy to clean surfaces.*

2.3 Completeness

A requirement must contain complete information in itself without needing extra elements to understand correctly the requirement. In the example (Req4), the requirement missed the agents who shall realize the actions, and in (Req5), *these* and *this* refer to some elements which can be identified with extra contextual information.

- (Req4) *In particular the received configurations shall be used and the communication signal shall be isolated.*
- (Req5) *If these systems are required for safety purpose, this requirement shall not prohibit the use of the supply systems.*

2.4 Singularity

A singular requirement must express a single idea and characteristic concerning what the system has to make. The (Req6) contains multiple actions *shall deliver* and *reload*, introduced by the use of the combinator *and*. The (Req7) expresses the main action, then justify why this action is required (*in order to...*). This last is not a part of the requirement.

- (Req6) *The system shall deliver data and reload the configuration checks performed and not performed.*
- (Req7) *Seats shall be selected at the discretion of each customer in order to [accommodate differences in operations and passenger preferences].*

2.5 Readability

A complex requirement makes difficult the comprehension on given requirements and increase the cognitive works of the reader. In (Req8), the quantifier *all* needs to be specified by a list to be easily readable. In (Req9), the three acronyms should be defined in a glossary and if not, the requirement will not be understandable without specific domain knowledge.

- (Req8) *All exterior graphics shall be applied to the vehicle in accordance with Customer specifications.*
- (Req9) *Static RAM or dynamic EPROM windows shall be covered with labels that are opaque at the UV erasing wavelengths.*

The above requirements (Req1)~(Req9) illustrate the counterexamples of high quality requirements, which do not respect the non-ambiguity, conformity, completeness, singularity and readability. Some of them will be reconsidered in §3.1 to describe the Requirements Grammar.

3 Requirements grammar and Errors patterns

As shown in §2, the requirements texts need to be qualified as unambiguous, conforming, complete, readable and singular. Such constraint of a requirement written in Natural Language form a specific linguistic genre that we call "requirements grammar". We consider in this work the five previously explained constraints for writing good requirements and define the corresponding rules in our requirements grammar. We also elaborate the types of most frequent language errors as errors patterns, and describe them in relation with the rules of requirements grammar. Table 1 describes a list of error patterns that we developed based on requirements grammar.

3.1 Ambiguity rules

Rule 1: A requirement should not contain ambiguous adjectives, adverbs, verbs and nouns which can lead it to several interpretations, such as *significant, flexible, sufficient, adequate, nearly, correctly, properly, minimize, optimize, malfunction, undesirable effects*, etc. All adverbs ending in *-ly* particularly make requirements unverifiable. These terms can be replaced or complemented by a value, a set of values or an interval. The example (Req1) shows the case that prohibits this rule. If the *standard operating temperature* is not defined in the text, it should be reformulated like *the standard operating temperature between 5°C and 10°C.*

Rule 2: A requirement should avoid the use of the combinator *or* and the combination of *and* and *or*. The conjunctions *or* and *and*, which coordinate two actions verbs and two subjects, are not acceptable as it raises a critical ambiguity problem (if they appear in a main clause, it is more critical than in a subordinated clause). The example (Req2) shows the case that the *or* is used between two main action verbs *shall set* and *shall send*.

3.2 Conformity rules

Rule 3: A requirement expresses an obligation that states what the system should realize. The modal *shall* is mainly used for mandatory requirements. Other modals verbs like *must, should, could, would, can, will, may, should* are not allowed in writing the main action of a requirement. The example (Req3) uses the modal verb *should* which expresses a recommendation rather than an obligation. It means that *it is recommended that Paint coatings assist in overall maintenance but not obligatorily*. The impact of not respecting this requirement can be critical for the system.

Rule 4: The negation markers should be avoided in a main clause as they states what the system does not do as we can see in *The system* <u>*shall not*</u> *transfer unauthorized data to the sub-systems*. This requirement should be reformulated like *The system shall transfer only authorized data to the sub-system.*

3.3 Completeness rules

Rule 5: A requirement should be written in the active voice because the majority of passive sentences do not include explicit agents to indicate exactly who perform the action. For example, in the requirement *It shall be tested in the following conditions:...*, we need extra information to identify what will be tested and who will test. The example (Req4) shows the same situation.

Rule 6: Referential ambiguities appear when the demonstrative and possessive pronouns like *it, they, them, their..* are used with unclear antecedents in requirements. These terms can refer to more than one element of the same sentence or of the previous sentence. In the example (Req5), the pronoun *these* probably refers to some elements introduced in the antecedent requirements. All elements that *these systems* refer to should be clearly specified in the given requirement.

3.4 Singularity rules

Rule 7: A requirement should express only one action and one idea (one subject) in a requirement. First, we find two types of erroneous structures introducing multiple actions in a requirement: 1) more than two action verbs enumerated in a list, 2) more than two action verbs coordinated by more than one *and*. Second, when the subject is expressed in using *and* like *X and Y shall...*, we consider the requirement as having multiple subjects and multiple thoughts.

The example (Req6) describe the performance of several actions and ideas in a requirement. In this kind of case, when one of the actions is updated, it can influence on the other action, consequently makes difficult the maintenance and validation of the requirement.

Rule 8: A requirement should contain appropriate information, not including the solution and the purpose of the given requirement. These extra information should be presented separately in another documents.

In the example (Req7), *in order to* introduces a new information: the reason why *seats are selected at the discretion of each customer*. The author should not include the justification part in the requirement. This problem often occurs using the following structures: *to, so as to, for the purpose of, so that, in order that*, etc.

3.5 Readability rules

Rule 9: The use of universal quantifiers like *every, all, each, several, a, some*, etc. should be avoided because they generates the scope ambiguity. For example, in the requirement *All sub-systems shall have their fire alarm*, the quantifier *all* does confuse readers if the meaning is that *all sub-systems share one alarm* or *all sub-systems has its own alarm*.

Rule 10: In principle, a requirement text should have available a glossary where the acronyms and abbreviations are defined in order to help the reader to understand the concepts related to them. Otherwise an acronym should have a definition inside of the requirement like *The APU (Auxiliary Power Unit) system*.

4 Experiments and Results

4.1 Building training data

We build training data by using POS tagging and syntactic parsing. We define five types of errors as described in §2: ambiguity (`AMBI`), conformity (`CONF`), completeness (`COMP`), singularity (`SING`), and readability (`READ`) and we write heuristic rules based on error patterns. We use the IOB format for error labels, in which `B-` for 'beginning' of the label, `I-` for 'inside', and `O` for 'outside': *e.g.* `B-AMBI` and `I-AMBI` for the beginning and the inside of the ambiguity label. Since we use the automatic method to build our training data, we want to minimize the error rate in our data. Therefore, we introduce the filtering method by using two different algorithms to filter out instances that we consider as errors for POS tagging and syntactic analysis. To so do, we simply use the consensus filtering method by the intersection operation as follows:

$$\hat{\mathcal{D}} = \mathcal{D}(\mathcal{M}_1) \cap \mathcal{D}(\mathcal{M}_2) \quad (1)$$

where $\mathcal{D}$ is raw text data, $\mathcal{M}_i$ is a learning algorithm to annotate raw text data, and $\hat{\mathcal{D}}$ is filtered annotated data. For POS tagging, we use a hidden Markov model (HMM) and conditional random fields (CRFs) in which we trained with POS information of English treebank data[6]. We use a TnT tagger (Brants, 2000) and Wapiti described in (Lavergne et al., 2010) for the HMM and CRF annotation, respectively. For syntactic parsing, we use two pretrained dependency parsing models for MaltParser (Nivre et al., 2006).[7] We use syntactic parsing results to detect the correct range of contaminator errors described in §3.1, in which `or` and `X'` are dependent of `X` in `X or X'` (for the `AMBI` error label). The length of `X` and `X'` can vary in the sentence and it would be difficult to detect them without syntactic analysis. Otherwise, error annotation rules are entirely based on POS tagging and lexical patterns and these rules are described in detail throughout §2 and §3. For raw text data, we use ukWaC (the largest English web-crawled resource), one of the WaCky corpora presented in (Baroni et al., 2009). We believe that ukWaC contains large numbers of texts written in technical English as it shows some lexical and structural similarity to requirements texts: use of the modal *shall*, action verbs, terms expressing needs, etc. Finally, after consensus between POS tagging and syntactic analysis, we obtain 82,847 sentences with 844,770 tokens for the training data set. For the error annotation based on heuristic rules, we give priorities for certain error patterns. Therefore, when there are several possibilities to annotate errors in the same word, we use the following error precedence:

[6]`https://catalog.ldc.upenn.edu/LDC99T42`

[7]`http://www.maltparser.org/mco/english_parser/engmalt.html`

Error patterns	Description	Impacts and rules
Combinators	This error pattern related to the use of combinators *or* and *and* concerns the rules 2 and 7, respectively. • `X or X'` where POSs (or phrase type) of X and X' are same. • `X and/or X'` where POSs (or phrase type) of X and X' are same. • `X and X'` where POSs (or phrase type) of X and X' are same. X= verb (infinitive form), verb phrase, noun, noun phrase, adjective, value followed by a unit of measurement	Ambiguity 2 Singularity 7
Pronouns	This error pattern related to the use of possessive and demonstrative pronouns concerns the rule 6. • `Pron(possessive), Noun`: *their application* • `Pron(possessive), NP`: *their proper development* • `Pron(demonstrative), modal(shall)`: *this shall, these shall*	Completeness 6
Lexicals	This lexical error pattern concerns the rules 1, 8, 9 and 10 of §3. Requirements containing one of the following lexical items: ambiguous terms (Rule 1), purpose expressions (Rule 8), quantifiers (Rule 9), acronyms (Rule 10), raises the problem of ambiguity, singularity and readability. Due to lack of space, we do not give its complete lists but the main items are mentioned in each rule.	Ambiguity 1 Singularity 8 Readability 9, 10
Passive construction	This error pattern related to the use of passive construction concerns the rule 5. We do not consider the passive construction followed by the preposition *by* which introduces the agent as being erroneous. • `modal(shall), be, AdvP, Verb(Action, PP)`: *shall be used, shall be properly used*	Completeness 5
Negations	This error pattern related to the negation marker concerns the rule 4. `modal` is only the mandatory modal *shall*. • `modal, Neg`: *shall not*	Conformity 4
Modals	This error pattern related to the use of different types of modal verbs concerns the rule 3. `modal` excepts the mandatory modal *shall*. • `modal, AdvP, Verb(Action, Inf)`: *would implement, should correctly implement*	Conformity 3

Table 1: Correspondence between errors patterns, impacts and rules

The	DT	O
analytes	NNS	B-AMBI
or	CC	I-AMBI
investigations	NNS	I-AMBI
covered	VBN	O
by	IN	O
the	DT	O
Scheme	NNP	O
shall	MD	B-COMP
be	VB	I-COMP
selected	VBN	I-COMP
on	IN	O
the	DT	O
basis	NN	O
of	IN	O
their	PRP$	B-COMP
clinical	JJ	I-COMP
relevance	NN	I-COMP
.	.	O

Figure 1: An example sentence from training data: *analytes or investigations* represents the ambiguity error, *shall be selected* is annotated as completeness error, and *their clinical relevance* has the completeness error.

$$\text{combinators} > \text{pronouns} > \text{lexical} > \text{passive construction} > \text{negations} > \text{modals} \quad (2)$$

Figure 1 shows an example sentence from our training data. In this figure, first, *analytes or investigations* represents the ambiguity error because of *or* as explained in the Rule 2 of §3.1. Second, *shall be selected* is annotated as completeness error because the information about who realize the required action is not specified as shown in the Rule 5 of §3.3. Third, *their clinical relevance* also has the completeness error because of the possessive pronoun *their*. It probably refers to one of the following antecedents: *analystes*, *investigations*, *the Scheme* but we need extra information to correctly identify the reference of *their* (see the Rule 6 of §3.3).

We use CRFs for training. Since we are heavily based on lexical and POS information, we use a simple feature set, in which ±2 word/POS window context, and bi-gram word/POS models.

label	number	average length
AMBI	138	1.69
CONF	88	2.36
COMP	88	2.94
SING	59	3.27
READ	243	1

Table 2: Error labels in the evaluation data set.

4.2 Evaluation data

To evaluate our proposed method and the model trained by automatically generated data, we build evaluation data. Our evaluation data are composed of 319 technical requirements (481 sentences with 10,324 tokens), extracted from 12 documents (over 200 pages) coming from four different companies, kept anonymous at their request. The main features considered to validate our data are as follows:

(1) requirements corresponding to various professional activities: product design, management, finance, and safety
(2) requirements following various kinds of business style and format guidelines imposed by companies
(3) requirements coming from various industrial areas: finance, telecommunications, transportation, energy, computer science.

To build evaluation data, we annotate POS labels using an HMM model and we correct them. Then, we manually assign error labels as defined in §3. Table 2 shows the number and the average length of error labels in the evaluation data set.

4.3 Results

Table 3 presents evaluation results based on the evaluation data that we described in §4.2. We also provide precision and recall for each error label. We obtain overall 79.17% F_1 score for our *automatic* error label annotation by using the CRF model learned from which we build training data.

4.4 Error analysis and discussion

READ error labels are entirely based on lexical information and we correctly annotate almost all of them because we have enough lexical information in training data. CONF error labels show only about 26% of precision because even though the expected modals

label	precision	recall	F_1
AMBI	45.65	82.89	58.88
CONF	26.14	82.14	39.66
COMP	73.86	84.42	78.79
SING	79.66	65.28	71.76
READ	100.00	99.18	99.59
total	71.59	88.55	**79.17**

Table 3: Evaluation results: We learned our model from the training data described in §4.1 and evaluated it using CRFs.

as erroneous should have been detected exclusively in the main clauses, many of them were identified in the subordinated clauses where their use is allowed. AMBI and SING error labels for the combinator error pattern are required parsing results, and we used them for building training data. However, our CRF model uses only lexical and POS information and it was difficult to spot the correct range of arguments of the combinators without syntactic information. Actually, by using our program that we introduced for building training data, which also used syntactic analysis, we can obtain up to 82.47%. Results on AMBI and SING labels for combinators error patterns by our heuristic rule-based program are especially better than by the CRF model. Note that our heuristic rule-based program are overfitted to our training/evaluation data and the proposed CRF model is better for the general usage of the error annotation. However, dependency information is difficult to be integrated in the CRF model with dependency distance. Moreover, dependency results are not often correct for conjunction marks such as *or* and *and*, which we use for the combinator error pattern.

5 Conclusion and Future Perspectives

We have presented a linguistic model for the requirements quality analysis. A tool helping to improve the requirements authoring quality allows to reduce multiple proofreading steps which are time consuming and costly but crucial in the whole life cycle of the Requirement Engineering. The accuracy of this kind of tools is obviously very important as technical authors (users) can reject to use them once they generate false positives of more than 20%. To reduce the rate of false positives, the model that we developed is based on the error patterns manually identified in the linguistic framework of the requirements grammar.

The results of our first experiments on the model developed in this paper show promising improvements and some directions for the future work. First, we need to improve the results of CONF and AMBI error patterns by increasing the accuracy of the dependency parsing results. For CONF, we can limit the identification of modal *shall* followed by an infinitive verb to those only preceded by the subject of the main clause. For AMBI, We are planning to effectively integrate syntactic analysis results in our learning model. Second, we can enrich the error patterns depending on the lexical information by adding more lexical items into our model. Third, the five constraints and the corresponding rules presented in the requirements grammar do not cover all of the potential errors of the requirements authoring. It is necessary to revise and complete the rules of the requirements grammar in order to detect another error types: (1) detection of incomplete terms (use of "TBD", "TBC", "etc."...) for the Completeness, (2) detection of over-specified elements (design/solution parts (how the system realize the required action) included in the requirements) for the Singularity, (3) detection of grammatical errors (e.g. ditransitive verbs missing one of arguments like *the system shall send the received configuration*) for the Completeness. There are also another types of constraints more ambitious such as the problem of consistency and of redundancy between requirements or sets of the requirements. For those errors, we need to consider contextual information over a requirement sentence and to understand semantic meaning of the requirements and the relation between them. Finally, the current model are based on automatically annotated training data. We can improve its quality by adding another language processing models to get the better result on error filtering method. We may also add eventually manual verification and we leave them as our future work.

References

[Alred et al.2012] Gerald J. Alred, Charles T. Brusaw, and Walter E. Oliu. 2012. *The Handbook of Technical*

Writing. Bedford/St. Martin's, New York.

[Arora et al.2013] Chetan Arora, Mehrdad Sabetzadeh, Lionel Briand, Frank Zimmer, and Raul Gnaga. 2013. Automatic Checking of Conformance to Requirement Boilerplates via Text Chunking: An Industrial Case Study. In *2013 ACM / IEEE International Symposium on Empirical Software Engineering and Measurement*, pages 35–44, oct.

[Baroni et al.2009] Marco Baroni, Silvia Bernardini, Adriano Ferraresi, and Eros Zanchetta. 2009. The WaCky wide web: a collection of very large linguistically processed web-crawled corpora. *Language Resources and Evaluation*, 43(3):209–226.

[Berrocal Rojas and Barrantes Sliesarieva2010] Allan Berrocal Rojas and Elena Gabriela Barrantes Sliesarieva. 2010. Automated Detection of Language Issues Affecting Accuracy, Ambiguity and Verifiability in Software Requirements Written in Natural Language. In *Proceedings of the NAACL HLT 2010 Young Investigators Workshop on Computational Approaches to Languages of the Americas*, pages 100–108, Los Angeles, California. Association for Computational Linguistics.

[Berry et al.2003] Daniel M. Berry, Erik Kamsties, and Michael M. Krieger. 2003. From Contract Drafting to Software Specification: Linguistic Sources of Ambiguity.

[Bourque et al.2004] Pierre Bourque, Alain Abran, Juan Garbajosa, Gargi Keeni, Beijun Shen, Alain April, Antonia Bertolino, Durba Biswas, Nabendu Chaki, Roger Champagne, Christof Ebert, Pierce Gibbs, Mira Kajko-Mattsson, Gerald Kotonya, Eda Marchetti, James McDonald, Xin Peng, Annette Reilly, Pete Sawyer, Michael Siok, Yanchun Sun, and Hengming Zou. 2004. *Guide to the Software Engineering Body of Knowledge (SWEBOK Guide)*. IEEE Computer Society.

[Brants2000] Thorsten Brants. 2000. TnT – A Statistical Part-of-Speech Tagger. In *Proceedings of the Sixth Conference on Applied Natural Language Processing*, pages 224–231, Seattle, Washington, USA. Association for Computational Linguistics.

[Fabbrini et al.2001] Fabrizio Fabbrini, Mario Fusani, Stefania Gnesi, and Giuseppe Lami. 2001. An Automatic Quality Evaluation for Natural Language Requirements. In *in Proceedings of the Seventh International Workshop on RE: Foundation for Software Quality (REFSQ'2001*, pages 4–5, Interlaken, Switzerland.

[Firesmith2003] Donald Firesmith. 2003. Specifying Good Requirements. *Journal of Object Technology*, 2:77–87.

[Fuchs2012] Norbert E. Fuchs, 2012. *First-Order Reasoning for Attempto Controlled English*, pages 73–94. Springer Berlin Heidelberg, Berlin, Heidelberg.

[Galin2003] Daniel Galin. 2003. *Software Quality Assurance: From Theory to Implementation*. Pearson.

[Glas2002] Robert L. Glas. 2002. *Facts and Fallacies of Software Engineering*. Addison-Wesley Professional.

[Gnesi et al.2005] Stefania Gnesi, Fabrizio Fabbrini, Mario Fusani, and Gianluca Trentanni. 2005. An automatic tool for the analysis of natural language requirements. *CRL Publishing: Leicester*, 20:53–62.

[Grady2013] Jeffrey O. Grady. 2013. *System Requirements Analysis*. Elsevier.

[Hull et al.2011] Elizabeth Hull, Ken Jackson, and Jeremy Dick. 2011. *Requirements Engineering*. Springer-Verlag London.

[Kuhn2013] Tobias Kuhn. 2013. A Principled Approach to Grammars for Controlled Natural Languages and Predictive Editors. *Journal of Logic, Language and Information*, 22(1):33–70.

[Lavergne et al.2010] Thomas Lavergne, Olivier Cappé, and François Yvon. 2010. Practical Very Large Scale CRFs. In *Proceedings of the 48th Annual Meeting of the Association for Computational Linguistics*, pages 504–513, Uppsala, Sweden. Association for Computational Linguistics.

[Nivre et al.2006] Joakim Nivre, Johan Hall, and Jens Nilsson. 2006. MaltParser: A Data-Driven Parser-Generator for Dependency Parsing. In *Proceedings of the Fifth International Conference on Language Resources and Evaluation (LREC'06)*.

[Stecklein et al.2004] Jonette M. Stecklein, Jim Dabney, Brandon Dick, Bill Haskins, Randy Lovell, and Gregory Moroney. 2004. Error Cost Escalation Through the Project Life Cycle. In *Proceedings of the14th Annual International Symposium*, Toulouse, France.

[Weiss1990] Edmond H. Weiss. 1990. *100 Writing Remedies: Practical Exercises for Technical Writing*. Greenwood.

[White and Schwitter2009] Colin White and Rolf Schwitter. 2009. An Update on PENG Light. In Luiz Pizzato and Rolf Schwitter, editors, *Proceedings of the Australasian Language Technology Association Workshop*, pages 80–88, Sydney, Australia.

[Zapata Jaramillo2010] Carlos Mario Zapata Jaramillo. 2010. Computational Linguistics for helping Requirements Elicitation: a dream about Automated Software Development. In *Proceedings of the NAACL HLT 2010 Young Investigators Workshop on Computational Approaches to Languages of the Americas*, pages 117–124, Los Angeles, California. Association for Computational Linguistics.

Designing CzeDLex – A Lexicon of Czech Discourse Connectives

Jiří Mírovský, Pavlína Synková, Magdaléna Rysová, Lucie Poláková

Charles University in Prague, Czech Republic
Faculty of Mathematics and Physics
Institute of Formal and Applied Linguistics
{mirovsky|synkova|magdalena.rysova|polakova}@ufal.mff.cuni.cz

Abstract

We present a design for a new electronic lexicon of Czech discourse connectives. The data format and the annotation scheme are based on a study of similar existing resources, and we discuss arguments for choosing the data structure and selecting features of the lexicon entries. A special attention is paid to a consistent encoding of both primary and secondary connectives. The data itself comes from exploiting the Prague Dependency Treebank, a large treebank manually annotated with discourse relations.

1 Introduction

Electronic lexicons of discourse markers[1] are not only a useful tool in theoretical research of text coherence/cohesion, they may also help in practical tasks such as discourse parsing, disambiguation of non-connective vs. connective usages of discourse markers, determining semantic type of discourse relations the markers convey, and also in selecting the correct counterpart of a discourse marker in translation from one language to another. Generally, systematic information on discourse markers contributes to processing discourse relations and in that way it helps NLP applications such as machine translation, text generation, information extraction, and others (cf. e.g. Meyer et al. (2011), Stede (2014) or Lin et al. (2014)).

Our goal has been to design and create an electronic lexicon of Czech connectives, having in mind especially the following objectives:

- to contribute to the theoretical understanding of Czech connectives, and more generally, to understanding how text coherence/cohesion is established in Czech,
- to help in NLP tasks such as discourse processing, text generation and machine-translation, and
- to make the lexicon readable to a non-Czech speaker and linkable to existing lexicons in other languages.

Once an annotation scheme of a lexicon is established, there are several options how to actually build the lexicon, i.e. how to fill it with data, from consulting existing printed lexicons, to using translation from lexicons in other languages or even just parallel texts, to exploiting existing (preferably discourse-annotated) corpora in the given language. We have chosen the last option, as a large discourse-annotated treebank – the Prague Dependency Treebank (see Section 1.2) – is available for Czech, and we are currently in the process of entering the data into the lexicon.

The subsequent text is organized as follows: First, in the rest of Introduction, we give an overview of main existing electronic lexicons of discourse markers that served as inspiration for our own work, and describe shortly the Prague Dependency Treebank with focus on its dis-

[1] We use "discourse markers" as a broader term for expressions generally structuring discourse, and "discourse connectives" as a narrower term for expressions signalling semantico-pragmatic relations between two abstract objects – see Section 2.1.

course annotation. Section 2 starts with delimiting the class of expressions we are interested in, i.e. the definition of connectives, their division into primary and secondary ones, and how we understand the terms compound connectives and modified connectives. We discuss issues related to nesting all these types of connectives in the lexicon (including their non-connective usages), as well as issues related to placement of connectives in their arguments. In Section 3, we discuss the selection of data for the lexicon and present the data format and annotation scheme for CzeDLex on two examples, and then we conclude in Section 4.

1.1 Existing Lexicons

Nowadays there are many corpora annotated with discourse relations but electronic lexicons of discourse connectives are much less common. We mention the most important ones.

DiMLex is a lexicon of German discourse markers; it was first introduced in Stede and Umbach (1998) and Stede (2002)(by then it was focused on syntactic properties of the connectives) and recently updated (Scheffler and Stede, 2016) with the annotation of discourse types – senses – from the Penn Discourse Treebank 3.0 (PDTB 3.0) sense hierarchy.[2] It is a computer-oriented resource, encoded in XML, with the main practical purpose to help NLP applications such as text generation and text understanding. It currently covers 275 German connectives.

LexConn is a lexicon of French discourse connectives (Roze et al., 2012), consisting of 328 connectives with their morphological categories, syntactic properties and discourse relations they convey according to the SDRT framework (Asher and Lascarides, 2003). Similarly to DiMLex, it is also a computer-oriented resource, encoded in XML, with the main practical purpose to help in NLP tasks that involve discourse parsing.

DPDE (Diccionario de partículas discursivas del español) is a dictionary of Spanish discourse markers (Briz et al., 2003). It consists of 229 entries and for each of them, it provides a definition, translation, ambiguous meanings, prosody, position, syntax, partial synonyms, idioms, register, and non-DM uses. Given its format (only HTML online) and annotation scheme (properties of markers are defined in plain language), its purpose is mostly for theoretical research.

1.2 Prague Dependency Treebank

The Prague Dependency Treebank (PDT) represents a richly annotated corpus with a multilayer annotation of approx. 50 thousand sentences of Czech newspaper texts. It contains morphological information and two layers of syntactic annotation, both of them in a form of dependency trees.

Annotation of discourse relations in the PDT was carried out on top of the deep-syntax layer (tectogrammatics) and covers explicit discourse relations, i.e. discourse relations anchored by a surface present connective. For sense annotation, a modified version of the PDTB 2.0 taxonomy was used, see Zikánová et al. (2015). The annotation proceeded in two phases. The first phase involved primary connectives (expressions like *však* [*however*] or *proto* [*therefore*]), arguments of these relations were limited to structures governed by a finite verb (mainly clauses or sentences). This annotation was published in the PDT 3.0 (Bejček et al., 2013). In the second phase, secondary connectives (expressions like *z toho důvodu* [*for that reason*], *to znamená* [*it means*]) were covered; the annotation of secondary connectives involved also relations with nominal phrases as arguments. Its publication is in process.

2 Theoretical Aspects

A crucial issue for building a lexicon of discourse connectives is a delimitation of this category. Since CzeDLex is based on the annotation of discourse relations in the PDT, it adopts also the PDT approach to discourse connectives.

2.1 Theoretical Delimitation

In the PDT, a discourse connective is defined as a predicate of a binary relation opening two positions for two text spans as its arguments and

[2] The PDTB 3.0 sense hierarchy is to be published later this year, for the PDTB 2.0 sense hierarchy see e.g. Prasad et al. (2008).

signalling a semantic or pragmatic relation between them.[3]

The two connected text segments are defined according to Asher (1993) as abstract objects expressing events, states, situations, etc. Syntactically, abstract objects (discourse arguments) can be represented by various structures ranging from whole sentences or their combination, over simple clauses to participial and infinitive constructions and nominal phrases. In the PDT, annotation of discourse arguments was syntactically restricted to verbal arguments (i.e. whose basis is a finite verb).[4] The same restriction has been adopted also for CzeDLex.

Primary and secondary connectives

Discourse connectives in the PDT are divided into primary and secondary, according to Rysová and Rysová (2014). They differ especially in the degree of their grammaticalization. Primary connectives are rather short and grammaticalized expressions belonging to certain parts of speech (mostly conjunctions, particles and some types of adverbs), such as (in English[5]) *while, because, however, therefore.* On the other hand, secondary connectives are especially multiword phrases like *for this reason, to follow, due to this* etc. that are not yet fully grammaticalized (see also Rysová and Rysová (2015)).[6]

Since the PDT contains detailed annotation of both primary and secondary connectives, we include both of these types also into CzeDLex. However, primary and secondary connectives differ in many important aspects that need to be reflected in the lexicon design: lemmatization, syntactic characteristics, part-of-speech appurtenance, placement of the external argument and argument integration (i.e. placement of a connective in the argument).

[3] A similar approach was used in the PDTB, cf. Prasad et al. (2008).

[4] with the exception of secondary connectives

[5] For simplicity, in the subsequent text we often present – when it is sufficient – only English equivalents of Czech expressions.

[6] The annotation and description of primary connectives in the PDT is given in detail in Poláková (2015) and of secondary connectives in M. Rysová (2015).

Generally, the difficulty of secondary connectives is that many of them may be inflected (*for this reason – for these reasons*; *the condition is – the conditions were* etc.) and they exhibit – at least in Czech – a high degree of variation (*důvod je* vs. *důvodem je* [*the reason is*: nominative vs. instrumental], both variants in Czech are equal). See Sections 2.2, 2.4 and 2.5 below.

Compound and modified connectives

Discourse connectives may be further divided into the following categories: compound vs. single and modified vs. non-modified. Compound connectives consist of two or more connective words all participating on expressing the given discourse relation type. Compound connectives occur in a single argument (*a proto* [*and therefore*]) or they may form correlative pairs (*buď_nebo* [*either_or*]). A compound connective may express the same or different semantic type than its individual parts.

Modified connectives contain an expression (often of evaluative or modal nature) that further specifies/modifies the discourse relation, without changing its semantic type (*hlavně protože* [*mainly because*] or *možným důvodem je* [*the possible reason is*]).

To sum up, all members of compound connectives participate on expressing the particular discourse relation (e.g. both parts of *a proto* [*and therefore*] express together a relation of reason–result, and both parts of *buď_nebo* [*either_or*] express a relation of disjunctive alternative), while in modified connectives, the modification (e.g. *mainly* in *mainly because*) does not participate on expressing a discourse relation type (in our example reason–result) but it only modifies it (it expresses the intensity of the relation). For more details see M. Rysová (2015).

Non-connective usages

Most connective expressions (or, in case of secondary connectives, certain parts of them) exhibit a functional homonymy with expressions that have different functions in the text. The non-connective uses of these homonymous expressions can be categorized into several groups with specific properties:

- From the perspective of a discourse analysis defining a discourse argument as an abstract object (Asher, 1993), expressions connecting mere entities (*mum **and** dad*) are not considered discourse connectives.
- Expressions in the role of expressive particles, reaching almost the role of interjections, are not treated as discourse connectives. They may function in discourse structuring, possibly within the wider category of discourse markers but they do not connect two abstract objects in our sense (***Tak** co s tím, nová rado? [**So** what (do you do) about it, new council?]*).
- Expressions (homonyms of primary connectives) in the role of sentence constituents, mostly moreover in the rhematic part of the sentence, are not considered connectives[7] (*Vana plechová se zahřeje rychle a rychle zchladne, vana litinová se chová **naopak**. [A metallic bathtub gets heated quickly and quickly cools, a cast-iron bathtub behaves **otherwise**.]*).
- Expressions functioning as answer particles are not considered connectives (*Půjdeš tam? **Ovšem**. [Will you go there? **Of course**.]*)

For each lexicon entry in CzeDLex, in addition to the list of connective usages, non-connective usages of the expression/phrase are listed at level two of the lexicon structure (see Section 2.2 just below), along with their syntactic characteristics.[8]

2.2 Nesting

On the first level of the CzeDLex structure, entries are nested according to a lemma of the connective.[9]

Lemma for secondary connectives

Selecting a representative lemma for primary connectives is a straightforward decision but for secondary connectives, a suitable similar approach needs to be found. For example, there are many secondary connectives containing the word "reason" (*for this reason, that is the reason why, the reason is* etc.), and we consider the word "reason" their common "core" word. In our approach, we extract these "core" words of secondary connectives, which are mainly nouns (*reason, condition, conclusion* etc.), secondary prepositions (*due to, because of, thanks to* etc.) and verbs (*to precede, to conclude, to sum up* etc.), and treat these "core" words (their lemmas) as umbrella lemmas for all individual variants.

Level-two nesting

There are two main options for nesting level-two entries in the lexicon – according to a lemma with a PoS tag (this principle has been adopted e.g. in DiMLex) or according to a lemma combined with a discourse semantic type (similarly to LexConn). For CzeDLex, we have chosen the latter option for these reasons: (i) part-of-speech annotation of discourse connectives in the PDT is outdated, (ii) part-of-speech appurtenance for connectives and expressions homonymous with them is often questionable and (iii) in machine-translation systems, links between lexicon entries in the involved languages need to be tied to discourse semantic types (the same preference comes also from text generation tasks).

If we followed this rule strictly, the depth of the lexicon scheme for secondary connectives would increase to three levels, as secondary connectives usually form several different syntactic structures (which need to be captured in separate entries), while still conveying the same semantic discourse type. To keep the scheme of the lexicon simpler and more unified for primary and secondary connectives, we cluster the level-two entries for secondary connectives not only by the semantic discourse type but also by the syntactic structure of similar surface realizations

[7] Secondary connectives (or their parts) are always sentence constituents (in contrast to primary ones). However, their "core" words may also have a non-connective function – cf. *the suggestion was rejected for procedural **reasons**.*

[8] A detailed analysis of "degree of connectivity" of frequent Czech connectives according to the PDT 3.0 annotation can be found in Zikánová et al. (2015, pp. 161–162).

[9] We use the morphological lemma rather than the tectogrammatical lemma, as many connectives are not represented as nodes on the tectogrammatical layer of the PDT (thus they do not have a tectogrammatical lemma).

of the connective.

To describe all possible realizations (in the PDT) of a secondary connective that conform to the same syntactic structure (and thus fall into the same lexicon entry), we establish a general pattern for such a structure, expressed by a linear text notation of the dependency representation of the structure on the surface-syntax layer of the PDT – see e.g. the scheme *(anaph. Sb) Pred ([(Atr)] důvod.1,7) AuxC*[10] for realizations such as *to je důvod, proč*; *to byl hlavní důvod, proč*; *to je důvodem, proč* [all meaning *that is/was the (main) reason why*]. See another example in the XML element *schema_dep* in Section 3.2.2.

PoS for secondary connectives

Another issue concerns the part-of-speech appurtenance of discourse connectives. Whereas we may relatively easily define the part of speech for primary connectives, the situation with secondary connectives is less simple, as they form whole syntactic structures (like *under these conditions*). At level one of the lexicon, we only define the part-of-speech category of the "core" word (i.e. of the lemma), and for each individual variant of the secondary connective (represented at level two), we state the global syntactic characteristics of the whole expression (e.g. *under these conditions* – prepositional phrase), see the XML element *syntactic_characteristics* in Section 3.2.2.

Compound and modified connectives

Single connectives (such as *a* [*and*], *ale* [*but*], *protože* [*because*]), in combination with their individual semantic types, are in the lexicon always treated as separate entries.

Within compound connectives, only those expressing a semantic type different from those expressed by the members of the compound connective themselves have a separate entry (e.g. *i když* [lit. *also if*, meaning *even though*][11]). Other compound connectives (like *a proto* [*and therefore*], *i proto* [lit. *also therefore*]) are listed under a semantically "stronger" connective (e.g. *proto* [*therefore*]). Including compound connectives into the lexicon is important for NLP applications, as processing them separately by the individual parts might lead to incorrect results.

Modified connectives are not treated as separate entries in CzeDLex, as they do not change the semantic discourse type. Instead, the modifications (that occur in the PDT) are listed under the relevant non-modified connective.

2.3 Semantics of Arguments

From the semantic point of view, there is a difference between symmetric and asymmetric discourse relations. Whereas for symmetric relations, the general semantic characteristics is shared by both arguments, asymmetric discourse relations hold between arguments that reveal different semantic characteristics. For example, if the arguments are in the asymmetric relation of reason–result, one of them expresses a reason, the other one a result.[12]

Typically, a connective is characterized by its placement in one specific part of the relation it signals. For example, coordinating conjunction *tedy* [*thus*] signals a result, while *totiž* [*because*] signals a reason. In CzeDLex, this characteristics of connectives in asymmetric relations is captured in the XML element *arg_semantics* (see Section 3.2).

2.4 Position of the External Argument

A connective and its position not only help determine the semantics of the arguments (and the whole relation), but also positions of the arguments. This characteristics is given by part-of-speech appurtenance for almost all primary connectives in Czech. Coordinating conjunctions, adverbs and particles are placed in the

[10] Where *anaph. Sb* means an anaphoric subject, *Pred* is a predicate, *Atr* is an attribute, *důvod.1,7* means the word *důvod* [*reason*] in nominative or instrumental, *AuxC* is a subordinating conjunction; elements in square brackets [ ] are optional, parentheses ( ) mark syntactic dependencies.

[11] The single primary connective *i* [*also*] signals mostly a conjunction, *když* [*if*] signals mostly a condition and together they express a relation of concession.

[12] This (a)symmetry has to be addressed one way or another in any approach to discourse relations (see e.g. Prasad and Bunt, 2015; Sanders et al., 1992; Prasad et al., 2007).

linearly second argument (so the external argument has to be searched for in the previous text), while subordinating conjunctions are not specific in this respect – the external argument can be placed before or after the clause with a subordinating conjunction. There are however exceptions to this rule, for example the connective particle *nejenže* [lit. *not only that*] always signals the linearly first argument of the gradation relation.

It is therefore important to capture information about placement of the external argument of the relation in the lexicon. In CzeDLex, the XML element is called *ordering* (the label has been adopted from DiMLex) and carries a value expressing whether the external argument is in the previous context, the later context, or that both options are possible.[13]

2.5 Placement of a Connective in an Argument

According to their origin and functions, Czech connectives are placed at different positions in the argument. Only subordinating conjunctions and several prototypical coordinating conjunctions are placed at the beginning of a clause or sentence, but mostly, Czech connectives are placed elsewhere. Some of them obligatorily at the clitic, i.e. second position of the sentence (e.g. *však* [*however*]), but the position can also vary between first and second (e.g. *proto* [*therefore*] or *ale* [*but*]). A specific case is represented by so called focus particles, which signal the focus of the sentence and their placement thus varies according to information structure of the sentence.

The placement of the connective in an argument is captured in the XML element *integration* (the name taken again from DiMLex), with values for "first", "second", "first or second" or "any" position, and also "N/A" (non-applicable). The last value is used for secondary connectives represented by a whole clause.

[13] There is a special (fourth) value for those types of secondary connectives that occur entirely between arguments as a separate syntactic unit (like *Důvod je jednoduchý.* [*The reason is simple.*]).

3 CzeDLex

3.1 Data Selection

Entries for the Lexicon of Czech Discourse Connectives (CzeDLex) are being selected on the basis of the Prague Dependency Treebank, a corpus annotated with discourse relations (see Section 1.2). For the first version of CzeDLex, approx. 100 most common connectives will be processed. As the lexicon is intended to be used in NLP tasks, throughout the whole process – from designing the lexicon to selecting the connectives and their semantic types – we only use 9/10 of the PDT, leaving the predefined etest data unseen for allowing correct testing of applications that will use the lexicon in the future.

3.2 CzeDLex Annotation Scheme

The annotation scheme for the lexicon of Czech connectives is presented in this section on two commented examples: one primary connective and one secondary connective. For space restrictions, less important parts have been left out. We have chosen XML as the data format, following the examples of DiMLex and LexConn; it also simplifies integration into the PDT annotation framework (Pajas and Štěpánek, 2008).

3.2.1 A Primary Connective

The following is a shortened schema for a lexicon entry of a primary connective, demonstrated on the connective *tedy* [*so, therefore*].

```
<lemma id="l-tedy"> (a level-one entry)
  <text>tedy</text> (the lemma itself)
  <type>primary</type> (vs. secondary)
  <struct>single</struct>
      (vs. continuous, discontinuous, correlative)
  <variants>
    <variant register="informal">teda</variant>
  </variants>
  <connective_usages>
    (list of connective usages, see below)
  </connective_usages>
  <non-connective_usages>
    (list of non-connective usages)
  </non-connective_usages>
</lemma>
```

One of the connective usages is described in the following example. The discourse type represented by this level-two entry is reason–result.

```
<connective_usage id="c-tedy-reason">
  <discourse_type>reason-result</discourse_type>
  <gloss>proto</gloss>
  <english>so, therefore</english> (English transl.)
  <pos>conjunction</pos> (part of speech)
  <subpos>coord</subpos> (a detailed POS)
  <arg_semantics>result</arg_semantics>
    (the argument associated with the connective
     represents the "result" part of the relation)
  <ordering>2</ordering>
    (the (same) argument is always second in the text)
  <integration>first or second</integration>
    (position in the argument)
  <modifications> (list of modifications)
    (N/A for "tedy")
  </modifications>
  <compounds> (list of compounds)
    <compound struct="discontinuous">
      <orig>a tedy</orig>
      <english>and therefore</english>
    </compound>
  </compounds>
  <examples>
    (list of a few examples from the PDT, see below)
  </examples>
  <usage>standard</usage> (vs. rare)
  <register>neutral</register> (vs. e.g. formal)
  <pdt>
    (PDT-related info, e.g. POS and sub-POS according
     to the PDT, statistics etc.)
  </pdt>
</connective_usage>
```

The following is a slightly shortened PDT example of a connective usage of lemma *tedy* with discourse type reason–result:

```
<example>
  <orig>Přitom právě u dlouhodobějších investic,
    jako je stavba bytových domů, právní nejistota
    výrazně zvyšuje úroky z úvěrů, čímž snižuje
    nabídku. Legislativní činnost je tedy
    nejlevnější cestou, jak nabídku stimulovat, ...
  </orig>
  <english>
    But especially in long-term investments such as
    the construction of residential houses, legal
    uncertainty significantly increases the interest
    on loans, thereby reducing the supply.
    A legislative action is therefore the
    cheapest way to stimulate the supply.
  </english>
</example>
```

3.2.2 A Secondary Connective

The following is a shortened schema of a lexicon entry for a secondary connective, demonstrated on a connective with the core word *důvod* [*reason*]. The level-one entry is almost identical to a level-one entry of a primary connective, with the exception of the element *struct*, which – for secondary connectives – has been moved to level-two entries.

```
<lemma id="l-důvod">
  <text>důvod</text>
    (a lemma of the core word of the secondary conn.)
  <type>secondary</type> (vs. primary)
  <pos>noun</pos> (PoS of the core word)
  <connective_usages>
    (list of connective usages, see below)
  </connective_usages>
  <non-connective_usages>
    (list of non-connective usages)
  </non-connective_usages>
</lemma>
```

One of the connective usages is described in the following example. The discourse type represented by this level-two entry is reason–result. As for secondary connectives, there may be several level-two entries for the same discourse type, the identifiers (attribute id) carry a suffix number (-1, -2, etc.). Again, the level-two entry is almost identical to a level-two entry of a primary connective, with these exceptions: the *struct* element has been moved here from the level-one entry, part-of-speech elements have been replaced by *syntactic_characteristics* and *schema_dep* and complemented by the *realizations* element, which gives the most frequent examples of actual secondary connectives described by the dependency schema.

```
<connective_usage id="c-důvod-reason-1">
  <discourse_type>reason-result</discourse_type>
  <gloss>proto</gloss>
  <english>therefore</english>
  <syntactic_characteristics>
    prepositional phrase
  </syntactic_characteristics>
  <schema_dep>
    z ((anaph. Atr) důvod.2)
  </schema_dep>
```

```
<realizations>
  <realization>
    <orig>z tohoto důvodu</orig>
    <english>for this reason</english>
  </realization>
  <realization>
    <orig>z uvedených důvodů</orig>
    <english>for the stated reasons</english>
  </realization>
</realizations>
<struct>single</struct>
<arg_semantics>result</arg_semantics>
<ordering>2</ordering>
<integration>any</integration>
<modifications>
  <modification_type="eval">
    <orig>z tohoto prostého důvodu</orig>
    <english>for this simple reason</english>
  </modification>
  <modification_type="modal">
    <orig>z tohoto možného důvodu</orig>
    <english>for this possible reason</english>
  </modification>
</modifications>
<compounds>
  <compound struct="discontinuous">
    <orig>a z tohoto důvodu</orig>
    <english>and for this reason</english>
  </compound>
</compounds>
<examples>
  (list of a few examples from the PDT, see below)
</examples>
<usage>standard</usage> (vs. rare)
<register>neutral</register> (vs. e.g. formal)
<pdt>(PDT-related info, statistics)</pdt>
</connective_usage>
```

And a slightly simplified PDT example:

```
<example>
  <orig>S ohledem na toto ustanovení by se hrubé
    chování muselo týkat vaší osoby a nestačí pouze
    nevhodné zacházení s předmětem darovací smlouvy.
    Z tohoto důvodu by byla vaše žaloba na vrácení
    daru u soudu zamítnuta.
  </orig>
  <english>With regard to this regulation, the rough
    behaviour would have to involve your person and
    not simply improper handling of the subject of
    the donation agreement. For this reason, your
    legal action on the return of the donation with
    the court would be rejected.
  </english>
</example>
```

4 Conclusion

We have presented the design of CzeDLex – a Lexicon of Czech Discourse Connectives. It is the first lexicon of Czech connectives and its uniqueness also lies in the fact that it includes secondary connectives (existing lexicons of connectives for other languages do not cover expressions like *for this reason, to conclude* etc.).

We are currently in the process of filling the lexicon with data. The first version of CzeDLex will contain approx. 100 most frequent Czech discourse connectives according to the annotation of discourse relations in the PDT. Building the lexicon on the ground of a discourse-annotated corpus brings a certainty that the selection of the connectives and their coverage in the lexicon is to a certain degree representative but at the same time it sets limits on both these aspects, as the treebank consists of newspaper texts only and, although it is large for a manually annotated treebank, its size is still limited.

CzeDLex is built not only for theoretical purposes. Given its rich annotation of the properties of the connectives (including the general scheme for secondary connectives and inclusion of compound connectives), it may be useful also for NLP tasks that involve discourse parsing, for machine translation, and for text generation.

Our aim was also to make the lexicon readable for non-Czech speakers, and simplify its possible interlinking with lexicons in other languages, which we try to achieve by using both human and computer readable format and by providing English equivalents for all Czech entries, and also by providing comprehensive morphological, syntactic and other characteristics both for the primary and secondary connectives.

Acknowledgments

The authors gratefully acknowledge support from the Ministry of Education, Youth and Sports of the Czech Republic (projects COST-cz LD15052 and Kontakt LH14011). The research reported in the present contribution has been using language resources developed, stored and distributed by the LINDAT/CLARIN project of the Ministry (project LM2015071).

References

Nicolas Asher. 1993. *Reference to Abstract Objects in Discourse.* Kluwer Academic Publishers.

Nicolas Asher and Alex Lascarides. 2003. *Logics of Conversation.* Cambridge University Press.

Eduard Bejček, Eva Hajičová, Jan Hajič, Pavlína Jínová, Václava Kettnerová, Veronika Kolářová, Marie Mikulová, Jiří Mírovský, Anna Nedoluzhko, Jarmila Panevová, Lucie Poláková, Magda Ševčíková, Jan Štěpánek, and Šárka Zikánová. 2013. *Prague Dependency Treebank 3.0.* Data/software, Univerzita Karlova v Praze, MFF, ÚFAL, Prague, Czechia, http://ufal.mff.cuni.cz/pdt3.0/.

Antonio Briz, Salvador Pons Bordería, and José Portolés. 2003. *Diccionario de partículas discursivas del español.* Data/software, www.dpde.es. Online since 2003.

Ziheng Lin, Hwee Tou Ng and Min-Yen Kan. 2014. A PDTB-styled end-to-end discourse parser. *Natural Language Engineering, 20, 2,* pp. 151–184. Cambridge University Press.

Thomas Meyer, Andrei Popescu-Belis, Sandrine Zufferey and Bruno Cartoni. 2011. Multilingual annotation and disambiguation of discourse connectives for machine translation. *Proceedings of the SIGDIAL 2011 Conference*, pp. 194–203. Association for Computational Linguistics.

Petr Pajas, Jan Štěpánek. 2008. Recent Advances in a Feature-Rich Framework for Treebank Annotation. In: *Proceedings of the 22nd International Conference on Computational Linguistics.* Coling 2008 Organizing Committee, Manchester, UK.

Lucie Poláková 2015. *Discourse Relations in Czech.* Ph.D. Thesis. Charles University in Prague, Czechia.

Rashmi Prasad and Harry Bunt. 2015. Semantic relations in discourse: The current state of ISO 24617-8. *Proceedings of the 11th Joint ACL-ISO Workshop on Interoperable Semantic Annotation (ISA-11)*, pp. 80–92,

Rashmi Prasad and Nikhil Dinesh and Alan Lee and Eleni Miltsakaki and Livio Robaldo and Aravind Joshi and Bonnie Webber. The Penn Discourse Treebank 2.0. *Proceedings of LREC 2008*, pp. 2961–2968, Marrakech, Morocco.

Rashmi Prasad, Nikhil Dinesh, Alan Lee, Eleni Miltsakaki, Livio Robaldo, Aravind Joshi, and Bonnie Webber. 2008. The Penn Discourse Treebank 2.0. In: *Proceedings of the 6th International Conference on Language Resources and Evaluation (LREC'08).* European Language Resources Association, Marrakech, 2961–2968.

Rashmi Prasad, Eleni Miltsakaki, Nikhil Dinesh, Alan Lee, Aravind Joshi, Livio Robaldo, and Bonnie L. Webber. 2007. *The Penn Discourse Treebank 2.0 Annotation Manual.* Philadelphia: University of Pennsylvania.

Charlotte Roze, Laurence Danlos, and Philippe Muller. 2012. LEXCONN: A French Lexicon of Discourse Connectives. *Discours [En ligne], 10/2012*, http://discours.revues.org/8645.

Magdaléna Rysová and Kateřina Rysová. 2014. The Centre and Periphery of Discourse Connectives. In: *Proceedings of the 28th Pacific Asia Conference on Language, Information and Computing.* Bangkok, Thailand, 452–459.

Magdaléna Rysová and Kateřina Rysová. 2015. Secondary Connectives in the Prague Dependency Treebank. In: *Proceedings of the 3rd International Conference on Dependency Linguistics (Depling 2015).* Uppsala University, Sweden, 291–299.

Magdaléna Rysová. 2015. *Diskurzní konektory v češtině (Od centra k periferii)* [*Discourse Connectives in Czech (From Centre to Periphery)*]. Ph.D. Thesis. Charles University in Prague, Czechia.

Ted Sanders, Wilbert Spooren, and Leo Noordman. 1992. Toward a taxonomy of coherence relations. *Discourse processes. 15, 1,* Taylor & Francis.

Tatjana Scheffler and Manfred Stede. 2016. Adding Semantic Relations to a Large-Coverage Connective Lexicon of German. In: *Proceedings of the 10th International Conference on Language Resources and Evaluation (LREC 2016).* European Language Resources Association, Paris, France.

Manfred Stede and Carla Umbach. 1998. DiMLex: A Lexicon of Discourse Markers for Text Generation and Understanding In: *Proceedings of the 17th International Conference on Computational linguistics.* pp. 151–184. Association for Computational Linguistics.

Manfred Stede. 2002. DiMLex: A Lexical Approach to Discourse Markers In: *A. Lenci, V. Di Tomaso (eds.): Exploring the Lexicon - Theory and Computation.* Alessandria (Italy): Edizioni dell'Orso.

Manfred Stede. 2014. Resolving connective ambiguity: a prerequisite for discourse parsing. *The Pragmatics of Discourse Coherence.* Amsterdam: John Benjamins.

Šárka Zikánová, Eva Hajičová, Barbora Hladká, Pavlína Jínová, Jiří Mírovský, Anna Nedoluzhko, Lucie Poláková, Kateřina Rysová, Magdaléna Rysová, and Jan Václ. 2015. *Discourse and Coherence. From the Sentence Structure to Relations in Text,* Prague: ÚFAL, Charles University in Prague.

Transitivity in Light Verb Variations in Mandarin Chinese -- A Comparable Corpus-based Statistical Approach

Menghan Jiang, Dingxu Shi, Chu-Ren Huang
Department of CBS, The Hong Kong Polytechnic University
menghan.jiang@connect.polyu.hk;
{dingxu.shi, churen.huang}@polyu.edu.hk

Abstract

This paper adopts a comparable corpus-based approach to light verb variations in two varieties of Mandarin Chinese and proposes a transitivity (Hopper and Thompson 1980) based theoretical account. Light verbs are highly grammaticalized and lack strong collocation restrictions; hence it has been a challenge to empirical accounts. It is even more challenging to consider their variations between different varieties (e.g. Taiwan and Mainland Mandarin). This current study follows the research paradigm set up in Lin et al. (2014) for differentiating different light verbs and Huang et al. (2014) for automatic discovery of light verb variations. In our study, a corpus-based statistical approach is adopted to show that both internal variety differences between light verbs and external differences between different variants can be detected effectively. The distributional differences between Mainland and Taiwan can also shed light on the re-classification of syntactic types of the taken complement. We further argue that the variations in selection of arguments of light verb in two Mandarin variants can in fact be accounted for in terms of their different degree of transitivity. Higher degree of transitivity in Taiwan Mandarin in fact show that light verbs are less grammaticalized and hence consistent with the generalization that varieties away from the main speaking community should be more conservative.

1 Introduction

In modern Chinese, there exists a kind of semantically bleached verbs which are called light verbs. They are similar to English light verbs (e.g., take rest, give advice) in the sense that the light verb does not contain any eventive information and the predicative content mainly comes from its taken complement (e.g., Jespersen, 1955; Zhu, 1985) while the light verb itself may only contributes aspectual information. LVC in English has been comprehensively studied in both theoretical (e.g., Butt and Geuder 2001, Cattell, 1984) and computational approaches (e.g., Tu and Dan, 2001), while in Chinese, the identification and differentiation of LVC especially the LVC variations between different language varieties may be more complicated. Due to the semantic versatility, Chinese light verbs usually do not have strong collocation restrictions, e.g.,進行/加以/搞/做研究 *jinxng/jiayi yanjiu* 'do research'. However, collocation constraints are sometimes found with these light verbs, e.g., 進行/*加以 会议 *jinxing/*jiayi huiyi* 'have a conference'; ?進行/加以考慮 *?jinxing/jiayikaolv* 'give considerarion'. The challenge is even greater when we compare different variants of the Mandarin, i.e., Taiwan and Mainland Mandarin. Huang and Lin (2013) have found that even with the very limited collocation constraints, light verb variations still exist: Taiwan light verbs tend to take more types of NPs and even VPs as its complements, for instance, LVC like 進行處理臨時提案 *jinxing/chuli/linshi/ti'an* 'to process the supplementary proposal' can only be found in Taiwan corpus. We should also note that light verbs in Chinese can take both verbs, deverbal nouns, and eventive nouns, while the morphological status of these categories are typically unmarked (Lin et al., 2014), that may make the identification more complicated. For example, we have found several inconsistencies in the POS tagging for the taken complements. In"國家語委現代漢語通用平衡語料庫" (CNcorpus), when either "戰鬥" *zhandou* "battle" or "鬥爭" *douzheng* "fight" is used individually, it is annotated as a Verb. But if they appear after the light verb, the annotation results are sometimes confusing, as shown below:

1. a. 每日/nt 都/d 在/p 進行/v 劇烈/a 的/u/連綿/a 的/u 戰鬥/v

meiri douzai jinxing juliede lianmiande zhandou

"Every day they are having fierce and continuous battles."

b. 進行/v 了/u 堅決/a 的/u 鬥爭/n
jinxing le jianjue de douzheng
"had a resolute fight"

In 1a&b, both "戰鬥" *zhandou* "battle" and "鬥爭" *douzheng* "fight" are modified by the attribute in De construction, but with different tagging. The inconsistent annotation results may bring a variety of inconveniences for grammatical analyses.

Another difficulty for identifying and differentiating Chinese LVC is that in Chinese the difference between light verbs as well as variations are very subtle and complex to be observed, and also this kind of differences are more tend to be frequency or preference difference instead of grammaticality dichotomies which is unlikely to be studied by using the traditional approach. Therefore, in our study, to identify the subtle tendency difference between different light verbs as well as light verb variations, a statistical corpus-based approach based on annotated comparable corpus is adopted, following the research paradigm set up in Lin et al. (2014) and Huang et al. (2014). Our current study further show that the variation differences can further imply the transitivity difference between different speaking communities and this result is also consistent with the generalization that a smaller speaking community away from the main speaking community tends to be more conservative.

2 Methodology

2.1 Data collection

The data for this study is extracted from Annotated Chinese Gigaword corpus (Huang, 2009) which was collected and available from LDC and contains over 1.1 billion Chinese words, with 700 million characters from Taiwan Central News Agency and 400 million characters from Mainland Xinhua News Agency.

Basically, in our study we focus on two pairs of light verbs, 進行 *jinxing* "proceed" and 加以 *jiayi* "inflict", 做 *zuo* "do" and 搞 *gao* "do". These four are among the most frequently used light verbs in Chinese (Diao, 2004) and previous studies have conducted several studies on distinguishing these two pairs (e.g., Zhou, 1987; Diao, 2004) while no clear conclusion has been drawn yet.

About 400 sentences are randomly selected for each light verb, half from the Mainland Gigaword sub-corpus and the other from the Taiwan Gigaword sub-corpus, which resulted in 800 sentences in total.

2.2 Feature annotation

For each sentence, we manually annotated 13 features which may help to distinguish different light verbs in each variant as well as the light verb variations among different variants (Zhu, 1985; Cai, 1982; Huang et al., 1995 among others). The features cover semantic (e.g., the semantic type of taken complements), syntactic (e.g., the syntactic type of taken complements) as well as discourse (e.g., the connotation of the context) levels. The detailed annotation schema and examples are shown in **Appendix 1**. To facilitate the annotation as well as statistical analyses, most of the factors have binary choices (yes or no). The annotator is a trained expert on Chinese linguistics. Any ambiguous cases were discussed with another two experts in order to reach an agreement.

3 Data analysis

In our study, we used Chi-square test to test for the significance of the co-occurrence of each factor with each individual light verb. The tool we used is SPSS v.21. All the results are transformed (Standardized pearson residuals $e_{ij}>$ or $<$ 1.9 (Agresti 2011)) into signs. The results of Chi-square test show that both differences among light verbs and variation difference can be detected by our statistical method and the features we selected are also effective in making the distinction.

Basically, two kinds of comparisons from different dimensions were conducted in our study. One is the variety internal comparison, and we are going to examine the subtle difference within the same pair (e.g., between 進行 *jinxing* "proceed" and 加以 *jiayi* "inflict"). Another comparison is the variety external comparison, in which we can investigate the variation differences of the same light verb in different varieties.

3.1 Difference between light verbs

For the variety internal comparison within each light verb pairs, our results show that both pairs in both varieties can be differentiated by most of the annotated factors (i.e., those where they have contrasting positive/negative tendencies to appear (P-value<0.05)). We can take the Mainland data as an example, the Chi-square test results are shown in table below (some features which do not show significant correlation would be omitted in the table).

3.1.1 Differentiation between 進行 and 加以

Features		進行	加以
Complement Types	Event noun	+	-
	De-verbal noun	-	+
Event complement at subject position		+	-
Take aspectual marker (le)		+	-
Take marker (guo)		0	0
Durative event		+	-
Formal event		-	+
Psychological event		-	+
Event involving interaction of the agent and patient		+	-
Accomplishment event		-	+
Attributive of the complement		+	-
Connotation ofthe Complement	Positive	0	0
	Neutral	+	-
	Negative	-	+

Table 1.comparison between ML 进行 and 加以

According to table 1, 進行 *jinxing* and 加以 *jiayi* in Mainland can be differentiated by most of the factors. For example, Mainland 進行 *jinxing* "proceed" has a preference of taking Event Noun (e.g., 進行會議/賽事 *jinxing huiyi/saishi* "have a conference/play a game) as the complement while 加以 prefers to take verbs (e.g., 加以提高/修改 *jiayi tigao/xiugai* "to improve/revise"). 進行 differs from 加以 *jiayi* "inflict" in that it also has preference in taking aspectual marker le (進行了激烈的戰鬥 *jinxing le jilie de zhandou* /"have a fierce fight"), taking durative events (進行會議 *jinxing huiyi* "have a conference"), interactive events (e.g., 進行磋商 *jinxing cuoshang* "have a negotiation") and complements which have attributives (進行長時間的討論 *jinxing changshijiande taolun* "have a long-time discussion"), whereas 加以 *jiayi* "inflict" shows dis-preference over these features. In contrast, 加以 *jiayi* prefers to take psychological event as the complement (加以考慮 *jiayi kaolv* "give consideration") while 進行 does not (??進行考慮 *jinxing kaolv* "give consideration").

3.1.2 Difference between 做 and 搞

The light verbs 做 *zuo*"do" and 搞 *gao*"do"can also be differentiated effectively by using the same method, as shown below:

Features		做	搞
Complement Types	Event noun	+	-
	De-verbal noun	-	+
VO complement		0	0
Take aspectual marker (le)		+	-
Take aspectual marker (guo)		0	0
Durative event		0	0
Attributive of the complement		+	-
Connotation of the Complement	Positive	-	+
	Neutral	+	-
	Negative	-	+

Table 2.comparison between ML 做 and 搞

做 *zuo* "do" and 搞 *gao* "do" are also differed in POS feature in the sense that 做 *zuo* has the preference in taking Noun as the complement (e.g., 做工作/手術/活動 *zuo gongzuo/shoushu/huodong* "do job/operation/activity") while 搞 *gao* tends to take verbal complement (搞批發/改革 *gao pifa/gaige* "do wholescale trade/make reform"). Moreover, 做 *do* also significantly prefers the complements which have attributive (e.g., 做了很長時間的工作 *zuole henchang shijiande gongzuo* "have been working for a very long time") while 搞 *gao* shows the opposite preference.

3.2 Difference between different varieties

With respect to the external comparison of the same light verb in different varieties of Chinese, the result of statistical analyses can also present the tendency differences. As shown in the tables below,

3.2.1 进行 in Taiwan and Mainland

Features		ML	TW
Complement Types	Event noun	0	0
	De-verbal noun	0	0
	VP	-	+
VO complement		-	+
Take aspectual marker (le)		+	-
Take aspectual marker (guo)		0	0
Event involving interaction of the agent and patient		+	-
Connotation of the Complement	positive	+	-
	neutral	-	+
	negative	-	+

Table 3.comparisonbetween 进行 in ML and TW

As presented in table 3, the usage of 進行 *jinxing* in Mainland and Taiwan have differences at semantic, syntactic as well as discourse level. The most obvious difference is that the Taiwan 進行 *jinxing* can take VPs as the complement, as in 處理 臨時提案 *chuli linshi ti'an* "process the interim proposal". This specific usage of Taiwan might shed light on the classification of light verb complements. It may indicate different status of taken complements in each variety is located in the process of de-verbalization. We will discuss this in detail in the following section.

Also, the result demonstrates that TW 進行 *jinxing* is more likely to take VO compounds, as in 進行開票/投票 *jinxing kaipiao/toupiao* "ballot-counting/voting". With respect to the semantic property of the taken complement, 進行 *jinxing* in Mainland tends to co-occur more with interactive complements like 磋商/商討 *cuoshang/shangtao* "hold a negotiation".

3.2.2 加以 in Taiwan and Mainland

加以 *jiayi* shows the similar tendency as 進行 *jinxing* between Mainland and Taiwan, as shown in table 4.

Features		ML	TW
Complement Types	Event noun	0	0
	De-verbal noun	+	-
	VP	-	+
VO		-	+
Durative event		-	+
Formal event		0	0
Psychological event		+	-
Accomplishment event		+	-
Connotation of the Complement	positive	+	-
	neutral	0	0
	negative	0	0

Table 4.comparisonbetween 加以 in ML and TW

Similar with 進行 *jinxing*, 加以 *jiayi* in two varieties also differ in that TW 加以 *jiayi* has preference in taking VP and VO complements while 加以 *jiayi* in Mainland shows the opposite preference. The examples like 加以調整實用性 *jiayitiaozhengshiyongxing* "make adjustment to the practicability" can only be found in Taiwan data. And also, Mainland 加以 *jiayi* tends to co-occur more with psychological (e.g., 加以考慮 *jiayikaolv* "give consideration") and accomplishment (e.g., 加以澄清 *jiayi chengqing* "make clarification") event while Taiwan 加以 *jiayi* prefers durative events (e.g., 加以學習/瞭解 *jiayi xuexi/liaojie* "to learn").

3.2.3 做 zuo in Taiwan and Mainland

The variation difference of 做 *zuo* mainly lies in the constraints of the taken complements. Taiwan 做 *zuo* almost has no constraints in taking the complements while the complements of Mainland 做 *zuo* are relatively limited in types. Examples show that Taiwan 做 *zuo* can take a wide range of complements compared to Mainland 做. LVCs as 做人身攻擊 *zuo renshengongji* "make personal attack", 做環保 *zuo huanbao* "protecting the environment", 做 競 賽 *zuo jingsai* "have competition" can only be found in Taiwan data.

Features		ML	TW
Complement Types	Event noun	+	-
	De-verbal noun	-	+
Event complement at subject position		+	-
Take aspectual marker (le)		+	-
Take aspectual marker (guo)		0	0
Durative event		0	0
Formal event		-	+
Accomplishment event		-	+

Table 5.comparison between 做 in TW and ML

The table suggests that the light verb 做 *zuo* in Taiwan has the similar preference of taking V as the objects (same with 進行 *jinxing* and 加以 *jiayi*, e.g., 做**表示/考量** *zuo biaoshi/kaoliang* "make official statement/give consideration**)**, while Mainland 做 *zuo* is more likely to co-occur with event noun as 工作/活動/手術 *gongzuo/huodong/shoushu* "do work/activity/operation".

TW 做 is also likely to take formal event as the complement (政府對上述事件做表示 *zhengfu dui shangshu shijian zuobiaoshi* "the government made official statement for this affairs") while more informal complements can be found in Mainland usages (做小生意/買賣 *zuo xiaoshengyi/maimai* "doing small business").

3.2.4 搞 gaoin Taiwan and Mainland

The difference of 搞 *gao* in two varieties show the opposite tendency compare to the light verb 做 *zuo* in the sense that 搞 *gao* in Mainland can take a quite wide range of objects while in Taiwan, 搞 *gao* can only appears in political context with the negative meaning.

Features		ML	TW
Complement Types	Event noun	-	+
	De-verbal noun	+	-
Event complement at subject position		+	-
Take aspectual marker (le)		+	-
Formal event		-	+
Event involving interaction of the agent and patient		+	-
Accomplishment event		**0**	**0**
Attributive of the complement		+	-
Connotation of the Complement	positive	+	-
	neutral	+	-
	negative	-	+

Table 6.comparison between 搞 in TW and ML

As shown in table 6, the taken complement of Taiwan 搞 *gao* has significant correlation with the feature "negative context".

Examples like 搞**形式主義/和平演變/分裂/抹黑** *gao xingshizhuyi/hebingyanbian/fenlie/mohei* "take formalism approach/make peaceful evolution/cause state disruption/throw mud"are typical usages which are frequently appeared in Taiwan corpus. In contrast, Mainland 搞 *gao* can take a variety of complements, including both formal (搞國有企業經營 *gao guoyouqiye jingying* "managing state-owned enterprises") and informal event (搞批發 *gao pifa* "do wholescale trade"), interactive events (搞辯論 *gao bianlun* "engage in debate") and complements with attribute (搞了很長時間的科技承包 *gaole henchang shijiande keji chengbao* "begin technology contract manufacturing for a very long time"). Also, the polarity of the context for Mainland 搞 *gao* can be both positive (搞先進性學習 *gao xianjinxing xuexi* "learn about advanced nature").

In general, for 做 *zuo* and 搞 *gao* in both Mainland and Taiwan, we can summarize as the usage of Taiwan 做 *zuo* is semantically much lighter than its Mainland counterparts in the sense that it can take a much wider range of complements under different context, whereas in Mainland 搞 *gao* may be semantically more bleached than its Taiwan counterparts because Taiwan 搞 *gao* can barely be used in other context except for political context with the negative meaning.

4 The syntactic type of taken complement

Agreement has been reached that only a small part of noun can be taken by light verbs (e.g., 會議/賽事 *huiyi/saishi* "conference/competition") while most of the complements taken by 進行 *jinxing* are originally verbs (e.g., 進行研究/改革 *jinxing yanjiu/gaige* "do research/make reform"). But unlike common verb, these taken complements, being in the object position, has already possessed some properties of nominal phrase in terms of its syntactic behavior (e.g., Zhu, 1985). Evidence as shown below,

a. The eventive complement usually cannot take another object：*進行**研究**這份文檔 *jinxing yanjiu zhefen wendang* "conduct research on this document";
b. The eventive complement cannot be modified by adverbial directly：*進行**在會議中**研究 *jinxing za ihuiyizhong yanjiu* "do research on the conference"；

c. The complement can be modified by the attribute：進行**長達十年的**研究 *jinxing changda shiniande yanjiu* "conduct a long-term research"；
d. It can be questioned by 什麼 *shenme* "what" instead of 怎麼樣 *zenmeyang* "how": 在進行**什麼**？"What is being proceeded?" *在進行**怎麼樣**？*zai jinxing zenmeyang* "*How is being proceeded?"

Previous studies have numbers of debates on which syntactic type do these verbal-like complements belong to. Some studies consider the taken complement as a 名動詞/動名詞 "nominal verb" which has both nominal and verbal properties (e.g., Zhu, 1985; Chen, 1987) while others hold the opinion that the complement has already been transferred from the original verb to a typical noun through the process of nominalization (e.g., Xiao, 1955; Li, 1990).

However, in our study based on large corpora, we find that the actual usages may be much more complex than what has been presented in the previous studies, especially when we take the variation differences into consideration. In Taiwan corpus, light verbs can be followed by a variety of NPs (e.g., 進行議程/君子之爭 *jinxing yicheng/junzizhizheng* "to carry out the assembly's agenda/having a gentleman's dispute"). Besides, although previous studies all claim that the light verb cannot take a Verb-Object phrase as the complement (e.g., Zhu, 1985; Hu and Fan, 1994; Qiu, 1994; Du, 2011 among others), in Taiwan corpora we have found examples like 進行處理臨時提案 *jinxing chuli linshi ti'an* "process the interim proposal" in which the complements taken by 進行 and 加以 can be a VO phrase. And the VO phrase can even by modified by adverbial (2):

2. 政府目前正 進行 **對中非共和國**<u>提供養魚、養蝦的技術</u>.
   Zhengfu muqianzheng jinxing dui zhongfeigongheguo tigong yangyu yangxia de jishu
   "The government is now providing the technology of fish and shrimp farming for the Central Africa Republic."

This may pose a challenge to the traditional classification. Therefore, in our annotation standard, we distinguish there types of taken complements in terms of their syntactic types: event noun, de-verbal noun and VP. And our comparative study show that there are also distributional variation differences between different varieties of Mandarin Chinese.

Event noun refers to a subtype of noun which lexically encodes eventive information, including event structure and time (Wang et al, 2011). The proportion of taking a noun as the complement is relatively small (e.g., for 進行, about 20.1% in Mainland). Taiwan can take more types of NPs (e.g., 進行感恩之旅 *jinxing gananzhilv* "have thanksgiving trips") with a little bit lower frequency (18.87%). Since the definition of an event noun is clear, we mainly focus on differentiation of the other two types (de-verbal noun and VP).

In our proposal, we argue that "研究" *yanjiu*"research" in "進行可行性研究" *jinxing kexingxing yanjiu* "do research on the practicability" and "進行研究可行性" *jinxing yanjiu kexingxing* "do research on the practicability" belong to different syntactic types. Generally speaking, the "研究" *yanjiu* "research" in the former one can be considered as a de-verbal noun which has undergone the process of de-verbalization. While in "進行研究可行性" *jinxing yanjiu kexingxing* "do research on the practicability", "研究" *yanjiu* "research" should still be considered as typical verbs. The whole phrase should be a VP. We will illustrate this issue in detail.

Shi (2011) differentiates two kinds of eventive phrases which can appear in the object position, by using a set of syntactic tests.

3. a. 我們需要注意**環境保護**。
   Women xuyao zhuyi huanjing baohu
   "We need to pay attention to
   b. 我們需要注意**保護環境**。
   Women xuyao zhuyi baohu huanjing
   "We need to pay attention to environmental protection."

He argues that due to its internal nominal structure and the typical nominal syntactic behavior, 保護 *baohu* "protect" in sentence 3a should be considered as a Noun (can be modified by attribute). But in sentence 3b, "保護" *baohu* "protect" here still has syntactic behavior of verbs (e.g., can take object and complement). The whole phrase "保護環境" *baohu huanjing* "protect the environment" still has the verbal internal structure (V-O structure) and can be used as predicate as in "我們要保護環境" *women yao baohu huanjing* "We need to protect the environment." (Shi, 2011).

With respect to light verb constructions, the variation differences we have observed in our data can be well classified by this standard. For the usage of Mainland LVC, the patient can only appear before the eventive complement, either before the light verb (4a) or between light verb and the taken complement with DE (b), which shows the typical properties of a Noun.

4. a. 對分配制度進行改革
Dui fenpeizhidu jinxing gaige
"making reforms of distribution system"
b. 進行分配制度的改革
jinxing fenpeizhidu de gaige
"having reformation of distribution system"

But in Taiwan specific usage, the object "改革" *gaige* "reform" can be followed by the patient "分配制度" *fenpeizhidu* "distribution system" (5a), which shows that "改革" *gaige* "reform" here still remains the property of a typical verb of taking another object. Moreover, "改革分配制度" *gaige fenpeizhidu* "make reforms of distribution system" as a VO phrase is considered as a VP in the sense that it has the verbal internal structure (V-O structure) and can be used as predicate (政府改革分配制度 *zhengfu gaige fenpeizhidu* "government is making reforms of the distribution system"). And also, the whole VO phrase as a VP can be modified by adverbial (5b). Hence, we use "VP" to distinguish it from a de-verbalized Nominal Phrase (分配制度的**改革** *fenpeizhidu de gaige* "the reformation of distribution system").

5. a. 進行改革分配制度
Jinxing gaige fenpeizhidu
"to make reforms of distribution system"
b. 政府目前正進行對有關部門改革分配制度
zhengfu muqian zheng jinxing dui youguanbumen gaige fenpeizhidu
"The government now is making reforms of distribution system in all relevant departments."

In this regard, we adopt Shi(2011)'s analysis and treat the 改革 *gaige* "reform" in mainland usage as a de-verbal noun which has been transferred from the verb through the process of de-verbalization. While in Taiwan specific usage, "改革" *gaige* "reform" keeps the verbal characteristic of taking another object (e.g., 進行改革分配制度 *jinxing gaige fenpeizhidu* "make reforms of distribution system"). Moreover, we have also found examples are showing that in Taiwan usages, the when eventive complement is modified by a prepositional structure, de is not always necessary (6).

6. . 進行 對大陸宣傳.
Jinxing dui dalu xuanchuan
"conduct propaganda to Mainland"

While in Mainland, in this context, "de" has to appear to license the sentence (e.g., 進行對大陸**的**宣傳 *jinxing dui dalu de xuanchuan* "conduct propaganda to Mainland"). As prepositional structure cannot modify an NP directly without de (e.g., Huang and Liao, 2007), what we found in Taiwan data is another evidence to prove that the taken complement in Taiwan usage can be a real verb.

In our study, we clearly differentiate three types of taken complements: event noun, de-verbal noun and VP which can cover all the examples we have observed in the corpus. This may also help with the annotation standard for POS tagging in the corpus. Back to the problematic annotation result we have mentioned in 1a and 1b, it would be very clear according to our analysis. Both "戰鬥" *zhandou* "battle" and "鬥爭" *douzheng* "fight" here should be treated as a de-verbal noun. But if they are followed by another object, it should be treated as a verb.

One thing should be addressed is that in Taiwan corpus, both constructions are commonly used, i.e., the patient can front the complement (進行可行性研究 *jinxing kexingxing yanjiu* "conduct research on the practicability") as well as follow it (進行研究可行性" *jinxing yanjiu kexingxing* "conduct research on the practicability") while in Mainland only the former construction is acceptable. This displays that Taiwan light verb has less constraints in taking the complements (can take both NP and VP, with and without de). There are more alternative patterns for LVC in Taiwan. Also, for the examples which VPs are taken as the complements, light verbs can be omitted without changing the grammatical acceptability of the sentences. The light verb itself can be totally redundant. As shown below:

7. a. 先 (進行)調整 國內有關法律以做好配合歐盟司法合作案件

Xian (jinxing) tiaozheng guonei youguan falv yi peihe oumeng sifa hezuo anjian

"make adjustment on relevant laws in order to cooperate with EU judicial cooperation cases"

In contrast, in Mainland usages, although light verb does not contribute to the eventive information, it is still compulsory in order to licenses the sentences structure.

b.*政府正對少年兒童 (進行) 正確消費教育

Zhengfu zhengdui shaonianertong (jinxing) zhengque xiaofei jiaoyu

"The government is educating the young children about consumption view."

5 Transitivity in Light Verb Variations

Based on their distributional differences in syntactic type of the taken complements between Taiwan and Mainland Mandarin, we further argue that the light verb itself may differ in its degree of transitivity between these two varieties. Taiwan light verbs may have a higher degree of transitivity compared to its Mainland counterparts. The most obvious evidence is that Taiwan light verbs have the tendency of taking more types of NP and VPs as the complements with less collocation constraints. It is 'more transitive' in the sense that it is more likely to be used transitively in different contexts.

Besides this, the semantic properties of the taken complements also demonstrate the higher transitivity of Taiwan light verbs. Hopper and Thompson (1980) have proposed 10 parameters to identify the degree of transitivity. According them, an action can be easier transfer to a patient which is individuated, Taiwan and Mainland light verbs do show variations in this property. Both previous study (Huang and Lin, 2013) and our data show that in Taiwan corpus, light verbs can be followed by more types of event nouns (e.g., 進行議程/君子之爭 *jinxing yicheng/junzizhizheng* "to carry out the assembly's agenda/having a gentleman's dispute"), this may indicate that the complements of Taiwan light verbs tend to be more highly individuated. Since the event noun, compared to either de-verbal noun or VP, may have more 'nouny' or 'referential' property, which may refer to higher degree of individuality. Also, as we have shown in section 3 and 4, Taiwan light verb has the preference of taking VP as the complements while the Mainland counterparts prefer de-verbal nouns. VP like "改革分配制度" compared to the de-verbal noun "改革", is obviously higher in individuality as the patient is overt. Also, as the patient is already there, the affectedness of the objects in Taiwan preference is also higher. These two both indicate the higher transitivity of Taiwan light verbs.

Another important issue we would like to address is that the higher degree of transitivity in Taiwan Mandarin in fact show that Taiwan light verbs are less grammaticalized, hence more 'verbal' and in fact more conservative in terms of bleaching of verbal properties. This is consistent with the generalization that varieties away from the main speaking community should be more conservative.

6 Conclusion

In the current study, we have showed that our comparable corpus-based statistical approach can identify comparative differences which are challenging for human analysis. Either internal comparison within one variety or external comparison between different varieties can be differentiated effectively. Furthermore, the semantic and syntactic feature set we used in our study could also be used for future studies on other light verbs as well as other lexical categories.

Based on statistical result, we also argue that the variation difference in collocation may due to their variation in the degree of transitivity. , Moreover, the higher transitivity of Taiwan light verbs also indicates the conservatism of Mandarin in Taiwan which is consistent with the generalization that the languages in immigrant speaking communities tend to be more conservative.

Acknowledgements

The work is supported by a General Research Fund (GRF) sponsored by the Research Grants Council (Project no. 543512).

References:

Agresti, A., &Kateri, M. (2011).*Categoricaldata analysis*.Springer BerlinHeidelberg.

Butt, M., &Geuder, W. (2001). On the (semi) lexical status of light verbs.*Semi-lexical Categories*, 323-370.

Cai, Wenlan. (1982). Issues on the Complement of 'jinxing' ("進行"帶賓問題).*Chinese Language Learning (漢語學習)* (3), 7-11.

Cattell, R. 1984. *Composite Predicates in English.Syntax and Semantics*. 17. Sydney: Academic Press. Australia.

Chen, Ningping. 1987. The Expansion of Modern Chinese Noun Class (現代漢語名詞類的擴大). *Studies of the Chinese Language (中國語文)* (5).

Diao, Yanbin. 2004. *Research on Delexical Verb in Modern Chinese (現代漢語虛義動詞研究)*. Dalian: Liaoning Normal University Press.

Du, Quner. 2010. *A Tentative Study on Dummy Verbs ofContemporary Chinese Language (現代漢語形式動詞研究)*. Shanghai: Shanghai Normal University.

Hopper, P. J., & Thompson, S. A. (1980).Transitivity in grammar and discourse.*Language*, 251-299.

Hu, Yushu& Xiao Fan. 1995. *Research on Verbs (動詞研究)*. Kaifeng: Henan University Press.

Huang Borong and Liao Xuduo (2007).*Modern Chinese*. Beijing Higher Education Press.

Huang, Chu-Ren. 2009. *Tagged Chinese Gigaword Version 2.0*. Philadelphia: Lexical Data Consortium, University of Pennsylvania. ISBN 1-58563-516-2

Huang, Chu-Ren and Jingxia Lin. (2013).The orderingof Mandarin Chinese light verbs.*Proceedings of the 13th Chinese Lexical Semantics Workshop*. D. Ji andG. Xiao (Eds.): CLSW 2012, LNAI 7717, pp. 728-735. Heidelberg: Springer.

Huang Chu-Ren, Jingxia Lin, and Huarui Zhang (2013).World Chineses based on comparable corpus: *Thecase of grammatical variations of jinxing. 《澳門語言文化研究》*, 397-414.

Huang, Chu-Ren, Lin, Jingxia, and Menghan Jiang and Hongzhi Xu.(2014). Corpus-based Study and Identification of Mandarin Chinese Light Verb Variations.*The Workshop on Applying NLP Tools to Similar Languages, Variations, and Dialects (VarDial)*, at the 25th International Conference on Computational Linguistics. Dublin, Ireland. 23 August.

Institute of Applied Linguistic Ministry of Education.(教育部語言文字應用研究所計算語言學研究室). 2009. *Introduction to CN corpus (國家語委語料庫科研成果簡介)*. [EB/ OL] [2007 - 10 - 15] . www. china2languange.gov. cn.

Jespersen, O. (1954). *A Modern English Grammar Vol 3 Syntax*. George Allen & Unwin Limited.

Li Linding. (1990). *Verbs in Modern Chinese (現代漢語動詞)*. China Social Science Press.

Lin, Jingxia, Hongzhi Xu, Menghan Jiang and Chu-Ren Huang.(2014). Annotation and Classification of Light Verbs and Light Verb Variations in Mandarin Chinese.*The Workshop on Lexical and Grammatical Resources for Language Processing (LG-LP 2014)*, the 25th International Conference on Computational Linguistics. Dublin, Ireland. 24 August.

QiuRongtang. (1994). Doubts on Nominal Verbs (名動詞質疑------評朱德熙先生關於名動詞的說法). *Chinese Learning (漢語學習)*, (6), 15-20.

Shi Dingxu. (2011). *Nouns and Nominals.(名詞和名詞性成分)*.Peking University Press.

Tu, Yuancheng and Dan Roth. 2011. Learning English light verb constructions: Contextual or statistical. In *Proceedings of the Workshop on Multiword Expressions: from Parsing and Generation to the Real World*. Association for Computational Linguistics.

Wang, S., & Huang, C. R. (2011).CompoundEvent Nouns of the'Modifier-head'Type inMandarin Chinese.*In PACLIC* (pp. 511-518).

Xiao Fu. (1955). Onlight verb jinxing ("進行"). *Chinese Knowledge (語文知識)*.

Zhou, Gang. (1987). Subdivision of Dummy Verbs(形式動詞的次分類).*Chinese LanguageLearning (漢語學習)*, 1, 11-14.

Zhu, Dexi. (1985). Dummy Verbs and NV inModern Chinese(现代書面漢語里的虛化動詞和名動詞).Journal of Peking University(Humanities and Social Sciences) *(北京大學學報(哲學社會科學版))*, 5, 1-6

Appendix A: Annotation schema for LVC

Feature	example
1. occur with other light verbs **Yes or no**	開始進行討論 ***kaishi*** *jinxing taolun*'start to discuss'
2. the complement of a light verb is in the V(erb)-O(bject) form **Yes or no**	進行投票 *jinxing* ***tou-piao*** proceed cast-ticket 'to vote'
3. take aspectual marker **Zhe, le, guo or no**	ASP.zhe/le/guo (進行著/了/過戰鬥 *jinxing-* ***zhe/le/guo****zhandou* 'is fighting'/have fight/fight)
4. Event complement of a light verb is in subject position **Yes or no**	比賽在學校進行 ***bisai****zaixuexiao jinxing* game at school proceed 'The game was held at the school')
5. The part-of-speech of taken complement **Event noun, deverbal noun or VP**	Event Noun/de-verbal noun (進行戰爭/戰鬥 *jinxing* ***zhanzheng/ zhandou***'tofight') VP (**進行處理臨時提案** jinxing **chulilinshiti'an** 'process interim proposal'
6.the complement is a Spontaneous/ controllable event **Yes or no**	**進行投票** jin4xing2/tou2piao4 'to vote'
7. the complement is durative event **Yes or no**	進行戰鬥 *jinxing* ***zhandou*** 'to fight'
8. the complement: is formal event **Yes or no**	進行國事訪問 *jinxing* ***guoshifangwen*** 'to pay a state visit'
9. the complement is psychological event **Yes or no**	加以反省 *jiayi****fanxing***'to retrospect')
10. the event denoted by the complement involves interaction **Yes or no**	進行討論 *jinxing* ***taolun***'to discuss'
11. the complement is accomplishment event **Yes or no**	進行解決 *jinxing* ***jiejue***'to solve'
12. Connotation of the Complement **Negative, neutral or positive**	進行破壞 (negative) *Jin4xing2/po4huai4* 'do harm to' 進行表揚 (positive) Jin4xing2/biaoyang2 'speak highly of'
13. Attributive of the complement **Yes or no**	進行一次長達八小時的比賽 *jin4xing2/bi3sai4* 'have an eight-hour competition'

The Interaction between SFPs and Adverbs in Mandarin Chinese —A Corpus-Based Approach

Yifan He
Department of Chinese and Bilingual Studies
The Hong Kong Polytechnic University
11 Yuk Choi Road, Hung Hom, Hong Kong
yifanhe324@yahoo.com.hk

Abstract

This paper proposes a new methodology in investigating the semantic and pragmatic properties of SFPs in Mandarin Chinese. A case study of the interaction and correlation between SFP-*Ne* and SpOAs--*Shenzhi, Qishi,* and *Nanguai* has been conducted. Two semantic features of [+unexpectedness] and [+intersubjectivity] have been summarized on SFP-*Ne*.

1 Introduction

Research on Sentence Final Particles (SFPs henceforth) has been a long-held issue in the field of Chinese linguistics. A voluminous body of literature has been devoted to the study of structural properties, historical development as well as the semantic or pragmatic properties of SFPs. Zhu (1982: 208) accurately observes the hierarchical structure of SFPs and proposes a three layer classification on them, which include: 1) Tense and Aspectual Information, e.g. *Le, Laizhe, Ne*$_1$; 2) Sentence Type Marker, e.g. *Ma, Ba, Ne*$_2$; 3) Speaker's Attitude, e.g. *Ou, A, Ne*$_3$. Three senses of *Ne* are listed in (1)-(3) and this paper concentrates on the outmost layer of *Ne*$_3$.[1]

(1) Ta1 zai jia kan dianshi ne.
He PROG home look television *ne.*
He is watching television at home.

(2) Ni mama ne?
You mum *ne*
Where is your mum?

(3)Ta chi le shi wan mifan ne.
He eat PERF 10 CL rice *ne.*
He has eaten ten bowls of rice.

Previous research on SFPs focuses on *Ne* alone, seldom do they take other constituents within the sentence into consideration. Moreover, the authors only explain the few examples they listed on the papers, seldom do the corpora data are involved.

According to our corpus investigation, we find the interaction and correlation between certain adverbs, namely, Speaker-oriented Adverbs (SpOAs henceforth) and SFP-*Ne* are not random. The goal of this research is to gain a comprehensive picture of the actual use of *Ne* and to unveil the mechanism of interaction between SpOAs and SFP-*Ne.*

2 Background Literature

2.1 Review on SFP-*Ne*

Previous research on SFP-*Ne* can be summarized as following two opposite directions, as Wu (2005: 48) put it, one is the "Meaning Maximalist" and the other is the "Meaning Minimalist". The former (Chao, 1968; Chu 1985) would enumerate all the possible meanings of SFP-*Ne* in the descriptive tradition, while the latter (Alleton, 1981; Li and Thompson,1981; King, 1986; Shao, 1996; Wu, 2005; Constant, 2014) endeavors to extract a general, unified core meaning or function of SFP-*Ne*. We take the basic stand of the latter and argue that the seemingly bewildering uses of SFP-*Ne* are in fact contextually derived.

[1] All the SFP-*Ne* below, if not specified, refers to *Ne*$_3$. The abbreviations used in this paper are glossed as follows: PROG: progressive aspect marker; CL: classifier; NEG: negative morpheme; PERF: perfective aspect marker. BI: comparative morpheme. DE: prenominal modifier maker, post-verbal resultative marker.

2.2 Review on SpOAs

The term of SpOAs, to the best of my knowledge, was firstly proposed by Jackendoff (1972: 56). He treats SpOAs as sentential adverbs, which express speaker's attitude or evaluation towards the propositional content. Later on, scholars (Bellert, 1977; Nilsen, 2004; Ernst, 2008, 2009) unanimously agree that SpOAs are used by the speaker to express his/her attitude or evaluation towards the proposition, or to be more specific, they refer to speaker's commitment to the truth of the proposition.

Review on the SFP-*Ne* and SpOAs indicates that both of them, at the semantic level, are used by the speaker to express his/her attitude towards the propositional content. And at the syntactic level, they are situated at the higher, periphery positions above the clause. Therefore it's reasonable and logical for us to investigate their correlation and interaction.

3 Preliminary Observation on *Ne*

3.1 Two Features

To begin with, we start with the minimal pair comparison between sentences with SFP-*Ne* and without SFP-*Ne*. [2]

(4) a. A: Zhe jian qunzi duo shao qian?
This CL dress more little money
How much is this dress?
B: san wan
30,000 (RMB)
B: san wan ne.
30,000 ne.(RMB)

b. A: Ta jia hen qiong, ni jiu
He family very poor, you then
bu yao gen ta laiwang
NEG want with he contact.
His family is very poor, so you'd better not have contact with him anymore.
B: Ta jia you ershi tao fang
He family have twenty CL house
His family owns twenty houses.
B: Ta jia you ershi tao
B: He family have twenty CL
Fang ne.
House *ne.*
His family owns twenty houses. (To your surprise)

[2] All the examples, if not specified, come from the CCL or BCC corpus.

In (4a), The first answer without *Ne* is just a statement of observation, of the fact that the cost of this dress is 30000 RMB. When *Ne* is added at the end, the speaker is informing or reminding the hearer of this unexpected or surprising cost of 30000 RMB for a single dress;

The same applies to (4b) as well, the first answer without *Ne* indicates a basic fact that "twenty houses are owned by his family." When *Ne* is appended at the end, the speaker reminds the hearer that the new information of owning twenty houses is unexpected to the hearer and the speaker to some extent is persuading the hearer to accept their relationship.

We further test the unexpectedness triggered by *Ne* by observing the co-occurrence between certain Chinese idioms with *Ne.*

(5) a. Zhong-suo-zhou-zhi, diqiu wei
As_everyone_knows, Earth surround
zhe taiyang zhuan (*ne)
ASP Sun revolve.(**ne*).
As everyone knows, the Earth revolves around the Sun.

b. Su hua shuo, meiyou
General utterance speak, NEG
Guiju bu cheng fang yuan (*ne).
rule, NEG become square circle (**ne*)
As old saying goes, no rule, no proper practices.

The idioms of "*zhong-suo-zhou-zhi* (As everyone knows)" and "*su-hua-huo* (As old sayings goes)" all indicate old information or the propositions follow it must be in line with the previous expectation, and hence the semantic clashes arises when *Ne* triggers the unexpected information, therefore it is infelicitous for *Ne* to appear at the end of the sentence.

We may summarize here that *Ne* is used to trigger unexpected information. It has the semantic feature of [+Unexpectedness].

We also find that *Ne* in general is used in interactive context, when the speaker takes the hearer's attention or attitude into consideration. This coincides with the notion of "Intersubjectivity" proposed by Traugott and Dasher (2001).

The Intersubjectivity encoded in *Ne* can be proved by the co-occurrence between degree modifier "*Ke* (so/such)", "*Zhen* (really/truly)" and "*Tai* (excessively/very)" and SFPs. We investigate the Chinese corpus created by center for Chinese Linguistics at Peking University (CCL in abbreviation) and all the data is shown in the figures below.

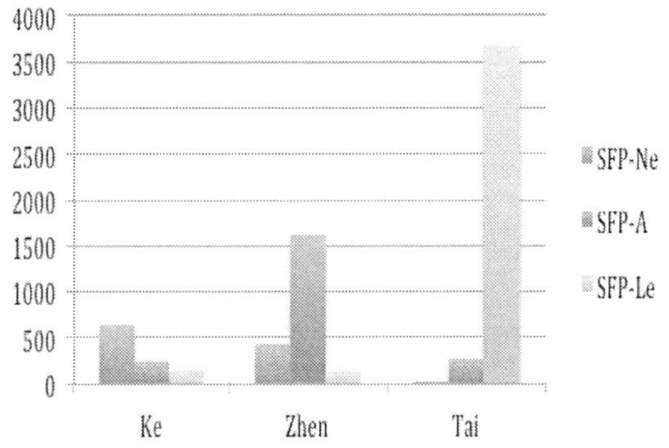

Figure1 Frequencies of the co-occurrence between Degree Modifiers and SFPs in CCL

Both corpora data indicate that *Ke* is in high frequency of co-occurring with *Ne,* whereas *Zhen* and *Tai* co-occurs with *A* and *Le* respectively. Typical examples of each are illustrated in (6).

(6) a. Xianggang xiatian ke re ne.
Hong Kong summer so hot *ne.*
It is so hot in summer in Hong Kong.

b. Xianggang xiatian zhen re a
Hong Kong summer really hot *a.*
It is really hot in summer in Hong Kong.

c. Xianggang xiatian tai re le .
Hong Kong summer very hot *le.*
It is excessively hot in summer in Hong Kong.

With respect to the "*Ke* X *Ne*" construction, we find the "X" can be gradable adjectives, psychological verbs and measurable verb phrases, which are listed in (7)-(9).

(7) "Jiaqian ke gui ne." ma wei shuo.
Price so expensive *ne.* Ma Wei speak
"It costs a lot." said Ma Wei.

(8) Women lingdao duiyu jiashu de jiating
We leader for subordinate DE family
wenti ke guanxin ne.
problem so care *ne.*
Our leader cares a lot about his subordinates' family issues.

(9) Nongchang jin wan zhe ge dianying
Farm today night this CL movie
Ke kai yanjie ne.
So open field of vision *ne.*
You may watch this movie tonight in the farm. It's quite eye-opening.

Ke here not only marks the degree of the predicate, but more importantly, it triggers the speech participants' expectation and assumption. This interactional context and intersubjectivity information need to be marked by SFP-*Ne.*

To sum up, based on our discussion in section 3, two semantic features can be summarized on SFP-*Ne,* one is the unexpectedness, the other is the intersujectivity.

The following co-occurrence data between certain SpOAs and SFP-*Ne* will further confirm our preliminary prediction.

3.2 Co-occurrence data

Chinese SpOAs forms a heterogeneous group. Due to the limit of space, we select twenty typical examples of disyllabic SpOAs from each category and investigate their interaction and correlation with SFP-*Ne* in the CCL and BCC[3] corpus respectively.

SpOAs	SFP-*Ne*			
	CCL		BCC	
	Tokens	%	Tokens	%
1.*Queshi* (Truly)	20	1.78	75	2.08

[3] BCC corpus is constructed by Beijing Language and Cultural University. The corpus has approximately 15 billion characters. See http://bcc.blcu.edu.cn
in the table refers to the absent of relevant data

2.*Genben* (Thoroughly)	4	0.35	6	0.17
3. *Jiujing* (On earth)	#	#	#	#
4.*Nanguai* (No wonder)	74	6.61	716	19.83
5. *Benlai* (Originally)	3	0.26	10	0.28
6. *Yiding* (Definitely)	6	0.53	8	0.22
7. *Dagai* (Probably)	15	1.34	5	0.14
8.*Qishi* (Actually)	538	48.03	1781	49.32
9. *Fanzheng* (In any case)	10	0.90	3	0.08
10.*Mingming* (Obviously)	#	#	4	0.11
11. *Yexu* (Maybe)	35	3.12	130	3.54
12. *Haoxiang* (Seem)	5	0.45	25	0.69
13. *Juran* (Surprisingly)	8	0.71	110	3.05
14. *Xingkui* (Fortunately)	2	0.18	5	0.14
15. *Shenz*hi (Even)	377	33.76	647	17.92
16. *Pianpian* (Persistently)	2	0.17	20	0.55
17. *Zhenghao* (Just right)	4	0.36	42	1.16
18. *Guoran* (As expected)	#	#	12	0.33
19. *Jianzhi* (Simply)	16	1.43	10	0.28
20. *Qiahao* (Just in time)	1	0.09	2	0.05
Total	1120		3611	

Table 1 Distribution of co-occurrence between SpOAs and SFP-*Ne*

Table 1 displays the distribution of the Chinese SpOAs along with SFP-*Ne* in both the CCL and BCC corpora. Corpus data clearly prove that co-occurrence between SpOAs and SFP-*Ne* is not random, certain adverbs are in high frequency of co-occurring with *Ne* while others never co-occur with *Ne.* Among all these twenty SpOAs, the top three adverbs that are in high frequency of co-occurrence are *shenzhi, qishi* and *nanguai.* Despite the seemingly disparate meanings and functions of these three SpOAs, we assume they are fundamentally linked by certain common features, and this explains their co-occurrence with SFP-*Ne.*

4 Co-occurrence between *Shenzhi, Qishi, Nanguai* and *Ne.*

4.1 *Shenzhi* and *Ne*

Shenzhi is a commonly-used adverb in Chinese, it in general triggers an additive ordering and designates the boundary information on the scale. Typical example of numeral ordering is illustrated below,

(10) Yang haizi zhe ge zeren,
Raise child this CL responsibility,
Hui peiban ni dao ershi
will accompany you reach twenty
sui, sanshi sui, shenzhi sishi sui.
age, thirty age, even forty age.
The responsibility of raising children will accompany you to 20,30 even 40.

Shenzhi in (10) firstly triggers a scale along the dimension of age, and at the same time designates the constituent following it "forty-year-old" to be the endpoint on this scale. With respect to the co-occurrence between *Shenzhi* and *Ne,* examples in (11) and (12) demonstrate their interaction.

(11)Ta suiran chuzhong biye ,
He although junior high school graduate,
Danshi ta tudi you
but he apprentices have
benkesheng, yanjiusheng, shenzhi boshi ne.
bachelor, master even Ph.D. *ne.*
Although he only graduates from junior high school, among his apprentices, there are bachelors, masters and even Ph.Ds.

(12) "Wo ye shoudao yaoqinghan le."
I also receive invitation PERF
Ta jiaoao de shuo, " renjia
She proudly DE speak, They
Shenzhi shang men qing wo ne.
Even up door invite I *ne.*
"I got the invitation as well," she said proudly, "They even invited me at my door."

In (11), noun phrases form an additive scale along the dimension of degree titles. *Shenzhi* still designates the constituent following it "Ph.D. title" to be the endpoint information on the scale.

Apart from this, this boundary information from the speaker's view is unexpected or surprised the hearer. Therefore *Ne* is used by the speaker to inform or remind the hearer of this unexpected information; It's more felicitous to use *Ne* than delete it in conversation as (12). The event of "invite me by my door" is still unexpected or surprised the hearer from the speaker's viewpoint, therefore *Ne* is used by the speaker to remind to inform the hearer of this unexpected information.

To sum up, *Shenzhi* designates the endpoint on a given scale and this boundary information is in general unexpected or surprised the hearer from the speaker's view, therefore SFP-*Ne* is added to inform or remind the hearer of this unexpected information.

4.2 *Qishi* and *Ne*

Qishi is used fundamentally to trigger a contrastive relation among propositions. It can be a natural contrast encoded in predicates or an evaluative contrast triggered by the background knowledge and current proposition, as exemplified in (13) and (14).

(13) Xianzai ting qi lai kexiao,
Now listen up come ridiculous
qishi dangshi hen xian suan.
Actually then very heart sour
Now it sounds like ridiculous, however it actually was very heart-breaking at that time.

(14) Shuo shi jia, qishi jia li
Speak BE home, actually home inside
Jiu wo yi ge ren
only I one CL person.
(While you may say) I have a family, but actually I am the only person in it.

The contrastive relation in (13) is triggered by the predicates between "*Kexiao* (ridiculous)" and "*Xinsuan* (heart-breaking)" and in (14) the contrastive relation is generated between the general world knowledge that family members must exceed one and the current statement of only one family member. Typical examples of co-occurrence between *Qishi* and *Ne* are extracted from the corpus data and illustrated in (15) and (16).

(15) Kan zhe women xiang getou yiyang
Look ASP we like height the same
Qishi wo bi ta ai shier limi ne.
Actually I BI she short twelve cm *ne.*
It looks like that we are in the same height, but actually I am 12 cm shorter than her.

(16) "Xiao yun, wo mei gaosu ni, qishi
Little Yun, I NEG tell you.
Qishi wo you wuwan duo de gupiao ne.
Actually I have 50000 more DE stock *ne.*
"Little Yun, I did not tell you this before, but I actually have stocks worth more than 50000RMB

The contrastive relation in (15) exists between the height in look and in reality, the speaker is informing or reminding the hearer to pay attention to this unexpected, contrastive relation, and hence *Ne* is add by the end. The conversation in (16) is held between boyfriend and girlfriend, the boy is persuading his girlfriend to keep the baby by informing her that he actually possesses stock investments. Therefore *Ne* is used by the speaker/boyfriend to inform the hearer/girlfriend to pay attention to this unexpected, surprising possession of money.

Therefore we may summarize that *Ne* is used in *Qishi* sentences to mark the unexpected contrastive relation among predicates or propositions.

4.3 *Nanguai* and *Ne*

Nanguai is used to introduce the effect part of the causality relation in Chinese. The speaker usually finds the observed event to be surprising or out of expectation. And it is not until the reason is discovered that the speaker suddenly realizes this cause and effect relation.

(17) Ta zi xiao shenghuo zai zhongguo,
She from little live in China,
Nanguai shuo yi kou liuli de hanyu.
no wonder speak one CL fluent DE Chinese.
She has been living in China since childhood.
No wonder she speaks fluent Chinese.

(18) Nanguai ta mei shang ke,

No wonder he NEG up class,
yuanlai shi bing le.
originally BE sick PERF.
No wonder he did not attend the class, it turns out that he is sick.

The speaker in (17) finds her fluency in Chinese to be surprising, and it is not until the speaker discovers that she actually lives in China since childhood that the speaker realizes this causality relation and no longer be surprised. In (18), the speaker finds his absent from the class to be abnormal, and it is not until the speaker knows his sickness that the speaker realizes this causality relation and no longer be confused. Co-occurrences between *Nanguai* and *Ne* are displayed in (19) and (20).

(19) Nanguai ta turan yun dao ne,
No wonder he suddenly faint down *ne,*
zuijin yizhi zai jian fei
recently always PROG minus fat.
No wonder he fainted suddenly, he has been on the diet recently.

(20) A: Baobei, duo chi huluobu dui
Sweetie, more eat carrot for
Shili hao.
Eyesight good.
A: Sweetie, eat more carrot, it's good for your eyesight.
B: o, nanguai tuzi bu dai
oh, no wonder rabbit NEG wear
yangjing ne.
glasses *ne.*
B: Oh, I see. No wonder the rabbits do not wear glasses.

In (19), the speaker finds his faintness to be unexpected or abnormal, the speaker is informing or reminding the hearer of this unexpected causality relation and when the speaker finds him to be sick recently, the speaker realizes the cause and effect. In a conversation between the mum and her daughter in (20), the mum is informing her daughter of eating more carrots, the daughter used to find rabbits not wearing glasses to be confused, upon hearing her mum's words, the speaker/daughter is reminding or informing her hearer/mum of this unexpected causality relation.

From this we may conclude that *Ne is* used by the speaker in *Nanguai* sentences to remind or inform the hearer of this unexpected causality relation.

5 Conclusion

This paper starts with a preliminary observation on SFP-*Ne* and two semantic features of [+unexpectedness] and [+intersubjectivity] are summarized accordingly. Following this line of analysis, we investigate the interaction between SpOAs and SFP-*Ne* in corpora data and pick out the top three SpOAs that are in high frequency of co-occurring with SFP-*Ne,* which include *Shenzhi, Qishi* and *Nanguai.* Despite the disparate meanings of these adverbs, we find they are fundamentally linked by the properties of unexpectedness, be it an unexpected boundary point on the scale, a contrastive relation or a causality relation.

Putting the pieces together, we conclude the semantic properties of *Ne* and more importantly, our proposal could be further confirmed through analysis upon the co-occurrence between SpOAs and SFPs. We hope the methodological innovation used in this paper may apply to future studies on SFPs both in other dialects across China and cross linguistically.

Acknowledgement

This paper is part of my doctoral thesis, special thanks goes to my supervisor Prof. Dingxu,SHI.
I would also like to thank the anonymous reviewers for their valuable comments and suggestions. All remaining errors are mine.

References

Alleton, Viviane. 1981. Final particles and expression of modality in modern Chinese. *Journal of Chinese linguistics*. 9: 91-115.

Bellert, Irena. 1977. On semantic and distributional properties of sentential adverbs. *Linguistic Inquiry*, 8(2): 337-351.

Chao, Yuen-Ren.1968. *A Grammar of Spoken Chinese.* Berkeley: University of California Press.

Chu, Chauncey. 1986. Yuyongxue yu hanyu jiaoxue—juwei xuzi ne gen me de yanjiu [Pragmatic and Chinese Teaching—Studies on final particle *Ne* and *Me*].

Zhongnan Minzu Daxue Xuebao [Journal of South-Central University for Nationalities] 3:28-37.

Constant, Noah. 2014. Contrastive Topic: Meanings and Realizations. Doctoral Dissertation, University of Massachusetts, Amherst.

Ernst, Thomas 2008. Adverbs and Positive Polarity in Mandarin Chinese. In *Proceedings of the 20th North American Conference on Chinese Linguistics (NACCL-20)* 1: 69-85.

Ernst, Thomas. 2009. Speaker-oriented Adverbs. *Natural Language & Linguistic Theory*. 27(3): 497-544.

Jackendoff, Ray.1972. *Semantic Interpretation in Generative Gramma*r. Cambridge: MIT Press.

King, Brian. 1986. NE---a discourse approach. *Journal of the Chinese Language Teachers Association*. 21(1): 21-46.

Li, Charles N. and Sandra A, Thompson. 1981. *Mandarin Chinese: A Functional Reference Grammar*. Berkeley: University of California Press.

Nilsen, Øystein. 2004. Domains for adverbs. *Lingua,* 114(6): 809-847.

Shao, Jing-Min.1996. *Xiandai Hanyu Yiwenju Yanjiu* [Research on Modern Chinese Interrogatives] Shanghai: East China Normal University Press.

Traugott, Elizabeth. C., and Dasher, Richard. B. 2001. *Regularity in Semantic Change*. Cambridge: Cambridge University Press.

Wu, Guo. 2005. The discourse function of the Chinese particle ne in statements. *Journal of the Chinese Language Teachers Association*. 40(1): 47-82.

Zhu, De-Xi. 1982. *Yufa Jiangyi* [Lecture Notes on Grammar]. Beijing: Commercial Press.

On the Semantics of Korean modalized question

Arum Kang
Korea University / Seokwan 110A, Anam-ro 145, Seongbuk-ku, Seoul, Korea
arkang@korea.ac.kr

Abstract

The goal of the current study is to suggest a novel paradigm of epistemic modal operator originated from the disjunction. Our main data is Korean disjunction operator *nka* which forms a non-factual question. Examining how the modal effect in question is induced by *nka*, I propose that the prerequisite of *nka* brings about non-homogenous nonveridical (i.e. modal) spaces partitioned in equipoised epistemic spaces, thus there is no bias between them. I furthermore show how the distinct notions of disjunction, question, and possibility modal can be captured under the theory of nonveridical equilibrium (Giannakidou 2013, Giannakidou and Mari 2016).

1 Introduction

In the standard theories of question (Hamblin 1973; Karttunen 1977; Groenendijk and Stokhof 1984), the meaning of the question denotes a set of propositions (i.e. alternative possible answers to the question). The general purpose of information-seeking questions is to receive a true answer from the addressee by posing such a set of alternatives for consideration. Surprisingly, however, the question marked by *nka* in Korean concerns speaker's knowledge and issues, thus it reports on the *speaker's* consideration of a set of alternatives. In (1a), for instance, based on the fact that John had a very subtle smile in the context, the speaker conjectures that 'John is the winner' has a good possibility while acknowledging the negative possibility at the same time. The statement is therefore marked by *nka*. It contrasts with the factual question marker *ni* in (1b) without such presumption by the speaker:

(1) *Context: Mary, a reporter, was waiting for John and Bill who were competing with each other for the win in the finals of the chess competition. After the match, John and Bill came out of the room. John had a very subtle smile and Bill had a poker face. Given their facial expressions, she raises the possibility that John might have won. Mary says:*

a. *Con-i* *wusungca-i-**nka**?*
John-Nom winner-be-NKA
'Could John possibly be the winner?'

b. *Con-i* *wusungca-i-**ni**?*
John-Nom winner-be-Q
'Is John the winner?'

I treat the *nka*-question in (1a) as a non-factual question (Jang 1999; C. Kim 2010, a.o.): as indicated in the use of 'possibly' in the translation, it is a question about the *possibility* of the content of the proposition, i.e., the speaker is asking whether it is possible that John won the game, rather than whether he actually won the game. The use of *nka* indicates the speaker's presumed awareness of asking a weaker question, and specifies the degree of certainty about the proposition in question, just like an epistemic modal. In this sense, I term the *nka*-question *modalized question* (MQ, henceforth). A MQ questions about the speaker's belief and knowledge, thus it raises a weaker inquiry than the regular unmodalized question.

I argue that the epistemic modality of *nka* is initiated from its original function of disjunction operator. As shown below, *nka* coordinates two DPs in (2a) or two TPs in (2b):

(2) a. *Wusungca-nun* *Con-**inka*** *Pil-i-ta.*
winner-Top John-or Bill-be-Decl
'The winner is possibly John or Bill.
b. *Con-i* *wusungca-i-**nka?***
John-Nom winner-be-NKA
'Could John possibly be the winner?'

As indicated in the use of *possibly* in the translation, *nka* disjunctions are modalized (Choi 2011, a.o.). I assume that *inka*-disjunction in (2a) is a disjunction without overt modals in the sense of Zimmermann (2001) and Geurts (2005), interpreted as a list of epistemic possibilities. It asserts that the winner might be John or the winner might be Bill in a world w if and only if the proposition contains at least one world that is permitted in w.

In fact, MQs are pervasive in diverse languages, not genetically or geographically connected, and some light is shed on the topic from previous studies examining them under various labels. The common semantic denominator of these MQs is that the epistemic uncertainty is produced by the interaction of modal ingredients occurring in questions. To name a few, there are *darou-ka* 'MOD+Q' in Japanese (*self-addressing* question; Hara and Davis 2013), as=*há=k'a* 'SBJN+YNQ+INFER' in St'át'imcets (*conjectural* question; Littell et al. 2009, Matthewson 2010), and *na* 'SBJN' occurring in the interrogative in Greek (*epistemic subjunctive question;* Giannakidou, to appear). Above MQs have *double-layered* epistemic modal because they are morphologically decomposed into overt question markers and modal ingredients which contribute to form modalized non-factual questions. In Salish and Japanese the modal component is a modal marker; in Greek it is a subjunctive marker; in English it is *possibly, probably, might*, etc. Unlike the above MQs, however, the Korean MQ is notable in that the double-layered modal is achieved by a single element, *nka.* Our discussion on *nka* crucially hinges on the question of (i) how the semantic categories of MQs can be distinguished within the traditional domain of modality, and how they can be defined, and (ii) how the seemingly distinct notions of disjunction, modal effect, and question are amalgamated in the single element *nka*.

To capture the semantics of double-layered modal, I argue that the *nka*-disjunction is based on modal-concord structure, positing an implicit possibility modal. The existence of default implicit modal in *nka*-MQs is evidenced by the fact that, when *nka* co-occurs with other modal verbs, it withdraws the otherwise strong modality of these verbs. For example, *nka* combines with biased (i.e. strong) possibility modal verbs such as evidential modal suffix *te* 'I saw that' (J. Lee 2008, a.o.) and strong possibility modal auxiliary verb *kes kath* 'look like' (Choi 1995, a.o), but no bias is indicated:

(3) *Con-i* *wusungca-i-**te-nka**?*
John-Nom winner-be-INFER-NKA
'Did I possibly see that John was the winner?'

(4) *Con-i* *wusungca-i-n-**kes kath**-un-**nka**?*
John-Nom winner-be-Rel-must-Rel-NKA
'Could John possibly look like the winner?'

I take this to argue that the function of *nka* is to constrain the modal base, just as modal adverbs do. The distinct feature of its restriction, however, lies in the fact that *nka* partitions the modal base into equal spaces, i.e. $p \vee \neg p$ (polarity partition), and nullifies the bias.

I thus propose that three seemingly distinct notions of disjunction, question, and possibility modal can be unified under the framework of *nonveridical equilibrium* (Gianankidou 2013; Giannakidou and Mari (GM) 2016). The epistemic weakening in *nka*-MQs is obtained by the creation of non-homogenous nonveridical (i.e. modal) states partitioned in equipoised epistemic spaces.

The paper proceeds as follows: In section 2, I provide a brief recapitulation of nonveridical equilibrium. Exploring the basic properties of *nka* in Korean in section 3, I show that its function is akin to the modal-verb modifier restricting modal base. In section 4, I offer the semantic analysis of MQs, showing how a more comprehensive picture of MQs that I provide fits into the framework of nonveridical equilibrium. In section 5, I conclude with theoretical implications.

2 Theoretical backgrounds

Nonveridicality is placed at the heart of mood and modality (Giannakidou 1994 et seq.). Giannakidou assumes Kratzerian semantics for modals (Kratzer 1981, 1991), where modals take modal bases and ordering sources, and add one ingredient, the *Nonveridicality Axiom* that all modal bases are nonveridical. From the epistemic domain, I can move to generalize veridicality and nonveridicality to all kinds of modal spaces (sets of worlds), involving various kinds of modal bases. All modal bases are nonveridical spaces in that they do not entail the truth of the prejacent proposition. The (non)veridicality can be defined in terms of the properties of modal spaces:

(5) Veridical, nonveridical modal spaces
(sets of worlds) (Giannakidou 2014: (31))
(i) A set of worlds M is veridical with respect to a proposition p iff all worlds in M are p-words (Homogeneity): $\forall w'(w' \in M \rightarrow p(w'))$
(ii) A set of worlds M is nonveridical with respect to a proposition p iff there is at least one world in M that is a non-p world. (Non-homogeneity):
$\exists w', w'' \in M\,(w' \neq w'' \wedge (p(w') \wedge \neg p(w'')))$
(iii) A set of worlds M is antiveridical with respect to a proposition p iff M and p are disjoint: $M \cap p = \varnothing$

Nonveridicality is a precondition on modalities, as shown below:

(6) Nonveridicality Axiom of modals (GM 2016: (27))
MODAL(M)(p) can be defined only if the modal base M is nonveridical, i.e. only if M contains p and non-p worlds.

This axiom guarantees that MODAL p will not entail p, since there are also $\neg p$ worlds in M, and the actual world may be one of those. The modal base M intersects with p, but also contains non-p worlds. Following Portner 2009, she assumes the ordering sources and Best worlds (GM 2016 (28)(29)):

(7) a. *Ordering of worlds* – Portner 2009, p.65
For any set of propositions X and any worlds w,v: $w \leq_X v$ iff (i) for all $p \in X$, if $v \in p$, then $w \in p$
b. For any set of propositions X, Best worlds as per X. $\text{Best}_X = \{w' : \forall q \in X(w' \in q)\}$

Given an epistemic modal base M(i), Best is a function over M(i), in the sense of Portner:

(8) For any set of propositions X, Best worlds is a function over M(i) (GM 2016: (30)):
$\text{Best}_S\text{M}(i) = \{w' \in \text{M}(i) : \forall q \in X(w' \in q)\}$

Best worlds consist of two basic parts: *support* and *bias*. Support is defined in (9). The Support function takes the modal base as its argument and returns a subset of it. The set of worlds returned is such that the propositions in the ordering source S are true.

(9) Support function (GM 2016: (31)):
$\text{Support}_S(\text{M}(i)) = X$ s.t. $X \subset \text{M}(i)$ & $\forall w' \in X$: $p(w')$

The support set is the inner domain of the modal base, and the modal base is its outer domain. The support function delivers the positive set of the nonveridical modal base.

The next is bias. Bias is defined in terms of a measure function μ, which takes sets as arguments and returns their sizes.

(10) A modal is biased iff (GM 2016: (32)):
$\mu(\text{Support}_S(\text{M}(i))) > \mu(\text{M}(i) \setminus \text{Support}_S(\text{M}(i)))$

This axiom guarantees that MODAL p will not entail p, since there are also $\neg p$ worlds in M, and the actual world may be one of those. The modal base M intersects with p, but also contains non-p worlds.

The nonveridical equilibrium is a state of fifty-fifty, and p and $\neg p$ are equal options. The nonveridical equilibrium can be generalized as follows:

(11) Nonveridical equilibrium
(with ordering sources) (GM 2016: (33))
A modal base M(i) is nonveridical equilibrium iff:
$\mu(\text{Support}_S(\text{M}(i))) \approx \mu(\text{M}(i) \setminus \text{Support}_S(\text{M}(i)))$

Nonveridical equilibrium characterizes possibility modals. It holds the nonveridical modal spaces, partitioned in equipoise, that are compatible with the speaker's belief, and indicates an equal possibility of its spaces given what the speaker's doxastic (or belief) world is: it conveys that the speaker considers both *p* sets and non-*p* sets equally possible. Ordering sources add information restricting sets of possibilities and creating support sets, thus privileging one subset of the modal base over its complement ($\neg p$). In the state of nonveridical equilibrium, however, there is no preference towards the *p* or non-*p* worlds, no best worlds, and no support of *p*.

Thus far, I have overviewed relevant theoretical ingredients, showing how the theory of nonveridicality can incorporate the distinct notions of question, disjunction, and possibility modal. In what follows, I investigate the nature of *nka*-disjunction and show how nonveridical equilibrium offers an elegant analysis to capture the meaning of *nka*-marked MQs.

3 Core property of *nka*-disjunction

Given the full range of phenomena that correlate with the occurrence of *nka*, I suggest the semantic properties of *nka*-disjunction and show how it forms a MQ in this section. The core property of *nka*-disjunction is double-layered, where *nka* is a modal-verb modifier restricting the modal base induced by an implicit modal operator. I examine each property in detail and show how the disjunction marker can function as a special subspecies of epistemic modal markers.

I take the empirical evidence that *nka*-disjunction involves double layers of modality to assume that *nka*-disjunction involves modal concord. Modal concord refers to the phenomenon that a sentence in which a modal verb and a modal adverb occur is interpreted as if it contained only one (Halliday 1970, Lyons 1977, Huitink 2012, Annad and Brasoveanu 2010, a.o.), as shown in (12). When a modal verb combines with a modal adverb, the modal adverb fortifies the meaning of the modal verb:

(12) **Possibly** John **may** be the winner of the competition.
(13) **Possibly** John is the winner of the competition.
(14) John **may** be the winner of the competition.

If both *possibly* and *may* express modality, it is expected by compositionality that (12) makes a doubly modalized statement, whereas (13) and (14) involve only one layer of modality. In order to make iterated modalities entail a single modality, the relationship underlying the modal expressions in modal concord would have to be transitive and dense (Huitink 2012, (4)-(5)):

(15) a. $\Diamond\Diamond p \rightarrow \Diamond p$
b. Transitivity: For all possible worlds *w, v, u*: if *wRv* and *vRu*, then *wRu*
c. Density: For all possible worlds *w, v, u*: if *wRv*, then there is a *u*, s.t. *wRu* and *uRv*.

Modal adverbs are devices for domain restriction that come with selection restrictions concerning the modal force of the quantifier they combine with. They are not assuming modal concord as the result of certain modals being semantically vacuous (Anad and Brasoveanu 2010; Huitink 2012; Giannakidou and Mari 2016).

Modal concord of *nka* can be captured by positing an underlying argument structure of modals. This structure is realized explicitly when *nka* is present. The existence of default implicit modal in MQs is evidenced by the fact that *nka* restricts the modality of co-occurring overt modal verbs, especially biased possibility modals including the evidential modal suffix *te* 'I saw that' (J. Lee 2008, a.o.) in (16) and the epistemic modal auxiliary *kes kath* 'it looks like' (S. Choi 1995, a.o.) in (17). These modals mark the speaker's strong bias toward the content of prejacent proposition based on concrete evidence available in the context, which is revealed by their incompatibility with the low degree of commitment expressed by low probability adverbs such as *ama* 'maybe' or *hoksi* 'maybe/by any chance':

(16) Con-i (*ama/*hoksi)
John-Nom maybe
wusungca-i-**te**-la.
winner-be-INFER-Decl
'(I saw that) John was the winner.'

(17) Con-i (*ama/*hoksi)
John-Nom maybe
wusungca-i-n-**kes kath**-ta.
winner-be-Rel-may-Decl
'John may be the winner; John looks like the winner.'

Surprisingly, however, when *nka* combines with them, no such bias is detected:

(18) Con-i (ama/hoksi)
John-Nom maybe
wusungca-i-**te**-**nka**?
winner-be-INFER-NKA
'Did I possibly see that John was the winner?'

(19) Con-i (ama/hoksi)
John-Nom maybe
wusungca-i-n-**kes kath**-un-**nka**?
winner-be-Rel-may-Rel-NKA
'Could John possibly look like the winner?'

Nka is thus an integral component of modality indeed. Nullifying the bias to the prejacent proposition is expected in MQs, because the MQ presupposes equipoised partitioned epistemic space.

4 Semantics of MQ

Given what I have said about the properties of *nka*-disjunction thus far, it is plausible to assume that the meaning of *nka*-MQ is best represented as a partitioned two possibilities of p and $\neg p$, containing epistemic modals.

(20) $[[\text{NKA}(p)]]^w = \{\{\text{that it is possible that p}\},$ $\{\text{that it is not possible that p}\}\}$

The speaker considers *p* and non-*p* worlds equally possible, and *no preference or bias* is given between them. I can argue that having 50% certainty can naturally be explained if the core reanalysis of *nka* necessarily occurs in a statement whose meaning consists of both *p* and non-*p*. As shown below, an *nka*-MQ is infelicitous in contexts with high possibility and low possibility, while felicitous in contexts with medium possibility:

(21) imsin-i-nka?
pregnancy-be-NKA
'Could it be possibly a pregnancy?'

(22) MQ and Degree of Certainty
a. High-possibility context (80-100%): It has been 1 year since my sister got married. One day, I visited her. She wanted to tell me about the surprise news. She showed me her pregnancy test kit. There were two lines on it. I say: continuation (21): #
b. Medium-possibility context (50%): It has been 1 year since my sister got married. One day, I visited her. She showed some symptoms that she was suffering from nausea and craved something sour. I say: continuation by (21): o.k.
c. Low-possibility context (0-20%): It has been 1 year since my sister got married. One day, I visited her. She told me that she wants a baby. I say: continuation by (21): #

The example in (22) suggests that in order for *nka* to be felicitous, the speaker must believe that the realization of the propositional content has a medium possibility given what she knows. The context is set up such that the speaker is uncertain about the truth of the proposition expressed by the sentence: the speaker does not know which of p (she is pregnant) and non-p (she is not pregnant) is true. However, if the evidence points too strongly, as in (22a), or too weakly, as in (22c), in favor of the proposition being true, *nka* becomes infelicitous. The contribution of *nka* thus involves approximately medium certainty. The speaker's presupposition on the medium possibility of the realization of the propositional content, I argue, is the reason why *nka* is used.

Given that *nka* yields medium possibility in speaker's epistemic states, I assume that the function of *nka* is a restrictor of modal base: there is an implicit modal which existentially quantifies over the set Bests (which is a subset of the modal base), and the modal base of MQs is partitioned into p and $\neg$p worlds with no ordering. Within the system of Giannakidou and Mari (GM 2016), the truth condition for *nka* will come out as follows:

(23) $[[\varnothing_{\text{epistemic}}(p)]]^{M,i}$ will be defined iff
(i) the modal base M(i) is nonveridical;
(ii) $\exists X \subset M(i)$ s.t. $\mu(X) \approx \mu(M(i) \setminus X)$
(nonveridical equilibrium)
if defined, $[[\varnothing_{\text{epistemic}}(p)]]^{M,i} = 1$ iff
$\forall w' \in X$ s.t. $X \subset M(i)\ p(w')$

I thus suggest that an appropriate interpretation of *nka* is obtained by considering the epistemic status of the speaker. The nonveridical modal base of *nka*-Q holds the nonveridical modal space, p and $\neg$p, which is compatible with the speaker's belief, and indicates an equal possibility of its spaces given what the speaker's doxastic (or belief) world is. That is, the MQ conveys that the speaker considers both p and ¬p equally possible. Here, the modal base already forms a state of nonveridical equilibrium.

I therefore assume that the function of *nka* is analogous to that of an epistemic modal adverb, and translated as 'maybe' or 'possibly' in English, maintaining the default of the existential modal (adapted from GM 2016: (63)):

(24) $[[\text{NKA}]]^{M,i,\text{S-adv}}$ is defined iff
$\mu(\text{NKA}_{\text{S-adv}}(M(i))) \approx \mu(M(i) \setminus \text{NKA}_{\text{S-adv}}M(i)))$
Maintaining the default of the existential modal: the Support set the modal base (p-worlds) is approximately of the same size as the set of non-support worlds (¬p-worlds).

Nka expresses the speaker's perspective towards p by determining the size of equilibrium in the modal base, and has no effect on the equilibrium, since it returns a modal base equally partitioned between p worlds and non-p worlds. It is characterized as equipoised epistemic space, as follows (adapted from GM 2016: (64)):

(25) $[[\text{NKA } \varnothing_{\text{epistemic}}(p)]]^{M,i}$ will be defined iff
(i) the modal base M(i) is nonveridical;
(ii) there is a set X, $X=\text{Support}_S(M(i))$ and $\mu(X) \approx \mu(M(i) \setminus X)$ if defined,
$[[\text{NKA } \varnothing_{\text{epistemic}}(p)]]^{M,i,\text{S-adv}} = 1$ iff
$\forall w' \in \text{Support}_{\text{S-adv}}(M(i)): p(w')$

$\text{NKA}_{\text{S-adv}}$ (M(i)) M(i) \ $\text{NKA}_{\text{S-adv}}$ (M(i))
p ¬p

Figure 1: Nonveridical equilibrium of MQ

The speaker has reduced the truth commitment by creating a nonveridical modal space, i.e. one that contains p and non-p worlds. The domains of non-veridical equilibrium are modal domains partitioned into p and non-p worlds. Unlike the typical partition, which is the result of an ordering (e.g. ordering sources with modals), the proposed semantics conveys that there is no best world in *nka*-questions, hence no ordering occurs.

5 Conclusions

In this paper, I identified a novel type of epistemic uncertainty on the proposition, i.e. MQs, and showed that the composite morpheme *nka* conveys a meaning more than just a possibility modal or a factual question marker: it is a modal-verb restrictor to maintain the default of the existential modal. I proposed that: (i) the epistemic constraints of MQs can be achieved by the presence of nonveridical modal space; and (ii) this modal space is partitioned in *equipoised epistemic space*. I furthermore showed how the challenge of capturing the precise semantics of such type of epistemic uncertainty can be met by capitalizing on the notion of nonveridical equilibrium. Korean facts importantly reveal that modalized questions do not form a uniform class with ordinary questions and that interrogative semantics alone cannot predict this epistemic uncertainty.

Acknowledgments

I would like to thank Anastasia Giannakidou for valuable discussions and suggestions about this material. I am also grateful to Ming Xiang, Allonso-Ovalle, Chungmin Lee, and Mark de Vries for their helpful comments, insightful suggestions and questions. Part of this paper has been presented the joint meeting of the International Circle of Korean Linguistics (ICKL) and the Harvard-International Symposium on Korean Linguistics (ISOKL) 2015 at University of Chicago, Linguistic Society of America's 90th Annual Meeting (LSA2016) in Washington D.C., the 18th Seoul International Conference of Generative Grammar (SICOGG18) in Seoul. All errors are my own.

References

Anand, Pranav and Adrian Brasoveanu. 2010. Modal concord as modal modification. In Martin Prinzhorn, Viola Schmitt, and Sarah Zobel (eds.), *Proceedings of Sinn und Bedeutung* 14, 19-36.

Choi, Soonja. 1995. The development of epistemic sentence-ending modal forms and functions in Korean children. In J. Bybee & S. Fleischman (eds.), *Modality in grammar and discourse*, , 165-204.

Choi, Yoon-Ji. 2011. Correlation between disjunction and modality: focused on *inka* (written in Korean). *Journal of Korean linguistics* 60. 146-181.

Geurts, Bart. 2005. Entertaining Alternatives: Disjunctions as Modals. *Natural Language Semantics* 13(4). 383-410.

Giannakidou, Anastasia. 1995. Subjunctive, habituality and negative polarity items. *Semantics and Linguistic Theory* 5. 94-111.

Giannakidou, Anastasia. 1999. Affective dependencies. *Linguistics and Philosophy* 22. 367-421.

Giannakidou, Anastasia. 2013. Inquisitive assertions and nonveridicality. In Maria Aloni, Michael Franke, & Floris Roelofsen (eds.), *The dynamic, inquisitive, and visionary life of ϕ, ?ϕ and possibly ϕ, A festschrift for Jeroen Groenendijk, Martin Stokhof and Frank Veltman*, 115-126.

Giannakidou, Anastasia. To appear. The subjunctive as evaluation and nonveridicality, epistemic subjunctive, and factive-as-emotive. In Blaszack et al. (eds.), *For: Mood, Aspect and Modality: What is a linguistic Category?* University of Chicago Press.

Giannakidou, Anastasia and Alda Mari. 2016. *The semantic roots of positive polarity: epistemic modal verbs and adverbs*. ms., University of Chicago.

Groenendijk, Jerson and Stokhof, Martin. 1984. *Studies in the Semantics of Questions and the Pragmatics of Answers*. University of Amsterdam Ph.D. dissertation.

Geurts, Bart. 2005. Entertaining alternatives: Disjunctions as modals. *Natural Language Semantics* 13(4). 383-410.

Halliday, Michael Alexander Kirkwood. 1970. Functional diversity in language as seen from a consideration of modality and mood in English. *Foundations of Language* 6. 322-361.

Hamblin, Charles Leonanrd. 1973. Questions in Montague grammar. *Foundations of Language* 10. 41-53.

Hara, Yurie and Christopher Davis. 2013. *Darou* as a deictic context shifter. In Kazuko Yatsushiro and Uli Sauerland (eds.), *Proceedings of Formal Approaches to Japanese Linguistics* 6 (FAJL 6), 41-56. Cambridge, MA: MITWPL.

Hara, Yurie. 2013. On the interaction among sentence types, bias, and intonation: a rating study. In *Proceedings of Glow in Asia IX*.

Huitink, Janneke. 2012. Modal concord: a case study of Dutch. *Journal of Semantics* 29. 403-437.

Jang, Youngjun. 1999. Two types of question and existential quantification. *Linguistics* 37. 847- 869.

Kang, Arum. 2015. *(In)definiteness, disjunction and anti-specificity in Korean: a study in the semantics-pragmatics interface*. University of Chicago Ph.D. dissertation.

Kang, Arum and Suwon Yoon. 2016. Two types of epistemic ignorance in Korean. In Patrick Farrell (eds.), *The proceedings of the Linguistic Society of America* Vol. 1 (2016), 21. 1-15 (DOI: http://dx.doi.org/10.3765/plsa.v1i0.3723), Linguistic Society of America.

Karttunen, Lauri. 1977. Syntax and semantics of questions. *Linguistics and Philosophy* 1. 3-44.

Kratzer, Angelika. 1981. The notional category of modality. In Hans-Jürgen Eikmeyer & Hannes Rieser (eds.), *Words, worlds, and Context*, 38-74. Berlin: de Gruyter.

Kratzer, Angelika. 1991. Modality. In von Stechow & Wunderlich (eds.), *Semantics: an International Handbook of Contemporary Research,* 739-650. Berlin: de Gruyter.

Kim, Chonghyuck. 2010. *Korean Question Particles Are Pronominals: A transparent Case of Representing Discourse Participants in the Syntax.* http://ling.auf.net/lingBuzz/001157/

Lee, Jungmee. 2008. The Korean evidential *-te:* a modal analysis. In *Empirical Issues in Syntax and Semantics* 7. 1-25.

Littell, Patrick, Lisa Matthewson and Tyler Peterson 2009. *On the semantics of conjectural questions.* Paper presented at the MOSAIC Workshop (Meeting of Semanticists Active in Canada), Ottawa.

Lyons, John. 1977. *Semantics.* Cambridge: Cambridge University Press.

Matthewson, Lisa. 2010. Cross-linguistic Variation in Modality Systems: The Role of Mood. *Semantics and Pragmatics 3*. 1-74.

Portner, Paul. 2009. *Modality.* Oxford University Press.

Zimmerman, Thomas Ede. 2001. Free choice disjunction and epistemic possibility. *Natural Language Semantics* 8. 255–290.

The Synaesthetic and Metaphorical Uses of 味 *wei* 'taste' in Chinese Buddhist Texts

Jiajuan Xiong
School of Foreign Languages for Business
Southwestern University of Finance and Economics
Chengdu, China
jiajuanx@gmail.com

Chu-Ren Huang
CBS
The Hong Kong Polytechnic University
Hong Kong
churen.huang@polyu.edu.hk

Abstract

This paper investigates the non-gustatory uses of the gustatory word 味 *wei* 'taste' in Chinese Buddhist texts, in particular, in the *Āgamas*. The non-gustatory uses of 味 *wei* 'taste' basically fall into two categories: the synaesthetic category and the metaphorical category. The former features the use of 味 *wei* 'taste' as an umbrella sensory term which can collocate with all the other sensory words, whereas the latter shows that 味 *wei* 'taste' can modify abstract and sublime Buddhist terms, such as 法 *fa* 'dhamma' and 解脱 *jietuo* 'enlightenment', for the sake of concretization. These two categories of uses have one sense in common: the sense of "pleasure and joy", which can be interpreted in both mundane and supra-mundane levels, depending on the context. Moreover, we find that the versatile uses of 味 *wei* 'taste' are most likely to be influenced by its equivalent in the *Pāli* Buddhist texts. This finding sheds light on the history of Chinese language development, specifically, how Chinese language has been influenced by Buddhist text translation.

1 The gustatory word 味 'taste'

In the Chinese Buddhist texts, 味 *wei* 'taste' is basically used as a gustatory word, referring to 'taste', as shown in (1).

(1) 我眼見色，我耳聞聲，我鼻嗅香，我舌嘗**味**，我身覺觸，我意識法。【雜阿含經】
Wo yan jian se, wo er wen
I eye see form I ear hear
sheng, wo bi xiu xiang, wo she
sound I nose smell smell I tongue
chang **wei**, wo shen jue chu,
taste taste I body feel tangible
wo yi shi fa. (Saṃyutta Nikāya)
I mind perceive object
'My eyes see the forms, my ears hear the sounds, my nose smells the smells, my tongue tastes the taste, my body feels tangible things and my mind perceives objects.'

In the Chinese Buddhist texts, the gustatory and olfactory words are clearly distinguished, as represented by 味 *wei* 'taste' and 香 *xiang* 'smell', respectively. Devoid of the convergence between gustatory and olfactory expressions, which is now shown in Modern Chinese, Chinese Buddhist texts feature some other special uses of 味 *wei* 'taste', as follows:

First, 味 *wei* 'taste' is attested to be able to collocate

with all the sensory words, i.e. 色 *se* 'form', 聲 *sheng* 'sound', 香 *xiang* 'smell', 味 *wei* 'taste', 觸 *chu* 'touch', to give rise to the Buddhist expressions such as 色味 *sewei* 'form-taste', 聲味 *shengwei* 'sound-taste', 香味 *xiangwei* 'smell-taste', 味味 *weiwei* 'taste-taste', 觸味 *chuwei* 'touch-taste'; Second, 味 *wei* 'taste' can follow some abstract, as well as philosophically important, terms to concretize their philosophical meanings, such as 義味 *yiwei* 'meaning-taste', 法味 *fawei* 'Dhamma-taste' and 解脫味 *jietuowei* 'emancipation-taste'. In Section 2, we present the synaesthetic uses of 味 *wei* 'taste'. The origin of the synaesthetic uses is reported in Section 3. Subsequently in Section 4, we examine the implicit synaesthetic uses of 味 *wei* 'taste' in collocation with *Five Aggregates*, which are apparently non-sensory but essentially sensory. Next, the metaphorical uses of 味 *wei* 'taste' are presented and analyzed in Section 5. Section 6 concludes this paper.

2 Synaesthetic Uses of 味 *wei* 'taste'

In this section, we analyze the uses of 味 *wei* 'taste' which transcend the gustatory sense *per se* but extend to other non-gustatory sensory meanings. The data are grouped into two types, viz. nominal and verbal types, along the grammatical line.

2.1 The nominal use of synaesthetic 味 *wei* 'taste'

We go through the uses of 味 *wei* 'taste' in *Āgamas* (CBETA 2015) and find out that 味 *wei* 'taste' is not limited to the TASTE use. Apart from being a gustatory word, it serves as an umbrella sensory word to collocate with all the sensory words. This is illustrated in (2). In this dialogue, a visiting Brahmin used the expression "tasteless" to refer to the Buddha's lack of conventional hospitality. The Buddha, in reply, uttered a statement, which is an apparent consent to the Brahmin's comment but a *de facto* refutation.

(2) 梵志復白：「瞿曇**無味**。」(*Madhyama Āgama* 157)
Fanzhi fu bai: qutan **wu** **wei**.
Brahmin reply say Gotama NEG taste
'Master Gotama lacks taste.'
世尊告曰：「梵志！有事令我**無味**，然不如汝言。若有**色味、聲味、香味、觸味**者，彼如來斷智絕滅拔根終不復生，是謂有事令我**無味**，然不如汝言。」
Shizun gao yue: fanzhi! You shi
Buddha reply say Brahmin have thing
ling wo **wu** **wei**, ran
make me NEG taste however
bu ru ru yan. Ruo you
NEG like you say if have
se-wei, **sheng-wei,** **xiang-wei,**
form-taste sound-taste smell-taste
chu-wei zhe, bi rulai duanzhi
touch-taste etc. that Tathagata break
juemie bagen zhong bu fu
destroy disroot finally NEG again
sheng, shi wei you shi ling wo
grow be call have thing make me
wu **wei,** ran bu ru ru yan.
NEG taste but NEG like you say
'The Buddha said: 'Brahmin! There are indeed things that make me tasteless. Suppose that there are form-taste, sound-taste, smell-taste and touch-taste, the Tathagata destroys them and makes them cease to be. Thus we say that there are things, different from what you said, that make me tasteless.'

According to the Brahmin, the Buddha's lack of taste is due to his observation that the Buddha does not follow the cultural convention to salute visitors. The Buddha, in order to eschew confrontation with the Brahmin, literally admits to the comment but reinterpretes it in a different way, i.e., the Buddha lacks taste with regard to forms, sounds, smells and tangibles, indicating the Buddha's disenchantment with sensory gratification. Crucially, in this passage, the gustatory word 味 *wei* 'taste' is applied to all the other sensory words, transcends the gustatory sense and refers to sensory gratification. With regard to this use of 味 *wei* 'taste', it functions as a noun.

2.2 The verbal use of synaesthetic 味 *wei* 'taste'

The example in (2) is not the single case of the non-gustatory use of 味 *wei* 'taste'. In the *Saṃyuttāgama*, 味 *wei* 'taste', together with 著 *zhuo* 'attach', is attested to function as a verb, meaning "attach to; attract", as exemplified in (3). The verb 味著 *weizhuo* 'attach to; attract' connects the six internal organs, viz. 眼 *yan* 'eye', 耳 *er* 'ear', 鼻 *bi* 'nose', 舌 *she* 'tongue', 身 *shen* 'body' and 意 *yi* 'mind', and the six external objects, viz. 色 *se* 'form', 聲 *sheng* 'sound',

香 *xiang* 'smell', 味 *wei* 'taste', 觸 *chu* 'tangible' and 法 *fa* '(mind)-object'. This connection is enforced by means of "attaching to" or "attracting" each other. According to the Buddha, the action instantiated by 味著 *weizhuo* 'attach to; attract' leads to bondage. As a result, the actor gets stuck by a magic hook.

(3) 爾時，世尊告諸比丘：「有六魔鉤。云何為六？眼味著色，是則魔鉤，耳味著聲，是則魔鉤，鼻味著香，是則魔鉤，舌味著味，是則魔鉤，身味著觸，是則魔鉤，意味著法，是則魔鉤。若沙門、婆羅門眼味著色者，當知是沙門、婆羅門魔鉤鉤其咽，於魔不得自在。」(Saṃyuttāgama 244)

Ershi, shizun gao zhu biqiu: you liu
then Buddha speak_to PL monk have six
mogou. Yunhe wei liu? Yan
mara_hook why be six eye
weizhuo se, shi ze mogou,
attach_to form be then mara_hook
er **weizhuo** sheng, shi ze mogou,
ear attach_to sound be then mara_hook
bi **weizhuo** xiang, shi ze mogou,
nose attach_to smell be then mara_hook
she **weizhuo** wei, shi ze mogou,
tongue attach_to taste be then mara_hook
shen **weizhuo** chu, shi ze mogou,
tongue attach_to tangible be then mara_hook
yi **weizhuo** fa, shi ze mogou.
mind attach_to thing be then mara_hook
Ruo shamen, poluomen yan weizhuose se
if ascetic Brahmin eye attach_to form
zhe, dang zhi shi shamen, poluomen
person should know this ascetic Brahmin
mougou gou qi yan, yu
mara_hook catch its pharynx at
mo bu de zizai.
Mara NEG get freedom

'At that time, the Buddha told the monks: "There are six types of additive hooks. What are the six? The eye-taste, due to its attraction to forms, is reckoned as an additive hook; the ear-taste, due to its attraction to sounds, is reckoned as an additive hook; the nose-taste, due to its attraction to smell, is reckoned as an additive hook; the tongue-taste, due to its attraction to taste, is reckoned as an additive hook; the body-taste, due to its attraction to tangibles, is reckoned as an additive hook; the mind-taste, due to its attraction to objects, is reckoned as an additive hook. As for an ascetic or a Brahmin, if their eye is attached to forms, gets stuck by the additive hook, and then they cannot be away from freedom.'

The examples of (2) and (3) converge to a focal point regarding the non-gustatory use of 味 *wei* 'taste', be it a noun or a verb. Crucially, 味 *wei* 'taste' transcends the gustatory sense but retains its sensual meaning. Specifically, it refers to "sensual gratification" or "get sensually gratified", depending on its part of speech.

3 The synaesthetic uses of 味 *wei* 'taste': inherent or induced?

味 *wei* 'taste', according to its uses in the *Āgamas*, can be semantically bleached, in the sense that the gustatory meaning recedes to give way to the general sensual meaning. Going beyond the gustatory meaning, 味 *wei* 'taste' can thus collocate with all the sensory words. The question that naturally ensues is why 味 *wei* 'taste', out of the inventory of sensory words, is selected as an umbrella term to signify "sensual gratification" or "get sensually gratified". Considering the fact that Chinese Buddhist scriptures were translated from South Asian languages, e.g., Sanskrit or Pāli, we need to figure out whether the choice of 味 *wei* 'taste' as an umbrella sensory term happened in the original South Asian languages or in Chinese language during the process of translating. To answer this question, we checked the uses of 味 *wei* 'taste' in Chinese *Nikayas* (CBETA 2015), which were translated from Pāli to Chinese via Japanese. Importantly, the original Pāli scriptures were translated independently to English in Modern time by Ven. Bhikkhu Bodhi. The availability of two versions from the same source enables us to compare the Chinese and the English versions to determine whether the use of TASTE for SENSUAL PLEASURE is induced by translation or inherent in Chinese language.

The example shown in (4) is extracted from *Anguttara Nikaya* (CBETA 2015) and the free translation is cited from the English translation provided by Ven. Bhikkhu Bodhi (2012). It is interesting to note that, in both Chinese and English versions, the gustatory word TASTE is used in this context.

(4)「尊瞿曇乃無色味。」Anguttara Nikaya (2012: 1125)

Zun qutan nai wu se wei.
Venerable Gotama indeed NEG form taste
'Master Gotama lacks taste.'

「婆羅門！有事由，依此事由之故，正說者謂我：『沙門瞿曇乃無色味。』婆羅門！色味、聲味、香味、味味、觸味者，此如來已斷其根本，如無根多羅樹令歸滅於無，而爲未來不生之法。婆羅門！有此事由，依此事由之故，正說者謂我：『沙門瞿曇者乃無色味。』」

Poluomen! You shiyou, yi ci shiyou
Brahmin have way by_means_of this way
zhi gu, zheng shuo zhe wei wo
DE reason rightly speak person say me
'Shamen qutan nai wu se wei.
ascetic Gotama indeed NEG form taste
Poluomen! Se-wei, sheng-wei, xiang-wei,
Brahmin form-taste sound-taste smell-taste
wei-wei, chu-wei zhe, ci rulai
taste-taste touch-taste these this Tathagata
yi duan qi genben, ru wugen
already abandon their basis like root-less
duoluoshu ling guimie yu wu,
palm_stump make annihilate at nothingness
er wei weilai bu sheng zhi fa.
then for future NEG arise DE Dhamma
Poluomen! You ci shiyou, yi ci
Brahmin have this way by_means_of this
shiyou zhi gu, zheng shuo zhe
way DE reason Rightly speak person
wei wo: shamen qutan zhe nai wu
say me ascetic Gotama person indeed NE
se-wei. *Anguttara Nikaya* (2012: 1125)
form-taste

'There is, brahmin, a way in which one could rightly say of me: 'The ascetic Gotama lacks **taste**.' The Tathagata has abandoned his **taste** for forms, sounds, odors, tastes, and tactile objects; he has cut it off at the root, made it like a palm stump, obliterated it so that it is no more subject to future arising. It is in this way that one could rightly say of me: 'The ascetic Gotama lacks **taste**.''

Since the Chinese version and the English version are not supposed to be influenced by each other, we come to a conjecture that the use of TASTE as "sensual gratification" derives from the Pāli source. In order to corroborate this conjecture, we checked the original Pāli scripture for the corresponding expressions, as shown in (5). This conjecture is borne out, as the Pāli word *rasā* 'taste' is proven to collocate with other sensory words, as illustrated by *rūparasā* 'taste of forms', *saddharasā* 'taste of sounds', *gandharasā* 'tatse of smells' and *phoṭṭhabbarasā* 'taste of tangibles'.

(5)

English	Pāli
taste	rasā
taste of forms	rūparasā
taste of sounds	saddharasā
taste of smells	gandharasā
taste of tangibles	phoṭṭhabbarasā

So far, we have established the fact that the gustatory TASTE in Pāli is versatile and capable of collocating with all the other sensory words. This feature, through the process of translation of Buddhist scriptures, has been adopted in Chinese language.

4. More on 味 *wei* 'taste' : synaesthetically-motivated uses of 味 *wei* 'taste' on *Five Aggregates*

To strengthen our understanding of 味 *wei* 'taste' in the *Āgamas*, we take a close look at the data and figure out an extended context in which 味 *wei* 'taste' occurs. Other than the sensory words, e.g., 色 *se* 'form', 聲 *sheng* 'sound', 香 *xiang* 'smell', 味 *wei* 'taste', 觸 *chu* 'tangibles', the words for "five aggregates", viz. 色 *se* 'form', 受 *shou* 'feeling', 想 *xiang* 'perception', 行 *xing* 'preparation', 識 *shi* 'consciousness', can collocate with 味 *wei* 'taste', when the five aggregates are understood in terms of the five sense faculties. As shown in (6), our understanding of the five aggregates relies on the six sense faculties, viz., 眼 *yan* 'eye', 耳 *er* 'ear', 鼻 *bi* 'nose', 舌 *she* 'tongue', 身 *shen* 'body' and 意 *yi* 'mind'. Dependent on our knowledge of the five aggregates gleaned from the sensory data, there arise pleasures, which are termed as the **taste** of the five aggregates.

(6) 爾時，世尊告諸比丘：我昔於**色味**有求有行，若於**色味**隨順覺，則於**色味**以智慧如實見。如是於**受、想、行、識味**有求有行，若於受、想、行、識味隨順覺，則於**識味**以智慧如實見。...云何**色味**如實知？謂色因緣生喜樂，是名**色味**，如是**色味**如實知。

Ershi, shizun gao zhu biqiu: wo
then Buddha speak_to PL monk I
xi yu **se-wei** youqiu
in_the_past at form-taste have_expectation
youxing, ruo yu **se-wei**
have_preparation if at form-taste
suishunjue ze yu **se-wei** yi zhihu
follow_naturally then at form-taste by wisdom
rushi jian. Rushi yu **shou, xiang,**

thus see thus at feeling perception
xing, **shi-wei** youqiu
preparations consciousness-taste have_expectation
youxing, ruo yu shou xiang,
have_preparations if at feeling perception
xing, **shi-wei** suishunjue,
preparations consciousness-taste follow_naturally
ze yu **shi-wei** yi zhihui rushi
then at consciousness-taste by wisdom as_such
jian. Yunhe **se-wei** rushi zhi? Wei
see why form-taste as_such understand such
se yinyuan er sheng xiyue, shi ming
form reason then arise pleasure thus call
se-wei, rushi **se-wei** rushi zhi.
form-taste thus form-taste thus understand

'At that time, the Buddha spoke to the monks: I used to have expectations and preparations with regard to the taste of forms; if I were in tune with the taste of forms without expectations, I see the taste of forms as it is with the help of wisdom. Likewise, with regard to feeling, perception, preparations, and consciousness, I used to have expectations and preparations; if I were in tune with the tastes of feeling, perception, preparations, and consciousness without expectations, I were in tune with the tastes of feeling, perception, preparations and consciousness as they are, I see the taste of consciousness as it is with the help of wisdom…Why do we see the taste of form as it is? Dependent on forms, there arise pleasures. This is called the taste of forms. It is in this sense that we see the taste of forms as it is.'

云何**受味**如實知？緣六受生喜樂，是名**受味**，如是**受味**如實知。

Yunhe **shou-wei** rushi zhi?
why feeling-taste as_such understand
Yuan liu shou sheng
dependent_on six feeling arise
xiyue, shi ming shou-wei,
pleasurebe called feeling-taste
rushi **shou-wei** rushi zhi.
as_such feeling-taste as_such understsand

'Why do we understand the taste of feelings as it is? Dependent on the six feelings, there arise pleasures. This is called the taste of feelings. It is in this sense that we see the taste of feelings as it is.'

謂眼觸生想，耳、鼻、舌、身、意觸生想，是名想，如是想如實知。云何想集如實知？...云何想味如實知？想因緣生喜樂，是名**想味**，如是想味如實知。

Wei yan chu sheng xiang, er,
call eye touch arise perception ear
bi, she, shen, yi chu sheng
nose tongue body mind touch arise
xiang, shi ming xiang, rushi
perception be call perception as_such
xiang rushi zhi. Yunhe
perception as_such understand why
xiang-wei rushi zhi? Xiang
perception-taste as_such understand perception
yinyuan sheng xiyue, shi ming
reason arise pleasure be call
xiang-wei, rushi xiangwei-wei
feeling-taste as_such perception-taste
rushi zhi.
as_such understsand

'Dependent on eye-touch, there arise perceptions. Dependent on ear-, nose-, tongue-, body- and mind-touch, there arise perceptions. They are called perceptions. It is in this sense that we understand perceptions as they are… Why do we understand the taste of perceptions as it is? Dependent on perceptions, there arise pleasures. This is called the taste of perceptions. It is in this sense that we see the taste of perceptions as it is.'

云何行如實知？…眼觸生思，耳、鼻、舌、身、意觸生思，是名為行，如是行如實知。…謂行因緣生喜樂，是名**行味**，如是行味如實知。

Yunhe xing rushi zhi?
Why preparations as_such understand
Yan-chu sheng si, er,
eye-touch arise mental_formation ear
bi, she, shen, yi-chu sheng
nose tongue body mind-touch arise
si, shi mingwei
mental_formation be call
xing, rushi xing rushi
preparations thus preparations as_such
zhi… wei xing yinyuan
understand call preparation reason
sheng xiyue, shi ming
arise pleasure be call
xing-wei, rushi **xing-wei**
preparation-taste thus preparation-taste
rushi zhi.
as_such understand

'Why do we understand preparations as they are? Dependent on eye-touch, there arises mental formation. Likewise, mental formation can be derived by ear-touch, nose-touch, tongue-touch, body-touch and mind-touch. This mental formation is called preparation. It is in this sense that we understand preparation as it is.

Dependent on preparation, there arise pleasures. This is called preparation-taste. It is in this sense that we understand preparation-taste as it is.'
云何識如實知？謂六識身——眼識身，耳、鼻、舌、身、意識身，是名為識身，如是識身如實知…云何**識味**如實知？識因緣生喜樂，是名識味，如是**識味**如實知。(雜含經卷第一)
Yunhe shi rushi zhi?
why consciousness as_such understand
Wei liu shi shen,
call six consciousness substance
yan-shi shen, er, bi,
eye-consciousness substance ear nose
she shen yishi-shen
tongue body consciousness-substance
shi mingwei shi-shen, rushi
be call consciousness_substance as_such
shi-shen rushi zhi…
consciousness_substance as_such understand
Yunhe **shi-wei** rushi zhi?
why consciousness-taste as_such understand
Shi yinyuan sheng xiyue, shi
consciousness reason arise pleasure be
ming shi-wei rushi
call consciousness-taste thus
shi-wei rushi zhi.
consciousness-taste as_such understand
'Why do we understand consciousness as it is? It is called the substance of the six consciousnesses. The substance of eye consciousness, that of the ear consciousness, that of the nose consciousness, that of the tongue consciousness, that of the body consciousness, and that of the mind consciousness, are collectively called the substance of consciousnesses. It is in this way that we understand consciousness as it is. Why do we understand the taste of consciousness as it is? Dependent on consciousness, there arise pleasures. This is called the taste of consciousness. It is in this way that we understand the taste of consciousness as it is.'

In addition to the nominal use of 味 *wei* 'taste' in collocation with the five aggregates, 味 *wei* 'taste' can be used as a verb, meaning "be gratified by sensual pleasures". This can be exemplified in (7) below.

(7) 爾時，世尊告諸比丘：若眾生於色不**味**者，則不染於色；以眾生於色**味**故，則有染著。如是眾生於受、想、行、識不**味**者，彼眾生則不染於識；以眾生**味**受、想、行、識故，彼眾生染著於識。
Ershi, shizun gao zhu
at_that_time Buddha speak_to PL
biqiu: ruo zhongsheng yu se bu
monk if beings at form NEG
wei zhe, ze bu ran yu se;
taste person then NEG delude at form
yi zhongsheng yu se **wei** gu,
by beings at form taste reason
ze you ranzhuo. Rushi zhongsheng
then have delusion thus beings
yu shou, xiang, xing, shi
at feeling perception preparation consciousness
bu **wei** zhe, bi zhongsheng
NEG be_gratified person those beings
ze bu ran yu shi,
then NEG delude at consciousness
yi zhongsheng **wei** shou,
because beings taste feeling
xiang, xing, shi
perception preparation consciousness
gu, bi zhongsheng ranzhuo
reason those beings delude
yu shi.
at consciousness
'At that time, the Buddha told the monks: "if beings are not gratified with regard to forms, they don't get deluded by forms; if beings are gratified with regard to forms, they are deluded by forms. With regard to feeling, perception, preparation and consciousness, if beings are not gratified, they don't get deluded by them. It is because beings are gratified with regard to feeling, perception, preparation and consciousness, they are deluded by them."'

The discussion above points to the fact that the Chinese word 味 *wei* 'taste' can transcend the gustatory meaning to refer to "sensual gratification" as a noun or "be gratified by sensual input" as a verb. Despite of this grammatical difference, these two uses have one feature in common: they are related to sensory meaning. Crucially, we find that these two uses in Chinese are derived from Pāli language, by which the original texts were composed.

5. The Metaphorical Uses of 味 *wei* 'taste'

Apart from the sensory uses of 味 *wei* 'taste', we identify another usage of 味 *wei* 'taste', which collocate with words of abstract meanings, such as 法

fa 'dhamma', 意 *yi* 'meaning' and 解脱 *jietuo* 'liberation'. Since these words are devoid of sensory meanings, 味 *wei* 'taste' in this use is said to be further semantically bleached.

(8) 如我今日說法，上中下言，皆悉真正，**義味**具足，梵行清淨。(長阿含經 佛說長阿含 第二分轉輪聖王修行經第二)
Ru wo jinri shuofa, shang zhong
like I today preach_dhamma up middle
xia yan, jiexi zhenzheng, **yi-wei**
down speech all authentic meaning-taste
juzu, fanxing qingjing.
endowed holy_practice clean
'As I am preaching Dhamma for now, the beginning, the middle and the end of the Dhamma is authentic and meaningful. And the holy practice is clean.'

(9) 比丘！行此十念者，便獲大果報，得甘露**法味**。(增壹阿含經卷第三十四七日品第四十之一（五）)
Biqiu! Xing ci shi nian zhe,
monk practice this ten thinking person
bian huo da guobao, de ganlu
then gain big benefit gain nectar
fa-wei.
dhamma-taste
'Monks! If you practice the ten thinking patterns, you will reap great benefits and gain the nectar taste of Dhamma.'

(10) 行法得樂果，**解脱味**中上，智慧除老死，是為壽中勝。(雜阿含經卷第五十)
Xing fa de le guo,
practice dhamma gain happiness fruit
jietuo-wei zhong shang, zhihui
liberation-taste in up wisdom
chu lao si, shi wei
rid aging death be as
shou zhong sheng.
life in superb
'The fruit of happiness gained by one's Dhamma practice is the upmost one in the taste of liberation; the elimination of aging and death by means of wisdom is the superb one in one's life.'

(11) 正如此，能得義味、法味、解脱味之有情少；相反者，不能得義味、法味、解脱味之有情更多。諸比丘！是故，今汝等應如是學，謂：我等欲得**義味、法味、解脱味**。諸比丘！汝等應如是學。(增支部；第十九 不放逸品）
Zheng ruci, neng de **yi-wei,**
right as_such can obtain meaning-taste
fa-wei, **jietuo-wei** zhi youqing
dhamma-taste liberation-taste DE being
shao; xiangfan zhe, bu neng de
few opposite case NEG can obtain
yi-wei **fa-wei** **jietuo-wei**
meaning-taste dhamma-taste liberation-taste
zhi youqing gengduo. Zhu biqiu
DE being more PL monk
shi gu jin ru deng ying rushi
thus reason now you PL should thus
xue, wei: wo deng yu de
learn call I PL want obtain
yi-wei, **fa-wei,** **jiatuo-wei**.
meaning-taste dhammat-taste liberation-taste
zhu biqiu! Ru deng ying rushi
PL monk you PL should as_such
xue.
learn
'... So too those beings are few who obtain the taste of the meaning, the taste of the Dhamma and the taste of liberation; more numerous are those who do not obtain the taste of the meaning, the taste of the Dhamma, the taste of liberation. Therefore, bhikkhus, you should train yourselves thus: 'we will obtain the taste of the meaning, the taste of the Dhamma, the taste of liberation.' It is in such a way that you should train yourselves.'

The above examples show that 味 *wei* 'taste' could fully transcend the sensory meaning. Moreover, 味 *wei* 'taste' of this use, unlike that in the sensory context, carries commendatory sense. As shown in (8)-(11), 義味 *yiwei* 'meaning-taste', 法味 *fawei* 'dhamma-taste', 解脱味 *jietuowei* 'liberation-taste' are positive qualities that Buddhist practitioners are encouraged to procure through diligent practice. Though "pleasure and joy" component of meaning is retained, this "pleasure and joy" are not derived from sensory input. As is well-known, sensual pleasures are something unwholesome in Buddhist teachings, 味 *wei* 'taste' derived out of sensory data is naturally negative in the sense that practitioners should forgo this kind of sensory taste. By contrast, "pleasure and joy" gained through one's knowledge of dhamma or one's experience of liberation, at the supra-mundane level, is something wholesome and thus commendatory.

This polarity value can be well captured by two types of emotional evaluation: the spontaneous emotion and the evaluative emotion (Xiong and Huang 2015). The synaesthetic uses of 味 *wei* 'taste' are usually associated with spontaneous or embodied emotion, as they are sense-related, whereas the metaphorical ones can be evaluative, as they are more abstract and less embodied.

6. Concluding Remarks:

This paper investigates the non-gustatory uses of 味 *wei* 'taste', which can be generally classified into two types: one is the synaesthetic usage and the other is the metaphorical usage. The former one features its collocation with all the other sensory words, directly or indirectly. The latter one is not sense-related but it inherits the "joy and pleasure" meaning, which is interpreted in the supra-mundane level and thus commendatory.

References

Ahrens, Kathleen. 2010. Mapping Principles for Conceptual Metaphors. In Cameron Lynne, Alice Deignan, Graham Low, Zazie Todd (Eds.), Researching and Applying Metaphor in the Real World. Amsterdam: John Benjamins. Pp.185-207.

Bardovskaya. A.I. 2002. Different approaches to synesthesia. In A. A. Zalevskaya (Ed.). Psycholinguistic researches: Word and text. pp. 16-22. Tver: University of Tver Press.

Bhihku Bodhi. 2000. *The Connected Discourses of the Buddha: A Translation of the Samyutta Nikaya*. Boston: Wisdom Publications.

Bhihku Bodhi. 2012. *The Numerical Discourses of the Buddha: A Translation of the Anguttara Nikaya*. Boston: Wisdom Publications.

Bhihku Nanamoli and Bhihku Bodhi. 1995. The Middle Length Discourses of the Buddha: A Translation of the Majjhima Nikaya. Boston: Wisdom Publications.

Bretones-Callejas, Carmen. 2001. "Synaesthetic meta phors in English", Technical Reports, TR 01-008, International Computer Science Institute, Berkeley, USA. Cacciari, Cristina. 2008. "Crossing the senses in metaphorical language", in Gibbs, R. W. (ed.), The Cambridge handbook of metaphor and thought, New York, Cambridge University Press, 425-443.

CBETA: Chinese Buddhist Electronic Text Association. 2015

Huang, Chu-Ren, Siaw-Fong Chung and Kathleen Ahrens. 2006. An Ontology-based Exploration of Knowledge Systems for Metaphor. In Rajiv Kishore, Ram Ramesh, and Raj Sharman Eds. Ontologies: A Handbook of Principles, Concepts and Applications in Information Systems. Pp. 489-517. Berlin: Springer.

Xiong Jiajuan and Chu-Ren Huang. 2015. Being Assiduous: Do We Have Bitterness or Pain. Springer: LNAI.

L2 Acquisition of Korean locative construction by English L1 speakers

Sun Hee Park
Department of Korean Studies
Ewha Womans University
Seoul, Korea
sunheepark@ewha.ac.kr

Abstract

Korean has locative construction as other languages do such as English. Although L2 acquisition of locative construction has been examined in L2 English research, few experimental investigations of Korean L2 acquisition have been conducted. The current study focused on the syntactic alternation among Figure Framed sentence, Ground Framed sentence, Figure only sentence and Ground only sentence. Forced choice task on 72 locative construction have been conducted by 21 Native Korean speakers and 20 advanced L1 English learners of Korean. L2ers showed different acceptability judgment on Korean locative construction which was distinct from their L1 argument structure. The results showed that these asymmetries were driven by L1 effect when the learnability problem arises due to insufficient input.

Introductions

Locative construction in languages imposes intriguing phenomenon in terms of case marking[1]. Locative verbs compose two different structures with a transitive verb. This phenomenon is known as 'figure/ground' alternation or locative alternation. Locative verbs denote a transfer of a substance or a set of objects (theme, content, or locatum) into or onto a container or surface (the goal, container, or location) as investigated in Pinker (1989). A substance or a set of objects are often referred as 'figure' and a container or surface is referred as 'ground' in the locative alternation studies. For example, English locative verb '*load*' can have two structures of figure direct object [Figure Frame, henceforth FF] as in (1a) and ground direct object [Ground Frame, henceforth GF] as in (1b).

(1) a. Irv loaded <u>hay</u> into the wagon. [Figure Frame]
b. Irv loaded <u>the wagon</u> with hay. [Ground Frame]

Semantically locative sentences which alternate between FF and GF have different interpretation, often called as 'holistic interpretation' [2]. Syntactically, FF locative constructions whose figure NPs are denoted as objects are argued as unmarked compared to GF. Since FF has unmarked case marking, they have canonical/unmarked

[1] In researches of error Analysis on L2 Korean case marking, there have been reports on high frequency errors among L2ers of Korean regarding 'ey' and 'ul/lul' substitution. The locative structure has very structural (or systematic) substitution among these two types of case marking in the alternation phenomenon. There have been researches on semantic interpretation on locative structures but since case marking and argument structures are quite important in Korean language as other agglutinative languages. It is worthy investigating what mechanism in L2 language of case marking alternation of Korean happens in the path.

[2] The holistic interpretation will be explained in chapter 2 of this research.

linking pattern (Larson 1988) [3] or canonical structural realization (Grimshaw, 1981).
Regarding to the L2 acquisition of Korean locative construction which is not often focused as target grammar items in the classroom, a question arises whether L2ers will conform to the canonical linking pattern or be affected by their L1 or even L2. L2ers may have diverse acquisition paths available when L2 argument structure is not identical to their L1 and target input is insufficient enough to acquire target knowledge.

Previous Studies

There have been a series of studies of locative structure in L2 acquisition but they were mostly on L2 English cases (Juff, 1996a; Juff, 1996b; Brinkmann 1997; Inagake, 2007; Kim, 1999; Joo, 2000; Bley-Vroman & Joo, 2001, Choi & Lakshmanan, 2002). In addition, the focus was not on the argument structure itself but on semantic interpretation, 'holism effect'.
Holism effect or holistic interpretation can be explained in (2). For example, verb 'load' can have two structures, FF and GF.

(2) a. Irv loaded hay into the wagon.
[Figure Frame]
b. Irv loaded the wagon with hay.
→ *Holistic interpretation* [Ground Frame]

GF Sentence (2b) has holistic interpretation compared to FF sentence (2a) [4]. The ground NP 'wagon' in (2b) is interpreted as fully filled with hay compared to 'wagon' in (2a), which is in _adverb phrase. The holistic interpretation is that the ground NP as in (2b) has been fully affected by the action of locative verbs.
There have been researches on L1 Korean acquisition research (Lee, 1997) and child bilingual (Kim et. al., 1999; Kim, 1999) for younger speakers. In this study, L2 Korean acquisition of English L1 young learners has been examined but these studies also focused on holistic interpretation not on syntactic alternation.
Few studies in L2 adult Korean acquisition of locative structure by L1 English speakers can be found. Syntactic locative alternation is left for further investigation in L2 acquisition research.

Cross-linguistic variation across Korean and English locative construction

Many studies have investigated the cross-linguistic variation in the mapping of locative construction among Korean and English including Kim et al. (1999), Kim (1999), Bley-Vroman and Joo (2001), Choi and Lakshmanan (2002), and Joo (2003).
One of the discrepancies is that the number of Korean locative verb classes is smaller than that of English. Also, the number of locative verbs that belongs to each category is not evenly distributed. The English locative verbs show 4 types of diversity in terms of syntactic alternation as in (3) ~ (6).

(3) Non-alternating Figure verbs in English
(e.g., *dribble, spill, slop, or ladle*)
a. John *poured* water into the glass. [FF]
b. *Josh *poured* the glass with water. [GF]

(4) Non-alternating Ground verbs in English
(e.g., *cover, decorate, or soak*)
a. *John *filled* water with the glass. [FF]
b. Sarah *filled* the glass with water. [GF]

(5) Alternating Figure verbs in English
(e.g., *spray, load, or, sow*)
a. John *piled* books on the table. [FF]
b. John *piled* the table with books. [GF]

(6) Alternating Ground verbs in English
(e.g., *paint, wrap, or stuff*)
a. John *stuffed* feather into the pillow. [FF]

[3] In the linking theories, Larson (1988:82) that Agent maps onto subject, Theme maps onto object, and Location maps onto oblique object. This syntactic and semantic hierarchies is called as Canonical linking pattern.
[4] Pinker (2013:92) explained that holistic interpretation is not confined to locative alternation. Holistic requirement on the ground framer, whereby the grammatical object must be completely affected (covered filled, etc.) by the action of the verb (see Andersen, 1971). Holistic effect is a characteristic of grammatical objects in general, not just of grammatical objects in the container-locative construction, which has been mentioned in Hopper and Thomson (1980) and Rappaport and Levin (1985).

b. John *stuffed* the pillow with feather. [GF]

However, Korean has mostly two types of locative verbs as in (7) and (8). For ground verbs, there are arguments over the availability of alternation among researchers and it is displayed by '?' mark in Table 1 below.

(7) Non-alternating figure verbs
a. John-*i* cengwen-*ey* mwul-*ul*
John-NOM garden-LOC water-ACC
wulyesseyo.
sprayed. [FF]
'John sprayed water on the garden.'
b. *John-*i* mwul-*lo* cengwen-*ul*
John-NOM water-INS garden-ACC
pwulyesseyo.
sprayed. [GF]
'John sprayed the garden with water.'

(8) Alternating Ground verbs
a. John-*i* cup-ey mwul-*ul*
John-NOM cup-LOC water-ACC
chaywuesseyo. [FF]
filled.
*'*John filled water into the cup.'*
b. John-i mwul-*lo* cup-*ul*
John-NOM water-INS cup-ACC
chaywuesseyo. [GF]
filled.
'John filled the cup with water.'

The distribution of English and Korean locative verbs can be summarized as in Table 1 below.

Table 1. English and Korean locative verbs

	English		Korean	
	Alternating	Non-alternating	Alternating	Non-alternating
Figure oriented	√	√		√
Ground oriented	√	√	√/?	?[5]

As shown in table 1, English has figure oriented[6] alternating, non-alternating, ground oriented alternating, and non-alternating verbs. In Korean, however, has figure verbs which do not alternate and most of the ground verbs are alternating except a few ground verbs, which is marked by '?'. Researchers have different judgments on the grammaticality of the structure of alternating ground verbs and non-alternating ones. Choi and Lakshmanan (2002) stated that Korean only has figure non-alternator verbs and ground alternator verbs. But Lee, H. (1997) reported that Korean has alternators (figure/ground), figure non-alternators, but very little number of ground non-alternators[7]. Since the defining the ground alternating and non-alternating verbs is not agreed upon and Korean native speakers show diverse spectrum of grammaticality[8], we will focus on the figure non-alternating verbs in the current research.

[5] These disagreements can be explained by two reasons. One is that the studies examined different group of locative verbs from each other. The other reason is that the grammaticality judgment task or researcher's individual grammaticality judgment was not decisive enough to draw conclusion.

[6] Figure oriented means that the figure verbs allow 1 argument sentence with figure object only but not with ground object only in the sentence. Verb 'pile' is an alternating figure verb. The verb 'pile' allows figure only sentence in (1a) below but not ground only sentence (1b). Pinker (1989) argued that there existed directionality from figure only object sentence (1a) to figure frame sentence (1c). (1d) is possible since 'pile' allows the ground frame, therefore verb 'pile' is a figure oriented alternator verb.

(1) a. He piled the books. [Figure only]
b. * He piled the shelf. [Ground only]
c. He piled the books onto the shelf. [FF]
d. He piled the shelf with the books. [GF]

[7] Only two verbs of 'telephita (*stain*)' and 'cangsikhata (*decorate*)' belong to ground non-alternating class in Korean.

[8] A norming test has been conducted on the 23 Korean native speakers' grammaticality judgment over the sentences of the ground alternating and ground non-alternating verbs. The verbs tested in the norming test were 6 verbs including 'chilhata (*paint*)', 'makta (*block*)', 'paluta (*spread*)', 'tephta (*cover*)', 'cangsikhata (*decorate*)', and 'chaywuta (*fill*)'. For each verb, 3 sentences in FF and GF were given to the participants. The table below shows that so called ground verbs in Korean do not have consistency in the grammaticality judgments performed by Korean native speakers.

	Grammaticality judgments (%)	
Sentences type	FF	GF
Chilhata	21.7 (94.34%)	19.7 (85.65%)
Makta	6.67 (29%)	21.3 (92.6%)
Paluta	22.7 (98.7%)	8.33 (36.22%)
Tephta	20.3 (88.26%)	19.7 (85.65%)
cangsikhata	15 (65.22%)	20.3 (88.26%)
chaywuta	20.67 (89.87%)	18.33 (79.7%)

Now let us turn to the other discrepancy. The discrepancy of grammaticality judgments of corresponding locative constructions between English and Korean. As we have seen in (7b), some Korean figure non-alternating verbs semantically correspond to alternating verbs in English. This may lead L2ers whose L1 is English to judge Korean sentence in GF to be grammatical, even though it is not grammatical in Korean.

The structural equivalence of the locative alternation in Korean and English may create a significant confusion/problem for language learners, since despite the affinity in their structural alternation (i.e. existence of alternation phenomenon between figure and ground argument structure), they are quite distinctive in their grammaticality of the semantically corresponding verbs.

We are interested in cross-linguistic variation of locative structures. Therefore, we will specify the verbs that will be examined in the research as in Table 2.

Table 2. Locative verbs classification in this research

	Korean
Grammaticality	Figure non-alternator
Identical with English	Type 1a hullita, *'spill'* pwusta, *'pour'* kelta, *'hang'*
Distinct from English	Type 1b ppwulita, *'spray'* ssahta, *'stock'* sitta, *'load'*

For Type 1a in Table 2, grammaticality judgments over FF and GF in English and Korean are identical. FF is grammatical but GF is ungrammatical in Type 1a. For Type 1b, grammaticality on the FF in English and Korean is ungrammatical. However, grammaticality on GF in Korean and English is distinct from each other. Korean GF is ungrammatical but English GF is grammatical.

The linguistic knowledge required for L1-English learners of Korean to learn ground frame by figure non-alternator verb (7b) is not easily accessible for them since it cannot come from their L1, nor is it easily induced from L2 Korean input alone, and it is not covered as target grammar in the Korean classroom. This (specifically figure non-alternator) causes learnability problem[9] in L2 adult acquisition of Korean locative construction. Therefore, we will focus on the figure non-alternator construction in the study.

1 The Study

1.1 Research Questions and Hypothesis

Research Question: Is there difference in acceptability judgment on Korean non-alternators among Native Korean speakers and L1 English learners of Korean (henceforth, L2ers)?

Hypothesis: The L2ers will show different acceptability judgments from Korean native speakers in the figure non-alternator construction, which is distinct from their L1 argument structure.

L2ers of Korean may choose to conform to L2, L1, or canonical linking pattern (or canonical structural realization) in acquisition of locative alternation. If figure non-alternating construction is easy to acquire without focused instruction, there will be no difference in grammaticality judgments of NKs and L2ers. However, Korean figure non-alternating verbs may cause learnability problem to the L1 English learners of Korean. If L2ers conform to L1 argument structure of figure non-alternator, they will show different acceptability judgments in GF from NKs when their L1 argument structure is distinct from L2 Korean. If L2ers follow canonical linking pattern, they will show preferences for FF and Figure only sentence (henceforth F) consistently in acceptability judgments.

1.2 Participants

The study participants consisted of two groups: 21 Korean Native speakers (NKs, age range=25~38) and 20 advanced L1 English learners of Korean (L2ers, age range=17-20). NKs were either current university students or graduates of universities in

[9] White (2003:8) argued that learnability problem is constituted by the situation where there is a mismatch between the adult knowledge and the data that the child is exposed to. In other words, the input is insufficient to alert the learners to the relevant distinction, learnability problem arises.

Korea. L2ers were current high school students of foreign school near Seoul. The proficiency of L2ers corresponds to level 5-6 in TOPIK (Test of Proficiency in level Korean) which is advanced level.

1.3 Task, Material & Procedures

The main task used in the experiment was a forced choice task. The participants were asked to indicate acceptability for the given sentences by choosing all the acceptable sentences.

The test material was composed of 72 Korean locative constructions along with 104 fillers of Korean causatives: There were 36 sentences of three non-alternating figure verbs (hullita, '*spill*'; pwusta, '*pour*'; kelta, '*hang*'). All of them were identical with the grammaticality of corresponding English sentences: all of the alternatives are grammatical. The other 36 sentences were composed of another three verbs (ppwulita, '*spray*'; ssahta, '*stock*'; sitta, '*load*') which have discrepancy in grammaticality between in English and in Korean: which is grammatical in English GF and Ground only sentences (henceforth G), but not grammatical in Korean.

For each verb, four types of sentences which are FF, GF, figure only sentence, and Ground only sentence were given for participants' choice.

(9) a. John-*i* khep-*ey* mwul-*ul*
John-NOM cup-LOC waater-ACC
pwuesseyo.
poured. [FF]
'John poured water into the cup.'

b. *John-*i* mwul-*lo* khep-*ul*
John-NOM water-INS cup-ACC
pwuesseyo. [GF]
poured.
'John poured the cup with water.'

c. John-*i* mwul-*ul* pwuesseyo.
John-NOM water-ACC poured.
'John poured water.' [Figure only]

d. *John-*i* khep-*ul* pwuesseyo.
John-NOM cup-ACC poured.
'John poured the cup.' [Ground only]

In order to help the participants to understand the sentences, pictures were provided along the sentences of one verb as in Figure 1.

Figure 1. Example of the experiment material

1.4 Statistical Analysis

The data collected were not applicable for parametric test such as *t*-test or MANOVA. In order to compare the scores of participants' choice over the acceptable Korean locative, Mann-Whitney U test has been used. The dependent variable in the analysis was the total scores of the acceptability judgment for the sentences which share the same argument structure. The independent variable was the Korean proficiency group of NKs and L2ers.

2 Results

In our data sets, there were two types of figure non-alternators: the verbs that have identical argument structure with English and the verbs that have distinct argument structure from English. We first compared the total score of forced choice task on each FF, GF, F, and G for the both of identical and distinct categories.

Table 2. Mann-Whitney *U* test of forced choice task scores of NKs and L2ers

L1-L2		*df*	*z*	*p*
Identical	FF	21.676	-1.361	.187
	GF	21.676	-1.361	.187
	F	29.117	-1.110	.276
	G	27.262	-.473	.640
Distinct	FF	28.637	-1.474	.151
	GF	22.711	-3.099	.005*
	F	28.637	-.783	.440
	G	21.522	-2.635	.015*

*p< .05

Table 2 demonstrates that NKs and L2ers showed statistically significant difference only in GF and G sentences of distinct category.

The descriptive statistics in Table 3 shows that L2ers have chosen the unacceptable sentence more than NKs in GF sentences and G only sentences. The range of L2ers' responses in GF and G of distinct context is marked by boxes in Table 3 below.

Table 3. Median and range of the forced-choice task scores on acceptable locative sentences

L1-L2			*median*	*Range (Min.~Max.)*
Identical	FF	NKs (21)	9	1 (8~9)
		L2ers (20)	9	1 (8~9)
	GF	NKs (21)	9	1 (8~9)
		L2ers (20)	9	1 (8~9)
	F	NKs (21)	9	1 (8~9)
		L2ers (20)	9	2 (7~9)
	G	NKs (21)	9	1 (8~9)
		L2ers (20)	9	2 (7~9)
Distinct	FF	NKs (21)	9	1 (8~9)
		L2ers (20)	9	1 (8~9)
	GF	NKs (21)	9	1 (8~9)
		L2ers (20)	9	3 (6~9)
	F	NKs (21)	9	1 (8~9)
		L2ers (20)	9	2 (7~9)
	G	NKs (21)	9	1 (8~9)
		L2ers (20)	9	2 (7~9)

Discussion

Korean figure non-alternating verbs may cause learnability problem in L1 English learners of Korean. They may choose to conform to L2, canonical linking pattern (or canonical structural realization), or L1.

First, it is assumable that since L2 locative alternation is not focused as target grammar in the classroom, L2ers may not be able to know all the figure oriented verbs are non-alternators in L2. This may have L2ers file to conform to L2 argument structure of locatives. Secondly, L2ers can choose to follow the canonical pattern (or argument structure) or conform to their L2, in which L2ers may simply regard all the FF and F sentences as acceptable and deny all the GF and G sentence as unacceptable.

However, the results showed that advanced L2ers did not conform to L2 argument structure nor did they to canonical linking pattern. They made the acceptability judgments based on their L1 argument structure by showing discrepancy over identical and distinct categories.

L2ers of Korean might have seen that some of Korean ground verbs could alternate, assuming that the alternators in their L1 correspond to L2 locative construction even when all the Korean figure verbs are non-alternators.

Conclusion

The current study investigated how the interlanguage of L1 English learners of Korean is shown in Korean figure non-alternating verbs' construction. 21 NKs and 20 advanced L2ers of Korean participated in the acceptability judgment tests which were composed of 4 types of locative construction (FF, GF, F, and G).

The results showed that advanced L2ers failed to acquire syntactic distinction in figure non-alternating constructions. They appeared to make their judgments in GF and G constructions in distinct argument structure category based on their L1. This may explain how L2ers depend on L1 knowledge when learnability problem arises.

Acknowledgments

This work was supported by the National Research Foundation of Korea Grant funded by the Korean Government (NRF-2014S1A2A1A01028163).

References

Andersen, S. A. 1971. On the role of deep structure in semantic interpretation. Foundation of Language, 6: 197-219.

Bley-Vroman, R. and Joo, H. 2001. The Acquisition and interpretation of English locative constructions by native speakers of Korean. Studies in Second Language Acquisition, 23: 207-219.

Choi, M. and Lakshmanan, U. 2002. Holism and locative argument structure in Korean English Bilingual Grammars. Proceedings of BUCLD 26: 95-106.

Ellis, S. L. 2009. The development and validation of a Korean C-Test using Rasch Analysis. Language Testing, 26(2): 245–274.

Grimshaw, J. 1981. Form, Function, and the Language Acquisition Device. In C. L. Baker and J. J. McCarthy, eds., The logical problem of Language Acquisition. MIT Press, Cambridge, MA.

Hopper, P. J., and Thomson, S. A. 1980. Transitivity in grammar and discourse. Language, 56: 251-299.

Joo, H-R. 2003. Second language learnability and the acquisition of the argument structure of English locative verbs by Korean speakers, Second Language Research, 19(4): 305–328.

Juffs, A. 1996a. Learnability and the lexicon: theories and second language acquisition research. Philadelphia, John Benjamins, PA.

Juffs, A. 1996b. Semantics-syntax correspondences in second language acquisition. Second Language Research, 12(2): 177-221.

Kim, C-S 2011. Korean Educational Model for International standards. National Institute of Korean Language. Seoul, Korea.

Kim, M., Landau, B., and Phillips, C. 1999. Cross-linguistic differences in Children's Syntax for Locative verbs. In *Proceedings of BUCLD 23*, ed. A. Greenhill, H. Littlefield, and C. Tano, 337-348. Somerville, MA: Cascadilla Press.

Kim, M. 1999. A Cross-linguistic perspective on the acquisition of locative verbs. Unpublished Ph. D. dissertation of the University of Delaware.

Larson, R. 1988. On the double object construction. Linguistic Inquiry 19. 335-392.

Lee, Hanjung. 1997. The meanings and acquisition of the Korean locative verbs. In Lee, H.J., Linguistic theories and Korean semantic and syntax acquisition I. Seoul: Mineum-sa, 103–26.

Pinker, S. 1989. Learnability and Cognition. MIT press.

Rappaport, M., and Levin, B. 1985. A case study in lexical analysis: The locative alternation. Unpublished manuscript, MIT Center for Cognitive Science.

White, L. 2003. Second language acquisition and Universal Grammar. Cambridge University Press.

Towards a Unified Account of Resultative Constructions in Korean

Juwon Lee
School of English, Kyung Hee University
26, Kyungheedae-ro, Dongdaemun-gu, Seoul 02447, Republic of Korea
happyjuwon@gmail.com

Abstract

This paper discusses predicative resultative constructions in Korean and argues that they are actually a kind of clausal resultative construction (see the two types of resultatives in Wechsler and Noh, 2001). In particular, I propose the following hypotheses: (i) the resultative predicate, X-*key*, is morpho-syntactically an adverb rather than an adjective, (ii) X-*key* forms a fully saturated clause (i.e., result clause) (sometimes with the predication subject omitted), and (iii) the result clause is a complement of the main verb in a resultative sentence. Based on these properties, a unified analysis of the resultative constructions is formalized in Head-driven Phrase Structure Grammar (HPSG) (Pollard and Sag, 1994; Sag *et al.*, 2003).

1 Introduction

This paper discusses what is referred to as predicative resultative constructions in Korean, exemplified in (1a), and argues that they are in fact a kind of clausal resultative construction like (1b) (see the different types of resultatives in Wechsler and Noh, 2001). It is normally understood that in (1a) the resultative predicate *ppalkah-key* 'red-Key' is predicated of the matrix object *mwun-ul* 'door-Acc' in a controlled structure. In (1b), however, the nominative NP *sinpal-i* 'shoes-Nom' and the resultative predicate *talh-key* 'threadbare-Key' constitutes a fully saturated result clause (Wechsler and Noh, 2001: 404). Despite some differences (e.g., (in)transitivity of the verb), these two sentences share the notion of resultative: as a result of the event denoted by the main verb, an argument undergoes a change of state denoted by the result predicate.

(1) a. *ku-ka mwun-ul ppalkah-key*
he-Nom door-Acc red-Key
chilhay-ss-ta
paint-Pst-Dec
'He painted the door red.'

b. *ku-ka [sinpal-i talh-key]*
he-Nom shoes-Nom threadbare-Key
talli-ess-ta.
run-Pst-Dec
'He ran so that (his) shoes became threadbare.'

There have been various clausal analyses of Korean resultative expressions such as that in (1a) in the literature (see Shim and den Dikken, 2007; Shibagaki, 2011 for TP adjunct analysis, Son, 2008 for small clause complement analysis, and Nakazawa, 2008 for adverbial clause adjunct account of Japanese resultatives). While I agree with the general idea that the resultative predicate forms a clause, particularly I propose the following hypotheses in this paper: (i) the resultative predicate, X-*key*, is morpho-syntactically an adverb rather than an adjective, (ii) X-*key* forms a fully saturated clause, result clause (sometimes with the predication subject omitted), and (iii) the result clause is a complement of the main verb. A unified analysis of the resultative constructions is then cast in the framework of Head-driven Phrase Structure Grammar (HPSG) (Pollard and Sag, 1994; Sag *et al.*, 2003).

2 Adverb vs. adjective

It is generally assumed in the literature that at least some resultative predicates are adjective (see, e.g., Wechsler and Noh, 2001: 420). However, in this section I provide three pieces of evidence supporting the claim that resultative predicates in Korean are adverb, but not adjective.

2.1 Coordination

Coordinated conjuncts are known to basically belong to the same syntactic category and the resultative predicate, Adj(ective)-*key*, [1] can be coordinated with a typical adverb modifying manner of action, as illustrated in (2) (cf. Wechsler and Noh, 2001). When the positions of the conjuncts in (2) are exchanged, the sentences are also grammatical, as expected.

(2) *Tom-i changmwun-ul*
Tom-Nom window-Acc
[*ppalkah-key kuliko*
red-Key and
chenchenhi / kupha-key] *chilhay-ss-ta.*
slowly / urgent-Key paint-Pst-Dec
'Tom slowly/urgently painted the window red.'

This coordination suggests that the resultative predicate is an adverb. Note, however, that according to Wechsler and Noh (2001: 410) a similar coordination like (3) sounds so weird that it is ungrammatical.

(3) ?*Tom-i changmwun-ul* [*ppalkah-key*
Tom-Nom window-Acc red-Key
kuliko wancenhi] *chilhay-ss-ta.*
and completely paint-Pst-Dec
'Tom completely painted the window red.'

I agree that the sentence in (3) sounds a little awkward, but it is at least marginally acceptable to some native speakers of Korean I consulted with. Based on the minimal pairs between the sentences in (2) and (3), we may hypothesize that the awkwardness of the coordination in (3) is derived from the degree adverb, *wancenhi* 'completely'. The sentence in (3) can have multiple meanings depending on whether the scale related to the degree adverb is the area of the window or the redness: the whole window was painted completely or the window was painted completely red. I do not go into detail about what exactly causes the differences between (2) and (3). What is important here is the fact that generally coordinations of a manner adverb and a resultative predicate, Adj-*key*, are permitted in Korean as in (2).

Some people may say that since many languages allow coordination of unlike categories, the coordination in (2) does not necessarily support the claim that the Adj-*key* is adverb. In fact, as illustrated in (4a), the NP *a Republican* and the AP *proud of it* are coordinated in English even though they belong to different syntactic categories (Beavers and Sag, 2004: 54) and similarly for the Korean coordination in (4b).

(4) a. Jan is [a Republican and proud of it].
b. *ku-nun* [*ttokttokha-ko* (*kuliko*)
he-Top smart-and and
yakwusenswu-i-ta].
baseball.player-Cop-Dec
'He is smart and a baseball player.'

However, it is important to keep in mind that not every unlike categories can be coordinated. Then, we must look into whether typical adverbs can be coordinated with any non-adverb. In (5) the conjuncts are *wh*-words and the coordinations of NP and AdvP are allowed in both English and Korean (see Whitman, 2004).

(5) a. [What and how] did Tom eat?
b. *Tom-i* [*mwues-ul kuliko*
Tom-Nom what-Acc and
ettehkey] *mek-ess-ni?*
how eat-Pst-Que
'What and how did Tom eat?'

However, if the conjuncts are not *wh*-word, such a coordination is not permitted in both English and Korean, as illustrated in (6).

(6) a. *Tom ate [the pie and quickly].
b. **Tom-i* [*phai-lul kuliko*
Tom-Nom pie-Acc and
chenchenhi] *mek-ess-ta.*
slowly eat-Pst-Dec
(lit.) 'Tom ate the pie and slowly.'

It appears that if adverbs are not *wh*-words, the adverbs can be coordinated only with adverbs. Unless a counterexample to this generalization is found, the coordinations in (2) can be used as

[1] There is an issue about whether lexemes like *ppalkah-* 'red' are adjective or stative verb in Korean (see, e.g., Yeo, 2008). I just assume here that they are adjectives since it seems irrelevant for the problem discussed in this paper. What is important here is which syntactic category resultative predicates (i.e., X-*key*) belong to.

evidence for the claim that the Adj-*key* is syntactically an adverb.

2.2 Modification of degree adverb

The Adj-*key* is parallel to clear adverbials with respect to degree adverb modification. The degree adverb *acwu* 'very' can appear either before or after a predicative adjective which it modifies:

(7) a. *soy-ka* [*acwu mwukep-ta*].
metal-Nom very heavy-Dec
'The metal is very heavy.'
b. *soy-ka* [*mwukep-ta acwu*].
metal-Nom heavy-Dec very
'The metal is very heavy.

Although (7a) is more natural than (7b), (7b) can be also used in a colloquial context. By contrast, when *acwu* 'very' modifies an adverb, it must appear before the adverb:

(8) a. *ku-ka* [*acwu chenchenhi*] *kel-ess-ta.*
he-Nom very slowly walk-Pst-Dec
'He walked very slowly.
b. **ku-ka* [*chenchenhi acwu*] *kel-ess-ta.*
he-Nom very slowly walk-Pst-Dec
(int.) 'He walked very slowly.

Based on this clear syntactic difference between adjective and adverb, we can now test whether the Adj-*key* is really adverb or adjective as follows:

(9) a. *ku-ka soy-lul* [*acwu*
he-Nom metal-Acc very
maykkunha-key] *twutulki-ess-ta.*
smooth-Key hammer-Pst-Dec
'Tom hammered the metal very smooth.'
b. **ku-ka soy-lul* [*maykkunha-key*
he-Nom metal-Acc smooth-Key
acwu] *twutulki-ess-ta.*
very hammer-Pst-Dec
(int.) 'Tom hammered the metal very smooth.'

In (9b) the degree adverb *acwu* 'very' cannot appear after the resultative predicate. This common property shared by manner adverb and Adj-*key* supports the claim that the Adj-*key* of a resultative construction is syntactically an adverb rather than adjective.

2.3 Morphological property

The topic marker -(*n*)*un* and delimiters like *-man* 'only' cannot be attached to predicative adjectives, but to adverbs, as shown in the following:

(10) a. *ku cha-ka mwukep(*-un/*-man)-ta.*
the car-Nom heavy(-Top/-only)-Dec
'The car is heavy.'
b. *ku-ka pwucilenhi(-nun/-man)*
he-Nom diligently(-Top/-only)
talli-ess-ta.
run-Pst-Dec
'He diligently ran.'

Just like adverbs, the Adj-*key* can have the topic marker or a delimiter:

(11) *ku-ka mwun-ul kem-key(-nun/-man)*
he-Nom door-Acc black-Key(-Top/-only)
chilhay-ss-ta.
paint-Pst-Dec
'He painted the door black.'

These morphological properties also indicate that the Adj-*key* is morpho-syntactically an adverb.

2.4 Participant-oriented adverb

If the resultative predicates are adverb rather than adjective, we should also claim that some adverbs take their predication subject to form a clause, which looks unusual. However, this unusualness does not constitute a convincing counter-argument to the adverbial analysis of resultative predicates. The Adj-*key* seems to belong to what is known as participant-oriented adverb (see Geuder, 2000; Himmelmann and Schultze-Brendt, 2005; Shibagaki, 2011). Unlike pure manner adverbs (*slowly* or *quickly*) describing how an action is performed, participant-oriented adverb (e.g., the 'resultative adverb' *heavily* in *They loaded the cart heavily* from Geuder, 2000: 69) characterizes an argument participant. Consider the following contrast:

(12) a. Tom loaded the cart heavily. So the cart became heavy. / #That is, the action of loading the cart was heavy.
b. Tom loaded the cart slowly. That is, the action of loading the cart was slow. / #So the cart became slow.

In (12a) *heavily* does not modify the action of loading the cart, but it describes a result state of the cart. In (12b) *slowly* modifies the action of loading the cart, but it does not describe a result state of the cart. Just like the English participant-oriented adverbs, the Adj-*key* of a resultative construction adds more information to an argument rather than to an action. Summarizing, we can say that the Adj-*key* serves as a resultative predicate characterizing a result state normally associated with the referent of the matrix object, albeit the Adj-*key* is morpho-syntactically an adverb like English resultative adverbs.

3 *Pro*-dropped clause vs. control

In this section I support the view that the Adj-*key* in (1a) forms a *pro*-dropped clause (a fully saturated clause), rather than a controlled structure (see, e.g., Shibagaki, 2011), with further evidence. In (13) the nominative NP *pancwuk-i* 'dough-Nom' appears and this functions as the predication subject of the resultative predicate, *napcakha-key* 'flat-Key' (cf. Wechsler and Noh, 2001).

(13) ?*Luke-ka pancwuk-ul pancwuk-i*
Luke-Nom dough-Acc dough-Nom
napcakha-key twutulki-ess-ta.
flat-Key pound-Pst-Dec
'Luke pounded the dough so that it became flat.'

Although the sentence in (13) sounds a little awkward, this awkwardness can be ascribed to the two contiguous NPs referring to the same referent. When the two NPs are separated as in (14a), the sentence sounds much better. In addition, when the accusative object is omitted as in (14b), the sentence sounds fine (see similar examples in Shim and den Dikken, 2007; Shibagaki, 2011), although the sentence only with the accusative NP (*Luke-ka pancwuk-ul napcakha-key twutulki-ess-ta*) is the most natural.

(14) a. *pancwuk-i napcakha-key Luke-ka*
dough-Nom flat-Key Luke-Nom
yelsimhi pancwuk-ul twutulki-ess-ta.
diligently dough-Acc pound-Pst-Dec
'Luke diligently pounded the dough so that it became flat.'

b. *Luke-ka pancwuk-i napcakha-key*
Luke -Nom dough-Nom flat-Key
twutulki-ess-ta.
pound-Pst-Dec
'Luke pounded the dough so that it became flat.'

Furthermore, the honorification marker *-si* (which targets nominative subject, but not accusative object functioning as notional subject) can be attached to a resultative predicate as in (15) (cf. Son, 2008), supporting the view that the nominative predication subject of the resultative predicate is omitted in the sentence.

(15) *nochin-ul pyenanha-si-key*
old.parents-Acc comfortable-Hon-key
pongyang-to mosha-ko...
support-also not.do-and
'I could not even support my old parents so that they were comfortable, and...'
(*Pioneer*, a novel by Kwangswu Lee)

The omitted nominative NP of a resultative construciton is normally interpreted as if it refers to the same referent of the matrix object, as illustrated in some examples above. However, it can also refer to the matrix subject as in (16a) or something not appearing in the sentence as in (16b). The referent of the omitted NP in (16b) is recoverable from the context in which the sentence is uttered.

(16) a. *Luke-ka chelphan-ul himtul-key*
Luke-Nom iron.plate-Acc tired-Key
twutulki-ess-ta.
hammer-Pst-Dec
'Luke hammered the iron plate so that he was tired.'

b. *Luke-ka chelphan-ul sikkulep-key*
Luke-Nom iron.plate-Acc noisy-Key
twultulki-ess-ta.
hammer-Pst-Dec
'Luke hammered the iron plate so that the whole house/the iron plate was noisy.'

In summary, the availability of the nominative predication subject of a resultative predicate supports the claim that the resultative predicate heads a result clause.

4 Complement vs. adjunct

I show in this section that result clause headed by Adj-*key* is a complement of the main verb (cf. Sells, 1996; 1998; Shim and den Dikken, 2007; Shibagaki, 2011). In the following *do-so* test, the Adj-*key* must not appear in the second sentence, suggesting that the Adj-*key* in the first sentence is a complement of the main verb:

(17) *Tom-i ppalkah-key changmwun-ul*
Tom-Nom red-Key window-Acc
chilhay-ss-ta. kuliko Alice-to
paint-Pst-Dec and Alice-also
(**ppalkah-key*) *kulay-ss-ta.*
red-Key do.so-Pst-Dec
'Tom painted a window red. And Alice did so, too.'

Shim and den Dikken (2007) argue that since the Adj-*key* can be "stranded" in an example like (18), it should be an adjunct.

(18) *Bill-i Sarah-lul ttayli-ess-ko, na-nun*
Bill-Nom Sarah-Acc hit-Pst-and I-Top
ku-ka aphu-key kulay-ss-ta-ko
he-Nom in.pain-Key do.so-Pst-Comp
sayngkakhay.
think
'Bill hit Sarah, and I think he did so (so that she is) in pain.'

However, since *kulay-* 'do.so' in (18) should correspond to the combination of the object and the verb in the first clause, the grammaticality of the following clause does not necessarily show that the Adj-*key* in the second clause is an adjunct.

Shim and den Dikken (2007) also tries to support the adjunct status of the Adj-*key* with the fact that it can be "iterated" with an adverb as in (19).

(19) *Tom-i changmwun-ul chenchenhi*
Tom-Nom window-Acc slowly
ppalkah-key chilhay-ss-ta.
red-Key paint-Pst-Dec
'Tom slowly painted the window red.'

However, they did not discuss an alternative account: (i) it is possible in (19) that the adverb *chenchenhi* 'slowly' modifies the combination of the Adj-*key* (complement) and the verb (head); the accusative object is also a complement of the verb, but in Korean binary branching (rather than ternary structure) seems to be more plausible due to scrambling (see Kim, 2004), or (ii) in Korean the coordination *kuliko* 'and' can be omitted and it may also be omitted in (19) (compare (19) to (2)). If the Adj-*key* is really adjunct and can be iterated, two Adj-*key* expressions should be able to occur around the verb of a sentence just like the adverbial adjuncts in (20a). But this is not the case as in (20b). This contrast can be accounted for if the Adj-*key* is complement: since the verb requires one Adj-*key* expression as a complement, the two Adj-*key* expressions is not permitted. Note that since the verb in (20b) appears in between the two Adj-*key* expressions, they cannot be coordinated.

(20) a. *Tom-i changmwun-ul chenchenhi*
Tom-Nom window-Acc slowly
takk-ass-ta cosimsulep-key.
clean Pst Dec careful-Key
'Tom slowly cleaned the window carefully.'

b. **Tom-i changmwun-ul ppalkah-key*
Tom-Nom window-Acc red-Key
chilhay-ss-ta yeyppu-key.
paint-Pst-Dec beautiful-Key
(int.) 'Tom painted the window red and beautiful.'

Nakazawa (2008) argues that the Japanese resultative predicate would be adjunct, since it can be coordinated with an adverbial adjunct. That is, if the Japanese resultative predicate is assumed to be complement, the coordination of complement and adjunct would cause a theoretical burden. However, we can find other cases where different syntactic functions (complement or adjunct) are coordinated like (21) in Korean (and in other languages such as English, e.g., *How and what does John eat?* from Whitman, 2004: 404).

(21) *Tom-i [halwu-tongan kuliko cal]*
Tom-Nom one.day-for and well
cinay-ss-ta.
live-Pst-Dec
(lit.) 'Tom lived well for one day.'

In (21) the temporal adverbial *halwu-tongan* 'for one day' is adjunct, but *cal* 'well' is the complement of the verb, *cinay-* 'live' (which can be verified by some tests like *do-so* test).[2] Thus this kind of coordination does not pose a serious challenge to the complement status of the Adj-*key* expression, although how to account for such the coordination is an interesting question (see more in Whitman, 2004). Summarizing, the *do-so* test and some syntactic property lead us to conclude that the result clause headed by a resultative predicate should be a complement of the main verb of a resultative construction.

5 Some consequences

If the resultative constructions in Korean are like English clausal resultative constructions in terms of having a result clause, it is expected that they allow various kinds of resultative predicates like English clausal resultatives. In fact, both weak and strong resultatives (see Washio, 1997 for the notions) are allowed in Korean (see also Wechsler and Noh, 2001: 411-412):

(22) *Hank-ka ku soy-lul napcakha-/*
Hank-Nom the metal-Acc flat-/
?yeyppu-/ kil-/ ccalp-/ yalh-/ tukkep-key
beautiful-/ long-/ short-/ thin-/ thick-Key
twutulki-ess-ta.
hammer-Pst-Dec
(lit.) 'Hank hammered the metal flat / beautiful / long / short / thin / thick.'

In (22) when the resultative predicate is, e.g., *napcakha-key* 'flat-Key', the sentence is called weak resultative since hammering the metal is closely related to the flatness of the metal. When the resultative predicate is, e.g., *yeyppu-key* 'beautiful-Key', the sentence is referred to as strong resultative because hammering the metal is not closely related to the beauty of the mental.

[2] An anonymous reviewer pointed out that it is generally assumed that an adverb is not a complement of a verb. However, it is well-known that some adverbs are actually a complement of a verb: e.g., *cal* 'well' is required as the complement of the verb *cinay-* 'live' in Korean and consider the following English sentences, *He is staying *(in a hotel)* and *He loves living *(in a city)*. I believe that the previous "popular" assumption itself does not really constitute a counter-argument to the view that Adj-*key* is a kind of adverbial complement, for which I explicitly provided several pieces of evidence in this paper.

6 Eventive resultative constructions

I show here that the so-called eventive resultatives (see Son, 2008) with V(erb)-*key* are parallel to the stative resultatives with Adj-*key* with respect to the three grammatical properties.

6.1 Adverb

First, V-*key* can be coordinated with manner adverb as in (23).

(23) *ku-ka Jane-ul [nemeci-key kuliko*
he-Nom Jane-Acc fall-Key and
ppalli] mil-ess-ta.
quickly push-Pst-Dec
'He quickly pushed Jane so that she fell.'

Second, when a degree adverb modifies V-*key*, the adverb cannot appear after it:

(24) a. *ku-ka Jane-ul [acwu nemeci-key]*
he-Nom Jane-Acc very fall-Key
mil-ess-ta.
push-Pst-Dec
'He pushed Jane so that she completely fell.'
b. **ku-ka Jane-ul [nemeci-key acwu]*
he-Nom Jane-Acc fall-Key very
mil-ess-ta.
push-Pst-Dec
(int.) 'He pushed Jane so that she completely fell.'

Third, the topic marker or delimiters can be attached to V-*key*, as in the following example:

(25) *ku-ka Jane-ul nemeci-key(-nun/-man)*
he-Nom Jane-Acc fall-Key(-Top/-only)
mil-ess-ta.
push-Pst-Dec
'He pushed Jane so that she fell.'

These three properties suggest that the V-*key* also belong to adverb in terms of morpho-syntax just like the Adj-*key*.

6.2 *Pro*-dropped clause

The nominative predication subject of V-*key* can explicitly occur in eventive resultative constructions as follows:

(26) a. *Jane-i nemeci-key ku-ka*
Jane-Acc fall-Key he-Nom
himkkes Jane-ul mil-ess-ta.
forcefully Jane-Acc push-Pst-Dec
'He forcefully pushed Jane so that Jane fell.'
b. *ku-ka Jane-i nemeci-key*
he-Nom Jane-Nom fall-Key
mil-ess-ta.
push-Pst-Dec
'He pushed Jane so that Jane fell.'

The honorification marker *si* can be attached to the V-*key* in (27).

(27) *kunye-ka apeci-lul ilese-si-key*
she-Nom father-Key stand.up-Hon-key
tangki-ess-ta.
pull-Pst-Dec
'She pulled his father so that he stood up.'

These grammatical features indicate that the V-*key* heads the result clause of an eventive resultative construction.

6.3 Complement

In (28a) the V-*key* must not appear with *kulay-ss-ta* 'do.so-Pst-Dec' and in (28b) the two resultative predicates cannot occur around the verb at the same time.

(28) a. *ku-ka Jane-ul ilese-key*
he-Nom Jane-Acc stand.up-Key
tangki-ess-ta. kuliko Sophia-to
pull-Pst-Dec and Sophia-also
*(*ilese-key) kulay-ss-ta.*
stand.up-Key do.so-Pst-Dec
'He pulled Jane so that Jane stood up. And Sophia did so, too.'
b. **ku-ka Jane-ul ilese-key*
he-Nom Jane-Acc stand.up-Key
tangki-ess-ta talli-key.
pull-Pst-Dec run-Key
(int.) 'He pulled Jane so that Jane stood up and ran.'

If one of the two V-*key* expressions is removed from (28b), the sentence becomes grammatical. In short, the resultative predicates (Adj-*key* and V-*key*) can be analyzed as the head of an adverbial complement clause.

7 An HPSG Formalization

I believe the adverbial complement clause analysis can be expressed in various frameworks. In this paper, HPSG is employed for generation of the Korean resultative constructions.

7.1 Main verb

The verbal lexeme *chilha-2* 'paint' in (29) (which will be used in a resultative construction) can be licensed from the normal transitive verb, *chilha-1* 'paint', by a lexical rule through which a result clause whose FORM value is *key* is added to the ARG(UMENT)-ST(RUCTURE) list of *chilha-1* 'paint' (cf. Lee, 2012).

(29) *chilha-2* 'paint':

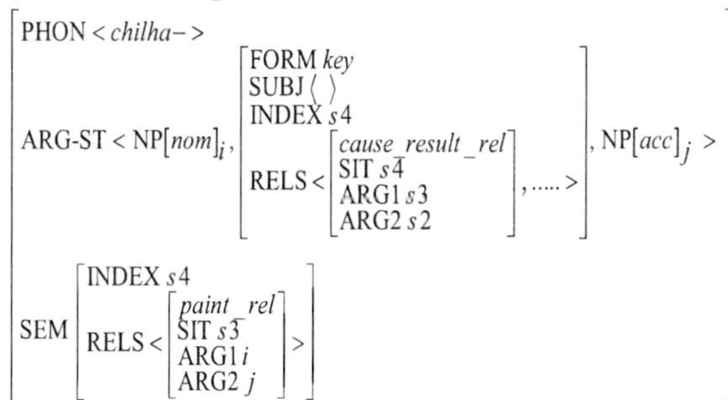

In (29) the INDEX value (*s4*) of the verb is identified with the INDEX value (*s4*) of the result clause, which guarantees that the INDEX value (*s4*) of the resultative predicate (the head of the result clause) is passed up to the VP of a resultative sentence. Also, the SIT(UATION) value (*s3*) of [*paint_rel*] is identical to the ARG1 value (*s3*) of [*cause_result_rel*]. This means that [*paint_rel*] corresponds to the causing subevent of a causation denoted by [*cause_result_rel*]. I assume that the semantics ([*paint_rel*]) of *chilha-2* 'paint' is the same as that of *chilha-1* 'paint', since a resultative meaning obtains basically due to the addition of a resultative clause.

7.2 Resultative predicate lexical rule

The resultative predicate, Adj-*key*, can be systematically licensed from an adjective lexeme by the lexical rule proposed in (30) below (cf. Lee, 2012; 2014). Since the Adj-*key* (e.g., *ppalkah-key* 'red-Key') is an adverb, it has a verbal expression as its MOD value; this constraint can be inherited from the type, *adv*(*erb*). In addition, the verbal expression requires an X-*key* expression (result clause) as a complement; this will prevent the Adj-*key* expression from modifying verbs like *chilha-ta-1* 'paint'. The Adj-*key* optionally selects a nominative subject (tagged [2]). In semantics, the meaning (tagged [3]) of the adjective lexeme becomes the result state in the meaning of the Adj-*key*. Since a transitive verb sentence becomes a resultative construction due to the addition of an Adj-*key* expression, the cause-result meaning (i.e., [*cause_result_rel*]) of the resultative sentence is posited to be in the semantics of the Adj-*key*. Following the causation event structure (e.g., Dowty, 1979), [*become_rel*] is also added to the REL(ATION)S list of the Adj-*key*. I assume, however, that [*cause_result_rel*] is different from CAUSE of a causation event structure: CAUSE represents a direct causation, but [*cause_result_rel*] does not necessarily do so (see the basic semantics of clausal resultatives in Wechsler and Noh, 2001: 402-403).

7.3 Generation of VP

The result clause in (31) below is licensed by the general rule, *hd-subj-ph* (see the grammar rule in Sag *et al*., 2003; Kim, 2004). The result clause has no value for the SUBJ list, which guarantees that the main verb of a resultative construction combines with the result clause. Note that in (29), *chilha-2* 'paint' requires an expression whose FORM value is *key* and whose SUBJ list is empty. When the SUBJ list of the resultative predicate is empty, it forms a *pro*-dropped clause and this clause can also combine with the main verb of a resultative construction.

In (32) below the verb combines with the result clause via *hd-comp-ph* (see the Head-Complement Rule in Sag *et al*., 2003; Kim, 2004). However, the MOD value of the resultative predicate is passed up to the result clause as in (31) due to the Valence Principle (Sag *et al*., 2003: 146) and so the result clause can combine with the verb via *hd-mod-ph* (see the Head-Modifier Rule in Sag *et al*., 2003; Kim, 2004). Then it is possible to overgenerate sentences like (33).

(33) **ku-ka* [*ppalkah-key* [[*mwun-i*
he-Nom red-Key door-Nom
ppalkah-key] *chilhay-ss-ta*]].
red-Key paint-Pst-Dec
(int.) 'He painted the door red.'

In (33) the COMPS value (a result clause) of the verb is passed up to *hd-mod-ph* of the verb and the result clause, and then it combines with another result clause (which in this case is a *pro*-dropped clause) via *hd-comp-ph*. While there seem to be different ways to solve this problem (e.g., positing *hd-comp-mod-ph* using multiple inheritance), I assume here that *hd-mod-ph* is reformulated so as to block the application of *hd-mod-ph* to the combination of the verb and the result clause in (33). It can be formally stated in *hd-mod-ph* using a kind of subtraction operation that a modifier only modifies an expression whose COMPS list does not include an element which modifies that expression. This subtraction operation should be a little different from the one defined in Sag *et al.* (2003: 431); the subtraction here is defined even if an element to be subtracted from a list is not included in the list (like set complementation).

If the VP in (32) combines with other required expressions (e.g., the matrix subject) at the higher level of the syntactic structure, a grammatical resultative sentence can be licensed. Intransitive resultatives like (1b) and eventive resultatives can be generated in much the same way.

8 Conclusion

I have argued that in Korean resultative constructions, (i) X-*key* is a resultative adverb, (ii) X-*key* forms a fully saturated clause, and (iii) the result clause is a complement of the main verb. This adverbial complement clause analysis of the resultatives may be applied to a range of other constructions with Adj-*key* or V-*key* expression (e.g., unaccusative resultative constructions and causative constructions). The resultative predicate in Korean can be X-*tolok* and this seems to have almost the same properties as X-*key*, examination of which is left to future research. In addition, this analysis would provide a basis for a cross-linguistic study of resultative constructions in, for example, Korean, Japanese, and English.

Acknowledgments

I am grateful to three anonymous reviewers for their helpful comments. Thanks also to Stephen Wechsler for discussion of some issues in this paper. I am solely responsible for any errors or shortcomings.

(30) Resultative predicate lexical rule:

INPUT ⟨ [1], [SYN [HEAD [*adj*, PRED +], ARG-ST < ([2]NP[nom]$_j$) >], SEM [RELS < [3][SIT s1, ARG1 *j*] >]] ⟩

OUTPUT ⟨ F$_{\text{-}key}$([1]), [*word*, SYN [HEAD [*adv*, PRED +], SUBJ ⟨ ([2]) ⟩, COMPS ⟨ ⟩, MOD ⟨ [HEAD *verb*, COMPS ⟨ [FORM *key*, RELS < [*cause_result_rel*], ...>], ... ⟩, RELS <[SIT *s*3]>] ⟩], SEM [INDEX s4, RELS < [*cause_result_rel*, SIT *s*4, ARG1 *s*3, ARG2 *s*2], [*become_rel*, SIT *s*2, ARG1 *s*1], [3] >]] ⟩

(31) Generation of a result clause, *mwun-i ppalkah-key* 'door-Nom red-Key':

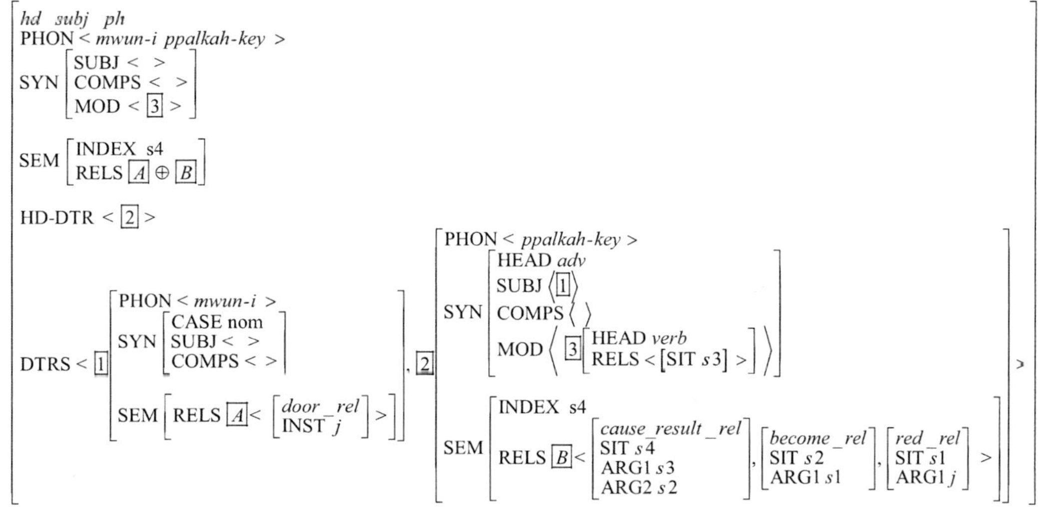

(32) Generation of a VP, *mwun-i ppalkah-key chilhay-ss-ta* 'door-Nom red-Key painted':

[*hd–comp–ph*
PHON < *mwun-i ppalkah-key chilhay–ss–ta* >
SYN [SUBJ < [3] >, COMPS < [4] >]
SEM [INDEX s4, RELS < [*door_rel*, INST *j*], [*cause_result_rel*, SIT *s*4, ARG1 *s*3, ARG2 *s*2], [*become_rel*, SIT *s*2, ARG1 *s*1], [*red_rel*, SIT *s*1, ARG1 *j*], [*paint_rel*, SIT *s*3, ARG1 *i*, ARG2 *j*] >]
HD-DTR < [1] >
DTRS < [2][PHON < *mwun-i ppalkah-key* >, SYN [HEAD *adv*, MOD ⟨ [1] ⟩]], [1][PHON < *chilhay-ss-ta* >, SYN [SUBJ < [3][*nom*] >, COMPS < [2][FORM *key*], [4][*acc*] >]] >]

References

Beavers, John and Ivan A. Sag. 2004. Coordinate Ellipsis and Apparent Non-Constituent Coordination. In *Proceedings of the 11th International Conference on Head-Driven Phrase Structure Grammar*, 48–69. Stanford: CSLI Publications.

Dowty, David. 1979. *Word Meaning and Montague Grammar – The Semantics of Verbs and Times in Generative Semantics and in Montague's PTQ*. Reidel, Dordrecht.

Geuder, Wilhem. 2000. *Oriented adverbs: Issues in the lexical semantics of event adverbs*. PhD thesis, Universität Konstanz.

Himmelmann, Nikolaus P. and Eva F. Schultze-Brendt. 2005. Issues in the syntax and semantics of participant-oriented adjuncts: an introduction. In Nikolaus and Schultze-Brendt (eds.), *Secondary Predication and Adverbial Modification: The Typology of Depictives*, 1-67. Oxford: Oxford University Press.

Kim, Jong-Bok. 2004. *Korean Phrase Structure Grammar*. [in Korean] Seoul: Hankook Munhwasa.

Lee, Juwon. 2012. Change of State Verb and Syntax of Serial Verb Constructions in Korean: An HPSG Account. *Coyote Papers: Working Papers in Linguistics* 20, *Special Volume for the West Coast Conference on Formal Linguistics*: 55-63.

Lee, Juwon. 2014. Multiple Interpretations and Constraints of Causative Serial Verb Constructions in Korean. In *Proceedings of the 38th Annual Meeting of the Berkeley Linguistics Society*, 288-306.

Nakazawa, Tsuneko. 2008. Resultative Phrases in Japanese as Adjuncts. Abstract.

Pollard, Carl and Ivan A. Sag. 1994. *Head-Driven Phrase Structure Grammar*. Chicago: University of Chicago Press.

Sag, Ivan A., Thomas Washow, and Emily M. Bender. 2003. *Syntactic Theory: A Formal Introduction, 2nd edition*. Stanford: CSLI Publications.

Sells, Peter. 1996. The Projection of Phrase Structure and Argument Structure in Japanese. In Takao Gunji (ed.), *Studies on the Universality of Constraint-Based Phrase Structure Grammars*, 39-60. Report of the International Scientific Research Program, Joint Research, Project No. 06044133. Osaka University, Graduate School of Language and Culture.

Sells, Peter. 1998. Structural Relationships within complex predicates. In Park, B-S. and J.H-S. Yoon (eds.), *Selected Papers form the 11th Meeting of the International Circle of Korean Linguistics*, 115-147.

Shibagaki, Ryosuke. 2011. *Secondary predication in Chinese, Japanese, Mongolian and Korean*. PhD thesis, University of London.

Shim, Ji Young and Marcel den Dikken. 2007. The Tense of Resultatives–The Case of Korean. In *Proceedings of the 38th Annual Meeting of the North East Linguistic Society*, 337-350. Amherst: GLSA.

Son, Minjeong. 2008. Korean resultatives revisited: Complementation versus adjunction. In Peter Svenonius and Inna Tolskaya (eds.), *Tromsø Working Papers on Language and Linguistics: Nordlyd 35, Special issue on Complex Predicates*: 89-113.

Washio, Ryuichi. 1997. Resultatives, compositionality and language variation. *Journal of East Asian Linguistics* 6:1-49.

Wechsler, Stephen and Bokyung Noh. 2001. On resultative predicates and clauses: Parallels between Korean and English. *Language Sciences* 23: 391-423.

Whitman, Neal. 2004. Semantics and Pragmatics of English Verbal Dependent Coordination. *Language* 80(3): 403-434.

Yeo, Seungju. 2008. Morphosyntax of predicates and syntactic categories in Korean. *Lingua* 118: 332-369.

The use of body part terms in Taiwan and China: Analyzing 血 xue 'blood' and 骨 gu 'bone' in Chinese Gigaword v. 2.0

Ren-feng Duann
Department of English
Wenzao Ursuline University of Languages
d94142001@ntu.edu.tw

Chu-Ren Huang
Department of Chinese
and Bilingual Studies
The Hong Kong Polytechnic Universit
churen.huang@polyu.edu.hk

Abstract

This article, examining the qualia roles retrieved from the metaphorically/metonymically used body part terms in news texts, addresses the similarities and differences of such uses in Taiwan and China. Analyzing the behavior of 血 xue 'blood' and 骨 'bone', two corporeal terms with relatively high visibilities compared with 肉 rou 'flesh' and 脈 mai 'meridian' (Duann and Huang 2015) in the Chinese Gigaword Version 2 (Huang 2009), this research have the following findings: (1) For the use of 血 xue 'blood', the agentive role predominates in both Taiwan and China, which is not in line with the argument in Duann and Huang (2015). (2) Regarding the use of 骨 gu 'bone', the telic role predominates. However, China uses it in personification much more often than Taiwan does. (3) The unique dimension of a place triggers the use exclusive to the place.

1 Introduction

Embodiment, referring to 'understanding the role of an agent's own body in its everyday, situated cognition' (Gibbs 2006: 1), is a manifestation of the significance of the human body in cognition. Embodiment, of which the tenet is that meaning stems out of 'the organic activities of embodied creatures in interaction with their changing environments' (Johnson 2008: 11), has been drawing scholars' attention for more than three decades. While providing cognitive accounts for meaning generation and functioning as the foundation of conceptual metaphor understanding and interpretation (e.g. Yu 2003, 2007; Lakoff and Johnson 1980, 1999; Johnson 2006), embodiment does not address what triggers conceptual metaphors, or the constraints which motivate the selection of a corporeal term to represent another concept.

Incorporating the theories of embodiment and of generative lexicon (Pustejovsky 1991, 1995), Duann and Huang (2015) proposes a method to uncover what constrains the use of a body part in the stead of a comparatively abstract notion. They focus on the qualia structure of the corporeal terms as the source concept and testify their approach with authentic corpus data. Examining the behavior of four atypical body parts, 血 xue 'blood', 肉 rou 'flesh', 骨 gu 'bone' and 脈 mai 'meridian' in Sinica Corpus (Chen et al. 1996), they contend that the visibility of these body parts and the telic role from the qualia structure constrain the selection. In this current research, we explore the metaphorical/metonymical uses of 血 xue 'blood' and 骨 'bone', the two corporeal terms with relatively high visibilities compared with 肉 rou 'flesh' and 脈 mai 'meridian' (Duann and Huang 2015) in the Chinese Gigaword Version 2 (Gigaword2, Huang 2009), and finds out: (1) Regarding the use of 血 xue 'blood', the agentive role predominates in both Taiwan and China, which differs from the argument in Duann and Huang (2015). (2) Concerning the use of 骨 gu 'bone', the telic role still predominates. However, China tends to use it in personification much more often than Taiwan. (3) The political ecology of Taiwan motivates the use unique to Taiwan. For the first finding we would like to amend the argument in Duann and Huang (2015): instead of the telic role only, we think both the telic and agentive roles constrain the selection, as these two roles represent eventive dimensions which reveal the interaction between the object/entity and human beings. For the second finding, we claim that China tend to use certain body parts in a more holistic way, which is attributable to the genre of the corpus. For the third finding, we argue certain dimensions of a place lead to the use exclusive to the place.

2 Research Questions and Hypotheses

This research aims to answer the following questions:

(1) What are the similarities and differences between the uses of identical body part terms in Taiwan and China?
(2) What qualia role dominates the use of the body part terms in the corpus at issue?
(3) Does a specific genre influence the metaphorical/metonymical use of body part terms?
(4) How do we explain the findings?

This research is conducted based on the following hypotheses:

(1) As Mandarin Chinese is the major/official language in both Taiwan and China, the metaphorical/metonymical uses of body part terms in Taiwan and China should be similar to a large extent.
(2) Genre plays a role in the uses of an identical corporeal term in Taiwan and China.
(3) There should be metaphorical/metonymical uses of a body part term exclusive to Taiwan or China.

3 Data and Method

3.1 Data

The corpus data comes from the Chinese Gigaword Version 2.0 (henceforth Gigaword2), which is a part-of-speech tagged corpus created by scholars at Academia Sinica (Huang 2009). This corpus, containing 831,748,000 Chinese words, is composed of news texts from three sources of news: Central News Agency (CNA, 501,456,000 words) in Taiwan, Xinhua News Agency (XIN, 311,660,000 words) in China, and Lianhe Zaobao (ZBN, 18,632,000 words) in Singapore. As we aim to compare the similarities and differences between Taiwan and China, we take the data from CNA and XIN. There are 4,670 occurrences of 血 xie 'blood' in CNA and 3,760 in XIN. Regarding the occurrences of 骨 gu 'bone', 1,006 hits are found in CNA and 1,198 in XIN. Table 1 below summarizes the two sub-corpora:

Sub-corpus	CNA	XIN
Total number of words	501,456,000	311,660,000
Total number of occurrences of 血 xue 'blood'	4,670	3,760
Total number of occurrences of 骨 gu 'bone'	1,006	1,198

Table1. Basic information of CNA and XIN in Gigaword2

3.2 Method

We searched 血 xue 'blood' and 骨 gu 'bone' in the two sub-corpora of Gigaword2 respectively through the Word Sketch function at http://158.132.124.36/. We go through the following four categories:

(1) and/or, which shows the words occurring in parallel with the body part
(2) Subject_of, which displays the behavior of the words functioning as the subject in the syntactic structure
(3) Object_of, which shows the behavior of the words when functioning as the object in the syntactic structure
(4) Measure, which lists the classifiers of these body parts

We manually examine all the hits of all the entries in each category, in order to check whether the body part terms are used literally or metaphorically/metonymically.

We then apply the modified version (Duann and Huang 2015) of metaphor identification procedure (MIP, Pragglejaz 2007) to identify the metaphorically/metonymically used words so as to better analyze Chinese data. The modified version focuses not only on the basic contemporary meaning of a lexical unit as a whole, but also on the meaning of the parts in compounds. Examining how the body part terms behave in compounds is important, because a word usually undergoes metaphorical or metonymical extension when functioning as a part of a compound.

For example, the contemporary meaning of 鐵骨 tiegu in the online dictionary of the Ministry of Education (MOE), Taiwan, is

> 比喻意志堅貞不變[1] '(Metaphorical) unyielding, uncompromising'[2]

According to the MOE dictionary, the meaning of the morpheme 骨 in the compound 鐵骨 deviates from its original definition:

> 動物體內支持身體的支架組織 'The frame inside the body of an animal which supports the body'

In other words, the morpheme 骨 gu 'bone' in the compound 鐵骨 has undergone meaning extension. Rather than the internal frame which supports the body, it represents where the specific personal trait resides.

After identifying the metaphorically/metonymically used words, we proceed to retrieve the qualia roles of the body part terms under discussion.

Following the steps described in Duann and Huang (2015), we retrieve the qualia roles of the corporeal terms:

(1) We first examine whether there is more than one sense of the body part at issue. E.g. in Gigaword2, two senses are found in 血 xie "blood":
    Sense 1 refers to the liquid circulating naturally inside human body, and sense 2 to the liquid flowing inside/out of human body due to injury or effort making.
(2) We spell out the qualia structure, i.e. the four roles, of the body part at issue according to the sense(s) found in step (1). The qualia structures of the two senses of 血 xie "blood" is shown below:

Sense 1
Constitutive=...
Formal= liquid, red
Telic= sustain life, carry ethnic tie, carry emotion and personal traits, etc.
Agentive: Natural kind

Sense 2
Constitutive=...
Formal=liquid, red, smell, coagulation
Telic=...
Agentive=X which causes blood to flow out of body/body parts

(3) We investigate the behavior of the body part term in a lexical form and see whether a specific role is highlighted.
(4) We then go beyond the lexical level into the clausal level to find out the role(s) of the body part which is/are specified at the clausal level.

In Example 1, no specific role is retrieved from 血 xie 'blood' at the lexical level. However, when the context, specifically 手 shou 'hand' and 沾滿 zhanman 'stained/covered with', is taken into consideration, it is found that 'blood' here realizes Sense 2, i.e. the liquid flowing inside/out of human body due to injury or effort making. Specifically, 'blood' here refers to blood flowing outside human bodies due to injury or killing (thus can stain/cover another's hands), the agentive role is retrieved. Moreover, the verb 沾 refers to liquid, which realizes the formal role.

Example 1
他的手沾滿阿富汗人民的**血**
'His hands are stained with Afghanistanis' blood.'

We proceed to practice the steps and retrieve the qualia roles from all the metaphorically/metonymically used 血 xie 'blood' and 骨 gu 'bone' of the four categories in Gigaword2, and obtain the results discussed in the following section.

[1] The other definition 鐵鑄的骨架 'framework made of iron' is discarded as it is not used on human being.
[2] The translation of the definition of all the entries in the MOE dictionary is done by the authors.

4 Results

4.1 Blood

Tables 2 and 3 show the metaphorically/metonymically used 血 in the two sub-corpora:

Sense (no. of hits)	Target	Qualia Role	Personification (%)
Sense 1 (25)	Essence: 13 Ethnic tie: 12	Telic: 25 Formal: 11	10 (0.214%)[3]
Sense 2 (79)	Wound: 32 Death: 38 Making effort: 9	Agentive: 79 Formal: 45	Null

Table2. Metaphorically/metonymically used 血 xue 'blood', its qualia role and personification in CNA

Sense (no. of hits)	Target	Qualia Role	Personification (%)
Sense 1 (6)	Close connection: 1 Essence: 1 Ethnic tie: 2 Emotion: 2	Constitutive : 1 Telic: 5 Formal: 2	2 (0.053%)
Sense 2 (67)	Wound:10 Death: 34 Making effort: 23	Agentive: 67 Formal: 58	9 (0.239%)

Table3. Metaphorically/metonymically used 血 xue 'blood', its qualia role and personification in XIN

According to Table 2, for Sense 1 of 血 xie 'blood' in CNA, there are 25 occurrences in total, among which 13 refers to the ESSENCE (Example 2) and 12 to ETHNIC TIE (Example 3). Regarding the qualia structure, the telic role is retrieved from 25 occurrences, and the formal role from 11 hits. (Please note that there is no one-on-one correspondence between a figuratively used body part and the qualia roles, as more than one qualia role may be retrieved, which is exemplified by Example 1 above.) Ten occurrences are personification. When it comes to Sense 2, there are 79 occurrences of metaphorically/metonymically used 血 xie 'blood' in total, among which 32 occurrences stand for WOUND (Example 4), 38 for DEATH (Example 5), and 9 for MAKING EFFORT (Example 6).

[3] We divide the frequency with the total number of hits of 血 xie 'blood' in CNA so as to reveal whether personification is significant in this corpus. In this case, it is 10/4,670=0.214%. Same for the rest personifications.

In terms of the qualia role, 79 occurrences are agentive and 45 are formal. There is no personification of the metaphorically used 血 of Sense 2 in CNA.

Example 2
ESSENCE IS BLOOD
佛教與儒、道二教，無一不是中國文化的**血**與肉、骨與髓
'All Buddhism, Confucianism and Taoism compose the blood and flesh, bone and bone marrow [i.e. essence] of Chinese culture.'

血 xie 'blood' here refers to essence. First of all, Chinese culture is personified. Then the essential parts of the personified entity are pointed out in parallel: blood, flesh, bone and bone marrow. We thus consider blood stands for essence in this examples.

Example 3
ETHNIC TIE IS BLOOD
大家都是流著中國人的**血**，有難相助
'Chinese blood is flowing in our bodies [i.e. we are all Chinese], and we should help whoever is in need.'

When blood collocates with 流 liu 'flow' and an ethnic group modifies blood, blood stands for ethnic tie.

Example 4
BLOOD FOR WOUND (in CNA)
看到這些八卦新聞令人吐**血**
'It makes me vomit blood when reading the gossips'.

Example 5
DEATH IS BLOOD
戈巴契夫兩手沾滿了立陶宛人的**血**
'Both hands of Gorbachev are stained/covered with Lithuanian's blood.'

Example 6
MAKING EFFORT IS BLOOD
每一處繁榮，無不浸透了中國人的**血**與汗
'The prosperity which is seen everywhere is soaked with the blood and sweat of Chinese people.'

Table 3 shows that, regarding Sense 1 of 血 xie 'blood' in XIN, there are 6 occurrences in total, among which 1 represents CLOSE CONNECTION (with something else), 1 ESSENCE, 2 ETHNIC TIE, and 2 EMOTION. In terms of the qualia role, there are 1 constitutive role, 5 telic and 2 formal roles. For Sense 2, there are 10 occurrences of WOUND, 34 of DEATH, and 23 of MAKING EFFORT. Regarding the qualia role, 67 occurrences are agentive and 58 are formal. There are 2 occurrences and 9 occurrences of personification of Sense 1 and Sense 2 respectively in XIN.

What merits attention is the diverging uses of 吐血 'to vomit blood' in CNA and XIN. Originally a symptom caused by a serious wound or disease, 吐血 can be regarded as a metonym of serious wound/disease. However, the use of 吐血 goes a step further to refer to a negative emotion, e.g. anger, aversion, depression, of a person in CNA. On the other hand, in XIN, 吐血 occurs to the personified corporate or group, as exemplified as Example 7 below:

Example 7
BLOOD FOR WOUND in XIN
罰得企業吐了**血**，誰來創造財富？
'Who can create prosperity if corporates vomit blood because of the penalties?'

The difference between this use of 血 in Sense 2 in CNA and XIN discloses that, XIN, with its less embodied way which is applied to personified corporates/groups, tends to take a more holistic manner, while CNA still uses this symptom in a more embodied manner, referring to the ongoing emotion of a human being.

What also draws attention is that Tables 2 and 3 reveal something which differs from the argument in Duann and Huang (2015): the agentive role predominates in the metaphorical/metonymical uses of 血 xie 'blood' in both CNA and XIN. We thus need to broaden the argument in Duann and Huang to include both telic and agentive roles motivating the figurative uses of body parts, as both involve the eventive dimension in which human beings interact with the entities/objects.

4.2 Bone

Tables 4 and 5 summarize the metaphorically/metonymically used 骨 gu 'bone' in the two sub-corpora:

Sense (no. of hits)	Target	Qualia Role	Personification (%)
Sense 1 (13)	Political orientation: 7 Met of body: 6	Telic: 13	3 (0.298%)

Table 4. Metaphorically used 骨 gu 'bone', its qualia role and personification in CNA

Sense (no. of hits)	Target	Qualia Role	Personification (%)
Sense 1 (80)	Met of body: 78 Personal trait: 2	Telic: 80 Formal: 43	74 (6.177%)

Table 5. Metaphorically used 骨 gu 'bone', its qualia role and personification in XIN

According to Tables 4 and 5, only one sense is activated in both sub-corpora, and the telic role of this body part predominates in both sub-corpora. In CNA, there are 13 occurrences in total, among which 7 refer to the POLITICAL ORIENTATION (Example 8), and 6 are used metonymically: BONE FOR BODY (Example 9). Three occurrences are personification. In the XIN sub-corpus, there are 80 occurrences in total, among which 78 are metonymically used and 2 refer to personal trait. Aside from the telic role, the formal role is also retrieved. Personification occurs extensively in the XIN.

The metaphorical/metonymical uses of bone present a more interesting case, though only Sense 1 comes into play in these uses.

First of all, elections in Taiwan triggers a use of 骨 gu 'bone' unique to Taiwan: it functions to represent one's political orientation. Though it can be subsumed under 'personal traits', this use is not found at all in the XIN.

骨 gu 'bone' representing a person's political orientation co-occurs with 皮 pi 'skin', and the typical structure is X 皮 Y 骨, in which X and Y usually refer to candidates, as exemplified in Example 8 below:

Example 8
POLITICAL ORIENTATION IS BONE (in CNA)
有中常委則說，黨內確實有不少是連皮某種**骨**

A central standing committee member said, there are quite a few members who are covered with the skin of Lien but carry the bones of other people [i.e. in favor of Lien on the surface but actually support other candidates].

This use, arising due to the political ecology in Taiwan, describes one's political orientation via the use of bone, which is inside the body and supporting it, in contrast to what s/he pretends to vote for, via the use of skin, the outmost part covering the whole body.

Another use is prominent: the metonymical use of 骨 gu 'bone', i.e. BONE FOR BODY, occurs in a less embodied manner; that is, it occurs in the personified industry, city, enterprise, etc, and this is significant in the XIN corpus (6.177%). Moreover, this specific use of 骨 gu 'bone' always co-occurs with 筋 jin tendon/meridian, as in 強筋壯骨 qiangjin zhuanggu 'to strengthen the body' as in Example 9 and 傷筋動骨 shangjin donggu 'to get seriously wounded' as in Example 10.

Example 9
BONE FOR BODY
電子業「強筋壯**骨**」見成效
'The electronic industry successfully strengthens his body.'

Example 9 presents several mappings. Firstly, the electronic industry is personified, i.e. THE ELECTRONIC INDUSTRY IS A PERSON. It is inferred from the context that the industry lacks competiveness, from which another mapping is retrieved: LACK OF COMPETITIVENESS IS WEAKNESS OF THE HUMAN BODY. Something needs to be done to boost the competiveness of the industry, which is regarded as strengthening the human body: REFORMATION OF THE INDUSTRY IS STRENGTHENING THE HUMAN BODY.

Example 10
BONE FOR BODY
在上海「傷筋動**骨**」的大改造中，約有三十萬市民必須搬出家園
'In the large-scaled/drastic reformation of Shanghai, around 300,000 citizens have to move out of their hometown.'

The mappings in Example 10 are more complicated than those of Example 9. Still, the city is personified: THE CITY IS A PERSON. There are problems in this city which need to be tackled, which is conceptualized as disease in a person: PROBLEM IN A CITY IS DISEASE IN A PERSON. The solution, or reformation in this case, will be drastic which will damage a bit to the city in the beginning. This is compared to a surgery, in which a person will be cut up at the first stage in order to settle the medical issue. The mapping thus emerges: SOLUTION TO PROBLEM (REFORMATION) IS SURGERY TO A PERSON.

In terms of the use of 骨 gu 'bone', the telic role still predominates. However, Taiwan and China present different pictures. Taiwan uses 骨 to represent a person's political orientation, which is not found in the XIN corpus. China uses 骨 in personified organization/industry/place much more often than Taiwan does. Overall, we argue that XIN takes a more holistic view, while CNA more analytical, in the use of 骨 gu 'bone'.

5 Conclusion

We have analyzed and compared the metaphorical/metonymical uses of two atypical body parts with comparatively high visibility, 血 xie 'blood' and 骨 gu 'bone', in Gigaword2, a corpus of news from Taiwan and China. We have found that the agentive role predominates the use of 血 in both Taiwan and China. We thus broaden the argument in the that work: instead of the telic role only, we think both the telic role and the agentive role constrain the selection, as these two roles represent eventive dimensions which demonstrate embodiment, i.e. the interaction between the object/entity and human beings. In terms of the use of 骨 gu 'bone', the telic role still ranks the highest. However, Taiwan presents a use unique to its political ecology, and China tends to employs it in a less embodied way than Taiwan does, which reveal Taiwan's inclination to use certain body parts in a more analytical way while China in a more holistic way. Whether it is the unique use of 骨 in the CNA sub-corpus, or it is the holistic use of 骨 in XIN, we argue it is attributable to the genre of this corpus, and to the specific dimension of a country.

For the future studies, we aim to explore the rest categories of 血 and 骨, and all the categories of

肉 rou 'flesh' and 脈 mai 'meridian', so as to get a complete picture of the constraints of the selection of the metaphorical/metonymical uses of these four body parts.

References

Chen, Keh-Jiann, Chu-Ren Huang, Li-ping Chang, and Hui-Li Hsu. 1996. Sinica Corpus: Design methodology for balanced corpora. In *Proceedings of the 11th Pacific Asia Conference on Language, Information, and Computation (PACLIC 11)*, pages 167-176, Seoul.

Duann, Ren-feng and Chu-Ren Huang. 2015. When embodiment meets generative lexicon: The human body part metaphors in Sinica Corpus. *The Proceedings of the 29th Pacific Asia Conference on Language, Information and Computation (PACLIC 29)*, 396-403.

Gibbs, Raymond W. 2006. *Embodiment and Cognitive Science*. Cambridge University Press, Cambridge and New York.

Huang, Chu-Ren. 2009. Tagged Chinese Gigaword Version 2.0 LDC2009T14. Web Download. Philadelphia: Linguistic Data Consortium.

Johnson, Mark. 2008. *The Meaning of the Body. Aesthetics of Human Understanding*. University of Chicago Press, Chicago and London.

Lakoff, George and Mark Johnson. 1980. *Metaphors we live by*. University of Chicago Press, Chicago.

Lakoff, George and Mark Johnson. 1999. *Philosophy in the Flesh: The Embodied Mind and its Challenge to Western Though*. Basic Books, New York.

Pragglejaz Group. 2007. MIP: A mhod for identifying metaphorically used words in discourse. *Metaphor and Symbol, 22*(1): 1–39.

Pustejovsky, James. 1991. The generative lexicon. *Computational Linguistics,* 17(4): 409-441.

Pustejovsky, James. 1995. *The Generative Lexicon*. The MIT Press, Cambridge, MA and London.

Yu, Ning. 2003. Metaphor, body and culture: The Chinese understanding of gallbladder and courage. *Metaphor and Symbol,* 18(1): 13-31.

Yu, Ning. 2007. The Chinese conceptualization of the heart and its cultural context. Implications for second language learning. In Farzad Sharifian and Gary B. Palmer, editors, *Applied Cultural Linguistics: Implication for Second Language Learning and Intercultural Communication*. John Benjamins Publishing Company, pages 65-85.

A POMDP-based Multimodal Interaction System Using a Humanoid Robot

Sae Iijima
Advanced Sciences,
Graduate School of
Humanities and Sciences,
Ochanomizu University
g1220503@is.ocha.ac.jp

Ichiro Kobayashi
Advanced Sciences,
Graduate School of
Humanities and Sciences,
Ochanomizu University
koba@is.ocha.ac.jp

Abstract

In recent years, with the spread of the household robots, the necessity to enhance the communication capabilities of those robot to people has been increasing. The objective of this study is to build a framework for a dialogue system dealing with multimodal information that a robot observes. We have applied partially observable Markov Decision Process to modeling multimodal interaction between a human and a robot. Through the experiments, we have confirmed that our proposed framework functions properly and achieves effective multimodal interaction with a robot.

1 Introduction

In recent years, with the spread of the household robots, the necessity to enhance the communication capabilities of those robot to people has been increasing. Furthermore, we expect those robots which can observe information from multimodal resources and perform proper actions based on the observed information in interaction with people. In this context, the objective of our study is to achieve effective interaction with a robot using the multimodal information observed by the sensors of the robot. As a concrete system, we have implemented a dialogue system with the framework of partially observable Markov decision process (POMDP) in a humanoid robot called "Pepper" which can observe various multimodal information by its own sensors. Through several experiments, we aim to confirm that our system can assist Pepper to achieve flexible multimodal interaction with people.

2 Multimodal dialogue with a robot

2.1 Observation of multimodal information

In the experiments, we use a humanoid robot called "Pepper"[1] produced by SoftBank Co. Ltd. The figure of Pepper and its sensors are shown in Figure 1. We obtain multimodal information through the sensors of Pepper and aim to achieve multimodal interaction between Pepper and a user with those observed information. As for the multimodal information observed by the sensors equipped with Pepper, we obtain visual information from RGB camera, voice from microphone, contact information from touch sensor, and distance information from laser and sonar sensor. Pepper has face recognition function and can estimate user's age and identify five kinds of user's emotion: i.e., *neutral, happy, surprised, angry*, and *sad*, from user's facial expression.

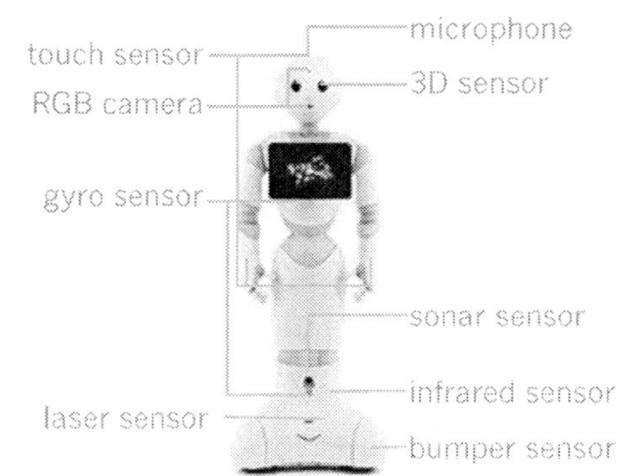

Figure 1: Pepper and its sensors

[1] http://www.softbank.jp/robot/

2.2 POMDP

In this paper, we use a framework of partially observable Markov decision process (POMDP) to represent uncertain states of the Markov decision process as stochastic states. The graphical model of POMDP is illustrated in Figure2.

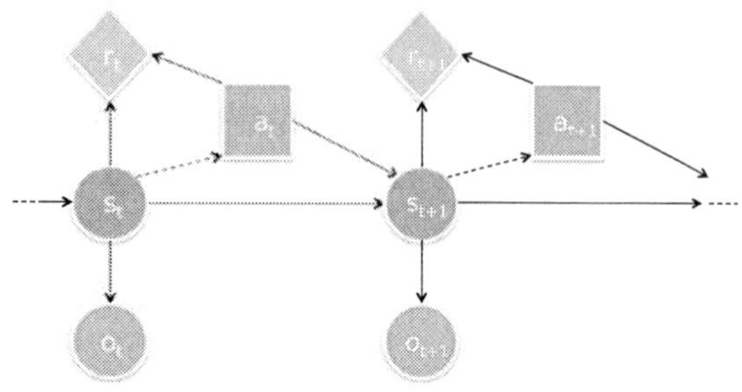

Figure 2: Graphical model of POMDP

A POMDP can be represented in the form of the following n-tuple:$\{S, A, T, O, Z, R, b_0\}$, where $s \in S$ denotes the state of a user, $a \in A$ is an action of the agent, $o \in O$ denotes an observation at state s. T is the probability of transitioning from state s to state s': $P(s'|s, a)$, Z is the probability of observing o' from state s' after taking action a: $P(o'|s', a)$, and $r(s, a) \in R$ is the reward signal received when executing action a in state s.

The process of POMDP is as follows: at each time-step, the target world is expressed as some unobserved state s. Because s is not known exactly, a distribution over states is maintained. This distribution is called "belief state" expressed as b, and its initial state is expressed as b_0. We represent $b(s)$ to indicate the probability of being in a particular state s. At each step, the belief state distribution b is updated as shown in equation (1).

$$b'(s') = k \times P(o'|s', a) \sum_s P(s'|s, a)b(s) \quad (1)$$

Here, k is regarded as a normalization constant to satisfy $\sum_s b'(s') = 1$.

2.3 Expansion to multimodal states

In the interaction between a user and an agent, we consider three states: s^e, s^p and s^l to represent user's emotional state, user's physical state, and user's intention by words, respectively. Here, o^e, o^p, o^l are the corresponding observations for those states, respectively. Figure3 shows the graphical model of the relation between states s and observations o.

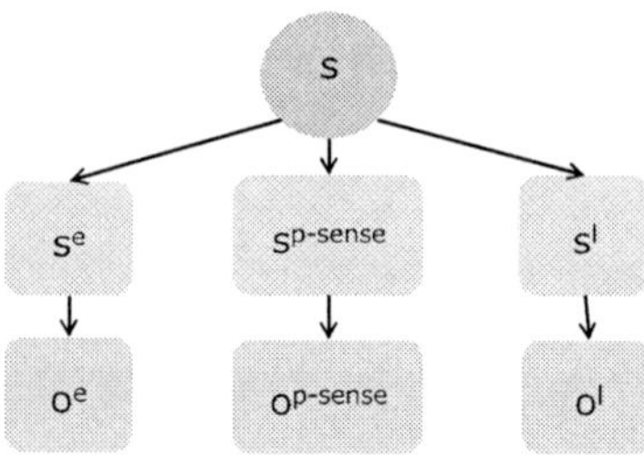

Figure 3: Graphical model of the relation between states and their observations

Here, a more detail about the multimodal states is explained as follows:

- Emotional state : s^e
  This factor indicates the state of user's emotion. We estimate this state based on the observation o^e observed by user's facial expression through an image recognition function equipped with Pepper.

- Physical state : $s^p(s^{p-dis}, s^{p-sense})$
  In our study, the physical state can be divided into two states. One is the distance state s^{p-dis} which represents the state of how far a user is from the agent, and the other is the state of sensing $s^{p-sense}$ which represents whether or not a user is touching the agent. We obtain observation o^{p-dis} from the laser sensor and the sonar sensor and $o^{p-sense}$ from the touch sensor equipped with Pepper.

- Linguistic state : s^l
  This factor indicates the state of user's intention provided by user's utterances. We obtain observation o^l through voice recognition system equipped with Pepper.

2.4 Stratified relation of states

In the case that it is difficult to obtain the optimal policy due to the increase of the state space in reinforcement learning, as one of the solution for this problem, the states are often reconstructed so as they are stratified (Dietterich, 2000). In the reinforcement learning employing stratified states in its decision process, a complex task is divided into several subtasks which correspond to each strata of the stratified interaction processes. The agent learns the local policy at each strata and then learns the global policy for the complex task by unifying those local policies (Yamada et al., 2015).

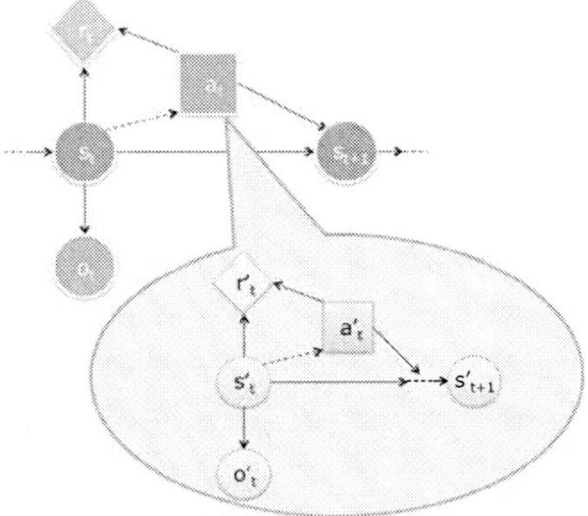

Figure 4: Stratified state in POMDP

2.5 Obtaining optimal policy by Q-learning

A plan to choose action a in state s is defined as policy π. Besides, π^* is defined as the optimal policy to choose optimal action a^* in state s. In POMDP, the states are represented in continuous states and therefore the number of states are monotonically increasing as the process unfolds. Therefore, Pineau et al. (2002) developed point-based value iteration algorithm to reduce calculation cost by transforming continuous values into discrete values at some points. In this paper, however, we assume that states s are regarded as being discrete for simplifying the model and then optimal policy π^* is obtained by Q-learning. The Q-values are updated as shown in equation (2). Here, α and γ indicate the learning rate and the discount rate, respectively.

$$Q(s,a) \leftarrow Q(s,a)+\alpha(r'+\gamma \max_{a'} Q(s',a')-Q(s,a)) \quad (2)$$

Figure 5 illustrates the introduction of Q-learning in the framework of POMDP to estimate the value of each state.

3 Experiments on multimodal iteraction

We conducted experiments employing a dialogue scenario in which Pepper and a user interact with

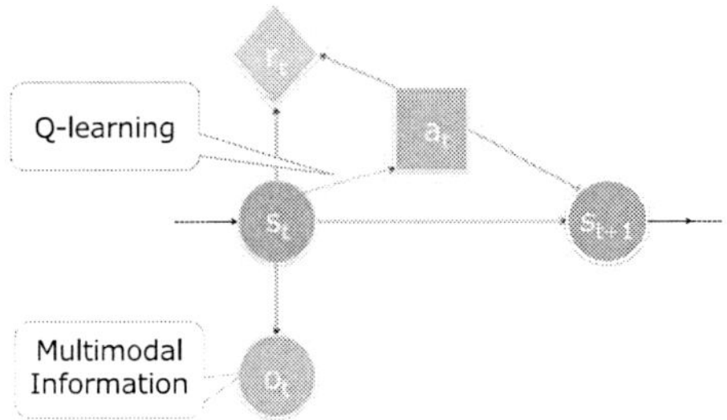

Figure 5: Q-learning in the framework of POMDP

multimodal information – the interaction is modeled by means of POMDP extended so as to be able to deal with multimodal information and to have stratified organization to represent the interaction. In the scenario, the task is stratified in accordance to the priority of interaction – here, user's location is the first priority to start interaction.

To build an interaction system, we improved the Python sample code[2] which implements a demo system for a spoken dialogue system with POMDP by (Williams et al., 2007) in the framework of PythonSDK[3] which is the software developer kit for Pepper.

3.1 The scenario of multimodal interaction

The scenario of multimodal interaction between Pepper and a user is shown in Table1.

Table 1: The scenario of multimodal interaction

Speaker	Interaction content	Observation	Action
User	(Far)	Distance	
Pepper	Come on, here!		Call
User	(Near)	Distance	
Pepper	Let's talk with me.		Speak to
User	Hello.	Voice	
Pepper	Hello.		Greet
User	(Sad face)	Picture	
Pepper	You look so sad! I will encourage you! (Pepper dancing)		Cheer
User	Thank you. (Patted head)	Voice Sensor	
Pepper	I am shy		Shy
User	(None)	Distance	
Pepper	(End of dialogue)		End

[2]https://github.com/mbforbes/py-pomdp
[3]http://doc.aldebaran.com/1-14/dev/python/index.html

3.2 Experimental settings

As for the interaction, in this study we represent the whole interaction in two stratified structure. The first strata represents the transition states of the physical location between Pepper and a user, and the second strata represents the dialogue interaction.

We show the detail settings of POMDP in the following – in this study, state transition probability, observed probability, reward, and the initial belief state are manually provided in advance.

- S : User's states

  S^{p-dis} : { None, Far, Near }
  S : { Greet, Sad, Fun, Happy, Unhappy }

- A : Actions

  A^{p-dis} : {None, End, Call, Speak to}
  A : { None, Greet, Cheer, Enjoy, Shy, Get down}

  Here, A^{p-dis} are the actions corresponding to S^{p-dis}.

- T : State transition probability, $P(s'|s,a)$
  The probabilities of transitioning from a state s to the next state s' for distance identification task and interaction task are shown in Table2 and 3, respectively.

Table 2: State transition probability for distance

s^{p-dis} / $s^{p-dis'}$	None	Far	Near
None	0.2	0.15	0.15
Far	0.2	0.15	0.15
Near	0.3	0.2	0.2

Table 3: State transition probability for dialogue

s / s'	Greet	Sad	Fun	Happy	Unhappy
Greet	0.2	0.25	0.25	0.15	0.15
Sad	0.2	0.15	0.15	0.25	0.25
Fun	0.2	0.15	0.15	0.25	0.25
Happy	0.3	0.2	0.2	0.15	0.15
Unhappy	0.3	0.2	0.2	0.15	0.15

- O: Observation information

  o^e : Observation of user's emotion from the facial expression through image recognition.
  o^{p-dis} : Observation of distance between Pepper and a user.
  $o^{p-sense}$: Observation of the sensing information of touch.
  o^l : Observation of user's voice.

- Z: Observation probability
  In accordance with the stratified relation of states, we consider two observation probabilities: $P(o'|\boldsymbol{s}',a)$ and $P(o^{p-dis}|s^{p-dis'},a)$.
  In the experiments, we set the observation probability of user's voice as 0.8, and the other observation probability as 0.7.

- R : reward, $r(s,a)$
  The rewards given after every action for the identification of the distance to a user from Pepper and for the dialogue interaction are shown Figure4 and 5, respectively.

Table 4: R^{p-dis} : reward for the identification of distance

s^{p-dis} / a^{p-dis}	None	End	Call	Speak to
None	-1	5	-10	-10
Far	-1	-10	5	-10
Near	-1	-10	-10	5

Table 5: R : reward

s / a	None	Greet	Cheer	Enjoy	Shy	Get down
Greet	-1	5	-10	-10	-10	-10
Sad	-1	-10	5	-10	-10	-10
Fun	-1	-10	-10	5	-10	-10
Happy	-1	-10	-10	-10	5	-10
Unhappy	-1	-10	-10	-10	-10	5

- ${b_0}^{p-dis}$ and b_0: The initial belief states
  ${b_0}^{p-dis}$ indicates the initial belief state of the distance between Pepper and a user, and b_0 indicates the initial belief state of a user.

$$
\begin{aligned}
{b_0}^{p-dis} &= (None: 0.2, Far: 0.2, Near: 0.2) \\
b_0 &= (Greet: 0.3, Sad: 0.2, Fun: 0.2, Happy: 0.15, Unhappy: 0.15)
\end{aligned}
$$

Table 6: Experimental result

Agent	Interaction Contents	Observation	$b(s)$	Action	reward
User Pepper	(Far) (None)	o^{p-dis}[Far]	None 0.182, Far 0.545, Near 0.273	None	-0.986
User Pepper	(Far) Come on, here!	o^{p-dis}[Far]	None 0.082, Far 0.735, Near 0.184	Call	1.100
User Pepper	(Near) Let's talk me.	o^{p-dis}[Near]	None 0.06, Far 0.222, Near 0.718	Speak to	0.819
User Pepper	Hello. Hello.	o^{l}[Greet]	Greet 0.8, Sad 0.05, Fun 0.05, Happy 0.05, Unhappy 0.05	Greet	2.541
User Pepper	(Sad face) How are you? I encourage you.	o^{e}[Sad]	Greet 0.046, Sad 0.727, Fun 0.156, Happy 0.035, Unhappy 0.035	Cheer	1.539
User Pepper	Thank you. (Patted head) I am shy	o^{l}[Happy] $o^{p-sense}$[Touch head]	Greet 0.045, Sad 0.035, Fun 0.035, Happy 0.729, Unhappy 0.156	Shy	1.965
User Pepper	(None) (None)	o^{p-dis}[None]	None 0.464, Far 0.298, Near 0.238	None	-0.989
User Pepper	(None) (End of dialogue)	o^{p-dis}[None]	None 0.796, Far 0.146, Near 0.058	None	1.964

- π^*: The optimal policy
  The optimal policy π^* shows the optimal action a^* in the belief state $b(s)$. It is represented in equation (3) by Q-value.

$$\pi^*(b(s)) = Q(b(s), a) \quad (3)$$

To find the optimal policy, we use ϵ-greedy method in Q-learning, and set the learning rate α as 0.2, and the discount rate γ as 0.9.

3.3 Experimental result

Table 6 shows an experimental result. Figure 6 shows the graphical model of POMDP for the scenario.

3.4 Discussions

Through the experiment, we have confirmed that our proposed multimodal interaction framework with a humanoid robot Pepper works well to interact with a user, and understood that the representation of the states in the interactive system tends to depend on the sensing functions and abilities of a robot. If each sensing function and ability is poor, it should be difficult to establish the interaction.

Furthermore, in this study we have built an interaction system with two strata in the framework of POMDP – we have set the first stratum so as it decides to start interaction based on the physical distance between Pepper and a user, and set the second stratum to control multimodal interaction. We have confirmed that the stratification of the whole interaction works well to reduce the dimension of states and then reduce calculation cost, and to make a good organization of the interaction.

In the experiment, we obtained the optimal strategy assuming that the states on the interaction are observed as being definite in order to reduce calculation cost. As a result, because the size of the scenario was short, there was not any problem in the interaction. However, we will have to take care of this problem, when we deal with a complicated and long interaction.

4 Related studies

As for employing POMDP in dialogue management, the essential features, e.g., how to model the inherent uncertainty in spoken dialog systems, why exact optimization is intractable, and how to describe the hidden information state model which does scale

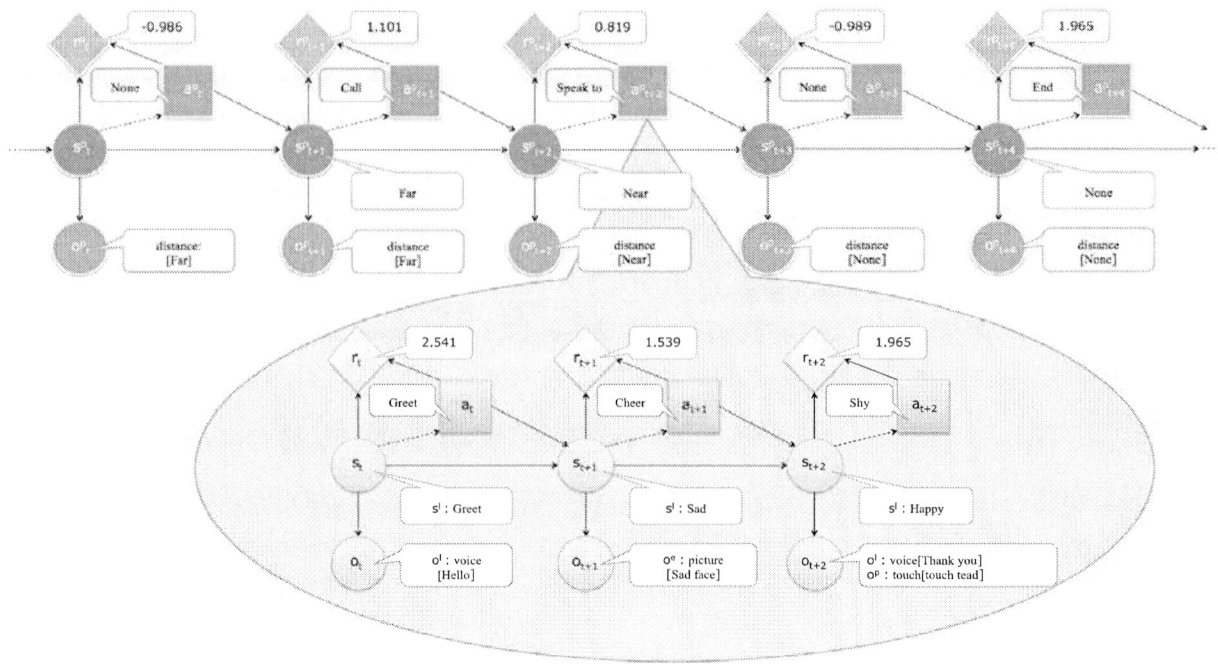

Figure 6: Overview of POMDP for the scenario

and which can be used to build practical systems, are studied in (Young, 2006; Young et al., 2007; Williams, 2006; Williams et al., 2007) – Young et al. (2007) partitioned the state space using a tree-based representation of user goals so that only a small set of partition beliefs needs to be updated at every turn to achieve the efficient calculation and showed a practical framework for POMDP-based spoken dialogue management system for the tourist information domain (Young et al., 2010).

Jurcicek (2011) proposed a reinforcement algorithm for learning parameters of dialogue systems modeled as POMDPs. Lison (2010) represented constraints on selecting actions with a small set of general rules expressed as a Markov Logic network in the framework of POMDP. He extended his idea to dialogue management based on the use of multiple, interconnected policies (Lison, 2010).

As for dealing with probabilistic states in a dialogue, a dialogue is modeled as Markov decision processes (MDPs) (Lemon, 2008; Lemon, 2011; Rieser, 2008; Rieser et al., 2009) and solved them by means of reinforcement learning (Sutton and Barto, 1998).

As a new trend in POMDP-based dialogue management, Gaussian Processes is applied to reinforcement learning Engel (2005) for optimal POMDP dialogue policies, in order to make the learning process faster and to obtain an estimate of the uncertainty of the approximation (Gasic et al., 2010; Gasic et al., 2013).

5 Conclusion

In this study, we have proposed a multimodal interaction system with a humanoid robot, expanding the framework of POMDP so as it can deal with multimodal information observed by the robot. In the system, we have achieved stratified interaction to reduce the increase of the user's belief states to deal with. Furthermore, we have also dealt with the estimated states as being definite so as to avoid the explosion of calculation cost. Through an experiment with a scenario, we have confirmed that our proposed method works well to achieve multimodal interaction between a user and a robot. As future work, we will consider the effective way to deal with continuous states in the framework of POMDP employing multimodal information, and make a good organization of stratified structure in the dialogue interaction.

Acknowledgments

We would like to express our appreciation for financial support by Tateishi Science and Technology Foundation.

References

B. Bonet 2002. *An e-optimal grid-based algorithm for par- tially observable Markov decision processes* In Proc. of ICML, pp. 51-58.

T.G. Dietterich 2000. *An Overview of MAXQ Hierarchical Reinforcement Learning*, Lecture Notes in Computer Science, pp. 26-44.

Y Engel, S Mannor, and R Meir 2005. *Reinforcement learning with Gaussian processes*, In Proc. of the International Conference on Machine Learning.

M. Gasic, F. Jurcicek, S. Keizer, F. Mairesse, B. Thomson, K. Yu and S. Young 2010. *Gaussian Processes for Fast Policy Optimisation of POMDP-based Dialogue Managers*, In Proc. of SIGDIAL 2010: the 11th Annual Meeting of the Special Interest Group on Discourse and Dialogue, pp. 201-204.

M. Gasic, C. Breslin, M. Henderson, D. Kim, M. Szummer, B. Thomson, P. Tsiakoulis and S. Young 2013. *POMDP-based dialogue manager adaptation to extended domains* In Proc. of the SIGDIAL 2013 Conference, pp. 214-222.

F Jurcicek, B Thomson, and S Young 2011. *Natural actor and belief critic: Reinforcement algorithm for learning parameters of dialogue systems modelled as POMDPs*, ACM Transactions on Speech and Language Processing.

O. Lemon, 2008. *Adaptive natural language generation in dialogue using reinforcement learning*, In Proc. of the Workshop on the Semantics and Pragmatics of Dialogue (SEMDIAL), pp.141-148, London, UK. SemDial.

O. Lemon, 2011. *Learning what to say and how to say it:joint optimization of spoken dialogue management and natural language generation*, Computer Speech and Language, 25(2):pp.210-221.

P. Lison 2010. *Towards Relational POMDPs for Adaptive Dialogue Management* In Proc. of the ACL 2010 Student Research Workshop, pp. 7-12.

P. Lison 2011. *Multi-Policy Dialogue Management* In Proceedings of the SIGDIAL 2011 Conference, pp. 294-300

J. Pineau, G. Gordon, and S. Thrun 2002. *Point-based value iteration: An anytime algorithm for pomdps* In Proc. of the International Joint Conference on Artificial Intelligence, pp. 1025-1032.

V. Rieser and O. Lemon 2008. *Learning Effective Multimodal Dialogue Strategies from Wizard-of-Oz data: Bootstrapping and Evaluation*, In Proc. of ACL-08: HLT, pp. 638-646.

V. Rieser and O. Lemon, 2009. *Natural Language Generation as Planning under Uncertainty for Spoken Dialogue Systems*, In Proc. of the Conference of the European Chapter of the Association for Computational Linguistics (EACL), pp.683-691, Athens, Greece.

N. Roy, J. Pineau and S. Thrun 2000. *Spoken Dialogue Management Using Probabilistic Reasoning*, In Proc. of the Association for Computational Linguistics.

R. S. Sutton and A. G. Barto, 1998. *Reinforcement Learning: An Introduction*, MIT Press, Cambridge, MA.

J. D. Williams. 2006. *Partially Observable Markov Decision Processes for Spoken Dialogue Management*. Ph.D. thesis, University of Cambridge.

J. D. Williams, S. Young 2007. *Partially observable Markov decision processes for spoken dialog systems*, Computer Speech and Language, Volume 21 , Issue 2, pp. 393-422.

Y. Yamada, T. Takiguchi, and Y. Ariki, 2015. *SPOKEN DIALOGUE SYSTEM FOR PRODUCT RECOMMENDATION USING HIERARCHICAL POMDP*, 2015 First International Workshop on Machine Learning in Spoken Language Processing (MLSLP), 6 pages.

S. Young. 2006. *Using POMDPs for Dialog Management*. In Proc. of IEEE/ACL SLT, Palm Beach, Aruba.

J.Young, W. K. Schatzmann, and H. Ye. 2007. *The Hidden Information State Approach to Dialog Management*. In Proc. of 2007 IEEE International Conference on Acoustics, Speech and Signal Processing - ICASSP '07 (Volume:4), Honolulu, Hawaii.

S. Young, M. Gasic, S. Keizer, F. Mairesse, J. Schatzmann, B. Thomson, and K. Yu 2010. *The Hidden Information State model: A practical framework for POMDP-based spoken dialogue management*, Computer Speech and Language, 24:pp. 150-174.

The Cloud of Knowing: Non-factive *al-ta* 'know' (as a Neg-raiser) in Korean

Chungmin Lee
Seoul National University
1 Gwanak-ro, Gwanak-gu, Seoul,
South Korea 151-742
clee@snu.ac.kr

Seungjin Hong
University at Buffalo, SUNY
609 Baldy Hall, Buffalo,
NY 14260, U.S.A.
shong23@buffalo.edu

Abstract

We distinguished the two different uses of factive and NonFactive (NF) in the verb *al-ta* 'know' in Korean and the distinction is crucially made by the different complement cases of factive *ul* ACC and NF *uro* Directional (oblique). The NF use is possible with nonveridical/negative contexts in English and other languages but it is possible with a positive sentence with the Directional case in Korean uniquely (Hungarian only is similar in this respect and Japanese has no NF 'know'). The NF *–uro al-ta* verb, however, is different from other weaker epistemic verbs meaning 'believe'/'think' in that it strongly tends to show some piece of evidence for JTB but the evidential justification may turn out to fall short of knowledge. We conducted experiments to clearly show that the NF *–uro al-ta* has the relation of neg-raising between the high neg S and the low (complement) neg S, which are truthconditionally equivalent. It implies that this NF verb *–uro al-ta* is identical in neg-raisability with other weaker epistemic verbs meaning 'believe' and 'think' in Korean. An exerpt from *Sejong* Corpus indicates that the NF 'know' in Korean typically accompies some piece of evidence that led the speaker to hold a firmer belief than other epistemic verbs meaning 'believe'/'think' in Korean.

1 Credits

We thank Sebatian Löbner and others at an earlier KSLI 2016 presentation and anonymous SALT 26 and PACLIC reviewers for their comments.

2 Introduction

Horn (2014) cites Hintikka's ambiguity of negating a *know* clause, as (1c) and its translations in contrast to its positive clause (1a). Here *p* is factive in (1c") but not in (1c'). He agrees with Hintikka on the conjoined (1c") reading being taken to be the appropriate one for "the most typical cases," especially third person examples. The third person condition is Horn's addition.

(1) a. a knows that p   a'. Kap
  b. a knows whether p   b'. Kap v ~Kap
  c. a does not know that p   c'. ~Kap
    c". p & ~Kap
  d. a does not know whether p
  d'. ~(Kap v Ka~p) ↔ ~Kap & ~Kap

Horn further cites Russell's imagined reaction to rumours of Wittgenstein's death, as in (2). He gives a simpler example in (3).

(2) I don't know that he is dead; the rumours may not be true, for all that I really know.
(3) I don't know that I can make it there on time.

Horn (2014) questions how factive is *know*, taking all the interesting cases of *know*-N(on)F(active) drawn from *not know* and questions (*not know*'s kin, i.e., nonveridical) such as 'Do you know that he is reliable?' He notes its correlate complementizer, near-obligatory in *not-know* NF, as in *I don't know **that** I can*, based on English. Other languages such as Greek and Bulgarian also require nonveridical elements like subjunctive complements for the NF use of 'know.'

In emotive factive predicates such as 'regret', however, their negation does not nullify their factivity. Observe (4). The complement 'she married a foreigner' is still true. The same holds in Korean.

(4) Mary does not regret that she married a foreigner.

Korean is different in the negation of the epistemic factive verb *al-ta* 'know'; the negation cannot make the verb non-factive at all, if the complement form of the factive verb *al-ta* is intact with ACC in the negative *al-ta* sentence. Examine (5) (cf. (7)).

(5) Na-nun chinkwu-ka cwuk-un
I-TOP friend-NOM die-PreN
kes-***ul*** al-ci mos hay-ss-ta
COMP-***ACC*** know-CI NEG PST-DEC
'I didn't know that my friend died.'

A question sentence cannot make *al-ta* 'know' with ACC NF in Korean either, unlike in English.

The Korean verb *al-ta* 'know' becomes non-factive in a purely positive sentence unlike in other languages if it takes the directional (DIR) (oblique) complementizer case. We try to characterize this phenomenon epistemologically.

3 The Non-factive Positive verb *al-ta* in Korean

This paper addresses the non-factive positive verb *al-ta* 'know,' as opposed to the factive positive verb *al-ta* 'know,' rather unique in Korean (Lee 1978), and shows how its negated complement clause can undergo neg-raising just like other non-factive epistemic verbs such as 'think' and 'believe.' It discusses how the distinction between the non-factive vs. factive uses of the verb *al-ta* occurs via difference in complementizer cases: DIR(ECTIONAL) vs. ACC. Consider the pairs.

3.1 Its form

(6) [non-factive]
Mina-nun chinkwu-ka cwuk-un
M-TOP friend-NOM die-PreN
kes-***uro*** al-ass-ta
COMP-***DIR*** know-PST-DEC
'Mina knew toward (literally) it that her friend died.'

(7) [factive]
Mina-nun chinkwu-ka cwuk-un
M-TOP friend-NOM die-PreN
kes-***ul*** al-ass-ta
COMP-***ACC*** know-PST-DEC
'Mina knew that her friend died.'

Because the factive verb *al-ta* 'know' is a transitive verb, it is natural to expect the ACC complementizer case, as in (7). The so-called complementizer *kes* 'thing' involved is a dependent nominal traditionally and can take cases. The ACC complementizer case with a factive presupposition gives the sense of hitting the target even cognitively, whereas the oblique DIR case with no factive presupposition does not and rather gives the sense of going astray. In motion, ACC is telic, whereas DIR is atelic.

3.2 Its epistemic nature

What would be the real difference in the epistemic states between the subject or the epistemic agent of (6) and that of (7)? How about between the speaker of (6) and that of (7)? For (7), at least the subject and the speaker must commonly know that P because it is factively presupposed. How about (6)? The speaker does not know that P but the subject = the epistemic agent of the verb in (6) may know that P possibly false so it can turn out to be false or true. Just like 'false belief,' 'false knowledge' may be involved, though like a contradiction in the traditional justified true belief (JTB) definition in (8).

(8) S knows that p iff
a. p is true; (if false, you cannot know p)
b. S believes that p;
c. S is justified in believing that p.

The NF 'know' can be caused by the Gettier Problem:

(9) --- the clock on campus (which keeps accurate time and is well maintained) stopped working at 11:56 pm last night, and has yet to be repaired.

On my way to my noon class, exactly twelve hours later, I glance at the clock and form the belief that the time is 11:56., thinking that I know the time--- JTB can still involve luck and thus fall short of knowledge. -[*Interenet Encyclopedia of Philosophy* ---Peer-reviewed]

Our 'false knowledge' may involve inductive fallacy as in white swans with no black ones attested leading to 'know' that swans are white. Because of this fallibility, we use hedges like 'As far as I know.' Our experience is limited for **justifying** our true belief. Knowledge entails belief, but not vice versa, a la Hinttikka (1962). The non-factive verb *al-ta* 'know' is used by its epistemic agent's epistemic state of more justification with some solid evidence than other belief type epistemic verbs such as *mit-ta* 'believe' and *sayngkakha-ta* 'think' by their epistemic agent's epistemic state of justification.

Contexts for (6) above, NF, may be either a or b: a. Mina saw her friend's name in the toll list (evidence), so (6), but later she got a call from him. So Mina's initial justified belief (which led her to use *al-ta* 'know') that he died has been falsified. b. Mina rushed to her friend who collapsed with cardiac arrest beyond the critical point, so (6). Transport with desperate continuing CPR could not save him. Death was confirmed. For (6), the complement proposition can turn out to be either false or factual.

3.3 Crosslinguistically scarce

The non-factivity of non-factive (NF) *al-ta* 'know' in Korean is not caused by nonveridicality or explicit negation of the epistemic verb 'know' as elsewhere. Japanese lacks any **NF 'know'** and has only factive *siru*, as in (10). Even if the negation of *siru*, *sirana-i* 'not know' replaces 'know' in (10a), the factive presupposition still holds. In (10b), 'thinks' cannot be replaced by 'know' because of the reportative complementizer '*-to,*' assuring NF.

(10) a.Mia-wa tomodachi-ga sinda-koto-**o** sitte-iru
M-TOPfriend-NOM die-COMP-ACC know
'Mia knows that her friend died.'
b. Mia-wa tomodachi-ga sinda-to omotte-iru
M-TOP friend-NOM die-COMP think
'Mia thinks that her friend died.'

In Greek and Bulgarian, subjunctive complementizers, which are nonveridical, make distinction. Hungarian *tud* 'know' with DELATIVE 'about' as NF and with Def ACC COMP as factive, alone behaves similarly to Korean (Kiefer 1978). NF *al-ta* takes an oblique DIRectional (atelic in space) case. It is opposed to factive *al-ta* (and emotive 'regret'), with the ACC marker (telic) attached to *kes*, event NOM/COMP. NF *al-ta*, though neg-raising, is different from the 'think'/'believe' type neg-raisers and the 'say' type that takes a reportative complementizer as a non-neg-raiser; the speaker's epistemic state of NF *al-ta* 'know' is justified with solider evidence than for *sayngkakha-ta* 'think' type verbs. The Sejong Korean corpus data attest this. A clause with *sayngkakha-ta*/*mit-ta* may lack evidence.

4 NF Neg-Raising

The high negation senence in (11) and the low negation sentence in (12), both NF, with the DIR COMP case, are in neg-raising relation. This synatactic relation semantically strengthens formal contradictory negation to contrariety (reading left to right) , i.e., $\neg f(X) \Leftrightarrow f\neg(X)$, as shown by Zwarts (1986), as cited by Horn. Horn objects to stricit syntatic derivational relation, based on properties of non-factive "know." (11) with high negation entails (12) with low negation. The high negation senence is argued to have the pragmatic effect of 'toning down' (Horn 2014).

(11) [NF]
Mina-nun chinkwu-ka cwuk-un
M-TOP friend-NOM die –PreN
kes-***uro*** alkoiss-ci- an-ess-ta
COMP-DIR know-CI-NEG-PST-DEC
'Mina didn't know toward (literally) it that her friend died.' [high negation]

(12) [NF]
Mina-nun chinkwu-ka an cwukun
M-TOP friend-NOM NEG die
kes-***uro*** alkoiss-ess-ta
COMP-DIR know-PST-DEC
'Mina knew toward (literally) that her friend didn't die.' [low negation]

5 A Formal Treatment

The factive presupposition and lack of it (NF) may be represented as below. In (13), f is like 'fact' in Kiparsky and Kiparsky (1970) (cf. Schueler (2016)).

5.1 Factive

(13) [[*al-ta*]] 'know' = λfλxλw. x knows f.
(14) a. [[chikwu-ka cwuk-un kes-***ul***]] = λw. Mina's friend died in w; where defined = the unique fact that Mina's friend died in w.
b. [[kes-***ul*** $_F$]] = λpλw. fact(p, w), where p(w) cannot be 0. (Kratzer: λpλe) [*kes* COMP -*ul* ACC]
(15) [[moru-ta]]=~[[*al-ta*]]=λfλxλw. x ~knows f.
(16) [[*hwuhoyha-ta*]] 'regret'= λfλxλw. x feels remorseful about f. (Schueler (2016))

If (14) matches (15), then it attains factive presupposition, as in (14) and in its higher 'not know' as well.

In (15), the lexial negative verb *moru-ta* 'not know' is semantically the negation of the factive verb *al-ta* 'know' and retains its factive presupposition all the time, taking the COMP ACC constantly. By contrast, the long form negation *–ci mos-ha-ta* 'do not know' can take the DIR NF *al-ta* freely. The lexial negative verb *moru-ta* 'not know' is an interesting case of fossilization in conventionalization, blocking the NF use.

5.2 Non-factive

If the verb *al-ta*, with no λf, takes the following complementizer:

(17) [[kes-***uro*** $_T$]] = λp.p (a la Kratzer 2006) [*kes* COMP -*uro* Directional]

Then, it becomes NF *al-ta*, as exemplified in (6) with its context given.

Overall, *al-ta* is identified as an epistemic factive or NF predicate, determined by its complement case marking. Its NF realization is not by nonverifical/negative contexts as in other languages. Its unique 'part time' (Beaver and Geurts 2011) or 'soft' predicate nature awaits further exploration. In English, In English, we see the following relation in the *know---as* construction (found in corpus). The *as* part here is not a full complement clause (as Larry Horn indicates, being against neg-raising, p.c.) needed for neg-raising and some view the negated one as marginal, although it is still a small clause and (18) and (19) are not truth-conditionally identical, as Ken Turner, Andrew Simpson, Bruce Wakdman (biologist), and ten American grad students confirmed. in contrast, the high neg S and the low neg S of the *regard---as* construction in (18') and (19') are in NR, being truth-conditionally identical. It is interesting to see the high neg S of the *know---as* construction alone is NF at least, adding one more item to the 'cloud' of not knowing in English. The NR relation between the *regard---as* construction in (18') and (19') has not been treated so far either, as far as we know.

The item *as* appears to be similar to one meaning from the DIRECTIVE COMP case in Korean. DIR 'toward' seems to develop to QUA 'as' (in Korean *–uro* is now lexically ambiguous between 'toward' and 'as'). In Korean, DIR *–uro* constitutes NF with a positive *al-ta* 'know.'

(18) I don't know him as being a good student. ---non-factive
(19) I know him as not being a good student. ---factive
(18') I don't regard him as being a good student.
(19') I regard him as not being a good student
:

6. Experiments

We show how native speakers react to the neg-raisability of the **NF** *al-ta* 'know' along with belief type epsistemic predicates and to (no) factive presupposition. We conducted an experiment with non-factive verb **NF** *al-ta*, factive verb *al-ta*, factive emotive verb *hwuhoyha-ta* 'regret', non-factive verb *mit-ta* 'believe,' and non-factive verb *sayngkakha-ta* 'think.' For Experiment 1, we constructed it with contexts given in (high negation) [-uro al-ta *al-ta p~*] (11) and asked a question in (low negation) [~-uro al-ta *al-ta p*] (12). 20 participants were asked to choose one of the three answers 'yes,' 'no,' and 'don't know' to indicate whether the two sentences had the same meaning or not.

(20) = (12) given in the context.
Q: Mina-nun chinkwu-ka an cwukun
Mina-NOM friend-NOM NEG die
kes-***uro*** alkoiss-ess-supnikka?
COMP-DIR know-PST-Q
'Did Mina know toward (literally) it that her friend died?'

The results of all the verbs are shown in figure 1. The results show that non-factive verb *al-ta* 'know' has the same patterns of non-factive verbs mit-ta 'believe' and *sayngkakha-ta* 'think' since the percentages of the answer 'yes (neg-raising, henceforth NR)' are about 40~50% and 'no (non-neg-raising, henceforth NNR)' are around 50~60%. It seems that the answer 'no (NNR)' is quite high (50~60%). That is because some subjects may have been sensitive to the pragmatic meaning difference of 'toning down' by raising. Therefore, non-factive verb *al-ta* 'know' is also a neg-raising verb along with *mit-ta* 'believe' and *sayngkakha-ta* 'think.' Also, factive verb *al-ta* 'know' has the similar pattern of the (factive) emotive verb *hwuhoyha-ta* 'regret.' The percentages of the anwer 'yes (NR)' of these verbs are over 90%. We can conclude that the factive verb *al-ta* 'know' is a non-neg-raising verb like emotive verb *hwuhoyha-ta* 'regret.' These results are indirectly supported by the experiments in Lee and Hong (2016) of reaction times of no significant difference between non-factive NR verbs and factive NNR verbs, implying the

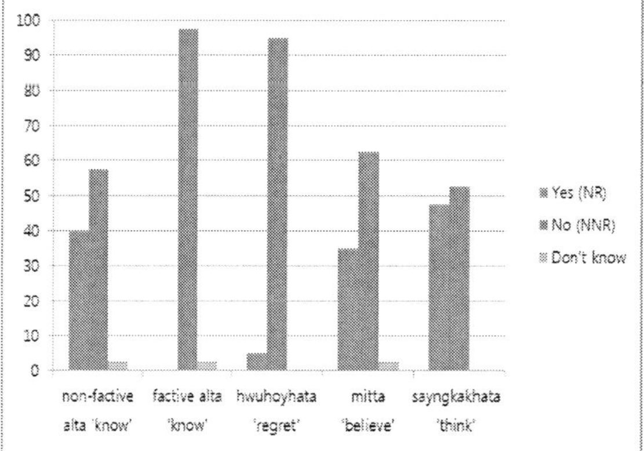

Figure 1. The neg-raisability of factive and non-factive verbs

participants' no difficulty deciding which verb is neg-raising and which not.

In this paper, another experiment was conducted to verify whether the non-factive verbs bear the presumption that can turn out to be false. The second experiment asked questions whether the P is true or not. Consider (20).

(20) = (6) given in the context.
Mina-nun chinkwu-ka cwuk-un
M-TOP friend-NOM die-PreN
kes-***uro*** al-ass-ta
COMP-***DIR*** know-PST-DEC
'Mina knew toward (literally) it that her friend died.'
Q: ku ttay chinkwu-ka cwuk-ess-supnikka?
At that moment friend-NOM die-PST-Q
'At that moment, did her friend die?

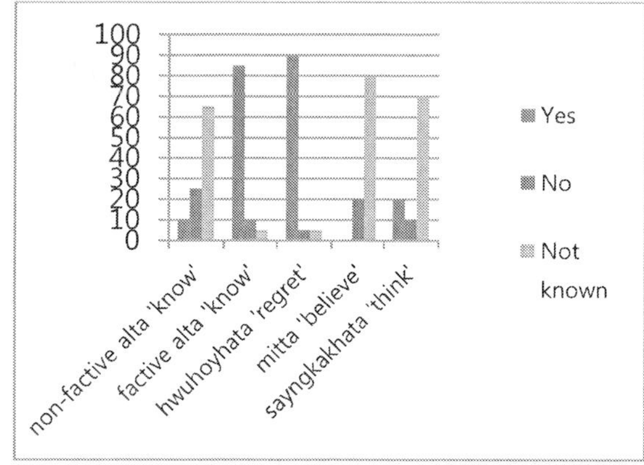

Figure 2. Bearing possibly false knowledge of the non-factive verbs and factive verbs

Figure 2 clearly shows that the non-factive verbs involve a possible 'false knowledge' presumption while the factive verbs do not.

For the non-factive verbs *al-ta* 'know,' *mit-ta* 'believe' and *sayngkakha-ta* 'think,' the answers are mostly 'not known' which means the presumption can be either true or false. For the factive verbs *al-ta* 'know' and the emotive verb *hwuhoyha-ta* 'regret,' over 80~90% of the answers are 'yes,' which indicate that the factive verb *al-ta* and the emotive verb *hwuhoyha-ta* only bear the presupposition that is granted to be true. Especially, the emotive verb *hwuhoyha-ta* has a stronger tendency of involving presupposition since its factive presupposition is far way from the at-issue assertion unlike epistemic verbs.

The results of the two types of experiments show that Korean *al-ta* 'know' bears two types of meanings, non-factive and factive, depending on the obligue/ACC cases. As a consequence, non-factive *al-ta* is a neg-rasing verb unlike factive *al-ta*.

A further expertiment will be conducted to verify that non-factive *al-ta* 'know' and *mit-ta* 'believe' can be contradicted if one of them negated in the same sentence. The experiment will be given contexts, asking about contradiction tests like "Mina-nun p-uro al-ass-una Mina-nun p-rako mit-ci ahn-ass-ta ('Mina knew toward p but did not believe p')", a sheer contradiction, and vice versa, puzzling.

7 Corpus and Acquisition Support

7.1 Corpus

Our claims are also supported by contextual data collected from *Sejong Korean Corpus* for factive and NF *al-ta*. In the corpus data, as in (13), *al-ta* with *–uro* is used to imply that the speaker has uncertainty or false belief about the complement content he/she is talking about but she has some piece of evidence for her belief unlike in the case of other neg-raising weaker epistemic verbs such as *mit-ta* 'believe.' Consider the following:

(21) e~ malchalyey-ka congkyeltoyessum-ul
Uh~ conversation turn-NOM finish-ACC
phyosihanun, malcharyey tanwi phyoci-ka
represent conversation turn unit sign-NOM
nathanaca, hyencay hwaca-uy palhwa-ka
appear present speaker-POSS utterance-NOM
kkuthnan kes-***uro*** alko mal-ul
finish **COMP-DIR** know utterance-ACC
sicakha-ciman hyencay hwaca-ka
start-but present speaker-NOM
mal-ul kyeysokhayse sayngkinun
utterance-ACC continue generate
kyepchimul malha-pnita.
overlap indicate-DEC

'Uh~ as soon as a conversation turn unit marker that indicates the utterance is finished appears, the next speaker is starting to talk 'knowing towards' it that the present speaker finished his/her utterance. Therefore, the utteraces of the present speaker and the next speaker overlap since the present speaker continues the utterances.'

In (21), *al-ta* with *–uro* is used to indicate that the next speaker misunderstood that the present speaker was finishing his/her utterance because of the unit marker, so the next speaker was starting his/her speech. Here, *uro* is used instead of *–ul* because the verb *al-ta* 'know' with *–uro* has a distinctive implicational meaning that the information is not confirmed and may be falsified. However, it must be noted that the speaker witnessed the piece of evidence i.e., turn unit completion marker. That's why *al-ta* with *–uro* has been employed rather than a weaker epistemic verb.

On the other hand, if the ACC marker *–ul* had been used in this context, the sentence would not contribute to the coherence of the discourse. Since *–ul* is for confirming the truth of the complement information, the sentence becomes contradictory. This example clearly shows that *al-ta* with *–uro* implies uncertainty of the complement information, which can turn out to be false. The speaker often uses the NF verb *–uro al-ta* after realizing she was mistaken. (21) is one such case.

In corpus, the occurrence rate of *–uro al-ta* NF DIR 'know' (90%, 18 out of 20) is far higher than that of *–ul al-ta* factive ACC 'know' (10%, 2 out of 20). The rarity of the latter should be this: when you know that p, you make an assertion that p. If you have some piece of evidence, you often use *al-ta* with *–uro* to justify your position often defensively. You also often use it out of politeness, even if you actually know, to mitigate the hardness of fact. For instance, if the hearer (often senior) firmly believes that Mia is too poor to be admitted to a college, and the speaker knows that she has been actually admitted, the speaker may use the following NF *al-ta* with *–uro*, avoiding the factive *al-ta* with ACC (or even the declarative assertion), not to stand against the hearer.

(22) Mia-ka iphak-ha-n kes-*uro* al-ko iss-um-ni-ta
M-NOM admitted-COMP-DIR know-DEC
'(I) know toward it that Mia has been admitted.'

7.2 Acquisition

Dudly et al (2015) reports the interesting experimental results, showing that some three-year-olds' can distinguish between *know* as factive and *think* as NF, whereas the remaining three-year-olds' treat both *know* and *think* as NF. They, therefore, suggest that early representations of *know* may be NF.

When we consider the developmental stages, the divergence of NF *al-ta* with DIR and factive *al-ta* with ACC is not surprising, typologically.

8. Concluding Remarks

In conclusion, we distinguished the two different uses of factive and NF in the verb *al-ta* 'know' in Korean and the distinction is crucially made by the different complement cases of factive *–ul* ACC and NF *–uro* Directional (oblique). The NF use is possible with nonveridical/negative contexts in English and other languages but it is possible with a positive sentence with the Directional case in Korean uniquely (Hungarian only is similar in this respect and Japanese has no NF 'know'). The NF *–uro al-ta* verb, however, is different from other weaker epistemic verbs meaning 'believe'/'think' in that it strongly tends to show some piece of evidence for JTB but the evidential justification may turn out to fall short of knowledge.

We conducted experiments to clearly show that the NF *–uro al-ta* has the relation of neg-raising between the high neg S and the low (complement) neg S, which are truthconditionally equivalent. It implies that this NF verb *–uro al-ta* is identical in neg-raisability with other weaker epistemic verbs meaning 'belive' and 'think' in Korean. An exerpt from *Sejong* Corpus indicates that the NF 'know' in Korean typically accompanies some piece of evidence that led the speaker to hold a firmer belief than other epistemic verbs meaning 'believe'/'think' in Korean.

This research sheds new light to the issue of knowledge and evidential justification.

References

Beaver, D & B. Geurts 2011. Presupposition. In Edward N. Zalta (ed.), *Stanford Ency-clopedia of Philosophy*, summer 2011 edn.

Dudley, R., N. Orita, V. Hacquard, and J. Lidz 2015. Three-year-olds' understanding of *know* and *think*. In S. Floria (ed.) *Experimental Perspectives on Presuppositions*. Cham: Springer.

Hintikka, J. 1962. *Knowledge and Belief.* Ithaca: Cornell U. Press.

Horn, L. 2014. The cloud of unknowing. In J. Hoeksema & D. Gilbers (Eds.), *Black Book. A Festschrift in Honor of Frans Zwarts* (pp. 178-196). Groningen: University of Groningen.

Kiefer, F. 1978. Factivity in Hungarian. *Studies in Language 2.(2).* (pp. 165-197).

Kiparsky, C. and Kiparsky, P. 1970. Fact. In: M. Bierwisch & K. Heidolph (eds.), *Progress in Linguistics*. The Hague: Mouton, 143-173.

Kratzer, A. 2006. Decomposing attitude verbs. Ms., University of Masachusetts at Amherst, Amherst, Mass.

Lee, C. 1978. An analysis of *al-ta* 'know' [in Korean]. *Maum* 1 'Mind' (A Journal of the Mind Philosophy Society Ywusimhoy).

Lee, S and Hong, S.J. 2016. An experimental study of neg-raising inferences in Korean. In P. Larrivée & C. Lee (Eds.), *Negation and polarity: experimental perspectives* (pp. 257-277). Cham: Springer.

Schueler, D. 2016. Factivity and Complement-Types. *Studia* Linguistica 70 (2). DOI: 10.1111/stul.12060.

Zwarts, F. 1986. *Categoriale Grammatica en Algebraïsche Semantiek:Een Onderzoeknaar Negatie en Polariteit in het Nederlands.* Doctoral dissertation, U. of Groningen.

Neural Joint Learning for Classifying Wikipedia Articles into Fine-Grained Named Entity Types

Masatoshi Suzuki[†], **Koji Matsuda**[†], **Satoshi Sekine**[§], **Naoaki Okazaki**[†], **Kentaro Inui**[†]
† Tohoku University §Language Craft Inc
{m.suzuki,matsuda,okazaki,inui}@ecei.tohoku.ac.jp sekine@languagecarft.com

Abstract

This paper addresses the task of assigning fine-grained NE type labels to Wikipedia articles. To address the data sparseness problem, which is salient particularly in fine-grained type classification, we introduce a multi-task learning framework where type classifiers are all jointly learned by a neural network with a hidden layer. In addition, we also propose to learn article vectors (i.e. entity embeddings) from Wikipedia's hypertext structure using a Skip-gram model and incorporate them into the input feature set. To conduct large-scale practical experiments, we created a new dataset containing over 22,000 manually labeled instances. The dataset is available. The results of our experiments show that both ideas gained their own statistically significant improvement separately in classification accuracy.

1 Introduction

Recognizing named entities (NEs) in text is a crucial component task of a broad range of NLP applications including information extraction and question answering. Early work on named entity recognition (NER) defined a small number of coarse-grained entity types such as `Person` and `Location` and explored computational models for automatizing the task. One recent direction of extending this research field is to consider a larger set of fine-grained entity types (Lee et al., 2006; Sekine et al., 2002; Yosef et al., 2012; Corro et al., 2015). Recent studies report that fine-grained NER makes improvements to such applications as entity linking (Ling et al., 2015) and question answering (Mann, 2002). Given this background, this paper addresses the issue of creating a large gazetteer of NEs with fine-grained entity type information, motivated by the previous observations that a large-coverage gazetteer is a valuable resource for NER (Kazama and Torisawa, 2008; Carlson et al., 2009). Specifically, we consider building such a gazetteer by automatically classifying the articles of Wikipedia, one of the largest collection of NEs, into a predefined set of fine-grained named entity types.

The task of classifying Wikipedia articles into a predefined set of semantic classes has already been addressed by many researchers (Chang et al., 2009; Dakka and Cucerzan, 2008; Higashinaka et al., 2012; Tardif et al., 2009; Toral and Muñoz, 2006; Watanabe et al., 2007). However, most of these studies assume a coarse-grained NE type set (3 to 15 types). Fine-grained classification is naturally expected to be more difficult than coarse-grained classification. One big challenge is how to alleviate the problem of data sparseness when applying supervised machine learning approaches. For example, articles such as "Japan", "Mt. Fuji", and "Tokyo dome", may be classified as `Country`, `Mountain`, and `Sports_Facility` respectively in a fine-grained type set whereas all of them fall into the same type `Location` in a common coarse-grained type set. Given the same number of labeled training instances, one may obtain far fewer instances for each fine-grained type. Another challenge is in that fine-grained entity types may not be *disjoint*; for example, "Banana" can be classified as `Flora` and `Food_Other` simultaneously.

To address these issues, in this paper, we propose

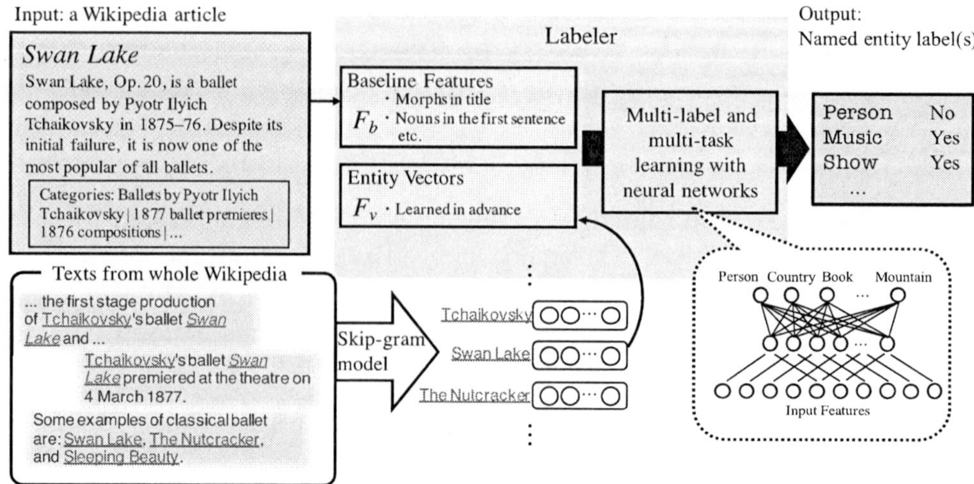

Figure 1: Automatic assignment of NE labels to Wikipedia articles based on multi-task learning and vector representation of articles

two methods (illustrated in Figure 1). First, we adopt the notion of multi-task learning (Caruana, 1997) and solve the whole task using a two-layered neural network. Our model learns all types of training instances jointly, which enables the model to learn combinations of input features commonly effective for multiple NE types with the hidden layer. By sharing effective feature combinations across different NE types, the data scarcity in minority NE types can be alleviated. Furthermore, this model can also naturally realize multi-label classification.

Second, we extend the feature set by exploiting the hyper-text structure of Wikipedia. The idea of using hyperlinks for Wikipedia article classification was first reported by Dakka and Cucerzan (2008). In this work, they represented local context of anchor texts of hyperlinks in Wikipedia as bag-of-words features. However, since its feature space was too sparse, they reported that the new context features had no effect on improving classification performance. Our proposal is to refine the context features using a distributed representation. To do this, we give each article a vector learned from all context words around hyperlinks (i.e. anchor texts) in Wikipedia using the Skip-gram model (Mikolov et al., 2013b). In the Skip-gram model, vector representations of words are learned so that two words similar in contexts have vectors with high similarity. In our intuition, articles in the same NE types are likely to be mentioned in similar contexts. Therefore, we adopt this model for learning article vectors.

We test our ideas on Japanese Wikipedia articles using the 200-NE type set proposed by Sekine et al. (2002). The results of our experiments show that the proposed methods achieve a 4.94-point improvement in entity-based F1 score. Our methods are particularly effective in labeling infrequent NE types.

Main contributions of this paper are as follows:

- We propose to apply a neural network-based multi-task learning method to the fine-grained multi-label classification of Wikipedia articles.
- We also propose to encode the local context of hyperlinks as vectors using the Skip-gram model. We make the obtained vectors publicly available[1].
- We created a new dataset by manually annotating over 22,000 Japanese Wikipedia articles with fine-grained NE types. The dataset is available if one contacts the authors.
- We tested our models on our new dataset and empirically showed their positive impacts on the accuracy of classification.

2 Related Work

The task of assigning labels of NE types to Wikipedia articles has been addressed in the context of automatic construction of an NE gazetteer

[1]http://www.cl.ecei.tohoku.ac.jp/~m-suzuki/jawiki_vector/

from Wikipedia articles. Toral and Muñoz (2006) proposed a method to classify Wikipedia articles into three NE types (Location, Organization, Person) using words included in the body of the article. They used WordNet as an external knowledge base for collecting hypernym information. They also applied weighted voting heuristics to determine NE types of articles. Dakka and Cucerzan (2008) classified articles into four NE types (PER, ORG, LOC, MISC) defined in ACE (Doddington et al., 2004) using supervised machine learning algorithms based on SVMs and naive Bayes. They used the bag-of-words in the target article as well as context words from the anchor text linking to the target article. Watanabe et al. (2007) focused on the HTML tree/link structure in Wikipedia articles. They formalized an NE categorization problem as assigning of NE labels to anchor texts in Wikipedia. They constructed graph-based representations of articles and estimated assignments of NE labels over the graphs using conditional random fields. In addition to these studies, there have been efforts toward automatic categorization, such as (Tardif et al., 2009; Chang et al., 2009). However, most of these studies assume a relatively small set of coarse-grained NE types (up to only 15 types).

In recent years, several projects such as YAGO (Suchanek et al., 2007) and DBpedia (Auer et al., 2007) have been devoted to provide Wikipedia articles with ontology class labels by applying simple heuristic or hand-crafted rules. However, these approaches heavily rely on metadata (e.g., infobox templates and category labels) and suffer from insufficient coverage of rules due to the lack of metadata, as reported by Aprosio et al. (2013).

Another trend of research which may seem relevant to our work can be found in efforts for automatically annotating entity mentions in text with fine-grained NE type labels defined in an existing type hierarchy such as Freebase (Ling and Weld, 2012; Nakashole et al., 2013; Shimaoka et al., 2016). While these studies focus on the identification and classification of individual mentions, our work aims at the classification of Wikipedia articles. The two tasks are related and may well benefit from each other. However, they are not the same; techniques proposed for mention classification cannot directly apply to our task nor can be compared with our methods.

The work closest to our study is done by Higashinaka et al. (2012), who proposed a supervised machine learning model for classifying Wikipedia articles into the 200 fine-grained NE types defined by Sekine et al. (2002). They conducted experiments to determine effective features extracted from article titles, body text, category labels, and infobox templates in Wikipedia. They train a logistic regression-based binary classifier for each type individually and the overall model chooses a single NE type receiving the highest score from the classifiers, ignoring the possibility that a Wikipedia article may belong to multiple NE categories. In contrast, our model learns classifiers for different NE types jointly and also addresses the issue of multi-label classification.

3 Data Preparation

3.1 Sekine et al.'s Fine-grained NE Type Set

In this study, we use the *Extended Named Entity Hierarchy*[2] proposed by Sekine et al. (2002) as our fine-grained NE type set. This ontology consists of 200 types, structured in a three-layered hierarchy. In this type hierarchy, a Wikipedia article may fall into multiple categories. Consider the following example:

> **Article title**: Godzilla
> **Article body**: Godzilla is a giant monster originating from a series of tokusatsu films of the same name from Japan. ... (excerpted from the English corresponding page of the same title)

It is reasonable to assume that the entity of this article belong to both Character and Movie).

3.2 Manual Annotation

From Japanese Wikipedia as of Nov. 23, 2015, we first extracted 22,667 articles that are hyperlinked at least 100 times from other articles in Wikipedia. We then manually annotated each of the 22,667 articles with one or more NE type labels from Sekine et al's type set[3].

Articles on abstract notions such as "Peace" and "Sleep" do not fall into any NE category particularly.

[2] https://sites.google.com/site/extendednamedentityhierarchy/

[3] The annotation was done by one annotator, supervised by the curator of Sekine et al's type set. Verification of the annotation accuracy is left for future work.

Table 1: 10 most frequent labels within the annotated dataset

Label name	Frequency	Example
Person	4,041	Isaac Asimov, Hillary Clinton, J. K. Rowling
Broadcast_Program	2,395	Sesame Street, Star Wars, Glee (TV series)
Company	1701	Sony, IBM, Apple Inc., Rakuten
City	975	New York, Tokyo, Melbourne
Product_Other	964	Microsoft Windows, Apple II,
Date	916	1977, January 3,
Book	909	Gutenberg Bible, The Lord of the Rings
Game	625	Lacrosse, Soccer, Table tennis
Pro_Sports_Organization	484	New York Yankees, Japan national baseball team
Position_Vocation	462	Physiotherapist, Prosecutor, Professor

Table 2: Infrequent labels within the annotated dataset

Frequency	Number of labels	Examples
0	55	URL, Temperature, Paintings
1	8	Ship, Star, Time
2-5	16	Canal, Market, Bridge
6-10	23	Earthquake, Treaty, School_Age
11-20	23	Public_Institution, Religious_Festival, Nationality

Table 3: Distribution of the number of labels per article

Number of labels assigned	Number of articles
1	21,624
2	850
3	187
4	14
6	2

We labeled such articles as CONCEPT. Wikipedia also includes articles or pages specific to Wikipedia like "List of characters in The Lion King" and "Wikipedia: Index". Those pages need to be discarded as well. We therefore decided to label such pages as IGNORED. Among our 22,667 articles, 2,660 articles are labeled as CONCEPT and 611 as IGNORED. Overall, our task is to classify Wikipedia articles into the 202 categories (Sekine et al.'s 200 types and the two additional categories).

Table 1 lists 10 most frequent labels that appear in the annotated articles and Table 2 shows examples of infrequent labels. As shown in these tables, the distribution of NE types in our data set is highly skewed. This makes the data sparseness problem salient particularly for the long tail of infrequent NE types.

Table 3 shows the distribution of the number of labels assigned to one article in the annotated data. Most of the articles have only one label whereas 4.6% of articles were assigned multiple labels. This figure may seem not to be a big deal. However, given that the error rate of our model is already below 20% (see Section 5.2), considering the 4.6% is inevitable to seek further improvements.

4 Proposed Methods

4.1 Joint Learning of Multi-Label Classifiers

As a baseline approach of multi-label classification, we construct a classifier for each NE type; each classifier independently decides whether an article should be tagged with the corresponding NE type. We model this setting using binary classifiers based on logistic regression (Figure 2a). We call this model INDEP-LOGISTIC.

While INDEP-LOGISTIC is a simple model, this model may not work well for infrequent NE types because of the sparseness of the training data. This problem is crucial particularly in our task setting because the distribution of our NE types in Wikipedia is highly skewed as reported above. To address this problem, we propose a method based on multi-task learning (Caruana, 1997) and jointly train classifiers of all NE types. Concretely, we construct a neural network with a hidden layer (Figure 2b) and train it so that each node in the output layer yields the prob-

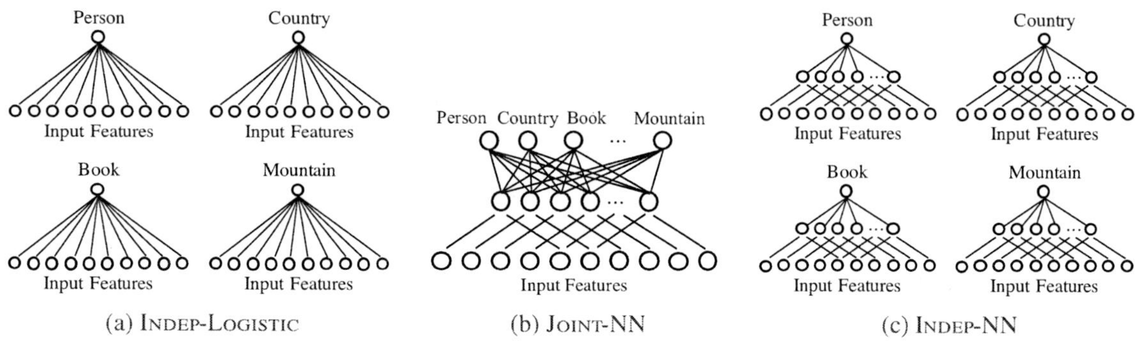

(a) INDEP-LOGISTIC (b) JOINT-NN (c) INDEP-NN

Figure 2: The three models for labeling types of articles.

ability of assigning the label of an NE type. Note that the activation function of the output layer is the singmoid function, not the softmax function. This means that this model can output mutiple labels of NE types for each article. In this method, we aim to learn effective combinations of input features which can also be used for labeling of infrequent NE types. We call this model JOINT-NN.

Note that there are two changes from INDEP-LOGISTIC to JOINT-NN: incorporating of a hidden layer and applying of joint learning. To examine the effect of each individual method separately, we also consider an intermediate model, INDEP-NN (Figure 2c). Similarly to INDEP-LOGISTIC, this model trains a classifier for each label, but has a hidden layer.

Formally, the INDEP-LOGISTIC model estimates the conditional probability that a given Wikipedia article represented by an n-dimensional feature vector $\boldsymbol{x} \in \mathbb{R}^n$ belongs to NE type c:

$$p_{\text{INDEP-LOGISTIC}}(y_c = 1|\boldsymbol{x}) = \sigma(\boldsymbol{w}_c \cdot \boldsymbol{x} + b_c), \quad (1)$$

where $\boldsymbol{w}_c \in \mathbb{R}^n$ and $b_c \in \mathbb{R}$ denote a weight vector and a bias term for NE type c, respectively. $\sigma(x) = \frac{1}{1+e^{-x}}$ is a sigmoid function.

The JOINT-NN model maps an input feature vector to a hidden layer with a matrix $\boldsymbol{W}$ whose parameters are shared across all the types:

$$p_{\text{JOINT-NN}}(y_c = 1|\boldsymbol{x}) = \sigma(\boldsymbol{w}_c \cdot \sigma(\boldsymbol{W}\boldsymbol{x} + \boldsymbol{b}) + b_c), \quad (2)$$

where $\boldsymbol{W} \in \mathbb{R}^{n \times k}$ and $\boldsymbol{b} \in \mathbb{R}^k$ denote a weight matrix and a bias vector of the k-dimensional hidden layer, $\boldsymbol{w}_c \in \mathbb{R}^k$ and $b_c \in \mathbb{R}$ denote a weight vector and a bias term, respectively, of the output layer, for each NE type c.

In contrast, the INDEP-NN model maps an input feature vector to a hidden layer by using a matrix W_c whose parameters are trained for each NE type independently:

$$p_{\text{INDEP-NN}}(y_c = 1|\boldsymbol{x}) = \sigma(\boldsymbol{w}_c \cdot \sigma(\boldsymbol{W}_c\boldsymbol{x} + \boldsymbol{b}_c) + b_c), \quad (3)$$

where $\boldsymbol{W}_c \in \mathbb{R}^{n \times k}$ and $\boldsymbol{b}_c \in \mathbb{R}^k$ denote a weight matrix and a bias vector, respectively, of the k-dimensional hidden layer for each NE type c. $\boldsymbol{w}_c \in \mathbb{R}^k$ and $b_c \in \mathbb{R}$ denote a weight vector and a bias term of the output layer for the NE type c, respectively.

The training data with N articles and C NE types is represented as $\{\boldsymbol{x}^{(i)}, \boldsymbol{y}^{(i)}\}_{i=1}^N$, where $\boldsymbol{x}$ is a feature vector of an article and $\boldsymbol{y} = \{y_c\}_{c=1}^C$ is an array of binary variables indicating if the article belongs to an NE type c. With this data set, we minimize the cross entropy loss $\mathcal{L}$ of each model by using ADAM gradient-based optimization algorithm (Kingma and Ba, 2014):

$$\mathcal{L} = -\sum_{x,c}\{y_c \log(p(y_c = 1|\boldsymbol{x})) + (1 - y_c)\log(1 - p(y_c = 1|\boldsymbol{x}))\} \quad (4)$$

4.2 Input Features

We used two sets of features for building the models; one is a reproduction of the previous study (Higashinaka et al., 2012), and the other is our novel proposal.

4.2.1 Baseline Features

As a baseline feature set, we reproduced the features proposed by Higashinaka et al. (2012). Table 4 lists all of the basic features.[4] We were not

[4]Note that although the features of "Last n character(s) in the title" are effective in labeling NE types of Japanese article titles,

Table 4: List of features used for learning

Features
Word unigram of the title
Word bigram of the title
POS bigram of the title
Character bigram of the title
Last noun in the title
Last single character in the title
Last three characters in the title
Last character type in the title
Last noun in the first sentence
Headings of the article
Direct categories defined in Wikipedia
Upper categories defined in Wikipedia

able to reproduce features T8, T12, T14, and M22 described in the original paper (Higashinaka et al., 2012) because those features require the authors' internal resources to implement. For similar reasons, we used MeCab (Kudo et al., 2004) as a morphological analyzer instead of JTAG (Fuchi and Takagi, 1998), which was unavailable to us. For extracting text from Wikipedia dump, we used Wikipedia Extractor (`http://medialab.di.unipi.it/wiki/Wikipedia_Extractor`). We denote this baseline feature set as F_b.

4.2.2 Article Vectors

To extend the aforementioned basic feature set, we hypothesize that the way how each article (i.e. named entity) is mentioned in other articles can also be a useful clue for classifying that article. To test this hypothesis, we introduce distributed representations of Wikipedia articles.

Consider an article "Mount Everest". This article is hyperlinked from other articles as follows:

(1) ... *After his ascent of Everest on 29 May 1953 ...*

(2) ... *reached the summit of Everest for the twenty-first time ...*

(3) ... *fatalities of the 2014 Mount Everest avalanche ...*

In this example, words near the anchor text, such as *summit* and *avalanche*, can be useful for estimating the semantic category of "Mount Everest" and assigning the label `Mountain` to the article "Mount Everest". While a number of approaches have been proposed for learning distributed representations of words, we simply adopt the Skip-gram model (Mikolov et al., 2013a) in this study.

Skip-gram trains a model so that it can predict context words from a centered word in a document. We apply this model to learn the embeddings of Wikipedia articles. To this end we need to address the following issues:

- An anchor text is not always identical to the article title to which the anchor refers. For this reason, we need to normalize an anchor text to the title of the article linked by the anchor.
- Article titles often consist of multiple words such as "White House". Therefore, we need a special treatment for tokenizing article titles.
- Not all of mentions to other articles are marked as anchor text in the Wikipedia articles. Typically, when an article mentions an entity multiple times, a hyperlink is inserted only at the first appearance of the mention to the entity[5].

To address these problems, we designed the following preprocessing steps. First, we replace every anchor text with the title of the article referred to by the hyperlink of the anchor text. Next, we assume all occurrences of the phrase identical to an anchor text to have hyperlinks to the article linked by the anchor text. This is based on the one-sense-per-discourse assumption. In addition, all white spaces in article titles are replaced with "_" to prevent article titles from being separated into words. In this way, we jointly learn vectors of words and articles. We use word2vec[6] to obtain 200 dimensional vectors.

We denote the 200-dimension article vector as F_v.

5 Experiments

To demonstrate the effectiveness of our models, we conducted experiments for labeling NE types to Japanese Wikipedia articles.

5.1 Settings

We tested the three classifier models (Indep-Logistic, Indep-NN, and Joint-NN) with two different feature sets (F_b and $F_b + F_v$). For each combi-

Higashinaka et al. (2012) reports that "Last two characters in the title" are not so useful in combinations with other features.

[5] `https://en.wikipedia.org/wiki/Wikipedia:Manual_of_Style/Linking`

[6] `https://code.google.com/p/word2vec/`

Table 5: Entity-based precision, recall and F1 of the models with different settings.

	F_b			$F_b + F_v$		
Model	Precision	Recall	F1	Precision	Recall	F1
INDEP-LOGISTIC	83.59	83.57	83.34	85.79	86.76	85.84
INDEP-NN	84.00	84.68	83.94	86.90	88.05	87.00
JOINT-NN (our model)	86.32	86.54	**86.14**	88.48	88.63	**88.28**

Table 6: NE labels whose weight vectors in output layers in (JOINT-NN, F_b) have high similarity to that of the NE label (in the header line of the table), accompanied with improvements of the label-based F1 score between (INDEP-NN, F_b) and (JOINT-NN, F_b). The number of articles assigned with an NE label is given in brackets.

	Label (# of articles)	$\Delta F1$	Label (# of articles)	$\Delta F1$	Label (# of articles)	$\Delta F1$
	Book (909)	5.28	Country (282)	1.38	Food_Other (57)	-0.13
Nearest Labels	Broadcast_Program (2395)	2.08	Nationality (14)	32.73	Flora (80)	5.04
	Movie (438)	3.64	County (126)	0.00	Dish (47)	10.36
	Show (43)	5.18	Clothing (12)	10.83	Compound (51)	8.12
	Name_Other (92)	0.53	River (58)	0.00	Mineral (12)	9.56
	Printing_Other (24)	4.64	Island (56)	3.72	Religious_Festival (12)	-5.92

nation of model and feature set, we evaluated classification performance by measuring entity-based/type-based precision, recall, and F1 value (Godbole and Sarawagi, 2004; Tsoumakas et al., 2009) over 10-fold cross validation. Entity-based precision, recall, and F1 value are calculated as below:

$$\text{Precision} = \frac{1}{N}\sum_{i=1}^{N}\frac{|Y^{(i)} \cap Z^{(i)}|}{|Z^{(i)}|} \quad (5)$$

$$\text{Recall} = \frac{1}{N}\sum_{i=1}^{N}\frac{|Y^{(i)} \cap Z^{(i)}|}{|Y^{(i)}|} \quad (6)$$

$$F_1 = \frac{1}{N}\sum_{i=1}^{N}\frac{2|Y^{(i)} \cap Z^{(i)}|}{|Z^{(i)}| + |Y^{(i)}|} \quad (7)$$

Here, $Y^{(i)}$ and $Z^{(i)}$ denote the set of correct labels and the set of predicted labels of article i, respectively. N denotes the number of documents. For type-based evaluation, we calculated precision, recall and F1 value of each named entity types.

For INDEP-LOGISTIC, we used scikit-learn (Pedregosa et al., 2011) to train classifiers. We used L2 penalty for regularization. For INDEP-NN and JOINT-NN, we used Chainer (Tokui et al., 2015) to implement neural networks. The dimension of the hidden layer was set to $k = 200$. When training the models, we used most frequent 10,000 baseline features (F_b) and 200-dimension article vectors (F_v) as input features of classifiers. For optimization, we used Adam with a learning rate of 0.001 and a mini-batch size of 10 and iterated over the training data until the cross-entropy loss per document gets smaller than 1.0×10^{-4}.

INDEP-LOGISTIC was implemented as a baseline model intended to reproduce the model proposed by Higashinaka et al. (2012). Note, however, that the results of our experiments cannot be compared directly with those reported in their paper because some of the features they used are not reproducible and the training/test data sets are not identical.

5.2 Results

The overall results are summarized in Table 5. We conducted binomial tests to determine statistical significance of the results, confirming that the improvement between any pair of settings is statistically significant $p < 0.01$ except that the improvement from (INDEP-LOGISTIC, F_b) to (INDEP-NN, F_b) was significant at $p < 0.05$.

Comparing the results between the baseline method (INDEP-LOGISTIC, F_b) and our full model (MULTI-NN, $F_b + F_v$), entity-based F1 score improved by about 5 points (83.34% to 88.28%), which is about 30% reduction of error rate. Table 5 also indicates that both of our two proposed methods, multi-task learning and article vector features, have

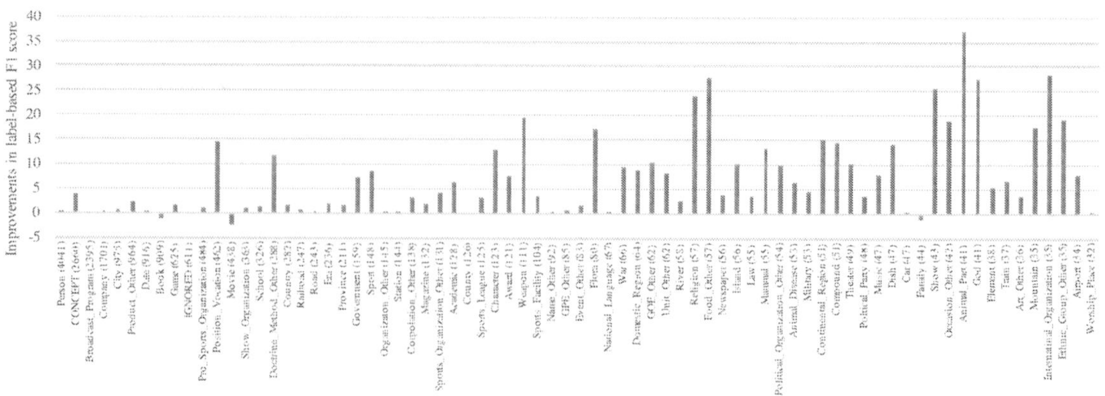

Figure 3: Improvement in F1 score per type between (INDEP-LOGISTIC, F_b) and (JOINT-NN, $F_b + F_v$). Only types with more than 30 (numbers are shown in brackets) articles are shown.

a separate significant gain.

To see the improvement in labeling performance per NE type, we compared label-based F1 score of each NE type between (INDEP-LOGISTIC, F_b) and (JOINT-NN, $F_b + F_v$). Figure 3 shows the improvement in F1 score for each NE type, where NE types are sorted by the number of articles in descending order. The figures indicate that our full model tends to obtain a larger gain particularly for infrequent NE types, which means our model addresses the data sparseness problem for infrequent NE types.

We made a deeper analysis of how our full model learns labeling of NE types. Our joint learning model is designed to learn combinations of features effective for multiple NE types. If two NE types share common combinations of features, they will have similar weight vectors at the output layer. So we observed clusters of the learned weight vectors at the output layer of (JOINT-NN, F_b) and discovered that many clusters comprise NE types that are semantically related with each other. Some example clusters are shown in Table 6. For example, the NE type `Book` has such neighbors as `Broadcast_Program`, `Movie` and `Show`. These NE types had similar weight vectors and gained considerable improvements with together. This demonstrates that our joint learning model learned combinations of input features and utilized them for multiple NE types effectively, which lead to the improvements observed particularly for infrequent NE types.

6 Conclusion

We have addressed the task of assigning fine-grained NE type labels to Wikipedia articles. To address the data sparseness problem, which is salient particularly in fine-grained type classification, we have introduced multi-task learning in which all the type classifiers are jointly learned by a neural network with a hidden layer. Additionally, to extend the input feature set, we have proposed to learn article vectors (i.e. entity embeddings) from Wikipedia's hypertext structure using the Skip-gram model and incorporate them into the input feature set. We created a new dataset containing over 22,000 manually labeled instances and conducted experiments on that dataset to evaluate the practical impacts of our ideas. The results show that both ideas gained their own statistically significant improvement separately in classification accuracy. The labeled dataset we created is available if one contacts the authors.

For future work, we aim to incorporate the hierarchy structure of NE types into classification. Also, each type in Sekine et al's NE type set has *attributes*. For example, `Mountain` has such attributes as *Height* and *People who reached the summit*. We aim to address a task of assigning correct attributes to each entity using the results of named entity classification.

Acknowledgments

This work was partially supported by *Research and Development on Real World Big Data Integration and Analysis*, MEXT and JSPS KAKENHI Grant 15H05318 and 15H01702.

References

Alessio Palmero Aprosio, Claudio Giuliano, and Alberto Lavelli. 2013. Extending the coverage of DBpedia properties using distant supervision over Wikipedia. In *Proceedings of ICON 2013*.

Sören Auer, Christian Bizer, Georgi Kobilarov, Jens Lehmann, Richard Cyganiak, and Zachary Ives. 2007. Dbpedia: A nucleus for a web of open data. In *Proceedings of ISWC'07/ASWC'07*.

Andrew Carlson, Scott Gaffney, and Flavian Vasile. 2009. Learning a named entity tagger from gazetteers with the partial perceptron. In *Proceedings of the 2009 AAAI Spring Symposium on Learning by Reading and Learning to Read*.

Rich Caruana. 1997. Multitask learning. *Machine learning*, 28:41–75.

Joseph Chang, Richard Tzong-Han Tsai, and Jason S. Chang. 2009. Wikisense: Supersense tagging of wikipedia named entities based wordnet. In *Proceedings of PACLIC 23*.

Luciano Del Corro, Abdalghani Abujabal, Rainer Gemulla, and Gerhard Weikum. 2015. FINET: Context-aware fine-grained named entity typing. In *Proceedings of EMNLP*, pages 868–878.

Wisam Dakka and Silviu Cucerzan. 2008. Augmenting wikipedia with named entity tags. In *Proceedings of 3rd IJCNLP*.

George Doddington, Alexis Mitchell, Mark Przybocki, Lance Ramshaw, Stephanie Strassel, and Ralph Weischedel. 2004. The automatic content extraction (ace) program tasks, data, and evaluation. In *Proceedings of LREC*.

Takeshi Fuchi and Shinichiro Takagi. 1998. Japanese morphological analyzer using word co-occurrence - jtag. In *Proceedings of ACL '98 and Proceedings of COLING '98*.

Shantanu Godbole and Sunita Sarawagi, 2004. *Advances in Knowledge Discovery and Data Mining: 8th Pacific-Asia Conference, PAKDD 2004, Sydney, Australia, May 26-28, 2004. Proceedings*, chapter Discriminative Methods for Multi-labeled Classification, pages 22–30. Springer Berlin Heidelberg.

Ryuichiro Higashinaka, Kugatsu Sadamitsu, Kuniko Saito, Toshiro Makino, and Yoshihiro Matsuo. 2012. Creating an extended named entity dictionary from wikipedia. In *Proceedings of COLING*.

Jun'ichi Kazama and Kentaro Torisawa. 2008. Inducing gazetteers for named entity recognition by large-scale clustering of dependency relations. In *Proceedings of ACL-08: HLT*, pages 407–415. Association for Computational Linguistics.

Diederik P. Kingma and Jimmy Ba. 2014. Adam: A method for stochastic optimization. *ICLR*.

Taku Kudo, Kaoru Yamamoto, and Yuji Matsumoto. 2004. Applying conditional random fields to japanese morphological analysis. In *Proceedings of EMNLP*, pages 230–237.

Changki Lee, Yi-Gyu Hwang, Hyo-Jung Oh, Soojong Lim, Jeong Heo, Chung-Hee Lee, Hyeon-Jin Kim, Ji-Hyun Wang, and Myung-Gil Jang. 2006. Fine-grained named entity recognition using conditional random fields for question answering. In *Proceedings of Information Retrieval Technology, Third Asia Information Retrieval Symposium, AIRS 2006, Singapore, October 16-18, 2006*, pages 581–587.

Xiao Ling and Daniel S Weld. 2012. Fine-grained entity recognition. In *In Proc. of the 26th AAAI Conference on Artificial Intelligence*. Citeseer.

Xiao Ling, Sameer Singh, and Daniel S Weld. 2015. Design challenges for entity linking. *TACL*, pages 315–328.

Gideon S. Mann. 2002. Fine-grained proper noun ontologies for question answering. In *Proceedings of SEMANET '02*.

Tomas Mikolov, Kai Chen, Greg Corrado, and Jeffrey Dean. 2013a. Efficient estimation of word representations in vector space. In *Proceedings of Workshop at International Conference on Learning Representations*.

Tomas Mikolov, Ilya Sutskever, Kai Chen, Greg S Corrado, and Jeff Dean. 2013b. Distributed representations of words and phrases and their compositionality. In C.J.C. Burges, L. Bottou, M. Welling, Z. Ghahramani, and K.Q. Weinberger, editors, *Advances in Neural Information Processing Systems 26*, pages 3111–3119. Curran Associates, Inc.

Ndapandula Nakashole, Tomasz Tylenda, and Gerhard Weikum. 2013. Fine-grained semantic typing of emerging entities. In *51st Annual Meeting of the Association for Computational Linguistics*, pages 1488–1497. ACL.

F. Pedregosa, G. Varoquaux, A. Gramfort, V. Michel, B. Thirion, O. Grisel, M. Blondel, P. Prettenhofer, R. Weiss, V. Dubourg, J. Vanderplas, A. Passos, D. Cournapeau, M. Brucher, M. Perrot, and E. Duchesnay. 2011. Scikit-learn: Machine learning in Python. *Journal of Machine Learning Research*, 12:2825–2830.

Satoshi Sekine, Kiyoshi Sudo, and Chikashi Nobata. 2002. Extended named entity hierarchy. In *Proceedings of LREC*.

Sonse Shimaoka, Pontus Stenetorp, Kentaro Inui, and Sebastian Riedel. 2016. An attentive neural architecture for fine-grained entity type classification. In *Proceedings of the 5th Workshop on Automated Knowledge Base Construction (AKBC) 2016*.

Fabian M. Suchanek, Gjergji Kasneci, and Gerhard Weikum. 2007. Yago: A core of semantic knowledge. In *Proceedings of WWW*, WWW '07, pages 697–706, New York, NY, USA. ACM.

Sam Tardif, R. James Curran, and Tara Murphy. 2009. Improved text categorisation for wikipedia named entities. In *Proceedings of ALTA Workshop*, pages 104–108.

Seiya Tokui, Kenta Oono, Shohei Hido, and Justin Clayton. 2015. Chainer: a next-generation open source framework for deep learning. In *Proceedings of Workshop on Machine Learning Systems (LearningSys) in The Twenty-ninth Annual Conference on Neural Information Processing Systems (NIPS)*.

Antonio Toral and Rafael Muñoz. 2006. A proposal to automatically build and maintain gazetteers for named entity recognition by using wikipedia. In *Proceedings of Workshop on New Text, EACL*.

Grigorios Tsoumakas, Ioannis Katakis, and Ioannis Vlahavas. 2009. Mining multi-label data. In *Data mining and knowledge discovery handbook*, pages 667–685. Springer.

Yotaro Watanabe, Masayuki Asahara, and Yuji Matsumoto. 2007. A graph-based approach to named entity categorization in wikipedia using conditional random fields. In *Proceedings of EMNLP-CoNLL*.

Mohamed Amir Yosef, Sandro Bauer, Johannes Hoffart, Marc Spaniol, and Gerhard Weikum. 2012. HYENA: Hierarchical type classification for entity names. In *Proceedings of COLING 2012: Posters*, pages 1361–1370, Mumbai, India, December. The COLING 2012 Organizing Committee.

MINING CALL CENTER CONVERSATIONS EXHIBITING SIMILAR AFFECTIVE STATES

Rupayan Chakraborty, Meghna Pandharipande, and Sunil Kumar Kopparapu
TCS Innovation Labs-Mumbai
Yantra Park, Thane West-400601, India
{rupayan.chakraborty, meghna.pandharipande, sunilkumar.kopparapu}@tcs.com

Abstract

Automatic detection and identifying emotions in large call center calls are essential to spot conversations that require further action. Most often statistical models generated using annotated emotional speech are used to design an emotion detection system. But annotation requires substantial amount of human intervention and cost; and may not be available for call center calls because of the infrastructure issues. Therefore detection systems use models that are generated form the readily available annotated emotional (clean) speech datasets and produce erroneous output due to mismatch in training-testing datasets. Here we propose a framework to automatically identify the similar affective spoken utterances in large number of call center calls by using the emotion models that are trained with the freely available acted emotional speech. Further, to reliably detect the emotional content, we incorporate the available knowledge associated with the call (time lapse of the utterances in a call, the contextual information derived from the linguistic contents, and speaker information). For each audio utterance, the emotion recognition system generates similarity measures (likelihood scores) in *arousal* and *valence* dimension using pretrained emotional models, and further they are combined with the scores from the contextual knowledge-based systems, which are used to reliably detect the similar affective contents in large number of calls. Experiments demonstrate that there is a significant improvement in detection accuracy when the knowledge-based framework is used.

Index Terms:Affective content analysis; mining call center audio; spontaneous emotional speech; knowledge-based systems; similar affective states

1 Introduction

Affective content [1] analysis of audio calls is important in recent days with the increasing number of call centers (Pang and Lee, 2008), (Liu, 2012), (Kopparapu, 2015). Perhaps, audio is the best possible modality that can be used to effectively analyze the call center conversations between customer and agent. However, manual analysis of such calls is cumbersome and may not be feasible because large number of recordings take place on daily basis. Therefore only a small fraction of such conversations are carefully heard by the human supervisors and addressed, thus resulting many of those unattended.

The difficulty of identifying the affective regions (or emotionally rich) manually in large number of calls is illustrated in Figure 1. The call duration is plotted on the x-axis, while different calls are shown along the y-axis. As represented in Figure 1, the calls are of different durations, and the gray color represents the actual length of the calls. The black color within the call shows the location of a specific affective state (highly correlated to the problematic regions in the calls). It is clear that the locations of such problematic regions are arbitrary, and the durations are of variable length. In spite of such challenges, automatic emotion analysis

[1] Affective content and Emotion will be used interchangeably in this paper

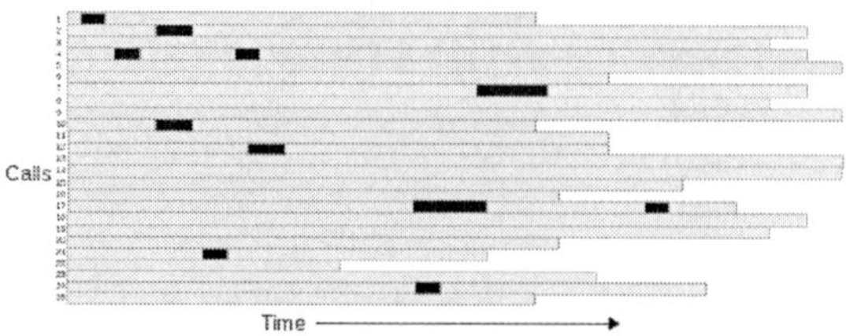

Figure 1: Call center calls (dark portions indicate problems)

of call center conversations has attracted the attention of researchers (for example (Petrushin, 1999), (Vidrascu and Devillers, 2007), (Gupta and Rajput, 2007), (Mishra and Dimitriadis, 2013), (Kopparapu, 2015), (Pappas et al., 2015)).

Affective content analysis is a technique that extracts emotions from spoken utterance [2], and thus useful to find the similar emotional utterances in call center calls. In general, affective contents are represented categorically in terms of the different emotion classes (e.g (Petrushin, 1999; Vidrascu and Devillers, 2007; Gupta and Rajput, 2007; Pappas et al., 2015)). Mostly in call center calls, four emotions (namely, *anger*, *happy*, *neutral*, *sad*) in the categorical space are addressed. Although in (Nicolaou et al., 2011), authors proposed to capture the time varying emotional information in the dimensional space using audio-visual cues. And in (Mishra and Dimitriadis, 2013), authors proposed an incremental emotion recognition system that updates the recognized emotion with each recognized word in the conversation. They make use of three features from two modalities (i.e. cepstral and intonation form audio and textual features from text), which are obtained at the word level to estimate the emotion with better accuracies. It has been observed that combining linguistic information with the acoustic features improves the performance of the system. As an example, in (Lee and Narayanan, 2005), authors proposed a combination of three information (i.e. acoustic, lexical, and discourse) for emotion recognition in spoken dialogue system and found improvements in recognition performance. Similarly in (Planet and Sanz, 2011), authors described an approach to improve emotion recognition in spontaneous children's speech by combining acoustic and linguistic features.

In this paper, we propose a novel framework that automatically extracts the affective content of the call center spoken utterances in *arousal* and *valence* dimensions. In addition, context-based knowledge (e.g. time lapse of the utterances in the call, events and affective context derived from linguistic content, and speaker information) associated with the calls are intelligently used to reliably detect the affective content in speech. Unlike (Mishra and Dimitriadis, 2013), we do not fully rely on the use of word recognition to determine the emotion. This makes our system feasible even for resource deficient languages that do not boast of a good automatic speech recognition (ASR) engine. In addition to the linguistic information like in (Lee and Narayanan, 2005), we also incorporate more knowledge like the time lapse of the utterance in calls, contextual information derived from linguistic content, speaker information etc. For each spoken utterance, the affective content extractor generates probability scores in *arousal* and *valence* dimensions, which are then probabilistically combined to label it with any of the predefined affective classes. The framework is motivated by the observation that there is significant disagreement amongst human annotators when they annotate call center speech; the disagreement largely reduces when they are provided with additional knowledge related to the conversation. Unlike (Mishra and Dimitriadis, 2013), the proposed system extracts affective information separately in dimensional space, thus reduces the classification complexity. Moreover in our proposed framework, emotions are extracted at discrete levels of affective classes (i.e. positive, neutral, negative in arousal and valence dimensions), instead of using affective information in continuous scale like in (Nicolaou et al., 2011), thus reducing the complexities related to the difficulties in annotation at continuous level of affective states, resulting less number classes in each dimension. In addition, detection of similar emotional content in large number of audio calls are performed by using the emotion models trained with the freely available acted emotional speech. Therefore the system is able to work even in a scenario if somebody does not have an annotated call center calls. Extensive experimentations on the acted dataset contaminated with 4

[2] The word utterance, turn, and spoken terms will be used interchangeably from here on

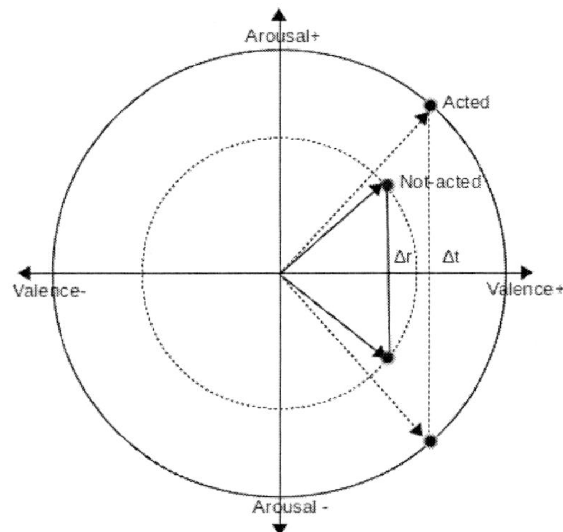

Figure 2: Error in emotion estimation for spontaneous call center calls

different types of noise (babble, F-16, machine-gun and volvo) from Noisex-92 dataset at different SNR levels has also been carried out. The main contributions of the paper are: (i) affective content extraction from large call center calls and also finding similar segments (ii) incorporation of the knowledge for reliable detection.

The rest of the paper is organized as follows. Section 2 presents the motivation of this work. In Section 3, we propose the framework for affective content extraction, using knowledge for reliable affective state identification and finding similar affective states. Section 4 describes the dataset, experiments, and results. We conclude in Section 5.

2 Motivation and challenges

Voice-based call center handle and record thousands of calls on daily basis. It is a difficult task for someone to identify manually the emotional segments from these large number of calls; and subsequently decide which of these recorded calls are to be selected for taking necessary actions regarding the issues related to customers dissatisfaction. In general, the calls are of variable duration, where time length varying from few seconds to few minutes depending on several factors, like the type of the call center, the type of the problems that the customers are facing, the prior affective state of the customer, the way agents handle the problem and behave etc. In such scenario, super agent (or supervisors) manually select at random few calls from a large number of calls, then listen and check if there are some abnormalities. In this way, very few calls are normally analyzed and addressed, thus resulting many calls unattended, ends up with a increasing dissatisfaction among the customers. Automatic detection of the equivalent emotional segments in large set of calls are useful to deal with such situation. Like in other pattern classification problems, most often the statistical models are generated using the annotated data and then used to detect the affective states in the audio calls.

It motivates us to think about a system that learns the pattern of different affective states from freely available acted emotional speech, and detect similar affective parts in large number of call center calls. Since, the classifiers trained and tested in different environments, are expected to give erroneous output. The difference of similar emotions in two different environments is elaborated in Figure 2 that represents the two affective dimensions of emotion, namely, *arousal* (also referred as activation) and *valence*. A point in this 2D space can be looked upon as a vector and is representative of an emotion. The acted speech in the training dataset exhibits higher degree of intensity, both in *arousal* and *valence* dimensions resulting in a larger radii emotion vector compared to the spontaneous speech. On the other hand, call center spontaneous speech has lesser intensity than the acted speech. For this reason, it is easy to mis-recognize one emotion for another in call center speech. Subsequently, if the first quadrant (Figure 2) represents emotion E_1 and the fourth quadrant represents emotion E_2, then the mis-recognition error is small (Δr) for call center speech but requires higher degree of error in judgment (Δt) to mis-recognize emotion E_1 as emotion E_2 and vice-versa for acted speech.

To handle such mismatch in train-test environments, the proposed system intelligently makes use of several knowledge for the reliable extraction of the affective content in call canter calls. For an audio segment in a call, the idea is to generate a probability matrix, whose elements are a joint probability estimate in the affective dimension of *arousal* and *valence* . Then all the knowledge-based information are used to modify the elements of the matrix. Simi-

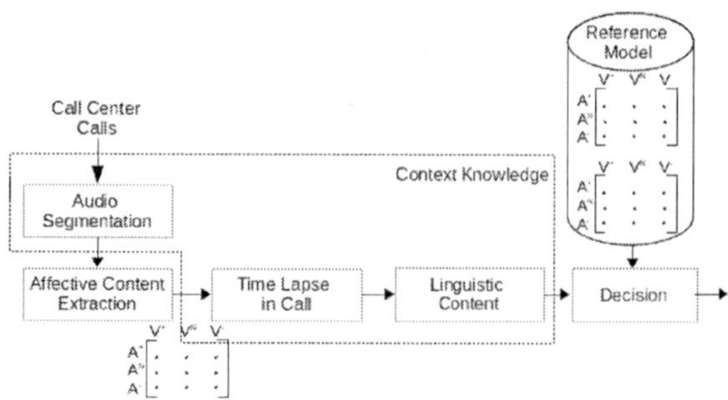

Figure 3: Call center call analysis framework

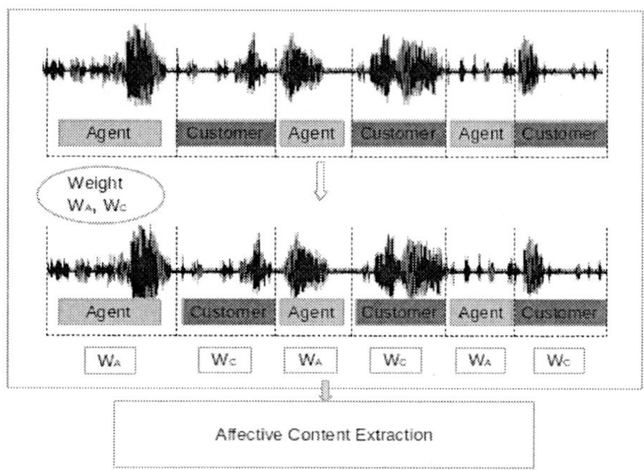

Figure 4: Audio segmentation based knowledge

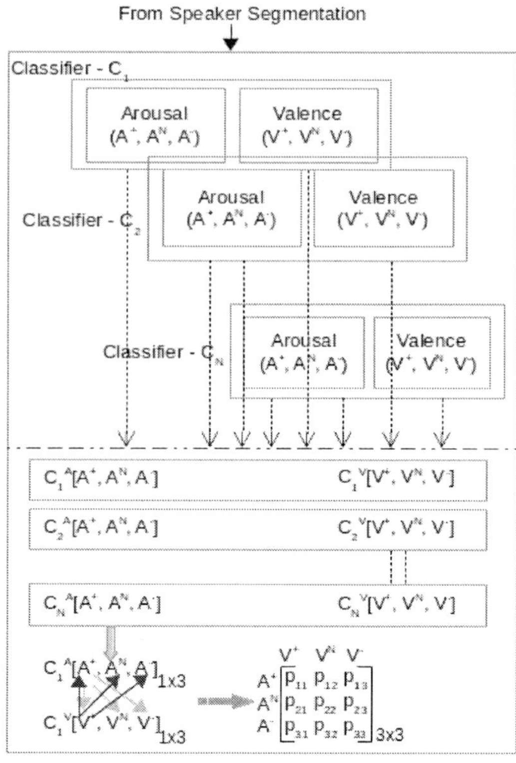

Figure 5: Affective content extraction

larities are measured by calculating the distances between the modified matrix and the reference matrices. In this way, similar segments are bucketed and it becomes easier for the supervisors to analyze the problematic calls depending on the labeled affective contents.

3 Mining similar audio segments

The proposed framework for mining similar audio segments consists of several blocks as shown in Figure 3. The blocks are (i) affective content extractor that gives scores for different affective states in the two dimensional (*arousal* (A) and *valence* (V)) space, (ii) three knowledge-based systems (audio segmentation, time lapse of the segment in the call, and voice to text analytics) (iii) decision block for deciding similar segments. As shown in Figure 3, when an audio call is fed to the framework for the analysis, it is passed through a speaker segmentation system which segments an audio call into different segments of agent's and user's voice. Call center calls consist of voice of the two speakers (agent and customer). Knowledge regarding the speaker (whether an agent or a customer) becomes useful while analyzing a continuous audio call (see Figure 4). As an example, super-agent might be interested to analyze of the customer's voice, not the agent's speech, then there is no need to process the agent's speech. On the other way, if super-agent has to check the performance of agents in terms of their expressed emotions (normal or elicited) in handling calls, the agent's voice are required only for analysis, not the customer's voice. As depicted in the Figure 4, depending on the requirement, the framework is able to pick up all the segments either from the agents or from the customers by selecting appropriate value to (w_A, w_c) pairs. The system choose (1,0) for agent's audio and (0,1) for customer's audio.

3.1 Affective content extraction

Let us assume that we have annotated data from a large corpus in two dimensions, namely A and V. Further, let there be three classes in each affective dimension, namely $E_A = \{A^+, A^N, A^-\}$ and $E_V = \{V^+, V^N, V^-\}$. Let us further assume that we have statistical models for A^+,A^N,A^-, V^+,V^N, and V^- such that we can compute for an audio segment S the following, $P(E_A|S)$ (namely, $P(A^+|S)$, $P(A^N|S)$, and $P(A^-|S)$) and $P(E_V|S)$ (namely, $P(V^+|S)$, $P(V^N|S)$, and $P(V^-|S)$). Therefore, we represent an audio segment S in the A-V space by a 3x3 matrix at the output of each classifier ($1 \leqslant k \leqslant C$),

$$\left\{ \begin{matrix} P(A^+|S)P(V^+|S) & P(A^+|S)P(V^N|S) & P(A^+|S)P(V^-|S) \\ P(A^N|S)P(V^+|S) & P(A^N|S)P(V^N|S) & P(A^N|S)P(V^-|S) \\ P(A^-|S)P(V^+|S) & P(A^-|S)P(V^N|S) & P(A^-|S)P(V^-|S) \end{matrix} \right\}$$

Affective content of a segment S is defined by

$$\epsilon^k_{A,V} = P(E|S) = P(E_A, E_V|S) \quad (1)$$

where $\epsilon^k_{A,V} = P(E_A, E_V|S)$ is the posterior score associated with S being labeled as emotion E_A and E_V, using a trained recognition system. The posterior can be represented as,

$$P(E_A, E_V|S) = \frac{P(S|E_A, E_V)P(E_A)P(E_V)}{P(S)}$$

where $P(S|E_A, E_V)$ is the likelihood, $P(E_A)$ and $P(E_V)$ are the priors. Assuming that affective contents at the *arousal* and *valence* dimensions are independent, we can write,

$$P(S|E_A, E_V) \approx P(S|E_A)P(S|E_V)$$

Note that S is defined as $\chi(x(\tau - \Delta\tau), x(\tau))$, where χ is the operator that extracts high level features from the audio signal between the time interval $(\tau - \Delta\tau)$ and τ. High level features are the statistical functionals and are constructed from the low level descriptors, which operates in the interval of $x(\tau - \Delta\tau)$ and $x(\tau)$ of the signal. From the output of each classifier, we construct a 3x3 matrix, whose elements are posterior probabilities ($\epsilon^k_{A,V}$) (as shown in Figure 5). According to the Equation 1, $\epsilon^k_{A,V}$ can have two set of elements, ϵ^k_A and ϵ^k_V respectively. As an example, lets say for the first set of classifiers, we have the scores $\epsilon^1_{A^+}$, $\epsilon^1_{A^N}$, and $\epsilon^1_{A^-}$ for the emotions in *arousal* scale. Similarly for the same (first) set of classifier, we have the scores $\epsilon^1_{V^+}$, $\epsilon^1_{V^N}$, and $\epsilon^1_{V^-}$ for the emotions in *valence* scale. Then $\epsilon^k_{A,V}$ (3x3 matrix) is obtained considering each pair from ϵ^k_A and ϵ^k_V. Then the recognition system outputs a posterior probability matrix for the utterance $x(\Delta\tau)$ by combining the scores from all the classifiers, which is given by

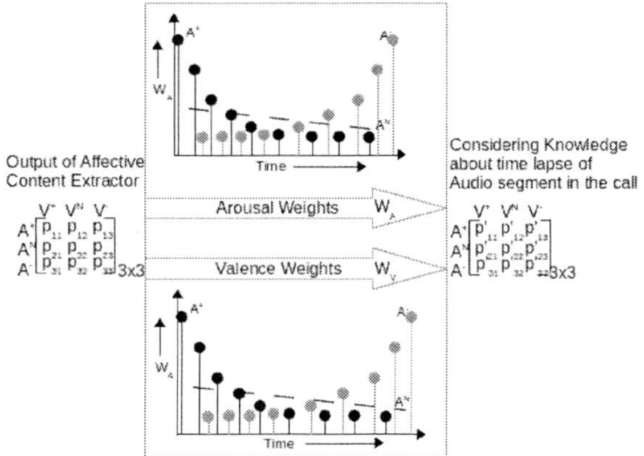

Figure 6: Knowledge regarding the time lapse of the segment in a call

$$\epsilon^{ER}(x(\Delta\tau)) = \sum_{k=1}^{C} \epsilon^k_{A,V} \quad (2)$$

where $\epsilon^k \in \mathcal{E}_{A,V}$ is the estimated joint probability scores of the utterance ($x(\tau - \Delta\tau)$,$x(\tau)$). This works well with acted speech where one has the luxury of annotated training data (namely, $(x(\Delta\tau), E_A E_V)$ pairs) to build classifiers. However, with the spontaneous speech like call-center calls, probability estimation may be erroneous. However, the estimations can be improved by using knowledge.

3.2 Knowledge about the time lapse of the audio segment in the call

The output probability matrices that we get from affective content extractor is passed through a knowledge-based system, which modifies the probability scores depending upon the time lapse of the segment in the audio call (as shown in Figure 6). We observed through analysis that the duration of the audio calls plays an important role in the induction (or change) in the user's affective state. In such scenario, we hypothesize that intensity of some of the affective states (namely, A^+, V^-) increases and some (namely, A^-, V^+) decreases. This hypothesis is valid only if no other events occur and change the affective state suddenly. The output can be represented as,

$$\epsilon_i^{lapse} = w_i \epsilon^{ER} \quad (3)$$

where ϵ^{lapse} is the output matrix we get after multiplying weight matrix w_i at the time index i. As shown in the Figure 6 , it is expected that weight values for (A^+,V^-) affective content close to the end of the call will be more in comparison to the beginning of the call. We hypothesize these weight components are expected to increase exponentially as time index i increases for A^+ and V^-, and decrease exponentially as time index i increases for A^- and V^+ (see Figure 6).

3.3 Speech to text analytics

The modified matrices are then passed through the last knowledge-based system (as shown in Figure 7), which converts the spoken utterances into the text format (by using an ASR), followed by the text analytics to generate a weight matrix w_t that consists of the probabilities of affective state given a spoken word or phrase. To analyze the affective state of customer's voice at any instant of time, just previous spoken words of the agent is considered. The same process is followed for analyzing the agent's voice. The hypothesis is that the spoken words from one speaker at any instant of time induce some specific affective state in the other user during a call conversation. This knowledge-based system consists of two sub-system, i) an ASR engine, and ii) a voice analytics. The ASR engine converts the spoken words in the textual format. And the voice analytics system learns and spots emotionally prominent words so as to improve the recognition of emotions. We consider affectively prominent word in audio segment with respect to an affective state is one which appears more often in that category than in other categories of affective states. Like in (Lee and Narayanan, 2005), we also used the prominence measure to find and associate words that are related to affective states in the speech data. With the affective prominence, we create the weight matrix w_t, where each element represent the affective prominence corresponds to each affective state. For each utterance, we have the measure of the affective prominence for each affective states, which forms the weight matrix weight matrix w_t to modify the output of second knowledge-based system (as shown in Figure 7).

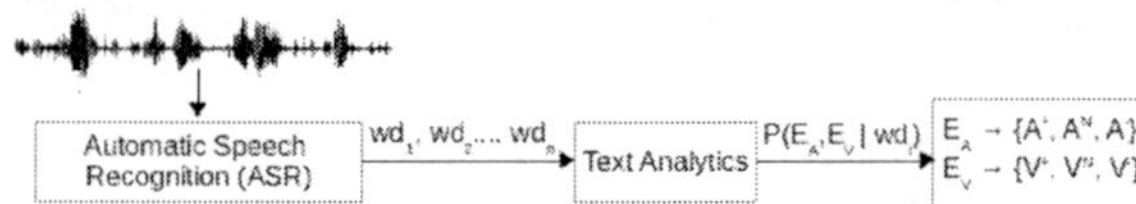

Figure 7: Speech to text analytics

< 0 - No Agreement; 0.0 – 0.19 - Poor agreement; 0.20 - 0.39 - Fair agreement; 0.40 – 0.59 - Moderate agreement; 0.60 – 0.79 - Substantial agreement; 0.80 - 1.00 - Almost perfect agreement		Kappa Score – Without any knowledge						Kappa Score – Using Knowledge (time Lapse of utterance + linguistic Content)					
		A^+	A^N	A^-	Raters	P_i	P_o	A^+	A^N	A^-	Raters	P_i	P_o
No of samples	U1	7	0	0	7	1.00	0.47	7	0	0	7	1.00	0.86
	U2	1	1	5	7	0.48		0	1	6	7	0.71	
	U3	3	0	4	7	0.43		7	0	0	7	1.00	
	U4	2	0	5	7	0.52		2	0	5	7	0.52	
	U5	2	0	5	7	0.52		0	0	7	7	1.00	
	U6	5	0	2	7	0.52		6	0	1	7	0.71	
	U7	4	0	3	7	0.43		0	0	7	7	1.00	
	U8	2	2	3	7	0.24		0	7	0	7	1.00	
	U9	2	1	4	7	0.33		7	0	0	7	1.00	
	U10	2	3	2	7	0.24		2	0	5	7	0.52	
	U11	5	0	2	7	0.52		1	0	6	7	0.71	
	U12	0	5	2	7	0.52		7	0	0	7	1.00	
	U13	1	2	4	7	0.33		0	0	7	7	1.00	
	Total	36	14	41	91	6.19		39	8	44	91	11.19	
	p_j	0.40	0.15	0.45		$K=(p_o-p_e)/(1-p_e)$		0.43	0.09	0.48		$K=(p_o-p_e)/(1-p_e)$	
	P_e	0.38				K=	0.14	0.43				K=	0.76

Figure 8: Kappa statistics in *arousal* dimension with and without knowledge

$$\epsilon^{vta} = w_t \epsilon^{lapse} \quad (4)$$

3.4 Decision based on similarity measures

We get the output matrix ϵ^{vta} for each audio segment and then find the distances from the reference matrix (i.e. the template for each affective state) to calculate the similarity measures. The distance d between ϵ^{vta} and $\epsilon_{A,V}$ are calculated as,

$$d = \parallel \epsilon^{vta} - \epsilon_{A,V} \parallel \quad (5)$$

Then the affective state is hypothesized as the output corresponds to the reference matrix that has the minimum distance from the output matrix. It is also possible to arrange the segments in the descending order, i.e. from the highest to the lowest distance. Therefore at the output, audio segment is labeled with the affective class, and its distances from all affective classes.

4 Experiments

4.1 Database

To validate our proposal, we considered call center conversations between the agents and the customers.

Table 1: Affective content detection accuracies for call center calls (%)

Description	Classifiers							
	SVM		ANN		k-NN		SVM + ANN + k-NN	
	Full Utterance	*400ms Split*	*Full Utterance*	*400ms Split*	*Full Utterance*	*400ms Split*	*Full Utterance*	*400ms Split*
Affective Content Extractor	32.3	62.7	36.1	63.8	31.3	63.2	39.8	65.8
+Time Lapse	49.3	78.3	53.9	78.9	44.2	72.5	59.7	81.9
+ASR and text analytics	56.8	80.9	56.2	82.1	45.1	76.1	61.2	85.2
+Time Lapse + ASR and text analytics	65.3	87.6	61.2	88.9	47	85.6	72.1	89.6

However the agents are trained to behave (and talk) normally in any given situation, how much adverse that might be, mostly suppressing their emotions while talking with the customers. On the other side, customers generally express their emotions while talking to the agents, which means that the customer speech are non-acted (natural). We have considered total 107 call center calls from three different sectors (37 calls from finance, 34 calls from telecommunication sector, and 36 calls from insurance sector). There are total 354 randomly selected audio utterances of the customer which are considered for testing our framework. Notice that each of the spoken utterance has a reference in the form of when in the call flow it was spoken, plus also the manual transcription of speech (temporal sequence of words and phrases transcribed along the duration of the calls). We asked 7 human evaluators to annotate the emotion expressed in each of the 354 utterances by assigning it an emotion label from the set of *arousal* (positive, neutral, and negative) and *valence* (positive, neutral, and negative). In the first set of experiments, we randomly sequenced the utterances (with some utterances repeated) so that the evaluators had no knowledge of the events preceding the audio and we then asked the evaluators to label the utterances; while in the second set of experiments, we provided the utterances in the order in which they were spoken along with the spoken words transcription. The motivation is to include knowledge related to the conversation because of our observation that there is significant disagreement amongst human annotators when they annotate call center speech; the disagreement largely reduces when they are provided with additional knowledge related to the conversation. We computed the Kappa score (Viera and Garrett, 2005) on the annotations in *arousal* dimension for each of the two settings. In the first set of experiments (refer Figure 8), we obtained a score of 0.14 (i.e. without knowledge), suggesting a very poor agreement between the evaluators. While in the second set of experiments we obtained a Kappa score of 0.76 (refer Figure 8) suggesting that there was fair degree of agreement between the evaluators (i.e. with the knowledge). This clearly demonstrates that there was a better consistency in the evaluator's annotation when they were equipped with prior information (knowledge) associated with the utterance. This observation form the basis for the proposed framework for reliable recognition of affective states in call center speech.

4.2 Experimental Results

We considered audio calls which are manually speaker segmented so that the segmentation errors do not propagate to the affective content extractor. Similarly for the speech to text conversion, instead of taking the ASR output, we considered the manual transcription of the audio calls. Affective content extraction system is trained with the acted speech utterances from EmoDB (Emo-DB, 2010). Since the EmoDB dataset has annotations in categorical space, we converted the labels into the dimensional space. All the audio samples in our experimentations are sampled at 8 kHz, 16 bit, and monaural. A low level descriptors (intensity, loudness, 12 MFCC, pitch, voicing probability, F0 envelope, 8 Line Spectral Frequencies, zero-crossing) followed by statistical functionals (maximum, minimum values, range, arithmetic mean, 2 linear regression coefficients, linear and quadratic error, standard deviation, skewness, kurtosis, quartile 1-3, and 3 inter-quartile ranges) are extracted as the meaningful and informative feature sets from each of the segment using the OpenSmile feature extraction toolkit (openSMILE, 2014).

Different classifiers SVM, artificial neural network (ANN), and k-NN have been used in the experiments. LibSVM toolkit is used for implementing SVM classifier (LibSVM, 2015). For ANN, we have used feed-forward multilayer perceptron (WEKA-Toolkit, 2015), and the network is trained with back-propagation algorithm. All the results are presented as an average detection accuracies over all classes. Two different approaches were adopted for extracting the features from the speech utterances, (1) considering the full utterances (2) splitting the audio in 400 ms like in (Pandharipande and Kopparapu, 2015). In the second case, classifier scores are combined to get the scores for the full utterance.

Table 1 represents the affective content detection accuracies for the segments using different classifiers (and their combination), and using different knowledge-based system. It is observed that combining classifier scores using add rule improves the recognition accuracies (Kuncheva, 2004). The recognition accuracies are improved by using only the knowledge of the segment's lapse in the audio call. Similar trend is observed when only the voice to text analytics knowledge is used, and the accuracies were better compared to the system when only time lapse based knowledge is used. Moreover, the better accuracies are obtained when all the knowledge are incorporated, and the best accuracies are obtained with the framework that segments the full utterance into 400 ms smaller segments compared to the system which uses full utterance for processing. A significant absolute improvement in accuracy of 23.8% is achieved when all the knowledge are used for the combined classifier, and full utterances were segmented into 400 ms smaller segments. We found an average SNR of 8.15 dB for call center calls.

Table 2 presents the affective content detection accuracies for the acted speech samples (from EmoDB dataset), which are contaminated by different levels (SNR level of -5dB to 20dB) of 4 different types of noise (babble, F-16, machine-gun, and volvo) from Noisex-92 dataset. The noise were added using FaNT Toolkit (Filtering and Tool, 2015). Noise contaminated acted speech samples (i.e utterances) are segmented in 400 ms smaller segments like we did in (Pandharipande and Kopparapu, 2015). As expected, for lower SNRs the accuracies are quite on the lower side, and improved with higher SNRs. Combining classifier scores improves the accuracy. Performance of the system degrades significantly when the signal is affected by babble noise, and comparatively lower degradation is observed with the machine-gun noise. However comparing results in Table 1 and 2, we can say that the knowledge-based information significantly helps in improving the performance of the system, even for spontaneous call center calls in real-life noisy environment.

Table 2: Detection accuracies for acted speech (EmoDB) contaminated by noise (Noisex-92)

		Classifiers			
Noise type	**SNR (dB)**	**SVM**	**ANN**	***k*-NN**	**SVM+ANN+*k*-NN**
Babble	-5	21.05	22.3	32.6	33.2
	0	22.1	22.8	32.9	33.9
	5	24.8	25.6	34.6	35.5
	10	28.9	30.1	35.2	37.2
	20	42.3	45.6	47.3	53.3
F-16	-5	20.8	20.8	28.3	30.6
	0	21.6	22.3	29.1	32.4
	5	22.7	23.8	30.5	39.6
	10	28.3	30.1	34.6	43.7
	20	30.7	33.4	38.6	45.2
Machine Gun	-5	22.8	34.6	41.1	47.1
	0	45.6	61.4	61.4	73.3
	5	70.8	71.2	63.2	75.4
	10	71.9	73.2	64.9	77.2
	20	72.3	76	68	80.2
Volvo	-5	20.3	22.8	32.9	37.3
	0	40.3	42.7	40.3	52.9
	5	49.1	49.8	42.1	57.6
	10	54.3	54.8	57.3	71.3
	20	66.7	66.9	72.7	77.3

5 Conclusions

In this paper, we propose a framework that provides an automatic way to extract the affective contents in audio segments of large call center audio calls in *arousal* and *valence* dimension. The system not only relies on the classifier trained with the available acted emotional speech samples, but also incorporates available knowledge related the speech utterances for reliable detection of the affective content. Thus the system provides the call center supervisors an easier way to identify and subsequently address the abnormal calls. Experimental validation suggests that the incorporation of the associated knowledge in terms of speaker information, time lapse of the segment in the call, and linguistic content has improved the performance of the system to reliably identify the affective states and to tag the similar emotional segments. This provides an efficient and useful way for identifying the problematic calls from a large set of recorded call center audio.

References

Emo-DB. 2010. http://www.emodb.bilderbar.info/.

Filtering and Noise Adding Tool. 2015. http://dnt.kr.hs-niederrhein.de/index964b.html?option=com_content&view=article&id=22&Itemid=15&lang=de.

Purnima Gupta and Nitendra Rajput. 2007. Two-stream emotion recognition for call center monitoring. In *INTERSPEECH*.

Sunil Kumar Kopparapu. 2015. *Non-Linguistic Analysis of Call Center Conversations*. Springer, India.

Ludmila I. Kuncheva. 2004. *Combining Pattern Classifiers: Methods and Algorithms*. Wiley-Interscience.

C M Lee and S S Narayanan. 2005. Towards detecting emotions in spoken dialogs. *IEEE Transactions on Speech and Audio Processing*, 13:293–303.

LibSVM. 2015. https://www.csie.ntu.edu.tw/~cjlin/libsvm/.

Bing Liu. 2012. Sentiment analysis and opinion mining.

Taniya Mishra and Dimitrios Dimitriadis. 2013. Incremental emotion recognition. In *INTERSPEECH*.

M. A. Nicolaou, H. Gunes, and M. Pantic. 2011. Output-associative rvm regression for dimensional and continuous emotion prediction. In *FG*, pages 16–23.

openSMILE. 2014. http://www.audeering.com/research/opensmile.

M. A. Pandharipande and S. K. Kopparapu. 2015. Audio segmentation based approach for improved emotion recognition. In *TENCON 2015 - 2015 IEEE Region 10 Conference*, pages 1–4, Nov.

Bo Pang and Lillian Lee. 2008. Opinion mining and sentiment analysis. *Found. Trends Inf. Retr.*, 2(1-2):1–135, jan.

D. Pappas, I. Androutsopoulos, and H. Papageorgiou. 2015. Anger detection in call center dialogues. In *CogInfoCom*.

V. Petrushin. 1999. Emotion in speech: Recognition and application to call centers. In *Artificial Neural Networks in Engineering (ANNIE)*, pages 7–10.

Santiago Planet and Ignasi Iriondo Sanz. 2011. Improving spontaneous children's emotion recognition by acoustic feature selection and feature-level fusion of acoustic and linguistic parameters. In *Advances in Nonlinear Speech Processing - 5th International Conference on Nonlinear Speech Processing, NOLISP 2011, Las Palmas de Gran Canaria, Spain, November 7-9, 2011. Proceedings*, pages 88–95.

Laurence Vidrascu and Laurence Devillers. 2007. Five emotion classes detection in real-world call center data the use of various types of paralinguistic features. In *PARALING*, pages 11–16.

A. J. Viera and J. M. Garrett. 2005. Understanding interobserver agreement: the kappa statistic. *Family Medicine*, 37(5):360–363.

WEKA-Toolkit. 2015. http://www.cs.waikato.ac.nz/ml/weka/.

Association for Computational Linguistics
209 N. Eighth Street
Stroudsburg, Pennsylvania 18360